A COMPANION TO THE

ENGLISH

PARISH

CHURCH

'Time passes. Listen. Time passes.'

(Dylan Thomas)

A COMPANION TO THE
ENGLISH
PARISH
CHURCH

STEPHEN FRIAR

ALAN SUTTON PUBLISHING LIMITED

First published in the United Kingdom in 1996
Alan Sutton Publishing Limited
Phoenix Mill · Far Thrupp · Stroud · Gloucestershire

British Library Cataloguing in Publication Data

A catalogue record for this book is available from the British Library.

ISBN 0-7509-0461-5 (case)

ISBN 0-7509-1284-7 (paper)

Title-page illustration: Branscombe church, Devon (see p. 433).

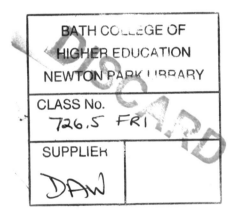
Typeset in 9/10 Times.
Typesetting and origination by
Alan Sutton Publishing Limited.
Printed in Great Britain by
Butler and Tanner, Frome, Somerset.

LIST OF PLATES

Monk's head corbel on the porch of Milton Abbey, Dorset.

INTRODUCTION

During a television interview, John Piper enquired of John Betjeman 'Why do you suppose that we all like churches so much?' Betjeman replied 'Because they're there whatever happens, aren't they?'

Three-quarters of Britain's Grade 1 listed buildings are ecclesiastical and the Church of England is responsible for most of these, including over 16,000 churches and forty-three cathedrals. But, as Graham Hutton observed in his introduction to the 1977 edition of *English Parish Churches*, 'At the present rate of extinction of historic parish churches solely in rural areas, by the year 2000 England will have lost one out of every six at present remaining: a grievous destruction of what by common consent of all authorities constitutes the nation's greatest collective heritage of art, architecture and craftsmanship. Indeed, broadly one-quarter of all existing parish churches in England are now threatened with demolition or conversion out of all recognition.'

Graham Hutton was writing nearly two decades ago but his exhortation is no less valid today. A report by Lord Templeman, commissioned in 1994 by the Bishop of London, recommended that twenty-four of the City's thirty-six churches should be 'mothballed'. Of course it can be argued that, as a result of recent legislation, the fabric of our historic churches is better protected than it was in the 1970s. But the Church of England is now experiencing serious financial difficulties and the Archbishop of Canterbury has warned that it cannot be expected to maintain all its churches because 'we have inherited so many buildings which do not reflect modern liturgical practices'.

It is of equal importance that the age-old relationship between church and community should also be preserved, a relationship which provides the warp and weft of this book. It will give me no satisfaction if the *Companion*, which is intended to celebrate the English parish church, should one day be read as its epitaph.

Every one of England's parish churches is unique: from St. Edwold's tiny church at Stockwood in Dorset and Bremilham in Wiltshire (twelve feet square and sitting in a farmyard) to the Gothic masterpiece of St. Mary Redcliffe in Bristol and the great monastic churches of Tewkesbury in Gloucestershire and Sherborne in Dorset. It is tempting to include, as others have elsewhere, a list of 'unmissable' churches: Fairford, Patrington, Blythburgh, Kilpeck . . . but to what purpose? Every church contains something which is unique, some object of beauty, some indefinable quality which invites even the most hard-bitten wayfarer to pause and experience the thrill of investigation and the delight of discovery.

England's parish churches are potent and sometimes enigmatic symbols of our heritage – the 'dark Satanic mills' of Blake's spectral landscape. Each is the repository of a community's soul and none can be considered in isolation from its congregation: that multitude of mostly anonymous parishioners who built, enlarged, decorated and maintained their church, who worshipped in it, were baptised and married in it, whose social life centred around it, and who are buried in its churchyard. From the wills, bequests, endowments and chantries of medieval benefactors to the churchwardens' accounts and vestry minutes of more recent centuries, we can begin to understand the nature of past worship and the pivotal role of the parish church in the life of a community. Indeed, for many parishioners, the parish church was their only point of contact with ideas and concepts which extended beyond the grinding reality of their daily lives and their only means of communicating with the outside world. Even today, there is a convention in rural parishes that public notices should be displayed in the church porch.

I have encountered a number of difficulties while writing the *Companion*, not least the length of the book's title which should be *A Companion to the English **and Welsh** Parish Church*. For this omission I beg forgiveness of my Welsh friends and colleagues. No slight is intended – numerous Welsh churches are referred to in the text and I have included an entry which deals exclusively with Christianity in medieval Wales.

Secondly, so many of our parish churches were originally monastic or collegiate foundations that I have included a number of entries which deal with the architectural components of a medieval monastery and with monasticism itself. It is impossible to appreciate the glories of former monastic churches such as Milton Abbey and Abbey Dore without considering first the composition and function of the original buildings and the history of their truncated remains.

Similarly, it is often impossible to separate the ecclesiastical and civic functions of parochial administration prior to the Local Government Act of 1894. In order that the reader should appreciate the complex relationships which once bound a community to its parish church, I have included material relating to various secular matters which were then administered by the churchwardens and vestries.

It is unfortunate that the latest review of local government should have coincided with the writing of the *Companion*. I have referred to the post-1974 counties throughout – with the exception of Herefordshire and Worcestershire which (mercifully) are to be restored.

The *Companion* is arranged alphabetically and consists of a number of primary entries (e.g. MONUMENTS) from which cross-references lead on to a larger number of secondary entries (e.g. BRASSES, EFFIGIES, WALL MONUMENTS). Many of the terms encountered when researching the history of a church or parish are also included, either as short individual entries or by cross-referencing. These include the terminology of associated subjects, such as architecture and heraldry, while entries on subjects such as MONASTICISM, the REFORMATION, etc. are intended to assist in placing local research in a wider historical context. The *Companion* is *not* a gazetteer (we have Betjeman, Harbison and many others to guide us) though an Index of Places is included in APPENDIX III.

Cross-references are indicated by CAPITAL LETTERS and, where necessary, these are picked out in *italic letters* in the entries to which the reader is referred.

Suggestions for further reading have been appended to appropriate entries, and a bibliography in APPENDIX I includes both gazetteers and books which are considered to be particularly suitable for beginners. The addresses of organisations referred to in the text will be found listed in APPENDIX II.

Stephen Friar
Caundle Wake, Dorset
November, 1995

ACKNOWLEDGEMENTS

The author acknowledges with gratitude the invaluable assistance of the following people in the preparation of this book: G.F.W. Adler, Clare Bishop, B. Breton, W.P. Burgess, Gill Capel, Sheila Chapman, Peter Clifford, B.G. Friar, E.M. Garrett, Sir Archie Hamilton MP, J.M. Hardman, C. Harrold, the Rev. Derek Hillier, A.L. Jones, the Right Rev. Richard Rutt, Janet Seeley, Jane Singleton, S. Slater, C.E.J. Smith, M. Stuchfield, C.A. Suter, Mrs. D. Treasure and Suzie Ward.

The author and publisher would like to thank the following for their permission to reproduce illustrations:

B.T. Batsford Ltd. (162, 173, 263, 286, 305); British Library, Add. Ms. 39810 (272); Hugh Collinson (x, 228, 229, 234, 392, 484); Paul Felix (colour plates 1, 4, 5, 10, 11, 12, 13); John Ferguson (21, 31, 40, 55, 73, 75, 105, 133, 227, 389, 391, 467, 492); Stephen Friar (47, 96, 144, 157, 164, 178, 182, 194, 202, 205, 219, 226, 262, 326, 387, 403, 446); Tom Friar (5, 10, 13, 18, 36, 38, 39, 67, 79, 88, 101, 125, 151–2, 163, 197, 200, 201, 215, 216, 221, 278, 282, 353, 388, 426, 435, 459, 461, 464, 468, 472, 496); Sir Archie Hamilton MP (260); Andrew Jamieson (30, 35, 37, 41, 130, 144, 145, 146, 148, 231, 232, 233, 237, 238, 275, 276, 291, 297, 339, 353, 414, 499); John Mennell (iii, 2, 7, 9, 14, 20, 34, 43, 58, 87, 119, 136, 139, 158, 165, 168, 171, 186, 213, 220, 230, 236, 237, 246, 264, 267, 274, 281, 299, 304, 341, 343, 351, 355, 357, 362, 368, 369, 385, 393, 427, 433, 437, 442, 451, 453, 455, 463, 469, 486, colour plates 2, 3, 6, 14); Michael Messer (483); L.E. Milton (484); Florence Morris (vi, 5, 74, 196, 306, 312, 327, 333, 335, 372, 379, 381, 384, 421, 425, 438, 441, 489); Stephen Slater (210, 229, 290, 342); Geoffrey Wheeler (59, 91, 131, 174, 175, 203, 214, 257, 295, 296, 327, 367, 383, 386, 407, 408, 429, 431, 448, 482, 491, 495, colour plates 7, 8, 9, 15); Anthony Wood (259, 260); Doreen Yarwood (286). The illustrations between pages 60–3 are taken from the Victoria and Albert Museum's publication *Catalogue of Rubbings of Brasses and Incised Slabs* (HMSO).

Brudenell tablet at Stonton Wyville, Leicestershire.

ABACUS The flat slab forming the upper section of a CAPITAL (*see* PIER).

ABBESS The superior of certain communities of Benedictine nuns and of orders of canonesses, especially those of the Franciscan Order (the Poor Clares).
See also ABBOT

ABBEYS An abbey was a major monastic establishment of the Benedictine orders or certain orders of the Canons Regular and superior to a priory, though in practice several priories attained religious eminence and economic prosperity which greatly exceeded that of many abbeys. Where an abbot was also a bishop, the administration of the community would be delegated to a prior and its church designated as a CATHEDRAL PRIORY: at Durham for example.

Following the DISSOLUTION OF THE MONASTERIES many abbey churches were acquired by local communities as parish churches. In most cases the cloistral and domestic buildings were demolished, or adapted for other purposes, and where an abbey church was considered too large for the needs of a parish, it was reduced in size by removing or shortening the nave, as at Abbey Dore in Herefordshire. Fortunately, many magnificent abbey churches have survived intact: Tewkesbury in Gloucestershire, for example, Selby in Yorkshire and Sherborne in Dorset which, in 1539, was purchased by the townspeople for the sum of £337. At the same time the adjoining parish church of All Hallows was demolished and in 1560 the Lady Chapel was acquired by the Governors of Sherborne School who converted it into a residence for the headmaster. There are also instances of abbey churches (now parish churches) which appear to have been reduced in size but, in fact, were never completed. Milton Abbey in Dorset, for example, was rebuilt after a disastrous fire (*totaliter inflammavit*) in 1309. But, by the time of the Dissolution, only the choir, crossing and transepts had been completed.
See also ANGLO-SAXON CHURCH, MINSTERS, MONASTIC BUILDINGS *and* PRIORIES
Further reading:
Thorold, H., *Guide to the Ruined Abbeys of England, Scotland and Wales*, London, 1993

ABBOT The superior (literally 'father') of a major religious establishment of one of the Benedictine orders or of certain orders of the Canons Regular. Normally elected for life by the monks of his abbey, an abbot exercised considerable authority in its governance. The second-in-command of an abbey was the prior (or prioress) and a religious house which was dependent on a larger, more important abbey was known as a priory.
See also MITRED ABBOT *and* PRIORIES

ABJURATION, OATH OF An oath imposed in 1701 by which the holders of spiritual, civil or military office renounced the Stuart dynasty and the temporal power of the Pope.

ABJURATION OF THE REALM *see* SANCTUARY, RIGHT OF

ABLUTIONS The washing of the chalice by the celebrant following the Eucharist.
See also PISCINA *and* LAVABO

ABRAIDING *see* STAINED GLASS

ABSOLUTION The formal pronouncement by a priest or bishop of Christ's forgiveness of sins to the penitent. Under the influence of the Anglo-Saxon and Celtic missionary monks, the early system of public penance, exclusion and reconciliation was replaced by the secret confession of sins, followed by absolution and then penance. By the thirteenth century, penance consisted of three elements: contrition (an awareness of one's sins and a desire to abandon them), confession (a thorough admission of those sins to a confessor – *see* CONFESSION), and satisfaction (a punishment or penance to be undertaken in expiation for the sin).
See also INDULGENCES *and* SHRINE

ABSTINENCE The penitential or disciplinary practice of abstaining from certain kinds of food, in contradistinction to FASTING. From very early times, Christians observed a Friday abstinence in memory of Christ's Passion. In the Middle Ages, abstinence was also practised on Wednesdays in Lent, Ember Days, Rogation Days and on the vigils of certain major feasts.

ABUTMENT A mass of masonry or brickwork against which an arch abuts or from which it springs. Structurally, an abutment resists the lateral thrust of an arch and may be a pier, wall or BUTTRESS.
See also ARCH *and* VAULTING

Cistercian Abbey Dore, Herefordshire, restored as a parish church by Lord Scudamore in 1634.

ACADEMIC COSTUME *see* BRASSES (MONUMENTAL)

ACANTHUS A stylised representation of a plant with thick scalloped leaves usually found as carved decoration in (e.g.) Corinthian capitals (*see* DECORATIVE MOTIFS).

ACCIDIE One of the 'Seven Deadly Sins' – restlessness preventing work or prayer.

ACCOLLÉ *see* HATCHMENTS

ACCUSATIONS The first 'reserved business' at a meeting of a monastic chapter was the revelation of breaches of discipline – the 'accusations'.

ACHIEVEMENT OF ARMS A pictorial representation of heraldic devices, usually in the form of the conventional COAT OF ARMS but not necessarily so.
See also ARMORIAL BEARINGS, FUNERAL HERALDRY, HATCHMENTS *and* HERALDRY

ACOLYTE A person assisting a priest: specifically one who is dedicated to service at the ALTAR (*see* MINOR ORDERS).

ACOUSTIC CHAMBERS *see* AMPLIFIERS

ACROTERION A pedestal or ornament at the top or side angle of a PEDIMENT.

ACTS OF PARLIAMENT *see* LEGISLATION

ADDORSED Two similar or identical figures placed back to back – as in heraldry and architectural decoration.

ADDRESS, FORMS OF
Archbishops of Canterbury and York
Letter: Dear Archbishop
                 Yours sincerely
Envelope: The Most Reverend and Right Hon. the
                 Lord Archbishop of . . .
Verbal address: Your Grace (formal) *or* Archbishop
                 (informal)

Bishop of London
Letter: Dear Bishop
                 Yours sincerely
Envelope: The Right Reverend and Right Hon. the
                 Lord Bishop of London
Verbal address: Bishop

Bishop (Diocesan and Suffragan)
Letter: Dear Bishop
           Yours sincerely
Envelope: The Right Reverend the Lord Bishop
           of . . .
    or The Right Reverend the Bishop of . . .
    or The Right Reverend John Jones (if an
           assistant bishop or retired)
Verbal address: Bishop

Dean
Letter: Dear Dean
           Yours sincerely
Envelope: The Very Reverend the Dean of . . .
Verbal address: Dean

Provost
Letter: Dear Provost
           Yours sincerely
Envelope: The Very Reverend the Provost of . . .
Verbal address: Provost

Archdeacon
Letter: Dear Archdeacon
           Yours sincerely
Envelope: The Venerable the Archdeacon of . . .
Verbal address: Archdeacon

Canon
Letter: Dear Canon *or* Dear Canon Jones
           Yours sincerely
Envelope: The Reverend Canon John Jones
Verbal address: Canon *or* Canon Jones

Prebendary
Letter: Dear Prebendary *or* Dear Prebendary
           Jones
           Yours sincerely
Envelope: The Reverend Prebendary John Jones
Verbal address: Prebendary *or* Prebendary Jones

Rural Dean
No special form of address unless an honorary canon
(see above).

Other Clergy
Letter: Dear Mr. Jones *or* Dear Father Jones (*see*
           FATHER. For beneficed clergy, Dear
           Rector or Dear Vicar may be used.)
           Yours sincerely
Envelope: The Reverend John Jones
Verbal address: Mr. Jones *or* Father Jones (*see*
           FATHER)

See also CLERGY (CHURCH OF ENGLAND) *and*
SIGNATURES (BISHOPS AND ARCHBISHOPS)
Further reading:
Montague-Smith, P., (Ed.), *Debrett's Correct Form*,
   Kingston-upon-Thames, 1976

ADIT An entrance or approach to a building.

AD LIMINA APOSTOLORUM Pilgrimages to the tombs of St. Peter and St. Paul in Rome – 'to the threshold of the Apostles' – were popular in the Middle Ages.

ADMINISTRATION *see* CHURCH ASSEMBLY, CONVOCATION, PAROCHIAL CHURCH COUNCIL, SYNOD *and* VESTRY

ADMINISTRATION, LETTERS OF *see* PROBATE

ADMINISTRATOR A non-member of a community, usually a layman, who was charged with the administration of the temporal affairs of a religious house. Enclosed communities were particularly dependent on lay administrators, as were communities of nuns. Administrators were also appointed to correct the business affairs of houses whose finances had become unmanageable, usually through the acquisition of debts.
See also LAY OFFICIALS

ADVENT The ecclesiastical season immediately before Christmas, beginning on the Sunday nearest to St. Andrew's Day (30 November). It is observed as a penitential season, not only for Christmas, but in anticipation of the Second Coming of Christ (*Parousia*). The first day of Advent (Advent Sunday) is also the first of the ecclesiastical year.

ADVENT SUNDAY *see* ADVENT

ADVERTISEMENTS Injunctions issued to the clergy in 1566 pursuant to the Act of Uniformity.

ADVOWSON The right of nomination or presentation to an ecclesiastical benefice. An advowson is held by a *patron*, who may be an individual or institution, clerical or secular. The patron presents the candidate to the appropriate bishop for institution and induction, though the nomination may be refused. An advowson is a form of property which may be bought, sold or given away and is subject to civil law.

ADVOWSON APPENDANT An ADVOWSON annexed to a manor or estate.

ADVOWSON IN GROSS An ADVOWSON in the gift of an individual.

AEDICULE Originally, a small room or sacred shrine, the term came to be used to describe an opening framed by columns or pillars and a PEDIMENT.

AFFINITY A relationship arising from a valid marriage which is held to create an impediment to

subsequent marriage between one party and certain blood relations of the other. In the Church of England, the PROHIBITED DEGREES of intermarriage are set out in the *Table of Kindred and Affinity*, first published in 1563, and customarily printed at the end of the *Book of Common Prayer*. These were amended in 1946 and again in 1969 when adopted children were added to the list. An extraordinary number of papal dispensations were granted in the medieval and Tudor periods. At one point, for example, the Pope was even inclined to approve a marriage between the Princess Mary and Henry, Duke of Richmond, half-sister and half-brother by Henry VIII, on condition that the King abandoned his projected divorce.
See also CONSANGUINITY

AFFRONTED In architecture, the term is similar to ADDORSED, but with the figures facing one another. In heraldry, the term *combatant* is used to describe two beasts *rampant* and face to face, *affronty* meaning that the figure is actually facing the observer (*see also* HERALDIC BEASTS).

AFFRONTY *see* AFFRONTED *and* HERALDIC BEASTS

AFFUSION This method of BAPTISM, whereby water is poured over the head of the candidate, has been in common use in England since the Middle Ages. The alternative methods of *immersion*, by which part of the body is submerged, and *submersion*, which requires the entire body to be covered by water, are known to have been used by the early Church.

AFTERGRASS *see* CHARITY MEADS

AGNOSTICISM The doctrine, which came into general usage in the nineteenth century, that only material phenomena can be the subject of real knowledge and that a First Cause and a supernatural world are beyond knowledge.
See also ATHEISM

AGNUS DEI *see* CHRISTIAN SYMBOLS

AGRARIAN REVOLUTION *see* EIGHTEENTH-CENTURY CHURCH

AILETTES Rectangular plates fastened upright on the shoulder and decorated with heraldic devices (*see* ARMOUR *and* BRASSES, MONUMENTAL).

AISLE From the Latin *ala* meaning 'wing', an aisle is a lateral extension of a NAVE from which it is divided by an ARCADE or COLONNADE. In some Anglo-Saxon churches, the nave wall was broken only by a doorway to provide access to the chambers beyond. Some Norman churches were built with aisles (St. Margaret-at-Cliffe in Kent and St. Peter's, Northampton, for example) but, for the most part, they were added to earlier buildings.

An aisle was intended to provide additional space for the congregation and, in larger monastic and collegiate churches, a processional route associated with the elaboration of the liturgy. Late-medieval aisles were often constructed to accommodate the activities of parish GUILDS or as CHANTRY CHAPELS and, in both cases, there is likely to be evidence of a subsidiary altar at the east end (*see* CHAPELS).

Occasionally, a TRANSEPT was incorporated into an aisle, and the aisles themselves were sometimes extended outwards, especially in the late-medieval period. This, of course, resulted in the nave windows being blocked by the roof of the enlarged aisle and, in order that sufficient natural light should be admitted to the nave, the nave walls and roof also had to be raised to accommodate a CLERESTORY. There are many instances of single aisles, including a number of former monastic churches where the presence of a CLOISTER precluded the construction of an aisle on the southern elevation of the nave. Several churches have double-aisles, providing five parallel chambers, while the aisles of HALL CHURCHES are of the same height as the nave, as at St. Mary's, Warwick.

In most cases, aisles were added to earlier naves and may reflect an (often transient) period of prosperity in a community's affairs or the generosity of a benefactor. Even the smallest of churches may boast a substantial aisle: the little fifteenth-century church of All Saints at Hilton in Dorset, for example, where the traceried windows of its north aisle were acquired from the nearby abbey of Milton following the Dissolution of the Monasteries. At some churches, such as Newland in Gloucestershire, unusually wide aisles create a wonderful feeling of spaciousness, while at Leominster Priory in Herefordshire the great north 'aisle' was the nave of the former (Benedictine) monastic church.

The term 'aisle' is often used erroneously to describe a passageway between rows of seats or benches.
See also AMBULATORY, MEDIEVAL ARCHITECTURE *and* RETRO-CHOIR

ALABASTER Calcium sulphate, a form of gypsum, found in certain strata of rocks in the north Midlands (notably at Chellaston in Derbyshire) and elsewhere. Alabaster was used in medieval sculpture (particularly in EFFIGIES) because of the ease and speed with which it could be carved. Dressed

North aisle at All Saints, Hilton, Dorset, removed from the cloister of nearby Milton Abbey in the 1530s.

alabaster is exceptionally smooth to the touch and is white with occasional flecks of red, though most medieval MONUMENTS were originally coloured and sometimes gilded.
See also PLASTERWORK *and* PURBECK MARBLE

ALB *see* VESTMENTS

ALBACIO Whitewash.

ALCOVE A vaulted recess or large niche.

ALEPH The first letter of the Hebrew alphabet.

ALEPLAYS *see* DRAMA

ALIAS The Latin word for 'otherwise'. An alias, or alternative name, may have been adopted for a variety of reasons, including the perpetuation of a family name. Commonly found in wills, memorial inscriptions etc.

ALIEN In a medieval context, one who was unable to hold or inherit titles or land.

ALIENATION The transfer of property.

ALIEN PRIORY A direct dependency in England of a continental religious house. There were two types of alien priory: conventual houses, in which a community followed a claustral life under a PRIOR, and (more commonly) manors, sometimes with an appropriated church, from which revenues were diverted to the mother house (*see* APPROPRIATION). Many alien priories originated in benefactions made by the followers of William I from their newly acquired English estates to monasteries at home. At one time there were over one hundred alien priories in England and, of the conventual houses, several churches have survived. Good examples are the Priory Church of St. Mary and St. Martin at Blyth in Nottinghamshire (from Rouen) and the Priory Church of St. Mary and St. Blaise at Boxgrove, Sussex (from Lessay). It is often difficult to determine the precise relationship between alien priories and parishes, particularly in those manors where there was an appropriated church, but it is known that at Ecclesfield in Yorkshire the 'custos' of the priory served the cure of the parish church.

During the Hundred Years War the alien priories were widely suspected of acting as conduits for money and intelligence and were rigorously suppressed. In some cases their personnel and resources were used for other religious purposes: for establishing chantries (*see* CHANTRY) and colleges (*see* CHANTRY COLLEGE) or for supplementing existing monastic foundations, for example. Some of the larger houses obtained charters of DENIZATION and became independent monasteries under English priors or dependencies of established English houses. By the second quarter of the fifteenth century, alien priories had ceased to exist.
See also DAUGHTER HOUSE *and* PRIORY

ALITURGICAL DAYS In the Roman Catholic Church, the Eucharist may not be celebrated on Good Friday and Holy Saturday which are aliturgical days.

ALL HALLOWS (HALLOWMAS) *see* ALL SAINTS' DAY *and* FEAST DAYS (FIXED AND MOVABLE)

ALL SAINTS' DAY (ALL HALLOWS *or* HALLOWMAS) The celebration of all Christian saints, known and unknown, originally observed on the first Sunday after PENTECOST but (since the eighth century) celebrated on 1 November.
See also FEAST DAYS (FIXED AND MOVABLE) *and* HALLOWE'EN

ALL SOULS' DAY The commemoration of the souls of the faithful departed, observed (since the mid-eleventh century) on 2 November, the day following ALL SAINTS' DAY.
See also FEAST DAYS (FIXED AND MOVABLE) *and* HALLOWE'EN

ALLUSIVE ARMS *see* HERALDIC CHARGES

ALMERY *see* CHEST CUPBOARD

ALMONER One who is responsible for distributing ALMS.

ALMONRY Monastic buildings often included an almonry from which ALMS were distributed. Several almonries had infirmaries or ALMS-HOUSES attached while others supported a school. At Durham, for example, there was an infirmary for the maintenance of four elderly women and lodgings for 'the children of the almonry'. A number of former monastic churches, now adapted for parochial use, retain evidence of almonries. At Dorchester (Oxfordshire), where the almonry was combined with a guest house, the *dole window* from which alms were distributed may still be seen, together with the almoner's seat.
See also BEDE-HOUSE, CHEST CUPBOARD, DOLE CUPBOARDS *and* DOLE TABLES

ALMS A donation of food or money given to the poor, to destitute wayfarers and to pilgrims. It has been estimated that one tenth of monastic income was devoted to alms-giving. No needy person who called at the gatehouse of a religious house was ever to be turned away, though there were usually appointed times for the distribution of alms. Alms could also include education or hospitality, and guest houses, infirmaries and hospices were often provided for that purpose (*see also* ALMONRY, BEDE-HOUSE, HOSPICE, INFIRMARY *and* ALMSHOUSES). Of course, spiritual alms, intercessory prayers for the souls of benefactors and founders and for all God's people, both living and dead, were the *raison d'être* of all religious houses.

ALMS BAG An embroidered purse, passed among a congregation during a service, for the collection of offerings. At one time, a parish may have possessed a number of alms bags of different colours, each corresponding with the liturgical colour appropriate to a particular season.

ALMS BASIN A large dish, usually of base metal and over 30 cm in diameter, in which a congregation's offerings ('the collection') are received and presented at the altar during a service.

ALMS BOXES (*also* POOR BOXES) Containers for the receipt of donations for the poor (*see* ALMS). Typically these date from the seventeenth and eighteenth centuries and may be inscribed with the words 'Remember the Poor' and a date. Earlier oak boxes were usually rectangular with a rounded lid, bound with iron straps and sometimes embellished with enamel tracery. The tall, pre-Reformation alms box at Blythburgh church in Suffolk has three traceried panels at the front while those at Cawston in London and Loddon, Norfolk are extraordinary for the ingenuity of their security systems! At Watton in Norfolk the seventeenth-century alms box is supported by the wooden figure of a beggar and at Pinhoe in Devon a singularly dapper gentleman describes himself as 'Ye Poor Man of Pinhoe 1700'. At Tunworth in Hampshire each side of the box is carved with a human face, the lips forming a slot through which offerings are made (one figure has its tongue out!). There are medieval stone alms boxes at the neighbouring churches of Bridlington Priory and Speeton in Yorkshire. Both were once accompanied by carved stone figures but only the brackets remain. After the DISSOLUTION OF THE MONASTERIES, relief of the poor became an urgent necessity (*see also* POOR LAW). But today most alms boxes have been replaced by metal containers, firmly embedded in a wall and used to collect payments for post-cards and guide-books and donations for the work of the Church and the parish fabric fund.

ALMS DISH *see* ALMS BASIN

ALMSHOUSES Medieval almshouses were established as charitable foundations by religious bodies, trade guilds, livery companies and individual benefactors to care for the elderly, poor and infirm and wayfarers such as pilgrims (*see also* ALMONRY). Each would have a warden, master or

prior and would comprise an infirmary hall and chapel, similar in plan to a monastic infirmary. Known as spital houses, bede houses or *maisons dieu*, some were devoted to the care of lepers or lazars (such as the lazar houses of the Order of St. Lazarus) and these would be divided into small cells or separate cottages instead of a corporate infirmary (*see also* HOSPITALS).

In the later Middle Ages many hospices became permanent homes for the poor and elderly, who were required to pray for the repose of the founder in return for board and lodging. In 1547 most were dissolved as places of worship. The Elizabethans, however, re-established many old hospitals as almshouses and, encouraged by their example, the wealthy and charitable of the seventeenth and eighteenth centuries founded new establishments, the inmates of which were carefully selected for their unquestionable virtue.

Typical of a number of medieval foundations which continue to operate today are the almshouses at Sherborne in Dorset, built in 1437 under royal licence at a cost of £80 raised (unusually) by public

The almshouse of St. John the Baptist and St. John the Evangelist at Sherborne, Dorset.

subscription. They were intended for 'twelve pore feeble and ympotent old men and four old women', cared for by a housewife who was required to share in the meals of the residents, presumably to ensure that they were properly fed.

Many post-Reformation almshouses are associated with parish churches. Typical of the seventeenth century are the beautiful brick almshouses at Wimborne St. Giles (also in Dorset), built by Sir Anthony Ashley in 1624 as ten single-storey, one-roomed tenements with a chapel above a central loggia, and attached to the north-west corner of the parish church. They were intended 'for the comfort in old age' of elderly widows from Sir Anthony's estate and are similar in design (though of superior quality) to the almshouses at nearby Milton Abbas. These date from *c.* 1674 but were removed to their present site following the obliteration of the original village by Lord Dorchester in 1779–80.
See also CHARITIES

ALMUCE *see* VESTMENTS

ALPHA AND OMEGA The first and last letters of the Greek alphabet and, in Christian symbolism, the beginning and the end of all things (*see* CHRISTIAN SYMBOLS).

ALPHYN *see* BEASTS (HERALDIC)

ALTARAGE Minor church income (*see also* MORTUARY *and* SURPLICE FEES).

ALTAR CANOPY A canopy (or *tester*) fixed or suspended above an altar and intended both to dignify the sanctuary and to amplify and direct a celebrant's voice (*see also* BALDACCHINO *and* SOUNDING BOARD). Few altar canopies remain but of those which have survived several have ornately decorated roofs, as at Clun church in Shropshire. A Canopy of Honour is a large altar canopy (*ciborium*) and is a feature of the later work of the architect Sir Ninian Comper (1864–1960).
See also ALTARS, CANOPY *and* CELURE

ALTAR CROSS It is not known precisely when the altar cross was introduced, but it has been suggested that it may have evolved from the medieval practice of placing the head of the processional cross on the altar during the service. The cross thereby became the focal point of worship, particularly at the Eucharist. Nevertheless, altar crosses and CANDLESTICKS were not widely used in parish churches until the nineteenth century (*see* NINETEENTH-CENTURY CHURCH). Crosses will be found in a variety of decorative forms and materials and are worthy of study, though many are locked away between services to discourage thieves and vandals.
See also ALTARS, CROSSES *and* CANDLES

ALTAR LIGHTS There is evidence to suggest that the practice of placing a candle or CANDLES on the altar dates from *c.* 1175. Before the Reformation, it was customary for a single candle to be placed on the altar or, at most, one on either side of the ALTAR CROSS. Thereafter any number was acceptable, and three (on each side) considered the most effective. The legality of this practice was contested in the nineteenth century but was confirmed in 1890. Strictly speaking, it is not correct to place anything else (such as flowers) on the altar.
See also LAMPS

ALTARPIECE (i) A DIPTYCH or TRIPTYCH placed on an altar or predella. (ii) An arrangement of large panels, often three in number, affixed to the wall behind a communion table in place of an east window. These are inscribed with religious texts, the lettering of which is usually in gold leaf on a black or varnished background. Altarpieces are characteristic of churches built in the Georgian period (*see* EIGHTEENTH-CENTURY ARCHITECTURE *and* REREDOS).

ALTAR RAILS *see* COMMUNION RAILS

ALTARS The term, with its sacrificial connotations, was adopted by the early Church to describe the Eucharist table which, at that time, was probably little more than a simple wooden table in a private house. It was also the custom to celebrate the Eucharist on the tombs of martyrs which may account for the later practice of constructing altars of stone. Strictly speaking, the term altar should be applied only to medieval stone altars though it is commonly used also to describe post-Reformation *communion tables*.

In Britain, most Celtic and early Anglo-Saxon churches had free-standing, wooden altars. But from the first decade of the sixth century stone was used, especially where altars were erected over the interred relics of saints. At that time it was customary to have only one altar in a church, usually on a raised platform (a *predella*) at the east end of the PRESBYTERY. The front was covered with a decorative cloth (*frontal*) or a carved and painted panel known as the *antependium* and a *retable* may have been fitted above the back of the altar. This was a frame for a decorative panel or a shelf on which ornaments could be placed (*see also* ALTAR CANOPY *and* REREDOS). Illustrations in several Dark Age and early medieval manuscripts suggest that altars may also have been covered by an arched roof (*ciborium*), supported at the corners by pillars.

Some altars must have been truly magnificent works of art. William of Malmesbury, writing in *c.* 1125, tells us that, on his return from Rome in

AD 700, St. Aldhelm brought with him 'An altar of shining white marble six feet long [1.8 metres], four feet deep [1.2 metres] and three palms thick [30 cm], with a lip projecting from the stone and beautifully carved round the edge. He gave the altar to Ine [King of the West Saxons] who placed it for the service of the Mother of God in a royal villa called Briwetune [Bruton in Somerset] where it stands to this day, a living proof of the sanctity of Aldhelm'.

From the early thirteenth century, the *High Altar* in the presbytery, where the priest celebrated the Sacrifice of the Mass, was concealed from the laity in the nave by the ROOD SCREEN. But, in many churches, the practice of saying private Masses (attended only by the celebrant and an ACOLYTE) resulted in the provision of subsidiary PRIVILEGED ALTARS, sometimes enclosed by a PARCLOSE (screen) and provided with a SQUINT in order that the celebrant could observe what was taking place at the high altar (*see also* CHANTRY *and* CHANTRY CHAPEL). Similarly, as more

monks entered the priesthood, so additional altars were required in the great abbey churches, many of which became parish churches following the DISSOLUTION OF THE MONASTERIES. These private altars were usually positioned at the eastern end of the church, as at the former Cistercian abbey of Dore in Herefordshire, where an eastern aisle gave access to a row of five chapels. Most churches also had a small porch altar located near the south door (*see* PORCHES).

Common features of medieval altars were the CELURE and the BALDACCHINO, a cloth canopy suspended above the altar, and *riddel curtains* (from the French *rideau* meaning 'curtain') which screened the altar table at the back and sides. The *ridel posts*, which were affixed to the four corners of the altar table to support the ridell curtain, developed into tall, slender pillars, each surmounted with the gilded figure of an angel. A PISCINA (wash-basin and drain) was always provided near an altar, usually in the south wall of the presbytery, together with a SIDILIA (seating) and AUMBRY (cupboard).

Saxon altar at the church of St. Laurence, Bradford-on-Avon, Wiltshire.

The doctrine of the Sacrifice of the Mass, and the medieval concept of the mystery of the *inner sanctum*, were rejected by the sixteenth-century reformers who brought the congregation into the chancel, or moved the altar into the nave, where the Eucharist was shared as a family at 'God's Board'. An Act of Edward VI (1547–53) required that all altar stones were to be removed and destroyed, though in many cases they were hidden by Roman Catholics in anticipation of better times. A few have been found intact and restored (though not always in their original position), the top (or *mensa*) almost invariably bearing five engraved crosses – one at each corner and another in the centre. A small number of stone altars have also survived *in situ*, often in free chapels (those not subject to a bishop's jurisdiction) such as the thirteenth-century chapel of St. Bartholomew at Corton in Dorset (*see* CHAPELS).

Elizabethan and Jacobean *communion tables* were usually splendidly carved in wood with bulbous legs, as at Carleton Rode in Norfolk and Minehead, Somerset. The accessibility of the new communion tables caused problems, however, particularly from stray DOGS, and rails to prevent profanation were widely introduced in churches from the early years of Elizabeth I's reign. These were disliked by the Puritans but were often restored following the Restoration of 1660 and became known as COMMUNION RAILS.

Many CHANCEL SCREENS were removed during Victorian restorations while, until recently, nearly every parish church possessed a communion table which followed the early designs of the ecclesiastical architect Sir Ninian Comper (1864–1960). These consisted of a table with antependium or embroidered frontal and *super frontal* (a fringed and embroidered 'pelmet') and RIDDEL CURTAINS or a triptych retable with riddel posts. In a small number of his later churches, Comper anticipated recent liturgical changes by moving the communion table from its eastern position into the nave, enclosed within communion rails (*see* CHANCELLI) and surmounted by a magnificent ciborium.
See also ALTARPIECE

ALTAR TOMB *see* TABLE TOMB

ALTERNATIVE SERVICE BOOK, THE (ASB)
see COMMON PRAYER, BOOK OF

ALURE A walk or passageway behind a parapet.

ALWITE In EFFIGIES and BRASSES, instances of splendid 'alwite' armour are numerous during the period *c.* 1410–60. The term was applied to plate armour which, although very plain, was extraordinarily beautiful. Contours were so perfectly crafted that reflected light rendered the armour almost white to the eye. A full harness of alwite armour was tailored for a particular client and was therefore enormously expensive. The finest harnesses were imported from Italy (notably from the Missaglia workshop in Milan), and it is hardly surprising that owners should wish to display such magnificence, not only in the field, but also in their memorials. For the most part, therefore, armour in brasses and effigies of the period was unadorned, without the JUPON of earlier periods or the later TABARD, the heraldry confined to crests (on helms, usually depicted beneath a figure's head) and to painted or enamelled SHIELDS, set within matrices or the interstices of TOMB CHESTS.

AMBO (i) A raised platform in a BASILICA from which the Scriptures were read and the liturgy conducted. Pulpits replaced ambos after the fourteenth century. (ii) Latinised place-name element meaning 'both'. Usually found added to the name of a single parish or village which was once two parishes or hamlets. (*See* LATIN)

AMBRY *see* AUMBRY

AMBULATORY A covered way for walking. A characteristic of Norman churches, the ambulatory is a semicircular AISLE enclosing an apsidal PRESBYTERY or chapel. By the mid-twelfth century, the apsidal form was less popular in England and was superseded by a square-ended eastern termination. As a result, the term is also applied to the right-angled conjunction of the north and south chancel aisles and RETRO-CHOIR found in many larger churches.
See also CHEVET

AMERCEMENT A money penalty.

AMICE *see* VESTMENTS

AMORINO (*also* PUTTO) A decorative cupid's head, or that of a winged cherub often found depicted on HATCHMENTS or carved on GRAVESTONES.
See also ANGELS

AMPHISBAENA A symbol of evil and the devil, this allegorical beast has dragon-like wings and a head at both ends of its scaly body, thereby enabling it to move with cunning in either direction. Found in medieval carving but rarely in heraldry.
See also CHRISTIAN SYMBOLS

AMPLIFIERS (*also* ACOUSTIC CHAMBERS *or* RESONATORS) Earthenware vessels, usually set in the eastern face of a chancel wall in order to amplify the voice of the priest during the mass. A set at Tarrant Rushton church in Dorset dates from *c.* 1458 and must have been effective, for in 1541 the churchwardens' accounts of nearby Wimborne Minster record: 'payd for 2 potts of cley for the wyndfylling of the Church 8p'. In many monastic churches *acoustic chambers* were intended to provide extra resonance and amplification during the singing of plainsong and to make 'hauteyn speche ring out as round as gooth a belle'. Those at Fountains Abbey in Yorkshire consisted simply of rows of ceramic jars laid on their sides, but elsewhere sophisticated drain-like series of boxes were constructed beneath choir STALLS for the same purpose. The twelfth-century set of acoustic chambers at St. Gregory's Priory in Canterbury, Kent is .9 metres wide (3 feet) and .6 metres deep (2 feet), with tiled floors and walls mortared with chalk and flint. They were built to allow the low notes of male voices to reverberate and supposedly added lustre to the sound. Acoustic chambers were clearly *de rigueur* in the Middle Ages though it is doubtful whether they were really effective.

ANATHEMA Literally, 'separated' or 'accursed'. In the early Church anathematisation was used against heretics and, from the sixth century, was distinguished from EXCOMMUNICATION: the former requiring total separation from the Church and the latter exclusion from the Sacraments.
See also BELL, BOOK AND CANDLE

ANCASTER STONE An easily carved, grey limestone from Wilsford Heath, Lincolnshire.

ANCESTOR A person from whom others are descended. In law, one from whom an estate was inherited.

ANCHOR Greek and Roman sailors often dedicated the largest (sheet) anchor of a ship to a deity, for it was their chief dependence in a storm. It is also found in Christian imagery where anchors represent God as man's 'last hope and refuge'. An anchor is the symbol of St. Clement of Rome who, in AD 80, was bound to an anchor and cast into the sea; and of St. Nicolas of Bari, the patron saint of sailors.

ANCHORAGE An anchorite's dwelling, often an endowed cell within a church or churchyard and usually inferior to that of a HERMIT. Anchorites' cells were very small apartments in which the ANCHORITE was effectively walled up for life (a special office was observed when this took place). They were usually located on the cold north side of a chancel with an aperture (through the church wall) to the altar and another overlooking the grave which was prepared in readiness outside. Evidence of former anchorages may be found at a number of churches, mostly in southern England: at Compton and Shere in Surrey, for example.

ANCHORESS A female ANCHORITE.

ANCHORITE (*Fem.* ANCHORESS) A religious recluse living a solitary life of silence, prayer and mortification. Unlike a HERMIT, an anchorite would be 'walled up for life' in a tiny cell (*see* ANCHORAGE). Anchorages could only be established with the consent of a bishop who had to be satisfied that the anchorite possessed both the spiritual integrity and the material resources to survive in his strictly enclosed quarters. Some lived by means of an endowment: the Black Prince maintained an anchorite, in the park of Restormel Castle above the Fowey river in Cornwall, who said masses for the souls of his benefactor's ancestors. At Durham, an anchorite's cell, consisting of an elevated chapel between two piers, overlooked St. Cuthbert's shrine; while a similar (twelfth-century) arrangement at the splendid parish church of St. Nicholas at Compton in Surrey may also have been an anchorage, attracting travellers from the nearby Pilgrims' Way.
See also COENOBITE

ANCIENT DEEDS Documents at the Public Record Office, mostly drawn from monastic and private muniments, relating to conveyances of land, covenants, bonds, wills etc. 'earlier in date than the end of Elizabeth I's reign' (1603).
Further information:
Descriptive Catalogue of Ancient Deeds (6 vols.)
   HMSO and publications of the List and Index Society (*see* APPENDIX 2).

ANCIENT USER *see* TIME IMMEMORIAL

ANELACE A short, two-edged tapering dagger sometimes depicted in effigial figures and brasses (*see also* MISERICORDE).

ANGEL BEAM The projection of a HAMMER BEAM, carved at the end with a representation of an angel.

ANGELS In the Bible, angels are represented as an innumerable multitude of beings, a heavenly court, intermediate between God and man. In the early Church, interest in angels was largely concerned with matters hierarchical and, in c. 500, the celestial host was arranged in three orders of three choirs each: Seraphim, Cherubim and Thrones; Dominations, Virtues and Powers; Principalities, Archangels and Angels.

The depiction, in Anglo-Saxon and medieval churches, of angels in stone, wood and glass was intended to be a constant reminder of their invisible presence at the Sacrifice of the Mass, especially in the vicinity of the high altar.

See also AMORINO and WEEPERS. For the attributes of the various orders of angels and archangels see CHRISTIAN SYMBOLS

ANGELUS BELL A bell rung to mark each stage of the Angelus, a devotion repeated three times daily (early morning, noon and evening) as a memorial of the Incarnation.

See also BELLS

ANGLICAN CHANT A simple type of harmonised melody used in the Anglican Church for singing unmetrical texts, principally the Psalms and Canticles. A short melody is repeated to each verse of the text, the varying numbers of syllables in different lines being accommodated by the use of a reciting note at the opening of each line.

See also CHURCH MUSIC (ANGLICAN), PLAINSONG and VERSICLES

ANGLICANISM The system of Christian doctrine and practice upheld by those in communion with the See of Canterbury. Anglicanism, as a doctrinal system, came into existence during the reign of Elizabeth I (1558–1603) and was at its height under the Stuarts in the seventeenth century. Decline, which began in 1790, was arrested by the rise of the OXFORD MOVEMENT in the early nineteenth century.

See also HIGH CHURCH

ANGLO-CATHOLICISM Dating from 1838, the term refers to the more advanced section of the HIGH CHURCH movement which stresses the Church of England's historical continuity with Catholic Christianity.

See also OXFORD MOVEMENT

ANGLO-SAXON ARCHITECTURE Anglo-Saxon church buildings in England date from two distinct periods with the calamitous Viking raids of the late eighth and ninth centuries intervening and effectively obliterating much of earlier Saxon culture.

THE EARLY PERIOD

The work of the seventh and early eighth centuries was concentrated in two areas: a Celtic tradition based in Northumberland and an Augustinian school in the Canterbury area. Very few stone churches were built before the eleventh century, most Anglo-Saxon buildings being constructed of timber and wattle and daub. It is surprising, therefore, that so much evidence has survived from this early period though, in most cases, it is fragmentary: blocked doorways and window openings incorporated into the fabric of later churches and rediscovered during nineteenth-century restorations, for example.

The first Northumbrian churches had tall naves without aisles and with simple rectangular sanctuaries, one of the finest examples being the church of St. John the Evangelist at Escomb in County Durham (c. 680) which stands in an ovoid churchyard (see CHURCH SITES). The remains of several other seventh-century Northumbrian churches suggest that, like Escomb, they were intended to accommodate no more than a priest and a few worshippers, and even the great monastic centres, such as the twin foundations of Jarrow and Monkwearmouth (Tyne and Wear), had churches (675) which conformed to the basic Celtic two-celled plan.

Following the Synod of Whitby (664) and the Councils of Hertford (673) and Hatfield (680), the liturgy of both traditions followed the Roman pattern, as did church architecture, and by the end of the century many northern churches were being constructed on the BASILICAN plan, such as those at Hexham, Ripon and York. This was the plan already adopted for the construction of seventh-century churches in the south-east of England, though, because of the inexperience of the builders, these were comparatively simple in form. There was usually an apsidal SANCTUARY at the eastern termination and a corresponding vestibule (narthex) at the west. The church of St. Peter and St. Paul, Canterbury and St. Peter-on-the-Walls at Bradwell in Essex are two examples, the latter constructed in 653 using materials quarried from the ramparts of the Roman fort (Othona) on which it stands.

Anglo-Saxon builders did not always understand the structural systems they were attempting to emulate and consequently, in many churches, there were no arcades or aisles, a single (often tentative) opening through the nave wall providing access to any chambers beyond. But there were notable exceptions: the magnificent Church of All Saints at Brixworth in Northamptonshire, for example, which was built by monks from Peterborough in 676 as an aisled basilica with an eastern apse. Brixworth was intended to impress: it is nearly 100 feet in length (30.5 metres) and is one of the largest Saxon

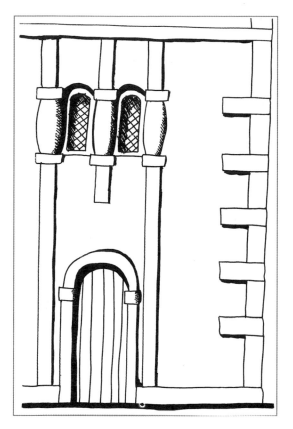

above ground supported by various columns and many side aisles, and adorned with walls of notable length and height surrounded by spiral stairs leading up and down . . .*

The church nave of St. Andrew at Greensted in Essex is believed to date from the mid-ninth century and is the only surviving example of an Anglo-Saxon wooden church with walls of solid oak. It is known that in 1013 the body of King Edmund rested there on its journey to Bury St. Edmunds, however recent tests suggest that the church, with its nave of split oak logs fixed to a wooden sill, may have been constructed 150 years earlier (though the present sill and brick plinth date from a restoration of 1848, as do the dormers in the nave roof).

THE LATER PERIOD

Numerous Anglo-Saxon churches date from the later period, though of the thirty Benedictine monasteries built during the tenth and early eleventh centuries (*see* ANGLO-SAXON CHURCH) most were rebuilt by the Normans and little Saxon work is extant above foundation level. Of the remaining smaller churches, many were remodelled following Viking incursions and most comprise a simple high nave with a narrow arch leading to a rectangular sanctuary, such as the church of St. Laurence at Bradford-on-Avon in Wiltshire. Remodelled from an early eighth-century building, its walls are constructed of large, well cut blocks of local stone. There is a simple high nave and rectangular sanctuary, separated by a narrow chancel arch. Some late-Saxon churches were also built with apsidal sanctuaries: Wing in Buckinghamshire (*c.* 700, rebuilt *c.* 950), Worth in Sussex (*c.* 1030–50) and Deerhurst in Gloucestershire, for instance. Deerhurst, built in *c.* 790, was an important pre-Conquest monastic site. It was twice destroyed by Vikings, rebuilt in *c.* 930 and altered in *c.* 1030 when the tower was added. The west wall of its tall, narrow interior is pierced with sharply pointed window openings, much photographed and 'evocative of a benighted, hence half-conscious, cruelty' (Robert Harbison). Nearby is a late-Saxon proprietary chapel built in 1056 by Odda, a kinsman of Edward the Confessor. Discovered in 1885, it remains immured within the half-timbered farmhouse to which it is attached.

SURVIVING SAXON WORK

Despite the loss of numerous timber churches and the Normans' enthusiasm for demolishing and reconstructing earlier buildings, no fewer than 400 churches contain visible Saxon stonework and many more contain fragments of late-Saxon decorative work or stand on Saxon foundations. Of the larger churches, Brixworth in Northamptonshire (*c.* 680),

buildings from this early period. The apse was destroyed by Vikings and rebuilt in *c.* 1000 when the porch was extended upwards to form the present tower. The blind arcading of the nave, which originally opened onto segmented aisles, consists of 8 foot (2.4 metres) sections of wall connected by round Roman arches.

The formation of internal divisions to provide subsidiary chapels and chambers (*porticus*) was a characteristic of several churches in the south-east and Midlands, such as Wing in Buckinghamshire (*c.* 700, rebuilt *c.* 950) and Breedon on the Hill in Leicestershire (*c.* 680), and may be found even in larger buildings constructed during the tenth and eleventh centuries. The abbey church of St. Andrew was one of four churches built at Hexham in Northumberland by St. Wilfrid in the late seventh century. Although only the Saxon crypt survives (*c.* 680), the *Life of Wilfrid*, written shortly after his death in 709, describes the architectural complexities of the church's interior:

My feeble tongue will not permit me to enlarge here upon the depth of the foundations in the earth, and its crypts and wonderful dressed stone, and the manifold building

St. Laurence, Bradford-on-Avon, Wiltshire.

Deerhurst in Gloucestershire (*c.* 790), St. Peter's at Barton-upon-Humber (*c.* 950, tower *c.* 990 – and sadly 'restored' by English Heritage) and Stow (*c.* 1020), both in Lincolnshire, Worth in West Sussex (*c.* 1030–50) and Breamore in Hampshire (*c.* 1010) are the most impressive. Unusually, the churches at Breamore and Stow were built on a cruciform plan with a central tower, while at Norton in Cleveland

the tower and transepts date from *c.* 990. But none of these churches has retained its architectural integrity and it is the smaller churches, such as those at Bradford-on-Avon in Wiltshire (*c.* 710), Escomb in County Durham (*c.* 680), Brigstock in Northamptonshire (*c.* 700), St. Martin's at Wareham in Dorset (*c.* 1030) and Bradwell in Essex (*c.* 640), which possess a timeless quality, evocative of late

Anglo-Saxon piety. Other good examples of late-Saxon architecture may be found at Boarhunt in Hampshire (*c.* 1060), Bosham in West Sussex (1040–50), Hovingham (*c.* 1020) and Ledsham in Yorkshire (800–1050 with Norman tower) and Great Paxton in Cambridgeshire (*c.* 1020).

Anglo-Saxon work may be recognised by:

(i) Narrow pilaster strips (*lesene*): these have the appearance of projecting, rectangular 'columns', without capital or base, attached to a wall. They are most often found in towers (see below).

(ii) *Long-and-short work*: a primitive method of strengthening corners by inserting long, vertical dressed stones (*quoins*) between horizontal ones.

(iii) Thin masonry or rubble walls (usually) without buttressing. Dressed stone (*ashlar*) was rarely used except for window and door openings, quoins and pilaster strips. Exterior walls were usually rendered.

(iv) Doorway and window openings (these sometimes in pairs) small with flat lintels or crude Roman semicircular arches or triangular architraves with imposts.

Most church ROOFS were thatched and (inevitably) no original Saxon examples have survived. TOWERS (at the west end) and BELLS, both of which are a characteristic of English churches, were added after *c.* 1000 and several have survived from this period, among them: Broughton, Humberside (*c.* 1000), Earl's Barton (*c.* 1020) and Barnack (*c.* 1030) in Northamptonshire, Sompting in Sussex (1040–60), St. Bene't at Cambridge (*c.* 1040), North Leigh in Oxfordshire (*c.* 1050), Barton-upon-Humber, Humberside (*c.* 950, tower *c.* 990) and Bolam, Northumberland (*c.* 1050). Many East Anglian churches have distinctive round towers which may have been built as refuges against Viking raids.

Further reading:

Harbison, R., *English Parish Churches*, London, 1992

Laing, L. and J., *Early English Art and Architecture*, Stroud, 1996

Randall, G., *Church Furnishing and Decoration in England and Wales*, London, 1980

——, *The English Parish Church*, London, 1982 (Spring Books 1988)

Rodwell, W., *Church Archaeology*, London, 1982

——, *The Archaeology of the English Church*, London, 1981

Taylor, H.M. and J., *Anglo-Saxon Architecture* (vols. 1 & 2), Cambridge, 1965

Taylor, H.M., *Anglo-Saxon Architecture* (vol. 3), Cambridge, 1978

Whitlock, D., *English Historical Documents 500–1042*, London, 1955*

Yarwood, D., *Encyclopaedia of Architecture*, London, 1985

ANGLO-SAXON CHRONICLE One of the prime historical sources for the Anglo-Saxon period, the *Chronicle* purports to run from AD 494 to 1154, the year of Henry II's accession to the throne. Much of the earlier material is almost certainly folklore and hearsay, but from the tenth century onwards it is very reliable. There are several versions since various monasteries kept annual records of what seemed to them to be significant events. Later chronicles, such as those of Henry of Huntingdon, Gervase of Canterbury, Ralph of Coggeshall and Roger of Howden, continued the tradition into the later medieval period.

ANGLO-SAXON CHURCH The Roman emperor Constantine's acceptance of Christianity in AD 312 was to have important consequences for the development of the Church in Britain. It ensured that Roman Britain was in part Christian before the end of Imperial rule (in 410) and it led to the conversion of Ireland by Roman missionaries in the fifth century and to the creation of a CELTIC CHURCH which was to be instrumental in later Pictish and Anglo-Saxon conversions. But the Roman Christians left little archaeological evidence of their faith, other than a number of (often enigmatic) Christian symbols in the fabric of their villas, notably at Chedworth and Cirencester in Gloucestershire, Frampton and Hinton-St-Mary in Dorset and Lullingstone in Kent.

Following the withdrawal of Rome, the Church survived in the west, in Cornwall, Ireland and Wales, isolated from the mainstream of Christianity and with its own customs, liturgy and a multiplicity of indigenous 'saints'. Elsewhere, successive waves of migration to Britain from north Germany and Scandinavia introduced a vigorous paganism, the potency of which was to affect significantly later Christian belief. The first Anglo-Saxon settlers were mercenaries who overthrew their British masters and founded their own independent states. Further settlers arrived during the fifth and sixth centuries and by the end of the seventh century three major political and military powers had emerged: Northumbria (in north-east England and the south of Scotland), Mercia (in the midlands) and Wessex (in the south and south-west).

In 597, a Papal mission of forty monks landed on the Isle of Thanet in Kent, led by Augustine (d. 604/5) who was destined to become the first archbishop of Canterbury. Sees were quickly established at Canterbury, London and Rochester and within a few months Christianity was adopted by Ethelbert (d. 616), King of Kent, whose wife, Bertha, daughter of the Frankish king Charibert, was already a Christian.

The year 597 also marked the death of Saint Columba (521–97) who, with his twelve companions, had travelled from Ireland in *c.* 563 and established a missionary base on Iona from where they embarked on the conversion of the far north. But while Christianity had managed to survive in those areas of sub-Roman Britain where Saxon culture had not penetrated, the administration and customs of the CELTIC CHURCH in the north and west differed fundamentally from the Augustinian model in the south. Its priests operated among isolated tribal communities, often in wild and inhospitable terrain, far removed from the influence of Rome. It was of necessity a Church of scattered MONASTERIES and itinerant missions in which the hieratic organisation of the Roman church, with its bishops and dioceses, had little relevance. In *c.* 603 Augustine attempted to reach agreement with representatives of the Celtic Church on differences in discipline and practice, but without success. By 627 Christianity had reached Northumbria and the Celtic Aidan was sent from Iona, at the request of the Northumbrian King Oswald, to be consecrated Bishop of Lindisfarne (Holy Island) in 635. It was from the efforts of Aidan and his followers that the Christianity of most of northern and midland England sprang (*see* SAINTS).

THE PROCESS OF CONVERSION

A remarkable feature of the period was the rapidity with which conversion was achieved. The conversion of a district usually began with the royal household (consequently new bishoprics were often conterminous with tribal territories) and with the founding of a missionary base (*see* MINSTERS): an early ninth-century charter to the minster at Worcester shows that it consisted of nine priests, four deacons and five clerks. Having been advised by Rome that the native population should not be alienated by the imposition of a raw Christian ideology on an already diverse and complex religious culture, the minster priests deliberately chose to preach at sites which had already acquired some local significance: at places of pagan worship (*see* CHURCH SITES) or the meeting places of legislative assemblies (*gemotes*), for example. As regular itineraries were established within an ever-expanding minster territory (*parochium*), so stone crosses were erected at preaching sites and many of these have survived, often beside the churches which replaced them (*see* CHURCHYARD CROSSES). But 'conversion' was rarely universal, for while the aristocracy may have adopted Christianity as its official religion, and while in 664 Bede was able to write 'if any priest happened to come to a village, the villagers immediately gathered together and sought from him the word of life', a formidable element of paganism survived in the customs and practices of the peasantry and is evident, for example, in the uninhibited vigour of later Romanesque carving (*see* HOLY WELLS *and* PAGAN SYMBOLS).

Throughout the first half of the seventh century, disputes concerning the observances of the Celtic and Roman traditions continued to hinder the work of the missions (*see* CELTIC CHURCH *and* EASTER). But, following the Synod of Whitby (664) and the Councils of Hertford (673) and Hatfield (680) common agreement was reached concerning the rights and duties of clerics and monks and the governance of the Church which was reformed on the Roman model, by dividing dioceses and extending the episcopate. The Councils were presided over by Archbishop Theodore (*c.* 602–90) who was appointed to the see of Canterbury in 668 and was chiefly responsible for the organisation of the missionary territories. As a result of his highly effective administration a 'national' Church was created long before the political unification of the country.

A REFORMED CHURCH

The second migration, of Vikings from Denmark and Norway, began with sporadic incursions in the late eighth century followed by systematic plundering and colonisation from *c.* 850. The English kingdoms of East Anglia, Northumbria and Mercia were eventually subjugated but during the tenth century the West Saxon kings retaliated and briefly created an English kingdom, theoretically unified but in practice divided into regions approximating to the old kingdoms and ruled by powerful overlords.

The invasions of the ninth century wrought destruction and disorder in the Church, but reconstruction was begun under Alfred the Great, King of Wessex (871–99) and the mid-tenth century saw a flowering of Anglo-Saxon culture (*see* DARK AGES) and the rejuvenation of large scale monasticism in England – a development which was to affect profoundly the subsequent nature of medieval society. Supported by the Anglo-Saxon monarchy, the Church was purged and strict Benedictine rule imposed by Dunstan (*c.* 909–88), son of a West Saxon nobleman, Abbot of Glastonbury (940) and Archbishop of Canterbury (959) under King Edgar (959–75), with whom he worked to reform both Church and State. The twin pillar of reform was Ethelwold (*c.* 908–84), Bishop of Winchester (963) and compiler of the *Regularis Concordia*, a code of monastic observance, approved by the Synod of Winchester in *c.* 970. A singularly powerful and influential cleric, ecclesiastically puritanical and yet an enthusiastic patron of the tenth-century artistic renaissance, Ethelwold's reformed monastic houses evolved into one of the wealthiest and most powerful forces in England and, under his influence, Winchester became the political and cultural centre of Anglo-Saxon society.

In such a climate, it is hardly surprising that there should be a parallel proliferation of church-building, inspired by the clergy and supported enthusiastically by landowners and magnates, which continued into the eleventh century. An inscription on a sundial at St. Gregory's Minster, Kirkdale in Yorkshire records that Orm rebuilt the church at the time of Edward the Confessor (1042–65) and Tosti, the Earl of Northumberland (1055–65):

> Orm, son of Gamal, bought St. Gregory's minster when it was all broken down and fallen, and he let it be made anew from the ground to Christ and St. Gregory, in the days of Edward the King and Tosti the Earl, and Haward wrought me, and Brand the Priest.

ORGANISATION

By the eleventh century, there were four types of church: headminsters, minsters, daughter churches (*chapelries*) and 'field churches' (*proprietary chapels*). *Headminsters* were the great ABBEYS and CATHEDRAL PRIORIES, centres of diocesan administration, culture and commerce which had grown out of the tenth-century renaissance. In those areas where the process of conversion was incomplete, the minsters (*monasteria*) continued to function as missionary centres where priests lived a communal life and from where they ventured out to preach, to celebrate the Mass and to baptise converts. Ancillary to the minsters, and dependent on them, were daughter churches or *chapelries*, each served by a single priest and strategically located within the minster territory (*parochium*). Chapelries were of two types: those with a burial ground and those without, a distinction which in some cases was perpetuated even into the nineteenth century. While many chapelries were later abandoned as settlements declined, a number continued as dependent churches for several centuries. Others became parish churches or continued as subsidiary chapels within the parochial system.

From the eighth century, landowners also began building chapels on their estates. Indeed, in late Anglo-Saxon England, possession of a proprietary chapel (sometimes described as a *thane's church*) was considered to be an attribute of rank (*see* CHAPELS). Most were served by a priest, who may also have acted as the lord's chaplain, and the estate retained the church's tithes and other dues while the lord exercised proprietorial rights, including the right to appoint a priest (*advowson*). Where proprietary chapels have survived as parish churches, they will often be found in close proximity to one another, especially in towns, or on the periphery of a settlement and close to a former fortified site, manor house or moated enclosure (*see* CHURCH SITES).

Within a district, the ancient pattern of minster and subsidiary chapelries may yet be discernible in surviving documents such as charters, monastic and cathedral records, court proceedings, land grants and bishops' records; in place-names (such as Yetminster, Iwerne Minster and Charminster in Dorset) and church dedications; in the delineation of ecclesiastical BOUNDARIES and in the structure and location of the churches themselves. In many areas, former minster churches retained exclusive rights of baptism and burial or continued to demand dues from their daughter churches even though they had attained parochial status. The former chapelries of Wayford, Seaborough and Misterton in Somerset, for example, continued until the nineteenth century to pay their dues and to bury their dead in the churchyard of the mother church at Crewkerne while, on the patronal feast-day of St. Bartholomew (24 August), the parishioners of Wayford would present the key to their church at the high altar at Crewkerne, thereby acknowledging their subsidiary status. At Bromyard in Herefordshire, late sixteenth-century records provide evidence, not only of the collegiate origins of the parish church (*see* CHANTRY COLLEGES), but also of the survival of the Anglo-Saxon *parochium*: 'the stalls in the choir were not only for the prebends there, but also for the fifteen other priests of the fifteen inferior churches thereabouts which came continuously once a year upon Whitsun monday to help to say service in the collegiate church confessing the same to be the Mother Church'.*

By the Norman Conquest the influence of the 'old minsters' had been superseded by that of the subsidiary churches they had created, and the parish was emerging as the fundamental unit of ecclesiastical administration

See also AUGUSTINIANS, MEDIEVAL CHURCH, PRIORIES, TOWNSHIP *and* WALES (MEDIEVAL CHURCH IN)

Further reading:

Aston, M., *Interpreting the Landscape: Landscape Archaeology in Local Studies*, London, 1985 *

Godfrey, J., *The Church in Anglo-Saxon England*, Cambridge, 1962

Mayr-Harting, H., *The Coming of Christianity to Anglo-Saxon England*, London, 1991

Rodwell, W., *The Archaeology of the English Church*, London, 1981

——, *Church Archaeology*, London, 1982

Thomas, C., *Christianity in Roman Britain to AD 500*, London, 1987

ANIMALS *see* ANTELOPES, APES, BEAKHEAD DECORATION, BEASTS (HERALDIC), BRASSES (MONUMENTAL), CHRISTIAN SYMBOLS, CREATURES, DOGS, DOVES, EAGLES,

EFFIGIES, ELEPHANTS, FISH, GARGOYLES, HART, LAMB, LIONS, PAGAN SYMBOLS, PASCHAL LAMB *and* STAGS

ANKH An Egyptian symbol for life, sometimes found in churches as a decorative motif.

ANNATES The 'first fruits' of an ecclesiastical benefice: the first year's revenues, together with one tenth of the income in all succeeding years, which were originally paid to the Papal curia in England but were transferred to the Crown in 1534 (*see* REFORMATION).
See also QUEEN ANNE'S BOUNTY

ANNEALING OVEN *see* GLASS

ANNO DOMINI (AD) Latin, meaning 'in the year of our Lord'. The current system of dating is based on the theoretical date of the birth of Christ though this is now generally considered to have been several years earlier.
See also GREGORIAN CALENDAR *and* JULIAN CALENDAR

ANNULET A decorative ring and, in heraldic cadency, the mark of a fifth son (*see* CADENCY, HERALDIC).

ANNULMENT *see* NULLITY

ANNUNCIATION OF THE BLESSED VIRGIN MARY A common theme in Christian art, the announcement by Archangel Gabriel to the Virgin Mary that she was to be the mother of Christ is commemorated in the festival of the Annunciation, otherwise known as LADY DAY, on 25 March.
See also FEAST DAYS (FIXED AND MOVABLE) *and* NEW YEAR'S DAY

ANTE-CHAPEL The western end of a (usually medieval) collegiate chapel, originally separated from the choir by a screen or pulpitum.

ANTE-CHURCH An extension at the west end of a church comprising several bays of both nave and aisles.
See also NARTHEX

ANTE-COMMUNION In the Anglican Church, that part of the service which precedes the Communion.

ANTELOPES An antelope may be depicted as a hind, hart, doe or STAG but in heraldry it has the face of an heraldic tiger, tusks, serrated horns, an antelope's body, a lion's tail and tufts down its spine.
See also BEASTS (HERALDIC)

ANTE-NAVE *see* NARTHEX

ANTEPENDIUM *see* ALTARS

ANTHEM In the liturgy of the Church of England there is a place reserved for the anthem, the Anglicised form of the ANTIPHON derived from the Latin motet. In most churches it is the only occasion during a service when the choir alone undertakes the duty of song and an anthem may include passages for solo voices, individually or in combination. The repertory of English anthems is large and contains many noble works as well as much that is banal.
See also CHURCH MUSIC (ANGLICAN)

ANTHEMION *see* DECORATIVE MOTIFS

ANTHROPOIDAL COFFINS *see* BURIALS

ANTI-CLERICALISM Opposition to organised religion, especially the power and privileges of the Roman Catholic Church. In England, it was evident in the fourteenth century when John Wycliffe (*c.* 1329–84) insisted that all men should enjoy a right of access to the scriptures. In the Tudor period, anti-clericalism arose from a variety of causes ranging from a genuine dislike of priestly powers and abuses to a desire to plunder the wealth of the monasteries (*see* DISSOLUTION OF THE MONASTERIES).

ANTIDISESTABLISHMENTARIANISM Opposition to the disestablishment of the Church of England.

ANTIPHON A piece of sacred music sung by two choirs alternately, with each choir (CANTORIS and DECANI) facing each other in the choir STALLS. Also the setting of sentences, usually from the

Scriptures, recited before and after the Psalms and Canticles in the Divine Office (*see* PRECES *and* VERSICLES).
See also ANGLICAN CHANT, CHURCH MUSIC (ANGLICAN) *and* PLAINSONG

ANTIPHONARIUM A collection of sacred chants and the book in which they are kept. This was normally placed on a lectern between the choir stalls.

ANTIPOPE One who proclaims himself pontiff in opposition to the canonically appointed pope.

APES The medieval symbol for a doctor, a chained monkey holding a bottle of urine, is found quite frequently in WOOD CARVING. Although the representation of apes in the fabric of churches is usually allegorical, reminding medieval man of his false pretensions by depicting apes as men 'aping' acts of virtue, their appearance in heraldry is not unknown. In the crest of the fourteenth-century Martyns of Athelhampton in Dorset, an ape is depicted admiring himself in a mirror. The family motto was: *He who looks on Martyn's Ape so Martyn's Ape shall look on Him.*
See also BEASTS (HERALDIC)

APEX STONE (*also* **SADDLE STONE)** The uppermost stone in a gable.

APOPHYGE The concave curve formed where the shaft of a column joins a capital (at the upper end) or base (at the lower).

APOSTASISE To abandon one's religious vocation.

APOSTASY Abandonment of Christianity, notably by one who has taken perpetual vows.

APOSTLES The twelve chief disciples of Christ: Peter, Andrew, James, John, Philip, Bartholomew, Thomas, Matthew, James (the Less), Thaddaeus, Simon and Judas Iscariot. Following Judas's suicide, his place was taken by Matthias. Paul and Barnabas are also referred to as apostles and several other saints have been included from time to time though, in total, there are never more than twelve. In the Church, the leader of a Christian mission may be so described, for example 'St. Patrick, the Apostle of Ireland'.
For the Apostles' emblems *see* CHRISTIAN SYMBOLS.

APOSTLES' CREED, THE A creed is a statement of faith, a formal summary of Christian beliefs or principles. By the end of the fourth century it was widely believed that this particular creed had been composed by the Apostles. By the early Middle Ages it was used in baptism and, at some time between the seventh and ninth centuries, it was adopted for use in the daily offices. In the *Book of Common Prayer* it is prescribed for use at Mattins and Evensong on most days of the year. As with other early creeds, it deals with God the Father, Jesus Christ and the Holy Spirit.
See also NICENE CREED, THE

APPAREL *see* VESTMENTS

APPARITOR An officer of an ecclesiastical court.

APPEALS In the Middle Ages, appeals (by both clergy and laity) to a judicial authority above that of a diocese, were directed to the Pope. From the mid-twelfth century, successive kings attempted to restrict appeals to Rome but they were not abolished until 1534 when Henry VIII made the Court of Delegates the final arbiter in such matters.

APPLIQUÉ Ornamental work in which material (usually fabric) is cut out and applied to the surface of another.

APPRENTICE SUNDAY *see* MOTHERING SUNDAY

APPROPRIATION The annexation of parish TITHES and other endowments to a religious house. Where an institution became rector it received the bulk of the revenues of the living while the parish church was served by a vicar who received a small income.
See also CARTULARY, IMPROPRIATION *and* MEDIEVAL CHURCH

APRIL FOOLS' DAY (ALL FOOLS' DAY) A non-Christian festival, celebrated (before noon) on 1 April, when practical jokes may be played with impunity. Its origins are obscure though there may be a link with *Lud* the Celtic god of humour whose festival occurred at this time.

APRON A shortened CASSOCK worn by bishops, deans and archdeacons.
See also VESTMENTS

APSE A polygonal or semicircular recess characteristic of the early basilicas of the Christian church and introduced into Anglo-Saxon architecture by missionaries from Rome at the end of the sixth century. There is a tall polygonal Saxon apse to the sanctuary of All Saints' church at Wing in Buckinghamshire. The apse was widely used by the Normans, in both domestic and ecclesiastical buildings, but was abandoned by the Cistercians of the twelfth century in favour of the square-ended chancel or chapel.

APSIDAL In the form of an APSE.

AQUAMANILE Ewer in which priests washed their hands during the Mass.

ARABESQUE *see* MORESQUE

ARCADE A range of arches resting on piers or columns. The term is also used to describe the arched division between the nave of a church and its aisles. A *blind arcade* is a decorative arcade attached to a wall.
See also ARCH, BAY, COLUMN, GALLERIES, PIER *and* TRIFORIUM

ARCH A curved series of radiating wedge-shaped bricks or blocks of stone (*voussoirs*) so arranged above an opening that they support one another and are capable of carrying a considerable weight (*see also* LINTEL). The uppermost central block is the *keystone* and the pair of horizontal blocks from which the arch rises on either side of an opening are the *springers*. Between the springers is the notional *springing line* which determines the geometry of the different types of arch. The walling or support on or against which an arch rests is the *abutment* and the width between abutments is termed the *span* (*see also* CAPITAL, COLUMN and PIER). The under-surface of an arch is the *soffit* and the height of the arch, measured between the soffit of the keystone and the centre of the springing line, is known as the *rise*.

Saxon arches were usually of the *triangular* or *mitre* type, formed by a pair of stone slabs joined in a mitre at the top. From the semicircular *classical arch* of ancient Rome derived the Romanesque arch of the early medieval period (popularly known as the 'Norman arch') which was either semicircular (with its centre on the springing line), *segmental* (with its centre below the springing line) or *stilted*

Blind arcading at Much Wenlock Priory, Shropshire.

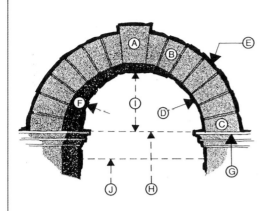

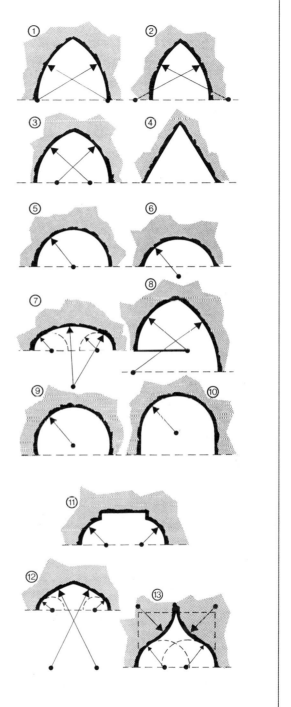

A   Keystone
B   Voussoir
C   Springer
D   Intrados
E   Extrados
F   Soffit
G   Impost
H   Springing line
I   Rise
J   Span

1   Equilateral
2   Lancet
3   Obtuse
4   Triangular
5   Semicircular
6   Segmental
7   Basket
8   Rampant
9   Horseshoe
10 Stilted
11 Shouldered
12 Four-centre
13 Ogee

(with its centre above the springing line). The classical arch is also found in Renaissance and Baroque architecture.

The essence of Gothic architecture was the *pointed arch* (the French *arc brisé* or 'broken arch') which originated in the Middle East and reached western Europe by the twelfth century (*see* VAULTING). Its principal forms were the tall narrow *lancet arch* associated with the Early English style of Gothic architecture; the *equilateral arch*, the radii of which were equal to the span; the *obtuse arch* with a span greater than its radius; the *ogee arch*, characteristic of the fourteenth century; and the *four-centred arch* which is commonly found in buildings dating from the late medieval and Tudor periods.

A *strainer* is an arch which spans an internal space to prevent walls from leaning (the finest examples are those above the crossing at Gloucester Cathedral); *interlacing* consists of semicircular arches which interlace and overlap, especially in Romanesque blind arcading (*see* ARCADE); the *Tudor arch* is an extreme form of the late fifteenth-century four-centre arch in which the upper curves are almost flat; and the *straight arch* is a rectangular opening the lintel of which is composed of radiating voussoirs. There are, of course, numerous other variations including the *rampant arch* in which the springing at either side of the opening is at different levels.

See also ARCHITECTURAL PERIODS *and* DOORS AND DOORWAYS

ARCHAEOLOGICAL EVIDENCE Archaeology, as opposed to antiquarian curiosity, is little more than a century old. Major advances in methodology in the second half of the nineteenth century provided the foundation for a scientific approach to archaeology which has subsequently developed at an increasing rate. Excavation, once practised in order to unearth artefacts, is now directed at the recovery of new evidence.

Antiquarians have studied and recorded evidence relating to the physical history of church buildings since the twelfth century. But it is only recently that full-scale archaeological studies of a select number of church sites have been attempted, bringing together a variety of specialist skills and services.

Just as archaeology is commonly perceived to be concerned with the excavation and recording of ancient remains, so it is taken for granted that those who study structures are architects and those who delve into documentary sources are ecclesiastical historians. But archaeology now embraces all these disciplines – and many more – and has become the 'total study of the material past'.

Similarly, there is no longer an assumption that equates age and rarity with importance. A Victorian chancel is, therefore, of equal significance to the modern archaeologist as a building's Anglo-Saxon foundations: each demands the same degree of meticulous investigation and recording. The practice of concentrating effort and resources on the earliest evidence, to the exclusion of the recent past, is no longer tenable. It is now acknowledged that it is rare for work of any period, no matter how recent, not to reflect influences from the past – including earlier features that have not survived. To consider the evolution of a building by studying the earliest evidence first invites the adoption of errors and omissions that may only become apparent in the later stages of an investigation. By beginning with the present and working back, by peeling away successive layers of history and by devoting equal care and resources to each layer, the archaeologist may arrive at a significantly more complete and accurate picture of a church's development.

But while stratigraphy reveals evidence of sequence, it should be remembered that an undisturbed series of layers, with the oldest at the bottom and the most recent at the top, is rare. More typical is a sequence which provides evidence of phases of rebuilding and periods of abandonment. Context, a term used by archaeologists to describe the position of a particular find in relation to other material, is of prime importance since it is only when such relationships are understood that progress can be made. And this approach is now applied, not only to archaeological excavations, but to all aspects of church investigation – to structures above ground level, to decorative features, monuments, furnishings and artefacts and to documentary and other historical evidence.

Investigations have revealed at least seventeen phases of church building at the church of St. Paul-in-the-Bail, Lincoln and twelve at St. Martin's church, Wharram Percy in Yorkshire. The church at Rivenhall in Sussex, which until recently was assumed to be Victorian, is now believed to be of Saxon origin and constructed on a Roman site. Furthermore, typology (the study of changes in the forms of tools, pottery etc.) may link artefacts from one site with those of another, and the sciences of palaeobotany (the study of vegetation), dendrochronology (growth-ring dating in timber), environmental archaeology (botany, zoology and ecology) and geophysics (notably magnetometry by which the earth's magnetic field is measured together with any effect that buried structures may have on it and resistivity by which the electrical resistance of the soil and any buried features are measured) contribute to the location, dating and interpretation of evidence, as do the techniques of radio-carbon dating, computer graphics, photography (both aerial photography and infra-red) and EDM (electronic distance measurer).

Today, an archaeological survey is a logistical exercise of considerable complexity requiring the services of numerous specialists: documentary historians, architectural historians, art historians, genealogists and armorists, palaeopathologists, radiographers, palaeo-environmentalists, geologists, photographers and conservators together with experts in stone, timber and glass, ceramics, metals and textiles and, of course, an experienced archaeologist responsible for co-ordinating the various stages of an investigation. Following preliminary meetings of incumbent, architect and archaeologist, a FACULTY is obtained and a research strategy agreed. As the investigation proceeds, material is systematically observed, recorded and analysed before a report is drafted and finally published.

Of course, very few parish churches are subjected to such rigorous (and costly) investigation and it is for this reason that the work of the NADFAS Church Recorders groups is invaluable. Their members are not usually experts, and they are able only to record what they see. Nevertheless, such is the thoroughness of their work that future generations of historians will be indebted to this tenacious and dedicated band of enthusiasts.

Further reading:
Brown, A., *Fieldwork for Archaeologists and Local Historians*, London, 1987
Rodwell, W., *Church Archaeology*, London, 1989 (includes a comprehensive bibliography)
——, *The Archaeology of the English Church*, London, 1981
Archaeology and the Church of England, Council for the Care of Churches, 1989
See also COUNCIL FOR BRITISH ARCHAE-OLOGY (CBA), NATIONAL ASSOCIATION OF DECORATIVE AND FINE ARTS SOCIETIES (NADFAS), NATIONAL MONUMENTS RECORD (NMR) *and* ROYAL COMMISSION ON THE HISTORICAL MONUMENTS OF ENGLAND (RCHME)

For the addresses of the above organisations, and of the Council for the Care of Churches, the Historic Buildings and Monuments Commission for England (English Heritage) and the Royal Commission on Ancient and Historical Monuments (Wales), *see* Appendix II.

ARCHAIC WORDS *see* INSCRIPTIONS

ARCHANGELS *see* CHRISTIAN SYMBOLS

ARCHBISHOP *see* CLERGY (CHURCH OF ENGLAND) *and* SIGNATURES, ARCHBISHOPS AND BISHOPS

ARCHBISHOP PARKER'S TABLE The table of prohibited degrees (*see* AFFINITY).

ARCH BRACE *see* ROOFS (TIMBER)

ARCHDEACON *see* CLERGY (CHURCH OF ENGLAND)

ARCHDEACONRY The administrative territory assigned to an ARCHDEACON by a bishop and from which he takes his title e.g. 'Archdeacon of Sherborne'.
See also PROBATE

ARCHDIOCESE A DIOCESE of which the holder is *ex officio* archbishop, e.g. York.

ARCHERY Long grooves may sometimes be found in the stonework of medieval churches, caused by the sharpening of arrow-heads (*see* PORCHES). Practice with the long bow was a statutory requirement in every town and village during the Hundred Years War in the fourteenth and early fifteenth centuries and the churchyard, or an adjacent enclosure, was often used for weekly archery practice at the butts. An English archer handled a bow differently from his European counterpart. Instead of keeping the left hand steady and drawing the bowstring with the right, he kept his right in position and pressed the weight of his body into the horns of the bow. Thus, archers were taught 'not to draw with strength of arms, as divers other nations do, but with the strength of the body'. With rapid advances in the use of firearms the long bow ceased to be strategically effective after Flodden Field in 1513 and yet, with the threat of a French invasion, the statute was revived in 1543 and obligatory practice at the butts on Sundays and holidays continued well into the next century. CHURCHWARDENS often arranged archery contests at the butts after Sunday mass as a means of raising funds for parochial purposes (*see also* CHURCH AND COMMUNITY). Archery butts usually comprised low mounds against which the targets were placed and although similar mounds may still be found in fields or closes, often in the vicinity of a parish church, the only surviving earthworks of certain provenance are those at Wold Newton in Yorkshire where they seem to have provided protection from stray arrows rather than targets. The popular proposition that the church precincts were commonly used for this purpose because of the proximity of yew trees which provided raw materials for bows and arrows is fallacious (*see* CHURCHYARDS). It is more likely that the church was the customary centre of a community's activities and that the enclosed churchyard or close afforded a reasonably safe place within which to practise.

ARCHES, COURT OF The CONSISTORY COURT of the Province of Canterbury which, at one time, met at Bow Church (the Church of St. Mary-le-Bow or St. Mary of the Arches) in Cheapside, London. The name derived from the stone arches of the original eleventh-century church.

ARCHITECTURAL ARCHIVES The principal collection in England of architectural drawings, plans, illustrations and other archival material is at the Royal Institute of British Architecture (*see* APPENDIX II *for address*). The collection includes complete files of architectural magazines and the papers of many architects and architectural organisations.
See also DRAWINGS (ARCHITECTURAL)
Further reading:
Colvin, H.M., *A Biographical Dictionary of English Architects 1660–1840*, London, 1978
Gray, A.S., *Edwardian Architecture*, London, 1985
Harvey, J., *English Medieval Architects, a Biographical Dictionary*, Hove, 1972
Yarwood, D., *Encyclopaedia of Architecture*, London, 1985

ARCHITECTURAL PERIODS The fluctuating fortunes of a community are invariably reflected in the architectural development of its parish church. Indeed, we are as much indebted to those parishes whose comparative poverty has ensured the survival of our oldest Saxon and Romanesque buildings as we are to those whose prosperity inspired the endowment of our great late-medieval churches. Contraction, perhaps in the form of blocked aisles and doorways, is usually indicative of economic decline; whereas expansion, epitomised by ornamentation and the addition of chantry chapels, aisles, transepts, clerestories and ornate towers, indicates the patronage of a prosperous society. Such periods of contraction and expansion may be dated from architectural and documentary evidence.

In 1817 the architect Thomas Rickman (1776–1841) published *An Attempt to Discriminate the Styles of English Architecture from the Conquest to the Reformation* in which he set out the architectural periods – Norman, Early English, Decorated and Perpendicular – which have subsequently become so familiar through repetition, despite repeated attempts to revise the classification. In the present context, Rickman's terms are used when referring to MEDIEVAL ARCHITECTURE, with the exception that *English Romanesque* is preferred to *Norman*.

Listed below are the terms most commonly used to describe architectural periods and styles. None is exclusive, all overlap and several are synonymous. Dates have been arrived at by consensus but they are by no means definitive.

For Saxon (600–1066) *and* early Romanesque (600–1189) *see* ANGLO-SAXON ARCHITECTURE.

For English Romanesque or Norman (1050–1189), Transitional Norman (1145–89), Gothic (1189–

1539), Early Gothic or Lancet (1190–1250), Early English or First Pointed (1170–1300), Decorated, Middle Pointed, Curvilinear, Flamboyant or Geometric (1275–1375), High Gothic (1290–1350) *and* Perpendicular (1350–1539) *see* MEDIEVAL ARCHITECTURE.

For Late Perpendicular, Late Gothic, Tudor Gothic or Gothic Survival (1539–1600), Tudor (1485–1603), Early Tudor (1485–1547), Renaissance (1547–1689), Late Tudor (1547–1603), Elizabethan (1558–1603), Early Stuart or Jacobean (1603–25), Renaissance (1603–89), Carolean (1625–49), Cromwellian or Puritan (1640–60), Classical (1530–1837), Restoration (1660–1770) *and* the introduction of Palladianism *see* SIXTEENTH- AND SEVENTEENTH-CENTURY ARCHITECTURE.

For Classical (1530–1837), Restoration (1660–1770), Baroque (1690–1730), Hanoverian (1689–1837), Queen Anne and Georgian (1702–1830), Palladian (1720–60), Neo-classical (1760–90), Classical Revival (1760–1820), Gothick (1750–1820) *and* Greek Revival (1780–1840) *see* EIGHTEENTH-CENTURY ARCHITECTURE.

For Classical Revival (1760–1820), Greek Revival (1780–1840), Regency (1811–30), Gothic Revival (from *c.* 1820), Victorian (1837–1901) *and* the influence of the Arts and Crafts Movement (from *c.* 1860) *see* NINETEENTH-CENTURY ARCHITECTURE.

See also CLASSICAL ORDER, ROCOCO *and* TWENTIETH-CENTURY CHURCHES
Further reading:
Addleshaw, G. and Etchells, F., *The Architectural Setting of Anglican Worship*, London, 1948
Child, M., *Discovering Church Architecture*, Aylesbury, 1976
Curl, J., *English Architecture: an Illustrated Glossary*, Newton Abbot, 1986
Fletcher, Sir B., *History of Architecture*, London, 1975
Harris, J. and Lever, J., *Illustrated Glossary of Architecture*, London, 1992
Yarwood, D., *Encyclopaedia of Architecture*, London, 1985

ARCHITRAVE (i) A moulded frame round a window or door. (ii) A horizontal beam resting on the tops of columns.

ARCHIVES Church archives, sometimes dating from the medieval period, provide demographic and historical evidence, not only of the evolution of a village community, but also of the gradual divergence of ecclesiastical and civil responsibilities within a parish, culminating in the Municipal

Corporations Act of 1835 and the Local Government Act of 1894. These established parish councils as minor authorities within the local government system in contradistinction to parochial church councils which, since 1919, have exercised (with the incumbent) responsibility for the administration of ecclesiastical parishes (*see* PARISH).

Today, as a consequence of the Parochial Registers and Records Measure of 1978, most DOCUMENTARY SOURCES have been removed from parishes and deposited where they will be better conserved and more accessible to public scrutiny, either in DIOCESAN REGISTRIES or in county record offices.

Archival material deposited at county record offices is usually available for inspection (possibly on microfilm or as transcripts of older material) and includes REGISTERS and the records of parish officials (such as CHURCHWARDENS' ACCOUNTS), TERRIERS, tithe records (*see* TITHES), tithe maps (*see* MAPS) and vestry MINUTES which include BASTARDY returns and the records of WORKHOUSES and OVERSEERS OF THE POOR prior to the Poor Law Amendment Act of 1834.

DIOCESAN RECORDS normally include BISHOPS' REGISTERS, BISHOPS' TRANSCRIPTS, COMPTON CENSUS returns, records of diocesan administration, faculties (*see* FACULTY), SUBSCRIPTION BOOKS, VISITATIONS (ECCLESIASTICAL) and records of ecclesiastical courts (*see* COURTS, ECCLESIASTICAL) together with wills, inventories and other PROBATE documents. Archives from parishes which were formerly dependencies of cathedral chapters or monastic and collegiate foundations or were proprietary churches of great estates will more often be found in national repositories such as the Public Record Office, the British Library, the Royal Commission on Historical Manuscripts, the Library of the House of Lords and the Bodleian Library, Oxford.

Where parish archives remain with an incumbent they should be available for inspection 'at all reasonable hours'. A research fee is usually required (as set out in the Parochial Registers and Records Measure of 1978) though this may be negotiable. Some incumbents are happy to undertake the research themselves but a fee should always be agreed beforehand. Similarly, the records of *church trustees* usually remain with the parish church and it is to the incumbent that an enquiry should be addressed. Other documentary sources which may be kept by a parish include visitors' books, registers of services, gift books, war memorial and churchyard records, parish magazines, village and church histories, collections of sheet music, inscribed Bibles and prayer books and (occasionally) church libraries.

The Society of Genealogists holds a large collection of registers (in transcript form) and Phillimore has published a very useful *National Index of Parish Registers*.

There are ECCLESIASTICAL LIBRARIES at various cathedrals and the archives of St. Paul's are deposited at the Guildhall Library in London. Archives relating to the Province of Canterbury are at Lambeth Palace, London (*see also* FACULTY) and those of the Province of York at the Borthwick Institute of Historical Research at the University of York.

Clerical records will be found in diocesan registries and early appointments of clergy are listed in the *Institution Books* deposited at the Public Record Office (*see also* INSTITUTION). Appointments for the period 1800–40 are listed in *Index Ecclesiasticus* by J. Foster and, from 1858, in Crockford's *Clerical Directory*.

For the addresses of these and other relevant organisations *see* APPENDIX II.

See also ARCHITECTURAL ARCHIVES, CENSUS OF RELIGIOUS WORSHIP (1851), COLLEGE OF ARMS, COUNCIL FOR THE CARE OF CHURCHES, ELECTORAL REGISTER, MAPS, MINUTES, NATIONAL MONUMENTS RECORD, NINETEENTH-CENTURY CHURCH, PARISH CHEST, PHOTOGRAPHS, ROYAL COMMISSION ON THE HISTORICAL MONUMENTS OF ENGLAND, VISITATIONS (HERALDIC) *and* WELSH RECORDS

Further reading:

Emmison, F., *Archives and Local History*, London, 1966

——, *Introduction to Archives*, Chichester, 1977

Foster, J. and Sheppard, J., *British Archives*, London, 1982

Friar, S., *The Batsford Companion to Local History*, London, 1991

Iredale, D., *Enjoying Archives*, London, 1973

Macfarlane, A., *A Guide to English Historical Records*, London, 1983

Richardson, J., *A Local Historian's Encyclopedia*, New Barnet, (rev. 1986)

Riden, P., *Local History: A Handbook for Beginners*, Chichester, 1983

Stephens, W., *Sources for English Local History*, London, (rev. 1981)

Tate, P., *The Parish Chest*, Cambridge, 1969

Thoyts, E., *How to Read Old Documents*, Chichester, 1980

West, P., *Village Records*, London, 1966

——, *Town Records*, London, 1983

ARCHPRIEST (i) In the early Church, a senior cleric who assumed some of the duties and responsibilities of a bishop in his absence. (ii) A term formerly applied to a cleric who presided over the Sunday Eucharist in a group of parishes.

AREA DEAN The urban equivalent of a rural dean (*see* CLERGY (CHURCH OF ENGLAND)).

ARGENT The heraldic term for silver, usually depicted as white.
See also COLOURS, HERALDIC

ARK In church decoration, an ark is that which Noah built to preserve life during the flood. As such it symbolises the Church, while the Ark of the Covenant, usually depicted as a rectangular box overlaid with gold, symbolises the Presence of God.

ARMARIUM A recessed book cupboard or a book store. The rule of St. Benedict stressed the importance of divine reading (*lectio divina*) in the life of a monastery, and time was set aside for this purpose. Most Cistercian *armoria* are in the vicinity of the CLOISTER where the best sunlight for reading would be found in the north alley.
See also AUMBRY and LIBRARIES

ARMARIUS The senior monastic officer (usually the PRECENTOR) responsible for the ARMARIUM and SCRIPTORIUM.

ARMATURE A metal structure used to reinforce tracery, canopies, slender columns or sculptural decoration.

ARMIGEROUS An *armiger* is one who is entitled to bear a COAT OF ARMS by lawful authority and is thereby armigerous.

ARMORIAL BEARINGS A complete heraldic achievement in which all the elements are present i.e. SHIELD, HELMET, MANTLING, WREATH, CREST and (where appropriate) CREST COR-ONET, CORONETS OF PEERS, SUPPORTERS and insignia.
See also ACHIEVEMENT, COAT OF ARMS and HERALDRY

ARMORIAL PANEL Panels of wood or canvas, erected on a church wall for the purpose of displaying heraldic devices. Armorial panels are of three types: MEMORIAL BOARDS, HATCH-MENTS and boards on which the ROYAL ARMS are depicted.
See also MEMENTO MORI

ARMORY (i) A system of personal identification by means of hereditary devices placed on, or associated with, a shield. Armory is generally (and erroneously) referred to as HERALDRY. (ii) A dictionary of coats of arms listed alphabetically by surname: notably Sir Bernard Burke's *General Armory of England, Ireland, Scotland and Wales*, published in 1842 and reprinted by *Heraldry Today* in 1984.
See also BLAZON

ARMOUR see BRASSES (MONUMENTAL) for illustrations showing the development of armour.

The following terms are most commonly used when describing the armour worn by figures in military brasses and EFFIGIES (* see also individual entries).

AILETTES *	shoulder protection
BASCINET *	pointed steel helmet
CAMAIL *	mail protection for neck and shoulders
CHAUSSES	mail leggings
CINGULUM MILITARE *	broad hip-belt
COIF *	mail hood
COUDES	elbow protection
CUIRASS *	back- and breast-plate
CUISSES *	padding for thigh
CYCLAS *	overgarment
FAULD *	protective 'skirt'
GAMBESON *	quilted protective garment
GORGET *	plate armour form of camail
GREAVES	shin-guards
GUIGE	strap supporting shield
HAKETON *	padded protective garment
HAUBERK *	long-sleeved mail shirt
JUPON *	short sleeveless tunic
LAMBREQUIN	see MANTLING
MISERICORDE *	thrusting dagger
PANACHE	crest of feathers
PAULDRON	shoulder-guard
POLEYNS	knee protectors
POMMEL *	rounded end of sword-hilt
REREBRACE	protection for upper arm
ROUNDELS *	protection for armpits
ROWEL *	star-shaped end of spur
SABATON	broad-toed mail 'slipper'
SOLLERETS *	pointed steel shoes
SURCOAT *	sleeveless cloth coat
TABARD *	heraldic coat with sleeves
TACES *	metal strips of 'skirt'
TASSETS *	metal plates to protect thighs
TORSE	see WREATH
TOURNAMENT HELM	see HELMETS
VAMBRACE	protection for forearm
VISOR *	hinged frontpiece of helmet

See also ALWITE, BRASSES (MONUMENTAL), CAMAIL PERIOD, COSTUME, CREST, EFFIGIES, FUNERAL HERALDRY, HELMETS, MANTLING, SHIELDS and WREATH
Further reading:
Borg, A., *Arms and Armour in Britain*, London, 1977
Kelly, F. and Schwabe, R., *A Short History of Costume and Armour 1066–1800*, Newton Abbot, 1972
For the Arms and Armour Society *see* APPENDIX II.

ARMS, COAT OF *see* COAT OF ARMS

ARMS OF OFFICE In HERALDRY, the vertical division of a shield to incorporate the arms of (e.g.) a bishopric to the dexter (the left when viewed from the front) and the personal arms of the incumbent to the sinister (the right).
See also HERALDRY (ECCLESIASTICAL) *and* MARSHALLING

ARMS, ROYAL *see* ARMORIAL PANELS, MEMORIAL BOARDS *and* ROYAL ARMS

ARRIS In architecture, the sharp edge produced at the meeting of two flat or curved surfaces.

ARROWS In Christian art, the symbol of St. Edmund the Martyr (*c.* 840–69), King of East Anglia who, captured by Danish invaders, refused to share his kingdom with a pagan chieftain and was made the target of the Danes' archery practice before being beheaded. In the tenth century his body was translated to Bury St. Edmunds (Suffolk) which became a place of pilgrimage.

ARROW SLITS Medieval castles were defended by means of the longbow and crossbow. Arrows and bolts were released from arrow loops in the towers and curtain walls, the massive thickness of which enabled the castle builders to provide both comparative safety for the defending archer and a wide range of view. This was achieved by constructing an embrasure inside the wall which narrowed to a vertical 'slit' in the exterior masonry. Arrow slits may be found in several church towers, notably the round towers of East Anglia and the defensive refuges of the Welsh and Scottish marches. They should not be confused with turnpike windows, which illuminated staircases, or ventilation slits which were intended to allow the free circulation of air and are commonly found both in church towers and in agrarian buildings such as TITHE BARNS.
See also TOWERS

ARTIFICIAL RUINS Most artificial ruins, 'church' towers, façades and crumbling gateways date from the eighteenth century when they were constructed as Gothic 'eye-catchers': focal points in landscaped parklands. These ornamental ruins, with their chivalric overtones, correspond to the Gothic Revival of domestic architecture and the Romantic Movement in literature, in which 'the classical, intellectual attitude gave way to . . . claims of passion and emotion' (Sir Paul Harvey). Being integral to the geometry of a planned landscape, they should not be regarded as follies. 'When a wide heath, a dreary moor, or a continued plain is in prospect, objects which catch the eye supply the want of variety; none are so effectual for this purpose as buildings. The Mind must not be allowed to hesitate; it must be hurried away from examining into the reality by the exactness and the force of the resemblance' (*Observations on Modern Gardening*, Whately, 1770). The illusion was often enhanced by 'an intermixture of a vigorous vegetation' which 'intimates a settled despair of their restoration' (*ibid.*) and served as a reminder of man's mortality and the transience even of his most noble creations.

Of the true follies, those man-made structures which have no apparent rationale other than to pronounce the eccentricity of the builder, the nineteenth-century replica of Dallington church steeple, Sussex, erected by 'Mad Jack' Fuller, who swore that he could see the original from his home and found that he could not, is just one example of many. Even Sir Thomas Tresham's Lyveden New Bield in Northamptonshire, described as 'the grand-daddy of the English folly', was originally intended as a garden house and banqueting hall though it is of ecclesiastical appearance. Built in the 1590s, this gaunt, roofless building is of cruciform plan which, with its numerous religious panels and inscriptions, provides an unambiguous architectural reference to Tresham's conversion to Roman Catholicism. Tresham's religious obsession is also reflected in his triangular Trinitarian Lodge, a true folly of 1593, the three-gabled walls of which are divided into three panels each decorated with trefoils and other symbols of the Trinity.
See also MAUSOLEUM
For the Folly Society *see* APPENDIX II.
Further reading:
Headley, G. and Meulenkamp, W., *Follies*, London, 1988
Jones, B., *Follies and Grottoes*, London, 1953
Lambton, L., *Beastly Buildings*, London, 1987
Mott, G., *Follies and Pleasure Pavilions*, London, 1989

ASCENSION The ascent of Christ into heaven, witnessed by the Apostles, is a popular motif in Christian art and (according to Acts 1:3) occurred on the fortieth day following the Resurrection. It is celebrated on Ascension Day which is the sixth Thursday (i.e. the fortieth day) after Easter.
See also FEAST DAYS (FIXED AND MOVABLE)

ASCETICISM The word means 'discipline' or 'training' – and was described by St. Benedict as 'the more perfect way' for those who follow God. Asceticism was a system of practices intended to combat vices and develop virtues through severe self-discipline, abstinence and austerity. Early ascetics tended to withdraw from the world, either as solitaries or in communities. In Britain, extreme asceticism was more often found in the Celtic Church than that of Rome. In the Middle Ages, ascetics sometimes joined formal religious orders such as the Cistercians or Austin Canons.

ASHLAR Smooth-faced MASONRY constructed of square-hewn FREESTONE. Also thin slabs of dressed stone used for facing walls over RUBBLE.

ASH WEDNESDAY The first day of LENT, so called from the ancient Roman Catholic custom of sprinkling ashes on the heads of public penitents who were required to commence their penance on this day. Possibly introduced by Pope Gregory 'the Great' (590–604), the ashes were those of the palms burnt on Palm Sunday. The penitents (*pessimi*) were sprinkled with ashes, though those who had committed lesser offences were merely marked on the forehead with the sign of the cross, the officiating minister saying 'Memento, homo, quia pulvis es, et in pulverem reverteris'. The practice was replaced by a general penance by a congregation, symbolised by the imposition of ashes on the heads of clergy and people.
See also QUINQUAGESIMA *and* SHROVE TUESDAY

ASP In Christian art, a small snake, often depicted in a tightly coiled position, and symbolising venal and sexual temptation.
See also CHRISTIAN SYMBOLS

ASPERGES (i) The ceremony of sprinkling consecrated water over the altar and congregation during the Mass. (ii) The sprinkler used for that purpose, usually a perforated ball finial attached by a silver stem to a wooden handle (*see* PLATE). *HOLY WATER* sprinklers and asperges buckets, in which the holy water was carried during the service, may still be found in some parish churches, though (for reasons of security) they are rarely on show. *Holy water* (which may contain a small quantity of salt) was similarly used for other purposes such as ceremonial cleansing, dedications, blessings and exorcisms.

ASPERGILLUM *see* PLATE

ASPERSION In exceptional cases, a method of BAPTISM by which the candidate is sprinkled with HOLY WATER, as opposed to AFFUSION, IMMERSION or SUBMERSION.

ASPIRANT One who aspires to a religious vocation.

ASSAY *see* HALLMARKS *and* PEWTER

ASSUMPTION OF THE BLESSED VIRGIN MARY The belief, dating from no earlier than the fourth century, that the Blessed Virgin Mary 'having completed her earthly life was in body and soul assumed into heavenly glory' (Pope Pius XLL, 1950). Formulated by Gregory of Tours (*c.* 1540–94), it appears to have been widely acknowledged in the western Church by the end of the seventh century. The Feast of the Assumption, which was celebrated on 15 August, disappeared from the *Book of Common Prayer* in 1549.
See also MARY, THE BLESSED VIRGIN

ATHEISM Denial of the existence of God. Before the term AGNOSTICISM came into general use in the nineteenth century, those who denied the possibility of proving the existence of God were also described as atheists.

ATTACHED *see* ENGAGED

ATTAINDER Made after a judgement of death or outlawry on a capital charge, a declaration of attainder by act of Parliament resulted in the absolute forfeiture of all civil rights and privileges. Frequently applied during the Middle Ages in association with charges of treason, when a declaration of attainder implied also a 'corruption of the blood', whereby goods, lands, titles and armorial bearings of an attainted person could not be inherited by his heirs until the attainder had been revoked, also by act of Parliament. Lands, and any rights in them, reverted to a superior lord subject to the Crown's rights of forfeiture. During the Wars of the Roses, acts of attainder were regularly used by one side to liquidate the other. But it is interesting to note that during the period 1453 to 1504, of 397 attainders, no fewer than 256 were reversed. Attainder was abolished as recently as 1870.

ATTIC BASE In classical architecture, a moulded base to a column, characterised by two convex rounded mouldings, the lower one larger than the upper, separated by a broad, concave moulding.

ATTRIBUTED ARMS 'The heralds of the medieval and post-medieval periods shared with artists and writers of the time a sense that the characters of "history" were somehow familiar contemporaries. Just as King Arthur, Charlemagne, Prester John and King David would be depicted in medieval costume and leading medieval lives, so too the heralds determined that, because all persons of consequence in their society were armigerous, so too were the characters of their religion and the heroes of legend and history' (Stephen Friar, *A New Dictionary of Heraldry*).
Coats of arms were devised and attributed to both persons and abstractions. The *Scutum Fidei* (the 'Arms of Faith'), for example, were devised as a symbol of the Trinity and consisted of a diagrammatic representation of the triune nature of

the Holy Trinity in silver on a red field, this being the colour of rulers and princes (*see* CHRISTIAN SYMBOLS). Religious concepts such as the Passion of Christ, the Precious Blood, and the Assumption of the Blessed Virgin Mary were provided with arms, as were the saints and martyrs, the apostles and disciples and the Old Testament prophets and kings. The early heralds were reluctant to attribute arms to Christ, however the Instruments of the Passion – the *Arma Christi* or *Scutum Salvationis* (Arms of Salvation) – were frequently depicted on shields and clearly these were considered to be His personal emblems: 'that gintilman Jhesus . . . Kyng of the londe of Jude and of Jues, gentilman by his Modre Mary, prynce of Cote amure' (*The Boke of St Albans*). The Archangel Michael bore a red cross on a silver field and, not to be outdone, Satan himself bore arms (as a former seraph he was assumed to be armigerous) and to him was attributed a red shield charged with a gold *fess* (horizontal band) between three frogs, a reference from the Book of Revelation: '. . . three unclean spirits like frogs come out of the mouth of the dragon . . . for they are the spirits of devils.' The post-medieval heralds were particularly systematic, beginning with Adam (a plain red shield) and Eve (plain silver). To King David they attributed a gold harp on blue and to Joseph, not a multi-coloured coat as one might expect, but a simple black and white chequered shield.

We should not mock the medieval mind: the need for symbolism was symptomatic of a desperate search for salvation. Great banners of Christ's Passion, the Trinity and the Blessed Virgin Mary accompanied the medieval army into battle and many a warrior emblazoned the *inside* of his shield with religious emblems. Our churches provide abundant evidence in glass and decoration, not only of medieval symbolism, but also of the continued use of many of those devices today.

Identification of attributed arms can be great sport – but beware! There are instances of medieval tombs on which the attributed arms of a patron saint or religious concepts are emblazoned together with inherited quarterings.

See also BADGES, CHRISTIAN SYMBOLS, GLAZIERS' MARKS, HERALDRY, MASONS' MARKS, MERCHANTS' MARKS *and* REBUS

AUDITORY CHURCH A church designed primarily to enable the congregation to see and hear the preacher.

AUGMENTATION, COURT OF Created in 1535, the Court of Augmentation administered the lands, possessions and revenues of the dissolved religious houses and succeeded in augmenting the royal income by £32,000 a year (*see* DISSOLUTION OF THE MONASTERIES). The Court's function was transferred to the Exchequer in 1554.

AUGMENTATION OF HONOUR Augmentations are 'additions' to coats of arms, usually awarded in recognition of signal service to the Crown. They are of two kinds: the first, now rare, being awarded 'by mere grace', the second being won by merit. In the first category are augmentations such as those granted by Richard II to his kinsmen Surrey, Exeter and Norfolk, who were permitted to add the attributed arms of Edward the Confessor to their own. In the second category there are many instances of augmentations granted as rewards for acts of valour or outstanding service. Such augmentations seem to have existed since the earliest days of armory and may appear to 'break the rules' in order to draw attention to the distinction.
See also COLOURS (HERALDIC) *and* HERALDRY
Further reading:
Huxford, J.F., *Honour and Arms*, London, 1984
Scott-Giles, C.W., *The Romance of Heraldry*, London, (rev. 1965)

AUGUSTINIANS (*also* AUSTIN *or* REGULAR CANONS) Communities of clerics who, from the mid-eleventh century in Italy and France, adopted the Rule of St. Augustine of Hippo (354–430) which required strict personal poverty, celibacy and obedience (*see* RULE). Their ethos was formally approved at Lateran synods in 1059 and 1063 and by the early twelfth-century members of these communities, which had spread throughout western Europe, came to be known as *Regular Canons*. Like monks, they were bound to the Divine Office (*Opus Dei*) and led a communal life. But, unlike monks, all canons were priests, their rule was less severe and they were not confined to their houses. The Augustinian habit consisted of a black cassock, white surplice and hooded black cloak and, as a result, they came to be known as the Black Canons. They are also referred to as *Austin Canons*, this being an early English form of Augustine.

The Augustinians arrived in England at the beginning of the twelfth century and by 1200 had established 140 foundations in England and Wales. (These were to rise in number to over 200 before declining to 170 at the Dissolution.) They appear to have selected ancient monastic sites for many of their houses and where there were survivors of an earlier community they sometimes joined it: at Bardsey Island in Gwynedd, for example. Each house was governed by a 'prelate', usually a prior, though there were some two dozen houses, mostly in the Midlands, which were ABBEYS. They appear to have had parochial responsibilities which may explain why so many Augustinian churches and dependent CHAPELRIES have survived, in whole or in part. Examples are Llanthony in Gwent, Cartmel in Lancashire, Bolton and Bridlington in Yorkshire and Waltham in Essex, while the cathedrals of

Bristol, Oxford, Carlisle, Portsmouth and Southwark were all Augustinian foundations (Carlisle became a CATHEDRAL PRIORY in 1133). The Augustinians were noted for their HOSPITALS, of which St. Thomas and St. Bartholomew's (London) were the first and, perhaps, the best known.

Independent Augustinian congregations include the *PREMONSTRATENSIANS* or 'White Canons' who adopted a particularly austere way of life. There were also Augustinian (Austin) Canonesses with over twenty houses in medieval England and Wales, most of which appear to have suffered from inadequate endowments. Most ranked as PRIORIES, though Burnham Canonsleigh in Buckinghamshire and Lacock in Wiltshire were abbeys.

The Augustinian Friars (usually referred to as Austin Friars or the Hermit Friars of St. Augustine) were constituted from three small congregations of English hermits in *c.* 1256. They established forty priories in England and Wales and worked as mendicants within the territories (*limites*) assigned to each house. Their constitution was modelled on that of the Dominicans (*see* FRIARS) and their habit consisted of a long black gown and hood over a white cassock – hence, the Black Friars.

Further reading:

Butler, L. and Given-Wilson, C., *Medieval Monasteries of Great Britain*, London, 1979

AUMBRY (or AMBRY) A secure chest or cupboard in which altar plate and other sacred items and relics were stored. Usually formed within a rectangular recess in a north wall near the altar, several aumbries retain their original oak doors: as at Great Walsingham, Norfolk and Rothersthorpe in Northamptonshire. Today, aumbries are often used to store the Blessed Sacrament (*see* RESERVATION). The term is also used to describe cupboards with more mundane uses: those for storing towels near the monastic LAVATORIUM, for example, and 'civerys' in which the FRATER table furnishings were kept.

See also ARMARIUM, CHEST CUPBOARD, CREDENCE, PISCINA *and* VEILS

AUMBRY LAMP A light, burned constantly in the sanctuary in honour of the Blessed Sacrament. This may be coloured red if suspended above an altar or white if the Sacrament is nearby (*see* LAMPS).

AUREOLE In Christian art, the background of gold which sometimes surrounds a figure as distinct from the NIMBUS (or halo) which surrounds the head.

AUSTIN CANONS *and* **AUSTIN FRIARS** *see* AUGUSTINIANS *and* FRIARS

AVOWESS *see* BRASSES (MONUMENTAL), EFFIGIES *and* VOWESS

AXIAL TOWER A tower located above the crossing of a cruciform church.
See also TOWERS

AZURE *see* COLOURS (HERALDIC)

BACKPLATE The metal plate by which a STOUP, SCONCE, BRACKET etc. is affixed to a wall. Backplates may be plain but are more often decorated in a style corresponding with that of the object which they support.

BACKSTOOL A term, used until the late eighteenth century, meaning a chair without arms. Inventories usually distinguish between the backstool and chair (which was either an *elbow chair* with arms or a *back chair* with sides) and the FALDSTOOL, lowstool and footstool.
See also CHAIRS (SANCTUARY)

BADGES A badge is a simple heraldic device, not associated with a shield or COAT OF ARMS. Some badges were adopted for decorative purposes or to mark personal property, while others (livery badges) were worn on the uniforms of retainers and borne on livery flags at tournaments and in battle (*see* FLAGS *and* LIVERY AND MAINTENANCE). Many

Hungerford

Nevill

badges were simply charges taken from a shield of arms (the white lion of Mowbray, for example) while others were adopted for their hidden meaning or in allusion to a name, title or office. Typical are the mill-sail device of the lords Willoughby, the gold 'drag' (sledge) of the Lords Stourton, the silver ape's clog of William de la Pole, Duke of Suffolk and various stylised KNOTS, the most familiar being that of the lords Stafford. Chimerical creatures were particularly popular (*see* BEASTS, HERALDIC) and many of these were later translated into CRESTS and SUPPORTERS. Magnates often adopted a number of badges: those of the fifteenth-century De Vere earls of Oxford, for example, included the silver five-pointed star (*mullet*) from their arms; a blue boar with gold tusks and bristles (which was also the De Vere crest) and a bottle with a blue cord which may have been a pun on the family name (*de verre* being 'of glass'), though elsewhere this has been attributed to the office of Lord High Chamberlain which was held by John de Vere, Earl of Oxford (*c.* 1443–1513).

Badges were sometimes combinations of devices obtained through marriage and seigniorial alliances or adopted for political purposes. The famous bear 'chained to the ragged staff' of Richard Nevill, Earl of Warwick ('Kingmaker'), is perhaps the most familiar example of two badges forming a single device, while Sir Walter de Hungerford combined his badges of a sickle and a Hungerford knot with the garb (wheatsheaf) of the Peverel family when he married the co-heiress of Thomas Peverel. (Lord Hungerford's seal of 1432 shows two of these devices combined and borne as a crest: *A Garb between two Sickles*.) The combined falcon and fetterlock (manacle) badges of the dukes of York signified the frustrated political aspirations of that house and it was not until Edward, Duke of York (1442–83) became King Edward IV of England (in 1461) that the fetterlock was unclasped and the falcon of York no longer confined.

ROYAL BADGES

Numerous badges have been adopted or inherited by British sovereigns and may be found in the glass and fabric of many parish churches, including those on the former estates of magnates who once enjoyed (or anticipated) royal patronage.

Henry II used the broom plant (*Planta Genista*), which is clearly a pun on the name Plantagenet, as did Richard I who also used the star and crescent device later adopted by King John. Both badges were used by Henry III and by Edward I who also inherited a golden rose device from Eleanor of Provence. Edward II adopted a golden castle (for Castile) and Edward III used many badges of which a sunburst, a tree stock (for Woodstock), a falcon and an ostrich feather were particularly favoured. Richard II also used these, but his favourite badge

Falcon and Fetterlock

White Hart

Rose en Soleil

was the ubiquitous white hart which he inherited from his mother, Joan of Kent.

The Lancastrian Henry IV used a monogram SS (*see* COLLARS), a fire-basket (*cresset*), a red rose and the silver swan of Bohun, each on liveries of white and blue. Henry V used a silver ostrich feather, a chained antelope with the motto DIEU ET MON DROIT and a chained swan. Henry VI adopted the antelope and added a spotted panther to the royal bestiary.

Edward IV's Yorkist badges included the falcon and fetterlock (see above), the sun in splendour, the white rose and the white lion of March, with liveries of blue and mulberry (*murrey*). At various times he also used the black bull of Clarence and the black dragon of Ulster and, following his marriage with the Lancastrian Elizabeth Woodville, he adopted a red and white rose *en soleil* (surrounded by rays of the sun). Richard III used the Yorkist badges to which he added his legendary white boar.

The Tudors, with their white and green liveries, introduced the portcullis of the Beauforts, the red dragon, the silver greyhound and the TUDOR ROSE, a political combination of the Lancastrian and Yorkist roses. Henry VII also used a crowned hawthorn bush, with the cypher HR, to commemorate his exploits at Bosworth Field. Henry VIII added a white cockerel and Mary I a pomegranate for Aragon which she sometimes combined with a Tudor Rose. Elizabeth I used a crowned falcon with a sceptre (for Boleyn), a phoenix, a golden harp for Ireland and a crowned Tudor Rose with the motto 'Rosa sine spina'.

James I inevitably introduced the Scottish thistle and a device which combined the Tudor Rose and thistle beneath the Royal Crown with the motto 'BEATI PACIFICI'. The two kings Charles also used these badges, though Charles II introduced several non-heraldic devices associated with his flight from Worcester, such as the oak wreath and crowned oak tree. Thereafter, successive sovereigns made use of former royal badges, notably combinations of the rose, thistle and shamrock and crowned CYPHERS.
See also HERALDRY, REBUSES *and* ROYAL ARMS
Further reading:
Fox-Davies, A.C., *Heraldic Badges*, John Lane, 1902
Friar, S., *Heraldry for the Local Historian and Genealogist*, Stroud, 1992

BAKEHOUSE (PISTRINUM) A monastic bakehouse was generally located in the outer court, usually near the granary and mill. Huge quantities of bread were required in the larger monasteries, not only to feed the community, but also for hospitality and alms. In addition to the great bakehouse, there was often provision within the church itself for the baking of the 'single bread' – the unleavened bread used at the Mass.
See also BREAD OVEN

BALDAC(C)HINO (*also* BALDACHIN, BALDAQUIN *and* UMBRACULUM) A cloth CANOPY above an altar or bishop's throne (*cathedra*). Sometimes (incorrectly) described as a *ciborium* which is a solid canopy or *tester* of wood, stone or metal. The baldacchino, originally a medieval feature, was re-introduced into the English church by the architect Sir Ninian Comper (1864–1960). From the Italian for a richly embroidered cloth, the word originated in *Baldacco* the Italian form of *Baghdad* where the fabric was made.
See also ALTAR CANOPY *and* ALTARS

BALDRIC In this context, a thick leather thong by which a clapper is attached to a bell.

BALE TOMB *see* TABLE TOMBS

BALLFLOWER ORNAMENT A decorative motif (especially from the medieval Decorated period) consisting of small, widely-spaced spheres in a concave moulding, each carved with a crude trefoil-like 'floret'.
See also DECORATIVE MOTIFS *and* MEDIEVAL ARCHITECTURE

BALUSTER A short pillar with a curving, convex outline. Used to describe the shape of vessels, the stems of candlesticks, incense boats, finials etc. and the balustrades of altar and communion rails, staircases, copings etc.
See also BALUSTRADE

BALUSTER FONT A font supported on a curvilinear shaft, usually dating from the late seventeenth or eighteenth century.

BALUSTRADE A series of short pillars or posts (*balusters*) supporting a rail and standing on a base (*string*) as in a parapet or altar rail, or in STAIRCASE construction.

BANGOR, USE OF No trace remains of the pre-Reformation liturgical 'Use of Bangor' referred to in the 1549 *Book of Common Prayer*. It seems likely that it would have retained at least some vestiges of the ancient Celtic liturgical tradition.
See also CELTIC CHURCH *and* SARUM, USE OF

BANNER *see* FLAGS

BANNERET *see* KNIGHT BANNERET

BANNEROL *see* FLAGS *and* FUNERAL HERALDRY

BANNER-STAVE LOCKERS The long staves of gonfannons and crucifixes, which were such a feature of medieval processions, were often stored in a tall, narrow recess formed for that purpose in a church wall. The best examples, some up to 3.6 metres (12 feet) high, are to be found in East Anglian churches, such as that at Barnby in Suffolk which retains its original door.
See also FLAGS

BANNS OF MARRIAGE An announcement in church, usually made on three successive Sundays, of an intended marriage in order to provide an opportunity for objection. Banns are usually read from the pulpit in the parish (or parishes) in which the parties reside and, since 1754, are recorded separately in the registers (or in separate volumes). The procedure (which is regulated by statute) is acknowledged in the *Book of Common Prayer* and was first ordered in England in 1200, in order to prevent possible consanguinity, and confirmed throughout Christendom by the Lateran Council of 1215.

See also GEORGE ROSE'S ACT, HARDWICK'S MARRIAGE ACT, MARRIAGE ACT, MARRIAGE LICENCES *and* REGISTERS

BAPTISM The sacramental rite by which a candidate is admitted to the Christian Church. Infant baptism may also be an occasion of *christening*: the giving of personal names (*christian names*). In the early Church baptism, which required total SUBMERSION, was normally conferred by a bishop. The ceremony was associated with CONFIRMATION and participation in the Eucharist and, from the second to the fourth centuries, was only conferred at Easter and Pentecost. Since at least the third century, children born of Christian parents have been baptised in infancy (*paedobaptism*) though in the fourth century it was also common for baptism to be deferred until death was imminent because of the perceived impossibility of the remission of post-baptismal sins. (This practice was superseded by the development of the penitential system and widespread infant baptism.) From the eleventh and twelfth centuries, submersion was replaced by IMMERSION (or, occasionally, ASPERSION) and this is reflected in the size and shape of contemporary FONTS, several of which have survived.

It has always been recognised in ecclesiastical law that a layman can baptise in an emergency, indeed in the Middle Ages midwives were licensed by bishops with that eventuality in mind and were advised that they should under no circumstances neglect baptism in the presence of witnesses if there was any likelihood of a child dying before the arrival of a priest.

Unlike the pregnancies of the peasantry, those of the medieval nobility and gentry were occasions for ceremonial, especially in the later stages. Some four to six weeks before the anticipated birth, the lady would 'take to her chamber' and was thereafter attended only by women. Midwives, including a number of experienced matrons, assisted in the labour – an anxious time since the risks for both baby and mother were considerable. For the same reason baptism usually took place on the day a child was born, the priest, GODPARENTS (*sponsors*) and guests having been summoned when labour began. In about 1482, Sir William Stonor set down the arrangements for his child's baptism: 'to lead the child my brother Thomas and my brother Rokys; to bear the salt Thomas Lyne; to bear the basin John Doyly; to bear the gifts Edmund Romsey . . .'. The baby would be carried from the 'birthing chamber' to be blessed at the font (*see* CHRISM *and* UNCTION), where it was undressed and immersed with the help of godparents, before being presented at the altar for confirmation. The mother would not be present: no woman was permitted to enter a church after she had given birth until she had been 'churched' (*see* CHURCHING OF WOMEN).

Like marriages and burials, baptisms were occasions for the re-affirmation of a family's status in society by means of ceremonial, heraldic display and lavish hospitality (*see* MATRIMONY *and* BURIAL). Many parents strove to strengthen or extend kinship by inviting powerful patrons to be godparents, usually two of the same sex as the child and one of the opposite sex. The chief godparents usually gave the child its name – often his or her own – though this was not an invariable practice, a popular alternative being to name a first male child after its father. Becoming a godparent created a spiritual kinship with the child and its parents which was recognised by the Church and precluded a future marriage among the parties. The mother remained in her chamber during the forty days following the birth before proceeding to the solemn ceremony of *churching*, a form of thanksgiving and purification after childbirth.

Since the Reformation, baptism has followed the order set out in the *Book of Common Prayer* (or, since 1980, in the *Alternative Service Book*) which is effectively a simplified version of the Roman catholic rite. AFFUSION is now more common than immersion though godparents continue to assume a responsibility for the Christian upbringing of the child and make the same promises of renunciation, faith and obedience in the child's name.

See also HOLY WATER *and* REGISTERS

BAPTISMAL SHELL A saucer-like vessel, shaped and decorated in the form of a shell, with which water is poured over the head in BAPTISM.

See also AFFUSION

BAPTISTERY That part of a church in which BAPTISM is administered. From the third century the baptistery was often a separate, polygonal building west of the church, containing a large basin below ground level in which the candidate was submerged. An increase in infant baptism from the end of the fourth century led to the widespread practice of AFFUSION and the use of FONTS which were placed within the church, usually (though not invariably) near the south door, though many were later removed to the space beneath a (west) tower.

BAPTISTS The Baptists are one of the largest Protestant bodies, tracing their origin from John

Smythe (1554–1612), a SEPARATIST exile in Amsterdam who, in 1609, reinstituted the 'Baptism of conscious [adult] believers' and thereby reaffirmed his belief in the individual's responsibility to work for the salvation of his soul. The first Baptist church in England (in Newgate Street, London) consisted of the members of Smythe's church who returned from the Continent in 1612 under the leadership of Thomas Helwys (1550–1616). From this derived a number of other churches, known as General Baptists, and in 1633 a group of Calvinistic London Separatists established the Particular Baptist churches whose members believed in predestination and individual redemption. During the seventeenth century many Baptists were associated with radical spiritual and political movements and were persecuted until the Toleration Act of 1698. With the formation of the New Connexion in 1770, the General Baptists divided, the Old Connexion becoming the *Unitarians*. In 1813, the Baptist Union encouraged greater co-operation among the various branches and in 1891 the Particular Baptists and the New Connexion formed the Baptist Union of Great Britain and Ireland.

BARBETTE *see* COSTUME

BARGE-BOARDS Possibly originating in the medieval *bargus*, meaning 'gallows', a barge-board is hung from the roof projection (the 'barge') on the gable-end of a building in order to protect the otherwise exposed ends of roof timbers. Medieval and Tudor barge-boards were often elaborately carved, though few originals remain, and similar ornamentation became a feature of the Gothic Revival of the mid-eighteenth and nineteenth centuries.

BARNS The word barn is derived from the Old English *bereærn* meaning 'barley house', for barley was the chief crop of the Anglo-Saxon farmer. Barns, constructed in a variety of sizes, styles and materials, are often difficult to date and may have other buildings added to them. Though intended primarily to store produce, they were used for a multiplicity of purposes and enabled farmhands to carry out many essential tasks under cover in inclement weather. They were used as shippens (for milking), for sheltering calves and for protecting

Medieval tithe barn at Bradford-on-Avon, Wiltshire.

ewes at lambing time. Others were provided with first-floor hay lofts and pigeon lofts, constructed within the roof gable, and some incorporated separate domestic quarters, complete with a hearth and chimney, as in the late medieval barn at Hales Hall, Hales in Norfolk.

Many parishes once possessed a tithe barn but these were rarely built of durable materials and few have survived (*see* TITHES). Most of the magnificent buildings which we now describe as tithe barns were constructed by monastic communities to store the produce of their estates and granges and the tithes of their appropriated parishes.

In the south and east of England medieval barns were usually of timber construction but elsewhere they were generally built of stone beneath a timber-framed roof with thatch or stone tiling and with narrow vertical openings in the walls for ventilation. Both in plan and elevation, these massive barns are similar to churches with their lofty 'naves', heavily buttressed walls, aisles and 'transepts' (*midstrays*) with tall double doors providing vehicular access to the threshing floor. This was usually constructed of closely fitted two inch planks of oak or elm and the draught between the pairs of doors served to reduce the dust during threshing and to separate the heavier grain from the chaff. The great fourteenth-century barn at Bradford-on-Avon in Wiltshire has two pairs of double doors, while the abbey barn at Glastonbury in Somerset is of cruck-frame construction. There are two notable fourteenth-century tithe barns in Oxfordshire at Church Enstone and Swalcliffe and splendid examples from the fifteenth century at Abbotsbury in Dorset, originally 82 metres (270 feet) in length, and Ashleworth in Gloucestershire.

Following the DISSOLUTION OF THE MONASTERIES, many monastic buildings were converted to agrarian use, such as the 'priory barn' at Latton in Essex which was created out of the ruins of the early fourteenth-century crossing of the priory church, abandoned in 1534. Long open-sided barns, often with magnificent thatched roofs and wooden floors supported on staddle stones (shaped like mushrooms to prevent vermin from entering), were popular throughout southern England from the sixteenth century to the eighteenth when they were used for storing straw after threshing. The Gothic Revival of the late eighteenth and nineteenth centuries inspired the construction of a number of 'tithe barns', the best known of which is Augustus Pugin's remarkable 'medieval' barn at Milford in Surrey. Recently, many ancient barns have been converted to domestic use – often with a conspicuous absence of architectural or historical sensitivity.

Further reading:

Hughes, G., *Barns of Rural Britain*, London, 1985

BARON *see* PEERAGE, THE

BARONET This hereditary English rank was created by James I in 1611 with the objective of raising money to support troops in Ulster. The 'honour' cost the first recipients £1095 and they were granted the prefix Sir and Lady (or Dame) with precedence above knights. In 1625 a baronetage of Scotland was established to provide funds for the colonisation of Nova Scotia and both creations lasted until 1707 when they were replaced by the baronetage of Great Britain. In 1619 the baronetage of Ireland was created and on 1 January, 1801 both the baronetage of Great Britain and that of Ireland were replaced by the baronetage of the United Kingdom. The helmet in a baronet's coat of arms is that of a knight, facing forward and with an open visor (*see* HELMETS (HERALDIC)). Baronets of England, Ireland, Great Britain and the United Kingdom have as their badge the 'bloody hand of Ulster', a red hand on a white shield or *canton*, borne as an augmentation in their arms. Baronets of Scotland wear a badge comprising the shield of arms of Nova Scotia and this is depicted suspended from a tawny-coloured ribbon beneath the shield in their coats of arms.

Further reading:

Cokayne, G., *Complete Baronetage*, London, 1906 (reprinted 1982)

Friar, S. and Ferguson, J., *Basic Heraldry*, London, 1993

Pendant badges of baronets of the United Kingdom (left) and of Scotland (right).

BAROQUE *see* EIGHTEENTH-CENTURY ARCHITECTURE

BARREL ROOF *see* ROOFS (TIMBER)

BARREL VAULT *see* VAULTING

BARTIZAN A nineteenth-century term coined to describe an embattled turret projecting from the top of a tower.

BARTON A place-name element from the Old English *bere* or *bær-*, meaning 'barley', to *beretun* or *bærtun*, meaning 'granary farm'. The term was widely applied to a demesne farm and in particular to a monastic GRANGE which may have supported a chapelry. The proximity of a 'barton' place-name to a parish church may, therefore, suggest that the latter originated in a dependent chapelry of a monastic foundation.

BASCINET A plain helmet with a pointed crown (*see* HELMETS (HERALDIC)).

BASE An architectural term used to describe the base of a COLUMN or PIER between the shaft and the pedestal or pavement.

In the CLASSICAL ORDER an *attic base* is a concave moulding (*scotia*) between two convex mouldings (*tori*). A *Tuscan base* is a concave moulding with a fillet above. A third type has two small convex mouldings (*astragals*) with a concave moulding above (*scotias*) and a large convex moulding below (*torus*).

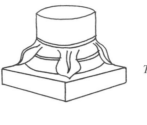

Twelfth Century

Thirteenth Century

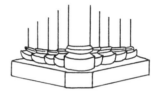

Fourteenth Century

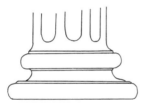

Attic Base

Eleventh-century Romanesque bases usually consisted of a quarter-round moulding on a square plinth. In later work, the angles between the square and rounded sections were sometimes filled by carved decorative foliage or even animals. Some resemble the classical attic base (see above), a style which was commonly used in the Early English period of Gothic architecture (*see* MEDIEVAL ARCHITECTURE). From this developed a variety of elaborately moulded bases set on deep pedestals which were often octagonal. In the early fourteenth century bases were composed of triple rolls which were later replaced by ogee mouldings. In the Perpendicular period, bases were tall and slender and finely proportioned, usually with roll mouldings at the top and a double ogee and further rolls beneath. Bell-shaped bases on octagonal plinths are a feature of this later period.
See also CAPITAL

BASE, IN *see* POINTS OF THE SHIELD

BASILICA An early form of church, entered by a narrow porch (*narthex*) and consisting of a nave and two (sometimes four) colonnaded aisles with a CLERESTORY above and an apsidal eastern termination with a raised altar. In a true basilica walls are not reinforced and are therefore unable to carry a stone vault. The original Basilica was one the the principal judicial and commercial buildings of ancient Rome. The term is commonly used to describe an aisled church with a clerestory.

BASILICAN In the present context, the term implies a simple rectangular plan with a nave that is both higher and wider than the aisles, from which it is usually divided by colonnades, and with an APSE at the eastern end.
See also ANGLO-SAXON ARCHITECTURE

BASILISK *see* BEASTS (HERALDIC)

BASKETWORK A decorative motif of interlaced lines.

BAS-RELIEF Sculpture or carving in low-relief.

BASTARD FEUDALISM *see* LIVERY AND
MAINTENANCE

BASTARDY

CANON AND COMMON LAW

Strictly speaking, a bastard was the base child of a
father of gentle or noble blood but the term is
applied more generally to an illegitimate child.

Bastardy was a fairly public fact of life in
medieval England. It is not unusual, therefore, to
find references in documents and monuments to a
noble illegitimate half-brother who was equally as
distinguished as any of the legitimate line. A bastard
was a child born out of wedlock or of a couple
whose marriage was later found to be invalid. Under
the law, a bastard was not of inferior status but, since
he was 'the son of no-one' (*filius nullius*), he could
not be heir to his parents, neither could he inherit
property, even if he was acknowledged as their child.
(One strange consequence of this principle was that
the illegitimate son of a villein was legally incapable
of inheriting his father's status and therefore became
a free man on his father's death.) There was also a
presumption at Common Law that children borne by
a wife were fathered by her husband and were
therefore legitimate. Because marriage was a
sacrament, the validity or otherwise of a marriage
was determined by Canon Law while questions of
inheritance were brought before the secular courts to
be determined according to the Common Law.
Inevitably, the two systems sometimes contradicted
one another. The Common Law, for example, held
that children born out of wedlock could not be
legitimated by the subsequent marriage of their
parents, while Canon Law decreed that this could be
so. Similarly, Canon Law held that, where a
marriage was entered into 'in good faith' but later
found to be invalid, any children born prior to the
nullification of the marriage were deemed to be
legitimate. In such cases, the Courts of Common
Law would seek to establish only whether a child
was born in or out of wedlock. The question of
legitimacy was determined by the Church courts,
even though the verdict may have been contrary to
the principles of the Common Law.

See also BETROTHAL

PAROCHIAL MEASURES

An act of 1576 enabled Justices to imprison the
parents of an illegitimate child and a further act, of
1610, provided for a mother to be imprisoned unless
she could provide securities for her good behaviour.
Usually, an illegitimate child would receive the same
settlement rights as its mother but, if the father was
from another parish, both child and mother would be
settled there if the parents subsequently married. An
act of 1733 obliged a mother to declare that she was
pregnant with an illegitimate child and to reveal the
father's name. Parish officers would then attempt to
obtain a bond of indemnity from the father which

*Marks of Distinction: 1 Sir John de Warren;
2 Bordure wavy; 3 Beaufort; 4 Scottish abatement;
5 Baton sinister*

would provide for maintenance to be paid, either as
a lump sum or by instalments. Vestry minutes often
contain records (*Bastardy Returns*) of proceedings
against fathers for the maintenance of illegitimate
children, as do the records of Quarter Sessions from
1844 when mothers were permitted to apply to the
courts for maintenance orders.

ILLEGITIMACY AND HERALDRY

The historical concept of bastardy and the use of
special heraldic devices (*marks of distinction*) to
signify illegitimacy continue to attract debate.
Although in England such marks are theoretically
'abatements of honour' which 'debruise' a coat of
arms, in the Middle Ages to be related (no matter
how tenuously) to the Crown or to the nobility was
considered a privilege worth advertising. Neither did
marks of distinction necessarily imply the
illegitimacy of the armiger who bore them: often

they were intended to indicate, not that he was personally illegitimate, but that he was not in legitimate line of succession,

Contrary to popular belief it is not the *bend sinister* which denotes bastardy but the *bordure wavy* which has been in use since the eighteenth century and which replaced the *bendlet sinister* for this purpose. Other charges have been used: the *canton* of Sir John de Warren, natural son of the Earl of Surrey (1347), for example, which bore his maternal arms. The *baton sinister* (erroneously called a 'bar sinister' by novelists) has almost invariably been used to denote illegitimacy in the English royal family, though there have been notable exceptions particularly during the Middle Ages when there were few established heraldic conventions relating to bastardy. The Beauforts, for example, the illegitimate line of John of Gaunt and Katherine Swinford, following their legitimation in 1397, adopted the royal arms within a *bordure* of the Lancastrian colours – silver and blue.

BATH STONE Oolitic limestone quarried in northern Wiltshire where it occurs in beds of up to 10 metres. When quarried it is damp (with 'quarry sap') and is easily cut and carved before being seasoned. This pale, golden stone was widely used for church building throughout the Middle Ages and the sixteenth century. In the eighteenth century Bath Stone was used in a number of major projects, notably the rebuilding of Bath as a fashionable neo-Roman city.

BATTER A wall with an inclined face.

BATTLEMENT A crenellated parapet at the top of a wall, the indentations being *embrasures* and the raised section *merlons*. Both were originally finished with a coping though these are sometimes missing.

BAY (i) A vertical section of wall between columns, piers or buttresses or a division of a vaulted or timber roof (*see* ARCADE, BUTTRESS, CLERESTORY, COLUMN, PIER *and* TRIFORIUM). The Normans introduced the concept into their larger churches where nave walls were articulated into bays, each separated by a tall vertical shaft which extended from floor to ceiling. With the introduction of stone vaults, this shaft (or group of shafts) terminated in a CAPITAL which supported the vault. The vault was also divided into bays by ribs which splayed upwards from the capital (*springing*) in a variety of forms (see VAULTING). (ii) A recess in a room, especially one formed by a projecting window.

BAYLEAF *see* DECORATIVE MOTIFS

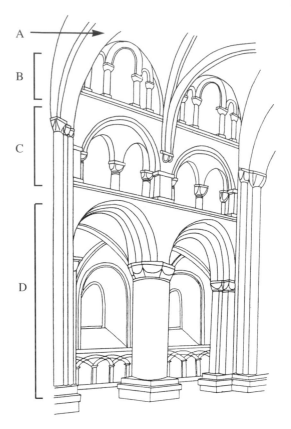

A Nave vault; B Clerestory; C Tribune or triforium; D Nave arcade

BEAD (i) Originally a prayer (also *bede*) but later applied to the component parts of a necklace which were used to assist the memory when reciting the ROSARY, hence 'telling beads' (*see* BEDESMAN). The famous 'Syon Beads', for example, were rosaries of either five or sixty-three beads which could be obtained from the Bridgettine double house of Syon (Twickenham, Greater London) in the fifteenth century (*see* INDULGENCES). Special prayers were prescribed for their use and various symbolic meanings ascribed to the number of beads and even to the number of words in the text of the devotions. In a manuscript, now in the British Library (Harley 494), five short prayers are given, each to be followed by a 'refrain' which was to be 'sayde on every bede':

O swete blessyd Jheus for thi holy name and thy bytter passion, save us from synne and shame and endless damnacion and bryng us to thi blysse. Amen.

In a further manuscript (Harley 541) there is also a

list of indulgences which accompanied the saying of additional prayers:

> The pardon of Syon Bedez. For every paternoster CCCC dayez
> For every Ave Maria CCCC dayez
> For every credo CCCC dayez
> The summe of the pardon to the hole Sawter is
> 1 x Mi vij et ijC dayez

(ii) A decorative motif (*see* DECORATIVE MOTIFS).

BEAD AND REEL *see* DECORATIVE MOTIFS

BEADSMAN *see* BEDESMAN

BEAKER A tall drinking vessel with a pronounced lip but no handle.

BEAKHEAD ORNAMENT Romanesque ornamentation consisting of mythical birds' and beasts' heads with pointed beaks or tongues (*see* MEDIEVAL ARCHITECTURE).

BEAM A long piece of timber (or other solid material) forming one of the main structural members of a building. (*For* collar-beam, hammer-beam, tie-beam, etc. *see* ROOFS (TIMBER).)

BEASTS (HERALDIC) The vigorous late-medieval interpretation of beasts, birds, fish, reptiles and chimerical creatures is, for many, the quintessence of HERALDRY. Heraldic beasts and monsters are commonly found carved and painted in the tombs, monuments and architectural features of our medieval and Tudor churches. When not associated with a shield they may be mistaken for allegorical or religious images or vernacular ornamentation. Heraldic beasts are depicted in a variety of postures (*attitudes*), the most common of which are illustrated on page 41.

THE LION
In the Middle Ages, the lion was considered to be the embodiment of courage, strength and nobleness, the King of Beasts and a fitting symbol of kings and princes. One of the earliest examples of hereditary arms is that of William Longespée, natural son of King Henry II, who bore six gold lions on a blue shield as did his grandfather, Geoffrey of Anjou. In early heraldry, what is now *a lion passant guardant* was described as a leopard (hence 'the leopards of England' in the royal arms), indeed any lion that was not *rampant* was blazoned *leopardé*. According to the bestiaries, lion cubs were born dead and remained so for three days whereupon their father breathed into their faces and gave them life. For this reason, the lion is associated with Christ risen from the dead and is often depicted in church carvings as fighting with the devil in a dragon's form. The lion is of such a noble and compassionate nature that he will not attack a stricken man and is angered only when wounded. He fears nothing except a white cockerel and if he is sick he is cured by eating a monkey. The winged lion represents St. Mark the Evangelist, being one of the four beasts 'round about the throne' which 'rested not day and night' (Revelation 4 vs. 6–7).

THE EAGLE
The eagle was the standard of the Roman legion. In heraldry it is considered to be pre-eminent among the birds, and Charlemagne is said to have adopted an eagle as his device when he was crowned Holy Roman Emperor in AD 800. Until recently, LECTERNS in the form of eagles were to be found in nearly every church; with wings open as in flight they carried forth the Word and the Light of the Gospel. The eagle's suitability for such a task is explained in the medieval *Book of Beasts*: 'When the eagle grows old and his wings become heavy and his eyes become darkened with a mist, then he goes in search of a fountain, and, over against it, he flies up to the height of heaven, even into the circle of the sun [symbolising Christ], and there he singes his wings and at the same time evaporates the fog of his eyes in a ray of the sun. Then at length taking a header down into the fountain, he dips himself three times in it, and instantly he is renewed with a great vigour of plumage and splendour of vision.' (trans. T.H. White, London, 1954)

CHIMERICAL CREATURES
Most chimerical creatures arrived in European heraldry through the medieval bestiaries and many originated in classical mythology. The *centaur*, for example, which has the body and legs of a horse and a man's trunk, arms and head (when holding a bow and arrow it is termed *sagittary* or *sagittarius*); the

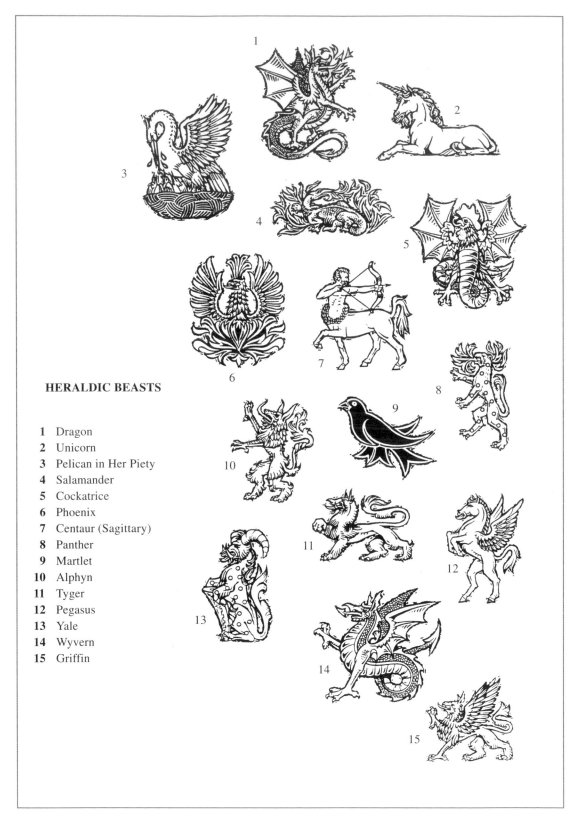

HERALDIC BEASTS

1 Dragon
2 Unicorn
3 Pelican in Her Piety
4 Salamander
5 Cockatrice
6 Phoenix
7 Centaur (Sagittary)
8 Panther
9 Martlet
10 Alphyn
11 Tyger
12 Pegasus
13 Yale
14 Wyvern
15 Griffin

Pegasus, the beautiful flying horse of the Knights Templar, which became the symbol of fame, eloquence and contemplation; and the *salamander* which, when frightened, would exude a milky substance that moistened its skin and enabled it to extinguish fire.

The *tyger* has the body of a wolf with a thick main, a lion's tail, massive, powerful jaws and a pointed snout. The tyger comes from Hyrcania and was famed for its swiftness by the Persians who named their river after it. The female tyger was a devoted mother but could be deprived of her young by placing looking glasses in her way 'whereat she useth to long to gaze . . . and so they escape the swiftness of her pursuit'. Because of this the tyger is often depicted gazing into a mirror. The *alphyn* is similar to the tyger but stockier and with tufts of hair on its body and a thick main. It has a long thin tongue, long ears and a knotted tail. The heraldic *antelope* has a tyger's head, tusks, serrated horns, an antelope's body, a tufted spine and a lion's tail.

The Egyptian *phoenix* was believed to live for five centuries. At the approach of death it would fly to Arabia and hide itself in a nest of sweet-smelling spices which burst into flames when fanned by the bird's wings. The phoenix was burned to ashes but after three days a small worm appeared which grew into a new phoenix. Inevitably, it was adopted as a Christian symbol of resurrection and immortality.

The *griffin* combines the attributes of the king of beasts and the king of birds. It has the body and ears of the lion and the head, wings and talons of the eagle. It was associated with the gods of Minos and Greece and was an animal of the sun and of justice and was the guardian of treasure. It has recently been suggested that the griffin may have originated in the beaked skeletons of the *Protoceratops*, a four-legged bird-like dinosaur which once inhabited the Gobi Desert, a region rich in gold deposits and crossed by ancient trade routes. There is in heraldry a separate beast called the *male griffin* which dates from the post-medieval period. This has no wings but spikes protrude from its body like rays.

The heraldic *panther* is termed *incensed*: having flames issuing from its ears and mouth. In the bestiaries it is described as being both beautiful and kind, and when it awakes from sleep 'a lofty sweet singing comes from his mouth and . . . a delightful stream of sweet-smelling breath' that all other animals follow – excepting the dragon, who runs away and hides in fear.

Traditionally, the *pelican* is devoted to her young and is frequently depicted piercing her breast (vulning herself) in order that they should be revived by her blood. Thus the pelican became a mystic emblem of Christ, whose blood was shed for

Couchant

Salient

Rampant

Passant

Sejant

Dormant

Statant

mankind, and of the Resurrection and the Eucharist. When depicted vulning herself, and nourishing her young while standing on the nest, the pelican is described as being *in her piety*.

The medieval *unicorn* of western Europe is an elegant and beautiful animal, like a horse but with cloven feet, a lion's tail, a goat's beard and a delicate spiralling horn on its forehead. It became a symbol of Christ because of its purity and virtue and to its horn were ascribed medicinal powers of healing and purification.

In a twelfth-century bestiary the *yale* is described as being the size of a horse and having the tusks of a boar and extremely long horns that could be moved as required – either singly or together – to meet aggression from any direction.

In appearance, the *martlet* is similar to the house martin, swallow and swift, but is depicted without feet or claws for the bestiaries claimed that it lived its entire life in the air and had no need to touch the ground.

Originally, all scaly creatures with bat-like wings were 'dragons': depicted as serpents, without legs or sometimes with just two. With the arrival in the late medieval bestiaries of a four-footed version, a distinction came to be made between the *wyvern* (with two legs) and the *dragon* (with four). The dragon probably entered British heraldry as the standard of the Roman cohort and remained in the symbolism of the post-Roman era, notably in the 'burning dragon' of Cadwallader. Dragons are often associated with water: the legendary *Gargouille*, a seventh-century river dragon who supposedly ravaged the city of Rouen, is commemorated in the water spouts of churches (*see* GARGOYLES). Although the dragon of western mythology typifies viciousness and envy, and became the emblem of pestilence and plague, in heraldry it is used as a symbol for overthrowing the tyranny of a demonic enemy.

The *cockatrice* is hatched on a dunghill from a cock's egg by a serpent. It is so venomous that its look or breath are lethal to all other creatures – except for the weasel. At the age of nine years, the cockatrice will lay an egg on a midden and a toad will come to hatch it and produce, not another cockatrice, but a *basilisk* which has a dragon's head at the end of its tail. So dreadful is its appearance that should it catch sight of its reflection it will instantly burst with horror.

During the post-medieval period many strange creatures were added to the heraldic zoo, often by the interbreeding of their medieval forebears to produce a singularly unattractive (and rare) collection of armorial hybrids.

See also ANTELOPES, APES, BADGES, CHRISTIAN SYMBOLS, DOVES, EAGLES, ELEPHANTS, FISH, HART, LIONS, PAGAN SYMBOLS, PASCHAL LAMB, REBUSES, STAGS *and* TORTOISE
Further reading:
Dennys, R., *The Heraldic Imagination*, London, 1975
Friar, S., *A New Dictionary of Heraldry*, Sherborne and London, 1987

BEATIFICATION The act by which a Pope permits the public veneration of a faithful Catholic after his death.

BEATING THE BOUNDS *see* PERAMBULATION

BEDE-HOUSE A form of ALMONRY attached to some secular colleges in the late Middle Ages.
See also ALMSHOUSES, CHANTRY COLLEGE, HOSPICE *and* HOSPITALS

BEDE ROLL A list of benefactors to a church for whom commemorative prayers are to be said. The roll was usually read from the pulpit on Sundays and at Michaelmas and Christmas (it is now replaced by the Bidding Prayer). Medieval guilds and fraternities made provision for prayers and masses to be said in perpetuity for those whose names were entered in the bede rolls.
See also CHANTRY CHAPELS

BEDESMAN (*also*** BEADSMAN)** One who is paid or endowed to pray for others. Tiny figures of bedesmen were often carved in medieval tomb chests as symbols of the perpetual prayers which were to be offered for the deceased and his family (*see* CHANTRY).
See also BEAD

BEDLAM A vernacular corruption of the Hospital of St. Mary of Bethlehem in Bishopsgate (London) which was founded in 1247. It is known that lunatics were admitted to the Bishopsgate hospice in the early fifteenth century and it is likely that thereafter the term gradually came to be associated with lunatic asylums in general.

BELFRIES A belfry is a structure in which BELLS are housed or the chamber in which they are rung. The term is most often used to differentiate between TOWERS containing peals of bells and smaller timber structures (other than BELL-COTES) in which just one or two bells are hung. Belfries of this type often appear to 'straddle' the roof of a nave, usually at the western end, and are especially common in those areas of England where timber was once plentiful, notably the south-east. Some have just a small pyramidal cap (as at Evesbatch in Herefordshire and Tortington in Essex) while others have a spire (*see* FLÈCHE), usually covered with wooden shingles, which may be of moderate height (as at Birdbrook in Essex and Brenzett in Kent) or tall and slender (as at Crowhurst in Surrey and Cowden in Kent).

For DETACHED BELFRIES *see* TOWERS.

BELL, BOOK AND CANDLE The ritual of ANATHEMA, the greater excommunication, introduced into the Church in the sixth century. After reading the Sentence a bell is rung, a book closed and a candle extinguished. From that moment, the anathematised person was separated from the body of the faithful, denied the Sacraments and excluded from all forms of divine worship.

See also EXCOMMUNICATION

BELL-CAGES Not all BELLS were hung in TOWERS, BELFRIES or BELL-COTES. The central tower of Romsey Abbey in Hampshire is crowned by a wooden bell-cage of 1625 while, at East Bergholt in Suffolk, there is a conical, timber-framed bell-cage at ground level which contains a fine peal of five bells.

BELL-COTES (*also* BELL-GABLES) Where there is no tower or timber belfry in which to hang BELLS, then an open bell-cote may have been provided, usually above or within the western termination of the nave. This may be an upward projection of the gable-end of the church (*bell gable*) or (more rarely) a separate structure, as at Brympton D'Evercy in Somerset. A bell-cote usually comprises a stone or brick arch, in which the bell is hung, beneath a pitched roof of slate or tiles. Double bell-cotes are similar in appearance but have a pair of bells, each hung within its own arch, beneath a single or double pitched roof. There are numerous examples: at Kelmscott in Oxfordshire and at Essendine in Rutland (a double bell-cote), for instance, and at Hermitage in Dorset where a charming Queen Anne bell-cote is crowned with an knob. Bell-cotes are usually indicative of churches which were built (or, more often, re-built) in parishes which enjoyed only limited resources. Many were donated by local benefactors whose generosity may be commemorated inside the church – often on a plaque in the porch. A bell-cote at the eastern termination of a

A double bell-cote at Sutton Bingham, Somerset

43

chancel (or above a chancel arch) will almost certainly house a SANCTUS BELL.
See also BELFRIES *and* TOWERS

BELL FLÈCHE A slender spire (usually of wood) rising from a tower or stair turret and containing a bell or bells.
See also TOWERS

BELL-HATCH (*or* BELL-HOLE) An opening in a tower vault through which bells were raised and lowered.

BELL LOUVRES Window-like openings in the walls of a tower in which sets of horizontal overlapping slats provide protection from the weather while not impeding the sound of the bells.
See also BELLS *and* TOWERS

BELL METAL An alloy of copper and tin.

BELLS Bells were introduced into the Celtic Church in the sixth century and came into general use in the eighth century.
MONASTIC BELLS
In the monasteries '. . . the sound of bells was rarely absent from the air, either the small bells of the dorter, frater, chapter and church or the greater bells of the tower. They seem to have punctuated every occasion throughout the day and they must have given an air of animation both within and without the monastery' (Crossley, *The English Abbey*, 1935). The great bells were rung to summon a community to prayer at the appointed Day Hours (*Diurnal*) of Lauds, Prime, Sext, None, Vespers and Compline. The onerous duty of ringing the great bell fell to a 'careful brother' selected by the Abbot, though in the later Middle Ages bells were controlled by clock mechanisms which had neither hands nor face. Of course, there was still a need for the bells to be rung in celebration (in some abbeys as often as forty times a year) and ringers were often rewarded with special rations or were replaced by paid servants.
MEDIEVAL BELLS
Throughout the land, the bells of parish churches marked the canonical hours and summoned the faithful to worship. They tolled the CURFEW and the ANGELUS, warned of invasion and alarm, and announced the death of a parishioner: '. . . three times three for a man and three times two for a woman, followed by the years of the dead person's age. When the bell stopped at eighteen or twenty a hush would come over the fields' (Ronald Blythe, *Akenfield*). Bells celebrated baptisms, weddings and feast days, they conveyed news of royal births and changing political fortunes, of glorious victories and humiliating defeats.

In the thirteenth and early fourteenth centuries, ringers experimented with new ways of hanging bells so that the sound could be controlled. Before the fourteenth century church bells were normally suspended on a single spindle but from *c.* 1300 they were mounted on wooden quarter-wheels, the spindle serving as the axle and with the rope attached to the rim of the wheel. It was then found that even greater control could be achieved when the bell was mounted on a half-wheel.

Amazingly, nearly three thousand medieval bells are still rung in England's churches, the oldest of which is believed to be the bell at Claughton in Lancashire which was cast in 1296. Individual bells were often dedicated to a saint and were inscribed with an appropriate prayer or biblical text. Initial letters, sometimes in the form of crosses, word stops, lettering and foundry marks are of great beauty and interest though, because of their lofty location, they remain inaccessible. In England, medieval bells are not usually dated but may be identified by their distinctive elongated shape. There are good examples of early bells at Caversfield and Goring in Oxfordshire and at Chaldon in Surrey.
THE POST-REFORMATION PERIOD
At the Reformation many church bells were either silenced or removed. The task of restoring them during and after the Elizabethan period usually necessitated re-hanging which provided an opportunity for experimentation. Most bells were now mounted on a complete wheel while the introduction of a slider and stay made it possible for the bell's movement to be halted at will. Additional bells were installed in many churches and responsibility for belfries transferred to the parishioners. Inscriptions on Tudor and post-Reformation bells tend to be secular in character. They are usually (though not invariably) in English and often incorporate the name of the bell-founder and of benefactors – squires, merchants, parsons and even princes. The bells of Sherborne Abbey in Dorset (now the parish church) are believed to be the heaviest peal of eight in the world. The tenor ('Great Tom') alone weighs two and a quarter tons, its inscription recalling Cardinal Thomas Wolsey (*c.* 1475–1530) who gave the bell to the abbey:

> By Wolsey's gift I measure time for all,
> To mirth, to grief, to church, I serve to call.

Also at Sherborne is the Fire Bell which is rung for conflagrations. It too is inscribed:

> Lord, quench this furious flame:
> Arise, run, help put out the same.

CHANGE-RINGING
'Ringing the changes' on peals of five, six, eight, ten or twelve bells, was introduced in the mid-

seventeenth century and is almost unknown outside England. The bells are rung in a series of different orders (*changes*): on eight bells, for example, 40,320 changes are possible (this is called 'accomplishing the extent') and some 1,600 changes can be rung in an hour. The earliest evidence of change-ringing (from *c.* 1618) is a carving on the tower door-post of Buxhall church in Suffolk:

1	2	3	4	5
2	1	3	4	5
2	3	1	4	5
2	3	4	1	5
2	3	4	5	1
	2	.	.	.

But it was the publication of Fabian Stedman's *Tintinnalogia* in 1668 and his *Campanologia* in 1677 which formalised a system by which the bells could make 'real music'. Stedman's method (which is still the most popular) requires an even number of bells though (paradoxically) the changes are rung on an odd number. Thus, in a 'ring of bells' of six, 'Stedman' would be rung on the 'front five' (2–1–4–3–5) with the largest bell (the tenor) coming in behind. Inevitably, numerous variations evolved from Stedman's system and the names of those who attempted to ring Grandsire Triples, Bob Major, Stedman Caters, Tittum Bob Royal and other sequences were painted on boards and proudly displayed in ringing chambers throughout England.

There are over five thousand English churches with rings of five or more bells – and many of these have six, eight or twelve bells, the greatest numbers being in the counties of Devon and Somerset. All bells are considered to be feminine and are 'raised' or 'turned over' to 'speak' their Pleasures, Tittums, Superlatives and Surprises. The essence of ringing in a peal is that each bell should turn through an almost complete revolution each time the bell-rope is pulled, beginning from an inverted position (a stay on the wheel prevents a bell from performing a complete revolution).

MANUFACTURE

Since the late seventeenth century, bells have been made by a small number of bell-foundries such as the famous Whitechapel Bell Foundry in London (now Mears and Stainbank), Abraham Rudhall of Gloucester (1684–1774) and Samuel Smith of York (1680–1730). But many early bellfounders were itinerant craftsmen who simply set up their casting equipment in a field adjacent to the churchyard. (In several villages such sites are still referred to as the 'Bell Field'.) The first stage in casting was the making of the core, usually of brickwork covered with soft clay. This was moulded with a curved compass (the *crook*) which defined the inner surface of the bell. In the same way, a larger mould

(*cope*) was shaped to form the outer surface. The moulds were then baked until hard and the cope fitted over the core leaving a space between the two and a hole at the top. An alloy of copper and tin was then prepared and poured into the space between the two moulds. When the alloy had cooled and hardened, the moulds were removed from the bell. Initially, an alloy of three parts of copper to one of tin was found to be the most effective, though over the years the quantity of tin has been reduced to give proportions of five to one. It is the tin which imparts the true ringing quality of the bell. If the alloy was too hot when poured it would split the bell and if it was too cold it would spoil it.

Tuning was achieved by chipping at the inside of the bell to flatten the tone and by chipping at the edge to sharpen it. Modern bells are scientifically tuned but in earlier centuries '. . . it was like a woman with a cake who could turn out four or five passable efforts to every one which was perfect' (*ibid.*). It is claimed that 'the sweetest bell in England' is the Lavenham tenor (in Suffolk) which was cast in 1625.

Then followed the 'hanging' of the bell in its frame, an extraordinarily difficult manoeuvre which must surely have required the involvement of the whole parish, for a tenor can weigh eleven hundredweight (559 kg) or more (the tenor at St. Paul's Cathedral weighs three and a quarter tons!). A bell-frame must be rigid and perfectly set otherwise it will affect the movement of the bell. Many timber bell-frames are between four and five hundred years old, though an increasing number of these are being replaced by iron and steel.

RINGING CHAMBERS

The bells are rung from a *ringing chamber* (or *hanging chamber*) within the tower, usually at ground level or midway up the tower where it may be reached by ladders or a turnpike stair (*vice*). At Hemingborough in Yorkshire and Somerby in Leicestershire the central position of the tower requires the ringers to stand in full view of the congregation, while at Crowland Abbey in Lincolnshire the bells are immediately above the porch so that worshippers are obliged to pass through the circle of ringers as they enter the church.

Ringing chambers often contain fascinating evidence of continuous use, sometimes dating from the seventeenth and eighteenth centuries, such as ringers' rhymes (almost invariably warning of a fine for wearing spurs or a hat in the chamber), lists of tower captains (the head ringers, also known as Bell Captains) and ringing boards on which are chalked the orders for the day. Societies of ringers (known as 'The St . . . Tower' and whose members are described as 'youths') also maintain records of their achievements. Those of the Ipswich Senior Society, for example, tell of an attempted peal of 6,144 Treble Bob Major at Woodbridge (Suffolk) in 1851: 'We attempt the difficult, but there is no virtue in what is easy'. The peal book of The Ancient Society of Painswick Youths at St. Mary's, Painswick in Gloucestershire (founded in 1687) contains many famous peals:

18 April 1737, a peal of Cators, 12,006 changes in 7 hours, 55 minutes.
14 February, 1920, a peal of Grand sires Cinques, 13,001 changes in 8 hours, 45 minutes.

Painswick's is one of the finest peals in England and each of the twelve bells is inscribed:

No. 1 'Non clamor sed amor cantat in ore Dei' ('Not noise but love is music in God's ear')
No. 2 'Pro deo, ecclesia at Regina' ('For God, Church and Queen')
No. 3 'When you me ring I'll sweetly sing'
No. 4 'Prosperity to all our benefactors'
No. 5 'The Gift of Edmund Webb, clothier 1687'
No. 6 'The Gift of William Rogers Esq. 1686'
No. 7 'Abraham Rudhall cast us all 1731'
No. 8 'A.R. 1732'
No. 9 'Prosperity to the Town of Painswick, A.R. 1731'
No.10 'John Downs, Vicar, 1831'
No.11 'Thomas Smith and William Barnfield, Churchwardens, A.R. 1731'
No.12 'I to the Church the living call and to the grave do summon all.'

The towers themselves (which may move during ringing) have an effect on the sound produced by the bells which hang within them. Old bricks soak up the sound and sweeten it, and the taller the tower, the quieter the bells in its immediate vicinity. In recent centuries, bells were usually hung about twelve feet (3.6 m) lower than the BELL LOUVRES in the tower walls so that the sound can rise and spread outwards.

Seventeenth- and eighteenth-century churchwardens' accounts demonstrate the importance of bell-ringing in the life of communities. Then as now, the cost of replacing ropes, sallies, baldrics and frames and of re-casting or replacing bells was a constant demand on the parish purse but one which, for the most part, was cheerfully met. Records of payments to ringers provide a vivid chronicle of the times and illustrate how rapidly news was spread, even to the more remote parishes.

The churchwardens' accounts for Crewkerne in Somerset *, for example, contain the following entries from the year 1665:

Two bell-ropes, the great bell and the fourth bell	6–0
Paid the ringers the 29th May	5–0
In beere to the Ringers at the over throw of the Dutch	5–0
A pint of oyle about the bells, clock and chimes	7
To the Ringers in beere at the rejoycing at the Dutch over throw	2–0
More to the Ringers at the same	1–0
To the ringers the 5th of November	6–0

The celebrations of 29 May marked both King Charles's escape after the battle of Worcester in 1651 and his restoration in 1660. The 'over throw of the Dutch' was a celebration in anticipation of victory in the second Dutch War of 1665–7 and 'the 5th of November' commemorated what is now known as the Gunpowder Plot of 1605.

* *From* Bettey, J., *Church and Parish*, London, 1987

See also BELFRIES, BELL-CAGES, BELL-COTES, BURGESS BELL, CARILLON, CLOCKS, SANCTUS BELL *and* TOWERS

Further reading:
Camp, J., *Discovering Bells and Bellringing*, Aylesbury, 1975
Cattermole, P., *Church Bells and Bell-ringing: A Norfolk Profile*, London, 1990
Elphick, G., *The Craft of the Bellfounder*, London, 1988
Walters, H., *Church Bells of England*, Oxford, 1977
For the Central Council of Church Bell Ringers *see* APPENDIX II.

BEMA In early churches, a raised platform on which a priest stood to speak.

BENCHES AND BENCH-ENDS Medieval congregations were rarely provided with seating: they simply stood or knelt – though stone benches were sometimes attached to the walls as a concession to the elderly and infirm (hence the expression 'gone to the wall'). But with the growing popularity of itinerant preachers (notably the FRIARS who arrived in England in the fourteenth century), so the need for seating increased (*see also* PULPITS). A number of examples of wooden benches have survived from the thirteenth and fourteenth centuries: at Dunsfold in Surrey, for example. With the introduction of an English LITURGY following the Reformation, most parish churches acquired some form of seating, often trestles which could be removed when the nave was required for other purposes (*see* CHURCH AND COMMUNITY). Nevertheless, by the late sixteenth century an increasing number of churches had installed permanent long-backed benches. These have backs with open rails or panels, bench-ends and bookrests for the benefit of those sitting on the bench behind. (Medieval bookrests are always horizontal while those from the post-Reformation period are usually sloping.) As the name implies, a bench front (*desk*) with bookrest is usually found at the front of each section of benches. Rows of benches are often (and erroneously) referred to as PEWS which are enclosed and of a much later date.

Bench-ends may be carved in a variety of sophisticated or vernacular styles and with a wide range of decorative, allegorical or heraldic subjects. They also reflect regional styles and fashions: notably those of East Anglia and the West Country.

East Anglian bench-ends usually terminate in a carved *POPPY HEAD* finial, similar in appearance to a FLEUR-DE-LIS, below which are carvings of human figures or animals which sometimes surmount small buttresses at the sides or ends. The finials themselves are often ingeniously carved: at Blythburgh in Suffolk, for example, a series of poppy-head finials depicts the Seven Deadly Sins. Bench-ends are sometimes panelled

and the backs pierced with delicate tracery. The best examples (among many) are at Wiggenhall (St. Mary the Virgin and St. Germans), Great Walsingham and Harpley in Norfolk and Fressingfield, Woolpit, Dennington, Stowlangtoft and Ufford in Suffolk.

Bench-ends in West Country churches are almost invariably square-headed. Figure carving (usually of secular subjects) and foliage are common motifs and decorative themes are sometimes carried through into the bench fronts. Local 'schools' of carvers may be identified: at a cluster of churches around the Quantock Hills in Somerset, for example, where the bench-ends are carved with traceried panelling and foliage (Bishop's Hull, Broomfield, Crowcombe, Milverton, Monksilver and Spaxton churches). In Cornwall and Devon (especially in the north of the county) heraldic devices, rebuses and CHRISTIAN SYMBOLS are common. A popular decorative theme, in both counties, is a border of foliated scroll-work, usually comprising long, pointed leaves with indented edges. There are almost complete sets of early long-benches at Abbotsham, Braunton, East Budleigh, High Bickington, Lapford and Lew

Bench-ends at Lansallos in Cornwall (left) and Brent Knoll, Somerset (right). The mitred pig is probably an unflattering reference to the Bishop of Rome.

Trenchard in Devon and Altarnum, Kilkhampton, Lanteglos-by-Fowey, Lansallos, Launcells, Mullion, Talland and St. Winnow in Cornwall. At Trull in Somerset a series of five bench-ends depicts figures in a religious procession, an unusual subject for post-Reformation decoration (*c.* 1560); while at Brent Knoll, in the same county, three bench-ends relate the fable of Reynard the Fox, though in this version Reynard is depicted as a mitred abbot and his cowled monks have heads of swine. Beneath his feet, two monkeys roast a pig on a spit and there can be little doubt that, in this Reynard, we have a singularly unflattering reference to the Bishop of Rome!

Some of the most delightful sets of bench-ends conform to neither period nor regional patterns. In the fifteenth-century church at Bradford Abbas in Dorset both square-headed bench-ends and poppy-head filials are carved with a rich variety of foliated, heraldic and vernacular motifs and figures including a pig and a bird eating acorns from a very strange oak tree. The front panels of a 'parson's pew' or reading desk, constructed of late-medieval bench-ends, are beautifully carved with a magnificent griffin and the figure of St. Paul, while the poppy-head filials of the side panels have elbow-rests fashioned into an owl, a monkey, a dog and a puppy.

See also PEWS (FAMILY) *and* PEW RENTING
Further reading:
Smith, J., *Church Woodcarvings: Misericords and Bench-ends*, Newton Abbot, 1974

BENCH MARKS *see* MAPS

'BEND SINISTER' *see* BASTARDY

BENEDICITE The song of praise 'Bless ye [the Lord]' attributed (in *Dan.* 3) to Shadrach, Meshach and Abednego as they stood together in the 'fiery furnace'. The canticle has been used in the Christian liturgy since the days of the early Church.

BENEDICTINES (The Black Monks) The Rule of St. Benedict of Nursia (*c.* 480–*c.* 550) provided a cohesive, inclusive and individual code by which monastic life, both spiritual and administrative, could be ordered (*see* RULE). It was a perfect expression of devout sobriety, neither excessive nor fanatical, and was to become the model for all subsequent forms of monasticism in Western Europe. But there was no *order* of St. Benedict: the Benedictine Rule was simply one of several from which an abbot selected the observances by which his community lived. Successive medieval Popes attempted to bring the Benedictine abbeys under a centralised constitution but the Benedictines themselves preferred to exercise reform through

independent local congregations.

Throughout the DARK AGES it was the Benedictines who maintained the ideals and practice of scholarship and liturgical worship. They '. . . provided stability in chaotic and restless times, regulation in anarchy and continuity in a time of dissolution'.* Indeed, their influence affected profoundly the subsequent nature of medieval society.

In England, the tenth-century clerics Dunstan, Oswald and Ethelwold reintroduced large-scale monasticism after a century of decline in the ANGLO-SAXON CHURCH. With the support of the Anglo-Saxon monarchy they introduced a strict Benedictine rule and established (or re-founded) a series of monasteries 'correcting the foolish with rods' and so antagonising the 'evil-living [secular] clerics', with their 'illegal wives' and partiality for gluttony and drunkenness, that there was even an unsuccessful attempt to poison Ethelwold in his hall at Winchester.

The Benedictines were known as the *Black Monks* because they wore a black cowl over a black, white or russet cassock, trimmed with black or white fur, and a black cape and hood (they were not referred to as Benedictines until the late Middle Ages). Prior to the DISSOLUTION OF THE MONASTERIES, there were (in England and Wales) fifty abbeys of Benedictine monks, over forty conventual priories, a similar number of lesser houses and cells, and more than sixty houses of Benedictine nuns: a total of nearly two hundred communities with some three thousand brethren and sisters together with numerous servants, employees and dependants. Several abbey and priory churches have survived as CATHEDRALS: Winchester Cathedral Priory, for example, and the 'new foundation' cathedrals of Chester, Gloucester, Peterborough and Westminster, while many others have been adopted for parochial use. Not all are as magnificent as the parish churches of Milton (where the nave was never built) and Sherborne in Dorset, Tewkesbury in Gloucestershire and Great Malvern in Worcestershire. The majority remain as simple parish churches in which at least some part of the monastic structure survives.

See also ABBEYS, CISTERCIANS *and* PRIORIES
Further reading:
Bottomley, *The Abbey Explorer's Guide*, Kaye & Ward, 1981*
Butler, L. and Given-Wilson, C., *Medieval Monasteries of Great Britain*, London, 1979

BENEDICTUS The song of thanksgiving for the birth of John the Baptist (Luke 1: 68–79) sung liturgically at Lauds and incorporated into the *Book of Common Prayer* for use at Mattins.

BENEFACTION BOARD *see* BEQUEST BOARD

BENEFACTORS Those who contributed to the building or extension of a monastery or church, or who granted lands to a religious community, in return for the prayers of the beneficiaries (*see* CHANTRY) and recognition as confrater or honorary member of the community (*see* CONFRATERNITY). The names of beneficiaries were often inscribed in a book or bede roll so that their generosity would be commemorated in perpetuity and, if they were armigerous, their heraldic devices might be incorporated in the fabric of the building they had helped to endow (there are 825 shields of arms of benefactors in the vault of the Canterbury cloister which was rebuilt in *c.* 1400). A relatively poor man could qualify as a benefactor but a substantial donation was required before he could be recognised as a 'founder'. It was not unusual for founders to join the communities they had endowed: Walter L'Espec, for example, who in 1154 ended his days as a humble monk at the Cistercian abbey of Rievaulx in Yorkshire.
See also FOUNDATION

BENEFICE An ecclesiastical office such as a RECTORY, DEANERY or VICARAGE. An amalgamation of discrete parishes.

BENEFIT OF CLERGY Exemption from trial by a secular court accorded to the medieval clergy. In England this provision was extended to all those whose literacy theoretically qualified them for holy orders. Prisoners were often required to read from the Scriptures in order to avoid a capital sentence for a minor offence. The test was abolished in 1706 and the procedure in 1827.
See also CANON LAW *and* CLARENDON, CONSTITUTIONS OF

BEQUEATH *see* DEVISE

BEQUEST BOARD (*also* BENEFACTION BOARD) A public record of a bequest (or bequests), usually painted on wood and dating from the eighteenth century, originally displayed on a church wall though now more often confined to some other, less accessible, place. Bequests, often of income arising from land rents or investments, were made for the benefit of 'the Poor of this Parish' who received an annual dole of bread and 'other Comforts' (*see* DOLE CUPBOARDS). Typical of its type is the splendid bequest board in the church at Milborne Port in Somerset. This lists a number of CHARITIES which had been established at various times for the benefit of the poorer inhabitants of the town and the surrounding villages, including the 'Commonalty Monies' (a sum of £22 14*s* 9*d*) which were paid half-yearly on St. Thomas's Day and Shrove Tuesday. The Commonalty was originally a medieval merchant GUILD which provided funds for distressed

members, its income derived from land and property. Payments from Prankerd's Charity were made annually to the poor of the ancient manor of Kingsbury Regis in the parish of Milborne Port. Thomas Prankerd died a bachelor in 1609 and willed the sum of £40 to the poor 'for ever', appointing overseers to distribute the interest raised on his investment. He was clearly proud of his charitable works for they were inscribed on his tomb in the nave of the church. The Horsey Gift was established in 1860 'for the benefit of the second poor for ever' by Anne Harris Hutchings who left instructions that the interest on £500 worth of government securities (*consols*) should be distributed to those who did not qualify for poor relief.

BESTIARY A medieval illustrated treatise on beasts, both real and imagined. Many of the creatures were imbued with medicinal and spiritual powers or endowed with allegorical significance. The reader was often exhorted to emulate the qualities of certain beasts and to shun others.
See also CREATURES *and* HERALDIC BEASTS
Further reading:
Barber, R. (trans.), *Bestiary*, Woodbridge, 1993

BETROTHAL A promise, freely given, of future marriage. In the Middle Ages, Canon Law differentiated between betrothal and PRE-CONTRACT which could be cited in cases relating to questions of inheritance, illegitimacy etc. The essential difference between betrothal and pre-contract was in the form of words used and the tense of the verb contained therein – 'I will marry you' was a betrothal whereas 'I marry you' was a pre-contract.
See also BASTARDY, ESPOUSAL *and* MARRIAGE LICENCES

BETWS In the Welsh, a chapel or oratory.

BEZEL The inner rim of a vessel by which a cover is held in place. A standing PATEN, for example, may have been provided with a bezel so that it would serve also as a lid for a matching communion cup.

BI-AXIAL The frame of a door, window, panel, tablet etc. in which the space enclosed is surrounded by ornament symmetrically on all sides. A *mon-axial* frame has ornamentation only at the upper and lower edges, that at the top forming a cresting feature.

BIBLE BOXES In 1538, Thomas Cromwell (as Vicar General) ordered that a copy of Coverdale's 'Great Bible' should be set up in every parish church. This was replaced by the revised 'Bishops'

Bible' of 1568 (*see* BIBLES). Large wooden Bible boxes, in which these valuable tomes were secured, may still be found in some churches, though often they are used for other purposes. Most date from the seventeenth century and many retain the original lock and hasp. Others doubled as lecterns or desks and have sloping tops with ornamental hinges and keyplates. Most Bible boxes have decorative carving on the front and sometimes a date.

BIBLES The Bible (in Latin) was the main instrument in the monastic process of spiritual formation and edification. It was used in the LITURGY: the DIVINE OFFICE (*Opus Dei*), which included a recitation of the PSALTER, and at the MASS which contains a variety of Psalms and extracts from Scripture (*lections*), mostly from the New Testament. The Bible was read at meetings of the CHAPTER, at COLLATION and in the FRATER where meals were taken in silence. It was used for private reading and contemplation, was the subject of commentaries and homilies, and much labour was devoted to the study of its historical, mystical and moral meaning.

In England, the earliest vernacular versions of biblical texts were Anglo-Saxon interlinear glosses of the Gospels and Psalms and (sometimes abridged) extracts translated from the Latin. From the mid-thirteenth century a number of Middle English metrical versions were made, notably of the Psalms, and in the fourteenth century several anonymous translations of New Testament books appeared. These included two versions of the 'Wycliffite Bible', the earlier of which was probably the work of Nicholas of Hereford (d. *c.* 1420) which was followed by a revised version completed in 1388 by John Purvey, a Wycliffite preacher. In 1407 the Council of Oxford prohibited further translations.

The first translations from the Greek and Hebrew were made by William Tyndale (*c.* 1494–1536) who completed the printing of his English New Testament at Worms in 1525. Tyndale, who spent the last years of his life in Antwerp, was strangled and burned for heresy in 1536 but his work later formed the basis of both the Authorised and Revised versions of the English Bible. It is interesting to note that, almost 500 years ago, Tyndale referred to divinity with a gender-neutral pronoun: 'All thyngs were made by it / and without it / was made noo thinge / that made was. In it was lyfe.'

In 1534, the Convocation of Canterbury petitioned Henry VIII that the whole Bible might be translated into English and, in the following year, Miles Coverdale (1488–1568), an Augustinian friar and Reformer who, like Tyndale, had been forced to reside abroad, produced the first complete English Bible which he dedicated to the King. Wherever possible Coverdale followed Tyndale's work, but for much of the Old Testament he translated from the German of Martin Luther (1483–1546) and others. (Coverdale's version of the Psalms has remained in constant use in the *Book of Common Prayer*.) In 1537 'Matthew's Bible' was published. This version, which was authorised by the King, was apparently edited by one Thomas Matthew, though this was an alias for John Rogers (1500–55) who again followed Tyndale and Coverdale but added a number of previously unpublished texts. Further revisions included Coverdale's 'Great Bible' of 1538, which Thomas Cromwell (1485–1540) ordered should be issued to every parish church.

It should not be imagined that the introduction of an English Bible was universally popular. Stephen Gardiner (1483–1555), Bishop of Winchester and leader of the conservative faction within the English Church, viewed Cromwell's legislation with considerable suspicion. Following Cromwell's attainder and execution in 1540, Gardiner suggested to Henry VIII that the Great Bible was not an impartial translation but a specifically protestant text. As a result, Archbishop Thomas Cranmer (1489–1556) was obliged to ask Convocation whether the English Bible could be retained '. . . without scandal, error and open offence to Christ's faithful people' to which a majority of the bishops replied that it could not and the Archbishop was forced to apportion the text for detailed examination by various committees and by the universities. In 1543 Gardiner succeeded in persuading the King to give his assent to an Act of Parliament which seriously curtailed the study of the scriptures in English. This was euphemistically termed 'the Act for the advancement of true religion' which, because of so many 'crafty, false and untrue' translations (including Tyndale's), restricted access to an educated few. Thereafter, noblemen and gentlemen were permitted to read translations aloud to their families, and merchants of substance and gentlewomen were allowed to read to themselves alone. But the common people were to be denied access to the Scriptures for, as Henry later complained to Parliament, the 'most precious jewel, the Word of God, is disputed, rhymed, sung and jangled in every alehouse and tavern'.

The brief and turbulent reigns of Edward VI (1547–53) and Mary I (1553–8) were followed by the relative stability of the Elizabethan Age, and in 1568 the Great Bible was revised and replaced by the 'Bishops' Bible'. It was this version which churchwardens were required to 'set up' in their churches in 1571.

As a consequence of the Hampton Court Conference of 1604, James I ordered that a new translation of the Bible should be made. No fewer than fifty-four experts were engaged for this purpose with instructions to work from the Bishops' Bible, retaining ecclesiastical terms (e.g. 'baptism' for 'washing') but omitting marginal notes unless they were required to explain Hebrew or Greek terms. The Bible of 1611 (known as the Authorised Version or King James Version) was destined to become 'the only familiar form of the Bible for generations of English-speaking people'.* 'The English Bible [is] a book which, if everything else in our language should perish, would alone suffice to show the whole extent of its beauty and power' (Macaulay).

In 1870, the Convocation of Canterbury appointed a committee to revise the 1611 Bible in order to reflect advances in scholarship and changes in English usage. But the committee was also instructed to introduce as few alterations as possible and to do so in a form of language that was compatible with the Authorised Version and earlier texts. This became the Revised Version which was published in 1881 (New Testament), 1885 (Old Testament) and 1895 (Apocrypha) and is the Bible which, until recently, was most often found in our parish churches. Unfortunately, the *New English Bible*, which was published in 1961 (New Testament) and 1970 (complete), while being a work of considerable scholarship, is written in language which is often banal and singularly lacking in inspiration. Nevertheless it is now used in most churches together with a plethora of similar 'modern' versions.

Several bibles acquired distinctive names as a result of typographical errors or the use of archaic words:
The Breeches Bible (1579), so called because Genesis 3:7 was rendered: 'The eyes of theme both were opended . . . and they sowed figge-tree leaves together, and made themselves breeches.'
The Idle Bible (1809), in which the 'idole shepherd' of Zechariah 11:17 is printed 'the idle shepherd'.
The Bug Bible (1551), in which Psalm 91:5 is translated 'Thou shalt not be afraid of bugges [bogies] by nighte.'
The Treacle Bible (1549), in which the word 'balm' is rendered as 'treacle'.
The Unrighteous Bible (1652), so called because of a printer's error in 1 Corinthians 6:9: 'Know ye not that the unrighteous shall inherit the Kingdom of God.'
The Vinegar Bible (1632), in which the heading to Luke 20 is given as 'The Parable of the Vinegar' instead of '. . . the Vineyard'.
The Wicked Bible or *The Adulterer's Bible* (1632), in which the Seventh Commandment is rendered as 'Thou shalt commit adultery.'
THE BIBLE IN WALES
In 1563 the bishops of Wales and Hereford were commanded to ensure that, by 1567, Welsh

versions of the Bible and Prayer Book would be available in every parish church in Wales. But the 1563 Act emphasised that English was 'the naturall mother tonge used within this Realme' and that the Bible and Prayer Book in English should also be available in Welsh churches. As a consequence of this legislation, a translation of the New Testament (*Epistol at y Cembru*) was published in 1576 by Richard Davies, bishop of St. David's. The translation (by William Salesbury) was based on the most correct texts of the Greek Testament and, although his Welsh has attracted criticism, Salesbury's scholarship has never been questioned.

In 1588 William Morgan, vicar of Llanrhaeadr-ym-Mochant, added his translation of the Old Testament to (what he described as) a 'cleansed' version of Salesbury's New Testament to provide the first complete Bible in Welsh. Nearly one thousand copies were printed, sufficient to meet the needs of every Welsh parish. And yet, within a generation, Richard Parry, the bishop of St. Asaph, declared that 'the majority of the Bibles in our churches have either been lost or have worn out.' In 1620 Parry published a new edition, an adaptation of the 1588 translation by John Davies of Mallwyd. The 'Parry Bible' was to influence generations of godly and literate Welshmen. It was published twenty-eight times between 1620 and 1800 and scores of further editions appeared in the nineteenth century. But it was a large book (about twice the size of the 1588 Bible) and was reprinted in a smaller form in 1630. The 'Little Bible', as it came to be known, was the first to reach the homes of the ordinary people.

Further reading:

Livingstone, E.A., *The Concise Oxford Dictionary of the Christian Church*, Oxford, 1977*
Metzger, B., (ed.), *The Oxford Companion to the Bible*, Oxford, 1994

BIER *see* BURIAL *and* LICH-GATES

BIER LIGHT A tall candle-holder, four of which would have been placed on the floor at the corners of a coffin when kept in a church for any length of time. Medieval bier lights were lit and placed at the corners of TOMB CHESTS to commemorate the birthday or saint's day of the deceased and when masses were said for his soul (*see* CHANTRY *and* EFFIGIES). Processional torches, which were carried on either side of the cross in processions, are of similar appearance and have heavy, removable bases so that they may be stored in an upright position or used as bier lights. Bier lights and processional torches were usually made of polished brass and most of those which have survived date from the mid-nineteenth century (*see* OXFORD MOVEMENT).

BIFURCATED Of a decorative motif when divided into two branches.
See also DECORATIVE MOTIFS *and* DOORS AND DOORWAYS

BILLET (i) An heraldic charge shaped like the rectangular face of a brick. (ii) Romanesque ornamentation consisting of a series of raised rectangular or cylindrical motifs alternating with spaces (*see* DECORATIVE MOTIFS *and* MEDIEVAL ARCHITECTURE).

BIRETTA A stiff square cap worn by a clergyman (*see* VESTMENTS).

BISHOP *see* ABBEYS, CATHEDRAL PRIORY, CLERGY (CHURCH OF ENGLAND), DIOCESE *and* SIGNATURES (ARCHBISHOPS AND BISHOPS)

BISHOPS' LANDS On 9 October 1646 an ordnance of Parliament effectively abolished the offices of archbishop and bishop and set their lands, the last TEMPORALITIES of the Church of England, over to trustees for disposal for the benefit of the Commonwealth.

BISHOPS' REGISTERS From the early thirteenth century, the Church began to exercise greater care in the ordering of its records. A series of Papal records, which begin in 1198, are an invaluable source for English ecclesiastical history, as are royal records and bishops' registers also dating from the thirteenth century. By the late Middle Ages diocesan administration had developed into a complex network that affected the lives of parishioners from the cradle to the grave. As a result, there are few aspects of parochial and manorial life that do not appear in the bishops' registers of the time. Entries relate to individual parishes and contain an extraordinary wealth of historical information: the identity of patrons and incumbents; priests ordained or instituted to parochial chapelries, free chapels, private oratories and chantries; licences to clergy to leave their parishes (to enter royal service or to undertake a pilgrimage, for example); entries concerning the re-dedication of a church or alterations in its patronal festivals; the consecration (required by Canon Law) of the extension or re-building of churches; details of the division or combining of parishes and the founding of chantries and oratories; records of TITHES and of disputes brought before a bishop. Such information provides invaluable evidence of demographic, political, agricultural and social change for a time when other sources are rare. There may also be incidental evidence of road and bridge building, harbour repairs, the provision of drainage and water supplies, repairs to the parish church and other communal works which were carried out, either in return for INDULGENCES (usually, of forty days) or by subscription, and recorded in the registers. Many registers have been published by local record societies and details of all the episcopal registers may be found in the *Guide to Bishops' Registers of England and Wales* (see below). Most of the early printed registers were produced in the original Latin but later volumes are generally translated into English and include summaries and calendars.
Further reading:
Owen, D., *Medieval Records in Print: Bishops' Registers*, London, 1982
Smith, D.M., *Guide to Bishops' Registers of England and Wales*, London, 1981

BISHOPS' TRANSCRIPTS From 1598 incumbents were required to provide their diocesan bishop with copies of entries in the parish registers. Unfortunately, in some cases the order was observed only sporadically and, in others, the returns were not scrupulously maintained. Consequently, the Bishops' Transcripts are often a poor substitute for the original registers, though they may prove invaluable where registers (or entries) are found to be missing.
See also ARCHIVES *and* REGISTERS
Further reading:
Gibson, J., *Bishops' Transcripts and Marriage Licences*, London, 1983

BLACK CANONS *see* AUGUSTINIANS

BLACK DEATH *see* PLAGUE

BLACK FRIARS *see* FRIARS

BLACKLETTER *see* LETTERING

BLACK LETTER DAYS The lesser saints' days which were printed in black in the *Book of Common Prayer*. The major festivals were printed in red (*see* RED LETTER DAYS).

BLACK MASS *see* REQUIEM

BLACK MONKS *see* BENEDICTINES

BLASPHEMY Contempt of God, expressed through grossly irreverent speech, action or even thought, was once both a mortal sin and a legal offence, as was blasphemy against the Church and its saints. In Britain, it remains so only if calculated to offend believers or is likely to cause a breach of the peace.

BLAZON To describe a coat of arms or other heraldic device using the conventions and terminology of HERALDRY. Such a description is itself termed a *blazon*. Familiarity with blazon facilitates the rapid and accurate recording of heraldic devices, enables the researcher to make effective use of reference works such as ordinaries, armories, peerages etc., and to communicate with those who specialise in the study of heraldry (*armorists*), of whom there is a growing number. An accurate blazon is concise and unambiguous and from it heraldic devices may be painted (*emblazoned*) or researched. The conventions of blazon are well established and logical. Relatively few terms are met with regularly and are learned best through practice. Blazons of arms may be obtained from works such as Burke's *General Armory*. This is essentially a list of armorial references, arranged alphabetically by surname, with blazons of arms for each, together with crests, supporters and mottoes where known.

See also BASTARDY, BEASTS (HERALDIC), CADENCY (HERALDIC), COLOURS (HER-ALDIC), HERALDIC CHARGES, MARSHALLING *and* POINTS OF THE SHIELD

Further reading:

Burke, Sir B., *The General Armory of England, Scotland, Ireland and Wales*, 1842 (reprinted Marlborough Today, 1984)

Friar, S., *A New Dictionary of Heraldry*, Sherborne and London, 1987

——, *Heraldry for the Local Historian and Genealogist*, Stroud, 1992

Friar, S. and Ferguson, J., *Basic Heraldry*, London, 1993

BLEMYA Apparently derived from the Blemmyae of Pliny's *Natural History*, these strange headless creatures, of human form but with eyes and mouth below their shoulders, are to be found in medieval carvings where they represent gluttony.

BLESSED SACRAMENT A term used to describe the Sacrament of the EUCHARIST, both the service and (especially) the consecrated elements of bread and wine.

See also HOST *and* RESERVATION

BLESSED VIRGIN MARY, THE *see* ASSUMPTION OF THE BLESSED VIRGIN MARY *and* MARY, THE BLESSED VIRGIN

BLIAUT *see* COSTUME

BLIND A term used to describe raised architectural features, such as arcading and vaulting ribs, between which the intervening spaces are closed.

BLIND ARCADE *see* ARCADE

BLOCK CAPITAL (*also* CUSHION CAPITAL) A Romanesque capital formed from a cube of stone the lower edges of which have been rounded off to meet the circular shaft below (*see* CAPITAL).

BLUE BOOKS *see* NINETEENTH-CENTURY CHURCH

BOARD OF GOVERNORS (*or* MANAGERS) In England and Wales, the governing body of a school. (*See* SCHOOLS)

BOARD OF GUARDIANS The governing body of a local workhouse or 'union' (*see* POOR LAW *and* WORKHOUSES).

BODY SNATCHERS (RESURRECTIONISTS) In 1745 barbers and surgeons decided to go their separate ways. Thereafter, the training of surgeons became increasingly rigorous and included the study of human anatomy. Bodies for dissection were obtained by means of legislation, enacted in 1752, which enabled the London medical schools to acquire the corpses of executed murderers. But demand outpaced supply, and a trade in corpses developed which, while singularly unethical, was not illegal. Though an action could be brought for trespass and the removal of items from a corpse (such as rings and gold teeth) was theft, there was no specific law relating to the exhumation and sale of corpses.

The first authenticated instance was the removal of the body of a Mrs. Jane Sainsbury from a burial ground near Gray's Inn, London, in 1777. Several earlier disappearances remain unexplained, including that of the body of Laurence Sterne, the author, who died in 1768 and was buried in the churchyard of St. George's, Hanover Square. There is a tradition that, within four days, Sterne's body had disappeared – only to re-appear on the slab of an eminent Cambridge surgeon whose audience included a former friend of the dead author! At about the same time, a team of body snatchers was operating in the churchyard of St. Sepulchre, also in London. It was believed at the time that corpses were stored in a nearby hostelry until required by the anatomists at St. Bartholomew's Hospital. In an attempt to prevent further abuses, a watch house was erected from which new graves could be observed. Watch houses (or *watch boxes* as they were known) were similar in appearance to sentry boxes, though some were specially designed and equipped to deter marauders.

The problem was not confined to London. At Warburton church in Cheshire a hole was cut in the oak door of the west tower to provide an unimpeded view of the churchyard at night, while in the churchyard of Pannal in Yorkshire an immense medieval stone coffin (known locally as the Resurrection Stone) was hired out at a guinea a fortnight and positioned over freshly-dug graves to deter body-snatchers. In some areas (notably in Edinburgh, where the trade acquired an unparalleled notoriety) bodies were sometimes buried in iron coffins and graves enclosed by protective railings (*mortsafes*).

An article in the *Lancet* of 1896 described the body snatchers' methods: 'Several feet, 15 or 20, away from the head or foot of the grave, the resurrectionist would remove a square of turf, about 18 or 20 inches in diameter. This he would carefully put by and then commence to mine. Most pauper graves were of the same depth and, if the sepulchre was that of a person of importance, the depth of the grave could be pretty well estimated by the nature of the soil thrown up. Taking a 5-foot grave, the coffin lid would be about four feet from the surface. A rough, slanting tunnel, some 5 yards long, would be constructed, so as to impinge exactly on the coffin head. This being at last struck (no very simple task) the coffin was lugged up by hook to the surface, or preferably the end of the coffin was wrenched off with hooks while still in the shelter of the tunnel, and the scalp or feet of the corpse secured through the open end and the body pulled out, leaving the coffin almost intact and unmoved. The body once obtained, the narrow shaft was easily filled up and the sod or turf accurately replaced. The friends of the deceased, seeing that the earth over the grave was not disturbed, would flatter themselves that the body had escaped the resurrectionists, but they seldom noticed the neatly-placed square of turf, some feet away.'

In the same year, a diary was published in which are described the activities of a gang of seven body snatchers who operated in London in the early years of the nineteenth century. The scale of the operation was quite extraordinary: during the period November 1811 to December 1812, for example, no fewer than 500 bodies were exhumed and sold to London hospitals. The gang's leader retired early and built a large hotel in Margate while another member left £6000 on his death, a considerable sum of money at that time. In 1814 three members of the gang were tried and acquitted after being found to be in possession of seven corpses. A further test case was brought at Lancaster Assizes in 1827 when a Warrington surgeon was charged (with others) of obtaining the body of a young woman from a Baptist churchyard. The surgeon agreed that he had paid £4 for the body and the case was referred to the Old Bailey in London where he was fined £20, not for stealing the body (which was not a criminal offence) but for having in his possession something which he knew to have been stolen.

The most infamous case concerned two Irishmen: William Hare, who ran a boarding-house in Edinburgh, and William Burke who, in 1827, became Hare's lodger. When an elderly sailor died in one of Hare's rooms, the two Irishmen sold the body for seven pounds and ten shillings to Dr. Robert Knox, an Edinburgh anatomist. Encouraged by the prospect of easy money, Burke and Hare proceeded to entice other poor men to lodging houses where they were plied with drink and suffocated. Fifteen bodies were sold for sums of between eight and fourteen pounds before the pair were apprehended in 1829. Hare turned King's Evidence and escaped the gallows but Burke was executed.

In 1830, two body snatchers were caught after stealing two corpses from the churchyard of Alderley in Cheshire but the only charges that were brought against them were trespass and the theft of a wedding ring from one of the bodies. Public opinion was so offended by the impotence of the Law to deal with such cases that, two years later, Parliament passed the Anatomy Act which required that anatomy schools should be licensed and that body snatching was to be punished by means of a fine and imprisonment.

An inscription in the churchyard of Mottram, Cheshire, commemorates the removal of the body of a fifteen-year-old boy who was buried there in October 1827:

Though once beneath the ground his corpse was laid,
For use of surgeons it was then convey'd
Vain was the scheme to hide the impious theft,
The body taken, shroud and coffin left.
To wretches who pursue this barbarous trade
Your carcasses in time may be convey'd
Like his, to some unfeeling surgeon's room
Nor can they justly meet a better doom.

See also CHURCHYARDS, MORTSAFE *and* VAULTS (BURIAL)

BONA NOTABILIA In documents, a term meaning goods worth five pounds or more.

BONDING The arrangement of bricks in a wall for structural and decorative purposes. Continuous vertical joints are structurally unsound and walls of more than 23 cm (9 inches) thickness require bonding by means of *headers* (bricks laid at right angles to the face of the wall). Early brickwork was haphazard but from the end of the thirteenth century English bond was widely used and from the mid-seventeenth century *Flemish bond* became popular. Many other types and combinations of bonding will be found, the most common of which are illustrated. *See also* BRICK

BOOKMARKER A coloured and embroidered ribbon, usually with a contrasting fringe at each end, used to mark a page in a Bible or prayer book. Most parish churches have sets of bookmarkers, each of a colour appropriate to a particular ecclesiastical season (*see* COLOURS, LITURGICAL).

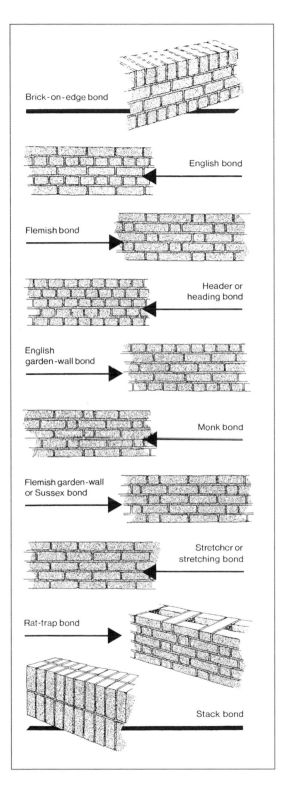

Brick-on-edge bond

English bond

Flemish bond

Header or heading bond

English garden-wall bond

Monk bond

Flemish garden-wall or Sussex bond

Stretcher or stretching bond

Rat-trap bond

Stack bond

BOOK OF HOURS Often the most impressive of all medieval written documents, Books of Hours were personal devotional books widely used by the devout laity from the thirteenth century. Most were embellished more or less elaborately according to the taste and pocket of the patron for whom they were prepared. Some were presented as gifts by calligraphers and illuminators in hope of patronage. Books of Hours provided a series of prayers appropriate to the eight canonical hours into which the day was divided, together with a calendar and various extracts from the Divine Office and Psalms. They were invariably exceedingly beautiful, the illustrations providing also a wealth of information on contemporary social life.

See also MANUSCRIPT ILLUMINATION *and* PRIMER

Further reading:

Harthan, J., *Books of Hours and their Owners*, London, 1977

BOOK OF REMEMBRANCE *see* DOCU-MENTARY SOURCES

BOOKPLATE (i) A decorative label pasted inside the front cover of a book for *ex libris* identification or to commemorate a gift (often a Bible) to a parish church. Bookplates may be dated by their decorative style and often include invaluable heraldic and genealogical information.

For The Bookplate Society *see* APPENDIX II.

Further reading:

Lee, B.N., *British Bookplates*, Newton Abbot, 1979

(ii) A sloping wooden or metal plate, with a projecting lower edge, to support an open book: as on a LECTERN, MISSAL STAND or PULPIT DESK.

BOOKS *see* ARCHIVES, BIBLES, BLUE BOOKS (*see* PARLIAMENTARY RECORDS), BOOK OF HOURS, BREVIARY, CALENDAR, CAPITULARY, CARTULARY, CATECHISM, COLOPHON, COMMON PRAYER (BOOK OF), CONCORDANCE, CUSTOMARY, DOCU-MENTARY SOURCES, DOMESDAY, ECCLESIASTICAL LIBRARIES, EVANGELIARY, FACULTY, FOLIO, HORN-BOOK, HYMNAL, HYMNARY, INVENTORY, LECTIONARY, LIBRARIES, LITANY, LITURGY, MANUALE, MANUSCRIPT ILLUMINATION, MAPS, MARGINAL INSCRIPTIONS, MARTYROLOGY, MINUTES, MISSAL, MONASTIC BREVIARY, MONASTICON ANGLICANUM, ORDINAL, ORDINARY (OF ARMS), PAPER, PARCHMENT, PHOTOGRAPHS, PONTIFICAL, PRIMER, PRINTING, PSALTERS, PSALTERY, REGISTERS, ROLL, RUBRIC, SACRAMENTARY, SCRIPTORIUM, SUBSCRIPTION BOOKS, TEMPORALE, TERRIER, TRACT, TRANSCRIPT, TRANSCRIPTION, TRENTAL, VELLUM,

VESPERALE, VICTORIA COUNTY HISTORY, VISITATIONS (HERALDIC), VULGATE *and* WELSH RECORDS

BOOKS, CHAINED *see* LIBRARIES

BOOK STAMP The book stamp, with an heraldic device, cypher or Christian symbol impressed and often gilded on the bindings of books in private or corporate collections and in churches, was the precursor of the BOOKPLATE and its use continues to the present day.

BOSSES A boss is a decorative termination in wood or stone where the cross-members of a roof or ceiling intersect. In a stone vault it is a projecting keystone at the intersection of ribs and is both functional and ornamental (*see* VAULTING). In the magnificent vault of Sherborne Abbey in Dorset there are no fewer than eight hundred stone bosses and CORBELS, all elaborately carved, painted and gilded with heraldic designs, rebuses and vernacular motifs. Most medieval churches have at least one or two bosses, often in a ROOD CELURE or in the vault of a porch or subsidiary chapel (*see* CHANTRY CHAPELS *and* PORCHES). The majority of bosses are late medieval, foliated decoration and simple quatrefoil and shield motifs being especially common. Unless foliated designs have acorns, haws or grapes they can be difficult to identify botanically. Popular subjects include devils and human faces; saints' emblems and symbols of the Passion (*see* CHRISTIAN SYMBOLS); the heraldic shields, BADGES, REBUSES and CYPHERS of benefactors and donors; MERCHANTS' MARKS; animals and symbolic beasts (such as 'Tanners' hares' which have shared ears) together with a profusion of sacred and secular legends mingled with (sometimes bawdy) everyday scenes.
Further reading:
Cave, C., *Roof Bosses in Medieval Churches*, Cambridge, 1948

BOUNDARIES The Anglo-Saxon colonisation of new land and its demarcation into private estates resulted in the creation of thousands of miles of boundaries, some of which corresponded with those of earlier Roman or even Iron-Age estates while others followed established trackways and natural features such as streams or were formed by the construction of linear embankments and lanes or 'meres' (from the Old English *mære* meaning 'boundary' – *see* MERE LANE). The practice was not universally welcomed, however, and according to Giraldus Cambrensis, writing in the twelfth century, the Welsh were particularly 'given to digging up boundary ditches, removing limits, disregarding landmarks and extending their property

in every possible way'. Some major boundaries had a lasting effect on the political landscape. In the thirteenth century, for example, Gilbert de Clare, Earl of Gloucester (1243–95), constructed the Shire Ditch on the crest of the Malvern Hills to mark the boundary between his hunting grounds to the east and those of the Bishop of Hereford to the west and for seven centuries the 'Red Earl's' ditch separated the counties of Hereford and Worcester.

Today, the boundaries of a civil PARISH are not always contiguous with those of an ecclesiastical parish or with earlier manorial estates and their constituent *TOWNSHIPS (vills)*. In many instances, nineteenth-century legislation resulted in the rationalisation of parishes, particularly those which consisted of two (or occasionally more) separate parts, and in such cases these 'islands' were absorbed into the parishes within which they were located and the ancient boundaries modified accordingly. Similarly, the reorganisation of local government in 1972–4 resulted in numerous adjustments being made to the administrative boundaries of civil parishes, districts, counties and parliamentary constituencies and these have been incorporated into the 1:25000 (*Pathfinder*) Ordnance Survey maps.

Nevertheless, numerous ancient boundaries have survived, not only in the delineation of many ecclesiastical parishes, but in the 'boundary markers', sunken lanes, earthworks and other topographical features of the traditional English landscape. By far the most satisfactory sources of information are the original land *charters*, the earliest dating from the seventh century, which refer to grants of estates to various men and to institutions such as monastic foundations; and major documents, such as the Forest Charter, granted in 1299/1300 by Edward I, which contain records of PERAMBULATIONS. Many of these documents have been published in printed form by local history or record societies but where charters have not been published, the amateur researcher will need guidance from county record offices both to locate the originals and to translate them. References to boundaries in the earliest charters are often frustratingly vague but many later grants describe the limitations of an estate in extraordinary detail, by (often obscure) reference to topographical features and place-names and to adjacent demesne lands. These 'boundary markers', which may include even single trees and boulders (*see* ROGATION), are usually (though not invariably) described in clockwise order: 'First into *Merecumb*, then into the green pit, then on to the tor at *Merecumbes* spring, then to Denewald's stone, then to the ditch where Esne dug across the road . . . from the stream down where the vixen's ditch meets the brook . . . thence on the old way towards the white stone, thence to the hill which is called 'at the holly', thence to the hoary stone . . . thence eastward into the fort . . . thence to the paved road, thence below the wood straight out to the reed pool, then up the Avon until the old swine-enclosure runs out to the Avon . . . thence along the 'wall-way' to the stone at the stream, from the stone on along the highway to the ditch, thence down to *Wealdenesford*, thence on to the hollow way, thence down the brook to *Hunburgefleot*, and there to the sea.'*

Of course, most areas have since been subject to intermittent manorial and parochial surveys and perambulations, some of which have been conducted in comparatively recent times. By correlating the information from these and earlier documents, and by studying available MAPS, an ancient boundary may be defined. The Royal Commission on Historical Manuscripts maintains a register of relevant documents (*see* APPENDIX II) and most county record offices have collections of nineteenth-century tithe maps and estate maps, usually dating from the seventeenth and eighteenth centuries, or are able to provide details of where they may be located. Large-scale Ordnance Survey sheets are essential; 1:25000 is the most useful scale to begin with and any research must culminate in field-work. Boundary banks, ditches, green lanes, footpaths, tumuli, standing stones, ponds and even surviving field boundaries suddenly acquire an entirely new significance and with perseverance obscure documentary references to boundary markers may be identified. A typical perambulation may be ten or twelve miles in length and can often reveal factors which are not evident from documentary sources, the 'dovetailing' of field boundaries following the division of a single estate into two parishes, for example.

(* From a grant of twenty hides of land in the South Hams of Devon dated 846: *see* W.G. Hoskin's *Fieldwork in Local History*, London, 1982.)

Further reading:
Winchester, A., *Discovering Parish Boundaries*, Princes Risborough, 1990

BOUNDS, BEATING THE *see* PERAMBULATION

BOWING *see* GENUFLEXION

BOXES *see* ALMS BOXES, BIBLE BOX CHESTS, FERETORY, PARISH CHEST *and* POOR BOXES

BOX PEWS *see* PEWS *and* PEW RENTING

BOY BISHOP A strange medieval custom whereby, in some monasteries, schools and rural parishes, a boy was elected to 'perform' the duties usually associated with a bishop during the three-week period from St. Nicholas's Day (6 December) to Holy Innocents' Day (28 December).

BRACE Diagonal subsidiary timbers added to a structure (e.g. a door or the frame of a roof) to increase its rigidity.
See DOORS AND DOORWAYS, LEDGE, MUNTIN, RAIL, ROOFS *and* STILE

BRACED COLLAR *see* ROOFS

BRACKET A flat-topped, right-angled projection of stone, wood or metal used to support a shelf, statue, candles etc. Not to be confused with a CORBEL, an architectural feature of similar appearance which carries the distributed downward thrust of a larger structure. Both may be elaborately carved, painted and gilded. A bracket in the form of a scroll is described as a *console*.

BRANDAE *see* SHRINES

BRASS An alloy of copper and zinc, sometimes including minor constituents such as tin. In the Industrial Revolution brass was fundamental to the extensive hardware manufacturing industry of the English midlands, to the engineering trade and, in its purest form, for coinage and to sheathe the bottom of ships. Brass artefacts, such as crosses, candlesticks, chandeliers, sanctuary lamps, pulpit desks and lecterns are commonly found in churches and mostly date from the late-Georgian and Victorian periods.

BRASSES (MONUMENTAL) A monumental brass is an engraved metal plate affixed as a memorial to the floor or wall of a church or to a tomb chest.

There are some 8,000 brasses in England, more than any other European country, though these represent only a small proportion of the brasses laid down between *c.* 1250 and *c.* 1650. About half of these are figure brasses (depicting a human figure) while others are engraved with heraldic devices (see below) and CHRISTIAN SYMBOLS such as chalices, stylised lilies, sacred hearts and crosses and brackets. A number of later brasses are engraved with religious scenes: the Annunciation (at Fovant in Wiltshire), the Nativity (Cobham in Surrey) and the Resurrection (Slaugham in Sussex), for example, all of which are from the early sixteenth century and were fortunate to escape the attentions of the reformist iconoclasts.

Figure brasses include men, women, children and infants in swaddling clothes (*see* CHRISM) as well as skeletons and shrouded figures (*see* CADAVER). Archbishops, bishops and abbots are usually depicted in their processional or mass VESTMENTS and monks and nuns in the habits of their orders (only 30 monastic brasses have survived). Members of the Major and Minor orders of the priesthood may often be identified by symbols (*see* CHRISTIAN SYMBOLS). Judges and notaries usually have coifs (close-fitting caps), hoods and fur-lined mantles, buttoned on the right shoulder. A notary in a brass at St. Mary Tower, Ipswich has a pencase and inkhorn suspended from his belt. Academics (of which there are some seventy-five examples) are usually depicted with a skull cap or raised cap, a hood (which is not always visible) and a gown, similar in appearance to a short CASSOCK. The gown worn by Doctors of Divinity was slit at the front to show the hands (see below).

By far the largest and most interesting category is the military brass, so called because figures are depicted in ARMOUR (see below); while, of numerous civilian brasses, those of wool merchants often include the symbols of their trade (such as woolsacks) and MERCHANTS' MARKS.

Decorative canopies are common to all periods and may be 'single', 'double' or 'triple', depending on the number of 'arches' depicted, and tend to reflect current architectural styles (see CANOPY).

FEMALE FIGURES

Female figures, although not so numerous, are of equal interest and most include an element of heraldry (*see also* EFFIGIES). Elizabeth Tendring, who died in 1466, desired that the arms of her family and those of her husband should be inscribed on her memorial at Holbrook, Suffolk and she left £20 for figures of herself and her husband 'in the dress which we wore in life' to be set in brass on the marble slab. There are many examples of female figures in heraldic kirtles and mantles from the medieval and Tudor periods. The earliest example is believed to be that of Margaret, Lady Camoys (*c.* 1310) at Trotton in Sussex but unfortunately all nine enamelled shields which were once set into Lady Margaret's gown are now missing. Other notable brasses include those of Joyce, Lady Tiptoft at Enfield, Middlesex (d. 1446, engraved 1470) and Lady Katherine Howard at Stoke-by-Nayland, Suffolk (d. 1452, engraved 1535). Both are examples of retrospective memorials, that of Lady Howard being laid down during the reign of Henry VIII to commemorate descent from a singularly distinguished medieval family.

There are also many examples of women depicted in the simple white widow's veil and wimple, sideless cotehardie and kirtle of a *vowess* (or *avowess*): a widow who had 'avowed to live a life of chastity and obedience to God's will' but had not necessarily entered a religious community. Some of these splendid ladies were widows of the nobility and it is interesting to observe how many of them chose also to be depicted wearing the symbols of their rank – the ducal coronet of a duchess, for example. Good examples of vowesses' brasses may be found at Frenze and Wotton in Norfolk and at Quinton in Gloucestershire.

MANUFACTURE

Medieval brasses were, in fact, made of an alloy of

Brass of Sir John D'Abernon at Stoke D'Abernon, Surrey.

copper (75–80 per cent), with 15–20 per cent zinc and small elements of lead and tin. In the Middle Ages this material was known as *latten*, and later *cuivre blanc* (white copper).

Brasses originated in the Low Countries in the thirteenth century and a number were imported into England, notably from the fourteenth-century manufacturing centre of Tournai on the river Scheldt. Typical of these large, elaborate imported brasses is that of Abbot Thomas de la Mare at St. Alban's, Hertfordshire which measures 2.8 × 1.5 metres (9 feet 3 inches × 4 feet 4 inches). There are

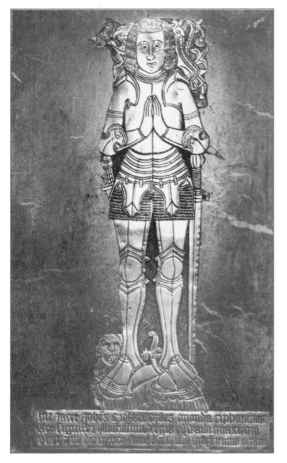

Brass of Sir John Crocker (d. 1471) at Yealmpton, Devon.

also good examples of Flemish brasses at King's Lynn in Norfolk, Newark in Nottinghamshire and Wensley in Yorkshire.

The majority of surviving English brasses originated from workshops established in the early fourteenth century at Norwich, York and London. The more ornate brasses were specially commissioned and engraved to a client's specification but each workshop also developed series of templates from which a cheaper 'off the peg' design could be selected and to which personal devices might be added. It may be possible to identify the different workshops from the characteristics of a particular brass but, as with effigies, early brasses portray only a stylised representation of a deceased person, not an accurate portrait.

Those who worked on monumental brasses were sometimes described as 'marblers', a possible reference to the craft of engraving INCISED SLABS from which the monumental brass developed. Indeed, it seems likely that several workshops which had traditionally produced lavishly expensive effigies turned also to the production of brasses as an alternative form of memorial which could be afforded by the average cleric, merchant or gentleman.

The first English brasses comprised a number of separate pieces, cut from a single sheet of metal, each of which was deeply engraved and set within an indentation (*matrix*) carved out of the stone slab so that the brass was flush with the surface. Each section was secured within its matrix in a bed of black pitch which also protected the metal from corrosion, though later brasses were often fixed by means of brass rivets driven into lead plugs which were compressed within holes in the slab. In many instances coloured enamels were let into the concave surfaces of the brass and this practice continued well into the sixteenth century.

The segmented nature of medieval brasses made them particularly vulnerable to vandalism and effacement and comparatively few complete brasses have survived. These are mostly in the south-east of England and East Anglia: in Kent, for example, there are 327 complete brasses, in Essex 237 and in Norfolk 232; while in the northern counties of Cumbria, Northumberland and Durham there are only eighteen.

DATING
It should be remembered that brasses do not always mark the place of interment: at Felbrigg in Norfolk, for example, the brass of Sir Simon Felbrigg was engraved (1416) in anticipation of his death and placed over the tomb of his first wife Margaret. But when Sir Simon died in 1442 he was buried at Norwich.

The illustrations between pages 60 and 63 are intended to assist with the dating of brasses. They include examples of military, civilian, ecclesiastical, academic and judicial styles from the thirteenth century to the seventeenth century. But they are only a guide: it is not possible in the available space to illustrate every stage in the complex development of costume and armour. Individual items such as MISERICORDES and sword belts (*see* CINGULUM MILITARE) are a useful guide to dating (*see also* CAMAIL PERIOD), as are INSCRIPTIONS.

There are also difficulties of interpretation for those who wish to date brasses or to trace the development of armour or costume through the study of monuments. Many brasses were not contemporary with the death of those they commemorate: some were retrospective, others were prepared in anticipation of death and the erection of others may have been delayed because of unreliable executors or contested wills.

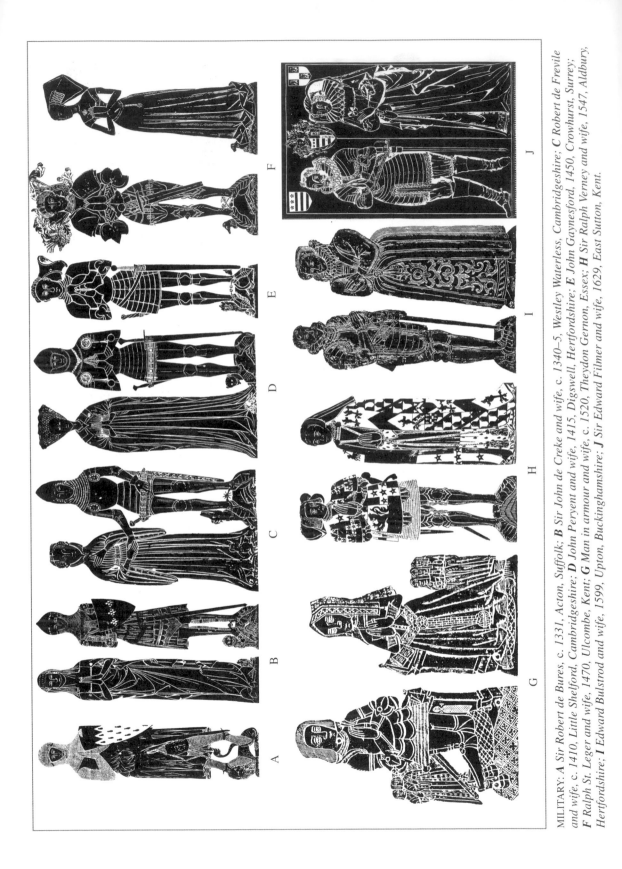

MILITARY: A *Sir Robert de Bures, c. 1331, Acton, Suffolk;* **B** *Sir John de Creke and wife, c. 1340–5, Westley Waterless, Cambridgeshire;* **C** *Robert de Frevile and wife, c. 1410, Little Shelford, Cambridgeshire;* **D** *John Peryent and wife, 1415, Digswell, Hertfordshire;* **E** *John Gaynesford, 1450, Crowhurst, Surrey;* **F** *Ralph St. Leger and wife, 1470, Ulcombe, Kent;* **G** *Man in armour and wife, c. 1520, Theydon Gernon, Essex;* **H** *Sir Ralph Verney and wife, 1547, Aldbury, Hertfordshire;* **I** *Edward Bulstrod and wife, 1599, Upton, Buckinghamshire;* **J** *Sir Edward Filmer and wife, 1629, East Sutton, Kent.*

CIVILIANS: *A Richard Torryngton and wife, 1356, Great Berkhampstead, Hertfordshire; B Sir Thomas Brook and wife, 1437, Thorncombe, Dorset; C William Maynwaryng, 1497, Ightfield, Shropshire; D Sir Thomas Nevell, 1542, Mereworth, Kent; E Civilian and wife, c. 1600, Harrow, Middlesex; F George Coles and two wives, 1640, Northampton, St. Sepulchre.*

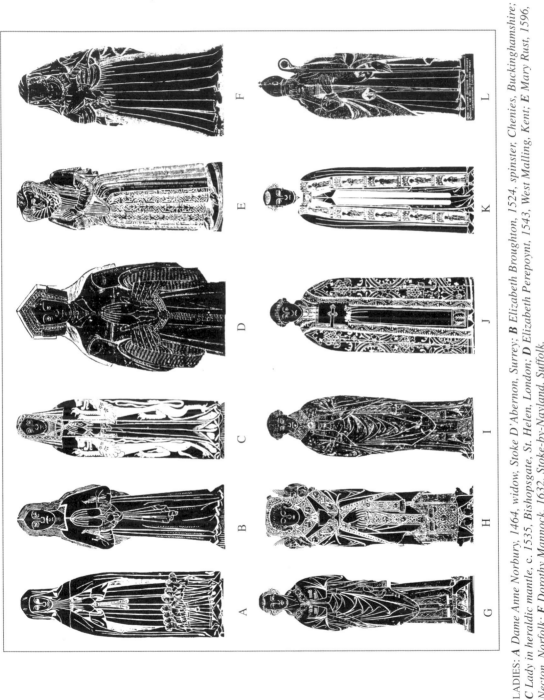

LADIES: **A** *Dame Anne Norbury, 1464, widow, Stoke D'Abernon, Surrey;* **B** *Elizabeth Broughton, 1524, spinster, Chenies, Buckinghamshire;* **C** *Lady in heraldic mantle, c. 1535, Bishopsgate, St. Helen, London;* **D** *Elizabeth Perepoynt, 1543, West Malling, Kent;* **E** *Mary Rust, 1596, Necton, Norfolk;* **F** *Dorothy Mannock, 1632, Stoke-by-Nayland, Suffolk.*
ECCLESIASTICAL: **G** *Laurence de St. Maur, 1337, Higham Ferrers, Northamptonshire;* **H** *Sir Simon of Wensley, c. 1375, Wensley, Yorkshire;* **I** *Robert Lond, 1461, Bristol, St. Peter, Gloucestershire;* **J** *Thomas Tonge, 1472, Beeford, Yorkshire;* **K** *William Ermyn, 1401, Castle Ashby, Northamptonshire;* **L** *Samuel Harsnett, 1631, Chigwell, Essex.*

ACADEMIC: *A Eudo de la Zouche, 1414, Cambridge, St. John's College; B Thomas Teylar, c. 1480, Byfleet, Surrey; C John Stonor, 1512, schoolboy, Wraysbury, Buckinghamshire; D Robert Hacombleyn, 1528, Cambridge, King's College; E Roger Lupton, 1540, Eton College, Buckinghamshire; F Edmund Geste, 1578, Salisbury Cathedral, Wiltshire.*
JUDICIAL: *G Sir John Cassy and wife, c. 1400, Deerhurst, Gloucestershire; H Sir John Juyn, 1439, Bristol, St. Mary Redcliffe; I Sir John Spelman and wife, 1545, Narborough, Norfolk.*
SHROUD: *J William Roberts and wife, 1484, Digswell, Hertfordshire.*

Brasses from the second half of the fifteenth century (notably from the period 1470–90) show a marked deterioration in drawing and balance. The whole figure is often out of proportion and details rendered without consideration to the constructive essentials of armour. Furthermore, brasses were a very much cheaper form of memorial than a stone or bronze effigy so that persons thus commemorated tended to come from the lesser gentry and merchant class who were largely unaffected by contemporary fashion. Thus we often find brasses in which figures are depicted in armour of an earlier period or in an ornate German or Italian harness which they were unlikely to have worn in real life (*see* ALWITE). Neither should it be assumed that all those who are depicted in armour were of a military disposition for it was customary for a man of note (*nobilis*) to be shown in death wearing the accoutrements of his feudal obligation of military service. Nobility and gentility were the hereditary prerogatives of the ancient warrior class: the shield was the symbol of that class and armour its uniform.

THE FOURTEENTH CENTURY

Many of the earliest brasses commemorate senior clerics who are depicted in their vestments and bearing the insignia of their office. These early figures are usually life-size or slightly smaller and may be set within a decorative engraved canopy with an inscription, usually composed of separate letters, set round the edge of the brass.

Knights of this period are usually shown cross-legged with a dog or lion at their feet, long SURCOAT and a shield on the left arm (*see* SHIELDS), while their ladies may have a pet dog playing in the folds of their costume. Invariably, military brasses contain heraldic devices which facilitate dating and identification and often provide genealogical and personal information not included in the inscription. Indeed, it was for this reason that HERALDRY was considered to be such an important component of most memorials for it declaimed both the authority and status of the deceased and the achievements which his descendants wished to commemorate.

The earliest military brass, now only a collection of gaping matrices, is at Aston Rowan in Oxfordshire and dates from *c.* 1314 while a series of military brasses, now dated from between 1320 and 1330, illustrates the use of heraldic devices on memorials. The brass of Sir John d'Abernon at Stoke d'Abernon in Surrey shows a knight bearing a shield and pennon on which there are traces of blue enamel from his arms *Azure* (blue) *a Chevron Or* (gold). This was once considered to be the oldest English military brass but has recently been re-dated to 1327. Three other splendid figures of this period are those of Roger de Trumpington at Trumpington in Cambridgeshire, Sir William de Setvans at

Chartham, Kent and Sir Robert de Bures at Acton, Suffolk. All three hold shields of their arms which are repeated on *surcoats* and *ailettes* (shoulder-guards): punning trumpets for De Trumpington and winnowing fans (*sept vans*) for De Setvans. (*See* HERALDRY *for* the dating of the Trumpington brass).

From *c.* 1330 brasses were manufactured in a variety of sizes, were usually exquisitely engraved and often included an ornate canopy. Marginal inscriptions were now incorporated within continuous strips of metal and PRECATORY SCROLLS and cross and bracket designs of great beauty were especially popular. In military brasses, the long flowing surcoat was gradually replaced by the short, tight-fitting JUPON. This was ideally suited to heraldic embellishment and yet during the period 1360–1460 only one tenth of military brasses have figures wearing heraldic garments. Of course, it may be that it is not the jupon which is depicted in these brasses but the waisted breast-plate (*cuirass*) which was increasingly in evidence from *c.* 1350 and (in two-dimensional form) would be of similar appearance (*see also* CAMAIL PERIOD).

With the emergence of a medieval middle class there was a significant increase in the number of civilian brasses and, from *c.* 1380, male civilian figures are often depicted wearing a short sword (*anelace*) which is suspended from the belt of the tunic. Civilians usually have long hair and beards until *c.* 1410.

THE FIFTEENTH CENTURY

Fifteenth-century brasses are still well-engraved but are generally smaller. Children are sometimes included, usually on separate plates below those of their parents. In 1426, William Hanningfield of Benacre in Suffolk, asked for a brass representing himself, his three wives and his twelve children to be prepared for his tomb – an early example of an entire family being depicted in a memorial.

Some of the most magnificent brasses of the period were to be found in monastic churches though, following the Dissolution of the Monasteries, fewer than thirty remain. Of these, the finest is that of Thomas Nelond, Prior of Lewes (1433), at Cowfold in Sussex. Prior Thomas is depicted in the habit of the Benedictines for he was head of the senior Cluniac monastery in England. There are further examples of monastic brasses at Denham in Buckinghamshire, Dorchester in Oxfordshire, Elstow in Bedfordshire, Nether Wallop in Hampshire, Norwich (St. Laurence) in Norfolk and the abbey of St. Alban, Hertfordshire.

Some seventy-five brasses, mostly in the collegiate chapels of Oxford and Cambridge, are of academics. As one might expect, most were in Holy Orders and are, therefore, depicted with tonsures. Academic gowns are similar in appearance to a cassock but shorter, while Doctors of Divinity wore the *cappa clausa*, a gown divided at the front to show the hands.

Lancastrian and Yorkist livery COLLARS are a characteristic of this period and a number of brasses are decorated with heraldic BADGES, either within the overall design (as at Wollaton, Northamptonshire where the slab of Richard Willoughby (1471) is inset with small brass whelk shells) or as collars (in the brass of Thomas, Lord Berkeley at Wotton-under-Edge in Gloucestershire, for example, which shows him wearing a collar of mermaids). There are numerous Garter brasses in which the figure wears the Garter on his left leg and may also be robed in the mantle of the Order. The military brass of Thomas Boleyn (father of Anne Boleyn) at Hever in Kent shows him in his full Garter robes.

From c. 1470, engraving is less precise, figures are exaggerated and shading (cross-hatching) is more in evidence. Figures in military brasses are often depicted wearing the plate armour of the period, uncovered and without embellishment, reflecting the current popularity (among the nobility at least) of the magnificent and expensive products of German and Italian armourers. But the figure is often out of proportion and details rendered without consideration to the constructive essentials of armour.

CRESTS and HELMETS are also represented in military brasses, particularly in those of the fifteenth and sixteenth centuries, when the helm is usually placed beneath or near the head of the figure. There are also examples from the late fourteenth century such as the hunting horn crest of Sir William de Bryene at Seal in Kent (1385) and the panache of feathers in the crest of Sir John Harsyck at Southacre, Norfolk (1384).

THE TUDOR PERIOD

During the early Tudor period (1485–1558) brasses become more numerous but, for the most part, they were poorly engraved with excessive cross-hatching on thin metal. Mural plates (set on walls or incorporated into WALL MONUMENTS) were increasingly popular, English replaced Latin in inscriptions and there was some attempt at portraiture.

From this time a number of brasses show figures dressed in heraldic TABARDS and these continued well into the sixteenth century, the complexity of QUARTERINGS increasing significantly in the Tudor period when descent from (or association with) an 'ancient' family (i.e. pre-Bosworth) was highly prized by the newly created Tudor aristocracy.

Numerous medieval brasses (notably those which were considered to be 'Popish') were torn from their matrices and discarded by the iconoclasts of the English Reformation, though many reappeared later as *palimpsests* (see PALIMPSEST). These were engraved on the reverse of the original (medieval) brass and the majority date from the second half of the sixteenth century when they could be obtained more cheaply than a new plate by those seeking a brass memorial.

To her credit, Elizabeth I (1558–1603) attempted to preserve monuments by means of legislation which required that, where possible, they should be repaired and restored to the churches from which they had been removed. From about 1570 the use of figures declined in popularity and designs were generally heraldic: often a central, multi-quartered coat of arms surrounded by separate shields representing hereditary and marital connections.

DESTRUCTION AND REVIVAL

Both sides in the Civil War (1642–9) destroyed thousands of brasses, often melting them down to make weapons. Those bearing religious symbols, such as the Trinity, and the beautiful cross and bracket brasses were especially vulnerable (there are bullet holes in a brass at Newnham Murren in Oxfordshire).

The monumental brass declined in popularity from the mid-seventeenth century and many were damaged or destroyed as a consequence of insensitive refurbishing and re-building schemes in the eighteenth and nineteenth centuries. But many were also saved (and even restored) during the Gothic revival of the nineteenth century, when the brass figure, set into a slab, and the brass wall monument with ornate Gothic inscriptions and the florid heraldry of the period enjoyed a revival.

For Church Monuments Society *and* Monumental Brass Society *see* APPENDIX II.

Further reading:

The Monumental Brass Society publishes an excellent series of guides arranged by counties.

Bertram, Fr. J. (ed.), *Monumental Brasses as Art and History*, Stroud, 1996

Borg, A., *Arms and Armour in Britain*, London, 1977

Bouquet, A., *Church Brasses*, London, 1956

Coales, J., (ed), *The Earliest English Brasses 1270–1350*, London, 1987

Chapman, L., *Brasses and Brass Rubbing*, Aylesbury, 1987

Clayton, M., *Brass Rubbings*, London, 1979

Cunnington, P., *A Dictionary of English Costume*, London, 1960

——, *Handbook of English Costume* (several vols.), London, 1973

Gittings, C., *Brasses and Brass Rubbing*, London, 1971

Haines, H., *A Manual of Monumental Brasses*, 1861 (reprinted 1970)

Kelly, F. and Schwabe, R., *A Short History of Costume and Armour 1066–1800*, Newton Abbot, 1972

Macklin, H., *Monumental Brasses*, 1905 (rev. J. Page-Phillips, London, 1975)

Macklin, H., *The Brasses of England*, London, 1975

Mayo, J., *The History of Ecclesiastical Dress*, London, 1985

Norris, M., *Monumental Brasses*, London, 1977–8 (3 vols.)

Page-Phillips, J., *Children on Brasses*, London, 1970

——, *Palimpsests: the Backs of Monumental Brasses* (2 vols.), London, 1980

BRATTISHING Late medieval ornamental cresting consisting of carved formalised flowers or leaves (sometimes within a crenellated form) on (e.g.) a screen, cornice or parapet.
See also DECORATIVE MOTIFS

BRAWLING Although the word is commonly used to describe a noisy quarrel or fight, brawling was a specific offence: that of causing a disturbance in a church or churchyard.

BRAY, THE VICAR OF *see* REFORMATION, THE

BREAD In the Christian Church, bread symbolises all food and exemplifies God's providence. It was baked in huge quantities to feed monastic communities, for almsgiving and for the sustenance of guests. In BENEDICTINE houses, the daily bread was distributed with extraordinary ceremony. At the commencement of a meal the loaves were placed in a basket suspended by ropes and pulleys above the abbot's table. When all were assembled the basket '. . . shall descend onto the abbot's table, in order that the rations of God's labourers may appear to descend to them from Heaven'. Of course, bread is associated with the Sacrament and in the western Church unleavened (unfermented) bread has always been used in the Eucharistic rite, though in the Church of England both leavened and unleavened bread are now permitted.
See also BREAD OVENS *and* DOLE CUP-BOARDS

BREAD OVEN In addition to the great monastic BAKEHOUSE, there was often provision within the abbey church itself for the baking of the 'single bread' – the unleavened bread (*obleys*) used at the mass – a task which was usually directed with great solemnity by the sacrist. Bread ovens may occasionally be found in churches: rectangular openings within the thickness of a wall, with well-constructed close-fitting stone or brick linings and an external flue. Before baking, the oven was pre-heated by a small fire, of faggot-wood or furze, lit in the base of the oven. When this had died down, the ashes were hastily removed and the door shut on the bread which gently baked in the diminishing heat, supplemented by latent heat from the chimney flue.

BREECHES *see* COSTUME

BRESSUMER (*also* BREASTSUMMER) A horizontal beam, often carved ornamentally, which carries the superstructure in timber-framed buildings and into which the first floor joists are tenoned. The term is also used to describe a heavy beam spanning a fireplace or other opening.

BREVIARY A liturgical book containing the text (and often the music) to be used in the DIVINE OFFICE together with certain additions such as prayers for the dead. So complex was the music that in many religious houses a number of quire books would be used during a single service: the Antiphoner, Graduale etc.

BRICK Since Roman times, the process of brick-making has consisted of obtaining clay from the ground, preparing and moulding it into shape and burning it. The methods used in this process changed little until the mid-nineteenth century: after excavation, the clay was 'puddled' to remove unwanted material and to provide an even consistency; the brick was then moulded to the required form, using a wooden mould, and dried to reduce shrinkage; final burning was carried out in a clamp in which the bricks were stacked together with faggots of brushwood as fuel. Clamp firing produced unevenness in size and colour (evident in the attractive variety of medieval and Tudor brickwork) and the system was eventually replaced by burning in kilns in which the bricks were stacked to allow the passage of hot air between them. Firing took about 48 hours, coal replacing wood as the principal fuel from *c.* 1700. A seventeenth-century innovation was the pug-mill, a mechanical device for puddling which until then had been done (literally) by foot. Pug-mills were at first horse (or donkey) powered but later water power and steam were used. The dimensions of bricks were first standardised in 1477 to conform to the grasp of the brick-layer's fingers and thumb.

There is little evidence of brickmaking following the Roman withdrawal until the earliest known English bricks appeared in the eastern counties in the mid-twelfth century, at Polstead church in Suffolk and Little Coggeshall in Essex for example. Roman 'bricks', elongated red tiles, were sometimes re-used by medieval builders but, contrary to practice in Europe, there was no real brick-building tradition in Britain until the seventeenth century.

It is surprising that the English for so long failed to recognise the obvious advantages of brick as a building material: baking bricks on site or using local kilns was considerably quicker and cheaper than quarrying, dressing and transporting stone. Eventually, it was the inexorable depredation of the forests for building timber, combined with the immigration of Flemish weavers into East Anglia during the fourteenth century, that encouraged a quickening appreciation of the brick architecture of the Low Countries and the development of a brick-making industry along the east coast in the fifteenth century. But even then the use of brick was mostly confined to domestic buildings while churches continued to be built or extended in stone. The fourteenth-century Holy Trinity church at Kingston-upon-Hull, Humberside is one of only a small number of notable medieval exceptions. There are, however, several churches with fine mellow brickwork dating from the Tudor period, notably in the county of Essex: at Chignal Smealy (where the entire church, including the font, is of brick) and Layer Marney, for example, and at Sandon (porch), Feering (porch) and Great Baddow (clerestory). There are splendid brick TOWERS at Castle Heddingham, Gestingthorpe, Great Holland, Ingatestone, Rochford and Wickham St. Paul, all in Essex, and at St. Mary-at-Elms in Ipswich, Suffolk.

Building regulations following the Great Fire of London of 1666 encouraged the rapid expansion of the brick manufacturing industry which, together with the gradual acceptance of classical architecture during the seventeenth century and the consequential development of a variety of new bonds (*for* illustration *see* BONDING), presaged the great age of English brick-building. By the end of the eighteenth century the brick making industry was perfecting techniques of mass-production in response to the demands of the Industrial Revolution and a rapidly increasing urban population. The Victorian appetite for civic pride and corporate rivalry satiated itself in a welter of architectural activity and civic, domestic, industrial and ecclesiastical buildings and structures were erected on a vast scale. The predominant material was brick which was available in an extraordinary range of qualities and colours: from extra hard 'engineering bricks' for use in viaducts, tunnels and factories to hand-made, textured bricks for churches and domestic buildings.

See also BRICK NOGGING, MASONRY, SLATES *and* TILES

Further reading:
Yarwood, D., *Encyclopaedia of Architecture*, London, 1985

BRICK NOGGING Late seventeenth- or eighteenth-century patterned brickwork placed between the vertical timbers (*studs*) of a timber-framed buildings to replace earlier lath and plaster or wattle and daub.

BRIDGES *see* CHAPELS

BRIDLEWAYS *see* FOOTPATHS AND BRIDLE-WAYS

BRIEF (i) Written consent from a bishop or senior ecclesiastical official authorising collections for charitable or other worthwhile causes. (*See also* BULL) (ii) A formal document, drawn up by the breviator of a religious community to record the death of a member. The brief, which requested that prayers be said for the soul of the deceased, was conveyed to the almoners of other religious houses who sometimes endorsed the document with Latin verses, praising the dead or expressing sympathy with the bereaved, before returning it.

BRISURE A mark of cadency (*see* CADENCY (HERALDIC)).

BRITANNIA METAL A silvery alloy of tin, antimony and copper. Closely resembling silver or polished pewter, Britannia Metal was in use from *c.* 1790 into the nineteenth century (*see* EPBM, EPGS AND EPNS).

BRITANNIA SILVER Precious metal consisting of 95.8 per cent pure silver (*see also* STERLING STANDARD).

BROACH SPIRE *see* TOWERS

BROACH STOP A diamond-shaped stop against a CHAMFER.

BRONZE An alloy of copper and tin.

BROTHER (i) In older wills, the term 'brother' included a brother-in-law or stepbrother. (ii) A lay member of a religious order (*see* FATHER).

BUCKET *see* ASPERGES *and* FIRE BUCKET

BUCRANE (*also* **BUCRANIUM**) Classical ornamentation comprising a garlanded ox skull (sometimes inverted) commonly used as a frieze decoration.

BUGIA (also PALMATORIUM and SCOTULA)
A portable candlestick with lighted candle.

BUILDING MATERIALS Old churches are usually constructed of local materials which is why they sit so comfortably in the landscape. The best building material is oolitic limestone which stretches in a great band across England from east Yorkshire to the Dorset coast at Lyme Regis. Within this band, the colour and texture of the stone is variable: in the eastern Cotswolds, for example, it is a rich, golden colour while in the Painswick area above the Severn Vale it is almost white. The superb stone spires of Northamptonshire are constructed of oolitic limestone as are the magnificent church TOWERS of Somerset. In the Fen Country of Norfolk, several splendid churches such as West Walton and Walpole St. Peter are built of stone transported by water from the oolitic limestone belt to the north-east.

Elsewhere in East Anglia, as in other chalk country, FLINT is almost universal with stone restricted to doorways, buttresses and window openings. In the chalk and clay of south-east England, the absence of good quality building stone has resulted in a large proportion of fairly modest churches, many constructed of flint and chalk, with timber (which was plentiful) used for BELFRIES and spires. The church at Greenstead in Essex is the oldest timber church in England while, in the same county, there is an abundance of fine brickwork, mostly dating from the Tudor period (*see* BRICK).

Sandstones vary in colour from white to the yellow, brown or red which indicates the presence of iron, and to a greenish shade which comes from the mineral Glauconite. Churches on the sandstone ridge which runs parallel with the chalk of the North and South Downs are of a light yellow sandstone while the pink or dull yellow sandstones of the north Midlands weather badly. Many Herefordshire churches (including the sublime little Norman church of St. Mary and St. David at Kilpeck) are built of Old Red Sandstone, a mysterious dark, almost maroon-coloured stone – 'imbrued with blood' according to a native Welsh tradition. New Red Sandstones appear in Cheshire, Devon and parts of Somerset. These vary in texture and are of a warmer, more vivid colour: as in the churches at Exminster in Devon and Combe Florey in Somerset.

'Magpie' churches, timber-framed and white-plastered, are a characteristic of the Welsh Marches as at Lower Peover and Marton in Cheshire and Melverley in Shropshire.

Churches in the far north-west of England, the south-west peninsular and the Welsh uplands although built of coarse materials nevertheless harmonise perfectly with the landscape and, because

of the extraordinary durability of the rock, possess an almost timeless quality. Most of these churches would have been white-washed, and many still are. The twelfth-century biographer of Gruffudd ap Cynan tells us that Gwynedd 'came to shine with white-washed churches, like stars in the firmament'. Granite is especially difficult to carve but there are several examples of well-fashioned granite churches, notably St. Mary Magdalene at Launceston, Cornwall.

Building materials are often mixed to good effect. In Northamptonshire, for example, ironstone and grey oolitic freestone may be found in decorative bands, as in the elegant perpendicular tower of St. Mary's, Whiston. In chalk areas, flint combined with limestone produces flushwork, a singularly beautiful form of ornamentation (*see* FLINT).

The material used for roof coverings also varies according to availability and local tradition. Red TILES are ubiquitous in the south of England, old grey SLATES in the south-west and stone tiles in the Cotswolds and parts of Dorset and Wiltshire. Red PANTILES may be found in East Anglia and the east Midlands, as at Bawburgh in Norfolk and Holme in Nottinghamshire, while there are several thatched churches, notably at Filby, Hales, Edingthorpe and Potter Heigham in Norfolk and Fritton in Suffolk.

See also ALABASTER, ANCASTER STONE, ASHLAR, BARGE BOARDS, BATH STONE, BRICK, BRICK NOGGING, CLAPBOARD (*see* WEATHERBOARD), CLUNCH, COADE STONE, COB, COTSWOLD STONE, DRESSED STONE, FACING MATERIALS, FLINT, FLUSHWORK (*see* FLINT), FOREST MARBLE, FREESTONE, FROSTERLEY MARBLE (*see* PURBECK MARBLE), GREENSAND, GYPSUM (*see* ALABASTER), IRONSTONE, KENTISH RAG, KETTON STONE, KNAPPING (*see* FLINT), LATH AND PLASTER, MARBLE, MASONRY, MOORSTONE, PANTILES, PEBBLEDASH, PLASTERWORK, PORTLAND STONE, PURBECK MARBLE, RAG and RAGSTONE, RAGWORK, ROOFING TILES (*see* TILES *and* SLATES), RUBBLE, RUSTICATION (*see* MASONRY), SHINGLES, SLATES, STONEWORK (*see* MASONRY), STUCCO (*see* PLASTERWORK), STUD, TILE HANGING, TILES, TOUCH, TOURNAI MARBLE (*see* TOUCH), WEATHER-BOARD *and* WELDON STONE
Further reading:
Parsons, D., *Stone: Quarrying and Building in England AD 43–1525*, London, 1990

BULLA An embossed metal disc, originally lead, attached to a document as a means of authentication (*see also* SEALS). Papal edicts were sealed in this manner – hence the term *papal bull*.

BULLARIUM A collection of papal bulls (*see* BULLA) and similar documents.

BULL'S EYE (*or* BULLION) *see* GLASS

BURGESS BELL A bell which rings for a few strokes three quarters of an hour before a service. The origin of the name is obscure: it may be a corruption of *expergiscere* meaning 'awake!' or simply a reference to the burgesses who dwelt at some distance from a church and for whose benefit the bell was rung.

BURIAL ACTS Legislation enacted between 1847 and 1906 giving local government authorities powers to act in matters concerning the overcrowding of churchyards and the supervision of burial grounds. Prior to the Cemeteries Clauses Act of 1847 and the Burial Acts of 1852 and 1853, most people were buried in church graveyards many of which were already overcrowded and insanitary by the seventeenth century (*see* BURIALS). Furthermore, demographic changes brought about by the Industrial Revolution resulted in a significant increase of population in many parishes and the overcrowding of churchyards which was becoming a serious health risk. The Act of 1852 applied only to London and the provision was extended to the rest of the country in the following year. Thereafter, local authorities were able to administer their own cemeteries through burial boards appointed by vestries. The Public Health (Interments) Act of 1879 was followed by the Local Government Act of 1894, which transferred the duties of the burial boards to parish and district councils, and the Cremation Act of 1902. The Local Government Act of 1972 abolished burial boards, simplified existing legislation and made provision for the maintenance of CLOSED CHURCHYARDS. The Local Authorities' Cemeteries Order of 1974 provided for the management, regulation and control of local authority cemeteries but this was revoked and replaced by a similar Order in 1977 which dealt with the functional administration of cemeteries. Burial registers and lists of grave-lots are normally kept in the superintendent's office at the larger cemeteries. The registers for cemeteries which were established before 1837 are kept at the Public Record Office in Chancery Lane, London.
See also CHURCHYARDS, OSSUARIES *and* PLAGUE

BURIAL IN WOOL ACTS 1667 AND 1678 Legislation, intended to promote the wool trade, requiring that corpses should be buried in wool. The 1678 Act stated that '. . . no corpse of any person (except those who shall die of the plague), shall be buried in any shirt, shift, sheet or shroud or anything whatsoever, made or mingled with flax, hemp, silk, hair, gold or silver, or in any stuff or thing other than what is made from sheep's wool only . . .'. Initially, the officiating priest was required to certify that a deceased person had been 'buried in wool' and, later, relatives of the deceased had to swear an affidavit within eight days of a 'woollen burial'. This was recorded in the REGISTERS. Failure to comply resulted in a fine of £5 which was levied on both the estate of the deceased and on those associated with the burial. Occasionally, a particularly conscientious churchwarden would acquire an additional register for the entry of 'burials in woollen'. The acts were repealed in 1814.
See also BURIALS

BURIALS
MONASTIC BURIALS
Stone coffins (or their lids) may sometimes be found at former monastic churches and these almost invariably contained the remains of distinguished members of the religious community who were granted the privilege of burial in the chapter house, east walk of the cloister or in the church itself. Most monks were buried (without coffins) in the monastery cemetery, usually to the east of the chapter house and south of the church and approached from the cloister via a SLYPE or, in Cistercian houses, through a door in the transept. Only in Carthusian monasteries was the cloister garth used for burials. The right to burial in a monastic cemetery was usually confined to brethren and confraters (*see* CONFRATERNITY) though urban monasteries sometimes provided a separate lay cemetery within its precincts. According to medieval practice, bones were exhumed after a time and conveyed to a charnel house near the cemetery. This was sometimes a CRYPT with a chapel above. Founders (*see* BENEFACTORS) and royalty were often afforded burial in or near monastic churches: at the Cistercian abbey of Ystrad Fflur (Strata Florida) in Dyfed, for example, which became the burial place of the thirteenth-century princes of Deheubarth. The south porch of Beaumaris church, Anglesey contains the splendid stone coffin of Princess Joan, illegitimate daughter of King John and consort of Llywelyn ab Iorwerth (Llywelyn Fawr, d. 1240). Joan was originally buried at nearby Llanfaes Friary (which was founded to commemorate her death) but, after various vicissitudes, her coffin finally came to rest in the parish church of Beaumaris in 1808. Her effigy is carved on the coffin lid, surrounded by Celtic-style tracery.
MEDIEVAL FUNERALS
In medieval society, a high mortality rate and the brooding presence of the DOOM served as constant reminders of the transient nature of life. This preoccupation was less concerned with obtaining a

speedy transition through the 'purifying pains' of Purgatory (which could be facilitated through the endowment of chantries and the receipt of indulgences) than with avoiding the eternal torments of Hell (*see* CHANTRY *and* INDULGENCE). The funeral was regarded as a preliminary to this process and it was necessary, therefore, that the making of a will, which paid obligations to God and to man (*see* PROBATE), should be followed by a 'good death', a funeral appropriate to the status of the deceased, and a Christian burial. But death was also regarded as a release from the trials and tribulations of a sinful world to a larger, fuller life in Heaven. The anniversary of a death (the 'year's mind') was therefore a greater reason for celebration than a birthday, and a funeral an occasion for solemn rejoicing that 'the soul of a good and faithful servant had detached itself from the body for a glorious reunion with God'**.

In the upper echelons of society testators sometimes required that there should be 'no worldly pomp' at their funerals, but most anticipated a ceremony befitting their status, and the funerals of those of noble and knightly rank were arranged in every detail by the Kings of Arms (*see* FUNERAL HERALDRY). Some wills simply specified the place of burial and the amount to be set aside for alms, torch-bearers, masses and other expenses, the details of the funeral being left to the executors to determine. Gentlemen and their ladies were normally buried within the parish church and it was also common for those of 'gentle rank' to be interred in the church of a monastery or friary. Interment was preceded overnight by VESPERS after which MATTINS and LAUDS (*Dirge*) were said and, in the morning, a REQUIEM MASS celebrated by the priest in black vestments.

In order to obtain 'perpetual remembrances' in the prayers of those who attended, and by the poor who received alms, the funerals of the great medieval and Tudor magnates were often magnificent occasions accompanied by heraldic pomp and ceremonial. On the death of his third wife, Jane Seymour (*c.* 1509–37), Henry VIII 'retired to a solitary place to see to his sorrows' while the Duke of Norfolk (as Earl Marshal) attended to the burial arrangements 'according to custom.'

First the wax chandler 'did his office' of embalming, then the Queen's corpse was 'leaded, soldered and chested' by the plumbers. The ladies and gentlemen of the court, with white veils covering their heads and shoulders, kept a perpetual watch around the royal hearse in 'a chamber of presence' lit by twenty-one tapers until the Vigil of the Feast of All Saints on 31 October. The entire chapel of Hampton Court, and all the chambers and galleries leading to it, were draped with black and

'garnished with rich images'. The hearse, after being incensed, was processed by torchlight and received in the chapel by Lancaster Herald who 'in a loud voice' invited all those present 'of their charity' to pray for the late Queen's soul. Thereafter, twelve priests watched over the coffin by night and twelve of the Queen's ladies kept watch by day until 12 November when the body was taken in solemn procession to Windsor, borne on a chariot by six horses and accompanied by nobles and heralds with banners. The poor who witnessed the procession were presented with alms and the coffin installed within St. George's Chapel. The next day the Queen was buried 'with great solemnity' in a vault beneath the choir 'and all finished by twelve o' clock that day'. By the standards of the day, Queen Jane's funeral was a comparatively simple affair.

For the more impoverished members of society, such niceties were of little consequence. Even so, a funeral was a complex and expensive occasion which must have placed an enormous financial burden on most families.

A single bell would toll across the fields, causing the field-workers to pause just long enough to offer up a silent prayer for the soul of the departed and to ponder on their own mortality (*see* BELLS). Meanwhile the cortège would pass through the village, preceded by the crucifer and acolytes, its approach heralded by the clerk or sexton ringing a handbell and the priest and his ministers robed in albs and singing psalms. Next came the bier, followed by the chief mourners in black cloaks and hoods and then the other relatives and friends of the deceased, all carrying tapers. On its arrival at the church the bier was placed at the entrance to the chancel (with the feet to the east) and covered with a pall. Candlesticks were placed at the four corners of the bier or, in wealthier churches, a HEARSE erected over the corpse. With the mourners standing in the nave and the priest occupying his stall the *Officium pro Defunctus* (the Office for the Dead) began.

In the Sarum Rite, Vespers of the Dead were sung on the preceding evening and the body remained in the church overnight. On the following morning, while the penitential Mattins and Lauds were being sung, the priest, dressed in his alb and stole (*see* VESTMENTS), went into the churchyard where he made the sign of the cross over the ground appointed for the burial, sprinkled it with holy water and marked out its length and breadth in the shape of a cross, reciting the words 'Open ye to me the gates of justice; I will go into them, and give praise to the Lord. This is the gate of the Lord; the just shall enter into it' (Psalm 107:19–20). This done, he returned to the church for the Requiem Mass. After the post-Communion prayer the priest removed his chasuble, put on his cope and walked round the corpse in an anti-clockwise direction while sprinkling it with holy water and censing it. The altar party and mourners then processed into the churchyard and on coming to the grave (which would have been dug during the Requiem Mass) the body was sprinkled and censed for a second time before being lowered into the shallow grave by the sexton and his assistants. The priest then placed either a simple lead cross or a scroll inscribed with the words of the Absolution on the breast of the shrouded corpse which was censed and sprinkled a third time. After the recitation of Psalm 131 and further prayers for the soul's repose, the priest began the infilling by spading the soil lightly onto the body in the form of a cross. The burial party then returned to the church singing the seven penitential psalms and leaving the sexton to complete his work. Thereafter masses were said every day for a month with special solemnity on the third, seventh and thirtieth days (*see* TRENTAL), though observation of this protracted liturgy was already in decline by the mid-fifteenth century, no doubt because the priest expected to receive a fee on each occasion.

The more affluent mourners were expected to make doles of money, food and mourning clothes to the poor on the day of the funeral and on the third, seventh and thirtieth days of mourning – though this practice was also replaced by a single feast for the chief mourners following the funeral, a custom which survives today

POST-REFORMATION FUNERALS

Much of the ritual which accompanied even the simplest medieval funeral was swept away with the introduction of the revised LITURGY of the Church of England (*see* REFORMATION). Gone were the crucifer and acolytes of the procession, many of the 'house offices' which preceded the medieval funeral were modified or omitted and the preliminary obsequies were performed at the 'church stile' or LICH-GATE before the shrouded body was transferred from the corpse-table to the parish bier and conveyed to the door of the church (*see* CORPSE ROADS *and* PORCHES). The second part of the service took place in the south porch before the cortège moved into the chancel for the final solemnities and then outside again for the committal (burial), usually in an unmarked grave on the south side of the church (*see also* CHURCHYARD CROSSES *and* CHURCH-YARDS).

Until the eighteenth century, corpses were usually buried in material, though many parishes kept a coffin in which the corpse was carried during the service. The parish coffin at Easingwold in Yorkshire (*c.* 1645) is believed to be the earliest to have survived complete with its lid. Following the BURIAL IN WOOL ACT of 1678, the priest was obliged to confirm that the shroud was made of wool and, with the churchwarden, to enter the fact in the church records. Inevitably, the absence of a coffin rendered a corpse vulnerable to abuse. John Aubrey, writing in his diaries in the second half of the seventeenth century, tells of those who could recall the practice of placing a penny in the mouths of corpses as a gratuity to St. Peter and also that '. . . it was a common fashion for the women to get a tooth out of a skull in the churchyard, which they wore as a preservation against the toothache' (*see also* BODY SNATCHERS).

Anthropoidal lead coffins (i.e. of human shape and form) were sometimes used but were so expensive that they were beyond the means of all but the nobility and gentry. Several have survived, mostly from the early seventeenth century, including those of two children in the Sackville vault at Withyham in Sussex.

While the great and good were interred and commemorated inside the church, all other members of society continued to be buried in the churchyard, 'uncoffined and anonymous corpses, wrapped in cloth [and] deposited in the ground, one on top of the other.' * Eventually, the level of the south side of the churchyard rose until overcrowding could no longer be concealed. The results are sometimes evident today, especially in the high banks at the sides of paths leading to the church porch, as at the church of St. Nicholas at Montgomery in Powys.

To the unconsecrated north side of the churchyard were committed the mortal remains of transgressors: usually those who had taken their own lives or the lives of others. An entry, dated 1667, in the parish register of Malpas in Cheshire recalls the death of 'Sarah Harrison who hanged herself' and 'was buried on the backside of the church'. The sinister nature of the north side of the churchyard persisted even when the more salubrious south side became overcrowded. Gilbert White, in a letter written in the 1780s, observed: 'All wish to be buried on the south side, which has become such a mass of mortality that no person can be there interred without disturbing or displacing the bones of his ancestors'. One solution to the problem of overcrowding was to erect a small charnel house (*see* OSSUARIES) in which 'undecayed relics of mortality' were stored. There is a good example, set against the churchyard wall, at Mere in Wiltshire. But these in turn proved inadequate and there are several recorded instances of bones being tipped into large pits (now referred to as *mortuary holes*) which may be mistaken for plague pits (*see* PLAGUE). It was the BURIAL ACTS of 1852 and 1853 which finally resolved the problem by permitting civil authorities to create burial grounds.

Between the late seventeenth century and the early

nineteenth, city and town churches were heavily used by the middle class for intramural burial – interment beneath the floor of the church (*see* INCISED SLABS *and* VAULTS, BURIAL). At Bath Abbey in Avon, for example, the walls are encrusted with memorial tablets to those who are buried nearby, while at the former church of St. Augustine in Bristol no fewer than 107 private chambers were revealed beneath the floor when the site was excavated in 1983. Several centuries of intramural burial at the church of St. Helen, Bishopsgate in London resulted in the floor being raised on several occasions. When, in 1892, the remains were removed to the City of London cemetery at Ilford, over one thousand bodies were counted.

The EIGHTEENTH-CENTURY CHURCH was preoccupied with the niceties of social behaviour and the funerals of those who aspired to gentility were splendidly formal occasions. Attendance at such a funeral was itself indicative of one's position in society and admission was strictly controlled. As a result, commercial stationers produced an impressive variety of engraved and embossed *funeral tickets* which could be 'personalised' by the addition of heraldic devices and suitably sombre inscriptions and illustrations.

The late nineteenth century was the golden age of the Victorian funeral: 'the horse-drawn cortège, the flower-decked funeral car with its encased burden, and sable mourning coaches containing weeping ladies swathed in crape and black bombazine, supported in their grief by stiff-lipped husbands, brothers and uncles, resembling the top-hatted beetles in contemporary caricatures by Griset. On the road, two dreadful mutes led the way, harbingers of death itself, whilst the tramp, tramp, tramp of the attendants' measured paces re-echo the clop, clop, clop of the horses' hooves. . .' **

See also GRAVESIDE SHELTERS *and* MAUSOLEUMS

CHURCHYARD SUPERSTITIONS

It was Pope Gregory I (*c.* 540–604) who advised that the dead should be buried in churchyards rather than CEMETERIES. It was hoped that those attending services would be minded to remember the dead in their prayers – having passed among them on their way to the church (*see* YEW TREES). But paganism often prevailed: it was believed by many that the Devil could claim the first body to be buried in a newly-consecrated churchyard and a dog was sometimes interred as a substitute before the first Christian burial took place. Elsewhere, it was believed that the most recently buried corpse assumed the duties of churchyard 'watcher', a singularly unpleasant vigil which was to be avoided whenever possible. Consequently, when two or more burials were scheduled for the same day, there was often an unseemly competition among the various groups of mourners in an attempt to outwit each other and avoid the last committal. Such superstitions have often persisted, even to the present day. In the nineteenth century, when a churchyard was in danger of becoming overcrowded, relatives of the deceased would go to extraordinary lengths to ensure that their loved one was not the last to be buried – and thereby assume the duties of the 'watcher' in perpetuity. To escape this awful fate, it was sometimes agreed that the body should be buried upside down so that it would be incapable of performing its duties.

Bodies were normally buried on their backs with their heads to the west and their eyes towards the east. Vestigial elements of pagan sun-worship are also evident in a number of funeral rites which, in more remote areas, persisted for many years. A cortège would approach the church only in an anti-clockwise or 'sunways' direction, for instance, a ritual which is still observed by a number of funeral directors today (though few will admit it). In one known case, villagers would carry a corpse three times round the churchyard cross before presenting it for Christian burial, much to the consternation of the incumbent who caused the cross to be destroyed and the fragments hidden. Anti-clockwise was, of course, considered to be unlucky and was known as 'going the back way'.

RIGHTS OF BURIAL

Every parishioner has a right of burial within his parish, though the responsibility for finding a burial space lies with the executors of a deceased person and neither a parochial church council nor any local authority is under a legal obligation to provide burial space. In the event of executors being unable to find a space or where, for example in the case of a vagrant, there are no executors, responsibility for the disposal of the body lies with the appropriate district council (or its successor authority) under Section 50 of the National Assistance Act, 1949 (*see also* CLOSED CHURCHYARDS). Providing two independent doctors' certificates have been obtained, a body may be taken to a burial plot and 'committed to the earth' without recourse to an undertaker or, indeed, a funeral service. It is also in order to bury up to two people in a back garden: permission is not required though it is advisable to inform a local authority. Of course, the value of a property may be reduced thereby and there is no guarantee that a new owner will not exhume a body for burial elsewhere. Less than one third of deaths now lead to burials: 70 per cent of Britain's annual 635,000 deaths are followed by CREMATION.

See also BURIAL ACTS, GRAVESTONES, HATCHMENTS, HEART BURIAL, MEMORIALS, MORTSAFE, REGISTERS, SEARCHER *and* SUICIDES

Further reading:

Curl, J., *Celebration of Death*, London, 1990

Gregory, D., *Yesterday in Village Church and Churchyard*, Llandysul, 1988 *

Litten, J., *The English Way of Death*, London, 1991 **

Southworth, E., (ed.), *Anglo-Saxon Cemeteries*, Stroud, 1989

BUTTERY *see* LARDER

BUTTRESS A projecting support constructed against a wall to counteract the weight of roofs and TOWERS and to compensate for the structurally weakening effects of window openings. The walls of Saxon and Norman stone buildings were invariably of considerable thickness with small windows and comparatively light timber roofs supported by tie and collar beams. Consequently they required little reinforcement and buttresses of this period are generally wide but of low projection. The thinner walls, larger windows and heavy stone vaults of Gothic architecture required substantial buttressing with projections of greater depth at the base, reducing in upward stages to the roof level (*see* BAY). During the thirteenth century *angle buttresses* were used at the corners of buildings where they met at 90 degrees (*see* illustration below). *Setback buttresses* are similar but are set back slightly to expose the corner of the building. Less common are the large, square *clasping buttresses* which enclose the corners of a tower or porch. In the fourteenth century *diagonal buttresses* were widely used. These are set diagonally at right angles to the corners of a tower or building. The *flying buttress* (or *arch buttress*) is one by which the thrust of a vault is carried from a wall to an outer buttress by means of an arch or series of arches. The lofty stone vaults, vast windows and slender walls (often little more than cages of stone ribs) which characterise the Perpendicular style of Gothic architecture of the late fourteenth and fifteenth centuries demanded extraordinary ingenuity in order that the downward and outward thrust of roof, tower and (sometimes) spire should be evenly distributed and counteracted. Mainly through trial and error, the abutment system developed by which arches, placed at the point of greatest thrust (found to be immediately below the springing line of a vault on an internal wall) transferred the pressure through buttresses to ground level and, by means of heavy pinnacles on the buttresses themselves, successfully offset the effect of the thrust. Buttresses were sometimes incorporated into the structure of larger buildings,

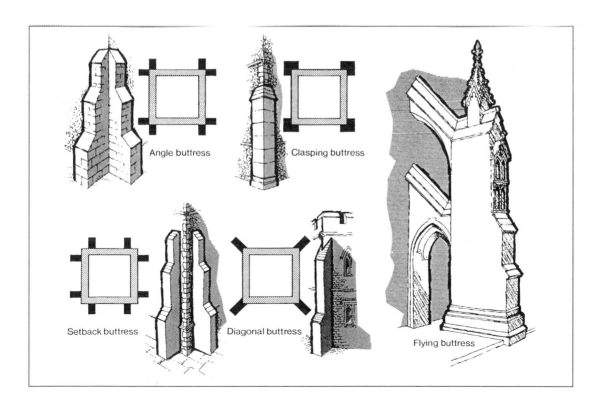

Angle buttress

Clasping buttress

Setback buttress

Diagonal buttress

Flying buttress

Flying buttresses and crocketed pinnacles at Milton Abbey, Dorset.

and may be visible from the interior, as at Gloucester Cathedral where massive 'flying' buttresses, constructed within the transept walls, transfer the outward thrust of the tower to ground level. Buttresses are not confined to medieval churches: the flying buttresses of Wren's St. Paul's Cathedral, London (1675–1711) are concealed behind high screen walls which themselves support the buttresses.

BUTTS *see* ARCHERY

CABLE FONT A font (usually Norman) having carved decoration in the form of a girdle of braided rope.

CABLE MOULDING (*also* ROPE MOULDING) Moulding imitating a twisted rope (*see* DECORATIVE MOTIFS).

CADAVER From the Latin *cadaver* meaning 'corpse', the name is applied to effigies of the dead when represented in emaciated form and on the verge of decay. Death, and the imagery of decay, haunted the medieval mind especially following the plagues and pestilences of the early fifteenth century. Death was personified as a grasping skeleton, often as the' Grim Reaper' with scythe and timeglass, and decay as worms: *humiliatus sum vermis* – 'by worms I am abused'. Examples of cadavers may be found at Fyfield church in Berkshire (Sir John Golafre d. 1442) and at Tewkesbury Abbey, Gloucestershire, where writhing worms and various snails, toads and mice feast on the corpse of a fifteenth-century abbot.

Skeleton brasses generally date from the mid-fifteenth century to the late sixteenth century and usually depict a skeleton in a knotted shroud as at Margate in Kent and Hildersham in Cambridgeshire. There is a true cadaver brass at Oddington in Oxfordshire in which Ralph Hamsterley is shown being consumed by worms. *Shroud brasses* are slightly different for they show a living figure wrapped in a SHROUD. Female shroud brasses are often strangely beautiful for the long hair is shown flowing down the outside of the shroud. There are good examples at West Firle in Sussex, Digswell in Hertfordshire and Yoxford in Suffolk.
See also BRASSES (MONUMENTAL) *and* EFFIGIES

CADENCY (HERALDIC) The medieval tenet 'one man one coat' often necessitated the 'differencing' of coats of arms in order that each male member of a family, and of its cadet branches, should possess distinctive arms, a practice known as cadency. Originally this was achieved by making minor alterations to the design: by varying the colours (*tinctures*) or charges, for example. Since the Middle Ages the three-pointed *label* has been borne by an eldest son during the lifetime of his father. In the fifteenth century, this was augmented by a system of symbols (*brisures*), each appropriate to a particular male member of a family. But in practice (and with the exception of the label) this system has been found to be singularly unsatisfactory and has generally been more honoured in the breach than the observance. During the Middle Ages cadency marks were also used to signify feudal tenure and even political allegiance, elements of one coat being transferred to another for this purpose.
See also BASTARDY *and* HERALDRY
Further reading:
Gayre, R., *Heraldic Cadency*, Harlow, 1961

Brisures used by eldest son (label, top), fifth son (annulet, middle) and third son (mullet, bottom). A crescent was used by a second son, a martlet by a fourth and a fleur-de-lis by a sixth.

CADET A younger son who is the progenitor of a subsidiary branch of a family.

CALEFACTORIUM (WARMING-HOUSE) A room in a medieval monastery in which a fire was maintained during the winter months for the benefit of the monks, especially those who were occupied in sedentary work in the cloister. The warming house was usually situated near the night stair and therefore also provided a little warmth to the DORTER above, though in Cistercian abbeys it was often an independent building adjoining the FRATER. Until the late Middle Ages the calefactorium was the only room (other than the kitchens and infirmary) which was heated but with the growth of private chambers (*camerae*) it became a common room for informal meetings and recreational conversation.

CALENDAR (i) The numerous medieval methods of calculating dates rendered calendars particularly important, and many liturgical manuscripts, private devotional works and official documents were prefixed by a calendar. Dating by reference to saints' days and religious festivals was popular in the Church and, from the thirteenth century, such dates are to be found in letters and documents. The Roman JULIAN CALENDAR, devised by Julius Caesar in

46 BC, remained in use until 1582 when it was replaced by the GREGORIAN CALENDAR, though its introduction into England was delayed until 1752.
See also FEAST DAYS (FIXED AND MOVABLE), NEW YEAR'S DAY *and* YEAR (LITURGICAL)
Further reading:
Cheney, C.R. (ed.), *Handbook of Dates*, London, 1970
Pickering, F., *The Calendar Pages of Medieval Service Books*, Cambridge, 1981
(ii) A catalogue of documents together with summaries of their contents.

CALLIGRAPHY *see* LETTERING

CALVINISM John Calvin (1509–64) was a French theologian and religious reformer who founded the Calvinistic branch of the Protestant Church. The first edition of his *Institutes of Christian Religion*, published in Basle in 1536, was the most systematic Protestant theological treatise of the REFORMATION, one which he constantly revised and extended. Unlike Luther (*see* LUTHERANISM), Calvin anticipated a complete restructuring of society in accordance with strict Christian principles. Private morality was monitored and EXCOMMUNICATION freely applied. Although Calvinism was austere and frequently brutal, Calvin's scholarship and his influence on Protestantism were immense.

CAMAIL PERIOD A term applied to military brasses and effigies in which the figures are depicted wearing the *camail* (mail protection for the throat and neck) which was introduced into English armour during the second half of the fourteenth century.
See also BRASSES (MONUMENTAL) *and* EFFIGIES

CAMBER A slight upward curve in an otherwise horizontal structure.

CAMPANILE A bell tower, usually detached from other buildings.
See also BELLS *and* TOWERS

CAMPANOLOGY The study or science of BELLS or bell-ringing.

CANCELLI Low, latticed railings in front of, or enclosing, a communion table, usually with a broad top surface to facilitate the taking of communion.
See also ALTARS *and* COMMUNION RAILS

CANDELABRUM A large branched candlestick or light-holder. There are various types, including the seven-branched Jerusalem candelabrum or *menorah*.
See also CHANDELIER *and* HEARSE

CANDLE AUCTION *see* CHARITY MEADS

CANDLE-BEAM *see* ROOD LOFT

CANDLE EXTINGUISHER A combined candle extinguisher and taper-holder will be found in most churches. This usually consists of a cone-shaped brass extinguisher, often with a rolled edge and decorative finial, to the back of which is attached a curved, cylindrical taper-holder. Both are attached by a brass ferrule to a rod, usually of oak. The taper is used to light the church candles before a service and the brass cone to extinguish them afterwards.

CANDLEMAS (2 February) The Feast of the Purification of the Virgin Mary and the presentation of Christ in the Temple. It was a festival at which childbirth was venerated: mothers who had borne children in the preceding year carried candles to church in thanksgiving. In order to suppress the medieval cult of the Blessed Virgin Mary, the sixteenth-century Reformers provided an alternative, the Presentation of the Christ in the Temple, when they compiled the *Book of Common Prayer*.

Old Candlemas Day was 14 February '. . . the day which was of great import to agriculturalists – the day of the Candlemas Fair. It was at this fair that new engagements were entered into for the twelve months following the ensuing Lady Day, and those of the farming population who thought of changing their places duly attended at the county town where the [hiring] fair was held.' (Thomas Hardy)
See also FEAST DAYS (FIXED AND MOVABLE) *and* LADY DAY

CANDLES It is self-evident that, in medieval churches, candles were necessary in order that a priest should be able to read. But the widespread adoption of candles as ornaments, especially associated with the altar, may have developed from the early use of processional lights which were stood beside or on the altar table (*see* PROCESSIONS). Liturgical candles were made of beeswax and were an expensive commodity, while candles used simply for illumination were of tallow. In the medieval period only one candle would be placed on the altar, others being offered as *votive lights* before images, shrines and tombs, often at enormous expense. A votive candle is one which is lit as a personal offering, usually in fulfilment of a vow or bequest.
See also ALTAR LIGHTS, CHANDELIERS, LAMPS, RUSHLIGHT HOLDER, SERGES *and* TRENDAL

CANDLESTICKS Altar crosses and candlesticks were once a common feature of parish churches but most are now locked away when not in use. They were not widely used on altars before the nineteenth century and many older candlesticks may have been donated to a church at that time, having originally been used for domestic purposes. Typically, a candlestick consists of a *nozzle* (in which the candle is secured), a *drip-pan* (which surrounds the nozzle and is intended to collect molten wax), a cylindrical *stem* with decorative *knops* (or *knots*) and *collets* (rings or collars) and a heavy or splayed *foot* (base). Some have a spike (*pricket*) within the nozzle on which the candle is impaled, while others have various means of ejecting spent candles. Many candlesticks date from the seventeenth and eighteenth centuries, and generally reflect the decorative styles of those periods, while others (mostly in brass) are Victorian. Early seventeenth-century examples in pewter or brass are often bell-shaped at the foot and have a drip-pan at the centre of the stem. Late seventeenth-century gilt or silver candlesticks may be in the ornate baroque style, with highly ornamented baluster stems and tripod feet, or a more restrained classical style with a fluted and reeded column on a high plinth and solid, square stepped foot. There are splendid seventeenth-century pairs at Buckland in Surrey and Harthill in Yorkshire. Early eighteenth-century examples, usually of silver or brass, have a reel-shaped nozzle and a shouldered, baluster stem with knops and a polygonal foot. This style became a model for brass candlesticks and, for this reason, is perhaps the most familiar. Silver or brass neo-classical candlesticks from the late-eighteenth century have a tapering, fluted stem on a high trumpet-shaped foot and a bell-shaped nozzle, often with leaf decoration. A number of early examples have survived, including four from the thirteenth century at St. Thomas's, Bristol.
See also ALTAR LIGHTS, BIER LIGHT, CANDELABRUM, CANDLES, CHANDELIER, CRESSET, HEARSE, LAMPS, RUSHLIGHT HOLDER, STRAP SCONCE, TRENDAL *and* TRIPLE CANDLESTICK

CANES *see* WINDOWS

CANON (i) An ecclesiastical law (*see* CANON LAW). (ii) A body of writings acknowledged as genuine. (iii) A list of canonised saints. (iv) A member of a body of clergy serving a cathedral or collegiate church. At first the term was applied to all clergy who were members of a diocesan staff but was later restricted to secular clergy belonging to a cathedral or collegiate church. Residentiary canons are permanent members of a cathedral staff who undertake administrative duties and are responsible for services. Non-residentiary canons are those who hold unsalaried posts associated with certain privileges and responsibilities.
See also CANON REGULAR *and* CLERGY, CHURCH OF ENGLAND

CANONESS REGULAR A member of a community of women living under a RULE which, since the twelfth century, was usually that of St. Augustine (*see* AUGUSTINIANS).

CANONICAL HOURS *see* HOURS, CANON-ICAL, MONASTERIES *and* SUNDIALS

CANONICALS The official dress of the clergy regulated by the Church canons.

CANONICORUM Latinised place-name element indicating that a manor was once owned by a medieval community of canons, as at Whitchurch Canonicorum in Dorset.
See also LATIN

CANONISATION (i) An act which is sanctioned by ecclesiastical authority. (ii) To enrol in the canon (list) of SAINTS. In the early Church, bishops controlled the cult of saints within their dioceses but, as the veneration of certain popular saints spread beyond local limits, so papal intervention increased until, in *c.* 1170, Pope Alexander III asserted that no-one should be venerated as a saint without the authority of the Roman Church.

CANON LAW Ecclesiastical law based on New Testament precepts. A digest of the formal decrees of various councils of the Church (*canons*) and patriarchal decisions (*decretals*) relating to doctrine and discipline. Before the Norman Conquest the courts heard all suits, both lay and ecclesiastical, with bishops and ealdormen sitting as joint judges. Such courts were disliked by the Papacy and William of Normandy was able to obtain papal approval for his conquest of Britain by promising to establish separate ecclesiastical courts to consider those matters which 'belong to the government of souls.' These courts dealt not only with offences against morality and the doctrines of the Church but also with secular matters such as legitimacy and matrimonial causes (*see* COURTS, ECCLESI-ASTICAL *and* PROBATE).

CANON REGULAR A member of a body of canons living under a RULE which, from the twelfth century, was usually that of St. Augustine.
See also AUGUSTINIANS, CANON, CLERGY (CHURCH OF ENGLAND), GILBERTINE *and* PREMONSTRATENSIAN

CANONRY The benefice of a canon.

CANONS, THE The *Book of Canons* was, until recently, the main body of canonical legislation in the Church of England following the Reformation. Approved by the Convocation of Canterbury in 1604 and by York in 1606 it was eventually superseded by legislation promulgated in 1964 and 1969.

CANOPY (i) A roof-like projection above a statue, tomb, memorial, etc. usually of stone but also of wood or metal (*see* CANOPY, MONUMENTAL). (ii) A similar structure of carved wood surmounting the stalls in a medieval cathedral, collegiate chapel or former monastic church (*see* STALLS). (iii) An ornate, tapering tower-like structure suspended above a font (*see* FONT COVERS *and* TABER-NACLE). (iv) An architectural or decorative motif which resembles any of the above (*see* BRASSES, MONUMENTAL). (v) A projecting or suspended hood (*tester*) above a pulpit or altar (*see* ALTAR CANOPY, BALDACCHINO *and* SOUNDING BOARD).

CANOPY (MONUMENTAL) A roof-like projection above a tomb or memorial, usually of stone but occasionally of wood or metal. This type of canopy may surmount a free-standing or recessed TOMB CHEST or a hanging WALL MONUMENT and there are examples of free-standing tomb canopies which have been adapted to form small CHANTRY CHAPELS. The undersides of these canopies were often vaulted with floreated and heraldic painting and gilding, though much of this original work may have been lost through neglect or vandalism.

Canopies developed in the thirteenth century, principally over the tomb chests of prelates, and may have originated in the roof-like structures which were sometimes placed above shrines. The overall design of a canopy followed contemporary architectural style and decoration, indeed that above the Despenser tomb at Tewkesbury Abbey in Gloucestershire contains the earliest example of fan vaulting (1378). Heraldry was a common theme, both in the miniature bosses and spandrels of the vaulting and in the ornamentation of the moulding. The canopy of Edmund Crouchback's tomb at Westminster Abbey, for example, contains no fewer than 150 shields of arms. Canopies above recessed tombs (those which were set within a church wall) are usually less ornate, the spandrels formed on either side of the arch containing simple shields of arms, though the canopies of late perpendicular recessed tombs often have decorative cornices with carved and gilded shields of arms and other devices such as BADGES, CYPHERS and REBUSES.

With the Renaissance, Gothic pillars and arches were superseded by Roman columns and classical pediments and entablatures which provided the 'new gentility' of the post-medieval period with an eminently suitable vehicle by which to display all, or at least the most significant, of the heraldic quarterings to which they laid claim (*see* MARSHALLING). Every available surface was utilised for this purpose: usually a central achieve-ment (containing all the principal quarterings) was flanked by two smaller ones above the pediment (usually of impaled arms) with the various arms acquired by marriage depicted individually in shields on the columns and pediments. Heraldic supporters were often modelled (not necessarily in stone) on either side of the central achievement or were incorporated into the overall design of the monument: flanking an obelisk, for example. Arches provided spandrels for further shields and the underside of the arch was often decorated with shields, badges and other devices. Smaller shields in a frieze along the base of the pediment, or on the back plate of a wall monument, were used to display the marriage alliances of children and ancestors and, where a monument was erected to the memory of two or more generations, the alliances of each generation would be shown. Where highly emblazoned canopies surmounted tomb chests the overall effect was even more splendid, for the chest itself would also be decorated with shields and might be surrounded by ironwork which included gilded pennants and scrollwork. Good examples are the tombs of Elizabeth, Lady Hoby (d. 1609) at Bisham, Berkshire, which is set against a wall, and that of Bishop Montague (d. 1618) at Bath Abbey.

From c. 1630 there was an increasing tendency towards a purer classical treatment with less decoration. Heraldry was, for the most part, confined to segmental pediments while the shield was gradually replaced by the cartouche. From the end of the seventeenth century, a single CREST or heraldic cartouche might be incorporated within the canopy and, during the eighteenth century, the canopy itself became an architectural feature, eventually being replaced by the wall monument and reappearing only briefly during the Gothic revival.
See also CELURE, MONUMENTS *and* ROOD CELURE

CANOPY OF HONOUR A large CANOPY (*ciborium*) above an altar (*see also* BALDA-CHINO).

CANTARIST A singer in a choir and, in the Middle Ages, a member of a foundation of secular clergy (*see* COLLEGE). Adult members of cathedral choirs are known as lay clerks.

CANTERBURY CAP A soft cloth cap sometimes worn by English clerics.

CANTICLE A prayer derived from the Bible (other than from the Psalms) used in the liturgy of the Church. Most familiar are the *Magnificat, Nunc Dimittis* and *Benedicite*.

CANTILEVER Horizontal projection with no visible support.

CANTLE A small piece of the holy loaf.

CANTOR A member of a choir who pre-intones and leads in liturgical music.

CANTORIS Literally 'of the cantor' whose stall was on the north side of the choir, the term is used to describe all those who in antiphonal singing sit on that side.
See also ANTIPHON, CHURCH MUSIC (AN-GLICAN), DECANI, STALLS *and* VERSICLES

CAPACITY In medieval PROBATE law, in order to make a will or testament, boys had to be over fourteen years of age and girls over twelve. A person had to be of full mental capacity and intent on making a will. Women (unless with their husband's permission) had to be unmarried or widowed. Traitors, outlaws and felons were unable to make wills, their property being forfeit to the Crown.
See also WILLS

CAPEL (Welsh) A chapel.

CAPELLA ANTE PORTAS The chapel at (or near) the gate of a religious house provided for the use of visitors, servants and employees. Such chapels sometimes became parish churches: at Merevale in Warwickshire, for example which was built for the benefit of pilgrims.

CAPITAL A capital is the head of a COLUMN, PIER or PILASTER. Shaped like an inverted bell, most capitals comprise a flat upper stone (*abacus*) and a tapering lower section (*necking*) which is usually separated from the shaft of the pier or column by a narrow moulding. The function of a capital is to provide an area, larger than the supporting column or pier, from which an arch may spring or on which an entablature may rest.

The decoration of a capital is often a useful guide to the period or style of architecture. Romanesque piers and capitals were of massive construction: clearly, contemporary builders felt that new notions of structure were no substitute for mass. In the earliest examples both neck and abacus were combined in a single square or round block of stone. Early carved decoration was crude (though interesting) and included interlacing. Typical of the Norman period is the *cushion* capital which is a cube of masonry, the lower parts of which were rounded off to conform with the circular shaft of the column, leaving a flat face (*lunette*) on each of the four sides. From this evolved the *scalloped* capital in which each of the lunettes is divided into cone-shapes, beneath a square abacus. Later Romanesque capitals are deeply carved with foliated motifs,

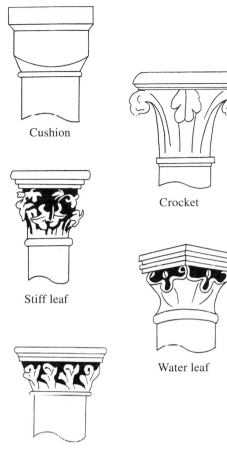

Cushion

Crocket

Stiff leaf

Water leaf

Natural leaf

animals, birds and (more rarely in England) figures. In Gothic architecture, capitals of the Early English period were generally moulded or splendidly foliated with a round or moulded abacus. There are good examples at Eaton Bray in Bedfordshire, Acton in Cheshire and East Hendred, Berkshire. Occasionally, human heads peep out from the foliage (*see* GREEN MEN). Specific types of foliated capital include the *crocket* capital which has stylised leaves forming 'scrolls' (*volutes*) beneath the abacus, the *stiff-leaf* capital (with long stalks) which developed from it and the *water-leaf* capital which has plain, broad leaves turned over beneath the angles of the abacus (*see* STIFF LEAF ORNAMENT). Characteristic of the Decorated period is the removal of the undercut hollow beneath the abacus to form a more unified capital, usually decorated with rolls of scroll moulding or foliage. By the fourteenth century foliated capitals of oak, ivy, maple and vine leaves were carved

in a more naturalistic manner and with a profusion of fruit and flowers (*see* NATURAL LEAF ORNAMENT). In the Perpendicular period of the fifteenth century octagonal capitals, often chamfered at the upper edge, were set on circular columns or groups of shafts and were, for the most part, moulded though foliated forms may be found in some West Country churches: at Broad Clyst, Molland and Wolborough in Devon, for example. Carved and foliated capitals are also a feature of several larger buildings where they are usually more stylised, of lower relief and sometimes include figures in the form of angels. After the Reformation the Gothic style was gradually superseded by Classical forms (*see* CLASSICAL ORDER).

CAPITILAVIUM From the Latin 'washing of the head', an early medieval name for PALM SUNDAY.

CAPITULARY A compilation of legislation published by bishops for the guidance of the clergy and laity in their dioceses.

CAPUCHON *see* COSTUME

CARDINAL A member of the Pope's council or Sacred College. Cardinals hold the next highest office to the Pope and are nominated by him. These ecclesiastical princes comprise six cardinal bishops, fifty cardinal priests and fourteen cardinal deacons. When required, on the death of a pope, they elect a successor. Their main responsibilities are advisory and administrative and, unless expressly excused or bishops of foreign dioceses, they reside in Rome. There have been comparatively few English cardinals, the best known being Cardinals Beaufort (1377–1447), Morton (*c.* 1420–1500), Wolsey (*c.* 1475–1530) and Newman (1801–90).
See also HERALDRY (ECCLESIASTICAL)

CARILLON More popular on the continent of Europe than in Britain, a carillon is a peal of BELLS played from a manual and pedal keyboard similar to those of an organ (*see* ORGANS) but with the whole hand (gloved in leather) being required to depress a single key. It is possible to play tunes, rather than changes, together with simple accompanying harmonies. There is usually a clockwork mechanism which triggers the sounding of the hours, halves and quarters but this is disengaged when the carillon is being played. There are a few carillons in English churches: at Yetminster in Dorset, for example, which was first played for Queen Victoria's Jubilee. It chimes every three hours by day and night using five of its six bells to play the National Anthem. There was once a much larger carillon at nearby Cattistock but this was destroyed by fire some years ago. Dedicated in 1899, it had thirty-five bells on which regular recitals were performed by visiting musicians. Perhaps the most celebrated carillon in England is that on the tower of Bournville Primary School, Birmingham, which is often played for the benefit of the nearby parish church of St. Francis.

CARMELITE ORDER *see* FRIARS

CAROL The term is now applied to traditional songs of a religious character, especially those associated with Christmastide. Until the early nineteenth century a carol was a song of joy which accompanied a dance and the distinction between carols and HYMNS was more clearly understood. The earliest English collection of carols was published in 1521.
See also CHRISTMAS

CARPENTRY *see* WOODWORK

CARRELS *see* CLOISTER

CARTHUSIANS The Poor Brothers of God of the Charterhouse (originally the *Grande Chartreuse* in Grenoble) were a strictly contemplative order, founded by St. Bruno in 1084, with a Rule dating from 1130 that required of them vows of austerity, humility and silence. Like the desert hermits of the past, each monk lived in his own cell, with its garden and patch of cultivated land, working and devoting several hours each day to prayer. His clothing was coarse and undyed and for three days a week he lived on bread and water. On other days he ate scanty rations of fish, eggs and vegetables: no meat was taken. The monks came together for the offices of Mattins, Lauds and Vespers, the other Hours being recited in their cells; and for meals only on feast days when conversation was permitted. In order that their priories should not become too large or well endowed, numbers were restricted to a prior and twelve monks, with eighteen lay brothers who had cells and an oratory of their own and were responsible for maintaining the meagre arable holdings, flocks and herds. The first Carthusian priory (or *Charterhouse*) in England was founded by Henry II in 1178 as part of his penance for the murder of Thomas Becket in 1170. The chosen site was then a remote and inhospitable one at Witham in Selwood Forest on the Somerset–Wiltshire border. Two further Charterhouses were established at Hinton near Bath in 1226 and Beauvale near Nottingham in 1320. Following the onset of the Black Death in 1348–50, at a time when the endowment of monastic communities was otherwise in decline, the Carthusians enjoyed both the respect and the financial support of the nobility. Several priories

were endowed by members of the medieval court circle, including the London Charterhouse in 1370. The latest (and largest) Carthusian foundation in England, the House of Jesus in Bethlehem at Sheen on the Surrey bank of the Thames, was founded by Henry V (1413–22) the most puritanical of the medieval English kings. Alone among the English monastic orders, the Carthusians may be distinguished by that integrity and courage of soul which compelled them to stand against Henry VIII at the Dissolution in 1536.
See also PLAGUE

CARTOON *see* STAINED GLASS

CARTOUCHE Scroll-like architectural decoration. Ornament in the form of a tablet or heraldic escutcheon enclosed in scrolls representing rolled-up paper.

CARTOUCHE TABLET A type of WALL MONUMENT popular in the seventeenth and eighteenth centuries. Cartouche tablets are usually made of marble and have the appearance of a sheet of paper with the sides curled up. Typically, the central section contains an inscription and, above it, a coat of arms or crest.
See also TABLET

CARTULARY A monastic or estate register-book containing details of deeds, charters, grants, property and other possessions. Also one who keeps the register and the place in which it is stored.
  Monastic cartularies provide invaluable information concerning appropriated churches (*see* MEDIEVAL CHURCH) and may even contain the earliest reference to a particular parish church, including the names of incumbents, dependent chapelries and the obligations (financial and otherwise) owed by a parish to a mother church, and the rights and emoluments established for a VICAR when a religious house became the RECTOR of the parish.
Further reading:
Davis, G., *The Medieval Cartularies of Great Britain*, London, 1958

CARYATID A female figure used as a column to support an entablature in classical architecture. Male figures are *Atlantes* (plural of *Atlas*), female figures carrying baskets on their heads are *Canophorae* and demi-figures which appear to emerge from the pedestal are either *Herms* (humans) or *Terms* (animals or mythical creatures).

CASKET TOMBS *see* TABLE TOMBS

CASSOCK A long garment worn by the clergy and by members of a church choir. The cassock originated in the full-length robe which was retained by the clergy when, in the sixth century, shorter garments evolved for secular use. Traditionally clergy of the Church of England wear black cassocks and bishops purple. Choristers' cassocks come in a variety of colours, though only the choirs of royal foundations should wear red.

See also FORTY-BUTTON MAN, SURPLICE *and* VESTMENTS

CAST In metalwork, a pattern made by running molten metal (or by pressing malleable material) into a mould.

CASTELLATED Surmounted with battlements (*see* BATTLEMENT).

CATAFALQUE A temporary tomb-like structure originally used at a Requiem Mass to represent the body in its absence. The term is now used to describe a platform on which is supported the coffin of a (usually distinguished) person during a funeral or lying-in-state.

CATCHLAND (*also* CATCHPOLE ACRE) Land on the boundaries of two (or more) parishes but belonging to neither. The land's tithe usually went to the first cleric to claim it.

CATECHISM In the *Book of Common Prayer*, the series of questions and answers to be learned by a candidate for Confirmation. These deal with Baptism, the Apostles' Creed, the Ten Commandments, the Lord's Prayer and the Eucharist.

CATECHUMENS Those undergoing religious instruction prior to baptism.

CATHEDRA *see* CATHEDRALS

CATHEDRAL CHAPTER The body of canons responsible for the administration of a cathedral (*see* CANON). Chapter records include information concerning the affairs of those parishes which came within their exempt jurisdiction (*see* PECULIAR). For example, records of the VISITATIONS of churches in the jurisdiction of the Dean and Chapter of York from 1362 to 1481 include details of defective church buildings, the inadequate provision of service books, and a variety of offences by clergy and laity including non-residence, adultery, witchcraft and heresy.

CATHEDRAL PRIORY The seats (*cathedra*) of early bishoprics were established in the churches of several of the more important monasteries (*headminsters*). The monastic church thereby became a cathedral and the bishop the titular abbot of the community which, in practice, was governed by a prior (*see* PRIORIES). Although accorded the style and honour of abbot, a bishop was not necessarily a member of the monastic community and exercised no authority within its CHAPTER (at Durham, in particular, the relationship was often acrimonious). It was the Benedictine archbishop Dunstan (909–88) who, with Edgar of Wessex, reformed both church and state and established the cathedral priory as the fulcrum of regional ecclesiastical government.

See also ANGLO-SAXON CHURCH, CATHEDRALS *and* MITRED ABBOT

CATHEDRALS A cathedral is a church which contains the *cathedra* or throne of the bishop of a DIOCESE. The *cathedra* was normally situated in an apse behind the high altar but was removed to the PRESBYTERY in the medieval period. A symbol of spiritual and temporal power, bishops' thrones were immense structures: that at Exeter Cathedral is almost 18 metres (60 feet) high. Originally, a cathedral was served by a bishop and his household but responsibility was later devolved to a separate body of clergy, an ecclesiastical corporation known as the CHAPTER. Some chapters were secular, others monastic (see below).

THE MIDDLE AGES

English dioceses have always been large and cathedrals, therefore, few in number. Consequently, the medieval cathedrals were able to exercise considerable regional influence and enjoyed patronage of such munificence that the scale and splendour of their architecture greatly exceeds that of most parish churches. This is particularly evident in the development of cathedrals to the east of the crossing where magnificent provision was made, not only for considerable numbers of clergy, but also for the shrines of saints, reliquaries, CHANTRY CHAPELS and royal and magnatial tombs. CHAPELS were often added to the ambulatory for these purposes and many cathedrals built *lady chapels* to the east of the high altar in response to the popularity of the cult of the Virgin during the fourteenth century. With the obvious exception of St. Paul's in London (rebuilt by Sir Christopher Wren 1675–1710) no major English cathedral is of a single, unified architectural style. Even at Salisbury, which was constructed within a period of sixty-four years (1220–84), the tower and spire were not completed until *c.* 1380.

Of the seventeen medieval cathedrals at the DISSOLUTION OF THE MONASTERIES, seven were BENEDICTINE monastic foundations: Canterbury, Durham, Ely, Norwich, Rochester, Winchester and Worcester, as was Bath which replaced Wells as a cathedral between 1090 and 1218 when the joint diocese was established. In these monastic cathedrals the bishop was also the titular abbot, though in practice responsibility for the

Salisbury Cathedral.

monastic establishment rested with the prior and that for the cathedral with a CHAPTER, so that they were known as CATHEDRAL PRIORIES. The remaining ten cathedrals were served by canons who were responsible (as they are today) for the maintenance of cathedral services. The *Canons Regular* lived in accordance with a fixed code (Latin *regula* meaning 'rule') and were, in England, AUGUSTINIAN (or Austin) Canons whose rule was monastic in character, for which reason their cathedral church at Carlisle was classified as a monastic foundation at the Dissolution. The other nine cathedrals were administered by *Secular Canons* who followed no rule and were free to live where they chose.

Of these cathedrals of the 'Old Foundation', five are of pre-Conquest foundation: Exeter, Hereford, Lichfield, London and York; and three date from the reign of William I (1066–87): Chichester, Sarum and Lincoln. The fourth, Wells, regained its former cathedral status from Bath in 1218 and in 1228 a new building at Salisbury replaced the old cathedral at Sarum – now Old Sarum – some two miles away. Secular Canons lived by means of *prebends* or benefices of income from endowed land, manors or even churches. Membership of a non-monastic cathedral chapter was restricted to prebendaries – holders of prebends – and each had his prebendal stall in the cathedral. In some cathedrals the ancient territorial titles of prebends have been retained, though not the endowments.

THE POST-REFORMATION PERIOD

At the Dissolution, the monastic foundations were reconstituted to become cathedrals of the 'New Foundation' and in the 1540s Henry VIII created six additional sees. The former Augustinian churches at Oxford and Bristol and the great Benedictine churches at Chester, Gloucester, Peterborough and Westminster all became cathedrals, though Westminster was 'demoted' again in 1550. No further sees were established until 1836 and of the twenty new anglican cathedrals created since then only five are of medieval foundation: St. Albans was a Benedictine abbey; Southwark an Augustinian priory; and Manchester, Ripon and Southwell were collegiate churches of secular canons.

Today, English cathedrals are normally administered by a chapter of residentiary canons presided over by a dean or, in recent foundations, by a provost: as at the former parish church of St. Philip in Birmingham which became a cathedral in 1905. There are also non-residentiary or honorary canons, who may have certain responsibilities and privileges; and minor canons who are responsible for assisting at musical services but are not members of a chapter. In cathedrals of the 'Old Foundation', the *precentor* (who is responsible for the direction of the choral services) is a member of the chapter, while elsewhere he is a minor canon as is his deputy, the *succentor*.

See also CHURCH MUSIC (ANGLICAN) *and* CLERGY (CHURCH OF ENGLAND)

Further reading:

Chamberlin, R., *The English Cathedral*, Webb and Bower, 1988

Clifton-Taylor, A., *The Cathedrals of England*, London, 1967

Livingstone, E.A., *The Concise Dictionary of the Christian Church*, Oxford, 1977

CATHOLIC Literally, 'general' or 'universal', the term may imply the universality of the Church in contradistinction to local Christian communities; it is used to imply orthodoxy as distinct from the 'heretical' or 'schismatical' and it may be used to describe the undivided Church before the schism of East and West in 1054, following which the Western Church referred to itself as 'catholic' and the Eastern Church as 'orthodox'. Since the Reformation Roman Catholics have come to use it exclusively of themselves, and it is used by those who claim to possess a historical and continuous tradition of faith as opposed to those who are Protestants.

See also ROMAN CATHOLIC CHURCH

CATHOLIC EMANCIPATION ACTS A series of acts by which Roman Catholics were freed from civil disabilities. The 1778 Act enabled Roman Catholics in Ireland to own land. The 1791 Act removed discrimination against Roman Catholic schools and those who worked in them. The Roman Catholic Relief Act of 1829 removed most other disabilities and enabled Roman Catholics to hold public office.

See also RECUSANCY

CAVETTO A hollowed moulding, the curvature of which is a quarter circle.

CEILINGS *see* PLASTERWORK, ROOFS *and* VAULTING

CEILURE A panelled and decorated section of a wagon roof above an ALTAR or ROOD.

CELEBRET In the Roman Catholic Church, a written authority to say Mass (literally 'let him celebrate').

CELIBACY OF THE CLERGY In the Middle Ages celibacy was required of all those in Holy Orders. In the Church of England, the obligation to celibacy of the clergy was abolished in 1549.

CELL (i) The rudimentary quarters of an individual monk in a semi-eremetical institution. (ii) A dependent house of a monastery, usually with no more than four religious. These small daughter houses were sometimes provided for convalescence, contemplation or penitentiary purposes and, as a result, were almost invariably in remote locations. The term is also applied to larger dependencies, though erroneously so.

CELLARER 'The second father of the house' was responsible for the provision of food, drink, fuel and all the day-to-day requirements of a monastic community. Through his staff he controlled the mills, malt-house, brew-house and bakehouse, he was responsible for collecting tolls and for the carriage of goods, for the staffing of granges, the production and storing of produce and the welfare of guests and CORRODIANS. He leased and sold land and appointed overseers for the monastic estates. Most importantly, it was the cellarer who was the chief means of communication between the monastery and the outside world.

See also LARDER

CELLARIUM The great storehouse of a monastery which often occupied the entire ground floor of the western range of claustral buildings. The entrance, which opened onto the great court, was often large enough to admit a horse and cart. The cellar at

Fountains Abbey in Yorkshire was 91 metres (300 feet) in length and vaulted in twenty-two double bays which sprang from a central arcade of columns. Originally, it was divided into store-rooms, offices and FRATER.

CELTIC CHURCH The term 'Celtic Church' is something of a misnomer for, while it had its own distinctive features, it was nevertheless an integral part of the universal Church – albeit a Church in which there was little uniformity of ritual or organisation. It would be more accurate to describe the 'Celtic Church' of the fifth and sixth centuries as 'the church of those who spoke the Celtic language'.

It has been argued that the Church of Dyfrig, Illtud and Dewi owed little to the Christianity of Roman Britain and that it developed from the work of peripatetic missionaries. However, it is more likely that its origins are to be found in a variety of influences and that it was in south-east Wales that these came together, notably under Dyfrig (Dubricius), a bishop who presided over a Roman form of organisation in the second half of the fifth century. Dyfrig is generally acknowledged to have been the first Celtic 'saint' and, according to legend, it was he who crowned King Arthur (*Artorius*). He was succeeded by Illtud, 'the renowned master of the Britons, learned in the teachings of the Church in the culture of the Latins and in the traditions of his own people.' Illtud was not a bishop but an abbot, which confirms that the monastic tradition had already taken root in Wales. That tradition possessed severely ascetic elements but was also characterised by scholarship and devotion. Illtud's monastery of Llanilltud Fawr (Llantwit Major, now in South Glamorgan) was very different from the remote houses of his successors. It was close to the ruined villa of Llantwit (it may be that Illtud was a descendant of its former owners) and only 18 kilometres from Dynas Powys, once the seat of the kings of Glywysing. Llanilltud Fawr became the axis of the Celtic Church: Samson studied there before leaving for Dol in *c.* 520 to become the 'father of Breton monasticism'; Paul Aurelian, one of Samson's fellow students, became a leading figure in the Church in Cornwall; and Gildas, another of Samson's contemporaries, was acknowledged by the Irish to be an authority on ritual and discipline.

THE AGE OF SAINTS
While Dyfrig was a bishop in an essentially post-Roman environment, the ascendancy of asceticism which was evident before his death in *c.* 612 reflected the final collapse of the economy which had sustained that environment. By the end of the sixth century, the desire of religious communities to retreat to remote and desolate places had become irresistible, no doubt encouraged by PLAGUE which reached western Britain in 549 and is believed to have been as virulent as the notorious fourteenth-century Black Death.

This was the 'Age of Saints' when Christianity consolidated its hold on the inhabitants of Wales. In particular, it was from this time that the *llan* entered the country's toponymy. The meaning now attributed to the word is 'church' but at that time a *llan* was a consecrated enclosure in which the dead were buried and it was not until several centuries later that many *llannau* acquired churches. Associated with the ubiquitous *llan*- place-names of Wales and the Marches are the names of numerous 'saints' whose principal (and, perhaps, only) claim to fame was a gift of land on which to locate a community's burial enclosure. Such men are often described as 'founders' but, in most cases, 'benefactor' would be more precise – though, inevitably, time and local pride have created legends round them. Of course, there were exceptions and there can be no denying the influence of 'saints' such as Deiniol, Padarn and Teilo (see below). But there is very little documentary or archaeological evidence relating to them and no way of knowing whether church dedications were contemporary or reflect a later cult.

ST. DAVID OF WALES
From *c.* 900 there is increasing evidence of the quite exceptional influence of David and his church, and it is not without significance that by the end of the twelfth century there were more than sixty churches dedicated to him in an area which extended from Pembroke to Hereford. *The Life of David*, written in *c.* 1090 by Rhygyfarch, the son of Julien, Bishop of St. David's, is the earliest of the lives of the Welsh 'saints' to which may be added material from Giraldus Cambrensis (in *c.* 1200) and the anchorite of Llanddewibrefi in (*c.* 1346). From these and other sources it would appear that David (*c.* 520–89) was of the royal house of Ceredigion, the son of Sant (*Dewi Sant*), and that he belonged to a severely ascetic branch of the monastic tradition. In his day, he was the most respected leader of the Christians of Wales and is reputed to have founded twelve monasteries including Glastonbury in Somerset and Menevia (later St. David's in Dyfed). The regime in all his houses was especially strict: his monks performed harsh austerities and hard manual labour, keeping no cattle to help them plough. They lived mainly in silence and on a frugal diet of vegetables, bread and water, indeed David's insistence on abstinence, and his habit of immersing himself in ice-cold water as a means of subduing the flesh, earned for him the nickname *Aquaticus* – 'Waterman'. Such was his reputation that he was summoned to speak at the Synod of Brefi in *c.* 550 and (according to Rhygyfarch) he so impressed the assembly by his preaching that he was unanimously elected

archbishop with authority over the whole of Wales. (This last detail is almost certainly a fabrication, intended by Rhygyfarch to invest his father's see of St. David with metropolitan status.) David died at his monastery of Menevia in *c.* 589. His cult received papal approval in *c.* 1120 and his relics were translated to a shrine in the cathedral of St. David 1131 and again in 1275 when the cathedral was rebuilt, financed largely from offerings at his shrine (*see* ST. DAVID'S DAY).

THE INFLUENCE OF ROME

Deiniol, Padarn and Teilo were contemporaries of David and were abbots, presiding over monastic communities and *clasau*, self-contained ecclesiastical communities consisting of an abbot (who might also be a bishop) and a group of hereditary canons, sharing a common income but living as secular clerks (*claswyr*). The *clasau* were originally pioneering instruments of conversion but, by the twelfth century, they had become well-endowed and self-indulgent communities (*see* CLAS).

When Augustine arrived in England in 597 he carried with him Pope Gregory's directive that he should exercise his authority '. . . over all the Christians of Britain' (*see* ANGLO-SAXON CHURCH). But when Augustine rather arrogantly sought to assert that authority in 603 he was rebuffed by the Welsh bishops who questioned the power of the Pope to impose upon them the jurisdiction of Canterbury, an archbishopric which had existed for less than a decade. Thus began the acrimonious relationship between Wales and Canterbury which was to last for more than thirteen centuries (*see* WALES, MEDIEVAL CHURCH IN). The most significant area of disagreement concerned the date of EASTER which, in the Celtic Church, was calculated by means of a system devised in 314 – unlike that of Rome which had been adopted in 457. Inevitably, the date of Easter became a symbol of freedom from the interference of Augustine and his successors. The Welsh stubbornly retained the old system until 768 but there can be little doubt that a century of isolation from the mainstream of Christendom severely weakened the influence and effectiveness of the Church in Wales.

Further reading:

Davies, J., *A History of Wales*, London, 1993

CELTIC CROSS The Celtic heritage persists most visibly in art and architecture and especially in numerous stone WHEEL HEAD CROSSES carved with magnificent interlaced patterns. In Wales, the best examples are to be found in Anglesey, Dyfed and Glamorgan, such as the massive eleventh century cross at Carew in Dyfed which is four metres high (13 feet) and is carved with a continuous, intricate fretted and interlaced pattern, 50 metres (164 feet) in length. Cornish crosses are generally smaller and of granite so that it was

impossible to pierce the space between the limbs of the cross and the encircling annulet. Since 1956 the traditional Celtic cross has also found its way into the official terminology of HERALDRY.

See also CHRISTIAN SYMBOLS *and* CROSSES

CELURE (i) A canopy (*see* CANOPIES). (ii) The painted, panelled or vaulted section of a roof immediately above an altar or ROOD (*see* ROOD CELURE).

CEMETERIES *see* BURIAL ACTS, BURIALS, CHURCHYARDS, CLOSED CHURCHYARD, OSSUARIES *and* VAULTS (BURIAL)

CENOTAPH A monument to persons buried elsewhere.

CENSER *see* THURIBLE

CENSUS Census returns are an invaluable source of information for those who wish to study demographic changes within a parish – though it should be remembered that figures relate to civil parishes which are not always conterminous with ecclesiastical ones. The first population census of England and Wales, the Channel Islands and the Isle of Man was taken in 1801. Since then a census has been taken every ten years, except in 1941 when the country was at war. Initially the purpose of the census was to provide population statistics so that most of the records from 1801 to 1831 do not provide details of individuals. From 1841 an increasing amount of information was gathered and this is available through the Office of Population Censuses (*see* APPENDIX II), the returns for each census becoming available for public inspection after a period of one hundred years. Microfilm copies of the records are widely available at local record offices.

See also CENSUS OF RELIGIOUS WORSHIP (1851)

Further reading:

FitzHugh, T., *A Dictionary of Genealogy*, Sherborne and London, 1989

Higgs, E., *Making Sense of the Census: The Manuscript Returns for England and Wales 1801–1901*, London, 1989

CENSUS OF RELIGIOUS WORSHIP 1851 Compiled in conjunction with the 1851 population CENSUS, the Census of Religious Worship is an indispensable source of information for the local historian. Returns were made from almost every place of worship (of all denominations) in each parish. The originals are maintained at the Public Record Office (*see* APPENDIX II) while copies are sometimes available at libraries and record offices. The Census provides details of accommodation, pew-renting, average attendances (for the previous twelve months), endowments and the number present at services on 30 March of that year. It also records the foundation of non-conformist chapels built (or adapted) after 1800. The Census was not without its detractors (several ministers refused to disclose attendance figures) and the reliability of many returns has been questioned. At Somerton in Somerset, a Congregational minister claimed that his eyesight was so bad that he was unable to count the number present beyond the front benches! By comparing the two sets of 1851 figures, an indication of the proportion of parishioners who attended the different places of worship within a parish may be calculated, and the strength of the various non-conformist churches and Catholicism assessed. It is also possible to identify 'closed' communities where a small number of landowners were able to impose their notions of religious observance on their tenants, and 'open' parishes populated by small proprietors and landless labourers who were less inclined to church-going and where there are likely to be more non-conformist chapels. At Belton in Lincolnshire, where almost the entire parish was owned by Lord Brownlow, there were no non-conformist chapels and more than seventy-four per cent of the population attended the parish church where a relative of the Earl (who was patron of the living) was the incumbent. On the same day, less than thirty per cent of the people of Crewkerne in Somerset attended one (or more) of the town's places of worship: Anglican, Methodist, Bible Christian, Unitarian and Mormon. The Census revealed statistics which were of little comfort to the ecclesiastical establishment. Throughout England, only twenty-one per cent of the population attended Anglican services and these figures were to fall even further in the second half of the century. Many returns also include remarks appended by the incumbent and these can be most revealing. In Lincolnshire, for example, several of the clergy observed that their parishioners often attended both Anglican and non-conformist services, while the vicar of Alton Pancras in Dorset commented: 'Well attended; many come from other places where Puseyism [the Tractarian Movement] scatters the congregation'.

See also NINETEENTH-CENTURY CHURCH
Further reading:
Bettey, J.H., *Church and Parish*, London, 1987

CENTAUR *see* BEASTS (HERALDIC)

CENTERING A wooden framework used in the construction of arches and vaulting and removed when the mortar has set.

CERE CLOTH A cloth impregnated with wax (Latin *cera*) which is laid on the surface of an altar to prevent the linen cloths from being soiled by the oils used when consecrating the MENSA.

CHAINED LIBRARY *see* LIBRARIES

CHAIRS (SANCTUARY) The throne (*cathedra*) of a bishop is usually located on the north side of the sanctuary in his cathedral while in parish churches an area is similarly designated as a place of honour for a visiting bishop. The chair which is reserved for this purpose is often of some antiquity (there are many Jacobean examples) though with thefts from churches becoming commonplace such valuable items of furniture are often locked away. The stone sanctuary chair at Beverley Minster in Yorkshire is of Saxon origin while the late sixteenth-century chair at Ledbury in Herefordshire is richly carved with scenes of the Journey of the Magi and the Entry into Jerusalem.
See also FALDSTOOL, GLASTONBURY CHAIR, SEDILIA *and* STALLS

CHALICE *see* PLATE

CHALICE VEIL A square of material, usually of the appropriate liturgical colour, used to cover the chalice and paten when they are not in use during the Eucharist.
See also COLOURS (LITURGICAL) *and* VEILS

CHAMBERLAIN *see* LAVATORIUM

CHAMFER To cut away the sharp edge (*arris*) of a block of stone or timber beam, usually at 45 degrees to the vertical and horizontal surfaces. A *hollow chamfer* has a concave surface; a *moulded chamfer* is cut in parallel mouldings; and a *stopped chamfer* is one in which the chamfer is carried part-way along the block or beam and is terminated by a carved splay.

CHANCEL A comparatively recent term (derived from the Latin CANCELLI meaning 'lattice' or 'grating') used to describe a PRESBYTERY which is separated from the NAVE by a screen (*see* CHANCEL SCREEN *and* ROOD SCREEN).
 A number of twelfth-century churches which have survived without enlargement or remodelling serve to demonstrate that, in the Anglo-Saxon and early medieval Church, there was no physical division between the presbytery and the nave or, indeed, between a priest and his people. Churches such as Winterborne Tomson in Dorset, Boarhunt in Hampshire and Kilpeck in Herefordshire are so small that close contact and liturgical intimacy between priest and congregation were inevitable. But, following the Fourth Lateran Council of 1215 (which pronounced the doctrine of transubstanti-

ation, thereby emphasising the sacredness of the MASS), it was considered necessary to enclose the presbytery by means of a screen both to preserve the mystery of the Eucharist (*see* LITURGY) and to isolate the SANCTUARY from the secular activities of the nave (*see* CHURCH AND COMMUNITY). It is this enclosed space which is now described as the chancel (*see also* CHOIR).

There is a unique, two-storeyed chancel (*c.* 1170) at Compton in Surrey where the space beyond the chancel arch is divided horizontally with a vaulted chamber below and a chapel above. The upper chapel, which is reached by a wooden staircase, has the oldest chancel screen in England and was probably used by travellers on the Pilgrims' Way. (The staircase also provided access to an anchorite's cell which may have contained a relic – *see* ANCHORAGE).

By the late Middle Ages, responsibility for the maintenance of the nave rested with the parishioners while the rector or patron was responsible for the chancel. For this reason there is often a startling discrepancy between the size and workmanship of the two areas. At Methwold in Norfolk, for example, the fourteenth-century chancel is completely overshadowed by a fine nave and a great tower and spire which were erected by the parish. At Addlethorpe in Lincolnshire, the chancel was demolished by an eighteenth-century incumbent who could not be bothered to repair it!

Following the REFORMATION the laity was brought into the chancel for the celebration of the Eucharist and, despite legislation which specifically stated that screens should be retained, many medieval screens were dismantled together with the figures of the ROOD and ROOD LOFTS. As a consequence of the Dissolution of the Monasteries, the chancels of several former religious houses were adopted for parochial use (their naves having been demolished): the church of St. Thomas of Canterbury at Upholland in Lancashire, for example, was once the chancel of a Benedictine priory founded in 1317.

See also ALTAR RAILS, ALTARS, AMPLIFIERS, AUMBRY, CHANCEL VENTILATOR, CRE-DENCE, FENESTELLA, MISERICORD, PISCINA, PORCHES, PRIEST'S DOOR, SACRISTY, SQUINT *and* SEDILIA

CHANCEL ARCH The arched opening in the eastern wall of a NAVE providing access to the CHANCEL (*see also* PRESBYTERY). In the late-medieval period a ROOD SCREEN was usually erected across the opening in order to separate the (often secular) activity of the nave from that of the chancel. The arch also defined the boundary between the parishioners' responsibility for the maintenance of the nave (including the screen) and that of the rector or patron who was responsible for the chancel.

Norman chancel arch at Kilpeck, Herefordshire.

The chancel arch is often the most striking interior feature of a parish church. At Worth Matravers in Dorset, for example, a massive Norman arch (of *c.* 1130) rests on six piers with heavy scalloped capitals, carrying three depths of Norman chevron mouldings. Some churches in Devon and Cornwall, and in the Craven area of Yorkshire, were built without any architectural division between the nave and presbytery, although in most of these cases a screen has been added to form a chancel.
See also TYMPANUM

CHANCELLOR (i) One of the four dignitaries of CATHEDRALS of the 'Old Foundation' whose responsibilities include the cathedral library and school. (ii) A Diocesan Chancellor is a professional lawyer who acts on behalf of the bishop in the administration of the diocese. The Chancellor is usually president of the CONSISTORY COURT and is chiefly responsible for considering applications for the granting of faculties (*see* FACULTY) and for hearing complaints against clerics brought under the Ecclesiastical Jurisdiction Measure of 1963 other than those concerning doctrine or ceremonial.

CHANCEL SCREEN (*also* CHOIR SCREEN) A carved stone, wood or ironwork screen separating the CHANCEL of a church from the NAVE. In the medieval period (as in several churches today) the nave was used for secular purposes, the parish church being the only public meeting place in a community (*see* CHURCH AND COMMUNITY). A screen was therefore necessary in order to preserve the dignity and mystery of the PRESBYTERY (*see also* CHANCEL ARCH *and* DOGS). Unlike the figures of the ROOD and ROOD LOFTS, the screens which supported them were specifically protected by sixteenth-century legislation (*see* REFORMATION). Many former ROOD SCREENS have therefore survived as chancel screens.

CONSTRUCTION

Typically, chancel screens are supported on a plinth with a chamfered top edge and are divided by vertical members (*posts*) into sections (*bays*), pierced by a central opening which may still have a gate or pair of gates. (West Country screens almost invariably had gates but East Anglian examples normally do not.) Each bay is usually panelled to a third of its height above which openings (*lights*), sometimes divided by delicate vertical members (*muntins*), terminate in pierced tracery within a pointed arch or arches. Such bays have vertical outer frame members (*stiles*) which are held within horizontal rails at the top (*head rail*) and bottom (*base rail*) and by an intermediate (*transom*) rail. A chancel screen may carry a heavy overhanging cornice supported by a coving or fan vaulting. In some cases these are part of the original medieval structure which carried the projecting base of a ROOD LOFT while others were added to earlier screens during nineteenth-century restorations.

If the screen has a rood it is known as a rood screen, though roods are invariably Victorian Gothic or early twentieth-century additions (*see* ROOD). Most cathedrals and major monastic churches had both a rood screen and a massive PULPITUM, though in many instances the latter has subsequently been demolished and replaced by a chancel screen and no cathedral rood screens have survived.

MEDIEVAL SCREENS

Medieval screens were generally coloured and gilded and a surprising number have survived the ravages of time and the depredations of over-zealous reformers and iconoclasts. The thirteenth-century painted screen at Stanton Harcourt in Oxfordshire is believed to be the earliest in England. A number of Devon churches contain magnificent examples of fifteenth-century wooden screens and several retain their original colouring: at Wolborough, for

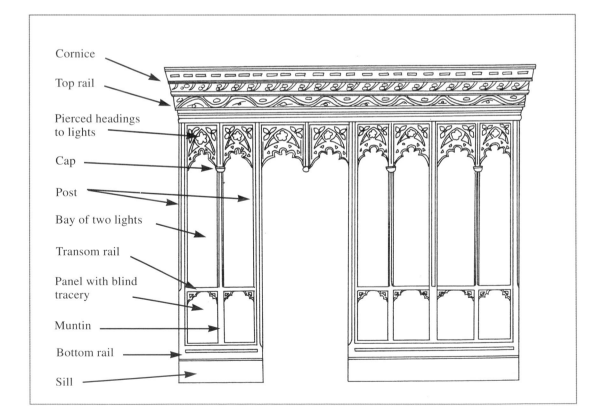

Cornice

Top rail

Pierced headings to lights

Cap

Post

Bay of two lights

Transom rail

Panel with blind tracery

Muntin

Bottom rail

Sill

example. The lower panels are often crowded with painted figures and the tracery is bold and the cornice ornately carved. Such screens may stretch from one side of the church to the other in a single, unbroken line. Many excellent Devonshire examples remain such as those at Ashton, Bovey Tracey, Cullompton and Lapford, and in Somerset at Dunster, Minehead and Banwell.

The fourteenth- and fifteenth-century wooden screens of East Anglian churches are somewhat different: they are lighter, higher and generally more finely executed than those in West Country churches. Tracery is not so conspicuous and sometimes there is no tracery at all, particularly when a screen is vaulted, as at Attleborough in Norfolk and Bramfield in Suffolk. Base panels are almost invariably painted and gilded: the Twelve Apostles is a favoured subject, as are obscure saints and martyrs, angels, prophets and kings. Often the backgrounds are alternately red and green or of rich *gesso* work (gold). Paint was generally oil based though water-soluble azurite blue and water-gilding were also used. There are fine screens at Barton Turf, Ludham, Hunstanton and Ranworth in Norfolk and at Eye, Westhall and Somerleyton in Suffolk. A section of unpainted (but original) panelling in an otherwise decorated medieval screen may suggest that a subsidiary altar once stood there, or a low bench at which the priest heard confession.

In the Welsh Marches there is a particularly fine fifteenth-century rood screen and loft at lonely Partrishow church in Powys (or, more properly, the church of Merthyr Issui at Patricio): vines, grapes, foliage and dragons are all superbly carved in honey-coloured oak.

Medieval stone screens are comparatively rare and in parish churches they are generally of similar design to contemporary wooden screens: that at Totnes in Devon is one of the finest and there are several in Wiltshire (Hilmarton and Compton Bassett, for example) and two interesting fourteenth-century examples at Stebbing and Great Bardfield in Essex, both of which support a (nineteenth-century) rood.

POST-REFORMATION SCREENS
Late sixteenth- and early seventeenth-century wooden screens are usually ornamented with round-arched arcading, geometrical patterns of interlaced 'straps' (called *strapwork*) and S scrolls, often with obelisks set on the cornice. Most Jacobean examples are screens to collegiate ante-chapels and halls, though there are chancel screens of this period, as at Croscombe and Rodney Stoke in Somerset. The church of St. Lawrence at Folke in Dorset was rebuilt in 1628 on the site of a former medieval church and contains a magnificent pair of Jacobean screens, the larger being a chancel screen and the smaller separating the north aisle from the nave, together with contemporary communion rails, table,

pulpit reading desk and bench ends. A common feature of this period was the inclusion in the design of the Royal Arms which surmount the centre of the screen, flanked by the arms of a patron or benefactor and those of a bishop impaling the arms of his diocese. A good example is the screen at Abbey Dore in Herefordshire.

In the eighteenth century, many screens were reduced to the level of the transom, usually as a result of wet rot caused by leaking roofs or simply in accordance with current liturgical practice (*see* EIGHTEENTH-CENTURY CHURCH). In the early Victorian period medieval polychrome was often disguised with brown oak graining, sometimes on top of eighteenth-century white lead paint, while (incredibly) caustic soda was used to strip many screens to bare oak, a practice associated with late nineteenth- and early twentieth-century 'restorations'.

Larger churches and cathedrals often have several screens (*see also* PARCLOSE *and* TOWER SCREEN) and these, whether in wood or stone, invariably reflect the architectural style of the period in which they were erected. Metal screens, often cast in bronze, are comparatively rare and usually of Victorian or Edwardian origin. One of the most magnificent is Sir Ninian Comper's three-bay iron rood screen at Wellingborough, Northamptonshire (1908–30) above which is suspended a gigantic golden God in Glory from which shooting rays fan out over the rood.

See also PULPITS, READING DESKS *and* RETURNED STALLS

Further reading:
Bond, F., and Camm, D., *Rood-screens and Rood-lofts* (2 vols), London, 1909
Bond, F., *Screens and Galleries in English Churches*, Oxford, 1908
Burman, P., (ed.), *Treasures on Earth*, Donhead, 1994

CHANCEL VENTILATOR (LOW-SIDE WINDOW) A small opening immediately beneath a window in the south wall of the presbytery, originally provided with a grille and shutters which could be opened to admit fresh air when the accumulated smoke of candles and censers became overpowering. There is a good example at Melton Constable in Norfolk which retains its original shutter. Sometimes a seat was also provided on which the priest could recuperate. Occasionally, ventilators may be found on both sides of the presbytery, though many have been glazed or blocked. At one time, chancel ventilators were believed to have been 'leper windows' through which lepers received the host at communion.

CHANCERY, COURT OF The appeal court of the Province of York.

CHANDELIER Although true 'evening' services were uncommon before the introduction of oil and gas lamps, many churches possess candelabra. The most imposing form is the chandelier, an ornamental branched support for a number of lights suspended from a ceiling. Typically, a (usually brass) chandelier consists of a central shaft of hollow ball and baluster turnings, held together by an iron hanging rod, and two or three tiers of curving arms (*branches*) springing from the shaft together with a top finial and a pendant finial. It is usually the top finial, between the hanging ring and the stem, which is particularly distinctive. Provincial manufacturing centres each had their own style of finial: a 'London Dove' (with feathered body and open wings) or a 'Bristol Dove' (with closed wings), for example. One of the finials may also be inscribed with the name of the donor and a date. Seventeenth-century chandeliers have the arms hooked into rings in the balusters, or into trays pierced with holes, and consequently appear to droop. During the eighteenth century arms became shorter, were fitted to the circumference of the spheres and were more erect. Branches were elaborate and covered with scroll-work and the flame finial was popular. Dutch chandeliers of the period have minimal decoration and no finials and the branches are attached to hollow trays by means of tenons and pins. Manufacturing of chandeliers ceased in England in the nineteenth century. Among numerous fine examples, those at Axbridge, Stogumber and Wedmore in Somerset, Ashburton and Braunton in Devon, Ightham in Kent, Lingfield in Surrey, Bourne in Lincolnshire and Mayfield in Sussex are exceptional.
See also CANDLES *and* CORONA LUCIS

CHANTRIES ACT (1547) *see* CHANTRIES

CHANTRY 'Three things helpen souls most out of penance, that is devout praying, alms-giving and mass-singing . . . right as meat and drink comforteth a man when he is feeble, right so the sacrament comforteth and strengtheneth the souls that it is done for.'

Strictly speaking, a chantry is an office, established for a special purpose, either with an endowment of land or rent, or celebrated for a specified period for which funds have been bequeathed. Freehold chantries and most stipendiary services were in the first category, while the second included OBITS and TRENTALS. But the term is generally applied more widely to a variety of pre-Reformation religious foundations established in cathedrals, chapels and parish churches (*see* MORROW MASS).

From the Old French *chanceries*, meaning 'to sing', a chantry was a private soul-mass, celebrated regularly for the repose of the soul of a testator and others nominated by him in his will (*see* PRIVILEGED ALTAR). It was the conviction that a regular offering of the Eucharist was the most effective means of redemption that encouraged medieval man to make financial provision in his will for a chantry or chantries (*see* PROBATE). This was particularly so during the fourteenth and fifteenth centuries when the LITURGY of the Catholic Church increasingly emphasised the importance of the MASS. Some chantries were endowed during the lifetime of the founder, and the mass-priest would be obliged to celebrate masses for his well-being on earth and his soul after death. Chantries were also endowed by guilds and fraternities for the benefit of their members. They were, in fact, a very cheap form of endowment for even the most humble testator could arrange for one or two masses to be said for his soul (*see* BEDE ROLL). However, it was those with the largest purses (and often the heaviest consciences) who were responsible for the erection of the magnificent late medieval CHANTRY CHAPELS and for the endowment of numerous charitable institutions such as the Hospital of All Saints (now known as Brown's Hospital) at Stamford in Lincolnshire, built in the reign of Henry VII to accommodate ten poor men, together with two poor women who were to be 'attentive and useful to the poor men in their necessities'. The residents of the Hospital of All Saints were required to recite three psalms a day for the soul of the home's founder Thomas Brown, a prominent wool merchant, and it was a condition of admission that a candidate should not only be 'lowly, devout and poor' but also fluent in chanting 'the Lord's Prayer, the Angelic Salutation and the Apostles' Creed'. Men such as Thomas Brown were prepared to make considerable and often posthumous investments to ensure that their souls did not remain too long in the dreadful limbo-land of PURGATORY, a concept which was popularly established in the twelfth century and which motivated the building of numerous social institutions as well as chantry chapels and other memorials. In the Suffolk town of Lavenham, Thomas Spring III (known as The Great Clothier) left money to build the superb tower of Lavenham's parish church, and in many of England's great cathedrals endowments were provided to maintain choirs whose tasks included praying for the souls of the departed: at York Minster, for example, where the choristers were known as the College of the Vicars Choral (*see* CHANTRY COLLEGES).

The dissolution of the chantries in 1547 was accompanied by the confiscation of those funds of guilds and corporations which (it was claimed) had been assigned to 'superstitious objects' (*see* REFORMATION, THE). This measure had a far greater impact on community life than the more spectacular DISSOLUTION OF THE MONASTERIES

The Beauchamp chantry chapel at Tewkesbury Abbey, Gloucestershire.

for many chantries were dependent on their investments for the maintenance of SCHOOLS, ALMSHOUSES, HOSPITALS and other charitable functions. Most significantly, the Chantries Act of 1547 confirmed official disapproval of the doctrine of purgatory and masses for '. . . them which be departed'. As a consequence (and because of the Crown's urgent need for resources) all chantry endowments, goods and valuables were transferred to the King. *Chantry Certificates*, which were issued in 1548 are housed at the Public Record Office, together with the *confiscation inventories* of 1552 (*see* APPENDIX II) and many of these have been published by local history societies. They provide an invaluable source of information concerning the nature of chantries, guilds, almshouses, schools, hospitals and other charitable foundations at the close of the Middle Ages, together with details of the plate, vestments and other valuables which parish churches had accumulated through medieval bequests and endowments.
See also LIGHTHOUSES

CHANTRY CERTIFICATES *see* CHANTRIES

CHANTRY CHAPELS By the fifteenth century most large churches, and many smaller ones, had at least one chantry chapel in which a priest was employed to sing masses for the soul of the founder and others nominated by him in his will (*see* CHANTRIES *and* PROBATE). Cardinal Beaufort (d. 1447) provided for three thousand masses to be said at the altar of his magnificent chapel at Winchester while successive members of the Hungerford family spent vast sums on bequests to the church so that, by the end of the fifteenth century, they had founded twelve chantries, seven anniversary masses (*obits*), a school and two almshouses. Like other forms of memorial, a chantry chapel does not necessarily mark the place of interment of the person in whose memory it was erected.

Some chantry chapels were large (Henry VII's chapel at Westminster Abbey is the most spectacular example) and often consisted of an aisle or side chapel built on to the main body of the church: the glorious Beauchamp chapel at the collegiate church of St. Mary, Warwick (*c.* 1450), for instance, and Cardinal Morton's chapel (*c.* 1500) in the north aisle of Bere Regis church in Dorset. Other chapels were created by extending an aisle (or aisles) in an eastward direction, parallel to the chancel, or to the north and south to create small transepts. Heraldic embellishment in these larger chapels is often sumptuous and may include BADGES, CYPHERS and REBUSES.

The majority of chantry chapels are very much smaller and usually comprise a gilded and painted rectangular PARCLOSE of ornate stone or metal and an intricately vaulted CANOPY. (The essential difference between a canopied monument and a small chantry chapel is the presence in the latter of an altar at which masses were celebrated.) Such chapels are generally found linking the piers of the chancel arcade or flanking the presbytery and their proximity to the high altar is usually an accurate guide to the status of those they commemorate. It is significant that the popularity of chantry chapels in the high Middle Ages should coincide with the flowering of the Perpendicular style of architecture for, almost without exception, the decorative detail is exquisite. At Tewkesbury Abbey in Gloucestershire, for instance, the chapel erected (*c.* 1378) for Edward Despenser (d. 1375) on the south side of the high altar contains the earliest example of fan vaulting in England. From within a lofty canopy on the roof of the chapel the kneeling figure of Edward stares out at the High Altar and to where the SACRAMENT HOUSE was once suspended. (There is no other known example of an effigial figure in this position.) The chapel is commonly known as the Trinity Chapel because on the east wall of the interior is a remarkable fresco representing the Holy Trinity, with portraits of Edward and his wife (Elizabeth de Burghersh) on either side of the central figures, kneeling behind angels with censers. In the corresponding north bay is a chapel within which stands the tomb of Robert Fitz Hamon, a descendant of William the Conqueror and the abbey's founder, who died in 1107. Fitz Hamon was first buried in the Chapter House of the Benedictine monastery but his body was moved to its present position in 1241 and the chantry erected by Abbot Parker in 1397. The finest of the Tewkesbury chantry chapels is that built by Isabel Despenser in memory of her first husband Richard Beauchamp, Earl of Abergavenny and Worcester (d. 1421). Begun in 1422, but not completed until 1438, it has an ornate and spiky canopy and a lovely miniature fan-vault within which is set a carved lady's head – presumably that of Lady Isabella herself. There are traces of original painting in the vaulting: peacock blue with ribs and pendants in red and gold. There are other notable examples at Newark in Nottinghamshire, Paignton in Devon, Boxgrove Priory in Sussex and Christchurch Priory, Hampshire.

At several churches an additional aisle was constructed to accommodate chantry chapels, as at Devizes in Wiltshire (another Beauchamp chapel), North Leigh in Oxfordshire and Tiverton and Cullompton in Devon. Many churches were extended in this way by guilds and fraternities who competed with one another in the opulence of their chapels: that of the Merchant Tailors in St. Ewen's church, Bristol, for example, which occupies the entire south aisle and was separated from the nave by carved wooden screens. An inventory of 1401 tells of tapestries depicting scenes from the life of

The Beauchamp chapel at St. Mary's, Warwick, in the mid-nineteenth century.

St. John the Baptist (the Guild's patron saint), of valuable vestments and plate, altar hangings, crosses and processional banners (*gonfannons*). There were nearly two hundred religious fraternities in the 107 parishes in and around London in the late Middle Ages and their chantries enabled even the poorest members of society to benefit from masses and to have their names entered in the BEDE ROLLS.

With the dissolution of chantries in 1547, many chantry chapels were used for other purposes: the superb Hungerford chantry at Salisbury Cathedral, for example, was converted into an exceptionally ornate mayoral pew.

See also CHANTRY COLLEGES, LIGHTHOUSES, PRIVILEGED ALTARS *and* SQUINT

CHANTRY COLLEGES In the fourteenth and fifteenth centuries the founding of a college of secular clergy (i.e. a chapter of canons or prebendaries) was often the ultimate ambition of members of the medieval establishment. The very rich, especially those who left no direct heir, might provide for the establishment of a college which was endowed primarily to provide masses in perpetuity for the souls of the founder and his family (*see* PROBATE). Apart from the landed endowment itself, a licence had to be obtained from the sovereign to grant land into *mortmain* (to a religious body), a long and costly process which was often aggravated by legal disputes following a testator's death. Sir John Fastolf (d. 1459), for example, planned to establish a college at Caister in Norfolk and was 'sore set thereupon' despite innumerable impediments. His will imposed on his executors the responsibility of carrying out his scheme but, as often happened, protracted legal wrangling following his death caused the project to be deferred and the endowment was eventually transferred to William Waynflete's foundation of Magdalen College, Oxford.

Ralph Nevill, Earl of Westmorland (1354–1425) was preoccupied with elevating Staindrop church, at the gates of his castle of Raby in County Durham, into a college of priests. His grandfather had endowed three chantries in the church for the repose of his parents, and Ralph Nevill obtained a licence from the Prior of Durham for a further foundation of a warden, twelve clergy, twelve poor gentlemen and six 'other poor persons'. For their support he gave two houses, twelve acres of land and the advowson of the church. He extended the nave and raised it to accommodate a clerestory, built a battlemented square tower in place of an early English spire and added a two-storeyed priest's dwelling to the north of the chancel. In the presbytery he provided twelve STALLS and a fine wooden screen, the only medieval chancel screen in the county. When he died in 1424, Westmorland left legacies to the friars, nuns and anchorites of the dioceses of York and Durham together with 300 marks to complete the work on his college. His splendid alabaster effigy, and those of his two wives, were placed on a great tomb chest before the altar at Staindrop where 'perpetual masses' were said for their souls (the tomb was subsequently removed from the chancel and has recently been restored).

Richard of Gloucester (later Richard III) obtained licences to establish COLLEGIATE CHURCHES at Barnard Castle, County Durham and Middleham in Yorkshire as perpetual chantries at which masses were to be celebrated for himself, his duchess and his family. A further scheme, for a college of 100 canons at York, was begun in 1483 but was never completed. One wonders whether this was to have been Richard's mausoleum?

ACADEMIC FOUNDATIONS

Many colleges developed as academic institutions though, in practice, there was little legal or constitutional difference between the two types of college. During the later fifteenth and early sixteenth centuries there was a significant expansion in the number of colleges at Oxford and Cambridge and many of these were endowed specifically for the better education of the clergy. Substantial endowments made provision for increasing numbers of undergraduates and for the teaching duties of fellows, while smaller bequests provided loans for the benefit of 'poor, virtuous scholars, not vicious nor wasters nor haunters of taverns or alehouses.' Only a minority of scholars graduated as a Bachelor of Arts after four years or as a Master of Arts after a further three. Many students were the sons of the nobility and gentry who were there at their own expense in order to improve their general education.

Of course, there were many educational foundations outside Oxford and Cambridge. Eton College, for example, was endowed by Henry VI as a religious college with a provost, fellows, clerks and choristers to sing at divine service and a school of twenty-five 'poor scholars' under the direction of a Master. Although such places have subsequently developed as centres of academic excellence, in the Middle Ages their essential function remained that of commemorating patrons by prayers and intercessory masses.

PARISH CHURCHES

Several parish churches have collegiate origins. The Collegiate Church of St. Mary, Warwick, for example, was served by a chapter of dean and seven canons from 1123 to the Reformation. It was Henry, the first Earl of Warwick, who established a PREBEND to provide for the needs of a priest. By 1123 his son, Roger, had given sufficient property to maintain six further prebends, together with houses in Warwick to accommodate the canons, several of whom came from the chapel of All Saints in the nearby castle. The chapter met together in the church to celebrate the Mass and the seven canonical offices, and in the chapter house where their business affairs were conducted. The chancel was reserved for the College (which later came to included vicars who deputised for absent canons), together with clerics in minor orders and boy choristers. The nave was divided from the chancel by a screen and contained a parish altar and side-chapels for the townspeople. In 1544 the college surrendered to Henry VIII who confiscated its estates, some of which were restored to the burgesses of Warwick by royal charter in 1545.

The wonderful set of twenty-eight MISERICORDS in the stalls of Ludlow parish church in Shropshire, suggest that this too was a collegiate foundation. But while a college-like establishment existed at Ludlow, it was not truly collegiate. Members of the influential Palmers' Guild, whose altar dedicated to St. John the Evangelist was in the north-eastern chapel, endowed a number of chantries within the church. The chaplains employed to administer these chantries (ten in the late fifteenth century) were accommodated in a lodging house in College Street and shared the daily offices and duties of the church with the secular clergy while attending also to their individual responsibilities.

THE REFORMATION

Chantry colleges were suppressed in 1547, though many were later re-founded as academic institutions and some even managed to survive the Dissolution in their original form. The College of St. Endellion in Cornwall, for example, is first mentioned in documents dated 1260 (*Ecclesia Sancte Endeliente*) as a college of secular clergy serving the church and shrine of the sixth-century Celtic saint (*see*

HERMIT). In 1547 the Rector was deprived of his living, the college members (*prebendaries*) all received their £5 pensions as dispossessed clerics and the College was presumed to be dissolved. And yet, unaccountably, there is a College of St. Endellion today, its fellows claiming corporate continuity from before the Reformation. Even more remarkable, the College received a grant of armorial bearings in 1950. Grants of arms are signed and sealed by the Sovereign's authority and the letters patent of 1950 would therefore appear to confirm the College's claim.

See also CHANTRIES, CHANTRY CHAPELS *and* HOSPITALS

CHAPEL OF EASE *see* CHAPELS

CHAPEL ROYAL *see* CHAPELS *and* CHURCH MUSIC (ANGLICAN)

CHAPELRY A term usually applied to the daughter church of a MINSTER but also used to describe a church serving a section of a large PARISH, sometimes with a resident priest who would be subordinate to the incumbent.

See also ANGLO-SAXON CHURCH *and* AUGUSTINIANS

CHAPELS Derived from the Latin *cappella*, diminutive of *cappa* meaning 'little cape', the term refers to the cloak of St. Martin of Tours which was preserved as a sacred relic by the Frankish kings. In time, the term was applied generically to sanctuaries where holy relics were preserved and prayers were said and, from *c*. 800, to sacred buildings which are less than churches.

PROPRIETARY CHAPELS
From the eighth century, landowners began building chapels on their estates to augment those of the MINSTERS (*see* CHAPELRY). Indeed, in late Anglo-Saxon England, possession of a proprietary chapel (sometimes described as a *thane's church*) was considered to be an attribute of rank. Most were served by a priest, who may also have acted as the lord's chaplain, and the estate retained the church's tithes and other dues while the lord exercised proprietorial rights, including the right to appoint a priest (*advowson*) (*see* ANGLO-SAXON CHURCH).

ORATORIES
Similarly, most medieval residences and castles contained private chapels (*oratories*), licensed for divine worship by a bishop, and built within the walls of a house or castle, or adjacent to it. Unique among these is the circular chapel of St. Mary Magdalene in the inner ward of Ludlow Castle in Shropshire. What remains today is the nave, the apsidal chancel having all but vanished. The

western, twelfth-century door is richly ornamented and an arcade of seven arches, alternately moulded and chevroned, extends around the inner walls on both sides of the entrance. Without documentary evidence it is often difficult to distinguish between a proprietary chapel, built in the vicinity of a manor house (for example), and an oratory in a similar location: either may now be a parish church. Chapels were sometimes built within the gatehouses of castles and walled towns, to provide for the spiritual needs of the constable and his garrison and (theoretically) to deter those whose consciences might prevent their attacking a consecrated place. There are good examples at Harlech Castle in Gwynedd (1283) and at Warwick where a chapel was built above the west gate in 1123.

HOSPICE CHAPELS
The gatehouse chapel of St. James at Warwick was later adopted by the town's guilds and incorporated into the Lord Leycester hospital for twelve 'poor and impotent persons' in 1571. Other notable examples of hospice chapels are those of Browne's Hospital (*c*. 1480) at Stamford in Lincolnshire and the almshouse of St. John the Baptist and St. John the Evangelist at Sherborne in Dorset (1437) (*see also* ALMSHOUSES *and* HOSPITALS).

MONASTIC CHAPELS
Most former monastic churches contain a number of minor chapels each of which would have been used by a priest to say mass, while others were dedicated to a particular saint or provided for a specific purpose. Of these, the LADY CHAPEL, dedicated to the Blessed Virgin Mary and located at the east end behind the high altar, is usually the largest. Others were built into the aisles, transepts or ambulatory and may have been CHANTRY CHAPELS (*see also* PARCLOSE *and* PRIVILEGED ALTAR).

A chapel was usually provided at (or near) the gate of a religious house for the use of visitors, servants and employees (*see* CAPELLA ANTE PORTAS) and at granges (*see* GRANGE) and these sometimes became parish churches, the best-known example being the church of St. Margaret at Westminster. The chapel of St. Michael on the summit of Glastonbury Tor in Somerset was built by the monks of the nearby Abbey for the benefit of pilgrims visiting one of the most sacred and historic sites in England. (It was on the Tor, in 1539, that the Abbot of Glastonbury was butchered for refusing to relinquish the Abbey plate following the DISSOLUTION OF THE MONASTERIES.) The Glastonbury chapel may have performed a function similar to that of the fourteenth century 'Shoe House' or Slipper Chapel at Houghton St. Giles in Norfolk which is situated about 1.6 kilometres (1 mile) from the shrine of Our Lady at Walsingham Priory. Here, the pilgrims would pause and meditate before embarking on the final stage of their journey – barefoot and penitent.

The chapel of King's College, Cambridge, begun in 1446 and completed in 1515.

PECULIARS

Free chapels (*peculiars*), such as the tiny thirteenth-century chapel of St. Bartholomew at Corton in Dorset, were not subject to a bishop's jurisdiction, though most of the rights and privileges of peculiars have now been revoked. Many were the chapels of former COMMANDERIES and PRECEPTORIES of the military and hospitaller orders of St. John of Jerusalem and the Knights Templar, usually described in documents (as recently as the nineteenth century) as *ex-parochial* and, as such, exempt from diocesan jurisdiction (*see* ST. JOHN OF JERUSALEM, ORDER OF *and* TEMPLAR, KNIGHTS). Chapels Royal (*Royal Peculiars*) are private chapels attached to the royal court and are exempt from any jurisdiction save that of the Sovereign, exercised through the Dean of the Chapels Royal. Other royal chapels include mausoleums which were often constructed for that purpose during a sovereign's lifetime. The most magnificent of these is Henry VII's chapel at Westminster Abbey which is itself a royal peculiar.

CHAPELS OF EASE

A Chapel of Ease was one which was provided for 'the ease and comfort' of those living at some distance from a parish church, and was subordinate to it. But such chapels did not usually have rights of burial so that parishioners were compelled to carry corpses to the mother church for interment (*see* COFFIN PATHS *and* LICH-GATES). Other chapels (many of them endowed by means of chantries) were built at the roadside, often near bridges and fords, at SHRINES and above HOLY WELLS. At the Severn crossing near Stourport in Worcestershire, the medieval hermits of Redstone Rock operated a ferry on the important saltway from Droitwich; and in Devon the Starcross ferry across the Exe was maintained by monks from the benedictine abbey of Sherborne in Dorset. Among the various legacies of Ralph Nevill, Earl of Westmorland (1354–1424) were bequests for the building of two bridges – over the Ure at Middleham, Yorkshire and over the Tees at Winston near Raby in County Durham. At these, and at other river crossings, chapels would have been provided both for the comfort of travellers and in 'perpetual memory' of those by whom they were endowed. Few have survived, a notable exception being the chapel of St. Twrog which was constructed on a rocky outcrop near Beachley, on the eastern bank of the river Severn, by the hermits who maintained a ferry across the Arlingham Passage. The tiny St. Brynach's Well chapel in Dyfed was already a ruin when Richard Fenton, the antiquarian, saw it in the early nineteenth century: 'Cross over a small brook to Brynach's Well, a redundant spring close to the ruins of an old chapel, having an upright rude stone pitched on end near it, marked with a cross.' Only the place-name and a gushing spring remain – and a great Dark Age stone which has been removed to the nearby church at Henry's Moat. At Rhos-on-Sea in Clwyd, the diminutive seaside well-chapel of Capel Trillo is in far better condition. Built from rounded beach boulders, it was restored and re-consecrated in 1935. The lonely Norman chapel on St. Alban's Head in Dorset may have been built as a chantry chapel, though its massive walls do not have an east-west orientation and there is no evidence of a PISCINA. The superb vaulting of the twelfth-century roof, supported by a massive central pier, and the fine Romanesque arched doorway are of the finest quality and it is known that medieval kings paid the chaplain 50*s* a year for his services. It is now known as St. Aldhelm's chapel, though there is no record of Aldhelm ever having been associated with the place, and the modern cross on its roof almost certainly replaced a cresset or signal beacon (*see* LIGHTHOUSES).

MORTUARY CHAPELS

There are numerous tiny Welsh chapels dedicated to a pantheon of local saints, such as the chapel of the enigmatic St. Govan, 'an empty, echoing building hidden at the foot of the cliffs' * at Bosherston, Dyfed (see CELTIC CHURCH). In several Welsh churchyards may be found *eglwysau-y-bedd*, 'churches of the grave'. These tiny mortuary chapels are usually located at some distance from their parish churches and provide evidence of the Celtic church's practice of building separate chapels for specific purposes.

POST-REFORMATION

Chapels were suppressed by the Chantries Act of 1547 and many were closed for public worship though several of the more remote chapels of ease escaped the attentions of the reformers and became parish churches. Others, such as St. Nyven's Chapel at Crick in Gwent and Poynton Chapel in Shropshire, were adapted for agricultural purposes. But for many others, only place-name evidence remains. Anglican chapels and oratories are now regulated by the PRIVATE CHAPELS ACT of 1871.

In 1786, after entertaining George III at his mansion at Lulworth in Dorset, Thomas Weld was given leave to build a Roman Catholic chapel in his grounds – providing it did not look like one – the first in England since the Reformation. Many of these private chapels were sumptuously decorated, such as the (Roman Catholic) Palladian oratory of Wardour Castle in Wiltshire which is said to be the model for Evelyn Waugh's chapel at *Brideshead*. The elegant chapel of St. Michael and All Saints at Great Witley in Worcestershire stands beside the gaunt Witley Court, a roofless ruin with trees growing inside. But the chapel, which is now the parish church, is a flamboyant celebration of the rococo style and dates from the eighteenth century when Lord Foley of Witley Court rebuilt the medieval chapel and furnished it with the stained glass, magnificent ceiling panels and organ case which he acquired from the oratory of Canons, the Edgware home of the first Duke of Chandos. Even the most modest of buildings may contain unexpected treasures. Rug Chapel in Clwyd, for example, was established as an estate chapel by Lord Salisbury in 1637 and boasts some of the finest carved and adorned woodwork in Wales. The atmosphere created by the extravagance of carving, painting and stained glass is wonderfully evocative.

For the Chapels Society see APPENDIX II.

See also CHANTRY CHAPELS

Further reading:

Davis, P. and Lloyd-Fern, S., *Lost Churches of Wales and the Marches*, Stroud, 1990

Hibbs, J., *The Country Chapel*, Newton Abbot, 1988 *

CHAPERON *see* COSTUME

CHAPLAIN (*CAPELLANUS*) The priest of a chapel. In the Middle Ages, chaplains were priests without benefices who ministered to private families or to bodies corporate such as hospices and guilds. It is clear from contemporary documents, such as the Paston Letters, that many chaplains acted as private secretaries, undertaking a variety of administrative, clerical, teaching and religious duties, and even donning 'jack and sallet' in defence of their master's interests.

See also CLERGY (CHURCH OF ENGLAND)

CHAPTER (i) A section of a monastic rule and the members of a religious house when assembled to hear a section read or for other purposes. (ii) The body corporate of a religious house or other ecclesiastical institution, e.g. the canons of a cathedral.

CHAPTER HOUSE A building used for meetings of a CHAPTER. The daily meeting of a monastic chapter commenced with a short reading (*capitulum*) from the rule of the order, or from the Scriptures, followed by public confession of sins and the remembrance of benefactors. Then followed the business of the day: reports from officers on various aspects of worship and domestic administration, and the management of the monastic estates, for the great foundations were endowed with considerable resources and property. The chapters of secular CATHEDRALS likewise met as a governing body in the chapter house which was always adjacent to the cathedral or abbey church and usually approached from the eastern alley of the CLOISTER.

The earliest chapter houses were rectangular as at Bristol and Ely, though that at Worcester was circular, and is still so within. From the early thirteenth century, most chapter houses were polygonal (probably because the acoustics were infinitely superior to those of the earlier rectangular buildings), though the Cistercians continued to build in rectangular form (as at Fountains Abbey in Yorkshire) because their rule demanded austerity. The first of the polygonal chapter houses was at Lincoln and this established an architectural fashion peculiar to England. Most were octagonal, though Lincoln's was decagonal with a diameter of 18 metres (59 feet). Exterior roofs were usually pointed and the walls buttressed at each corner. As at Lincoln, most chapter houses had wooden roofs which were replaced with stone in the mid-thirteenth century. The chapter house at Wells in Somerset (*c.* 1319) is the finest in England, though by no means the largest. Below the windows is an arcade of fifty-one stalls with beautifully carved canopies and above, springing from a single, slender column, is a superb vault, quite unsurpassed in its architectural exuberance. The chapter house at Westminster Abbey was used by the early House of Commons as its meeting place and it remains under the jurisdiction of Parliament.

See also MONASTERIES

CHARITABLE DONATIONS With the DISSOLUTION OF THE MONASTERIES in 1536, parishes were made responsible for the care of the 'impotent poor'. Able-bodied vagrants risked whipping or mutilation if they did not work and private alms-giving became an offence which carried a penalty of ten times the amount given (though priests and churchwardens were permitted to solicit charitable donations on Sundays.) From 1547 a vagrant who refused to work was branded with a letter V (for vagabond) and adjudged to be a slave for two years. If he absconded during that period he was again branded (this time with an S) and adjudged a slave for life.

See also POOR LAW

CHARITIES In the Middle Ages, INDULGENCES could be obtained through acts of charity. In the mid-fifteenth century, for example, the Archbishop of York granted an indulgence of forty days to all who assisted in the rebuilding of a flood-damaged bridge on the river Trent at Kelham in Nottinghamshire; while in 1488 a similar indulgence was granted to those who contributed to the refurbishing of the church of St. Mary-le-Strand in London which had been desecrated by thieves. Medieval parishes were heavily dependent on charitable gifts, bequests, endowments and CHANTRIES for which early CHURCH-WARDENS' ACCOUNTS provide an invaluable source of information. The dissolution of the chantries in 1547 resulted in significant changes, both in the affairs of parish churches and in the activities of GUILDS, fraternities and other charitable corporations which were dependent on investments for the maintenance of their HOSPITALS, SCHOOLS, ALMSHOUSES and other institutions.

Changes effected as a result of the REFORMA-TION included a marked increase in the secular responsibilities of parish priests who were required, for example, to exhort their parishioners to provide for the relief of the poor. It was at this time that the parish ceased to be a purely ecclesiastical unit and began to develop administrative functions within the local government system (*see* VESTRY). The CHURCHWARDENS in particular were required to undertake a variety of tasks, many of which had hitherto been administered by the chantries, including the care of the poor and infirm and the maintenance of highways and bridges. During the reign of the first Elizabeth, the growth of Puritanism (*see* PURITANS) led to a dilution of traditional parochial activities, many of which had charitable objectives (*see also* CHURCH AND COMMUN-ITY).

PAROCHIAL CHARITIES

In the seventeenth century, the administration of parochial charities became an integral part of the vestry system. Together with the churchwardens' accounts, vestry minutes provide a fascinating insight into the charitable activity of parishes at that time, and of the diverse claims which demanded attention. At Cerne Abbas in Dorset, for example, the accounts for 1686 include allocations for the repatriation of sailors who had been captured by Turkish pirates, for the relief of fourteen men who claimed to have been shipwrecked off the Dorset coast, for the French Protestants who were suffering persecution and for 'Mary Francis and Benjamin Cimber and their children begging who had lost all their goods by fire'.

In the eighteenth century, parochial charities (including many which had survived the Chantries Act of 1547) continued to provide food, clothing, fuel and money for the poor and these were distributed by the parson and his churchwardens and overseers, especially to those who attended regularly at church or were numbered among the 'second poor' who did not normally receive poor relief (*see also* BEQUEST BOARDS, DOLE CUPBOARDS *and* POOR LAW). Details of parochial benefactions may be found, not only in churchwardens' accounts and vestry minutes, but also in charity books which were kept for that purpose. These sources also include lists of *briefs*, issued in the seventeenth and eighteenth centuries by the Privy Council, by which national collections were authorised for the relief of calamities, to support worthwhile causes (*see* Cerne Abbas, above) and for the rebuilding of churches. The briefs, which set out the circumstances of an appeal, were read out by the parson during a service at the conclusion of which the churchwardens would collect donations from the congregation in the church porch. The system seems to have been effective for it continued into the nineteenth century despite widespread concern regarding the activities of professional 'undertakers', who were employed to collect the money, and the obvious remoteness of many of these good causes from those who were expected to contribute to them.

PATERNALISM

Numerous charitable ALMSHOUSES and SCHOOLS were founded in the eighteenth century as the result of endowments and 'improvement schemes' introduced by paternalistic estate-owners and industrialists. It was at this time that many of Britain's most prestigious charitable foundations were established or revived, notably hospitals such as the Radcliffe Infirmary at Oxford and Addenbrooke at Cambridge, Westminster, Guy's, the Foundling Hospital, Queen Charlotte's and the Royal Maternity Hospital in London.

The nineteenth-century Evangelical Revival inspired an unprecedented proliferation of charitable foundations, both national and parochial. Numerous church schools, Sunday and day schools, orphanages, parish halls, public LIBRARIES, 'institutes' and reading rooms were provided for the benefit of the 'labouring classes', while enormous sums of money were donated for the building and restoration of parish churches, usually in the fashionable early Gothic style (*see* NINETEENTH-CENTURY CHURCH).

DOCUMENTARY SOURCES

From 1786 charities were required to register with Clerks of the Peace who forwarded detailed returns of their activities to Parliament. Copies of these returns are usually held in the Quarter Session records at county record offices. For the early nineteenth century, an invaluable source of information is the series of reports of the Charity Commissioners for 1819–40. These were published as Parliamentary Papers, for which there is an index (*Analytical Digest, 1843, XVIII*). In the same century, numerous printed histories were produced, each containing details of charities, both large and small, which had existed in a particular area. These histories quite often include the only surviving records of early charities. The vestries continued to administer local charities until the civil and ecclesiastical components of their authority were finally separated by the Municipal Corporations Act of 1835 (*see* PARISH). Thereafter, responsibility for parochial charities was divided between the new (civil) parish councils and the (ecclesiastical) parochial church councils which were established in 1919 (*see also* MINUTES). Today, many early charities continue to flourish, often in modified form (*see* CHARITY MEADS) or absorbed into the accounts of the bodies which administered them, while others have become moribund. The *Charity Commission for England and Wales* (established 1853) supervises the activities and accounts of all registered charities, including many schools, hospitals and almshouses. Its archives contain records relating to nearly 150,000 charities (*see* APPENDIX II). Several Community Councils now employ an officer with responsibility for collating information relating to parochial charities.

See also DORCAS MEETINGS, FRIENDLY SOCIETIES *and* POOR LAW

CHARITY BLANKET A euphemism for poor relief (*see* POOR LAW).

CHARITY BOARDS *see* BEQUEST BOARDS

CHARITY COMMISSION *see* CHARITIES

CHARITY MEADS Lands vested in the parish for the upkeep of the poorhouse. The aftergrass of a mead is that which grows after the first crop has been mown for hay. At Leigh in Dorset nine acres of aftergrass at Alton Mead and two at Beer Mill Mead are sold annually by means of a candle auction, a custing from at least 1732. Bids are made as a candle slowly burns down, the successful bid being that last made before the flame dies. The purchaser is entitled to graze his livestock on the aftergrass from LAMMAS Day (13 August) to CANDLEMAS (2 February) in the following year, though the candle auction is usually delayed until MICHAELMAS (29 September) in order that the aftergrass should have time to grow. The proceeds of the Leigh Candle Auction are now used for charitable purposes within the parish.

CHARNELS *see* BURIALS *and* OSSUARIES

CHARTER A document conferring rights on a body corporate or on an individual. A royal charter was a formal instrument by which a sovereign granted or confirmed lands, liberties, titles or immunities on his subjects in perpetuity. Charters were used particularly for grants of land and transactions of the Anglo-Saxon period, whereby land was granted to both monasteries and individuals. These charters also record BOUNDARIES and therefore contain early place-name references. There are two types of *Charter Roll*, the first recording grants and the second confirmations. Both relate to the period 1199 to 1516 after which charters were succeeded by letters patent (*see* PATENT).

CHARTERHOUSE *see* CARTHUSIANS *and* PLAGUE

CHASING A technique in metalwork whereby a pattern is created by surface hammering rather than by removing material. Flatter in appearance than engraving and especially appropriate to brass.

CHASUBLE An outer garment worn by priests when celebrating the Eucharist (*see* VESTMENTS).

CHAUSSES *see* ARMOUR

CHECKER (*also* CHEQUER) A monastic office, controlled by the Cellarer, where accounts were tallied and payments made and recorded. A cloth or board marked with squares was used to assist calculation.

CHEMISE *see* COSTUME

CHERUB *see* AMORINO

CHERUBIM *see* ANGELS

CHEST CUPBOARD (*also* ALMERY *and* HUTCH) Chest cupboards, which were used for storing valuables and documents, were usually fitted with a heavy door or pair of doors, secured with bars and padlocks. They were usually located at the west end of a church, unlike an AUMBRY which is more likely to be in the vicinity of the chancel. Not to be confused with later DOLE CUPBOARDS (which usually have ventilation holes in the doors), chest cupboards are now comparatively rare in churches, a notable exception being that at Louth in Lincolnshire which dates from *c.* 1500.

CHESTS From the medieval period to the seventeenth century, chests and coffers were numerous in parish churches where they were used for storing linen, VESTMENTS, documents and valuables. Surviving examples have become highly desirable antiques and most small chests (*coffers*) are now locked away for 'reasons of security'. Many chests were originally items of household furniture which were later transferred to churches as bequests or when new fashions in joinery (such as the settle and the chest of drawers) made them redundant for domestic purposes. It follows, therefore, that many surviving chests may pre-date the legislation which resulted in their acquisition for parochial use. Most have been adapted in some way (by the addition of locks and iron bands, for example), while advances in constructional techniques and in the introduction of decorative motifs invariably overlapped and were rarely as clear cut as may be suggested by the following summary.

LEGISLATION
In 1166 Henry II required that a chest should be placed in every parish church for the collection of money for the Crusades. Many of these chests were later used as alms boxes. A mandate, issued in 1206 by Pope Innocent II, exhorted the faithful to place alms in 'a hollow trunk', while in 1287 the Synod of Exeter ordered that a chest should be provided in every parish church for the safe custody of books and vestments. Thomas Cromwell's directive of 1538 required that a 'secure coffer' should be kept in every church as a repository for parish registers and other documents (see PARISH CHEST). This was later confirmed at the Hampton Court Conference of 1604. It was not uncommon for the valuables of institutions such as GUILDS to be secured in parish chests, together with charters and other civil documents.

MATERIALS
The majority of chests were made from cleft or sawn oak, though some elm chests have survived and elm and other native timbers were sometimes used for the backs and undersides of chests. Cedar, cypress and camphorwood were often used for vestment and linen chests: the aroma perfumed the contents of the chest and repelled moths. Records exist of pine chests but these were both expensive and rare.

CONSTRUCTION
The oldest and simplist chests were 'dug-out' logs, roughly squared and with a slice removed to serve as a lid: there are examples at several Warwickshire

churches, notably Curdworth. Chests of this type deteriorated rapidly as the timber dried out and had to be reinforced with iron bands held in place with nails which further weakened the trunk.

Boarded chests (commonly known as '*six plank chests*') consisted of four wide, sawn boards flanked by a pair of uprights (*stiles*) which extended below the chest to raise it from the damp. Base boards were usually nailed in place and lids were hinged. Later examples of these chests, which were common from the thirteenth century to the fifteenth, are often carved with decorative roundels, usually on the central section or above the stiles: as at Earl Stonham in Suffolk and Stoke D'Abernon in Surrey. Warping and shrinkage usually caused the boards to split in line with the nails or pegs so that, in the fourteenth century, the heavy oak boards were often clamped and bound with ironwork which provided both strength (Selworthy in Somerset and Warbleton in Sussex) and an opportunity for scroll-work decoration (Icklingham in Suffolk and Church Brampton in Northampton-shire). Some fourteenth-century examples are elaborately carved, especially those in which the stiles and the central section are treated differently. The stiles of chests at Saltwort in Kent and Wath in Yorkshire are divided into horizontal panels, carved with grotesques and beasts, and with traceried central sections. The chest at Dersingham in Norfolk is carved with the symbols of the Four Evangelists while those at Crediton in Devon and Faversham in Kent have splendid traceried panels.

In the early fifteenth century the mortise and tenon joint was introduced into England from the Netherlands (*see* WOODWORK) and by 1450 joiners were using the technique to make framed and panelled chests (joynt chests) which were stronger, lighter and not susceptible to shrinkage. These chests consisted of a timber framework (*stiles, rails* and *muntins*) and wooden panels secured in grooves within the frame. At first, a separate framework was used for each side of the chest and these were nailed together at the corners. Eventually, corner posts were added into which the top and bottom rails were mortised. These posts extended beneath the chest to serve as feet. This type of construction provided considerable scope for decoration: the edges of stiles, rails and muntins were moulded and panels decorated with carving, inlay or applied mouldings (*see* LINENFOLD). In the sixteenth century Renaissance motifs such as arcading, pilasters, stylised fruits and foliage were introduced, often in vernacular forms.

Mule chests, introduced in the early seventeenth century, were a hybrid form of the framed and panelled chest. These had a row of (usually crudely made) drawers beneath the body of the chest in which items such as candles, herbs and valuables were stored.

From the mid-seventeenth century, dovetailing encouraged the re-introduction of wide boards – but without the attendant problems of splitting and warping. Dovetailed chests were usually supported on plinths, the flat sides of the chest provided further scope for decorative carving.

SECURITY

Old chests are usually secured with bolts and at least three locks (the incumbent and his two wardens each having a different key) which can be of the most ingenious construction. Lifting rings, for a chain or rope attached to a carrying pole, may be fitted to the ends of the chest.

See also BOXES *and* COPE CHEST.

Further reading:

Tracy, C., *English Medieval Furniture and Woodwork*, London 1988

CHEST TOMB *see* TABLE TOMB (not to be confused with TOMB CHEST)

CHEVET The eastward apsidal termination of a church, often with radiating chapels.

CHEVRON (i) A zig-zag motif characteristic of late Romanesque carving used especially in the deeply recessed mouldings of arches, as at Iffley in Oxfordshire. *See* DECORATIVE MOTIFS *and* MEDIEVAL ARCHITECTURE (ii) One of the most common charges in HERALDRY consisting of a broad, inverted V across the centre of the shield.

CHIEF, IN *see* POINTS OF THE SHIELD

CHILDERMAS *see* HOLY INNOCENTS' DAY

CHIMERE A silk or satin gown worn by bishops and doctors of divinity.

CHIMNEYS Occasionally a chimney flue may be found rising from the side wall of a parish church or, as at Cerne Abbas in Dorset, piercing the wall itself. If in the vicinity of the chancel or a side chapel, such an opening may be a CHANCEL VENTILATOR, while there are several examples of post-Reformation flues which once served the fireplaces of private pews (*see* FAMILY PEWS). School-rooms were sometimes accommodated in church towers and these were often provided with fireplaces.

CHINOISERIE European interpretation of a Chinese decorative motif, consisting of interlaced lines, especially popular in the second half of the eighteenth century.

CHIP CARVING *see* DECORATIVE MOTIFS

CHI-RHO *see* CHRISMON *and* CHRISTIAN SYMBOLS

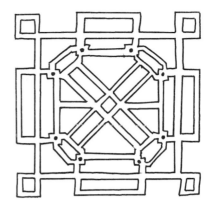

Chinoiserie

CHIROGRAPH *see* INDENTURE

CHOIR (*also* QUIRE) (i) An organised group of singers. In the worship of the early Church all music was rendered by the clergy and congregation. From the fourth century bodies of singers, comprising clerics in minor orders and boys, assisted in the music of divine services. A *schola cantorum* was established in Rome by Pope Gregory the Great (d. 604) and the custom spread through western Christendom so that the medieval cathedrals and monastic churches became centres of musical excellence and almost the only places at which a musical education could be obtained. It was not until the fifteenth century, when harmonised music began to supplement PLAINSONG, that lay singers sometimes augmented these choirs. *See also* CHURCH MUSIC (ANGLICAN), GALLERIES, MISERICORDS, ORGANS *and* STALLS (ii) That part of a cathedral or monastic or collegiate church, between the PRESBYTERY and the PULPITUM, furnished with STALLS and occupied by the members of the body corporate during the Divine Office. The term is not applicable to the CHANCEL of a lesser church, indeed it was the Victorian clergy who first introduced stalls for singers into the chancels of their parish churches. Several Norman churches had an additional space between the nave and sanctuary (Studland in Dorset and Stewkley in Buckinghamshire, for example) and this is sometimes (erroneously) referred to as a choir.

It is almost invariably in the choirs of the great abbeys and cathedrals that MEDIEVAL ARCHITECTURE enjoys its most glorious manifestation: at Gloucester, for example, which was restructured during the second quarter of the fourteenth century and marks a turning point in architectural history. Here is the first flowering of the peculiarly English perpendicular style of Gothic architecture which lasted from the mid-fourteenth century to the early sixteenth century. At Gloucester, the eastern apse and presbytery roof were removed and a lofty cage of delicate perpendicular tracery erected within the great Norman arcade, with an immense window (the Crécy window) to the east of the high altar and a delicate lierne vault above (*see* VAULTING). The result is breathtakingly beautiful.

See also AMBULATORY, AMPLIFIERS, MONASTIC BUILDINGS, RETRO-CHOIR *and* RETURNED STALLS

CHOIR SCREEN *see* CHANCEL SCREEN, PULPITUM *and* ROOD SCREEN

CHOIR SISTER A nun who is required to attend choir offices in contradistinction to a lay sister who attends only certain services.

CHOIR STALLS *see* CHURCH MUSIC (ANGLICAN) *and* STALLS

CHRISM (*also* CHRYSOM) A mixture of olive oil and balsam used in baptism, confirmation and the consecration of churches, altars and sacred vessels. Chrism may only be consecrated by a bishop and, according to current Latin usage, only at a special Mass of the Chrism celebrated on MAUNDY Thursday. The CHRISMATORY in which the chrism was stored was covered by a silk *chrism-cloth* when carried from the AUMBRY to the font.

Linen *chrisom-cloths* (note the different spelling of the word) were worn for a month following BAPTISM in order to protect the baptismal chrism (which remained on the infant's head) and as a token of innocence and the cleansing of sin. Images of chrisom-children, swathed in their chrisom-cloths, are commonly found in MONUMENTS (notably in BRASSES of the Tudor period) where they may signify death in infancy. Chrisom-cloths were no longer used in the English Church from 1552.

See also CONSECRATION CROSSES *and* UNCTION

CHRISMATORY A small vessel in which holy oil is kept. Also a set of Holy Oil Stocks containing the oil of the CATECHUMENS, the oil of the sick and CHRISM.

See also PLATE (CHURCH)

CHRISMON The symbol for Christ based on the Greek letters *khi* and *rho*. It is sometimes found drawn at the beginning of early medieval documents and inscriptions as a symbol of sacred protection.

See also CHRISTIAN SYMBOLS

CHRISOM-CHILD (CHRISOMER) *and* **CHRISOM-CLOTHS** *see* BAPTISM, CHRISM, BRASSES (MONUMENTAL), EFFIGIES *and* WEEPERS.

CHRIST-CROSS-ROW (*also* CRISS-CROSS-ROW) The alphabet. A term derived from the practice of placing a cross at the beginning of an alphabet in a child's hornbook (a single leaf set in a frame and protected with a thin plate of transparent horn).

CHRISTENING *see* BAPTISM

CHRISTIAN SYMBOLS

CROSSES

The cross is the universal Christian symbol (*see also* CRUCIFIX). It is widely used in HERALDRY where it has been estimated there are over four hundred different forms, though of these only twenty or so are in regular use (*for* illustrations *see* CROSSES). In churches the most common forms are:

The Christus Rex, Christ on the Cross, crowned and robed.

The *Rood*, a large crucifix suspended or fixed beneath the chancel arch and flanked by the figures of the Virgin Mary and St. John the Baptist (*see* ROOD).

The *Latin* or *Passion* cross which has an elongated upright.

The *Greek* cross which has arms of equal length.

The *Calvary* cross which is a Latin cross mounted on three steps, symbolising Faith, Hope and Charity.

The *Celtic* or *Iona* cross in which the circle symbolises Eternity.

See also CELTIC CROSS, VOTIVE CROSS *and* WHEEL HEAD CROSS

THE ARCHANGELS

The company of archangels varies in number from four to twelve, but of these only three appear regularly in church decoration: Michael, warrior, enemy of Satan and weigher of souls, usually depicted bearing a sword or scales; Gabriel, the Messenger of God and ever-present in scenes of the Annunciation, sometimes depicted with long hair and multi-coloured wings and often holding a sceptre or lily; and Raphael, who is especially associated with healing and travellers and may be represented in symbolic form by a lion or snake. When a fourth is required (in order to balance a window, for example) it is often the unfamiliar figure of Uriel who is pressed into service. The least important of the four major archangels, Uriel (in Hebrew, 'Light of God') was vividly described by Milton as 'Regent of the Sun: the sharpest-sighted spirit of all in heaven' and may occasionally be found holding a flaming sword or orb and the book of an interpreter, foreteller of God's will on earth.

THE ANGELS

In the Middle Ages nine Orders of Angels were identified in three hierarchical 'choirs':

Seraphim

Cherubim

Thrones

Dominations
Virtues
Powers
Principalities
Archangels
Angels

Seraphim and cherubim are often represented crowned with fire and with six wings which may be strewn with eyes. Thrones are sometimes depicted as winged scarlet wheels, often with eyes, and all three principal orders may be depicted as warriors or judges. Angels usually have a pair of wings and a nimbus, and may hold scrolls, Instruments of the Passion (see below) or musical instruments.

DEVILS

The antithesis of good and the enemy of God, the devil in his many forms is prominent in the decoration of early churches: a constant reminder of medieval man's preoccupation with the daily struggle between damnation and salvation. Just as God was depicted in symbolic form, so too the devil assumes the guise of a multitude of beasts and serpents culled from the imagery of the Old Testament and the medieval bestiaries. Many are depicted being trampled beneath the feet of Christian saints, notably St. Michael and St. George (see also AMPHISBAENA, APES, ASP *and* DOOM). Of course, many of these beasts are also found in heraldry where they do not possess the same demonic connotations (see BEASTS, HERALDIC). Satan was the supreme embodiment of evil. Nevertheless, as a former seraph, he was considered to be armigerous (*see* ATTRIBUTED ARMS).

CHRISTIAN CONCEPTS

Although Christ is frequently depicted in Christian art, most often by means of a CRUCIFIX or *Vernicle* (the head of Christ), it was considered blasphemous to represent God in pictorial form so a variety of symbols was adopted, the most common of which are:
The Ray of Light
The Father supporting the Crucifix
The hand raised in blessing, encompassed by a nimbus (*Manus Dei*)
Three crowned figures
A Trinity
Three interlaced fishes

A *ship* represents the Church
The *Tree of Jesse* (see JESSE WINDOW) is usually found in stained glass and is intended to depict Christ's descent from Jesse, the father of King David.
The *Tree of Life* is often found on Romanesque fonts or on a tympanum above a church door and recalls the sentence in Revelation: 'Blessed are they that

doeth his commandments, that they may have right to the tree of life, and may enter in through the gates into the city.' (*see* TREE OF LIFE).
The *fish* was used by early Christians as a secret sign, the letters of the Greek word for 'fish' being the initial letters of 'Jesus Christ, Son of God, Saviour' (*see* ICHTHUS).
The *Agnus Dei* (the *Lamb of God* or *Paschal Lamb*) represents Christ. It is usually depicted supporting a banner of victory and has a halo charged with a cross.
A *dove* is frequently found on fonts where it represents the Holy Spirit at baptism. Seven DOVES represent the Seven Gifts of the Holy Spirit.

THE PASSION

The Instruments of the Passion include:
The Title (*INRI* – see below)
The Crown of Thorns and Nails
The Dice
The Seamless Robe
The Scourges
The Cross and Sheet
The Ladder and Sponge
The Lantern of Gethsemane
The Five Wounds of Christ
The Cockerel of Peter's Denial
The Thirty Pieces of Silver
The Hammer and Pincers

THE STATIONS OF THE CROSS

1 Jesus is condemned to death
2 Jesus receives the Cross
3 Jesus falls for the first time beneath the cross
4 Jesus meets his mother
5 Simon of Cyrene bears the cross
6 Veronica wipes the face of Jesus
7 Jesus falls the second time
8 Jesus meets the women of Jerusalem
9 Jesus falls the third time
10 Jesus is stripped of his garments
11 Jesus is nailed to the cross
12 Jesus dies on the cross
13 Jesus is taken down from the cross
14 The body is laid in the sepulchre

MONOGRAMS

These consist of two or more letters interwoven to form a symbol:
The *Labarum* comprises the first two letters of the Greek word for Christ (*Chi* and *Rho*); *IHS* the first three letters for *Jesus* (also *IHC*); *MR* was a popular medieval monogram for *Maria Regina* as was the crowned *M* and the letters *MARIA*. *INRI* are the Latin initials for *Jesus of Nazareth, King of the Jews; XP* or *HPC* is an abbreviation of the Greek word for *Christ* and *Alpha* and *Omega*, the first and last letters of the Greek alphabet, signify that Christ is both the beginning and the end.

CHRISTIAN SYMBOLS

GEOMETRICAL SYMBOLISM

To the medieval mind every number had a mystic significance and was easily translated into a geometrical shape:

Equilateral triangle represents the Trinity.

Two interwoven triangles form the six-pointed Star of David

The Triquetra is an ancient symbol whose three equal arcs represent the Trinity and its continuous form Eternity.

Baptismal fonts are often octagonal, the number eight representing resurrection and new life.

Stars: Star of Epiphany (5 points), Creator's Star (6), The Seven Gifts of the Spirit (7), Regeneration (8), the Nine Fruits of the Spirit (9), the Twelve Tribes of Israel (12)

SEVEN

Seven was a holy number: there were seven days of creation, seven phases of the moon, seven spirits before the throne of God (Michael, Gabriel, Lamael, Raphael, Zachariel, Anael and Oriphel), seven Joys of the Virgin (the Annunciation, Visitation, Nativity, Adoration of the Magi, Presentation in the Temple, Finding Christ amongst the Doctors and the Assumption), seven Virtues (faith, hope, charity, prudence, justice, fortitude and temperance) and seven Spirits of God (wisdom, understanding, counsel, power, knowledge, righteousness and divine awfulness).

The Seven Deadly Sins, the Seven Sacraments and the Seven Works of Mercy are often depicted in the stained glass and decorative carving of medieval churches. The Deadly Sins are pride, wrath, envy, lust, gluttony, avarice and sloth. The Sacraments are baptism, confirmation, mass, penance, extreme unction, ordination and matrimony. The Seven Works of Mercy are feeding the hungry, giving drink to the thirsty, hospitality to the stranger, clothes to the naked, visiting the sick and those in prison, and burying the dead.

The Seven Champions of Christendom were devised by Richard Johnson who lived in the late sixteenth and early seventeenth centuries. These are: St. George of England, who was seven years imprisoned by the Almi'dor, the black king of Morocco; St. Denys of France, who lived seven years in the form of a hart; St. James of Spain, who was dumb for seven years because of his love for a fair Jewess; St. Anthony of Italy, who (with the other champions) was enchanted into a deep sleep in the Black Castle and was released by St. George's three sons; St. Andrew of Scotland, who delivered six ladies who had lived for seven years in the form of white swans; St. Patrick of Ireland, who was immured in a cell where he excavated his own grave with his nails; and St. David of Wales who slept seven years in the enchanted garden of Ormandine.

OLD TESTAMENT FIGURES AND CONCEPTS

Aaron	rod and serpent
Abel	crook and lamb
Abraham	knife and shield
Adam	flaming sword, spade
Amos	crook
Atonement, Day of	young bullock and censer
Bodily decay	beetles, lizards and snails
Cain	plough
Canaan, entry into	cluster of grapes
Daniel	ram with four horns
David	harp and lion
Earthly life	caterpillar
Elijah	fiery chariot
Esau	bow and arrows
Ezekiel	a closed gate
Eve	distaff
Fall of Man	apple
Gideon	torch within a pitcher
God, presence of	Ark of the Covenant
Hosea	mantle
Isaiah	saw
Isaac	cross of bundles of wood
Israel's captivity	lash and bricks
Jacob	sun, moon and twelve stars
Jeremiah	large stone
Jonah	whale
Joseph	many-coloured coat
Joshua	sword and trumpet
Micah	temple on a mountain
Moses	basket of bulrushes, burning bush, horns, tablets
Nahum	feet protruding from a cloud
Noah	ark or oar
Old Testament worship	Menorah (seven branch candlestick)
Passover	paschal lamb, doorposts and lintel
Peace and forgiveness	dove with olive sprig
Pentecost	scroll and wheatsheaf
Pestilence	dragon
Ruth	head of wheat
Samson	jawbone of an ass, pillars
Seth	thread wound three times round thumb
Sinful nature of world	serpent coiled round globe
Solomon	model of Temple
Soul, escape of	butterfly
Torah (Five Books of Moses)	scroll
Victory over evil	dragon trampled underfoot
Zephania	sword suspended over Jerusalem

THE MAGI

Caspar (Europe)	old man with long beard
Melchoir (Asia)	middle-aged with short beard
Balthazar (Africa)	young man, usually negroid

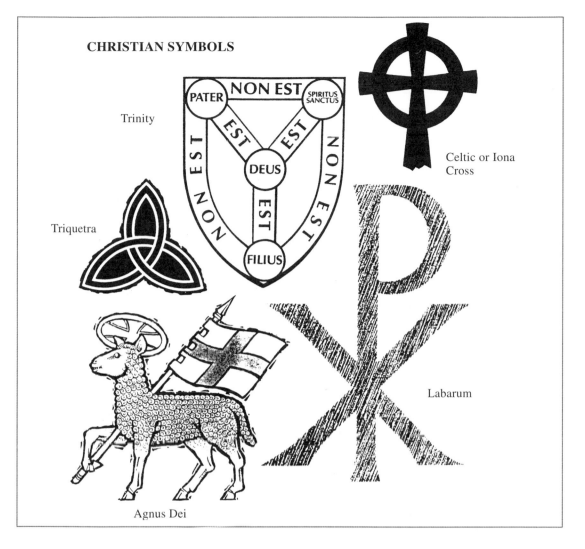

CHRISTIAN SYMBOLS

Trinity

Triquetra

Celtic or Iona Cross

Labarum

Agnus Dei

THE TWELVE APOSTLES

There are always twelve, but not always the same saints. Jude, Simon and Matthias are those most often omitted.

St. Andrew	saltire
St. Barnabas	roses on shield or gospel
St. Bartholomew	flaying knife
St. James Major	scallop shell and pilgrim's staff
St. James Minor	fullers' club (long, and bent at one end)
St. John the Evangelist	chalice with dragon emerging
St. Jude	halberd, lance, boat
St. Luke the Evangelist	winged ox
St. Mark the Evangelist	winged lion
St. Matthew the Evangelist	angel, sword (scimitar)
St. Matthias	axe (or scimitar)
St. Paul	sword
St. Peter	keys
St. Philip	loaves or baskets of loaves
St. Simon	fish (or oar or saw)
St. Thomas	spear

THE FOUR EVANGELISTS

St. Matthew	angel
St. Mark	winged lion
St. Luke	winged ox
St. John	eagle

THE FOUR LATIN DOCTORS

St. Gregory	pope in tiara
St. Jerome	cardinal
St. Augustine	bishop or doctor
St. Ambrose	bishop

ROYALTY

Constantine	holding labarum
Edmund	with sceptre mounted by a dove or a wolf and an arrow
Friedeswide	queen in habit of abbess
Louis IX of France	in royal robes or Franciscan habit and crowned with thorns
Oswald	holding large cross

CLERGY

In brasses the figures of clerics in MINOR ORDERS are sometimes accompanied by symbols:

acolyte	candle
doorkeeper (sexton)	key
exorcist	holy water vessel
lector	book
subdeacon	basin and ewer

RELIGIOUS

Benedictines	all black
Carmelites	white cloak over brown habit
Carthusians	white serge
Cistercians	white or grey
Dominicans	white tunic, black cloak
Franciscans	brown (sometimes grey)
Templar, Knights	white with red cross
St. John, Knights of	black mantle with white cross, red surcoat with white cross

SYMBOLS AND ATTRIBUTES

Martyrs usually hold a palm, hermits a T-shaped staff and rosary, pilgrims wear a hat with a shell and carry a staff and wallet. Founders usually hold models of the buildings they founded, bishops or abbots hold a crozier or pastoral staff, and popes wear the triple tiara, cope and pallium and carry a triple cross.

anchor	Clement
anvil	Adrian
apple	the fall of man
arrow (piercing breast or hand)	Giles
arrows(s) enfiling crown	Edmund
arrow(s) piercing body	Sebastian
axe	Matthias
balls (3)	Nicholas
banner with red cross	Ursula
basket of fruit or flowers	Dorothea
basket of loaves	Philip
bedstead	Faith
beehive	Ambrose
beggar or cripple	Martin (offering cloak)
bell	Anthony
birds	Francis of Assisi
boat	Jude
bones	Ambrose
book and crook	Chad
bottle	James the Great
box of alabaster	Mary of Magdela
breasts (on a plate)	Agatha
builder's square	Thomas
bundle of rods	Faith
candle and devil	Genevieve
caldron of oil	Vitus
chains (held by)	Leonard
chalice containing dragon	John the Apostle
children (two carried by)	Eustace
children (three in a tub)	Nicholas
cloak (half)	Martin
cock	Peter and Vitus
comb (iron)	Blaise
cow	Bridget
cross (red on white)	George
cross (saltire)	Andrew
cross (inverted)	Peter
cross – T (carried)	Anthony
cross – T	Philip
devil with bellows	Genevieve
devil underfoot	Michael
distaff	Eve's expulsion
dog with wounded leg	Roch
dogs with torches in mouths	Dominic
doorpost and lintel	Passover
dove	Pope Gregory
dove on sceptre	King Edmund
dove on shoulder	David of Wales
doves in cage	Joseph
dragon	George, Archangel Michael, Martha, Satan and sin
dragon and cross	Margaret of Antioch
dragon led by chain	Juliana
dragon under foot	victory over evil
eagle with nimbus	John the Evangelist
eyes in a dish	Lucy
fleur-de-lis	Virgin Mary
flowers in a basket	Dorothy
gridiron	Laurence
halberd	Jude
head (crowned)	Cuthbert or Denis
head (man's, at feet of)	Catherine of Alexandra
head carried before altar	Winifred
heart (flaming/ transfixed by sword)	Augustine or Mary
hermit	Anthony
hog	Anthony
hook (iron)	Faith or Vincent
horseshoe	Eloy
idols (broken)	Wilfred
keys	Peter
knife and skin	Bartholomew
lamb	Agnes, Francis and John the Baptist

Lamb (Paschal)	Passover
lamb of God on a book	John the Baptist
lash and bricks	Israel's captivity
lily	Virgin Mary and Joseph
lion	Adrian or Jerome
lion (winged) with nimbus	Mark the Evangelist
lion and raven	Vincent
loaves and fishes	disciples
man (winged) with nimbus	Matthew the Evangelist
manacles	Leonard
money bag	Matthew
mule (kneeling)	Anthony of Padua
musical instruments	Cecilia
olive branch	Agnes
organ (portable)	Cecilia
otter	Cuthbert
ox (winged) with nimbus	Luke the Evangelist
palm	Agnes
pagans being baptised	Wilfred
partridge	Jerome
pelican	Sacrifice of the Cross
pen, ink and scroll	Mark or Matthew
phoenix	resurrection
pig	Anthony
pincers	Agatha or Dunstan
pincers and tooth	Apollonia
pomegranate	resurrection and unity
pot and ladle	Martha
ring (held by)	Edward the Confessor
roses (crown of)	Cecilia, Dorothy or Teresa
saw	Simon
scallop shell	James the Great
scourge	Ambrose
scroll	the Five Books of Moses
serpent	Satan
shears	Agatha
sheep	Genevieve
sieve (broken)	Benedict
stag	Adrian, Eustace or Hubert
stone(s)	Stephen
swan and flowers	Hugh of Lincoln
sword	Paul or Barbara
sword (flaming)	Adam's expulsion
sword through breast	Euphemia
sword through neck	Lucy
tooth in pincers	Apollonia
tower	Barbara
tree (beneath foot of)	Boniface
tree (sleeping beneath)	Etheldreda
unicorn	Virgin Mary
vase of ointment	Mary Magdalene
weighing souls	Michael
wheel (spiked)	Catherine
windlass	Erasmus
wolf	King Edmund
Wounds of Christ	Francis of Assisi

See also ATTRIBUTED ARMS, BEASTS (HERALDIC), CREATURES, COLOURS (LITURGICAL) *and* PAGAN SYMBOLS

Further reading:

Benedictine Monks, *The Book of Saints*, London, 1989

Child, H. and Colles, D., *Christian Symbols Ancient and Modern*, London, 1979

Ellwood Post, W., *Saints, Signs and Symbols*, London, 1964

Hall, J., *Dictionary of Subjects and Symbols in Art*, London, 1987

Hume, E., *Symbolism in Christian Art*, London, 1975

Whittemore, C.E., *Symbols of the Church*, London, 1959

CHRISTINGLE A lighted candle set in an orange representing Christ as the Light of the World. The children's ADVENT service, at which each child is presented with a Christingle, originated in the Moravian Church and has recently become popular in England.
See also CHRISTMAS

CHRISTMAS The commemoration of Christ's nativity. The earliest known reference to 25 December is in the Philocalian Calendar, a list of popes down to Liberius (352–66), which represents Roman practice in 336. The date may have been chosen as a celebration of the birth of the 'Sun of Righteousness' in opposition to the pagan festival of the *Natalis Solis Invicti* – the 'Birthday of the Unconquered Sun'. In the Western Church it is celebrated by the three masses: of the night, of the dawn and of the day. In the gradual transition from darkness to light, these again echo the pagan belief in the sun's rebirth after the winter solstice. Indeed, a remarkable number of pagan traditions were absorbed into Christmas festivities in the early medieval period and many lingered on, even to the present day. The *Twelve Days of Christmas*, for example, which originated in the Norse *Yule* (*jól*), a twelve-day celebration of rebirth when logs were burned and Yule candles lit to represent fire and light. The (sacred) mistletoe, holly and other evergreens, which were believed to be a refuge for woodland spirits when other trees lost their leaves, were gathered to decorate the medieval hall while, in the fifteenth century, a candlelit Christmas tree was erected in a London street, though Prince Albert is usually credited with having introduced the custom into England in 1841. Much to the consternation of the Church, medieval festivities sometimes followed the licentious Roman *Saturnalia* (when masters and servants changed roles) and a servant, crowned as Lord of Misrule, would hold a wild court over the Christmas period (*see* MISRULE, LORD OF). Minstrels performed mumming plays, their central theme the conflict between darkness and light, and toasts were drunk from an elaborate wassail cup to the accompaniment of wassail songs (from the Old Norse *ves heill*, a greeting meaning 'be in good health'). Such traditions continued well into the nineteenth century, especially in rural communities.

Christmas has always provided an opportunity for family gatherings, especially in the Victorian period, and for feasting. In wealthier homes, the boar's head was the centrepiece of the festive table, a further translation of the Norse Yule celebrations when the sacrificial boar was a sacred beast. In the sixteenth century good luck could be guaranteed for a twelve month if a mince pie was eaten on each of the Twelve Days of Christmas. At this time turkey first appeared on the dinner table, along with the traditional goose and beef, and the flaming Christmas pudding, a stiffened form of the earlier plum porridge, was introduced *c.* 1670. In medieval England, the Christmas season concluded on Twelfth Night (6 January) an occasion for parties and games when the Twelfth Night King and Queen were chosen. Until well into the nineteenth century every family had its Twelfth Cake which contained a dried bean and a pea: the man who found the bean became King and the girl who discovered the pea was Queen. Christmas decorations are now removed on TWELFTH NIGHT (*see also* EPIPHANY), for fear of inviting bad luck, though in earlier centuries it was considered safe to leave them in place until Candlemas (2 February). A representation of the crib (*manger*) in which the Christ Child was laid at his birth is often placed in churches on Christmas Eve. St. Francis of Assisi is believed to have made the first model of the crib at Greccio in 1223.

In England, Father Christmas was not the St. Nicholas of medieval Europe but the personification of Christmas: a genial red-robed old man who appeared in many sixteenth-century masques and mumming plays. Neither was he the bringer of gifts but acquired that characteristic from St. Nicholas in the nineteenth century when there was a revival of 'traditional' Christmas festivities.

Perhaps the most vivid account of Christmas in mid-nineteenth century rural England is to be found in Thomas Hardy's *Under the Greenwood Tree*, first published in 1872.

See also CAROLS, CHRISTINGLE *and* FEAST DAYS (FIXED AND MOVABLE)
Further reading:
Cullen Brown, J., (ed.), *Figures in a Wessex Landscape*, London, 1987

CHRONOGRAM A phrase (usually in a memorial inscription) the Roman numeral letters of which provide a date when added together. For example:

LorD	haVe	MerCIe		Vpon	Vs	
50+500	+5	+1000+100+1		+5	+5	= 1666.

CHRYSOM *see* CHRISM

CHURCH The term is used to describe (i) the Christian community and (ii) a building used for public Christian worship. The *New Testament* teaches that the Church is not merely an association of individual disciples but an organic society established by Christ and endowed by Him with the Holy Spirit at PENTECOST. It is also a tenet of the Christian faith that in addition to the Church on earth there is the invisible Church of the faithful departed. One consequence of the REFORMATION was a reformulation of the concept of the Church which no longer sought to claim its being through sacramental relationships but through the Word of God. This is reflected in changes in the internal arrangements of parish churches.

CHURCH ALES Major community festivities by which funds were raised for the parish church. There were several types of ale-feast including bride-ales, clerk-ales, give-ales, lamb-ales, leet-ales, Midsummer-ales, Scot-ales and Whitsun-ales. Here 'ale' does not mean the drink, but the feast at which good stout ale was supplied (*see* CHURCH AND COMMUNITY *and* CHURCHWARDENS' ACCOUNTS). The term *taberna cerevisiae* is sometimes applied to church ales, though a more precise meaning is simply 'alehouse'.

CHURCH AND COMMUNITY Before the Reformation the church was usually the only public building in a parish which could accommodate large numbers of people. It is hardly surprising, therefore, that while the CHANCEL was the *sanctum sanctorum* the nave was the parish hall.

Unconsecrated, and effectively beyond the jurisdiction of the parish priest or bishop, the nave was a focal point of community life, second only to the church porch (*see* PORCHES). On weekdays business was transacted there, agreements negotiated, disputes resolved (or otherwise) and, in many parishes, it was the meeting place of the manor court. Such activities were even advertised from the pulpit on Sundays: William Paston (d. 1444), who raised his family into the ranks of the Norfolk gentry, ordered the parish priest to give notice of meetings of the manor court from his pulpit and to make it abundantly clear that every tenant was expected to attend. In the seventeenth and eighteenth centuries, parliamentary candidates were often formally adopted in the church nave.

Medieval parish churches must have been wonderfully colourful, noisy places. Pillars and walls were brightly painted (*see* WALL PAINT-INGS) as were memorials, doors and furniture, though at that time church naves rarely contained BENCHES or pews. When the weather was fine, disputants would repair to the north (unconsecrated) side of the churchyard to settle their differences. But in inclement weather, or when public witness was required, they would join with others in the nave and the noise of protestation, negotiation and (on occasion) altercation must have been far removed from the hushed calm of today's parish churches. Towers were often pressed into service as school-rooms and in some the old benches and fireplace remain.

Of course, difficulties sometimes arose as a result of secular use. At the back of the nave, between the south door and the base of the tower, stood the font. This was unconsecrated ground and fonts were subject to occasional vandalism or misuse. Consequently, in many churches, covers were fitted and secured by padlocks so that the holy water could not be removed and used for superstitious purposes (*see* FONT COVERS *and* FONTS).

CHURCH HOUSES

Aisles were sometimes added to the nave to accommodate the activities of parish GUILDS whose functions were as much secular as they were religious, and by the fifteenth century many parishes had built *church houses*, usually in the vicinity of the churchyard, which were maintained by the CHURCHWARDENS for parish festivities, especially PATRONAL FESTIVALS and 'church-ales'. But so unbridled were these activities at times that they were roundly condemned by the Puritans and the magistracy and many church houses had disappeared by the mid-seventeenth century. It is clear from CHURCHWARDENS' ACCOUNTS that church houses were not usually lived in and that 'housekeepers' were engaged to brew the ale and to maintain the stores and equipment. In some cases, it appears that redundant church houses were rented to former housekeepers who continued to brew and sell ale. Several of these independent taverns have survived, usually in close proximity to the church and often with quasi-religious names such as the Cross Keys (for St. Peter) and the Lamb and Flag (*see* PASCHAL LAMB). At Sandford in Devon, for example, there is both a Lamb Inn and a small building (known as the Vestry) which may once have been a church house. One of the finest surviving church houses, at Crowcombe in Somerset, was given to the parish in 1515 and was used for the brewing and selling of church ales and other social functions. It later became an almshouse and is now used once again as a church hall.

CHURCH ALES

With the exception of the chancel (and any CHANTRY CHAPELS), the day-to-day maintenance of the church was the responsibility of the parish. Late medieval documentary sources, such as churchwardens' accounts, provide ample evidence of the methods used to raise money for the repair and development of the tower, the porch and the nave. The yearly round of festivals, the 'ritual year' which ended on 28 June with the midsummer celebration of St. Peter's Eve, was in reality an ingenious exercise in fund-raising which included many traditional activities which, until recently, were believed to have been pagan survivals (such as apple wassailing and morris dancing). One of the most interesting (and popular) practices was the 'Church ale', a festival of sports, dancing, drama and general merrymaking accompanied by the drinking of strong ale:

The churches much owe, as well we all do knowe
For when they be drooping and ready to fail.
By a Whitsun or Church-Ale up again they shall go,
And owe their repairing to a pot of good ale.

The 'pot of good ale' was provided by the churchwardens who begged or bought the malt for brewing the liquor. In the Tudor period, certain villagers (variously known as *Hognells, Hogglers, Hogans, Hogners* or *Hoggells*) were empowered to gather financial contributions on behalf of the churchwardens. Tariffs varied from parish to parish: 'By way of enticement to the populace the churchwardens brewed a strong ale to be ready on the day appointed for the festival, which they sold to them: and most of the better sort, in addition to what they paid for the drink, contributed towards the collection' (Joseph Strutt, *The Sports and Pastimes of the People of England*, 1800). Four ales were brewed annually at Elvaston and Ockbrook in Derbyshire '. . . and every inhabitant of Ockbrook shall be at the several ales, and every husband and wife shall pay two pence, and every cottager one penny to the use and behoof of the said church of Elvaston.' The Whitsun ale was usually the most successful – probably because it could be held out of doors in the churchyard. In Oxfordshire, Woodstock's Whitsun ale lasted longer than most of the ales that once flourished in villages up and down the county . . . at least in its later days it seems to have lost its early character as a practical money-raising event . . . and to have become far more a boisterous festival. The people danced and sang, ate, drank and sometimes got drunk, set up their summer bowers in the churchyard, played games and loudly welcomed the Morris dancers in their ribbons and bells' *.

Despite an edict of Henry VIII, in which he expressed the wish that there should be no more eating and drinking in churches, the practice seems to have flourished. Bride's ales became popular in many areas, as did wakes and bid-ales (*see* WAKE). Wedding guests were expected to pay generously for the ale which the bride's father had provided and, by so doing, contributed significantly to the marriage dowry – though when impoverished young couples married, it was often the churchwardens who provided the ale. In 1644, one Margaret Atkinson left instructions in her will that, on the Sunday after her funeral, '. . . there be provided two dozen of bread, a kilderkin of ale, two gammons of bacon . . . desiring that all the parish as well rich as poor to take part thereof and a table to be set in the midst of the church with everything necessary thereto . . .'. Bid-ales were sometimes organised by the church-wardens for the benefit of parishioners who had suddenly fallen on hard times.

The growth of Puritanism in the early seventeenth century was to have a debilitating effect on traditional communal activities such as parish revels, play-acting, pageants and church ales. Church ales in the church itself or in the churchyard were expressly forbidden in an act of 1603, though the publication of James I's *Book of Sports* in 1617 sanctioned the holding of church ales on Sundays – providing they did not conflict with divine worship (*see* SPORTS, THE BOOK OF). In the following year, the King ordered all clergy to read the declaration from their pulpits but this caused such an uproar that it was withdrawn. Thereafter, and despite several unsuccessful attempts to legislate against the practice, church ales and similar festivities continued to raise funds for both church and parish (*see also* ARCHERY). Indeed, there was a general reluctance to relinquish activities which had become necessities in many people's lives: in the more remote parishes, villagers 'went nimbly dancing' even through the prohibitions of the Civil War. Seasonal customs gave meaning to the passing of the years and regular periods of carnival and misrule provided a diversion from the daily struggle for subsistence. In the mid-seventeenth century, 'clerk's ales' were held with the laudable purpose of providing the PARISH CLERK with a salary. But by the eighteenth century church-wardens' accounts contain far fewer references to such congenial methods of parochial fund-raising and '. . . by the nineteenth century, with only a few exceptions, the whole custom was . . . no more than a fading memory.'

(*For* churchyard games *see* CHURCHYARDS *and* PLAISTOW.)

PAROCHIAL RESPONSIBILITIES
Before the days of the Welfare State, the parish church tended to the needs of the aged, the infirm, the poor and those who experienced bereavement or unexpected misfortune (*see* CHARITIES, FRIENDLY SOCIETIES *and* POOR LAW). It was the churchwardens (elected by parishioners at the annual meeting of the VESTRY) who made the decisions, and their officers (such as the constable and overseers of the poor) who implemented them. And it is in the churchwardens' accounts that the payments are recorded: two shillings and sixpence in 1660 'to a poor woman who had leprosy all over her', one shilling to 'a poor child who had the King's evil', two shillings and sixpence in 1673 to a man 'for the rebuilding of the house that fell upon his wife and children suddenly in the night', two shillings to 'three poor men who had their corn destroyed by the great hail storm' of 1684, three

shillings to a woman '. . . her husband being formerly a minister, but now melancholy and almost distracted' and two shillings in 1723 to 'a poor woman and her 5 children on going to New England'. From time to time, the churchwardens were also responsible for administering the dictates of central government. Statutes of Henry VIII and Elizabeth I, for example, required that the already hard-pressed wardens should reward those parishioners who brought to them the heads of vermin which, in some areas, included small birds (in 1786 some 708 dozen were killed in one Cheshire parish) and even the poor hedgehog!

Until recently, items such as constables' truncheons and beadles' maces, dog tongs, thatch rakes or fire hooks (for removing burning thatch), mud-scrapers (for clearing the roads), the parish bier, weaponry for the local militia and numerous other reminders of a community's past were stored in the parish church (*see* PARISH CONSTABLES *and* DOGS). But, with increasing vandalism and theft, many of these have been transferred to local museums for safe-keeping, though the occasional 'find' will delight the unsuspecting visitor: at Puddletown in Dorset, for example, where a number of leather fire-buckets remain, suspended beneath the gallery. At nearby Burton Bradstock, the vestry minutes record an agreement of 1813 that 'The Fire buckets belonging to the Parish and furnished by the Sun Fire Office be placed in the Church, and that they be painted and lettered at the expense of the Parish'. Even the parish fire-engine was sometimes stored in the church: at Crewkerne in Somerset and Worlingworth in Suffolk, for example, where (as elsewhere) the cost of maintaining the 'pump' and of keeping the leather pipes greased fell on the churchwardens. At Fenny Stratford in Bucking-hamshire six 'popgun' cannons (the 'Fenny poppers') are brought out from the church for the St. Martin's Day celebrations, while the town DUCKING STOOL is still retained in the north aisle of Leominster Priory in Herefordshire.

See also DRAMA, FESTIVALS AND SOCIAL CUSTOMS *and* HOCK-TIDE

Further reading:
Bettey, J., *Church and Parish*, London, 1987
Davies, J., *The Secular Use of Church Buildings*, London, 1968
Hammond, P., *Food and Feast in Medieval England*, Stroud, 1994
Hole, C., *A Dictionary of British Folk Customs*, London, 1975 *
Hutton, R., *The Rise and Fall of Merry England: The Ritual Year 1400–1700*, Oxford, 1994
Pounds, N.J.G., *The Culture of the English People: Iron Age to the Industrial Revolution*, Cambridge, 1994
Reeves, C., *Pleasures and Pastimes in Medieval England*, Stroud, 1995

CHURCH ASSEMBLY The National Assembly of the Church of England, established by the Convocations in 1919 and superseded in 1970 by the General Synod (*see* SYNOD). It consisted of a House of Bishops, a House of Clergy and a House of Laity and its principal function was to prepare ecclesiastical measures for presentation to Parliament under the Enabling Act of 1919.

CHURCH COMMISSIONERS Formed in 1948 from the ECCLESIASTICAL COMMISSIONERS and QUEEN ANNE'S BOUNTY, the Church Commissioners for England manage the estates and revenues of the Church of England. The Commission consists of the Archbishops and Bishops of England and three lay Church Estates Commissioners together with a number of other persons, both clerical and lay.

CHURCH DEDICATIONS *see* CHURCH SITES *and* DEDICATION OF CHURCHES

CHURCH HATCH *see* LICH-GATES

CHURCH HAY The churchyard.

CHURCH HOUSE The building at Westminster, completed in 1940, in which the Convocation of Canterbury (*see* CONVOCATION) and the General Synod of the Church of England meet (*see* SYNOD). Also the headquarters of a number of Anglican organisations.

CHURCH HOUSES *see* CHURCH AND COMMUNITY

CHURCHING OF WOMEN, THE A form of thanksgiving made by Christian women following childbirth. The religious ceremony by which a woman was 'released back into the world' after childbirth.
See also BAPTISM *and* PORCHES

CHURCH LANDS *see* TEMPORALITIES

CHURCH MUSIC (ANGLICAN) In the worship of the early Church all music was rendered by the clergy and congregation. But, following the foundation of a *schola cantorum* in Rome in the late sixth century, choirs of trained singers were gradually introduced into major churches throughout western Christendom (*see* PLAINSONG).
THE POST-REFORMATION
At the REFORMATION, the new Church of England services, although vernacular, were little different from the Roman Catholic liturgy which preceded them (*see* COMMON PRAYER, BOOK OF). Before this time there was a clear distinction between the musical customs of the major monastic and cathedral churches, which had large choirs and organs, and those of urban and rural parishes which rarely had choirs but sometimes possessed a primitive organ. Following the DISSOLUTION OF THE MONASTERIES a small number of abbey or priory churches were retained as CATHEDRALS where, after making the necessary liturgical changes, the elaborate type of service was perpetuated. This, of course, was the age of great English composers: Thomas Tallis (*c.* 1505–85), William Byrd (*c.* 1542–1623), Thomas Morley (1557–*c.* 1603), Thomas Weelkes (*c.* 1575–1623) and Orlando Gibbons (1583–1625), all of whom learned their art as cathedral organists and (with the exception of Weelkes) were Gentlemen of the Chapel Royal. Service settings (i.e. elaborate musical settings of the CANTICLES) continued after the Reformation but in modified form. They had now to be set in the vernacular, without lengthening by repetition of phrases and on the principle of one syllable to a note (though this last requirement seems to have been almost universally disregarded). Some sixteenth-century communion services exist in two forms: the Latin Mass and an adaptation which conformed with the new conditions. The new forms were sometimes described by composers as 'The Short Service' and the lengthy and complex older forms as 'The Long Service'. Antiphonal singing (by the DECANI and CANTORIS sides of the choir) is a feature of service music (*see* ANTIPHON *and* STALLS) while the traditional Anglican settings of the PRECES and VERSICLES are adaptations by John Merbecke (1510–85) of the ancient plainsong. Various Elizabethan composers made 'harmonised' versions of the responses, a form now generally known as Festal Responses. From this golden age flowed the magnificent body of distinctively Anglican church music which remains in the repertoire of cathedral and collegiate choirs today.
ORGANS
Organs were generally small instruments and (by modern standards) clumsy to manipulate (*see* ORGANS). Even in the major churches there was no repertory of organ music and no independent 'organ parts' in anthems or service music. The instrument simply augmented the choir voices and occasionally accompanied plainsong unisonally. In parish churches, where the music was simpler, the organ can have had little function other than to assist priest and people in the performance of the plainsong.

At the Reformation a substantial number of parishes tended towards thorough reform, on Calvinistic lines. In 1536 the Lower House of Convocation declared that the playing of organs was one of the 'eighty-four Faults and Abuses of Religion' and many organs were removed from parish churches or allowed to decay. The clerks (either lay clerks or clerks in minor orders) who had previously assisted the priest in the responsive parts of the service were now reduced in number to a single PARISH CLERK who was responsible for leading the people's verses of the prose PSALMS and responses. The degree of ritual in churches varied considerably as did observance of the official *Prayer Book*. Many unsuitable appointments were made to country livings, some parsons being almost illiterate and incapable of preaching, and it is not unreasonable to assume that the standard of music in many churches was similarly afflicted. The decline was temporarily reversed by the appointment of Archbishop William Laud (1573–1645), a high-churchman who opposed the prevailing Calvinist theology and sought to restore something of pre-Reformation liturgical practice (*see* LAUDIAN). But his reforms were widely resented and he was impeached by the Long Parliament, imprisoned in 1644 and executed in the following year. The pendulum now swung rapidly in the opposite direction. Services naturally tended to informality and Parliament decreed that all church organs should be silenced and that church music should be reduced to its simplest form. The parish church became in some places Independent and in others Presbyterian and there was no music other than metrical psalms, sung by the congregation. Of the few surviving organs, those in some cathedrals and collegiate chapels were occasionally played for secular purposes and (perhaps) for an occasional voluntary following a service.

THE PARISH CLERK

With the restoration of the Monarchy in 1660 the Church of England became episcopal once again. Independency and Presbyterianism suffered wide-spread persecution, the *Book of Common Prayer* was restored and organs and choirs were heard again in cathedrals and collegiate chapels. But in most parish churches, music was still confined to congregational metrical psalms, led by the parish clerk, and very few organs were restored. From the mid-seventeenth century the practice of 'lining-out' was widely adopted whereby the parish clerk read out each line of a psalm before it was sung by the congregation. Inevitably, this curious and mannered way of singing, and the excessively slow tempo, invited parody. In 1692, TATE AND BRADY published their *New Version of the Psalms*, a versification of the Psalter which accorded with the artificial tastes of the period and was widely used until the early nineteenth century.

English literature in the eighteenth and nineteenth centuries is littered with observations concerning the character of church music: Isaac D'Israeli, for example, in 1793 tells of 'a mixed assembly roaring out confused tones, nasal, guttural and sibilant' and, as late as 1840, De Quincey complained 'There is accumulated in London more musical science than in any capital in the world' and yet 'the psalmody in most parish churches is a howling wilderness'.

THE WEST GALLERY CHOIR

The absence of organs in most parish churches resulted, in the later eighteenth century, in the remarkably widespread custom of employing musicians to accompany the metrical psalms or HYMNS and to perform the occasional anthem. Together with a small choir, these 'bands' of local musicians (who also provided the music for community festivities and dances) occupied the west galleries of churches which became the focus of a significant musical tradition (*see* GALLERIES). There are records of some twenty-four different instruments having been used in various church orchestras at this time, including flutes, clarinets, bassoons, trombones, serpents, violins and cellos (*see* MUSICAL INSTRUMENTS). Base instruments were considered to be especially efficacious: nine bassoons were played simultaneously in one Sussex band. The same raw enthusiasm seems to have pervaded contemporary choral music. In 1790, the Bishop of London complained of the monopolising of the psalmody in rural parishes by 'a select band of singers who have been taught by some itinerant master to sing in the worst manner a most wretched set of psalm tunes in three or four parts, so complex, so difficult, so totally devoid of true harmony, that it is impossible for any of the congregation to take part with them; who, therefore, sit absorbed in silent admiration, or total inattention, without considering themselves in any degree concerned in what is going forward.'

Some urban churches also had their orchestras. In the 1770s, Sheffield parish church had 'no solemn loud pealing organ, but before the west window, high over the gallery, was a kind of immense box hung in chains, into which, by the aid of a ladder, musicians and singers, male and female, contrived to scramble, and with the aid of bumbasses, hautboys, fiddles, and various other instruments, accompanying shrill and stentorian voices, they contrived to make as loud a noise as heart would wish.' But in the majority of town churches there was an organ and a choir of 'charity children of the parish'. These were either the children from the free schools for the poor or Sunday school children who, having received their weekly instruction in reading, writing, the Catechism and the Bible, were marched into church to join in the service. The same Bishop of London, this time commenting on London's numerous choirs of 'charity children', declared that services were often 'a contest between [the children] and the organ which shall be the loudest and give most pain to the ear.' It was the introduction into churches of the barrel organ and then the harmonium which signalled the gradual demise of the church orchestra. Barrel organs first appeared in churches in the late eighteenth century while the harmonium was introduced from France in the 1840s and was followed by the American organ or melodeon.

THE NINETEENTH CENTURY

In many nineteenth-century parish churches, a stultifying preoccupation with decorum resulted in the diminution of musical originality and variety. This was accentuated by the OXFORD MOVEMENT which was, in part, responsible for the introduction into parish churches of male, surpliced choirs for the chanting of the responses and the psalms. This was clearly an attempt to impose on parishes a tradition which had hitherto been associated with cathedral and college choirs, even in the removal of the singers from the west gallery to STALLS erected on either side of the chancel in the collegiate fashion.

A stimulus to the development of music in the larger parish churches was provided by the Revd. Walter Hook (1798–1875) who, as Vicar of Leeds parish church (1837–59), instituted a professional choir performing daily 'cathedral' services. This was also the age of the 'second wave' of great English composers, notably Thomas Walmisley (1814–56), Sir Hubert Parry (1848–1918), Sir Charles Villiers Stanford (1852–1924) and Sir Edward Elgar (1857–1934), all of whom wrote sacred music. But, for most of the new 'surpliced choirs', musical expectations exceeded performance. Elsewhere, the old forms of service survived until the turn of the century, often with 'a few children in charity attire placed beside the organ' or 'no choir, unless seven poor boys may be regarded as such.' It would seem that, even where there was no choir, an organ was used and the ANGLICAN CHANT was retained at least for the canticles and, in some cases, for the psalms. It is equally clear that, by the second half of the nineteenth century, hymn books had everywhere replaced the metrical psalter, though anthems and service settings of the canticles were still comparatively rare.

THE TWENTIETH CENTURY

In the present century there seems to be a general acceptance of the distinctive character of 'cathedral' and 'parish' music. In the former (and in certain collegiate chapels), the choir is expected to sing the entire service (with the exception of hymns) and usually does so with consummate skill and panache. In parish churches, the congregation is encouraged to participate in the whole of the musical part of the service while choirs (if such there be) tend to lead the singing rather than attempt to perform music which may be beyond their competence. In all this, the Royal College of Organists (founded 1864) and the Royal School of Church Music (1927) have exercised a considerable influence on both the selection of music and the standard of performance (*for addresses see* APPENDIX II).

Further reading:

Scholes, P., (ed. Ward, J.O.), *The Oxford Companion to Music*, Oxford, 1991

CHURCH OF ENGLAND The English branch of the Western or Latin Church which, having rejected the Pope's authority since the Reformation, has the sovereign as its titular head.

Following the Synod of Whitby in 664, unification of the Celtic and Roman traditions was finally achieved under Theodore of Tarsus (*c.* 602–90), Archbishop of Canterbury from 668, who reformed the government of the Church by dividing dioceses and extending the episcopate (*see* ANGLO-SAXON CHURCH *and* CELTIC CHURCH). The Norman Conquest of 1066, and the influence of reforming bishops and abbots from the continent of Europe, led to a restructuring of ecclesiastical administration, the introduction into England of CANON LAW and an extraordinary period of religious activity and church building. Thereafter, and despite regular disputations with the Papacy, the English Church remained part of the Western Catholic Church until the sixteenth century when, against a background of religious dissatisfaction and growing national self-awareness, HENRY VIII failed to obtain a divorce from Catherine of Aragon and subsequently repudiated papal supremacy, bringing the Church under the control of the Crown (*see also* DISSOLUTION OF THE MONASTERIES). Many of the King's advisers were deeply influenced by the Protestant Reformation which, in England, culminated in the Act of Supremacy of 1534 (*see* REFORMATION). This confirmed to Henry VIII and his successors the title of 'the only supreme head in earth of the Church of England'. Under Edward VI, Archbishop Thomas Cranmer (1489–1556) produced the First and Second *Books of Common Prayer* in 1549 and 1552 which (with some modifications) became the service book of the Church of England in 1559 (*see* COMMON PRAYER, BOOK OF). A further Act of Supremacy in 1559 declared Elizabeth I to be 'the only supreme governor . . . as well in all spiritual or ecclesiastical things or causes as temporal' and, in 1571, the THIRTY-NINE ARTICLES were adopted as the doctrinal formulary of the English Church.

Episcopacy and Anglicanism were important issues in the English Civil War of 1642–9 and led to Presbyterian reform and Independency under the Commonwealth. But with the Restoration of Charles II in 1660 the Church of England was again confirmed as the established Church and repressive measures were taken against dissenters. The formal separation of the Methodist movement from the Church of England in 1791 was followed by an Anglican Evangelical revival and, in the nineteenth century, by administrative reform and the creation of new parishes and bishoprics which reflected demographic changes' brought about by the Industrial Revolution. At the same time, the OXFORD MOVEMENT sought to emphasise the Catholic and apostolic character of the established church. The Enabling Act of 1919 gave to the Church Assembly authority to present legislation to Parliament and in recent years the Church of England has exercised a considerable degree of control over its services through the Prayer Book (Alternative and Other Services) Measure of 1965 and the Church of England (Worship and Doctrine) Measure of 1974.

For the Church in Wales *see* WALES, THE CHURCH IN

See also CLERGY (CHURCH OF ENGLAND) *and* DEFENDER OF THE FAITH

CHURCH OF ENGLAND (WORSHIP AND DOCTRINE) MEASURE (1974)

Legislation which repealed the Prayer Book (Alternative and Other Services) Measure of 1965 and delegated authority to the General Synod to regulate the forms of service used in the Church of England and the forms of assent and subscription to doctrine required of the clergy.

CHURCH RATES These were levied on property (both freehold and leasehold) and were assessed by reference to the size of the land-holding. Church rates, which were abolished in 1868, were used specifically to defray the expenses of the parish church and to maintain its building and ceremonies.

CHURCH RECORDERS *see* NADFAS

CHURCH SCHOOLS *see* SCHOOLS

CHURCH SITES A large number of churches are located on sites for which there is no apparent rationale. At Knowlton in Dorset the lonely ruins of a twelfth-century church stand at the centre of a circular Neolithic embankment and ditch. The large-scale map reveals that the earthwork is the last surviving of a series, known locally as Knowlton Rings, and that the church, abandoned in the eighteenth century when its roof fell in, was once the parish church of a medieval settlement located in a river valley a mile to the south-west. Whatever its original purpose, the earthwork was almost certainly used in successive centuries for ceremonial purposes, and its religious associations perpetuated in the founding of an early church on the site.

In 601 Pope Gregory instructed Abbot Mellitus (later Bishop of London) that such sacred places should not be destroyed but rather that they should be sanctified and Christian altars set up in the place of pagan ones, thereby ensuring that the powerful religious associations of a site would be sustained in the minds of the people and a continuum of worship guaranteed. Throughout Britain (and especially in Wales and the West of England) there are numerous instances of pagan sites being adopted as places of Christian worship and these are often characterised

by circular churchyard enclosures (*see* CHURCH-YARDS). The churches at Edlesborough, Taplow and West Wycombe in Buckinghamshire, Ludlow in Shropshire, Avebury in Wiltshire, St. Issey in Cornwall, and many others, are all situated within or near prehistoric earthworks or burial mounds. At Berwick in Sussex and Maxey in Northamptonshire the churches were built near large barrows, while at Rudston in Yorkshire a huge prehistoric monolith, some 5.8 metres high (19 feet), stands next to the church. Undoubtedly, many other ancient sites await identification (*see also* HOLY WELLS and PAGAN SYMBOLS).

In the sixth and seventh centuries, wooden crosses were erected to mark missionary centres which were visited by peripatetic priests from the MINSTERS. Quite often, the sites were selected because they were already well-established centres of pagan worship and, if the missions proved successful, the wooden crosses were replaced by more permanent stone structures around which Christian burials were clustered. Most of these early stone crosses therefore pre-date the foundation of churches on sites which, because of their pagan origins, are often associated with prominent or unusual topographical features such as promontories and isolated hillocks (*see also* YEW TREES). Similarly there is evidence to suggest that many of our churches occupy sites which were already established as centres of local administration long before the arrival of the minster priests (*see* CHURCHYARD CROSSES).

Many ancient churches were built on Anglo-Saxon estates, or by Norman manorial lords, as proprietary (private) CHAPELS or to serve newly established settlements (*vills*). The church at Kilpeck in Herefordshire, for example, was built in the 1130s on a site which had already been established as a seigniorial complex of castle and attendant township during the reign of William I (1066–87). The castle at Kilpeck is first mentioned in 1134 when 'the [proprietary] chapel of St. Mary of the castle' was granted to the monks of St. Peter's abbey at Gloucester, together with the parish church of St. David. Of the motte and bailey castle and township only earthworks remain. Neither is there any trace of the castle's chapel – but it is not without significance that the celebrated little church is now dedicated to both St. David and St. Mary. Kilpeck is not alone: the presence of a MOTTE in the vicinity of a remote church is nearly always indicative of a failed medieval town, the former streets delineated by field boundaries and lanes and house plots (*tofts*) evident in the rectangular platforms and hollows of adjacent paddocks (*see* DESERTED VILLAGES).

The absence of a reference in *Domesday Book* (*see* DOMESDAY) does not necessarily mean that a church did not exist, for the commissioners were primarily concerned with fiscal matters and their methods varied from one area to another. In Suffolk, for example, most churches were recorded, whereas in Essex and Staffordshire very few were noted by the commissioners.

Churches may be found in close proximity to a manor house, as at North Cadbury and Brympton D'Evercy in Somerset and Wickhamford in Worcestershire, or occasionally attached to it, as at Nevill Holt in Leicestershire and Wyke Champflower in Somerset. In dispersed communities of hamlets and farmsteads, churches were often built in apparent isolation: at the intersection of routeways, on ancient boundaries, at river crossings or in the vicinity of a holy well or spring (*see also* CHAPELS *and* HOLY WELLS). Many were originally chapelries of minsters and evolved as parish churches from the end of the eleventh century (*see* ANGLO-SAXON CHURCH).

CHURCH DEDICATIONS

Early sites may sometimes be suggested through a Saxon or Celtic dedication (*see* DEDICATION, CHURCH *and* RELICS): the hilltop church at Oldbury-on-Severn in the county of Avon, for example, is dedicated to a local Saxon saint, Arilda, and stands within an even earlier circular earthwork high above the village. Dedications to St. Lawrence, who died on a gridiron, are common to many churches with pre-Christian associations, suggestive perhaps of pagan sun-worship and sacrificial flames; and churches dedicated to the saints Catherine, Edward and Michael are frequently sited on eminences and in high places. There are over six hundred English churches dedicated to St. Michael, and seventy in Wales, of which a considerable number are on hilltop sites. It may be that many of these sites are of pagan origin and that the warrior-Archangel Michael was considered an appropriate saint to stand guard over ancestral remains, pagan and Christian alike. Having driven Lucifer out of Heaven the saint was apparently invoked against dragons, one of which was believed to have inhabited the wild and lonely hills of Radnor Forest in mid-Wales where there is a significant cluster of churches dedicated to St. Michael.

But dedications can be deceptive. Different dedications were fashionable at different times and old dedications may have been forgotten, corrupted or changed where no official record has survived. Many dedications were changed during the Middle Ages and the names of more fashionable (and efficacious) saints adopted. In such cases it may still be possible to discover an earlier dedication from medieval wills, charters, monastic cartularies or bishop's registers or from place-name and field-name evidence. Earlier this century, for example, the original dedication to St. Cosmos and St. Damien was restored to the church of St. Michael and All Angels at Sherrington in Wiltshire following the discovery of the will of John Carter, rector of Sherrington, dated 1553, in which he desired that he

should be buried in 'the chauncell of Cosmos and Damien of Sherryton.' In Shropshire, the Saxon church at Wistanstow was dedicated to the Mercian saint, Wistan, who was martyred in 849 (*Wistanstow* = 'Wistan's holy place'). But, while the manor of *Wistanestov* is mentioned in *Domesday Book*, by 1086 the church had already been completely rebuilt and re-dedicated to the Holy Trinity.

Sometimes, where an earlier dedication has been lost, the PAROCHIAL FESTIVAL has remained unaltered, and reference to the Roman calendar may assist in discovering both the original dedication and when the church was first constructed on the site.

When the provenance of an original dedication can be substantiated it may also serve to link clusters of churches with similar dedications to a mother church and, thereby, identify former *parochia* or early parishes which have subsequently been fragmented. There are also many instances of church dedications being used as place-name elements to differentiate between villages with otherwise identical names: Donhead St. Andrew and Donhead St. Mary in Wiltshire, for example. But even here dedications can be deceptive: in Essex, the village of Belchamp St. Paul has a church dedicated to St. Andrew!

Some dedications are unique, such as that to St. Eata (d. 685) at Atcham in Shropshire, and suggest that the churches may have been founded by the saints themselves. This is particularly so in Wales and the Marches where there are many churches which possess both a unique or rare dedication and a site for which there is no apparent explanation. Celtic dedications are usually indicative of a foundation which pre-dates the Synod of Whitby in 664 at which the Celtic tradition was forced to concede to that of Rome. But it is often difficult to differentiate between myth and reality. In the CELTIC CHURCH the term 'saint' was applied to all who were by vocation religious and there is little evidence to support the notion (favoured by Victorian ecclesiologists) that by identifying sites with similar dedications one can trace the journeys of Celtic missionaries and evangelists.

ISOLATED CHURCHES

So many ancient churches occupy apparently illogical and inconvenient sites, that it is not unreasonable to conclude that they were left in splendid isolation following the re-settlement of communities on more favourable sites, or as the result of 'emparking' in the seventeenth and eighteenth centuries (*see* DESERTED VILLAGES). The prospect of 'removing' a village's most substantial stone building must have been daunting indeed, and there must also have been a natural reluctance among a superstitious people to disturb the sanctity of hallowed ground and its ancestral associations. The solitary church of St. Andrew at Bolam, Northumberland, for example, now stands where once there was a castle and a town with '. . . two hundred slated houses enclosing a green'. Other churches were late arrivals and sited on the periphery of a village, as at Long Stanton in Shropshire, or occupy a clearly defined croft within a regular village plan, suggesting either that an earlier church was moved to accommodate the new plan or even that it was the first church to have been provided for the community. Clues to abandoned sites may sometimes be found in place-names, such as St. Peter's Place and Church Knapp, and in local Ordnance Survey maps where a pattern of converging footpaths and bridleways may serve to locate the focal point of earlier parochial activity. In the gently rolling countryside of south Herefordshire the churches are often located well away from their tiny riverside settlements, the inhabitants of which would withdraw to higher ground whenever the river Wye flooded. The church at Holme Lacy, for example, stands in the meadows outside the village while further upstream at Monnington-on-Wye and Byford the Wye has been known to rise more than 6 metres (20 feet) in a single night.

DOUBLE PARISHES

There are also several instances of churches sited in close proximity to one another for no apparent reason. At sequestered Bywell in Northumberland, for example, the ancient churches of St. Andrew and St. Peter stand in a silvan loop of the Tyne together with a vicarage, a medieval market cross, a hall and a pele tower – all that remain of a once-flourishing town. There are several instances in the eastern counties of England: at South Walsham in Norfolk (one church is now in ruins), and at Willingdale Doe and Willingdale Spain in Essex, for example, and at Trimley in Suffolk, while three churches once shared the same churchyard at Reepham in Norfolk.

In most cases, the presence of two churches within close proximity of one another is usually indicative of a 'double parish'. The village of Aldwincle in Northamptonshire has two churches which stand some 450 metres apart (500 yards). There is no historical evidence of over-population (today there are just over two hundred houses in the civil parish) and no obvious need, therefore, for two churches. But in the Middle Ages there were two manors (Aldwincle All Saints and Aldwincle St. Peter), one belonging to the Aldwincle family who presented to the living of All Saints, and the other held by the Benedictine abbey of St. Peter at Peterborough which built the parish church of St. Peter for its tenants. Despite the two manors and the two parishes, the tax collectors of the Exchequer took a different view of Aldwincle. For clerical purposes there were, of course, two units to be assessed; but for all the lay subsidies for which records have survived there was only a single assessment. The two parishes were combined in 1879.

Monastic houses often built parish churches in close proximity to their own: at Sherborne in Dorset, for instance, where the parish church of All Hallows was attached to the western end of the abbey nave, and at Evesham in Worcestershire where both the abbey church and the parish church remain today within the same precinct.

See also NINETEENTH-CENTURY CHURCH *and* TWENTIETH-CENTURY CHURCHES

Further reading:

Aston, M., *Interpreting the Landscape: Landscape Archaeology in Local Studies*, London, 1985

Morris, R., *Churches in the Landscape*, London, 1989

CHURCH SOCIETY, THE The Church Association was founded in 1865 by evangelical churchmen with the aim of maintaining the protestant ideals of faith and worship in the Anglican Church. In 1950 the Association joined with the National Church League to form the Church Society.

CHURCH TOWERS *see* TOWERS

CHURCHTOWN A west-country term for a hamlet, village or town which contains a church.

CHURCH TRUSTEES' RECORDS *see* ARCHIVES

CHURCHWARDENS (CUSTODES ECCLESIAE *also* **CHURCHMEN, CHURCH REEVES** *or* **KIRKMASTERS)** Until the separation of the civil and ecclesiastical components of vestral authority in 1894 (*see* PARISH *and* VESTRY) the role of the churchwardens in parochial life was of even greater significance than that of the parson. The usual arrangement was for two churchwardens to be appointed annually at the Easter meeting of the vestry, though there were local variations both in the number of wardens chosen and in the method of selection. In some parishes, for example, the office was filled by 'house-row': by appointing the occupiers of certain properties in turn. Until recently, most parishes appointed two: a vicar's warden and a people's warden, their staffs of office bearing a mitre and crown respectively (*see* CHURCHWARDENS' STAFFS). But at one time, in many large parishes, there were often three or four churchwardens appointed to represent different townships or wards, administrative divisions of a parish which levied a separate poor rate and appointed their own constables (*see* TOWNSHIP). In such cases, appointments were sometimes made by a PATRON or local land-owner, or (occasionally) by a corporate body such as a borough council or GUILD. At Prestbury in Cheshire, for example, there were four wardens: two appointed by the people and one each by the patron and incumbent.

CHURCHWARDENS' RESPONSIBILITIES

When one considers the extraordinary range of parochial responsibilities which were delegated to the wardens, it is quite remarkable that annual vestry meetings almost invariably succeeded in filling the office. Once appointed, the corporate life of a local community was vested in the wardens who exercised considerable authority, aided by parish officials who were also appointed at the annual vestry meeting. These included the PARISH CONSTABLE, the Overseer of the Poor (see POOR LAW) and the Surveyor of Highways. At one time the churchwardens were responsible for presenting offenders against ecclesiastical law and even today they are empowered to remove a person's hat during divine service. Their other duties have, from time to time, included the management of parish property and finances including the collection of rents and the upkeep of the fabric of the church (see CHURCHWARDENS' ACCOUNTS); the provision of facilities for worship, including the allocation of pews (see PEW RENTS); with the Overseers, supervision of the education and relief of the poor and orphans, the sick and the needy (see CHARITIES, POOR LAW and SCHOOLS); the upholding of law and order, both civil and ecclesiastical; the maintenance of public buildings and of fences and boundaries (see PERAMBULATIONS); the condition of parish munitions and the payment of members of the militia; fund-raising and the organisation of community festivities; the removal of vagrants from the parish and the extermination of vermin (see CHURCH AND COMMUNITY and DOGS). On occasions, a warden may even have acted as pawnbroker, depositing pledged articles in the PARISH CHEST.

The churchwardens also represented the views of parishioners, both corporately and severally, in parochial matters and were responsible for encouraging church attendance and ensuring that the young were baptised. At the annual audit, the churchwardens took possession of property left to the parish in the previous year, received contributions from the people, each according to his occupation, and arranged for the distribution of surplus goods to those they believed to be in greatest need. The audit was one occasion when almost the entire parish would be present to witness the administration of their affairs. Gifts and bequests (which were mostly in kind) varied enormously: large bequests were often of land (which thereafter produced annual rents) and among the smaller gifts, frequently mentioned in the accounts, were swarms of bees to provide valuable wax for the church candles.

Churchwardens were expected to be rigorous in upholding standards of behaviour: parishioners who were guilty of moral transgressions were reported to the archdeacon's courts, the punishment for sexual offences being a period of penance in the church porch where they were required to stand in a white sheet. One Thomas Parr, whose grave in Westminster Abbey records his death in 1635 at the remarkable age of 152, was made to undertake just such a penance in his church at Alberbury in Shropshire (the porch has since been demolished) for fathering an illegitimate child in his hundredth year. The line between diligence and officiousness was often finely drawn: some wardens are known to have patrolled the church during a service, tapping on the head with a long wand those whose attention appeared to be wandering. In a Yorkshire parish, it was the custom during morning service for the wardens to leave the church, following the second lesson, and to visit the inns in the neighbourhood to ensure that the parishioners were behaving themselves, before returning to the church for the sermon. In the parish of St. Peter at Congleton in Cheshire, the churchwardens came upon a young woman who so upbraided them for interfering with her liberty that she was at once arrested and taken to the magistrate who ordered that a bridle be put upon her head and that she be paraded round the town as an example to all those who failed to recognise the dignity of the wardens' office.

Churchwardens are now chosen (traditionally on Easter Tuesday) by the joint consent of the incumbent, those who are recorded in the Church Electoral Role and the local government electors who reside in the parish.

See also HOCK-TIDE, PARISH CLERK, SEXTON and SIDESMEN

Further reading:

Bettey, J., *Church and Parish*, London, 1987

Gough, R., *The History of Myddle*, London, 1981

Tate, W., *The Parish Chest*, Cambridge, 1969

CHURCHWARDENS' ACCOUNTS Churchwardens' accounts, some dating from the medieval period, may be found in county record offices. They are an invaluable source of information, not only for church historians but also for those who wish to study wider historical and demographic changes in society. Churchwardens' accounts first appear in the late medieval period, a time when the Church's involvement in all aspects of community affairs was at its height. Churchwardens were the most important lay officials in a parish (see CHURCHWARDENS). They were responsible for the maintenance of the church, for the provision of books, furnishings, vestments and equipment and for raising the money with which to finance these, and many other, activities. From the sixteenth century, they acquired additional responsibilities for parochial matters such as poor relief (though overseers' accounts were usually kept separately) and highway maintenance. Churchwardens' accounts show how their affairs were managed (often through the appointment of parish officials such as the SEXTON and PARISH CLERK), how building works were organised and how money was raised through gifts, bequests, fees and community activities such as Church Ales (*see* CHURCH AND COMMUNITY). The earliest surviving accounts are those of St. Michael's church in Bath which begin in 1349.

MEDIEVAL RECORDS

Unfortunately, only a small number of medieval statements of account have survived but these are sufficient to demonstrate the care with which the records were kept and the diversity of the churchwardens' duties. Occasionally, they include inventories of church goods and even contracts made with masons and other craftsmen for work carried out in the church.

Perhaps the most revealing aspect of many of these accounts, is the extraordinary concern of wardens and parishioners for the care and development of their churches. It is evident that the enlargement and rebuilding of many late-medieval churches was entirely due to the generosity and enthusiasm of benefactors and parishioners, and that churchwardens were often quite willing to borrow heavily in order that a major project might be completed. Incredibly large sums were raised even from poor and sparsely populated parishes. At Bodmin in Cornwall, for example, the Norman church was demolished in the late fifteenth century and a splendid new building constructed in the latest architectural fashion – the largest church in the county. The Bodmin accounts show that money was raised by selling material from the demolished church (window glass was purchased by the nearby parishes of Helland and St. Kew), by public sub-scription and by fund-raising activities, several of which were organised by the local GUILDS as part of their annual Whitsuntide festivities. The churchwardens arranged for stone for the building to be transported by water from the quarries at Pentewan to Lostwithiel on the Fowey river in order to avoid the difficult overland journey across central Cornwall. Much of the timber for the roof and scaffolding was donated by local landowners, and most of the building work was carried out voluntarily by local people. Specialist masons, carpenters and glaziers were employed for the construction of the roof, windows and doorways. The total cost was in the region of £270, excluding the materials and labour contributed by local people, an enormous sum for a late fifteenth-century rural parish.

POST-REFORMATION RECORDS

Many more churchwardens' accounts have survived from the sixteenth century and these provide a graphic picture of the profound effects of the REFORMATION on the religious and social life of communities. This was a time of constant change

and yet the records show that, throughout the country, the legislative requirements of successive governments were almost immediately complied with by the churchwardens. During the brief reign of Edward VI (1547–53) they supervised the institution of new practices and the abolition of numerous ancient traditions and rituals. With the accession of (the Catholic) Mary I (1553–8) they were obliged to expend large sums in order to replace all the church books, vestments, plate, ornaments and furnishings which had been destroyed only a few years before. And again, in 1558, they were required to revert to the practices of the new Church (and to remove all vestiges of the old) when Elizabeth I succeeded to her father's title as 'the only supreme governor' of the English Church (*see* CHURCH OF ENGLAND).

In his book *Church and Parish*, J.H. Bettey sets out the following extracts from the churchwardens' accounts of St. Mary's church at Devizes in Devon to illustrate the bewildering rapidity of change at that time:

Edward VI
1551	Paid for . . . plucking down of the [stone] Altars	1s 2d
Mary I		
1553	Paid for . . . setting up the great Altar	8d
1555	Paid for defacing the Scriptures on the walls	2s 4d
	Paid for . . . putting in the Roodloft	6s 0d
1557	Paid for tymber to make the pyctor [picture] that standeth by the Rode [rood] named Mary and John	2s 0d
Elizabeth I		
1561	Paid for taking down of the Roodloft	6s 0d

Such disruption and expense must have caused considerable and widespread resentment: but on this the churchwardens' accounts are silent. There are occasional references to valuables being hidden in anticipation of further changes in the religious climate, but whether this was for purely economic reasons or because of an attachment to the beauty and craftsmanship of items which were, in effect, community heirlooms, is not clear. It may be that in those churches where a ROOD LOFT or stone altar has survived the parishioners did indeed regret the passing of the 'former ways'. If so, we should be grateful that their transgressions were somehow overlooked, even during the iconoclastic orgy of the Interregnum (1649–60) (*see* SEVENTEENTH-CENTURY CHURCH).

As a consequence of sixteenth-century legislation the responsibilities of churchwardens for parochial affairs increased significantly, while successive acts of Parliament also encouraged the development of secular parochial authority through the VESTRY system. Seventeenth- and eighteenth-century account books refer repeatedly to gifts of money collected for the relief of soldiers maimed in the wars, for providing apprenticeships for orphans and food and clothing for the destitute. Numerous minor payments are recorded for community activities, such as bell-ringing, for the provision of lock-ups, stocks and pillories and the building of POUNDS for stray animals. But as local communities became less isolated and the dictates of central government increasingly impinged on the lives of parishioners, so the authority of the churchwardens waned (*see* PARISH).

See also ARCHIVES, CHARITIES, PERAMBULA-TIONS and PEW RENTS

Further reading:

Bettey, J., *Church and Parish*, London, 1987

Cox, J., *Churchwardens' Accounts*, London, 1913

Salzman, L., *Building in England*, London, 1967

Tate, W., *The Parish Chest*, Cambridge, 1969

CHURCHWARDENS' STAFFS Until recently, churchwardens' staffs (or *wands*) were to be found in most churches, next to the wardens' seats in the nave. The wooden staffs are usually surmounted by a brass or silver mitre (for the vicar's warden) and a crown (for the people's warden), although other emblems may also be found: at Whiston in Northamptonshire, for example, where a pair of cats commemorates the Catesby family's rebuilding of the church in 1534.

See also CHURCHWARDENS

CHURCHYARD CROSSES Some churchyards contain ancient tree-standing stone crosses, or fragments of crosses, usually located to the south of the church or occasionally found incorporated within the fabric of the building itself, following rebuilding.

EARLY CROSSES

In the sixth and seventh centuries, wooden crosses were erected to mark local centres of worship which were visited regularly by peripatetic priests from the MINSTERS (*see* CHURCH SITES). If a mission proved successful, the wooden cross was replaced by a more permanent stone structure at which masses were celebrated and around which Christian burials were clustered. These early crosses almost invariably pre-date the foundation of churches on the same sites. When a church was built it was usually positioned so that its shadow would not fall on the cross. This may be the reason why so many churches occupy the northern part of a churchyard and why the larger (and more salubrious) southern section is used for Christian burial – though there are exceptions: at Grosmont in Gwent, for example, where both churchyard and (medieval) cross are to the north of the church. The heads of these early crosses are likely to have been of a simple cruciform shape though many Celtic or wheel-headed crosses have survived, notably in Wales and the West Country: the celebrated Carew Cross in Dyfed, for example, which was erected in memory of Maredudd

ab Edwin, ruler of Deheubarth in the eleventh century. Other beautifully sculpted 'high crosses' include those at Nevern, also in Dyfed, and Llangan in Glamorgan (*see* CELTIC CROSS *and* WHEEL HEAD CROSS). The cross at Penmon Priory, Anglesey had one arm removed in the thirteenth century so that it could be used as a lintel to support one of the refectory windows (it is now kept inside the church). Several early Anglian crosses, often with vine-scroll decoration on the shaft, are to be found in the north of England. There are magnificent examples of early stone crosses at Bewcastle and Gosforth in Cumberland, Bakewell and Eyam in Derbyshire and at Rothbury and Hexham in Northumberland. An eighth-century biography of St. Willibald describes how, in Somerset, a visiting priest would preach and celebrate the Mass at a cross erected outside a lord's hall, suggesting that many of our churches occupy sites which were already established as centres of local administration long before the arrival of the minster priests.

MEDIEVAL CROSSES

Other churchyard crosses are generally of medieval origin and, in these, tabernacles are more common than cross-heads and wheel-heads. They were to be found in most churchyards before the REFORMATION and were intended both to sanctify the churchyard and to provide a corporate memorial to the anonymous dead of the parish (individual GRAVESTONES became fashionable in the late seventeenth century). They were also used for liturgical purposes, the churchyard cross being the second of the processional Stations of the Cross on Palm Sunday and the one at which the Mass was celebrated. After the celebration, the cross itself was wreathed in 'palms' which were usually branches of yew (*see* YEW TREES). Many survive only as a shaft and polygonal stepped base, the tabernacle, with its niches containing 'Papist' images of Our Lady and Child and a crucifix (*rood*), having been destroyed by Tudor or Cromwellian iconoclasts (see below). A vacant niche was usually provided for the pyx (vessel) in which the Host was reserved in the Palm Sunday mass and this may be located at the foot of the shaft as at Weobley in Herefordshire where the churchyard cross has five steps rather than the usual three (*see* PENITENTIAL CROSSES). There are notable examples of medieval crosses at Ampney Crucis in Gloucestershire and Somersby in Lancashire.

Inevitably, churchyard crosses came to be used for a variety of other purposes, many of them secular. For centuries they were used by itinerant preachers (hence 'preaching crosses') and in times of war or threatened invasion they served as mustering points for the local militia. It was at the churchyard cross that parishioners would assemble to learn of the accession of kings and the death of princes, to hear proclamations and churchwardens' announcements.

Churchyard cross at Snowshill, Gloucestershire.

At lonely Partrishow, deep in the mountains of Powys, a stone bench on the outside of the church wall provided comfort for the aged and infirm who assembled at the churchyard cross to hear visiting preachers, among them Archbishop Baldwin and his chaplain, Gerald of Wales, who arrived there in 1188 'preaching the Cross' and recruiting for the Third Crusade – 'During this long, laborious and praiseworthy mission, about three thousand men were signed with the cross . . . if only the Crusade itself had proceeded as quickly, and achieved as much success.' The churchyard cross also served as the focal point of community festivities (*see* CHURCH AND COMMUNITY) and was considered by merchants and tradespeople to be an ideal place at which to conduct business (*see* MARKET CROSSES).

POST-REFORMATION

The widespread mutilation of churchyard crosses dates from the English Reformation of the sixteenth century and from seventeenth-century legislation which required that any remaining shafts should be reduced in height to four feet and six inches (1 m 37 cm). It was at this time that a great many of these truncated shafts were pressed into service as SUNDIALS, the old vertical 'scratch-dials' (which may still be found on the southern elevation of many churches) having been superseded by the more efficient horizontal plate which fitted neatly on top of the broken shafts of churchyard crosses. A surprising number of crosses has survived, mostly in remoter areas where the commissioners and their agents were least effective.

Of course, it is sometimes difficult to distinguish between different types of cross. There are instances of isolated missionary crosses surviving where no church was built and of churchyard crosses which stand at some remove from the present churchyard. Some villages possess more than one cross: Leigh in

Dorset, for example, which boasts both a splendid fifteenth-century WAYSIDE CROSS and the remains of a medieval churchyard cross. Conversely, there are also instances of wayside and market crosses having been removed to a churchyard in order to protect them from traffic or development. Bristol's famous fourteenth-century market cross, which was removed to Stourhead in Wiltshire in 1733, is perhaps the most extreme example. In recent times, many large 'reproduction' stone crosses, usually of the wheel-head type, have been erected in churchyards: to commemorate benefactors, as war memorials or (as at Holwell in Dorset) as rather grandiose tombstones.

See also CHURCHYARDS

CHURCHYARDS There can be little doubt that, long before Christianity reached the shores of Britain, burial places had been used '. . . for communal and secular no less than religious purposes in an age when the two were essentially one and indivisible' (Mortimer Wheeler). They served '. . . as religious meeting places, the scenes of seasonal activities of a simple agricultural people [whose] cultural association with the tombs was one much concerned with rebirth' (Jacquetta Hawkins). This notion of spiritual regeneration by association with the dead persisted for many centuries, not only in the adoption of pagan sites for Christian worship but also in their continuing use as centres of community activity. The value of religious and cultural continuity was recognised by Pope Gregory when (in 601) he advised that pagan shrines should not be destroyed 'but rather that they should be purified with holy water so that in time they [would] become temples of the true God' (*see* PAGAN SYMBOLS). For this reason, numerous ancient burial sites were adopted by missionary priests as centres of worship (*see* CHURCHYARD CROSSES) and, once established, they were used as Christian burial grounds and eventually acquired permanent churches (*see* CHURCH SITES). Consequently many churchyards are of greater antiquity than the church buildings they contain.

CIRCULAR CHURCHYARDS
In the Saxon period, churchyards continued to be used as places of assembly and moot courts (*gemotes*) were sometimes held there. In sixth-century Wales an open space or enclosure (*llan*) was set aside for religious purposes and for burials. These sites may have been associated with pagan burial grounds, or with the cemeteries of early monastic settlements, and consequently they were often enclosed by an earlier embankment, the distinctive circular or oval shape of which may have survived to the present day (*see also* YEW TREES). These enclosures usually preceded the building of a church on (or near) the same site, indeed the word *llan* came to mean 'church' (*see* WALES,

CHRISTIANITY IN). There are numerous circular churchyards in Wales: at Old Radnor in Powys, for example, where the original Norman church was constructed within a prehistoric earthwork. Today the (fourteenth-century) church, churchyard and prehistoric embankment are all surrounded by a circular stone wall. At Ysbytty Cynfyn, also in Powys, the church stands at the centre of a Bronze Age burial chamber which itself was once surrounded by an embankment and a series of lofty standing stones, five of which have been incorporated into a low, circular wall. One of the best examples in England is the isolated twelfth-century church at Knowlton in Dorset (abandoned in the eighteenth century) which stands within a circular Neolithic henge, one of a group of similar earthworks known locally as Knowlton Rings. Significantly, an adjacent 'ring' is described in documents as 'the Old Churchyard' (*see also* TRENDEL).

A raised churchyard may be a further indication of antiquity, for repeated BURIALS will have raised substantially the level of earth above that of adjacent land (*see also* OSSUARIES). There are several instances of ancient churchyards being shared by neighbouring parishes and a small number may even contain two churches, as at Swaffham Prior in Cambridgeshire (*see* CHURCH SITES). From the Saxon period, churchyards have generally been of rectangular shape and may conform to the crofts (the enclosed areas of land adjacent to dwellings) within a regular village plan.

SECULAR ACTIVITIES
The churchyard was often the venue for village festivities and social gatherings, for dancing, games and commercial transactions: much to the consternation of the ecclesiastical establishment (*see* CHURCH AND COMMUNITY). In many parishes, the unconsecrated north side of the churchyard was effectively the village recreation field (*see* PLAISTOW). Quoits, ninepins, marbles, wrestling, hammer-throwing and football may have incurred the displeasure of the diocesan authorities, but many a country parson enthusiastically participated in these events and churchwardens' accounts from the seventeenth and eighteenth centuries sometimes provide details of the amenities (such as benches) which were provided for participants and spectators. Even the church building was used for games, an external section of wall between two buttresses (with the windows shuttered) being ideally suited to the game of fives which (the records suggest) was the most popular of churchyard sports. Parson Woodforde, writing in 1764, tells us that his '. . . guests plaid at Fives in the churchyard this evening and I lost there at betting 0.1.6.' In several churches the iron hinges and stays for the shutters have survived, though rarely the shutters themselves, while at Craswall in Herefordshire the rectangular

outline of a level 'court' may still be seen in the ground to the north of the chancel.

The increasing influence of Puritanism in the sixteenth and seventeenth centuries appears to have caused little more than a sporadic reaction to such activities and, in some areas, churchyard games continued well into the nineteenth century. Nevertheless, by the mid-eighteenth century, Methodism was already influencing opinion: at Nantwich in Cheshire, for example, where in 1776 the playing of fives was specifically forbidden, and at Llanfair Discoed in Gwent where the following inscription may still be seen in the church porch:

> Whoever hear on Sunday
> Will Practis Playing at Ball
> it May Be before Monday
> The Devil Will Have you All.

Another popular churchyard 'sport' was cockfighting which, like fives, provided an opportunity for gambling. Henry VIII was especially enthusiastic and, as a result, cockfighting came to be known as the 'royal diversion'. 'In later Stuart times the cock-fight was the most popular sport of all, on which all classes staked their money even more than upon horse-racing' (Trevelyan). There can be little doubt that, in most parishes during the seventeenth century, the churchyard was used for this purpose and there are even recorded cases of cock-fights being held in church naves. Behind St. Mary's church at Craswell in Herefordshire is a grassy hollow where local men gathered to watch the cockfighting and, in the north wall of the church, the projecting beam-ends to which spectators tethered their horses. Cockfighting was prohibited by Parliament in 1849, as was *cockthreshing*, a notably unruly entertainment by which a cockerel was tethered by one leg and bombarded with missiles.

At lonely Glascwm in Powys, the church porch was once used as one of the 'goals' for an annual inter-village football match, the other being over four miles away, across the hills, at the church at Disserth. Such games were a regular feature of life in many parishes and, because there was no restriction on the number of participants, they were singularly unruly affairs: 'The lads and young men by the hundreds kicking the football in all their pants and shirts and belabouring each other more like dogs fighting for a bone than men bearing the name of Christian. The old men acting as spectators, encouraging and urging on every man his party; sticks in hand, they shouted and swore in a manner which made them look hideous. The women in scores contended and yelled at the tops of their voices; in their excitement and wild rage they would cast off their shawls, their hats and caps, more formidable in aspect than hags.'

The same account, written in Anglesey in 1799,

tells us that 'The common people delighted in nothing but empty sport and carnal pleasures, playing with dice and cards, dancing and singing with the harp, playing football, tennis, mock-trials and hostages and many other sinful sports too numerous to be mentioned. They used the Sundays like a market day to gratify every wicked whim and passion; old and young . . . they flocked in crowds to the parish churches on Sunday morning; not to listen to the word of God . . . but to entice each other to drink at the wash-brew house of the devil's market'. It was the influence of Methodism which finally led to a significant decline in such excesses. But, while there can be little doubt that standards of conduct and morality improved as a result, the poor were also deprived of many simple and harmless pleasures which served to relieve the harshness of everyday life.

BURIALS

Burial in the churchyard is the right of every parishioner irrespective of his beliefs or station in life (*see* BURIALS). Today, the freehold of both the church and the churchyard are the prerogative of the incumbent, in joint possession with the parochial church council: the churchyard is maintained by the council and its use controlled by the parish priest (*see also* CLOSED CHURCHYARDS). At one time, and in certain parishes, the owners or occupiers of particular houses or farms were required to accept responsibility for maintaining specified sections of the 'churchyard rails' (i.e. the fence or wall surrounding the churchyard). GRAVESTONES were a seventeenth-century innovation and most date from the eighteenth century or later. Each gravestone or memorial is owned by the person who erected it, or by his successors, and anyone who removes or defaces a memorial trespasses thereby. By custom all the grass contained within a churchyard belongs to the incumbent as part of his endowment, though in the past it was frequently grazed by the sexton's animals, the graves being provided with a protective trellis of osier and bramble. Although the entire churchyard is now consecrated ground this was not always so and there persisted into the last century the practice whereby the virtuous received burial on the salubrious south side of the church while felons, outcasts and unbaptised infants were consigned to perpetual shadow on the north (*see also* SUICIDES).

Some churchyards contain ancient free-standing crosses or fragments of crosses, usually located to the south of the church or occasionally found incorporated within the fabric of the building itself, following rebuilding (*see* CHURCHYARD CROSSES). Others, such as Painswick in Gloucestershire (*see* TABLE TOMBS) and Mells in Somerset, are renowned for their collections of memorials. Painswick churchyard is also noted for its ninety-nine yew trees which, for over two

hundred years, have received an annual clipping – an event which is entirely unrelated to Painswick's famous Clipping Service which is also held annually in the churchyard (*see* CLIPPING).
See also BODY SNATCHERS, BURIALS, EPITAPHS, INCUBATION, INSCRIPTIONS, LICH-GATES, MAUSOLEUM, MEMORIALS, OSSUARIES, POOR SOUL'S LIGHT, PORCHES, SUNDIALS *and* VAULTS (BURIAL)
Further reading:
Bailey, B., *Churchyards in England and Wales*, London, 1987
Burgess, F., *English Churchyard Memorials*, London, 1979
Greenwood, D., *Who's Buried Where in England?*, London, 1990
Gregory, D., *Yesterday in Village Church and Churchyard*, Gomer (Llandysul)
Hutton, R., *The Rise and Fall of Merry England: The Ritual Year 1400–1700*, Oxford, 1994
Stapleton, H. and Burman, P., (eds.), *The Churchyards Handbook*, London, 1988

CIBORIUM (i) A vessel, shaped like a chalice and with a lid, used to retain the Sacramental Bread of the Eucharist (*see* PLATE). (ii) A large canopy or tester of wood, stone or metal above an altar or bishop's throne (*cathedra*). Originally a medieval feature, the ciborium was re-introduced into the English church by the architect Sir Ninian Comper (1864–1960).
See also ALTARS, ALTAR CANOPY *and* BALDA-C(C)HINO

CINGULUM MILITARE A broad hip-belt of ornamental gold or metalwork from which depended a sword and MISERICORDE (*see* ARMOUR). Popular in the period *c.* 1360–1450.

CINQUEFOIL A figure having five radiating stylized 'petals' found both as an architectural motif and an heraldic device (*see* FOILS).

CIRCARIES The visitation districts of a medieval monastic foundation.

CIRCATOR (*also* CIRCAS) The monastic official responsible for security.
See also LANTERN

CIRCULAR CHURCHES A small number of circular (*centrally planned*) churches were built in Britain, mainly in the twelfth century, and these reflected the traditions of earlier cultures, notably that of the Roman mausoleum. They were built in an Anglo-Romanesque style with an inner ring of arcaded columns supporting triforium walling and clerestory beneath a conical roof, and with a lower roof at triforium level above a circular aisle. For the

The Temple Church, London, (c. 1185) before rebuilding.

most part, circular churches were built by the military and hospitaller orders of knights (*see* TEMPLAR, KNIGHTS *and* SAINT JOHN OF JERUSALEM, ORDER OF), apparently following the plan of the Rotunda of Constantine's Church of the Holy Sepulchre in Jerusalem. The most notable examples are the church of the Holy Sepulchre (*c.* 1130) at Cambridge and the Temple Church in London (*c.* 1185) which was substantially reconstructed after the Second World War.
See also MEDIEVAL ARCHITECTURE

CIRCUMCISION, THE FEAST OF THE *see* FEAST DAYS (FIXED AND MOVABLE)

CIRCUMSCRIBED To be enclosed within a line or inscription.

CISTERCIANS The Cistercian Order (the White Monks) was founded in 1098 at Cîteaux (in Latin, *Cistercium*) in Burgundy by Robert of Molesme who, with others, sought to establish a strict form of Benedictinism (*see* BENEDICTINES *and* RULE). After a precarious start, the order spread rapidly during the first decades of the twelfth century, inspired by the energy and personality of St. Bernard of Cîteaux (1090–1153), so that by 1200 some 500 houses had been established throughout Europe. The Cistercian life was one of simple communal worship, private devotion, study and meditation; and of asceticism in sequestered surroundings, far from the distractions of the outside world. There were strict rules of silence and diet, worship included none of the liturgical intricacies associated with that of the Cluniacs, and the Cistercian rule prescribed manual labour. Churches were to be devoid of all ornament and the monks wore habits of undyed wool: hence they became known as the 'white monks'. The order's constitution, the *Carta Caritatis*, provided for self-regulation subject to the ordinances of the annual General Chapter of Cîteaux at which each community was represented. Supervision was by means of a mutual system of visitations among the 'mother' and 'daughter' houses. The constitution also laid down strict rules for the formation and location of new houses. They were to be founded in places 'remote from the habitations of men', as colonies, or 'daughters', of existing houses, each with an abbot and at least twelve choir monks (those in full monastic orders). Unlike the Benedictine rule, that of the Cistercian's forbade receipt of the customary revenues in cash or kind (such as tithes, rents and fees) drawn from the society they had renounced, but gifts of hitherto uncultivated 'desert' land were acceptable: indeed, an effective agriculture was an economic necessity if a community was to survive. Although the choir monks were obliged by their rule to undertake some manual work, a substantial labour force was required to work a community's often extensive arable and grazing lands and to maintain its buildings.

The illiterate LAY BROTHERS (*conversi*), whose religious commitment was manifested through their labours, often outnumbered the choir monks by two to one. They would work either in the vicinity of the abbey or on outlying *granges* which were (in theory) located within a day's journey of the abbey, though some were more distant. These granges were not individual cells (as in the Benedictine model) but agrarian estates, each with a farmstead and oratory, and were staffed only by lay brothers. The *conversi* lived as part of the full community, though their rule was less severe, and the domestic arrangements provided for the two divisions of a Cistercian community are evident in the architecture of their abbeys.

Enthusiasm for the Cistercians caused some benefactors to endow lands which were hardly 'desert places' and the monks were often obliged to depopulate such areas, and to degrade villages into granges, by evicting tenants and demolishing their houses and even parish churches.

Cistercian abbeys, which were always dedicated to the Blessed Virgin Mary, are architecturally severe by comparison with those of other orders: presbytery, transepts etc. are usually square-ended,

chapter houses are rectangular rather than polygonal, windows contained plain glass and ornamentation of all kinds was minimal. Despite this austerity, provision was always made for a 'warming house' in the vicinity of the refectory so that the brethren could dry their clothes and warm themselves.

The first Cistercian house in England was founded at Waverley in Surrey in 1128 but it was the foundation in 1132 of Rievaulx in the Rye Valley of Yorkshire which aroused the enthusiasm of the English for the Cistercian combination of compassion and asceticism. By the fourteenth century the prohibition on learning was relaxed and the architectural influences of the Gothic age become more apparent. It was also becoming difficult to recruit sufficient men who were prepared to enter into a life of such austerity as that endured by the lay brothers. Hired labour was increasingly used and there was a move from arable farming (which was labour-intensive) to sheep breeding on a sometimes vast scale.

See also MONASTERIES

Further reading:

Butler, L. and Given-Wilson, C., *Medieval Monasteries of Great Britain*, London, 1979

Knowles, D., *The Monastic Order in England*, 2nd edn., Cambridge, 1966

CITATION MANDATE *see* VISITATIONS, ECCLESIASTICAL

CIVIL WAR *see* INTERREGNUM

CLADDING *see* FACING MATERIALS

CLAPBOARD *see* WEATHERBOARD

CLARENDON, CONSTITUTIONS OF (1164) A written statement compiled by Henry II at Clarendon (near Salisbury in Wiltshire) of the relationship between Church and State which had been established under his predecessors. The most controversial clause related to BENEFIT OF CLERGY and required that if a clerk in holy orders was convicted of a crime in an ecclesiastical court he should then be transferred to the secular authorities for punishment. This was vigorously opposed by Archbishop Thomas à Becket (*see* SAINTS).

CLAS The *clasau* were the ancient mother churches of early medieval Wales, self-contained ecclesiastical communities consisting of an abbot (who might also be a bishop) and a group of hereditary canons, sharing a common income but living as secular clerks (*claswyr*). The *clasau* were originally pioneering instruments of conversion but, by the twelfth century, they had become well-endowed and self-indulgent communities. Nevertheless, *clasau* such as Tywyn in (modern) Gwynedd

and Llandinam in Powys continued to dominate the ecclesiastical life of their respective districts well into the thirteenth century. It has been suggested that the *glas-* element in a number of Welsh place-names is indicative of a former *clas* (*glas* is normally interpreted as 'blue'): Glascwm in Powys, for example, which might have been 'The Valley of the Clas' rather than 'Blue Valley'.
See CELTIC CHURCH *and* WALES, THE MEDIEVAL CHURCH IN

CLASSICAL ORDER The classical Orders were introduced by the Greeks, and later adopted by the Romans, as a set of architectural standards for the design of temples and public buildings. The Orders regulated the proportions and relationships of the three principal elements of their buildings: the *stylobate* (the base), the *column* (the structural pillar) and the *architrave* (the beam carried by the columns). Classical columns are divided into capital, shaft, base and plinth (*see* BASE *and* COLUMN). The first three Orders devised by the Greeks were the *Doric* (the simplest and most widely used), *Ionic* (rather more elegant) and *Corinthian* (the most florid and least used). The Romans adapted these Orders to their own, less restrained, taste and added the *Tuscan* (a clumsy version of the Greek Doric) and the *Composite* (an extravagant and unsatisfactory version of the Greek Ionic and Corinthian).

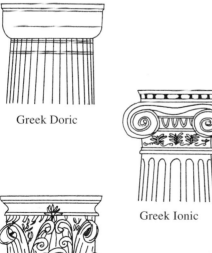

Greek Doric

Greek Ionic

Greek Corinthian

There have been successive revivals of classical architecture from the Renaissance to the present day. By the early seventeenth century, the term 'classic' was applied to exemplary literature and drama, especially that of ancient Greece and Rome. But the Greek and Roman architectural orders were not at that time fully understood and it was believed that Rome was the fount of classical architecture and Italy its natural successor. Indeed, the term 'Renaissance' implied a rebirth of the classical culture of ancient Rome and architectural Classicism was to remain Roman until the so-called Greek Revival of the late eighteenth century.
See also SIXTEENTH- AND SEVENTEENTH-CENTURY ARCHITECTURE *and* EIGHTEENTH-CENTURY ARCHITECTURE

CLAUSTRAL (or CLOISTRAL) Pertaining to the domestic buildings of a monastery, many of which were arranged round the CLOISTER. The CLAUSURA was that part of the buildings from which those of the opposite sex (and sometimes lay persons) were excluded.

CLAUSTRAL PRIOR The disciplinary officer of a monastery, responsible (to the Prior) for maintaining the Rule and for correcting breaches of conduct.

CLAUSURA (i) The practice of excluding members of the opposite sex from designated areas of a religious house or, in some instances, of excluding also those of the same sex who were not members of the community. (ii) That part of a religious house from which such persons were excluded.

CLAVI *see* VESTMENTS

CLAY LUMP A traditional East Anglian building material consisting of large rectangular blocks of compressed straw and clay, hardened naturally in sunlight.

CLERESTORY In larger churches, the upper storey of a nave pierced by a series of windows (*for illustration see* BAY). Clerestories were sometimes added (especially during the Perpendicular period) in order to increase the amount of light entering a building.
See MEDIEVAL ARCHITECTURE

CLERGY, BENEFIT OF *see* BENEFIT OF CLERGY

CLERGY (CHURCH OF ENGLAND) An *archbishop* is responsible for a PROVINCE of the Church of England: either Canterbury, which covers the dioceses south of the river Trent, or York which includes those to the north. The Archbishopric of Wales was established in 1920; before that time

Wales fell within the province of Canterbury (*see* WALES, THE CHURCH IN). The Archbishops of Canterbury and York (Primate of All England and Primate of England and Metropolitan respectively) are privy councillors and have seats in the House of Lords. Before the Reformation, archbishops of Canterbury were often appointed cardinals by the Pope (*see* CARDINAL).

BISHOPS

Bishops, whose appointment is vested in the Crown, have jurisdiction over dioceses (*see* DIOCESE). A bishop's throne (*cathedra*) is located in the cathedral of his diocese and before the Reformation bishops were appointed by a council of canons (*see* CATHEDRALS). The Bishop of London is also a privy councillor and, with the bishops of Durham and Winchester, sits in the House of Lords with precedence over all other bishops who, until 1841, also had seats (with the exception of the Bishop of Sodor and Man). Since then only twenty-one bishops sit in the Lords, a vacancy being filled by the senior diocesan bishop without a seat. In the late Middle Ages it was common practice for one or more *suffragan bishops* to be appointed (usually by the Pope) to assist the diocesan bishops. An Act of 1534 made provision for the appointment of suffragan bishops by the Crown and the original list of twenty-six suffragan sees was adopted for this purpose. At that time, these suffragan sees did not relate to the dioceses though some became diocesan sees and others were later adopted by the Roman Catholic Church. The office lapsed in 1592 and no further suffragans were appointed until 1870 when the suffragan bishops of Nottingham and Dover were consecrated. Suffragan bishoprics are not always named after major towns in the dioceses; often the name of an ancient ecclesiastical centre has been used, such as Ramsbury in Wiltshire and Dunwich in Suffolk, or a well-known district name such as Sherwood.

A *vicar-general* is a deputy of an archbishop or bishop, an office previously held by an archdeacon (see below). In the 1990s, a number of *Provincial Episcopal Visitors* (derogatorily known as 'Flying Bishops') have been appointed to minister to those who are irreconcilably opposed to the ordination of women.

CATHEDRAL AND COLLEGIATE CLERGY

A *dean* presides over the chapter of a cathedral or collegiate church. But there are exceptions. The incumbent of a cathedral which has been raised from parochial status (such as Birmingham) is usually a *provost*, though Truro and Manchester have deans. Similarly, some collegiate churches have a provost rather than a dean: Eton is an example. In monastic Britain, *canons* were clerks in holy orders who lived according to a rule; a monk, on the other hand, was simply someone who vowed to follow a life of austerity, meditation and prayer. Today, a canon is

either residentiary with cathedral duties, or has been appointed as a non-residentiary honorary canon in recognition of service to a diocese or as a conjunct to another diocesan appointment (such as Diocesan Director of Education). A cathedral's statutes may require that certain honorary canonries be given to the holders of specified diocesan offices: at Truro, for example, the Bishop of St. German's is by statute created an honorary canon. Cathedral statutes differ from one another in many details but most allow a bishop to appoint some canons from outside the diocese. A minor canon is a clergyman attached to a cathedral or collegiate church to assist in services and is not a canon: the *precentor*, for example, who is responsible for the direction of choral services, and his deputy the *succentor* (though, in cathedrals of the 'Old Foundation', the precentor is a member of the chapter). In certain cathedrals (such as Wells in Somerset) prebendal stalls are reserved for honorary canons. In the Middle Ages the endowment of most non-monastic cathedrals was divided into *prebends*, each intended to support a single member of the chapter. Holders of prebends became known as *prebendaries* and in some English cathedrals the territorial titles have been retained, but not their incomes.

DIOCESAN CLERGY

An *archdeacon* is a senior clergyman having administrative authority delegated by a bishop. He is responsible for the parishes within his archdeaconry which may itself be sub-divided into rural deaneries, each the responsibility of a *rural dean* (see below). In the pre-medieval Church, an archdeacon was a bishop's principal assistant ('the eye of the bishop') and the senior *deacon*. At that time deacons were accorded a rank next below that of presbyter (*see* PRIEST) and were chiefly responsible for collecting and distributing alms. During the Middle Ages the deacon was one of the three sacred ministers at the High Mass (*see* MASS *and* SUBDEACON) but the influence of the diaconate declined and the term is now applied to those who have reached an advanced stage in preparation for the priesthood. In the early Church, a *deaconess* was responsible for caring for the poor and sick of her sex and for assisting in the baptism of women. With the increasing popularity of infant baptism in the fifth century, the office declined in importance until its revival in the nineteenth century in modified form. The office of *rural dean* is also an ancient one but its duties were gradually subsumed by those of an archdeacon. It was revived in 1836 and the rural dean now presides over the Ruridecanal Chapter, which comprises the incumbents and clergy of a deanery, and is co-chairman of a deanery synod. An *area dean* is the urban equivalent of a rural dean.

A *rector* was originally an INCUMBENT who received the 'Great Tithes': all the customary offerings and dues of his PARISH. He was responsible for the chancel and the rectory and for providing service books and VESTMENTS. In many instances, benefices were annexed by corporate bodies such as monastic or collegiate foundations who then received the Great (or Rectorial) Tithes, the Lesser (or Vicarial) Tithes going to a *vicar* who was appointed by them to administer the parish. Following the Dissolution of the Monasteries, many monastic estates became the property of laymen who also acquired the right to nominate vicars (subject to a bishop's approval), together with responsibility for maintaining the chancel and vicarage. TITHES were virtually abolished in 1936 and a vicar is now appointed to all new livings, the designation rector being applicable to the incumbent of a new joint benefice or united parish or on the creation of a team ministry. A PARSON was originally a rector, though the term is now applied also to a vicar. Before the seventeenth century a *curate* was any minister who had the cure of souls, especially a deputy who was in full charge of a parish but could be removed by his employer. Since then the term has come to mean an assistant to the incumbent or an unbeneficed clergyman. A PERPETUAL CURATE was the minister of a parish in which the great tithes had been annexed by an ecclesiastical body or lay person.

CHAPLAINS
Chaplains were 'chapel priests' without benefices who ministered to royal and magnatial households or bodies corporate such as hospitals and nunneries. Today, they perform a similar function in relation to the armed forces and prisons or are the private secretaries of bishops.

See also ADDRESS (FORMS OF), CHURCH OF ENGLAND, CROCKFORD, HERALDRY (ECCLESIASTICAL), MAJOR ORDERS, MINOR ORDERS, SIGNATURES (BISHOPS AND ARCHBISHOPS) *and* VESTMENTS
Further reading:
Hinnels, J.R., *Dictionary of Religions*, London, 1984
Livingstone, E., *The Concise Oxford Dictionary of the Christian Church*, Oxford, 1983
Wilson, A.N., (ed.), *The Faber Book of Church and Clergy*, London, 1992

CLERGY (PRE-REFORMATION) *see* MEDIEVAL CHURCH, MAJOR ORDERS, MINOR ORDERS, REFORMATION *and* WALES, THE CHURCH IN

CLERGY RESIDENCES REPAIR ACT (1776) *see* DIOCESAN RECORDS

CLERICAL COLLAR *see* VESTMENTS

CLERICAL RECORDS *see* ARCHIVES

CLERK IN HOLY ORDERS The formal designation of a bishop, priest or deacon in the Church of England.

CLIPPING A festive ceremony, almost certainly of pagan origin, in which parishioners (or the children of the parish) form an unbroken human chain round their church to protect it against the power of the Devil (from the Old English *ycleping* meaning 'embracing'). Clipping often took place on Shrove Tuesday, though the ceremony at Painswick in Gloucestershire is still held annually on the Sunday following 19 September and is accompanied by the singing of a clipping hymn and the 'doling out' of clipping buns. Similar Shrove-tide ceremonies were held at Ellesmere and Wellington in Shropshire until the nineteenth century. At Wellington, a boys' band gathered in the town centre before making its way to the church, 'each lad blowing lustily on his tin trumpet' – presumably to drive away the evil spirits before the clipping of the church. (Visitors to Painswick should note that the clipping service has nothing to do with the annual trimming of the ninety-nine YEW TREES which grace the splendid churchyard.)

CLIPSHAM STONE A honey-coloured stone quarried in the Clipsham region of the county of Rutland.

CLOCHERIUM A detached belfry.

CLOCK JACKS *see* CLOCKS

CLOCKS Clocks are a feature of many parish churches where a dial or dials may be found on one or more faces of a church tower. Indeed, the sound of a distant church bell intoning the hours and quarter-hours is, for many, a powerful evocation of rural England. And yet, in most parishes, striking clocks are a comparatively recent innovation.

In the Middle Ages, the demands of the monastic timetable (*see* HORARIUM), and its division into canonical hours (*see* HOURS, CANONICAL), led to the development of time-keeping devices and, in particular, to mechanical clocks. These were large, weight-driven structures fitted into towers (*turret clocks*) or positioned in the transept of an abbey church near the night stairs which led to the monks' dormitory (*dorter*). They had no dial or clock-hands but sounded a signal which alerted a keeper to toll a bell. In England, the first mechanical clock was installed at Canterbury in 1292; while in *c.* 1320, Richard of Wallingford, a Benedictine monk of St. Albans, constructed a clock which not only indicated the time in hours and minutes but also showed the tides, the phases of the moon and the position of the sun and planets. Striking clocks were a fourteenth-century development of the turret clock and, by the end of the fifteenth century, most major monastic churches and cathedrals possessed one, as did several large town churches. Striking clocks used a weighted arm (*foliot*) as an oscillating fly-wheel controlled by a toothed wheel and an escapement mechanism.

A sophisticated (and charming) development of the striking clock was the clock jack (or *Jack of the Clock*) in which the bells which mark the hours and quarter hours are struck by carved and painted figures. In Britain, the earliest example is believed to be the late fourteenth-century clock jack at Wells Cathedral where two 'quarter jacks' strike the quarter hours and 'Jack Blandifer' the hours. The clock jack at St. Mary Steps, Exeter, is one of the most delightful. On the clock face the hours are marked by a circle of numerals and, within the circle, a sun on a rotating dial indicates the hour. The minutes are shown by a clock hand, one end of which is tipped with a crescent moon. In a niche above the dial stand two quarter jacks, each holding a pike and hammer with which the quarters are struck, and between them a seated figure nods his head with each stroke of the hour. There are other splendid examples (all working still) at Rye in Sussex, St. Thomas at Salisbury, Wimborne Minster in Dorset and All Saints, Leicester.

For the most part, country parishes depended on a simple sundial, scratched on the south wall of the church, to remind the faithful of their obligations (*see* SUNDIALS) and, from the seventeenth century, horizontal sundials were sometimes affixed to the truncated shafts of CHURCHYARD CROSSES. Of course, there was no such thing as universal time: most people rose with the sun and retired when it set. Consequently, even in the few villages which possessed a striking clock, the sundial was the only reliable time-keeper. Very few clocks had dials before the seventeenth century and even then most had only an hour hand until *c.* 1780. Roman numerals were used for the hours, often within an outer circle of minutes in Arabic numerals, until after 1800. At West Acre in Suffolk the dial bears the words 'Watch and Pray' – twelve letters instead of numerals. For some reason there is a convention that dials should be painted black and that numerals and hands should be gilded though, of course, there are exceptions.

Elaborate projecting clocks became popular in the seventeenth century and Sir Christopher Wren (1632–1723) incorporated them most effectively in many of his towers: at St. Mary-le-Bow in Cheapside and St. Magnus, London Bridge for example. Clocks of various styles may also be found within the church itself, most often in a vestry, ringing chamber or former school-room (*see* TOWERS). For the most part these date from the nineteenth century, earlier (and more valuable) examples having been removed for reasons of security.

See also BELLS
Further reading:
Beeson, C., *English Church Clocks 1280–1850*, Chichester, 1971

CLOISTER A number of former monastic churches, now adopted for parochial use, have retained at least some vestige of their cloisters. From the Latin *claustrum* meaning 'an enclosed place' (hence claustrophobia), the cloister is a rectangular court surrounded by a covered and colonnaded passageway, the outer elevation of which is formed by the walls of surrounding buildings. The length of passageway on each side of the quadrangle is known as an *alley*, and the open area contained within is the *cloister garth*. This usually incorporates a well and would have been laid out with vegetable beds and herb gardens (though the Carthusians used the cloister garth as a burial ground). The cloister was usually on the salubrious south side of the monastic church (though not invariably – see Gloucester below). It was covered with a lean-to roof set against the south aisle of the church and surrounding cloistral buildings. In some instances the upper storeys of these buildings project over the cloister to form the roof. Early Cistercian cloisters were built of wood, later to be replaced with stone. The arched openings in the colonnade were filled with a combination of glass and wooden shutters, and the northern side, with its abundance of natural light, was often provided with *carrels* for individual study. Carrels were usually wooden cubicles, often made draft-free by the provision of doors and canopies, each containing a desk and bench and a clear or unglazed south-facing window by which to work. At monasteries with strong academic traditions, additional carrels were sometimes provided in the eastern or western alleys of the cloister, and a recessed *armarium* for the storage of books. *Scriptoria* (for the writing and illumination of manuscripts) were usually located in the south alley which benefited from pure, northern light. One of the finest cloisters in England is that at the former Benedictine monastery of St. Peter (now the Cathedral) at Gloucester. Built to the north of the abbey church in 1375–1410 (because the town cemetery lay to the south), the cloister has one of the earliest fan-vaults in England. In the south alley are twenty recessed stone carrels of the *scriptorium* and along the western half of the north alley is a superb *LAVATORIUM*, with its own miniature fan-vault: a stone trough for the washing of hands before meals (taken in the adjacent FRATER) and a nearby *aumbry* (recessed cupboard) which contained a supply of dry towels.

CLOSE *see* PRECINCT

CLOSED CHURCHYARDS A closed churchyard

is one which is no longer able to accommodate burials and has been closed by an Order in Council. In England, a PAROCHIAL CHURCH COUNCIL is responsible for 'keeping [a closed churchyard] in decent order and its walls and fences in good repair.' However, a parochial church council may serve a written request on the appropriate minor authority (either a parish council, a community council or the chairman of a parish meeting) to accept responsibility for the maintenance of the churchyard. A parish or community council, or a parish meeting, may then resolve to transfer this responsibility to a district council, providing that such a resolution is communicated to the parochial church council and district council within the expiration of three months. (*Local Government Act 1972*, section 215).
See also BURIALS *and* MINUTES

CLOSE ROLLS These contain registered copies of private letters and documents of the royal Court of Chancery, such as conveyances, writs of summons to Parliament and orders to royal officers. Letters Close were 'closed' (folded and secured with a seal) unlike Letters Patent which were 'open' and addressed 'To all and singular . . .'. Copies of these documents were made on parchment sheets which were stitched together and stored in rolls: one or more for each regnal year. They are housed at the Public Record Office (*for* address *see* APPENDIX II).

CLUBS *see* FRIENDLY SOCIETIES

CLUNCH Chalk for building quarried from the hard, grey-coloured beds of the Lower Chalk, sawn into blocks and dried. Often used in conjunction with brick dressings in buildings dating from the Middle Ages to the nineteenth century.

CLUNIACS Founded by William of Aquitaine in 910, the monastery of Cluny in Burgundy was that most venerated by the Norman kings (*see* RULE). Cluniac monasticism of the late eleventh century was marked by a preoccupation with the liturgical: effectively to the exclusion of all intellectual, artistic or educational aspirations. The abbey was described as 'a world in itself, given wholly to the worship of God in a setting of incomparable splendour and untouched by secular intrigue'. The first Cluniac priory in England was founded in 1077 by William de Warenne at Lewes in East Sussex. Thereafter, a further thirty-five houses were founded, many as cells of Norman priories; but none, other than that at Burmondsey (1087), was to rival Lewes.

King Stephen (1097–1154) was buried in his Cluniac abbey at Faversham, Kent. No doubt he had in mind the Cluniacs' reputation as 'ferrymen of departing souls': it was they who instituted All Souls Day (2 November) as an appropriate sequel to All Saints Day (1 November). The importance of the Cluniacs in medieval England lay not in the size or number of their houses but in the prominence and influence attained by so many of their brethren.
Further reading:
Cowdrey, H., *The Cluniacs and the Gregorian Reform*, Oxford, 1970.

COADE STONE Artificial 'stone', with the appearance of hard-grained limestone, made in the late eighteenth century and early nineteenth century by Coade and Seely of London. Coade stone is fired in a kiln and is, therefore, stoneware. When removed from its mould, the material is fairly soft but becomes 'leatherhard' in contact with air. It is ideally suited to detailed decorative work (especially heraldry) for, unlike most natural stone, it is easily incised with a stylus before firing and, when used out of doors, is not susceptible to weathering. Repeat motifs can be moulded separately, applied to the surface by means of slip (liquefied clay) and fixed in place by firing.

COAT OF ARMS Correctly, this term should be applied only to the shield of arms, the design of which was sometimes repeated on the surcoat or jupon of a medieval armiger: hence 'coat' of arms. But it is now used conventionally to describe the combined elements of SHIELD, HELMET, WREATH, MANTLING, CREST and (where appropriate) CREST CORONET, CORONETS OF PEERS and SUPPORTERS which form an heraldic ACHIEVEMENT OF ARMS. When describing a coat of arms using the terminology of ARMORY (*blazon*), the left side (when viewed from the front) is the *dexter* and the right, the *sinister*. A charge placed in the upper portion of a shield is said to be *in chief* and one in the lower portion is *in base*.
See also HERALDIC CHARGES *and* HERALDRY

COB An ancient building material, formed of mud, marl, chalk or gravel with dung and some form of binding material such as hair or chopped straw, used in the construction of buildings and walls from the Dark Ages to the present century. Cob walls were built in 'wet' layers of about 60 cm (2 feet) on a foundation of moorstone or boulders, each layer being allowed to set for at least seven days before the next was applied. Cob was often strengthened by the addition of horsehair or cowhair and the walls limewashed for protection and provided with a water-repellent 'skirt' of tar at the base. A sound roof of thatch or tile is necessary to prevent a cob wall washing away into the earth from whence it came and eaves protrude to ensure that rainwater from the roof is projected away from the surface of the wall and does not accumulate at the base. Cob buildings are particularly common in Cornwall, Devon and Dorset where local chalk, pebbles or flint are often included to add substance to the cob. Most surviving cob buildings date from the seventeenth to the early nineteenth centuries and include an occasional parsonage.

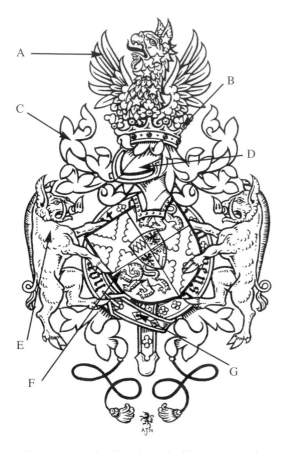

The arms of John Tiptoft, Earl of Worcester and Knight of the Garter (c. 1427–70). Sometime Constable of England, scholar, humanist, patron of Caxton and avant-courier of the Renaissance, Tiptoft's ruthless and bestial cruelty earned him the sobriquet 'Butcher of England'. The Tiptoft arms, Argent a Saltire engrailed Gules, are quartered with those of his mother, heir of Edward, Lord Chorleton, Or a Lion rampant Gules. On an escutcheon of pretence are the arms of his first wife Cecily, daughter of Richard Nevill, Earl of Salisbury (4 Gules a Saltire Argent and a Label gobony Argent and Azure), and Alice, daughter and heir of Thomas Montacute, Earl of Salisbury (1 Argent three Lozenges in fess Gules) and heir of Monthermer (2 and 3 Or an Eagle displayed Vert).

A Crest
B Crest coronet
C Mantling
D Helmet
E Supporters
F Shield of Arms
G Garter Insignia

COCKATRICE see BEASTS (HERALDIC)

COCKFIGHTING and COCKTHRESHING see CHURCHYARDS

CODICIL An addition to a will, explaining, modifying or revoking it in whole or in part (*see* PROBATE).

CODICOLOGY The study of the materials, techniques and personnel in manuscript and book production.

COENOBITE An ANCHORITE who occupies a separate dwelling, and observes a rule of silence, within a monastic community.

COFFER A small chest, usually for securing money or valuables (*see* BOXES and CHESTS).

COFFERING Decoration of a ceiling or vault, or the underside of an arch, with a pattern of sunken square or polygonal ornamental panels.

COFFIN PATHS see CORPSE ROADS

COFFINS see BURIALS and MORTSAFE

COFFIN STONE see CORPSE ROAD, LICH-GATE and MORTSTONE

COFFINS (STONE) Distinguished members or confraters (*see* CONFRATERNITY) of religious communities were sometimes buried in a stone coffin which was sunk in the floor of an abbey church, chapter house or cloister so that its lid (often finely carved) was level with the floor. These may occasionally be found where they were buried though in most monastic ruins they have been removed and the lids separated from the (now empty) stone coffins.
See also MORTSAFE

COFFIN STOOLS A pair of simple (usually three-legged) stools on which a coffin was placed before and during a burial service. Thomas Hardy (in *The Woodlanders*) tells how, in the late nineteenth century, 'It had been customary for every well-to-do villager, whose tenure was . . . in any way more permanent than that of a mere cotter, to keep a pair of these stools for the use of his own dead; but changes had led to the discontinuance of the custom and the stools were frequently made use of . . .' for more domestic purposes.

COIF (i) A close-fitting cap or hood (*see* COSTUME). (ii) A similar cap of mail or leather (*see* ARMOUR). A *coif-de-mailles* is a Balaclava-type hood of mail.

COLLAR BEAM A horizontal beam spanning a roof and tying the principal RAFTERS together (*see* ROOFS (TIMBER)).

COLLAR PURLIN A timber running the length of the centre of a roof beneath the COLLAR BEAMS (*see also* PURLIN *and* ROOFS(TIMBER)).

COLLARS From the late fourteenth century, collars incorporating heraldic devices, and sometimes with pendant livery BADGES, were worn to indicate adherence to a royal or noble house, and (by implication) to a political cause.

It seems likely that collars were originally granted as marks of favour and that some became insignia of office: the collar of SS is still worn by certain officers of the Crown, for example, including the Kings of Arms.

This famous collar is of obscure origin. It is composed of, or studded with, esses and was probably worn and given as livery by 'time-honoured Lancaster', John of Gaunt, and later by Henry IV, with the swan of De Bohun as a pendant. Between Henry's return from exile and his seizure of the throne he distributed 192 collars of SS to his retainers and later ordained that '. . . all the sons of the king, dukes, earls, barons and baronets, might use the livery of our Lord the King of his collar as well in his absence as in his presence; and all other knights and esquires should use it only in the presence of the King'. The collar comprised a strip of leather, silk or velvet set with SS in silver gilt, silver or latten, and ending in two buckles linked by an ornamental trefoil from which a badge could be suspended. The SS letters were of several different shapes, sizes and styles, sometimes reversed or horizontal, and were set at varying distances from each other. In earlier versions the SS appear to have been attached to the material, possibly by rivets, and the collar fitted tightly over the camail when worn with armour. Later collars were made entirely of metal with the SS elaborately strung or linked together. The collar of SS remained the cognizance of the House of Lancaster for fifty years and the Tudors adapted the device, alternating the Lancastrian SS with Beaufort portcullises and with a Tudor Rose or portcullis as a pendant. There are over one hundred late medieval brasses and effigies in which the SS collar shows that those they commemorate owed allegiance to the House of Lancaster, and yet the meaning of the SS badge itself remains a mystery.

The corresponding Yorkist collars are composed of alternate suns and roses with a white lion pendant (for Mortimer) or, under Richard III, a white boar. There are nearly 100 examples of effigies and brasses with Yorkist collars but only one boar pendant has survived – that of Sir Ralph Fitzherbert at Norbury in Derbyshire.

Yorkist collar on effigy of Lord Saye and Sele (d. 1471) at Broughton, Oxfordshire.

Lancastrian collar on effigy of Elizabeth Wykham, Broughton, Oxfordshire.

These fifteenth-century Yorkist and Lancastrian collars are of particular interest to historians for they are indicative of preferment and allegiance, though their depiction in an effigy or brass does not necessarily mean that they were actually presented and may imply simply long service to a particular royal house (*see* BRASSES *and* EFFIGIES).

The Massyngberd brass at Gunby in Lincolnshire is interesting in that it is possible to discern that the brass was made without a collar and was later cut for its insertion. Tudor SS collars were generally more substantial and were essentially chains of office rather than symbols of allegiance.

A pair of effigies, apparently husband and wife, at Broughton, Oxfordshire provides the local historian with a fascinating instance of mistaken identity. The 'husband' wears a Yorkist collar of suns and roses while his 'wife' has a Lancastrian SS collar: hardly a recipe for matrimonial bliss! However, research will reveal that the effigies have been moved and are of Elizabeth Wykeham and the second Lord Saye and Sele who was killed at Barnet in 1471 and was probably the husband of Elizabeth's grand-daughter.

Plain collars may also be found on several

fifteenth century effigies and (more often) on brasses. These are likely to be erased Lancastrian or Yorkist collars, while others were never completed, suggesting that a family may have been 'hedging its bets' when commissioning a memorial at a time of political uncertainty. It has also been suggested that some plain collars represent strips of leather or cloth on which livery colours were enamelled or painted: that on the brass of John Leventhorp at Sawbridge-worth, Hertfordshire, for example.

It seems likely that magnates also had their own collars and pendants but very few of these have survived in effigies or brasses. The brass of Thomas, Lord Berkeley at Wotton-under-Edge in Gloucester-shire (*c.* 1417), for example, shows him wearing a collar of mermaids and it is known that this device was used by the Berkeleys from at least 1322. But 'Mermaids of the Sea' are also referred to in the Black Prince's will and it is possible that the Berkeley collar may therefore be indicative of Thomas's attachment to the Black Prince.

Further reading:
Friar, S., *A New Dictionary of Heraldry*, Sherborne and London, 1987
——, *Heraldry for the Local Historian and Genealogist*, Stroud, 1992

COLLATION (i) A light meal permitted on days of fasting. (ii) Institution to an ecclesiastical benefice when the ORDINARY (usually a bishop) is himself the PATRON or when a patron has failed to carry out his responsibilities within six months of the vacancy occurring.

COLLECT A short prayer, of one sentence and conveying one petition, usually read on an appointed day. In the Church of England, the collects are set out in the *Book of Common Prayer* and mostly derive from medieval sources, though some were Thomas Cranmer's original compositions.

COLLEGE A chapter of secular clergy who held services in a COLLEGIATE CHURCH. University colleges also supported scholars through their studies.
See CANTARIST, CHANTRY COLLEGES *and* UNIVERSITIES

COLLEGE OF ARMS The Corporation of the Officers of Arms in Ordinary, comprising the thirteen kings, heralds and pursuivants of arms, is part of the Royal Household and exercises authority in England, Wales and Northern Ireland for matters heraldic. Royal officers of arms have acted as a body corporate since the early fifteenth century but did not receive a charter until 1483/4. The College was reincorporated in 1555 at Derby House, near St Paul's Cathedral, and maintains a magnificent collection of heraldic and genealogical records and documents. There is no public access to these, however, and enquiries should be addressed to the Officer-in-Waiting.
For address *see* APPENDIX II.
See also FACULTY *and* HERALDRY
Further reading:
Wagner, Sir A., *The Records and Collections of the College of Arms*, 1952
——, *Heralds of England*, 1967 (re-issued 1985)
Catalogue of Manuscripts in the College of Arms: Collections (Vol. II), London, 1988

COLLEGIATE CHURCH A church which is endowed for a chapter of canons and/or prebendaries but is not a cathedral.
See also CHANTRY COLLEGES

COLLET A decorative ring or collar: on the stem of a candlestick or chalice, for example.

COLONNADE A row of columns supporting arches or an ENTABLATURE.

COLONETTE A diminutive column.

COLOPHON A brief passage at the conclusion of a hand-written document, usually giving the name of the scribe and sometimes including an expression of relief and thanks that the task has been concluded.

COLOURS (HERALDIC) The metals, colours and furs used in HERALDRY are known as tinctures.

The metals are *Or* (gold, often depicted as yellow) and *Argent* (silver, usually depicted as white).

The colours are *Gules* (red), *Azure* (blue), *Sable* (black), *Vert* (green), *Purpure* (purple) and *Murrey* (mulberry). The so-called 'stains' are *Sanguine* (blood-red) and *Tenné* (tawny). These supposedly 'stain' the nobility of arms and are rare.

The most common furs, each of which is possessed of several variations, are *Ermine* (white with black 'tails') and *Vair* (white and blue 'pelts').

Where a charge is represented in its natural colours it is described as *proper*.

Metals and colours are subject to the tincture convention. This is the fundamental 'rule' of heraldry: **that metal shall not lie on metal, nor colour on colour**. This convention seems to have been universally accepted from the earliest times and is clearly intended to facilitate the accurate identification of heraldic devices at a distance. A blue lion on a silver background (*field*) is clearer than a blue lion on black, for example. The convention applies only to charges that are placed **upon** a field or another charge. It does not apply to varied fields (composed of a number of different metals and colours), to borders (*bordures*) or to furs.

HERALDIC TINTURES AND TRICKING

Hatching

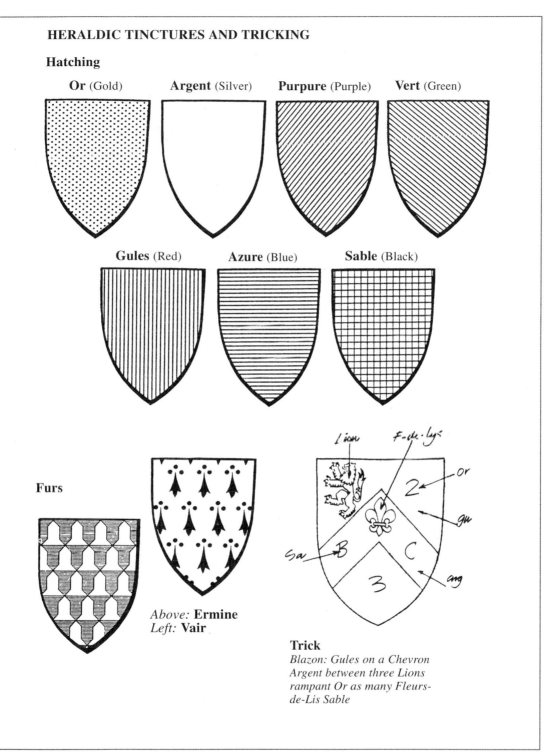

Or (Gold) **Argent** (Silver) **Purpure** (Purple) **Vert** (Green)

Gules (Red) **Azure** (Blue) **Sable** (Black)

Furs

Above: **Ermine**
Left: **Vair**

Trick
Blazon: Gules on a Chevron Argent between three Lions rampant Or as many Fleurs-de-Lis Sable

Exceptions will be found and these are usually BRISURES or AUGMENTATIONS OF HONOUR. As such they are intended to draw attention to the coat of arms.

The tinctures of uncoloured coats of arms (those engraved on silver or in bookplates, for example) may often be determined by reference to the system of *hatching* developed by Sylvester Petra Sancta, a seventeenth-century writer on heraldry (*see illustration*). In documents the tinctures may be shown by means of a 'trick' – a line drawing in which abbreviations are substituted for tinctures and numbers or letters for charges.

COLOURS (LITURGICAL) Colours used in vestments, altar frontals etc. to mark the liturgical seasons and festivals:

White: Signifying joy: Christmas, Easter, Corpus Christi, the Feast of St Mary, Trinity and All Saints day (1 November) and feasts of saints who were not martyrs.
Red: Associated with fire: Whitsunday (Pentecost), Palm Sunday, Holy Cross Day and feasts of saints who were martyrs.
Green: Signifying life and hope: the periods following Trinity and Epiphany and on weekdays when no other feast or fast is kept.
Violet: Signifying penitence: Advent and Lent (in some churches unbleached linen is used during Lent to represent penitence), Rogation and Ember days.
Black: Good Friday and All Souls' Day (2 November), funerals and requiems.

COLOURS, REGIMENTAL *see* FLAGS

COLUMN An upright masonry or brick support used for structural purposes or architectural adornment. Unlike a PILLAR (or *pier*) a column invariably has both a BASE and CAPITAL. A column may be used singly, in pairs or in groups (*see* ARCADE *and* COLONNADE) or it may be wholly or partly attached to a wall or to another column. Pairs of columns are described as *coupled* and a column which has part of its surface attached to a wall is said to be *engaged, applied* or *attached*. A central shaft surrounded by a number of slender columns (not necessarily attached to each other) is described as *grouped, clustered* or compound. Twisted BAROQUE columns are sometimes described as 'barley-sugar' or *Solomonic* (after their alleged use in the Temple of Solomon) and when entwined with vine leaves they are *wreathed*. In the CLASSICAL ORDER, a column is divided into capital, shaft, base and plinth. A *fluted shaft* is one which is cut in vertical channels and columns and

piers may be *annulated* with narrow bands encircling the shaft.
See also BAY

COMBATANT *see* AFFRONTED *and* BEASTS (HERALDIC)

COMMANDERY A manorial estate and hospice belonging to the military order of the Knights Hospitaller of St. John of Jerusalem, usually staffed by a small complement of knights with a chaplain and servants. Such manors enjoyed certain privileges: the parish of the commandery at Dinmore in Herefordshire is entirely free of tithe, the owners of the estate benefiting from immunities granted to the Hospitallers by Pope Paschal II in 1113. Dinmore is known as an ex-parochial or *peculiar* parish for, although it possesses a parish church (one of only four dedicated to St. John of Jerusalem), it forms no part of a diocese neither do the bishop or the ecclesiastical authorities have any jurisdiction there; indeed until the mid-nineteenth century the parishioners were exempted from paying local rates. The commandery at Dinmore ranked as third or fourth in importance among the fifty or so similar Hospitaller commanderies established in England and Wales in the twelfth and thirteenth centuries. Each was in the charge of a knight of the Order, the gift of a commandery being the usual reward for outstanding service in the Crusades. In addition to providing income for the Order by the management of the estates, commanderies were regional military training centres and *hospices* or places of rest for those who returned injured or invalided from the Holy Land. They also afforded shelter and refreshment to travellers and sustenance to the sick and needy. Commanderies accumulated extensive tracts of land, acquired both from the Templars following their suppression in 1310 and from the endowments of *corrodians*: those who were not members of the Order but enjoyed residential benefits in return for their generosity (*see* CORRODY). At Dinmore, as at other commanderies, local field-names evoke its past in Knights' Grove, Great St. John's Meadow etc. In the same county, at Hereford, the ruins of the fourteenth-century commandery were converted to ALMSHOUSES (the Coningsby Hospital) in 1640 by Sir Thomas Coningsby who had acquired the nearby Dominican friary at the Dissolution.

The parallel order of the Knights Templar possessed similar establishments called *preceptories* though, following the suppression of the Templars in 1312, these were transferred to the Knights Hospitaller who also adopted the term to describe some of their later commanderies. Typically, the Hospitaller preceptory at Chibburn in Northumberland was built around a central courtyard approached through an arched gateway in a northern two-storey range of domestic buildings, and with a chapel to the south and dwelling house to the west. (*See also* ST. JOHN OF JERUSALEM, ORDER OF *and* TEMPLAR, KNIGHTS)

COMMEMORATION Until recently, when two ecclesiastical feasts fell on the same day, the lesser of the two was 'commemorated' by including some of its prayers in the service – following the corresponding prayers of the feast being observed. *See also* FEASTS (ECCLESIASTICAL)

COMMENDAM A vacant benefice could be held temporarily by an individual (who might be a layman) who would receive the revenues of that benefice *in commendam*. The term came to be applied to those benefices which were held more or less permanently by a bishop or other dignitary.

COMMENDATOR A system, dating from the eighth century, whereby a layman was appointed to the title and income of a monastic superior in return for military protection. Once the original purpose was lost, the system was often abused as a means of rewarding the favourites of a king or pope.

COMMISSARY COURT A diocesan court concerned with matters of PROBATE which fell entirely within the diocese.

COMMISSIONERS' CHURCHES *see* NINETEENTH-CENTURY ARCHITECTURE

COMMON PRAYER, BOOK OF (BCP) The official service book of the Church of England and one of the finest works in the English language. The BCP contains the daily offices of Morning and Evening Prayer, the forms for the administration of the SACRAMENTS and other rites, the PSALTER and (since 1552) the ORDINAL. The book was compiled in response to Thomas Cranmer (1489–1556) and others who wished to simplify and condense the Latin service books of the medieval Church (*see* SARUM, USE OF) and to produce in English a convenient and authoritative guide for priest and people.

The first BCP (Edward VI) was authorised by the Act of Uniformity in 1549 but was revised, following Protestant criticism, and a second version issued in 1552/3 (also Edward VI). Although, with the accession Queen Mary (1553–8), it was never actually brought into use, the 1552 Prayer Book marks the establishment of Protestantism in the territories of the Crown of England. It abandoned TRANSUBSTANTIATION, thereby confirming the distinction between the MASS and the communion service which is the essence of the distinction between Protestantism and Roman Catholicism. The 1552 Prayer Book was reissued in 1559 (Elizabeth I)

in a slightly amended form and with the Ornaments Rubric attached (a ruling that the ornaments of the Church and its ministers should be those in use 'by the authority of Parliament in the second year of the reign of King Edward VI'). During the Commonwealth the BCP was replaced by *The Directory of Public Worship*, but at the Restoration the Act of Uniformity (1662) authorised a BCP which including the 1611 (King James) Authorised Version of the BIBLE for the Epistles and Gospels, and this has remained in use (almost without alteration) to the present day.

A Welsh translation of the main texts of the Prayer Book (Kynniver Llith a Ban) was published in 1551. This was the work of William Salesbury who, in the previous year, had translated the Old Testament into Welsh (*see* BIBLES)

In 1906 a Royal Commission on Ecclesiastical Discipline recommended that the Prayer Book should be revised but the Convocations decided to retain the 1662 book and to incorporate all changes in a new book, the use of which should be entirely permissive. Although the new book was approved by the Church Assembly, it was rejected by the House of Commons in 1927 and again (following further minor revisions) in 1928. In 1955 the Archbishops appointed a Liturgical Commission to prepare a revision of the BCP and, in 1965, the Prayer Book (Alternative and Other Services) Measure authorised experimentation. This was repealed by the Church of England (Worship and Doctrine) Measure of 1974 which allows the use of alternative services on a permanent basis. These are set out in *The Alternative Service Book* (ASB) of 1980. The decision, whether or not to adopt the new services, is a matter for parochial church councils, subject to the advice of the incumbent.

In 1994, the Synod agreed that a new 'core' Prayer Book should be published by the year 2000. This is to include elements of both the *Book of Common Prayer* and the *Alternative Service Book*. *See also* LITURGY, RUBRIC, STATE SERVICES *and* WALES, THE MEDIEVAL CHURCH IN *For* the Prayer Book Society *see* APPENDIX II. *Further reading:*
Taylor, N., *For Services Rendered: An Anthology in Thanksgiving for the Book of Common Prayer*, Cambridge, 1995

COMMONWEALTH, THE *see* SEVENTEENTH-CENTURY CHURCH

COMMUNION *see* EUCHARIST

COMMUNION IN BOTH KINDS *see* EUCHARIST

COMMUNION LINENS Liturgical cloths which include the *Communion Veil* (c. 45 cm square), the

Purificator for cleansing the chalice (*c.* 26 cm), the stiffened *Palla* with which the chalice is covered (*c.* 15 cm), the *Corporal* on which the bread and wine are placed and consecrated (*c.* 50 cm) and the *Lavabo Towel* for the washing and drying of the celebrant's fingers after the offering of the oblations in the EUCHARIST (60 × 27 cm).

See also CHRISM, PLATE *and* VESPERALE

COMMUNION PLATE *see* PLATE

COMMUNION RAILS Communion rails were introduced after the REFORMATION to protect the COMMUNION TABLE when it became more accessible and therefore vulnerable to profanation, especially by stray DOGS. Communion rails were particularly popular in the seventeenth century at a time when the Church, led by Archbishop Laud, was resisting the removal of communion tables into the nave, as advocated by the Puritans. Many examples are therefore of the early seventeenth century and of wood or date from the early twentieth century when CANCELLI were re-introduced into the English church by Sir Ninian Comper (1864–1960). They usually extend across the chancel but sometimes enclose the communion table on three sides, as at Elmsett in Suffolk, or (rarely) on four sides, as at Lyddington in Leicestershire. The balusters may provide a clue to dating: the twisted type are usually from the second half of the seventeenth century, as at Branscombe, Devon.

COMMUNION TABLES *see* ALTARS *and* REFORMATION, THE

COMMUNITY, USE OF CHURCH BY *see* CHURCH AND COMMUNITY

COMPLINE (COMPLETORIUM) The last of the Canonical Hours observed before a religious community retired for the night. Compline was established in the Benedictine Rule and included the *Nunc Dimittis*, a short lesson, psalms and a hymn, *Te lucis ante terminum*. It was preceded by confession and concluded by the singing of an anthem of Our Lady and the sprinkling of holy water as the brethren filed through the cloister to the dormitory (*dorter*) – usually at eight thirty or an hour earlier during the winter months. The essential elements of Compline were incorporated into the service of Evensong in the *Book of Common Prayer*.

See also VESPERALE

Jacobean communion rails at Cerne Abbas, Dorset.

COMPOSITE *see* CLASSICAL ORDER

COMPOUND PIER *see* COLUMN

COMPRECATION The intercession of saints on behalf of the Church.

COMPTON CENSUS In 1676 parish priests were required to return a census of parishioners to their archbishop, together with details of those who absented themselves from worship. Where they have survived, these returns are now deposited among DIOCESAN RECORDS.

COMPURGATION A system by which an accused person might call upon twelve 'oath helpers' to vouch (on oath) for his innocence or good character.

CONCORDANCE A reference book containing all the quotations from the Scriptures in which a particular word is found. The best known concordance is that compiled by Alexander Cruden (1701–70) in 1737.

CONCORDAT An agreement between ecclesiastical and civil authorities regarding a matter of mutual concern.

CONDUCTIO SEDILIUM *see* PEW RENTS

CONDUCTUS A type of sacred or secular choral composition of the twelfth and thirteenth centuries, the precursor of the MOTET. At this time, the art of musical composition was that of adding voice-parts to an existing melody, the *canto fermo*. In the *conductus*, the words sung were confined to the voice singing the *canto fermo* while other voices (usually two in number) vocalised on the principal vowel of each word.
See also PLAINSONG

CONDUIT A trough or pipe for conveying water, usually from a central conduit house where a raised tank provided water pressure. There are good examples at Durham and at Beaulieu in Hampshire and Monkton Farleigh in Wiltshire. Monastic water and drainage systems were often complex and extremely efficient. Stone-lined conduits may have been revealed by the subsequent removal of conventual buildings: as at Tintern Abbey in Gwent. The well-known 'Conduit' in the market place at Sherborne in Dorset was constructed as a LAVATORIUM in the cloister of the nearby abbey in the early sixteenth century and moved, following the Dissolution in 1539, to form a small market house and public fountain. Friaries (which were usually established in towns) were especially noted for providing public conduits of running water.
See also DRAINS

CONFEDERATION An obit roll of *c.* 1230, recording the death of the first prioress of Hedingham, was conveyed to 120 religious houses all of which acknowledged its receipt with the words: 'May the soul of Lady Lucy, prioress of Hedingham and the souls of all the faithful departed, by the mercy of God, rest in peace. We concede to her the benefits of our church. We pray for you; pray for us.' Thus, confederations of abbeys formed spiritual unions, the members of which were visited annually by special messengers (*rotularius*) from each house, bearing lists of those for whom prayers were desired and exchanging expressions of greeting and mutual support.
See also CONFRATERNITY

CONFESSION (i) The tomb or shrine of a MARTYR or CONFESSOR or the church containing such a shrine. (ii) A declaration of religious belief. (iii) An acknowledgement of sin, either by an individual penitent in private or in the hearing of a priest (*auricular confession*), or by a congregation during an act of worship (*see* SHRIVE). The Fourth Lateran Council of 1215 made confession an annual obligation for all Christians. In religious communities, both the Mass and the offices began with a general confession and there were opportunities for confession of more particular offences (especially breaches of the Rule) before the community in Chapter. There were also provisions for auricular confession and spiritual council which were available to members of the community and to others. Following the REFORMATION, incumbents supervised public confessions which were required, not only by the ecclesiastical courts, but also by Quarter Sessions.

CONFESSIONAL (*or* SHRIVING PEW) An enclosed recess or stall within which a priest sits to hear confessions. Although now rarely used in the Church of England, such stalls may occasionally be found in churches. Confessional pews provide privacy and anonymity for the priest (and sometimes for the penitent) and are characterised by the presence (usually in one of the sides) of a latticed grille through which confession is made.

CONFESSOR (i) A priest who hears confessions. (ii) In the early Church, one who suffered for confessing his or her faith, but excluding those who were martyred (*see* MARTYR). The term was later applied also to holy men, especially those who were pronounced as such by the Pope.
See also SHRINES

CONFIRMATION A religious rite, confirming a baptised person as a member of the Church and thereby conveying '. . . in fuller measure the grace of the Holy Spirit'. There is evidence to suggest that by the third century the rite of confirmation was considered to be separate from that of BAPTISM. In the late medieval Church, confirmation usually took place shortly after the seventh birthday. Candidates renewed their baptismal vows and the bishop, extending his hands over them, prayed that they might receive the Holy Spirit. He then traced the sign of the cross in CHRISM on the forehead of each candidate (*see also* UNCTION). This practice was continued by the Church of England following the Reformation, though the use of oil ceased in 1549 and the sign of the Cross in 1552. The *Book of Common Prayer* requires that none is to be admitted to Communion until he is confirmed 'or ready and desirous to be confirmed'.

CONFISCATION INVENTORIES *see* CHANTRIES

CONFRATERNITY A rare honour and privilege by which a benefactor was granted honorary membership of a religious community. By becoming 'one of the family', a *confrater* could reasonably anticipate redemption through association with the piety, self-sacrifice and prayer of a religious house. He (or she) was usually allocated a place in the chapter house and granted a right of burial in the monastic cemetery: King John (1199–1216), for example, who made a late entry into the confraternity of Worcester, was buried in the priory church, clothed in a Benedictine habit. Wealth was not necessarily a prerequisite: long-serving employees were sometimes admitted to a confraternity.
See also BENEFACTORS, COFFINS (STONE) *and* CONFEDERATION

CONGREGATION (i) A body of people who habitually attend a particular church (*see* MEDIEVAL CHURCH). (ii) A religious society in contradistinction to a strict religious order. (iii) A group of monastic houses, formed since the end of the medieval period.

CONGREGATIONALIST A member of a church which originated in an early Puritan sect established by Robert Browne (*c.* 1550–*c.* 1633) in 1580. Browne denounced the established Church and suffered imprisonment before accompanying his followers to the Netherlands. He later returned to accept a benefice in the Church of England. The *Brownists* (or *Independents*) opposed state intervention in religious matters and maintained the autonomy of each local Church. As early as 1550 groups of Independents began meeting together as SEPARATISTS. They formed the backbone of Oliver Cromwell's model army and were forced into non-conformity at the Restoration. They expanded in the nineteenth century and in 1831 established the Congregationalist Union of England and Wales. In 1972 they joined with the PRESBYTERIANS to form the United Reform Church. Congregationalist registers are now at the Public Record Office, Chancery Lane and the central repository for their records is the Congregational Church of England and Wales in London (*see* APPENDIX II).

CONJUROR One who was reputedly a 'white witch'. This probably meant that he was skilled in treating sick animals – and sometimes people – using methods which may have been considered unconventional at the time. Inevitably, an aura of superstition surrounded such people: Conjuror Minterne, a seventeenth-century squire of Batcombe in Dorset, is said to have leapt on his horse from the surrounding downs and in so doing removed one of the pinnacles of the church tower. When he died he left instructions for his burial half in and half out of the church, the problem being solved by placing him beneath a wall. The truth is more likely that he was merely a homely quack called in by farmers when their beasts were ill.
See also WITCHCRAFT

CONSANGUINITY Persons who are descended from the same ancestor and are therefore related by blood. Within certain degrees consanguinity renders marriage unlawful (*for* the Table of Kindred and Affinity *see* AFFINITY).

CONSECRATION In the Christian Church, the term is possessed of a number of meanings: (i) To make or declare something sacred and thereby to dedicate it to a divine purpose. (ii) The act whereby the bread and wine of the Eucharist become the Body and Blood of Christ. (iii) The act whereby a bishop bestows on others some aspect of the inherent authority of his office (*see* ORDINATION). (iv) The solemn act of reserving Eucharistic vessels, altars and churches exclusively to the service of God.

CONSECRATION CROSSES In this context, the term *consecration* implies the dedication of a newly founded church to the exclusive service of God. Consecration crosses were, in the Middle Ages, a visible declaration of this dedication, symbolising the victory of Christ through the Passion and providing a defence against demonical powers. A full set of consecration crosses numbers twenty-four: three on each of the interior walls and a further twelve outside. These small red-painted crosses, each depicted within a circle, were usually incised in stone or cast in metal and affixed to the walls at a height of about 2.4 metres (8 feet), safe from defilement. When a bishop consecrated the church he would ascend to each cross in turn and anoint it with CHRISM: *Sanctifecetur hoc templum* – 'blessed be this church'. Each interior cross was provided with a candle bracket: twelve crosses with lighted candles symbolising the world's enlightenment through the twelve apostles. Some churches still possess one or two consecration crosses and at Edington in Wiltshire there are twenty-one: eleven inside and ten outside. Other notable (though incomplete) collections include those at Crosthwaite in Cumberland, Carleton Road in Norfolk and Holnest in Dorset. Exterior crosses are more susceptible to erosion and most have disappeared, though there are examples at Moorlynch in Somerset, Uffington in Berkshire and Ottery St. Mary in Devon. Consecration crosses may occasionally be found on surviving pre-Reformation altars: as at Partrishow in Powys where each of three altar stones bears an cross, despite sixteenth-century prohibition. Crosses on door-jambs are not consecration crosses, though these were also intended to ward off the devil.

Consecration cross at Sutton Bingham, Somerset.

CONSISTORY COURT A bishop's court concerned with diocesan ecclesiastical administration.
See also PROBATE *and* TWENTIETH-CENTURY CHURCHES

CONSOLE (i) The frame of an organ containing the keyboard(s), stops, pedals etc. The gallery in which the console is located is known as the *organ-loft* and, in larger churches, this may be reached by a stair (*see* ORGANS). (ii) A scroll-shaped BRACKET.

CONSTABLES *see* CHURCH AND COMMUNITY, LOCK-UP *and* PARISH CONSTABLE

CONSTITUTIONS Ecclesiastical regulations adopted by a provincial synod.

CONTEMPLATATIVE LIFE Descriptive of the austere life required of certain religious living under vows, which included a considerable element of contemplation and prayer.

CONVENT From the Latin *convenire* meaning 'to assemble', a convent is a religious community or the building in which it lives. Historically the term may be applied to communities of either sex, though current usage generally implies a house of nuns (*nunnery*).

CONVENTICLE A meeting of monks, though in the seventeenth century also a meeting (usually unlawful) of non-conformists.

CONVENTICLE ACTS (1593, 1664 and 1670) The Conventicle Act of 1593 imposed penalties on those who did not attend Anglican churches, while the Act of 1664 declared illegal all acts of worship attended by more than five persons (in addition to the members of a household) other than those prescribed in the *Book of Common Prayer*. A further Act of 1670 increased the penalties for attendance at unlawful assemblies.
See also SEVENTEENTH-CENTURY CHURCH

CONVENTUAL A conventual is one who belongs to a religious house. A conventual mass is a public mass attended by all members of a religious community.

CONVERSI *see* LAY BROTHERS

CONVOCATION The convocations of Canterbury and York are the two ancient provincial assemblies of the English Church. Originally, they consisted only of prelates but in 1225 Archbishop Langton (d. 1228) summoned representatives (*proctors*) of the cathedral and monastic chapters. From the end of the thirteenth century, bishops, abbots (until the Reformation), deans, archdeacons and representatives of the clergy of each diocese and cathedral chapter attended, sitting together as one House. Since the fifteenth century, the bishops and lower clergy have sat as two Houses. Until 1664 ecclesiastical legislation and clerical taxation were determined by the Convocations but, with the SUBMISSION OF THE CLERGY in 1532, their powers were restricted and in 1717 they were prorogued. Thereafter, their work was entirely formal until, in 1852, the Convocation of Canterbury was reactivated, followed in 1861 by the Convocation of York. In 1969, most of the functions of the Convocations were transferred to the General Synod, though they continue to meet separately (*see* SYNOD).

COPE *see* EMBROIDERY *and* VESTMENTS

COPE CHEST A horizontal quadrant-shaped wardrobe in which a cope is stored (*see* VESTMENTS). Usually of sturdy timber construction with panelled sides, legs and a lid opening in two halves decorated with foliated hinges.
See also EMBROIDERY

COPING A protective capping intended to disperse rainwater from the top of a wall.

COPPERPLATE (i) A polished copper plate for engraving or etching. (ii) A print produced from such a plate. (iii) A contemporary form of cursive handwriting properly known as script.

CORBEL A projection of stone, wood or brick supporting an arch, beam, parapet or moulding. Corbelling refers to receding courses of stone, brick etc. supporting a projection such as a chimney stack or oriel window.
See also BRACKET

CORBEL-TABLE A series of corbels (see above), occurring immediately below the roof eaves, both internally and externally. The Normans were especially fond of corbel-tables which were often elaborately carved in the forms of monsters and grotesque figures. There are wonderful examples at Kilpeck in Herefordshire, Elkstone in Gloucestershire, Berkswell in Warwickshire and Worth Matravers in Dorset.
See also FIGURE SCULPTURE *and* MEDIEVAL ARCHITECTURE

CORINTHIAN *see* CLASSICAL ORDER

CORNICE A moulded projection surmounting a wall, arch or building. A plaster moulding round a ceiling (*see* PLASTERWORK).

CORONA LUCIS A crown-shaped wrought iron or brass CHANDELIER. Most surviving examples are from the nineteenth-century Gothic Revival. Typically, a lower (larger) circlet supports a series of drip-pans and candle-sockets on its upper rim while the outer face may be embellished with enamelled shields and decorative pendant finials. This is suspended by chains from a smaller circlet attached to the ceiling. Evidence of earlier examples includes the mechanisms by which they were raised and lowered, as at Ubbeston in Suffolk (*see* LAMPS). In medieval churches, a *corona lucis* was often the principal source of artificial light. The Benedictine

abbey of Canterbury, for example, had two huge wheel-like chandeliers, each bearing twenty-four candles.

CORONET (HERALDIC) *see* CORONETS OF PEERS, CREST *and* CREST CORONETS

CORONETS OF PEERS The presence in a COAT OF ARMS of a ceremonial cap of red velvet, lined with ermine and contained within a decorative gold circlet indicates that the arms are those of a peer (or peeress) of the realm, the design of the rim corresponding with one of the five ranks of the peerage (*see* PEERAGE *for* illustration). These coronets of rank should not be confused with CREST CORONETS which (as the name suggests) are part of the CREST and are not indicative of rank.

CORPORAL *see* COMMUNION LINEN

CORPSE ROADS (*also* COFFIN PATHS, CORPSEWAYS, LYCHWAYS *or* LICKWAYS) Trackways in remote upland areas along which corpses were borne for burial at a distant churchyard. Medieval parishes in such districts were usually large and composed of widely scattered settlements. Although these hamlets were sometimes provided with subsidiary chapels of ease, the right of burial was usually reserved for the mother church (*see* CHAPELS). As a result bereaved families from remote farmsteads were obliged to arrange for bearers to carry a corpse many miles for interment: an arduous and sometimes hazardous commission, especially in the depths of winter. Journeys of up to 25 kilometres (15 miles) and lasting two days were recorded in the Yorkshire Dales as recently as the eighteenth century. A corpse road to Lydford, on the edge of Dartmoor, crossed the river Tavey by means of a series of large stepping stones, each of sufficient size to accommodate two pairs of bearers and their uncomplaining companion. Although corpse roads are sometimes described as 'coffin paths', it was not until the eighteenth century that coffins were available to any but the more affluent members of society (*see* BURIALS). In some areas rough-hewn coffin stones (*mortstones*) were provided along the route on which the corpse (or coffin) was laid while the bearers rested.
See also LICH-GATE *and* WAYSIDE CROSSES

CORPSE TABLE *see* LICH-GATE

CORPUS CHRISTI ('Body of Christ') (i) The feast commemorating the institution and gift of the Eucharist, observed on the Thursday following TRINITY SUNDAY. By the fourteenth century, the feast of Corpus Christi was universally celebrated in the western Church and in many towns was an occasion for the performance of religious plays (*see* MYSTERY PLAYS). (ii) A representation of Christ Crucified (*see* CRUCIFIX).

CORRODIAN The recipient of a CORRODY.

CORRODY The right to board and lodging exercised by certain benefactors of religious houses or their nominees. The term was later applied to pensions and other benefits granted by a monastery. *See also* COMMANDERY *and* MONASTICISM

COSMATI WORK Marble panels inlaid with mosaic, stones and gilding.

COSTUME *see* BRASSES (MONUMENTAL) *for* illustrations of academic, civilian, ecclesiastical, judicial, monastic and women's costume.

The following terms are those most commonly used when describing the costume worn by figures in monuments (* *see also* individual entries):

BARBETTE	linen chin-strap
BLIAUT	figure-fitting tunic
BREECHES	leg-coverings tied at waist
CAPUCHON	woman's loose-fitting hood
CHAPERON	stylised hood: padded role with liripipe
CHEMISE	long linen shirt
COIF *	close-fitting cap
COTEHARDIE	waisted tunic
COTTE	ankle-length under-garment
CRESPINE	headdress: fillet, fret and barbette
CYCLAS *	type of surcoat
DOUBLET	short padded jacket
FARTHINGALE	underskirt reinforced by circular hoops
FILLET	narrow band of material
FRENCH HOOD	headdress: tight-fitting, falls over neck
FRET	interlaced work
GABLE HOOD	headdress: shaped over face like gable
GARDECORPS	long open sleeves
GORGET	linen wrap for throat
HENNIN	exaggerated conical headdress
HORNED	headdress with two raised 'horns'
HOSE	covering for the legs and feet
HOUPPELANDE	voluminous circular gown
JUPON *	short, close-fitting sleeveless jacket
KENNEL	headdress: *see* gable hood
KIRTLE	close-fitting, tight-sleeved gown
LIRIPIPE	the long tail of a hood
MANTLE	cloak
PELLISE	woman's loose-fitting over-garment
RUFF *	starched and plaited frill round neck
STEEPLE HEADDRESS	*see* hennin
SURCOAT *	long, sleeveless garment
TABARD *	a thigh-length, sleeved tunic
TIPPET *	a long band of cloth or fur
WIDOW'S VEIL	*see* VOWESS
WIMPLE	a draped gorget

See also ARMOUR, BRASSES (MONUMENTAL), EFFIGIES *and* VESTMENTS
Further reading:
Cunnington, P., *Handbook of English Costume* (various vols.), London, 1973
Kelly, F. and Schwabe, R., *A Short History of Costume and Armour 1066–1800*, Newton Abbot, 1972
Mayo, J., *The History of Ecclesiastical Dress*, London, 1985

COTEHARDIE *see* BRASSES *and* COSTUME

COTSWOLD STONE The band of oolite which runs south-west from the Humber to the Dorset coast is at its widest and reaches its greatest elevation in the Cotswolds, a range of limestone hills, largely in Gloucestershire but extending east into Oxfordshire and south-west into Wiltshire and the county of Avon. Noted for sheep pastures and formerly a centre of the woollen industry, the wide Cotswold landscape is complemented by its buildings as in no other area of Britain. Manor houses, churches, farmsteads, cottages and entire villages are constructed of oolitic limestone or 'Cotswold Stone', the colour of which varies from the richest orange-brown in the east to pale creamy greys in the south and west. High quality freestone (*see* ASHLAR) is to be found in deep strata which are accessible only in the steep north-western escarpment. 'Cotswold' is derived from *Cod's wald* or forest.
Further reading:
Bailey, B., *Stone Villages of England*, Hale, 1982
Brill, E., *Life and Tradition in the Cotswolds*, London, 1973

COTTE *see* COSTUME

COUCHANT *see* BEASTS (HERALDIC)

COUDES *see* ARMOUR

COUNCIL FOR BRITISH ARCHAEOLOGY (CBA) The CBA has a Churches Committee which provides advice on all matters relating to church archaeology. It also maintains a network of Diocesan Archaeological Consultants and publishes pamphlets on a variety of subjects. These include: *How to Record Graveyards* (Jones, 1984), *Historic Churches: A Wasting Asset* (Rodwell, 1977), *The Archaeological Study of Churches* (Addyman and Morris, 1976), *The Church in British Archaeology* (Morris, 1983) and *The Anglo-Saxon Church* (Butler and Morris, 1986). *For* address *see* APPENDIX II.

COUNCIL FOR THE CARE OF CHURCHES (CCC) Formerly the Council for Places of Worship, the CCC works closely with the Council for British Archaeology, diocesan advisory committees and other organisations concerned with the care and maintenance of parish churches, including those which have been designated as redundant. One of its most important functions is the compiling of reports on all Anglican churches for which redundancy is proposed under the provisions of the *Pastoral Measure* of 1983. It has issued an important series of publications including *Churches and Archaeology* (1978) and *The Churchyards Handbook* (1988). *For* address *see* APPENDIX II.

COUNTER-FLORY *see* FLEUR-DE-LIS

COUNT PALATINATE *see* PALATINATE

COUNTY HISTORIES County histories have been compiled for many of the English and Welsh counties, many dating from the nineteenth and early twentieth centuries. These often contain details of church furnishings, monuments, architectural features etc. which have not survived, or have been badly restored, and are therefore invaluable source of information. Heraldic references and genealogical charts dating from this period are not always reliable, however.
Further reading:
Currie, C., and Lewis, C., (eds.), *English County Histories: A Guide*, Stroud, 1994

COUPLED ROOF *see* ROOFS (TIMBER)

COURSE A single horizontal row of masonry, brick or flint.

COURSED RUBBLE Walling of roughly dressed stone or flints set in courses (*see* COURSE). Uncoursed rubble consists of unhewn stones or flints not laid in regular courses.

COURT OF ARCHES *see* ARCHES, COURT OF

COURT OF AUGMENTATION *see* AUGMENTATION, COURT OF

COURT OF CHANCERY *see* CHANCERY, COURT OF

COURT OF DELEGATES *see* DELEGATES, COURT OF

COURTS (ECCLESIASTICAL) The Norman kings established separate courts for the hearing of judicial cases under CANON LAW: the Bishops' Courts and the Archdeacons' Courts. These dealt with matters such as church attendance, behaviour at services and in the churchyard, the condition of buildings and furnishings, parish boundaries, the conduct of clerics and church officials, the payment of parish dues, marriage, immorality, slander, usury and perjury. Heresy was dealt with only in the Bishops' Courts. A large number of cases arose from ecclesiastical visitations (*see* VISITATIONS, EC-CLESIASTICAL) and many ecclesiastical courts achieved reputations as 'Bawdy Courts' because of their apparent preoccupation with cases of adultery and fornication. The ecclesiastical courts also had jurisdiction over a wide range of cases which affected the laity, especially the enforcement of TITHES, mortuaries, sexual offences, matrimonial and testamentary affairs (*see* PROBATE), and perjury.
ARCHDEACONS' COURTS
Archdeacons' Courts were held once every three weeks at a central location and usually occupied the western end of an aisle in the parish church. The courts were presided over by the Archdeacon or his Official Principal and cases were of two types: Office Causes, which were brought by the Office of Judge against a defendant, and Causes of Instance which were brought by one person against another. Witnesses were required to testify under oath and a defendant might be given an opportunity to purge himself by producing (usually six) *compurgators* who would swear to his innocence. If found guilty by the judge (there was no jury), the offender would be required to undertake a penance which (until the sixteenth century) might be accompanied by castigation and a fine. Serious offences were punishable by EXCOMMUNICA-TION as was *contumacy*, the crime of failing to appear to answer a citation. Causes of Instance began with the appointment of Proctors to represent the two sides. There then followed a formal procedure which was conducted under oath: the *Libel of Articles* was the prosecution case which was followed by the *Responsions* for the defence. The *Attestations* were the statements made by witnesses for the prosecution, and the *Interroga-tories* the cross-examination of those witnesses by the defence. The same procedure was then followed by the opposite side, though on occasions, the defence would attack the credibility of the prosecution witnesses in *Articles of Exception*. Once judgment had been made, the Registrar would record the case in a Correction Book (for Causes of Instance) or in an Act Book (for Office Causes),

though these are often singularly lacking in substance and may be of limited interest to the historian. Non-judicial business was recorded in separate volumes for matters such as faculties, licences, probate records and inventories. These records are kept in DIOCESAN REGISTRIES which may now be in county record offices.

CONSISTORY COURTS
Appeal from the archdeacons' courts lay with the bishop's consistory (or diocesan) court. The medieval English Church consisted of the two provinces of Canterbury and York, each divided into dioceses with consistory courts presided over by a chancellor (*see* DIOCESE). Appeals from the consistory courts were brought before the *Court of Arches* (in the Province of Canterbury which included Wales) or the *Court of Chancery* (in the Province of York), the former presided over by the *Dean of Arches* and the latter by the *Official Principal* of the Court of Chancery. Appeal from the provincial courts to the Pope in Rome was restricted by the fourteenth-century *Statutes of Praemunire* and abolished in 1532. Thereafter appeals were determined by an *ad hoc Court of Delegates* which consisted of three judges and three Doctors of Civil Law.

RECENT LEGISLATION
The Ecclesiastical Courts Commission was established by Parliament in 1830 to consider legal procedures within the Church of England. It recommended that the Court of Delegates should be replaced by the Privy Council as the final court of appeal in matters ecclesiastical. A further commission of 1881–3 recommended a radical revision of the ecclesiastical courts but no action was taken.

Nevertheless, several aspects of Canon Law were transferred to the civil courts during the nineteenth century: since 1833 appeals on matters of conduct have been brought before the Judicial Committee of the Privy Council; in 1857 matrimonial causes were transferred to the new *Divorce Courts* and matters concerning wills and probate to the new *Probate Courts*, both of which were incorporated into the *Supreme Court of Judicature* in 1873 and finally into the Family Division of the High Court in 1970. But the Church Courts remain to deal with disciplinary and moral matters within the Church of England, including those relating to the conduct of priests and certain lay-people such as churchwardens and parish clerks, and with matters concerning the demolition or alteration of church premises. Such courts are not courts of common law.

See also ARCHES (COURT OF), ARCHIVES, AUGMENTATION (COURT OF), CHANCERY (COURT OF), CHAPTER, COMMISSARY COURT, CONSISTORY COURT, DELEGATES (COURT OF), DIOCESAN RECORDS, ECCLESI-ASTICAL JURISDICTION MEASURE 1963, FACULTIES (COURT OF), PROBATE *and* QUARE IMPEDIT

Further reading:
Chapman, C., *Ecclesiastical Courts, their Officials and their Records*, Chichester, 1992
Tarver, A., *Church Court Records*, Chichester, 1995

COURTS (MONASTIC) Abbots were feudal lords and as such exercised their authority through their own courts. There is a court room above the abbey gate at Ely in Cambridgeshire and in a separate building (*Tribunal*) in the main street at Glastonbury. Many monastic gatehouses also contained a prison: at Bury St. Edmunds in Suffolk, for example.

COUSIN In medieval usage, any relative other than parent, brother, uncle or aunt.

COUSIN GERMAN A first cousin.

COVE *and* COVING A concave moulding at the junction of a ceiling and a wall.

COVERED PATEN *see* PLATE

COWL A hooded garment worn by monks.

CREATURES *see* AMPHISBAENA, ANTELOPES, APES, ASP, BEAKHEAD DECORATION, BEASTS (HERALDIC), BESTIARY, CHRISTIAN SYMBOLS, DOVES, EAGLES, ELEPHANTS, FISH, GARGOYLES, HART, LAMB, LION, PAGAN SYMBOLS, PASCHAL LAMB *and* STAGS.

CREDENCE A niche or shelf, sometimes within a FENESTELLA, on which the elements of the Eucharist were placed before consecration.
See also CREDENCE TABLE *and* PISCINA

CREDENCE TABLE A small side table in the sanctuary on which the bread, wine and water were placed during the EUCHARIST, together with accessories required for the service. Before the REFORMATION a CREDENCE was used for this purpose.
See also AUMBRY *and* PISCINA

CREED *see* APOSTLES' CREED *and* NICENE CREED

CREMATION Disposal of a corpse by reducing it to ashes was anathema to the early Church because the practice appeared to contradict fundamental Christian belief in the resurrection of the body. It was revived in the nineteenth century and formally recognised by the Church of England in 1969.

CRENELLATED From *crenel* meaning 'embrasure', an embattled parapet or a wall with loopholes (*see* BATTLEMENTS, EMBRASURE *and* MERLON).

CRESPINE *see* COSTUME

CRESSET The carved holes in *cresset stones* into which cooking fat or grease and floating wicks were placed to provide multiple lamps. Some cresset stones were portable and contained three or four such holes; larger ones were too heavy to move and had perhaps twelve or more cressets. Cresset stones are sometimes found in monastic buildings or preserved in churches. There are good examples at Collingham and Westow in Yorkshire and Lewannick in Cornwall.

CREST A three-dimensional device affixed to a helmet and so depicted in a COAT OF ARMS. During the Middle Ages, crests were considered to be the perquisites of the knightly class: those who possessed both the rank and the resources which enabled them to participate in tournaments where crests were used. Crests were made of light materials (paste board, cloth or boiled leather over a basketwork frame) and were fastened to the helm by means of laces or rivets, the unsightly join concealed beneath a WREATH of twisted silk (*torse*) or a CORONET. To this was attached a decorative mantling (*lambrequin*) which covered the back and sides of the helm. Crests of the post-Tudor period were often ridiculously complex and few could have been affixed to a real helm: *A Ship in distress on a Rock proper* (Pellew), for example. Crests are often depicted on a wreath or coronet but without the other elements of a coat of arms, notably in memorials and stained glass.

See also HELMETS *and* PANACHE

Further reading:

Fairbairn, J., *Crests of the Families of Great Britain and Ireland*, 1905 (reprinted The Heraldic Book Company, 1983)

Crest depicting a freeminer of the Forest of Dean in the brass of Robert Greymdour at Newland, Gloucestershire.

Pellew

CREST CORONETS Not to be confused with CORONETS OF PEERS, crest coronets are ornamental circlets which form part of the CREST in some coats of arms. Confusingly, nearly all crest coronets are described as 'crowns'. Those most commonly found in heraldic memorials, stained glass etc. are:

1	*Ancient Crown*	A recent addition to heraldry and usually indicative of armigers who have antiquarian interests.
2	*Astral Crown*	Associated with distinguished members of the Royal Air Force, eminent aviators and institutions associated with aviation.
3	*Crown Vallary*	From the Latin *vallare*, to fortify. Most commonly found in the arms of those associated with the magistracy and judiciary.
4	*Ducal Coronet*	Composed of four strawberry leaves on a chased rim. Despite its name it has no nobiliary significance.
5	*Eastern Crown*	Associated with distinguished service in the Near or Far East.
6	*Mural Crown*	Widely used in civic heraldry and in the arms of distinguished soldiers where such a crown may be an AUGMENTATION OF HONOUR.
7	*Naval Crown*	Usually reserved for distinguished sailors and local authorities which have naval traditions (such as Devon).
8	*Palisado Crown*	The origin of this coronet is the defensive palisade and it is to be found in the arms of, for example, towns with Roman associations or those constructed within ancient fortifications.

CRIB *see* CHRISTMAS

CRIPPLEGATE *see* HOLY WELLS

CROCKET In MEDIEVAL ARCHITECTURE, carved leaf-like decorative features projecting at regular intervals on the sloping sides of spires, gables, pinnacles etc.
See also BALLFLOWER, DIAPER, DOGTOOTH *and* QUATREFOIL

CROCKFORD Short for *Crockford's Clerical Directory*, a reference book of Anglican clergy first published in 1860. J. Crockford, nominally the first publisher, died in 1865.

CROP MARKS It was William Camden (1551–1623) who observed of Richborough, the Fort of the Saxon Shore in Kent, 'Age has erased the very tracks of it . . . it is at this day a cornfield, wherein, when the corn is grown up, one may observe the draughts of streets crossing one another (for where they have gone, the corn is thinner) . . .'. Such crop marks are produced by variations in the quality of plant growth caused by differences in the soil and subsoil. The presence of buried walls and foundations just beneath the soil's surface will produce weak plants which are vulnerable to dry conditions while deeper pits and silt-filled trenches retain moisture and allow for the development of a substantial root structure and more luxuriant growth. From the air such variations of vegetation (usually in a cereal crop) become more evident and may delineate the former walls and buildings of archaeological sites. Aerial photography of crop marks is particularly effective when a low sun shines across a field, the different levels of vegetation casting shadows which clearly trace the structures beneath.
Further reading:
Beresford, M. and St. Joseph, J., *Medieval England: An Aerial Survey*, Cambridge, 1979
Muir, R., *History from the Air*, London, 1983

CROSIER (*also* CROZIER) Literally 'cross-bearer', the term has come to mean the cross itself, the symbol of episcopal jurisdiction, a staff of office carried by bishops and formerly by abbots and abbesses. Crosiers usually take the form of an ornate shepherd's crook though (as the name suggests) a cross is more appropriate. Crosiers (both crooks and crosses) are also found in heraldry: in the coats of arms of bishops and abbots, in the arms of former monastic churches and in the civic devices of towns

HERALDIC CROSSES

1	Cross-crosslet fitchy	8	Flory	15	Potent quadrate
2	Potent	9	Maltese	16	Formy-fitchy at the foot
3	Patriarchal	10	Bottony	17	Fleuretty
4	Tau (St. Anthony's)	11	Saxon	18	Cross-crosslet
5	Recercely	12	Patonce	19	Formy-fitchy
6	Fylfot or cramponed	13	Celtic or wheel-head		
7	Formy or paty	14	Moline		

with ecclesiastical traditions. The arms of Sherborne Abbey in Dorset, for example, include a golden crosier which commemorates St. Aldhelm (d. 709), its eighth-century bishop.

CROSSES The use of the cross for decorative purposes pre-dates Christianity by many centuries but it was to become the universal symbol of the Christian Church. The preponderance of crosses in HERALDRY reflects both the influence of the Crusades on the knightly classes and medieval man's preoccupation with his religion. According to various sources there are between three and five hundred different types of cross to be found in heraldry, though of these only about twenty are in regular use and are here illustrated. There can be little doubt that the earliest heraldic crosses were of the simplest kind and that the proliferation of variants resulted from casual embellishment and the desire of the post-medieval heralds to define forms which had been arrived at by artistic licence. A cross on which is depicted the body of Christ Crucified is a CRUCIFIX.
See ALTAR CROSS, CELTIC CROSS, CHRISTIAN SYMBOLS, CHURCHYARD CROSSES, CONSECRATION CROSSES, CROSIER, ELEANOR CROSSES, GABLE CROSSES, MARKET CROSSES, PENITENTIAL CROSS, PILGRIM CROSSES, PROCESSIONAL CROSS, ROOD, SANCTUARY CROSSES, VOTIVE CROSSES, WAYSIDE CROSSES, WEEPING CROSS *and* WHEEL HEAD CROSS

CROSSING In larger churches, the space formed at the intersection of nave, chancel and transept, often vaulted and with an axial tower above.
See also MEDIEVAL ARCHITECTURE

CROSS-STAFF *see* CROSIER

CROWN GLASS *see* GLASS

CROWN POST A vertical post at the centre of a TIE BEAM to support a COLLAR BEAM or COLLAR PURLIN to which it is usually connected by means of diagonal braces (*see* ROOFS *and* KING POST).

CROWNS (HERALDIC) *see* CORONETS OF PEERS, CREST *and* CREST CORONETS

CROW STEPS Steps on the coping of a gable.

CRUCIFER One who carries a cross, usually before a procession.

CRUCIFIX An image of Christ crucified, usually in the form of a three-dimensional model. A figure with the eyes open is termed 'Christ in Agony', but if they are closed it is a CORPUS CHRISTI. Crucifixes were widely used as objects of devotion in the medieval period, as they are today in the Roman Catholic Church. Since the Reformation, they have generally been replaced by the cross in the Church of England.
See also CROSSES *and* ROOD

CRUCIFORM In the shape of a cross.

CRUETS Vessels, usually of glass or precious metal, in which wine and water are carried to the altar for the EUCHARIST.
See also CREDENCE, PISCINA *and* PLATE

CRUSADES The Wars of the Cross, to free the Holy Land from the Saracens, began with much optimism and high ideals. They occupied the best of Western Christendom's military, religious and chivalric fervour for three centuries. Yet they achieved virtually nothing, largely because of lack of organisation arising from jealousies among the leaders, and failure to come to terms with the terrain, the climate and the need for hygiene.

First Crusade	1095–99
Second Crusade	1146–49
Third Crusade	1188–92
Fourth Crusade	1202–04
Fifth Crusade	1217–21
Sixth Crusade	1228–29
Seventh Crusade	1245–69

(*See also* HEART BURIAL, MOS TUTONICUS, ST. JOHN OF JERUSALEM, ORDER OF *and* TEMPLAR, KNIGHTS)
Further reading:
Billings, M., *The Cross and the Crescent*, London, 1987
Hallam, E., (ed.), *Chronicles of the Crusades*, London, 1989
Riley-Smith, J., *The Crusades*, London, 1987
Runciman, Sir Stephen, *A History of the Crusades*, West Drayton, 1965 (reprinted 1985)
Tyerman, C., *England and the Crusades: 1095–1588*, Chicago, 1988

CRUTCHED FRIARS *see* FRIARS

CRYPT A vaulted underground chamber, usually constructed beneath the chancel of a church to accommodate tombs and the relics of saints. Some larger crypts (particularly those of the great abbeys and cathedrals) also contain altars which were provided for the use of individual priests or for the benefit of pilgrims who wished to pay homage at an adjacent shrine. An *undercroft* is a similar chamber beneath a church or monastic building, wholly or partially underground and originally used for offices or storage, though often (in the present century) adapted for administrative and commercial purposes.

CUIRASS A waisted back- and breast-plate of metal or leather (*see* ARMOUR).

CUISSES (or CUISHES) Quilted or leather padding for the thigh (*see* ARMOUR).

CULVERY *see* DOVECOTES

CUM A Latinised place-name element meaning 'with'.
See also PLACE-NAMES

CUPBOARDS *see* AUMBRY, CHEST CUP-BOARDS, CREDENCE *and* DOLE CUPBOARDS

CUPOLA A small circular or polygonal DOME crowning a roof or turret.

CURATE *see* CLERGY (CHURCH OF ENGLAND)

CURE OF SOULS Responsibility for the spiritual well-being of the common people.

CURFEW From *couvre-feu*, meaning 'cover the fire', the curfew bell warned villagers to dowse the fires in their thatched hovels before retiring to bed at the end of each day (*see* BELLS). At Presteigne in Powys the curfew bell is still rung from the church tower at eight o'clock each night.

CURIA (i) The papal court and its functionaries. (ii) The outer precincts of a religious house (*see* PRECINCT).

CURSIVE Descriptive, not only of handwriting with joined characters, but also of any flowing, repetitive pattern.

CURTILAGE (*also* COURTLEDGE) The monastic department responsible for the production of vegetables (*see also* LARDER).

CURVILINEAR *see* WINDOW TRACERY

CUSHION CAPITAL *see* BLOCK CAPITAL

CUSP In architectural decoration the point at which two curved shapes intersect. In Gothic TRACERY a projecting point between two lobes of a trefoil, quatrefoil etc. (*see* FOIL).

CUSPING A decorative feature consisting of a projection formed at the intersection of two arcs.

CUSTOMARY (*LIBER ORDINARIUS*) (i) The book containing the rules and customs of a cathedral or of a religious order or community. (ii) The book containing the rites and ceremonies for services. Sometimes the two were combined in a single book.

CYCLAS A SURCOAT cut short at the front and long at the back (*see* ARMOUR *and* COSTUME).

CYPHER A cypher is a monogram: two or more letters interwoven to form a symbol, sometimes ensigned with a coronet of rank (*see* CORONETS OF PEERS), and used as a personal or household device. Cyphers were particularly popular during the eighteenth and nineteenth centuries when the use of heraldic BADGES was in decline and the new rich of the Industrial Revolution perceived a need for some means of personal identity.
See also REBUS

D

DAGGER In Gothic TRACERY, a quatrefoil with one elongated and pointed lobe.

DAILY ROUND *see* HORARIUM

DALMATIC *see* VESTMENTS

DANCE OF DEATH An allegorical representation of Death, often depicted as a skeleton, leading various characters to their graves. It has been suggested that such paintings were inspired by the *danse macabre*, a symptom of the bubonic plague which entered England in 1349 (*see* PLAGUE), though the earliest example, a mural in a Parisian cemetery, is from *c.* 1425. The wild procession often included popes, kings, merchants and beggars, thereby emphasising the equality of all men before Death.
See also WALL PAINTINGS

DANELAW The north-eastern area of Britain occupied by the Danes in the ninth and tenth centuries comprising the kingdoms of Bernicia, York and East Anglia and the federation of the *Five Boroughs* of Derby, Lincoln, Nottingham, Leicester and Stamford. It was in the Five Boroughs that the Danes established their administrative and military headquarters. Following the Conquest, the Normans attempted to rationalise the often disparate practices of the Danelaw and Saxon administrations. In the Danelaw, divisions had been created out of the former Viking military districts, each with its central borough, wapentake sub-divisions and a Danish lord (*jarl*) responsible directly to the English king. But in the Saxon shires, administrative and judicial practices, which originated in the laws of Ine, King of Wessex (688–726) and his successors, were effected through shires and hundreds with an ealdorman and shirereeve representing the king and people.

DARK AGES The sixth-century British cleric Gildas described the destruction of his country by the German barbarians:

> Swords glinted all around, and the flames crackled. Foundation stones of high walls that had been torn from their lofty base, holy altars, fragments of corpses, covered as it were with a purple crust of congealed blood, looked as though they had been mixed up in some dreadful wine press.

It was inevitable that centuries of conquest and bloody resistance should acquire the epithet 'barbarous'. But this is the obverse side of the sun and, obscure though our vision of the *Dark Ages* may be, that which has been revealed to us is of a brilliant intensity.

The ancient kingdom of Northumbria was 'a land of art and culture, a haven of learning and skill' which in the seventh century became the force that first united England into a single realm. Most of this cultural creativity emanated from the Church and from the monastic foundations in particular. The monasteries of Northumberland and Kent produced the finest illuminated manuscripts using pigments imported from as far afield as the Himalayas. In churches, Anglo-Saxon artists established a unique and highly influential school of sculpture while England's first poets created epic poetry that marked the beginnings of English literature. This was the age of the *Codex Amiatinus*, the world's oldest surviving Latin bible. Weighing 75 lb and requiring the skins of 500 calves for its vellum pages, it was (probably) made at the monastery of Monkwearmouth (Tyne and Wear) as a gift for the Pope in 716 AD. This was the age of England's first major historian, the Venerable Bede, who produced his *History of the English Church and People* in 731 AD; of the magnificent illuminated *Lindisfarne Gospels* and of the mystical St. Cuthbert, whose beautifully carved wooden coffin may still be seen at Durham Cathedral together with an array of superb Anglo-Saxon treasures: the products, not of obscurity and barbarity, but of a highly sophisticated and cultured people.
See also ANGLO-SAXON CHURCH *and* CELTIC CHURCH
Further reading:
Delaney, F., *A Walk in the Dark Ages*, London, 1989
Pollington, S., *The Warrior's Way*, London, 1989

DATE STONE Occasionally date stones were inserted in the masonry of walls, particularly in the seventeenth and eighteenth centuries, to commemorate repairs or alterations to a church. They often include the initials of the incumbent and church-wardens.

DAUGHTER HOUSE A subsidiary house of a major monastic community. Early daughter houses were established as a result of successful missions (usually consisting of twelve monks and a superior) which achieved, not only conversion, but the active support of native ruling families whose endowments provided for the building of a monastery and the means to maintain it. In the Middle Ages, many daughter houses were founded simply because a mother house had expanded beyond its resources, appeals to the medieval establishment almost invariably resulting in substantial benefactions and endowments. Initially, a mother house retained control over the activities of her daughters, which usually began as priories, though many eventually became independent and some achieved even greater prestige and influence than the houses which founded them. A number of parish churches are associated with former daughter houses: the Benedictine abbey of St. Alban in Hertfordshire, for example, had eight daughter houses (and two dependent houses of nuns) of which Binham in Norfolk (the nave) and Hatfield Peverel in Essex (part of the nave) remain in use as parish churches.

See also ALIEN PRIORIES *and* MONASTERIES

DAY HOURS The services of LAUDS, PRIME, TERCE, SEXT, NONE, VESPERS and COMPLINE.

DAY STAIR *see* DORTER

DEACON *see* CLERGY (CHURCH OF ENGLAND), SUB-DEACON *and* VESTMENTS.

DEACONESS *see* CLERGY (CHURCH OF ENGLAND)

DEAN *see* CLERGY (CHURCH OF ENGLAND)

DEANERY The official residence or office of a DEAN and the group of parishes within his jurisdiction.

DEATH'S HEAD In memorials, a sculptured or engraved skull symbolising death and, by implication, both its commonality and ultimate victory through resurrection. Most death's heads date from the late fifteenth century to the eighteenth, during which period there was a preoccupation with the inevitability of death and an almost culpable desire to acknowledge, *in memoriam,* the transient nature of privilege and wealth. Many variations are to be found: some have bats' wings and others are carried by figures of children to indicate infant mortality.

DECALOGUE *see* TEN COMMANDMENTS, THE

DECANI Literally, the place 'of the dean', the term is used to describe those who, in antiphonal singing, occupy the stalls to the south of the choir.

See also ANTIPHON, CANTORIS, CHURCH MUSIC (ANGLICAN), STALLS *and* VERSICLE

DECORATED INITIAL In MANUSCRIPT ILLUMINATION, an initial capital which has been embellished by the use of coloured inks and gilding.

DECORATED PERIOD *see* ARCHITECTURAL PERIODS *and* MEDIEVAL ARCHITECTURE

DECORATIVE MOTIFS (*see* illustrations on pages 151 and 152)
Those marked with an asterisk will also be found as individual entries.

1   ACANTHUS *
2   ANTHEMION
3   BALL FLOWER *
4   BAY LEAF
5   BEAD
6   BEAD AND REEL
7   BIFURCATED *
8   BILLET (ROUND) *
9   BILLET (SQUARE)
10 BRATTISHING *
11 CABLE *
12 CHEVRON *
13 DENTIL *
14 DIAPER *
15 DOG TOOTH *
16 DOUBLE CONE
17 EGG AND TONGUE
18 EGG AND DART
19 EMBATTLED *, BATTLEMENTED, CASTELLATED or CRENELLATED
20 FLUTING *
21 FOUR LEAF FLOWER *
22 FRET, LATTICE or KEY *
23 GADROONING *, LOBING, or NULLING
24 GOUGING, CHANNELLING, ADZED or SCOOP
25 GUILLOCHE
26 HUSK *
27 LATTICE
28 LOZENGE *
29 LUNETTE
30 MORESQUE *
31 NAILHEAD
32 OVOLO
33 PATERA
34 PEARDROP
35 REEDING
36 RIBBON *
37 ROSETTE *
38 SCALLOPED
39 SHELL
40 STRAPWORK *
41 SWAG *
42 TRELLIS
43 TUDOR ORNAMENT
44 TUDOR ROSE *
45 VINE *
46 VITRUVIAN SCROLL or RUNNING DOG
47 WATERLEAF

See also AMORINO, BEAKHEAD ORNAMENT, BUCRANE, CHINOISERIE, FESTOON, FLEUR-DE-LIS, FOILS (*for* trefoil, quatrefoil, etc.), GROTESQUE, SCROLL *and* TRACERY

DECORATIVE MOTIFS

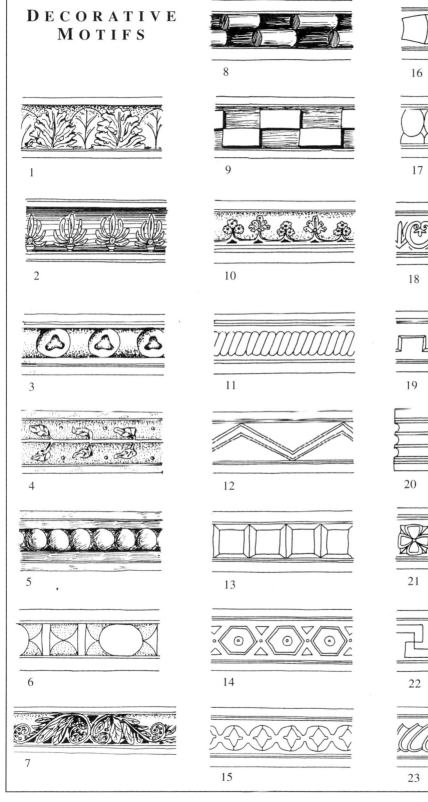

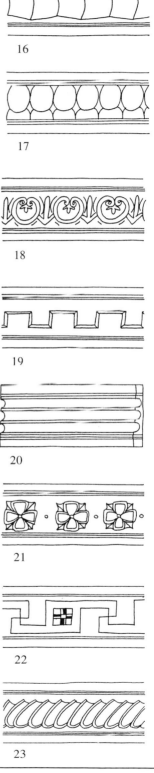

8

16

1

9

17

2

10

18

3

11

19

4

12

20

5

13

21

6

14

22

7

15

23

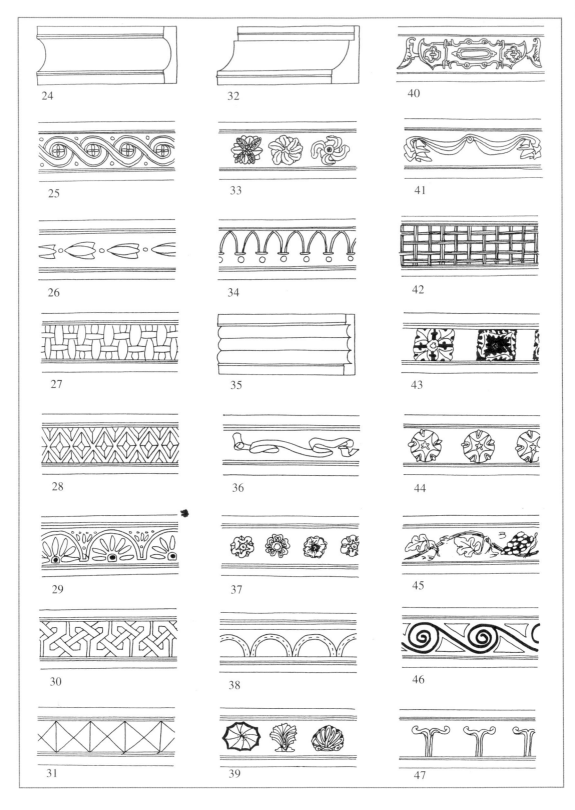

24

32

40

25

33

41

26

34

42

27

35

43

28

36

44

29

37

45

30

38

46

31

39

47

DECRETALS *see* CANON LAW

DEDICATION, CHURCH The practice of dedicating a church to a particular saint or saints, to a group (e.g. the English Martyrs) or a religious concept (Holy Cross) or event (the Assumption) dates from the early fourth century. From that time there developed an elaborate form of solemn consecration consisting of six ritualistic elements, followed by the Eucharist. A Feast of the Dedication was celebrated annually to mark the dedication of a particular church. In 1536 it was determined that this should take place on the first Sunday in October though, in practice, this is usually adopted only by those churches for which the date of dedication is unknown.

Providing a church with an identity was especially useful in towns where it would otherwise be difficult to distinguish between different churches. Even so, it was sometimes necessary to add a further physical or geographical description such as 'St. Peter on the Wall' (at Bradwell-on-Sea, Essex) or the delightful 'St. Mary in the Marsh' (at Brookland in Kent). Different dedications were fashionable at different times and in particular areas, and old dedications may have been forgotten, corrupted or changed where no official record has survived. Many dedications were changed during the Middle Ages and the names of more fashionable and (apparently) efficacious saints adopted. In such cases it may still be possible to discover an earlier dedication from medieval wills, charters, monastic cartularies or bishop's registers or from place name and field-name evidence (*see also* CHURCH SITES *and* RELICS). Some dedications were changed for political reasons. Lapford in Devon is one of the few churches to have retained its dedication to St. Thomas (Becket) of Canterbury, a martyr who represented the supreme victory of the Church over the State and whose memory was, therefore, repugnant to Henry VIII. Consequently, most St. Thomas of Canterbury dedications were changed to St. Thomas the Apostle in the 1530s.
See also CELTIC CHURCH

DEED POLL A deed made by a single party and therefore requiring no duplicate. Unlike an INDENTURE, it was not necessary to indent the edge which was cut in a straight line (*poll*). It is by deed poll that a change of surname is usually effected.

DEFENDER OF THE FAITH (*FIDEI DEFENSOR*) Pope Leo X conferred the title on HENRY VIII in 1521 in recognition of his treatise defending the doctrine of the Seven Sacraments. It was confirmed by Parliament as an official title of the English sovereign in 1544 and has remained so to this day.

DE HAERETICO COMBURENDO A statute of 1401 by which those found guilty of heresy in an ecclesiastical court were handed over to the secular authority to be burned at the stake.

DELEGATES, COURT OF The court which considers appeals against decisions of the Prerogative Courts of Canterbury and York (*see also* ARCHES, COURT OF *and* CHANCERY, COURT OF)

DENIZATION The granting of the privileges of naturalisation to an alien, including the right to purchase and devise land (which was forbidden to aliens) but excluding the right to inherit land or to receive grants of land from the Crown. Denization records are available for inspection at the Public Record Office (*see* APPENDIX II) and these usually show an immigrant's place of origin.

DENTIL Small, square blocks used in a series of classical cornices.
See DECORATIVE MOTIFS

DESERTED VILLAGES Thousands of deserted villages (or, more correctly, abandoned settlements) have been identified: many more await discovery. Not all are as manifest as Tyneham in Dorset, reluctantly surrendered to the army in 1943 as part of the Lulworth artillery range 'for the duration of the hostilities' or the drowned farmsteads of Elan and Clywedog in Mid-Wales.

Following the withdrawal of Rome in 410 AD, Romano-British settlements, and those of immigrant Saxons, tended to be scattered hamlets or farmsteads. A small number of early Saxon 'villages' developed but these generally occupied poor sites and most appear to have been abandoned by the mid-seventh century. The development of the open-field system in the eighth and ninth centuries, and the building of parish churches to serve a rapidly expanding rural population, provided the stimulus for the creation of what we today perceive as a village: a permanent cluster of dwellings with an identifiable nucleus, providing the focal point for outlying hamlets and farmsteads, many of which pre-date the village itself, and (usually) a parish church. But how permanent were these villages? Some expanded to become towns and even cities: many others declined and were eventually abandoned.

Documentary evidence of deserted villages is meagre before the compilation of Domesday Book in 1086. The destructive Norman *chevauchées* of 1069–71 in the north of England (the 'Harrying of the North') inevitably caused the disintegration of numerous rural communities, but little is known of these. The CISTERCIAN clearances of the twelfth and thirteenth centuries are well documented, however, and resulted in the effective depopulation of those areas identified by the Order as being sufficiently sequestered to meet the stringent requirements of its rule. By 1152 there were fifty-one Cistercian foundations in England, and dozens of rural communities had been dispersed, especially in northern England, in order to satisfy the Cistercians' demand for solitude and exclusiveness and to accommodate the expansion of their estates. *See also* GRANGE

Deteriorating climatic conditions, particularly severe in the fourteenth century, resulted in the gradual abandonment of many of the subsistence communities, created out of the rural population explosion of the previous century, on the margins of the heaths and moors. Such starveacre places were subject to recurring soil exhaustion and severe over-grazing and simply could not survive the changing climatic régime.

'PLAGUE VILLAGES'
Undoubtedly the most popular reason given for the abandonment of a village, and that which persists most strongly in the received traditions of many communities, is the fourteenth-century pestilence known as the Black Death (*see* PLAGUE). There is no doubting the virulence of this terrifying disease and the debilitating effect it could have on a small, rural community. But documentary and archae-ological evidence strongly suggest that very few settlements were abandoned *permanently* and, as in the case of villages decimated by civil war, most were re-colonised or replaced by planned villages on adjacent sites. Of course, some villages were lost entirely (such as Tusmore in Oxfordshire which in 1357 was '. . . void of inhabitance since their death in the pestilence'), but of the 2,000 deserted villages that have been recorded, mostly in the Midland counties and eastern parts of England, final abandonment was the result of gradual decline over many decades. Of eighty deserted medieval villages identified in Northamptonshire, for example, only two (Hale and Elkington) are true 'plague villages'. The real effect of the Black Death, and of subsequent recurrences of the plague which lasted into the seventeenth century, was to accelerate a decline in the rural population which was already evident by the middle of the thirteenth century. It was this decline, and the consequential reduction in the availability of peasant labour, which was to result in the eventual abandonment of many medieval rural settlements.

Undeterred by legislation intended to curtail their new-found bargaining power, labourers repeatedly demanded more favourable conditions of service, wages rose substantially and landlords sought means by which they could reduce their labour force and more profitably exploit their lands. Inevitably, in a flourishing wool market, they turned to sheep and during the late fifteenth and early sixteenth centuries open fields were enclosed, estates cleared and villagers evicted on an unprecedented scale, creating appalling poverty and almost universal resentment. Hardest hit were the east Midland counties, Norfolk, the Lincolnshire Wolds and the former East and North Ridings of Yorkshire. In the 1480s, the priest and antiquarian John Rous noted fifty-eight depopulated villages within twelve miles of his native Warwick.

EMPARKMENT
The late Tudor and Elizabethan periods witnessed the dismantling of the last remnants of the feudal system. Magnatial and dynastic strongholds were adapted or replaced by fashionable country mansions and medieval deer parks extended to incorporate open fields and common waste in vast areas of empty but equally fashionable parkland. Villages were generally considered to be obtrusive in such sylvan settings and were removed, sometimes to be rebuilt outside the park for the benefit of estate tenants. In other cases the unfortunate peasantry was abandoned together with its villages. The little market town of Milton in Dorset developed in the shadow of its tenth century abbey until 1780, when its proximity to his new mansion so offended the sensibilities of Joseph Damer (later the first Earl of Dorchester), that he demolished the entire town, save for one thatched cottage, and removed those inhabitants he was unable to drive away to a new 'model village' in a deep combe half a mile to the south. The earthworks and hollow ways that mark the crofts and streets of the former town are still evident in the fields to the south of the abbey church. Unlike most medieval desertions, many 'emparked' villages retained their parish churches which, although isolated from the congregations they were built to serve, remain in defiant juxtaposition to the splendid mansions that caused their decline (as at Milton Abbey).

IDENTIFICATION
Amazingly, many medieval village sites have escaped the plough and are still evident in apparently haphazard areas of humps and hollows often covering several acres. Upon closer inspection, former streets and back lanes may be identified as HOLLOW WAYS of varying width, with adjacent house platforms surrounded by low banks and ditches marking the boundaries of closes or tofts. There may be evidence of former ponds or moats, or the artificial mound of a motte and bailey castle or windmill; and at the village edge, the ridge and furrow pattern of ancient open fields is often discernible. The mounds and undulations in the fields at Abdon, in Shropshire, show where a medieval village once prospered before the decline of local quarrying and agriculture caused its depopulation; while at nearby Heath, the tiny Norman church stands forlornly in a field, similarly bereft of the settlement which once it served. Medieval sites in

areas of arable cultivation are usually visible only from the air as CROP MARKS.

Parish churches were sometimes plundered for building materials, except those that occupied ancient, venerated sites (often of pagan origin) or were themselves built of freely available materials, such as the flint churches of Norfolk. In such cases the church, or its dilapidated shell, may remain in splendid isolation (*see* CHURCH SITES).

Clues to the identity of a deserted village may be evident in the double-barrelled names of some civil parishes, such as Knayton-with-Brawith in Yorkshire (Brawith is a deserted village); or in an unusual configuration of parish boundaries, particularly those with a 'dumb-bell' shape, indicative perhaps of the annexation of a former parish by its neighbour.

From the mid-nineteenth century relatively few villages were abandoned: usually as the result of industrial decline (the closure of a colliery for example) or to create reservoirs or military training areas such as those on Salisbury Plain in Wiltshire.

Further reading:

Beresford, M.W., and Hurst, J.G., *Deserted Medieval Villages*, Cambridge, 1971

Friar, S., *The Batsford Companion to Local History*, London, 1991

Muir, R., *The Lost Villages of Britain*, London, 1984

DESKS In churches, the term 'desk' is generally applied to a piece of furniture comprising a sloping surface on which an open bible or other large book is supported and angled towards the reader. The most common form of LECTERN consists of an eagle carrying a desk on its outspread wings, while others may have double desks, back-to-back and with decorative gabled ends and candle-holders. PULPITS also have desks, though these are usually smaller and are more correctly described as *bookplates*. They are quite often attached to an adjustable stem which is affixed to the inside of the pulpit drum. In three-decker pulpits, desks were provided for the pulpit, the parson (*see* READING DESK) and the PARISH CLERK. Pulpit desks often support a FALL of the appropriate liturgical colour. A *litany desk* is intended for the recitation of the LITANY and incorporates a kneeler, as does a PRIE-DIEU which is a small prayer-desk for private devotions.

See also CREDENCE *and* MISSAL STAND

DETACHED BELFRIES *see* TOWERS

DEVIL, THE *see* ATTRIBUTED ARMS, CHRISTIAN SYMBOLS, DOOM *and* WALL PAINTINGS

DEVISE Personal property is bequeathed by will, but landed property is devised.

DEXTER *see* POINTS OF THE SHIELD

DIAPER (i) In MEDIEVAL ARCHITECTURE, diaperwork is a surface decoration of diamond-shaped patterns (*see* DECORATIVE MOTIFS). *See also* BALLFLOWER, CROCKET, DOGTOOTH *and* QUATREFOIL (ii) In heraldry, diaper is a method of decorating plain surfaces by filling them with a pattern, usually in a shade of the same colour. When applied in too heavy a fashion, diaper may be mistaken for an heraldic device. (iii) The term may also be applied to the artistic embellishment of the interstices in tiles, seals etc. which may allude to the heraldry contained therein.

DIMIDIATION *see* MARSHALLING

DIOCESAN ADVISORY COMMITTEE (DAC) There is a DAC for each diocese, its principal function being to advise the diocesan Chancellor on the granting of faculties (*see* FACULTY).

DIOCESAN BANNER *see* FLAGS

DIOCESAN RECORDS Diocesan records will usually be found in the record office of the county in which the diocesan office is located. For example, a nineteenth-century faculty for a Dorset parish will be found, not in the Dorset County Record Office at Dorchester, but at the Wiltshire County Record Office at Trowbridge which is where the records of the diocese of Salisbury are housed.

The earliest diocesan records, dating from the sixteenth century, provide a fascinating (though complex) insight into the activities and attitudes of clergy and parishioners at that time. Of these, the records of visitations (periodic inspections of parochial affairs) are an especially rewarding source of information (*see* VISITATIONS, ECCLESIASTICAL). Although established in the tenth century, following the Reformation the visitations became an effective method of implementing change and conformity in the reformed Church (*see* REFORMATION *and* SUBSCRIPTION BOOKS). Inevitably, not all diocesan officials were as scrupulous as they might have been and there are many omissions. Nevertheless, the PRESENTMENTS compiled by CHURCHWARDENS often contain a wealth of detail concerning the communities in which they lived and the churches they served. It should be borne in mind, however, that in those dioceses where the visitation records have survived not all parishes will be represented, neither will their reports invariably contain useful information.

The records (*act books*) of *ecclesiastical courts* provide a further invaluable source of information though they are so numerous and so complex that many local historians have been reluctant to approach them. Nevertheless, for those who are willing to delve into these extraordinary documents, '. . . written in cramped and hurried hands, in very abbreviated and technical Latin . . . ill-sorted and mostly un-listed, unindexed and sometimes broken in pieces' (G.R. Elton), they provide a unique insight into the daily lives of all levels of society. The evidence of witnesses was recorded in English (sometimes *verbatim*) and includes often lurid accounts of startling clarity, confirming that there was little privacy in sixteenth- and seventeenth-century society. Moral offences, slander, heresy, witchcraft, absence from services, non-payment of tithes and the misdemeanours of the clergy are all dutifully recorded, as are the most intimate aspects of a miscreant's personal affairs.

Visitation returns and BISHOPS' REGISTERS remain an important source of information for the eighteenth and nineteenth centuries, and are especially useful when attempting to identify the changes that were taking place in society (*see* EIGHTEENTH-CENTURY CHURCH *and* NINETEENTH-CENTURY CHURCH). They provide details of church services, the frequency of Communion, the number of Dissenters and Catholics in each parish and the founding of SUNDAY SCHOOLS. Diocesan records for the period also include details of the licensing and consecration of places of worship, lists of candidates presented for confirmation, licenses issued to curates (together with their personal details), terriers and inventories of church furnishings and plate, and details of faculties (*see* FACULTY) and mortgages relating to the repair and maintenance of churches and parsonage houses. Nineteenth-century faculties often refer to major restoration schemes, alterations or even re-building and the diocesan records may include the corresponding estimates, invoices and even plans and sketches of the proposed work. The *Clergy Residences Repair Act* of 1776 enabled clergy to raise the necessary funds for the repair or rebuilding of their parsonage houses by mortgaging the income from their benefices, usually through QUEEN ANNE'S BOUNTY. Mortgage deeds, dating from this period when so many substantial and elegant parsonages were built, may be found among the diocesan records, together with surveys of the houses they replaced. Bishops' records include correspondence concerning diocesan administration, records of ordinations and institutions and certificates issued to meeting houses. Directories, handbooks and calendars were published by many dioceses from *c.* 1850 and these contain information concerning parish churches, church schools, the clergy and their parishioners.
See also ARCHIVES, DOCUMENTARY SOURCES *and* PARLIAMENTARY RECORDS
Further reading:
Bettey, J.H., *Church and Parish*, London, 1987

Elton, G.R., *Sources of History: England 1200–1640*, London, 1969
Purvis, J.S., *Introduction to Ecclesiastical Records*, London, 1953

DIOCESAN REGISTRY The official archive of a diocese which may now be held at a county record office. Material includes details of church and cathedral administration, chapter books, bishops' transcripts, visitation books, tithes, land holdings, probate, Compton Census returns and marriage licences.

DIOCESE A diocese is an ecclesiastical administrative territory comprising archdeaconries, rural deaneries and parishes, all subject to the jurisdiction (*bishopric*) of a bishop. In the Church of England the Crown gives a Dean and Chapter leave to elect a bishop, and nominates the person to be elected. A *see* is the official 'seat' of a bishop and is normally located in the CATHEDRAL (*cathedra* = 'throne') of the diocese.
MEDIEVAL DIOCESES
By the beginning of the ninth century episcopal sees had been established at Iona, Abercorn, Whithorn, Lindisfarne, Hexham, York, Sidnacester, Lichfield, Hereford, Leicester, Elmham, Worcester, Dorchester (Oxfordshire), Dunwich, Sherborne, Winchester, London, Rochester, Selsey and Canterbury.

Following the Norman Conquest, a conciliar decree of 1075 required that sees should be removed from rural sites to urban centres. Sherborne, for example, was transferred to Old Sarum, an ancient hill-top site to the north of present-day Salisbury, where a new cathedral and castle were built as part of scheme which effectively remodelled an already thriving Saxon burgh to form a Norman city. Similarly, the cathedral church at remote North Elmham in Norfolk was abandoned in favour of Thetford and then Norwich. (Elmham's humble cathedral was converted into a moated hunting lodge the scant remains of which were unearthed as recently as 1903.)

At the end of the thirteenth century the English dioceses comprised: Canterbury (founded in 597), London (604), Rochester (604), York (625), Winchester (662), Lichfield (669), Hereford (676), Worcester (*c.* 680), Bath and Wells (909), Durham (995), Exeter (1050), Lincoln (1072), Chichester (1075), Salisbury (1078), Sodor and Man (before 1080), Norwich (1091), Ely (1109) and Carlisle (1133); and in Wales: Bangor, St. David's and Llandaff (all *c.* 550) and St. Asaph (1143) (*see* MEDIEVAL CHURCH *and* WALES, THE MEDIEVAL CHURCH IN).
POST-REFORMATION DIOCESES
Following the DISSOLUTION OF THE MONASTERIES a number of the English dioceses were sub-divided to create a further five: Chester

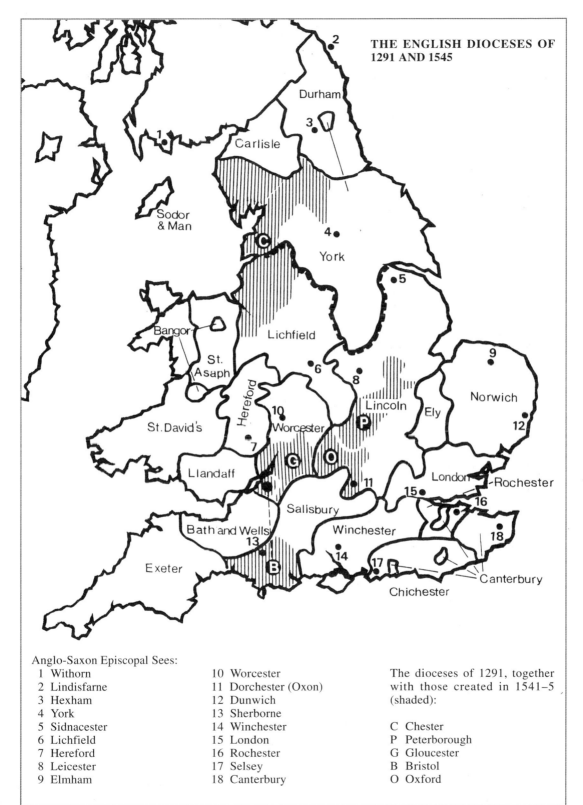

THE ENGLISH DIOCESES OF 1291 AND 1545

Anglo-Saxon Episcopal Sees:

1 Withorn	10 Worcester	The dioceses of 1291, together
2 Lindisfarne	11 Dorchester (Oxon)	with those created in 1541–5
3 Hexham	12 Dunwich	(shaded):
4 York	13 Sherborne	
5 Sidnacester	14 Winchester	C Chester
6 Lichfield	15 London	P Peterborough
7 Hereford	16 Rochester	G Gloucester
8 Leicester	17 Selsey	B Bristol
9 Elmham	18 Canterbury	O Oxford

(1541), Peterborough (1541), Gloucester (1541), Bristol (1542) and Oxford (1545). Of these, Chester encompassed the western third of the dioceses of York and Lichfield; the creation of Peterborough and Oxford in a narrow, diagonal band across the vast diocese of Lincoln effectively divided it in two, much of the southern half being incorporated in the later diocese of St. Alban's (1877). Gloucester was created out of the southern half of the diocese of Worcester and the new diocese of Bristol comprised a small area north of the city together with a large detached 'island' to the south, transferred from the diocese of Salisbury, and corresponding almost exactly to the old county of Dorset. A sixth diocese, with the Abbey of Westminster as its cathedral, lasted for only a decade from 1540–50.

No further sees were established between 1546 and 1836 but since then twenty new dioceses have been created in response to the rapid expansion of the urban population during the Industrial Revolution and the proliferation of suburban conurbations in the present century.

PROVINCES

An association of dioceses is a *province* over which one of the diocesan bishops presides as archbishop. There are two English provinces: that of Canterbury consisting of all the dioceses south of the river Trent, and that of York which includes the remaining dioceses to the north. The Province of Wales was created out of the Province of Canterbury in 1920, and two new dioceses formed (*see* WALES, THE CHURCH IN).

DIOCESAN RECORDS, deposited in the archives of diocesan registries, have mostly been transferred to county record offices.
See also CLERGY (CHURCH OF ENGLAND)

DIPTYCH (i) An ALTARPIECE consisting of a folding pair of pictures or tablets depicting religious themes and often recording genealogical and heraldic information. Many of the finest medieval diptychs originated as portable altars in royal and magnatial households (*see* TRIPTYCH). (ii) Lists of names of living and departed Christians for whom prayers are offered. (iii) A double-folding writing table.

DIRGE A lament for the dead, the term originated in the Office of the Dead which included the antiphon 'Dirige Domine Deus . . .' (Psalm 5:8).

DISCALCED Bare-footed.

DISPENSATION A licence, granted by an ecclesiastical authority, exempting the applicant from the consequences of an otherwise canonically illegal act or granting the remittance of a penalty for such an act. Most dispensations were granted in matters relating to vows, marriage and divorce. By

the late fifteenth century, the granting of dispensations had become a papal prerogative, one which was transferred to the archbishops of Canterbury in 1534 though was seldom used.

DISSENTERS Non-conformists, members of those Christian bodies which do not conform to the doctrines of the Church of England. Before the 1662 Act of Uniformity 'dissenters' or 'puritans' were frequently persecuted. The oldest non-conformists are the BAPTISTS, Independents (CONGREGATIONALISTS) and (in England) the PRESBYTERIANS. The METHODISTS date from 1738 but did not consider themselves to be non-conformist until later.
See also NINETEENTH-CENTURY CHURCH
Further reading:
Stell, C., *An Inventory of Non-Conformist Chapels and Meeting Houses in Central England*, RCHM, 1987

The first non-conformist chapel in England built at Horningsham, Wiltshire, in 1556 for workpeople on the Longleat estate.

DISSOLUTION OF THE CHANTRIES (1547)
see CHANTRIES

DISSOLUTION OF THE MONASTERIES
Monastic communities were by no means immune to criticism in the late Middle Ages, but it was in order to appropriate their considerable wealth and to facilitate the establishment of the royal supremacy that Henry VIII demolished the entire system (*see* AUGMENTATION, COURT OF).

THE LESSER MONASTERIES

In 1536 the Act for the Dissolution of the Smaller Monasteries required the suppression of all religious houses with fewer than twelve monks or nuns and an annual value of less than £200 so that 'His Majesty should have and enjoy . . .' all their possessions. The annual revenues recorded in the VALOR ECCLESIASTICUS of 1535 varied considerably from one religious house to another. In Wales, for example, the abbey of Tintern was assessed at £192 while the tiny priory of Caldey was assessed at only £5. Gilbertine Houses were specifically exempted from the 1536 Act and others (over seventy) were allowed to purchase exemptions at some considerable cost: in both instances the reprieve was short-lived. Government policy was not necessarily one of oughtright confiscation; commissioners deliberately sought out vulnerability and exploited it so that monastic communities were steadily persuaded to surrender. Confessions of sinful conduct and incompetent management were the usual instruments by which surrender was effected and should not be taken at face value: '. . . for asmuch as manifest sin, vicious, carnal and abominable living is daily used and committed among the little and small abbeys, priories and other religious houses of monks, canons and nuns . . .'. The commissioners themselves were often under considerable pressure from members of the nobility and gentry who happened to covet a particular monastic estate and who were known to enjoy royal patronage. At the same time, the often rich and famous SHRINES were being dismantled: that of St. Thomas a Becket at Canterbury was stripped of its encrusted gold, silver and jewels which were carried away in wagon-loads.

THE GREATER MONASTERIES

The Act for the Dissolution of the Greater Monasteries (of 1539) vested in the Crown all the properties so far surrendered and all remaining eligible monasteries and their vast estates. The Act did not in fact sanction dissolution *per se*, but rather safeguarded the Crown's title to the proceeds. Those who would not comply soon found themselves isolated and facing expulsion, attainder and even execution. Many were themselves tried and convicted of stealing from their own abbeys: On 15 November, 1539, Richard Whyting, abbot of the most venerable monastic foundation in England, was hanged, drawn and quartered on the summit of Glastonbury Tor for refusing to release the abbey plate. After a short and often brutal finale, the process of dispossession and dispersal was completed in 1540 and most of the religious brethren pensioned off (though the FRIARS were not) or provided with licences to become incumbents of parish benefices.

Perhaps the most significant aspect of the Dissolution was that it was effected with so little opposition (the principal exception being the northern rebellion of 1536–37 known as the 'Pilgrimage of Grace' which was chiefly concerned with the conduct and policies of the government of which the suppression of the lesser monasteries was but one element). No doubt the fact that the breach with Rome was essentially unopposed by the monastic orders in England facilitated the process: the dispersed brethren were not perceived as loyal adherents to the Papacy and the laity readily accepted the Dissolution. It is also significant that, although there was nothing to prevent the re-formation of a conventual community, no existing foundation managed to survive after 1540.

DESTRUCTION AND ADAPTATION

By 1539 explicit orders had been given for the total destruction of all newly surrendered monastic buildings and for the systematic removal of all lead and other materials. Total demolition (an expensive operation) was not always achieved: comprehensive ruination invariably was. Many dilapidated buildings provided accessible supplies of ashlar and rubble for local builders, particularly in those areas (such as East Anglia) where supplies of building stone were scarce. Because of their inherent remoteness, many of the great CISTERCIAN abbeys, such as Tintern in Gwent and Fountains in North Yorkshire, were less vulnerable to plundering and remain as gaunt, skeletal memorials to monastic exclusiveness. The twelve pre-Norman monastic cathedrals retained both their diocesan status and their lands which were administered by a dean and chapter. Westminster Abbey became a collegiate royal PECULIAR with a dean and secular canons, and from 1540–50 a diocesan cathedral. The new dioceses created out of the Dissolution ensured the survival as CATHEDRALS of the great medieval abbey churches of Bristol, Chester, Gloucester, Oxford and Peterborough (*see* DIOCESE). Nearly a hundred monastic churches, whose naves had long been parish churches, were retained whilst others, such as Tewkesbury in Gloucestershire and Sherborne in Dorset, were purchased by local benefactors or acquired for parochial use through diocesan intervention. But such churches were invariably deprived of their cloistral and domestic buildings and at some transepts, chapels and even choirs were demolished. When monastic buildings were sold into private hands, the great church was often the first component to be destroyed. Only rarely was a church small enough to provide comfortable domestic accommodation, as at Buckland in Devon. Elsewhere, the Tudor gentry, attracted as their monastic predecessors had been to fertile, sheltered and beautiful locations, adapted former abbots' lodgings and gatehouses as family residences and retained the monastery kitchens, cellars, barns and outhouses as at Beaulieu in Hampshire and Forde Abbey in Dorset. The buildings of Malmesbury

Abbey in Wiltshire were acquired by a clothier and converted into a factory!

MONASTIC REVENUES

Despite the declared intention of the 1536 Act of Suppression that the wealth acquired by the monasteries 'for the maintenance of sin' should be 'converted to better uses', the policy of retaining monastic holdings to provide a reliable source of income for the Crown was never maintained. The only real beneficiaries were the 'new' Tudor gentry: the post-medieval class of ambitious and successful men who through the acquisition of monastic estates were able more quickly to establish their credentials. Estates were valued at twenty times the assessed value of the lands, properties and tithes to be sold, and were transferred to their new owners with comparative ease. Most were already organised in manors administered by professional bailiffs who were unaffected by the change: few were demesne lands. When Elizabeth I ascended the throne in 1558, only a quarter of the estimated £150,000 income once available annually to the religious foundations remained in Crown hands.

See also REFORMATION, THE

DISTAFF DAY (*or* ST. DISTAFF'S DAY) The day after Twelfth Day (*see* EPIPHANY) on which day (7 January) women resumed their normal employment following the holiday.

DISTINCTION, MARKS OF *see* BASTARDY

DIURNAL The service book containing the DAY HOURS.

DIVINE OFFICE Described by St. Benedict as the *Opus Dei* (God's work), the divine office was the duty owed to God by all members of a religious community. Inspired by Psalm 119:164 'Seven times a day do I praise thee', it consisted of the Day Offices (services) of PRIME, TERCE, SEXT, NONES, VESPERS and COMPLINE to which were added the long night office of NOCTURNS or MATTINS and LAUDS at daybreak.

See also BREVIARY, HORARIUM, HOURS, CANONICAL *and* LITURGY

DIVINE RIGHT OF KINGS, THE The doctrine by which a monarch in the hereditary line of succession exercises authority directly from God and therefore enjoys a divine and indefeasible right to kingship. For a subject to rebel against that authority was considered to be a sin against God and the most grievous of political crimes. For this reason, conviction on a charge of treason was punishable by (an often barbarous) death and ATTAINDER.

DIVINE SERVICE A term used to describe any authorised form of Christian worship though, strictly speaking, it should be applied only to MATTINS and EVENSONG.

DIVORCE (i) The dissolution of the marriage bond. (ii) The legal termination of a marriage.

The estate of MATRIMONY is indissoluble in CANON LAW and divorce (in the first sense) is therefore not permitted in the Roman Catholic Church, though unconsummated marriages have been dissolved by papal authority. Divorce is also contrary to the canons and formularies of the Church of England. In the second sense, the Divorce and Matrimonial Causes Act of 1857 created a new court to exercise jurisdiction in matters matrimonial previously exercised by the ecclesiastical courts, and to grant divorces without the need for private acts of Parliament which only the very rich could afford. Thereafter, the 1878 Matrimonial Causes Act empowered magistrates to grant a legal separation with maintenance (i.e. not divorce) to wives whose husbands had been convicted of assault upon them. The clear division between secular legislation and Christian doctrine was recognised in the Divorce Reform Act of 1969 and both the Roman Catholic and Anglican churches permit the legal termination of a marriage for grave causes e.g. adultery.

See also AFFINITY, CONSANGUINITY, NULLITY *and* PROHIBITED DEGREES

DOCTORS OF THE CHURCH Saints whose doctrinal writings have special authority.

See also CHRISTIAN SYMBOLS

DOCUMENTARY SOURCES *see* ANCIENT DEEDS, ARCHITECTURAL ARCHIVES, ARCHIVES, BISHOPS' REGISTERS, BISHOPS' TRANSCRIPTS, 'BLUE BOOKS' (*see* NINETEENTH-CENTURY CHURCH), BOOKS, CENSUS, CENSUS OF RELIGIOUS WORSHIP (1851), CHANTRY CERTIFICATES (*see* CHANTRY *and* REFORMATION), CHARITIES, CHURCH TRUSTEES' RECORDS (*see* ARCHIVES), CHURCHWARDENS' ACCOUNTS, CLERICAL RECORDS (*see* ARCHIVES), CLOSE ROLLS, COLLEGE OF ARMS, COMPTON CENSUS, CONFISCATION INVENTORIES (*see* REFORMATION), COUNCIL FOR THE CARE OF CHURCHES, COUNTY HISTORIES, DIOCESAN RECORDS, DOMESDAY, ECCLESIASTICAL COURT RECORDS (*see* COURTS, ECCLESIASTICAL), ECCLESIASTICAL LIBRARIES, ECCLESIASTICAL TAXATION RECORDS, ELECTORAL REGISTER, FACULTY, INVENTORY, LIBRARIES, MANOR, MAPS, MINUTES, NATIONAL MONUMENTS RECORD, NATIONAL RECORDS, ORDINARY (OF ARMS), PARISH CHEST, PARISH REGISTERS (*see*

REGISTERS), PARLIAMENTARY RECORDS (*see* NINETEENTH-CENTURY CHURCH), PEDIGREE, PHOTOGRAPHS, POOR LAW, PRESENTMENTS (*see* VISITATIONS, ECCLESIASTICAL), PROBATE INVENTORIES, QUEEN ANNE'S BOUNTY, RECUSANCY, REFORMATION, REGISTERS, ROYAL COMMISSION ON THE HISTORICAL MONUMENTS OF ENGLAND, SCHOOLS, SETTLEMENT AND REMOVAL RECORDS, STAINED GLASS, SUBSCRIPTION BOOKS, TERRIER, TITHE MAPS (*see* MAPS), TITHE RECORDS (*see* TITHES), TRANSCRIPTS, TRUSTEES (CHURCH), VALOR ECCLESIASTICUS, VESTRY MINUTES (*see* MINUTES), VICTORIA COUNTY HISTORY, VISITATIONS (ECCLESIASTICAL), VISITATIONS (HERALDIC), WELSH RECORDS *and* WILLS (*see* PROBATE)

See also APPENDIX II *for* addresses of organisations several of which maintain archives of documentary records.

Not to be overlooked are the many mundane documents of parochial life. These include: (i) *Parish magazines*, which vary in size from a single duplicated sheet to splendidly illustrated journals, lovingly produced by bands of enthusiastic volunteers. All contain invaluable information concerning services, entries in the parish registers and community activities, while the larger publications often include articles written by local historians, correspondence columns which may reflect tensions within a local community, and financial reports which provide information concerning the fabric of a church or the condition of its churchyard. Some parish magazines have survived from the nineteenth century. (ii) *Guide Books* (and sometimes *Village Histories*) are available at many parish churches and, again, these vary considerably both in size and quality. But they should always be treated with circumspection: not all compilers are experienced historians, archaeologists, genealogists or armorists and, as a result, research is sometimes minimal and myths can easily be perpetuated. (*See also* HORN-BOOKS) (iii) *Visitors' books*, containing details of visitors to a church, are usually kept by an incumbent. They are a comparatively recent phenomenon and may be of interest to students of demography. (iv) *War memorial books* contain the names of those who subscribed to the erection of WAR MEMORIALS. Most will have found their way to county record offices but some are still kept by incumbents. (v) Similarly, some parishes retain *books of remembrance* in which are inscribed the names of those members of the community who died in the World Wars of 1914–18 and 1939–45 (in some cases, more recent campaigns have also been added).

Most incumbents are pleased to assist researchers, indeed a long-serving parson can often be relied upon to provide detailed or anecdotal information which may not be available from other sources. A telephone request for an appointment is essential – and a contribution to church funds is always appreciated.

Local newspapers are also an invaluable source of information. In the nineteenth century, for example, they contained regular reports on Church affairs, church restorations and parochial fund-raising (including lists of benefactors), while national journals such as *The Builder* (from 1834) and *The Ecclesiologist* (1841–68) published detailed articles on new churches and restoration schemes.

Further reading:

Bryant Rosier, M., *Index to Parishes in Phillimore's Marriages*, Chichester, 1991

Church, R. and Cole, J., *In and Around Record Repositories in Great Britain and Ireland*, Chichester, 1991

Edwards, P., *Rural Life: Guide to Local Records*, London, 1993

Friar, S., *The Batsford Companion to Local History*, London, 1991

Gibson, J., *Bishop's Transcripts and Marriage Licences*, Chichester, 1992

Gibson, J. and Peskett, P., *Record Offices and How to Find Them*, London, 1991

Humphery-Smith, C., *The Phillimore Atlas and Index of Parish Registers*, Chichester, 1984

Munby, L., *Reading Tudor and Stuart Handwriting*, Chichester, 1988

Riden, P., *Local History: A Handbook for Beginners*, London, 1983

——, *Record Sources for Local History*, London, 1987

Stephens, W., *Sources for English Local History*, Cambridge, 1981

Stuart, D., *Manorial Records*, Chichester, 1992

Tate, W., *The Parish Chest*, Cambridge, 1979

Thoyts, E., *How to Read Old Documents*, London, 1980

Trice Martin, C., *The Record Interpreter*, London, 1982

Webb, C., (ed.), *The National Index of Parish Registers* (series), Chichester

West, J., *Village Records*, London, 1984

——, *Town Records*, London, 1983

'DOG COLLAR' *see* VESTMENTS

DOGRAIL A grille-like section of ornate ironwork at the lower edge of a gate or railing intended to prevent dogs from passing through (*see* DOGS).

DOGS The driving of livestock from the cab of a tractor is a recent innovation. At one time, men and working dogs were constantly together, even on

Sundays, and at the parish church measures had to be taken to deal with noises and fights which inevitably disturbed the solemnity of the occasion. COMMUNION RAILS were introduced after the REFORMATION to protect the communion table when it became more accessible and therefore vulnerable to profanation, especially by stray dogs, and from this time owners were discouraged from taking their animals into church. At Grappenhall in Cheshire the vestry ordered '. . . that the wardens of this parish shall cause the church during the time of divine service to be kept clear from all dogs and bitches by hiring a person to whip and drive them out of church'; and in the vestry minutes for Wrexham, an entry for 1663 states that 'Hee that keeps ye dogs out of church is ordered to have 2/6 quarterly and 5/- for arrears'. Persons appointed to perform this duty were known as *dog whippers, knocknobblers* or *sluggard walkers*. But, as usual, there were exceptions: until *c.* 1830, just inside the chancel arch of Northope church in Lincolnshire, there was a small enclosed pew, known as the Hall Dog Pew, where the dogs from the great house were kennelled while the squire's family and household servants attended the service.

In Wales and the border counties many 'dog-whippers' were provided with dog tongs (*gefail gwn*) which were usually kept in the church. These tongs consisted of three pairs of bars which moved freely on pivots so that, when the handles were brought together, the tongs expanded to their full length and would restrain the animal at a safe distance. Most dog tongs were made of oak (and consequently bore the teeth marks of many generations of parish dogs) though at Clynnog Fawr in Gwynedd an iron pair is preserved, 1.4 metres (3 feet 9 inches) in length and with four spikes set within each of the grips. In the eighteenth century, the dog-whippers of Wrenbury in Cheshire were provided with splendid blue gowns with yellow tippets, and their duties also included the restoring to consciousness those who dozed during the sermon. For this purpose each officer carried a white wand at one end of which was a knob and at the other a fox's brush – the former for tapping the offending male members of the congregation on the head and the latter for tickling the ladies' nostrils! In order to emphasise the dignity of their office, the title of dog-whipper was changed to that of beadle in 1826.
See also CHURCHWARDENS' ACCOUNTS *and* DOGRAIL
For dogs depicted in monuments *see* BRASSES (MONUMENTAL) *and* EFFIGIES.

DOG TONGS *see* DOGS

DOGTOOTH ORNAMENT A form of architectural ornamentation typical of the Gothic work of the late twelfth and early thirteenth centuries (*see*

DECORATIVE MOTIFS). It consists of a horizontal band of raised saltires, the four limbs of which are shaped like leaves (or pointed teeth). Not to be confused with the QUATREFOIL.
See also MEDIEVAL ARCHITECTURE

DOLE CUPBOARDS *and* **DOLE TABLES** Similar in appearance to a CHEST CUPBOARD or AUMBRY, but open-fronted or pierced with holes to admit air, a dole cupboard contained bread and other food (*doles*) for distribution to the poor. Dole cupboards may still be found in several churches and usually date from the sixteenth century or later. There are good examples at All Saints, Hereford and Milton Ernest in Bedfordshire. Doles, which were often donated by a benefactor or acquired by the churchwardens (*see* CHARITIES) were also distributed from dole tables. Pre-Reformation *dole tables* are singularly rare: that in the churchyard at Powerstock in Dorset dates from the thirteenth century when charitable doles of bread were distributed to the poor. The colloquial usages 'to dole out . . .' and 'on the dole', both of which imply a sparing distribution of resources, are derived from this practice.
See also ALMONRY

Dole cupboard at the church of St. Martin, Ruislip.

DOLE-WINDOW *see* ALMONRY

D.O.M. *Deo Optimo Maximo* (Latin = 'to God, the best, the greatest'). Once a favourite Roman dedication to Jupiter, especially for a work of art, but it acquired a Christian application and may sometimes be found carved in the fabric of churches.

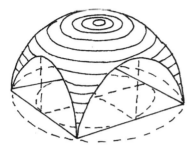

Sail vault

DOME A convex, rounded roof with a circular, elliptical or polygonal base. In Renaissance (and especially BAROQUE) architecture the dome was a fundamental characteristic of design and a variety of constructional forms was adopted. Among these was the use of the *pendentive* which enabled a dome to be carried on free-standing piers. A pendentive is a spherical triangle formed by the intersection of a dome with two adjacent arches (*see illustration*). The domical structure created thereby is known as a *sail vault* because it has the appearance of a sail when anchored at the four corners.
See also CUPOLA *and* SQUINCH

DOMESDAY Following the Conquest of England in 1066, Duke William of Normandy was crowned King and most of the lands of the native nobility were granted to his followers. In 1085 '. . . at Gloucester in midwinter . . . the King had thorough and deep discussion with his counsellors about this country, how it was occupied and with what sort of people' and he sent his men '. . . all over England into every shire . . . to find out . . . what or how much each landholder held . . . in land and livestock, and what it was worth.' (*Anglo-Saxon Chronicle*).

The Commissioners were instructed to ascertain and record all taxable holdings and anything which added to the annual value of a manorial estate (*manerium*), tithing or township, including disputed lands. The entire realm, which did not then include Cumberland and Westmorland (present-day Cumbria), was divided into seven circuits and visited county by county, hundred by hundred and township by township. Evidence was taken on oath '. . . from the Sheriff; from all the barons and their

Frenchmen; and from the whole hundred, the priests, the reeves and six villagers from each village.' The *Inquisitio Eliensis* (the Ely volume of returns) also tells us that the Commissioners were required to establish:

The name of the place.
The names of those by whom it was held, before 1066 and since.
The extent of taxable ploughland (expressed as hides, carucates or other local units of land measurement), and the number of ploughs, before and after 1066.
The number of villagers, cottagers, slaves and free men (but not details of their families).
The number of mills and fishponds and the extent of meadow, pasture and woodland (it is unclear whether this was coppiced woodland or open wood pasture).
The extent to which fiscal potential had been reduced or increased since 1066.
The value of holdings enjoyed by each free man.

Details were verified by four Frenchmen and four Englishmen from each hundred, whose names were also recorded, and yet many details were omitted, including several churches and an occasional castle! Because it was essentially a means by which feudal law and tenure could be maintained, those that were exempt from taxation were generally excluded: in particular lands owned by religious houses. But it was not exclusively a tax assessment: its purpose was that every man '. . . should know his right and not usurp another's'. A second group of commissioners was charged with the task of checking their predecessors' returns in '. . . shires they did not know' and 'where they were themselves unknown.'

The survey was completed within a year and so pervasive and authoritative was its ambit, establishing every landholder's inescapable liability, that its consequences were likened to those of Domesday itself – the Last Judgement. At Winchester, the returns (written in a form of Latin shorthand) were corrected, abridged and catalogued by reference to landowners, before being copied by a scribe into a single volume. The surveys of Essex, Norfolk and Suffolk were also collated and copied, unabridged, into a further volume dated 1086, but those of Durham and Northumberland and of several towns (notably, London and Winchester) were not transcribed. Domesday Book – *Liber de Wintonia* – describes, in minute detail, England 'under new management'

The Domesday survey was the product of an experienced and sophisticated administration and was undoubtedly unique in early medieval Europe, both in its scope and execution. But problems and anomalies exist, especially for the novice who is unaccustomed to interpreting such information and may be unnerved by the complexities of the terminology and format. For example, the listings by land-owner often result in references to a single parish being found under a number of owners; and a Domesday reference to a present-day village does not necessarily imply its existence as a *village* in 1086: only the names of manorial estates, tithings and townships were recorded and even these may be concealed in a single entry. The original survey (which has recently been rebound) is at the Public Record Office (*see* APPENDIX II).

Further reading:

Darby, H., (ed.), *Domesday England*, Cambridge, 1977

Hallam, E., *Domesday Book Through Nine Centuries*, London, 1986

Jones, M., *England Before Domesday*, London, 1976

Morris, J., (ed.), *History from the Sources: Domesday Book*, in county volumes, Chichester

Versey, G., *Domesday Gazetteer*, Cambridge, 1975

Welldon Finn, R., *Domesday Book: A Guide*, Chichester, 1973

Wood, M., *Domesday: A Search for the Roots of England*, London, 1986

DOMINICANS *see* FRIARS

DOMUS CONVERSORUM The domestic quarters of the lay brethren (*conversi*) of a Cistercian community, usually the west range of conventual buildings.

DONATIVE PARISH (DONATIVE BENEFICE) *see* PARISH

DONOR WINDOW A window donated to a church by a benefactor or group of benefactors (*see* STAINED GLASS).

DOOM In most medieval parish churches the CHANCEL and NAVE were separated by a screen supporting the figure of Christ Crucified (the ROOD). The rood screen also separated the clergy from the laity – medieval sanctity from pagan superstition – and in order to concentrate the minds of the latter the wall above the chancel arch, or a wooden or plaster TYMPANUM fixed above the rood screen, was often painted with a lurid representation of the Doom. Typically, this depicted Christ presiding in majesty over the Last Judgement in which the naked souls of the dead rose from their graves to be weighed by St. Michael and received by the angels into eternal paradise or forked by devils into the gaping and fiery mouth of *Hades*. Such a *Hell Mouth* was often depicted as the open jaws of a gigantic whale – the great *Leviathan* of the Book of Job – or the mythical sea-tortoise of the bestiaries, *Aspido Chelone*, who enticed the wicked into his

A painting of the Last Judgement above the chancel arch at the church at St. Thomas of Canterbury, Salisbury.

mouth in the midst of their depravity, as at Wiggenhall St. German in Norfolk. Such creatures symbolised the devil himself and served to stimulate the medieval preoccupation with salvation and eternal damnation. Usually, only the mouth is depicted in Doom paintings, though in a fifteenth-century window at Fairford Church, Gloucestershire the whole terrifying creature is shown.

Satan, as one might expect, is prominent as is his riotous crew of horned and hairy demons. The damned are confined in chains, suspended in gibbets, boiled in caldrons and transported to hell in wheelbarrows and farmstead carts. All levels of medieval society are represented: from popes and kings to peasants and poachers. Most are shown stumbling beneath the burden of their sins: the greedy merchant with his money bags, the malingerer on her knee pads and hand stools, feigning crippledom (as at Hornton in Oxfordshire) and the dishonest ale-wife with her pitcher of watered-down ale and seductive bodice.

The transitional state of Purgatory, where souls reconciled to God suffered for an indeterminate period, was of little interest to medieval artists: probably because a speedy passage could be guaranteed by obtaining an indulgence (*see* INDULGENCES), endowing a CHANTRY or joining a crusade or pilgrimage.

Most of these murals were painted by local jobbing artists and are singularly vernacular both in style and execution. Medieval pigments of mud, rock and ochre were applied straight on to limewash with brushes of squirrel or hog hair. The wonderful simplicity of line which characterises the earliest paintings was achieved simply because the artist had no second chance once the pigment was applied. There is evidence to suggest that many were routinely repainted every fifty years or so. When, at the Reformation, the laity was permitted into the chancel for the Eucharist, many Doom paintings were removed or painted over. Victorian 'restorations' also took their toll: rood screens were often dismantled and most surviving Doom paintings destroyed. Nevertheless, some sixty medieval examples have survived, among them murals at Lower Oddington, Gloucestershire and Clayton, Sussex (twelfth century); Pickworth, Lincolnshire and North Cove, Suffolk (fourteenth century); Chesterton, Cambridgeshire and Salisbury (St. Thomas's), Wiltshire (fifteenth century); Wenhaston, Suffolk and Dauntsey, Wiltshire (early sixteenth century).

See also BURIALS, HARROWING OF HELL *and* WALL PAINTINGS

Further reading:

Tasker, E., *Encyclopaedia of Medieval Church Art*, London, 1994

Early twelfth-century west doorway to the circular chapel of St. Mary Magdalene at Ludlow Castle, Shropshire.

DOORCASE The framework lining a doorway and on which the door is hung.

DOOR-KEEPER The lowest of the MINOR ORDERS, with responsibilities similar to those of a VERGER.

DOORS AND DOORWAYS In most medieval churches, the west door was used for ceremonial purposes (*see* WEST DOORWAY) while the south door was that by which the congregation usually entered from the churchyard. Inevitably it was on the south door of the parish church that public notices were displayed, a tradition which persists in the publishing of electoral registers and notices of elections in church PORCHES today. When studying church doors and doorways, it should be borne in mind that an entire doorway may have been moved and set in a later wall, and that most ancient doors will have been repaired many times and may therefore contain timber and fittings (*door furniture*) which are not original. VOTIVE CROSSES, MASONS' MARKS and other graffiti may be found scratched in the stonework of a doorway or in the door itself, and many ancient door-latches have been engraved with a '*witches mark*' (typically, a saltire within a rectangle) intended to deter witches from entering the church.

SAXON DOORS AND DOORWAYS

Saxon doorways were narrow with heavy triangular or round arches, often supported on large, square impost stones, as at Barnack in Northamptonshire. Doors were constructed of thick oak boards, placed vertically on the outside and horizontally inside, and secured by long wrought-iron 'clout' nails with ornamental heads, driven through and clenched on the inside. Of the few surviving Saxon doors, that at Hadstock in Essex is perhaps the best (*see* ANGLO-SAXON ARCHITECTURE)

MEDIEVAL DOORWAYS

Romanesque doorways were often the most richly ornamental feature of a building and were deeply recessed and moulded, the space (*tympanum*) between the usually square-topped door and the round arch above being vigorously carved in high relief (*see* MEDIEVAL ARCHITECTURE). Undoubtedly the best example is the south doorway at Kilpeck in Herefordshire (*c.* 1170–90), though there are numerous others, notably at Barford St. Michael and Iffley in Oxfordshire, Windrush in Gloucestershire, Tutbury in Staffordshire,

Heckingham in Norfolk and Adel, Alne, Fishlake, Kirkburn, Stillingfleet and Wighill in Yorkshire. Some of the best tympana are found in Cotswold churches: at Elkstone, for example, where a figure of Christ in Majesty is surrounded by symbols of the Evangelists, at Quenington where (in one of two splendid examples) there is a Harrowing of Hell, at Siddington and at Moreton Valence in the Vale of Berkeley. There are other good examples at Brinsop and Stretton Sugwas, both of the same 'Herefordshire School' of carving as Kilpeck, at Dinton in Buckinghamshire, Aston Eyre in Shropshire and Barfreston and Patrixbourne in Kent. Many early doorways are carved with PAGAN SYMBOLS as at Leominster Priory in Herefordshire where the inner faces of the capitals of the west door are a riot of bug-eyed fertility gods spewing grapes and grain.

See also FIGURE SCULPTURE

MEDIEVAL DOORS

Medieval doors were usually made of interlinked vertical planks bound on the inside with horizontal members (*ledges*) and with prominent, often decorated, metal hinges, locks and handles. The hinges usually have bi-furcated ends (divided into two curving branches) and stamped work. The twelfth-century door in the north wall of Maiden Newton church in Dorset is considered by many to be the oldest medieval church door in England, though there are better preserved early examples at Little Hormhead in Hertfordshire, Old Woking in Surrey, Edstaston in Shropshire and Stillingfleet in Yorkshire.

Thirteenth-century doors are to be found at Skipworth in Yorkshire and Eaton Bray and Turvey in Bedfordshire and there is a magnificent fourteenth-century example, with ironwork of leaf-scrolls and leopards, at St. Saviour's church at Dartmouth in Devon. (There are also numerous nineteenth-century copies the detail of which is almost invariably more precise than a medieval original.)

In the fourteenth century, decorative ironwork deteriorated in quality and was superseded by carved wooden mouldings and cover beads (linear reinforcement covering joints in the door timbers) and tracery (at the head of the door) which was either carved into the woodwork or applied with glue and nails and often reflected the style of contemporary WINDOW TRACERY, as at Wellow in Somerset and Addlethorpe in Lincolnshire.

Even where an ancient door has been replaced, the medieval furniture may remain: the thirteenth-century door-handle and knocker at Baltonsborough in Somerset, for example, or the extraordinary handles at Adel in Yorkshire and Dormington in Herefordshire both of which are clasped in the mouths of demonic monsters. Interior doors have often survived from the medieval period, especially those to ROOD STAIRS and TOWERS, as at Stogumber in Somerset and Blewbury in Berkshire.

In doorways, the Gothic pointed arch predominated and, in larger buildings, was often moulded and carved in the contemporary ornamental style. As the Gothic period progressed, the shape and proportion of the arch itself became flatter and wider culminating in the four-centre style of the late fifteenth century (*see* ARCH). These later Perpendicular and Tudor doorways had a square hood-mould above the arch and spandrels filled with carved ornamentation.

POST-MEDIEVAL DOORS

Until the late seventeenth century, most church doors continued to be constructed of long oak planks held together within a framework and strengthened by means of diagonal members (*braces*) and horizontal members (*ledges*). Such doors are usually described as *framed and braced* (having a diagonal member within a timber frame) or *ledged and braced* (having a series of horizontal and diagonal members). There was a brief revival of decorative metalwork in the late seventeenth century (see below) which was followed by the introduction of the 'classical' six-panelled door with prominent mouldings in the early eighteenth century. Typically, this type of door consists of an outer frame of horizontal and vertical members (*rails* and *stiles*), strengthened by means of additional rails and vertical members (*muntins*). In churches, panelled doors were often hung in pairs, each door at least 1.8 metres high (6 feet) and .9 metres wide (3 feet) with the top two panels smaller and rectangular (not square, as in many sham-Georgian examples). Often the bottom two panels were combined and increased in thickness to save that part of the door from wear and tear. Early eighteenth-century doorcases sometimes incorporated columns or pilasters supporting rounded arches (with projecting key-stones), flat cornices or elaborate hoods or canopies. From *c.* 1720 glass fanlights were introduced into these 'temple' Palladian doorcases and by the end of the century these had become complex with Robert Adam and others using profuse delicate tracery. Some eighteenth-century doors were made from seasoned oak or imported mahogany and waxed, but most were of close-grained pine, painted in dark colours, 'graining' being introduced in the early nineteenth century. From 1832 (when Continental 'plate' glass was introduced by Lucas Chance) decorative and colourful stained glass panels became popular and by 1840 fanlights were no longer fashionable.

DOOR FURNITURE

Door furniture dating from all periods will be found in churches, though locks, keys and latches are not always contemporaneous with the doors on which they are found or, indeed, with each other. Hinges are generally more permanent, though even these should not be relied on for dating purposes, earlier styles having been revived and copied, especially during the Victorian period.

1. The grave of the Dorset poet and novelist Thomas Hardy (1840–1928) at St. Michael's, Stinsford. Hardy had specifically willed that he should be buried at Stinsford, '. . . unless the Nation strongly desires otherwise'. A Westminster Abbey funeral was arranged but Hardy's second wife, Florence, was 'nagged by doubts'. Eventually, it was agreed that Hardy's ashes should be buried in the Abbey and his heart at Stinsford, a final irony that would have been appreciated by Hardy, and one which was met with local cynicism and even ribaldry: 'Almighty, 'e'll say, "'ere be 'eart, but where be rest of 'e ?"' According to some sources, the grave also contains the remains of a village cat which, on the night before the funeral, discovered the heart in a biscuit tin and ate it.

2. *Nineteenth-century lich-gate at Charlton Horethorne, Somerset. One of a group of gates constructed by a 'school' of south-Somerset craftsmen and characterised by carved wooden brackets representing death and resurrection.*

3. *Detail: head of a female mourner.*

4. The thatched church of St. Edmund at Acle, Norfolk. The round tower is typical of many East Anglian churches, the octagonal upper section being a late medieval addition, as was the two-storey south porch.

5. Set within the ramparts of an Iron Age hill fort, the medieval church of St. Laurence at West Wycombe, Buckinghamshire, was partly rebuilt in the eighteenth century for Sir Francis Dashwood, traveller, dilettante and reputed Satanist. Its fourteenth-century tower is surmounted by an immense golden ball within which the members of Dashwood's infamous Hell Fire Club met for drinking sessions. Made of wood and covered with fabric and lead, the ball is provided with seats for up to ten people.

6. Norman chevron and beakhead moulding in the west doorway of the former priory church of St. Mary and St. Bega at St. Bees, Cumbria.

7. Doom painting above the chancel arch in the Guild Chapel of the Holy Cross at Stratford-upon-Avon, Warwickshire. The outline of the rood, and the corbels which once supported it, are clearly visible. Built in 1269, the chapel was much altered in the mid-fifteenth century.

The earliest surviving medieval hinges are reminiscent of Nordic designs: crescent-shaped with snake-head, tendril or floriated terminals. Indeed, the twelfth-century hammered ironwork on the door of All Saints church at Staplehurst in Kent is strangely evocative of a craft which is older than Christianity itself. Twelfth- and thirteenth-century strap-hinges (which extend horizontally across the surface of the door) are composed of bi-furcated, geometrical patterns of stems and leaves, while finely executed scroll-work is a characteristic of the late thirteenth century (see above). One of the finest examples, on a mid-thirteenth-century door at Eaton Bray in Bedfordshire, is believed to be the work of the eminent medieval smith, Thomas de Leighton. Concealed butt hinges were widely used from the late seventeenth century as were simple, tapering wrought-iron strap-hinges with (often crude) surface decoration and ornamental finials such as fleurs-de-lis.

Many of the locks and keys used in our older parish churches are from the late eighteenth and nineteenth centuries, typically the Old Stock lock with its heavily bound wooden casing, key operated bolt and integral latch. A number of sixteenth-century iron lock-plates have also survived and these are usually square (or nearly so) with a prominent keyhole and external ratchet device. Eighteenth-century door furniture was considerably smaller than modern brass reproductions and made of sheet-iron, painted black or lead-colour. At the rectory, the knocker was of great importance, most bell-pulls dating from the late nineteenth century and electric bells from *c.* 1900. Postmen always knocked twice and other callers had distinctive knocks which must have been familiar to the servants.

DORCAS MEETING A women's church association, popular in the nineteenth century, primarily concerned with the making of clothes for the poor (*see* Acts 9: 36–43).

DORIC *see* CLASSICAL ORDER

DORMANT *see* BEASTS (HERALDIC)

DORMER A projecting upright window in a sloping roof, having also its own independent roof.

DORSAL (*or* DOSSAL) A fabric screen at the back of an altar.

DORSE The reverse side of a document.
See also ENDORSEMENT

DORTER In the cloistral buildings of a monastery, the dorter was the first-floor monks' dormitory, usually situated on the south side of the cloister from which it was reached by means of a *day stair*. A *night stair* lead from the dorter to the transept of the abbey church and it was by this that the monks descended to attend the early offices. The dorter was a long open room, with a series of low windows, probably one for each bed-stead. Privacy was considered to be an unnecessary luxury in many orders, as was any form of heating in the dormer, though several monastic houses eventually divided the dormitories to form cubicles and warming houses were sometimes provided in the vicinity of the stair so that the rising heat would give some relief from the cold and damp of the dorter above. Adjacent to the dorter, and usually at right-angles to it, was the *reredorter* or 'house of easement' (otherwise known as the *necessarium* or 'necessary house'). This was the monks' privy, usually a long, narrow room furnished with divisions and wooden seats, venting into a channel beneath which was cleansed by flowing water. The lay brothers' dormitory was often located at the opposite side of the cloister or in an entirely separate building. Regrettably, the second storeys of most cloistral buildings were demolished following the Dissolution and few dorters or reredorters have survived.
See also LAVATORIUM *and* MONASTERIES

DOSSAL *see* DORSE

DOUBLE CONE *see* DECORATIVE MOTIFS

DOUBLE MONASTERY A religious house for both men and women and having a common superior. The two sexes lived in separate but contiguous establishments and worshipped in distinct parts of the common church.

DOUBLET *see* COSTUME

DOVECOTES (*also* CULVERY *and* DOVECOT) In medieval nucleated settlements the parish church, manor house, home farm and tithe barn are often found in close proximity to one another, forming an attractive cluster of ancient buildings which may also include the site of a former mill and a dovecote.

South of St. Michael's church at Garway in Herefordshire is a fine circular dovecot built by the Knights Templar in the early fourteenth century with nesting spaces for 666 birds. A few monastic dovecotes have also survived, at Penmon on Anglesey, for example, where the former priory church is now the parish church (though it may be that the dovecote was built in the sixteenth century after the priory had been dissolved).

The Romans obtained fresh protein from birds which nested in tower-like dovecotes similar to those which were introduced into England from Normandy in the eleventh century. Medieval dovecotes are usually square or rectangular free-standing buildings of stone or brick or, from the thirteenth century, cylindrical with a conical roof and 'lantern' through

Churchyard dovecote at Stoke-sub-Hamdon, Somerset.

century there were over 25,000 dovecotes in England and an act of 1761 enabled freeholders and landlords to erect dovecotes and to license their use by tenants. Church towers were occasionally used as pigeon-houses and many large farms continued to use dovecotes until the introduction of the new turnip husbandry of the eighteenth century provided for the overwintering of cattle.

Further reading:

Hansell, P. and J., *Doves and Dovecotes*, Millstream Books, 1988

DOVES The dove is the Christian symbol for peace and reconciliation. It is a device commonly found in the fabric and ornamentation of churches, and in vestments, plate and religious illustrations where it represents the Holy Spirit and the soul regenerated by baptism. The Eucharistic Dove is a receptacle in the shape of a dove in which the Blessed Sacrament is contained.

See also CHRISTIAN SYMBOLS

DOWER *and* DOWAGER Originally, a dower was a gift (*dowry*) from a husband to his bride on the morning of their marriage, but from the twelfth century the term came to mean a portion of an estate (generally one-third) claimed by a widow in her lifetime or until she remarried (*see* PROBATE). Similarly, a residence assigned from an estate to a widow for life is a *dower house*. A *dowager* is a woman with property or a title derived from her late husband.

DRAGON *see* BEASTS (HERALDIC) *and* CHURCH SITES

DRAINS Monastic communities produced vast quantities of liquid waste, especially from the kitchens, INFIRMARY (*farmery*), LAVATORIUM (wash-house) and reredorter (*see* DORTER). This was collected in a main drain which usually traversed the site, its route dictated by the gradient. Those buildings which produced the most waste were carefully sited along its course so that when water was reused, that which was most heavily polluted entered the drain at its lowest level. Rain water from roofs was collected and fed into the system following use. Collection and drainage systems are often extraordinarily sophisticated and were provided with CONDUITS, sluices and subsidiary drains, syphons and balancing tanks. The main drain was often constructed of fine masonry: at Monk Bretton and Fountains in Yorkshire and at Tintern in Gwent, for example.

DRAMA From the tenth century, the death and resurrection of Christ were commonly celebrated in churches by means of vernacular drama, usually mime and dialogue, performed during or after the liturgical rites on feast days which were also public holidays (*see* CHURCH AND COMMUNITY).

which the pigeons (domesticated rock-doves with an instinct for nesting on cliff faces) could come and go as they pleased. The cylindrical shape accommodated a ladder (or pair of ladders) which revolved on central pivots to provide access to the rows of nesting holes that lined the walls. This mechanism, or *potence* (from OE *potent* meaning 'crutch'), was often so well-balanced that it could be turned at the touch of a finger and enabled the culverer to remove the *squabs* (young birds not fully fledged) with a minimum of fuss. The general impression inside a dovecot was of a circular brick wall with alternate bricks removed from floor to roof level. In fact, each hole was larger than two bricks and was several feet deep to provide ample space for roosting and nesting accommodation for the succession of two-egg clutches produced through most of the year. Many culveries contained more than one thousand nesting holes and with two pigeons and two young to each there could be up to four thousand birds feeding freely on the tenants' crops! This no doubt accounts for the fact that dovecotes in the medieval period were restricted to demesne and monastic lands where they represented a significant element in the domestic economy by providing fresh meat and eggs during the winter and a constant supply of droppings (*guano*) which was used as fertilizer. Later dovecotes were more varied: sometimes octagonal or rectangular with lectern-shaped vents above the roof or simple box-like structures of brick, stone or timber-framing with polygonal roofs and an attractive variety of vented cupolas (*glovers*). At the close of the seventeenth

From this 'praiseworthy custom' developed *aleplays*, which were performed to raise money for church funds, and the MYSTERY PLAYS (or miracle plays) of the medieval period, the most impressive of which were the Passion Plays. CORPUS CHRISTI processions also provided opportunities for the elaborate representation of the Gospel stories. Mystery plays were usually performed on temporary open-air stages or on wagons which were moved through the streets along established routes, halting at regular intervals to entertain (and to educate) the audiences who awaited them. The plays were usually performed by members of trade GUILDS (which were also religious fraternities) and individual dramas gradually merged to form cycles of plays, the best-known collections being named after the towns where they were performed: Chester, Coventry, Wakefield and York. In the fifteenth and sixteenth centuries, the mystery plays were superseded by MORALITY PLAYS in which a moral truth was inculcated by the personification of abstract qualities. Thereafter, vernacular drama became increasingly secular in character and was repudiated by the more puritanical Reformers, though vestiges of ancient religious customs lingered in many rural areas, even into the nineteenth century.
See also CHURCH AND COMMUNITY
Further reading:
Anderson, M., *Drama and Imagery in Medieval Churches*, London, 1963

DRAWINGS (ARCHITECTURAL) Architectural drawings (sometimes accompanied by a scale model) will often be found in churches which were the subject of Victorian restoration (*see* NINETEENTH-CENTURY ARCHITECTURE). These drawings are especially useful for they usually include 'before and after' plans, elevations and sketches. They are not always on public display, however, and it is often best to enquire by post or telephone before visiting a church. Others may have been removed to public record offices.
See also ARCHITECTURAL ARCHIVES

DRESSED STONE Worked and smoothly finished stone used in architectural features such as doorways and window openings.
See also MASONRY

DRESSER WINDOW In monastic buildings, the serving hatch between kitchen and frater on either side of which was a serving table (*dresser*). There are good examples at Mattersey Priory in Nottinghamshire, where fragments of masonry from the former priory have been incorporated into the parish church, and at Muchelney in Somerset where the parish church forms part of a group with the ruins of the adjoining Benedictine abbey.

DRESSINGS Stones worked to a smooth or moulded edge and set round an architectural feature such as a doorway or window opening.

DRIP COURSE A projecting course to catch and throw off rainwater.

DRIPSTONE (*also* DRIP-MOULDING, HOOD-MOULDING *and* LABEL) A projecting moulding above an arch, doorway or window to throw off rain. The dripstone corbels (*label-stops*) of exterior windows are often carved as human heads and may assist in dating that part of the building. At Beaumaris, Anglesey, for example, a charming label-stop depicts a woman's head with a wimple, hood and veil and hair bunched at the temple – all in the style fashionable in the reigns of the Edwardian period (1270–1330) when the church nave was built.
See also FIGURE SCULPTURE

DRUIDISM Esoteric Celtic priesthood in Gaul, Britain and Ireland. Current perceptions of the Druids are based almost entirely on a brief canon of classical literature comprising no more than twenty references, chiefly in the *De Bello Gallico* of Julius Caesar (100–44 BC) and the equally hostile *Annals* of the Roman historian Tacitus (b. 56 AD). Caesar states that the Druids originated in Britain and that they combined judicial and priestly functions, enjoyed a reputation for natural philosophy and astronomy and were charged with the education of young Gaulish noblemen, which they achieved by means of oral poetry. We are told that they propounded the transmigration of souls, sacrificed murderers, worshipped in forest clearings (*groves*) and believed in the sanctity of mistletoe which was removed with a golden sickle when discovered (as it rarely is) growing from an OAK which they also sanctified. Tacitus records the slaughter of the Druids of Anglesey in AD 60 and the symbolic clearance of their ancient groves. Indeed, Roman suppression of Druidism was ferocious and unrelenting and clearly suggests that it was perceived as a potential focus for opposition to Roman rule. Druidism is evident in the pre-Christian Irish sagas and even then appears to have contained elements of older, pagan faiths.
See also CELTIC CHURCH
Further reading:
Kendrick, T., *The Druids*, London, 1994

DRUM A common term used to describe a cylindrical artefact or architectural feature e.g. a receptacle for liquids, a round vertical wall supporting a dome, the body of a pulpit, a section of a cylindrical column.

DUKE *see* PEERAGE, THE

DUCKING STOOL A punishment, usually reserved for scolding women and dishonest tradespeople, by which the victim was harnessed in a makeshift seat at the end of a pole and immersed several times in a convenient pond or river. The last recorded use of a ducking stool in England was at Leominster, Herefordshire in 1809 when one Jenny Pipes was paraded through the town and ducked in the river near Kenwater Bridge. The Leominster ducking stool was provided with wheels and was so large that it had to be kept in the priory church where it may still be seen today.

DUPLEX QUERELA In the Church of England, the form of action available to a cleric whom a bishop refuses to institute to a benefice for which he has been selected.

DUPLICATES Transcripts of parish REGISTERS furnished annually or triennially to a bishop or archdeacon by the churchwardens of a parish.

DURHAM, PRINCE BISHOPS OF see HERALDRY (ECCLESIASTICAL) and PALATINATE

EAGLES In the Christian Church, the four beasts 'round about the throne' (*Revelation* 4: 6–7) represent the four evangelists, and of these St. John the Evangelist is symbolised by the eagle, 'because his gaze pierced further into the mysteries of heaven than that of any man'. Until recently, LECTERNS in the form of eagles were to be found in nearly every church: with wings open as in flight they carried forth the Word and the Light of the Gospel.
See also BEASTS (HERALDIC) *and* CREATURES

EARL see PEERAGE, THE

EARLY ENGLISH see ARCHITECTURAL PERIODS and MEDIEVAL ARCHITECTURE

EARLY GOTHIC see ARCHITECTURAL PERIODS

EASTER The Feast of the Resurrection of Christ, the oldest and greatest feast of the Christian Church, celebrated on the Sunday following the first full moon after the vernal equinox (the Paschal Full Moon). Easter therefore falls between 21 March and 25 April.

Originally, the Celtic Church calculated the date of Easter by a method which differed from that which had been adopted by Rome in 457. Eventually, the Christians of southern Ireland accepted the Roman Easter in 630, the Northumbrians in 664, Strathclyde in 688, the north of Ireland in about 697, the Church of Iona in 716 and, after a long and debilitating struggle, Wales in 768 (*see* CELTIC CHURCH).

The name is said to be derived from Eostre, a pagan goddess who symbolised the rebirth of the natural world in the spring, a time of rejoicing following the long days of winter. Inevitably, Christ's crucifixion and resurrection mirrored primitive rites and symbols of regeneration (*see* ANGLO-SAXON CHURCH). In the southern Marches of Wales, there persisted into the present century a tradition of dressing the churchyard graves with wildflowers and greenery on Easter Eve – in anticipation of natural and spiritual regeneration.

In the early Church, a vigil was kept throughout the night of Holy Saturday and Easter Sunday and this was closely associated with baptism. In the Roman Catholic Church the Paschal Vigil Service remains the principal celebration of Easter (*see also* PASCHAL CANDLE).

In many parts of the country feasting took place in the church on Easter Day, a practice which did not attract universal approbation. At Berrington in Shropshire, for example, the bishop attempted to interfere with the traditional Easter revels. According to the records of 1639 '. . . there hath been time out of mind an ancient custom used within the parish . . . that the parson . . . hath yearly on Easter Day feasted all the parishioners and landholders with a love-feast, the solemnization of which was ever yet performed in the church.' After much wrangling, the parishioners were allowed to continue with their feast, still paid for by the parson, but not in the church and not on Easter Day.

Easter Monday is traditionally a day of festivities and games: the Bottle-Kicking at Hallaton in Leicestershire, for example, and the Hare-pie Scramble which recalls the mythical association of Easter with the goddess Eostre one of whose emblems was a hare. At several parishes in the counties of Cheshire, Shropshire and Staffordshire, the custom of Lifting or Heaving took place on Easter Monday and Tuesday. On the Monday, pairs of village lads would seek out young women and lift them off the ground in a make-shift 'chair' formed by the coupling of hands and wrists. Once secured, the young lady would be returned to the ground only on payment of a forfeit. On the Tuesday, the roles were reversed and it was the men who were obliged to be lifted – though a chair, decorated with flowers and ribbons, was usually provided for the purpose. Once again, vestiges of the Resurrection and of pagan ritual are evident in this charming custom.

See also EASTER EGGS, EASTER SEPULCHRE, FEAST DAYS (FIXED AND MOVABLE), GOOD FRIDAY, LENT, MAUNDY, PALM SUNDAY, PASSIONTIDE *and* SHROVE TUESDAY

EASTER DUES The CHURCH RATES paid at Easter.

EASTER EGGS It is no coincidence that the great Christian festival of EASTER should coincide with the pagan celebration of the coming of Spring for there can be little doubt that the one was deliberately grafted onto the other, just as pagan sites were adopted for christian use by the early Church (*see* CHURCH SITES). Both festivals celebrate rebirth: for Christians through the Resurrection of Christ and in pagan mythology through the annual rejuvenation of the natural world personified in the goddess Eostre. And for pagan and Christian alike, the egg was a symbol of rebirth. The Church insisted on self-denial during LENT and this included the eating of eggs, the last of which were beaten into pancakes on SHROVE TUESDAY. Thereafter, cooking with eggs was forbidden until Easter when they were given pride of place in the festivities, though the traditional *Pace eggs* (from the Old English *pasch* meaning 'Easter'), hard-boiled and painted, have now been replaced by the chocolate variety. Edward I's household accounts include an item of one shilling and sixpence for the decoration and distribution of 450 pace-eggs. Easter egg-rolling ceremonies were held in many parishes, especially in Lancashire where they were known as *pace-egging.* Pace eggs were wrapped in onion skins and hard-boiled so that the shells acquired a golden, mottled appearance. They were eaten for breakfast on Easter Sunday, retained as ornaments or given to the Pace-eggers for their sport. Pace-eggers were once a common sight in Lancashire villages at Easter time and several of their traditions clearly originated in mumming plays which, elsewhere, were usually performed during Christmas festivities. Groups of black-faced mummers wearing animal skins, coloured ribbons and streamers, processed through the streets singing the Pace-eggers' song and collecting eggs and cash as tribute. Typically, the procession at Burscough included such characters as the Lady Gay, the Noble Youth, the Soldier Brave and Old Tosspot, a buffoon who wore a long straw tail stuffed with pins which was intended to punish any by-stander who was foolish enough to grab hold of it. At Preston, the Easter Monday egg-rolling on the slopes of Avenham Park still attracts thousands of spectators. Today, the children who take part do so for fun but at one time the egg-rolling was a serious competition in which contestants attempted to roll their eggs further than those of rivals – without cracking them. In rural Cheshire, children are still encouraged to visit neighbouring farms to ask for 'an egg for Easter' and, at Great Budworth, the eggs are blessed at an afternoon service on Easter Day before being sent to local hospitals.
See also PALM SUNDAY

EASTERN RANGE In a monastery, the range of buildings which extends beyond the east TRANSEPT of the church. This usually includes the SLYPE, CHAPTER HOUSE and warming house on the ground floor with the day stair (in the CLOISTER) and the night stair (in the transept) leading to the DORTER and reredorter on the floor above.

EASTER SEPULCHRE In a number of churches evidence remains of an Easter sepulchre which was located on the north side of the altar, usually in the sanctuary. It was here that the Blessed Sacrament was kept from Good Friday to early on Easter Sunday when it was returned to the altar with considerable ceremony. The sepulchre at St. Mary Redcliffe in Bristol is said to have included a representation of Heaven '. . . made of Stained clothes' and of Hell '. . . made of timber and iron-work thereto, with Divels to the number of 13'. At

Easter sepulchre at Patrington, Yorkshire.

the parish church of All Hallows at Sherborne in Dorset (which was dismantled when the town acquired the adjoining abbey church) watchmen were employed to guard the Easter sepulchre and were provided with ale and a brazier to keep them warm. Most sepulchres were temporary structures though several richly carved examples in stone have survived (mostly from the fourteenth century), notably those at Hawton in Nottinghamshire, Ledbury in Herefordshire, Northwold in Norfolk, Patrington in Yorkshire and Heckington and Navenby in Lincolnshire. Carving usually depicts the Resurrection and, above, the Ascension. The lovely early sixteenth-century Easter sepulchre at Tarrant Hinton in Dorset is inscribed with the words *Venire et Videte Locum Ubi Positus erat Dominus* ('come and see the place where the Lord lay') and, while its recess has a Tudor four-centred arch, the flanking columns are early Renaissance.

EASTWARD POSITION The practice of the celebrant at the EUCHARIST standing on the west side of the altar and facing east was introduced into the Roman Church during the eighth or ninth centuries. Before that time the WESTWARD POSITION was preferred, as it is in many churches today.

EAVES Underpart of a sloping roof overhanging a wall.

ECCLESIASTICAL CLOTHING *see* VEST-MENTS

ECCLESIASTICAL COMMISSIONERS The body responsible for managing the estates and revenues of the Church of England from 1835 to 1948 when it was combined with QUEEN ANNE'S BOUNTY as the CHURCH COMMISSIONERS for England.

ECCLESIASTICAL COURTS *see* COURTS (ECCLESIASTICAL)

ECCLESIASTICAL COURTS COMMISSION *see* COURTS (ECCLESIASTICAL)

ECCLESIASTICAL HAT *see* HERALDRY (ECCLESIASTICAL)

ECCLESIASTICAL HERALDRY *see* HER-ALDRY (ECCLESIASTICAL)

ECCLESIASTICAL JURISDICTION MEAS-URE 1936 This measure was intended to clarify and simplify ecclesiastical jurisdiction in the Church of England. It established the Court of Ecclesiastical Causes Reserved which considers matters of doctrine, ceremonial and ritual. Appeals are heard by a Royal Commission consisting of two bishops and three Lords of Appeal. Other cases involving clerics are considered by the CONSISTORY COURTS.

ECCLESIASTICAL LIBRARIES *see* ARCHIVES, DOCUMENTARY SOURCES *and* LIBRARIES
For the addresses of the following ecclesiastical libraries *see* APPENDIX II: Canterbury Cathedral, Carlisle Cathedral, Church Commissioners, Exeter Cathedral, Gloucester Cathedral, Hereford Cathedral, Lambeth Palace, Norwich Cathedral, Peterborough Cathedral, St. George's Chapel (Windsor Castle), St. Paul's Cathedral (London), Salisbury Cathedral, Winchester Cathedral, Worcester Cathedral *and* York Minster.

ECCLESIASTICAL TAXATION *see* TAXATION (ECCLESIASTICAL)

ECCLESIASTICAL VISITATIONS *see* VISITATIONS (ECCLESIASTICAL)

ECCLESIASTICISM (i) Preoccupation with the trappings of ecclesiastical practice and administration. (ii) Opinion founded entirely on consideration of the Church as an organisation.

ECCLESIOLOGY The study of church buildings, furnishings and decoration.

ECUMENIC (-AL) Belonging to the universal Christian Church.
See also OECUMENICAL

EDUCATION *see* SCHOOLS, SUNDAY SCHOOLS *and* UNIVERSITIES

EFFIGIES Figures representing a deceased person have been incorporated in church MONUMENTS since the twelfth century. The earliest effigies were of eminent ecclesiastics, carved in low relief and depicted in a standing position. In the thirteenth century, lay figures were also represented, usually recumbent and three-dimensional, while two-dimensional figures continued in the form of INCISED SLABS and monumental brasses (*see* BRASSES, MONUMENTAL). The earliest known military effigy is that of an unidentified knight at the Temple Church in London. Other early examples include those of King John (d. 1216, monument dated 1230) at Worcester Cathedral and William Longespee, Earl of Salisbury (d. 1226) at Salisbury Cathedral.

Through the thirteenth to the fifteenth century most monuments were carved in stone (usually Caen stone or ALABASTER), though there were some notable exceptions including the late twelfth century oak effigy of Robert, Duke of Normandy (d. 1134) at Gloucester cathedral. In parish churches, only eight wooden effigies have survived (mostly in Essex) including a good example from the fifteenth century at Wingfield in Suffolk.

Early effigies (other than those in magnesium limestone) were usually coated with *gesso* (a mixture of size and whiting) and painted. At Combe Florey in Somerset three cockleshells of paint were discovered behind an effigy some five centuries after the craftsmen had departed. The effigy of Henry III (d. 1272) at Westminster Abbey was the first of a series of gilt bronze effigies created for members of the English royal family, a fashion later emulated by Richard Beauchamp, Earl of Warwick (1382–1439) in his effigy at the collegiate church of St. Mary, Warwick. This magnificent tomb still retains its gilded *hearse*, a barrel-shaped metal cage originally intended to support candles and a PALL which was removed only on special occasions. There is evidence to suggest that, while most effigies and brasses were simply stylised representations of a deceased person, splendidly lavish examples such as these were 'based on a likeness'. Indeed, when the fifteenth-century tomb of Sir Richard Croft at Croft Castle in Herefordshire was recently restored, the skulls of Sir

Richard and Lady Eleanor were discovered and it was found that their bone structure corresponded precisely to the stone faces of their effigies.

The medieval practice of HEART BURIAL is evident in a number of *miniature effigies* each erected over the place at which a heart was interred. Such a miniature recumbent knight, complete with hauberk, surcoat, sword and heater-shaped shield, set within a recess of an aisle wall at Mappowder church in Dorset, is just 45 cm long (18 inches) and clasps what appears to be a casket, presumably that in which his heart was buried. Such effigies are usually of thirteenth-century origin and many show signs of having been painted and gilded.

Medieval effigies provide invaluable evidence for the development of COSTUME and ARMOUR, though it should be remembered that effigies and brasses were often commissioned in anticipation of death or erected some considerable time after interment and therefore reflect the fashion of the time in which they were made rather than that of the person they commemorate. (*For* illustrations showing the development of costume and armour *see* BRASSES (MONUMENTAL).)

Effigy, at Ickenham, Middlesex, of Robert Clayton who died 'within a few houres after his birth'.

HERALDRY

Heraldic display was particularly important for it proclaimed identity, lineage and status (*see* HERALDRY) and, with the loss of so many inscriptions, a carved crest or shield of arms is often the only surviving clue to the identity of an effigial figure.

Until the middle of the fourteenth century a knight's effigy usually bore a shield (*see* SHIELDS) and was clothed in an embroidered SURCOAT, CYCLAS or JUPON on which the arms were carved and painted. The detail of arms carved on shield and tunic may still be visible, depending on the depth of the original carving and the effects of defacement and erosion. Effigies were often richly painted but surviving contemporary medieval paintwork and gilding is rare, many figures having been refurbished (sometimes inaccurately) at a later date. The early wooden effigy of Robert of Normandy (see above) is coloured, but examination of the shields on the sides of the TOMB CHEST reveals that the heraldry is not contemporary and it is known that the chest was replaced and the effigy refurbished in the fifteenth century, and again following the Civil War.

From the mid-fourteenth century, shields of arms are more often incorporated into the fabric of the tomb chest or CANOPY and often display multiple QUARTERINGS. The importation into Britain of magnificent German and Italian armour during the fifteenth century encouraged a fashion among the nobility for discarding any form of heraldic overmantle and effigies of the period often reflect this. There was a brief period during the late fifteenth and early sixteenth centuries when the TABARD became popular. This garment was emblazoned on sleeves and body and will be found in some contemporary effigies. The use of heraldry in medieval and Tudor effigies was not merely decorative: heraldic devices were outward and visible symbols of authority and

The gilded bronze effigy of Richard Beauchamp, fifth earl of Warwick (d. 1439) at the collegiate church of St. Mary, Warwick. The effigy lies on a tomb chest of Purbeck marble and is enclosed within a hearse which once carried candles and a velvet pall. Contained within niches in the sides of the tomb chest are fourteen gilded bronze 'weepers', each a distinguished relative or companion of the dead earl, including Richard Nevill, the 'Kingmaker'.

Alabaster figures of Nicholas Fitzherbert (d. 1473) and Ralph Fitzherbert (d. 1483) and his wife, Elizabeth Marshall at Norbury, Derbyshire, where the family held lands from 1125.

power and accumulated quarterings and BADGES conveyed details of ancestry more proudly than any inscription.

Women too bore their marital arms on a *kirtle* (gown or outer petticoat) or *mantle* (cloak) and these appear in effigies as they would have been worn in life. The earliest example is the effigy of Matilda, Countess of Salisbury (d. 1281) in Worcester cathedral. She was daughter and heiress of Walter de Clifford and her cloak is powdered with small shields bearing her paternal arms. Between 1280 and 1330 it was usual for women to display their arms on a mantle which was worn on ceremonial occasions. In effigies (and brasses) the sides of the garment fall forward from the shoulders and the quartered or impaled arms are emblazoned with the husband's arms on the dexter (the left when viewed from the front) and the woman's paternal arms on the sinister (the right) – the reverse of when the garment was actually worn for it was intended to be viewed from the back. Sometimes there are 'missing' quarterings and one may reasonably assume that these are simply not visible. Thereafter, for the remainder of the fourteenth century, a close-fitting kirtle was worn beneath a sleeveless *cote-hardie*, the female equivalent of the jupon, and this was often emblazoned with the impaled marital arms (*see also* COSTUME). There are also instances of both mantle and kirtle being used for heraldic display and in such cases it is always the mantle which bears the husband's arms 'in dominion' over the woman's paternal arms which were embroidered on her kirtle. In the Tudor period heraldic kirtles and over-mantles continued to be depicted in monuments, though kirtles were now loose-fitting and without a waist. But it seems unlikely that such garments continued to be worn after the mid-sixteenth century, even for ceremonial purposes, and their use in effigies and brasses is seen to decline rapidly from this time. Of course, it should be remembered that heraldic costume, as depicted in effigies and brasses, was intended primarily as a vehicle for heraldic display and does not necessarily illustrate a contemporary fashion. Many female effigial figures are dressed in the simple white widow's veil and wimple, sideless cote-hardie and kirtle of a VOWESS, though it is not unusual to find that symbols of rank have been retained – the ducal coronet of a duchess, for example.

The shield and heraldic garment were not the only vehicles for heraldic display: recumbent effigies, both male and female, often have their heads resting on cushions which may incorporate heraldic devices in the embroidery. From the fourteenth century a knight's head normally rested on a helm to which was attached his CREST with wreath and mantling. Most effigies are depicted

with their feet resting on a beast: usually a lion for a man and a dog for a woman. These figures are more often symbolic than heraldic however the use of other animals is almost certainly of significance. At Puddletown in Dorset, for example, effigies of the Martin family of Athelhampton rest their feet on an ape which was the family crest.

Victorian antiquaries attributed all manner of explanation to the detail of effigial figures: cross-legged knights, for example, were said to have been castration by the Saracen while those who were depicted drawing their swords must surely have died in battle.

Many effigies also include the insignia of chivalric orders, of which the most common is the Order of the Garter. During the first half of the fifteenth century the SS collar of the House of Lancaster appears on many figures, and again during the early Tudor period, often with a pendant of the Portcullis badge. The collar of suns and roses of the House of York is found on effigies dating from the latter half of the fifteenth century, though many were defaced after Tudor's victory at Bosworth in 1485 (*see* COLLARS).

For the dating of effigies and brasses *see* ALWITE, ARMOUR, BRASSES (MONUMENTAL), CAMAIL PERIOD, CINGULUM MILITARE, COSTUME *and* MISERICORDE.

See also CHRISM *and* WEEPERS

Further reading:

Borg, A., *Arms and Armour in Britain*, London, 1977

Crossley, F., *English Church Craftsmanship*, London, 1941

Cunnington, P., *Handbook of English Costume* (various vols.), London, 1973

Greenhill, F., *Incised Effigial Slabs*, London, 1976

Humphery-Smith, C. (*et al*), *The Colour of Heraldry*, The Heraldry Society, 1958

Kelly, F. and Schwabe, R., *A Short History of Costume and Armour 1066–1800*, Newton Abbot, 1972

Mayo, J., *The History of Ecclesiastical Dress*, London, 1985

Stone, L., *Sculpture in Britain: the Middle Ages*, London, 1955

Tummers, H., *Early Secular Effigies in England: the Thirteenth Century*, London, 1980

Whinney, M., *Sculpture in Britain: 1530–1830*, London, 1964

For Church Monuments Society *see* APPENDIX II.

EGG AND DART *and* EGG AND TONGUE *see* DECORATIVE MOTIFS

EGLWYS The Welsh for 'church'. Like the Cornish place-name element *eglos*, derived through the Romano-Britons from the Latin *ecclesia*.

EIGHTEENTH-CENTURY ARCHITECTURE

Eighteenth-century architecture reflected a highly civilised age – 'The Age of Enlightenment' – characterised by refinement and an accepted standard of architectural good taste. Both the emparked Baroque mansion and the *Georgian* terraced town house flourished in a society that believed in the philosophy of materialism and reason. It was a time when the prodigious wealth of the aristocracy and gentry contributed to unprecedented architectural activity, not only in the creation of country houses and mansions with their ornamental parks, classical monuments, temples, obelisks, mausoleums and grottoes, but in the provision of numerous public buildings, churches and urban housing schemes at prosperous trading centres like Norwich and Bristol and fashionable spa towns such as Bath, the magnificent (though incomplete) creation of John Wood (1704–54) and his son, also John (1728–81).

Of the 16,000 parish churches in England over half have been built since the seventeenth century. Most of these were auditory churches, intended to accommodate a rapidly increasing urban population and often built by public subscription. There are few towns where there is not a large, classical church dating from this period, with box pews, galleries, lofty pulpits and elaborate altarpieces (*see* ALTARPIECE). Unfortunately, these churches were often built in areas which have long since lost their residential character and many have consequently become redundant.

THE BAROQUE

The Baroque is a classical form of architecture which originated in Italy and was prevalent in southern Europe in the seventeenth and eighteenth centuries. Originally the term was applied in a derogatory sense to the often bizarre and bulbous shapes that characterise this singularly vigorous and dynamic style of architecture. It was paralleled by a departure in art, music and literature from the humanism of the Renaissance and a return to the spiritual values of the Roman Church – 'evidence of man's need for belief in something greater than himself' (Yarwood). In Britain, classical architecture succumbed to Baroque influences for a relatively brief period between c.1690 and 1730 before turning to the greater order and discipline of Palladianism (see below). Baroque influences are evident in the (later) work of Christopher Wren (1632–1723), and in that of his pupil and friend Nicholas Hawksmoor (1661–1736) and in the churches of Thomas Archer (1668–1743), John James (1672–1746) and James Gibbs (1682–1754), once described as 'the inheritor of Wren's mantle'. Notable London churches include (among many) Christ Church, Spitalfields (1729) (one of John Betjeman's favourite churches), St. Anne's, Limehouse (1724) and St. Mary Woolnoth (1727) (all by Hawksmoor); St. Mary-le-Strand

(Gibbs, 1717), the church of St. John, Westminster (Archer, 1728, restored 1965–8 and now a concert hall), and St. Paul's, Deptford (also Archer, 1730). Archer's magnificent Baroque church of St. Philip, Birmingham (1725) acquired a fine rectangular chancel in c. 1883 (with superb windows by Burne-Jones) and became the city's cathedral in 1905.

John James is best known for the Church of St. George in Hanover Square which he designed in 1720 and which established the pattern for later London churches with its impressive free-standing pedimented portico of six Corinthian columns. Hawksmoor, for example, incorporated a similar portico in the church of St. George, Bloomsbury as did James Gibbs in his rebuilding of St. Martin-in-the-Fields, London (1722), a superb building which was to influence the design of Anglican churches in Britain and (especially) in America.

Another of James's churches, St. Lawrence Whitchurch at Little Stanmore (Edgware, London) which was built in 1715 for the Duke of Chandos, is one of the finest small Baroque churches in England. The exterior is plain brick with a crumbling medieval tower, but the interior is a 'startling embodiment of religion as theatre' (Harbison): far closer to Rome than Middlesex. Characteristic Baroque features are the imitation sky in the retro-choir, lit by a concealed window; the *trompe l'oeil* statues with their dramatic poses; and the illusionistic paintings which cover the walls and ceiling. The drama is accentuated by its theatrical design: three boxes at the west end, with painted curtains held by naked cherubs, and at the east end, set within a proscenium arch, the altar – and behind the altar, the splendid organ, itself a shrine to music and to George Fredrick Handel (1685–1759) whose *Chandos Anthems* were composed for the church's patron, James Brydges, first Duke of Chandos (1674–1744). The splendid woodwork (including the carved organ case) is by Grinling Gibbons. Even more startling is the adjoining Chandos mausoleum, described by Robert Harbison in his *English Parish Churches* as '. . . an extravagant pinnacle of English pseudo-Baroque.'

CLASSICAL REVIVAL

With the deaths of Wren and his contemporaries there was a return to the understatement favoured by English society and exemplified in the rigid *Palladian* principles introduced by Inigo Jones (1573–1652) in the previous century (*see* SIXTEENTH- AND SEVENTEENTH-CENTURY ARCHITECTURE). English Palladianism thrived in the period 1720–60 under the patronage of Lord Burlington (1694–1773) and Colen Campbell (1676–1729) and architects such as William Kent (1685–1748) and Capability Brown (1716–83). But it was essentially a revival of domestic architecture, most eighteenth-century Palladian churches being adjuncts of major rebuilding schemes.

Renewed interest in the antique, together with a reaction to the excesses of the late Baroque and ROCOCO styles, resulted in the Classic Revival of the second half of the eighteenth century which was viewed with horror by the Palladian movement who thought the style barbaric and primitive. Robert Adam (1728–92) was the chief proponent of the *Neoclassical* style, though he was responsible for very few churches: the small Adam church of St. Andrew in the park of Gunton Hall, Norfolk (1769) is exceptional, as is St. Mary's church at Croome D'Abitot in Worcestershire (1763), though even this was a collaborative scheme with Capability Brown and the church was built in the Gothic style (see below).

The classical churches of this period are often of brick, with clear glass, plasterwork and little decoration. One of the best examples is at Avington in Hampshire where the church of St. Mary (built by the Marchioness of Caernarvon in 1771 and adjoining her house) has a simple, sturdy tower, rectangular nave and coved plaster ceiling. Its interior furnishings in Spanish mahogany (said to

have been salvaged from an Armada galleon) are complete and unspoilt and include a reredos, three-decker pulpit with tester, family pews, gallery, font, communion rails and (working) barrel-organ. Other notable late eighteenth-century churches include All Hallows Church, London Wall (George Dance, 1767, now a library), All Saints at Newcastle upon Tyne (David Stephenson, 1786), St. Chad's at Shrewsbury, Shropshire (George Steuart, 1790) and St. Mary's, Paddington Green, London (John Plaw, 1791), a late Palladian gem.

A number of eighteenth-century provincial architects are associated with particular towns: the Hiorns of Daventry, John Carr of York and Thomas White of Worcester, for example. In Dorset, it was the Bastard brothers (John Bastard 1688–1770) who reconstructed the centre of Blandford Forum following a disastrous fire in 1731 and created the finest small Georgian town in England, including the splendid parish church of St. Peter and St. Paul (1735–9). In 1893 the apsidal sanctuary was moved on rollers to newly prepared foundations and a

St. Swithin's, Worcester, described by Betjeman as 'A perfectly preserved example of an 18th-century church with all its furnishings intact'.

chancel inserted. One of the most spectacular eighteenth-century churches is St. George Reforne, located high on the treeless Isle of Portland, also in Dorset. Designed and built by Thomas Gilbert, a local mason, during the years 1754–66, it is reminiscent of a style which was current in London some forty years earlier. The architecture is not faultless, but Gilbert's conception was one of true grandeur and his church is a magnificently imposing building – an eloquent testimony to the legion of enthusiastic amateur architects whose work is too often overshadowed by that of their more eminent colleagues.

From c. 1780 a Greek Revival school also developed and many of the simple, functional, often severe classical buildings of the late eighteenth and early nineteenth centuries are attributable to its influence.

THE GOTHIC REVIVAL

Also during the second half of the eighteenth century, a romantic form of medievalism was introduced into architectural ornamentation. Occasionally described as GOTHICK, this offered an alternative for those who reacted to the restrictive formality of Classical styles and, although it played only a minor role at this time, its influence was to increase significantly in the Gothic Revival of the following century (*see* NINETEENTH-CENTURY ARCHITECTURE). Whole buildings in the style are rare for, at this time, it was effectively an English variant of rococo with picturesque medieval motifs executed in wood and plaster and painted in pastel colours. Notable examples include St. Paul's, Portland Square in Bristol (1794) and the church of St. John the Evangelist at Shobdon in Herefordshire (see below).

PROPRIETARY CHAPELS

The Georgian aristocracy provided us with a wonderful legacy of classical and romantic Gothic chapels which, although technically parish churches, were built on country estates as proprietary chapels for the benefit of the owner and his employees. The opulent Baroque church of St. Michael and All Saints at Witley Court in Worcestershire (1735) continues as a parish church even though the great house to which it was attached has long been a gaunt ruin with trees growing inside its walls. As at the church of St. Lawrence Whitchurch (see above) many of its features came from Canons, the Edgeware house of the first Duke of Chandos. The magnificent stained glass windows (by Joshua Price, 1719) and painted plaster ceiling panels (Louis Laguerre?) were purchased on the Duke's death in 1744 by Lord Foley of Witley Court and installed in his new chapel. The nearby church of St. John the Evangelist at Shobdon, Herefordshire is the most extravagantly Gothic Revival church in England. Built by The Hon. Richard Bateman of Shobdon Court in 1756, it has carpeted and cushioned white-painted pews, a three-decker pulpit with canopied sounding board, elaborately plastered ceilings and

two tiny transepts containing the family and servants' pews. The remains of carved arches from its Romanesque predecessor may still be found in a field close by. Many of these chapels were provided with fireplaces in the family pews and private access from the adjacent house. Indeed, several were actually incorporated within the fabric of the house itself, though these should not be confused with the many fine private Roman Catholic chapels of the period, such as that at Wardour (New) Castle, in Wiltshire (James Paine, 1768).

CHURCH INTERIORS

Many ancient churches were enlarged and remodelled in the eighteenth century, sometimes with startling effect as at St. Mary's church at Whitby in Yorkshire where the medieval nave was replaced in 1764 in order to accommodate a growing population. The interior furnishings at Whitby are beyond compare: box pews and galleries everywhere and an elegant three-decker Georgian pulpit with tester and a pair of 'vamping horns' or ear-trumpets. (When two Whitby whaling ships were lost in 1826, a congregation of three thousand people attended the memorial service at St. Mary's.) Unfortunately, many of these remodelled churches suffered from later restorations, though several (mostly rural) examples remain intact. The church of All Saints at Minstead in Hampshire, for example, is second only to Whitby in its wealth of seventeenth- and eighteenth-century furniture including a double west gallery, two private pews (one with a fireplace) and a magnificent three-decker pulpit (*see also* EIGHTEENTH-CENTURY CHURCH).

For the Georgian Group *see* APPENDIX II.

Further reading:

Harbison, R., *English Parish Churches*, London, 1992

Summerson, J., *Georgian London*, London, 1988

Yarwood, D., *Encyclopaedia of Architecture*, London, 1985

EIGHTEENTH-CENTURY CHURCH The *Industrial Revolution* brought about a transformation of British society, during the second half of the eighteenth century and the first half of the nineteenth, in which the majority of the working population shifted from agricultural to industrial occupations. It was preceded by the *Agrarian Revolution* which effected a drastic reduction in the agricultural labour force and a corresponding increase in the urban population. This in turn stimulated an enormous demand for cheap, mass-produced goods and provided a substantial supply of manual labour for the new mills and factories. The two 'revolutions' may indeed be regarded as a single force by which society was reconstructed in order to feed, clothe and employ a population that was increasing with prodigious rapidity. The Industrial Revolution was caused by unprecedented scientific and technological innovation and in particular by the application of steam-power. Industry itself created a demand for machines and for the tools to manufacture and maintain them, thereby stimulating further mechanisation. The transportation of raw materials and coal to manufacturing centres and the distribution of finished goods to markets, both at home and abroad, required a massive investment in road improvements and in the construction of canals, railways and steamships. Britain became the most powerful industrial nation in the world but the profound social and economic problems which resulted from such a fundamental transformation of society were to dominate domestic politics for over a century.

THE ECCLESIASTICAL ESTABLISHMENT

The Church's response was one of quite extraordinary complacency. It remained subservient to the civil government, it regarded change with extreme suspicion, and it was incapable of addressing the demographic changes that were taking place because of the rigidity and inefficiency of its administration. Bishops were almost invariably political appointees who were expected to devote themselves to maintaining the Government in the House of Lords; numerous non-resident and pluralist clergy, appointed by lay patrons, enjoyed the income of their benefices while paying miserable stipends to their curates; and, above all, the Church doggedly protected the *status quo* while vehemently rejecting any resurgence of religious 'enthusiasm' which was identified with 'popery' and which the pious Dr. Johnson defined as 'a vain belief of private revelation; a vain confidence of divine favour or communication' (*Dictionary*, 1755). The Church's comfortable round of services and sermons, which emphasised the importance of maintaining the established order, provided neither inspiration for the commonalty of church-goers nor a spiritual alternative to the increasingly materialistic pressures of society in general. It was perceived as an institution whose chief responsibilities were the preservation of moral values and the reforming of manners in a society which was increasingly preoccupied with public order. But, for the most part, it failed to deal with the causes of unrest: exploitation and social deprivation. Parish records, such as CHURCHWARDENS' ACCOUNTS, vestry minutes (*see* VESTRY) and the accounts of overseers of the poor (*see* POOR LAW), visitation returns (*see* VISITATIONS, ECCLESIASTICAL) and the records of Church courts (*see* COURTS, ECCLESIASTICAL), invariably confirm that, in the majority of parishes, the maintenance of the social fabric and the preservation of order were of greater concern than the spiritual and social welfare of parishioners.

THE PARISH CHURCH

Of course, the impact of the Established Church on each of the 9,500 parishes in eighteenth-century England varied enormously. In rural communities, especially in the south and east, it continued to exercise considerable influence. But in the expanding industrial areas of the north and the Midlands, and in the valleys of South Wales, it failed to adapt to demographic change, thereby inviting the spread of nonconformity and the provision of Unitarian and Independent chapels, precursors of the ubiquitous nonconformist chapels of the next century. Even so, the parish church continued to touch the lives of people in a variety of ways. Baptism was widely regarded as essential for a child's future well-being, even by those who rarely attended church, and most parishioners were married in the parish church and buried in its graveyard. CHURCHYARDS remained the focus of many village activities (*see also* CHURCH AND COMMUNITY) and CHARITIES continued to provide for the destitute and infirm, especially those who attended church and who were prepared 'humbly to acknowledge their station in life'. There was also a reaction within the Church itself and this led to the creation of the Evangelical movement which was to play a leading role in the social reforms of the next century (*see* EVANGELICAL-ISM *and* NINETEENTH-CENTURY CHURCH).

THE CLERGY

The Church offered the prospect of an attractive career for the younger male members of gentry families, especially when the families were themselves patrons of one or more benefices. The demands of a rapidly expanding urban population led to increased agricultural production, higher prices and rising land values so that the value of TITHES almost doubled during the eighteenth century, providing a comfortable living for the benefice clergy in return for minimal duties. Their opulent life-style, evident in the grandeur of so many Georgian rectories, was in stark contrast to the miserable stipends paid to the unbeneficed clergy and yet, in the absence of the incumbent, it was upon their shoulders that the cure of souls so often rested. GLEBE terriers provide an invaluable source of information concerning clerical incomes, glebe lands, parsonage houses, tithes and parochial dues and the visitation records contain numerous references to absentee clergy. A visitation of 1743 in the Diocese of York revealed that, of the 836 parishes in the diocese, 393 had non-resident incumbents and that only 383 parishes had more than one service on a Sunday.

In the visitation record for the parish of Worth Matravers, Dorset (then in the Diocese of Bristol – *see* DIOCESES), it was observed that the incumbent was '. . . wicked, mad, now on board a man of war. His wife and 4 children receive the income [of the living]. Mr. Pope of Corfe Castle serves the parish for 5s 0d a week to their satisfaction.' Curates such as Mr. Pope were often responsible for a number of parishes and were hard-pressed to conduct a service in each church on a Sunday. Indeed, in most churches, Communion was celebrated no more than three or four times a year and the number of communicants was often pitifully small. Many incumbents were engaged in agriculture, farming their glebe lands for profit and, on occasions, advocating innovative methods of crop production and animal husbandry. Others served as magistrates and took a leading part in local affairs while many aspired to scholarship as historians, antiquarians, archaeologists or naturalists. The rector of Langton Herring in Dorset was a fellow of King's College, Cambridge and tutor to Lord Milton's sons at Eton. And, of course, there was the ubiquitous hunting cleric, epitomised in James Woodeforde's *Diary of a Country Parson* (5 vols. 1924–31), he who lived the life of a rural squire, readily accepted into local society and confining his religious activities to Sunday services and the occasional office.

DOCUMENTARY EVIDENCE

To determine to what extent, if at all, the foregoing was true of a particular parish, the researcher has access to an often bewildering array of documentary and other sources. Indeed, far more evidence survives for this than for any previous century, including material relating to RECUSANTS and dissenters and to the religious beliefs and moral attitudes of parishioners in general (*see* ARCHIVES *and* DOCUMENTARY SOURCES).

John Ecton's *Liber Valorem et Decimarum* of 1711 is a directory of ecclesiastical benefices, arranged under dioceses and deaneries, compiled in response to the formation of QUEEN ANNE'S BOUNTY in 1704. This was followed by further editions including *Thesaurus Rerum Ecclesiasticarum* (Browne Willis, 1742) and *Liber Regis* (John Bacon, 1786) both of which give details of incumbents, patrons, income, appropriations and dedications (*see* APPROPRIATION, INCUMBENT *and* PATRON). BISHOPS' REGISTERS and SUBSCRIPTION BOOKS provide further details, as do the records of Ecclesiastical Visitations which include information concerning the effect on parochial activity of non-resident clergy.

CHURCH INTERIORS

It is, perhaps, too easy to condemn the Established Church of the eighteenth century and to overlook the fact that, of the 16,000 parish churches in England, over half have been built since 1700 (*see* EIGHTEENTH-CENTURY ARCHITECTURE). This was, after all, the Age of Enlightenment and the focus of worship in the parish churches of Hanoverian England was far removed from that of the MEDIEVAL CHURCH. The dark, eucharistic mystery of the sanctuary had long ago been superseded by promotion of the Word – both the Word of God and that of the Church as guardian of the established order – and it was now the three-decker PULPIT, with its prayer-desk, lectern, pulpit, SOUNDING BOARD and HOUR GLASS, which dominated liturgical proceedings and demanded the congregation's attention, often for hours on end (*see also* SEVENTEENTH-CENTURY CHURCH).

Faculties were obtained so that churches could be enlarged or rebuilt and provided with GALLERIES to accommodate additional worshippers and the elaborate family pews and MONUMENTS of the aristocracy and gentry (*see* PEWS, FAMILY). Private, high-sided box PEWS were also available for those members of the congregation who were prepared to pay pew rents in return for draught-free accommodation and a fillip to their social aspirations (*see* PEW RENTING). Those who could not afford pew rents occupied benches at the back of the nave and in the aisles or galleries (*see also* BENCHES AND BENCH-ENDS). The rigid structure of contemporary society was clearly delineated in the provision of accommodation in the eighteenth-century parish church and was regarded as a matter of considerable importance by those who valued such things (*see also* BURIALS).

There can be little doubt that many of the poorer members of society were attracted to nonconformist worship because of its relative freedom from such snobbery, though concern for social status was eventually to afflict the chapel as it had the church. In many rural parishes, the poor were squeezed out of their churches as over-zealous CHURCH-WARDENS attempted to increase income by installing more and more private pews, and even in larger churches space was often at a premium as families insisted on 'due and proper accommodation' commensurate with their status.

Registers of faculties (*see* FACULTY), vestry minutes and churchwardens' accounts are invaluable sources of information concerning the changes that took place at this time and of the churches that were enlarged or replaced. From these and other sources it is evident that church interiors were usually whitewashed in order that light might be shed even into the darkest corner and that religious texts and sentences of scripture might be painted thereon. The usual practice was for the Commandments, the Creed and the Lord's Prayer to be displayed at the east end of the church in the vicinity of the communion table. This preference for whitewash, which was both cheap and easy to apply, is reflected in the number of white-painted pews and other furnishings which have survived from this period, as at the church of St. Mary at Whitby in Yorkshire and the tiny Church of the Assumption at Holnest in Dorset. There may also be evidence of provision having been made for singers and musicians who, from the mid-seventeenth century, were sometimes engaged to accompany the services (*see* CHURCH MUSIC (ANGLICAN), GALLERIES *and* ORGANS).

Mercifully, many eighteenth-century church interiors escaped the attentions of Victorian restorers and now serve to illustrate the setting and atmosphere of worship at that time, notably at Breedon-on-the-Hill in Leicestershire, Chaddleworth in Berkshire, Hinton St. George in Somerset, Tibenham in Norfolk, Tong in Yorkshire, and Whalley in Lancashire.

Writing in the 1830s, the Revd. George Rundle Prynne recalled his childhood at Fowey in Cornwall:

I can remember the grand old church to which I was taken every Sunday, and the great square pew in which I was boxed up, and the seats all round from which the family circle looked at each other, or when they knelt, turned their backs on each other. The whole church was fitted with pews of a similar character. I remember the parson's desk, and the clerk's desk, and their alternate reading of the verses and the psalms in which very few of the congregation ever joined, for the clerk's responses, though in a monotone, were not musical or easy to join in. The altar was blocked out of site altogether by the high square pews, but the Holy Communion was celebrated there once a month, I was told. There was a high gallery at the west end of the nave which was reached by a steep flight of stairs, and to this gallery, which had the Royal Arms in front of it, the clerk went to give out some verses of one of the metrical psalms composed by Messrs. Tate and Brady. Hymns of any kind were not considered orthodox or correct in those days. The aged vicar then went to the pulpit in a black gown and read a sermon, and so the service ended. It was certainly not a lively function . . .

For the Lord's Day Observance Act of 1781 *see* SUNDAY.

Further reading:

Bettey, J.H., *Church and Parish*, London, 1987

Purvis, J.S., *An Introduction to Ecclesiastical Records*, London, 1953

Randall, G., *Church Furnishing and Decoration in England and Wales*, London, 1980

——, *The English Parish Church*, London, 1982 (Spring Books, 1988)

Tate, W.E., *The Parish Chest*, Cambridge, 1960

ELEANOR CROSSES Wayside memorial crosses constructed to mark the progress of the body of Queen Eleanor of Castile, first wife of Edward I, who died at Harby in Nottinghamshire on 29 November, 1290 and was buried at Westminster Abbey (though her bowels were first removed and interred at Lincoln cathedral). From 1292–4, in accordance with her will, a series of elaborate crosses was erected by the King's masons at resting

Eleanor cross at Hardingstone, Northamptonshire.

places along the route to Westminster. Only three survive of the original eleven: at Geddington and Hardingstone in Northamptonshire and at Waltham Cross in Hertfordshire.

ELECTION (MONASTIC) Superiors of religious houses were elected by the members of the community, with the sovereign's permission and usually in consultation with the founder (or his successor) or patron. The new superior was usually chosen from the more experienced and senior members of the community, though on occasions political appointments were made (usually by the Crown as patron) and members of other communities might also be appointed. Other officials were nominated by the superior.

ELECTIONER One who was qualified for election to a parochial office by virtue of his holding in a parish.

ELECTORAL REGISTERS The Reform Act of 1832 required the parochial registration of every person qualified to vote, and the publication of the registers. Entries show the name and abode of each elector and identify the property (freehold or leasehold) which qualified him to vote. Electoral registers are housed in county record offices.

ELECTRIC LIGHTING In the splendid introduction to his *Guide to English Parish Churches* (1958), John Betjeman rails against the introduction of electric light into parish churches: 'It is a light too harsh and bright for an old building, and the few remaining delicate textures on stone and walls are destroyed by the dazzling floodlights fixed in reflectors in the roof, and a couple of spotlights behind the chancel arch which throw their full radiance on the brass altar vases and on the vicar when he marches up to give the blessing. At sermon time, in a winter evensong, the lights are switched off, and the strip-reading lamp on the pulpit throws up the vicar's chin and eyebrows so that he looks like Grock. A further disfigurement introduced by electrical engineers is a collection of meters, pipes and fuses on one of the walls. I have even seen electric heaters hung at intervals along the gallery of an eighteenth-century church and half way up the columns of a medieval nave.' He concludes by suggesting that 'The mystery of an old church, however small the building, is preserved by irregularly placed clusters of low-powered bulbs which light service books but leave the roof in comparative darkness. The chancel should not be strongly lit, for this makes the church look small, and all too rarely are chancel and altar worthy of a brilliant light.' Of course, technology has moved on since then and it is now possible to install lighting which does not detract from 'the delicate textures on stone and wall', neither does the installation have to be intrusive. Unfortunately, the best practice is not always the cheapest.

ELECTROPLATE A thin coating of of silver, chromium etc. applied by electrolysis. Similar to SHEFFIELD PLATE and metallic in appearance with straight seams. Used for church PLATE from the mid-nineteenth century.

ELEPHANTS When found in the fabric of churches, elephants are most likely intended to represent Adam and Eve with whom (according to the medieval bestiaries) they shared a carnal naïvety and mated only once during a lifetime. Elephants are also found in HERALDRY, notably in the punning arms of the Elphinston family and in the civic arms of the city of Coventry, where a single elephant with a castle on its back symbolises strength and sagacity.

ELEVATION An external face of a building. The *façade* is the principal elevation of a (usually classical) building. An elevational drawing is one showing an external face of a building, made in projection on a vertical plane.

ELEVATION, THE The raising of each of the sacred elements (the *Host*) at the EUCHARIST immediately following consecration, a practice which is believed to have originated in the thirteenth century.

EMBATTLED A decorative or heraldic motif in the form of a crenellation (*see* DECORATIVE MOTIFS).

EMBER DAYS From the Old English *ymbryne* meaning 'period', four groups each of three days which were observed as days of fasting, abstinence and prayer: the Wednesday, Friday and Saturday following (i) St. Lucy (13 December), (ii) the first Sunday in LENT, (iii) WHITSUNDAY and (iv) Holy Cross Day (14 September). Their original purpose is obscure and at one time there may have been only three such groups, possibly derived from pagan religious observances at seed-time, harvest and autumn vintage. More recently, Ember Days have come to be associated with ordination.
See also FEAST DAYS (FIXED AND MOVABLE)

EMBLAZON To depict ARMORIAL BEARINGS in colour. Not to be confused with the term *blazon*, which is to describe heraldic devices using the terminology of ARMORY.

EMBOSS To raise an ornamental motif in relief.

EMBRASURE (*also* CRENEL *or* CRENELLE) (i) An opening between the MERLONS of an embattled parapet (*see* BATTLEMENT). (ii) The bevelling of a wall at the sides of a window etc. (*see* SPLAY).

EMBROIDERY In the Middle Ages ecclesiastical VESTMENTS (such as copes, chasubles and maniples) were often embroidered, bishops and abbots enjoying the right to embroider their coats of arms on the orphreys of a cope or on the back of a chasuble. Of the thirteenth- and fourteenth-century *Opus Anglicanum*, once the finest collection of ecclesiastical needlework in western Europe, very little remains. But that which has survived, usually as fragments made into altar frontals, provides evidence of the wonderful craftsmanship which created the vestments and hangings of the pre-Reformation Church. Such reminders of the Mass were anathema in protestant England and as such were frequently destroyed, though a number of copes (which were not Mass vestments) have survived and are now mostly in museums (*see also* COPE CHEST). The most celebrated example is the late thirteenth-century Syon cope which once belonged to the nuns of Syon Abbey at Isleworth, formerly in Middlesex, and is now at the Victoria and Albert Museum (*see* APPENDIX II). Examples of early embroidery may be seen (usually by appointment) at Chipping Campden (a cope and a pair of altar frontals) and Cirencester (cope) in Gloucestershire, Barnstable in Devon and Hullavington in Wiltshire (chasubles), Buckland in Gloucestershire, Careby in Lincolnshire, Culmstock in Devon, East Langton in Kent, Forest Hill in Oxfordshire, Great Bircham and Lyng in Norfolk, and Othery in Somerset (fragments of copes). Altar frontals may be seen at Alveley in Shropshire and Baunton in Gloucestershire, while at Sutton Benger in Wiltshire there is a desk hanging composed of orphreys. There are also medieval palls (hearse cloths) at Dunstable Priory in Bedfordshire and the church of St. Peter at Sudbury in Suffolk.

Embroidery from the earliest times was regarded as an occupation suitable for the women of noble families and for nuns, but by the mid-thirteenth century other women also worked as lay professionals. Perhaps the best known of these was one Mabel of Bury St. Edmunds whose skill was highly regarded by Henry III (there are at least two dozen references to her during Henry's reign). By the end of the thirteenth century there were at least six large professional workshops in London employing some sixty or seventy embroiderers and producing both ecclesiastical and secular work. Only the finest materials were used, especially cloth of gold and velvet with great quantities of gold and silver thread. CHRISTIAN SYMBOLS were popular subjects for embroidery, as were scenes from the life of Christ and the saints, and HERALDRY which was ideally suited to this medium (see also BADGES). It was Henry VII who bequeathed to the Abbot, Prior and Convent of Westminster '. . . the hoole sute of vestiments and Coopies [copes] of clothe of gold tissue, wrought with our badges of rede Roses and Poortcoleys [portcullises], the which we of late at our propre costs and charges caused to be made, bought and provided at Florence in Italie: that is to say, the hoole Vestements for the Preist, the Deacon and Subdeacon, and xxix Coopes of the same clothe and worke.' Such vestments and copes were extraordinarily expensive. In this instance the cloth of gold was woven into shape in Florence and made up and embroidered in England by embroiderers (mostly women who were paid significantly less than men) under the direction of senior craftsmen in the royal workshops. But the importation of richly woven cloths, especially those from Italy, and the haste with which royal commissions had to be completed, served to undermine the embroiderer's craft in the late Middle Ages so that embroidery was increasingly concentrated in particular areas, such as the orphreys, instead of being applied to the entire outer surface of the garment as in the thirteenth century.

A great deal of more recent embroidery is also of a high standard of workmanship and design, not least that which emanated from the nineteenth-century Gothic Revival (see NINETEENTH-CENTURY ARCHITECTURE). By contrast, vernacular heraldry may be found in abundance in colourful embroidered kneelers, cushions and chair backs, favourite subjects including the arms of lords of the manor, past patrons of livings, benefactors and monastic or lay rectors, diocesan arms and the ATTRIBUTED ARMS of saints.

Further reading:
Dean, B., *Ecclesiastical Embroidery*, London, 1958
Staniland, K., *Embroiderers*, London, 1992

ENAMELLING Artefacts have been embellished with coloured enamels since at least the thirteenth century and include such items as goblets, ciboria and lamps. Memorials, notably monumental brasses (*see* BRASSES, MONUMENTAL), were also enriched by the addition of coloured enamels, and in the Gothic Revival of the nineteenth century the technique was widely used on memorial and commemorative plaques and in architectural decoration.

Enamel is a vitreous glaze, or combination of glazes, fused on a metallic surface. The base substance of enamel is a clear, colourless vitreous compound called flux, containing silica, red lead and potash. The material is coloured by the addition of metallic oxides while in a liquid state, so that the flux is stained through its entirety. The material is fired at varying temperatures into solid lumps: the higher the temperature, the harder the enamel. The brilliance of enamel depends on the materials which are added to the flux, and their proportions, whilst the colour is affected by the constituents of the flux and the added oxides. Turquoise blue, for example, is obtained from the black oxide of copper by using a large proportion of sodium carbonate in the flux.

The process begins by pulverising the lumps of prepared enamel, the resultant powder being washed in distilled water to remove contaminants. The pulverised enamel is then spread over the metal surface of the artefact which has been cleaned with acid and dried. The piece is then gently warmed before being introduced to the furnace which is then raised to the necessary temperature for vitrification – a process which takes only a few minutes. When the enamel is seen to have obtained an even sheen it is removed and allowed to cool. There are, of course, several methods of enamelling, each using different techniques. For example, raised metal ridges (*cloisons*) may separate different elements of a design (a technique known as *cloisonné*), or the work may be overlayed with a transparent enamel glaze. *See also* PLATE

ENCAUSTIC TILES *see* TILES

ENCLOSURE (MONASTIC) *see* PRECINTS

ENCLOSURE AWARD MAPS *see* MAPS

ENCYCLICAL A letter widely circulated to all the churches in an area. At one time the term was applied to communications from a bishop but in the Roman Catholic Church it is now confined to those emanating from the Pope.

ENDORSEMENT That which is written on the back (*dorse*) of a document.

ENFEOFFMENT *see* PROBATE

ENGAGED Descriptive of columns or piers which are attached to, or partly sunk into, a wall (*see* COLUMN *and* PIER).

ENGLISH BOND *see* BONDING

ENGLISH ROMANESQUE *see* ARCHITECTURAL PERIODS *and* MEDIEVAL ARCHITECTURE

ENGRAILED A decorative edge formed of a series of curves with outward-facing points.

ENGROSS (i) To copy a document in a formal hand or in distinct characters. (ii) To write out a document in legal form for signature. (iii) To name in a legal list or document.

ENGROSSMENT The combining of two or more holdings.

ENROLMENT The *Statute of Enrolment* of 1535 encouraged the registration of a conveyance, title or lawful act in an official document such as a Close Roll (*see* CLOSE ROLLS). The requirement that certain deeds should be enrolled was abolished by the Law of Property Act of 1925.

ENTABLATURE In Classical architecture the horizontal members above a column i.e. the ARCHITRAVE, FRIEZE and CORNICE.
See also CLASSICAL ORDER

ENTAIL To bequeath an estate inalienably to a specified succession of beneficiaries.

ENTASIS In architecture, an almost imperceptible deviation from a straight line. Used on Greek columns and some spires to prevent an optical illusion of concavity.

EPBM, EPGS *and* **EPNS** Church PLATE finished in Electroplated Britannia Metal (EPBM), Electroplated German Silver (EPGS) and Electroplated Nickel Silver (EPNS) is commonly found in churches. Electroplate is a thin coating of silver, chromium etc. applied by electrolysis, a commercial process which dates from the mid-nineteenth century. EPBM is usually post-1850 and has only one vertical seam through which the copper base may be visible. Some areas may be cast in PEWTER and makers invariably stamped their names and catalogue numbers on the item. EPNS is usually post-1840 and is also marked, most recently with (e.g.) crossed arrows, crossed keys, a bell, hand or pineapple. Unfortunately, for reasons of security it is now necessary to remove such items from public view and anyone wishing to inspect church plate is advised to do so by appointment.

EPIGRAPHY The study of inscriptions.

EPIPHANY (*also* TWELFTH-TIDE) From the Greek 'manifestation', Epiphany is the annual celebration (on 6 January) of Christ's manifestation to the Gentiles personified by the Magi. The feast originated in the Eastern Church in the third century as a celebration of Christ's baptism and was introduced into the Western Church in the fourth century.
See also CHRISTMAS, DISTAFF DAY, FEAST DAYS (FIXED AND MOVABLE) *and* TWELFTH NIGHT

EPISCOPACY (i) A system of Church government by bishops. (ii) The office of bishop and the period during which such an office is held. (iii) The bishops collectively.

EPISCOPATE The office of bishop.

EPISCOPI Latinised place-name element applied to a manor which was once held by a bishop. Bishops Caundle in Dorset, until recently Caundle Bishop (the last road sign was removed in 1989) and before that Caundle Episcopi, was once held by the Bishop of Sarum. (*See* LATIN)

EPISTLE (i) A letter, especially one written to an individual or church from one of the Apostles. (ii) The first of two readings at the Eucharist, customarily an extract from one of the apostolic epistles, but not necessarily so.

EPITAPHS

Famed little John a terror was to many a boxing blade,
But now alas an insult brooks from sexton's dirty spade;
For coward Death waiting the time till Jack was weak and low
The moment seized and spite of art put in his favourite blow.

Epitaph to John Marsh, the pugnacious landlord of the Red Lion at Madley in Herefordshire (1793).

The foregoing is typical of many amusing epitaphs which may be found in parish churches and churchyards – though John Marsh's memorial seems to have disappeared from Madely churchyard since the epitaph was first recorded.

From the Greek *epitaphion* (*epi* 'upon' and *taphos* 'a tomb'), epitaphs are commemorative INSCRIPTIONS on GRAVESTONES and MONUMENTS and are of interest, not only for the genealogical information they contain, but also because they epitomise contemporary social and religious attitudes.

Medieval tombs were themselves indicative of a man's status and dignity: the heraldry on EFFIGIES and BRASSES declaring his identity, lineage and authority more effectively than any epitaph. Inscriptions were usually in Latin (though some early brasses are inscribed in Norman French) and contained the briefest of details – name, dates and a religious aphorism – all modestly contained within the overall design of the monument. Those who were not armigerous sometimes included personal devices such as MERCHANTS' MARKS or the symbols of favourite saints (*see* CHRISTIAN SYMBOLS). Medieval man acknowledged the commonality of death and was preoccupied with salvation. This is reflected in the monuments of the period, which are often rich but rarely ostentatious, and in simple expressions of piety and humility.

The materialism of late Tudor society is evident in many sixteenth-century monuments which became increasingly elaborate with exaggerated heraldic display and lengthy florid epitaphs, often written in verse. Implicit in many of these memorials is an assumption that earthly gentility would find its reward in heaven. Some of the verse was of the highest quality (Shakespeare himself is said to have composed the epitaph on the tomb of Sir Thomas Stanley (d. 1576) in Tong church, Shropshire) and many early seventeenth-century monuments, though architecturally insensitive, contain epitaphs which accurately reflect the lyricism of contemporary poetry.

While many eighteenth-century monuments are singularly ostentatious, some are also exceedingly graceful, though all too often out of keeping with their medieval surroundings. But the epitaphs inscribed thereon frequently make the most preposterous claims for the self-righteous dead in doggerel which was unlikely to enhance a poet's reputation. Biographical detail was sometimes of a singularly intimate nature, as in Bridget Applewhaite's lengthy epitaph at Bramfield in Suffolk which recalls the 'Fatigues' of her first marriage ('Born by her with incredible Patience/For Four Years and three Quarters, barring three weeks), the 'glorious Freedom' of her widowhood and her decision to 'run the Risk of a Second Marriage-Bed' as well as the full medical details of the 'Apoplectick

Dart' which after 'Terrible Convulsions, Plaintive Groans or Stupefying Sleep' eventually dispatched her, at the age of 43, on 12 September, 1773. Not all epitaphs would have been welcomed by the churchwardens: at Burford in Oxfordshire, a monument to Lord Chief Justice Tanfield, erected by his widow, complains bitterly of the inconvenience caused by having to bury him in such a backwater.

The religious upheaval of the late eighteenth and early nineteenth centuries resulted in a reaction against such commemorative excesses. Memorials, and the inscriptions they bore, became stylised and bland just as religious observance declined into social convention. In 1843, the Rev. F.E. Paget, Rector if Elfield in Staffordshire, published his *Tract Upon Tombstones* in which he stated that the erection of a tombstone should be 'a Christian act and one that shall benefit the living. The tombstones in the

The hunting horns are the only reference to John Peel's sporting prowess in his memorial at Caldbeck, Cumbria.

churchyard are, as it were, a book, from whence [visitors] draw their reflections on man's mortality and in which every new inscription is a fresh page.' A proper epitaph, he continued, 'should be characterised by Christian humility, kindness, and by a disposition to say too little rather than too much.'

In the present century there is evidence of increasing conflict between those who oppose the cliché and the banal and others who consider epitaphs to be a reflection of personal taste and, therefore, of contemporary society. In 1994, a Consistory Court ruled that colloquial references to 'dad', 'nanna' and 'grandad' were undignified and inappropriate, a judgment supported by the *Churchyards Handbook* * which suggests that gravestones should be raised for the benefit of posterity rather than the transient gratification of a bereaved family. Censorship of inscriptions is nothing new. In 1797 at the church of St. Anthony-in-Meneage, Cornwall, the widow of Richard Roskruge suggested an epitaph for her murdered husband 'Doomed by a cruel ruffian's hand to die!'. The vicar was not impressed and substituted '. . . a neighbour's erring hand' as 'breathing more of Christian charity'. Certainly, there is little to recommend the ubiquitous 'in loving memory of . . .' and 'RIP' (*Requiescat in Pace* – 'may he rest in peace'). Infinitely preferable is the dignified epitaph 'Here to the earthly remains of . . .', inscribed on a seventeenth-century memorial at Folke in Dorset.

Epitaphs are collected and recorded by many of the family history societies whose addresses may be obtained from county record offices.
See also CHURCHYARDS, ESQUIRE, GENTLEMAN, MEMORIALS *and* WALL MONUMENTS
Further reading:
Rees, N., *Epitaphs: A Dictionary of Grave Epigrams and Memorial Eloquence*, London, 1993
Stapleton, H. and Burman, P., (eds.), *The Churchyards Handbook*, London, 1988 *

EQUILATERAL ARCH *see* ARCH

ERASMUS, DESIDERIUS (*c.* 1469–1536) Dutch Renaissance theologian, humanist, publisher and commentator and the most renowned scholar of his age. His Greek versions of the New Testament showed for the first time that contemporary Latin translations were defective. He is best remembered for his merciless satires on monasticism and the corruptions of the Church, notably his *Praise of Folly* (1509) which he dedicated to his friend Sir Thomas More (1478–1535). Although sympathetic to the sources implicit in the Reformation movement, Erasmus disliked violent political and religious upheaval and never openly joined the reformers, preferring instead the stability of the Church.

EREMITICAL Reclusive, like an ANCHORITE or COENOBITE.
See also HERMIT

ERMINE *see* COLOURS (HERALDIC)

ESCUTCHEON (i) In HERALDRY, a shield. (ii) Any shield-shaped decorative motif. (iii) A small metal plate pierced by a key-hole.

ESCUTCHEON OF PRETENCE A small shield charged with the arms of an heraldic heiress and placed at the centre of her husband's arms where it is said to be in pretence. Correctly an inescutcheon of pretence, this method of MARSHALLING can have alarming artistic consequences.

ESPOUSAL An engagement to be married which, before the seventeenth century, was considered to be of equal significance as the marriage itself.
See also BETROTHAL *and* MATRIMONY

ESQUIRE In the Middle Ages, an attendant (*escutifer* = shield bearer) to a knight. An esquire's feudal service required him to maintain his master's shield and armour, though his responsibilities and duties were considerably wider than this and were, in part, intended to train him in the martial and courtly arts and chivalric code. Many esquires were themselves of noble birth and in practice pages tended to perform the more menial duties. By 1400 sons of peers and the eldest sons of knights were deemed to be esquires and in the sixteenth century the title was applied to officers of the Crown. It was thereby considered superior to that of GENTLEMAN, though only by association with a royal office which provided added distinction.

From the mid-seventeenth century the style was widely adopted, not only by Crown officers (such as military and naval officers and justices of the peace) but also by those who unashamedly nurtured aspirations of gentility. It is to be found in numerous epitaphs of the period, often in the abbreviated form 'Esq.' or 'Esqre'.

The rural '*Squire*' is generally a lord of the manor or major land-owner, and the term is entirely colloquial.
Further reading:
Wagner, A., *English Genealogy*, London, 1960

ESTATE MAPS *see* MAPS

EUCHARIST (*also* COMMUNION, HOLY COMMUNION, THE LORD'S SUPPER *and* THE MASS) The Eucharist (meaning 'thanksgiving') is the central act of Christian worship. The institution of the Eucharist was recorded by St. Paul (1 Corinthians 11: 23–5) and references in the Acts of the Apostles confirm that it was a regular part of

Christian worship from a very early date. The term is applied to both the sacrament in which bread and wine are consecrated and consumed and to the consecrated elements themselves which are referred to doctrinally as the Body and Blood of Christ. Inevitably there was debate within the Church as to the sacrificial nature of the Eucharist and concerning the presence or otherwise of Christ at Communion. Belief in the doctrine of *transubstantiation* (by which the whole substance of the consecrated elements of the Eucharist are converted into Christ's body and blood, only the appearances (*accidents*) of the blood and wine remaining) was defined and confirmed at the Fourth Lateran Council in 1215. At this time, the celebrant received *Communion in Both Kinds* (or *Communion in Both Species*), other communicants receiving the bread only (*see* HOST).

The nature of the Eucharist caused considerable controversy at the REFORMATION. Martin Luther (1483–1546) defended a doctrine of *Consubstantiation* by which both the bread and wine and the body and blood of Christ co-existed each within the other at the Eucharist. Others, notably Ulrich Zwingli (1484–1531), maintained that the Eucharist was a purely commemorative act, while John Calvin (1509–64) advocated the doctrine of *Virtualism* by which the faithful received the power of the body and blood of Christ through the bread and wine, while denying that any change in the elements took place. The sixteenth-century reformers insisted that there was no scriptural justification for denying communicants *Communion in Both Kinds* and the practice was restored in Protestant churches at the Reformation.

In 1548, the *Order of the Communion*, a form of words (in English) for the administration of Communion, was inserted in the Latin MASS between the Communion of the priest and that of the people. It included the *General Confession and Absolution*, the *Comfortable Words* and the *Prayer of Humble Access* and was incorporated into the *Book of Common Prayer in 1549* (*see* COMMON PRAYER, BOOK OF). References to the nature of the Eucharist in the *Book of Common Prayer* are ambiguous and have allowed the co-existence of a number of doctrines within the Church of England. In the Roman Catholic Church, the final session of the Council of Trent (at Trento in northern Italy, 1562–3) reaffirmed the doctrine of transubstantiation and confirmed that the Sacrifice of the Mass was expiatory.

Although in the Middle Ages church attendance at the LITURGY was general, Communion was infrequent (the Fourth Lateran Council ordered Communion at least once a year). Most post-medieval revivals have sought to increase the frequency of Communion and weekly Communion is now common in both the Roman Catholic Church and the Church of England.

The word Mass is derived from the Latin *mittere* meaning 'send forth', a reference to the dismissal of the congregation following the Eucharist. Until recently, the Low Mass (a simplified form without music) was that which was most commonly celebrated.

See also ABLUTIONS, AUMBRY, COMMUNION LINEN, CREDENCE, EVENING PRAYER, FENESTELLA, LAMPS, LAVABO, MATTINS, PISCINA, PLATE, PRESBYTERY, PYX, RESERVATION, SEDILIA, SQUINT, TABERNACLE *and* VESTMENTS

EVANGELIARY A book containing the four Gospels or those portions of the Gospels which are read at the Eucharist in accordance with the ecclesiastical calendar.

EVANGELICALISM An evangelist was a missionary, and in the Church the term is used to describe the authors of the four Gospels (*see* GOSPEL). The Protestant churches are described as 'evangelical' because their teaching is based essentially on the Gospel. Since the eighteenth century, the Evangelical movement within the Church of England has emphasised personal salvation by faith in the Atonement (the reconciliation of God and man through the incarnation and death of Christ). It was formed at a time when the Church was preoccupied with maintaining the established order (*see* EIGHTEENTH-CENTURY CHURCH) and in the nineteenth century played a leading part in social reform and in the work of missionary societies (*see* NINETEENTH-CENTURY CHURCH).

EVANGELICAL REVIVAL *see* NINETEENTH-CENTURY CHURCH

EVANGELISM Promulgation of the Gospel with an emphasis on the need for a new birth or conversion. The evangelistic fervour of John Wesley (1703–91) and others aroused the great missionary spirit of the late eighteenth and nineteenth centuries.

EVANGELISTS, SYMBOLS OF THE *see* CHRISTIAN SYMBOLS

EVENING PRAYER (EVENSONG) The service of Evening Prayer as set out in the *Book of Common Prayer* combines elements of the evening offices of VESPERS and COMPLINE: the appointed Psalms and lesson from the *Old Testament*, the *Magnificat*, a lesson from the *New Testament*, the *Nunc Dimittis*, the Apostles' Creed and prayers. There may also be hymns and a sermon. At one time Evening Prayer was said daily in most churches, even in the absence of a congregation, but is now usually observed only on Sundays except at cathedrals and some collegiate

chapels where Choral Evensong is held also on weekdays. Recently, of the six Easter Day services held in the seven churches of a Dorset benefice not one was Evensong or MATTINS. And yet, for many, Evensong remains the quintessence of all things English. The 'mindless outpourings' of the afternoon congregation at Thomas Hardy's 'Mellstock', while familiar and somehow comforting, are far removed from the exquisite singing of today's cathedral and collegiate choirs. To sit in the candle-lit stalls of Gloucester Cathedral or Magdalen College, Oxford on a grey February afternoon, and to absorb the soaring splendour of Gibbons, Tallis and Byrd is to experience a sense of elation and spiritual renewal quite without equal. And then there is the *Alternative Service Book* (1980) and the ubiquitous guitar . . .
See also EUCHARIST

EVENSONG *see* EVENING PRAYER

EWER A vessel in which liquid is carried. A font ewer contains the HOLY WATER to be used at BAPTISM.
See also PLATE

EXCOMMUNICATION The act of expelling from the communion of the Church and of imposing other deprivations on those whose actions have attracted ecclesiastical censure. In the Roman Catholic Church those who have been excommunicated (*excommunicatus toleratus*) may neither receive nor administer the Sacraments and, if pronounced *excommunicatus vitandus* by the Pope, may not hold any office or dignity within the Church. Social intercourse is also discouraged. As recently as 1969 the Church of England confirmed that excommunication remains a valid form of censure.
See also ANATHEMA *and* BELL, BOOK AND CANDLE

EXECUTOR The person (or persons) appointed by a TESTATOR to see that the terms of a will are carried into effect (*see* PROBATE).

EXORCISM The practice of driving out evil spirits by means of invocation and prayer.

EXORCIST A member of the MINOR ORDERS whose duties included EXORCISM, although this power was not confined to exorcists alone.

EXTRA-PAROCHIAL An area of land located in a civil or ecclesiastical PARISH other than that to which it belonged. Extra-parochial land might be acquired (for example) by a neighbouring parish which required an additional consecrated burial ground, its own being full. Extra-parochial land was not subject to the jurisdiction of the parish which owned it, no poor or church rates were paid to the parish in which it was located and (in theory) tithe money was due to the Crown. In 1894 all extra-parochial lands were incorporated into the parishes where they were located or, if of sufficient size, became parishes in their own right. The term is also applied to uninhabited land outside the boundaries of a parish and exempt from church rates.

EXTREME UNCTION *see* UNCTION

FABRIC LANDS Land donated to a parish to provide funds for the maintenance of its church.

FAÇADE *see* ELEVATION

FACING MATERIALS Facing is the finish applied to the exterior surface of a building. When a building is described as *cased* the facing is of high-quality material, usually finer than that of which the building is constructed. *Rendering* is a covering of plaster mix or mortar (*see also* PARGETING) and is usually applied in two coats. Gravel, shingle or similar material may be cast on render before it hardens. This is known as *rough-cast* and is intended both as decoration and to provide protection. *Pebbledash* is similar but requires an additional layer of rendering in order that the pebbles or flints may be affixed to it before it dries. *Cladding* is a thin covering of stone, tiles or slate applied to the exterior of a building.
See also BUILDING MATERIALS, FLINT, GALLETING, MASONRY *and* RAGWORK

FACULTIES, COURT OF A court established in 1534 when the granting of licences, dispensations and faculties in the provinces of York and Canterbury passed from Papal jurisdiction to that of the Archbishop of Canterbury.
See DISPENSATION *and* FACULTY

FACULTY (i) Authorisation by an ecclesiastical superior for the granting of a dispensation permitting someone to hold an office or to perform a function which would otherwise be forbidden by law (*see also* FACULTIES, COURT OF). (ii) A licence, issued on behalf of a bishop (usually by the Diocesan Chancellor or Archdeacon), permitting

alterations or additions to be made to church buildings or churchyard for which the diocesan bishop is ultimately responsible. Under the *Faculty Jurisdiction Measure* of 1938 and subsequent legislation, permission is required for all works of repair or alteration in parish churches, including the erection of monuments inside the church. (It is also necessary to apply to the COLLEGE OF ARMS for the erection of an heraldic monument.) Archaeological investigation also requires a faculty if the fabric of the church is likely to be disturbed or excavation is anticipated. There is a Diocesan Advisory Committee for each diocese which advises the Chancellor on the granting of faculties. (*See also* DOCUMENTARY SOURCES, NINETEENTH-CENTURY CHURCH *and* TWENTIETH-CENTURY CHURCHES.) (iii) The Faculty Office of the Master of Faculties of the Archbishop of Canterbury is responsible for the administration of applications for marriage licences received from parties living in different provinces of the Church of England. Records of the licenses issued since 1660 are now housed at the Lambeth Palace Library in London (*see* APPENDIX II). Earlier records were destroyed in the Great Fire of London.
See also ARCHIVES

FAIENCE Decorated glazed earthenware.

FAIR LINEN CLOTH The white linen cloth, usually with lace or embroidered edgings, which covers the top surface of the communion table and overhangs the sides.

FAIRS AND MARKETS In the centuries that followed the withdrawal of Rome, Saxon chieftains built their strongholds and the monks their abbeys and, inevitably, such places attracted a scattered but increasingly gregarious populace, anxious to join with others in the celebration of saints days and holy days and to witness the administration of justice and the settlement of disputes in the lord's courts. For itinerant merchants, travel was both slow and dangerous, so that these large gatherings of people, enjoying the security of monastic or magnatial patronage, provided ideal opportunities for trade. Edward the Elder (900–925) decreed that all buying and selling should take place openly in a market place and within the jurisdiction of a town reeve. As permanent communities developed in the vicinity of abbeys and castles so markets and fairs flourished and by the late tenth century tolls were exacted by the nobles and clerics who organised and controlled the movement of goods between their estates.

During the Middle Ages fairs emerged as seasonal gatherings, sometimes on the periphery of towns or at prominent sites in the surrounding countryside, whereas markets were held weekly and always in towns or villages where the parish church was the focus of community activity (*see* CHURCH AND COMMUNITY *and* CHURCHYARDS). After the Conquest many of these customary markets and fairs were recorded in DOMESDAY Book and eventually regularised under the Norman kings by the granting of charters which permitted the receipt of revenues (see below). The acquisition of a market charter was obviously of great financial advantage to a manorial lord, who would receive the tolls and taxes and the fines exacted for breaches of trading regulations, and to the Crown from whom the privilege was almost invariably purchased.

Restrictions, aimed at alleviating the problems of inequitable competition, included the staggering of market days throughout a week in a particular area, the prosecution of *forestallers* or *regrators* (merchants who traded before reaching a market and sold on at a profit) and the imposition of limits on the proximity of markets. (A reasonable day's journey for an unmounted man was considered to be 20 miles which, when allowing time to walk to market, time to do business and time to walk home again, was divided by three to give six and two-thirds miles: the statutory distance between markets in the fourteenth century. 'And all these things it will be necessary to do by day and not by night on account of the snares and attacks of robbers.')

Despite these restrictions, medieval markets were essentially places where free trade was encouraged and a large wooden hand or stuffed glove was sometimes prominently displayed to signify that strangers were welcome. At Chester, such a glove was suspended from the church wall to advertise a twice-yearly fair, a practice which continued into the 1860s, while at the church of St. Oswald at Lower Peover (also in Cheshire) a wooden hand, now kept within the church, once signalled a welcome to those who wished to trade within the churchyard.

CHARTERS
Many market charters were granted by the Norman kings, but the greatest proliferation took place during the thirteenth century when some 3300 markets were authorised, with a further 1560 grants in the fourteenth century before the advent of economic decline. While many markets have been held on the same weekday for five or six centuries, the aspirations of numerous medieval entrepreneurs exceeded the commercial potential of their markets which eventually foundered, usually because they were geographically unsustainable or as a result of intense competition or the ravages of plague. Consequently, there are many tiny boroughs whose medieval charters have guaranteed continuing political and legal privileges not enjoyed by larger and more prosperous communities. Bishops Castle in Shropshire, for example, was the smallest borough in England until 1967 when it lost that distinction but none of its quaintness. But as others prospered so provision was made for permanent stalls, the

location of which may be evident in street names today: the *shambles*, for example, being the area of a market where fish and flesh were sold. Names such as Cheap Street and Sheep Street are indicative of early markets, so too is Chipping in place-names, derived from the Old English *ceping* or *cieping* meaning 'market' or 'market town', as in Chipping Norton in Oxfordshire.

ADMINISTRATION

A medieval market usually fell within the jurisdiction of a lord of the manor whose steward presided over the Court of Pie Powder (a corruption of *pieds poudreux*, meaning 'dusty footed' travellers). This court met in a building called a *tolbooth* or *tolsey* and was responsible for both the general administration of the market and the maintenance of law and order. Local traders often traded first while outsiders (known variously as *stallingers, censers* or *chensers*) either waited their turn or paid a supplementary fee in order to jump the queue. From the late sixteenth century expanding trade encouraged competition among many smaller market towns. This resulted in the erection of market halls, administrative offices supported on pillars to provide a covered space beneath for stalls. Here goods were weighed by the Ponderator and scrutinised and stored by the Overseers of the Market and other officials. From 1640 the senior official was the Clerk of the Market, appointed by the lord of the manor or town mayor. On market days the Clerk announced the commencement of trading at ten and its cessation at sunset.

FAIRS

Medieval fairs were generally annual occasions and of greater significance to a local populace than markets. They usually took place (or commenced) on the *feriae*, the feast or holy days of the local church to whose patronal saint the fair was often dedicated (*see* PATRONAL FESTIVAL). On such days men were freed from labour (holy day became holiday) to engage in both the business and sociability of the fair. Most fairs originated in the thirteenth and fourteenth centuries in the new towns and seigniorial boroughs and were concerned, not only with trade and commerce, but with entertainment and the propagation of news and ideas. Many fairs grew to national (even international) importance, lasting for several days. And because they were held regularly at a fixed time and fixed place, they became centres of banking and commerce and contributed to the intellectual and cultural development of medieval Europe.

The exclusive right to hold a fair was established through a royal or magnatial charter which specified the day or days on which it was to be held, though some smaller fairs possibly originated in village wakes (*see* WAKE). Enterprising manorial lords or burgesses who obtained charters profited from the revenues which could be raised through farming out stalls or 'pitches' to lessees. Often, booths, utensils etc. were provided and these were stored in a 'Fair House' when not required. Fairs inevitably attracted merchants who were able to offer exotic and high quality goods not normally available at markets and for this reason many continued to be held until the distribution of merchandise was transformed by the advent of the railway age and an efficient postal service in the nineteenth century. But the anticipated profits which encouraged many medieval magnates to apply for charters did not always materialise: establishing a fair was a speculative business and while many fairs flourished or specialised others became moribund.

Sheep fairs (such as Tan Hill Fair on the Marlborough Downs in Wiltshire) and others of medieval origin, at which goods and beasts were sold, were known as charter fairs. Statute fairs derived from legislation enacted during the reign of Elizabeth I (1533–1603) which required district or hundred meetings to be convened annually for the appointment of employees and the settlement of wages and contractual disputes. These 'hiring fairs' were often held in anticipation of CANDLEMAS DAY (2 February) and those wishing to find new employment would carry symbols of their trade: shepherds their crooks, maids their mops and so on. Indeed, many statute fairs survive today as 'mop fairs' or 'pack [pact?] fairs'. Woodbury Fair, near Bere Regis in Dorset, lasted for five days: the first was called 'Wholesale Day', the second 'Gentlefolks' Day', the third 'Allfolks' Day', the fourth was the sheep fair and the Friday was 'Pack and Penny Day', when remaining goods were sold off cheaply.

CHURCHES AND CHURCHYARDS

At first, parish churches were used as repositories for documents and valuables, trading taking place in the porch and churchyard (*see also* MARKET CROSSES). In 1285, however, a statute was passed forbidding the holding of fairs in churchyards and by 1448 the clergy was so incensed by 'the abominable injuries and offenses done to Almighty God because of fairs and markets upon their high and principal feasts', that trading was finally removed into the space beyond the churchyard wall and fairs prohibited on Good Friday, Ascension Day, Corpus Christi, the Assumption of the Virgin Mary, All Saints and on any Sunday except the four at harvest time. But the prohibition does not appear to have been particularly successful for, in many areas, churchyards continued to be used for the purpose until the end of the sixteenth century.

Further reading:

Verlinden, C., *Markets and Fairs*: *Cambridge Economic History of England* Vol. 3, Cambridge, 1963

FALCON AND FETTERLOCK *see* BADGES

FALDSTOOL An occasional stool with folding legs. The term is also used (erroneously) to describe a litany desk (*see* DESK) or PRIE-DIEU.
See also BACKSTOOL *and* CHAIRS (SANCTUARY)

FALL The cloth which depends from the front of a book-rest on a pulpit or lectern. Usually embroidered with a simple motif (such as a cross) on a background of the COLOURS (LITURGICAL).

FAMILY PEWS *see* PEWS, FAMILY

FANLIGHT A window above a door which, in the eighteenth century, was usually semi-circular with radiating glazing bars in the form of a fan.

FAN VAULT *see* MEDIEVAL ARCHITECTURE *and* VAULTING

FARM A comparatively recent term derived from the Latin *firma*, a fixed money rent applicable to a consolidated holding created by means of sixteenth-century piecemeal enclosure of open fields.
See also GLEBE

FARMERY A monastic INFIRMARY.

FARTHINGALE *see* COSTUME

FASTING A penitential discipline intended to strengthen the spiritual life through self-denial. In particular, to abstain from taking food (or specified foods) for a given period. The first full meal taken thereafter was the break-fast. In the early Church, fasting was observed on Fridays and sometimes on Wednesdays or Saturdays. Initially, fasting implied complete ABSTINENCE from food throughout the fast day though, in the medieval period, a light meal (*collation*) was sometimes taken in the morning and evening. The eating of flesh meat was prohibited and fish was usually substituted. The medieval church imposed fasting on all, except the very young and the elderly and infirm, usually at times which alternated with the great feasts of the liturgical year such as ADVENT and EASTER. The fast of LENT, for example, is still observed for a period of forty days before Easter and (even for many non-Christians) it remains an occasion for abstaining from some small personal pleasure (*see also* SHROVE TUESDAY). Fasting is recognised in the 1969 Canons of the Church of England but there are no instructions for its observance.

FATHER (i) God as the first person of the TRINITY. (ii) An ordained member of a religious order, with the exception of the Society of St. Francis in which all members are brothers (*see* BROTHER). (iii) The title of a Roman Catholic priest (the term is also used by Anglo-Catholic members of the Church of England).

(iv) In medieval England CONFESSORS were referred to as 'ghostly fathers'. (v) When found in documents or monumental inscriptions, 'father in law' may actually mean a stepfather.
For Father Christmas *see* CHRISTMAS.

FATHER-GENERAL The senior monk of an order which has many houses.

FAULD An protective 'skirt' of overlapping steel hoops (*see* ARMOUR).

FEAST DAYS (FIXED AND MOVABLE) The Church's influence on medieval society was so great that people's lives were regulated by the liturgical calendar. In addition to attending church on Sunday they were also expected to observe numerous religious feast days or holy days of which there were some forty or fifty throughout the year, depending on local custom. On these '. . . total or partial abstention from servile work was required and the laity were expected to observe the Sunday pattern of attendance at mattins, Mass and evensong, fasting on the previous eve.'* Only essential work was permitted on holy days so that, once their religious observance was complete, most workers were free to enjoy their leisure time (hence 'holiday'). Many recreational and fund-raising activities were organised by GUILDS and CHURCHWARDENS (*see also* CHURCH ALES, CHURCHYARD *and* PLAISTOW).

The early Church wisely chose to graft many of its festivals onto earlier pagan ones, both Celtic and Roman (*see* ANGLO-SAXON CHURCH). The Celtic calendar, which was based on the agricultural year, began on 1 November and the great feast of *Samain*. At this time of year, surplus livestock was slaughtered for winter food and sheep were mated to provide stock for the following year. It was also a time when natural laws were suspended, evil spirits ventured abroad and huge bonfires were lit in order that life should be sustained through the long winter. In 835 the Church re-dedicated the day to its saints (ALL SAINTS' DAY also *All Hallows* or *Hallowmas*) though vestiges of Samain lingered in HALLOWE'EN (All Saints Eve) with its tradition of bonfires and witches and, more recently, in Guy Fawkes' Day (5 November).

The Celtic festival of *Imbolc* (1 February) marked the beginning of the lambing season and anticipated the coming of Spring. In the Church, the festival of CANDLEMAS (the Purification of the Blessed Virgin Mary) occurs on the following day and, for centuries, was an occasion for the veneration of childbirth when mothers who had borne children in the preceding year carried lighted candles to church.

According to St. Bede, the English name for the EASTER festival is derived from *Eostre*, the goddess of Spring, whose feast was celebrated at the vernal equinox. Rogationtide, when the priest led the people through the fields, blessing the growing crops, originated in the Roman festival of *Terminus*, the god of fields and landmarks (*see* PERAMBULATION *and* ROGATION).

The return of Summer was marked on 1 May by the feast of *Beltane* at which fires were lit, homes were decorated with flowers and greenery and the people celebrated with dancing and song (*see* MAY DAY). This was followed by the great MIDSUMMER festival of St. Peter's Eve on 28 June, while *Lugnasad* marked the beginning of harvest on 1 August: the Christian festival of the *First Fruits* when the first corn was ground and made into loaves. The Saxons called the day *hlaf-maesse* (loaf-day), now known as LAMMAS (*see also* GREEN MEN, PAGAN SYMBOLS *and* WELL-DRESSING).

In the fifteenth century, four-fifths of the population worked on the land. Ploughing, sowing, sheep-shearing, and the hay and corn harvests marked the passing of the agricultural year – punctuated by religious festivals and seasonal customs which gave meaning to the passing of the years.

After the twelve-day holiday of CHRISTMAS, which ended at EPIPHANY (6 January), work on the land began in earnest (*see* TWELFTH NIGHT). Tillage began on Candlemas (2 February) and with it an end of free-grazing on the previous year's stubble. Ploughing, sowing and harrowing continued until Easter and sheep shearing was usually completed by St. John's Day (24 June), after which the hay was ready for mowing.

Lammastide (1 August) marked the beginning of Harvest, the busiest time of year for those working on the land, the completion of which was celebrated with sports and fairs (*see* HARVEST THANKSGIVING). MICHAELMAS (29 September), was traditionally the end of both the farming and accounting years.
See also CHURCH AND COMMUNITY, HOCKTIDE *and* QUARTER DAYS AND RENT DAYS

THE CHURCH CALENDAR
The *Calendar* of *The Alternative Service Book* (1980) provides comprehensive lists of *The Seasons, Principal Holy Days, Festivals and Greater Holy Days, Lesser Festivals and Commemorations, Special Days of Prayer and Thanksgiving, Days of Discipline and Self-Denial* and *A Table of Moveable Feasts and Holy Days*. Provision is also made for 'Holy Days which may be observed locally'.

The following feast days are to be found (with others) in the *Calendar* of the *Book of Common Prayer* (see COMMON PRAYER, BOOK OF) and are those which have been observed in our parish churches since before the Reformation. The feast of the ASSUMPTION OF THE BLESSED VIRGIN MARY (15 August) was omitted from the *Book of Common Prayer* in 1549.

(Those marked with an asterisk will also be found as individual entries.)

1 January	Circumcision of Christ
6 January	Epiphany *
13 January	St. Hilary the Bishop
25 January	Conversion of St. Paul
2 February	Purification of the Blessed Virgin Mary and the Presentation of Christ in the Temple (Candlemas *)
14 February	St. Valentine *
24 February	St. Matthias
1 March	St. David *
12 March	St. Gregory
17 March	St. Patrick
18 March	St. Edward, King of the West Saxons
25 March	Annunciation of the Virgin * (Lady Day * or Ladymas)
4 April	St. Ambrose
23 April	St. George *
25 April	St. Mark
1 May	St. Philip and St. James the Less.
26 May	St. Augustine, first Archbishop of Canterbury
24 June	Nativity of St. John Baptist
29 June	St. Peter * and St. Paul
2 July	Visitation of the Blessed Virgin Mary *
22 July	St. Mary Magdalene
25 July	St. James the Apostle
1 August	Lammas Day * or Lammastide (prior to 1753)
6 August	Transfiguration *
10 August	St. Lawrence
13 August	Lammas Day * (from 1753)
24 August	St. Bartholomew the Apostle
8 September	Nativity of the Virgin Mary *
14 September	Holy Cross Day * (Holy Rood Day or Roodmas)
21 September	St. Matthew the Apostle
29 September	St. Michael and All Angels (Michaelmas *)
30 September	St. Jerome
18 October	St. Luke
25 October	St. Crispin
28 October	St. Simon and St. Jude the Apostles *
1 November	All Saints * (Hallowmas or All Hallows)
2 November	All Souls *
11 November	St. Martin (Martinmas)
22 November	St. Cecilia*
30 November	St. Andrew *
6 December	St. Nicolas
8 December	Conception of the Blessed Virgin Mary
21 December	St. Thomas the Apostle
25 December	Christmas *
26 December	St. Stephen
27 December	St. John the Evangelist
28 December	Holy Innocents * (Childermas)
29 December	St. Thomas à Becket

MOVABLE FEAST DAYS (see also individual entries*)*

Septuagesima	The third Sunday before Lent
Sexagesima	The second Sunday before Lent
Quinquagesima	The Sunday before Ash Wednesday
Shrove Tuesday	The Tuesday before Ash Wednesday
Ash Wednesday	The first day of Lent
Palm Sunday	The Sunday before Easter and the sixth Sunday in Lent
Maundy Thursday	The day before Good Friday (*also* Sheer Thursday)
Good Friday	The Friday before Easter Sunday
Easter Sunday	The first Sunday following the first full moon after the vernal equinox (between 22 March and 25 April)
Rogation Sunday	The fifth Sunday after Easter
Rogation Wednesday	The Monday, Tuesday and preceding Ascension Day
Ascension Day	The Thursday following Rogation Sunday (between 30 April and 3 June)
Whitsunday	Pentecost, the seventh Sunday after Easter
Trinity Sunday	The Sunday following Whit Sunday and the eighth after Easter
Corpus Christi	The Thursday after Trinity Sunday
Advent Sunday	The Sunday nearest to 30 November
Ember Days	The Wednesday, Friday and Saturday following:

i) the first Sunday in Lent
ii) the Feast of Pentecost (Whitsunday)
iii) 14 September (Holy Cross Day)
iv) 13 December (St. Lucy)

See also EMBER DAYS, PASCHAL CANDLE, PASCHALTIDE, PASSIONTIDE, PATRONAL FESTIVAL, RELIC SUNDAY *and* SPY WEDNESDAY

For Apprentice Sunday, Mid-Lent Sunday, Refection Sunday, Rose Sunday *and* Simnel Sunday *see* MOTHERING SUNDAY.

For education and law terms *see* HILARY, MICHAELMAS *and* TRINITY.

Further reading:

Duffy, E., *The Stripping of the Altars: Traditional Religion in England 1400–1580*, London, 1992

FEET OF FINES From the Latin *finis* meaning 'conclusion', a fine in this context was a formal conveyance of land. Such an agreement was itself legal but the 'dispute' which it determined was fictitious so that a fine was essentially a means of ensuring that all such transactions should be registered in the courts. The practice dates from the reign of Henry II (1154–89) and originally each party received a copy of the agreement. But from 1195 a third copy, the 'foot of the fine', was filed by the Treasury. Such documents, which are maintained by the Public Record Office, provide a wealth of local detail and many have been published.

FELONY A generic term formerly applied to a class of crimes which were regarded by the law as being of greater severity than those described as misdemeanours. The class (which included murder, wounding, rape, arson and robbery) comprised those offences for which the penalties formerly included forfeiture of land and goods. Forfeiture was abolished in 1870 but in English Law procedural differences were maintained until the distinction between felonies and misdemeanours was abandoned in 1967. No such distinction ever existed in Scotland.

See also OUTLAWS *and* SANCTUARY

FENESTELLA A canopied niche in the south wall of a presbytery containing a PISCINA and often an AUMBRY or CREDENCE and SEDILIA. The decorative moulding of a fenestella is usually compatible with the architectural style of contemporary window arches and doorways.

Fenestella with piscina and sedilia. Here, the sanctuary floor was raised during a nineteenth-century restoration making the seats of the sedilia appear uncomfortably low.

FENESTRATION The disposition of windows on a building.

FERETORY A shrine, above ground level, in which the relics of a saint were deposited and at which they were venerated (*see* SHRINES) or a chapel containing such a shrine. A feretory was usually located in a bay behind the HIGH ALTAR, separated from the PRESBYTERY by an elaborate screen. The custodian of a feretory, and of its treasures, was called a *feretrar*.

FERIAL From the medieval Latin *ferialis* meaning 'festival', the term was used to name the days of the octave of EASTER: *feria prima, feria secunda* etc. (first festival day, second festival day, etc.). From this the designation was transferred to the days of ordinary weeks and, in ecclesiastical usage, to any day, other than a Sunday, on which no feast was celebrated. It is sometimes used erroneously to describe an 'ordinary' Sunday on which no other feast is celebrated.

FERRAMENTA Metal ornamentation and furniture e.g. of a door.

FERRIES *see* CHAPELS

FERRULE A metal ring or cap affixed to the foot of a pole to provide additional strength and protection.

FESS POINT *see* POINTS OF THE SHIELD

FESTIVALS AND SOCIAL CUSTOMS *see* ADVENT, ALL SAINTS' DAY, ALL SOULS' DAY, APPRENTICE SUNDAY (*see* MOTHERING SUNDAY), ASCENSION DAY, ASH WEDNESDAY, BOY BISHOP, CANDLEMAS, CHRISTMAS, CHURCH ALE, CHURCH AND COMMUNITY, CHURCHYARDS, CORPUS CHRISTI, DISTAFF DAY, DRAMA, EASTER, EASTER EGGS, EMBER DAYS, EPIPHANY, FAIRS AND MARKETS, FEAST DAYS (FIXED AND MOVABLE), FOOLS (FEAST OF), GOOD FRIDAY, GOSPEL OAK (*see* ROGATION), GUILDS, HALLOWE'EN, HALLOWMAS, HARVEST THANKSGIVING, HOCK-TIDE, HOLY CROSS DAY, HOLY INNOCENTS, HOLY SATURDAY, HOLY WEEK, HOLY WELLS, INCUBATION, KING CHARLES' DAY, LADY DAY, LAMMAS, LENT, MAUNDY, MAY DAY, MICHAELMAS, MID-LENT SUNDAY (*see* MOTHERING SUNDAY), MIDSUMMER, MOTHERING SUNDAY, NAVE, NEW FIRE, OAK APPLE DAY, PALM SUNDAY, PANCAKE TUESDAY (*see* SHROVE TUESDAY), PASCHAL CANDLE, PASCHALTIDE, PASSIONTIDE, PATRONAL FESTIVAL, PENTECOST, PERAM-BULATION, PLAISTOW, PLOUGH MONDAY, PORCHES, PRESENTATION OF THE BLESSED VIRGIN MARY, QUARTER DAYS AND RENT DAYS, REFECTION SUNDAY (*see* MOTHERING SUNDAY), RELIC SUNDAY, ROGATION, ROSE SUNDAY (*see* MOTHERING SUNDAY), *for* SAINTS' DAYS *see* FEAST DAYS (FIXED AND MOVABLE), *for* the traditions associated with particular saints *see* SAINTS (ANDREW, CECILIA, CLEMENT, DAVID, GEORGE, PETER, SIMON AND JUDE, SWITHIN *and* VALENTINE), SEPTUAGESIMA, SEXAGESIMA, SHEER SUNDAY, SHROVE TUESDAY, SIMNEL SUNDAY (*see* MOTHERING SUNDAY), STIR-UP SUNDAY, TRINITY SUNDAY, TWELFTH NIGHT, VISITATION OF OUR LADY, WAKE, WHITSUNDAY, YEW SUNDAY *and* YEW TREES

FESTOON A floral decoration, usually a carved garland of flowers or fruit suspended between two points to which it may be fastened with ribbons. A *swag* is similar, but composed of draped fabric.

FETTERLOCK *see* BADGES

FEUDAL OBLIGATIONS Like other great land-holders, the medieval Church owed feudal obligations to the Crown. For three centuries after the Norman Conquest, many abbeys (as feudal tenants) were obliged to provide knight service to the king by whom all land was held. In the eleventh century, for example, the Benedictine priory of Ely provided forty armed men while, in the twelfth century, the abbot of Peterborough had to equip sixty knights and the abbot of Bury, forty. But the obligation was at variance with the nature of a religious house and was eventually commuted to a cash payment (*scutage*). Archbishops, bishops and royal abbots were tenants in chief and held baronies. They owed knight service and were required to attend Parliament and to provide hospitality for others of equal rank. For this reason, the accommodation provided for religious superiors was often sumptuous and far removed from that of the humble monk.
See also HERALDRY (ECCLESIASTICAL) *and* PALATINATE

FFYNNON A Welsh word meaning a spring or well (*see* HOLY WELLS).

FIELD CHURCH *see* ANGLO-SAXON CHURCH

FIELD NAMES *see* PLACE-NAMES

FIGURE SCULPTURE (EXTERIOR) Roman-esque doorways were often the most richly orna-mental feature of a building and were deeply recessed and moulded, the space (*tympanum*) between the usually square-topped door and the round arch above

FIGURE SCULPTURE (INTERIOR)

being vigorously carved in high relief (*see* MEDIEVAL ARCHITECTURE). Undoubtedly the best example is the south doorway at Kilpeck in Herefordshire (*c.* 1170–90), though there are numerous others (*see* DOORS AND DOORWAYS). The Normans were especially fond of elaborately carved CORBEL TABLES, series of small corbels, occurring immediately below the roof eaves, each corbel fashioned in the form of a monster or grotesque figure. There are notable examples at Berkswell in Warwickshire, Bossall in Yorkshire, Elkstone in Gloucestershire, Kilpeck in Herefordshire, Steeple Langford in Wiltshire and Worth Matravers in Dorset. A corbel table may also be found at the top of a tower, supporting a thirteenth-century stone spire, and many later TOWERS have a similar band of ornamentation immediately beneath the parapet. Raised horizontal bands of masonry (*string-courses*) may be carved with foliage or figures, as at Adderbury in Oxfordshire, while some of the most charming figure sculpture (and the most common) is to be found in the carved heads, either human or animal, worked into the terminations (*label stops*) of hood-moulds (*see* DRIPSTONE). These little figures provide an invaluable insight into the medieval sculptor's art and yet they have been largely overlooked and are disappearing rapidly through decay or clumsy 'restoration'. Many are Victorian replacements or additions, though even these may be so badly weathered that their age is not immediately apparent. For the most part, however, a Victorian face will rarely be taken for a medieval one, though a number of more recent examples are very much closer in spirit to their medieval predecessors.

Before the REFORMATION nearly every parish church possessed a carved representation of the Madonna and Child, usually in a hooded niche in the outside wall of a tower. These figures were particularly detested by the reformers and surviving examples, such as that at Cerne Abbas in Dorset, are rare. Sculpted figures (or the niches which once contained them) are a particular feature of many West Country towers. There are figures of Christ surrounded by angels on the towers of Chewton Mendip and Batcombe in Somerset; representations of the Holy Trinity and St. Michael at Minehead in the same county and, at Hartland in Devon, a large figure of the patron saint, St. Nectan. Other notable figure sculptures have survived on the towers of Isle Abbots in Somerset and Fairford in Gloucestershire, while at St. Stephen's church, Clanfield in Oxfordshire the figure of St. Stephen holds a book and the stones by which he was martyred.

There are also occasional oddities such as the Roman statue of a local pagan god (*genius*) inserted in an exterior wall of St. Giles' church at Tockenham in Wiltshire. A recent investigation into the figure's origins led to the discovery of a major Roman site in a nearby field.

See also GABLE CROSSES, GARGOYLES, MOULDING *and* PAGAN SYMBOLS.
Further reading:
Stone, L., *Sculpture in Britain: the Middle Ages*, London, 1955
Meyer, F., *Handbook of Ornament*, Dover, 1957
Ware, D., and Stafford, M., *An Illustrated Dictionary of Ornament*, London, 1974
Whinney, M., *Sculpture in Britain: 1530–1830*, London, 1964

FIGURE SCULPTURE (INTERIOR) The essential difference between architectural moulding and sculpture is that, while the former is repetitive, the latter is unique. In the Middle Ages, stone figure sculpture was usually covered with a thin coating of lime or plaster to which polychrome paint and gold leaf were applied.

Rare twelfth-century figure of St. Michael defeating an amphisbaena (Revelation 12:7) inserted into a fourteenth-century porch at the church of St. Michael the Archangel, Mere, Wiltshire.

See BENCHES AND BENCH-ENDS, BOSSES, CAPITAL, CORBEL, EFFIGIES, FONTS, GREEN MEN, MISERICORDS, PANELLING, SCONCE, SCREENS, WEEPERS *and* WOOD CARVING
For further reading see also FIGURE SCULPTURE (EXTERIOR)

FILIATION The creation of subsidiary 'cells' or 'hives' of a (usually Cistercian) monastery, each consisting of twelve monks and a superior. The daughter (*filia*) was an independent community but was visited by the superior of the mother house.

FILIGREE Ornamental metallic lacework, usually of gold or silver, or a delicate structure resembling this.

FILLET (i) A narrow band between mouldings or running down a shaft. (ii) A narrow head-band (*see* COSTUME).

FINIAL A carved ornament on top of a pinnacle, gable or spire: for example a sphere (*ball finial*) or a foliated fleur-de-lis.

FIRE BUCKETS, FIRE-ENGINES *and* FIRE HOOKS *see* CHURCH AND COMMUNITY

FIRST POINTED *see* ARCHITECTURAL PERIODS *and* MEDIEVAL ARCHITECTURE

FISH 'And he saith unto them, Follow me, and I will make you fishers of men' (Mat. 4:19). At times of persecution, a fish was used as a secret sign of commitment to the early Church, the Greek word ICHTHUS ('fish') being composed of the initial letters of the Greek 'Jesus Christ, Son of God, Saviour'. In Christian art, it is the symbol of Christ and of the EUCHARIST (*see* CHRISTIAN SYMBOLS). It is often found, in an abstract form, as a pair of shallow arcs, joined at one end and intersecting at the other. Fish was eaten as an alternative to meat on days of ABSTINENCE which, in the medieval period, were known as 'fish-days'. At the time of Elizabeth I (1558–1603), Protestants often refused to eat fish on Fridays in order to demonstrate that they were not Papists. In folklore, the Devil is sometimes referred to as the 'Fisher of Souls'.

FISH PONDS The medieval method of preserving meat in brine was so unreliable (and the results so unpalatable) that most religious houses possessed their own DOVECOTES, warrens and fish ponds from which they obtained a regular supply of fresh protein. Of these the fish pond was of particular importance for it provided a reliable source of food for the numerous 'fish days' when no 'flesh' (i.e. red-blooded meat) could be eaten. ABSTINENCE was especially important in religious communities whose rules determined that the forgiveness of sins and the attainment of everlasting life were contingent on austerity and self-denial. Consequently even the most insignificant of religious houses possessed its own fish pond and many were retained when monastic buildings were converted to private homes or adopted for parochial purposes following the DISSOLUTION OF THE MONAS-TERIES. Carp were the most popular fish, though pike, perch, bream, roach, tench, trout and elvers were also farmed. Today, most medieval fish ponds are dry, their leats silted and their sluices long abandoned. Typically, they are rectangular and flat-bottomed with retaining embankments raised 1 metre (3.3 feet) above ground level and with two or three adjacent *stew ponds* where young fish were raised. The grid-like outlines of ancient fish ponds are sometimes evident as CROP MARKS or as linear undulations in the vicinity of former abbey churches. They may also be marked on Ordnance Survey 'Pathfinder' maps.

FISTULA In the Middle Ages, a silver tube (*fistula*) was occasionally used to administer communion from the chalice.

FIVE MILE ACT, THE (1665) An Act which prevented a clergyman who refused to conform to the Act of Uniformity (1662) from preaching or coming within five miles of any place where he had previously officiated without first taking an oath by which he agreed not to attempt to alter the government of Church or State.
See also UNIFORMITY, ACTS OF *and* SEVENTEENTH-CENTURY CHURCH

FIVES *see* CHURCHYARDS

FIVE WOUNDS OF CHRIST, THE The expletive 'Zounds!' (God's wounds), in common usage for at least two centuries after the REFORMATION, reflected an earlier medieval obsession with the notion that contemplation of of Christ's wounds (Isaiah: 'the wells of salvation') would provide protection against sudden un-confessed and unabsolved death. This was of particular significance during the second half of the thirteenth century when the Black Death decimated the population (*see* PLAGUE). Consequently, representations of the Five

Wounds of Christ are ubiquitous in the fabric of late medieval churches, depicted in stained glass, stone and wood. There are numerous variations but most show five disembodied wounds or Christ's heart, hands and feet, pierced and imbrued. They are sometimes crowned or contained within shields and may be mistaken for heraldic devices.
See also CHRISTIAN SYMBOLS

FLAGON A large vessel from which other vessels are filled.
See also PLATE

FLAGS Three types of flag are to be found in churches: heraldic flags, military colours, and the flags of parochial organisations. It is also customary for the national flag (or, more correctly, the diocesan banner) to be flown from church towers on certain occasions.
HERALDIC FLAGS
An heraldic *banner* is a square or oblong flag emblazoned with the arms (i.e. the devices which appear on the shield, but not the shield itself or the CREST and its appendages). This was the principal personal flag used by the medieval nobility down to the knights banneret. Banners of member knights of the orders of chivalry are hung above their stalls in the chapels of the orders: St. George's Chapel at Windsor Castle (the Most Noble Order of the Garter) and Henry VII's chapel at Westminster Abbey (the Most Honourable Order of the Bath), for example. On his death, a knight's banner is removed and by custom is conveyed to the king of arms of the order as his perquisite, though in practice it is usually given to the family to be hung in their parish church. These ceremonial banners are easily recognised: they are usually 1½ m square (5 ft.) and heavily embroidered and fringed. Few early banners have survived and those which are now displayed in churches are mostly from the nineteenth and twentieth centuries. There is a good example at Minterne Magna in Dorset where the banner of Lord Digby (*Azure a Fleur-de-lis Argent*) hangs above the west gallery.

While the banner accompanied armigerous commanders in battle, the mustering and rallying functions, during military campaigns and at tournaments, were performed by the livery flags: the long, tapering *standard* and the smaller, more manoeuvrable *guidon*. These bore the colours (*liveries*) and BADGES familiar to retainers and soldiery, and of which their uniforms were composed. Heraldic standards and guidons are rarely used today (except in Scotland) though there are examples in churches of civic standards, at the church of St. Mary Magdalene at Launceston in Cornwall, for example.

The foregoing heraldic flags should not be confused with those which were produced by the COLLEGE OF ARMS for use at the heraldic

funerals of the nobility and gentry (*see* FUNERAL HERALDRY). These included banners (usually oblong in form) and various standards, guidons (or *guydons*) and *pennons* (small, triangular or swallow-tailed flags), the size and function of which were strictly regulated according to the rank of the deceased. Unique among funerary flags was the *bannerol*, a banner of increased width on which were displayed the accumulated coats of arms (*quarterings*) of the deceased and his ancestors (*see* MARSHALLING). Having been carried in the funeral procession, the flags and other heraldic accoutrements were displayed in the church, often supported on brackets of a type provided by the College of Arms. Considering the multitude of flags produced for this purpose by the College between the late fifteenth and the late eighteenth centuries, surprisingly few have survived. There are notable examples of seventeenth- and eighteenth-century standards and bannerols of the Shirley family in the chancel of Staunton Harold in Leicestershire, while in the Sackville chapel at St. Michael's, Withyham in Sussex there is a magnificent collection of seventeenth-century banners, bannerols and standards (on painted canvas) relating to the earls De la Warr and the earls of Dorset.
MILITARY FLAGS
In 1747 regulations were introduced concerning the design of military uniforms and flags which, in part, were intended to prohibit the practice of using personal heraldic devices for military purposes: 'No colonel to put his arms, crest, devices or livery on any parts of the appointments of the regiment under his command'. Royal Warrants of 1751 and 1768 defined the colours, standards and guidons to be used by infantry and cavalry and these definitions have remained to the present day. These new flags bear little resemblance to their medieval or funerary predecessors and are essentially symbolic and ceremonial. The Colour represents the regiment, is carried into battle in the centre of the line and is defended to the last man. Infantry regiments have two colours: the First (or Queen's) Colour, a square version of the Union Flag at the centre of which is the regiment's title surmounted by the Imperial Crown, and the Second (or Regimental) Colour which bears the title, badges, mottoes, distinctions and battle honours of the regiment. The Household Cavalry and Dragoon Guards carry rectangular standards, while a (modern) guidon is carried by Dragoons and Light Dragoons. This too is rectangular but the fly is divided and has rounded corners. Hussars, Lancers and Rifle regiments do not carry standards, guidons or colours, neither do corps such as the Royal Artillery, Royal Signals, Royal Engineers etc. The company colours of the Welsh Guards are similar in appearance to medieval standards but are only 1 metre (3 feet 3 inches) in length.

Regimental flags are sometimes found in parish churches, usually in those counties where there is no cathedral. At Sherborne Abbey in Dorset, for example, the thirty-five Colours of the former Dorsetshire Regiment are suspended from the walls of the north aisle and ambulatory. Many of the older flags have all but lost their original colouring, only the gauze remaining. In churches where regimental colours have been 'laid up' there may also be WAR MEMORIALS donated by a regiment, often in the form of screens, reading desks or altar frontals.

Not all military flags commemorate famous regiments. In the north aisle of St. Mary's, Warwick hang the tattered remnants of the colours of Volunteers, raised in 1794 when it was expected that the French were about to invade England. Indeed, fears of a French invasion during the 1750s resulted in the Militia Act of 1757 and with it the effective creation of a territorial army which, at that time, numbered some 32,000 men. This was followed, in 1758 and 1759, by legislation permitting the raising of volunteer companies. These tended to comprise men of more independent means than those who served in the compulsory militia. They also preferred to train separately and to maintain their own headquarters, and an Act of 1782 formalised this distinction. But the volunteer companies were required only during wartime or when the peace was threatened. They were therefore disbanded in 1783, re-formed in the 1790s and disbanded again after the Peace of Amiens in 1802, only to be re-formed in the following year after which their popularity declined until the late 1850s when relations with France were once more becoming strained. In 1807, the Local Militia Act raised battalions of local militia within each county but, unlike the county militias, they were not required to serve beyond their own or adjacent counties and they were disbanded at the conclusion of the Napoleonic Wars in 1816. Annual 'Militia Sunday' parades were a popular feature of life in the eighteenth and nineteenth centuries and these invariably included a service in the parish church.

PROCESSIONAL FLAGS

Far more numerous are the flags of organisations such as the Mothers' Union which are often kept in the chancel of a parish church and used for processional purposes (*see* PROCESSIONS, LITURGICAL). Most are in the form of a GONFANNON, a flag which was especially favoured by the medieval GUILDS because of its suitability for carrying in processions (*see also* BANNER STAVE LOCKERS). Today, gonfannons are usually embroidered with religious or vernacular motifs appropriate to a particular organisation or church dedication (*see* CHRISTIAN SYMBOLS).

The heavy wooden 'poleheads' of FRIENDLY SOCIETIES may occasionally be found: a pair of rare early nineteenth-century heart-shaped boards at Stogursey in Somerset, for example. These were carried round the parish in an annual procession which culminated in a church service and a feast. Typically, they depict figures and inscriptions such as 'God Save the King', 'Britannia' and 'Success to Trade' and are a reminder of the church's continuing involvement with CHARITIES and the relief of the poor.

CHURCH TOWERS

The rules for hoisting the Union and National flags on public buildings are set out in *Appendix I* of *Debrett's Correct Form* *, though these do not refer specifically to parish churches. The (mildly) controversial question of which flag is appropriate to the tower of an English parish church was exacerbated by a warrant of 1938 which permitted the cross of St. George with the diocesan arms on a shield in the first quarter to be used for this purpose in the provinces of Canterbury and York. In Wales, a banner of the arms of the Church in Wales is flown (*Argent* [white] *on a Cross Azure* [blue] *a Celtic Cross Gold*). Some churches, usually of ancient foundation, possess their own arms and these are flown in the form of a banner on patronal festivals and other commemorative occasions. The arms of the former Benedictine Abbey and eighth-century cathedral of Sherborne in Dorset (*Gules* [red] *a Cross Argent* [silver] *over all on the dexter side a Crozier Gold*) are still flown on high days and holidays.

Further reading:

Friar, S., *A New Dictionary of Heraldry*, Sherborne and London, 1987

Montague-Smith, P., (ed.), *Debrett's Correct Form*, Kingston-upon-Thames, 1976 *

FLAMBOYANT The final phase of French Gothic architecture in which WINDOW TRACERY is composed of wavy undulating lines. To be found in English buildings of the Perpendicular period where the resulting motif resembles interwoven curves ('flames').
See also MEDIEVAL ARCHITECTURE

FLASHING A strip of lead or other material used to protect joints against damp.

FLÈCHE (*also* SPIRELET) A slender wooden spire at the centre of a roof.
See also BELL FLÈCHE

FLEMISH BOND *see* BONDING

FLEUR-DE-LIS (*also* FLEUR-DE-LYS) One of the most common decorative and heraldic motifs. Its origins remain a subject of debate, but it is generally believed to be a stylised lily – probably the Madonna Lily (*Lilium candidum*). The lily is a symbol of

apparent ordinariness, this extremely hard and fissile mineral was of singular importance in the development of civilisation: it provided Neolithic man with implements and, when struck, it would produce fire. The Anglo-Saxons knew it as *firestone*.

In the absence of other suitable materials, and because of its strength and durability, flint is frequently found as a building material in chalk districts of south and east England and has continued in use for this purpose from the Iron Age to the present day. Before the fourteenth century, whole flints were embedded in the mortar of walls which were further strengthened with stone and flint rubble and lacing courses of stone or brick. But from the late thirteenth century split and shaped (*knapped*) flints, with their dark facets outwards, were often used in conjunction with brick or stone to form chequer-work and other geometrically patterned surfaces (*knapping*).

A special decorative technique called *flushwork* also developed at this time. Knapped flint, set in mortar within the matrices of intricately carved freestone facings, is a feature of many East Anglian churches and continued, there and elsewhere, into the sixteenth century by which time a high standard of craftsmanship had evolved. In Dorset, flushwork is usually set in broad horizontal strips whereas in East Anglia it consists of thin vertical strips or squares. Flushwork motifs include simple geometrical or heraldic devices, CHRISTIAN SYMBOLS (such as the crowned M for St. Mary), monograms and inscriptions. There are celebrated examples in Suffolk at Eye and Southwold (towers), at Framsden and Kersey (porches) and Cavendish and Coddenham (clerestories).

Churchyard walls of knapped flint (often with brick or stone quoins) are commonly found in the southern counties of England and in some areas flint courses may alternate with horizontal bands of brick or stone. *See also* BUILDING MATERIALS *and* FACING MATERIALS
Further reading:
Muir, R., *The Stones of Britain*, London, 1986

FLOOR TILES *see* TILES

FLORIATION Decoration in the form of flowers.

FLORY (i) A decorative motif consisting of projecting FLEURS-DE-LIS. (ii) An heraldic device decorated with, or terminating in, fleurs-de-lis.

FLUSHWORK *see* FLINT

FLUTING Vertical channelling in the shaft of a COLUMN or PIER (*see* DECORATIVE MOTIFS).

'FLYING BISHOP' *see* CLERGY (CHURCH OF ENGLAND)

purity and has long been associated with the Virgin Mary. As the emblem of France (the punning 'Flower of Louis') it was first borne by Louis VII (1137–80) on a royal seal. The French arms *Azure Semy-de-Lis* (now termed France Ancient) were quartered with the lions of England by Edward III in 1340 (to emphasise the English claim to the throne of France) and the fleurs-de-lis remained in the arms of English sovereigns until 1801 (*for* illustration *see* ROYAL HERALDRY). The terms *flory* and *fleury* are synonymous and are used to describe an heraldic charge the limbs of which terminate in fleurs-de-lis (*see* CROSSES). *Flory-counter-flory* is descriptive of charges which are decorated with *fleurs-de-lis* alternately on either side, as in the *double tressure* in the royal arms of Scotland. *Floretty* (or *fleuretty*) is a field over which *fleurs-de-lis* are scattered, though the term *semy-de-lis* is more usual. Several of these terms are also used to describe decorative motifs, though as such they appear to be interchangeable. POPPY HEAD finials on bench ends are similar in appearance to the fleur-de-lis (*see* BENCHES AND BENCH-ENDS).
Further reading:
Ibbett, V., *Flowers in Heraldry*, London, 1977

FLEURON A flower-shaped ornament.

FLINT Flint is variety of quartz, consisting of irregular nodules of nearly pure silica, dark grey or black in colour, occurring in association with chalk which provides it with its white coating. Despite its

FLYING BUTTRESS *see* BUTTRESS *and* MEDIEVAL ARCHITECTURE

FOILS (i) Decorative figures in Gothic tracery consisting of a number of leaf-shaped curves (*lobes*) formed by small arcs separated by cusps (*see* CUSP). Most commonly used are the *trefoil* (3 lobes), *quatrefoil* (4) and *cinquefoil* (5). (ii) Similar figures in HERALDRY which include also the *sixfoil* (6) and the *octofoil* (8). These may be plain, pierced or *slipped* (having a stem).

Trefoil

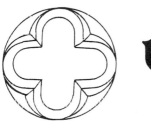

Quatrefoil   Heraldic cinquefoil

FOLDED CHASUBLE *see* VESTMENTS

FOLIATION A decorative motif consisting of carved leaves or leaf-like shapes.

FOLIO A leaf of paper folded once, thereby making two leaves of a book. Also a book composed of such sheets.

FOLLIES *see* ARTIFICIAL RUINS *and* MAUSOLEUM

FONT COVERS In order to avoid the lengthy process of sanctification before each christening, a supply of baptismal water was retained in the font, the lead lining of which prevented seepage through the porous stone. The practice of removing holy water for 'medical' and other, more sinister, purposes was so commonplace by the thirteenth century that an ecclesiastical statute required that lids should be fitted to FONTS and secured by means of iron bars and padlocks. The remains of the staples, by which the bars were held in place, may still be found on many fonts, inserted in lead-filled matrices in the stonework on either side of the bowl.

Early font covers were simple timber lids, braced on the underside to provide additional strength and shaped to fit securely within the top of the bowl. Several of these are still in use today. The covers of later hexagonal or octagonal fonts were often of a more elaborate conical design (known as *cone covers*). The ribs at each angle of the six- or eight-sided cone were sometimes straight (as at Monksilver in Somerset), gently curved (Ashbocking in Suffolk) or of ogee form (Colebrooke in Devon) and usually crowned with an elaborately carved finial. These forms continued in use after the Reformation, with Jacobean ornamentation replacing medieval crockets and pinnacles, as at Banwell and Rodney Stoke in Somerset, Astbury in Cheshire and Lanreath in Cornwall. The spaces between the ribs were usually filled with boarding, though not invariably so. The fine Jacobean font cover at Bolton Percy in Yorkshire, for example, has open ogee trusses radiating from beneath a bulb finial in the form of a crown (hence the term *crown cover*) and is supported above a shallow enclosed drum by means of a turned central shaft.

By the fifteenth century, earlier lids were sometimes replaced by magnificent tapering canopies (*see* TABERNACLE), carved and fashioned in the intricate architectural forms of the late Middle Ages and heavily painted and gilded. The best examples are to be found in East Anglia: at Castle Acre, Sall and Worstead in Norfolk, at Hepworth, Sudbury (St. Gregory), Worlingworth and (finest of all) at Ufford in Suffolk. There are also two splendid north-country tabernacles at Thirsk (restored) and Well in Yorkshire. Many of these lofty, soaring canopies almost reached the ceiling and were so heavy that they had to be suspended from a *font beam* (as at Sheringham in Norfolk) and raised by means of a *font crane* (Sall) which telescoped the lower section over the narrower upper section by means of a counterpoise mechanism. Sometimes the entire canopy was raised: at Ewelme in Oxfordshire and Pilton in Devon, for example.

The celebrated fifteenth-century oak canopy at Trunch in Norfolk is one of only four of its type in England. Erected on six piers above and around the font, its magnificent painted and carved panels, miniature flying buttresses and elaborate, pinnacled top are decorated with vines, flowers, monkeys and a wild man fighting a dragon. Regrettably, the font cover, which once telescoped into this canopy, has not survived. At Swimbridge in Devon and Terrington St. Clement in Norfolk there are good examples of another type of cover which completely encloses the font, a pair of doors providing access.

Post-Reformation fonts, especially those in newly built churches, were usually provided with simple cupola-shaped canopies, octagonal or hexagonal in shape and with subdued ornamentation. A number of nineteenth-century Gothic Revival fonts have elaborately painted and gilded canopies, encrusted with heavy 'medieval' motifs and enamelled shields, crests and cyphers (*see* NINETEENTH-CENTURY ARCHITECTURE). There are also several fine ornate canopies by the ecclesiastical architect Sir Ninian Comper (1864–1960), that at Wimborne St. Giles in Dorset, for example, which was commissioned by the ninth earl of Shaftesbury (d. 1961) as a memorial to his three sisters.

FONTS A font is a receptacle for baptismal water, normally (though not invariably) made of stone. In the early Church these were large basins, set below ground level, in which the candidate was submerged in baptismal water (*submersion*). It was not until the early Middle Ages, when infant baptism, *immersion* (partial submersion) and AFFUSION (the pouring of HOLY WATER over the head) became the general practice, that fonts were raised above floor level (*see* BAPTISM). In the Christian Church the Mass and Baptism are considered to be pre-eminent among the Seven Sacraments, baptism emphasising entry into the Christian life and the purging of sin. Consequently, every medieval church possessed its font which was symbolically located near the entrance, at the western end of the nave (*see* BAPTISTERY). In England and Wales, most surviving fonts were intended for infant baptism and are shallow and raised on pedestals or plinths to a convenient height. At baptism, the priest came into close personal contact with every family in his parish and the font was, therefore, an important symbol of the pastoral authority of the parish church. It was for this reason that in so many churches the ancient font has survived, even in those churches which have lost all other traces of their medieval origins. It follows, therefore, that the font is often a most effective guide to the age of a church.

SAXON AND CELTIC

Many Saxon fonts resemble an upturned drum and for that reason are known as *drum fonts*. They are usually lined with lead, stepped at the base and decorated with crude but vigorous motifs (such as Latin crosses), arcading and cable mouldings. There are notable examples at Curdworth in Warwickshire, Deerhurst in Gloucestershire and Little Billing, Northamptonshire. The dark stone font at Partrishow in Powys bears the inscription 'Menhir made me in the time of Genillin', a reference to Prince Cynddyllin of the old Welsh princedom of Powys. Perhaps the most extraordinary Saxon font is at Melbury Bubb in Dorset. Cylindrical and slightly tapered, the combined shaft and base are deeply carved with wild, entangled strands and interlinked animals – all upside down. The font's origins remain a mystery though it may once have been part of a circular pre-Conquest cross-shaft. The font at Penmon Priory, Anglesey was originally the base of an early eleventh-century cross which was adopted as a font in the nineteenth century.

MEDIEVAL

Twelfth-century Romanesque fonts, constructed at a time of ubiquitous church building, may be elaborately carved with CHRISTIAN SYMBOLS and biblical scenes such as the Baptism of Christ and the Crucifixion. Norman *pedestal fonts* are often square and set within the carved capital of a short octagonal stem and drum-shaped pedestal. In some instances, the font seems to have been constructed upon a figure of the devil, often in the form of a strange and mythical creature which is 'oppressed' both by the weight of the masonry and by the sacrament of baptism itself, as at Castle Frome in

Twelfth-century Romanesque font and 'oppressed' devil-creature at Castle Frome, Herefordshire.

Herefordshire (twelfth century). The fonts at Southrop in Gloucestershire and Stanton Fitzwarren in Wiltshire have carved figures of vices trampled beneath virtues, the names of the vices being inscribed backwards. Another type of font of the same period has a large *cup bowl* supported on a substantial cylindrical stem and four angle shafts, all rising from a square plinth and having the appearance of an orchestral *timpano*.

There are many wonderful examples of elaborately carved Norman fonts, notably those at Cottam, North Grimstone, Reighton and Thorpe Salvin, all in Yorkshire; at Burnham Deepdale,

Fincham, Sculthorpe, South Wootton, Shernborne and Toftrees in Norfolk; Cowlam in Humberside, Lenten in Nottinghamshire, Bridekirk in Cumbria, Chaddesley Corbett in Worcestershire, Coleshill and Stoneleigh in Warwickshire, Hook Norton in Oxfordshire, Luppitt in Devon, Strottesdon in Shropshire and Great Kimble in Buckinghamshire. The twelfth-century font at Eardisley is a splendid example of the work of that inspired Hereford School of craftsmen who were responsible for the sculpture at Kilpeck and other churches in the same county (*see* DOORS AND DOORWAYS). Even after eight centuries the carving of two battling warriors in flowing garments is razor-sharp, with enormous energy flowing from their movements, a writhing mass of tendrils ensnaring them and, in the bowl of the font, a huge lion lashing his tail round his body.

In Cornwall, two groups of late Norman fonts include Bodmin, Roche and St. Austell, all of which have carved cup-bowls supported on massive stems and angle shafts at each corner, and Altarnum, Laneast and St. Thomas-by-Launceston which are similar in appearance to massive Norman capitals, with circular motifs on the sides of the bowl and carved heads at each corner.

There is also a group of thirty fonts made entirely of lead, numerous others having been melted down for armaments and other purposes or destroyed by fire. The group includes fonts at Ashover in Derbyshire, Brookland in Kent and Dorchester Abbey in Oxfordshire. The magnificent twelfth-century font at the church of Lady St. Mary at Wareham in Dorset is the only hexagonal lead font to have survived. Cast in one piece, each side is ornamented by a pair of semicircular arches supported on fluted columns, each enclosing a standing figure of one of the twelve Apostles. A further group of seven richly ornamented fonts in TOURNAI MARBLE includes a wonderful example at East Meon in Hampshire.

Another type of font, dating from the transitional period between Norman and Early English (*see* MEDIEVAL ARCHITECTURE), is similar in appearance to the cup-bowl font described above but is of PURBECK MARBLE and has a square bowl supported on a large central pillar and smaller shafts at each corner. There are good examples at Eaton Bray, Leighton Buzzard and Studham in Bedfordshire and North Newbald in Yorkshire. Fonts of the Decorated period usually have an octagonal bowl with niches containing figures (often, of saints) as at Hitchin and Ware in Hertfordshire, Fishlake in Yorkshire and Tysoe in Warwickshire, or ornamented with tracery as at Brailes, also in Warwickshire.

EAST ANGLIAN FONTS
It was in the fifteenth century, and in East Anglian churches, that the elaborately carved font reached its apogee. These magnificently crafted fonts are often

Fifteenth-century font at Framlingham, Suffolk.

raised on steps (notably at Laxfield in Suffolk and Little Walsingham, Norfolk) and are of two types. In the first, the stem is surrounded by lions and sometimes by hirsute 'men of the woods' (*see* WODEHOUSE), the panels of the bowl carved alternately with angels, holding musical instruments or heraldic shields, and beasts (usually lions) or Christian symbols. Among many fine examples are those at Acle, Happisburgh, Surlingham and Upton in Norfolk and Chediston and Saxmundham in Suffolk. The second type (and by far the most beautiful of any) is known as the *Seven Sacraments* font. This is octagonal, seven of the panels depicting the Seven Sacraments (*see* CHRISTIAN SYMBOLS) and the eighth (typically) the Crucifixion or Baptism of Christ. No two fonts of this type are the same and collectively they provide a wealth of information concerning contemporary vestments and costume, together with illustrations of baptism by immersion and the confirmation of infants (at Sloley in Norfolk). The best preserved panels (in which some of the original colour remains) are at Walsoken and Great Witchingham in Norfolk and Westhall in Suffolk. There are other splendid examples at Badingham in Suffolk and Gresham in Norfolk. In all, there are twenty-two Seven Sacrament fonts in Norfolk and eleven in Suffolk, though a number of these have been defaced. Elsewhere, there are only two: at Farningham in Kent and and Nettlecombe, Somerset. There are also two Norfolk examples with sculpture of a later period: at Hemblington and Stalham.

POST-REFORMATION

Of several interesting post-Reformation fonts, that at Rothbury in Northumberland has a bowl of 1664 seated on a splendidly carved Saxon cross-shaft of *c.* 800; while at Essendon in Hertfordshire there is an elegant Wedgewood font of 1778. Constructed of black basalt-ware, this celebrated font is similar to that at Cardington in Bedfordshire.

By the greatest good fortune, many medieval fonts were spared the worst excesses of the reformist iconoclasts and continued in use, even to the present day. But many others were considered overtly 'primitive' by the Gothic Revivalists and were replaced in the nineteenth century by fonts which were (with only a few notable exceptions) pale and unworthy imitations of their medieval predecessors (*see* NINETEENTH-CENTURY ARCHITECTURE). *See also* FONT COVERS *and* PORCHES

FONT TAPERS A levy made by churchwardens, originally for the taper used at BAPTISM, but continued after the Reformation as a customary fee.

FOOLS, FEAST OF A mock-religious festival celebrated during the first week of January in the medieval period. Being an occasion for irreverence and buffoonery, it was suppressed in the sixteenth century.

FOOTBALL *see* CHURCHYARDS

FOOTPATHS AND BRIDLEWAYS More can be learned of the historical development of a locality from its network of ancient paths and bridleways than from any other feature. Some paths may be the remnants of prehistoric routeways while others once linked the settlements of Celtic and Anglo-Saxon Britain. Some were long-distance routes, used by medieval pack-horse trains and generations of drovers. Others form radial networks of paths linking outlying hamlets and farmsteads with a village nucleus (often with the tower of the parish church at its hub) and with each other. Many converge on fords, ferries and bridges or were adopted to delineate the boundaries of demesne lands or ecclesiastical and civil parishes. More recently, paths have been created out of the diversions of perambulating postmen where they were obliged to abandon the metalled road in order to service remote farms and country houses.

A *right of way* is a legal concept and a highway the strip of land to which it is applied. The nature of the right is dependent on the type of way which, under common law, may be a footpath (over which the public has a right of passage on foot only) a bridleway (rights of passage on foot, on horseback or leading a horse) or a carriageway (rights of passage on foot, on horseback or by means of a wheeled vehicle). All three are clearly marked on Ordnance Survey 'Pathfinder' maps (1:25 000). The term 'Queen's (or King's) Highway' refers to the notion of royal protection enjoyed by all travellers on a public road and of the inviolable nature of the road itself. This ancient principle is amply illustrated at Walpole St. Peter in Norfolk where, during re-building, the churchwardens of St. Peter's church were obliged to accommodate an ancient right of way by means of a passage beneath the chancel.

In 1555, the Highways Act required that a 'Surveyor of the Highways' should be appointed (usually in Easter week) by the churchwardens, constable and representatives of each parish. (The surveyor was alternatively known as *boonmaster, stonewarden, waymaker, wayman* and *waywarden*). In 1662 the law was amended so that the surveyor was elected by a majority of parishioners and from 1691 he was appointed by the justices from a list of eligible landholders in a parish. The office was unpaid and, from 1691, usually filled by rotation. The Surveyor was obliged to inspect the highways at least three times a year and to organise the statute labour or arrange commutations. Each able-bodied householder or tenant was obliged to provide four days 'statute' labour a year (from 1691 this was increased to six), to provide a substitute or pay a fine. Certain other parishioners were required to provide a cart for road repairs. Before 1835, therefore, the upkeep of the highway was generally a manorial or parochial responsibility. But in that year an act empowered quarter sessions to appoint paid district surveyors, to bring together groups of parishes 'for the better maintenance of the highway' and for a highway rate to be levied. The Highway Act of 1862 extended this authority and highway boards were established, charged with the responsibility of administering the highways within these groups of parishes. (These were abolished in 1894 but their records remain with county record offices.) The Local Government Act of 1888 transferred responsibility for the maintenance of highways to the newly established county councils, and the Local Government Act of 1894 brought minor roads within the jurisdiction of local authorities.

Many rights of way have been extinguished or diverted in recent years, and a (significantly smaller) number created. This practice is generally intended to 'rationalise' a local footpath network, usually by redirecting paths round field boundaries, thereby obliterating many networks which are of considerable antiquity. All such extinguishments, diversions and creations of rights of way are recorded by the highway authorities and these records are available at county council offices, together with copies of definitive maps for each parish. Analysis of extinguishment and diversion orders may assist in identifying ancient networks of footpaths and bridleways which once radiated from a parish church, linking it with outlying hamlets and farmsteads.

See also HOLLOW WAYS

Further reading:

Clayden, P. and Trevelyan, J., *Rights of Way: A Guide to Law and Practice*, London, 1983

FORDS *see* CHAPELS

FOREST MARBLE A limestone ideally suited to the manufacture of stone roofing slates.

FORTIFICATION Religious houses relied heavily for protection on their status and on the principle by which 'The precincts of monks' houses and granges . . . like cemeteries and churches are all by apostolic authority to be free and undisturbed by any invasion, terror or violence.' But principle was a poor defence against the unprincipled, especially in the disputed territories of the Welsh and Scottish Marches (from the Old English *mearc* meaning 'boundary'). In 1235, the house of Holmcultrum, near the Scottish border, was permitted to arm its servants and later to erect a small castle to protect its grange at Raby, County Durham.

Most monastic sites were enclosed within a wall and ditch, and provided with a gatehouse at which visitors could be interrogated by a gate-keeper or porter (*portarius*) before entering or leaving the PRECINCTS. At the Cistercian abbey of Cleeve in Somerset, the gatehouse wall is inscribed with the words: 'Stay open gate and close to no honest person.' But in the more volatile regions of the Borders, gatehouses were heavily fortified (as at Alnwick, Northumberland) and many outlying monastic estates were provided with pele towers for their defence (Nunnikirk, West Ritton and Greenleighton in Northumberland) and even castles (Carrycoats, Filton and Rytton). The monastery of Tynemouth (Tyne and Wear) is the largest to be located within the walls of a castle, while monastic sites at Hulne (Northumberland) and Lanercost (Cumberland) were heavily defended. So too was the priory of Ewenny (Glamorgan) in the southern March of Wales, a dependency of the Benedictine Abbey of Gloucester. The nave of the priory church remains in parochial use, while its great defensive walls, with gates and towers, have also survived.

The numerous fortified church TOWERS of the middle and northern Marches of Wales were built as refuges into which widely scattered communities could retreat whenever the bells warned of impending danger. The massive Norman tower at Clun in Shropshire is one of the finest examples and has a double pyramid timber roof, typical of medieval churches in this part of the Marches. Many of the border towers are detached from their churches and were clearly intended as fortresses. That at Bosbury in Herefordshire, built in the thirteenth century, is nearly nine metres (29 feet) square and heavily constructed of red sandstone.

See also MOTTE

Pele tower in the churchyard at Corbridge, Northumberland. Once a place of refuge, it is now the church vestry.

Mitred abbots and bishops were ecclesiastical magnates who exercised considerable political (and sometimes military) influence. It is hardly surprising, therefore, to find that many of their palaces were protected by walls and gatehouses, some of which (the moated Bishop's Palace at Wells in Somerset, for example) have defensive devices comparable with those of contemporary castles. They also provided an ostentatious manifestation of the status and influence of the superior.

Further reading:

Friar, S., *The Batsford Companion to Local History*, London, 1991

FORTY-BUTTON MAN A (somewhat derogatory) colloquialism meaning an Anglo-Catholic parson.

FORTY MARTYRS English and Welsh Roman Catholics who died between 1535 and 1680 and were canonised in 1970.

FOUNDATION (MONASTIC) The minimum requirement for an independent monastic foundation was usually a community of twelve brethren and a superior together with an endowment to provide for their needs and a site on which to establish a religious house. It was the size of the endowment which often determined the nature and vigour of a community: the Benedictine foundation of Peterborough, for example, had an establishment of 110 in 1240, while Cistercian Beaulieu (in Hampshire) was founded in 1204 with only thirty.
See also BENEFACTORS

FOUNDER *see* BENEFACTORS *and* BURIAL

FOUNDLINGS Foundlings, the abandoned infants of unknown parents, were usually a charge on the poor rate (*see* POOR LAW) details of which were recorded in vestry minutes, now held by local record offices. Foundlings also appear as such in parish registers.

FOUR-CENTRE ARCH *see* ARCH

FOUR EVANGELISTS *and* **FOUR LATIN DOCTORS** *see* CHRISTIAN SYMBOLS

FOUR-LEAF ORNAMENT Medieval architectural ornament consisting of petals radiating symmetrically from a raised or depressed centre (*see* DECORATIVE MOTIFS *and* MEDIEVAL ARCHITECTURE).

FOURTEEN HOLY HELPERS A group of saints venerated for the supposed efficacy of their intercessions on behalf of human necessities.

FRANCHISE A liberty, privilege or exemption by grant or prescription.

FRANCISCANS *see* FRIARS

FRANKALMOIGN Land granted by a lay person for the benefit of an ecclesiastical body, usually conditional upon the provision of a CHANTRY.

FRANKLIN A free tenant or farmer, usually enjoying reasonable prosperity and often a manorial steward or bailiff (*see* YEOMAN).

FRATER (*or* REFECTORIUM) The common dining room of a religious house. Correctly, the term should be applied to a monastic 'common room', the hall in which meals were taken being the *refectorium*. But, to the medieval monk, the fraternal breaking of bread was of the utmost significance and it is hardly surprising that the two terms have subsequently been perceived as complementary.

Behaviour in the frater and was strictly controlled, as was the food which was eaten there. The monks arrived in procession and washed at the nearby laver before taking their places (*see* LAVATORIUM). Once grace had been sung, the meal was eaten in silence while a reader read aloud from the frater pulpit. The end of the meal was marked by a bell, and by the singing of grace, before the monks departed in an ordered procession. The official responsible for ensuring order and cleanliness was the *Refectorian* (or *Fraterer*). Among his several duties, he had to arrange for the provision of fresh rushes for the floor, sweet-smelling flowers and herbs for the table and, in summer, fans or 'fly-traps' (*muscatorias*) for the brethren and guests. There was usually a high table (*mensa major*) at which sat the abbot, prior or sub-prior and invited guests who, in the interests of courtesy and hospitality, were permitted to converse with their hosts, but 'sparingly . . . and in a low tone.' The other tables were set at right angles to the dais, with the junior members of the community seated nearest to the door. Novices sat at their own table, where they were supervised by the novice-master, or in a separate room. Dishes were served through a DRESSER WINDOW by *servitors* who were appointed by rotation and took their meals with the reader and kitchen staff.

The frater was usually parallel to the CLOISTER on the side opposite the church, either on the ground floor or raised above an undercroft though, from the late twelfth century, Cistercian refectories were often constructed on a north–south axis beyond the cloister in order to accommodate a kitchen which also served the adjacent frater of the lay brethren (the *conversi*). In importance, the frater was second only to the church, for meals were perceived to be sacramental in character and symbolised the fraternal nature of the community. Consequently, they were usually imposing buildings (that at Fountains Abbey in Yorkshire was 33 metres long (110 feet) and 14 metres wide (46 feet)), without aisles but with lofty timber roofs and devotional paintings on the east wall. Of the few refectories which have survived, that at the Cistercian abbey of Cleeve in Somerset has a splendid hammer-beam roof with carved angels, while at Beaulieu in Hampshire (also Cistercian) the almost intact frater now serves as a parish church, complete with FRATER PULPIT.
See also LARDER

FRATERNITY A religious brotherhood, a guild or group of people sharing a common interest or belief.

FRATER PULPIT A raised lectern or balcony, set in the wall near the high table of the FRATER, from which passages of scripture were read during meals. A frater pulpit is all that remains of the conventual buildings at Shrewsbury Abbey in Shropshire, while at Beaulieu Abbey in Hampshire the frater has survived intact and is now the parish church. Its frater pulpit, which is approached by a narrow, vaulted stairway, is still used during services.

FRATRUM see LATIN

FREEMASONRY In the fourteenth century, groups of skilled and emancipated itinerant stonemasons established exclusive religious fraternities in order to protect their privileges and the 'mysteries' of their craft. Although abolished in 1547, the brotherhood was later re-formed for convivial and educational purposes and with a wider membership. Free-masonry professes an undoctrinal Christianity but its secret rituals and exclusiveness are considered by many to be perversely anachronistic. The church of St. Edmund at Rochdale in Lancashire is one of several 'masonic' churches. Built in 1873 at enormous expense, the structure is riddled with references to the Craft, even the dimensions of the plinth on which it stands are similar to those of Solomon's temple. This bizarre but singularly memorable church is appropriately located at the centre of a circus.

FREESTONE Easily sawn stone, usually oolitic limestone such as PORTLAND STONE or particular types of sandstone. Freestone has a fine grain, does not possess strongly marked laminations and may, therefore, be 'freely worked' with a saw and chisel. *See also* MASONRY

FRENCH HOOD see COSTUME

FRESCO A wall painting in which pure powder pigments mixed in water are applied to a wet, freshly-laid ground of lime plaster. The pigments which have penetrated the surface become fixed and insoluble to water as the plaster dries. The painter therefore has to work rapidly in order that his paint is applied before the surface dries. Once completed, a fresco will last as long as the wall on which it is painted. In England, a *secco* technique was considered more appropriate. In this, dry plaster was used and consequently the pigments remained soluble. As a result, very few WALL PAINTINGS have escaped the destructive effects of dampness.

FRET (i) A DECORATIVE MOTIF, sometimes described as a *key* or *lattice* motif, consisting of continuous combinations of straight lines joined at right angles. (ii) In heraldry, a device consisting of a voided diamond interlaced by two diagonal lines (*a mascle interlaced by a bendlet and a bendlet sinister*).

FRIARS Greyfriars, Whitefriars and Blackfriars are common place-names in towns and cities where medieval friaries once stood. But their churches were non-parochial and very few survived the dissolution of the friaries in 1538 (*see* FRIARY).

The two great orders of friars, the *Franciscans* (the Grey Friars or Friars Minor) and the *Dominicans* (the Black Friars or Friars Preacher) originated in the thirteenth century as adherents to the precepts of St. Francis of Assisi (1181/2–1226) and St. Dominic (1170–1221). A Spaniard by birth, Dominic's objective was to prepare a team of preachers capable of counteracting the spread of heresy in southern France and he took the institutions of the Augustinian canons as his model (*see* AUGUSTINIANS). In 1220 he is said to have met with Francis whose influence persuaded him to adopt the Franciscan ideal of absolute poverty, both several and corporate, which had been adopted by the early Franciscans as the *Regula Bullata* (the First Rule) in 1209. The Dominican Order was established at two general chapters at Bologna in 1220 and 1221, while the Franciscans recast their First Rule in 1221 and brought it into its final form in 1223.

The Franciscans and Dominicans, unlike the monastic orders, were international brotherhoods of individuals whose members were itinerant preachers, ministering to the needs, and dependent on the charity, of those who employed them or from whom they begged. Both were MENDICANT orders (Latin *mendicare* = 'to beg') whose members did not belong to a particular religious house or community, as did the monks, the properties needed for the administration of the orders being held on their behalf by the Pope or some other patron. The Dominicans divided Europe into a number of provinces, each under the jurisdiction of a prior. A provincial chapter, comprising representatives of the constituent houses, met annually to elect a *diffinitor*, by whom they would be represented at a general chapter (which also met annually), and four *diffinitores* responsible for the administration of the chapter. For two years of a three-year cycle the general chapter was attended by the *diffinitores* and for the third by the provincial priors. A master-general of the Order was elected (for life) by an *ad hoc* general chapter. By the 1240s the Franciscans had adopted a constitutional organisation very similar to that of the Dominicans.

The Dominicans arrived in England in 1221 and within fifty years had established some 46 houses. The Franciscans followed in 1224 and by 1255 had 49 houses, more widely dispersed than those of the Dominicans who preferred to concentrate their activities around the universities. Ironically, the

Franciscans attracted to their number many of the most brilliant men of the age and this resulted in the effective usurpation of the Dominicans' role as intellectuals and scholars and the diminution of Franciscan principles.

Other orders included the Order of the Hermits of St. Augustine – the *Austin Friars* – (an order distinct from the Austin Canons) who, as their name suggests, began as communities of hermits (in the mountains of Italy) dedicated to the Augustinian rule. Like the Dominicans, they became scholars and preachers but the order grew slowly in England starting in small country towns and eventually moving into the larger urban centres with some 34 houses. The *Carmelites* (or White Friars) also originated as a hermit community located on Mount Carmel in Palestine. They were the most contemplative of all the friars with 37 English houses, some of which were remote from towns. Like the Carmelites, the smaller orders of Friars of the Holy Cross (the Crutched Friars), the Friars of the Penitential Sack and the Pied Friars were all under Dominican influence and their function was to teach and preach as priests and instructors among the urban laity.

The popularity of the friars in thirteenth-century England was in part attributable to their preference for going into the world instead of withdrawing from it, and partly because their poverty contrasted with the rapidly increasing wealth of the monastic foundations. But of even greater significance was the concentration of pastoral work in the towns where the friars must have been a familiar and reassuring sight and where enormous crowds were attracted to their preaching. (The sermon was the principal medieval means of mass-communication and several urban churches, with long hall-like naves, were constructed by the Dominicans to accommodate congregations.) It was this popularity which bred increasing resentment and hostility among the lay clergy and the monasteries. Parish priests, for the most part poorly trained and held in low regard by their parishioners, were unable to compete with the sermons of the mendicants or with their competence in hearing confessions. They were also losing valuable revenues from burial fees as people opted in increasing numbers for burial in the friars' churchyards rather than those of their parishes. The poverty and humility of the friars were characteristics with which the populace readily identified, whilst the unremitting acquisition of wealth which typified many of the monastic foundations was thrown into sharp relief by the comparison. The response of the late medieval 'establishment' was predictable. Misinformation found its way into the works of Chaucer and Langland and even influenced the redoubtable Wycliffe. There can be little doubt that there was some justification for criticism of the friars during

the fourteenth and fifteenth centuries: observation of the First Rule had become lax and many friars employed decidedly dubious devices to extract money from patrons or to persuade young people to join their orders. Nevertheless, such criticism was by no means universal, indeed there is considerable evidence to suggest that there was no significant decline in the number or quality of bequests and benefactions to the mendicant orders until the Reformation.

See also RELIGIOUS ORDERS IN THE ANGLICAN CHURCH
Further reading:
Brooke, R., *The Coming of the Friars*, London, 1975

FRIARY The religious house of one of the orders of FRIARS together with its church which, unlike monastic churches, was designed to accommodate large numbers of people attracted by preaching. Most friary churches were effectively open halls, without screens or divisions, allowing uninterrupted views of the altar and preacher. A subsidiary church, reserved for the friars' private offices, was usually separated from the main church by a passage above which was a tower. Friary churches were not parochial, however, and few survived the dissolution of the friaries in 1538. Of those that did, the church of the Black Friars at Norwich is perhaps one of the most impressive (Norwich had convents of all four orders). Its nave, over 200 feet in length (61 metres), is indicative of the size of congregations attracted by the more popular preachers. The grounds of a friary were considered by many to be especially holy and were, therefore, popular places of burial.

FRIDAY A weekly commemoration of Christ's Passion is traditionally observed on Fridays by various forms of penitence, notably abstinence from meat.
See also ABSTINENCE, FASTING *and* GOOD FRIDAY

FRIENDLY SOCIETIES Societies formed to provide mutual aid and insurance against sickness. Most friendly societies began as GUILDS or as informal groups of parishioners who paid regular contributions into a communal fund. Village 'clubs', as they were often called, were a feature of nineteenth-century rural life and most retained close links with the parish church (*see* NINETEENTH-CENTURY CHURCH). In many ways their social activities replaced the earlier CHURCH ALES (*see* CHURCH AND COMMUNITY) for they often included traditional celebrations such as MAY DAY dances and PERAMBULATIONS. One such club was the Besom Club of West Harnham in Wiltshire. Unlike many similar societies, this was not a 'slate club' but kept continuing accounts. Members paid a shilling a month and drew an allowance when they were ill, and when a member or his wife died every member contributed a shilling towards the funeral expenses. On Whit Monday the club met at the church, each member carrying a banner, besom (broom) or stave with coloured streamers (see FLAGS). After attending a service, they processed round the parish (preceded by a brass band) before repairing to a field near the village inn where they feasted, drank and danced until nightfall. One incumbent, in the 1880s, was so distressed by these goings-on that he collected the children together in a farm waggon and took them off for a picnic and games! Several societies prospered and expanded as a result of judicious investments and from 1793 registers of Friendly Societies were kept by the Clerks of the Peace together with details of the societies' meeting places and rules. After 1846 these records were transferred to the Registrar of Friendly Societies. But, despite their apparent success, in many areas membership of the friendly societies was beyond the reach of the labouring poor. In 1831 it was estimated that the ratio of the number of persons in friendly societies to every 100 of the population was 4½ in Hampshire, 5 in Dorset, 8 in Wiltshire, 12½ in Devon and 17 in Lancashire.

See also CHARITIES and POOR LAW

Further reading:

Gosden, P., The Friendly Societies in England 1815–1875, London, 1961

FRIEZE In classical architecture, a horizontal band of sculpture filling the space between the ARCHITRAVE and the CORNICE (see ENTABLATURE). Also a horizontal decorative band along a wall near the ceiling.

FRONTAL (ALTAR FRONTAL) A panel placed in front of an altar or communion table. Most churches possess a number of embroidered cloth frontals which are interchangeable according to the liturgical season or feast day (see COLOURS, LITURGICAL). Other frontals may be of wood or metal, ornamented with carving or enamel.

FROSTERLEY MARBLE see PURBECK MARBLE

FUNERAL ARMOUR see FUNERAL HERALDRY

FUNERAL CERTIFICATES see FUNERAL HERALDRY

FUNERAL HATCHMENTS see HATCHMENTS

FUNERAL HERALDRY Funerals of the late medieval and Tudor nobility were often magnificent spectacles, not least the processions which preceded the committal in which the deceased's heraldic accoutrements were solemnly paraded in the cortège. These included his spurs, gauntlets, crested helm, shield (known in this context as a *targe*), sword, tabard, pennons and banner (see FLAGS). After the service these symbols of chivalry would be laid up in the church but regrettably very few early examples remain, the best known being the helm, scabbard, gauntlets, shield and embroidered surcoat of Edward the Black Prince (d. 1376) at Canterbury Cathedral (these are kept near his tomb, those which hang above it being replicas).

In the sixteenth and seventeenth centuries, the Kings of Arms organised the heraldic funerals of the nobility and gentry and the records of these magnificent occasions are contained in eighteen volumes in the archives of the College of Arms in London (see APPENDIX II for address). These *funeral certificates* contain much useful information including the date and place of death and details of the deceased's descendants and of his family's heraldry. A list of fees payable to the College for the entering of certificates was issued by the Earl Marshal in 1618. A fee of £45 was charged 'for a duke, duchess or archbishop' and this was reduced incrimentally according to rank, a 'gentleman' paying only £2. The herald-painters also charged for executing the various escutcheons, standards, bannerols, pennons and other items which were required by the heralds for a particular funeral. Again, these 'achievements' were strictly regulated according to the rank of the deceased. For example, banners and bannerols were confined to peers and their ladies, standards (but not banners) to knights, and pennons (but not standards) to esquires. Mere gentlemen had no pennons, only 'scocheons [escutcheons] of arms', small panels on which the arms were painted (the prototypes of later HATCHMENTS).

Not only was every detail of the heraldic funeral controlled by the heralds, but also the formalities of mourning and the precedence accorded to those who participated in the ceremonial. Of Thomas Howard, the 2nd Duke of Norfolk, it was stated that '. . . no nobleman was ever to be buried in such style again.' Following his death in May, 1524, the Duke's body lay in state for a month in the chapel of Framlingham Castle, Suffolk, in which were hung funereal drapes and numerous shields of arms. The Duke's coffin, drawn on a chariot and embellished with gold shields, was accompanied on its 24 mile progress to Thetford Priory in Norfolk by 900 mourners including heralds, gentlemen of his household and numerous black-robed torch-bearers. At Thetford the coffin was placed on an enormous black and gold catafalque, adorned with 700 lights, black-robed wax effigies holding eight bannerols (see FLAGS), and 100 richly emblazoned shields of arms. The service included a procession of heralds

Funeral accoutrements above the monument to Admiral Sir William Penn (d. 1670) in St. Mary Redcliffe, Bristol.

carrying achievements of the Duke's arms and the dramatic entry of a mounted knight, wearing the dead Duke's armour and carrying his inverted battleaxe.

Several less grandiose examples of funeral accoutrements have survived and from these may be traced the gradual evolution of the heraldic funeral from the practical equipment of medieval warfare and tournament through the stylised, artificial helms, crests, tabards and flags of the sixteenth and seventeenth centuries to the heraldic substitute, the funeral hatchment of the seventeenth, eighteenth and nineteenth centuries. At the great church of St. Mary Redcliffe in Bristol the memorial to Admiral Sir William Penn (d. 1670) (whose son founded Pennsylvania) is surmounted and flanked by his

breastplate, crested helm, gauntlet, spurs, shield, banner, standards and pennons.

But for the most part, only odd items remain. At Swinbrook, Oxfordshire, for example, there are two imitation helms with the griffin crests of the Fettiplace family while at St. Michael's church at Aldershot in Hampshire stylised funeral helms bear the crests of Sir John White (d. 1573) and his son Richard (d. 1599). Some funeral helms incorporate bits and pieces of genuine helmets while others may have been specially commissioned from expert armourers. At the Dorset County Museum in Dorchester there is a fine fifteenth-century tilting helm from the church at Melbury Sampford where it was probably erected as a funerary helm in memory of William Browning, Lord of the Manor (d. 1472). A later helm of *c.* 1540 from the tomb of Sir Nicholas Heron at Croydon is now in the Museum of London, while at Lydiard Tregoze in Wiltshire there is a splendid helm, complete with a gilded falcon crest, adjacent to the tomb of Sir John St. John (d. 1594). But the majority of post-medieval funeral helms were fabrications, obtained either from the College of Arms or locally by undertakers or executors and consequently they are to be found in a variety of materials and vernacular styles. Similarly, pieces of ARMOUR above tombs may have been manufactured for the purpose and may include one or two genuine items from an earlier period. For this reason, funeral accoutrements often form a mixed collection of indeterminate date and provenance, while some may even have been placed over the wrong tomb. Of course, armour and weapons were stored in parish churches for use by the local militia and items from these collections are sometimes displayed in churches where they may be mistaken for funerary armour.

The erection in churches of heraldic monuments is now subject to both the approval of Garter King of Arms and to the granting of a FACULTY by the diocesan authorities.

See also BURIALS, MASS PENNY and PALL
Further reading:
Litten, J., *The English Way of Death*, London, 1991

FUNERAL PALL *see* PALL

FUNERALS *see* BURIAL, BURIAL ACTS, BURIAL IN WOOL ACTS, CHURCHYARDS, CORPSE ROADS, CREMATION, FUNERAL HERALDRY, HATCHMENTS, LICH-GATES OSSUARIES *and* PALL

FUNERAL TICKETS *see* BURIALS

FURS *see* COLOURS (HERALDIC)

G

GABLE The triangular upper part of a wall supporting the end of a ridged roof.

GABLE CROSSES Carved stone crosses above the eastern gable of a nave or chancel may be original, though several have been erected in recent years to commemorate events such as the retirement of a popular parson: at Painswick in Gloucestershire, for example. Some are crucifixes and are of undoubted antiquity, as at Haslingfield in Cambridgeshire, Tilty in Essex and Skelton in Yorkshire.

GABLE HOOD see COSTUME

GADROONING (also LOBING or NULLING) Ornamentation consisting of a series of lobe-shaped motifs (see DECORATIVE MOTIFS).

GALILEE A vestibule reserved as a chapel for penitents at the western end of a church in the early Middle Ages. Derived from the NARTHEX of Byzantine churches, the term was sometimes extended to include the western section of the nave which was considered to be less sacred than the remainder of the church. The term may have originated in the 'Galilee of the Gentiles' of Matthew 4:15. Galilees were not a feature of English medieval parish churches (entry was normally through a southern porch – see PORCHES) but there are examples at some cathedrals, notably Ely and at Durham where a line across the floor marks the limit beyond which women could not pass. The term was later applied to the vestibules of Stuart and Georgian churches of the seventeenth and eighteenth centuries.

GALLERY (i) In major medieval churches there was often a broad passageway constructed within the space above an aisle. This gallery, which usually opened onto the nave through an ARCADE, is known as the *tribune*. It should not be confused with the TRIFORIUM which is a narrow wall passage or area of blind arcading immediately below the CLERESTORY. There are splendid examples at several parish churches (mostly former monastic foundations) such as Romsey Abbey in Hampshire, Selby Abbey in Yorkshire and Blyth Priory in Nottinghamshire. (ii) In a more general context, a gallery is a tiered upper storey constructed to provide additional seating. There are medieval galleries of this type at several churches, including Cawston and Worstead in Norfolk, but for the most part they were erected following the destruction of ROOD LOFTS or as a consequence of the act of 1644 which banned ORGANS from churches (see also CHURCH MUSIC). Most are located within the space beneath a west tower (hence, *west gallery*) and were intended to accommodate bands or 'choirs' of village musicians playing traditional instruments such as viols, hautboys, flutes and serpents. At Strensham in Worcestershire the panels of the medieval rood-loft were incorporated into the new west gallery, while at Trentishoe in Devon there remains to this day a hole in the panelling through which protruded the bow of the double-bass. These choirs compiled 'psalm books' of music, much of which was composed by members of the community, and established a tradition of instrumental playing and part-singing which continued from one generation to the next until the second half of the nineteenth century (see NINETEENTH-CENTURY CHURCH). They were extraordinarily popular with the commonalty if not with the clergy. John Foster, a renowned eighteenth-century musician from Ecclesfield in Yorkshire, attracted over five thousand mourners to his funeral; and a Shropshire blacksmith is reputed to have built his own iron cello so that he could join his village choir.

A Suffolk clergyman, writing in 1764, described the arrangements in East Anglian churches at that time:

> The Performers are placed in a Single Seat, sometimes a raised seat like a stage. Here they form themselves into a round Ring, with their faces to each other and their Backs to ye Congregation. Here they murder anthems, chuse improper Psalms, leave off in ye middle of a sentence, sing Psalms of all kinds to new jiggish tunes. If ye Minister offers to direct them, 'He may mind his Text; he may sing himself, they will sing as they list or not at all.' They frequently leave their own Parish Church, and go in a Body to display their Talents in other Churches. I have known them stroll six or seven miles for this purpose, sometimes with a young female singer or two in their train.

The Victorian clergy, always enthusiastic in their search for greater respectability, drove out many west gallery choirs: that at Puddletown in Dorset was replaced by a barrel organ in 1845, for example. (The devastating effect on a choir of the introduction of an organ or harmonium is described vividly in Thomas Hardy's *Under the Greenwood Tree*, first published in 1872). Some of the instruments used by these bands have also survived (see MUSICAL INSTRUMENTS). There are particularly good, early seventeenth-century galleries at East Brent in Somerset, Moreton Say in Shropshire and Puddletown in Dorset, while a splendid Jacobean gallery at Lyme Regis, also in Dorset, extends across the full width of the church and is inscribed in gold leaf with the words: 'John Hassard built this to the glory of almighty God in the eightieth year of his age Anno Domini 1611'. Unfortunaty, the additional words 'seven times Mayor' have been lost.

Not all west galleries were intended for musician or, indeed, for the benefit of the congregation. That at the fine eighteenth-century baroque church of St. Lawrence Whitchurch, Little Stanmore was built as a family pew for the Duke of Chandos and his family (see PEWS, FAMILY).

Side galleries, to the north and south of the nave, are much in evidence in eighteenth-century 'auditory' churches where they were intended to accommodate large (mostly urban) congregations and to concentrate attention on the pulpit and reading desk (see EIGHTEENTH-CENTURY ARCHITECTURE). These galleries extended the interior of a building outward, beyond the arcade and above the aisles, into the space which in larger medieval churches is occupied by the tribune. Thomas Archer (1668–1743) incorporated side galleries into his magnificent baroque church of St. Philip, Birmingham (now the cathedral), while at Portland in Dorset the fine ashlar cruciform church of St. George Reforne (Thomas Gilbert, 1766) was provided with three galleries for a congregation which, in the present century, was so reduced that the church is now redundant. Many older churches were also adapted to accommodate side galleries, often with quite extraordinary effect. Those at Whitby in Yorkshire, for instance, have created within the great rectangular nave '. . . a sense of agitated dynamic space' (Robert Harbison) while at humble Cameley in Somerset, a lofty south gallery, installed in 1819 'For the free use of the inhabitants' is entered by an external stair and dominates the ancient twelfth-century nave.

GALLETING Pebbles (French *galet* = a pebble) or stone chips applied to mortar for decorative purposes or to reduce the amount of mortar required and increase durability. A common technique found in buildings in south-east Norfolk and parts of Kent, Surrey and Sussex.
See also FACING MATERIALS

GAMBESON A padded or quilted protective garment usually worn beneath the SURCOAT and over the HAUBERK (*see* ARMOUR).

GAMBREL ROOF *see* ROOFS

GAMES IN THE CHURCHYARD *see* CHURCH AND COMMUNITY, CHURCHWARDENS *and* CHURCHYARDS

GARB (i) In HERALDRY, a stylised wheatsheaf. (ii) A 'tithe of garbs' was a tithe of white corn, part of the greater tithe (*see* TITHES).

GARDECORPS *see* COSTUME

GARDEROBE A medieval latrine or privy, usually a single cell at the end of a short, crooked passage within the thickness of a wall from which a shaft vented to a cesspool beneath. Others consisted of stone benches in cubicles (*gonges*) which jettied out on corbels high above a moat. Most latrines must have been exceedingly draughty, though those in private chambers were usually provided with braziers to heat water for washing and a degree of privacy. The monastic equivalent was the *domus necessaria* ('necessary house') or *reredorter* (*see* DORTER).

GARGOYLE The legendary *Gargouille* was a seventh-century river dragon who supposedly ravaged the city of Rouen (*see* BEASTS (HERALDIC)). From the Old French *gargouille* meaning 'throat', a gargoyle is a projecting gutterstone, usually (though not necessarily) incorporating a lead water-spout and often carved to depict a grotesque visage, beast or figure. Celtic warriors were inclined to remove the heads of their defeated enemies for public display and this may account for the popularity of gargoyles, many of which are certainly endowed with pagan characteristics. There may also be some truth in the notion that such figures on the exterior walls of Romanesque churches were intended to warn of the inevitability of Purgatory and Hell, but the function of a gargoyle was to traject rainwater away from the walls and footings of a building. This was particularly necessary when, in the fourteenth century, ornamental traceried parapets were developed as a means of finishing off a wall. With no eaves to carry rainwater away from the building, it was necessary to provide lead bow-gutters behind the parapets and gargoyles to discharge the rainwater at regular intervals.

Most medieval churches have one or two surviving gargoyles (though beware Victorian replacements!) while there are splendid collections at Denford in Northamptonshire, East Markham in Nottinghamshire, Evercreech and Monksilver in Somerset, Malpas in Cheshire, Patrington in Yorkshire and Winchcombe in Gloucestershire. Many gargoyles have a rain-spout projecting from a human mouth, as at Thaxted in Essex, and there are numerous examples of singularly grotesque or unusual gargoyles, indeed no two gargoyles are ever the same. At Welford in Northamptonshire, for instance, a pair of figures hold the lead spout between them, and at Lillington in Dorset, from the corner of the tower, a huge bird with outspread wings casts a dark shadow over the churchyard. At nearby Nether Cerne, the gargoyles are vigorously carved in the form of winged angels.

Medieval gargoyles are a wonderful source of inspiration for those who wish to study vernacular figure sculpture. It would appear that most were fashioned by itinerant masons who, freed from the constraints of dressing building stone, were allowed to let their imaginations run riot – and not always in the best of taste. At a time when the nobility and gentry were busily endowing chantries and extending and rebuilding churches one might reasonably expect any number of heraldic references to have been incorporated in the fabric of refurbished towers, aisles and chancels. It is quite extraordinary, therefore, that so few gargoyles are of heraldic significance. It may be that stonemasons enjoyed an inalienable right to design the gargoyles on which they worked, immune from the strictures of the Church and the blandishments of the aristocracy.

GARLAND (i) A decorative motif (*see* FESTOON). (ii) In heraldry, a circular wreath of leaves. When depicted with a flower (usually a rose) at each quarter, it is termed a *chaplet*. (iii) An anthology, usually of medieval or Tudor origin.

GARNISHING THE CHURCH Decorating the church with flowers and foliage for major festivals.

GARTER, THE MOST NOBLE ORDER OF THE Edward III (1327–77) and his court rejoiced in the chivalric ethos of the Arthurian legends. Pageants (called 'Round Tables') included tournaments at which two teams, each of twelve knights, fought under the leadership of the king and his eldest son, and these were followed by feasting at a circular table. It is likely that from these festivities evolved the notion of a brotherhood of young men, a fellowship in which all were equal, 'to represent how they ought to be united in all Chances and various turns of Fortune, co-partners in both Peace and War, assistant to one another in all serious and dangerous Exploits and through the whole Course of their Lives to show Fidelity and Friendliness towards one another'. The informal creation of the Round Table after the great tournament at Windsor in 1344 was translated, probably on St George's Day 1348, into the Order of

Gargoyle at Mappowder, Dorset.

Effigy of Sir Rhys ap Thomas, in Garter robes, at Carmarthen, Dyfed.

illustrations of its use by men) and it seems likely that it was adopted because of its suitability both as a device (in stylised form) and for its prominence when worn below the knee of a mounted knight. Although modelled on the principles of chivalric egalitarianism and humility, the Order of the Garter was essentially élitist, membership being the ultimate reward for loyal service to the sovereign or utilised for the purposes of international diplomacy. The insignia of the Order are to be found in the architecture and decoration of churches throughout England and Wales, in illuminated manuscripts and documents and on seals, monuments, memorials and hatchments (*see* BRASSES (MONUMENTAL), COLLARS *and* EFFIGIES).

See also KNIGHTHOOD, ORDERS OF

Further reading:

Friar, S., *A New Dictionary of Heraldry*, Sherborne and London, 1987

GARTH Derived from the Old Norse *garćr* meaning 'an enclosure', the term was originally applied to any small enclosed space as in churchyard/churchgarth. A *cloister garth* was the area enclosed within the CLOISTER of a monastery, generally used as a vegetable and herb garden or (by the Carthusians) as a burial ground.

See also LAVATORIUM

GASOLIER By the 1840s gas lights were to be found in even the smallest rural towns and in many churches. The most common type of gas-lamp was the gasolier which comprised a wall-mounted (often ornate) bracket terminating in an up-standing burner and spherical glass globe. Most have been replaced with electric lighting, though a few examples remain *in situ*.

GATEHOUSES *see* FORTIFICATION, MONASTIC BUILDINGS *and* PRECINCTS

GENERAL (i) The title usually given to the head of a religious order or congregation, hence the Master General was head of the Dominican Order and the Minister General was the head of the Franciscans. (ii) General chapters of the integrated monastic orders (such as the Cistercians) were convened at four-yearly intervals so that order and uniformity might be maintained. General Chapters were convened by a mother house and attended by the superiors of the daughter houses.

GENERATION For the genealogist, a generation is the period between the births of one male-line ancestor and the next. Suggested average generation spans have varied from twenty-five to thirty-five years but much depends on the normal age of marriage at a particular time, the socio-economic status of the family, and so on.

the Garter: twenty-four young men together with the king and his eldest son, Edward Plantagenet, the Black Prince. These were the founder knights 'foreshadowing a distinguished line of noble successors throughout the history of English chivalry'. The symbol of the blue garter is traditionally said to have been suggested by an incident at a ball at Calais in the autumn of 1347 when the young Countess of Salisbury, Joan of Kent (later to be Princess of Wales) dropped her garter, which the king retrieved and tied below his knee with the now famous words, *Honi soit qui mal y pense* – 'Shame on him who thinks evil of it' – and a promise that the garter would become highly honoured. There may be an element of truth in this, but the garter was not an exclusively female accoutrement (there are numerous contemporary

GENTLEMAN 'Gent.', the customary abbreviation for gentleman, is commonly found in documents, EPITAPHS and MEMORIALS. A statute of Henry V required that in certain legal documents the 'estate, degree or mystery' of a defendant must be stated, and the style 'gentleman' came into use to signify a condition between ESQUIRE and YEOMAN. Derived from the Latin *gentilis* meaning 'of the same *gens* or stock', the term *les gentiles* was used in an act of parliament of 1429 to describe men holding freehold property of forty shillings a year or more. Although lineage was considered to be an important factor (which explains the plethora of fake genealogies compiled for those who had abruptly risen from obscurity), from the sixteenth century the term seems to have been applied to all those who were not required to labour and who employed servants. Members of professions, military and naval officers, barristers etc. were considered to be gentlemen, some of them being entitled also to the designation esquire.

GENUFLEXION To genuflect is not simply to bow. It is a momentary kneeling on one knee, while the body remains erect, as a sign of reverence before the Blessed Sacrament. Until recently, it was the custom of many Anglicans to bow before the altar and 'at the name of Jesus' during the liturgy. Philippians 2:10 is quoted as the authority for this practice, though the requirement that 'every knee shall bow' suggests genuflexion rather than a respectful nod of the head.

GEOMETRICAL SYMBOLISM *see* CHRISTIAN SYMBOLS

GEORGE ROSE'S ACT (1812) This Act required that incumbents should keep two specially printed registers in which to record details of baptisms and burials in addition to the registers for marriages (*see* HARDWICKE'S MARRIAGE ACT 1754). Baptismal entries were to include the parents' names, addresses and occupations while burial entries were to state the name, age, address and occupation of the deceased.

GERMAN Brothers and sisters german have both parents in common while a cousin german is a first cousin, being the issue of an uncle or aunt.

GESSO SOTTILE *see* MANUSCRIPT ILLUMINATION

GILBERTINE ORDER Founded by Gilbert of Sempringham (*c.* 1089–1189) in 1131, the religious communities of nuns of the Gilbertine Order (the only truly English monastic order)

initially followed a simplified version of the Benedictine Rule but as their numbers grew, and lay brothers and sisters joined them, their direction was entrusted to Canons Regular following the Augustinian Rule. The communities then took the form of DOUBLE MONASTERIES.
Further reading:
Foreville, R. and Keir, G., *The Book of St. Gilbert*, London, 1986

GILD (i) To cover thinly with gold. The architect Sir Ninian Comper (1864–1960) used mercurial gilding (a mixture of gold and mercury) in many of his decorative schemes, a practice which was banned when it was found to be injurious to health.
See also MANUSCRIPT ILLUMINATION
(ii) *See* GUILDS

GIRDLE *see* VESTMENTS

GLASS *see* GLAZIERS' MARKS, STAINED GLASS *and* WINDOWS

GLASTONBURY CHAIR The type of chair most commonly found in the chancels of parish churches, the earliest examples are from the mid-seventeenth century though there are many copies. Glastonbury chairs are prefabricated, the components consisting of shaped planks which are assembled by means of wooden pins. The X-shaped legs are joined by a crossbar and the curved arms link the front of the seat with the upper rail of the panelled back.

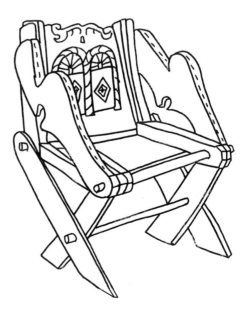

GLAZIERS' MARKS With the exception of a very small number of medieval examples, the marks and signatures found in STAINED GLASS windows are mostly from the nineteenth and twentieth centuries. Marks may identify a glazier, designer or both: the figure of a hooded friar is combined with a designer's initials in windows by the Whitefriars Glass company, for example. Monograms and signatures are widely used as are heraldic devices and rebuses: Geoffrey Webb (1879–1954) used a spider's web, Joseph Nuttgens (1892–1982) a hazelnut, Alfred Bell (1832–95) a bell and Barbara Batt (1909–present) a bat, for example. Some are more complex: a stylised flower may be a woodruff and therefore the mark of Paul Woodroffe (1875–1954) while a wheel, half cartwheel and half ship's wheel, were used by Harry Stammers (1902–69) whose father and father-in-law were respectively a wheelwright and a mariner. One of the best known glaziers' marks is that of Sir William Comper (1864–1960) who 'signed' his work with a strawberry leaf mark, apparently in memory of his father who was sharing strawberries with a group of children when he died. These, and many more delightful glaziers' marks, are to be found in a splendid catalogue of *Stained Glass Makers' Marks*, edited by Joyce Little and published in 1993 by the Church Recorders section of NADFAS (*for* address *see* APPENDIX II).

Comper's strawberry mark.

GLAZING BARS The vertical and horizontal wooden bars which secure pieces of glass within a window frame. Not to be confused with MULLIONS and TRANSOMS which separate the lights within a window opening.
See also WINDOWS

GLEBE From the Latin *glæba* meaning 'soil', glebe land was that which was anciently set aside for the maintenance of the parish priest (*see also* PARSONAGE). The income of most medieval priests was dependent on the receipt of TITHES which included payments made by parishioners on important occasions (*altarage*), the receipt of the second-best beast of a deceased person (*mortuaries*) and the produce of glebe land. Glebe lands varied considerably in quality, acreage and location. In some parishes the glebe was sufficiently profitable or extensive for the priest to sub-let part of it, and former parsonage buildings may still be found to include a barn and yard which once serviced the glebe lands. But in most cases the parson's labours would of necessity equal those of his parishioners. Clues to former glebe land may be found in place-names and field names and in enclosure patterns of strip-shaped fields which, because of the special status of glebe land, survived the informal re-allocation of land in the period before parliamentary enclosures. Unlike other holdings, glebe land was rarely sold or exchanged so that post-medieval maps in which glebe land is shown may also provide clues to the distribution of strips in the former open fields. Glebe lands were also known by the Latin term *sanctuarium* from which has derived the entirely spurious notion that a parish church enjoyed special rights of (*see* SANCTUARY, RIGHT OF).

Surveys of the endowments, possessions and profits of benefices were undertaken in 1571 and at intervals thereafter, the information being compiled in Glebe terriers which, when available in series, provide an invaluable insight into the changing value and disposition of glebe lands and of farming practice. Glebe terriers, which also give details of parsonage houses and clerical incomes, are now filed with the DIOCESAN RECORDS.

GLORIA PATRI The familiar ascription of praise to the TRINITY beginning with the words 'Glory be to the Father . . .' recited (or sung) at the conclusion of the Psalms. Its use dates from the fourth century and thereafter it is found in metrical form at the end of hymns in the Offices.

GLORIOUS REVOLUTION, THE The events leading to the deposition of James II and the accession of his daughter Mary and her husband William of Orange in 1688. This was confirmed by the *Bill of Rights* in October 1689 which also guaranteed the Protestant succession and set out the principles of parliamentary supremacy.

GLOSS A commentary on a text, usually added in the margin or inserted between the lines of text.

GNOMON *see* SUNDIALS

GODBOTE A fine imposed by the Church in respect of an offence against God.

GODPARENTS (*SUSCEPTORES also* SPONSORS *or* TESTES) Witnesses at a BAPTISM who undertake to accept responsibility for the Christian upbringing of the person baptised and avow renunciation, faith and obedience on behalf of an infant.

GOG AND MAGOG The powers represented in the Apocalypse as the forces of Satan at Armageddon (*Revelations* 20:8). Also, in medieval mythology, the last survivors of a race of giants who inhabited ancient Britain.

GOLD MARKS *see* HALLMARKS

GONFANNON From the Norse *Gunn-fane* meaning 'war flag', a flag supported by means of a horizontal pole suspended by cords from the top of a staff. Probably (in shape) a descendant of the Roman *vexillum*, and often with 'tails' at the lower edge, it was popular with medieval GUILDS because of its suitability for use in processions and parades. It is now to be found in the vernacular form of ecclesiastical 'banner' adopted by organisations such as the Mothers' Union.
See also BANNER-STAVE LOCKERS *and* FLAGS

GOOD FRIDAY Good Friday, the Friday before EASTER and the day of the Crucifixion, is traditionally a day of fast, abstinence and penance. Many people would refrain from using nails or iron tools in remembrance of their use on Calvary and, until recently, the day was considered by many to be unlucky: fishermen would not put to sea and miners were reluctant to go underground. In the Church of England, the Three Hours' Service is usually held on Good Friday during the hours of the Lord's Passion from noon to 3.00 pm. At this service the SEVEN WORDS FROM THE CROSS are separately considered.
See also EASTER, EASTER EGGS, FEAST DAYS (FIXED AND MOVABLE), LENT, MAUNDY THURSDAY, PALM SUNDAY, PASSIONTIDE *and* SHROVE TUESDAY

GORGET (i) A linen wrap for the throat (see COSTUME). (ii) The plate armour replacement of the CAMAIL to protect the neck (*see* ARMOUR).

GOSPEL (i) The teaching of Christ. (ii) A narrative of the life of Christ, notably the New Testament Gospels of Matthew, Mark, Luke and John the authority of which was established by the mid-second century. (iii) The stated portion of these to be read (or sung) at the Eucharist by the *gospeller*. Traditionally, the Gospel is read by the DEACON.

GOSPEL OAK *and* GOSPEL TREE *see* ROGATION

GOTHIC The style of architecture prevalent throughout western Europe from the twelfth century to the sixteenth century, characterised by the pointed ARCH (*see* ARCHITECTURAL PERIODS *and* MEDIEVAL ARCHITECTURE).

GOTHICK (NEO-GOTHICK) A derogatory term used to describe the excesses of romantic medievalism in late eighteenth- and nineteenth-century literature, architecture etc. Gothick is occasionally used to describe the early Gothic Revival period of *c.* 1750–1820.

GOTHIC LETTERING *see* CALLIGRAPHY

GOTHIC REVIVAL *see* NINETEENTH-CENTURY ARCHITECTURE

GOTHIC SURVIVAL The continuation of the Gothic style in the sixteenth and seventeenth centuries, often in order to complete an earlier building in conformity with its original style. *See* SIXTEENTH- AND SEVENTEENTH-CENTURY ARCHITECTURE

GOTHIC TRACERY *see* WINDOW TRACERY

GOTHIC VESTMENTS Eucharistic VESTMENTS introduced in the mid-nineteenth century the style of which was supposed to follow the medieval pattern.

GOUGING (*also* CHANNELLING, ADZED *or* SCOOPED) *see* DECORATIVE MOTIFS.

GRADINE A raised ledge behind an altar on which the cross is sometimes placed.
See also TABERNACLE

GRADUAL In the Eucharist, the ANTIPHONS sung immediately following the first Scriptural lesson. Since 1969, a Psalm may be sung instead.

GRAFFITI Graffiti, writing or drawings scratched on walls, tombs, memorials, benches and other hard surfaces, come in a variety of shapes and sizes and from all periods. Graffiti are a useful, though as yet incoherent, source of historical evidence which includes GLAZIERS' MARKS, MASONS' MARKS, MERCHANTS' MARKS and carpenters' and plumbers' marks. The value of masons' marks is in the contribution they can make to detailed studies of individual buildings and the various phases of construction. Carpenters' marks, both signatures and assembly marks, are invaluable when considering the construction of a roof, spire or timber floor; while plumbers' and glaziers' marks serve to identify individual craftsmen or workshops and to date their work.

Some graffiti are of genuine artistic merit while most are simply vernacular and a few deliberately vulgar and offensive. Medieval VOTIVE CROSSES are especially common and will usually be found near a south door in the vicinity of a (former) HOLY WATER STOUP. A pilgrimage was often the most significant event in a person's life, and it seems likely that many of these humble crosses were earnestly carved by pilgrims who, having renewed their baptismal vows at a porch altar (*see* PORCHES), wished to commemorate the occasion either before their departure or on returning from some distant shrine. They are often described as Pilgrims' Crosses, though not all were inscribed for this purpose.

Effigies and monumental brasses are particularly vulnerable to vandalism, though not all graffiti were surreptitiously inscribed. Workshop sketches have been found on the backs of brasses and even on the surfaces of effigies. Recent restoration work on the limestone effigy of Sir John de Buslingthorpe of Lincolnshire (d. c. 1340) led to the discovery of a number of early graffiti scratched on his shield. These included an unidentified coat of arms and several helms with crests, one of which is a bearded head with a brimmed helmet known as a kettle hat. The helms are of the type worn in the fourteenth century and it seems likely, therefore, that the graffiti are workshop sketches which were eventually covered when the shield was painted.

At Ashwell in Hertfordshire, a (singularly literate) medieval mason vented his frustration near the south door with somewhat ungodly vigour: *Cornua non sunt arto compungente – sputo* ('The corners are not pointed properly – I spit on them!') while at Burford in Oxfordshire the name of Anthony Sedley, one of the dissident Levellers imprisoned in the church tower by Cromwell in 1649, is scratched across the ancient font cover.

From the early nineteenth century, at Puddletown church in Dorset, an innocent little graffito in the book rest of a bench near the gallery steps must have caught Thomas Hardy's attention. The signature HENERY (sic) was that of Hardy's grandfather whose name he adopted for the character Henery Fray in his novel *Far From the Madding Crowd*, published in 1874 and set in the countryside round Weatherbury (Puddletown).

See also SUNDIALS

GRAIL, THE HOLY Although never recognised by the Church, the mystical vessel (*Sangrail*) of the medieval romances commands a potent place in the Christian tradition. While the origin, nature and significance of the Grail are unknown, it is most often identified with either the paten or the chalice used by Christ at the Last Supper. According to legend, Joseph of Arimathea preserved the chalice and received into it some of Christ's blood at the Crucifixion. He brought it to England, but it disappeared. Thereafter, the quest for the Holy Grail became the fertile source of the adventures of the Knights of the Round Table. In some of the tales it is the chalice and in others the paten. It was the impeccable Sir Galahad who discovered the grail, and each of King Arthur's one hundred and fifty knights caught sight of it though, unless pure of heart and holy of conduct, it disappeared from their view.

Further reading:
Godwin, M., *The Holy Grail*, London, 1993

GRANGE The Cistercian monasteries of the twelfth and early thirteenth centuries accumulated vast endowments of land from Norman magnates whose admiration of Cistercian piety conveniently matched their own preoccupation with salvation. Many of these lands were so remote and fragmented that it was impossible for them to be worked directly from the abbey itself and a system of outlying farms (*grangia*) and subordinate lodges developed, staffed by lay brethren and administered centrally by the abbey cellarer. Furness Abbey in Cumbria, for example, had eighteen granges located at strategic sites throughout its estates, and at Kilnsey in Wharfedale (one of the granges of Fountains Abbey in Yorkshire) there were seven subordinate lodges, each manned by one or two lay brothers together with a cowman or shepherd. So successful was the system in its early days that other monastic orders adopted it for their own estates. But during the thirteenth century endowments of land to monastic foundations declined. There was also a significant reduction in the recruitment of lay brothers, aggravated in the fourteenth century by the Black Death and a more competitive labour market. The monastic foundations were increasingly perceived as being avaricious and corrupt and, although the Cistercian rule required that monasteries should be detached from the evils of everyday life, the occupants of the granges inevitably experienced daily contact with local communities and were ill-equipped to cope with the numerous conflicts of interest that ensued. Difficulties in recruiting sufficient lay brothers lead to the employment of local peasant labour and granges were increasingly leased to laymen with a consequential weakening of the monastic system.

Granges varied considerably: some were substantial complexes of purpose-built agricultural and domestic buildings with a barn and chapel. Others were small farmsteads, adapted to accommodate two or three staff. Several developed as settlements or were converted to domestic use following the Dissolution, though not all 'Grange' place-names are genuine.

See also BARTON

GRAVESIDE SHELTER (*also* **HUDD**) A portable wooden shelter, similar in appearance to a sentry box, which in the eighteenth and early nineteenth centuries was positioned in a churchyard to provide shelter for the priest while he officiated at a committal (*see* BURIALS). There is a splendid black oilskin-covered shelter in the church porch at Beaumaris, Anglesey and another at Wingfield in Suffolk.

Graveside shelter at Beaumaris, Anglesey.

GRAVESTONES The nobility and gentry have almost invariably been commemorated, and frequently interred, inside their parish churches. Inspired by the grandeur, both of execution and sentiment, of these MONUMENTS, the new breed of self-conscious yeoman farmers, tradesmen and master-craftsmen of late seventeenth-century England commissioned memorial headstones to be erected over the churchyard graves of those whose lives, aspirations and achievements they wished to commemorate. With the exception of a number

Celtic gravestones, some of which date from the sixth century (at Penmachno in Gwynedd, for example), the oldest churchyard memorials are from this time. (Although a small number of gravestones may appear to be of an earlier date it is likely that these were raised retrospectively.) In many parishes, the earliest concentration of gravestones will often coincide with a period of commercial prosperity (*see* TABLE TOMBS) or the parliamentary enclosure of land from which many of the wealthier parishioners benefited both economically and socially. Churchyard headstones tended to imitate the style of earlier memorials found within the church and these in turn reflect contemporary religious and architectural fashion. Significant regional variations also occur: the eighteenth-century headstones of slate and freestone areas being particularly suited to the carving of classical forms, for example.

Frederick Burgess * identified four phases in the development of gravestone design. Still in evidence in the late seventeenth and early eighteenth centuries was the medieval and Tudor preoccupation with mortality and corruption exemplified by such devices as the Death's Head, Hour Glass and Reaping Hook. This was followed, in the later eighteenth century, by symbols of the Resurrection and, influenced by the spread of Methodism, a concern with a means of salvation expressed through allegorical figures such as Faith, Hope and Charity. Early nineteenth-century gravestones returned to the image of the Cross (which previously had been considered Popish) before being overtaken by a welter of mass-produced sentimentality and neo-Gothic symbolism in the Victorian era.

Churchyard inscriptions (*see* EPITAPHS *and* INSCRIPTIONS) are collected and recorded by many of the family history societies whose addresses may be obtained from county record offices. Early gravestones were often inscribed with both the identity of the deceased and the name of the person who erected the stone. Inscriptions can sometimes be a source of humour: on the headstone of a notoriously heavy drinker are the words 'THIS ONE'S ON ME' while, elsewhere, 'AT LAST' was substituted for 'AT REST'.

See also BURIALS *and* CHURCHYARDS

Further reading:

Burgess, F., *English Churchyard Memorials*, London, 1963 *

Jones, J., *How to Record Graveyards* (3rd edn), London, 1984

GRAVEYARDS *see* BURIALS, CHURCHYARDS *and* OSSUARIES

GREAT ROOD *see* ROOD

GREAT SCHISM The period 1378–1417 during which the western Church was divided by the

Generations of the Allin family in the churchyard of Sutcombe, Devon.

election of antipopes. The schism also caused bitter political dissent: the Avignon papacy was supported by France, Scotland, Castile, Aragon and some German princes; while the Pope in Rome was supported by the Emperor, England, Scandinavia and most Italian states.

Further reading:
Ullman, W., *The Origins of the Great Schism*, London, 1972

GREAVES *see* ARMOUR

GREEN MEN One of the most powerful and enduring symbols of pagan mythology (*see* PAGAN SYMBOLS), Green Men are to be found in a variety of forms in the foliated stonework and ornamental wood carving of medieval churches throughout Europe. These male heads wreathed in foliage, which is often depicted growing from their mouths, eyes, ears and nostrils, are ideally suited to the ornamentation of capitals, corbels, bosses, misericords, candle sconces etc. Originally a Celtic symbol of creative fertility in nature, the Green Man

is closely associated with Cerunnos, the stag-horned deity who lived deep in the greenwood and who controlled all living things. Indeed, a number of figures (known as Green Beasts) are more animal than human and have pointed ears: there is an example at Withycombe in Somerset. The Green Man is the May King (Man-in-the-Oak or Jack-in-the-Green) of MAY DAY ceremonies who, wreathed in garlands of oak and hawthorn (may tree), feigned death and then came to life to comfort and dance with his disconsolate May Queen. In Christian imagery, the Green Man became a symbol of Easter and Resurrection. With only a few exceptions, the medieval masons depicted the Green Man as a gentle and benevolent deity, as at Crowcombe and Withycombe in Somerset, though the head which crowns a pillar at Broomfield (also in Somerset) is more ethereal and frightening. Green men are also found in heraldry: in the allusive arms of the Wood and Woodhouse families, for example.

See also SHEELA-NA-GIG *and* WODEHOUSE
Further reading:
Anderson, W., *The Green Man*, London, 1991

GREENSAND A cretacious sandstone carrying the green iron-bearing mineral glaucomite.

GREGORIAN CALENDAR The 'New Style' calendar was introduced by Pope Gregory XIII who in 1582 declared that 5 October should be 15 October. This was generally adopted in Catholic countries but in England the calendar was not changed until 1752 when 3 September became 14 September. Eleven days were thereby lost from the fiscal year, the beginning of which was moved from 25 March to 6 April to compensate and NEW YEAR'S DAY changed from 25 March to 1 January. Correctly, reference to dates falling between 1 January and 25 March prior to 1753 should be referred to as e.g. 28 January, 1748/9. Pope Gregory also decreed that of the centesimal years only those exactly divisible by 400 should be counted as leap years.
See also JULIAN CALENDAR

GREGORIAN CHANT *see* PLAINSONG

GREYFRIARS *see* FRIARS

GRIFFIN (*also* **GRYPHON**) *see* BEASTS (HERALDIC)

GRISAILLE Thirteenth- and fourteenth-century window glass to which a delicate silvery-grey coating of paint was applied often with lightly painted leaf and stem patterns on a background of cross-hatching and interlaced strapwork. Such glass remains translucent and enhances the coolness and tranquillity of an interior. In the fourteenth century colourful painted and STAINED GLASS motifs, including human figures and armorial devices, were often inserted in the grisaille.

GROIN VAULT *see* VAULTING

GROTESQUE (i) A decorative motif in the form of a comically distorted visage. (ii) Decorative interweaving of foliage with human and animal forms.

GROZING IRON *see* STAINED GLASS

GUEST HOUSE (HOSPITIUM) The Benedictine rule declared that 'All guests who come shall be received as though they were Christ, for He himself said "I was a stranger and ye took me in."' Hospitality was therefore an essential element of monastic life and accommodation was provided for guests at even the smallest of religious houses. The usual stay was for two days and two nights though guests who were ill were usually granted an extension in order to recuperate. In the late medieval period, there were three classes of guest: magnates,

Grotesque

both noble and ecclesiastical, were the personal guests of the superior and shared his lodgings; those of lesser rank stayed in the cellarer's hospice or guest-house; and the poor and passing wayfarers were accepted into the ALMONRY or HOSPICE. There were several notable exceptions: at Durham, for example, all guests were treated with equal liberality. In large communities, the guest-house was a building of considerable size, administered by the Guest-Master who was responsible for the welfare of guests, though subordinate to the CELLARER. Of the few monastic guest houses that have survived, the Guesten Hall of Sherborne Abbey in Dorset is one of the most impressive, though it has been modified for use by Sherborne School.
See also BEDE-HOUSE *and* HOSPITALS

GUIDE BOOKS *see* DOCUMENTARY SOURCES

GUIDON *see* FLAGS

GUIGE A shoulder-strap supporting a shield (*see* ARMOUR).

GUILDS (*also* **GILDS**) Many parish churches have CHAPELS or AISLES which were built, not to accommodate additional worshippers, but to provide for the activities of guilds (*see also* PORCHES). Guilds originated in the twelfth century as religious fraternities which evolved round a church, monastery or hospice to which they attached themselves and whose saint they adopted as their patron. Members of those fraternities who lived together often worked together in a common trade or craft. They made provision for the poor, sick and needy of their communities, they endowed chantries for their members and their families (*see* CHANTRY) and promoted the interests of their 'mystery' or craft, granting apprenticeships and exercising the power of search which gave each company the right to inspect all goods handled by its members. This provided the guilds with an effective weapon against competition and enabled them to maintain high standards so that membership became a privilege. The medieval guilds were therefore as much concerned with secular matters as with religious observance, indeed there was often a significant overlapping of civic and religious functions within a community (*see also* CHURCH AND COMMUNITY).

By the late fourteenth century, guilds varied considerably in size and influence, and in their customs and organisation. Some were simply local societies of tradespeople who came together for social and charitable purposes, their members benefiting from prayer, fellowship and a common purse upon which they could draw for subsistence in times of hardship. At Milborne Port in Somerset, for example, a medieval merchants' guild (later known as the Commonalty) established a number of CHARITIES which continue to this day; while at nearby Bradford Abbas in Dorset, a fifteenth-century guild assisted in the rebuilding of the parish church to which they added a fine south aisle for their own use. In the major sea-ports and trading cities of England the guilds developed into great livery companies, so named because of the distinctive colours (liveries) worn by their members: the Worshipful Company of Vintners of the City of London, for example, the Company of Merchant Taylors in the City of York and the Company and Fellowship of the Merchant Adventurers of the City of Bristol whose influence was to extend throughout the world.

By far the most common type of guild was that which was formed in response to the Church's teaching which emphasised the need to prepare oneself for the afterlife. No one knew exactly how long a soul could be expected to remain in PURGATORY but it was widely believed that prayers for the souls of the departed could ease the pains of torment suffered there. Most individuals could not afford to pay for 'remembrances' for their souls but they were able to join a group, usually known as a guild, which had been formed for that purpose. Providing they paid the entrance fee, the value of which varied considerably, membership of a guild was normally available to anyone – including 'Bachelers and Maydons'. Guild meetings were one of the few gatherings at which a spinster (as opposed to a widow) could attend in her own right. Members were expected to attend the funerals of former guild members and commemorative masses throughout the year. An annual meeting was held on the parochial feast day, at which officers were appointed and income and expenditure accounted for, and this was often followed by a dinner and festivities (*see* CHURCH AND COMMUNITY).

Where available, guild records and accounts provide evidence of the appearance, furnishings and decoration of the churches which benefited from their support and of the significant contribution they made to community life. Medieval wills frequently included bequests to local guilds, both of money and of land, together with gifts of plate, books, furnishings and other valuables with which they embellished their chapels and guild halls (*see* PROBATE).

See also FRIENDLY SOCIETIES

GUILLOCHE *see* DECORATIVE MOTIFS

GULE OF AUGUST, THE The first day of August (*see* LAMMAS).

GULES *see* COLOURS (HERALDIC)

GUTTAE (i) A decorative motif consisting of stylised droplets. (ii) In heraldry, a *goutte* is a stylised droplet and *goutty* is a pattern of droplets of a specified colour.

GYPSUM *see* ALABASTER *and* PLASTERWORK

HABIT The distinctive dress worn by monks, nuns, canons and friars as members of various religious orders. The habits of the older orders consisted of a tunic and girdle, a SCAPULAR, a hood (or a veil for women: *see* VEILS) and a mantle. The habit was intended to be an outward and visible sign of dedication to a religious life. Colours and details of design varied from one order to another: for example the Benedictines and Dominicans wore black, the Cistercians white and the Franciscans grey (now brown).
See also VESTMENTS *and* entries for individual orders

HADES Although in several versions of the New Testament Hades is translated as 'Hell', it was the place where departed Christians waited for judgement.
See also DOOM *and* PURGATORY

HAGIOGRAPHY *and* **HAGIOLOGY** Hagiography is the study of the lives and legends of the saints. *Hagiology* is the body of literature arising there from.

HAGIOSCOPE *see* SQUINT

HAGODAY *see* SANCTUARY

HA-HA A sunken wall and outward-sloping ditch constructed at the perimeter of a churchyard to prevent livestock from entering. The top of the wall is at ground level so that from within the churchyard the view into the surrounding countryside is unimpeded. The term probably originated in the Old English *haya* meaning 'hedge', though it has been suggested that it is derived from an eighteenth-century French interjection intended to deter adventurous ruminants.

HAIL MARY A form of prayer addressed to the Blessed Virgin Mary (*see* MARY, THE BLESSED VIRGIN). Based on Gabriel's greeting (Luke 1:28) and that of Elizabeth (Luke 1:42).

HAKETON A padded garment intended to protect the body from the chafeing of the heavy HAUBERK (*see* ARMOUR).

HALF-BAPTISED Said of a child who has been baptised privately and not in a church.

HALF SHAFT (*also* **ENGAGED SHAFT**) A pier or column partially attached to, or let into, a wall.

HALL CHURCH A church (such as St. Mary's, Warwick) in which the NAVE and aisles are of approximately the same height.

HALLMARKS A mark used at Goldsmiths Hall and by assay offices in the United Kingdom to indicate the standard of gold, silver and (since 1975) platinum, to secure a uniform quality and to prevent fraud. Hallmarking dates from a statute of 1300 which required the Goldsmiths Guild to use the leopard's head hallmark (the *King's Mark*) as an indication of quality. (As an important customer of the London goldsmiths, Edward I had a strong interest in maintaining the standard of their products.) The Worshipful Company of Goldsmiths (established in 1150 as a fraternity of gold and silversmiths) has been responsible for the assaying and marking of PLATE since receiving its royal charter of incorporation in 1327, together with various provincial assay offices, notably at Edinburgh, Birmingham and Sheffield (all still functioning); Norwich (closed in 1702), York (1856), Exeter (1883), Newcastle (1884), Chester (1962) and Glasgow (1964). With certain exceptions

(such as Royal Plate), all gold, silver and platinum articles are required to be hallmarked before being offered for sale. The death penalty for counterfeiting the British hallmark was reduced to fourteen years' transportation as recently as 1773. The marks impressed in the metal include symbols indicating the maker, standard, assay office and date.

Since 1363 it has been compulsory for the maker to stamp his mark on a piece of silver plate before sending it to the assay office. At first marks were devices such as a bird, a hart, a cross etc., many of which were heraldic or alluded to the maker's name. A silver chalice, with a maker's mark of a gloved hand, eluded identification until the possibility of an heraldic pun was considered: a gauntlet for Gaunt or a glove for Glover, perhaps? Further research confirmed that the maker was indeed one John Glover, a freeman of the Goldsmiths Company who died in 1598. Towards the end of the sixteenth century makers began using cyphers and monograms and from 1739 they were required by law to use the initial letters of their Christian and surnames. It was in response to this regulation that many silversmiths began to re-register their marks: Paul de Lamerie (the finest of the London smiths) incorporated a crown to indicate royal patronage, for example. The practice continues today, though most marks are those of firms rather than individual craftsmen.

The standard mark follows that of the maker. The lion device indicates that the metal has been passed as sterling silver (i.e. 92.5 per cent pure silver). The earliest mark was a *lion passant guardant* (from the English royal arms) with its face looking outward. Since 1822 it has been *a lion passant* (i.e. looking straight ahead). From 1697–1720, the lion was replaced by the image of Britannia and the silver standard raised to 95.84 per cent. On sterling silver assayed at Sheffield and Chester, the lion has always been *passant reguardant* (i.e. looking over his left shoulder). The Irish office used a crowned harp. At Edinburgh a thistle was used prior to 1975 when the *lion rampant* (i.e. a lion rearing on his hind legs) of the former Glasgow office was adopted.

Town marks indicate the assay office responsible for testing the article. Most English-made silver is sent to London for hallmarking which complicates the identification of provincial silver. The leopard's head continues to be the London mark, though from 1478–1821 it was crowned and the *lion's head erased* (i.e. cut off at the neck) appears on Britannia standard silver from 1697–1720 (and remained valid for fine silver until 1975). A crown was used by Sheffield from 1773–1975, the Tudor Rose gold mark now being used also on silver and platinum. The Birmingham office has used an anchor since 1773: in the upright position for silver and on its side for gold. Edinburgh uses a castle on both gold and silver items. All the important former offices used devices based on their civic arms: a ship sailing from the port of a castellated town for Bristol; a castle above a lion for Norwich; five lions on a cross for York; a triple-towered castle for Exeter; three castles for Newcastle; a sword between three wheat-sheaves (the arms of the county of Cheshire) for Chester and (somewhat optimistically) . . . *on a Mount an Oak Tree surmounted by a Salmon with a Signet Ring in its mouth, on top of the tree a Redbreast and in the sinister an Ancient Handbell* . . . for Glasgow.

The date letter indicates the date on which the object was assayed (which is almost invariably the date when it was made). Date stamps on London-made silver, indicating the day to the nearest twelve-month, have been used for over four hundred years without repetition. For twenty consecutive years the twenty letters from A to U (excluding J) are used with the same style of shield and letter throughout. After U has been reached the styles of both shield and letter are changed. The Birmingham and Edinburgh offices also use all the letters excepting J, but Sheffield adopted a different cycle and the former assay offices used less regular systems of date-marking.

See also PEWTER (*for* touch marks) *and* PLATE
Further reading:
Banister, J., *English Silver Hallmarks*, Slough, 1970

HALLOWE'EN All Saints' Eve (31 October). Either by design or coincidence, the early Church chose to graft many of its festivals onto earlier pagan ones. The Celtic calendar began with the great autumnal feast of *Samain* at which the dead were honoured and huge bonfires lit in order that life should be sustained through the long, dark winter (*see* FEAST DAYS (FIXED AND MOVABLE)). Appropriately, the Church adopted the first two days of November for the commemoration of its saints (ALL SAINTS' DAY, also All Hallows or Hallowmas) and the souls of the faithful departed (ALL SOULS' DAY). But potent images of Samain lingered in the celebration of All Hallow E'en (All Saints' Eve), a time when evil spirits ventured abroad and concealed themselves within the smoke of the bonfires. Eventually, the Church acknowledged its inability to suppress the flames of superstition and sanctioned the All Hallow E'en fires by providing them with a new function, one which accorded well with the traditions of Samain and was well received by those whose ancestors would have celebrated similar rites. Each year, on the eve of All Saints' Day, the bones which had accumulated in parish charnel houses (*see* OSSUARIES) were removed and cast into the fires in order to make room for new supplies of bones from the churchyards.

Inevitably, pagan and Christian customs merged: the feast of Samain honoured the dead and on All Saints' Day money was collected to pay for the saying of masses on All Souls' Day, thereby easing the passage of souls through PURGATORY. The medieval custom of 'Souling' (which, in some parts, survived into the present century) involved groups of parishioners collecting money for this purpose, though food and drink was later substituted for cash:

> Soul! Soul! for a soul cake
> I pray, good missus, a soul cake
> An apple, a pear, a plum or a cherry
> Any good thing to make us merry.
> One for Peter, two for Paul,
> Three for Him who made us all.

In the 1880s, the Rector of Malpas in Cheshire wrote to a local newspaper to complain of the activities of 'Soul-cakers' whose behaviour was far removed from that of their sombre medieval predecessors: 'I have just heard three middle-aged men with a concertina singing a really sweet chant with words to the effect that all they souled for was cakes and strong beer.'

All Hallow E'en was also a night for divination and prophecy. As recently as the late eighteenth century, parishioners would often wait in a church porch at midnight in order to overhear, from within the church, the catalogue of those who were to die in the coming year.

Further reading:
Gregory, D., *Yesterday in Village Church and Churchyard*, Llandysul, 1987

HALLOWMAS *see* ALL SAINTS' DAY *and* FEAST DAYS (FIXED AND MOVABLE)

HALO (or NIMBUS) In Christian art, a disc or circle of light depicted behind the head as though surrounding it. Originally, the device was restricted to representations of Christ but from the fifth century its use was extended to the Blessed Virgin Mary, angels and saints. Later, other important Christians were so depicted, a square-shaped nimbus being reserved for those who were living at the time they were portrayed. A circle surrounding the intersection of a cross is also termed a nimbus. Not to be confused with the AUREOLE which surrounds the entire body.

HAMLET Historically a hamlet was a small settlement in which there was no constable, overseer, parish church or separate rate. It was, therefore, neither a TOWNSHIP nor a PARISH. Many VILLAGES have developed from the amalgamation of adjacent hamlets and townships while, in other areas, the hamlet continues to represent the principal component of an ancient rural settlement pattern.

But this is not an entirely satisfactory definition. It was only towards the end of the Saxon period that larger villages began to develop where now they predominate: particularly in the English midlands and other areas where open fields were introduced. It is undoubtedly true that a number of hamlets developed as secondary settlements (often enlarged farmsteads) as a result of the rapid expansion of villages in the early Middle Ages. But it is equally true that most hamlets were already established by the twelfth and thirteenth centuries and that their pedigrees may extend back to the Roman period and beyond. The term itself implies a place of permanence and security for an extended family group: as in Arlingham (Gloucestershire), derived from *erlingeham* – 'the *ham* of the people of the earl' – a remote settlement situated in a loop of the Severn and with its own parish church. Many hamlets merged or expanded to become villages and even TOWNS: Gillingham in Dorset, for example – 'the *ham* of Gylla's people'. Others declined to become solitary farmsteads or were abandoned entirely (*see* DESERTED VILLAGES). But in many areas the ubiquity and stability of these ancient hamlets remains a characteristic feature of the countryside. Most are little altered in size or form since they were first established some sixteen centuries ago.

HAMMER-BEAM *see* ROOFS (TIMBER)

HAPENCE Easter dues.

HARDWICKE'S MARRIAGE ACT (1754) Lord Hardwicke's act was intended to prevent clandestine marriages which had previously been regulated by CANON LAW. The Act required that no marriage should be performed other than by a clergyman of the Church of England (Jews and Quakers were exempt) and only following the publication of BANNS OF MARRIAGE, usually in the church of one of the parties where the marriage was to be celebrated. There was also a statutory obligation that the banns should be recorded, either at the back of a register or in a book reserved for that purpose, and printed forms were introduced for registration purposes (*see* REGISTERS). Minors were also required to obtain the consent of their parents or guardians before marrying.
See also GEORGE ROSE'S ACT, MARRIAGE ACT *and* MARRIAGE LICENCES

HARMONIUM *see* CHURCH MUSIC (ANGLICAN), GALLERIES *and* ORGANS

HARROWING OF HELL The descent of Christ into Hell, referred to in the APOSTLES' CREED and a common theme in medieval mystery plays, resulted in the defeat of the powers of evil and the release of its victims. In this context, hell means 'the enclosed world' in which the souls of non-Christians awaited the message of the Gospel. In some English counties, 'to hell the building' means to enclose it within a roof, the thatchers or tilers being described as 'helliers'.
See also DOOM *and* PURGATORY

HART The ubiquitous hart or stag is to be found depicted in the fabric of churches and emblazoned in heraldry. In Christian art, it is the emblem of solitude and purity of life and as such is especially associated with St. Eustace, St. Hubert and St. Julian. It may be represented in its old age fighting a snake or dragon whose flesh, when devoured, will restore the hart to health and vigour: a thirteenth-century allegory of Christ destroying the devil. Legendary white harts, marked out for royal protection by a gold collar, once haunted the forests and chases of England – Blackmoor Vale in Dorset is still known as the Vale of the White Hart. A white hart was the favourite device of Richard II, inherited from his mother Joan of Kent and worn as an indication of royal preferment by countless of the king's sycophantic courtiers.

HARVEST THANKSGIVING The familiar and popular Harvest Festival, at which thanks are offered for the safe ingathering of the harvest, originated in the nineteenth century when it replaced the traditional (but secular) Harvest Home. Usually held on a Sunday in September or October, the produce of field and orchard is brought to the church where it is blessed and afterwards distributed to local charities. The centre piece is usually a huge 'harvest loaf', fashioned in the form of a wheatsheaf (complete with harvest mouse) and displayed on or near the altar. In many churches, symbols of commerce and industry also have their place, as does the harvest of the sea. Despite its apparent authenticity, the harvest thanksgiving is not recognised by the Church of England as an official religious festival.
See also LAMMAS

HASSOCK A firm cushion on which to kneel during prayer. Hassocks are often colourfully embroidered with CHRISTIAN SYMBOLS, MONOGRAMS, REBUSES or HERALDRY. The arms of dioceses and cathedrals are especially popular as are those of manorial lords or armigers who are buried (or commemorated) within the church. Heraldry on hassocks is not always accurate, however, for it may have been interpreted incorrectly or obtained from an unreliable source. Benches often have integral wooden kneelers with *bench runners* which may be embroidered with similar motifs. Quite often, decorative themes are repeated in hassocks and altar rail kneeling pads. A pair of hassocks, usually of velvet with silk embroidery, may be reserved for weddings.

HATCHING *see* COLOURS (HERALDIC)

HATCHMENTS A hatchment is a diamond-shaped heraldic panel usually found in a church where it may be affixed to a wall or removed to a ringing chamber, vestry or some other equally inaccessible quarter.

A hatchment comprises a shield of arms (often with helm, CREST and mantling and, where appropriate, a peer's CORONET and SUPPORTERS) painted on a wooden panel or on canvas within a wooden frame. Occasionally a frame will carry a brief inscription and some hatchments include initials and a date. The word itself is a corruption of 'achievement', suggesting that it originated in the elaborate funeral heraldry of the medieval nobility. Like the earlier 'scocheon of arms' (*see* FUNERAL HERALDRY), a hatchment was carried in procession to the church where it remained following interment. Alternatively, it may have been returned to the deceased's house following the service and hung above the door during a period of mourning before being returned once again to the church. (It is uncertain how long a hatchment would remain outside a house: exposure to the weather would have caused rapid deterioration of the flimsy fabric.) In Scotland two hatchments were painted: one for the house and the other for the church, while in England there are several examples of hatchments for the same individual being erected in the churches of his various estates.

HISTORICAL DEVELOPMENT

The earliest hatchments date from *c.* 1627, though the rectangular MEMORIAL BOARD, erected to the memory of an individual and bearing both his arms and (unlike hatchments) a more detailed inscription, is usually of sixteenth-century origin and is clearly related to the 'scocheon' of heraldic funerals. Early hatchments are generally small, no more than one metre square (3 feet) with narrow frames decorated with symbols of mortality such as hourglasses, MORTHEADS and crossbones. They were painted in a vigorous style, unlike those of the nineteenth century which, for the most part, are of poor artistic quality.

Late eighteenth- and nineteenth-century hatchments are larger, their wider frames often covered with black cloth and decorated in the corners with rosettes. Although the College of Arms was responsible for confirming the authenticity of hatchments, many were painted for minor gentry, usually by local craftsmen who rarely appreciated the niceties of heraldry, and errors of interpretation are therefore not uncommon.

The use of hatchments was at its peak in the mid-nineteenth century but declined rapidly during Victoria's reign. Of the 4500 hatchments recently recorded in England, only 120 are of the present century.

INTERPRETATION

It is the treatment of the background which makes the hatchment unique: essentially, this is coloured black beneath those parts of a coat of arms which relate to the deceased (*see illustration*). The system was well established by 1700 but there are numerous traps for the unwary, especially in early hatchments. At Marnhull in Dorset, for example, the death of a nine-year-old girl is commemorated in a hatchment

Funeral hatchment above the door of Horsington House, Somerset, c. 1900.

Funeral Hatchments

1 Husband (wife surviving)
2 Wife (husband surviving)
3 Bachelor
4 Widow
5 Widower
6 Spinster

7, 8, 9 & 10 Husband (second wife surviving)

227

of the arms of her *living* parents together with the child's initials (MAS) and date of death (1663).

When a wife is an heraldic heiress her arms are correctly shown on a small shield at the centre of her husband's (in pretence). But because this cannot be reflected in the colour of the background, the arms are sometimes placed side by side (*impaled*) or both impaled and in pretence and the appropriate background used. This demonstrates the need for caution when interpreting hatchments, for the conventions of MARSHALLING are not always applicable. The impalement of a blank half-shield indicates that a wife was not armigerous; or alternatively no impalement is shown but the background of the hatchment is divided as though there were. (It is therefore possible to interpret a hatchment as being that of a bachelor when, in fact, it commemorates a man whose death followed that of his non-armigerous wife: both would show a single shield and an all-black background.) Several methods are used to indicate two or more wives (*see illustration*), and again these usually defy the normal conventions of marshalling. The sinister half of the shield (that to the right when viewed from the front) may be divided with the arms of the first wife at the top and those of the second wife below. Alternatively, the shield may be divided vertically

into three with the husband's arms in the centre between those of his first wife to the dexter (the left when viewed from the front) and his second wife's to the sinister (the right). This may be confused with another method in which the husband's arms appear in the dexter and those of his former wives successively to the sinister. A further (and less confusing) method was to depict the husband's personal arms in the centre and the impaled arms of his various wives on small shields set in panels on either side. The backgrounds of each panel would be appropriately coloured to indicate which of the marital partners had died. In a hatchment at Moulton in Lincolnshire, the impaled arms of of Henry Bolton (d. 1828) and his fifth wife are surrounded by shields of the impaled arms of her four predecessors. Similar practices were (rarely) adopted by ladies who had two or more husbands.

Hatchments erected to commemorate knights of the orders of chivalry will usually contain two shields side by side and slightly overlapping (known as *accollé*). The knight's personal arms, together with the insignia of his order (to which his wife is not entitled), are to the dexter and the impaled marital arms to the sinister, with the appropriate black and white background (*see* KNIGHTHOOD, ORDERS OF). Where an archbishop, bishop,

Cavendish hatchments at Cartmel Priory near the family estate at Holker Hall, Cumbria. The impalement is Lowther and the escutcheon of pretence Compton.

college warden etc. impales his personal arms with those of his office, the background behind the arms of office (to the dexter) will be white (to indicate the continuation of the office after his death) or, when married, the shields may again be depicted accollé. In a number of (usually later) hatchments, a peer's arms will be found depicted in front of a *manteau*, a ceremonial robe which may also be surmounted by a coronet of rank.

Non-heraldic devices appear in hatchments of all periods: cherubs' heads are frequently found above the lozenges in women's hatchments; skulls fill the vacant corners beneath motto scrolls whilst flags, sometimes bearing battle honours, embellish the hatchments of many military or naval men. Mottoes in hatchments are most unreliable. Many refer to mortality (e.g. *Resurgam* or *In Coela Quies*) and should not be confused with family mottoes which may also appear in a hatchment, but rarely so.

SURVIVING HATCHMENTS

Eighteenth- and nineteenth-century illustrations and engravings and the records of antiquarian county histories indicate that there were once many more hatchments in our parish churches than there are today. Canvas and wood (or, in one known case, carpet fabric) are unlikely to survive centuries of damp and neglect or the over-enthusiastic 'restorations' of the nineteenth century. At Shrewsbury in Shropshire two churches contain twenty and twenty-one hatchments respectively but in Britain this is exceptional. There is a notable collection of seventeen hatchments at Stanford in Northamptonshire, while at Thornton Watless in

Yorkshire there are eleven, mainly to the Dodsworth family, and ten at Bridlington Priory, also in Yorkshire. But most churches, if they have any, have one or two, the group of four to the Compton family at Compton Wynyates in Warwickshire being particularly fine examples from the seventeenth and early eighteenth centuries. Royal hatchments are rare and may easily be mistaken for the ubiquitous armorial boards, emblazoned with the royal arms and hung in churches since 1534 (*see* ROYAL ARMS IN CHURCHES).

Hatchment at Farley, Wiltshire, for Georgina Lennox, eldest daughter of Charles, second duke of Richmond and Lennox, who was created Baronesss Holland of Holland, Lincolnshire, in 1762. Her husband, Henry Fox, was created Baron Holland of Foxley, Wiltshire, in 1763. Husband and wife therefore each held titles in their own right – hence the two baronial coronets and the arms accollé.

As in most aspects of heraldry there is room for the vernacular: at Stourton Caundle church in Dorset a 'hatchment' of the arms of the Worshipful Company of Blacksmiths of the City of London, surmounted by a winged hourglass and what appears to be a golden goose sitting on a nest (clearly a misinterpretation of the Company's phoenix crest), commemorates one John Biddlecombe, village blacksmith and clock-maker, who died in 1741.

Further reading:

Friar, S., *Heraldry for the Local Historian and Genealogist*, Stroud, 1992

Summers, P.G., *Hatchments in Britain* (10 volumes), Colchester. (This superb series records all the 4,500 hatchments traced in Britain since Peter Summers began his survey in 1952. Counties are grouped together in each volume.)

See also ARMORIAL PANEL and BURIALS

Punning arms of Rabbet in a hatchment at Bramfield, Suffolk. The widow's arms are depicted on a white background, though the crest is clearly that of her late husband.

HAUBERK A shirt with long sleeves and made entirely from mail (*see* ARMOUR).

HEADER The narrow face of a brick. A *bull header* is made especially for circular work and has one end wider than the other.
See BRICK

HEADMINSTER *see* ANGLO-SAXON CHURCH.

HEADSTONES *see* EPITAPHS *and* GRAVESTONES

HEARSE (*also* HERSE) (i) A triangular stand holding fifteen candles. A hearse was used at a special form of Matins and Lauds known as *Tenebrae*, celebrated on the last three days of HOLY WEEK, during which the church candles were extinguished one by one (Latin *tenebrae* = 'darkness'). (ii) A barrel-shaped metal cage erected above an effigy and intended to support candles and

a PALL which was removed only on special occasions (*see* EFFIGIES). One of the most magnificent examples is that above the gilded bronze effigy of Richard Beauchamp, fifth earl of Warwick (d. 1439) at St. Mary's, Warwick. (iii) A cage-like structure over a bier, though in modern usage the term has come to mean a vehicle in which a coffin is conveyed to a funeral (*see* LICH-GATE).

HEARSE HOUSE Accommodation for a church bier (*see* BURIAL, LICH-GATE *and* PORCHES).

HEART *see* SACRED HEART

HEART BURIAL The medieval practice of interring a man's heart, the seat of love and piety, in a place other than that in which his body was buried was particularly common during the thirteenth and fourteenth centuries. The separate burial of the heart and body is sometimes described in documents as 'partly buried'. Frequently, such heart burials took

Heart burial at Mappowder, Dorset. The thirteenth-century figure of an unidentified knight is approximately 46 cm long (18 inches) and holds a representation of the casket in which the heart was placed.

place in monastic churches, notably the sequestered abbeys of the Cistercian order such as Sweetheart Abbey (*Dulce Cor*) in the county of Dumfries and Galloway where the heart of its founder John Baliol was buried. Similarly, the heart of a thirteenth-century Bishop of Hereford was interred at Cistercian Abbey Dore in Herefordshire, the spot being marked with a miniature effigy of the bishop.

In many localities, tradition links these miniature effigies with the heart burial of a local crusading knight: a not unreasonable assumption when the difficulties of transporting a rapidly deteriorating corpse from the Holy Land are considered. There are good examples at Mappowder in Dorset (*see* EFFIGIES) and Horsted Keynes in Sussex (probably the work of the same sculptor) and at Bottesford, Leicestershire and Halesowen Abbey in Worcestershire. At Burford in Shropshire, a half-size effigy to the medieval adventurer Edmund Cornewall is depicted clasping a heart in his hands. The epitaph reads: 'travelling to known Foreign Countries [he] died at Cologne, the xivth year of Henry VI, and willed his servant to bury his body there and to enclose his Heart in lead and carry it to Burford to be buried.'

Not all heart burials were commemorated in such a tangible way: the heart (or, more probably, the intestines) of the tragic Prince Arthur was buried somewhere within the church of St. Laurence at Ludlow in Shropshire but no contemporary memorial has survived.

Perhaps the most controversial heart burial was that of the Dorset poet and novelist Thomas Hardy (1840–1928). Hardy had specifically willed that he should be buried at Stinsford in Dorset, 'out there' with his parents, sister and his first wife. Despite this, a Westminster Abbey funeral was arranged and only after the local vicar interceded was it decided that Hardy's ashes should be buried in the Abbey and his heart at Stinsford. It was a final irony that would have been appreciated by Hardy but which met with local cynicism and even ribaldry: 'Almighty, 'e'll say, "'ere be 'eart, but where be rest of 'e?"'

See also MOS TUTONICUS

HEARTH PENNY A penny paid annually on MAUNDY Thursday by free householders to a MINSTER church.

HEIR One who has inherited, and enjoys possession of, a title, property or arms. The term is often mistakenly used to mean an *heir apparent* who is one whose right of succession is inalienable. An *heir presumptive* is one whose right of succession is dependent on the absence of an heir apparent.

HEIRESS (HERALDIC) An heraldic heiress is a daughter who has inherited arms from her deceased father, there being no brothers or surviving issue of

brothers. The arms of an heraldic heiress are shown on an *escutcheon of pretence*, a small shield at the centre of her husband's shield. Both her arms and those of her husband are transmitted to their children as quarterings (*see* QUARTERING), her husband's arms being in the first quarter. When there is more than one daughter, all are co-heiresses and all transmit their father's arms on equal terms. An *heiress in her issue* is one through whose issue arms descend when all male lines of her father have failed. In this way, it is possible for descendants of the daughter of an armiger to inherit his arms several generations after her death.
See also MARSHALLING

HELL and HELL-MOUTH *see* DOOM, HARROWING OF HELL *and* WALL PAINTINGS.

HELMETS (HERALDIC) Stylized helmets are to be found in BRASSES and EFFIGIES and in COATS OF ARMS on TOMBS, MEMORIALS and HATCHMENTS.

In the thirteenth and fourteenth centuries, when the helmet was an essential component of a knight's equipment, the cylindrical barrel or great helm, with a flat or rounded top, eye slits (*sights*) and ventilation holes (*breaths*), was invariably used in seals and other forms of heraldic display (*see* illustrations 1–2–3). From the end of the fourteenth century this was superseded by the ubiquitous tilting helm (4) which had no visor and was permanently

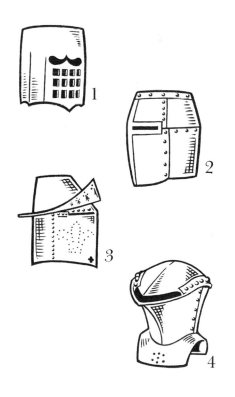

'closed', with only a slit for the eyes. It was, therefore, effective only when leaning forward in the tilting position. Tilting helms carried the ornate tournament crests of the period (*see* CREST) and were therefore associated with chivalric superiority – both in the lists and in coats of arms.

With the wholesale adoption of crests by the 'new gentility' of the Tudor period the nobility perceived a need for further differentiation in their arms and an extraordinary variety of bizarre and impracticable headgear began to appear in heraldry towards the end of the sixteenth century. By the early seventeenth century, these had been codified into a system in which different types of helm were assigned to armigers of different ranks. These were also stylised forms of tournament helms and, while they remain in use today, considerable artistic licence will be encountered, reflecting the heraldic tastes of intervening centuries. The tilting helm (4) was retained in the arms of gentlemen, esquires and corporations; the barriers helm (9), a fifteenth-century visored bascinet, was adopted for baronets and knights; and the mêlée helm (5), with its wide aperture for the face and protective bars or laticed grill, was reserved for peers. The late fifteenth-century 'basket helm' (6), armet (8) and sallet (or salade) (7) may also be found, particularly in Scottish heraldry where the sallet is now used in civic heraldry.

5

6

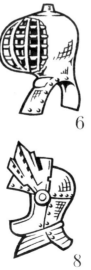

7

8

9

HELM ROOF *see* TOWERS

HENNIN *see* COSTUME

HENRY VIII (1491–1547) King of England 1509–47 whose attempts to dissolve his marriage with Catherine of Aragon led to England's break with the Church of Rome and, ultimately, to the establishment of the CHURCH OF ENGLAND. The *Act of Supremacy* of 1534 did not create the sovereign's title 'supreme head on earth of the Church of England'. It merely acknowledged his right to it and defined and sanctioned the legal powers which it entailed. The Act was repealed by Mary I in 1554 but the royal supremacy was revived by Elizabeth I (under the title 'Supreme Governor') in 1559. Although Henry repudiated papal authority, his religious views remained orthodox and it was not until after his death that doctrinal Protestantism became official policy in England.

The popular image of 'bluff King Hal' is far removed from the historians' verdict. R.W. Chambers, for example, said of him 'Henry VIII destroyed more things of beauty, and more things of promise, than any other man in European history.'
See also DEFENDER OF THE FAITH, DISSOLUTION OF THE MONASTERIES, REFORMATION *and* SIX ARTICLES, THE

HEPTATEUCH The first seven books of the Old Testament.

HERALDIC BEASTS *see* BEASTS (HERALDIC)

HERALDIC BOARDS *see* ARMORIAL BOARDS

HERALDIC CADENCY (MARKS OF DIFFERENCE) *see* CADENCY (HERALDIC)

HERALDIC CHARGES Of the numerous devices (*charges*) used in HERALDRY a comparatively small number will be encountered regularly. Most coats of arms rely on combinations of charges for their uniqueness, and on variations of background (*field*), line and colour (*tincture*) (*see* COLOURS (HERALDIC)). Two or more coats of arms may be combined in a single shield to indicate marriage, inheritance or tenure of office e.g. a bishopric *see* MARSHALLING). If a coat of arms is to be described (*blazoned*) or painted (*emblazoned*) accurately it is necessary to master the conventions and terminology of BLAZON.

Charges are of three types:
   (i)   those which are part of the original design
   (ii) those which have been added to indicate CADENCY
   (iii) those which have been added as AUGMENTATIONS OF HONOUR.

These include bold geometrical shapes (*ordinaries* and *sub-ordinaries*), beasts in a variety of attitudes (*see* BEASTS, HERALDIC) and stylised representations of objects both natural and man-made.

INTERPRETATION
The popular perception of heraldry is that all charges are possessed of some hidden significance or symbolism. While it is true that all arms are unique, charges may have been selected for purely aesthetic reasons while the significance of others is immediately apparent. An open book is a universal symbol of learning, for example, and wavy blue divisions invariably represent water. Others demand some understanding of classical allusions: the Rod of Aesculapius, for instance, which is generally associated with members of the medical profession. Historical references are also popular: the twentieth-century arms of Cooke of Athelhampton (*Quarterly Sable and Or four Hawk's heads in cross counterchanged*) are a direct reference to the arms of the De Pydele family (*Quarterly Argent and Sable four Hawk's heads counterchanged*) who were lords of the manor of Athelhampton, Dorset, in the late fourteenth century. Here, the significance of the hawk's heads remains a mystery but the historical rationale for the Cooke arms is obvious.

Arms often allude to the name, title, office or property of an armiger and these are correctly termed *allusive arms* or *armes parlantes*. The punning arms of Sir Thomas Harris of Shropshire, for example, are *Or three Herrisons* [hedgehogs] *Azure*, and his crest is a golden hedgehog (1622). *Canting arms* are a strict form of allusive arms in which the entire design of a shield is devoted to a pictorial pun on the name or title of the armiger. The arms of Sir Cecil Chubb, first Baronet of Stonehenge, (*Per fess Azure and Vert two Pales surmounted by a Chief Argent*) represent a pair of sarsen stones and a stone lintel on a background of sky and grass and refer to Chubb's gift of Stonehenge to the nation in 1918. Examples are numerous in early armory, indeed the frequency of allusive arms in the thirteenth and fourteenth centuries suggests that many exist which have yet to be identified, the allusion being obscure to the twentieth-century mind. Well known early examples are those of De Ferres (*Argent six Horseshoes* [ferrs] *Sable*) and Tremain (*Gules three dexter Arms conjoined in triangle Or*).

CRESTS and, of course, MOTTOES may also be allusive. The arms of the Dymoke family, from 1377 hereditary Champions of England, include a punning motto PRO REGE DIMICO ('I fight for the king') and a punning crest of two donkey's ears (*deux mokes*) which was later changed to those of a hare by disapproving members of the family. Notable events may also be commemorated heraldically: the *Saracen's Head* crests in the arms of the Lygon, Stapleton, Warburton and Willoughby families recall crusading ancestors, though it should not be assumed that all *Saracen's Head* devices originated in this way and most were adopted several centuries after the event, often replacing earlier and simpler *panache* or cockscomb crests. The almost identical *Moor's Head* crests of the Moore and Mordaunt families clearly allude to the names and have no further significance.

See also ATTRIBUTED ARMS, BADGES, CORONETS OF PEERS, CREST CORONETS, HELMETS (HERALDIC), KNOTS *and* REBUS.
For the 'Red Hand of Ulster' *see* BARONET
Further reading:
Elvin, C., *A Dictionary of Heraldry*, 1889 (reprinted London, 1969)
Friar, S., *A New Dictionary of Heraldry*, Sherborne and London, 1987
——, *Heraldry for the Local Historian and Genealogist*, Stroud, 1992

HERALDIC COLOURS *see* COLOURS (HERALDIC)

HERALDRY To most people, heraldry is synonymous with ARMORY. But, in fact, heraldry is concerned with the various duties and responsibilities of the heralds of which armory is but one.

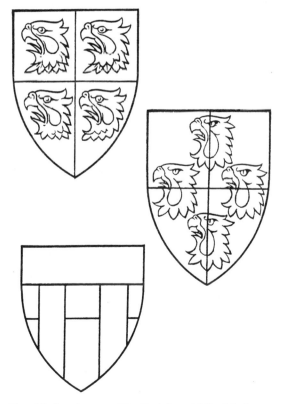

Top: Medieval arms of De Pydele; middle: Modern arms of Cooke; bottom: Arms of Sir Cecil Chubb

THE ORIGINS OF HERALDRY

It is clear that throughout the Ancient World symbols were used to represent authority and affiliation as they are today. The territorial districts of ancient Egypt, for example, possessed devices by which civil and military authority was recognized. But it is in the pages of the Old Testament that we first find mention of hereditary devices associated with individuals and their extended families:

Every man of the children of Israel shall pitch by his own standard, with the ensign of [his] father's house . . . And the children of Israel . . . pitched by their standards and so they set forward, every one after their families, according to the house of their fathers.

(Numbers 2: 2 and 34)

The Venerable Bede, writing in the early eighth century, describes the banners of King Edwin of East Anglia which 'were not only borne before him in battle, but even in time of peace, when he rode about his cities, towns or provinces . . . the standard bearer was wont to go before him'. Clearly, these banners bore the symbols of Edwin's dynastic and territorial authority, though Bede does not describe them in detail.

Most of the flags depicted in the Bayeux Tapestry (c. 1077) are of cloth and are small, semicircular or square with a number of 'tails' attached to the fly. That the devices borne on these flags were of territorial or even personal significance has long been a matter of dispute, but it is now generally accepted that the Normans had not, at that time, adopted the proto-heraldic system evident in the lance pennons of their Flemish allies.

It is most likely, therefore, that the origins of British heraldry are to be found, not in Normandy, but in the system adopted by certain ruling families descended from the Emperor Charlemagne who ruled the Frankish Empire of northern Europe from 768 to 814. These families perpetuated much of the administrative organisation of the Carolingian Empire, including the use of dynastic and territorial emblems on seals, coinage, customs stamps and flags, indeed 'wherever officialdom needed to identify itself both in peace and war'*. There is evidence to suggest that these devices were common to families or groups linked by blood or feudal tenure, and were, of necessity, hereditary. With the redistribution of lands following the Norman Conquest, the cadets in England of Flemish families (who were of Carolingian descent), and the devices used by them, became integrated in Anglo-Norman society.

The traditional theory, that heraldry originated in the decoration of shield and surcoat in order that heavily armoured knights should be identified more easily in battle, is of doubtful validity. Common sense suggests that the mud and debris of warfare would quickly obliterate the battered surfaces of shields, rendering them unrecognisable. Within the feudal system every man who held land subject to military service was 'known' or 'noted' (in Latin, *nobilis*) and while these obligations were frequently commuted to other services, or to the payment of fines, the feudal *nobilis* retained its clearly defined superiority within a two-tier society in which there was an enormous gap between the upper and lower classes: the 'gentle' and the 'simple'. Armigerous status (in Latin, *armiger* means 'arms-bearer') acknowledged the exclusive right of members of the twelfth-century military élite to possess emblems by which their feudal pre-eminence might be recognised.

The extraordinarily rapid adoption of heraldry throughout western Europe in the early twelfth century was almost certainly a result of what is now known as the Twelfth-Century Renaissance. The exuberance of spirit inspired by this movement

Thirteenth-century Giffard effigy at Boyton, Wiltshire: 'Gules three Lions passant Argent a Label of five points for difference.'

expressed itself in a self-confident delight in personal adornment and visual decoration of which the adoption of heraldic symbols and colours was an obvious manifestation. Promoted by the military households (the *familia regis*) of the Angevin kings, popularised by the tournament, communicated throughout Europe by itinerant knights, minstrels and scholars, it was inevitable that the principles of heraldry should eventually be consolidated as an essential element of the law of arms.

Clearly, it was considered both convenient and desirable that an heir, on coming to his estate, should adopt the same heraldic device as his father as a symbol of familial and feudal continuity. Although there is evidence to suggest that, in northern Europe, proto-heraldic devices were often adopted by succeeding generations of the same family (on seals, for example), the emergence of an hereditary system based on the shield (in other words, armory as it is now defined) is said to date from 1127 when Henry I of England invested his son-in-law, Geoffrey Plantagenet, with a blue shield charged with gold lions. The same shield later appears on the tomb (at Salisbury Cathedral) of Geoffrey's bastard grandson, William Longespée, Earl of Salisbury (d. 1226) and the device would therefore seem to have acquired an hereditary significance.

Originally, arms were largely self-assumed by members of the knightly class, though there are examples (including that above) of their being conferred as gifts of feudal superiors or in recognition of military leadership. Arms were (and remain) personal to the armiger and he alone displayed them on his shield and lance pennon and, from the early thirteenth century, on his banner and surcoat (hence a 'gentleman of coat armour' and the term 'coat of arms'). It became necessary, therefore, to ensure that each coat was sufficiently distinctive to avoid confusion with those of men related by blood, by seignioralty or who had simply adopted similar devices from the comparatively small number of figures available at that time. The 'differencing' of arms for this purpose, and the MARSHALLING of two or more coats on one shield to signify marriage alliances, inheritance or the holding of an office to which arms appertained, became an essential (and increasingly complex) element of heraldic practice.

THE HERALDS

By the beginning of the thirteenth century, admission to the tournament was established as the prerogative of the knightly class. Heralds were attached to royal or magnatial households as advisers and emissaries and it was they who were responsible for arranging and supervising tournaments which often lasted for several days and attracted knights from all the countries of western Europe. The heralds thereby acquired an expertise which was peculiarly their own. This was concerned, not only with the management of ceremonial and protocol, but also with the ordering and recording of the personal devices used at tournaments, on seals and in warfare and, because it was they who exercised this expertise, it became known as 'heraldry'. Theirs was the motivating force which enabled heraldry to develop systematically, it was they who devised its conventions and terminology, and it was they who benefited most from the approbation of the medieval establishment (*see also* COLLEGE OF ARMS).

INTERPRETATION

At Felbrigg in Norfolk the brass of a knight and his lady provides an eloquent example of how much information may be obtained by close observation of heraldic devices (*see also* MONUMENTS). The two figures are contained within a beautiful double-arched canopy above which are five shields. The armour is of the Lancastrian period (1410–30) and, in fact, the brass dates from 1416, the year after Henry V's victory at Agincourt. There is a garter buckled below the knight's left knee and this tells us that he was a Knight of the Garter – the most prestigious medieval order of chivalry. Our knight was, therefore, a man of considerable 'worship' (influence) and must have been closely associated with the royal household and with the king himself. This is confirmed by the banner which he supports in the crook of his right arm which is emblazoned with the (attributed) arms of St. Edward the Confessor impaling the ROYAL ARMS as used in the reigns of Edward III and Richard II. This most unusual combination was adopted only by Richard II (1377–99) and the presence in this brass of the king's banner suggests that the knight was indeed in the royal service, almost certainly as the king's banner-bearer. We now need to identify the shield of arms which occupies the principal, central position above the canopy. This is an impaled shield with the arms of the husband on the left and those of his wife on the right. Identification of the husband's arms will provide us with the family name and identification of his wife's arms will enable us to determine precisely which member of that family she married. Reference to an ORDINARY OF ARMS reveals that this is a memorial to Sir Simon Felbrigge, Lord of the Manor of Felbrigg in the County of Norfolk, appointed banner-bearer to Richard II in 1395 and created a Knight Companion of the Most Noble Order of the Garter in 1397; and to his wife who was Lady-in-Waiting to Richard's first queen, Anne, daughter of the Emperor Charles IV. The rationale for the four remaining shields is now apparent: that above Sir Simon bears the arms of the king in whose service he distinguished himself, that above Lady Felbrigge is emblazoned with the Imperial arms of her former mistress; and the two lower shields are charged with the FETTERLOCK device of the Felbrigge family (*see* BADGES).

A further example is to be found in the famous Trumpington brass at Trumpington in Cambridgeshire which for many years was attributed to the first Roger de Trumpington (d. 1289). However, it was later noted that the small shields on the sword scabbard, and the arms on the ailettes (shoulderguards), were crudely engraved with a five-pointed label, the CADENCY mark of an eldest son. These, it was concluded, had been added after the original brass had been engraved and the question of dating was re-examined. It is now believed that the brass was commissioned in anticipation of death by the son of Roger I, Sir Giles de Trumpington (d. 1332), and that it was appropriated, and the arms hastily changed, for the tomb of *his* son, Roger II, who predeceased his father in *c.*1326 and whose arms were distinguished by the addition of a silver label.

Detail from the Trumpington brass at Trumpington, Cambridgeshire.

REFERENCE WORKS

Shields of arms may be identified by using an ordinary of arms which lists blazons (written descriptions) alphabetically by their principal charge. The best known is *Papworth's Ordinary of British Armorials* by J.W. Papworth, 1898 (reprinted Five Barrows, 1977). Unusual charges may be identified by reference to the illustrative index in C.N. Elvin's *A Dictionary of Heraldy* (1889), reprinted in 1977 by Heraldry Today.

Crests may be identified by reference to the illustrative index in *Fairbairn's Book of Crests of the Families of Great Britain and Ireland* by J. Fairbairn, 1905 (reprinted The Heraldic Book Company, 1983). Fairbairn also lists mottoes, as does C.N. Elvin in his *Handbook of Mottoes*, 1860 (reprinted Heraldry Today, 1986).

Blazons of arms may be obtained from works such as *The General Armory of England, Scotland, Ireland and Wales* by Sir Bernard Burke, 1842 (reprinted Heraldry Today, 1984). This is essentially a list of armorial references, by surname and alphabetical, with blazons of arms for each, together with crests, supporters and mottoes where known.

See also ACHIEVEMENT, ARMIGEROUS, ARMORIAL BEARINGS, ARMORIAL BOARDS, ARMORY, ATTRIBUTED ARMS, BARONET, BASTARDY, BEASTS (HERALDIC), BLAZON, BRASSES (MONUMENTAL), CADENCY (HERALDIC), COAT OF ARMS, COLLARS, COLLEGE OF ARMS, COLOURS (HERALDIC), CORONETS OF PEERS (*for* illustration *see* PEERAGE), CREST, CREST CORONETS, CROSSES, CYPHER, EFFIGIES, FLAGS, FUNERAL HERALDRY, HATCHMENTS, HELMETS (HERALDIC), HERALDIC CHARGES, HERALDRY (ECCLESIASTICAL), KNIGHT BACHELOR, KNIGHT BANNERET, KNIGHTHOOD (ORDERS OF), KNOTS, LIVERY AND MAINTENANCE, MANTLING, MARSHALLING, MONUMENTS, MOTTOES, ORDINARY OF ARMS, PEERAGE, PLATE (CHURCH PLATE), POINTS OF THE SHIELD, REBUS, ROYAL ARMS, SEALS, SEIZE QUARTIERS, SHIELDS, STAINED GLASS, SUPPORTERS, TRICK, VISITATIONS (HERALDIC) *and* WREATH

See APPENDIX II *for* addresses of heraldry societies etc.

Further reading:

Friar, S., *A New Dictionary of Heraldry*, Sherborne and London, 1987

——, *Heraldry for the Local Historian and Genealogist*, Stroud, 1992

Friar, S. and Ferguson, J., *Basic Heraldry*, London, 1993

Platts, B., *The Origins of Heraldry*, London, 1980 *

Wood, A., *Heraldry, Art and Design*, Crayford, 1996

Above: Archbishopric of Canterbury. Archbishopric of York; below: Arms of Office: George Law, Bishop of Bath and Wells.

HERALDRY (ECCLESIASTICAL) The Lords Spiritual are armigerous as are their sees and the chapters and bodies corporate of cathedrals and major abbeys. Sherborne Abbey in Dorset, now a parish church, continues to use the arms of its medieval foundation (a silver cross and golden crozier on a red field), for example.

In the Middle Ages, archbishops, bishops and royal abbots were tenants in chief and held baronies. They were ecclesiastical magnates, responsible for the administration of vast estates, and held office as privy advisers in the King's Council (*Curia Regis*). Many accomplished clerics were elevated to the great Offices of State and their services rewarded with the emoluments of a bishopric – a device by which the Crown was spared the payment of a substantial pension. Bishops were addressed as 'My Lord', as they are today, and many of them were also warriors wielding, not the sword (which drew blood), but the mace (which, apparently, did not!). Their offices, and those of the senior pre-Reformation abbots, generated huge numbers of documents all of which required SEALS by which they were authenticated. Ecclesiastical seals are generally oval in shape and, by the thirteenth century, were predominantly heraldic. Religious motifs from early seals were often incorporated into coats of arms: the elaborate, enthroned figure of Christ in the arms of the See of Chester, for example, first appeared in a seal of Bishop Sigefrid (1180–1204).

BISHOPS AND ARCHBISHOPS

All Anglican bishops use a MITRE instead of a CREST in their coats of arms, and sometimes crossed croziers are depicted behind the shield. During their terms of office diocesan bishops impale their personal arms (on the sinister side) with those of their see but on translation to another bishopric the impaled arms of office are changed accordingly. The arms of the Archbishopric of Canterbury, which date from *c.* 1350, are charged with a white *pallium* on which four *crosses fitchy* [pointed at the foot] represent the pins by which it was attached to the vestment. Behind the *pallium* is a gold archiepiscopal staff and the background of the shield is blue. The earliest arms of the Archbishopric of York are of a similar design but with a red field, and these may occasionally be found on monuments. The present arms, which date from *c.* 1398, are red with silver cross keys (the Minster is dedicated to St. Peter) and a gold imperial crown which probably evolved from the papal tiara.

Impaled personal and diocesan arms are invaluable when attempting to establish how long a

Montagu heraldry in the west door of Bath Abbey commemorates James Montagu, Bishop of Bath and Wells 1608–16 and of Winchester 1616–18. The arms of office (top left) are those of the See of Winchester. The great oak doors were given to the Abbey by Lord Chief Justice Sir Henry Montagu in 1616.

Above: Arms of the Prince Bishops of Durham;
below: Arms and ecclesiastical hat of Cardinal
Newman.

particular incumbent held office, especially when they appear on seals, the use of which can provide precise dating. They will also be found on the tombs of bishops and abbots most of whom were buried in their cathedrals and abbey churches. Although, before the Reformation, most bishops were elected by chapter, it was usual for the Pope to confirm the appointment of a king's nominee. One effect of this system was that prominent members of the royal household were frequently appointed as bishops and members of the *curia regis*. The extraordinary influence of these few families, in matters ecclesiastical and secular, is evident in the ubiquity of their personal arms alongside those of the offices which they held.

Unique among the Lords Spiritual were the prince bishops of Durham who were appointed by the king as counts palatine, head of church and state in a vast territory which included St. Cuthbert's seventh century bishopric of Lindisfarne. The PALATINATE was effectively a kingdom within a kingdom and, as defenders of the realm in the north, the prince bishops were charged with the defence of the Scottish border and maintained a standing army. The (circular) Great Seal of the prince bishops had, on the obverse, an enthroned figure of a bishop and on the reverse the bishop as an equestrian figure in full armour. By the fourteenth century the Palatinate was at the height of its military power and its warrior-bishops are uniquely commemorated in the ducally-gorged mitre and crossed sword and crozier in the arms of all subsequent bishops of Durham.

ECCLESIASTICAL HATS

Cardinals, who belonged to the highest ecclesiastical rank (and were sometimes referred to as 'old red hat'), displayed above their arms a scarlet *ecclesiastical hat*: a domed hat of felt with a wide brim from which depend cords, interlaced with gold thread, and tassels. These hats, which were worn by cardinals for official engagements, were instituted by Pope Innocent IV in the thirteenth century.

RECTORS

The arms of rectors will often be found in churches, but the term does not necessarily imply an individual. A rector was originally an incumbent who received the 'Great Tithes': all the customary offerings and dues of his parish. But in many instances benefices were annexed by corporate bodies, such as monastic or collegiate foundations, many of which were armigerous.

DIOCESES AND CATHEDRAL CHAPTERS

Both dioceses and cathedral chapters have their own arms and, although they may allude one to the other, they are not the same. The arms of the Dean and Chapter of Hereford Cathedral, for example, are *Or five Chevronels Gules* (five red chevrons on gold) – a reference to the Clare earls of Hereford before 1313 who bore three red chevrons on gold – while the arms of the bishopric of Hereford are entirely different (see below).

INTERPRETATION

Ecclesiastical heraldry is distinctive for the manner in which colours and devices are frequently used to reflect religious concepts. As one might expect, the symbol of the cross is commonly found in ecclesiastical heraldry, though by no means exclusively so (*see* CROSSES). References to saints are common: the escallop shell in the arms of Rochester, for example, was the device of St Augustine, who founded the cathedral in 604, while the *saltire* on which it is placed is the familiar 'cross of St Andrew' to whom the church is dedicated.

Many diocesan arms contain local allusions: those of Birmingham (granted in 1906) for instance, are divided *per pale indented* (vertically by an indented line) and refer to the nineteenth-century arms of the City of Birmingham which, in turn, were based on the arms of the medieval De Bermingham family. Similarly, the arms of the diocese of Truro include, on a black border, the fifteen *bezants* (gold roundels) of the Duchy of Cornwall.

Several diocesan arms contain references to the personal devices of former abbots or bishops. Those of the See of Hereford, for instance, are derived from the arms of Thomas de Cantelope who was bishop from 1275 to 1282. The bishop's personal arms were *Azure* (blue) *three Leopard's Faces inverted jessant-de-lis Gold* (upside down and with fleurs-de-lis projecting from their mouths) but, in the diocesan arms, the field was changed to *Gules* (red).

Composite arms are of particular interest: those of Lincoln College, Oxford, for example, refer to the college's history. They are *tierced in pale* (divided vertically into three) with the arms of the founder, Richard Fleming (1427), to the left and those of Thomas Scott (*alias* Rotherham), who re-endowed the College in the late fifteenth century, to the right. Both men were bishops of Lincoln and the diocesan arms are depicted between those of the two benefactors.
See also CLERGY (CHURCH OF ENGLAND)

HERALDS' VISITATIONS *see* VISITATIONS, HERALDS

HERESY The formal denial of the authorised teaching of the Church. The Roman Catholic Church distinguished between 'formal heresy' (the wilful denial of doctrine by a baptised person) and 'material heresy' (adherence to heretical beliefs 'in good faith'), the former being a sin and subject to possible EXCOMMUNICATION.

HERMIT From the Old French *ermite*, the popular perception of the medieval hermit is one of a solitary (*eremitical*), religious recluse. But unlike an ANCHORITE or COENOBITE, a hermit was committed to public service as a guide, ferryman or river pilot, providing frugal hospitality and shelter to travellers (*see* CHAPELS *and* HERMITAGE).

Hermits, anchorites and ceonobites were a characteristic feature of the Celtic Church and were invariably referred to as saints. The Cornish saints Nectan and Endellion, for example, were but two of a remarkable brood of twenty-four children fathered by a sixth-century Welsh chieftain. All became hermits or anchorites and all died as martyrs or confessors for the faith, while their father, Brychan, was also celebrated as a saint in the Celtic traditions of Cornwall and Devon (the ancient kingdom of Dumnonia). In the church of St. Neot in Cornwall there is a window depicting St. Brychan enfolding in his lap ten of his hermitical progeny.

Welsh hermits lived either individually, as did Wechelen, the hermit of Llowes in Elfael, or in communities as did the culdees of Beddgelert (Gwynedd), Ynys Lannog (Priestholm in Anglesey) and Enlli (Bardsey Island). Welsh law accorded special status to such men (*diofrydogion*), not dissimilar to that of holy men and anchorites in other societies. Even Gerald of Wales conceded that '. . . nowhere will you find hermits and anchorites of greater spirituality than in Wales.'

At Partrishow in Powys, a grille in the west wall of the church of Merthyr Issui at Patricio overlooks an ancient, narrow chapel – the site of a cell built by the Celtic St. Issui, a hermit who was murdered by one of his guests and who worked various healing miracles after his death.
See also CHRISTIAN SYMBOLS

HERMITAGE Many of the sites to which the term 'hermitage' is traditionally ascribed were in fact ANCHORAGES or the cells of solitary CEONOBITES and religious mystics. Because of the nature of the hermits' calling, most hermitages were located in the vicinity of routeways: at bridges, fords, ferries and causeways, and where tracks entered inhospitable country. The buildings themselves were not necessarily insubstantial, indeed some were subsidiary houses of monastic foundations. Many hermitages were created within rock piles or out of natural caves, such as the twelfth-century chambers of Blackstone Rock above the river Severn at Bewdley in Worcestershire. Some hermitages incorporated a small CHAPEL and accommodation for travellers. Perhaps the best example is the fourteenth-century two-storey hermitage of the Holy Trinity, cut into a sandstone cliff above the river Coquet at Warkworth in Northumberland. This comprises a sacristy and small chapel within the rock to which a hall, kitchen and solar were added in masonry. There is evidence that the hermit kept a small farm and orchard above the cliff. Place-names, such as Armitage in Staffordshire, may be indicative of former hermitages. But place-names can be misleading: in the twelfth century, the hamlet of Hermitage in Dorset was known as Rocombe and the 'hermitage' was a minor Augustinian priory.

During the eighteenth and nineteenth centuries, neo-Gothic 'hermitages' added to the romanticism of several landscaped parks, perhaps the best example being that at Fonthill Park in Wiltshire. The 'Hermit's Sanctuary' in the woods of Burley House in Leicestershire was the home of a nineteenth-century hermit, employed by the Earl of Nottingham for the delectation of his guests. At Longleat in Wiltshire, a hermit was dismissed when he failed to make his customary appearance before Lord Bath's house-party and was later found to be drunk at the local inn.

HERRINGBONE A decorative zig-zag pattern in a wall or floor, similar in appearance to the bones of a herring, formed by alternate rows of diagonally laid stones, bricks or tiles.

HERSE *see* HEARSE

HETERODOXY Heretical opinion as opposed to conventional belief.

HIGH ALTAR The principal altar of a church, usually located at the east end.
See also ALTARS

HIGH CHURCH First used in England in 1703 to describe the Church party which insisted upon the enforcement of laws against the DISSENTERS. Since the early nineteenth century it has chiefly referred to the ANGLO-CATHOLIC wing within the Church of England which stresses historical continuity with Catholic Christianity and thereby upholds the 'high' conception of the episcopate and of the nature of the Sacraments.
See also ANGLICANISM, LOW CHURCH *and* OXFORD MOVEMENT

HIGH MASS *see* MASS

HIGHWAYS *see* FOOTPATHS AND BRIDLE-WAYS

HILARY The education and law term beginning in January near the feast day of St. Hilary on 13 January (14 January in the Roman Catholic calendar). St. Hilary (*c.* 315–*c.* 367) was Bishop of Poitiers and the leading Latin theologian of his age.
See also MICHAELMAS *and* TRINITY

HINGES *see* DOORS AND DOORWAYS

HIP The external angle made by the conjunction of two sloping surfaces.

HIPPED ROOF A roof with sloping ends instead of gables (*see* GABLE *and* ROOFS).

HISTORIATED INITIAL In documents, an initial capital letter within which is an illustration, usually associated with the text.

HISTORICAL DEVELOPMENT OF THE CHURCH *see* ANGLO-SAXON CHURCH, CELTIC CHURCH, MONASTICISM, MEDIEVAL CHURCH, REFORMATION, CHURCH OF ENGLAND, SEVENTEENTH-CENTURY CHURCH, EIGHTEENTH-CENTURY CHURCH, NINE-TEENTH-CENTURY CHURCH, TWENTIETH-CENTURY CHURCHES *and* WALES, THE MEDIEVAL CHURCH IN

HOCK-TIDE The second Monday and Tuesday following EASTER which, from the twelfth century, were public holidays. Rent Days, when quarterly or half-yearly rents were paid, usually fell on the QUARTER DAYS. But in many areas, half-yearly tenancies were renewed on MICHAELMAS and Hock Tuesday and anyone who was subject to Hock-tide payments was said to be 'in hock'. On these days, it was also the custom for young men to seek out young women and to bind them lightly with cords, release being obtained on payment of a 'toll' which was handed over to the churchwardens. In many parishes the traditional 'binding' rituals lasted into the eighteenth century.
See also CHURCH AND COMMUNITY *and* FESTIVALS AND SOCIAL CUSTOMS

HOGANS, HOGGELLS, HOGGLERS, HOGNELLS *and* HOGNERS *see* CHURCH AND COMMUNITY

HOLIDAYS *see* CHURCH ALES, CHURCH AND COMMUNITY, CHURCHWARDENS, CHURCH-WARDENS' ACCOUNTS, CHURCHYARDS, FAIRS AND MARKETS, FEAST DAYS (FIXED AND MOVABLE), FESTIVALS AND LOCAL CUSTOMS, HOCK-TIDE *and* PLAISTOW

HOLLOW WAY Commonly found in the vicinity of rural churches, hollow ways are lengths of sunken track, usually on sloping ground, worn into soft rock such as chalk or limestone by the constant passage of cattle, pack-horses, tranters' wagons and other traffic. Many ancient hollow ways are still used for driving farm animals and by ramblers and local pedestrians, while others have been abandoned following the creation of alternative routes such as turnpike and enclosure roads or the re-siting of a bridge.
See also FOOTPATHS AND BRIDLEWAYS

HOLOGRAPH A manuscript written entirely in the author's own handwriting.

HOLY COMMUNION *see* EUCHARIST *and* MASS

HOLY CROSS DAY (*also* HOLY ROOD DAY *and* ROODMAS DAY) The Exaltation of the Holy Cross, observed on 14 September to commemorate the exposition in 629 of the (supposed) true Cross at Jerusalem following its recovery from the Persians.
See also FEAST DAYS (FIXED AND MOVABLE)

HOLY GRAIL *see* GRAIL, THE HOLY

HOLY INNOCENTS' DAY (*also* CHILDERMAS) Observed on 28 December to commemorate Herod's slaying of the infants of Bethlehem (Matthew 2: 16–18).

HOLY LOAF Bread which has been blessed but not consecrated. The Holy Loaf was distributed among parishioners in the chancel following Mass as a sign of fellowship.

HOLY OILS *see* CHRISM, CHRISMATORY, PLATE *and* UNCTION

HOLY ORDERS A 'clerk in holy orders' is one who belongs to the higher grades (*major orders*) of

the Christian ministry: a bishop, priest or deacon.
See also MAJOR ORDERS, MINOR ORDERS *and* PRIEST

HOLY ROOD DAY *see* HOLY CROSS DAY

HOLY SATURDAY The day before Easter Sunday on which is commemorated the resting of Christ's body in the tomb.
See also EASTER *and* LENT

HOLY SEE The papal bishopric of Rome.

HOLY WATER Water which has been blessed for religious purposes, and to which small quantities of salt may have been added. In the Church, water represented life and purity. Holy water was a 'sacramental': matter which could effect the assimilation of religious truths.
See also ASPERGES, BAPTISM *and* HOLY WATER STOUP

HOLY WATER SPRINKLER *see* ASPERGES

HOLY WATER STOUP A receptacle for holding HOLY WATER, usually a stone basin set into a niche or stocle (plinth) near the church door (*see* PORCHES). Those entering the church would sign their bodies with holy water from the stoup as an act of self-consecration and spiritual cleansing. Stoups, which have no drain, were replenished regularly with holy water, which was mixed with salt, exorcised and blessed. Plinths were often ornately carved: that at Caldecote in Hertfordshire, for example, which also has an elaborate canopy. The word is correctly *stop*, meaning a pail or basin, and the practice was suppressed following the Reformation.

HOLY WEEK The week before EASTER, observed as a period of devotion to Christ's Passion.
See also HEARSE, GOOD FRIDAY, HOLY SATURDAY, MAUNDY THURSDAY, PALM SUNDAY *and* SPY WEDNESDAY

HOLY WELLS Places where water wells from the ground have always been venerated as sources of life: hence their almost invariable female dedication. The Neolithic practice of casting precious and sacrificial offerings into rivers and meres was, in some cultures, maintained well into the Iron Age and is even echoed in the Arthurian legends. SPRINGS were identified with Iron Age deities who possessed powers of healing and could foretell the future. In Celtic society the after-life was often portrayed as being beneath or beyond the water, while islands were regarded as the last refuges of the dead.

With the gradual introduction of Christianity into Britain, the worshipping of pagan water gods was repeatedly forbidden, but pragmatism prevailed and numerous sacred wells were re-dedicated to Christian saints so that the populace could continue to benefit from their supposed restorative properties. Particularly popular were the saints Agnes, Anne and Helen, the last two probably substituted for the Celtic goddesses Annis and Elen, and in Cornwall alone there are more than one hundred holy wells, many of them bearing the names of local missionary-saints. Medieval holy wells often provided a source of revenue for local religious and monastic foundations. Some were consecrated for baptismal purposes while others established reputations for healing specific ailments: St. Cynhafel's well near Denbigh was believed to cure warts, for example. Many were established as curative centres, complete with reservoirs, well-houses and ancillary chapels, and attracted pilgrims who lodged at their hospices.

St. Winefride's Well, at Holywell near Flint, has been described as one of the 'Seven Wonders of Wales' and is still the site of an annual open-air celebration of the Mass. Winefride was a local princess, niece of the hermit St. Beuno who built a chapel on the site in the early seventh century. When Prince Caradoc tried to seduce her, Winefride ran to her uncle's chapel for sanctuary but was decapitated in the attempt. A spring of water burst out of the ground and St. Beuno, hearing the commotion, hurried from his chapel and picked up his niece's head. He washed it in the spring and placed it back on her shoulders – and she lived on, to become an abbess and to die peacefully in *c.* 650. The dark, bubbling waters of the little well, in its ornate crypt beneath the hillside chapel (endowed by Lady Margaret Beaufort in 1490), has been a place of pilgrimage since the Middle Ages. It is but one of an estimated 1,000 sacred wells in Wales and there are probably a further 1,000 in England and Scotland, though many are little more than nettle-covered holes in the ground with little sign of the stone structures which often surrounded them.

With the Reformation holy wells were deprived of their saintly attributes but continued to attract those who wished to 'take the waters'. The curative properties of natural springs were first investigated scientifically during the seventeenth and eighteenth centuries and this led to the discovery of several new wells or 'spas': a term suitably devoid of religious connotations, derived from the sulphur springs at Spa near Liège. Several holy wells continue to be 'venerated'. At Bisley in the Gloucestershire Cotswolds, for example, and at Tissington, one of several villages in the Derbyshire Peak District where the wells are 'dressed' each year with religious pictures composed of natural objects impressed into clay panels, a tradition dating from the eighteenth century but probably of pagan origin.

PLACE-NAMES

The Old English *well, wiell* or *wæll* meaning 'well', 'spring' or 'stream', is commonly found in place-names, often as a second element to variants of 'Holy-', suggesting the site of a holy well. But the cult of the water gods was not a prominent one during the Saxon period and many 'holywells' have a different meaning or date from a later time. In Lincolnshire, the first element of Holywell is the Old English *hæl,* meaning 'omen', so that the name translates as 'wishing well'; and whereas Holwell near Weymouth in Dorset means 'holy spring or stream' another Holwell, near Sherborne in the same county, is said to derive its name from the Old English *holh* meaning 'hollow' and *walu*, meaning 'a ridge of earth or stone' which accurately describes the topography of the original settlement. Nevertheless, there is a 'well of unknown period' recorded in the county listings of archaeological sites and this, with its flight of steps, is still in evidence at Holwell today.

Cripplegate place-names are often associated with springs and wells, the waters of which were reputed to possess curative properties. A chapel (1807) at Cripplestyle, near Cranborne in Dorset, marks the place where medieval pilgrims rested before embarking on the final stage of their journey to nearby Holywell. Until recently, the annual spring-cleaning of the chapel was an occasion for festivities and an outdoor service held on Whit Thursday: 'Friends gathered from every direction . . . some years nearly a thousand were present'.

HONOUR POINT *see* POINTS OF THE SHIELD

HOOD-MOULD *see* DRIPSTONE

HOPTON WOOD STONE A grey, Derbyshire limestone used especially in highly polished floors.

HORARIUM The daily round of a Christian community, governed by observance of the Canonical Hours (*see* HOURS, CANONICAL). The horarium varied in different religious orders and according to the time of year, there being different timetables for summer and winter. At the Benedictine monastery of Canterbury, the winter horarium in the late eleventh century consisted of eight hours of services (*office*), three hours of reading and (at most) four hours of work:

2.30	Rise. Prayers with psalms. NOCTURNS and prayers for the royal house. MATTINS and Lauds of the dead. Mattins of All saints.
5.00–6.00	Reading.
6.00–6.45	LAUDS. Psalms and prayers for the royal house. Anthems.
6.45	PRIME. Seven penitential psalms. Litany of the saints.
7.30–8.00	Reading.
8.00	Seven psalms. TERCE. Psalms for the royal house. Chapter or Morrow Mass. Chapter meeting followed by psalms for the dead.
9.45–12.00	Work.
12.00	SEXT. Psalms and prayers for relatives etc. High Mass.
1.30	NONE. Psalms and prayers for relatives etc.
2.00	Dinner.
2.45–4.30	Reading or work.
4.30	VESPERS. Psalms and anthems. Vespers of All Saints. Vespers of the dead.
5.30	Reading.
6.15	COMPLINE. Psalms.
6.30	Retire.

See also MONASTICISM

HORN-BOOKS From the sixteenth century to the eighteenth, a page of reading matter was often placed between two thin sheets of (transparent) horn and the whole clamped within a wooden frame with a handle. Known as 'horn-books' they were used for instructional purposes and may occasionally be found to contain a church guide today, though the horn will usually have been replaced by Perspex.

HORNED HEADDRESS *see* COSTUME

HORSE BLOCKS, HORSE STEPS *and* **HORSE STONES** *see* UPPING STOCKS

HOSPICE (*HOSPITIUM*) A lodging for travellers, especially one maintained by a religious order. Hospices were usually located in the outer precinct of a monastery or friary and were sometimes administered independently. They provided a chapel for worship, a FRATER where meals were taken and a DORTER in which to sleep. Some university colleges originated as hospices or 'halls', supervised by a warden or master.
See also ALMSHOUSES, GUEST HOUSE, HOSPITALS *and* INFIRMARY

HOSPITALLER, KNIGHTS *see* ST. JOHN OF JERUSALEM, ORDER OF *and* COMMANDERY

HOSPITALS Also known as *mallardies* and *masendews* (a corruption of *Maison Dieu*), medieval hospitals were charitable institutions, founded by religious houses, GUILDS and private individuals or groups of benefactors, and were concerned as much with housing the elderly and infirm as tending the sick (*see also* ALMSHOUSES). The majority of hospices were established as a form of CHANTRY where the residents were required to pray for the souls of those on whose charity they depended. Some served the needs of specific groups of people such as pilgrims (*see also* HOSPICE) and lepers (*lazar-houses*). Typically, the Leper Hospital of St. Margaret and St. Antony at Wimborne in Dorset was founded in the thirteenth century, encouraged by the Pope who granted an indulgence of a year to anyone who contributed to its building or to its maintenance. Christ's Hospital in London was founded by Edward VI (1547–53) on the site of the Grey Friars, originally as a foundling hospital (for deserted and illegitimate children) though it soon became the famous Blue Coat School. There were also monastic hospices (*see also* INFIRMARY), but most of these were dissolved following the Dissolution of the Monasteries in 1536/9, St. Bartholomew's ('Bart's'), St. Thomas's and the Bethlehem hospital for the insane ('Bedlam') being notable exceptions which were refounded under lay control.

See also ALMONRY, AUGUSTINIANS, BEDE-HOUSE, CHARITIES, GUEST HOUSE *and* PRECEPTORY

Further reading:

Prescott, E., *English Medieval Hospitals*, London, 1992

HOST The consecrated wafer of the EUCHARIST (*see also* RESERVATION).

HOSTELLER In a religious house, the guest-master or his assistant who was responsible for the administration of the HOSPICE, GUEST HOUSE or ALMONRY.

HOUPPELANDE *see* COSTUME

HOUR GLASSES *see* PULPITS

HOURS, CANONICAL (i) The services (*canonical offices*) appointed to be said (or sung) at specified hours according to the BREVIARY. The day hours were PRIME, TERCE, SEXT, NONE, VESPERS and COMPLINE while the night hours were NOCTURNS or MATTINS followed by LAUDS at dawn. To the Canonical Hours, which came to be known as the Great Hours, were added various commemorative and festive services, prescribed private prayers and a daily service in the CHAPTER HOUSE, following Prime, called *Pretiosa* at which prayers were said for 'departed brethren' and benefactors.

See also CLOCKS, DIVINE OFFICE, HORARIUM *and* MONASTICISM

(ii) The hours wherein marriage may take place in an English parish church: formerly 8.00 a.m. to 12 noon, these were extended in 1886 to 3.00 p.m. and in 1934 to 6.00 p.m.

HOUSEL A medieval English name for the EUCHARIST. A long 'houseling cloth' of white linen was held in front of (or sometimes by) communicants as they received the Sacrament. Such cloths are still used at a very small number of churches (usually to cover the top of a HOUSELING BENCH), notably at Wimborne Minster in Dorset. In the Middle Ages, to die 'unhouseled' was to die without receiving the Sacrament.

HOUSELING BENCHES Long wooden flat-topped 'stools' used as communion rails and sometimes with a kneeler along one side.

HOUSELING BREAD The small wafers used at communion.

HOUSELING CLOTH *see* HOUSEL

HOUSELING PEOPLE Parishioners who are of sufficient age to take communion.

HOUSE (RELIGIOUS) A religious community of men was a monastery; of women a nunnery; of either, a convent; of friars, a friary; of Knights Templar, a commandery and of Knights Hospitaller, a preceptory. The terms abbey and priory denote rank: an abbey was of superior status to a priory, though there are exceptions. All Cluniac houses were dependencies of Cluny and, therefore, priories. Carthusian houses and those of regular canons are usually priories, while large Benedictine abbeys to which cathedrals are attached are usually called cathedral priories because they are administered by a prior, a bishop being the titular abbot.

HOUSE ROW Any parochial system of rotation among the inhabitants e.g. for the appointment of parish officers.

HUDD *see* GRAVESIDE SHELTERS

HUGUENOT A member of the Calvinistic French Protestants who were in constant conflict with the Roman Catholic majority throughout the latter part of the sixteenth century. Of disputed origin, the term was in popular use by 1560 and came to include also Protestant refugees from Spanish persecution in the Low Countries. Calvinistic French communities increased rapidly following a synod held in 1559 but a series of internal religious wars, culminating in the Massacre of Bartholomew in 1572, caused many Huguenots to flee to Protestant countries, including England. The *Edict of Nantes* of 1598 provided for religious and political freedom, but the Catholic Church in France maintained its pressure against the

Huguenots and in 1685 Louis XIV revoked the *Edict*, forcing many to apostatise or flee from France. Those who came to England were required to apply for either naturalisation or denization. Most became members of the numerous Huguenot churches in England and subsequently many French surnames have become anglicised or even translated. *For* The Huguenot Society *see* APPENDIX II.

HUMANISM (i) Belief in the human nature of Christ. (ii) The cultural movement of the Renaissance which turned away from medieval scholasticism and its preoccupation with theology.

HUMERAL VEIL *see* VEILS

HUSK CHAIN A motif in plaster, wood or stone consisting of looped chains of barley or corn husks (*see* DECORATIVE MOTIFS).

HYMNAL A collection of HYMNS, usually in the form of a book.

HYMNARY A medieval book containing the metrical hymns of the DIVINE OFFICE arranged according to the liturgical year.

HYMN BOARDS Wooden display boards, usually mounted on the pillars of the chancel arch. A hymn board consists of a framework into which numbered cards are inserted to denote the hymns and psalms to be sung during a service.

HYMNS From the Greek *hymnos* meaning 'song of praise', a hymn is a song used in Christian worship. St. Augustine defined a hymn as 'the praise of God by singing', to which might be added '. . . by a congregation'. Hymns are characterised by non-biblical texts in metrical and stanzaic form. Hymnody in the Church derives from the singing of psalms in the Hebrew Temple. It developed systematically following the legalisation of Christianity by the Emperor Constantine in 313, notably in the Byzantine Church. In the West, during the second half of the fourth century, St. Hilary of Poitiers composed a book of hymn texts (*c.* 360) and St. Ambrose of Milan instituted the congregational singing of psalms and hymns. These early hymns, which were sung to simple 'folk' melodies, derived from contemporary Christian Latin poetry. Hymns were a fixed part of the Benedictine monastic office, though they were not generally used in the Roman liturgy until the thirteenth century. By the late fifteenth century, liturgical music was sung by trained choirs (*see also* CHURCH MUSIC, ANGLICAN) though congregational singing was re-established by the Lutheran Church in Germany at the Reformation. The early German hymn melody (*chorale*) was unharmonised and unaccompanied,

though harmonised versions, used by combinations of congregation, choir and organ, appeared later. While some were new compositions, others drew on a variety of plainsong, vernacular and secular sources. Important early collections of hymn texts include those of Martin Luther (1524), Johann Gottfried Walther (1524) and George Rhau (1544). French, Scottish and English Calvinism later promoted the singing of metrical translations of the PSALMS, unaccompanied and in unison. The English psalter used only a few metres, while the common metre 8–6–8–6 (representing the number of syllables in each line) remains the archetypal English hymn metre.

The Congregationalist hymn writer Isaac Watts (1674–1748) provided the impetus for the development of English hymnody in the late seventeenth century. His *Horae Lyricae* (1706), *Hymns and Spiritual Songs* (1709) and *Psalms of David Imitated* (1719) included such well-known hymns as 'Jesus shall reign where'er the sun', 'When I survey the wondrous cross' and 'O God, our help in ages past'. The evangelical revival of the mid-eighteenth century under John Wesley (1703–91) and Charles Wesley (1707–88), the founders of Methodism, finally established hymnody in England, Charles Wesley's poems employing a variety of experimental metres and John Wesley's translations introducing a number of fine German hymns.

The Church of England officially recognised hymn singing in 1820 following a controversy concerning the singing of hymns at a Sheffield church. The OXFORD MOVEMENT stimulated new compositions, the use of plainsong melodies and translations of medieval hymns. *Hymns Ancient and Modern*, edited by H. W. Baker (1821–77) in 1861 (and subsequently revised on many occasions) incorporated many of the traditional office hymns and was characterised by an austerity of style and conformity to the *Book of Common Prayer* (*see* COMMON PRAYER, BOOK OF). Two influential collections which were published at the turn of the century were the *Yattendon Hymnal* (1899), compiled by the poet Robert Bridges (1844–1930) and *The English Hymnal* (1906), edited by Percy Dearmer and the composer Ralph Vaughan Williams (1872–1958), which contains many plainsong and traditional folk melodies. *Songs of Praise* (Vaughan Williams and Martin Shaw), first published in 1925, was a 'national' hymnal intended for use by Christians of all denominations. Theologically, it was markedly liberal, even more so in the second edition published in 1931. Since that time numerous hymnals have appeared, few of them succeeding in rising above the banal. Perhaps the most widely used is *Come and Praise*, a BBC hymnal for primary schools which contains several (somewhat enigmatic) songs by the admirable Sidney Carter.

I

ICHTHUS The Greek for 'fish', composed of the initial letters of 'Jesus Christ, Son of God, Saviour' (*see also* FISH).

ICONOCLASM The antithesis of the veneration of images. An *iconoclast* is one who destroys or defaces religious images.

ICONOGRAPHY *see* CHRISTIAN SYMBOLS

IHS A MONOGRAM formed by abbreviating the Greek word for Jesus (*see* CHRISTIAN SYMBOLS).

ILLEGITIMACY *see* BASTARDY

ILLUMINATION, MANUSCRIPT *see* MANUSCRIPT ILLUMINATION

IMBREX *see* TILES

IMBRICATED Overlapping. An architectural term applied to (e.g.) tiles or decorative motifs. In HERALDRY an imbrication is a charge added as a mark of CADENCY or AUGMENTATION OF HONOUR.

IMMACULATE CONCEPTION OF THE BLESSED VIRGIN MARY, THE The dogma that 'from the first moment of her conception the Blessed Virgin Mary was . . . kept free from all stain of original sin' was a matter of dispute throughout the medieval period. The feast day (8 December) was officially recognised by the Church in 1476.
See also MARY, THE BLESSED VIRGIN

IMMERSION *see* AFFUSION, ASPERSION *and* BAPTISM

IMPALEMENT In HERALDRY, the vertical division of a shield to incorporate two different coats of arms: the husband's (or that of an office such as a bishopric) to the dexter (the left when viewed from the front) and the wife's (or that of the holder of the office) to the sinister (the right).
See also MARSHALLING

IMPOST A wall bracket on which rests the end of an arch.

IMPROPRIATION The annexation or assignment of an ecclesiastical benefice to a lay proprietor or body corporate. When, as a consequence of the DISSOLUTION OF THE MONASTERIES, many benefices which had formerly been appropriated to monastic houses passed to LAY RECTORS, it became necessary for 'perpetual curates' to be appointed in order to undertake the duties of impropriated benefices (*see* PERPETUAL CURATE).
See also APPROPRIATION

INCENSE A spice or gum which gives off a sweet smell when burning. The smoke of incense symbolises prayer. In the western Church, incense has been used since the sixth century for ceremonial purposes though the legality of its use in the Church of England has long been a matter of dispute.

INCENSE BOAT A boat-shaped dish with a hinged lid in which incense is kept.

INCIPIT The opening words of a text.

INCISED SLABS Among the earliest examples in Britain of these engraved stone MEMORIALS is a collection of over two hundred, dating from the eighth to the tenth centuries, at Clonmacnois in Ireland. But it was during the period from the eleventh century to the mid-fourteenth century that coffin-shaped slabs, usually incised with a simple cross (*cross-slabs*), became numerous. These were usually of hard sandstone, though there were regional variations: Purbeck and other marbles in the south of England, gritstone in Derbyshire and Northumberland, and Bath and Ham stone in the south-west, for example. In the western Highlands of Scotland a vigorous Celtic school developed using mica-schist and by the Reformation alabaster was widely used in the English midlands. Human figures first appeared in the twelfth century. These were often of priests though there were also early military figures, such as that of a knight at Sollers Hope in Herefordshire. Unlike brasses (*see* BRASSES (MONUMENTAL)) and EFFIGIES, British incised slabs rarely depict heraldic figures, most armorial display being confined to coats of arms or small shields. One of the earliest heraldic slabs, at Gilling-on-Rydale in Yorkshire, is incised with a cross, gauntlets and a shield of arms. There are occasional examples of heraldic figures, such as those of Sir Johan de Botiler (*c.* 1285) at St. Brides Major in West Glamorgan and of John Foljambe (d. 1499 monument *c.* 1515) at Sutton Scarsdale, Derbyshire. In the Foljambe memorial the figure is depicted in full armour and emblazoned tabard, with the head resting on a crested helmet and the feet on a chatloup, a chimerical creature granted to the family as a badge in 1513 (*see* BADGES). Such slabs, which were almost invariably laid in the church floor, were clearly liable to excessive wear and many were eventually lifted and set upright against a wall or raised onto a plinth. An even greater number have been lost or their detail defaced. Some incised slabs may have been embellished with inlaid materials, especially those imported from the Low Countries. Regrettably, little remains of the pitch and painted lead (and occasionally copper or enamel) with which the figures were coloured.

During the seventeenth century incised slabs, depicting full-length figures, were replaced by *ledger stones.* These were usually of black marble (*see* TOUCH) or local stone such as slate and bore a simple but finely carved inscription and a deeply incised roundel containing a coat of arms or other device (*for* dating *see* SHIELDS). Ledger stones, which remained popular to the mid-nineteenth century, are indicative of intramural burials (*see* VAULTS (BURIAL)). They are the capping stones of brick-lined burial shafts which could accommodate up to six coffins stacked one above the other and separated by horizontal iron bars. Consequently, a ledger stone may have been chipped at the edges when raised with crowbars for the reception of further deposits. A number of ledger stones may also be found on TOMB CHESTS and TABLE TOMBS. Many East Anglian churches contain particularly good examples of finely executed and engraved ledger stones and there is a notable collection at Holy Trinity church in Hull, Humberside.
Further reading:
Greenhill, F., *Incised Effigial Slabs* (2 Vols.), London, 1976

Ledger stone at Swanton Morley, Suffolk.

INCORRUPT Unaffected by decay.

INCREASE Profit on the church 'stock' lent by churchwardens to GUILDS and other parochial organisations.

INCUBATION Of pagan origin, the practice of sleeping in a church, or within the precinct of a church, in anticipation of experiencing a divine revelation or of being cured of disease. Inevitably, certain churches acquired reputations for efficacious incubation.

INCUMBENT The holder of an office. In the present context, the holder of a BENEFICE: a RECTOR, a VICAR or (until 1968) a PERPETUAL CURATE. An incumbent was customarily chairman of the VESTRY. The office or tenure of an incumbent is an *incumbency.*
See also CLERGY (CHURCH OF ENGLAND) and PAROCHIAL CHURCH COUNCIL

INCUNABULUM An early printed book, especially one dating from before the sixteenth century.

INDENT A matrix in a slab from which a monumental brass (or a section thereof) is missing. *See* BRASSES (MONUMENTAL)

INDENTURE A formal inventory or agreement the text of which is repeated on a single sheet of paper or vellum and the two (or more) identical texts separated by cutting in an irregular manner so that the indentations of each party's document complement those of the other, thereby making it impossible to substitute a forged agreement or to alter the original. Sometimes the word *chirograph* was written across the indented line to show that there were several copies of the same text.

INDUCTION The concluding stage in the appointment of an INCUMBENT to his benefice. Following INSTITUTION by the bishop, the new incumbent is inducted (usually) by the archdeacon who, on conveying to him the key of the church door, requires also that he should toll the church bell. By these acts he acquires legal possession of the tithes, rights, endowments and other revenues of the parish.

INDULGENCE (i) Exemption of an individual from ecclesiastical law. (ii) Remission by the Church of temporal penalties still due after PENANCE and ABSOLUTION. The practice of granting indulgences presupposes that sin is punishable either on earth or in PURGATORY even when a sinner has been reconciled to God. There are several degrees of remission: plenary indulgences remit all temporal punishment (*see* PRIVILEGED ALTAR), partial indulgences remit a portion, temporal indulgences last only for a given time, indefinite or perpetual indulgences last until revoked, personal indulgences apply only to a specified person or confraternity, and local indulgences are obtainable only at a particular place. From the twelfth century, the granting of indulgences became commonplace, plenary indulgences being especially susceptible to abuse (*see also* SHRINES).

A number of religious houses acquired reputations for the granting of indulgences: the Bridgettine double house of Syon (Twickenham, Greater London) for example, which was popular for the many indulgences it could offer to pilgrims. In 1425, at the request of Henry V, the Pope granted the house the so-called Vincula indulgence, remission of punishment for sins equivalent to those available at Rome on the feast-day of St. Peter ad Vincula (1 August). Visitors could obtain indulgences of 500 days on the fourth Sunday in Lent and at Lammastide (1 August) and the brethren also blessed special rosaries (known as 'Syon Beads'), a practice which existed in the mid fifteenth century but was not confirmed by the Pope until 1500 (*see* BEAD).

INDUSTRIAL REVOLUTION *see* DIOCESES, EIGHTEENTH-CENTURY CHURCH *and* NINETEENTH-CENTURY CHURCH

INDUSTRY Evidence of former industrial activity may be found in the vicinity of several parish churches which once served monastic communities. From the twelfth century, wool, metals, agricultural surpluses and a variety of manufactured goods were offered for sale at FAIRS AND MARKETS. Coal was mined at Monk Seaton (a cell of the Benedictine priory of Tynemouth, Northumberland), the mighty cathedral priory of Durham had mines at Ferryhill and Gateshead, while a mine at Finchale (a dependency of Durham) had its own horse-powered pumping station in 1486. There were iron-workings at Jarrow Priory in County Durham and Kirkstall Abbey in Yorkshire and iron was mined at St. Bees Priory in Cumberland (now a parish church) and Byland Abbey in Yorkshire. Kirkstead Abbey in Lincolnshire had four forges for smelting and working iron while Bolton Priory (also in Yorkshire and, in part, a parish church) owned several lead mines. TILES were manufactured commercially at Repton Priory in Derbyshire and at Great Malvern Priory in Worcestershire (now a magnificent parish church). Medieval floor tiles from Malvern are still to be found in cathedrals and parish churches throughout southern England and beyond. By the fifteenth century, the wealth created through the responsible management of these and numerous other industrial enterprises contributed significantly to the resources of the Church which, at that time, possessed nearly one third of the total wealth of England.

INESCUTCHEON *see* ESCUTCHEON OF PRETENCE

INFANT BAPTISM *see* BAPTISM

INFIRMARIAN, INFIRMARER *or* **MASTER OF THE FARMERY** The monastic official responsible for the administration of the farmery (*see* INFIRMARY).

INFIRMARY (FARMERY) A monastic infirmary was a religious house in miniature with its own chapel, DORTER and FRATER (*misericord*), and its own kitchen where 'more subtle and delicate meats' could be prepared for the aged, sick and convalescent. It was to the infirmary that elderly monks retired, there to be treated with special consideration. These were the *sempectae* or *stationarii* – monks who had been professed for fifty years and whose age demanded some relaxation of the monastic rule. They, and the other inmates of the infirmary, were allowed a fire, given special diets (including meat) and permitted a modified office. The infirmary was usually located to the east of the CLOISTER, away from the noise of the CURIA. Most infirmaries had the same simple church plan as medieval HOSPITALS, the 'nave' being the hall and the chancel containing the chapel, though several (later) farmeries had separate chapels and were sometimes grouped round a cloister. In the hall, the beds were usually arranged along the walls, facing a central fireplace. This large (and draughty) communal space was often divided by partitions into 'wards' so that the occupant of each cubicle enjoyed a degree of privacy and, in some instances, the warmth of his own fireplace. Many religious houses (notably those of the Cistercians) also maintained infirmaries for the benefit of the sick and infirm beyond their walls. The parish church of St. Thomas at Ramsey in Huntingdonshire, for example, which was once the chapel of an infirmary located outside the gatehouse of the Benedictine abbey. The presence of a thirteenth-century font suggests that the chapel was also used for parochial purposes at that time.

INHIBITION The suspension from duty of an INCUMBENT by order of a bishop.

INHUMATION The act of burial in the ground.

INJUNCTIONS Orders issued by an ecclesiastical authority, or by the Crown, to clergy and churchwardens. Of the Royal Injunctions, those of Henry VIII (1536) required observance of anti-papal legislation, the abandonment of certain practices and the use of the English language for instruction. These were followed (in 1538) by injunctions which provided for the setting up of the Great Bible in all churches (*see* BIBLES). Edward VI's injunctions of 1547 required the clergy to promote the royal supremacy and to preach against the papal authority, while those issued by Queen Mary in 1554 required that married priests should be removed or divorced. In 1559, Elizabeth I issued a series of injunctions which effectively re-enacted those of 1547 (though the extreme anti-Romanism of the earlier injunctions was much reduced) to which she added a number of instructions concerning, for example, the conduct of services.

INK Most medieval and early modern texts were written in inks made from a mixture of oak-galls, iron sulphate and gum Arabic, though natural dyes and walnut juice were also used and a darker but less stable ink was produced from carbon, gum and water.
See also PARCHMENT, PENS *and* VELLUM

INLAY (also DAMASCENE, INTARSIA and PARQUETRY) A form of ornamentation created by embedding pieces of wood, metal, ivory etc. in another material so that the surfaces are level. *Damascene* is an inlay of metal (especially gold) on steel etc.. *Intarsia* is a form of decorative wood inlay, developed in fifteenth-century Italy. *Parquetry* is a flooring of wooden blocks arranged to form a pattern.

INNS *see* SHRINES

INQUISITION, THE An ecclesiastical court established for the detection and punishment of heretics in *c.* 1232. The officials of the Inquisition were chiefly Dominicans and Franciscans whose methods of interrogation rarely included torture (though this was accepted practice in judicial procedures of the time). Those accused of heresy were tried before an inquisitor assisted by a jury of clerics and laymen. Penalties for heresy included confiscation of goods, imprisonment and (in capital cases) surrender to the secular authorities for execution by burning. In 1542 the Inquisition was assigned by Pope Paul III to a church department, known as the *Holy Office* or *Congregation of the Inquisition*. This became the final court of appeal in trials for heresy and ultimately an organ of papal government.

INSCRIPTIONS The reading of inscriptions is often a difficult task which requires not only a knowledge of Latin and French but also an ability to decipher the LETTERING itself. On monumental BRASSES, for example, Norman French in Lombardic script was generally used during the period 1250–1350, Latin inscriptions in Blackletter usually date from the period 1350–1500 while English, in Tudor Blackletter or capitals, was used from 1500–1650. But, of course, there are many exceptions. At Brightwell Baldwin in Oxfordshire an inscription in English commemorates one 'John ye Smith' who died in 1370, while many of the clergy continued to commission MONUMENTS with Latin inscriptions long after the Reformation.

Norman French inscriptions are usually short with a name and a brief prayer: *Sire: John: Daubernoun: Chivalier: Gist: Ici: Deau: Sa: Alme: Eyt: Mercy*, for example, on a brass at Stoke d'Abernon in Surrey. Such an inscription requires only a rudimentary understanding of modern French and a little guesswork ('gist' would now be 'gît'). But Latin inscriptions in Blackletter are often very difficult to decipher. Vowels are usually omitted while a bar is placed above a preceding letter (or elsewhere) to indicate the omission. Dates are almost invariably inscribed in Roman numerals and most Latin inscriptions of the period begin with the words 'here lies' and end with an abbreviated prayer, 'on whose soul may God have mercy'. Where an inscription is set in a continuous metal strip or inscribed round the edge of a monument, the first word is usually that in the top left-hand corner and may be marked with a cross. Common phrases include: *hic jacet* ('here lies'), *orate pro anima* ('pray for the soul of'), *cui' aie ppiciet de' ame* (an abbreviation for 'on whose soul may God have mercy').

English inscriptions are, of course, easier to read though spelling can be erratic. Often, these EPITAPHS rhyme and some are exceedingly beautiful, such as the touching memorial to young Meneleb Rainsford, inscribed on a brass (1633) at Henfield in Sussex:

Great Jove hath lost his Ganymede I know
Which made him seek an other here below
And finding none, not one, like unto this
Hath ta'ne him hence into eternall bliss
Cease then for thy deer Meneleb to weep
God's darlinge was too good for thee to keep
But rather joye in this great favour given
A child on earth is made a Saint in Heaven

Ganymede was Jove's cup-bearer, the 'most beautiful boy ever born'.

Common abbreviations are:

AMDG	(*ad majorem Dei Gloriam*)	To the greater Glory of God
HIS	(*hic iacet sepultus*)	Here lies buried

HMP	(*hoc monumentum posuit*)	He erected this monument
INST	(*in nomine Sanctae Trinitatis*)	In the Name of the Holy Trinity
MS	(*memoriae sacrum*)	Sacred to the memory
RIP	(*requiescat in pace*)	May he rest in peace

The most common archaic words to be found in commemorative inscriptions are:

almys	alms
armiger	one entitled to bear arms
auncynt	ancient
aungeles	angels
awtere	altar
bles	bliss
capellanus	chaplain
certes	certainly
cheyffe	chief
comes	earl
consul	councillor
crysten	christian
decanus	dean
deptyd	departed
dominus	master
eccles	church
eke	also
elemosinarius	almoner
erchdiakn	archdeacon
eyre	heir
ſadyr	father
ffro	from
generosus	gentleman
gent	gentleman or gentlewoman
halud	hallowed
hem	them
maden	made
mci	mercy
mede	merit
miles	knight
moder	mother
or	our
p	per, pro or prae
pannarius	draper
pelliparius	tanner
pish	parish
prepositus	provost
pson	parson
quere	choir (chancel)
redecion	redemption
relict	widow
sowlys	souls
steven	staves of music
s'teyne	certain
thred	third
twey	two
wen	think
whylom	once
wot	know
XPS	Christus
yat	that
yistis	gifts
ys	this

See also LAPIDARY, PRECATORY SCROLLS *and* WALL MONUMENTS

INSIGNIA *see* COLLARS *and* KNIGHTHOOD, ORDERS OF

INSTALLATION The induction of a CANON or PREBENDARY to a stall in a cathedral or collegiate church.
See also CLERGY (CHURCH OF ENGLAND)

INSTITUTION The admission by a bishop of a new incumbent to the spiritual responsibilities of a parish. Institution is usually followed by INDUCTION.

INSTITUTION BOOKS *see* ARCHIVES

INSTRUMENTS, MUSICAL *see* MUSICAL INSTRUMENTS

INSTRUMENTS OF THE PASSION *see* CHRISTIAN SYMBOLS

INTERDICT An ecclesiastical punishment whereby the faithful are excluded from all matters spiritual, other than the Communion of the Church (*see also* EXCOMMUNICATION). A general interdict applied to an entire population or that of a defined district, a local interdict was confined to a particular place and a personal interdict was directed only at a specified person or persons.

INTERRED Strictly speaking, the term implies burial without Christian rites though it is commonly used as a synonym for burial.

INTERREGNUM, THE *see* BISHOPS' LANDS *and* SEVENTEENTH-CENTURY CHURCH

INTERSTICES (i) The intervening spaces between a decorative or heraldic motif and the border which surrounds it (*see, for example,* SEALS). (ii) According the CANON LAW, the period of time which must elapse between the conferment of different ORDERS upon the same person.

INTESTATE Not having made a valid will before death. One who has died without making a will.
See also LETTERS OF ADMINISTRATION *and* PROBATE

INTINCTION The practice of dipping the

Eucharistic bread into the wine, adopted by the western Church but abandoned by *c.* 1200. It has since been used occasionally as a means of administering Communion to the aged and infirm.

INTRAMURAL BURIALS *see* BURIALS *and* VAULTS (BURIAL)

INTRINSECA *see* PLACE-NAMES

INTROIT The opening act of worship in the Mass, usually the singing of a psalm or a part thereof.

INTRUDER A puritan minister installed in a benefice following the expulsion of the lawful incumbent during the Interregnum.

INVENTORY A list of possessions, goods and chattels, often with a valuation.

INVESTITURE The ceremonial giving of an office or benefice.

IONIC One of the three CLASSICAL ORDERS of architecture.

IRONSTONE (i) Limestone or sandstone which has been coloured brown or green by the presence of iron oxide. (ii) A hard, white pottery.

ITALIC *see* LETTERING

JACKS OF THE CLOCK Carved and painted human figures which strike the bell of a clock. In Britain, the earliest example is believed to be the late fourteenth-century jack-clock at Wells Cathedral where two 'quarter jacks' strike the quarter hours and 'Jack Blandifer' the hours.
See also CLOCKS

JAMB (i) The side of a doorway, window, archway or fireplace. (ii) In HERALDRY the lower part of a beast's leg, cut off at the second joint (*also* gamb).

JESSE TREE Christ's descent from Jesse, the father of King David, depicted in a church window, wall painting etc. in the form of a *Tree of Jesse*. This springs from the recumbent body of Jesse and

terminates in the Virgin and Holy Child, with the intermediate descendants represented on foliage scrolls branching out from each other. Of several fine examples those in the Shropshire churches of St. Mary the Virgin at Shrewsbury and St. Laurence at Ludlow are two of the best. Although restored, the fifteenth-century Ludlow window is still beautiful, with Jesse lying on his side and a tree of life flowing upwards, laden with kings and prophets, all gazing on the figure of Christ at the top. The fourteenth-century Shrewsbury window was probably transferred from a friary church in the town.
See also CHRISTIAN SYMBOLS *and* REREDOS

JESSE WINDOW *see* JESSE TREE

JESUIT A member of the Society of Jesus, an order of priests founded in Paris in 1534 by Ignatius Loyola and others. Although established as a missionary order, the Society became the spearhead of the Counter-Reformation. Members saw themselves as a disciplined force, effective in the defence of the Roman Church, and their success as missionaries, preceptors and scholars was, indeed, formidable. The arrival of the Jesuits in England in *c.* 1580 added impetus to RECUSANCY which contemporary statesmen regarded as insidious and dangerous. Remarkably, tombstones may occasionally be found in Anglican churches marking the graves of Jesuit priests. At Hampreston in Dorset, for example, there are two such memorials, each inscribed with the tell-tale post-nomial initials 'S.J.' and dated 1745 and 1750: a time of intense Catholic persecution.
Further reading:
Edwards, The Rev. F., *Elizabethan Jesuits*, London, 1981

JOINERY *see* WOODWORK

JUBE *see* ROOD LOFT

JUBILATE Psalm 100, the first words of which are 'Make a joyful noise unto the Lord'. According to the *Book of Common Prayer*, the Jubilate may be sung or said as an alternative to the BENEDICTUS at Morning Prayer. In the *Alternative Service Book* it is offered as an alternative to the VENITE.

JULIAN CALENDAR The calendar introduced by Julius Ceasar in 46 BC in which the standard year has 365 days and every fourth year is a leap year of 366 days. The GREGORIAN CALENDAR was introduced in 1582 to compensate for the ten days which had accumulated as a result of the Julian calendar being 11 minutes and 10 seconds too long, although the change was not effected in England until 1752.
See also NEW YEAR'S DAY

JUPON The successor to the SURCOAT: a short, sleeveless coat worn over ARMOUR and emblazoned with a coat of arms. Popular from the mid-fourteenth to the mid-fifteenth century, at which time plate armour became so highly embellished and valuable that it was fashionable for it to be worn without covering. The later TABARD was worn for purely heraldic purposes.
See also COSTUME

JUXTA *see* PLACE-NAMES

KEEIL Small stone-built rectangular chapels in the Isle of Man dating from the seventh century into the early Middle Ages. Several are located near HOLY WELLS (*chibbyr*) and most are dedicated to Irish saints.

KENNEL HEADDRESS *see* COSTUME

KENTISH RAG A grey-green sandy limestone quarried in Kent. Used extensively for architectural dressings and as facing stone because of its hard, impervious characteristics.

KETTON STONE A cream-coloured limestone quarried in Rutland.

KEY ESCUTCHEON The pierced metal plate affixed to a door to protect a keyhole.

KEYS *see* DOORS AND DOORWAYS

KEYSTONE *see* ARCH *and* BOSSES

KINDRED AND AFFINITY, TABLE OF *see* AFFINITY

KING CHARLES' DAY In copies of the *Book of Common Prayer* published before this century, 30 January was set aside as a day of prayer in memory of 'the martyrdom of the blessed King who was delivered up into the hands of cruel and unreasonable men' (1649).

KING JAMES VERSION *see* BIBLES

KING OF ARMS The senior rank of officers of

arms. Only a king of arms has authority to grant armorial bearings, and in England and Wales this is subject to the formal approval of the Earl Marshal in the form of a warrant.
See also FUNERAL HERALDRY *and* HERALDRY

KING POST A central vertical post rising from a tie beam to the ridge piece of a timber roof (*see* ROOFS). A *queen post* consists of two vertical posts instead of one.

KINGS AND QUEENS *see* CHRISTIAN SYMBOLS *and* RULERS OF ENGLAND AND OF THE UNITED KINGDOM

KING'S BOOKS, THE *see* VALOR ECCLESIASTICUS

KIRTLE *see* COSTUME *and* EFFIGIES

KITCHENER (COQUINARIUS) In a religious house, the official responsible for the kitchens, for the work of the cooks and their (often numerous) assistants and for planning meals 'according to traditional allowances.'

KNAPPING *see* FLINT

KNEELERS *see* HASSOCKS

KNIGHT BACHELOR The lowest degree of knighthood but also the most ancient. Knights were originally required to perform military service in exchange for the lands granted to them but this duty was gradually commuted to a money payment (*scutage* = 'shield money'). A knight bachelor was not a member of an order of chivalry and, in a medieval army, would command the smallest unit, perhaps consisting of only a few personal retainers. He displayed his arms on a pennon, the tails of which were removed to form the banner of a KNIGHT BANNERET if he was promoted in the field of battle. Since the Tudor period, the helmet in the coat of arms of a knight bachelor usually faces the front and has an open visor (*see* HELMETS (HERALDIC)).

KNIGHT BANNERET The highest degree of knighthood in the medieval period. A knight banneret was normally one who had performed some outstanding personal service to his sovereign or shown exceptional bravery on the battlefield. He was permitted to lead large contingents of troops in battle under his own *banneret* (a small banner), a right normally restricted to senior members of the nobility (*see also* KNIGHT BACHELOR).

KNIGHTHOOD, ORDERS OF Knights of the orders of chivalry may be identified through various devices which are added to their coats of arms. A knight's helm, for example, faces the front and has a raised visor, though it should be remembered that peers who are also knights use the helm appropriate to their noble rank (*see* HELMETS (HERALDIC)). Knights companion of the Garter, Thistle and St. Patrick are entitled to SUPPORTERS, as are knights commander of the other British orders.

Particular orders may be identified by reference to the circlet which surrounds a shield of arms. That of the Order of the Garter, for example, is dark blue with the enigmatic motto HONI SOIT QUI MAL Y PENSE ('shame on him who thinks evil of it') in gold letters (*see* GARTER, THE MOST NOBLE ORDER OF THE). The Most Ancient and Most Noble Order of the Thistle, which was 'revived' by James VII of Scotland (James II of England) in 1687, has a green circlet inscribed in gold with the motto NEMO ME IMPUNE LACESSIT ('no one invokes me with impunity'), while the circlet of the Most Illustrious Order of St. Patrick bears the words QUIS SEPARABIT, MDCCLXXXIII ('who will sever us, 1783), a reference to the political considerations which led to its institution in 1783 (no appointments have been made since 1934). The Most Honourable Order of the Bath, established by George IV in 1725, was modelled on 'a degree of knighthood which hath been denominated the Knighthood of the Bath' by Henry IV in 1399, the designation acknowledging the ritualistic purification undertaken by a knight-elect prior to his receiving the accolade. The maroon circlet bears the motto TRIA JUNCTA IN UNO ('three joined in one'), a reference to the kingdoms of England, Scotland and Ireland (or France). The Most Distinguished Order of St. Michael and St. George was founded by George III in 1818 and has subsequently become an honour for members of the Diplomatic Service. The blue circlet bears the motto AUSPICIUM MELIORIS AEVI ('token of a better age'). The Royal Victorian Order, instituted by Queen Victoria in 1896 and bestowed on members of the royal household and those who have rendered personal service to the sovereign, has a circlet inscribed with the word VICTORIA. The Most Excellent Order of the British Empire, instituted in 1917 and by far the largest of the British orders, has a rose-pink circlet with the motto FOR GOD AND THE EMPIRE.

Other officers and members of the various orders are entitled to depict the badge of their order suspended on a ribbon beneath the shield in their coats of arms.
See also BARONET, KNIGHT BACHELOR *and* KNIGHT BANNERET
Further reading:
Friar, S., *A New Dictionary of Heraldry*, Sherborne and London, 1987

KNIGHTS HOSPITALLER (*also* KNIGHTS OF MALTA *and* KNIGHTS OF RHODES) *see* ST. JOHN OF JERUSALEM, ORDER OF

KNIGHTS TEMPLAR *see* TEMPLAR, KNIGHTS

KNOBSTICK WEDDING *see* MATRIMONY

KNOCKNOBBLER *see* DOGS

KNOP A carved motif: an ornamental knob or the stylised bud of a flower.

KNOTS Intertwined cords in the form of slackened, symmetrical knots were particularly effective as heraldic BADGES. They are generally named after the families who adopted them and are often used in conjunction with other badges acquired through marriage or inheritance. Several have assumed somewhat spurious territorial designations as a result of their use as charges in the civic HERALDRY of a particular locality: the so-called 'Staffordshire Knot', for example, which was originally the badge of the earls of Stafford but is now ubiquitous as a charge in the heraldry of that county.
See also CYPHER *and* REBUS

KYRIE ELEISON *see* TEN COMMANDMENTS, THE

LABEL (i) A small, stylised 'scroll' inscribed with a religious aphorism or prayer and located, for example, near the head of a figure in a monumental brass (*see* PRECATORY SCROLL). (ii) *For* architectural label *see* DRIPSTONE. (iii) *For* heraldic label *see* CADENCY.

LABEL STOP Carved architectural decoration at the termination of a label (*see* DRIPSTONE).
See also FIGURE SCULPTURE

LADY CHAPEL A subsidiary chapel dedicated to the Blessed Virgin Mary, usually located at the eastern termination of a church beyond the high altar. From the eleventh century onwards many larger churches were constructed or remodelled to a cruciform plan with the lower, elongated limb of a Latin Cross forming the NAVE, the upper limb the

CHANCEL and the lateral limbs the north and south TRANSEPT. The PRESBYTERY around the altar was usually apsidal but many were rebuilt after c1150 to provide a square termination, and in larger churches a RETRO-CHOIR or AMBULATORY was added with radiating CHAPELS. Of these, the most important is often a lady chapel, usually of late medieval date, its size and architectural splendour reflecting a contemporary cult-like veneration of the Blessed Virgin Mary (*see* MARY, THE BLESSED VIRGIN).

LADY DAY (LADYMAS) The Feast of the Annunciation of the Virgin held on 25 March and, until 1752, New Year's Day (*see* GREGORIAN CALENDAR *and* NEW YEAR'S DAY). In the rural calendar, Lady Day was the day on which yearly contracts, entered into on the preceding CANDLEMAS DAY (2 February), became effective. In many areas *Old Lady Day* (6 April) was used for this purpose. In Victorian Dorset 'These annual migrations from farm to farm were on the increase . . . . When [her] mother was a child the majority of the field-folk . . . remained all their lives on one farm, which had been the home also of their fathers and grandfathers; but latterly the desire for yearly removal had risen to a high pitch. With the younger families it was a pleasant excitement which might possibly be an advantage. The Egypt of one family was the Land of Promise to the family who saw it from a distance, till by residence there it became in turn their Egypt also; and so they changed and changed.' Thomas Hardy, in *Tess of the D'Urbervilles*, goes on to describe in detail the *house ridding* and the 'preliminaries of the general removal, the passing of the empty waggons and teams to fetch the goods of the migrating families; for it was always by the vehicle of the farmer who required his services that the hired man was conveyed to his destination. That this might be accomplished within the day was the explanation of the reverberation occurring so soon after midnight, the aim of the carters being to reach the door of the outgoing households by six o'clock, when the loading of their movables at once began. A wet Lady Day was a spectre which removing families never forgot; damp furniture, damp bedding, damp clothing accompanied it, and left a train of ills. The day being the sixth of April, the Durbeyfield waggon met many other waggons with families on the summit of the load , which was built on a wellnigh unvarying principle, as peculiar, probably, to the rural labourer as the hexagon to the bee. The groundwork of the arrangement was the family dresser, which, with its shining handles, and finger-marks, and domestic evidences thick upon it, stood importantly in front, over the tails of the shaft-horses, in its erect and natural position, like some Ark of the Covenant that they were bound to carry reverently. Some of the households were lively, some mournful. . . .'
See also FEAST DAYS (FIXED AND MOVABLE) *and* SETTLEMENT AND REMOVAL RECORDS)

LAIRSTAL A grave located within a church. The stone covering of such a grave may be described as a *lairstone*.

LAITY Members of the Church other than those who belong to the clergy.

LAMB A symbol of Christ commonly found in religious art and derived from biblical references such as John 1:29 and Revelation 5:12.
See also CHRISTIAN SYMBOLS *and* PASCHAL LAMB

LAMBREQUIN *see* CREST *and* MANTLING

LAMMAS Lammas Day was the first day of August (the *Gule of August*) on which it was customary to consecrate bread made from the first ripe corn of harvest – the 'first fruits'. The Saxons called the day *hlaf-maesse*, meaning 'loaf-mass'. Lammas land (*also* Half Year Land) was common meadow on which manorial tenants were allowed to graze their livestock from Lammastide until the next sowing. The Lugg Meadows on the outskirts of Hereford are the largest surviving area of lammas land (132 hectares), and that where medieval practice is still most closely followed.
See also FEAST DAYS (FIXED AND MOVABLE)

LAMPLANDS Lands, the rent from which provided for the maintenance of the altar lights in the parish church.

LAMPS The practice of burning a sanctuary lamp (with a red light) before the altar, and to indicate the presence of the reserved Sacrament (a white light), dates from the thirteenth century (*see* RESERVATION). A further lamp (with a blue light) was also burned before images of the Mother and Child. Lamps of this type (sometimes described as *aumbry lamps*) are usually suspended from the ceiling by means of a chain and ring from which three shorter chains support an ornamental drip-pan with pendant finial. Sanctuary lamps are generally of highly polished brass, the red, white or blue light emanating from a slow-burning candle or oil lamp within a cylindrical funnel of coloured glass.
See also ALTAR LIGHTS, BIER LIGHT, CANDELABRUM, CANDLES, CANDLESTICKS, CHANDELIER, CORONA LUCIS, CRESSET, ELECTRIC LIGHTING, HEARSE, LANTERN, PRICKET, SERGES, STRAP SCONCE, TRENDAL *and* TRIPLE CANDLESTICK

LANATUS Buried in wool.

LANCET *see* ARCH, MEDIEVAL ARCHITECTURE *and* WINDOWS

LANTERN (i) A circular or polygonal turret-like structure, often surmounting a dome, for the purpose of admitting light and air. In churches, a lantern will usually be found above the CROSSING and may be a series of windows in the upper story of a central tower. (ii) A portable lamp, the windows of which were originally made of sliced animal horn, hence 'lant-horn'. In religious houses, night-time processions were led by a junior monk carrying a lantern. The CIRCATOR also carried a lantern when patrolling the conventual buildings in search of monks who were not at VIGIL. If he discovered a sleeping brother, he would wake him by placing the lantern before his eyes. The errant monk was then obliged to take the lantern, find another brother in a similar condition, and repeat the process.
See also LIGHTS *and* POOR SOUL'S LIGHT

LAPIDARY That which is engraved on stone.

LAPPETS *see* VESTMENTS

LAPS AND ROLLS The usual method of constructing a lead roof is for lengths of lead to be laid with their edges overlapping. The 'laps' are then 'rolled' to make them waterproof.

LARDER A medieval domestic department. In medieval households and large monastic establishments, the *larderer* was responsible for the acquisition and storage of provisions including meat which was, of course, cooked in the kitchens. Bread was the province of the *pantry* and there were other departments responsible for the preparation of poultry and game (the *poultry*) and spices and dressings (the *saucery*). Utensils and equipment were maintained by the *scullery* and table linen by the *napery*. Wine was the concern of the *buttery* and vegetables were provided by the *curtilage*. In the monastic hierarchy, the CELLARER was responsible for all these departments, together with the produce of the dairy and the brewhouse, while the *Kitchener* managed the serving of meals in the monastic refectories, the administration of which was the responsibility of the *Refectorian* or *Fraterer* (*see* FRATER).

LAST JUDGEMENT *see* DOOM *and* WALL PAINTINGS

LATCHES *see* DOORS AND DOORWAYS

LATH AND PLASTER Material used for ceilings, and for the internal walls of timber-framed buildings, consisting of a framework of interlaced or parallel laths (usually split hazel or willow) covered with layers of plaster which often contained a bonding agent such as horse-hair.

LATIN An Indo-European language of the Italic group and the ancestor of all Romance languages. Latin was originally the dialect of small communities living along the lower Tiber, a district of Italy known as Latium. With the increase of Roman political control, the language spread throughout Italy and into western and southern Europe and the western Mediterranean coastal regions of Africa. It became the official language of the Roman Empire and remained the international medium of communication in western Europe throughout the Middle Ages, notably in matters of law, scholarship and the liturgy. It remained the official language of the Roman Catholic Church until the mid-twentieth century.
See also BIBLES, COMMON PRAYER (BOOK OF) *and* PLACE-NAMES
Further reading:
Morris, J., *Latin Glossary for Family Historians*, Chichester, 1989

LATIN CHURCH, THE The Western Church.

LATIN CROSS A plain cross with an extended lower limb.

LATIN DOCTORS, THE FOUR *see* CHRISTIAN SYMBOLS

LATITUDINARIAN In seventeenth- and eighteenth-century England, a member of that section of the Church of England favouring breadth ('latitude') of thought in religious beliefs and practice. In the eighteenth century, the Church was in danger of becoming an adjunct of the government when latitudinarians were given preferment by successive Whig administrations as a means of weakening the HIGH CHURCH which was then synonymous with the Tory party.

LATTEN *see* BRASSES (MONUMENTAL)

LATTICE *see* DECORATIVE MOTIFS

LAUDIAN (i) Any feature which is characteristic of the reforms introduced by Archbishop William Laud (1573–1645) who opposed the prevailing Calvinist theology and sought to restore elements of pre-Reformation liturgical practice. A member of the High Commission, which was responsible for enforcing the new forms of public worship, his attempts to impose liturgical uniformity were singularly unpopular among the PURITANS. He was impeached by the Long Parliament, imprisoned in 1641 and executed in 1645. *See* SEVENTEENTH-CENTURY CHURCH *and* SIXTEENTH- AND

SEVENTEENTH-CENTURY ARCHITECTURE. (ii) Descriptive of that which encloses an altar or communion table, e.g. communion rails. (iii) Specifically, a loose (three- or four-sided) cover for a communion table, usually fringed at the lower edge and with an embroidered motif on the frontal.

LAUDS A short office, observed at dawn, which (until 1911) included five groups of psalms sung antiphonally. The fifth of these comprised Psalms 148–150, known as the *Laudes*, in which the word *laudate* ('praise ye') recurs. In the *Book of Common Prayer*, elements of Lauds and MATTINS were combined to form the service of Morning Prayer.
See also DIVINE OFFICE, HORARIUM *and* HOURS (CANONICAL)

LAVABO The washing of a priest's fingers following the offering of the OBLATIONS at the EUCHARIST. The lavabo was usually carried out at a PISCINA in the PRESBYTERY, indeed a second piscina was sometimes provided for this purpose and the term is often applied to this. There is a rare twelfth-century example of a double piscina at Ledbury in Herefordshire.
See also ABLUTIONS, COMMUNION LINEN, CREDENCE *and* FENESTELLA

LAVATORIUM (LAVER) The monastic lavatorium was usually located in (or adjacent to) the CLOISTER and near the entrance to the FRATER. It was here that the monks performed their morning ablutions (after PRIME), washed their hands before meals and celebrated the weekly MAUNDY. There were two types. The first consisted of a long trough, usually recessed within an alcove, lined with lead and fed by brass piping: as at Kirkham Abbey in Yorkshire and Hexham in Northumberland (where the lavatorium is now in the police station!). The second type was an independent circular or polygonal structure, projecting into the cloister GARTH and built round a large, central basin. One of the best examples is the 'Conduit' at Sherborne in Dorset, a sixteenth-century hexagonal lavatorium which was removed from the Abbey at the Dissolution and set up as a public fountain in the nearby market place. Both types of lavatorium were often embellished with ornate architectural decoration: the wonderful fan vaulting at Gloucester, for example. Larger houses were often provided with several lavers (there were four at Canterbury) and some were reserved for specific purposes. Towels were kept in a nearby cupboard (*see* AUMBRY), sometimes a recess in an adjacent wall, and were changed on Sundays and Thursdays. The lavatorium was the responsibility of the *chamberlain* whose many and diverse duties included the provision of hot water and soap when required, together with a whetstone and a supply of sand so that the brethren could clean and sharpen their knives.
See also CONDUIT *and* DRAINS

LAVER *see* LAVATORIUM

LAWLESS PARSON A cleric who was willing to marry couples at times or places not prescribed by Canon Law.

LAY One who is not ordained into the clergy. A member of the LAITY.
See also LAY BROTHER, LAY CLERK, LAY FEE, LAY READER, LAY RECTOR *and* LAY SUBSIDY

LAY ABBOT A layman who was appointed to the title, revenues and privileges of an abbacy. An abuse of royal or papal authority which almost invariably resulted in economic and spiritual dissipation (*see also* COMMENDATOR).

LAY BROTHER Lay brothers were accepted as members of religious orders from the eleventh century, a time when an increasing number of monks were ordained as priests and, therefore, excused manual labour. Lay brothers were not bound to the recitation of the DIVINE OFFICE and were generally occupied in manual work, though they were usually required to attend a daily Mass and to recite a short office.

In CISTERCIAN houses, there were often twice as many *conversi* (laymen who had 'turned' to the service of God) as there were quire monks. The conversi, who included skilled craftsmen such as masons, dedicated themselves to a simple life of work and prayer. They lived according to the Cistercian constitution (the *Carta Caritatis*), though with a simplified office and modified HORARIUM, and were provided with their own FRATER, DORTER, INFIRMARY and church. In the late twelfth century there were 70 monks and 120 conversi at Waverley Abbey in Surrey, while at mighty Rievaulx in Yorkshire there were 140 monks, 240 conversi and 260 lay servants. Small priories of *conversi* managed outlying granges (*see* GRANGE) and were attached to houses of Cistercian nuns where the sisters were unable to undertake heavy manual work. Although they took the monastic vows of poverty, chastity and obedience, the conversi were not permitted to become quire monks and for this reason were denied a literary education. Conversi wore a modified form of the Cistercian habit: a white cloak and tunic with a cowl which was shorter than that of a monk and which covered only the shoulders and chest.

From the mid-fourteenth century, lay brethren began deserting the monasteries in large numbers, attracted by improved wages and working conditions as a consequence of a labour shortage following the Black Death (*see* PLAGUE).
See also MONASTIC BUILDINGS

LAY CLERK An adult male member of certain cathedral or collegiate choirs.
See also PARISH CLERK *and* VICAR CHORAL

LAY FEE Land held of a lay person in contradistinction to that which is held of an ecclesiastical body.

LAY OFFICIALS In the late medieval period, many religious houses employed laymen to administer their estates. Chief among these were the offices of steward, bailiff and receiver. It was the steward who exercised the authority of a community's superior in matters which were brought before non-ecclesiastical courts.
See also ADMINISTRATOR

LAY READER Since 1866, the Church of England has licensed lay persons to conduct certain services. Lay readers are admitted to their office by their diocesan bishop and, since 1969, have included women.

LAY RECTOR A layman who is in receipt of the rectorial tithes of a benefice and is legally responsible for the repair of the chancel of the church. A lay rector may be an individual or a body corporate.
See also ADVOWSON *and* PORTIONISTS

LAY SUBSIDY A tax on movable items levied on laymen over the age of sixteen from the thirteenth century until 1623. The tax was also known as 'tenths and fifteenths' – town-dwellers paid one tenth and countrymen one fifteenth of the value of their movables.

LAZAR HOUSE A hospital for lepers (*see* HOSPITALS). The term is derived from St. Lazarus, the patron saint of lepers, and from the nursing order of that name.

LEAD A heavy, soft grey-coloured metallic element widely used in the glazing of churches, as a roof covering or sealant, as piping and as a lining in fonts. In Britain, lead was first used by the Romans for water pipes because of its durability and resistance to corrosion. In the medieval period it was used in the complex plumbing systems of religious houses (the Franciscans were acknowledged to be expert in the use of lead piping) and to replace the vast timber roofs of abbey churches which were especially vulnerable to destruction by fire. Lead was a particularly expensive commodity and at the Dissolution was an obvious target for Henry's commissioners (together with brass and bell-metal). A lead roof was stripped and rolled in sections and melted into ingots, using wooden furnishings from the church as fuel (*see also* LAPS AND ROLLS).

The ingots were then stamped with the King's crowned Tudor rose device and stacked in the roofless nave to await collection. At Rievaulx Abbey in Yorkshire, the over-zealous commissioners failed to secure the nave walls, the upper sections of which collapsed, burying the lead ingots beneath tons of rubble. They were discovered during excavations in 1920 and used for the re-glazing of the Five Sisters window at York Minster in 1923.

LEADED LIGHTS *see* WINDOWS

LECTERNS A Lectern is a bookstand to support liturgical books. Medieval lecterns were usually (though not invariably) located on the north side of the high altar, where they supported the *Gospels* during the Mass. In some churches, early stone lecterns may still be found protruding from the north wall of the chancel (as at Crich and Etwall in Derbyshire). In monastic churches, several lecterns were provided for different purposes: that in the middle of the quire, for example, was used by the *cantors* during the office. Following the REFORMATION most lecterns were replaced by reading DESKS in the nave from which the lessons were read at Mattins and Evensong. These desks often formed the middle 'deck' (above that of the parish clerk) in a 'three-decker' pulpit (*see* PULPITS), but from the eighteen forties, many congregations followed the example of the cathedrals and re-introduced separate lecterns, usually on the northern (or 'Gospel') side of the nave in front of the chancel arch. Most lecterns used today reflect the neo-Gothic style of the Victorian period and are of nineteenth- or twentieth-century origin. In many churches, however, the lectern has been removed as a consequence of changing liturgical practices.

There are three types of lectern: (i) a revolving two or four-sided reading desk supported on a pillar, (ii) a similar one-sided desk which is usually of nineteenth- or twentieth-century origin and (iii) an eagle (or, rarely, a pelican – the mystical emblem of Christ) with outstretched wings, usually standing on a sphere supported by a baluster stem and circular moulded base. They are generally made of wood, latten or brass though there are exceptions: at Caundle Marsh in Dorset, for example, where there is a complete (Victorian) set of altar, pulpit and (swivelling) reading desk, all in stone.

Several desk lecterns are medieval (usually those with four-sides, such as the splendid wooden lectern at Detling in Kent) and once supported the large books used for antiphonal singing. There are also good examples in brass at Yeovil in Somerset and in the chapel of Merton College, Oxford.

Medieval eagles are comparatively rare (though Victorian and later versions are legion) and mostly

Eagle lectern at Fotheringhay, Northamptonshire.

date from the fifteenth and early sixteenth centuries. The eagle's outstretched wings support the book which is often 'protected' by three beasts (representing the Evangelists) fashioned at the base of the column (*see* CHRISTIAN SYMBOLS). Just over forty medieval brass eagle lecterns remain (as at Wolborough and Bovey Tracey in Devon and Clare in Suffolk) and some twenty carved in wood (at Astbury in Cheshire and Ottery St. Mary in Devon, for example). These early eagle lecterns are often austere in appearance and brass examples are usually composed of several parts slotted together. Many originated in the workshops of a fifteenth-century 'school' of East Anglian craftsmen who exported throughout Europe, including a lectern at St. Mark's, Venice. Many post-Reformation eagle lecterns are flanked by single bracket candle holders with tulip-shaped glass shades. The eagle is the symbol of St. John the Evangelist whose words (in the *Fourth Gospel* and *The Revelation*) 'soared up into the presence of Christ' just as the eagle of the medieval bestiaries renewed itself by flying into the sun.

See also EAGLES, FRATER PULPIT, LITANY DESK *and* MISSAL STAND

LECTIO DIVINA *see* ARMARIUM

LECTIONARY A book containing extracts from the Scriptures which are to be read at services on specific days. Originally, such passages were marked in the margins of Bibles but were later collected in separate books, each relating to a particular service: the MISSAL for the Mass, for example.

LECTOR A reader and, as such, a member of one of the MINOR ORDERS.

LECTURER A stipendiary minister appointed by parishes, town corporations and (occasionally) laymen in the late sixteenth and early seventeenth centuries to provide regular preaching according to the tenets of Protestantism.

LEDGE A horizontal timber to provide rigidity to a door.
See also BRACE, DOORS AND DOORWAYS, MUNTIN, RAIL *and* STILE

LEDGER STONES *see* INCISED SLABS *and* VAULTS (BURIAL)

LEDGER TOMBS *see* TABLE TOMBS

LEGATE A papal ambassador.

LEGISLATION *see* ABJURATION (OATH OF), ANGLO-SAXON CHURCH, ANNATES ACT (1534) (*see* REFORMATION), BANNS OF MARRIAGE, BENEFIT OF CLERGY, BIBLES, BURIAL ACTS (1852, 1853, 1894 and subsequent legislation), BURIAL IN WOOL ACTS (1667 and 1678), BURIALS, CATHOLIC EMANCIPATION ACTS (1778, 1791 and 1829), CHANTRIES ACT (1547) (*see* CHANTRIES *and* REFORMATION), CHARITIES, CHESTS, CHURCH OF ENGLAND, CHURCH OF ENGLAND ASSEMBLY (POWERS ACT) (1919) (*see* PAROCHIAL CHURCH COUNCIL), CHURCH OF ENGLAND (WORSHIP AND DOCTRINE) MEASURE (1974), CHURCH TEMPORALITIES ACT (1919) (*see* WALES, THE CHURCH IN), CHURCHWARDEN'S ACCOUNTS, CLARENDON (CONSTITUTIONS OF), CLOSED CHURCHYARD, COMMON PRAYER (BOOK OF), CONVENTICLE ACTS (1593, 1664 and 1670) (*see* CONVENTICLE *and* SEVENTEENTH-CENTURY CHURCH), DIOCESAN RECORDS, DISSOLUTION OF THE MONASTERIES, DIVORCE, ECCLESIASTICAL JURISDICTION MEASURE (1963), EDUCATION ACTS (*see* SCHOOLS), EIGHTEENTH-CENTURY CHURCH, FAIRS AND MARKETS, FIVE MILE

ACT (1665), FLAGS, FOOTPATHS AND BRIDLEWAYS, GILBERT'S ACT (1782) (*see* POOR LAW), GEORGE ROSE'S ACT (1812), HARDWICKE'S MARRIAGE ACT (1754), INSPECTION OF CHURCHES MEASURE (1953) (*see* TWENTIETH-CENTURY CHURCHES), KNATCHBULL'S GENERAL WORKHOUSE ACT (1723) (*see* POOR LAW), LAW OF SETTLEMENT ACT (1662) (*see* POOR LAW), LOCAL GOVERNMENT ACT (1894) (*see* PARISH *and* VESTRY), LORD'S DAY OBSERVANCE ACT (1781) (*see* SUNDAY), MAPS, MARRIAGE ACTS (1823 and 1836), MARRIAGE LICENCES, MEDIEVAL CHURCH, METROPOLITAN BURIAL ACT (1852) (*see* VAULTS, BURIAL), METROPOLITAN INTERMENTS ACT (1850) (*see* VAULTS, BURIAL), MILITIA ACT (1757) (*see* FLAGS), MILLION ACT (1818) (*see* NINETEENTH-CENTURY ARCHITECTURE *and* NINETEENTH-CENTURY CHURCH), MORTMAIN, MORTUARY, NEW PARISHES ACT (1843) (*see* PEEL PARISH), NINETEENTH-CENTURY CHURCH, OCCASIONAL CONFORMITY ACT (1711), ORDINANCE OF 1644/5 (*see* REGISTERS), PARISH, PARISH CHEST, PARISH CLERK, PAROCHIAL CHURCH COUNCIL, PARSONAGE, PASTORAL MEASURE (1968, amended 1983) (*see* TWENTIETH-CENTURY CHURCHES), PASTORAL REORGANISATION MEASURE (1949) (*see* PARISH), PEEL PARISH, PLURALITIES ACT (1838), POOR LAW ACTS (1563, 1597/8, 1601) and POOR LAW AMENDMENT ACT (1834) (*see* POOR LAW), POPERY, PRAYER BOOK (ALTERNATIVE AND OTHER SERVICES) MEASURE (*see* COMMON PRAYER, BOOK OF), PRIVATE CHAPELS ACT (1871), PROBATE, PUBLIC WORSHIP REGULATION ACT (1874), QUEEN ANNE'S BOUNTY (1704), RECUSANCY, REDUNDANT CHURCHES ACT (1969) (*see* TWENTIETH-CENTURY CHURCHES), REFORMATION, REGISTERS, ROMAN CATHOLIC CHURCH, ROMAN CATHOLIC RELIEF ACT (1829) (*see* CATHOLIC EMANCIPATION ACTS *and* RECUSANCY), ROOT AND BRANCH BILL (1641) (*see* SEVENTEENTH-CENTURY CHURCH), SACRAMENT CERTIFICATE, SANCTUARY (RIGHT OF), SCHISM ACT (1714), SCHOOLS, SETTLEMENT ACT (1697) (*see* POOR LAW *and* SETTLEMENT AND REMOVAL RECORDS), SEVENTEENTH-CENTURY CHURCH, SIX ARTICLES, THE (1539), SPORTS (THE BOOK OF), STAMP ACT (1783) (*see* REGISTERS), STATUTE OF MORTMAIN (1391), SUBMISSION OF THE CLERGY (1532), SUPREMACY, ACTS OF (1534 and 1559) (*see also* HENRY VIII *and* REFORMATION), SYNOD, SYNODICAL GOVERNMENT MEASURE (1969)

(*see* PAROCHIAL CHURCH COUNCIL *and* SYNOD), TAXATION, TEST ACTS (1673 and 1678), THIRTY NINE ARTICLES, THE (1563), TITHE ACT (1925) (*see* TITHES), TITHE COMMUNICATION ACT (1836) (*see* TITHES), TOLERATION ACT (1689), TRIERS (1654), UNIFORMITY, ACTS OF (1549, 1552, 1559 and 1662) (*see* UNIFORMITY, ACTS OF), UNIFORMITY, ACT OF, AMENDMENT ACT (1872), VALOR ECCLESIASTICUS, VESTRY, VISITATIONS (ECCLESIASTICAL), VISITATIONS (HERALDIC), WESTMINSTER CONFESSION (1647) (*see* SEVENTEENTH-CENTURY CHURCH), WITCHCRAFT ACT (1735) (*see* WITCHCRAFT) *and* WORKHOUSES

LENT The period of forty days before EASTER, a period of penitence, ABSTINENCE and FASTING during which Christians recall Christ's suffering in the wilderness. The name is derived from the Anglo-Saxon word *lenct*, meaning 'spring', a period of enforced frugality in agricultural communities when the winter stores of food were running low. In the early Church, the period of abstinence did not usually exceed three or four days but, from the fourth century, it appears gradually to have been extended to forty days. At first, abstinence was rigorous: only one meal a day was permitted and the eating of flesh (including fish) was forbidden. In monastic communities a strict fast was prescribed (though in the later Middle Ages this was sometimes supplemented by raisins and figs) and this could not be broken before VESPERS. Eventually, the penitential character of Lent came to be expressed through abstinence from pleasurable activities, alms-giving and increased religious devotion rather than strict observance of a lengthy and rigorous fast. Even so, for centuries Lent has been a time for moderation in all things, for a frugal diet and self-denial. The festivities of SHROVE TUESDAY, which included the consumption of any foodstuffs that could not be preserved for forty days, was followed by ASH WEDNESDAY, the first day of Lent. Traditionally, it is considered unlucky to marry during Lent.
See also COLOURS (LITURGICAL), EASTER EGGS, FEAST DAYS (FIXED AND MOVABLE), QUADRAGESIMA *and* VEILS

LENTEN VEIL In the medieval church, the SANCTUARY was usually veiled from sight during LENT. The hooks from which the veil was hung have survived in some churches (at Alfriston in Sussex and Shillington in Bedfordshire, for example), while at Ubbeston in Suffolk, pulleys by which both the veil and a CORONA LUCIS were raised and lowered may still be seen in the roof space.
See also ROOD SCREEN *and* VEILS

'LEPER SQUINT' *see* SQUINT (HAGIOSCOPE)

'LEPER WINDOW' *see* CHANTRY VENTIL-ATOR

LESENE A shallow pier, with neither capital nor base, attached to a wall.
See also ANGLO-SAXON ARCHITECTURE *and* PILASTER STRIP

LETTERING The word calligraphy is derived from the Greek *kalos* and *graphos* meaning 'beautiful writing'. The writing found in medieval manuscripts and elaborately decorated books of hours varies from the formal 'book hands' of professional and monastic scribes to informal or cursive handwriting used for personal business purposes. (*Cursive*, from the Latin *curro* meaning 'to hasten', is the running characteristic of writing done at speed and is usually accompanied by a slope to the right.)

Uncial is a form of writing in large, rounded characters commonly found in manuscripts from the fourth to the eighth century, such as the magnificent seventh-century Lindisfarne Gospels in which both uncials (capital letters) and half-uncials (lower case letters) are used. Medieval book hands were mostly varieties of 'Textur' (known as *Blackletter* from c. 1600), a narrow angular hand which forms a rich pattern on the page. With the exception of Italy, Blackletter was the staple book hand of medieval Europe and Scandinavia, though it is often described as Old English or Gothic. In manuscripts, upper case letters are referred to as *majuscules* and lower case letters are *minuscules*, though for most other purposes the terms capital letters and lower case letters will suffice. A *serif* is a short cross line at the end of a stroke in a letter: hence the term *sanserif*, a style of lettering in which serifs are omitted. A *versal letter* is an ornamental capital letter at the beginning of a verse or paragraph in an illuminated manuscript. Significantly larger than the letters of the accompanying text, a versal is often colourfully embellished and gilded with floriated or decorative motifs and may include scenes and figures from contemporary life (*see also* MANUSCRIPT ILLUMINATION).

With the spread of literacy in the fourteenth century, the cursive element in writing became more common. Documents of the period continued to be written in varieties of Blackletter, including a less formal version known as *Gothic Cursive* or *Bastard Hand*. The introduction of PRINTING and, in England, the demise of the monastic *scriptoria* following the DISSOLUTION OF THE MON-ASTERIES, resulted in a rapid decline in the writing and decoration of manuscripts. But legal, ecclesiastical and state documents continued to be hand-written, either in a new humanist hand from Italy (*Renaissance Italic*) or in modified versions of

Blackletter

Gothic Cursive

Renaissance Italic

Engrossing Hand

Foundational Hand

earlier hands such as *Tudor Blackletter*. (The term *Italic* is now used generically to describe writing which slopes towards the right.)

Copperplate (*script*) originated in the Italian practice of engraving on copper plates in order to improve reproduction in the printing process and to obtain longer print runs than those provided by wooden blocks. These plates were engraved with a *burin*, a small triangular chisel, which produced lettering of such a distinctive style that calligraphers began to cut their quill pens in long, flexible points which enabled them to copy the new letters. *Copperplate* has been widely used since the sixteenth century and from it developed a number of similar styles. In the eighteenth century, variations of an ornate German hand (*Engrossing Hand*) became popular with professional calligraphers and was used in conjunction with varieties of Copperplate in formal documents such as deeds and indentures. *Foundational Hand* is a twentieth-century hand developed by the eminent calligrapher Edward Johnson (d. 1944). As the name suggests, Johnson's Foundational Hand possesses all the qualities of balance, rhythm, proportion and legibility necessary to provide a sound basis for formal writing.

Contemporary calligraphic styles are reflected in the lettering of monumental INSCRIPTIONS, as are the numerous typefaces which evolved with the development of printing. Most popular of these is *Roman* which is characterised by plain, upright letters in the classical tradition.

Lettering is formed by means of a variety of techniques, the most common being flat, applied, incised and raised. *Flat lettering* is painted or gilded directly onto a surface while *applied lettering* is that which is first carved in gilded wood, bronze, brass or lead, and then applied. *Incised lettering* is cut into

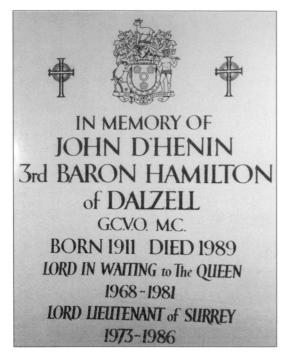

IN MEMORY OF
JOHN D'HENIN
3rd BARON HAMILTON
of DALZELL
G.C.V.O. M.C.
BORN 1911 DIED 1989
LORD IN WAITING to The QUEEN
1968-1981
LORD LIEUTENANT of SURREY
1973-1986

Memorial plaque in Bramley parish church, Surrey. Chemical engraving on brass. Designed by Anthony Wood (1994) in traditional classic Roman and italic letters.

the surface and (usually) gilded or painted or filled with lead or mastic. *Raised lettering* is that from which the background has been cut away, leaving the letters in relief.
Further reading:
Johnston, E., *Writing and Illuminating and Lettering*, London, 1906 (reprinted 1980)
Knight, S., *Historical Scripts: a Handbook for Calligraphers*, London, 1984
Stribley, M., *The Calligraphy Source Book*, London, 1986

LETTERS CLOSE Private documents which may be opened only by the breaking of a seal.
See also LETTERS PATENT

LETTERS OF ADMINISTRATION Instructions issued by a PROBATE court to the next-of-kin or other person granting them authority to administer the estate of a person who died INTESTATE. Letters of Administration-with-Will-Annexed may be granted where an executor has not been specified in a will or is unwilling or unable to act.
See also PROBATE INVENTORIES

LETTERS OF ORDERS A certificate, signed and sealed by an officiating bishop, issued to those who

have been ordained. Before 1977, candidates for ORDINATION into the Church of England were required to present *Letters Testimonial* to the bishop. These confirmed the ordinand's 'good life and conversation'.

LETTERS PATENT In 1516, letters patent replaced charters as the form in which royal grants are made (*see* CHARTER). They are 'open' documents intended for public consumption (Latin *patere* = 'to open'), often addressed 'To All and Singular to whom these Presents shall Come . . .' Armorial bearings, for example, are granted by means of signed letters patent to which the seals of the granting kings of arms are appended. Patent rolls, which contain copies of letters patent, were begun in 1201 and are still maintained today.
See also LETTERS CLOSE

LETTERS TESTIMONIAL *see* LETTERS OF ORDERS

LEVELLERS A radical but short-lived seventeenth-century anti-monarchist party which advocated republicanism, freedom in religion and a wide extension of suffrage.

LEWN(E) A church rate.

LEY LINES Generations of youngsters have been charmed by Alfred Watkins' notion 'that mounds, moats, beacons and mark stones fall into straight lines throughout Britain, with fragmentary evidence of [prehistoric] trackways on the alignments'. To these, of course, may be added churches many of which occupy sites which were selected precisely because of their pagan associations (*see* CHURCH SITES).
    The sixty-five-year-old Watkins 'perceived the existence of a ley system in a single flash' while riding across the hills near Bredwardine on the Welsh border. But when his theory was published, first in *Early British Trackways* (1922) and later in *The Old Straight Track* (1925), it caused violent controversy in archaeological circles. While it remains an anathema to the archaeologist and historian, the ley line theory has expanded into a supernatural cult. We are now asked to believe that ley lines form a kind of invisible national grid along which passes a mystical force which may be experienced through the standing stones and other 'markers' along its course.
    All of this is most unfortunate, for Watkins's original idea may contain an element of truth. We know that late Neolithic, Bronze and Iron Age peoples communicated and traded with each other, sometimes travelling considerable distances through inhospitable and unfamiliar terrain to do so. It is not unreasonable to assume that they followed

routeways which were waymarked by cairns and sky-line notches as they are in mountainous regions today. A society which was capable of constructing the great earthworks and barrows of the period was surely sufficiently advanced to recognise the benefits of waymarking (and, therefore, controlling) the routeways through its territory? To do so they may have used the 'smoke signal' method of aligning 'markers' and this would indeed produce multi-point alignments *on the map*, especially if intermediate waymarks were added later. But this does not imply that the tracks themselves were also straight and invariable. Travellers, then as now, would have selected the most appropriate route between one 'marker' and the next having regard to prevailing conditions and the gradients which lay before them. No doubt many of these ancient 'signposts' have survived while others may lie buried beneath the church towers which replaced them. But the landscape contains an enormous accumulation of topographical features, many of which lend themselves to such an interpretation. It is little wonder, then, that so many apparent 'alignments' may be identified.

Further reading:

Pennick, N. and Devereux, P., *Lines on the Landscape*, London, 1989

Watkins, A., *The Old Straight Track*, London, 1925 (Abacus 1970)

Williamson, T. and Bellamy, L., *Ley Lines in Question*, London, 1983

LIBRARIES

MONASTIC LIBRARIES

All religious houses possessed libraries, the size of which reflected the status of the monastery though not necessarily its size. They were administered by the ARMARIUS who was also responsible for the SCRIPTORIUM. Initially, collections were small and were usually housed in a cupboard (*armarium*) in the north-east corner of the CLOISTER. Later monastic libraries occupied whole rooms, together with ancillary book cupboards strategically placed in the church and conventual buildings. BOOKS, which were the common property of the house, were usually borrowed and copied in the scriptorium or donated by benefactors. Individual members of the community could borrow books *'ad usum'* for a fixed period but these had to be returned, checked and re-issued on the first Monday of Lent.

MEDIEVAL COLLECTIONS

Medieval books were, of course, extremely rare and usually written on continuous rolls of parchment or vellum which only later may have been cut and arranged into folio form (*see* MANUSCRIPT ILLUMINATION). Even in the century after the Mainz-born Gutenberg produced the first printed Bible and Psalter in 1456, significant collections of books were to be found only in the libraries of major religious and academic houses and of the most eminent magnates (*see* PRINTING). Not all these collections were private, however. During the fifteenth century a number of 'public' libraries were established: Duke Humphrey's at Oxford, the University Library at Cambridge, Whittington's at Grey Friars in London and another at Guildhall, for example. Just as today books are protected from theft by sophisticated electronic devices, so the librarians of the medieval and later periods looked to the security of their extremely valuable collections.

CHAINED LIBRARIES

The famous chained library at Hereford Cathedral is the largest of its kind to have survived. Each of its 1,500 handwritten and printed books has a chain attached to the front edge of one cover and to a rod on the bookcase. Only by turning a key to release the rod may a book be removed or added. Wooden desks and benches, placed conveniently between the oak bookcases (installed in 1611), facilitate study without the necessity of releasing the books from their fetters. All Saints' Church, also in Hereford, has a notable library of over three hundred books and there are other 'chained libraries' at Cartmel Priory in Lancashire, Grantham in Lincolnshire and Wimborne Minster in Dorset (all now splendid parish churches). Most medieval missals, psalters, gospels and other liturgical books are now in museums though individual chained books may still be found in parish churches: at Cumnor in Berkshire, Kingsthorpe in Northamptonshire and Sherborne St. John in Hampshire, for example.

POST-REFORMATION

One of the many consequences of the DISSOLUTION OF THE MONASTERIES (1536/39) was the fragmentation of several monastic libraries and the destruction of many irreplaceable manuscripts. In part, this was the result of contemporary attitudes to the old libraries: most beneficiaries of the Dissolution preferred the *de rigueur* printed folios of Caxton and his successors to the inconvenient and archaic manuscripts of the early Church.

The Injunctions of 1559 required that every parish church should acquire copies of Erasmus's *Paraphrases*, Foxe's *Book of Martyrs* and Bishop Jewel's *Apology* so that 'parishioners may most commodiously resort to the same and read it.' In many cases, these books became the nucleus of larger collections which were added to by benefactors who, before the Reformation, would have endowed a chantry or made gifts of church plate and vestments. Such books were highly valued and continue to appear at regular intervals in churchwardens' inventories. Three hundred volumes in the chained library at St. Wulfram's church at Grantham in Lincolnshire (see above) were donated by a neighbouring clergyman in 1598 while, at Langley Marish in Buckinghamshire a collection

The chained library at Hereford Cathedral.

was bequeathed to the church by Sir John Kederminster in 1623 and housed in the transept beside his family chapel.

By the end of the seventeenth century many churches had libraries, notably at St. John's, Bedford; All Saints, Bristol; All Saints, Northampton and St. Botolph's at Boston in Lincolnshire.
See also ARCHIVES, DOCUMENTARY SOURCES, ECCLESIASTICAL LIBRARIES *and* PORCHES.
Further reading:
Ker, N., *Medieval Libraries of Great Britain*, London, 1964

LICH-GATE (*also* LYCH-GATE) Many CHURCH-YARDS are entered by means of a roofed structure known as a lich-gate. The term, which was adopted by Victorian ecclesiologists, is derived from the Old English *lich* meaning 'corpse'. Indeed, 'corpse gate' (*lich-gate*) was in common usage until comparatively recently, though it was applied to any opening or stile by which a cortège might gain access to a churchyard.

FUNCTION
Although there were many covered churchyard gateways in the Middle Ages, it was the requirement in the 1549 Prayer Book that the priest, 'metyng the corpse at the church style', should there commence the *Order for the Burial of the Dead*, that encouraged the provision of shelters for that purpose. (The 'church style' was later defined in the 1662 Prayer Book as the entrance to the churchyard.) Sometimes the cortège had to wait for the arrival of the parson and this brief respite must have been welcomed by the bearers who often had to carry a corpse for many miles along rutted tracks from outlying hamlets and farmsteads (*see* CORPSE ROAD). Before the eighteenth century it was usually the shrouded corpse which was set down on the *corpse table* in the lich-gate (or, sometimes, on an adjacent wall), coffins being available only to the more affluent members of society (*see* BURIALS).

As roads improved so many parishes acquired a *bier* for shorter journeys and for transferring the coffin to the graveside where it was 'made readi to be laid into the earth'. This was usually either a wooden framework with four handles, turned legs and rollers (there is a splendid example at Lillington in Dorset) or a wheeled contraption of wicker-work within a wooden frame. Later examples (many of which may still be found gathering dust in crypts and redundant farm buildings) were sprung and had solid rubber 'tyres' and rollers on which the coffin was secured. (Strictly speaking, a HEARSE is a structure placed over a bier though in modern usage the term is used to describe the vehicle which conveys a coffin to a funeral.)

Corpse tables or *coffin stones* were wooden or stone plinths on which the corpse (or coffin) was placed at the entrance to the churchyard. Regrettably, few have survived: those at Bolney in Sussex, Chiddingford in Surrey and Atherington and Ashprington in Devon being notable exceptions. At Maltby in Yorkshire a fourteenth-century table tomb was removed to the lich-gate for this purpose while in many parishes a pair of simple three-legged COFFIN STOOLS was used. In some areas, rough-hewn coffin stones may sometimes be found at resting places along the route taken by a cortège from a remote dependent church to a mother church which retained parochial burial rights.

DATING

Few medieval lich-gates have survived without structural alteration, particularly to the timber framework, though several fourteenth-century examples still have original barge-boarding characteristically decorated with scrolls and floral motifs. There are fine medieval examples at Whitbourne in Worcestershire, Anstey and Ashwell in Hertfordshire and Boughton Monchelsea in Kent. Most lich-gates are from the seventeenth and eighteenth centuries, though many appear to be of some antiquity and are often difficult to date. That at Painswick in Gloucestershire, for example, is a substantial plaster and timber-frame building supporting a small gabled 'parish room'. Its timbers, particularly the decorative barge-boards on which are carvings of bells, are clearly very old but it was built as recently as 1901 by local craftsmen using timbers removed from the belfry. Occasionally, early church stiles and seventeenth- or eighteenth-century lich-gates are found side-by-side, as at Llanfaglan in Gwynedd, and some churchyards have two or more lich-gates of different dates, as at Troutbeck in Cumbria where there are three. Not all parishes could afford a covered entrance and the provision of a lich-gate is often indicative of the generosity of local benefactors. Many nineteenth-century lich-gates were erected to commemorate local worthies or as the final flourish of a church restoration or rebuilding, while more recent examples have served as war memorials, paid for by public subscription. There is an unusual revolving 'turnpike' lich-gate at Cruwys Morchard in Devon.

The four-gabled lich-gate at Monnington-on-Wye, Herefordshire.

CONSTRUCTION

Bearing in mind the rich variety of Britain's vernacular architecture, lich-gates are surprisingly uniform in design and there are few regional variations. They are frequently found constructed of materials which are used neither in the church nor in adjacent walls, indeed many pre-date the walls of which they are now a part. There is clear evidence to show that lich-gates served a purpose entirely distinct from that of a simple gateway (*church hatch*) in a boundary wall and in many cases they were sited in isolation. Most early examples have open timberwork with curved braces and additional wind braces in the roof. These were followed by timber structures, usually supported on masonry footings or in-filled with stone or brick. Footings gradually increased in height to become low walls and these remain the most common form of structure, usually with timber framing supporting the roof.

Lich-gates are generally defined by the structure of their roofs, by far the most common types being the longitudinal or 'porch' roof, the ridge of which corresponds to the passageway beneath, and the latitudinal or 'shed' type, in which the ridge is set at

Parish bier at Glanvilles Wootton, Dorset.

right-angles to the passageway. Occasional examples may also be found of gates where two roof ridges intersect at right-angles in a symbolic cruciform shape with four gables, as at Painswick (see above) and Clun in Shropshire (dated 1733). There are also pyramidal roofs as at Pulborough in Sussex and More in Shropshire. Most are tiled but there are thatched examples as at Fleet in Lincolnshire. Some lich-gates are built entirely of stone, the unique seventeenth-century gate at Astbury in Cheshire, for example, has battlements and pinnacles in keeping with its fourteenth-century church. Many lich-gates are provided with bench seats for the convenience of bearers and these are usually of stone or slate. At Mylor in Cornwall a modern (1928) commemorative lich-gate has been erected over an ancient granite coffin stone flanked by stone seats and a Cornish stepping-stone 'style' on either side.

Unlike domestic gatehouses, surprisingly few lich-gates were adapted for other purposes. Nevertheless there are several unusual exceptions, including the combined lich-gate and belfry erected at Great Bourton in Oxfordshire in 1882 and the medieval gate at Anstey in Hertfordshire, part of which was once used as the village lock-up. At Wykeham in Yorkshire the tower of a former church was retained as a lich-gate to the new building and at Egham in Buckinghamshire a fifteenth-century porch was similarly preserved.
See also GRAVESIDE SHELTER

LICK-WAYS *see* CORPSE ROADS

LIERNE *and* LIERNE VAULT *see* VAULTING

LIGHT A stipendiary endowment in the medieval church.

LIGHTHOUSES Medieval chantries were often established for the benefit of sea-farers, notably a number of beacons or lighthouses which were erected above chantry chapels and maintained by chantry priests (*see* CHANTRY). The best-known examples are the rocket-shaped fourteenth-century lighthouse and chapel on St. Catherine's Down on the Isle of Wight and the lonely Norman chapel on St. Aldhelm's Head in Dorset which once supported a fire basket on its roof (*see* CHAPELS).

LIGHTS *see* ALTAR LIGHTS, AUMBRY LAMP, BIER LIGHT, CANDELABRUM, CANDLES, CANDLESTICKS, CHANDELIER, CORONA LUCIS, CRESSETS, GASOLIER, HEARSE, LAMPS, LANTERN, LIGHTHOUSES, POOR SOUL'S LIGHT, PRICKET, ROOD BEAM *and* RUSHLIGHT-HOLDER

LIGHTS (WINDOW) The openings between the MULLIONS and TRANSOMS (*see* WINDOWS).

LIMEWASH Quicklime (unslaked lime) boils with intense heat when water is added. For centuries limewash was made by packing coarse waste fat in a tub of quicklime and adding water, the effect of which was to heat and distribute the fat. When used as an external wall-covering to a building, the fat content of limewash did not dissolve in the wet thereby making the coating waterproof.

LINENFOLD Sixteenth-century wooden PANEL-LING carved with stylised fabric in vertical folds, one piece of 'linen' filling each panel.

LINENS *see* CHRISM, COMMUNION LINENS *and* VEILS

LINTEL A horizontal stone or beam spanning an opening and supporting the wall above (*see also* ARCH).

LION According to the bestiaries, lion cubs were born dead and remained so for three days whereupon their father breathed into their faces and gave them life. For this reason, the lion is associated with Christ risen from the dead and is often depicted in church carvings as fighting with the devil in a dragon's form. Confusingly, the lion may also be found as a symbol of evil: trodden underfoot like the dragon and the serpent of the Psalms. The winged lion represents St. Mark the Evangelist, being one of the four beasts around the throne 'which rested not day and night' (Revelation).
See also BEASTS (HERALDIC)

LIRIPIPE *see* COSTUME

LITANY A form of prayer comprising a series of supplications said or sung by a priest, deacon or CANTOR to which the congregation responds. The Anglican Litany is a free translation and adaptation of the chief Roman Litany. It first appeared in English as a separate book in 1544 and in Henry VIII's *Primer* of 1545 in which it was described as

the 'Common Prayer of Procession', the rhythmical alternation of prayer and refrain being especially appropriate for processional use. In the *Book of Common Prayer*, the Litany is a 'general supplication' to be said or sung after Morning Prayer on Sundays, Wednesdays and Fridays.
See also MATTINS *and* VERSICLES

LITANY DESK *see* DESKS

LITERATE One who has been admitted to Holy Orders without a university degree.

LITTEN A burial ground.

LITURGICAL COLOURS *see* COLOURS (LITURGICAL)

LITURGICAL MOVEMENT A movement whose objective is to promote the active participation of the laity in worship. In the Church of England, the *Ritualistic Movement* which, in the early twentieth century, emphasised the importance of sacramental worship (*see also* TRACTARIANS *and* OXFORD MOVEMENT). In recent times, changes in the pattern of Sunday worship have tended to replace morning services with a 'Parish Communion' and to adopt ceremonial which stresses the corporate nature of the LITURGY.

LITURGY Derived from the Greek for 'a public work', the liturgy is the form of service used in the celebration of the EUCHARIST (*see also* MASS). But in ordinary English usage the term has come to imply all forms of service authorised by the Church, in contradistinction to private devotional worship. It is also used to describe the texts by which services are ordered and the study of such texts. In England, the evolution of the liturgy has affected significantly the development of the parish church, its architecture, art, music and ritual.

Before the Reformation, all the countries of western Europe shared a common (Roman) liturgy, though there were numerous local modifications. In England, for example, the rites (*uses*) practised at Salisbury differed from those of York and Hereford, though by the late Middle Ages it was the Salisbury rite (the *Use of Sarum*) which had been adopted for use in most English cathedrals and parish churches and this was to provide much of the material for the first *Book of Common Prayer (1549)* (*see* COMMON PRAYER, BOOK OF *and* SARUM, USE OF).
    The liturgy followed that of the Benedictines: a daily celebration of High Mass and the seven canonical offices (*see* DIVINE OFFICE) which were observed throughout the Middle Ages by a rapidly increasing number of clergy, chaplains and chantry

priests (*see* CHANTRY). But for the laity, there were usually three services on Sundays and Holy Days: MATTINS followed by MASS in the morning and EVENSONG in the afternoon. The Mass was of special significance: increasingly so following the Fourth Lateran Council of 1215 which pronounced the doctrine of TRANSUBSTANTIATION, thereby emphasising the sacredness and mystery of the Mass. This resulted in a weakening of the intimate relationship between priest and people, so evident in Anglo-Saxon and Norman churches where there was no screen between the SANCTUARY and the nave (*see* CHANCEL), and as belief in the potency of the Mass increased, so the sacrament was received less often. Communion was administered only after CONFESSION which was then so thorough that it was normally made only once a year, before Easter. Nevertheless, a regular reaffirmation of faith was required and this was achieved by witnessing the ELEVATION of the Host (see below). Consequently, High Mass on Sunday was the best attended service of the week, the other offices attracting modest congregations and, in many instances, none at all. Of course, in the Middle Ages, the laity was denied the Precious Blood of Christ (the wine) and received only the Host (the consecrated wafer of the Eucharist).

Neither was there a *Book of Common Prayer* which conveniently set out the liturgy in a single volume. In the Middle Ages, there were so many services, and so many variations and accretions, that several books were provided, one for each service or part thereof (*see* BOOKS). These included the MISSAL, or Mass book, which set out all the variations of the service required for Sundays, saints' days and festivals and, in the great abbey churches and cathedrals, this would be supplemented by other books containing specialised elements of the rite: the Epistle Book, the Gospel Book and the GRADUAL (or Grail) which contained the music. The MANUALE *(or Ritual)* set out the offices of baptism, marriage, visitation of the sick and the burial of the dead, while the BREVIARY attempted to provide an abbreviated edition of the daily offices and the main prayers and collects, though even this ran to four volumes, one for each season of the year, and contained 'optional extras' such as the *Placebo* and the *Dirige*, the evening and morning offices for the dead. Two of the more convenient service books which were used by both the clergy and the congregation were the PSALTER, which brought together the Old Testament psalms, and the BOOK OF HOURS which was a compendium of the most frequently used liturgical material. There was also the PONTIFICAL which set out the services and prayers to be used only by bishops: at confirmation and ordination, for example.

It should be remembered that, for many of those who occupied the nave, the ritual of the liturgy would be hardly visible or audible. The PRESBYTERY was separated from the nave by a CHANCEL SCREEN while much of the service was spoken *sotto voce* by the celebrant – and in Latin. It was the Elevation of the Host which was the culmination of the Mass, for it signified that transubstantiation had taken place (*see also* SQUINT). There were no hymns and only occasional sermons and, before the fifteenth century, no seating other than a stone bench at the foot of the nave wall for those who were too weak to stand (hence the saying 'gone to the wall'). Only during liturgical PROCESSIONS, was the congregation able to witness the proceedings at close quarters, and AISLES were often added for this purpose. The effect was to create a sense of mystery and symbolism, reinforced by the ritualistic movements of the celebrant beyond the screen, by the brilliance of the PLATE and VESTMENTS, and by the messages conveyed in sculpture, paint and stained glass. There can be no doubt that, while the doctrines of the Church were, for the most part, beyond the understanding of the commonalty, the regular performance of ritual, augmented by the special ceremonies associated with the various feast days, provided medieval communities with a sense of stability and security and created an intense attachment to the parish church.

By the thirteenth century, increasing ritual, and the need to accommodate additional priests, deacons and ACOLYTES, resulted in the building of numerous new chancels or the enlarging of existing ones. This was usually achieved by extending the chancel at its eastern termination, a process which may have been repeated several times and which often resulted in building elements which are perceptibly out of alignment with one another (*see also* SQUINTS). Evidence of liturgical elaboration, and of the burgeoning numbers of celebrants and acolytes, may also be found within the church (in the EASTER SEPULCHRE, SEDILIA and PISCINA, for example) and in surviving inventories of church possessions (*see also* BISHOPS' REGISTERS).

By the fifteenth century, even the most remote country church had at least one priest in addition to the incumbent, and some had two or three. In many town churches, and those where chantries and colleges had been established, the numbers were even greater. At the church of St. Thomas of Canterbury in Salisbury, for example, there were no fewer than 21 priests, 16 deacons, 11 sub-deacons and 9 chantry priests in 1432, all serving a population of less than 3,000 souls.

The liturgy changed significantly in the post-medieval period, notably as a consequence of the English REFORMATION and of the Evangelical Revival of the nineteenth century (*see* NINETEENTH-CENTURY CHURCH).

See also ANGLO-SAXON CHURCH, COMMON PRAYER, BOOK OF, MONASTICISM, MEDIEVAL CHURCH, SEVENTEENTH-CENTURY CHURCH, EIGHTEENTH-CENTURY CHURCH *and* WALES, THE CHURCH IN
Further reading:
Wordsworth, C. and Littlehales, H., *The Old Service Books of the English Church*, London, 1904

LIVERY AND MAINTENANCE Emoluments provided by a lord to his retainers (*livery*) and patronage exercised through the manipulation of the legal system (*maintenance*). The practice of paying and protecting large numbers of retainers in return for domestic and military services (known as *Bastard Feudalism*) was common throughout Europe in the Middle Ages, particularly in England during the fourteenth and fifteenth centuries when a magnate's influence was judged by the number of men wearing his BADGE and uniform (*liveries*) and his willingness to protect them when necessary in the courts of law. The ability of a magnate to summon to the field of battle large retinues of men whose allegiance was bought through the practice of livery and maintenance was a major factor during the civil wars of the period. This was recognised by successive sovereigns who attempted to legislate against abuses of the system, thereby reducing the effectiveness of the nobles' private armies. It was not until 1540 that the practice was finally suppressed, the private army abolished and the MIDDLE AGES brought to a close. Nevertheless, in late sixteenth-century Wales, the aristocracy continued to expect their tenants to follow them in military service; in the year of the Armada (1588) the earl of Pembroke was able to muster an army of eight hundred men.

LLAN- *and* LAN- Common place-name elements *llan-* in the Welsh and *lan-* in Cornish, meaning 'church'. In sixth-century Wales the word was used to describe a clearing or enclosure which had been set apart for religious purposes, including burial, and inevitably many *llannau* were considered to be suitable sites for later churches (*see* CHURCHYARDS). The *llan* element is often followed by the name of the founder or the donor of the land on which the *llan* stood (*see* CELTIC CHURCH). *Llan-*place-names are not confined to Wales: there are numerous examples in the border counties of England such as Llanwarne in Herefordshire which means 'church by the swamp'.
See also CLAS

LOCKS *see* DOORS AND DOORWAYS

LOCK-UP Before the formation of police forces in 1856, each parish elected an unpaid, petty constable whose responsibilities included the supervision of

The thirteenth-century town bridge at Bradford-on-Avon, Wiltshire. Modified in the seventeenth century, its tiny chapel was pressed into service as a lock-up.

watch and ward, the apprehension and detention of suspected criminals and the maintenance of the village stocks and lock-up (*see* PARISH CONSTABLE). The lock-up was a gaol where drunks and trouble-makers were locked up for the night and where felons were detained by the constable pending their removal to court. Most were little more than a secure shed, made available for the purpose by a local farmer and performing other functions when not required by the constable. But in some places more substantial buildings were used. At Stratton in Cornwall, for example, the solid timber door to the south porch of the parish church retains to this day 240 nails spelling out the colloquialism 'Clink' (*see* PORCHES), and at Bradford-on-Avon in Wiltshire the ancient oratory on the river bridge was commandeered as a gaol, as was part of the medieval lich-gate at Anstey in Hertfordshire.
Further reading:
Friar, S., *The Batsford Companion to Local History*, London, 1991

LOCULUS (i) A recess in an altar in which relics were kept. (ii) A recess in a vault for holding a coffin or urn (*see* VAULTS, BURIAL).

LOGGIA A covered verandah, open on at least one side.

LOLLARD A term of contempt, of Dutch origin, meaning 'mutterer' or 'mumbler', conferred on those who professed to follow John Wycliffe (*c.* 1330–84) in his opposition to the established order within the English church (*see* WYCLIFFE, JOHN). They rejected priestly authority and advocated evangelical poverty in imitation of Christ and the studying of the scriptures in the vernacular (*see* BIBLES). Official attitudes to the Lollards varied considerably, but they were generally considered to be heretics and were often violently suppressed.

LONG AND SHORT WORK Typical of Anglo-Saxon structures, alternate long vertical and short horizontal stones set in the termination of a wall to provide additional strength: to the corners of a tower or a doorway jamb for example.
See also ANGLO-SAXON ARCHITECTURE *and* QUOIN

LORD (i) The abbreviated style of a peer below the rank of Duke. (ii) An honorary prefix used by the younger sons of dukes and marquesses.
See also PEERAGE, THE

LORD OF THE MANOR Following the Conquest of 1066 England was divided among the followers of William I who remained, in theory, the owner of the kingdom. The smallest holding within these granted estates has subsequently become known as the 'manor'. The highest level of tenancy, held of the king, was the tenancy in chief (*lordship in fee*). Magnates in this category sometimes let to lesser lords (*mesne tenants*) who, on occasion, let to their followers who thereby became *tenants-in-demesne*. The 'lord of the manor' could belong to any of these categories but was always the tenant on whom the actual feudal obligation rested. Thereafter, overlordships of manors tended to become forgotten and after 1290, when the statute of *Quia Emptores* forbad further subinfeudation, qualifying clauses were inserted in conveyances to prevent future claims of overlordship. The term itself means 'landlord' and a lord of the manor was not necessarily titled or even armigerous. The identity of manorial lords and the service (*fees*) by which the manors were held, may be obtained from the *Book of Fees* (or *Feudal Aids*) and *inquisitions post mortem*. Since 1926 all matters relating to the ownership of manors and the location of manorial records have to reported to the Master of the Rolls and this information may be obtained from the National Register of Archives (*see* APPENDIX II). In the late twentieth century, manorial lordships have become marketable commodities despite the fact that they bring with them little more than an archaic title.

See also MANOR
For the Manorial Society *see* APPENDIX II.

LORD'S DAY OBSERVANCE ACT (1781) *see* SUNDAY

LORD'S PRAYER, THE The most familiar and sacred of prayers (that which begins 'Our Father . . .') which was taught by the Lord to the Apostles. The form used by the Christian Church is that in Matthew 6: 9–13 though a slightly different version may be found in Luke 11: 2–4. A concluding doxology, the GLORIA PATRI, was added (probably) by the fourth century. The prayer consists of the address followed by three petitions for the glorification of God and four petitions for the physical and spiritual needs of mankind.

LOUVRE (*or* LOUVER) (i) An opening in a wall in which a series of overlapping slats is arranged to admit air and to exclude rain. (ii) An erection on a roof, the side-openings of which provide ventilation to the space within.

LOW CHURCH The LATITUDINARIAN wing of the Church of England, close to Protestant nonconformity, which in the seventeenth and eighteenth centuries attached less importance to the sacraments, the priesthood and the episcopate than did the HIGH CHURCH. Since the mid-nineteenth century the term has been associated with EVANGELISM within the Church of England.
See also OXFORD MOVEMENT, THE

LOW MASS *see* MASS

LOW SIDE WINDOW *or* LOW SOUTH WINDOW *see* CHANCEL VENTILATOR

LOZENGE A rhombus, a diamond-shaped figure in e.g. heraldry.
See also DECORATIVE MOTIFS

LUCARNE A dormer window in a church spire.

LUNETTE (i) A semicircular opening, sometimes containing a painting or sculpture. (ii) *See also* DECORATIVE MOTIFS

LUSTRE A period of five years.

LUTHERANISM Martin Luther (1483–1546) was a German Protestant theologian, reformer and writer whose lifelong struggle against the doctrines of the medieval Church permanently changed the face of Christianity in Europe. In 1505 he entered an Augustinian community, was ordained in 1507 and became a lecturer at the new university of Wittenberg in 1508. Luther's studies as professor of

Scripture, the influence of Augustine and late medieval German mysticism, and his own experience of the religious life brought him to a belief in the Pauline doctrine of justification by faith. For Luther, this implied that Scripture was the sole rule of faith and that all men were equal before God. He advocated translation of the Scriptures and the restoration of the chalice to the laity, and castigated a system in which priests mediated with God on men's behalf. His nailing of the *95 Theses* to the church door at Wittenberg in 1517 precipitated Luther's break with the Church and condemnation by the Pope in 1520. Despite his opposition to the Peasants' Revolt (1524–6) his religious reforms won widespread public support and his teaching found systematic expression through the publication of *Catechisms* in 1529 which, together with other formularies, were combined in the *Book of Concord* of 1580.
See also CALVINISM, EUCHARIST *and* REFORMATION

LYCH-GATE *see* LICH-GATE

LYCHWAYS *see* CORPSE ROADS

MACE *see* CHURCH AND COMMUNITY

MADONNA (Italian = 'My Lady') The Blessed Virgin Mary when represented in statues and paintings.

MAGDALENES From St. Mary Magdalene, the term was often adopted as a title by medieval religious communities of penitent women.

MAGI, THE *see* CHRISTIAN SYMBOLS

MAGNA A place-name element meaning 'greater' as in Minterne Magna in Dorset. Minterne Parva, or 'lesser Minterne', is located half a mile to the south.
See also PLACE-NAMES

MAGNIFICAT From St. Luke's Gospel (1:39–55), the hymn sung by the Blessed Virgin Mary when her cousin Elizabeth greeted her as the mother of Christ ('My soul doth magnify the Lord . . .'). The Magnificat is a canticle in the office of VESPERS

and was incorporated into the Anglican Evening Service in the *Book of Common Prayer*. Together with the NUNC DIMITTIS, the Magnificat has been set to music by numerous composers and is regularly sung in cathedral and collegiate chapels at choral evensong.

MAINPORT A small offering (e.g. of bread) to a rector in lieu of TITHES.

MAJESTAS A representation of Christ in Majesty. The majestas was one of the few images allowed by the CISTERCIAN rule and was usually placed in a prominent position as a reminder of the Last Judgment and, therefore, of the purpose of the religious life.

MAJOR ORDERS The senior grades of the Christian ministry: bishops, priests and deacons (*see* CLERGY, CHURCH OF ENGLAND). From the thirteenth century, the office of SUBDEACON was considered to be the lowest of the major orders in the Roman Catholic Church until it was suppressed in 1972.
See also MINOR ORDERS

MAJUSCULE *see* LETTERING

MALLARDY (*also* **NURCERY**) A medieval hospice, specifically for the sick.

MANDATUM *see* MAUNDY THURSDAY

MANDORLA An oval panel or a work of art contained therein.
See also VESICA PISCIS

MANGER *see* CHRISTMAS

MANIPLE *see* VESTMENTS

MANOR A feudal estate (from the Latin *mansus*) and, for five hundred years after the Conquest, the essential unit of local government, though it is likely that several important elements of the 'manorial system' had been established long before 1066. A fundamental principle of the *land law*, introduced, applied and expanded by successive Norman kings, was 'no land without a lord and no lord without land.' A manor was held of the king by a manorial lord (literally, 'landlord') either directly or through one or more *mesne lords* (*subinfeudation*). Many held several, often widely dispersed, manors, the day-to-day management of each being entrusted to an elected officer known as a *reeve* and the administration of a manorial court (or group of courts) to a *steward* (see below). In practice, the term '*manorial system*' is fallacious, for there was no such thing as a 'typical' manor. Generalisations are inevitably misleading, therefore, and historians prefer to study individual manors, recognising that each was possessed of characteristics and customs which rarely conformed to a 'system' and were often unique.

A manor itself might encompass a number of TOWNSHIPS and farmsteads; it may have been reorganised around a new and more substantial village (*see* VILLAGES) or it may have retained the boundaries of an earlier Saxon (or even Roman) estate. A manor could be part of a PARISH, contiguous with its boundaries, or it could be spread over a number of parishes (*see* CHURCH SITES). It would usually comprise the lord's demesne lands and the common ploughland, meadowland and waste. Over much of England, the arable land of a manor consisted of three or more large open fields in which the inhabitants held scattered strips according to their relative tenements. The lord's demesne land might similarly be distributed within the open fields or contained in a consolidated block of the most fertile strips. From the produce of these demesne lands was derived the wealth of the manor, together with a variety of feudal dues, rents and fines exacted by the manorial court. The earliest manors were worked by *villeins*, who laboured on the demesne lands in return for their tenements (known as *villein tenure*), together with one or more *franklins* who were free tenants. As the feudal system decayed, villein tenure increasingly became commuted to money payments, a form of tenure known as *copyhold*.

ADMINISTRATION

The manor was governed by a manor court, a periodic meeting of tenants convened and presided over by the lord of the manor or his steward who was usually a man of some substance and often trained in law. Manorial custom determined both the frequency and the conduct of these meetings which were usually held at intervals of between six weeks and six months. Though the procedure was judicial, the manorial courts considered both judicial and administrative matters, such as the transfer of property (*alienationes*), sitting either as *courts baron* or *courts leet*. The overriding principle was that of custom by which the rights and responsibilities both of the lord and the tenantry were determined: 'Justice shall be done by the lord's court, not by the lord.' Many customs were already of 'ancient foundation' at the time of the Conquest and were to form the basis of Common Law. The manor court was not entirely autonomous, however, for it was subject to the authority of the royal courts in certain areas such as the rights of free tenants. All tenants were obliged to attend manorial courts and were eligible for election as jurors. Defaulters who failed to attend or refused to serve as jurors were fined, unless they were able to demonstrate 'good cause' to the satisfaction of the court. Manorial officers (other than the bailiff who was appointed by the steward as

his manager) were elected at an annual meeting of the court. These included the *reeve*, the *beadle*, *constable*, *hayward*, *ale-taster* and two *affeerors* who were responsible for determining the amounts to be paid in fines. When the lordship of a manor changed hands a special *Court of Recognition (Curia Prima)* was held at which the new lord was formally 'seized' of his tenants' service and received their renewed oaths of fealty. A *Court of Survey* was also convened at which were recorded all the manorial lands and the customary dues by which they were held.

The records of manorial courts are an invaluable source of information. Of these, the most significant are the *Court Rolls* which were compiled by the steward's clerk as minutes of proceedings, including disputes and changes in the occupancy of holdings. The customary rights and responsibilities of a lord and his tenants were set out in the *Custumal* and details of the location and size of the various holdings were recorded in the *Terrier*. Jury Verdicts were retained in a separate record and details of rents due and paid were kept in the *Rental*. In the *Valor* were recorded the financial value of holdings and the *Extent* was a document in which were summarised the customs, valuation and tenancies of a manor at a given time.

DOCUMENTARY SOURCES

Since 1926 all manorial records and changes of ownership of lordships of manors have to be reported to the Master of the Rolls. The Royal Commission on Historical Manuscripts (*see* APPENDIX II) maintains a *Manorial Documents Register* from which may be ascertained the names of the manor or manors in each parish and the last-known location of manorial records. In many cases these are held by the solicitors of families holding manorial lordships (*see* LORD OF THE MANOR) but many have been deposited at county record offices. There are also notable collections of manorial records at the Public Record Office, the British Library and Birmingham Reference Library (*see* APPENDIX II).

Further reading:

Friar, S., *The Batsford Companion to Local History*, London, 1991

Harvey, P., *Manorial Records*, British Record Association, 1984

Stuart, D., *Manorial Records*, Chichester, 1992

MANSARD ROOF *see* ROOFS (TIMBER)

MANTLING (*also* LAMBREQUIN) The mantling is a protective cloth affixed to the helmet and, in a COAT OF ARMS, is depicted as flowing from beneath the CREST, sometimes terminating in tassels and scalloped or 'slashed' in stylised form. Almost certainly, the mantling originated in the Holy Land where it was worn by crusading knights to absorb the sun's heat, thereby preventing the helmet from becoming unbearably hot. It is surprising, therefore, that the lighter colour (silver or gold) is always depicted on the **inside** of the mantling. A succession of sumptuary laws from 1363 to 1532 sought to limit the wearing of 'sumptuous apparel' by forbidding 'the untitled commonality' to wear items such as gold chains and collars or cloth of gold, purple silks and crimson velvet. Interestingly, the use of ermine was reserved for the nobility and, as a token of royal favour, by concession to other magnates close to the Crown. It may be that the extensive use of ermine in the heraldic mantlings of many of the Garter knights of the period (together with crimson linings) was therefore intended to indicate their privileged position in medieval society. *See also* WREATH

MANUALE (Latin = 'a book of convenient size') A medieval book containing the forms prescribed for the administration of the Sacraments.

MANUSCRIPT ILLUMINATION A manuscript is a book or document written by hand. Although paper-making was known in Spain and Italy by the twelfth century, PARCHMENT and VELLUM were the chief materials used for writing throughout medieval Europe until the development of PRINTING in the late fifteenth century. Parchment was ideally suited to ornamentation as well as writing, and some of the finest artistic works of the Middle Ages are the illuminated manuscripts produced in the *scriptoria* of monastic houses.

A manuscript which is described as illuminated is one which is decorated in colours and gold. When the page is bent, and the gold is caught by the light, it appears to possess a lustrous quality unequalled by other forms of decoration. The gold is applied either in the form of a powder mixed with a suitable water-based medium and used as a pigment or in the form of leaf, either directly to the working surface or on a plaster ground of *Gesso Sottile* (deactivated calcium sulphate, lead carbonate, an animal glue and sugar). This plaster ground is either applied with a quill pen or painted on and dries hard, flexible and raised. The leaf is then applied and polished with an agate burnisher.

In Britain, the early medieval schools of Ireland and Northumbria produced manuscripts of extraordinary skill and originality in the interlacing and counterpointing of geometrical and animal patterns and subtle variations of colour. The best known of these Celtic manuscripts are the *Lindisfarne Gospels* and the *Book of Kells*. In Europe, the Byzantine tradition, with its florid use of gold and vermilion, continued into the Carolingian period to produce works in which the emphasis was on illuminated ornamental motifs. In England, the (incomplete) twelfth-century *Winchester Bible*

contains the work of five different artists and, in its obvious Byzantine influences and its emphasis on naturalistic elements, is one of the finest and most innovative products of the illuminator's art.

From the end of the twelfth century the art of the miniaturist flourished, notably in the production of the great bibles. (The work of the *miniaturist* is not concerned with that which is small but with the use of red lead for colouring, the latin verb *minire* meaning 'to colour with red lead'.) In the later Middle Ages increasing use was made of enlarged and ornamented initial letters in which illustrations of biblical and naturalistic scenes were inserted. Beautifully illuminated breviaries, psalters, missals and books of hours were commissioned by medieval magnatial families as gifts to superiors and as benefactions to religious houses. These contained exquisitely executed illustrations of the agrarian year, biblical scenes, devotional texts and the lives of saints and martyrs, often identified as the patron saints of recipients. Not all illumination was confined to religious manuscripts: genealogies, romances and many official documents were also illuminated and almost invariably embellished with heraldry.
See also LETTERING
Further reading:

Alexander, J., *Medieval Illuminators and their Methods of Work*, New Haven and London, 1994
De Hamel, C., *A History of Illuminated Manuscripts*, London, 1994
Pacht, O., *Book Illumination in the Middle Ages: an Introduction*, London, 1986
Tymms, W., *The Art of Illumination*, London, 1988

MANUS DEI The Hand of God in blessing, often surrounded by a nimbus.

MAPS Churches cannot be studied in isolation and a map of an appropriate scale to show, for example, the topographical features of a parish or the relationship of an ancient minster to its subordinate churches, is an essential tool of the local historian. The conventional mapping symbol for a church is a cross, though on the smaller scale Ordnance Survey maps (see below) a church with a tower is depicted as a black square surmounted by a cross, one with a spire (or dome) as a black circle surmounted by a cross, and one with neither a tower nor a spire as a simple cross. It should be borne in mind, however, that these symbols are described simply as 'places of worship' which may be of any denomination.
EARLY MAPS
While pictorial symbols were used to denote settlements with churches on many sixteenth- and seventeenth-century maps, the early cartographers were unable to provide sufficient detail or accuracy to satisfy the needs of the twentieth-century researcher. Nevertheless, cartography improved

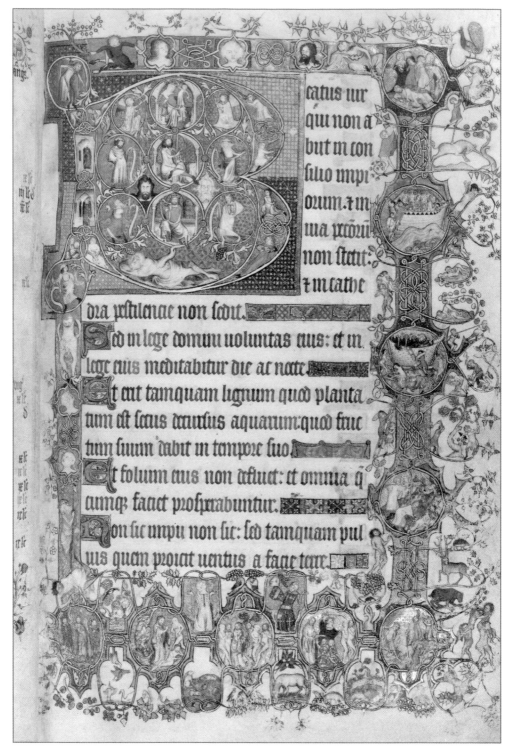

The Beatus page from the St. Omer Psalter, executed c. 1325 for members of the St. Omer family of Mulbarton, Norfolk, whose portraits appear in medallions beneath the text.

significantly towards the end of the seventeenth century, notably in the work of the prolific Robert Morden (d. 1703) and of John Ogilby (1600–76). Ogilby's *Britannia* (1675) contained one hundred plates of road maps, each printed to look like a series of six or seven vertical strips of parchment on which a main road was depicted together with towns, villages, junctions and roadside features, familiar to the seventeenth-century traveller, such as inns, churches, bridges, windmills, beacons and even gallows. Although of a small scale, these maps are of great interest, especially when compared with later Ordnance Survey maps. Also of interest are the *Britannia Depicta* or *Ogilby Improv'd* (1720) of Emmanuel Bowen (d. 1767), which contains 270 plates of road and county maps, and the *New and Correct English Atlas* (1787) of John Cary (1754–1835) which is notable for its accurate depiction of roads.

LOCAL MAPS
Numerous localised maps have been produced for specific purposes and these can be of inestimable value to the researcher.

Estate maps usually encompass a manor, park or farm or sometimes just a group of fields or the grounds of a country house. Although late sixteenth- and seventeenth-century estate maps are known, most date from the eighteenth century or later. They are usually very detailed, and may even delineate precisely every feature of a particular area, including the parish church and its churchyard. Many are retained in the archives of large landowners while others have been transferred to county record offices. Indexes of estate papers are maintained by the Royal Commission on Historical Manuscripts (*see* APPENDIX II).

Enclosure Award maps show only those parts of a parish which were subject to reorganisation as the result of parliamentary enclosure in the late eighteenth and early nineteenth centuries. In those areas of late enclosure (such as the Midlands) the old strips and areas of land described as 'ancient enclosures' are also shown. Of particular interest are field names (and acreages), which may be identified from numbers on the map and the corresponding entries in the award, and the location of GLEBE land. The Enclosure Acts provided that copies of the award should be deposited with the Clerk of the Peace for the county and the archives of the parish concerned. If extant, these, together with accompanying maps, will be found in the local or county record offices.

Tithe maps for England and Wales were produced between 1838 and 1854 as a result of the Tithe Commutation Act of 1836 by which payments in kind and MODUS were commuted to money settlements based on the ownership of property (*see* TITHES). Detailed parish maps, accompanied by registers (*terriers*) of land-holdings, were deposited

with the Tithe Redemption Commission (whose archives are now with the Public Record Office at Kew – *see* APPENDIX II) and the appropriate diocesan and parochial authorities. Unlike enclosure maps, tithe maps cover an entire parish and are often very large. In most maps, all properties are shown, including houses (which are numbered) and gardens as well as larger land-holdings and remaining areas of common. In many cases, the tithe map may be the earliest complete cartographical record of the parish since enclosure maps were often limited to those areas still in common. It will also delineate the boundary of the 'ancient' (ecclesiastical) parish which may differ from that of the civil parish. The commutation awards provide details of landowners (in alphabetical order) and tenants, types of dwelling, field names and land use. Most tithe maps are now held by county record offices.

ORDNANCE SURVEY MAPS
During the second half of the eighteenth century, when Britain was faced with the threat of invasion from France, accurate maps of the south coast of England were needed by the British Army. A survey was carried out by the Board of Ordnance, a Crown organisation mainly responsible for artillery, with offices in the Tower of London. The Board's work followed the example of a pioneering Scottish cartographer General William Roy, who had produced military maps at the time of the Scottish rebellion in 1745. Once the survey of the south coast had been completed at a scale of 1 inch to one mile, the new style of map-making was in considerable demand, the Industrial Revolution in particular creating a need for good quality mapping so that major engineering and constructional projects could be defined and demographic and social changes recorded.

The First Edition or *Old Series* of one-inch maps is an interesting though perplexing historical instrument because of the complexity of its development. The Trigonometrical Survey of England and Wales was founded in 1791 and the first regular sheet (Essex) published in 1805. But the national one-inch map was not completed until the publication of the last sheet (the Isle of Man) in 1873. After this date *Old Series* maps remained in print and were not universally superseded by the *New Series* sheets until the early 1890s, a century after the scheme was conceived, during which time numerous modifications were made progressively, not only to newly published sheets but also to existing copper plates. *Old Series* maps are therefore subject to considerable variation and the delay between survey and publication varies from a few years to twenty. After 1847, railway revisions were effected and special map series produced such as the *Index to the Tithe Survey* and the *Geological Survey*. Dating the content of these early maps is often difficult, nevertheless the facsimile series of post-1860 *Old Series* one-inch sheets (published by

David and Charles) provides a fascinating view of the late nineteenth-century landscape and, with its copious notes, enables the historian to trace the complex development of a particular map. The Third Edition was published by the beginning of the twentieth century and the seventh edition by 1961.

Since the original Trigonometrical Survey, maps at a variety of scales have been produced using a network of over 20,000 *trigonometrical stations*, pillars ('trig points') set in elevated positions in open countryside or on tall buildings such as church towers. Trig points were shown on maps as small blue triangles, each containing a spot-height (see below), the symbol for a trig point on a church tower being the conventional black square and cross contained within a blue triangle. Surveyors measured the angle and distances between these points to provide a base from which shorter distances could be measured and locations plotted accurately. Heights above (Cornish) sea level are also recorded and shown on maps as *spot-heights*, each of which correspond to a bench mark (an arrow beneath a horizontal line) carved at the foot of a church tower, on a milestone or other permanent structure. Today, aerial photography is used in map revision and the Ordnance Survey has compiled a library of over half a million aerial photographs, copies of which are available to the public. All information is stored in digital form on computer and may be used either to make a printing plate or to draw out any part of a map required by a customer.

Urban areas are surveyed, in considerable detail, at 1:1250 scale (50 inches to 1 mile). Rural areas are surveyed at 1:2500 scale (25 inches to 1 mile), while mountain and moorland areas are shown in maps at 1:10000 (6 inches to 1 mile), as are a growing number of towns and cities. The *Landranger* series covers the whole of Britain in 204 maps at 1:50000 (1¼ inches to 1 mile) while the *Pathfinder* series at 1:25000 (2½ inches to 1 mile) provides more detailed information such as field boundaries and rights of way.

For the Close Society, Ordnance Survey *and* the London Map Centre *see* APPENDIX II.
Further reading:
Barringer, C., *Maps and the Local Historian*, London, 1994
Hindle, P., *Maps for Local History*, London, 1988
Owen, T. and Pilbeam, E., *Ordnance Survey: Map Makers to Britain since 1791*, HMSO, 1992
Smith, D., *Maps and Plans for the Local Historian and Collector*, London, 1988

MARBLE A granular crystalline limestone, though the term is loosely applied to any stone of a similar appearance which takes a high polish. A rich and costly material, marble was frequently used for embellishing major medieval churches, notably in altars, colonnettes, flooring and screens. Both imported and local English marbles were used, the best known being the almost black marble obtained from quarries on the Isle of Purbeck in Dorset (*see also* PURBECK MARBLE *and* TOUCH).

MARGINAL INSCRIPTION An inscription contained within the margin of (e.g.) a monumental brass. The opening word of such an inscription is usually preceded by a cross.
See also INSCRIPTIONS

MARKET CROSSES It has been suggested that market crosses were intended to sanctify commercial transactions or were erected to commemorate the granting of a market's charter. In effect, they declared the authority of the market and, in their size and elaboration, its status (indeed, many markets had more than one cross). But like the CHURCHYARD CROSS, which is of similar design, they were probably possessed of a variety of functions not least of which was to provide a focal point from which the assembled traders and townspeople could be addressed by corporation or market officials and itinerant preachers. Indeed, many churchyard crosses were also market crosses, for commercial transactions often took place within a churchyard (*see* FAIRS AND MARKETS). Most market crosses are of medieval origin though of many only the stepped base and a broken shaft remain to tell of a community's former aspirations. In several of the more successful commercial centres, late medieval and Tudor benefactors provided for the construction of polygonal roofed shelters, or *butter crosses*, their walls pierced by arches and with a lantern or cross crowning the

Bench mark.

canopy. John Leland (*c.* 1505–52) described the late fifteenth-century cross at Malmesbury in Wiltshire as 'a right fair and costely peace of worke in the market place made al of stone & curiously voultid for poore market folkes to stande dry when rayne cummith.' In some less prosperous towns, such as Castle Combe in Wiltshire, the original cross had a shelter constructed around it, while at Sherborne in Dorset the former *lavatorium* was removed from the Abbey to the market place where it served both as a conduit and market shelter.

MARKETS *see* FAIRS AND MARKETS *and* MARKET CROSSES

MARKS, MAKERS' *see* HALLMARKS

MARKS, MASONS' *see* MASONS' MARKS

MARKS, MERCHANTS' *see* MERCHANTS' MARKS

MARKS OF DIFFERENCE *see* CADENCY

MARKS OF DISTINCTION *see* BASTARDY

MARKS, PEWTER *see* PEWTER

MARKS, PLATE *see* HALLMARKS

MARKS, WINDOW *see* GLAZIERS' MARKS

MARQUESS (*or* MARQUIS) *see* PEERAGE, THE

MARQUETRY Inlaid work in wood, ivory etc.

MARRIAGE *see* MATRIMONY

MARRIAGE ACTS (1823 and 1836) The Marriage Act of 1823 declared that while clandestine marriages (those without banns or a licence) were valid, any minister who officiated at such a marriage was a felon. The Marriage Act of 1836 empowered superintendent registrars to issue MARRIAGE LICENCES in registrars' offices and non-conformist chapels.
See also BANNS OF MARRIAGE, GEORGE ROSE'S ACT, HARDWICKE'S MARRIAGE ACT *and* REGISTERS

MARRIAGE LICENCE A licence allowing a marriage to take place without banns (*see* BANNS OF MARRIAGE). Such licences have been granted by bishops since the fourteenth century or, more recently, by their surrogates. Before a licence can be granted, one of the parties is required to swear that he/she knows of no impediment to the marriage and that the church or chapel in which the marriage is to be solemnised is that which is normally attended by one of the parties (or that one of the parties has resided in the parish during the preceding fifteen days). In exceptional circumstances, the Archbishop of Canterbury may grant a special licence permitting a marriage to be solemnised at any time and at any place.
See also FACULTY, GEORGE ROSE'S ACT, HARDWICKE'S MARRIAGE ACT, MARRIAGE ACTS *and* REGISTERS

'MARRIAGE LINES' A marriage certificate confirming that a lawful marriage ceremony has taken place.

MARSHALLING The practice of arranging heraldic devices to signify marriage, inheritance or the holding of an office. An understanding of the basic principles of marshalling is essential for those who are recording monumental effigies, brasses, stained glass and other memorials in which HERALDRY is present. For example, the combined arms of a husband and wife are unique and therefore enable the researcher to identify an individual member of a (possibly numerous) family.
EARLY PRACTICE
Early forms of marshalling are evident in a number of twelfth-century SEALS where a figure is depicted between shields bearing arms of alliance or where a geometrical arrangement of related shields surrounds that of the principal house. Another early method was to combine charges from several different

Arms of John de Dreux.

shields to form an entirely new one: John de Dreux, Duke of Brittany and Earl of Richmond, for example, whose mother was a daughter of Henry III, bore a shield charged with the gold and blue chequers of De Dreux within a red border charged with the gold lions of England and *over all a Canton Ermine* for Brittany.

From *c.* 1300 different coats were marshalled in the same shield, at first by means of *dimidiation*: the dexter half of a husband's arms (those to the left when viewed from the front) being joined to the sinister half of his wife's. But this practice often resulted in alarming visual ambiguities and it was abandoned in favour of *impalement*, by which two complete coats were placed side by side in the same shield (again, with those of the husband to the *dexter*).

IMPALEMENT AND ESCUTCHEONS OF PRETENCE

Impalement generally signifies a temporary or non-hereditary combination of arms, such as ARMS OF OFFICE and those of a husband and a wife who is not an heraldic heiress but whose father is armigerous. But a woman who has no brothers living and no nephews or nieces from deceased brothers becomes her father's *heraldic heiress* upon his death. While he lives her arms are impaled with her husband's, but when her father dies they are displayed on an ESCUTCHEON OF PRETENCE, a small shield placed over the centre of her husband's shield. If she has sisters, each is a co-heiress, and each transmits her father's arms on equal terms.

QUARTERING

After a woman's death, her husband ceases to bear his wife's escutcheon of pretence, and her children quarter their arms by dividing the shield into four and placing the paternal arms in the first and fourth quarters and the maternal arms in the second and third (*see also* CADENCY). Thereafter, further inherited arms may be added as 'quarterings', usually in order of acquisition – though not invariably so.

Many armigers accumulated a large number of coats, sometimes adding ones which were already present in their arms through earlier marriages with heiresses of the same family. It is not necessary to retain all the coats (*quarterings*) that have been acquired in this way, indeed it is often impracticable to display more than four. But when a selection is made it is necessary to include those coats by which the selected ones were acquired. For example, were an armiger able to prove Mowbray descent through a fairly humble ancestor called Smith, and thereby entitlement to the Mowbray arms, it would be necessary to include the Smith coat in order to justify the use of the more illustrious arms of Mowbray.

WIDOWS AND WIDOWERS

A widow continues to use her late husband's arms, but on a lozenge (a diamond-shaped 'shield') and without helm or crest, and with her own arms either

1   *Dimidiation*
2   *Impalement*
3   *Inescutcheon of Pretence*
4   *Quartering*

impaled or in pretence. If she is the widow of a peer she may continue to use supporters and the appropriate coronet of rank (*see* CORONETS OF PEERS). If a widow re-marries, she no longer uses the arms of her first husband.

A widower ceases to use his late wife's arms except on memorials and HATCHMENTS. If he remarries he may use the arms of *both* wives, for commemorative purposes, in the sinister half of his shield: either one above the other, with the arms of his first wife *in chief* (at the top), or side by side, with his first wife's arms to the *dexter*.

UNMARRIED WOMEN

Unmarried women are entitled to bear their father's arms in a lozenge, but not his crest. A divorced woman reverts to her maiden arms which, again, are borne in a lozenge, and these may be charged with a *mascle* (a voided diamond) to indicate that she is a divorcée.

See also BLAZON *and* SEIZE QUARTIERS

MARTINMAS *see* FEAST DAYS (FIXED AND MOVABLE)

MARTLET *see* BEASTS (HERALDIC)

MARTYR From the Greek meaning 'witness', the term was originally applied to the Apostles who

were witnesses of Christ's life and resurrection. Later, it came to mean those who were persecuted for their faith and, ultimately, those who suffered death in His name. In the Middle Ages, martyrs were venerated as potent intercessors, as were their relics (*see* SHRINES).
See also CHRISTIAN SYMBOLS

MARTYRIUM (*also* MARTYRION) A building or memorial constructed above the tomb (or relics) of a MARTYR, or (rarely) a church erected to the memory of a martyr.

MARTYROLOGY An official register of Christian martyrs (*see* MARTYR). The earliest examples are calendars, containing details of the martyr's name and place of death and the date on which he/she was commemorated. From the ninth century, it was the practice in most religious houses for the day's entry in the martyrology to be read during the office of PRIME.
See also NECROLOGY

MARY, THE BLESSED VIRGIN (BVM) In the Greek, *Theotokos*, 'the God-bearer', Mary, mother of Christ, daughter of Joachim and Anne, and betrothed to Joseph at the time of the Annunciation. The doctrine of the ASSUMPTION OF THE BLESSED VIRGIN MARY was formulated in the sixth century and the feast day (15 August) was widely observed in the Middle Ages, though omitted from the *Book of Common Prayer* in 1549. But while belief in the Assumption roused little opposition in the pre-Reformation period, the doctrine of the IMMACULATE CONCEPTION was the subject of vigorous disputation. Reformers, while acknowledging Mary's humility, also reacted strongly against what they perceived to be the excessive devotion of the Roman Catholic Church.

Belief in the humanity and intercessory powers of Christ's mother was apparent even in the early fourth century, while in the medieval period it reached almost cult-like proportions, promoted by her special devotees the Cistercians and the Franciscans. The cult found popular expression in the HAIL MARY, ROSARY and Angelus (*see* ANGELUS BELL), in the rededication of churches and the building of LADY CHAPELS and in pilgrimages to SHRINES such as Lourdes in south-west France. As a consequence of the nineteenth-century OXFORD MOVEMENT, several Anglican theologians continued to emphasise the importance of the Marian doctrine. Other feast days are the NATIVITY OF THE BLESSED VIRGIN MARY (8 September), the ANNUNCIATION OF THE BLESSED VIRGIN MARY (25 March), the Purification of the Blessed Virgin Mary (CANDLEMAS, 2 February) and the VISITATION OF OUR LADY (2 July).

MASONRY In Britain, most of the stone buildings which have survived from before the sixteenth century are of rubble construction. *Rubble* is not a derogatory term but describes stones of different sizes, laid in a variety of ways and bound with lime mortar. *Square coursed rubble*, for example, is walling of roughly square stones laid in horizontal courses (also described as *regular coursed rubble*), while *square-snecked rubble* is walling in which small stone blocks (*snecks*) are inserted to prevent a wall being weakened by long, vertical joints. The term *random rubble*, on the other hand, describes stones of differing shapes and sizes laid without any discernible pattern, while *coursed random rubble* consists of similar unshaped stones laid in horizontal courses. Cut and squared (*dressed*) stone was exceedingly expensive and, in medieval churches, was used only for facings and *dressings* such as mouldings, quoins, sills, window tracery, lintels and arches. Like most FLINT walling, rubble walls were generally plastered inside and out, the stone quoins and other dressings being kept proud of the rubble face to allow for the thickness of the plaster. Often the plaster has been stripped by Victorian restorers.

Very often, redundant buildings would be 'quarried' for building materials: at Tockenham in Wiltshire, for example, where the rubble walls of the parish church contain several *intrusions*, large dressed stones and tiles, removed from a nearby Roman building which remained undiscovered until 1994.

From the late sixteenth century, an increasing number of churches were built entirely of blocks of finely dressed stone laid in regular courses and with carefully worked joints. The most sophisticated stonework was *ashlar* which was cut precisely in vertical and horizontal faces, smoothly finished and laid in horizontal courses with vertical joints. Only high quality FREESTONE was suitable for such work and for carved decorative work and dressings (*see also* RAG).

A characteristic of eighteenth- and nineteenth-century classical architecture was *rustication*. Introduced by Inigo Jones (1573–1652) from Renaissance Italy, rustication was a method of providing contrasting textures in stonework by projecting square ashlar or decorative blocks of stone forward from the recessed mortar courses, usually at basement level or in the lower storeys of buildings and on columns. These projecting blocks were usually ornamented: banded, chamfered, diamond-pointed, frosted and rock-faced (all of which may be easily identified) and vermiculated which is carved to represent the random path of worms.

Walls which are constructed without mortar are described as *drystone walls*, some of those which enclose churchyards being even older than the churches themselves. There are numerous regional traditions of drystone construction, but common to all is the first principle that each stone should 'do its duty by its neighbour' and be placed in exactly the right position to secure adjacent stones and be secured by them.

See also ANCASTER STONE, BATH STONE, BRICK, BUILDING MATERIALS, CLUNCH, COADE STONE, COB, COTSWOLD STONE, FACING MATERIALS, FLINT, FOREST MARBLE, FROSTERLEY MARBLE (*see* PUR-BECK MARBLE), GREENSAND, IRONSTONE, KENTISH RAG, KETTON STONE, MARBLE, MOORSTONE, PORTLAND STONE, PURBECK MARBLE, RAG AND RAGSTONE, TOUCH *and* WELDON STONE

Further reading:

Parsons, D., *Stone: Quarrying and Building in England AD 43–1525*, London, 1990

MASONS' MARKS Devices used by stone masons to mark their work. Each mason had his distinctive mark which could be passed from father to son. They were usually hastily and shallowly incised and measure about 5cm (2 inches) in height. The marks were numerous and varied and include simple cyphers, geometrical patterns and runic-type symbols. Registers of marks were maintained by the medieval masons' guilds both to avoid duplication and to ensure that bad workmanship could be traced. Most medieval masons were peripatetic craftsmen who often worked in teams. It is therefore possible to trace the movements of a particular mason or group of masons from one commission to the next through the identification of their marks. Masons' marks may also assist in the dating of buildings and in studying the various phases of construction.

See also BADGES, CYPHER, GLAZIERS' MARKS, GRAFFITI *and* MERCHANTS' MARKS

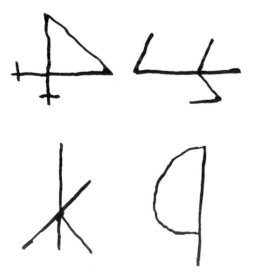

MASS A title for the EUCHARIST or Holy Communion, dating from at least the fourth century, and that most widely used during the Middle Ages. The word Mass is derived from the Latin *mittere* meaning 'to send forth', a reference to the dismissal of the congregation following the Eucharist. Medieval theology emphasised the propitiatory and sacrificial nature of the Mass and priests were expected to say the Mass each day. One consequence of this was a significant increase in the numbers of monks entering the priesthood and a corresponding increase in the celebration of masses. This in turn affected the development of ecclesiastical archi-tecture, notably in the provision of numerous side ALTARS, and the institution of CHANTRIES (*see* PRIVILEGED ALTAR).

The Mass, so men believed, was a re-enactment of Christ's supreme sacrifice and, as such, was an effective means of attracting God's mercy. Every testator in the fourteenth and fifteenth centuries therefore endeavoured to provide in his will for the celebration of soul-masses on the anniversary of his death, 'for the well-being of the living and for the repose of the dead', and in order to curtail the trials of PURGATORY. These private masses were celebrated by chantry priests at side altars and in the CHANTRY CHAPELS and CHANTRY COL-LEGES of the magnatial classes.

The High Mass (*Missa Solemnis*) was the normal form of the Mass at which the celebrant was always assisted by a deacon and subdeacon. But it was the Low Mass, without music and incense and with the assistance only of a single server, which was most commonly observed in the parish churches of medieval England (*see* LITURGY *and* MEDIEVAL CHURCH). At that time, of course, the laity was denied the Precious Blood of Christ (the wine) and received only the consecrated wafer of the Eucharist (the Host).

In religious houses, the Morrow Mass (*Mass Matutilanis*) at 8.00 or 8.30 a.m. (Mass was not permitted before dawn) was followed by High Mass (*Missa Major*) at noon. In some communities, the Morrow Mass was known as the Lady Mass because it was celebrated in honour of the Blessed Virgin Mary at the Lady altar. In houses other than those of the Benedictine and Cistercian orders, it was known as the Chapter Mass (*Missa Capitularis*) for it preceded the daily meeting of the CHAPTER. In the later Middle Ages, the Morrow Mass was attended by half the community's priests, the other half saying private masses (*missa familiaris*) at side altars scattered throughout the monastic church. There were also occasional masses for the dead (*Requiem*), and to mark special occasions such as visitations, while daily masses were celebrated in the INFIRMARY and for the lay brethren.

See also ABLUTIONS, ALTAR, AUMBRY, COMMUNION LINENS, CREDENCE, FENES-

TELLA, LAVABO, PLATE, PISCINA, PRESBY-
TERY, RESERVATION, SANCTUARY, SEDILIA,
SQUINT *and* VESTMENTS

MASS-DIALS *see* SUNDIALS

MASS PENNY At medieval funerals, a 'mass
penny' was paid to the celebrant by the chief
mourner during a small ceremony (the Offering)
which took place between the reading of the Gospel
and the public recitation of the Creed. The practice
continued after the Reformation, payment of the
'mass penny' interrupting the office of the Burial of
the Dead, following the lesson from the first Epistle
to the Corinthians.

MATERIALS *see* BUILDING MATERIALS,
FACING MATERIALS, MASONRY *and* PLASTER-
WORK

MATRIMONY To the medieval Church, marriage
was the next best thing to chastity, '. . . a good and
necessary institution ordained by God for the
procreation of children, the avoidance of lechery and
the comfort of man and woman.' But such a
sacramental view of marriage as an indissoluble
partnership inevitably invited disputation. For
example, what precisely constituted a valid
marriage? What were the obligations of one partner
to the other? And by what impediments might a
valid marriage be prevented or dissolved? Such
questions generated a substantial and elaborate
element of CANON LAW, much of which was
excessively ingenious and arbitrary, though for the
most part it was administered humanely by the
courts. Marriage was forbidden between those
related within the 'fourth degree' (a common great-
great-grandparent), a requirement which would have
placed an impossible restriction on the nobility who
sought marriages with those of equal or superior
rank, notably heiresses who brought with them titles
and land. The usual remedy was to seek a
dispensation from the Pope – for many, a costly and
convoluted experience. Other common causes of
litigation included an alleged absence of 'free
consent', which could not be obtained from a girl
until she was twelve years of age or a boy before he
was fourteen, and the principle of 'pre-contraction'
by which *verba de presenti* (words in the present
tense spoken with intent) were sufficient to
constitute an irrevocable marriage. Thus 'I take you
for my wife' was sufficient, even though the
statement might be made in the absence of a priest
or witnesses.

But, like BAPTISM and BURIAL, marriage
ceremonies were usually witnessed by large numbers
of friends and relatives and, for members of the
nobility and gentry, involved a degree of public
display appropriate to the families' status in society.
First, there was a formal exchange of contracts at the
church door (*see* PORCHES) and this was followed
by the blessing and a celebration of the MASS.

MARRIAGE SETTLEMENTS

At most levels of society, marriage involved property.
A widow or heiress could bring her land to her
husband for his lifetime or, when she had no land to
bring, her family would provide a dowry of money
and goods which would become the property of the
groom or, if he was a minor, his parents. In return,
the groom's parents would settle a *jointure* on the
couple – lands which benefited their son's wife
during her lifetime – and, on the death of her
husband, she was entitled to a third of his estate. It
was often the case, therefore, that a marriage would
be preceded by lengthy negotiations to determine the
precise relationship between a dowry and jointure.
Many marriage settlements have survived and from
these it is clear that the acquisition of property was of
considerable importance, as was a spouse's position
in society. There were also instances of heirs and
heiresses being 'sold' into marriage. Wardships of
minors were highly marketable commodities,
especially when they brought with them titles and
land. The young Anne Mowbray, for example, was
married at the age of five to the four-year-old
Richard, Duke of York, in order to secure the vast
estates of the Duchy of Norfolk for the Crown.

THE STATUS OF WOMEN

In the Middle Ages, the legal status of a married
woman was inferior to that of any free man.
Although responsible for her own criminal actions,
she could neither make a will without her husband's
consent nor enter into contracts in her own right. Her
personal goods were his property, as were any lands
or property she might inherit, and he was responsible
for all her debts. But once widowed, a woman
enjoyed the same private rights as a man. She had
absolute rights in her own property, and in the large
portion of her late husband's goods left to her, and
received at least a third of his estates for life.
Although a nobleman's widow would usually have
to petition the king before re-marrying (and pay a
sizable sum for a licence), she was free to follow her
own inclinations in choosing a second husband – or
a third, or fourth. . . .

A pregnant woman who was compelled by the
churchwardens to marry, and who was attended by
them in state, was said to have had a '*knobstick
wedding*' – from the staves carried by the wardens as
their insignia of office.

See also AFFINITY, BANNS OF MARRIAGE,
DIVORCE, FACULTY, GEORGE ROSE'S ACT,
HARDWICKE'S MARRIAGE ACT, HOURS,
CANONICAL, MARRIAGE ACTS, MARRIAGE
LICENCE *and* REGISTERS

MATRIX A cavity within which a thing is
embedded e.g. the hollow in a slab to receive a

monumental brass (*see* BRASSES (MONU-MENTAL)).

MATTINS (*or* MATINS) From the Latin *matutinus*, meaning 'of morning', the Breviary office for the night which, until the eleventh century, was known as *vigilae* from the VIGILS of the early Church (*see* DIVINE OFFICE). Originally it was observed at midnight but the Benedictine rule prescribed it for the 'eighth hour of the night' (2.00 am.). In importance Mattins was equal to all the day offices together and, for many centuries, was known as *Nocturns*, being composed of several divisions each defined as a *nocturn*. The number of nocturns varied according to the ecclesiastical calendar: three on Sundays and major feast days, for example, and a single nocturn on weekdays (*feria*). Each nocturn consisted of three psalms with their antiphons, versicle, paternoster and a short prayer (*Absolutio*) together with three lessons, each preceded by a benediction. The term Mattins is now more commonly used to describe the service of Morning Prayer in the Church of England which, as set out in the *Book of Common Prayer*, is essentially an abbreviated form of the medieval office with supplements from *Prime*. The BCP service includes the *Venite*, *Te Deum* (or *Benedicite*) and *Benedictus* (or *Jubilate*) together with prayers and the psalms and lessons appointed for the day.
See also EUCHARIST *and* EVENING PRAYER

MAUNDY (*also* SHEER THURSDAY) The maundy ritual of washing the feet of the poor is an act of love and humility which commemorates Christ's washing of the Apostles' feet at the Last Supper (*John 13*). In most religious houses a daily maundy (*Mandatum* or *Pedilavium*) was observed, during which a monk (selected by rotation from the brethren and supervised by the almoner) washed the feet of a specified number of the poor. At a weekly maundy, the brethren who were on duty in the kitchen and FRATER washed the feet of the superior and brethren, usually in the CLOISTER and in the vicinity of the LAVATORIUM. (At the Cistercian abbey of Strata Florida in Powys a stone-lined basin, with steps at either end and located at the centre of the crossing, may have been used for this purpose.) The annual ceremony of the Great Maundy was held in Benedictine houses on the Thursday of EASTER week when the poor, equal in number to the brethren, were admitted to the abbey church. After the singing of the psalms and collects for the day, they were taken to the lavatorium, cloister or chapter house, where each monk would wash a pauper's feet, kiss his mouth and eyes and then served him with a meal.

In the Middle Ages, the annual Maundy Thursday ceremony (which originated in the sixth century or even earlier) was also performed by royal or other eminent persons and was commonly followed by the distribution of clothing, food or money. Except in the Roman Catholic Church, all that remains in Britain of this ritual is the distribution by the sovereign of specially minted silver (*Maundy Money*) at a Maundy service (usually) held at a cathedral. From the time of Henry IV (r 1399–1413), the number of recipients has corresponded to the number of years of the sovereign's age. In the county of Shropshire, it was the custom to dip one's head in the waters of a holy well on Maundy Thursday.
See also FEAST DAYS (FIXED AND MOVABLE), FESTIVALS AND SOCIAL CUSTOMS *and* REPOSE, ALTAR OF

MAUSOLEUM A large and magnificent dynastic tomb or monument. The term was derived from the marble tomb of Mausolus, a fourth century King of Caria in Asia Minor, which was accounted one of the Seven Wonders of the World. The mausoleum designed by Nicholas Hawksmoor (1661–1736) at Castle Howard in Yorkshire took more than ten years to build (it was begun in 1731) and is probably the earliest (and certainly the finest) of many such classical structures to be erected in the landscaped parklands of the eighteenth- and early nineteenth-century aristocracy. It was described by Horace Walpole as 'a mausoleum that would tempt one to be buried alive.' There are other splendid examples at Blickling in Norfolk and Trentham Park, Staffordshire.

While many mausoleums were intended as memorials rather than tombs, the aristocratic perception of death as a dignified withdrawal from the plebeian gaze is evident in the cool classicism and romantic isolation of most of the mausoleums of this period. But the distinction between several later mausoleums and follies is often difficult to detect. The nineteenth-century Petersons' Tower in the New Forest in Hampshire, built by a retired judge from India, was both a folly and a mausoleum. Having completed the building of his house, Thomas Peterson was reluctant to put his labour-force out of work so he devised a work-creation scheme for the construction of a thirteen-storey 'campanile' which was to be the tallest concrete tower in the world. Inspired by a local spiritualist group (the New Forest Shakers) he is said to have been supported in his scheme by the posthumous attentions of Sir Christopher Wren and the tower was eventually completed in 1885. When Peterson died twenty-one years later, at the age of ninety-three, his ashes were placed in a crypt beneath his folly. The building was deconsecrated in 1968 and sold for £100.

There are several examples of mausoleums in churchyards: the extraordinary Lowther family mausoleum (1857) at Lowther in Cumbria, for example. Others have been demolished and only appear in records: the former Drax mausoleum at Holnest in Dorset, for instance, which once completely dominated the tiny church. Described by one critic as 'of marvellous hideousness', its appearance was reminiscent of an ornate Victorian pumping station.

See also VAULTS (BURIAL)

MAY DAY While the Church designated 1 May as the feast day of St. Philip and St. James the Less, it was the pagan festival of *Beltane* which, as May Day, was celebrated throughout Merry England, encouraged by the medieval churchwardens as a particularly effective (and popular) method of raising funds for their parish churches (*see* CHURCH AND COMMUNITY). The Celtic ceremony of Beltane celebrated the end of Winter with great bonfires in honour of the strengthening sun, while men and women looked forward with optimism to the fecundity of their fields and the fertility of their beasts (*see also* ROGATION DAYS). Until comparatively recently, young people decorated their homes with greenery and flowers collected from the woods and fields as a means of ritually conveying the fertilizing powers of nature into the community. May Day rites, which were revived in the Victorian period by John Ruskin (1819–1900) and the Arts and Crafts movement, include the crowning of the May Queen (usually accompanied by Jack O'the Green or a similar male figure) and dancing round the maypole. Maypoles are often painted with stripes and decorated with foliage to represents the stripped tree (usually a white hawthorn) which was selected by the young people of a village for particular homage as a phallic symbol of fertility and the potency of the natural world. A number of local May Day traditions have been translated into Christian festivals: at Barwick in Elmet (Yorkshire), for example, where the maypole is considered to be the oldest and tallest in England. Every third year, on Easter Monday, the pole is lowered by three 'pole men', painted and garlanded with flowers, and then raised again for the maypole dances on Whit Monday.

See also FEAST DAYS (FIXED AND MOVABLE), FESTIVALS AND SOCIAL CUSTOMS *and* GREEN MEN

MEAD *see* CHARITY MEADS

MEDALLION (i) A bas-relief of circular, oval or rectangular form. (ii) A circular tablet, ornament or panel. (iii) A small decorative panel of stained glass in a traceried window.

MEDIEVAL ARCHITECTURAL ORNAMENT *see* BALLFLOWER ORNAMENT, BEAKHEAD

ORNAMENT, BENCHES AND BENCH-ENDS, BLIND ARCADING (*see* ARCADE), BRATTISHING, CAPITAL, CORBEL TABLE, CROCKET, DECORATIVE MOTIFS, DIAPER, DOGTOOTH ORNAMENT, DOORS AND DOORWAYS, FIGURE SCULPTURE, FOILS, FOUR-LEAVED FLOWER, MEDIEVAL ARCHITECTURE, TREE OF LIFE *and* TUDOR FLOWER

MEDIEVAL ARCHITECTURE The familiar classification of medieval architecture – *Norman, Early English, Decorated* and *Perpendicular* – was devised by Thomas Rickman (1776–1841) and first published in his book *An Attempt to Discriminate the Styles of English Architecture from the Conquest to the Reformation* (1817). Other forms of classification have been advocated but those which attempt to apply specific dates to what was essentially an evolutionary process ignore both transitional elements, which are present in the gradual movement of one architectural phase to the next, and significant regional variations (*see* ARCHITECTURAL PERIODS). Furthermore, architectural features were frequently added to those of an earlier period: at

Norman south door at Kilpeck, Herefordshire.

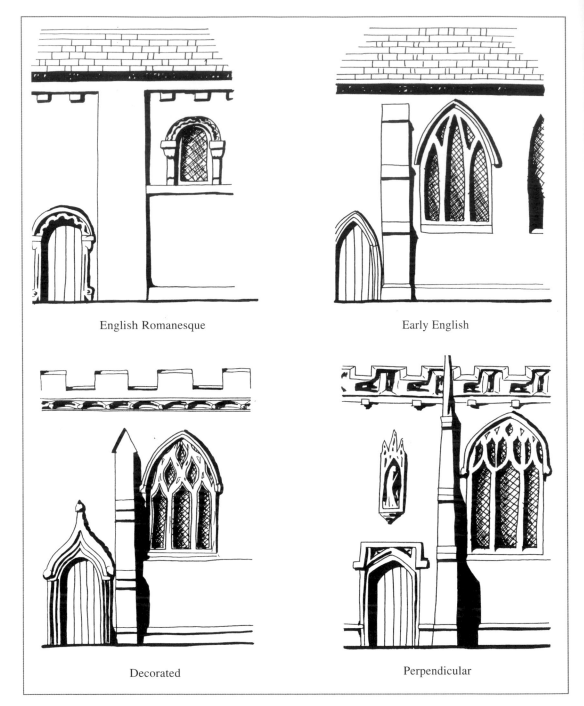

English Romanesque

Early English

Decorated

Perpendicular

Gloucester Cathedral, for example, where a fourteenth-century remodelling of the eleventh-century choir resulted in the construction of a spectacular Perpendicular stone-ribbed 'cage' which masked the original Norman arcade and was extended upward into a magnificent new clerestory and vault. Very few medieval churches have survived which are of a single architectural style: most have been altered, extended or rebuilt and therefore have features from a variety of periods.

ENGLISH ROMANESQUE

Rickman's *Norman* phase is that which is now described as *English Romanesque* and is easily recognised through the builders' preoccupation with solidity, exemplified by massively thick walling, small window openings and (in larger churches such as Tewkesbury Abbey in Gloucestershire and Wimborne Minster in Dorset) arcades of immense piers (*see* PIER) supporting semicircular arches (*see* ARCH).

Romanesque was a style of art and architecture prevalent in Europe *c.* 1050–1200 which reached its fullest development in central and northern France. As the name suggests, Romanesque architecture was inspired by the classical buildings of ancient Rome and the basilican plan with its nave, aisles and apsidal termination which was adopted in Romanesque churches. In central Europe, Romanesque masons developed variations of classical themes, using the semicircular arch, arcading and tunnel vaults, and their buildings were vigorously decorated with foliated and other motifs (*see* DECORATIVE MOTIFS). In northern and western Europe a more austere Romanesque style reflected Carolingian influences rather than those of classical Rome, and from this developed a distinctive Norman style which was evident in English church-building even before the invasion of 1066.

Early Norman churches, although built of stone, were modest structures, almost indistinguishable from many of their Saxon predecessors which the Norman establishment considered to be inadequate for the needs of a reformed Church (*see* ANGLO-SAXON ARCHITECTURE). They were constructed on a simple BASILICAN two-cell plan with a short, dark NAVE and apsidal SANCTUARY, as at Farleigh and Pyrford in Surrey, Buncton and Hardham in Sussex, Hales in Norfolk and Fritton, Suffolk. From this basic, two-cell church there developed the three-cell church (consisting of a nave, PRESBYTERY and sanctuary), the cruciform church (nave, presbytery with PORTICUS and sanctuary) and the larger aisled church (with nave, aisles and sanctuary). Three-cell and cruciform churches often had a central tower above the presbytery.

Eleventh-century masonry was massive, with walls of up to 7.3 metres (24 feet) at the base to provide structural stability and to compensate for poor-quality mortar and wide jointing. Window openings were small, so that the walls should not be weakened, and decoration was minimal (*see* WINDOWS). But in the twelfth century there occurred an extraordinary intensification in the scale and complexity of church-building. By *c.* 1130 walls were less massive, windows larger and the masonry more finely jointed, naves were longer and sometimes aisled, sanctuaries had square terminations and there was an increasing use of carved ornament.

Early *mouldings* had been cut very sparingly with shallow hollows, fillets and chamfers but later Romanesque work was profusely carved, mostly in geometrical forms the most common of which are the familiar zig-zag (*chevron*) decoration used in the deep mouldings of round arches (as at Iffley in Oxfordshire and Selby Abbey in Yorkshire), cylindrical motifs (*billets*) alternating with spaces in hollow moulding and, from *c.* 1130, blind arcading (*see* ARCADE). Sculptural decoration in doorway arches, capitals and tympana included floreated and animal forms, human figures, biblical scenes and monsters (*see also* FIGURE SCULPTURE). Typically English is *beak-head ornament* in which the heads of birds and beasts were carved in hollow mouldings so that the beaks or tongues overlapped into adjacent round mouldings (*see* DECORATIVE MOTIFS). Anglo-Norman sculpture was an extraordinary pot-pourri of influences: from Scandinavian to Levantine and from Celtic to Byzantine. Many of the sinuous and diabolical creatures depicted in British Romanesque carvings are of Celtic origin, while others were introduced through the importation of highly decorated eastern silks. This merging of Christian and pagan motifs, which was to continue well beyond the Romanesque period, is best observed in the ornamental carving of smaller churches such as Adel and Birkin in Yorkshire (both *c.* 1160), Elkstone in Gloucestershire (*c.* 1170) and Brinsop and Kilpeck (*c.* 1130–40) in Herefordshire (*see also* MOTTE). Of the carvings executed by the celebrated Herefordshire School (at Brinsop, Kilpeck, Rowlstone, Shobdon and Stretton Sugwas in Herefordshire and Llanbadarn Fawr in Powys) those at Kilpeck are by far the best preserved: a magnificent TREE OF LIFE tympanum above the south doorway, a curious doorpost with Celtic (?) warriors hidden among interlaced vines and an exceptionally varied (and occasionally *risqué*) carved CORBEL-TABLE. Brinsop, described by Harbison * as 'one of the enchanted places of England', has a spectacular image of St. George carved in the tympanum, while at Rowlstone a fine Christ in Majesty has survived, thanks to the protection afforded to the tympanum by the church porch. The south porch of Malmesbury Abbey in Wiltshire contains '. . . the richest ensemble of Romanesque carving in England . . . a great carved Pentecost broken into two halves, each with six Apostles. Almost nowhere else in England does one find figures on such a scale or in such profusion' (Ibid.). In Wales, the integration of Celtic and Romanesque motifs in the south door of Penmon Priory and the chancel arch of Aberffro (both in Anglesey) is indicative of an accelerating process of cultural assimilation.

COMPONENTS OF A MEDIEVAL CHURCH

In their simplest form, most surviving medieval churches consist of two cuboids: the larger being the nave and the smaller (at the east end) the presbytery. If separated from the nave by a screen the presbytery is normally referred to as a CHANCEL (*see also* CHANCEL SCREEN *and* ROOD SCREEN). Occasionally there is also a sanctuary to the east of the chancel and this may be apsidal. The nave may have an AISLE or aisles, possibly with a CLERESTORY above the ARCADE. There may also be a SACRISTY, adjacent to the chancel, which has subsequently been converted for use as a VESTRY. TOWERS were usually erected to the west of the nave or, more rarely, above the chancel arch or in the south-west corner between the nave and south porch. From the late twelfth century PORCHES become more numerous and these often contained an altar and a stoup of holy water (*see* HOLY WATER STOUP). The BAPTISTERY was usually located between the south porch and the west end of the nave, though FONTS were sometimes removed to the space beneath a tower. There are sometimes additional CHAPELS, usually extending to the north and/or south of the nave or adjacent to the chancel.

From the twelfth century, many cathedrals and large monastic churches were constructed or remodelled on a *cruciform* plan with the lower, elongated limb of a *Latin Cross* forming the nave, the upper limb the CHOIR and presbytery, and the lateral limbs the north and south TRANSEPT (*see* MONASTIC BUILDINGS). The presbytery in the vicinity of the high altar was usually apsidal but many were re-built after *c.* 1130 to provide a square termination, and a RETRO-CHOIR or AMBULATORY added from which radiated ancillary chapels (*see also* ALTARS, LADY CHAPEL *and* SHRINES). To the west of the presbytery, the STALLS of the body corporate lined the walls of the choir, separated from the nave by a massive PULPITUM (*see also* RETURNED STALLS). One bay to the west of the *pulpitum* was the rood screen and in front of that, the nave altar (the *Jesus Altar*), at which the laity participated in the Eucharist.

The naves of large medieval churches usually consist of three storeys: an arcade, separating the nave from the aisles, a TRIFORIUM or TRIBUNE, and a clerestory forming an upper level above the aisle roofs. In most cases, towers were constructed above the CROSSING, where the four limbs of the building meet, and these sometimes carry a spire (*see* TOWERS). During the twelfth and thirteenth centuries many timber ROOFS were replaced with stone vaults (*see* VAULTING) which, together with the weight of the tower, required considerable structural support and the provision of buttresses both at ground level and within the buildings themselves (*see* BUTTRESS).

A small number of churches followed the Rotunda of Constantine's Church of the Holy Sepulchre in Jerusalem, notably those of the Knights Templar and Knights Hospitaller. Of these, only four remain: the Temple Church in London (1185), the churches of the Holy Sepulchre at Cambridge (*c.* 1130, restored 1840) and Northampton (*c.* 1125 and much extended) and Little Maplestead in Essex (*c.* 1340, restored 1850). Originally, these churches were circular (or, at Little Maplestead, hexagonal) with an inner ring of arcaded piers, a central conical roof and a lower roof above the circular, outer aisle. The church at Garway in Herefordshire, extraordinary for its eccentric spatial organisation, massive linked tower and remote location, was once a circular Templar church though very little evidence remains of its former shape.

(*See also* CIRCULAR CHURCHES)

GOTHIC

Gothic was the architectural style current in medieval Europe from the late twelfth century to the mid-sixteenth century. The term was first used by the sixteenth-century painter, architect and historian Giorgio Vasari (1511–74) to imply disapprobation of all things medieval. For him, Gothic architecture symbolised barbarism and that of the Renaissance intellect: the verticality of faith versus the horizontality of enlightenment.

Rickman identified three phases of the Gothic style – Early English, Decorated and Perpendicular – each dependent on that which preceded it and fashioning that which followed. Each phase grew further away from the solidity which characterised Romanesque architecture and closer to the 'seemingly ethereal fragility' ** of the late fifteenth century. Above all, the medieval architect was attempting to achieve an appearance of lightness and elegance, 'a space enclosed by glass', in direct contrast to the heavy sturdiness of the Romanesque and, unlike Classical and Renaissance buildings, the great medieval churches were therefore conceived from within. How the medieval builders would have rejoiced in Sir Joseph Paxton's splendid Crystal Palace, constructed in Hyde Park for the Great Exhibition of 1851! Larger than Wren's St. Paul's, the luminescence of its 900,000 square feet of glass and the pure functionalism of its construction were precisely the architectural objectives which motivated medieval church builders for four centuries. It was this relentless quest for unattainable perfection (equated in the medieval mind with the greater glorification of God) which inspired architecture of the most extraordinary ingenuity and audacity and in particular the development of the stone vault and abutment (*see* VAULTING). The 'heavenward thrust' of glass and stone created that feeling of ascension which is the essence of Gothic architecture. And yet these great medieval buildings are essentially functional: every piece of stone is critical to the equilibrium of the building and (as at Richard Roger's twentieth-century Lloyd's building in London) no part of the structure is deliberately concealed. Like a house of cards, weight is distributed, and structural stability maintained, by translating the outward thrust of an arch into the downward thrust of a corresponding pier or buttress. Nothing is superfluous: even a PINNACLE is part of the structural equation, adding its weight to a buttress or corner tower. As the Middle Ages progressed so too did man's understanding of structure and his ability to apply new engineering techniques. Buildings became larger, higher, lighter and the geometry ever more complex.

The *Early English* phase (also *First Pointed* or *Lancet* from the characteristic narrow, pointed *lancet window*), is endowed with a certain austerity of form and a beauty of proportion best seen (in its most developed form) at Salisbury Cathedral in Wiltshire, built between 1200 and 1275. The vaulting has plain quadripartite ribbing; tiers of lancet windows pierce the walls of the aisles, clerestory and transepts in pairs and threes; and the tall piers of the nave have clustered shafts of black Purbeck marble and simple moulded capitals in a characteristic inverted bell form. Decoration is minimal and consists mostly of finely carved but formal stiff-leaf foliation, mainly in capitals and in window and doorway mouldings, together with DIAPER and DOGTOOTH ornament and CROCKETS.

The need for *tracery* (ornamental stone mouldings within a window) arose from the Early English practice of grouping two or more lancet windows beneath a single arch head (DRIPSTONE or *hood-mould*) which was intended to direct rainwater away from the openings. This created an awkward space (*spandrel*), between the window openings and the arch head, which at first was carved and pierced to provide the earliest form of tracery (*plate tracery*). From this simple device developed a variety of forms by which the Gothic phases are most readily identified. From the mid-thirteenth century single windows were divided by slender stone 'bars' (*bar tracery*) to provide larger areas of glass, one of the earliest forms being *Y-tracery* in which a Y-shaped mullion divide the window into two narrow vertical lights and a smaller top light. This later developed into *intersecting tracery* in which two or more mullions intersect each other in curves at the head of the arch. There are good Early English parish churches at West Walton in Norfolk and Kirkstead, Lincolnshire.

The *Decorated* phase (also *Curvilinear, Flamboyant* or *Geometric*) refers to the *middle pointed* style of window tracery which lasted from *c.* 1275 to *c.* 1375. The increased width of buildings, achieved through advances in vaulting, had created a need for greater internal illumination: windows became larger and wider and clerestories higher. This in turn increased the height of the nave and resulted in the development of the *arch buttress* (or *flying buttress*) which conveys the thrust of the vault and main roof over and beyond the aisles (*see* BUTTRESS). The increase in window size was accommodated by an equilateral arch and several mullions giving three, five, seven and even nine lights and ever more complex tracery. At first this was essentially geometrical with circles, quatrefoils and trefoils (*see* CUSP *and* FOILS), but in the fourteenth century *flowing* or *curvilinear tracery* evolved, based on the OGEE form of double-curving lines producing flowing flame-like shapes. *Reticulated tracery* was a development of this, circles forming a lattice of ogee shapes. Decoration also became more elaborate in the form of stone carving, coloured window glass (*see* STAINED GLASS) and painted and gilded stonework. Carved ornament became increasingly vigorous and dynamic with intense and detailed naturalism evolving into more stylised forms, the symmetrical *four-leaved flower* and BALLFLOWER ORNAMENT, for example. The nave of Exeter Cathedral (1275–1369) is a superb example of this period as are the parish churches of Heckington in Lincolnshire and Patrington in Yorkshire.

English medieval architecture reached its apogee in the *Perpendicular* style of the late fourteenth and fifteenth centuries, a time of almost frenetic architectural activity when numerous parish churches were refurbished, extended and even re-built (*see* MEDIEVAL CHURCH). In most cases, parishioners and patrons combined their resources, but the nave was now the responsibility of the parishioners while the rector or patron maintained the chancel, and consequently there is sometimes a startling discrepancy in the size and workmanship of the two components: at Methwold in Norfolk, for example, where the parishioners raised huge sums of money to refurbish the nave and to erected a great tower and spire, the magnificence of which is quite out of keeping with the modest, fourteenth-century chancel.

Perpendicular was a truly sumptuous and audacious style, characterised by the delicate vertical tracery of windows and stone panelling (from which the term 'perpendicular' is derived) with regular horizontal divisions and slender fluted piers leading upward into an exuberance of intricate fan-shaped vaulting (*fan vaulting*) exemplified in the magnificent vaults of Sherborne Abbey, Dorset (1425–85) and the Chapel of King's College, Cambridge (1446–1515). Windows of the period are significantly wider and the arches flatter, those of the late Perpendicular and Tudor Gothic periods being of the *four-centre* type. *Rectilinear* or *panel tracery* features both in windows and in wall panels and is characteristic of British architecture of the

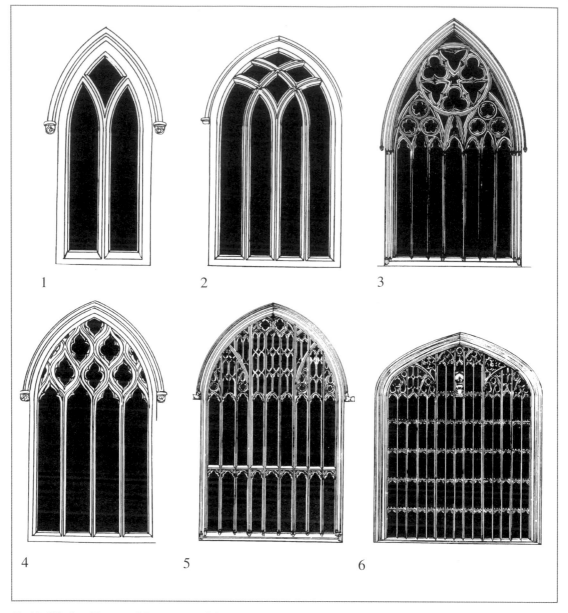

Gothic Window Tracery. 1 Y-tracery (13th century); 2 Intersecting tracery (13th century); 3 Geometrical tracery (early 14th century); 4 Reticulated tracery (14th century); 5 Panel tracery (late 14th century); 6 Panel tracery (late 15th and early 16th centuries).

period. This form of tracery incorporates both mullions and transoms thereby creating rows of small glass 'panels' (*lights*) with more complex tracery confined to the upper tiers within the arch. There are numerous wonderful examples of Perpendicular parish churches, notably St. John the Baptist at Cirencester in Gloucestershire (described by Betjeman as 'the largest and most splendid of the Cotswold 'wool' churches'), Walpole St. Peter in Norfolk ('the best of them all') and St. Mary Redcliffe at Bristol ('the most splendid parochial church in England').

The late Gothic builders very nearly achieved the perfection sought by their thirteenth-century predecessors. Their buildings are lofty, spacious and brilliant with a minimum of masonry supporting a maximum area of glass. But technical virtuosity and decorative richness seem almost to have become an end in themselves and ultimately they failed to attain that ideal.

See also SIXTEENTH- AND SEVENTEENTH-CENTURY ARCHITECTURE

Further reading:

Harbison, R., *English Parish Churches*, London, 1992 *

Harvey, J., *English Medieval Architects*, Stroud, (rev.) 1989

Little, B., *Architecture in Norman Britain*, London, 1985

Platt, C., *The Parish Churches of Medieval England*, London, 1981

Randall, G., *The English Parish Church*, London, 1982 (Spring Books 1988)

Tasker, E., *Encyclopaedia of Medieval Church Art*, London, 1994

Yarwood, D., *Encyclopaedia of Architecture*, London, 1985 **

MEDIEVAL CHURCH, THE The extraordinary proliferation of churches in the twelfth century was indicative of both the Norman establishment's enthusiasm for its reformed Church and the vitality of the Church itself. With the gradual demise of the old MINSTERS (*see* ANGLO-SAXON CHURCH), thousands of newly established parishes acquired their own churches, many of which occupied earlier Anglo-Saxon or Celtic sites (*see* CHURCH SITES). In the towns, there was a corresponding increase in the number of churches: by the end of the twelfth century there were over 100 in London, 35 in Lincoln and fourteen in York. Church-building was also considered to be a sound investment, producing both financial and spiritual rewards.

Most new churches were paid for by manorial lords (or groups of land-holders) who endowed land (*see* GLEBE) and a PRIEST'S HOUSE and thereafter claimed a major proportion of the TITHES and other revenues of the parish and exercised the right to select the priest (*see* ADVOWSON *and* PATRON). Even those churches which in *Domesday Book* (*see* DOMESDAY) are shown to be attached to specific estates may have shared their profits among a number of land-holders. Similarly, in the towns, an apparent multiplicity of churches may be explained by the building and endowment of churches for the benefit of groups of wealthy burghers or for the extended households of successful merchants. A church was regarded as the property of the patron and as such it could be rebuilt or enlarged, regardless of the wishes of the parishioners, or even demolished and removed to a new site. In particular, a church and its revenues could be bequeathed to a religious house, a practice known as APPROPRIATION. It has been estimated that, by 1200, one quarter of English parish churches had been annexed to monastic houses and that this number had more than doubled by the end of the fifteenth century (*see also* CARTULARY).

MEDIEVAL ENDOWMENTS

The medieval cathedrals exercised considerable regional influence, both ceremonial and commercial, while many abbeys promoted themselves as cult centres, with saints' SHRINES and reliquaries attracting pilgrims, sometimes in great numbers, and thereby stimulating local economies. The corporate ownership of property, and particularly the endowment of land, had ensured the continuing affluence of the cathedrals and monasteries up to the end of the thirteenth century, but the fourteenth and fifteenth centuries witnessed a gradual decline in this support and a corresponding diversion of patronage into the building and remodelling of parish churches.

In part, this was attributable to the piety of individual parishioners, anxious by their good deeds to secure eternal rest (*see* CHANTRY). It was also inspired by rivalry, both individual and corporate. In the neighbouring wool and cloth producing communities of Cullompton and Tiverton in Devon, for example, architectural emulation reached ostentatious proportions, while at Swaffham Prior in Cambridgeshire, the rival manorial churches of St. Mary and SS. Gyriac and Julia stand within each other's shadow, sharing a common churchyard.

Inevitably, civic pride reflected that of the individual and *vice versa*: the magnificent Perpendicular churches of East Anglia and the Cotswolds are indicative, not only of the prosperity of local industry, but also of the pre-eminence of the merchants and manufacturers whose MONUMENTS and CHANTRY CHAPELS rivalled those of the nobility and whose HERALDRY eloquently advertised the pervasive authority of the late-medieval establishment, even in death. In such areas, there were few churches which did not benefit in the fifteenth century from an endowment for the addition of a tower, clerestory or aisle while numerous benefactors, both individual and corporate (*see* GUILDS), provided for the building of HOSPICES, ALMSHOUSES and SCHOOLS, many of which may still be found in the vicinity of a parish church.

Of course, not all parishes prospered and there is ample evidence of abandoned churches following depopulation or contraction (*see* CHURCH SITES *and* DESERTED VILLAGES) and of churches which were neither rebuilt nor enlarged because of the declining influence of their patrons or the reduced circumstances of their parishioners. Throughout the Middle Ages, the Welsh Marches suffered deprivation, as did parts of East Anglia and Yorkshire in the late medieval period. Demolished chancels, aisles and chapels at churches such as Ovingdean in Sussex, Merton in Oxfordshire,

Chepstow in Gwent and Cley-next-the-Sea in Norfolk, and even the reduction of naves (maintenance of which was the parishioners' responsibility), are vividly indicative of the fluctuating fortunes of many medieval communities and those upon whose patronage they depended (*see also* CHURCHWARDENS' ACCOUNTS).

ORGANISATION

From 1072 the diocesan structure was reorganised under Archbishop Lanfranc of Canterbury (*c.* 1010–89). Those Saxon bishoprics which were located in remote, rural areas were removed to major towns such as Lincoln (from Dorchester-on-Thames), Chichester (from Selsey) and Chester (from Lichfield), while Sherborne in Dorset and Ramsbury in Wiltshire were combined and a new bishopric created at Old Sarum (to the north of present-day Salisbury). The see of Elmham in Norfolk was transferred to Thetford (and later to Norwich), and in Somerset Wells was moved to Bath. At the beginning of the twelfth century, the creation of two further dioceses, Carlisle and Ely, completed the pattern of diocesan administration which was to last, almost without alteration, until the REFORMATION (*see* DIOCESE).

Also during the eleventh century, Canon Law defined more clearly the financial and other parochial obligations of the laity (*see also* TITHES) while parish BOUNDARIES were delineated more precisely so that every man knew in which church he should attend the MASS, where his children should be baptised and his daughters married, and in which churchyard he should be buried. By the twelfth century, dioceses were sub-divided for administrative purposes into archdeaconries, rural deaneries and parishes while Church discipline was organised through a series of ecclesiastical courts (*see* COURTS, ECCLESIASTICAL).

The 'regular' clergy (in contradistinction to the 'secular' clergy) included monks and nuns (*see* MONASTICISM), CANONS REGULAR, FRIARS and members of the military orders (*see* TEMPLAR, KNIGHTS *and* ST. JOHN OF JERUSALEM, ORDER OF), all of whom lived according to rules imposed by the heads of their orders and were subject to the ultimate authority of the Pope. Members of the regular clergy (with the obvious exception of nuns) could be ordained priests and could become bishops – but not archdeacons or parish priests. All regular clergy were celibate, as were the secular clergy above and including the office of subdeacon, though this requirement was not strictly enforced until the end of the eleventh century. All clergy were were subject to CANON LAW which, on occasion, came into conflict with the civil law.

THE SECULAR CLERGY

Before the Reformation, there were over 9,000 parishes in England, each with its rector or vicar. A rector was a parish priest whose TITHES were not impropriate (*see* IMPROPRIATION), whereas a vicar had identical responsibilities but in a parish where the tithes were subject to appropriation (see above). Most parish priests performed their religious duties reasonably assiduously, either in person or by means of a deputy, and assisted by members of the MINOR ORDERS. They were responsible for 'the cure of souls', for celebrating the MASS and observing the Canonical Hours (*see* DIVINE OFFICE) and the various FEAST DAYS and festivals, and for visiting the sick and providing instruction. While many university-trained priests found employment as CHAPLAINS in the households of the nobility and gentry, most parish priests came from the lower classes of society and received only an elementary education, though standards improved during the fifteenth century. Each was 'presented' to his living by a PATRON who might be an eminent layman, a bishop or abbot or even the King. Few benefices provided an income of any substance and the majority of parish priests enjoyed a standard of living little better than that of a better-off peasant. The vicars of appropriated parishes suffered particularly badly, the rectorial tithes (those which were profitable and easily collected, such as corn and hay) being the prerogative of a religious house (*see also* LAY RECTOR), while the vicarial tithes (such as garden produce, milk and cheese) were more difficult to assess and of less value. Those priests who accepted appointments as domestic chaplains were often rewarded with a rectory and engaged a curate to perform the duties while continuing to receive the revenues of the living – for a patron, an economical way of rewarding service. The Paston letters of 1479 describe the Oxnead rectory in Norfolk as having a 'little and reasonably pleasant church', a 'well repaired parsonage' two orchards, a dovecote and 22 acres of land which, together with tithes, produced about £10 a year from which the rector would be obliged to deduct alms and payments for the repair of the chancel and his curate's stipend. 'It is but an easy cure to keep for there are not 20 persons to be yearly houseled [given the sacraments]', the implication being that there would be adequate time for more lucrative activities.

By far the most useful sources of information relating to the medieval clergy are the BISHOPS' REGISTERS. These include records of ordinations, inductions, patrons, changes of benefice and an extraordinary wealth of detail concerning the day-to-day work of a diocese and its parishes. Here too are the wealthy pluralists (*see* PLURALITY) and non-residents, many of them eminent administrators or Crown servants, and the wrong-doers who (by the nature of things) feature more prominently in the records than their more virtuous (and numerous) colleagues.

CHURCH INTERIORS

One of the pleasures of entering an ancient church is to experience the delicate play of light on mellowed stone and burnished wood, the reassuring texture of flint, brick and alabaster, and the hushed calm of continuity. But it was not always so. In the late Middle Ages the interiors of parish churches would have been very different from the quiet, sober places they are today. Then, they blazed with brilliantly painted stone and woodwork, brightly coloured glass, lurid WALL PAINTINGS, gilded SCREENS and candle-lit ROODS, a profusion of LIGHTS, pyxes, statues and ALTARS, a flamboyant conjunction of the sensual and the spiritual, primitive faith concealing a desperate need of salvation. Indeed, the vigour and intensity of medieval vernacular decoration convey an extraordinary sense of insecurity, a pervasive preoccupation with the transitory nature of life and the inevitability of death:

> For under the sunne a man may se
> Thys world ys butte a vanyte
> Grace passeth gollde
> And precyous stoon,
> And god schal be god
> When goolde ys goon.

Even the smallest church was liberally decorated with wall paintings in which the glory of redemption was contrasted with the horrors of hell and eternal damnation (*see* DOOM *and* PURGATORY), while numerous late-medieval chantries (*see* CHANTRY), endowments and benefactions provide ample evidence of man's attempts to secure salvation for himself and his family at a time when 'visitations of pestilence, famine and fire' were regular occurrences. For the most part, the tenets of the Christian faith (the incarnation, atonement, redemption, the sacrifice of the Mass and so on) were incomprehensible, especially as the ceremonies of the Church were conducted in Latin, and the religious and allegorical themes of paintings, STAINED GLASS and even play-acting (*see* DRAMA) were intended to instruct and to edify. But when the theology of Rome failed to satisfy, or was beyond a plain man's understanding, then dimly perceived images of past traditions were summoned in its place. Vestiges of paganism are evident in many surviving wall paintings, and in the carved images of monsters and demons so characteristic of English Romanesque stonework. For, just as many churches occupied earlier pagan sites, so the fabric of medieval worship was composed of two, sometimes conflicting, sometimes interchangeable, strands: the theological warp of Rome and the weft of an obscure primitive past.

For medieval church buildings *see* LITURGY *and* MEDIEVAL ARCHITECTURE.

See also CHURCH AND COMMUNITY, MAJOR ORDERS, PRIVILEGED ALTAR, ROMAN CATHOLIC CHURCH *and* WALES, THE MEDIEVAL CHURCH IN

Further reading:

Bainton, R., *The Medieval Church*, London, 1962

Brooke, R. and C., *Popular Religion in the Middle Ages*, London, 1984

Cook, G., *The English Medieval Parish Church*, London, 1955

Duffy, E., *The Stripping of the Altars: Traditional Religion in England 1400–c. 1580*, New Haven and London, 1992

Harper-Bill, C., *The Pre-Reformation Church in England: 1400–1530*, London, 1989

——, (ed.), *Religious Beliefs and Ecclesiastical Careers in Late Medieval England*, Woodbridge, 1991

Platt, C., *The Parish Churches of Medieval England*, London, 1981

Southern, R., *Western Society and the Church in the Middle Ages*, London, 1970

MEMBRANE A sheet of parchment sewn with others to form a roll.

MEMENTO MORI Literally, 'remember to die' (though, more aptly, 'remember that you must die'), a *memento mori* is a human skull or any other object serving as a reminder of the transient nature of life and of the inevitability of death. Frequently found carved in MEMORIALS, tombs and GRAVE-STONES and painted on HATCHMENTS and other types of ARMORIAL PANEL.
See also CADAVER *and* MORTHEAD

MEMORIAL (i) An object, institution or custom estab-lished to preserve the memory of a person or event.
See also BRASSES (MONUMENTAL), BURIALS, CARTOUCHE TABLETS, CENOTAPH, CHANTRY, CHANTRY CHAPELS, CHANTRY COLLEGES, (*see* CHEST TOMBS) TABLE TOMBS, CHURCHYARDS, EFFIGIES, EPITAPHS, GABLE CROSSES, GRAVESTONES, HATCHMENTS, INCISED SLABS, INSCRIPTIONS, LEDGER STONES (*see* INCISED SLABS), LETTERING, MASS, MAUSOLEUM, MEMENTO MORI, MEMORIAL BOARDS, MONUMENTS, OBELISK, STAINED GLASS, TABLETS, TABLE TOMBS, TOMB CHESTS, WALL MONUMENTS, WAR MEMORIALS *and* WEEPERS
(ii) A formal petition addressed to the Earl Marshal requesting that a warrant be issued to the kings of arms thereby enabling them to grant ARMORIAL BEARINGS to the petitioner.

MEMORIAL TABLETS *see* WALL MONUMENTS

MEMORIAL BOARD (i) An inexpensive form of heraldic WALL MONUMENT painted on wood or canvas and mostly dating from the seventeenth century. Memorial boards mark the transition from the 'scocheons' of FUNERAL HERALDRY to HATCHMENTS with which they may be confused. Unlike hatchments (which are invariably diamond-shaped), they are usually oblong and between 60 cm and 2 metres in diameter (2 and 6 feet), though occasional diamond-shaped examples may be found. As the name suggests, memorial boards are commemorative and usually have a text which includes such phrases as 'In Loving Memory of . . .' and 'Near Here Lies Buried . . .' together with biographical details and a biblical quotation or even a verse praising the character of the departed. Symbols of mortality (*memento mori*) such as death's heads (*mortheads*), cross-bones and bat-winged hour-glasses were also popular as decoration.
See also ARMORIAL PANELS *and* ROYAL ARMS
(ii) *For* a later type of memorial board, *see* WAR MEMORIALS.

MENDICANT Mendicant FRIARS were members of those orders which were forbidden to hold property. Consequently they worked or begged for a living and were not bound to a particular religious house (Latin *mendicare* = 'to beg'). In the Middle Ages they worked mainly in towns and enjoyed extensive privileges, including exemption from episcopal jurisdiction and faculties for preaching and hearing confession.

MENORAH *see* CANDELABRUM

MENSA (Latin *mensa* = 'table') In the early Church, a large stone tablet in the vicinity of a grave on which a meal could be taken in memory of the deceased. The term is now used to describe a flat stone altar-top.
See also ALTARS

MERCHANTS' MARKS In the broadly illiterate society of Medieval England, the ownership of trade goods was ascertained by reference to identification marks which were stamped on bales, casks and other containers or on the goods themselves. For safety reasons a consignment of items for dispatch by sea was often dispersed among a number of vessels. In such circumstances it was essential that the cargo should be properly marked to avoid confusion, and within the Hanseatic League merchants' marks on trade items were regarded as proof of legal ownership. A merchant's mark had to be recognisable, unambiguous and capable of being drawn, painted or scratched quickly. The majority of marks were built on the foundation of a single vertical 'stem': some combined a merchant's initials in an elementary form of cypher while others were runic in appearance. Merchant marks came to be used by non-armigerous men in much the same way as COATS OF ARMS were used by gentlemen. Members of the same family could sometimes be distinguished one from another by the adoption of small but distinctive variations in the family merchant mark, just as the cadet branches of armigerous families may be identified by the cadency marks added to their arms.

Seventeenth-century heraldic memorial boards at Lydiard Tregoze, Wiltshire. Ayliffe impaling St. John (top) and St. John (below).

With increasing prosperity, merchants proudly displayed their marks in the fabric and artefacts of their homes and in the window glass, tombs and memorials of the churches which benefited from their patronage. They were often displayed within a shield for this purpose; indeed, there are several examples of non-armigerous merchants who, having married heraldic heiresses, impaled their merchant marks with their wives' arms. The merchants who attained armigerous status invariably continued to use their familiar and respected merchant marks alongside their newly-acquired (and less familiar) arms. On the magnificent Canynge tomb at St. Mary Redcliffe, Bristol, for example, the family arms are flanked by their merchant marks. Although there were related classes of marks, indicating places of origin and craftsmanship, there is as yet no evidence to suggest that the marks of merchants from the same guild, town or trade contained any common elements or that they were subject to any form of systematic registration or control, unlike those used used by goldsmiths, masons and armourers.

See also ATTRIBUTED ARMS, BADGES, BRASSES (MONUMENTAL), CYPHERS, GLAZIERS' MARKS, GRAFFITI, MASONS' MARKS *and* REBUS

Further reading:

Elmhurst, E., *Merchants' Marks*, The Harleian Society, 1959

Girling, F., *English Merchants' Marks*, London, 1964

MERE (*or* MEARE) LANE Wide grass strips which once served to divide the open fields of adjacent estates or parishes (from the Old English *mære* meaning 'a boundary'). Mere lanes tend to follow parish BOUNDARIES, though modern civil and ecclesiastical parishes do not necessarily conform with their medieval predecessors.

See also PERAMBULATION

MERLON (*also* COP) The solid, up-standing part of an embattled parapet between two EMBRAS-URES (*see also* CRENELLATED).

METALS (i) *See* BELL METAL, BRASS, BRITANNIA METAL, BRITANNIA SILVER, BRONZE, ELECTROPLATE, EPBM EPGS AND EPNS, LEAD, NICKEL SILVER, ORMOLU, PEWTER, PLATINUM, SHEFFIELD PLATE, SILVER GILT, SILVER PLATE *and* STERLING STANDARD. *See also* METALWORK, HALL-MARKS, PLATE *and* WROUGHT IRON.

(ii) *For* the heraldic metals (*Argent* and *Or*) *see* COLOURS, HERALDIC.

METALWORK *see* ALTAR CROSS, BELLS, BRASSES (MONUMENTAL), CANDELABRUM, CANDLE STICKS, CAST, CHANCEL SCREENS, CHASING, CORONA LUCIS, DOORS AND DOORWAYS, EMBOSS, ENAMELLING, HATCH-ING (*see* COLOURS (HERALDIC)), HEARSE, LAPS AND ROLLS, LEAD, METALS, PAR-CLOSE, PLATE, REPOUSSÉ *and* WROUGHT IRON

METHODISTS A protestant denomination which originated in the eighteenth-century evangelistic movement inspired by John Wesley (1703–91) and Charles Wesley (1707–88) who, in 1738, began a ministry which propounded individual communion with God without the need for the intervention of a priest. Although within the Church of England, the movement was denied the use of anglican churches and was forced to hold meetings out of doors. The Methodist Society (known as the '*Holy Club*') was established in 1740 and, later, a governing body, the Methodist Conference. The movement formally separated from the Church of England in 1791 but there were several secessions. The first of these was the Methodist New Connexion which broke away in 1797 and joined with the United Methodist Free Churches in 1907 to form the United Methodist Church. The Independent Methodists were formed in 1805 and the Primitive Methodists in 1808. The Bible Christians (*Bryanites*) seceded in 1815 and joined the United Methodist Church in 1907. It was not until 1932 that most of the methodist groups were united, together with the original or 'Wesleyan' Methodist Church, as the Methodist Church in Great Britain. The supreme authority of the Methodist Church is the Conference which comprises equal numbers of ministers and laymen. Peculiar to Methodism is the class-meeting by which 'All members shall have their names entered on a Class Book, shall be placed under the pastoral care of a

Class Leader, and shall receive a Quarterly Ticket of Membership.' At the weekly class-meeting for 'fellowship in Christian experience' enquiry is made into the conduct and spiritual progress of individual members. Early Methodist registers are housed at the Public Record Office (*see* APPENDIX II).

In Wales, a Calvinistic form of Methodism was established by Howell Harris (1714–73) and others, who formed their first Association in 1743. Although they wished to remain within the Church of England, they were obliged to seek the protection of the *Toleration Act* and to register their meeting houses as dissenting chapels.

Further reading:

Stell, C., *An Inventory of Non-Conformist Chapels and Meeting Houses in Central England*, RCHM, 1987

METOPES In classical architecture, the square spaces between TRIGLYPHS in a Doric frieze, often decorated with sculptural groups.

METROPOLITAN The title of a bishop who exercises both diocesan and regional authority.
See also ARCHBISHOP *and* PRIMATE

MEZZANINE In a building an additional story between two others, usually entered from a half-landing.

MICHAELMAS (i) A quarter day: the Feast of St. Michael and All Angels on 29 September (*see* QUARTER DAYS *and* FEAST DAYS (FIXED AND MOVABLE)). This date coincides with the end of harvesting when the amount of fodder available for feeding livestock during the winter could be calculated. This assessment often resulted in the disposal of surplus stock and Michaelmas was, therefore, a time of great fairs and animal sales. (ii) The academic and law term beginning near Michaelmas (*see* HILARY *and* TRINITY).

MICHAEL, THE ARCHANGEL In the Bible, Michael is the helper of the Chosen People (Daniel 10:13 ff and 12:1) and guardian of the body of Moses (Jude 9). In the Middle Ages he was invoked by those who sought protection in battle against the heathen and by individuals against the Devil, especially at the time of death. As such he is depicted in religious art as fighting the Devil in the form of a dragon, a reference to Revelation 12:7–9. St. Michael's feast day is 29 September (*see* MICHAELMAS).

MIDDLE AGES, THE Traditionally, the Norman Conquest of 1066 is taken to be the 'beginning' of the Middle Ages in England and the accession of the Tudor dynasty in 1485, to be the 'end'. But, 'unlike dates, historical periods are not facts. They are retro-spective conceptions that we form about past events, useful to focus discussion, but very often leading historical thought astray.' (G.M. Trevelyan). Nevertheless, our common perception of medieval-ism would lead many to agree with Fossier when he suggests: 'We . . . should tread carefully; Henry V was medieval, Henry VIII was not: these are our limits.'

Today, definitions are as diverse as they are numerous. Archaeologists now use the term 'medieval' to describe the period, of about 1000 years, from the end of the Roman occupation to the time of the Tudors, with the Norman Conquest separating the 'early medieval' period from the 'high medieval'. Robert Fossier, in his *Illustrated History of the Middle Ages*, considers medievalism in a European context beginning in 1250 and lasting until 1520. H.R. Loyn's *The Middle Ages: A Concise Encyclopaedia* encompasses the eleven centuries from *c.* 400 to *c.* 1500, while the *Oxford Reference Dictionary* (1986) defines the Middle Ages as being 'the period in Europe after the Dark Ages (*c.* 1000–1400) or in a wider sense *c.* 600–1500.'

Some scholars have argued that the introduction of PRINTING in 1476 marked the end of the medieval period in England, or that it ended with the final battle of the Wars of the Roses at Stoke Field in 1487 and the suppression of livery and maintenance (see below). Others point to the diversion of resources from defence to domesticity, 'from castles to palaces', which was apparent during the reign of Edward IV (1461–83); while Neville Williams, in *Henry VIII and his Court*, suggests that the destruction of the Palace of Westminster in 1512 was '. . . a seminal event in the development of the court, a dividing line between medieval and modern kingship . . .'.

An essential characteristic of the Middle Ages was feudalism which, in the late medieval period, evolved into 'Bastard Feudalism' (*see* LIVERY AND MAINTENANCE). The earliest castles of Dové-laontaine and Langeais in northern France date from the second half of the tenth century which is where one would place the first establishment of a feudal society and therefore the beginning of the Middle Ages in Europe.

As to its close, Henry VII (1485–1509) is often credited with transforming England into a 'new monarchy' and thereby guiding the kingdom into a new age. But he did little more than revitalise government machinery which had changed little in its essentials since Edward I (1272–1307). Indeed, it was Edward IV (1377–99) who was chiefly responsible for rendering that machinery effectual and there is very little political or constitutional significance attached to the date 1485.

For the purposes of this book, the medieval period is taken to be the five centuries from the Norman

Conquest of 1066, following which the English Church entered the mainstream of western Christendom, to the mid-sixteenth century and the separation of the English Church from that of Rome (*see* REFORMATION, THE). The Dissolution of the Monasteries (1536 and 1539), the Dissolution of the Chantries (1545–7) and the introduction, through the *Book of Common Prayer*, of a revised LITURGY had a profound effect on the people and institutions of England. It was Thomas Cromwell and Archbishop Cranmer, not Henry Tudor, who brought the Middle Ages to a close.

Further reading:

Davies, R., *The Age of Conquest: Wales 1063–1415*, Oxford, 1987

Ford, B., *The Cambridge Cultural History: (Vol 2) The Middle Ages*, Cambridge, 1992

Fossier, R., *The Cambridge Illustrated History of the Middle Ages*, Cambridge, 1986

King, E., *Medieval England*, London, 1989

Le Goff, J., *Medieval Civilization*, London, 1989

Loyn, H., (ed.), *The Middle Ages: A Concise Encyclopaedia*, London, 1989

Saul, N., *Companion to Medieval England*, London, 1983

Thomson, J.A.F., *The Transformation of Medieval England: 1370–1529*, London, 1983

Williams, N., *Henry VIII and his Court*, London, 1971

MIDDLE POINTED *see* ARCHITECTURAL PERIODS *and* MEDIEVAL ARCHITECTURE

MID-LENT SUNDAY *see* MOTHERING SUNDAY

MIDSUMMER In the Celtic calendar Midsummer Eve (23 June) was observed by the lighting of sacrificial bonfires in honour of the sun, a ceremony which persisted until the last century in the custom (in some rural areas) of men and beasts passing through the embers of bonfires to ward off disease and bad luck. It was also a night when girls practised simple magic in order to discover the identity of their future husbands (*see* Thomas Hardy's *The Woodlanders*, chapter 20). The Midsummer Ale (24 June) was one of the most popular CHURCH ALES of the parochial year (*see* CHURCH AND COMMUNITY). *See also* FEAST DAYS (FIXED AND MOVABLE) *and* FESTIVALS AND SOCIAL CUSTOMS

MILITANT, THE CHURCH The body corporate of all Christians on earth, in contradistinction to those in Heaven or PURGATORY.

MILITARY ORDERS Founded in response to the capture of Jerusalem by the Saracens in 1076, members of the military orders were warrior-monks whose institutions exercised considerable political influence throughout medieval Europe (*see* TEMPLAR, KNIGHTS *and* ST. JOHN OF JERUSALEM, ORDER OF).

MILITIA *see* FLAGS

MILLION ACT (1818) *see* NINETEENTH-CENTURY ARCHITECTURE *and* NINETEENTH-CENTURY CHURCH

MILLS Like DOVECOTES and FISH PONDS, mills for grinding corn into flour were an essential part of the medieval economy and there is often evidence, usually documentary or archaeological, of a former manorial or monastic mill in the vicinity of a parish church.

Milling soke was a feudal monopoly exercised by most (though not all) lords of the manor. In practice many mills were leased to tenant millers and manorial custom required that the peasants should have their corn ground in the lord's mill on payment of a toll (*multure*), usually one-sixteenth of the grist ground, though from the thirteenth century the toll was usually commuted to a money payment. The lord, who was responsible for major repairs, had first claim on his mill for grinding corn from the demesne lands while the peasants could be fined for grinding their corn at home or for patronising a rival mill. No fewer than eighty mill stones (*querns*), confiscated in 1274 from the recalcitrant tenants of the Abbot of Cirencester (Gloucestershire), were later used to pave the abbey floor.

Windmills were numerous by the end of the twelfth century but, for the most part, these were primitive fixed structures which could only be operated when the wind was blowing from a particular quarter. Later *post mills* had box-like weatherboarded bodies which could be rotated on a strong central post to catch the prevailing wind. The characteristic mill mound, in which the post was embedded, may be mistaken for a tumulus.

Some six thousand watermills were recorded at the time of the DOMESDAY survey (though there were undoubtedly many more). Medieval watermills were of four types: the *click mill* (positioned horizontally across a stream), the *undershot mill* (a vertical wheel, the lower section of which came into contact with the water), the *overshot mill* (in which water was directed to the top of the wheel) and the *breastshot mill* (in which water was directed into 'buckets' at a point level with the wheel's axle). There were also *tidemills*, dating from the late fourteenth century, a type of undershot mill driven by water impounded at high tide.

Early references to mills are not always reliable for many are contained in documents which were forged by monastic houses in order to establish claims to ancient privileges which did not exist. The earliest authentic record is that of an 'adultarine' mill (one which operated unlawfully in direct competition to manorial mills) at Bury St. Edmunds, Suffolk, in 1191. There are many references to thirteenth-century mills in contemporary documents and several illustrations in manuscripts such as the *Windmill Psalter* of *c.* 1270.

Further reading:

Brown, R., *Windmills of England*, London, 1976

Friar, S., *The Batsford Companion to Local History*, London, 1991

Wailes, R., *The English Windmill*, London, 1954

Wenham, P., *Watermills*, London, 1989

MINIATURE A full-page illustration, originally in red lead (*minium*) but later coloured and often illuminated (*see* MANUSCRIPT ILLUMINATION).

MINISTER (Latin *minister*, meaning 'servant') One who is charged with the performance of spiritual functions within the Church. In the Church of England, one who administers at a service – not necessarily a priest.

MINISTER OF DELIVERANCE Present-day euphemism for an Anglican EXORCIST.

MINOR CANON A cleric attached to a cathedral or collegiate church. Minor canons were not members of a CHAPTER.

See also CLERGY (CHURCH OF ENGLAND)

MINORITES The Franciscan Friars Minor (*see* FRIARS).

MINOR ORDERS The ranks of the Roman Catholic ministry below the MAJOR ORDERS. Before 1972 these were ACOLYTES, DOOR-KEEPERS, EXORCISTS and LECTORS.

See also CHRISTIAN SYMBOLS *and* SUB-DEACON

MINSTERS (*MONASTERIUM*) Anglo-Saxon minsters were religious communities, usually comprising a priest and a group of monastic or secular assistants (collectively known as *familia*), which served as centres of conversion and administration from the seventh century prior to the development of a system of ecclesiastical parishes (*see* ANGLO-SAXON CHURCH). In Wales, *clasau* performed a similar function, though these were usually staffed by an abbot and hereditary canons (*see* WALES, THE CHURCH IN). A minster settlement usually consisted of a church and thatched outbuildings surrounded by a wooden palisade or wall of turf and stone. They were almost invariably established on Saxon royal estates and served vast territories (*parochium*), their missionaries protected by royal or thegnal patronage in recognition of the administrative and cultural services provided by the minster staff.

Gradually the peripatetic clergy of the minsters were replaced by priests attached to proprietorial *chapelries*, strategically located daughter churches ancillary to the minsters and dependent on them. Chapelries were of two types: those with a burial ground and those without, a distinction which in some cases was perpetuated even into the nineteenth century. While many chapelries were later abandoned as settlements declined, a number continued as dependent churches for several centuries. Others became parish churches or continued as subsidiary chapels within the parochial system.

Evidence of former minsters remains, not only in surviving documents such as charters, monastic and cathedral records, court proceedings, land grants and bishops' records, but also in place name elements such as the *eccles-* of Ecclesfield in West Yorkshire and Eccleston in Cheshire, derived from the Latin *ecclesia* or 'church' (Welsh: *eglwys*). More obviously, Kidderminster in Worcestershire was 'Cydda's minster' and Sturminster in Dorset was 'the minster by the river Stour'. Many others are as yet unidentified though remnants of Saxon stonework (which was used only in major buildings) may be indicative of a church's former minster status. Even when no Saxon work remains, the historical relationship of a group of churches may indicate that one was traditionally superior to the others and this may well have been a Saxon minster.

Some historians use the term 'minster' in its vernacular sense when describing 'family monasteries': small communities established by noblemen on their estates, governed by relatives and administered by dependants.

MINUSCULE *see* LETTERING

MINUTES The official records of VESTRY meetings and (more recently) those of PAROCHIAL CHURCH COUNCILS and deanery synods are invaluable sources of information. So too are the minutes, reports and correspondence of (civil) parish councils, who may have agreed to maintain a churchyard or church clock (for example), and district councils who are obliged to accept responsibility for CLOSED CHURCHYARDS. The minutes of the managers or governors of voluntary aided and voluntary controlled SCHOOLS are often illuminating, as are the punishment books, attendance records, log books and inspectors' reports which often accompany them. The minutes of meetings of the trustees of CHARITIES and FRIENDLY SOCIETIES may also be found in county record offices.

MIRACLE PLAYS see MYSTERY PLAYS

MISERICORDE Longer than an ANELACE, the misericorde was a thrusting dagger, carried on the right hip and used especially for the *coup de grace* through a visor. Often found depicted in brasses and effigial figures dating from the late fourteenth and fifteenth centuries (*see* ARMOUR *and* CINGULUM MILITARE). The earliest example is believed to be that in the brass of William de Aldeburgh (*c.* 1360) at Aldeburgh, Yorkshire.

MISERICORDS (i) A misericord is a hinged wooden seat which, when tipped up, presents a corbel-like projection for the user to rest on when in a standing position. Usually found in the choir STALLS of cathedrals and former monastic and collegiate churches, most date from the mid-thirteenth century to the late fifteenth (*see also* RETURNED STALLS). Their function was to provide support and relief for the monks or canons who were able to rest without sitting as they stood through interminable divine offices (*misericordia*: 'mercy'). Where misericords have survived, every stall seems originally to have been provided with one, suggesting that it was not only the elderly and infirm who had need of them.

By the mid-fifteenth century, the enigmatic imagery of the carved misericord had acquired a tradition of its own. Many designs are unique but others, or variations of them, were widely used by carvers who appear to have worked from design

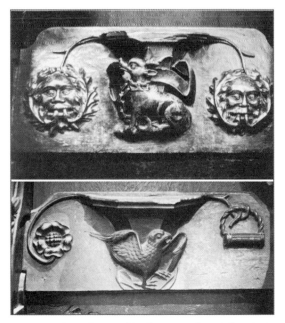

Misericords at Tansor, Northamptonshire (above), with Yorkist badges of falcon, fetterlock and white rose, and at Ludlow, Shropshire (below), with antelope of Henry VI between the two pagan 'Green Men'.

books. These would be submitted to the patron or chapter who would then select those designs which were considered appropriate to a particular church, at the same time commissioning others which were entirely new. Each collection therefore has its own unique flavour and reflects the tastes of a period as well as local influences and even contemporary political allegiances. Fifteenth-century Ludlow in Shropshire, for example, was thrust into the forefront of national politics, being one of the principal strongholds of Richard, Duke of York. In Ludlow church, Yorkist BADGES (such as the Falcon and Fetterlock and the white rose) are much in evidence among the thirty two misericords and in the splendid bosses of the chancel roof immediately above the stalls.

Most misericords consist of a raised central motif (beneath the corbel) between two subsidiary carvings (known as *supporters*) which are generally different in design and subject matter from the centrepiece. Heraldic symbolism was ideally suited to such carvings, as were images culled from the medieval bestiaries and from folklore and legend, moral allegories and cautionary tales. Sacred subjects are comparatively rare while sports, jesters, romances, satires (notably on monks and musicians) and domestic scenes were especially popular: carvings on the misericords at Ripple in Worcestershire depict the Labours of the Months, for example. Many themes are singularly abstruse. Typically, at Beverley Minster in Yorkshire, there is a misericord in which a man is depicted shoeing a goose – an illustration of the (then) popular maxim that, if you meddle in something you don't understand, you may as well try to shoe a goose. Wood carvers used a system of identification similar to that of the masons: several of the misericords at Ludlow are distinguished by a carver's mark of an uprooted plant, for example.

There can be little doubt that following the Reformation many sets of monastic and collegiate stalls provided fuel to melt the roofing lead salvaged by Henry VIII's commissioners. Fortunately many others were retrieved for use in parish churches: at Tansor in Northamptonshire, for example, where the mid-fifteenth-century misericords originated in the collegiate chancel at nearby Fotheringhay, and an exceptionally fine set of early fifteenth-century misericords and richly carved and canopied stalls at Whalley in Lancashire which were rescued from the abbey church. The church of St. Botolph at Boston, Lincolnshire ('the largest and most important parish church in England'), has a fine set of sixty-four late fourteenth-century misericords beneath a nineteenth-century canopy. There are also numerous instances of misericords which have been removed from their original stalls and re-arranged during restoration.

Misericords in stalls from Fotheringhay church, now at Tansor, Northamptonshire.

Further reading:
Laird, M., *English Misericords*, London, 1986
Smith, J., *Church Woodcarvings: Misericords and Bench-ends*, Newton Abbot, 1974

(ii) The word misericord may also be applied to a monastic dining room which was set apart for the use of those whose health or age required some relaxation of the strict rule. The terms 'loft', 'deportum', 'seyny' and 'oriel' were also used to describe monastic dining rooms for the aged and infirm. By the fifteenth century there were some religious houses where the numbers dining in the misericord exceeded those in the FRATER.

MISRULE, LORD OF (*also* ABBOT *or* MASTER OF MISRULE) In the medieval period, one who was chosen on All-Hallow's Eve (31 October) to preside over the CHRISTMAS revels which lasted until the Feast of Purification (2 February). In magnatial households, the Lord of Misrule was often a youthful servant or retainer who was provided with numerous officers, musicians, hobby-horses and dragons. The practice was prohibited in 1555.

MISSAL A liturgical book containing the words and ceremonial directions for the celebration of the MASS and, from the tenth century, combining in one book the devotions which had previously appeared in several. Development of the missal was encouraged by the medieval practice of saying private masses. Many were presented as gifts to benefactors and are exquisitely illuminated.

MISSAL STAND A sloping book-stand used by the priest at the altar. Two types are especially common: the wooden ledger stand with scrolled and foliated end panels and a scalloped bookplate edge, and the brass pedestal stand with a revolving bookplate and trumpet-shaped base.
See also DESKS *and* LECTERNS

MISTLETOE With its Druidical associations (mostly dating from the eighteenth century!) mistletoe is still revered for its magical qualities and its powers of inducing fertility. In the counties of the lower Severn, where mistletoe is more common than elsewhere, decorated boughs were taken into the house at Christmas-time where they remained for the ensuing year to ward off evil spirits. Norse mythology tells us that mistletoe provided a refuge for woodland spirits until other trees regained their leaves and that it was so sacred that it could only be cut by a priest using a golden sickle.

MISTRESS From the fourteenth century, the female correlative of 'Master' and thereafter a title of courtesy applied to a married woman, particularly one who employed servants or was head of a house or family. May be found abbreviated as Ms. in monumental inscriptions etc.

MITRE The liturgical head-dress of an archbishop or bishop and (until the Reformation) of certain MITRED ABBOTS. A tall cap, shaped at the front and back like an inverted shield, and deeply cleft from one side to the other. Mitres are usually covered with embroidered satin and have two fringed *infulae* or *lappets* (ribbons) at the back. The mitre is also a symbol of episcopal or abbatial dignity and Anglican archbishops and bishops ensign their ARMS OF OFFICE with a *mitra pretiosa* of precious metal, either jewelled or chased and jewelled. This was the mitre used by pre-Reformation bishops, while the *mitra simplex*, a plain white mitre, is that depicted in the heraldry of abbots of the Roman Catholic Church. Uniquely, in the arms of the Bishop of Durham the mitre is depicted within a ducal coronet as a symbol of the temporal jurisdiction exercised by the medieval prince bishops of the Palatinate.
See also ECCLESIASTICAL HAT *and* VESTMENTS

MITRE ARCH *see* ARCH

MITRED ABBOT The head of a major monastic house who was permitted (by papal authority) to wear a MITRE and other episcopal insignia and to carry a CROZIER. The privilege, which required confirmation by the metropolitan and diocesan bishops, was extended also to the priors of CATHEDRAL PRIORIES. By the late fifteenth century there were twenty-nine mitred abbots, most of whom were Benedictines.

MOCK OF THE CHURCH Banns of marriage which were announced but were not followed by a wedding. In many parishes, a customary fine would be imposed as a consequence.

MODELS (ARCHITECTURAL) *see* DRAWINGS (ARCHITECTURAL)

MODILLION In Classical architecture, a small bracket or series of brackets arranged in pairs to support a Corinthian or Composite CORNICE.

MODUS A private arrangement agreed between a vicar and a parishioner for the commutation of tithes paid in kind to a cash payment.

MONACHORUM Latinised place-name element meaning 'of the monks', suggesting that a manor was once possessed by a monastic foundation.
See also PLACE-NAMES

MONASTERIA *see* ANGLO-SAXON CHURCH *and* MINSTER

MONASTERIES *see* ABBEY, ALIEN PRIORIES, ANGLO-SAXON CHURCH, AUGUSTINIANS, BENEDICTINES, CARTHUSIANS, CATHEDRAL PRIORIES, CISTERCIANS, CLUNIACS, CONVENT, CONVERSI, COURTS (MONASTIC), CORRODY, DAUGHTER HOUSE, DISSOLUTION OF THE MONASTERIES, DIVINE OFFICE, DOUBLE MONASTERY, GILBERTINES, GRANGE, HORARIUM, LAY BROTHER, LITURGY, MEDIEVAL ARCHITECTURE, MEDIEVAL CHURCH, MINSTERS, MONASTIC BUILDINGS, MONASTICISM, MONK, NUN, PLACE-NAMES, PLAINSONG, PRIORY, REFORMATION, SHRINES *and* WALES, THE CHURCH IN

MONASTIC BREVIARY The BREVIARY used in religious houses which followed the Benedictine Rule.

MONASTIC BUILDINGS Many former abbey and priory churches escaped demolition at the DISSOLUTION OF THE MONASTERIES and became cathedrals and parish churches. In a number of cases, traces of conventual buildings have also survived: at Sherborne Abbey in Dorset, for example, where the former 'guesten hall' and undercroft now serve as libraries for Sherborne School and the former Abbot's Hall is the school's chapel.
Celtic and Anglo-Saxon monasteries were austere habitations, enclosed within a protective wall or bank and consisting of little more than a church and a few ancillary buildings (*see* ANGLO-SAXON CHURCH *and* CELTIC CHURCH). By the eleventh

century the CLUNIACS had established a regular plan for their monasteries which, with modifications to accommodate the peculiarities of a particular site and the needs of the various orders, became the model in England.

At the beginning of the thirteenth century there were over one thousand English monasteries, the richest being early English foundations which had acquired undeveloped land before the twelfth century, and those of the CISTERCIANS which were invariably situated in remote areas where there were fewer constraints on development. The monasteries varied considerably, both in resources and structure. Many monastic churches were less than 30 metres in length (100 feet) while others, such as Winchester and St. Albans, were five times that size.

THE SITE

A site had to be comparatively level with a reliable water supply, not only for drinking but also for cooking, washing and drainage, building works and FISH PONDS. As monastic sites became permanent, complex systems of CONDUITS and stone-clad DRAINS and sewers were constructed many of which are still in evidence, as at the Cistercian abbey of Tintern in Gwent. Space for expansion and quietude was essential: at Thetford in Norfolk the Cluniac priory became so beleaguered by urban housing that it had to be moved to a new site outside the town. The availability of substantial quantities of firewood was also an important consideration: Byland Abbey in North Yorkshire was moved four times in fifty years before a satisfactory site was found.

THE PRECINCT

The enclosed monastic PRECINCT was entered by means of a gatehouse at which visitors could be identified and their credentials checked before being admitted (*see also* FORTIFICATION). Many gatehouses had separate side entrances for pedestrians while a central vaulted gates passage was of sufficient height to allow for the movement of heavily laden wagons. Chambers above the gatehouse were often used as a courtroom or schoolroom and occasionally a small prison was incorporated into the building, as at the Benedictine priory at Ely in Cambridgeshire. Some gatehouses were crenellated while others (notably those of the Cistercians) included a chapel for the use of LAY BROTHERS. At Westminster, a parish church (St. Margaret's) was built outside the Abbey gatehouse for the benefit of the lay community. Having passed through the gatehouse the visitor entered the *curia*, a busy outer court where the monastic world met the secular. Here were located all the conventual buildings of a self-sufficient and self-contained community: a great BARN (often of considerable size), granary, bolting-house (where corn was sieved), bakery, malthouse, brewery, smithy and stables, together with a house and dining hall for monastic servants. Beyond the *curia*, and separated from it, were the cloistral buildings, to which only the brethren were permitted access, and the abbey church.

THE CLOISTRAL BUILDINGS

As the name suggests, the cloistral (or claustral) buildings were arranged around the CLOISTER, a covered and colonnaded passageway surrounding a rectangular open space or GARTH. Adjacent to this court were the most important domestic and administrative buildings of the monastery: the chapter house, dormitory (*dorter*), refectory (*frater*), the abbot's lodgings, the infirmary (*farmery*) and the great storehouse of the monastery (*cellarium*) which often occupied the entire ground floor of the western range. The SCRIPTORIUM was often accommodated in the cloister.

The CHAPTER HOUSE was normally within, or connected to, the eastern range of cloistral buildings in the upper storey of which was the DORTER or monks' dormitory with the latrines (*rere-dorter*) on the same floor and, in most Benedictine monasteries, a CALEFACTORY (warming-house) below. The refectory or FRATER was usually on the south side of the cloister, again on the upper storey though in a few houses it was on the ground floor, and in several (such as Rievaulx in Yorkshire) it was set at right-angles to, and south of, the cloister alley. In several cloisters, at the foot of the frater stairs, was the LAVATORIUM where the monks washed after rising and before meals. The monastery's *kitchens* were also near the frater, either in the adjacent western range of the cloister (*see also* CELLARIUM) or in a separate building to reduce the risk of fire. Chimney flues and ovens were set within the thickness of walls (though there may also have been a central hearth) and around the kitchens ancillary buildings housed the pantry, buttery, bakery and other domestic offices.

The guests' chambers and *abbot's* (or Prior's) *lodgings* were usually in the western range of the cloistral buildings. The lodgings would normally include a parlour, dining room, bedchamber and chapel, but as many abbots rose to positions of political influence, so their responsibilities for entertaining eminent guests (and their households) increased. Separate dining halls were provided at several monasteries, adjacent to the abbot's chambers and with suites of guests' rooms beneath. From the thirteenth century, a number of abbots had three-storeyed houses built, with dining halls on the middle floor and a parlour and bedchamber above. Some even had their own kitchens, the most splendid of which was the Abbot's Kitchen at Glastonbury Abbey in Somerset. Such opulence was not always of the abbot's choosing but was expected of him by the magnates and prelates who relied on the monasteries for hospitality.

The abbot's lodging at Muchelney Abbey, Somerset. Similar in size and comfort to many contemporary manor houses, the abbot's lodging survived the Dissolution because it made a convenient and attractive home for the abbey's new owner. The window openings of the south cloister walk were blocked to provide additional ground floor accommodation.

In Cistercian monasteries, however, the western range of cloistral buildings was originally used to accommodate the *conversi* (*see* LAY BROTHERS) who were provided with a common room and refectory on the ground floor and a dorter above. As the numbers of lay brothers declined in the fourteenth century, their quarters were often adapted for use as accommodation for guests (*see* CORRODY) and for administrative purposes.

The INFIRMARY (*farmery*) was usually built to the east of the eastern cloistral range and was intended both for the sick and infirm and for those who were too old or too deranged to cope with the astringent demands of monastic life. Dietary rules were relaxed for those in the infirmary and as these often included guests, food was usually obtained from the abbot's kitchen. The great hall of an infirmary contained at least one large fireplace and its own lavatorium and latrines. The beds were arranged between pairs of high windows in the side walls and faced a central space, as in a modern hospital ward. Many infirmaries were of considerable size, indicative of the practice of *phlebotomy* or blood-letting which was considered to be a medical necessity. Following phlebotomy, a monk was required to rest for three days during which time he could enjoy rich food and relaxation in the monastery gardens, could rise late and was excused choir. Consequently the frequency of blood-letting was, in most orders, restricted: four times a year for Cistercians, five times for Carthusians and eight for the Austin canons.

While eminent members of the monastic community might be buried beneath INCISED SLABS in the chapter house or cloister (or, from the fifteenth century, in the abbey church itself), most brethren shared a common grave in the monastery's cemetery which was approached by means of the SLYPE, a wide covered passageway from the cloister. The slype was generally used for conversation, which was forbidden in the cloister itself, and in some monasteries it developed into a library, though books were generally stored where they were needed: in the SACRISTY, the choir, the cloister or the frater (*see* LIBRARIES).

THE CHURCH

The cruciform-shaped church usually stood on the north side of the cloister (though not invariably so), the longer (western) arm of the nave providing shelter to the cloistral buildings without cutting off the sunlight. Although the interiors of Anglo-Saxon and Romanesque churches were often dark, later Gothic buildings were constructed to admit as much natural light as possible (*see* MEDIEVAL ARCHITECTURE). The principal door was at the west end and was often set within an imposing façade and sometimes flanked by twin towers, as at Durham. Eastward was the NAVE, with AISLES to the north and south separated by ARCADES of massive PIERS (*see also* ARCH) above which rose the TRIBUNE or TRIFORIUM and CLERESTORY. Some naves were of extraordinary length: that at Norwich, for example, is 76 metres long (250 feet). At the eastern end of the nave, were the ROOD SCREEN, the CROSSING and PULPITUM, and above the crossing the tower (*see* TOWERS). East of the pulpitum, and at a higher level than the nave, was the CHOIR with its wooden STALLS, each provided with a MISERICORD and a desk for service books. The stalls were raised on a stone base as protection against damp and this sometimes contained an acoustic chamber (*see* AMPLIFIER). At the west end of the choir were the LECTERN and abbot's stall, which was usually on the south side (*see* RETURNED STALLS), and to the east were the PRESBYTERY and the raised SANCTUARY in which was the high altar (*see* ALTAR). In larger churches, CHAPELS to the east of the sanctuary were linked by an apsidal aisle or AMBULATORY, as at Tewkesbury Abbey in Gloucestershire, or *retrochoir* (*see* CHOIR), screened from the high altar by a REREDOS. Of these chapels, the most important is the LADY CHAPEL, usually of late medieval date, its size and architectural splendour reflecting a contemporary cult-like veneration of the Blessed Virgin Mary (*see* MARY, THE BLESSED VIRGIN).

English monasteries were rich in relics, particularly of native saints, and these were often retained in ornate canopied SHRINES, few of which survived the Dissolution. Kings, princes and magnates sought burial in or near the sanctuaries of the great abbeys and numerous CHANTRY CHAPELS were erected for this purpose in the fourteenth and fifteenth centuries. Many shrines and royal tombs became so popular that additional accommodation had to be provided for the thousands of pilgrims who travelled from all over Britain and Europe to offer prayers and supplications and to swell monastic coffers. In the *TRANSEPT*, the northern and southern arms of cruciform building, were side chapels and subsidiary altars. A door in the north wall of the northern transept led to the community's burial ground, and from the southern transept a door opened on to the *NIGHT STAIRS* by which the monks descended from their first-floor dormitory (*dorter*) to attend the night office. A further door led from the transept to the cloister and was used as a processional entrance before high mass on Sundays and feast-days.

Further reading:
Aston, M., *Monasteries*, London, 1993
Butler, L. and Given-Wilson, C., *Medieval Monasteries of Great Britain*, London, 1979
Coppack, G., *Abbey and Priories*, London, 1993
The Ordnance Survey Map of Monastic Britain, Ordnance Survey

MONASTIC, CANONICAL AND MENDICANT ORDERS *see* AUGUSTINIANS, BENEDICTINES, CANONS REGULAR, CARTHUSIANS, CISTERCIANS, CLUNIACS, FRIARS (*for* Austin Friars, Carmelites, Crutched Friars, Dominicans, Franciscans, Friars of the Holy Cross), GILBERTINES, MILITARY ORDERS, MONASTICISM, PREMONSTRATENSIAN *and* RELIGIOUS ORDERS IN THE ANGLICAN CHURCH

MONASTIC DECLINE The history of western monasticism is one of alternating decline and revival, not only of individual houses but also of entire orders. In the ninth and tenth centuries many monastic communities suffered from repeated Viking incursions: their buildings were sacked and destroyed and their brethren slain or dispersed in a land where lawlessness was endemic. Furthermore, the religious communities of Britain were at that time isolated both from the mainstream of European religion and from one another. The Benedictine Rule, in particular, was susceptible to laxity because of its very moderation, and many abbots exploited their autonomy, not for the advancement of their houses, but in order to attract the patronage of powerful lords. That monasticism survived was due to a small number of determined and able men who set out to restore moral values by first reforming the monasteries (*see* ANGLO-SAXON CHURCH *and* BENEDICTINES).

The CISTERCIANS, whose sacrificial quality of life attracted numerous benefactions and endowments, acquired vast estates which they managed so efficiently that they became the victims of their own success. As landlords they could not avoid being part of feudal society, they became institutionalised and, as their administrative responsibilities multiplied, so they were forced to increase their establishments with CONVERSI and paid officials. By contrast, the arrival of the FRIARS in the thirteenth century brought renewed vigour and an innovative form of religious commitment with which the monasteries could not compete. At that time, many religious houses had already begun to relax their original principles of austerity and, in the face of increasing public hostility, monasticism suffered an acute crisis of identity in a society which was endowed with a superfluity of religious houses.

The economic and psychological repercussions of the PLAGUE were evident in the monasteries as elsewhere. From the mid-fourteenth century, lay brethren began deserting in large numbers, attracted by improved wages and working conditions as a consequence of a labour shortage following the Black Death. Society generally became increasingly acquisitive and materialistic. Endowments were diverted from the monasteries to parish churches where numerous additions and improvements were effected by benefactors whose generosity reflected their status in society as much as their religious devotion. A recent account of monastic life in the fifteenth century * paints an appalling picture of drunkenness, gluttony, licentiousness and racketeering at (of all places) the abbey of Westminster. Presumably, this cannot have been exceptional.

Ironically, towards the end of the fifteenth century, there were signs of renewed vigour in the Church and of a willingness to acknowledge the need for monastic reform. What the outcome might have been is a matter for conjecture (*see* REFORMATION).

Further reading:

Harvey, B., *Living and Dying in England 1100–1540: The Monastic Experience*, Oxford, 1993 *

MONASTICISM Monks followed an ascetic, disciplined life devoted to prayer and work, secure from worldly distraction (*see* MONK). Their objective was to achieve personal sanctification in fulfilment of the solemn threefold vow of poverty, chastity and obedience. They were not required to become priests and only the clerical order could administer the SACRAMENTS. Like the ordained clerks, monks received the *tonsure*, the circular shaved patch on the crown of the head, which signified commitment to the Church (though not necessarily ordination). From the sixth century, as a result of papal influence, a distinction was made between the clerical order, which served the spiritual needs of lay people under the authority of a diocesan bishop, and the monastic order which was devoted to a cloistered existence. In practice, however, the distinction was frequently blurred: many monks were also priests (or even bishops) and, by the beginning of the seventh century, were exercising significant influence beyond the precincts of their monasteries.

From the eighth to the twelfth centuries, Benedictine monasticism was the only form of religious life in Western Europe (*see* BENEDICTINES *and* ANGLO-SAXON CHURCH). Thereafter there was a proliferation of monastic, canonical and mendicant orders (*see* individual entries), the most significant period of monastic expansion lasting from the Conquest of 1066 to *c.* 1220 (*see* MEDIEVAL CHURCH). Although from that time the religious houses remained numerous and their prosperity increased, their popular credibility declined in an age of deprivation

and uncertainty, exacerbated by the Black Death of the mid-fourteenth century (*see* MONASTIC DECLINE *and* PLAGUE).

During the thirteenth century, one third of a typical monastic community consisted of quire monks and two thirds of lay brethren paying guests (*corrodians*), visitors and servants. The largest community in England was that of the Benedictine abbey of St. Alban in Hertfordshire where there were one hundred monks. But elsewhere, at the great Cistercian and Benedictine houses, establishments usually numbered between sixty and seventy and in the houses of other orders, perhaps no more than thirty. Of a population in thirteenth-century England of about three million, one out of every one hundred and fifty persons was a monk, canon or nun. There were some 4,000 Benedictines, 3,000 Cistercians, 500 Cluniacs and 200 Carthusians: monks who were not clerics but men who had vowed to pursue a life of austerity, contemplation and prayer 'outside the gates of the world.' Of canons, who were clerks in holy orders and lived according to a RULE, there were some 3000 Augustinians, 1,000 Gilbertines and 800 Premonstratensians (*see* CANON REGULATOR). In addition there were about 7,000 nuns of the various orders and 500 knights Templar or Hospitaller (*see* MILITARY ORDERS).

LAY BRETHREN

LAY BROTHERS (and, in Gilbertine houses, lay sisters) were an important element of the monastic population. They were not bound to the recitation of the DIVINE OFFICE and were generally occupied in manual and domestic work, though the Cistercian CONVERSI included many skilled craftsmen. In the mid-twelfth century the *conversi* outnumbered the monks in Cistercian houses by three to one, and the Carthusians, Austin Canons and Benedictines also recruited lay brothers in large numbers. But during the thirteenth century their numbers steadily declined so that by 1350 few remained in the monastic communities. In part, this was the result of 'market forces', but in many monasteries the often tense relationship between monks and lay brethren had proved to be incompatible with the objectives of monastic life. As the numbers of lay brethren decreased so a veritable army of wage-earning servants moved in. It is estimated that in the thirteenth century there were 40,000 servants in religious houses (twice the number of monks, canons and nuns), many of whom lived with their families in the PRECINCT. Their tasks ranged from curers of herrings to keepers of the wax and cressets (lamps) and Worcester Priory even maintained a crew of five boatmen on the river Severn.

Of course, domestic help was needed not only to free the monks of routine chores but also to provide for the numerous guests who comprised about one sixth of a monastery's population. Many temporary guests were accommodated without charge but others generated a substantial income through *corrodies*: annuities of land or money made over to a monastic foundation in return for guaranteeing the comfort and security of the benefactor in old age.

SUPERIORS

Ironically, it was the possession of vast tracts of land (obtained through corrodies and endowments) and numerous manorial estates and GRANGES which eventually diverted monastic energy away from quiet contemplation and prayer to the administration and commercial exploitation of property and promoted many an abbot to the dual status of spiritual leader and magnate, responsible to the brethren by whom he was elected, to the tenants of his estates and (if he was called upon to hold office) to the Crown. His instructions came as from God and in his monastery he was both good shepherd and autocrat, elected for life. But in practice, many abbots lived as ecclesiastical magnates with their own households and retinues, dispensing patronage and exercising political and judicial authority. In such cases responsibility for the day-to-day life of a monastery and the welfare and conduct of the monks was delegated to an abbot's deputy-general, the *prior* (*see also* PRIORIES).

OBEDIENTIARIES

The *obedientiaries*, or monastic officials, usually numbered between fifteen and twenty depending on the size of the monastery, though Cistercian houses were not organised on hierarchical principles. The senior obedientiaries were the PRIOR and *sub-prior*(s); the SACRISTAN, who with the *sub-sacristan*, was responsible for the abbey church; and the CELLARER who, with the *sub-cellarer*(s), was responsible for the properties of the monastery, including all revenues, rents and patronage. The cellarer also exercised supervision over the various domestic departments and was responsible for the maintenance of the monastery buildings; for the acquisition of food, drink, clothing, fuel and livestock and for tenants, lay brethren and servants. Responsible to the cellarer were the *kitchener* who ensured that meals were of a suitable quality and served on time; the *refectorian* who organised the refectory (*see* FRATER); the *hosteller* who ran the guests' house and the *infirmarian* who had charge of the INFIRMARY. The *almoner* provided for the needs of the poor and infirm who could not leave their homes and gave food, clothing and money to pilgrims, beggars and lepers who called at the monastery gate. The PRECENTOR maintained the monastery library and was responsible for its music.

ADMISSION

By 1200, the practice of offering children in infancy to be educated as *oblates* in religious communities had been abandoned and thereafter the age at which a POSTULANT could make application for admission to a monastery or nunnery was generally between seventeen and nineteen. Once admitted, a postulant became a NOVICE and was required to give all his possessions to the monastery or to the poor, though his clothing was kept so that he could re-enter the world if he so wished or if he was required to leave. The NOVICE MASTER instructed the novices in the Rule and prepared them for the demands of monastic life. He also gave lessons in reading, singing and comportment. The noviciate lasted for a year, at the end of which time the novice (if accepted) made his vows and swore obedience to the Rule.

THE DAILY ROUND

Spared the necessity of domestic chores, a monk's life was nevertheless one of discipline and routine. The primary responsibility of a monastic community was to recite the DIVINE OFFICE, the eight CANONICAL HOURS or services of the LITURGY, and each day's pattern was determined by the hours of daylight. At the March and September equinoxes, for example, when night and day each last twelve hours, the brethren rose from a seven-hour sleep at two o'clock to attend the 'night watch' meditation of NOCTURN and MATTINS. The Day Hours began with LAUDS ('praises') which was recited at first light and PRIME at sunrise. Then followed TERCE (third hour), SEXT (sixth hour), NONE (ninth hour), VESPERS (at sunset) and COMPLINE (sung to 'complete' the hours before retiring at dusk). All eight hours consisted of Psalms, hymns, lessons, antiphons, versicles, responses and prayers, led by the *precentor* and his deputy the SUCCENTOR, and sung in PLAINSONG. The Hours did not include CONFESSION, which was made at the daily meeting of the CHAPTER before the abbot and brethren, and High Mass which was celebrated each Sunday (*see* MASS). During services, the quire monks occupied the STALLS and the lay brothers the nave and each had their own entrance to the church. The intervals between the Hours were devoted to work, with a two-hour rest period following None and the daily meal taken after Vespers (*see* HONORARIUM).

F.H. Crossley, in his *The English Abbey* *, describes monastic life in terms which make its apparent popularity difficult to comprehend. 'They [the monks] spent their time in innumerable services and study, living a dull existence in silence, shut away from the world and its excitement, for they lived on a low diet and suffered much from indigestion, a prey to habits which cut across the precepts of good health, and the constant and periodical bleeding were weakening. The average life of a monk was 55 years. The picture of a monk's life during an English winter is not to be envied, with no heating in the monastery, the dorter icily cold when he rose for the long night service, going half asleep in the dark to a freezing church, perhaps filled with a clinging fog, and being expected to sing and pray with fervour for an hour and a half.' No wonder that a medieval monk wrote: 'I cannot endure the daily tasks. The sight of it revolts me. I am tormented and crushed down by the weight of the vigils and I often succumb to the manual labour. The food cleaves to my mouth, more bitter than wormwood. The rough clothing cuts through my skin and flesh down to the very bones. More than this, my will is always hankering after other things, it longs for the delights of the world and sighs unceasingly for its loves and affections and pleasures.'

See also MONASTIC BUILDINGS and RELI-GIOUS ORDERS IN THE ANGLICAN CHURCH
Further reading:
Bottomly, F., *Abbeys, Monasteries and Churches*, London, 1981
Butler, L. and Given-Wilson, C., *Medieval Monasteries of Great Britain*, London, 1979
Cook, G., *English Monasteries in the Middle Ages*, London, 1961
Crossley, F.H., *The English Abbey*, London, 1935 *
Knowles, D., *The Monastic Order in England*, London, 1966

MONASTICON ANGLICANUM A collection of monastic charters and other sources relating to English monasticism and medieval collegiate churches compiled between 1655–73 by Sir William Dugdale (1605–86).

MONASTIC PLACE-NAMES *see* PLACE-NAMES

MON-AXIAL *see* BI-AXIAL

MONK In its early form, the term was used to describe a religious who lived a solitary life (*see* COENOBITE) but it came to include all members of a closed religious community of men, living according to a RULE and subject to a tripartite vow of poverty, chastity and obedience. It should not be applied to CANONS REGULAR or to members of the MENDICANT or MILITARY ORDERS. There were two classes of monk: quire monks (*see* CHOIR) and LAY BROTHERS. Of these, the quire monks were the senior brethren whose principle function was to observe the DIVINE OFFICE. They were, of necessity, literate and were often the younger sons of the nobility and gentry. Many monks were also ordained priests but not necessarily so.
See also MONASTICISM *and* NUN

MONOGRAM Two or more letters interwoven to form a symbol. *For* sacred monograms *see* CHRISTIAN SYMBOLS.

MONSTRANCE From the Latin *monstrare* meaning 'to show', a monstrance is the (usually ornate) receptacle containing a glazed roundel in which the consecrated Host is exposed for the adoration of the people (*see* PLATE).

MONUMENTAL BRASSES *see* BRASSES (MONUMENTAL)

MONUMENTAL INSCRIPTIONS *see* INSCRIPTIONS *and* LETTERING

MONUMENTS Monuments, erected within a church to perpetuate the memory of an individual, invariably reflect the fashions and foibles, aspirations and *folies des grandeurs* of a particular class at a particular time. They can provide a wealth of information concerning the fluctuating fortunes of individuals and communities, the way people lived, their appearance and clothing, how and at what age they died, and how they (or their relatives) hoped they would be remembered. Monumental INSCRIPTIONS and HERALDRY are invaluable sources for the researcher (*see also* EPITAPHS), while changing artistic and architectural styles reflect both contemporary tastes and attitudes to religious observance. MEMORIALS vary in size from large, elaborate, canopied monuments to modest TABLETS affixed to a wall, and even the most mundane of parish churches, which at first may appear to be rebuilt and ordinary, will often contain memorials from an earlier, usually medieval, building. Monuments do not necessarily mark the place of interment which may be some distance away (*see* VAULTS (BURIAL)) or even at another church. Many have been moved – to accommodate an organ, for example. In all that follows, it should be remembered that only the 'great and good' of society enjoyed the privilege of being commemorated within their parish churches. *For* the commonalty *see* CHURCHYARDS *and* GRAVESTONES.

THE MEDIEVAL PERIOD
Memorials developed from the practice of carving designs on stone coffin lids and on grave covers which were exposed in a church floor. The earliest surviving lids are from the eleventh century and are carved in shallow relief with simple decorative designs, usually foliage or Christian symbols such as the fish and key. The tapering grave cover, engraved with a cross, at Studley in Warwickshire is typical of a style which lasted into the thirteenth century. Many others have survived (though not always in their original locations) and may be even older than the buildings which house them.

It is likely that depiction of the human form was reserved, in the twelfth century, for eminent ecclesiastics, the earliest known example in England being that of Abbot Gilbert Crispin (d. 1117) at

Westminster Abbey. In these early monuments the image was recessed into the slab, but from the beginning of the thirteenth century it was often placed on a TOMB CHEST and carved in a three-dimensional effigial form (*see* EFFIGIES). Throughout the medieval period, painted ALABASTER or PURBECK MARBLE effigies were widely used to commemorate members of the nobility and eminent knights and clerics, the familiar recumbent attitude signifying mortality and humility. Before the mid-fourteenth century, legs and arms were depicted in a variety of positions but thereafter legs are rigidly straight and hands closed together in veneration and prayer. One of the earliest military effigies is that of William Longespée, Earl of Salisbury (d. 1226) in Salisbury Cathedral which provides evidence of the early systematic use of hereditary armorial devices (*see* HERALDRY). The heads of effigies may rest on pillows (sometimes held by angels) or on HELMETS and their feet on beasts, usually (though by no means invariably) a lion for a man or a pet dog for his lady. Tiny BEDESMAN may also be found, carved in the folds of clothing or at a figure's feet.

Tomb chests were also highly decorated and usually reflect contemporary architectural styles, though many were subsequently replaced and are therefore of a later date than the effigies they bear. Tomb chests, with or without effigies (or, occasionally, with brasses) could be free-standing or recessed within a wall and were sometimes surmounted by an ornate CANOPY, as at Ewelme in Oxfordshire where the late fifteenth-century monument to the Duchess of Suffolk (complete with CADAVER) is possibly the finest of its type in England. (Free-standing canopied tomb chests were the precursors of the late medieval CHANTRY CHAPELS.) Two-dimensional figures continued to be engraved in INCISED SLABS and, from the late thirteenth century, in monumental brasses (*see* BRASSES (MONUMENTAL)). The figures in effigies and brasses are generally stylised, for it was the accompanying heraldry which announced the identity, lineage and status of the deceased, though some of the more lavish examples are idealised portraits – 'based on a likeness'. It became the practice to place man and wife (or wives) side by side (and sometimes holding hands) but their children were not usually represented, except as

Magnificent monument to Thomas Howard, third duke of Norfolk (c. 1554) at Framlingham, Suffolk.

WEEPERS around the sides of the tomb chest or by SHIELDS, illustrative of marital alliances. The figures carved on a tomb chest may help in dating: weepers occur from the late thirteenth century, angels from the late fourteenth century and saints in the fifteenth century.

The development of ARMOUR and COSTUME may be traced through effigial figures and brasses (*for illustrations see* BRASSES, (MONUMENTAL)), though it should be remembered that memorials are not necessarily contemporaneous with the death of those they commemorate: many were prepared years (or even decades) beforehand while others were commissioned retrospectively and may be in a later style. Similarly, dating a memorial by reference to the armour or costume of a figure can be fraught with difficulties. An effigy, at St. David's Cathedral in Powys, alleged to be that of The Lord Rhys of Deheubarth (d. 1197), is of a knight in fourteenth-century armour, for example.

THE SIXTEENTH CENTURY

Throughout the ages, a substantial portion of the surplus wealth of communities has been expended on the burial places of their leaders. But from the mid-fifteenth century there are signs of increasing expenditure on the commemoration of less distinguished members of society, indicative of the notion that everyone has the right to be interred beneath masonry. In the Tudor period, great families and those of the 'new gentility' and the merchant class were often commemorated in sumptuous monuments. The recumbent figure continued into the sixteenth and seventeenth centuries, but may be somewhat stiff in appearance. There was also a proliferation of undevotional postures reflecting, no doubt, changes in religious attitudes brought about by the Reformation: reclining casually on an elbow, for example, as in a Fettiplace monument at Swinbrook in Oxfordshire. Kneeling figures (often at a prayer desk) and demi-figures are also in evidence and these may be contained within a WALL MONUMENT which has no tomb chest. There are numerous splendid monuments from this period, notably those to the Howards at Framlingham in Suffolk, at Brington (the Spencer family) and Fawsley (the Knightley family) in Northamptonshire and at Layer Marney in Essex where a terracotta monument to Lord Marney combines Gothic and Renaissance detail. Two distinctive types of memorial which date from the late sixteenth and early seventeenth centuries are the TRIPTYCH, a hinged set of three painted panels, and the OBELISK, a tall, four-sided tapering pillar, usually placed on a plinth. Renaissance forms and decoration superseded the Gothic, characterised by STRAPWORK, grotesques, cherub-heads and allegorical figures.

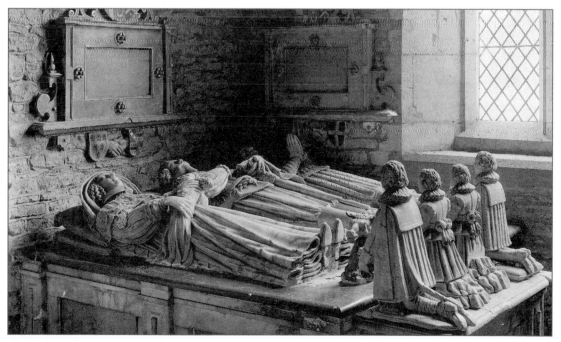

Finely carved monument (1631) to the Savage family at Elmley Castle, Worcestershire. On a tomb chest, beneath a simple heraldic wall monument, lie the effigies of William Savage (d. 1616), his son Giles, and the latter's wife, cradling an infant in her arms. At her feet are the kneeling figures of William's four surviving grandchildren.

MONUMENTS

THE SEVENTEENTH CENTURY

Many Jacobean monuments are singularly impressive, lavishly coloured and adorned with heraldry, the armour and costume of kneeling or recumbent figures being particularly striking. Children are often included, usually carved in relief or painted on a frieze with the boys in descending order on one side of their deceased parent(s) and the girls on the other. The monuments at Brewood in Staffordshire contain nearly fifty children, many of whom are depicted in their chrisom-robes (see CHRISM). A skull held by a child is also indicative of early mortality. Of numerous fine examples, that to the Knollys family at Rotherfield Grays in Oxfordshire is exceptional, as are the Bourchier monuments at Tawstock in Devon and those to the Hoby family at Bisham in Berkshire and to the Fermor family at Easton Neston in Northamptonshire.

During the late sixteenth and early seventeenth centuries heraldry proliferated, often ostentatiously so, reflecting the changing nature of armory from the practical to the ceremonial and symbolic. It was now necessary to provide artificial helms, gauntlets, tabards and other items of FUNERAL HERALDRY which, in the previous century, would have been readily available; and it was at this time (c. 1627) that the funeral HATCHMENT was introduced as an inexpensive substitute for the elaborate trappings of the heraldic funerals of the nobility and gentry (see also MEMORIAL BOARDS). Unfortunately for the genealogist, heraldic errors abound: from elementary mistakes committed by restorers with little understanding of armorial practice to multi-quartered shields which are either inaccurate or incomplete. For example, many contemporary coats of arms (either by accident or design) include the arms of wives who were not heraldic heiresses (see HEIRESS and MARSHALLING).

The seventeenth century witnessed the development of Classical architecture which, inevitably, influenced the design of church monuments. Tomb chests became unfashionable, columns and pediments predominated and, while kneeling effigies remained in hanging monuments, figures were carved in more natural poses. Indeed, at the church of St. Michael at St. Alban in Hertfordshire, Francis Bacon is depicted in a seated position and appears to be fast asleep while, at Culford in Suffolk, Lady Bacon is also seated – surrounded by her family and with her first husband recumbent beneath her feet! One of the finest examples of contemporary sculpture (by Nicholas Stone) is to be found in the effigial figures of Arthur Coke and his wife and child at Bramfield in Sussex.

EIGHTEENTH CENTURY

Black and white MARBLE superseded alabaster at the end of the seventeenth century and colour was confined to an occasional (and diminutive) heraldic motif. The ostentatious sculpted memorials of the period often dominate the churches in which they were erected, standing figures (indicative of self-glorification rather than humility) reflect the spirit of the times, and of the EIGHTEENTH-CENTURY CHURCH in particular, while contemporary EPITAPHS relate in the most pompous and verbose manner the innumerable merits of the deceased. There are also many memorials which reflect the flamboyant Baroque style of late seventeenth- and early EIGHTEENTH-CENTURY ARCHITECTURE. Imposing figures were often modelled to capture a significant moment in the deceased's life and ornate carved fruits, garlands and cherubs' heads were incorporated into designs, particularly in wall monuments. Typical of the period are the monuments to the Clayton family at Bletchingley in Surrey, the Poley family at Boxted in Suffolk and the Spencers at Yarnton, Oxfordshire.

The Damer monument at Milton Abbey, Dorset.

As the eighteenth century progressed, there was an inevitable reaction against the excesses of the Baroque and a reversion to more classical styles, indeed figures were often depicted in classical costume (or armour) surrounded by images of ancient Rome. From *c.* 1750 the architectural canopy was superseded by the two-dimensional pyramid, a large slab of black or grey marble set vertically against a wall, while the earlier tomb chest was reintroduced as the SARCOPHAGUS which often had figures of the deceased, his family or allegorical characters sitting or leaning against it. The area at the base of the monument was usually devoted to biographical or genealogical details or incorporated a frieze depicting a scene from the deceased's life, particularly of those who had enjoyed successful military or naval careers. Busts, small portrait medallions, amorini, urns, cartouches and symbols of mortality are ubiquitous.

Many eighteenth-century monuments appear extraordinarily vulgar to our modern eye: at Strensham in Worcestershire, for example, the figure of Sir Francis Russell reclines on his sarcophagus while his weeping widow hovers over him and points upwards to (what she assumes to be) her late husband's deserved destination. But many memorials, while no less ostentatious, are exquisitely sculpted. At Milton Abbey in Dorset, Caroline Damer (d. 1775), recumbent and cushioned in white marble, is watched over pensively by her widower, Lord Milton, who leans nonchalantly, on his right elbow. The Damer monument, wonderfully sculpted by Agostino Carlini to Robert Adam's design, is pathetic rather than vulgar and is greatly enhanced by its location in the north transept of the former abbey church where its scale is entirely in keeping with the massive fifteenth-century transept walls and memorial window.

NINETEENTH CENTURY

In the nineteenth century the classical Roman style was superseded by a restrained neo-classicism inspired by Greek designs, again in black and white marble (white was increasingly popular). The two-dimensional pyramid motif was replaced by the STELE, a rectangular slab surmounted by a low, triangular pediment, and recumbent effigies are again in evidence. The size of nineteenth-century monuments varied from small inscribed TABLETS to large hanging monuments with an inscription in the base and a sculpted relief figure, usually an angel or the deceased, in classical Greek dress, resting against an urn or sarcophagus.

Not all monuments were erected within a church. The eminent architect James Wyatt (1746–1813) designed an extraordinary classical monument (1804) to the poet Thomas Gray which was erected beyond the churchyard at Stoke Poges in Buckinghamshire. It is one of the most grotesque (and inappropriate) memorials imaginable, consisting as it does of a massive casket surmounting an equally overbearing pedestal.

The Greek revival continued into the second half of the century when it was overtaken by the Gothic Revival (*see* NINETEENTH-CENTURY ARCHITECTURE). Inevitably, there was a return to the 'medieval' tomb chest and alabaster effigy, sometimes surmounted by a canopy, and to the figured monumental brass. But most Victorian effigies combine a variety of medieval influences and rarely reproduce accurately the style of a particular period. Brass wall monuments and plaques were also popular, with their now familiar 'Gothic' lettering and decorative capital letters.

TWENTIETH CENTURY

From the end of the nineteenth century, large funeral monuments became unfashionable and, in most cases, impracticable. A notable exception is the tomb chest and effigy of T.E. Lawrence (Lawrence of Arabia, d. 1935) finely sculpted in marble by Eric Kennington and now in the Saxon church of St. Martin at Warcham, Dorset. But, for the most part, twentieth-century memorials take the form of simple commemorative wall tablets and window glass, or the provision of church furniture and fittings as bequests 'in memoriam'.

See also HEART BURIAL, STAINED GLASS *and* VAULTS (BURIAL)

For the Church Monuments Society, the Royal Commission for Historic Monuments *and* the Monumental Brass Society *see* APPENDIX II.

Further reading:

Collinson, H., *Country Monuments, Their Families and Houses*, Newton Abbot, 1975

Darke, J., *The Monument Guide to England and Wales*, London, 1987

Esdaile, K., *English Church Monuments 1510–1840*, London, 1946

Kemp, B., *English Church Monuments*, London, 1980

——, *Church Monuments*, Aylesbury, 1988

RCHM, *Inventories of Historical Monuments*

MOORSTONE A granite quarried in the west of England and used for buildings, paving and monuments.

MORALITY PLAY Popular in the fifteenth and sixteenth centuries, the morality play (*or* morality) was a development of the earlier MYSTERY PLAYS, a form of DRAMA in which a moral truth was inculcated by the personification of abstract qualities.

MORESQUE Sixteenth-century term for an interlaced decorative motif which was perceived to be Moorish in origin (*see* DECORATIVE MOTIFS).

MORNING PRAYER *see* MATTINS

MORROW MASS The early morning mass celebrated between TERCE and CHAPTER (*see* HORARIUM). A chapel at Newland in the Forest of Dean, Gloucestershire, was founded in the fifteenth century for a priest who was required to say morrow mass twice a week for the local miners before they began their long and dangerous day underground.

MORSE *see* VESTMENTS

MORTGAGE DEEDS *see* DIOCESAN RECORDS

MORTHEAD A death's head, a symbol of mortality and the transient nature of life, either painted (as in a HATCHMENT) or sculpted in (e.g.) the form of a skull.

MORTISE (*also* MORTICE) A cavity in a wooden member, cut with precision to receive the projection (*tenon*) of another member, thereby forming a *mortice and tenon* joint (*see* WOODWORK).

MORTMAIN Mortmain means, literally, 'dead hand' and, in the present context, it is the hand of the Church. Land which was granted by laymen to ecclesiastical bodies became free of escheats and reliefs, thereby reducing the revenues of the manorial lord. (Escheated estates were those which reverted to a lord when a tenant died without heirs or committed a felony which incurred the forfeiture of his estate.) Various medieval Statutes of Mortmain prohibited the transfer of land without a lord's consent and restricted the ability of the Church to acquire property in this way. Current practice relies on The Mortmain and Charitable Uses Act of 1888 and subsequent amendments.

MORTSAFE (i) A heavy grating intended to safeguard a corpse against resurrectionists (*see* BODY SNATCHERS). (ii) A coffin in which a corpse was temporarily deposited pending burial. In the eighteenth century these were usually wooden, earlier ones being of stone and without lids.

MORTSTONE A wayside stone on which a bier was placed when the bearers rested (*see* CORPSE ROAD).

MORTUARY (i) A customary levy (*soul scot*) received by a parish priest from the estate of a deceased parishioner. In the medieval period this often consisted of a deceased person's second-best chattel which was taken by an incumbent as recompense for TITHES and other dues which (theoretically) remained unpaid. Legislation of 1529 restricted mortuaries to moderate payments based on the value of an estate. (ii) A building in which corpses are temporarily stored. (iii) Descriptive of death or burial.

MORTUARY HOLES *see* BURIALS

MOS TUTONICUS The separation, by dismemberment and boiling, of bodily fat and bones in order that the skeleton of a deceased person might be returned home for interment (e.g. from the Crusades) while the remainder of the corpse was buried at the place of death. At the end of the thirteenth century, Pope Boniface VIII (*c.* 1234–1303) attempted to prohibit the practice because the chapels of churches were sometimes used as 'appropriate kitchens' for this purpose. The body of Henry V (1387–1422) was dismembered, boiled and well spiced before it was returned from the castle of Bois de Vincennes (on the outskirts of Paris) for burial in Westminster Abbey.
See also HEART BURIAL

MOTET A form of unaccompanied polyphonal chant which superseded that of the CONDUCTUS, though both were in use from the thirteenth century to the early sixteenth century. The motet was not a setting of any part of the ordinary of the MASS but was the equivalent of what (in the Protestant Church) we now call an ANTHEM. Motets (*sanctiones sacrae*) were introduced into the service at the Offertory, the Elevation of the Host and during processions and other ceremonies for which the LITURGY did not prescribe any other text to be sung. The motet reached its apotheosis at the end of the sixteenth century in the work of Giovanni Palestrina (*c.* 1525–94), William Byrd (1542–1623) and others.
See also CHURCH MUSIC (ANGLICAN) *and* PLAINSONG

MOTHERING SUNDAY (*also* APPRENTICE SUNDAY, MID-LENT SUNDAY, REFECTION SUNDAY, ROSE SUNDAY *and* SIMNEL SUNDAY) The fourth Sunday in LENT was once known as Rose Sunday, a great religious holiday when the Pope blessed the Golden Rose, an ornament of gold and gems, which was bestowed on 'the royal lady whose zeal for the Church hath most shown itself by pious deeds or pious intentions'. Strangely, both Julius II and Leo X sent the Rose to Henry VIII! (The Golden Rose is now presented occasionally as a mark of favour to an individual or community.)

But, to most Christians, the day was also Mothering Sunday – now erroneously described as 'Mothers' Day'. This was the day on which apprentices and domestic servants were permitted to visit their parents (and to feast on 'mothering cakes'), a tradition which originated in the ancient custom of presenting an Easter offering at the altar of a mother church on the fourth Sunday of Lent. In Lancashire, simnel cakes are eaten on this day (known as Simnel Sunday) while, in Somerset, they are known as simlin cakes. Both words are derived from the the Old French *simenel*, 'bread made of fine flower', and the custom commemorates both the banquet given by Joseph to his brethren (which forms the first lesson for the day) and the feeding of the five thousand (which is the Gospel for the day). For this reason it was also known as Refection Sunday (*dominica refectionis*).

MOTHERS' UNION Founded by Mary Elizabeth Sumner in 1876, the Mothers' Union is a women's organisation within the Church of England whose objectives are to uphold the sanctity of marriage and to encourage in mothers a sense of responsibility in the training of their children. Incorporated in 1910, the Mothers' Union was granted a royal charter in 1926.

MOTTE A raised, conical earthwork usually associated with early medieval fortifications.

MOTTO An aphorism, the interpretation of which is often obscure but may allude to a charge in a coat of arms or to some event in a family's history: 'TOUCH NOT THE CAT BOT A GLOVE' (referring to the cat crest of The Mackintosh) and 'I SAVED THE KING' (Turnbull), for example. Mottoes, accompanying signatures, will be found in medieval documents and first appear in HERALDRY in the fourteenth century, though they were not in general use until the seventeenth century when coats of arms became stylised. Researchers should be aware that mottoes in English and Welsh coats of arms may be changed at will and are therefore singularly unreliable clues to identity.
See also HATCHMENTS *and* KNIGHTHOOD, ORDERS OF
Further reading:
Elvin, C.N., *Handbook of Mottoes*, 1860 (re-printed 1986, Marlborough)
Pine, L., *A Dictionary of Mottoes*, London, 1983

MOUCHETTE A decorative motif having the shape of a curved dagger.

MOULDING A modelled surface to (e.g.) an arch, panel, capital or entablature which may be purely decorative, intended to define or accentuate the architectural character of a building, or designed to protect a vertical surface by projecting outwards in order to deflect rain and snow, as in (e.g.) a cornice or hood-mold. In some instances (notably in MEDIEVAL ARCHITECTURE) mouldings are both functional and decorative and may be carved ornamentally and/or painted. In most cases, mouldings are characteristic of certain periods of building and are useful when attempting to identify a particular architectural style.
See also DECORATIVE MOTIFS

MOUNTING BLOCKS *see* UPPING STOCKS

MOURNING *see* WIDOW'S WEEDS

MOVABLE FEASTS Annual ecclesiastical festivals which do not occur on a fixed day in the secular calendar (*see* FEAST DAYS (FIXED AND MOVABLE)).

MOZETTA *see* VESTMENTS

MULE CHEST *see* CHEST

MULLION A vertical bar dividing the lights of a window.
See also GLAZING BARS, TRANSOM *and* WINDOWS

MULTIFOIL Composed of a number of FOILS e.g. the head of a traceried window light.

MUNIMENT A title deed. Documentary evidence of a right or privilege.

MUNTIN A vertical framing piece between door panels, openings (*lights*) in screens etc. Not to be confused with a window MULLION.
See also BRACE, CHANCEL SCREEN, DOORS AND DOORWAYS, LEDGE, RAIL *and* STILE

MURAL Appertaining to a wall. A mural painting is a painting executed especially in distemper colours upon the wall of a building (*see* WALL PAINTINGS)
See also FRESCO

MURAL CROWN *see* CREST CORONETS

MURAL TABLET *see* TABLETS

MUSICAL INSTRUMENTS For the most part, the instruments which were commonly used by church bands in the eighteenth and nineteenth centuries belonged to the musicians and their families (the bands were in great demand for secular purposes) though some of the larger and more expensive instruments may have been provided by the churchwardens (*see* GALLERIES). Consequently, very few remain in churches and these are usually locked away for reasons of security. Many are now owned by collectors or museums who encourage their use by expert musicians, occasionally to accompany services. Most instruments bear the name of the maker and a serial number.

Clarinets, flutes, flageolets and oboes were simply tubes, usually of boxwood and with a minimum of keys. The bassoon (or base horn), ophicleide or *serpent* were low-sounding instruments, with long tubes either folded (bassoon) or curled (serpent) intended to sound a regular base note rather than a melody. The *vamping horn*, a huge type of trumpet, was used to fill out an insufficient body of sound from other instruments by 'humming' harmonies (to *vamp* is to improvise) and was popular from the late seventeenth to the nineteenth centuries. Key bugles and trombones (or *sackbuts*) were brass wind instruments, with padded keys (the key bugle) or an extendable slide (the trombone). Early stringed instruments which were occasionally played in churches in the eighteenth century included various viols (notably, the base viol) which were similar to the instruments of the violin family but had six strings, a fretted fingerboard and (usually) a flat back. The violin, cello and double-bass sometimes had wire strings (or both gut and wire) and home-made versions were not uncommon. In the absence of a band, a pitch-pipe was often used to provide the correct note for a choir.

At the time of writing, there are examples of pitch-pipes at Moreton Morrell in Warwickshire and Ditchling in Sussex, vamping horns at Braybrook in Northamptonshire and East Leake in Nottinghamshire, bassoons at Harringworth in Northamptonshire and Good Easter in Essex, a bass fiddle at Giggleswick in Yorkshire and a clarinet at South Muskham in Nottinghamshire.

INSTRUMENTS IN RELIGIOUS ART

The variety of musical instruments in Christian art makes identification especially difficult, though (with the exception of the Old Testament *shofar*) contemporary instruments were depicted by medieval artists, irrespective of the subject matter.

Of the stringed instruments, the *psaltery*, *lyre*, *harp*, *rebeck* and *tromba marina* are the most common. The *psaltery* is similar to a dulcimer and has a large number of strings stretched over a shallow sound-box which is played in an upright position. The *lyre* is a plucked string instrument in which (usually) five strings are fixed to a cross-bar supported by a pair of curved arms. The ('Celtic') *harp,* the symbol of St. Cecilia (the patroness of church music), is similar in appearance to the orchestral harp but is very much smaller and was held between the shoulder and knee. The medieval *rebeck* was an early form of violin but with a long neck, pear-shaped body, arched back and only three strings, while the *tromba marina* had a single string and a long, tapering sound-box.

Early wind instruments included the *shawm*, the *crumhorn, cornett, buisine* and *shofar* (all of which have a mouth-piece at one end), and the familiar *bagpipes* and *panpipes*. The *shawm* (the predecessor of the oboe) had a bell-shaped opening while the *crumhorn* was shaped like an inverted walking stick and the *cornett* a graceful ogee. The *buisine* was a straight, medieval trumpet and the *shofar* was the ancient synagogue horn of the Jews. *Bagpipes* and *panpipes* are common, as are the *pipe and tabor*, a simple combination of wind and percussion played by a single musician, the pipe having only three holes which could be played with one hand while the other beat the drum. The *portative organ*, a portable organ with keyboard and bellows, is a common motif and (in stylised form) an heraldic charge known as a *clarion*.

See also CHURCH MUSIC (ANGLICAN) *and* ORGANS

Further reading:

Hindley, G., *Musical Instruments*, London, 1971
Remnant, M., *Musical Instruments: an Illustrated History*, London, 1989
Scholes, P. (ed. Ward, J.O.), *The Oxford Companion to Music*, Oxford, 1991

MUSIC, CHURCH *see* AMPLIFIERS, ANGLICAN CHANT, ANTHEM, ANTIPHON, ANTIPHONARIUM, ANTHEM, BELLS, CAMPANILE, CANTICLE, CANTOR, CANTORIS, CARILLON, CAROL, CHURCH MUSIC (ANGLICAN), CHOIR, CONDUCTUS, DECANI, DIVINE OFFICE, EVENING PRAYER, GALLERY, GRADUAL, GREGORIAN CHANT (*see* PLAINSONG), HYMNAL, HYMNARY, HYMN BOARD, HYMNS, INTROIT, LAY CLERK, LITURGY, MOTET, ORGANS, PARISH CLERK, PLAINSONG, PRECENTOR, PSALMS, PSALTERS, REQUIEM, RESPONSES, STALLS, SUCCENTOR *and* VERSICLE

MUTULES Flat (often ornamented) blocks of masonry beneath a projection in classical architecture.

MYSTERY PLAYS Popular in the medieval period, mystery plays (*or* miracle plays) were a form of religious DRAMA which is believed to have developed from dramatic elements of the LITURGY, though they may also have been compiled from biblical and other sources. Performed out of doors on temporary platforms or carts, the best-known series was the Passion Plays though the CORPUS CHRISTI processions also provided an opportunity for the elaborate re-enactment of the Gospel stories.

See also GUILDS

MYSTIC One who practised mysticism, a form of deeply spiritual meditation through which divine truths were revealed.

N

NADFAS (NATIONAL ASSOCIATION OF DECORATIVE AND FINE ARTS SOCIETIES)

The Church Recorders group of NADFAS celebrated its twentieth anniversary in 1993. A very important part of the Association's work is to record the contents of parish churches. Often uncatalogued until now, a rich store of treasure has been unearthed by groups of church recorders working locally and detailed records have been made of monuments, stained glass, plate and metalwork, carvings, textiles, ecclesiastical archives, bells and musical instruments. The church authorities are delighted by some of the discoveries the recorders have made and the police have found the records of great use when investigating theft or vandalism. Over 550 records have been completed to date with many more in the pipeline.

For address see APPENDIX II.

NAME AND ARMS CLAUSE

A clause in a will requiring a beneficiary to assume the name and arms of the testator as a condition of inheritance. To comply, the beneficiary must apply to the Crown for a royal licence within a year of the testator's death. Both name and arms may then be used in addition to, or instead of, his own.

NAPERY *see* LARDER

NARTHEX

In early churches, a vestibule which extended transversely across the western end of the building, separated from the nave by a screen or wall. Also known as a *galilee* or *antenave*, in the Middle Ages it was often set aside for the exclusive use of women and penitents.

See also ANGLO-SAXON ARCHITECTURE

NATIONAL MONUMENTS RECORD (NMR)

A section within the ROYAL COMMISSION ON THE HISTORICAL MONUMENTS OF ENGLAND which holds the national archives of architectural and archaeological records. Its photographic collection is of particular importance.

For address see APPENDIX II.

NATIONAL RECORDS *see* ARCHIVES, DOCUMENTARY SOURCES *and* PARLIAMENTARY RECORDS

NATIVITY OF OUR LORD, FEAST OF THE *see* CHRISTMAS

NATIVITY OF ST. JOHN THE BAPTIST

Celebrated since the fourth century on 24 June to commemorate the birth of John the Baptist (Luke 1).

NATIVITY OF THE BLESSED VIRGIN

Since the eleventh century, the feast day of the Blessed Virgin Mary (*see* MARY, THE BLESSED VIRGIN) observed on 8 September.

NATURAL LEAF ORNAMENT

Architectural ornament characteristic of the late thirteenth and fourteenth centuries, particularly in the treatment of CAPITALS. Unlike earlier STIFF LEAF ORNAMENT, the carved foliage of ivy, vine, oak, rose and other plants is characterised by its naturalness and rich, undulating form.

See also MEDIEVAL ARCHITECTURE

NAVE

From the Latin *navis* meaning 'ship', the nave is the main body of a church which, from the late twelfth century, was usually separated from the CHANCEL by a ROOD SCREEN or CHANCEL SCREEN or, in monastic churches and cathedrals, from the CHOIR by a rood screen and PULPITUM (*see also* PRESBYTERY).

In the pre-Reformation church, the MASS was celebrated in the *sanctum sanctorum* to the east of these screens while sermons were preached in the nave and parishioners gathered for worship, assisted in their supplications by the terrifying images of the DOOM and other salutary WALL PAINTINGS. Most medieval congregations stood in the body of the nave, though a stone ledge was sometimes provided so that the elderly and infirm could 'go to the wall' to rest (*see also* BENCHES AND BENCH-ENDS). Some naves were hardly large enough to accommodate more than a few people: at St. Edwold at Stockwood in Dorset, for example, where the tiny nave measures just 6 by 3.6 metres (20 by 12 feet). When of sufficient size, the nave of a parish church also performed a variety of other functions: it was a venue for guild plays and processions (*see* GUILDS), for parochial assemblies and the CHURCH ALES which the Puritans found so distasteful, and might even be used for transacting business which would be concluded in the church porch (*see* CHURCH AND COMMUNITY *and* PORCHES).

Many naves were extended laterally by the addition of an aisle or AISLES and sometimes vertically by the raising of a CLERESTORY, many of which date from the fifteenth century. Several churches (know as *hall churches*) have aisles which are as large as the adjoining nave: the collegiate church of St. Mary at Warwick, for example, much of which was rebuilt (by William Wilson) following a fire in 1694, and the spacious thirteenth- and fourteenth-century church of All Saints at Newland in the Forest of Dean, Gloucestershire, known as 'the Cathedral of the Forest'. Hannington in Northamptonshire has a double nave while at Leominster Priory in Herefordshire there are three 'naves': to the north is the old monastic church with a fine Norman ARCADE, in the centre is the nave of the thirteenth-century parish church and to the south a large fourteenth-century aisle embellished with superb Decorated ornament. At Milton Abbey in Dorset, the projected nave was never built – possibly as a consequence of the PLAGUE which reached Milton in 1349 – and the great fourteenth- and fifteenth-century church (now a daughter church of nearby Milton Abbas) consists only of choir, TRANSEPT and tower. At Sherborne, also in Dorset, a second nave was added at the west end of the Abbey in the late fourteenth century to provide a large chapel-of-ease (All Hallows) for the townspeople. This was demolished at the DISSOLUTION OF THE MONASTERIES when the abbey church was acquired for parochial use, though the springing for the arches is still visible in the masonry of the west wall of the abbey nave. Elsewhere, several former monastic churches were found to be much too large for parochial purposes and their naves were either truncated or demolished.

Milton Abbey, Dorset, where the building of the nave was abandoned, possibly as a consequence of the Black Death.

At Abbey Dore in Herefordshire, for example, where nothing remains of the once magnificent early thirteenth-century nave which fell into disrepair following the abbey's suppression in 1536, though the choir and transept were restored in the early seventeenth century. At Upholland in Lancashire, the chancel of the former Benedictine priory now forms the nave of the parish church.

The BENEDICTINES and AUGUSTINIANS generally admitted the laity to the naves of their churches and these sometimes became parish churches, as at Brecon Priory (now the Cathedral), Binham and Wyndonham priories in Norfolk, Shrewsbury Abbey in Shropshire and Tynemouth Priory in Northumberland. In these larger churches a nave altar (the *Jesus Altar*) was located in front of the rood screen, one bay west of the pulpitum (*see also* RETRO-CHOIR). In some cases parishioners exchanged their rights in the nave for use of the chancel and transept: at Boxgrove Priory in Sussex and the Augustinian priory of St. Bartholomew, Smithfield, for example. This willingness to share their churches with a wider lay community explains the survival of so many Benedictine and Augustinian churches, but parochial rights were rarely granted in the churches of Cistercian, Cluniac or Premonstratensian foundations, hence their almost universal destruction following the Dissolution of the Monasteries. In Cistercian churches the nave was the church of the CONVERSI. It had its own nave altar and was separated from the rest of the building by stone screens, both at the eastern termination and between the pillars of the nave arcades. The churches of the FRIARS were entirely different: their naves were designed for preaching, and to accommodate large congregations, and were therefore provided with wide aisles and broad arcades.

The naves of many of the great medieval abbeys, priories and cathedrals are extraordinarily long: 76 metres (250 feet) at Norwich, for example, and 87 metres at St. Albans (285 feet). They are also very tall, with each BAY consisting of three vertical stages (ARCADE, TRIBUNE or TRIFORIUM and CLERESTORY) so that as much light as possible should be admitted to the interior, while complex VAULTING was required to support (and distribute) the weight of the roof. The nave at Westminster Abbey (begun by Henry III in the thirteenth century but not completed until after 1375) is 31.4 metres high (103 feet) and 11.75 metres wide (38½ feet). It is the tallest vault in Britain and its extraordinary French Gothic proportions inspire that feeling of spiritual elation which is the essence of medieval architecture.

For the development of the nave *see* ANGLO-SAXON ARCHITECTURE, MEDIEVAL ARCHITECTURE, SIXTEENTH- AND SEVENTEENTH-CENTURY ARCHITECTURE, EIGHTEENTH-CENTURY

ARCHITECTURE *and* NINETEENTH-CENTURY ARCHTECTURE.
See also BAPTISTERY, CROSSING *and* NARTHEX

NAVE ALTAR (*also* JESUS ALTAR) An altar set up in the NAVE of a church, to the west of the CHANCEL, at which the laity take communion. The practice has come to be associated with recent liturgical changes but there are numerous precedents, both medieval and post-Reformation (*see* ALTARS).

NECROLOGY A list of the dead to be remembered in the prayers of a religious house. A general necrology was a similar list used in groups of houses within a particular order.
See also MARTYROLOGY

NEEDLE SPIRE *see* TOWERS

NEOCLASSICISM An artistic and architectural style which originated in Rome in the mid-eighteenth century. Neoclassicism combined a reaction against Palladianism and the excesses of the baroque and rococo with a renewed interest in the antique. The Greek revival at the end of the eighteenth century was the final development of neoclassicism (*see* EIGHTEENTH-CENTURY ARCHITECTURE *and* ROCOCO).

NEPOTISM Favouritism shown to relations, especially by the bestowal of patronage in the form of offices and sinecures.

NEWEL POST *see* STAIRCASES

NEW FIRE, THE In the medieval church, a flame was kindled and blessed (usually in the church porch) on the Saturday of Holy Week to symbolise a community's renewal of faith. There can be little doubt that the tradition contained an element of paganism.
See also PORCHES

NEW FOUNDATION *see* CATHEDRALS

NEW PARISHES ACT (1843) *see* PEEL PARISH

NEWSPAPERS *see* DOCUMENTARY SOURCES

NEW YEAR'S DAY The Roman civil year began on 1 January which remained in use until the seventh century. But its pagan associations (and, in particular, its proximity to the feast of Saturnalia) led to the formulation of a Christian year (*annus gratis* or *annus domini*) based on the Dionysian Easter Table of *c.* 525 which calculated from the Incarnation (AD 1). This was rapidly adopted by every western European Christian country (except Spain) and either Christmas, the Annunciation or Easter was used to determine at what point the calendar year should begin. Christmas was adopted for this purpose by the papacy (to 1098), by the BENEDICTINES and by the English royalty until the Plantagenets (1154). The use of 25 March (*see* ANNUNCIATION OF THE BLESSED VIRGIN and LADY DAY), calculated from Christmas, was possibly the result of Cluniac influence and was adopted by the CISTERCIANS. Known as the *secundum consuetudinem* or *secundum et computationem ecclesiae Anglicanae*, it spread to France and the papal chancery (after 1098) and persisted in England from the late twelfth century until the adoption (in England) of the GREGORIAN CALENDAR in 1752. New Year's Day has no liturgical significance although it coincides with the Feast of the Circumcision which is observed on the eighth day after Christmas.
See also CALENDAR

NICENE CREED A creed is a statement of faith, a formal summary of Christian beliefs or principles. There are two Nicene creeds, the longer of which is found in the THIRTY-NINE ARTICLES and is used in the EUCHARIST.
See also APOSTLES' CREED, THE

NICHE A shallow recess in a wall.
See AUMBRY, BANNER STAVE LOCKER, BREAD OVEN, CREDENCE, EASTER SEPULCHRE, FENESTELLA, FIGURE SCULPTURE, PISCINA, SEDILIA, SQUINT *and* STOUP

NICKEL SILVER (EPNS) An alloy of copper, zinc and nickel with the appearance of silver (*see* EPBM, EPGS AND EPNS).

NIECE In older wills, the term 'niece' could mean a male or female descendant.

NIELLO INLAY A decorative technique in which engraved lines or indentations are filled with a black composition.

NIGHT OFFICE *see* MATTINS *and* NOCTURN

NIGHT STAIR In MONASTIC BUILDINGS, a staircase providing direct access from the DORTER to the church (usually via the south transept) for those attending the Night Office. Few night stairs have survived, though there is a splendid example at Hexham Priory in Northumberland. Occasionally, where space was restricted, the night stair was reduced to a spiral staircase as at Ewenny Priory in Glamorgan, where the nave has survived as a parish church.

NIMBUS *see* HALO

NINETEENTH-CENTURY ARCHITECTURE

The nineteenth century witnessed a period of church-building unparalleled since that which followed the Norman Conquest. By 1858 over three thousand new churches had been built in a period of fifty years during which the population of England had doubled (*see* EIGHTEENTH-CENTURY CHURCH). In part this was attributable to the Million Act of 1818 by which Parliament allocated one million pounds for the building of churches in new districts. Promoters of the Bill saw these churches not only as 'bulwarks against the rising tide of Dissent' but also as a 'thank offering to God for defending them from French free-thinking'* and the consequences of the French Revolution. The Lords Commissioner of the Treasury who were responsible for administering the fund required the new churches to be built as economically as possible, '. . . with a view to accommodating the greatest number of persons at the smallest expense within the compass of an ordinary voice, one half of the number to be free seats for the poor.' Many of these *Commissioners Churches* (known also as *Waterloo Churches*) were built for less than £10,000, there being a limit of £20,000 on buildings to accommodate congregations of two thousand. The finest is the Greek Revival church of St. Pancras in London (see below) which cost £70,000, the balance being met by private subscription and a levy on the rates. Designs were approved by the Commissioners who set out such stringent conditions that it is surprising to find that the scheme was supported by so many eminent architects of the time (*see* NINETEENTH-CENTURY CHURCH). The Commissioners' funds were also used for reconstruction: at the church of Lady St. Mary at Wareham in Dorset, for example, where the great (but dark and dilapidated) Saxon nave was replaced in 1842. It is apparent from the pages of the *Dorset County Chronicle* that those concerned with the decision were blissfully unaware of the antiquity and historical importance of the old nave for it was reported to be 'no more than 200 years old'. The replacement is airy, though characterless, and the splendid fourteenth-century chancel (with its wonderful sedilia and double piscina) was retained.

THE REGENCY PERIOD

During the early decades of the nineteenth century, most architects designed in both Classical and Gothic styles, though the latter was still not taken very seriously (see below). The period 1790–1830, known in architecture as the Regency Period (though the regency of the Prince of Wales (later George IV) lasted only from 1811–20) was a time of transition from the Georgian to the Victorian, characterised by some splendid architecture, light-hearted, romantic and experimental. Regency architects worked

empirically, aiming to create a style of their own rather than slavish copies of the original. Eminent architects such as John Nash (1752–1835) and Sir John Soane (1753–1837) drew on a variety of classical and other sources, often with considerable flare and imagination. Nash was an ebullient extrovert, but (regrettably) his work included very few churches, the best-known being All Souls, Langham Place in London (1822–5). The work of Sir John Soane, on the other hand, was more subdued but still original, though his three Commissioners' churches, Holy Trinity at Marylebone, St. John, Bethnal Green and St. Peter at Walworth (all in London) have suffered subsequent alteration and enlargement. The leading architect of the Greek Revival (a severe form of neo-classicism) was Sir Robert Smirke (1780–1867) who designed four Commissioners' churches, the best of which is St. Mary's in Wyndham Place, London (1821–3). Henry Inwood (1794–1843), also a notable exponent of the Greek Revival style, is best remembered for his wonderful St. Pancras church in London (1819–22) which consists of a large galleried hall with an apse at one end and a portico at the other, modelled on James Gibbs's early eighteenth-century masterpiece, the church of St. Martin-in-the-Fields, London (1722–6).

THE GOTHIC REVIVAL

Gothic influences have always been present in post-medieval British architecture. Although subdued by classicism during most of the seventeenth and eighteenth centuries, Gothic buildings continued to be constructed, usually to complement or complete earlier medieval structures such as Christ Church College, Oxford where Christopher Wren added the famous Tom Tower in 1681, and Westminster Abbey, the western towers of which were designed by Nicholas Hawksmoor just before his death in 1736.

During the second half of the eighteenth century romantic medievalism became fashionable as an alternative to Palladian formality, and in 1750 Sir Horace Walpole created a Gothic country villa at Strawberry Hill, Twickenham and thereby fashioned also an epithet 'Strawberry Hill Gothic' which was to become synonymous with charm and elegance and superficial medievalism (*see* GOTHICK). James Wyatt (1746–1813), the principal architect of his day, was also the most successful and adventurous exponent of the romantic Gothic, though his over-enthusiastic attitude to 'restorative improvements' (notably at Durham, Hereford, Lichfield and Salisbury cathedrals) earned for him the epithet 'Wyatt the Destroyer'. Wyatt designed very few churches, his 'Perpendicular Gothic' church at East Grinstead in Sussex (completed in 1813) being an exception. Drawings of Fonthill Abbey in Wiltshire (1795), an immense house of cruciform plan, some 91.4 metres in length (300 feet) with a 84.7 metre tower above the 'crossing' (278 feet) and a great hall

24 metres high (80 feet), provide a dramatic illustration of what Wyatt might have achieved had he been commissioned to build a Gothick cathedral! (Fonthill was demolished after the tower collapsed in 1825.)

The Gothic Revival began in earnest with the rebuilding after fire of the Palace of Westminster in 1834. The architects, Sir Charles Barry and Augustus Pugin, created a neo-Gothic masterpiece, of immense authority and containing ornamentation and craftsmanship of the highest quality. At this time there was a reaction against what the Victorians in particular perceived to be eighteenth-century vulgarity, both liturgical and architectural. The classical style was denounced as 'pagan' and, therefore, decadent and the Gothick ridiculous. Instead, there was a return to the 'true architecture of Christianity' – that of the thirteenth and fourteenth centuries. (Twelfth-century Romanesque was considered to be crude and fifteenth-century Perpendicular excessive, though both will be found in a small number of Victorian churches: the fine Italian Romanesque church by Thomas Wyatt (1807–80) at Wilton in Wiltshire (1846), for example, and J.P. Seddon's church at Hoarwithy in Herefordshire (1880) which has a tall and slender campanile.)

The Gothic Revival was not simply an architectural movement, it was inspired by idealists such as John Ruskin (1819–1900) who believed that only those who lived a good and moral life could create anything truly worthwhile. They revered all things medieval, espousing the art and architecture of that time as the epitome of human endeavour. They abhorred the artificial, especially the sham-gothic work of preceding generations with its cast iron and plaster. Rigid guidelines for Gothic design were set out in *The Ecclesiologist*, the journal of the Ecclesiological Movement which promoted the 'Middle Pointed' period of the late thirteenth and early fourteenth centuries as the only pure architectural style (*see* MEDIEVAL ARCHITECTURE). But, despite this preoccupation with authenticity, most Gothic Revival buildings are immediately recognisable and do not possess the vitality of their prototypes. Gothic architecture took over four centuries to evolve: the setting in place of every stone was innovative and dependent on the cumulative experience of generations of skilled craftsmen. The Gothic Revival took place at a time when there was an unprecedented demand for urban housing and for cheap, mass-produced materials. The skills of Pugin's specially trained craftsmen who worked on the Palace of Westminster were of little relevance in such a market.

THE VICTORIANS

In 1834 Augustus Welby Northmore Pugin (1812–52) was converted to Roman Catholicism which he embraced as passionately as he did the 'Second Pointed Style' of medieval architecture (*c.* 1280–1340). He regarded the Middle Ages as the zenith of human achievement, a time when the building of the great abbey churches and cathedrals reflected man's absolute commitment to the greater glorification of God. He detested the fake medievalism of Strawberry Hill Gothic and complained that the work of architects such as Wyatt lacked authenticity and employed spurious materials. A small number of Anglican churches are by Pugin: St. Lawrence at Tubney in Berkshire, for example. But the influence he exercised on his contemporaries was immense, especially through his writing: notably his *True Principles of Pointed or Christian Architecture* (1841), *The Present State of Ecclesiastical Architecture* (1843) and *Glossary of Ecclesiastical Ornament* (1844). Pugin's fascination with the medieval was not exclusively architectural. He designed numerous splendid artefacts and furnishings in wood, stone, metal and glass many of which remain in our churches, both Roman Catholic and Anglican.

Sir Charles Barry (1795–1860) was the leading architect of his day and the most versatile. His career began with a number of Commissioners' churches including the Gothic church of St. Peter at Brighton (1828), the Italian Renaissance St. Andrew's at Hove (1828) (both in Sussex) and the church of All Saints at Stand in Lancashire (1826). Other Barry churches include Trentham in Staffordshire (1844), a large ashlar building in which he incorporated late-Norman arcades, a screen of 1633 and a Georgian west gallery.

Despite the devastating blow delivered by the 1851 CENSUS OF RELIGIOUS WORSHIP, the *High Victorian Gothic* period from 1855 to 1885 was a time of ubiquitous architectural activity. Eminent ecclesiastical architects of the time included George Gilbert Scott, William Butterfield and George Street but, with some notable exceptions, the architectural precepts of the Ecclesiological Society inevitably gave way to pragmatism, and throughout the land town halls, universities, churches and railway stations, public baths and reading rooms, hotels and country houses were constructed in a pastiche of Romanesque and Gothic styles. (It was at this time that many medieval church towers acquired a fashionable set of 'Gothic' pinnacles and, perhaps, a castellated parapet.)

Sir George Gilbert Scott (1811–78) 'represents the quintessence of High Victorian Gothic architecture'**. He was responsible for a prodigious number of buildings but, unlike several of his contemporaries, his work lacked individuality. His first notable church, St. Giles in Camberwell, London (1844) was one of his best and established his reputation as a leading exponent of the Gothic Revival. Other

Interior of St. Bartholomew-the-Great, West Smithfield, in the City of London, splendidly restored in the late nineteenth century.

churches include St. Matthias at Richmond, Surrey (1858) and St. George at Doncaster in Yorkshire (1854) where the detail is particularly fine – notably a glorious east window and the carvings of the sculptor John Birnie Philip (including a delicate caterpillar, quietly minding its own business on the carved foliage of the stone reading desk).

William Butterfield (1814–1900) was a man of austere principles both in his faith and in his architectural views. His work is characterised by a strong massing of shapes, tall steeples and the use of strong colour in high-quality brick, tile, mosaic, stone, marble and alabaster. His first major commission was All Saints in Margaret Street, London (1859), a lofty and dramatic church of red brick decorated with bands of stone and black brick. Other Butterfield churches include Baldersby St. James in Yorkshire (1856) and All Saints at Babbacombe in Devon (1860).

George Street (1824–81) was also a deeply religious man and an architectural perfectionist. Consequently his churches are characterised by a consistently high standard of workmanship and design though the architecture is often excessively

severe. In 1853, following a period of work in Italy, he published *The Brick and Marble Architecture of Northern Italy*, a work which was to have a profound influence on the architecture of his day. His finest churches are St. James the Less in London (1861) and St. Philip and St. James, Oxford (begun in 1852). Others include St. Mary's at Wheatley in Oxfordshire (begun in 1855), All Saints at Clifton in Bristol (1868), the church of St. John at Torquay in Devon (begun 1861) and St. Mary's at the tiny village of Fawley in Berkshire (1864), familiar to Thomas Hardy as the parish church at 'Marygreen' in his novel *Jude the Obscure* (1895).

By the 1860s the embellishments of the Anglo-Catholic 'High Church' had become fashionable, especially in London and the south-east, and many of the new churches were suitably imposing. This was also the time of the Arts and Crafts Movement which sought to revive, in an industrial age, the ideals of handcrafted objects and simplicity of design. The influence of William Morris (1834–96), Edward Burne-Jones (1833–98), Ford Madox Brown (1821–93) and others was considerable and is evident in the fabric, glass and furnishings of many churches of the period. In the manifesto of his Society for the Protection of Ancient Buildings, William Morris excoriated '. . . those who make the changes wrought in our day under the name of Restoration . . . have no guide but each his own individual whim to point out to them what is admirable and what contemptible.' A close friend of Morris and Burne-Jones was the architect George Bodley (1827–1907) whose churches (mainly of late Gothic derivation) are distinguished by a professional quality and refinement of taste, especially in decorative detail. Two of Bodley's best churches are at Clumber Park in Nottinghamshire (1889) and Holy Trinity, London (1901).

Considered retrospectively, Gothic Revival architecture was essentially imitative and two-dimensional. In only a few churches, such as Pugin's (Roman Catholic) cathedral at Birmingham (1839), and in the craftsmanship of individual features, such as G.F. Bodley's rood screen at the Church of the Holy Angels, Hoar Cross, Staffordshire and Burne-Jones's magnificent sanctuary windows of Birmingham's anglican cathedral, can the Victorians compare with their medieval predecessors. Indeed, many medieval churches were demolished only to be rebuilt in a 'Gothic' style which mocked the prototypes. Even more were heavily 'restored' in a wave of architectural vandalism unmatched even by the excesses of Cromwell's iconoclasts. But nineteenth-century churches can be as interesting (or as dull) as those which preceded them and they should be considered in the context of the period in which they were built. It is through these buildings, and their fittings and decoration, that one is able to appreciate the religious aspirations of the Victorian Age.

See also EIGHTEENTH-CENTURY ARCHITEC-TURE and TWENTIETH CENTURY CHURCHES

For the Victorian Society see APPENDIX II.

Further reading:

Betjeman, J., Guide to English Parish Churches, (revised N. Kerr 1993), London *

Curl, J., Victorian Churches, London, 1995

Orbach, J., Blue Guide to Victorian Architecture, London, 1988

Randall, G., Church Furnishing and Decoration in England and Wales, London, 1980

Randall, G., The English Parish Church, London, 1982 (Spring Books 1988)

Yarwood, D., Encyclopaedia of Architecture, London, 1985 **

NINETEENTH-CENTURY CHURCH The economic and social revolution which marked the second half of the eighteenth century continued unabated into the nineteenth. But while the EIGHTEENTH-CENTURY CHURCH had been incapable of responding to demographic change, in the new century the Church of England was to be transformed by the disparate influences of the OXFORD MOVEMENT and the Evangelical Revival (see EVANGELICALISM).

WATERLOO CHURCHES

At the turn of the century, the growing popularity of nonconformity reflected widespread antagonism towards the established Church, especially among the labouring classes (see DISSENTERS). In 1818 the Government attempted to counter the rising tide of dissent by allocating one million pounds towards the building of 'Waterloo churches' in the new industrial heartlands (see NINETEENTH-CENTURY ARCHITECTURE). The Lords Commissioner of the Treasury who administered the fund required that the new churches should be capable of 'accommodating the greatest number of persons at the smallest expense within the compass of an ordinary voice, one half of the number to be free seats for the poor.' The instructions issued to architects are illuminating: 'The site must be central, dry and sufficiently distant from factories and noisy thoroughfares; a paved area is to be made round the church. If vaulted underneath, the crypt is to be made available for the reception of coals or the parish fire engine. Every care must be taken to render chimneys safe from fire; they might be concealed in pinnacles. The windows ought not to resemble modern sashes; but whether Grecian or Gothic, should be in small panes and not costly. The most favourable position for the minister is near an end wall or in a semicircular recess under a half dome. The pulpit should not intercept a view of the altar, but all seats should be placed so as to face the preacher. We should recommend pillars of cast iron for supporting the gallery of a chapel, but in large churches they might want grandeur. Ornament should be neat and simple, yet variable in character.' What was required, therefore, was a cheap box-like auditorium with the communion table located at one end in a shallow chancel, a high pulpit on one side and a reading desk on the other. Galleries were to be set against the north, west and south walls (with an organ in the west gallery and a font beneath) and two rows of windows inserted in the side walls, the lower to light the aisles and nave and the upper to light the galleries. Most northern industrial towns have at least one example of a Commissioners' Church and several were built in London, often with additional funding raised by public subscription. They provided worship for five million people and were the last auditory buildings to be built by the Establishment for over a century. Of course, as the Bishop of London admitted at the time, church building was then 'a work of prudence no less than charity'. For, despite the clergy's enthusiasm for countering nonconformity, the Government was far more concerned with arresting lawlessness and civil disorder in the industrial slums than it was with philanthropy or commemorating victory at Waterloo. Today, we are able to appreciate the architectural dignity and coherence of the Commissioners' churches but they proved singularly unpopular with the Victorian middle classes who, increasingly, were attracted to the fashionable piles of the Gothic Revival.

THE OXFORD MOVEMENT

The Victorian Age was one of great contrasts: pomp and splendour and appalling squalor; whimsical architectural romanticism and innovative feats of engineering. The romantic movement, which found beauty in rusticity and medievalism, had at first expressed itself in Gothick 'ruins' and fashionable curiosities such as the *cottage ornée* and the Gothick library and music-room. But the social evils of the Industrial Revolution created in many a need to seek out what were perceived to be the more wholesome characteristics of an earlier age. Inspired by idealists such as John Ruskin (1819–1900), who believed that only those who lived a good and moral life could create anything truly worthwhile, they attempted to encourage the making of artefacts by hand and regarded as worthless all things made by machine. In particular, they admired Gothic architecture for its structural honesty, but failed to apply that quality imaginatively to contemporary buildings and instead imitated the sombre detail of the Early English style (*see* NINETEENTH-CENTURY ARCHITECTURE).

This desire to return to the principles of an earlier, golden age was paralleled in the Church by the Oxford Movement whose leaders sought to counter the spread of 'liberal theology' and to re-assert the authority of the Anglican Church which had become excessively susceptible to secular influences. The potency of the Oxford Movement, and of the Evangelical Revival, inspired a fresh sense of professionalism and responsibility among many of the clergy and a re-defining of the Church's social conscience. Numerous church schools, orphanages, parish halls, church missions and reading rooms were built, mostly by public subscription or through the commitment of Victorian philanthropists, and many of these buildings have survived to the present day. New dioceses and parishes were created in the industrial conurbations (*see* DIOCESE) while nearly two thousand churches were consecrated during the first half of the nineteenth century and a further two thousand in the years 1851–70. The scale of the challenge which faced the Church became apparent when statistics relating to church attendance, obtained from the 1851 census, revealed that on Sunday, 30 March only 7,261,032 out of a total population of 17,927,609 had attended any form of religious service and of these only fifty two per cent had been to an anglican church (*see* CENSUS OF RELIGIOUS WORSHIP 1851).

VICTORIAN PHILANTHROPY

Funds for church-building and for the 'restoration' of numerous medieval churches (many of which were so dilapidated that they were no longer used) were raised in part by the extraordinary energy and enthusiasm of the clergy and their parishioners. But it was the beneficiaries of the Victorian Age who were particularly conspicuous in their generosity: industrial magnates, ironmasters and mill-owners, railway barons and the affluent, share-holding gentility. In many places, architecture and furnishings which did not accord with the restorer's notions of 'correctness' were ruthlessly removed, leaving interiors which were often so bereft of character and atmosphere that they are virtually indistinguishable from one another.

Even in the smallest parishes, funds were raised to provide new furnishings, pews, stained glass windows and bells, while ORGANS (or various form of harmonium) and surpliced choirs replaced the old church bands. (When an organ was installed at Purton, Wiltshire in 1851 the entire band picked up their instruments and walked out in protest – *see* GALLERIES.) In many parishes the system of PEW RENTING was abolished and more lively services introduced (not always without controversy) with a greater emphasis on ceremonial and increased congregational participation, especially through hymn-singing (*see* CHURCH MUSIC). Altar crosses and candlesticks appeared in many churches for the first time, as did VESTMENTS which complemented the Church's increasingly elaborate rituals and processions. Theological debate between and within the two movements became a popular activity, especially through the correspondence columns of national newspapers where subjects ranged from Original Sin and Predestination to the theory of evolution and the literal truth (or otherwise) of the Old Testament.

Parochial activity also increased. Sunday and day schools, adult classes, youth organisations, clubs, CHARITIES and FRIENDLY SOCIETIES proliferated, though there was a corresponding reaction against many of the traditional sports and social activities which hitherto had been associated with the parish church and its churchyard (*see* CHURCH AND COMMUNITY). Nationally, the founding of five new theological colleges contributed significantly to improving standards of professionalism among the clergy, while a further measure of the Church's revitalised missionary enthusiasm was the rapid development of organisations such as the Church Building Society (founded in 1818), the Church Pastoral Aid Society (1836) and the National Society for the Education of the Poor in the Principles of the Church of England which, within two years of its foundation (in 1811) was providing education for 40,000 children.

DISSENTION

But the new age of enlightenment was not universally welcomed. The introduction of ritual, vestments, lighted candles, ornaments and ceremonial were perceived by many to be 'papist' and the cause of considerable controversy (*see* PUBLIC WORSHIP REGULATION ACT). Numerous suits were brought before the ecclesiastical courts and, in many places, there was even armed insurrection: at Brighton in Sussex, for example, which by the mid-nineteenth century had become a leading centre of Anglo-Catholic activity. Furthermore, in many remote rural parishes the foundations of village communities remained firmly set in the mid-eighteenth century. A letter of 1830, addressed '. . . to the Members of Parliament for Dorsetshire on the Subject of Poor Relief and Labourers' Wages', encapsulated the attitude of many: 'After all that Legislation has done, or may do, the Poor must be left very much to the care and kindness of their more wealthy and natural Protectors. The Poor must live, to use their own forcible and homely expression, "from hand to mouth". Their lives are lives of casualties and expedients; their Protectors must guard them from the evils of the one, and guide them through the difficulties of the other.' In the absence of such 'natural protectors', the agricultural labourer invariably found himself bound to the soil which no longer offered him a living while, in some areas, the Church remained so entrenched that it was incapable of addressing the political and social injustices and economic hardships which led inexorably to the (often violent) riots of the 1830s. Inevitably, nonconformity was associated with the labouring class and was, therefore, perceived to threaten the *status quo*. Similarly, for most agricultural workers, the Church of England was the bulwark of the Establishment, overtly so when landowners and clergy joined forces to resist the spread of dissent and the building of nonconformist chapels. Many dissenters continued to be married and buried according to the Anglican rites while attending nonconformist meetings on Sundays.

DOCUMENTARY SOURCES

To determine to what extent, if at all, the foregoing was true of a particular parish, the researcher has access to an often bewildering array of documentary and other sources (*see* ARCHIVES *and* DOCUMENTARY SOURCES). First it is necessary to consider the demographic changes which may have affected parochial life. Population growth and decline and the proliferation of new settlements may be deduced from CENSUS returns (from 1801), as may the way in which the ancient parochial system was adapted to meet the demands of the nineteenth century (*see* PARISH). This system of dioceses, archdeaconries, deaneries and parishes, each with its own church and clergy, was characterised by long-established vested interests (patrons, incumbents, tithe- and rate-payers and so on) none of whom welcomed change. Furthermore, it was essentially a rural system, comfortable, inflexible and ill-equipped to accommodate the needs of the industrial age.

BISHOPS' REGISTERS and the returns of Ecclesiastical Visitations (*see* VISITATIONS, ECCLESIASTICAL) contain details of services (including, for example, attendance figures and the standard of musical accompaniment), of alterations to a church building and its furnishings, of the numbers of Catholics and Dissenters in a particular parish and evidence for the founding of Sunday schools and other institutions. The bishops' records may contain copies of the correspondence of bishops, archdeacons and rural deans, records of ordinations and institutions and details of the clergy in individual parishes. Those DIOCESAN RECORDS which relate to faculties (*see* FACULTY) and mortgages are especially useful when tracing the history of a church, churchyard or parsonage house. Earlier faculties usually refer to minor works such as the installation of private pews and galleries or the erection of monuments. But nineteenth-century faculties are more often concerned with major alterations or restorations (the rebuilding of a church, for example, or an extension to a churchyard) and may include plans, sketches and even specifications. Diocesan documents also include records of the licensing and consecration of new places of worship and from these it is sometimes possible to identify the location of a temporary church which was provided for the benefit of an expanding urban community while funds were raised for a more permanent parish church. (Sadly, the few remaining galvanised iron churches do not enjoy the statutory protection they deserve.)

A major source for the nineteenth century is the series of parliamentary reports known as *Blue Books*, copies of which (on disc or microfiche) are now available in many of the larger libraries and record offices. The material contained in these papers includes evidence collected by Parliamentary Commissioners, Royal Commissions and parliamentary accounts, together with statistics relating to local churches and church attendance obtained in conjunction with the 1851 Census (*see* CENSUS OF RELIGIOUS WORSHIP 1851). Although difficult to use (there is no detailed index to local evidence) the *Blue Books* are an invaluable source of information for they contain an enormous amount of detailed material relating to every aspect of life in even the most remote and (apparently) insignificant of parishes. A number of guides to the *Blue Books* have been published (see below) but the most useful starting point is a pamphlet *Local History from Blue Books: A Select List of the Sessional Papers of the House of Commons* by W.R. Powell, published by the Historical Association in 1962 (*for* address *see* APPENDIX II).

The nineteenth century produced an entirely new range of documentary sources, in addition to the statutory parish REGISTERS, VESTRY minutes and CHURCHWARDENS' ACCOUNTS. These include parish magazines, calendars or 'almanacs', local histories, journals and diaries compiled by energetic incumbents, confirmation and Sunday school records, church school log books and punishment books and the minute books and accounts of numerous parochial charities and organisations – though much material was lost during the salvage campaigns of the Second World War. Local newspapers are also an invaluable source of information, for they contained regular reports on church affairs, church restorations and parochial fund-raising (including lists of benefactors), while national journals such as *The Builder* (from 1834) and *The Ecclesiologist* (1841–68) published detailed articles on new churches and restoration schemes.

Further reading:

Bettey, J., *Church and Parish*, London, 1987

Bond, M.F., *The Records of Parliament: A Guide for Genealogists and Local Historians*, London, 1964

——, *Guide to the Records of Parliament*, London, 1971

Riden, P., *Record Sources for Local History*, London, 1986

Storey, R. and Madden, L., *Primary Sources for Victorian Studies*, London, 1977

Tate, W., *The Parish Chest*, Cambridge, 1969

NOCTURN An early name for the office of MATTINS derived from the units (*nocturns*) of which it was composed and which varied in number according to the significance of the day in the ecclesiastical calendar.

NOGGING *see* BRICK NOGGING

NOMBRIL POINT *see* POINTS OF THE SHIELD

NONCONFORMITY *see* DISSENTERS *and* NINETEENTH-CENTURY CHURCH

NONE A short office, the last of the Little Hours of the BREVIARY. The ninth hour of prayer (about 3.00 p.m.) consisting of a hymn followed by psalmody, a short reading, response and closing prayer.

See also TERCE *and* SEXT

NORMAN ARCH *see* ARCH *and* MEDIEVAL ARCHITECTURE

NORMAN ARCHITECTURE *see* ARCHITECTURAL PERIODS *and* MEDIEVAL ARCHITECTURE

'NORTH END', THE Members of the Evangelical wing of the Church of England (*see* EVANGELICALISM) sometimes choose to occupy a position to the north of the communion table when celebrating the EUCHARIST thereby demonstrating that the celebrant's function is neither priestly nor mediatorial.

NOTARY A professional scribe. Each notary authenticated the documents for which he was responsible by drawing a distinctive notarial symbol at the foot.

NOVICE When a POSTULANT was admitted to a religious house he or she was required to serve a probationary period as a novice. In some houses the novices were provided with their own communal accommodation where they might 'meditate, eat and sleep'. In most houses there would be no more than six novices at any time. They wore the habit of the order and followed its Rule (with some concessions to their age) and were able to leave at any time without penalty. All members of the community were expected to advise or reprove the novices, though it was the *Novice Master* who was responsible for their material, intellectual, social and spiritual needs. Novices were required to leave CHAPTER immediately after the sermon, to make frequent confession and to spend even more time in the abbey church than the monks. They were educated in the monastic school (usually in the west alley of the cloister) until they had acquired a basic understanding of the services and scriptures and of the minutiae of monastic behaviour (including, for example, how to sit correctly in the rere-dorter). This was followed by more advanced teaching from the Novice Master or tutor, while those who showed particular promise 'and had a pregnant wit withal' might be sent to study advanced divinity at a university. From the mid-twelfth century, the novitiate generally lasted for one year at the end of which, 'if the brethren approve of his behaviour and he of their way of life', the novice would appear before Chapter and, if elected, would read his formal profession 'before the high altar in the church in the presence of all the community'. There followed a solemn blessing of the cowl and investment by the superior: 'May the lord clothe thee with the new man who is created according to God in righteousness and the sanctity of truth.'

See also OBLATE

NOVICE MASTER *see* NOVICE

NOWY A straight line having a convex curvature at the centre.

NULLITY In Canon Law, the absence of legal validity from a contract, owing to an impediment or the omission of a legal requirement. For example, a marriage might be annulled as a consequence of the parties being related within the PROHIBITED DEGREES.

See also AFFINITY, CONSANGUINITY *and* DIVORCE

NUMERALS Roman numerals were used throughout the medieval period. In numbers such as *ii*, *iii* and *vii* the final stroke was often shown as a *j* to confirm that the sequence was completed. Arabic numerals occur in England from the thirteenth century but were not commonly used before the seventeenth.

NUNS and NUNNERIES A nun is a member of a religious order of women. In the medieval period, a nun could live within a community or (in exceptional cases) as an anchoress (*see* ANCHORITES). Communities of nuns which, in most respects, were similar to MONASTERIES, are known as nunneries (*convents* were religious communities of either sex). In the Middle Ages, about twenty per cent of religious were women. Nunneries increased in number from twelve in 1066 to 152 in the early fourteenth century. At the Dissolution of the Monasteries there were some 136 nunneries and 2,000 nuns (also known as *monachae*, *nonnae* or *sanctimoniales*). With the exception of the GILBERTINES and lay sisters, nuns appear to have been recruited almost exclusively from the upper classes of medieval society. Several nunneries established 'finishing schools' for young ladies of gentle birth while others acquired reputations as refuges for widows of noble rank and the relicts of traitors whose titles, lands and possessions had been forfeited through attainder. The spiritual and liturgical life in nunneries was similar to that of men in the same order. But, because nuns could not provide priests from their number, chaplains had to be appointed, either from the ordained brethren of a DOUBLE MONASTERY or by means of a PREBEND or CHANTRY. A *custos* or lay steward was usually engaged to administer a convent's lands and properties while men were employed as servants or admitted as lay brothers to undertake heavy manual work.

NUNC DIMITTIS The *Song of Simeon* (Luke 2 29:32): 'Lord, now lettest thou thy servant depart in peace.' Part of the office of COMPLINE from which it passed into the service of Evensong in the *Book of Common Prayer* where it follows the second (New Testament) lesson (*see* EVENING PRAYER). In Compline, the Nunc Dimittis has its traditional plainsong but in the Anglican service it is usually spoken responsively or sung to an Anglican chant. Together with the MAGNIFICAT, the Nunc Dimittis has been set to music by numerous composers and is sung in this form in most cathedrals and collegiate chapels.

OAK APPLE DAY The annual commemoration on 29 May of King Charles's escape following the battle of Worcester in 1651 and his restoration in 1660.

OBEDIENTIARIES The officers of a religious house who exercised departmental responsibilities ('obediences'). Most obedientiaries managed their own revenues and maintained accounts which were presented at quarterly meetings of CHAPTER. Their terms of office ended with the appointment of a new superior to whom they surrendered their keys. Some offices were particularly demanding and in such cases the Rule was often relaxed: obedientiaries might be excused certain services and permitted to leave the monastery precinct, for example. At the Austin Priory of Barnwell, Cambridgeshire, there were a prior, sub-prior, third prior, precentor, succentor, sacrist, sub-sacrist, cellarer, sub-cellarer, granger, receiver, fraterer, kitchener, chamberlain, hosteller, infirmarer and almoner in addition to a number of minor or rotational offices. It is likely that, in smaller houses, the majority of the brethren would hold office of some sort and that a number of offices may have been held by a single person. *See also* MONASTICISM

OBELISK A tapering usually four-sided stone pillar, named *obeliskos* ('little spit') by the Greeks after the copper-capped pyramidions of Egyptian pillars. These belonged to the Sun God and were placed before Egyptian temples where they reflected the rays of the sun. Many were carried off as trophies and inspired a variety of similar forms throughout the ancient world, eventually arriving in Britain in the Classical architecture and church MONUMENTS of the eighteenth century.

OBIT The office for a dead person (*see* CHANTRY). An anniversary or other commemoration of a death. An *obituary* was originally a monastic register of deaths but has come to mean a biographical account of a deceased person or a published record of his death.

OBITUARY *see* OBIT

OBLATE From the mid-sixth century, the Church permitted parents to dedicate their infants to a religious life by placing them in a monastic community where they were cared for until the age of fifteen. These *pueri* or *infantes* were taught reading and singing, were excused the night office and had their own CHAPTER. The child was presented as an oblation (an offering) at the offertory in the Mass, a petition (promising stability, conversion and obedience) being bound in its right hand by an altar cloth. Once the dedication was made, there could be no release – even when the young person reached maturity. The practice continued until the end of the twelfth century. Later, the term came to be applied to laity who lived in a monastery but who did not take full religious vows.

OBLATIONS (i) The bread and wine offered for consecration in the Eucharist. (ii) An offering presented at the Mass for the benefit of the clergy, the poor, the infirm etc.

OBTUSE ARCH *see* ARCH

OCCASIONAL CONFORMITY ACT (1711) The Act required that military or civil officers, who were obliged to receive communion in the Church of England in order to qualify for Government appointments, should be fined and removed from office if subsequently they attended a nonconformist conventicle. The Act was repealed in 1719.

OCCASIONAL OFFICES Those offices in the *Book of Common Prayer* which are used only as occasion requires e.g. Baptism and Visitation of the Sick.

OCTEOCHOS *see* YEAR, LITURGICAL

OCULUS (*also* OEIL-DE-BOEUF) From the Latin meaning 'an eye', a round or oval window usually with radiating glazing bars. Not to be confused with a ROSE WINDOW or WHEEL WINDOW.

OECUMENICAL An oecumenical council is a world-wide assembly of bishops and other ecclesiastical representatives whose decisions are binding on all Christians. According to CANON LAW, an oecumenical council of the Roman Catholic Church may be convened only by a pope and its decrees promulgated by the Holy See. They are thereby infallible.
See also SYNOD

OEIL-DE-BOEUF *see* OCULUS

OFFERTORY (i) The worshippers' offering of bread and wine to be consecrated at the EUCHARIST. This was often commuted to an offering of money (*see* PRAYER DESK). (ii) The offering of gifts (usually money) during a service.

OFFICE, DIVINE *see* DIVINE OFFICE

OGEE A double continuous curve (like an S). An *ogee arch* has two ogee curves meeting at the apex. *See also* ARCH

OGIVE (i) A diagonal ogee-shaped rib in a vault (*see* VAULTING). (ii) An OGEE arch above a door or window opening. (iii) An ogival compartment is a space delineated by a border consisting of two ogees.

OLD ENGLISH Old English (or Anglo-Saxon) is the language which developed from the composite dialects of Germanic-speaking tribes of Angles, Saxons and Jutes who settled in Britain from the mid-fifth century. It was an inflected language, though these endings gradually decayed until most of them had been lost by the fifteenth century. It was also essentially a spoken language, though by the time of Alfred the Great (849–99) a standard literary version was emerging. In addition to native Celtic elements and words surviving from the Roman occupation, vocabulary expanded through the spread of Christian culture and the influence of Scandinavian invaders in the ninth and tenth centuries. By the late tenth century the Wessex dialect had become dominant.

Following the Norman Conquest of 1066 Anglo-Norman was quickly established as the language of the aristocracy and LATIN that of the administration. It has been estimated that some 33,000 Old French words were absorbed into the English language in the centuries following the Conquest. From the fourteenth century English was again the standard and, despite the influence of French, the Germanic nature of the language has been maintained, even though the original native English element is probably now a minor one. The last will to be drawn up in French is dated 1431 and the last parliamentary petitions drafted in French were written in 1447. By that time (with the exception of the extraordinary language known as 'law French') Chaucer's English had become the vernacular of government and by the sixteenth century most vowels were pronounced as they are today.

The traditional historical phases of linguistic development are *Old English* (up to *c.* 1150), *Middle English* (*c.* 1150–*c.* 1500) and *Modern English* (from *c.* 1500) which derives from the east Midland dialect and that of London. But in practice the language evolved gradually and with considerable regional variations.
Further reading:
Robinson, M. and F., *A Guide to Old English*, Oxford, (rev.) 1989

OLD FOUNDATION *see* CATHEDRALS

OLD LADY DAY *see* LADY DAY

OLD SHEFFIELD PLATE *see* SHEFFIELD PLATE

'OLD-STYLE' Usually a reference to the CALENDAR prior to its reform in 1752, by which New Year was defined as 1 January and the English calendar brought into line with those of European countries by the omission of the days from 2 to 14 September 1752.

OLD TESTAMENT FIGURES AND CONCEPTS *see* CHRISTIAN SYMBOLS

OMBRELLINO (i) The papal 'umbrella' and a symbol of papal authority. A stylised representation of the ombrellino may occasionally be found in the heraldry of senior Roman Catholic churchmen such as cardinals. (ii) A small, umbrella-like canopy beneath which the Blessed Sacrament was moved from one place to another.

OMEGA *see* ALPHA AND OMEGA

OPEN STRING *see* STAIRCASES

OPUS DEI *see* DIVINE OFFICE

OR *see* COLOURS (HERALDIC)

ORATORY Oratories are places of worship other than parish churches though in the Church of England the term is most often applied to the CHAPELS of private houses. Canon Law defines three types of oratory (public, semi-public and private) and specifies the function of each. In the medieval period (and in the twelfth and thirteenth centuries in particular), oratories were often built to serve remote and inaccessible areas of large parishes. These oratories had to be licensed and consecrated by a diocesan bishop and their functions defined in order to safeguard the rights and dues payable to the parish church. Consequently bishops' registers and monastic cartularies often include details of medieval oratories and of the special conditions applied to each. Anglican oratories are regulated by the PRIVATE CHAPELS ACT of 1871.

ORDERS (ARCHITECTURAL) (i) In Gothic architecture, the series of recessed stages in an arch, often moulded or carved (*see* MEDIEVAL ARCHITECTURE). (ii) *For* Classical and Renaissance architecture *see* CLASSICAL ORDERS.

ORDERS (ECCLESIASTICAL) *see* CANON REGULAR, CLERGY (CHURCH OF ENGLAND), FRIARS, HOLY ORDERS, MAJOR ORDERS, MEDIEVAL CHURCH, MENDICANT, MILITARY ORDERS, MINOR ORDERS, MONASTICISM, MONASTIC ORDERS, ORDINATION, RELIGIOUS ORDERS IN THE CHURCH OF ENGLAND *and* RULE

ORDERS OF KNIGHTHOOD *see* GARTER, THE MOST NOBLE ORDER OF THE *and* KNIGHTHOOD, ORDERS OF

ORDINAL (i) A medieval manual intended to acquaint a priest with the offices to be recited in accordance with the variations of the ecclesiastical year. (ii) In the Church of England, 'The Form and Manner of Making, Ordaining and Consecrating of Bishops, Priests and Deacons' (*see* ORDINATION).

ORDINAND A candidate for ORDINATION.

ORDINARY (i) An ecclesiastical superior, e.g. a bishop. (ii) In HERALDRY, an ordinary is one of a number of bold rectilinear charges also known as the Honourable Ordinaries. (iii) An ordinary of arms is a reference book which lists the heraldic descriptions (*blazons*) of shields of arms alphabetically by the charges they contain. Proficiency in the use of BLAZON is essential if an ordinary is to be used to identify arms. The best known ordinary is J.W. Papworth's *Ordinary of British Armorials*, first published in 1874 and reprinted in 1977 (pub. Five Barrows).

ORDINATION Admission to the Christian ministry through the ceremonial laying-on of hands by a bishop. References to ordination occur in the New Testament (e.g. Acts 6: 1–6 and 13: 1–3) and to prayer and the laying-on of hands. In the early Church, a distinction was made between the 'missionary' ministry of prophets and apostles and the 'settled' ministry of bishops, presbyters and deacons. By the mid-thirteenth century, the ministry was arranged in orders which, by the end of the medieval period, were generally accepted to be seven in number, a distinction being made between the three MAJOR ORDERS of bishop, priest and deacon and the four MINOR ORDERS of acolyte, exorcist, lector and doorkeeper. (Bishops and priests were sometimes considered to be a single major order to which were added deacons and sub-deacons.) Traditionally, qualifications for admission to the ministry include a sound moral character and vocational conviction. Furthermore, a candidate (*ordinand*) should be a baptised and confirmed member of the Church, of 'due age' and seeking a 'title' to the cure of souls.

Ordination has always taken place in the context of the EUCHARIST and may be performed only by a duly consecrated bishop. The medieval form of ordination (which usually took place on one of the EMBER DAYS) was extremely elaborate, while that of the Anglican Church was first set out in 'The Form and Manner of Making, Ordaining and

Consecrating of Bishops, Priests and Deacons' (the *Ordinal*) of 1550 which was based on the (medieval) rites of the *Sarum Pontifical*. This was followed by further ordinals in 1552, 1559 and 1662, none of which makes provision for the minor orders. In the consecration of bishops, the medieval practices of anointing, of the putting on of gloves and of the receiving of a ring and MITRE were omitted, while in the Ordering of Priests the *Tradition of the Instruments* (the solemn delivery of the paten and chalice) was replaced in 1552 by the presentation of a Bible (deacons receive a book of the Gospels). In all the ordinals, the formula which accompanies the laying-on of hands includes the words 'Receive the Holy Ghost' and 'Whose sins thou dost forgive, they are forgiven; whose sins though dost retain, they are retained.'

ORDNANCE SURVEY MAPS *see* MAPS

ORGAN LOFT *see* CONSOLE

ORGANS The old Scottish name for an organ, 'kist o' whistles' (chest of whistles), describes very accurately the fundamental construction of all organs before the introduction of the pipeless electric version in the 1930s. Pipes of varying lengths are placed upon a box (*wind chest*). When in rows (*ranks*), each row of pipes possesses a special tone-character etc.. The box is furnished with an even supply of wind from a *bellows* by means of *feeders* or, in modern organs, by an electrically driven rotary fan. So that all the ranks do not sound together, wooden *sliders* are made to pass beneath the mouths of the pipes, each slider controlling a single rank. Holes in the sliders correspond with the mouths of the pipes so that when the slider is pushed in the rank is 'stopped'. Hence, the knobs which control this operation are known as *draw-stops*, or merely *stops*. (The set of pipes controlled by a draw-stop is also known as a *register*.) In modern organs the sliders are usually replaced by valves and the draw-stops by balanced slips of ivory.

In order that the pipes of a rank should not sound together, the mouth of each pipe is provided with a hinged 'lid' (*pallet*) controlled by a series of articulated rods (*trackers* and *stickers*) collectively known as the *action*. The action in a modern organ is usually controlled pneumatically (common from 1880–1930), electronically or by a combination of the two. The action is connected to a hand keyboard (*manual*) or (for certain ranks) a foot keyboard (*pedal board*). The organist therefore selects the required tone-colours by pulling out the appropriate stops, thereby placing certain ranks on 'standby'. He then depresses those keys which, either singly or in combination as chords, will open the mouths of those pipes through which he wishes the air to pass, thereby allowing them to 'speak'.

Collectively, the arrangement of keyboards and stops is known as a CONSOLE and, in larger organs, there may be several manuals, each of which controls what is effectively a separate organ. These organs are usually linked by means of *couplers* so that two or more manuals (and the pedal organ) can be operated simultaneously from a single keyboard. The most important manual is the Great Organ which has the solid-sounding, louder stops. The Swell Organ is enclosed in a *swell-box*, one side of which consists of movable shutters which can be opened and closed by means of a special pedal. (The swell-box principle is now applied to most manuals, usually with the exception of the Great Organ.) The Choir Manual contains a number of softer, sweet-toned stops which are ideally suited to accompaniment, while the Solo Organ contains certain stops of an orchestral quality which are most effectively used by themselves against an accompaniment on another manual. In the largest organs there may be an Echo Organ devoted to delicate stops with a 'distant' sound. The organs of most parish churches have just one or two manuals (the Great and Swell) and a pedal organ.

While the chief stops of a manual are 8 feet in length, the normal pitch of a pedal organ is an octave below that of the manuals and its pipes are therefore significantly longer, ranging from 16 feet to (very rarely) 64 feet. Some church organs are immense: that at Wakefield Cathedral, for example, has six manuals and a pedal organ with several 64 foot stops. Pipes are made of metal (usually zinc or an alloy of tin and lead) or wood which is commonly used for the larger pipes. While most of the pipes are located within the body of the organ (*organ case*), the visible front pipes are usually arranged in groups of short pipes (*flats*) or in projecting clusters (*towers*) of longer pipes. These are often elaborately decorated with diaper patterns and arranged according to their length to form an attractive composition. Where the tin content is high, the pipes may have a mottled appearance known as *spotted metal*.

HISTORICAL DEVELOPMENT
Of course, the instruments used in churches today are far removed from their medieval predecessors, though the fundamentals remain unchanged. An organ is recorded at Malmesbury, Wiltshire in the eighth century and, by the tenth century, 'portative organs' accompanied the singing of plainsong in most monastic churches and were carried in processions. These were portable instruments consisting of a single rank of pipes and a small keyboard and their use continued throughout the Middle Ages. *Positive organs* were those which could not be moved, the greatest of which (allowing for poetic hyperbole) was at Westminster in the tenth century. This had two manuals (played by two performers) each of twenty notes, each note having

ten metal pipes, making 400 pipes in all. It is said to have required seventy 'blowers' to operate the 26 bellows and the 'keys' were so heavy that they had to be depressed with the fist. A fourteenth-century document at Worcester records payments to a musician 'to thump the organs, teach the quire boys and instruct any of the monks who wishes to learn the art of organ-thumping.' Such organs merely thundered out the plainsong melodies and so led the singing.

By the end of the fifteenth century most parish churches possessed an organ and many abbey churches had several, each with a different function and, therefore, with different characteristics. At Durham, for example, there were three 'paires' of organs in the quire, one near the great rood (for the Jesus Mass) and another for public services in the Galilee.

In the sixteenth century, the new Church of England services, although vernacular, were little different from the Roman Catholic liturgy which preceded them (see COMMON PRAYER, BOOK OF). Before this time there was a clear distinction between the musical customs of the major monastic and cathedral churches, which had large choirs and organs, and those of urban and rural parishes which rarely had choirs but (surprisingly) often possessed a primitive organ (see CHURCH MUSIC (ANGLICAN)). Following the DISSOLUTION OF THE MONASTERIES several abbey or priory churches were retained as CATHEDRALS where the elaborate type of service was perpetuated. But, even in the major churches, there was no repertory of organ music and no independent 'organ parts' in anthems or service music. The instrument simply augmented the choir voices and accompanied PLAINSONG unisonally. In parish churches, where the music was much simpler, the organ can have had little function other than to assist priest and people in the performance of the plainsong.

At the Reformation a substantial number of parishes tended towards thorough reform on Calvinistic lines. In 1536 the Lower House of Convocation declared that the playing of organs was one of the 'eighty-four Faults and Abuses of Religion' and many organs were removed from parish churches or allowed to decay. The decline was temporarily reversed by the appointment of Archbishop William Laud (1573–1645), a high-churchman who opposed the prevailing Calvinist theology and sought to restore something of pre-Reformation liturgical practice. But his reforms were widely resented and he was impeached by the Long Parliament, imprisoned in 1644 and executed in the following year. The Puritans considered that instrumental music distracted the mind and soul from divine worship and in 1644 an act of Parliament required the removal of organs from churches. In many areas implementation of the act

was rigorous: organs were smashed and the pipes carried off to be used for more mundane purposes.

The restoration of Charles II in 1660 resulted in a revival of the craft of organ-building and the arrival in England of several eminent organ-builders from the continent of Europe, notably Bernhard Schmidt ('Father Smith', 1630–1707) together with his two nephews from Germany, and Renatus Harris (of English parentage, 1652–1724) from France. This revival was stimulated by the rebuilding (by Christopher Wren and others) of London's churches following the Great Fire of 1666. At that time, the churches of the City of London competed with each other in the excellence of their organs, both in the tone of the instruments and in the beauty of their cases. Despite the bombing of the last war, many of these have survived, notably at St. Clement's, Eastcheap and St. Magnus, London Bridge, St. Stephen's, Walbrook and St. Sepulchre's, Holborn.

Many congregations, especially in rural areas, had reacted to the 1644 Act by erecting west galleries in their churches to accommodate 'choirs' of instrumentalists to lead the singing (see GALLERIES and MUSICAL INSTRUMENTS). The re-introduction of organs following the Restoration had little effect in many of these parishes where the popularity of the 'choirs' was translated into a musical tradition which lasted for more than two centuries. Despite often stubborn resistance, many 'choirs' were eventually replaced by harmoniums and organs in the second half of the nineteenth century when the old 'psalm books' were burned and galleries demolished by zealous clergymen who sought to impose their own brand of liturgical respectability on their rural congregations (see NINETEENTH-CENTURY CHURCH). Most organs in parish churches date from this time and (although adapted for electricity) some still have the handle by which air was pumped through the bellows, usually by a 'poor boy of the parish'. They were often played by an 'outsider' (such as the vicar's wife or the schoolteacher) and, with the introduction of Hymns Ancient and Modern in 1861 (see HYMNS), served to divide congregations and, indeed, communities. In his novel Under the Greenwood Tree, Thomas Hardy describes vividly the effect on the Mellstock string choir of the arrival of an organ, acquired by the progressive Parson Maybold to impress the comely Miss Fancy Day. The traditional music of the west gallery became that of the non-conformist chapel and of the village band which continued to celebrate Christmas, Easter and Harvest by performing musical perambulations around the parish.

The most important nineteenth-century organ-builders were Hill, Willis, Gray and Davison and Walker (there is usually a name-plate on the console) and there are several examples of organ cases which were designed by eminent Victorian architects such as Bodley, Pearson, Pugin and Scott (*see* NINETEENTH-CENTURY ARCHITECTURE). Many organs were squeezed into side chapels or aisles and are often singularly obtrusive and ugly, while others were erected in the west galleries whose 'choirs' they replaced. With the exception of the organs in some London churches (see above), and a number of cathedrals and collegiate chapels, very few early organs have survived though many rebuilt organs incorporate parts from earlier instruments. There are, however, many notable organ cases: the church at Old Radnor in Powys has an early sixteenth-century panelled case and there are fine seventeenth-century examples at Stanford-on-Avon in Northamptonshire, Framlingham in Suffolk (originally at Pembroke College, Cambridge) and Winchcombe in Gloucestershire. At Wotton-under-Edge in the same county the noble eighteenth-century organ was acquired from the church of St. Martin-in-the-Fields, London.

See also CARILLON

Further reading:

Baker, D., *The Organ*, Aylesbury, 1991

Clutton, C. and Niland, A., *The British Organ*, London, 1963

Oriel window above the porch of the Abbot's Hall at Cerne Abbas, Dorset.

ORIEL A curved or polysided window projecting from an upper floor. Unlike a bay window an oriel window does not reach the ground but is either cantilevered or supported by means of a corbel or bracket.

ORIENTATION Tradition has it that medieval churches were invariably constructed with the CHANCEL to the east for symbolic reasons: that Jerusalem is in the east, that the rising sun represents Christ, the Sun of Righteousness, and that the second coming would be from that quarter. Inevitably, this tradition was compounded by Victorian ecclesiologists, many of whom were obsessed with symbolism. It was they who devised the notion of the 'weeping chancel', one which inclines slightly to the north of the east-west axis and supposedly represents the head of Christ on the Cross. But such deviations are entirely due to medieval masons not caring too much about geometrical niceties when altering or extending earlier buildings. (There are also chancels which 'weep' to the south, though these are rare.) More recently it has been suggested that, because so many churches were built on pagan sites, the eastern orientation reflects the pagan practice of praying towards the sunrise.

The reason for the eastern orientation of churches remains a mystery. The practice was consistent and is likely to have been symbolic. But it was also practical: in these northern climes, natural early morning light was needed for the Mass which was celebrated at dawn in the chancel or adjacent chapels (*see* MEDIEVAL ARCHITECTURE). In some cases, the exigencies of a site made an eastern orientation impossible: at Rievaulx in Yorkshire, for example, where the abbey church is aligned more nearly north and south than east and west.

ORMOLU Gilded BRONZE or copper alloy.

ORNAMENT *see* DECORATIVE MOTIFS *and* MEDIEVAL ARCHITECTURE

ORPHREY *see* VESTMENTS

OSSUARIES Charnel houses where the bodies or bones of the dead were kept. Ossuaries are most often associated with churches where overcrowded graveyards could no longer provide for the needs of a (usually urban) community (*see* BURIALS *and* CHURCHYARDS). In some instances endowed charnel-chapels were also provided in which prayers were offered for the souls of the dismembered dead. The medieval ossuary and chapel in the churchyard of Old St. Pauls, London were revered by the populace as exemplifications of immortality. Crypts were often used as ossuaries: at Mitcheldean church in Gloucestershire the rood loft stair continues downwards into a vaulted ossuary, complete with a

Skulls in the ossuary of St. Leonard's at Hythe in Kent.

Ossuary at Mere, Wiltshire.

chute for the bones, while at Thaxted in Essex there are charnel steps (*c.* 1520) in the south-east corner of chancel. Most of these ossuaries were hygienically cleared in the nineteenth century and their doorways blocked as part of church restorations. A number of churchyard ossuaries have survived, and these were usually erected against the churchyard wall, as at Mere in Wiltshire.

The antiquary John Aubrey, writing in the seventeenth century, described the ossuary beneath the cathedral at Hereford: '. . . the largest Charnel-house for bones that I ever saw in England. In 1650 there lived amongst these bones a poor woman that, to help out her fire, did use to mix deadmen's bones: this was thrift and poverty: but cunning alewives putt the ashes of these bones in their Ale to make it intoxicating.'

OSTENSORY A receptacle in which an object of religious devotion was displayed (*see also* MONSTRANCE).

OUTLAWS Those who were literally 'outside the law' were usually men or women who had either absconded or escaped from custody before being brought to court in order to answer criminal charges. If thereafter they failed to appear before a court, having been summoned to do so on four occasions, they were declared outlaws, their goods forfeited and, denied the protection of the realm, they could be killed on sight. With nothing to lose, most fugitives joined with others to form outlaw bands living by petty crime in remote areas where they were effectively beyond the law. Of course, the archetypal outlaw was Robin Hood, but in answer to the question 'Who was he?' the answer must be 'There were more than one'. This still allows for an original, but his identity is lost in the 'obscurity created by his own fame. Real people move in the shadows, their crimes revealed before the courts, but by borrowing [Robin Hood's] reputation they dissolved his identity.' (Holt) From 1547 many vagrants turned to outlawry as an alternative to branding and servitude (*see* POOR LAW). Outlawry was abolished as recently as 1879.

See also SANCTUARY, RIGHT OF

Further reading:

Holt, J., *Robin Hood*, London, 1989

OVENS see BREAD OVENS

OVERSEERS OF THE POOR (*SUPERVISORES PAUPERUM*) Unpaid parochial officials, appointed annually by a VESTRY, responsible for the administration of the POOR LAW.
See also ARCHIVES

OVOLO see DECORATIVE MOTIFS

OXFORD MOVEMENT A nineteenth-century movement in the Church of England which aimed at restoring HIGH CHURCH principles at a time of increasing theological 'liberalism'.

The 1830s must have been a distressing time for many churchmen. Few could have anticipated how helpless the Church would be when faced by a state determined to reform it and to redistribute its property. They could not tolerate the notion that authority for the reforms lay, not in the Church of England, but in Parliament, insisting that the Church's authority derived from the fact that its bishops were of the apostolic succession. To the zealous Protestant, this savoured of popery.

The movement began in July 1833 when, in the university church at Oxford, John Keble (1792–1866) preached a sermon criticising a bill for the suppression of ten Irish bishoprics. Between 1833 and 1841 Keble, Edward Pusey (1800–82), John Newman (1801–90) and Richard Hurrell Froude (1803–36) issued a series of pamphlets (*Tracts for the Times*) stating their position. They believed that the Church of England was threatened by secular power and that the Reform Act of 1832 would strengthen the position of 'liberals and dissenters'. They sought to defend the Anglican Church as a divine institution and to reassert its authority. They defended the doctrine of the Apostolic Succession and of the *Book of Common Prayer* as a rule of faith. The movement (the members of which were known as *Tractarians*) emphasised ministry and ceremonial in the Church, thereby demonstrating the continuity of the Catholic faith, and contributed significantly to social work and to scholarship. Although it gained influential support, the movement was attacked by the bishops and by liberals within the university and there were a number of conversions to the Roman Catholic Church, including that of John Newman in 1841 (Newman became a cardinal in 1879). With the withdrawal of Newman, leadership of the movement devolved on Pusey (his followers were known as *Puseyites*), the principal champion of the High Church Movement, who advocated union with the Roman Catholic Church and was devoted to the founding of religious orders within the Anglican Church (*see* RELIGIOUS ORDERS IN THE ANGLICAN CHURCH). Despite defections and continuing opposition from the press and

Government, the majority of Tractarians remained within the Church of England where they exercised considerable influence.
See also ANGLICANISM, ANGLO-CATHOLICISM *and* CHURCH MUSIC (ANGLICAN)

P

PACE-EGGING see EASTER EGGS

PADRE From the Latin *pater* meaning 'father', the term is popularly used to describe a clergyman and, in particular, a chaplain in the armed forces.

PAGANISM see ANGLO-SAXON CHURCH, CHURCH SITES, DRUIDISM *and* PAGAN SYMBOLS

PAGAN SYMBOLS In AD 601, just four years after the arrival of St. Augustine in Canterbury, Pope Gregory the Great wrote to Abbot Mellitus, a missionary-priest, advising him that pagan shrines should not be destroyed but purified with holy water so that in time they would 'become temples of the true God'. The early missionaries took great care not to alienate the native population by attempting to impose a raw Christian ideology on an already diverse and complex religious culture. Elements of pagan worship were adapted or incorporated into the practices of the early Church: Christian altars and relics replaced pagan idols and native festivals were assimilated into the great feast-days of the Church, notably Christmas and Easter (*see* ANGLO-SAXON CHURCH). Many early churches were built within or adjoining pagan religious sites (*see* CHURCH SITES) and the wells and springs of native water gods were re-dedicated to missionary saints (*see* HOLY WELLS). This policy of gradual religious substitution was effective but it created an enduring cultural ambivalence. At Codford St. Peter in Wiltshire, for example, a fragment of a ninth-century cross shaft is carved with the vigorous image of the pagan 'mallet god' *Sucellos*, bringer of happiness. Pagan gods are commemorated in the days of the week and in innumerable field and place-names and a formidable sub-culture of pagan belief persisted throughout the Middle Ages.

There is a fallacious tradition that pagan symbols, and grotesques and monsters from the medieval bestiaries, were carved in the exterior fabric of churches in order that a sinful peasantry should be alerted to the need to seek redemption. But this was also the function of the DOOM and other WALL PAINTINGS which are found *inside* churches and which depict images of eternal damnation no less horrific than the iconography of the pagan imagination. The fusion of pagan and Christian imagery is particularly evident in the ornamentation of the English Romanesque period (*see* MEDIEVAL ARCHITECTURE) but later medieval masons also delighted in the carving of pagan symbols, notably in GARGOYLES, roof-bosses, corbels and in the capitals of pillars, even in the most sophisticated of urban churches. These carvings included fertility-cult symbols as well as mythical creatures and humorous and obscene images of medieval life. How, despite prohibition by the Church and the denunciations of the clergy, such a tradition was sustained throughout the Middle Ages remains a mystery, but there is no doubting the extraordinary tenacity with which paganism maintained its hold on the medieval mind. Many of these carvings have been destroyed in successive restorations, particularly during the nineteenth century when pre-Christian fertility symbols were considered to be improper. But many examples have survived, notably the hideous SHEELA-NA-GIG and the ubiquitous GREEN MAN and TREE OF LIFE images.

See also CHRISTIAN SYMBOLS, FIGURE SCULPTURE, GARGOYLES *and* WOOD CARVING

Further reading:

Ashe, G., *Mythology of the British Isles*, London, 1990

Green, M., *Symbol and Image in Celtic Religious Art*, London, 1989

Weir, A. and Jerman, J., *Images of Lust: Sexual Carvings on Medieval Churches*, London, 1993

PAINTINGS *see* DOOM *and* WALL PAINTINGS

PALAEOGRAPHY
The reading, dating and localisation of handwriting. Palaeography is more than the study of how to read old documents. An understanding of scribal rules and conventions and of the peculiarities associated with particular places and periods can facilitate the identification of specific writers and assist in ascertaining the provenance of a document from the evidence of the script. The amateur historian will rarely have recourse to an original document and in any event will require expert advice both in its interpretation and in determining its provenance and, indeed, its authenticity. Most important historical documents have been transcribed and are available, often with explanatory notes, through libraries and record offices or by appointment with the archivists of specialist collections. For the most part, the interpretation of handwriting in more mundane

documents and maps (such as those which accompany tithe and enclosure awards) is a matter of patience and common sense. It is at the parochial level that most researchers will at some time experience difficulties, for there is little one can do to remedy retrospectively the calligraphic idiosyncrasies of a Georgian rector or a semi-literate parish clerk.

Further reading:

Grieve, H., *Examples of English Handwriting 1150–1750*, London, (reprinted 1978)

Hector, L., *The Handwriting of English Documents*, Dorking, (Second Edition 1980)

Richardson, J., *The Local Historian's Encyclopedia*, Historical Publications, 1986 (for a useful list of palaeographic terms and abbreviations and examples of various scripts)

PALATINATE
The word *palatine* means 'pertaining to a palace' and the palatine counties were those over which Norman magnates and their successors exercised royal jurisdiction. The original counties were those of the Welsh March (ruled by the earls of Chester, Shrewsbury and Hereford) and the Scottish borders (ruled by the Prince Bishop of Durham). The Palatinates were necessary for the defence of the Conqueror's new realm but elsewhere holdings were dispersed to prevent the concentration of magnatial power.

The *prince bishops* of Durham are unique in the history of England. They were appointed by the king as *counts palatine*, head of church and state in a vast territory which included all the lands between the rivers Tyne and Tees, land around Crayke and Northallerton in Yorkshire and an area along the river Tweed in Northumberland known as 'North Durham': Norhamshire, Islandshire, including Holy Island, and Bedlingtonshire. This was St. Cuthbert's diocese: the seventh-century bishopric of Lindisfarne which, from 995, was administered from Durham, the customary dues of its vast estates recorded in 1183 in what is now called the *Boldon Book*. The Palatinate was effectively a kingdom within a kingdom and, as defenders of the realm in the north, the prince bishops were charged with the defence of the Scottish border. By the fourteenth century the Palatinate was at the height of its military power, its warrior-bishops uniquely commemorated in the ducally-crowned mitre and sword in the coats of arms of all subsequent bishops of Durham. They had their own chancellors, exchequer and mint; they administered the civil and criminal law; granted charters for markets and fairs and exercised rights of forfeiture. Inevitably, the bishops' authority was reduced under the Tudor kings, nevertheless in 1585 the Bishop of Durham was the largest land-holder in the country with eighty manors worth £2,500 annually. The failure of the Northern Rising in 1569 succeeded in suppressing local opposition to the

bishops' traditional domination of local affairs and single-faction politics continued in County Durham until the mid-nineteenth century. The bishops' powers were finally vested in the Crown in 1836 and the palatinate courts abolished by the Courts Act of 1971.
See also HERALDRY (ECCLESIASTICAL)

PALIMPSEST A manuscript on which the original writing has been effaced to make room for new material. Also a monumental brass which has been turned and re-engraved on the reverse (*see* BRASSES, MONUMENTAL).

PALL (i) A small linen cloth (*palla*) with which the chalice is covered at the Eucharist. In its modern form it is usually stiffened by a means of a piece of board. (ii) A large cloth, usually purple or white and with a central embroidered motif, which is spread over a coffin during a funeral service. At one time, many parishes had at least one pall for general use while special palls of rich black Genoese or Utrecht velvet could be hired from the College of Arms for funerals of the gentility (*see* FUNERAL HERALDRY). These fell just below the sides of the coffin but larger palls, measuring about 4.3 metres by 3 metres (fourteen by ten feet), were also available for special occasions such as the funeral of Sir Philip Sydney in 1588. These were decorated with nine 'scocheons' (shields of arms), three along each side, one at each end and a ninth on the top, painted on canvas rectangles which were attached by tacking stitches to facilitate their removal, thus allowing the College to re-use the pall on future occasions. Livery companies and a small number of magnatial families possessed their own palls which were embroidered with coats of arms and other heraldic devices. A *pall-bearer* was one of the mourners at a funeral who held the corners of the pall. The term is now used to describe those who carry the coffin. (iii) In HERALDRY, a geometrical figure (an *ordinary*) consisting of a broad Y, its limbs extending to the edge of the shield. A.C. Fox-Davies, in his *Complete Guide to Heraldry*, suggests that '. . . there can be little doubt that originally the pall itself was the heraldic symbol in this country of an archbishop.' Its shape is certainly that of the PALLIUM (*see* VESTMENTS) and its application in heraldry is often ecclesiastical, though not invariably so.

PALLA *see* PALL

PALLADIAN *see* SIXTEENTH- AND SEVENTEENTH-CENTURY ARCHITECTURE *and* EIGHTEENTH-CENTURY ARCHITECTURE

PALL-BEARER *see* PALL

PALLIUM A circular band of white material with two pendant strips, the whole embroidered with six purple crosses, worn on the shoulders of the Pope and granted by him to archbishops (and occasionally to certain bishops) in the Roman Catholic Church. The *pallium* is not used in the Church of England though it has survived in its heraldic form in the arms of the archbishopric of Canterbury (*see* PALL *and* VESTMENTS).

PALM SUNDAY (*also* YEW SUNDAY) The commemoration of Christ's triumphal entry into Jerusalem on the Sunday before EASTER. In the Middle Ages, the blessing of the palms was an elaborate rite, similar in structure to that of the MASS. This was followed by a procession which left the nave by the north door and proceeded round the churchyard before returning by the south door. Although abolished in the Church of England in 1549, vestiges of the medieval observance remain even today in the distribution of palms which may be carried in a procession. For Christians, Palm Sunday announces the approach of Easter but it is also a celebration of the arrival of Spring and, until recently, churches were often decorated with willow or yew and the churchyard graves adorned with spring flowers. In the Middle Ages, Palm Sunday was known as Yew Sunday.
See also EASTER EGGS, FEAST DAYS (FIXED AND MOVABLE), GOOD FRIDAY, LENT, MAUNDY THURSDAY *and* SHROVE TUESDAY

PANACHE An early type of CREST consisting of a plume of feathers.

PANE An alley or covered way: in a monastic cloister, for example.

PANELLING From the thirteenth century, the interior walls of major buildings were often lined with wooden boards (*wainscoting*) which were placed vertically and overlapping one another as in a clinker-built ship. (Wainscot was usually oak imported from the Baltic coast and used also for wagons or 'wains', hence 'wagon boarding' in wainscot chests or tables.) During the fifteenth century panel and frame construction (*joined* woodwork) was introduced from Flanders. The panels, thin sheets of wood, were usually tapered on all four sides and fitted into grooves within a framework of thicker wood, the panel being either raised (*fielded*) or sunken (*coffered*). The horizontal and vertical strips of the frame (*rails* and *stiles*) were united by mortise and tenon joints and fastened by square oak pegs inserted into round holes. This type of panelling was used for centuries on walls and ceilings and in doors and furniture. Early panelling was rarely carved but was sometimes painted in coloured designs.

From the late fifteenth century until about 1550 *lignum undulatum* ('wavy woodwork') decoration was popular, each panel being carved with a representation of a piece of material folded vertically. (From the nineteenth century this style of decoration has been described as *linenfold* and has been much copied). Later examples may have a decorative 'punched' border to represent embroidery and a further variation of the design, known as *parchemin*, resembles a curled piece of parchment.

Early sixteenth century panels were often pierced with gothic motifs or decorated with a central roundel, incorporating heraldic and other devices, and from about 1550 a profusion of English Renaissance motifs appeared. At this time inlays (usually of bog oak, holly and laburnum) and painted and gilded ornamentation were also used. From the 1630s entire walls, together with window and door openings, were incorporated into classical designs comprising entablature, pilasters and plinth. During the seventeenth and eighteenth centuries panels were usually plain or raised at the centre (*fielded*) and by the eighteenth century pine or deal had replaced oak and this was painted in a light colour with ornamentation picked out in gilt or ormolu. Nineteenth- and twentieth-century panelling is often decorated with applied gothic tracery.

PANTHER *see* BEASTS (HERALDIC)

PANTILES *see* TILES

PANTOCRATOR An image of Christ enthroned.

PANTRY *see* LARDER

PAPAL BULL *see* BULLA

PAPER Paper was first used in England as a writing surface from the fourteenth century but was not manufactured here until the late fifteenth century and even then only in small quantities. In the late seventeenth century, Huguenot immigrants specialised in its production.

PARAPET A low wall erected along the outer edge of a structure for reasons of safety or to conceal guttering etc. A parapet may be plain, battlemented, pierced or carved ornamentally and was a characteristic of the perpendicular period of MEDIEVAL ARCHITECTURE. Battlemented parapets were sometimes added to churches in the nineteenth century as 'Gothic' features, despite the fact that contemporary architects disliked such elaboration and preferred the simplicity of the Early English style (*see also* PINNACLE).

PARAPET SPIRE *see* TOWERS

PARCHMENT A writing surface made from the treated skins of sheep or goats. The lighter 'flesh' side was preferred for formal documents but both sides were used in the writing of rolls and books. *See also* VELLUM

PARCLOSE A stone, timber or metalwork screen separating a chapel or shrine from the body of a church. More specifically, a screen or a set of railings enclosing a CHANTRY CHAPEL.

PARDONER A 'pardon' was an alternative name for an INDULGENCE. In the Middle Ages, shares in indulgences were hawked by pardoners, a practice which was denounced by Geoffrey Chaucer, John Wycliffe and others.

PARGETING Decorative PLASTERWORK, popular in the sixteenth and seventeenth centuries, particularly on the external walls of timber-framed buildings in the eastern counties of England. Some pargeting was incised but most remaining examples comprise panels of high relief ornamentation, usually foliage, flowers and heraldic and geometrical designs. These were made by applying moulds to the wet plaster and finishing by hand. The term may derive from the medieval practice of throwing coarse mortar at a wall to provide a protective covering, hence '*pour jeter*'.

PARISH The term is derived from the Anglo-Saxon *parochium*, the missionary territory of a MINSTER (*see* ANGLO-SAXON CHURCH). Dating from the ninth and tenth centuries, when parish churches superseded the minster system, the parish remains the smallest unit of ecclesiastical administration. An ecclesiastical parish possesses its own church or churches (*see* CHAPELRY) and burial rights (*rights of sepulture*) and is served by an INCUMBENT to whom parishioners once paid ecclesiastical dues and TITHES and to whose religious ministrations all residents of a parish are entitled (*see also* GLEBE *and* PARISHIONER). Many of the first parish churches were provided by Saxon lords, the boundaries of whose estates almost invariably corresponded with those of the parishes, and by Anglo-Norman lords who created small parishes which were often conterminous with the equally new units of manor or knight's fee (*see* BOUNDARIES).

Some parishes are therefore of considerable antiquity, while others may have been merged following the extinction of a neighbouring settlement (*see* DESERTED VILLAGES) or 'rationalised' as the result of legislation. A parish may also once have contained one or more medieval manors, each with its own manorial court, while sometimes a single manor encompassed several parishes (*see* DOMESDAY). A *donative parish* (also known as a PECULIAR) is one which is exempt from diocesan jurisdiction.

An incumbent is nominated by the PATRON of the BENEFICE (with, in modern times, certain rights of preference being available to the parochial church council) and may be removed only in exceptional circumstances. The incumbent is a RECTOR or VICAR, the distinction being of an historical nature. If, formerly, all the tithes were attached to the benefice for the maintenance of the incumbent it is a rectory, otherwise it is a vicarage (*see also* CLERGY, CHURCH OF ENGLAND). (The foregoing does not apply to team rectors, which were created by the Pastoral Measure 1968, and many clergy are now being appointed to parochial benefices on fixed-term licences.) The REGISTERS of baptisms, marriages and burials are in the custody of the incumbent but modern regulations for their preservation usually cause those not in current use to be deposited, usually in county archives.

Persons dying in a parish or resident there before death or having a close relative buried in the churchyard have a legal right to burial there (*see* BURIALS). But if they are unbaptised, suicides in their right mind or excommunicated, there can be no service from the *Book of Common Prayer*. The freehold of the churchyard is vested in the incumbent, who enjoys the rights of herbage, but its maintenance is the responsibility of the parochial church council and may be paid for out of the rates by the (civil) parish council (*see* CHURCHYARDS). It is a criminal offence to strike anyone in a church or churchyard.

Successive acts of Parliament, particularly in the sixteenth and seventeenth centuries, encouraged the development of secular parochial authority administered through *vestries (see* VESTRY). Early parishes levied a church rate, but legislation enabled them to levy additional rates for poor relief (*see* POOR LAW) and for the maintenance of the highway. At this time also, the manor courts were in decline and for a while there was an overlapping of manorial and vestral interests. Most were *open vestries* at which any male ratepayer could attend and vote, but in populous areas where the open vestry system could become unmanageable many parishes succeeded in establishing *select vestries* which, although self-perpetuating and undemocratic, were often more effective. A vestry was responsible for appointing the CHURCHWARDENS, Sexton, Overseer of the Poor, Surveyor of Highways and constables, and for organising the annual PERAMBULATION of the parish boundary.

Many ecclesiastical parishes were re-defined in the nineteenth century (*see* PEEL PARISH) and the civil and ecclesiastical components of vestral authority were finally separated by the Municipal Corporations Act of 1835, which consolidated urban parishes into boroughs, and the Local Government Act of 1894 which established (civil) parish councils

of elected members in rural areas with parochial populations exceeding 300 (or between 200 and 300 if agreed by a parish meeting). Since 1919 the administration of ecclesiastical parishes is vested in parochial church councils. One consequence of these changes is that the boundaries of ecclesiastical and civil parishes may not always be conterminous. Today's ecclesiastical parishes were delineated by the Pastoral Reorganization Measure of 1949 though there have been many subsequent amalgamations as 'group parishes'.

See also ARCHIVES, DOCUMENTARY SOURCES, FOOTPATHS AND BRIDLEWAYS *and* PLURALITIES ACT (1838)

Further reading:
Battey, J.H., *Church and Parish*, London, 1987
Tate, W., *The Parish Chest*, Chichester, 1983

PARISH CHEST Church records were once stored in the 'parish chest': a large, usually wooden coffer, bound with iron and secured with several locks. Thomas Cromwell's directive of 1538 required that each parish should obtain a 'secure coffer' in which to keep its records (*see* CHURCHWARDEN). The legislation also formalised the authority of parishes and the vestries which administered them and required that accurate records should be kept concerning the administration of poor relief, parochial accounts and charities, the appointment of parish officials and the maintenance of the church fabric. Parish chests may still be found in churches, often pressed into service as receptacles for cleaning materials or old prayer books. There is a splendid chest at Little Gaddesden in Hertfordshire and another in the north aisle of Bradford Abbas church in Dorset. Both are secured by padlocks, the two churchwardens and the rector each holding a different key so that the chests can be opened only when all three persons are present. The term is sometimes used by local historians when referring to the ARCHIVES of a particular community.

See also CHESTS *and* REGISTERS

Further reading:
Tate, P., *The Parish Chest*, Cambridge, 1969

PARISH CLERK (*CLERICUS PAROCHIALIS*) A layman who assisted the parish priest in the administration of the church and in the performance of minor duties during services such as leading the singing, reading the Gospel or Epistle, announcing the metrical psalm and making the congregational responses (*see* PULPITS). Clerks were often entrusted with making up the parish REGISTERS though, in fact, delegation of this responsibility was unlawful. They are often maligned by historians as being uneducated and reactionary. And yet their office was an ancient one and they made a significant contribution to the development of church music in England. Parish

Medieval parish chest at Bradford Abbas, Dorset

clerks were usually men, though there were rare exceptions such as the formidable Betty Howell who was clerk and sexton of St. Saviour's church at Puxton in Somerset in the early nineteenth century.

Originally, the word 'clerk' was used only of men in holy orders (including MINOR ORDERS). Thus '. . . the server at Mass used to be called the "clerk", because he did clerk's work, just as the boys at Mass [were] called "acolytes", though not really so, because they do acolytes' work.' (*Catholic Dictionary*, 1883). After the REFORMATION the term was applied to a number of minor functionaries in the Church, indeed the male members of most cathedral choirs are still referred to as lay clerks (*see also* VICARS CHORAL). Of the three salaried officials of a parish church, the Clerk was superior to the SEXTON but inferior to the rector or vicar. He was effectively the parochial equivalent of the cathedral PRECENTOR, providing the note for the psalm tune (or the four notes for the four voices) on an adjustable pitch-pipe, training the choir or band (*see* GALLERIES) and sometimes playing a 'finger organ' to lead the singing. He was, in many parishes, the leading musical functionary and in larger

churches was able to exercise considerable influence. John Playford (1623–87), for example, was both clerk at the Temple Church in London (not a parish clerk for the Temple Church is extra-parochial) and one of the most eminent music publishers of his day. Benjamin Payne, Clerk of the church of St. Anne at Blackfriars in London and author of *The Parish Clerk's Guide* (1685), described Payne as '. . . one to whose memory all parish clerks owe perpetual thanks for their furtherance in the knowledge of psalmody.'

The London guild of parish clerks was incorporated by Henry III in 1232 and became a Livery Company of the City of London. When their charter was renewed by James I (and later by Charles II) it was stipulated that 'Every person that is chosen Clerk of a Parish shall first give sufficient proof of his abilities to sing at least the tunes which are used in parish churches.' In 1762, William Riley (in his *Parochial Music Corrected*) stated that this test no longer applied, though the London clerks were not forgetful of their musical responsibilities for they continued to hold weekly meetings at their hall 'where they sing psalms, accompanied by an organ, for about an hour'. The *Parish Clerk's Guide* (see above) was a periodical journal in which were listed the metrical psalms best suited to each Sunday in the year so that they might enforce the precepts of the Collect, Epistle and Gospel. These official lists were published by the Company of Parish Clerks on whose shield of arms are two 'pricksong books'. Also described as 'pricking books', these contained 'pricksong', music which was 'pricked down' or composed – in contradistinction to unison plainsong and descant performed extemporaneously. (It has been suggested that the name derives from the medieval practice of PRICKING – the ruling the staves by reference to rows of pin pricks in the margins of the parchment.)

In 1844 an act of Parliament deprived the parish clerks of nearly all their duties (which were transferred to curates) while another of 1894 left them with few responsibilities other than the care of certain documents and maps which are now handed to that purely secular functionary, the clerk of the parish council.

A memorial at Bakewell in Derbyshire provides a fitting epitaph to the ancient office of parish clerk and to one Philip Roe (d. 1815) in particular:

The Vocal Powers here let us mark
Of PHILIP, our late Parish Clerk.
In Church none ever heard a Layman,
With a clearer Voice say Amen.
Who now with Halleluja's Sound
Like Him can make the Roof rebound?
The Choirs lament his Choral Tones,
The Town – so soon Here lie his Bones.
Sleep undisturbed within thy peaceful shrine
Till Angels wake thee with such notes as thine.

See also CHURCH MUSIC (ANGLICAN) *and* CHURCHWARDENS

PARISH CONSTABLES The constable was originally an officer appointed by a (manorial) court leet with responsibility for a wide range of duties which have, from time to time, included the collection of rates and special taxes, supervision of watch and ward, maintenance of stocks, pillories, lock-ups etc., the inspection of ale houses, supervision of jury service, the apprenticing of pauper children, poor relief and the supervision of intinerants and beggars, the collection of maintenance from fathers of illegitimate children, the training of local militia and the suppression of riot and unlawful assembly, the apprehension of escaped prisoners or suspected criminals, the organisation of relief at times of shipwreck, the convening of parish meetings and the supervision of church attendance. In the absence of a *pinder* (a minor manorial official responsible for the *pinfold*

or pound), the ubiquitous constable was even required to impound stray animals and care for the parish bull! A constable's jurisdiction (*constable-wick*) was usually equivalent to a TOWNSHIP or TITHING.

As parochial authority grew and that of the manor diminished, the VESTRY assumed many of the duties previously associated with the constable, indeed it was not unknown for both bodies to appoint constables within the same parish. Petty constables were elected annually by the vestries and were responsible for the punishment of parishioners referred to them by the CHURCHWARDENS. Penalties were imposed for a range of misdemeanours but the most common miscreants appear to have been vagrants, drunkards and scolds (*see also* WITCHCRAFT). In some parishes, whipping posts and stocks were erected for this purpose against the churchyard wall. There are examples at Painswick in Gloucestershire (though not in their original position) and at Holwell in Dorset (heavily restored). Several were subsequently removed and stored within the church, usually beneath the tower, as at Llywel in Powys. At nearby Llanfryant, the first occupant of the eighteenth-century stocks was the hapless carpenter who had manufactured them. Having received his wages he proceeded to indulge in an excess of alcohol and was arrested by the parish constable! Although most parishes elected petty constables, it was not until 1842 that such parochial responsibilities were legally conferred on vestries, subject to the approval of the justices.
See also CHURCH AND COMMUNITY *and* LOCK-UP
Further reading:
Friar, S., *The Batsford Companion to Local History*, London, 1991

PARISHIONER The inhabitant of a PARISH. During the thirteenth century a convention was established whereby parishioners were responsible for the upkeep of the church NAVE (*see* CHURCH AND COMMUNITY). This was formalised in 1282 when the Synod of Exeter determined that parishioners should be answerable to the Church courts for contributions to the repair of their churches 'according to the quality of land they possess in each parish'. Clearly, ownership of land was then considered to be a qualification and a man could therefore be a parishioner of two or more parishes. With the creation of civil parishes in 1894, the term has acquired a dual meaning. A parishioner is now one who resides in either an ecclesiastical or civil parish, though others (such as those whose place of work is in a parish other than that in which they reside) may also qualify for inclusion in the Register of Electors.

Stocks at Holwell, Dorset.

PARISH MAGAZINES *see* DOCUMENTARY SOURCES *and* NINETEENTH-CENTURY CHURCH

PARISH PRIEST Correctly, an unbeneficed clerk to whom the cure of souls is deputed by the parson.

PARISH REGISTERS *see* REGISTERS

PARLIAMENTARY RECORDS *see* CENSUS OF RELIGIOUS WORSHIP (1851) *and* NINETEENTH-CENTURY CHURCH

PARLOUR A room in a religious house where the rule of silence was relaxed to allow necessary conversation (*parler*), including the preparation of CHAPTER business. There were often two parlours: one which was reserved for the use of the community and another in which meetings took place with merchants, artificers, etc. from the outside world.

'PARLOUR PEWS' *see* PEWS, FAMILY

PAROCHIAL Derived from the Anglo-Saxon *parochium*, the missionary territory of a MINSTER, the term is now used to describe matters concerning a civil or ecclesiastical PARISH.
See also ANGLO-SAXON CHURCH

PAROCHIAL CHURCH COUNCIL (PCC) The Church of England Assembly (Powers Act) of 1919 required that each parish in the Church of England should elect a council through which lay members would be able to participate in the administration of parochial affairs. Parochial church councils and parish councils are entirely separate bodies and the BOUNDARIES of the two jurisdictions are not necessarily the same. A PCC is charged with the administration of an ecclesiastical parish while a parish council is a minor authority responsible for the affairs of a civil parish. Parochial church councils exercise considerable authority. No incumbent may use the services of the Alternative Service Book in preference to those of the Book of Common Prayer without their consent, for example. The *Synodical Government Measure* of 1969 provides for PCCs consisting of:

(a) All clerks in Holy Orders beneficed in or licensed to the parish, including in the case of a team ministry all vicars in the team.

(b) Any deaconess or woman worker licensed to the parish or any male lay worker licensed to the parish and receiving a stipend.

(c) The churchwardens being communicant members of the Church of England and whose names are on the roll of the parish.

(d) Any reader whose name is on the roll of the parish (subject to agreement by the annual meeting).

(e) All persons whose names are on the roll of the parish and who are lay members of any deanery or diocesan SYNOD or of the General Synod.

(f) Such number of representatives of the laity as the annual meeting shall determine.

(g) Co-opted members (not exceeding in number one fifth of the representatives of the laity) and being either clerks in Holy Orders or lay communicant members of the Church of England of seventeen years of age or upward.

In a group ministry, the incumbents of all benefices within the group are entitled to attend meetings of the PCCs of the parishes in the area for which the group ministry is established.

PAROCHIAL SOURCES *see* ARCHIVES, CENSUS, CHURCH AND COMMUNITY, CHURCH-WARDENS' ACCOUNTS, DIOCESAN RECORDS, DOCUMENTARY SOURCES, EIGHTEENTH-CENTURY CHURCH, GLEBE, MAPS, MEMORIAL BOARDS, MINUTES, NINETEENTH-CENTURY CHURCH, PARISH, PARISH CHEST, PARSONAGE, PHOTOGRAPHS, REGISTERS, SEVENTEENTH-CENTURY CHURCH, TITHES, VESTRY, VISITATIONS *and* WAR MEMORIALS

PAROCHIUM *see* ANGLO-SAXON CHURCH, MINSTER, PARISH *and* PAROCHIAL

PARSON Specifically, a RECTOR – the holder of an ecclesiastical benefice who has full possession of its rights. Since the seventeenth century the term has been applied more generally to any clergyman of the Church of England.
See also CLERGY (CHURCH OF ENGLAND) *and* REFORMATION

PARSONAGE The revenue, obtained from a number of sources, for the maintenance of an incumbent. Information concerning TITHES, dues, offerings and other clerical incomes, the extent and disposition of GLEBE lands, the size of parsonage houses and other local matters are to be found in the glebe *terriers*, inventories of the possessions, profits and endowments associated with a BENEFICE which were first required in 1571 and thereafter were compiled periodically in each diocese.

PARVA *see* MAGNA *and* PLACE-NAMES

PARVIS (*also* PARVISE) Literally, 'Paradise', the term was originally applied to the atrium in front of St. Peter's in Rome. Thereafter it was used to describe the court between the west end of a large church and the outer wall of its precinct. The word is also used to describe the western portico of a church and a porch with a room above, though such use is possibly erroneous (*see* PORCHES). These rooms were used for a variety of purposes: to house a chantry priest, for example, or as a schoolroom. The elaborate, three-storeyed south porch at the church of St. John the Baptist, Cirencester in Gloucestershire was built in *c.* 1490 and adopted for use as a town hall in the seventeenth century.

PASCHAL CANDLE A lighted candle carried through a darkened church at the Paschal Vigil Service, the main celebration of EASTER observed during the night of Holy Saturday/Easter Sunday.

PASCHAL LAMB (*AGNUS DEI*) *see* CHRISTIAN SYMBOLS

PASCHAL MONEY A levy for the cost of the paschal taper which was lighted at EASTER and again at Whitsuntide.

PASCHALTIDE In the ecclesiastical year, the period from EASTER Sunday to PENTECOST or, in the Church of England, to the Saturday before TRINITY SUNDAY. The word *paschal* is derived from the Hebrew *pesah* meaning 'pass over' and refers to the Jewish feast of the Passover at which a lamb was sacrificed (*see* Exodus 12: 11 ff and 1 Corinthians 5:7).
See also TRIPLE CANDLESTICK

PASSANT *see* BEASTS (HERALDIC)

PASSION, INSTRUMENTS OF THE *see* CHRISTIAN SYMBOLS

PASSION SUNDAY The fifth Sunday in LENT (*see* PASSIONTIDE).

PASSION, THE The sufferings of Christ on the Cross. A narrative of this derived from the Gospels or a musical setting based on such a narrative.
See also CHRISTIAN SYMBOLS

PASSIONTIDE The last two weeks of LENT when the ROOD and all crucifixes, sacred pictures and images were veiled in purple.
See also EASTER, FESTIVALS (FIXED AND MOVABLE), GOOD FRIDAY, HOLY WEEK *and* MAUNDY THURSDAY

PASTOR One who exercises spiritual guidance. A *pastorate* is a pastor's office or a body of pastors.

PASTORAL LETTERS Official letters addressed by a bishop to all members of his diocese. ENCYCLICAL letters are those which are addressed only to the clergy.

PASTORAL STAFF A stave, surmounted by either a cross or a shepherd's crook, carried for ceremonial purposes by a bishop and (in the medieval period) by a senior abbot or abbess (*see* CROSIER).

PATEN *see* PLATE

PATENT *see* LETTERS PATENT

PATERA *see* DECORATIVE MOTIFS

PATINA An encrusted or glossy surface acquired by an object as a result of age or chemical changes following burial.

PATRON The right to nominate a clergyman to a living (*see* ADVOWSON) is exercised by a diocesan bishop or by some other person or body corporate, either lay or clerical, known as the patron. Even though a candidate may have been nominated by a patron for INSTITUTION and INDUCTION he may still be rejected by the bishop in whose diocese the vacancy has occurred (*see* QUARE IMPEDIT). During the thirteenth century a custom was established by which the RECTOR or patron was responsible for the upkeep of the CHANCEL while the parishioners maintained the NAVE.
See also PARISH

PATRONAL FESTIVAL (FERIAE) At one time every church had a patronal festival on which was commemorated either the dedication of the church or the birthday of the saint in whose name it was dedicated. On the eve of the patronal day there would be a candle-lit procession to the church followed by a vigil of thanksgiving and, on the day itself, a public holiday with numerous diversions such as plays (*see* DRAMA), dancing and games accompanied by eating and drinking (*see* CHURCH AND COMMUNITY). All this took place in the north side of the churchyard which was usually unconsecrated (*see* CHURCHYARDS). It is likely that such occasions were intended originally to supplant the pagan festivities which preceded them (*see* ANGLO-SAXON CHURCH) and therefore they should not be confused with CHURCH ALES. Instead of the gluttony, drunkeness and licentiousness which apparently characterised pre-Christian festivities, there was to be moderation and 'good Christian charity one to another'. But, inevitably, such optimism was ill-founded and the religious purpose of the celebrations was invariably lost in the secular pleasures which accompanied them. From a tenth-century source, quoted by Joseph Strutt in his *Sports and Pastimes of the People of England* (1800), we learn that '. . . the people fell to lechery, and songs and dances, with harping and piping and also to gluttony and sin, and so turned the holiness to cursedness; wherefore holy fathers ordered the people to leave that waking and to fast the evening'. Matters became so bad that congregations of young people would leave the church during the vigil to dance wildly in the churchyard, only to return at dawn to find the priest still chanting his Latin office. In 1240, the Bishop of Worcester ordered 'Let none come to such vigils save for reasons of devotion and willingness to abstain from such practices.'

Of course, patronal holidays provided opportunities for relaxation and enjoyment in a society where the lot of the average parishioner was one of unrelieved hardship and drudgery. And, with celebrations taking place at different times in neighbouring parishes, it was possible for the villagers of one parish to take part in the revels of several others. Many festivals proved so popular that the large crowds attracted itinerant entertainers and tradespeople who set up their stalls along the churchyard wall. Indeed, in some cases they developed as FAIRS AND MARKETS many of which, even today, are held on (or near) a patronal feast day. Other fairs occur on the first weekend of October as a consequence of a Convocational order of 1536 which required that all patronal feasts should be held on the first Sunday of October, a ruling which was widely disobeyed. The term WAKE seems originally to have applied to the religious procession and vigil which preceded the patronal festival and, later, to the feast day itself.

It is hardly surprising that the riotous activities which accompanied patronal festivals should have offended the sensibilities of Victorian society. In 1837 an Act of Parliament forbade the announcement of parish wakes from the pulpit and in 1840 the Society for the Suppression of Sunday Wakes was formed. With the parallel suppression of church ales, by the end of the nineteenth century one thousand years of 'Merry England' came to an end.
See also FESTIVALS AND LOCAL CUSTOMS *and* MOTHERING SUNDAY
Further reading:
Hammond, P., *Food and Feast in Medieval England*, Stroud, 1994
Hutton, R., *The Rise and Fall of Merry England: The Ritual Year 1400–1700*, Oxford, 1994

PATRON SAINT A saint selected as the special intercessor in heaven of an individual or body corporate. The symbols of patron saints are often found in the memorials and CHANTRY CHAPELS of the medieval aristocracy and in the chapels of GUILDS and fraternities.

PATTENS Wooden over-shoes. The wearing of pattens in church was discouraged because of the mud which clung to them. Notices requiring their removal may still be found in church porches, together with shelving on which they were deposited.

PAULDRON *see* ARMOUR

PAWN A strip of parchment containing a list of names.

PAX BREDE (OSCULATORIUM) A small tablet of ivory, wood etc. on the surface of which was a representation of some sacred subject such as the ROOD. It was held by means of a handle on the reverse and used to convey the 'Kiss of Peace' by the celebrant at the Eucharist who would kiss it before inviting others to do so in turn.
See also PLATE

PEBBLEDASH *see* FACING MATERIALS

PECTORAL CROSS A cross, often of precious metal, worn on the breast and suspended by means of a chain round the neck. In the Church of England, use of the pectoral cross is now generally confined to bishops.
See also VESTMENTS

PECULIAR A church or parish (or group of parishes) which is exempt from the jurisdiction of the bishop in whose diocese it is situated. Peculiars usually derived from the possession of land in one diocese by a senior church dignitary who held office in another or from privileges granted to special groups of religious such as the Knights Templar (*see* COMMANDERY). The *Royal Peculiars* are churches connected with royal palaces or castles: St. George's Chapel at Windsor Castle and Westminster Abbey, for example, which are exempt from any jurisdiction other than that of the sovereign. Most of the privileges associated with monastic and cathedral peculiars have been abolished. The term *testamentary peculiar* refers to PROBATE jurisdiction when exercised by a peculiar.

PEDESTAL A base to support a column, statue or decorative feature such as an urn. In classical architecture, a pedestal consists of a *cornice* (the top), a *dado* (the central section) and a *plinth* (the base).

PEDESTAL TOMBS *see* TABLE TOMBS

PEDIGREE A genealogical table illustrating descent through the male line. The term is said to have originated in the practice of writing the names of forebears in groups of circles which, when joined by curved lines, were thought to resemble a crane's foot: in French, a *pied de gru*. A chart which records all direct line ancestors, both male and female, is a *birth brief*, *blood descent* or *total descent*.

PEDILAVIUM *see* MAUNDY THURSDAY

PEDIMENT In classical architecture, the triangular gable above a the ENTABLATURE of a PORTICO or a decorative feature over a door, window or niche. The horizontal base moulding may be incomplete (*broken pediment*), the apex of the triangle may be omitted (*open*) or the top members may be curved and scrolled (*segmental*).
See also TYMPANUM

PEEL PARISH A parish established by the New Parishes Act of 1843 (or a subsequent act) when Sir Robert Peel (1788–1850) was Prime Minister.

PEERAGE, THE Derived from the medieval Latin *paragium*, the term 'peerage' means simply 'a company of equals' and was originally applied to those of similar rank within the nobility (*see also* LORD). From 1321, the term was used to describe those senior barons of England who normally received writs of summons to Parliament and, later, to the lords spiritual. The British peerage now comprises five separate peerages: those of England, Scotland, Ireland, Great Britain (from 1707) and the United Kingdom (from 1801).

Although coronets of rank and helmets appear in the coats of arms of medieval and Tudor peers, these were not standardised until the seventeenth century (*see* illustration *and* HELMETS (HERALDIC)). Peers are also entitled to use hereditary SUPPORTERS in their arms.

A *dukedom* is the senior rank of the British peerage. Derived from the Latin *dux*, meaning 'leader', the rank was introduced into England in 1337 although the style had been known before that date, William the Conqueror being referred to as *Ducis Normannorum et Regis Anglorum*, for example. The first English non-royal dukedom was granted to Henry, Earl of Lancaster, Derby, Lincoln and Leicester in 1351 while in Scotland, David, the eldest son of Robert III, became Duke of Rothesay in 1398. The wife of a duke is a duchess.

A *marquess* (or *marquis*) belongs to the second rank of the British peerage. Although introduced from Europe in 1385, the term *marchiones* had previously been used by lords of the Welsh and Scottish marches. The wife of a marquess is a marchioness.

Several of the lords who followed Duke William in his conquest of England held substantial territories (*comtés*) in the Low Countries and France and,

Duke

Earl

Marquess

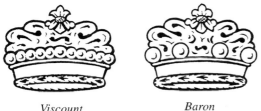

Viscount   *Baron*

although granted English lands and titles by the Conqueror, they retained the superior title of *comté, county or count*. The English equivalent of count is *earl*, a title which originated in Scandinavia and appeared in England in the early eleventh century as *eorl*, an Old English form of *jarl*. Prior to 1337, when the Black Prince was created a duke, it was the senior rank of the nobility. The earliest known charter creating an hereditary earl is that of *c.* 1140 by which King Stephen created Geoffrey de Mandeville Earl of Essex. An earldom is now the third rank of the British peerage and the wife of an earl (or one who holds an earldom in her own right) is a countess.

A *viscount* belongs to the fourth rank of the British peerage, the first creation being of 1440, though the title itself is considerably older. In the days of the Carolingian empire the *vice-comtés* were the deputies of the counts and gradually assumed hereditary rights. The wife of a viscount is a viscountess.

The word 'baron' is of uncertain origin: it was introduced into England following the Norman Conquest of 1066 to identify the 'man' (vassal) of a great lord, though prior to the Conquest a *barony* was simply a chief's domain. Following the Conquest, tenants-in-chief of the king below the rank of earl were often referred to as barons, and from the thirteenth century the title appears to have been reserved for those magnates summoned by writ to parliament: greater barons being those who were summoned by direct writ to the king's council and

summoned by the county sheriffs. During the reign of Edward IV (1461–83) a new and powerful merchant class emerged (principally as a result of Edward's encouragement of trade and commerce) and this was to bring about the eventual dissolution of the feudal baronage. The style itself was introduced by Richard II in 1387 and it is now the fifth and lowest rank of the British peerage. The Life Peerage Act of 1958 enabled the Crown to create non-hereditary peerages with the rank and style of baron.

See also BARONET, GARTER, THE MOST NOBLE ORDER OF THE, KNIGHT BACHELOR, KNIGHT BANNERET *and* KNIGHTHOOD, ORDERS OF

Further reading:
Friar, S., *A New Dictionary of Heraldry*, Sherborne and London, 1987

PEGASUS *see* BEASTS (HERALDIC)

PELICAN *see* BEASTS (HERALDIC)

PELL A parchment document in which a money payment is recorded.

PELLISE *see* COSTUME

PENANCE *see* ABSOLUTION, SEVENTEENTH-CENTURY CHURCH, SHRINES *and* VISITATIONS, ECCLESIASTICAL

PENDANT Dependent or suspended from.

PENDENTIVE *see* DOME

PENDLE *see* SLATES

PENITENTIAL CROSS An unusual form of CHURCHYARD CROSS, of which few examples have survived. A penitential cross is distinguished by the grooves worn into its base by the knees of penitents as they knelt in supplication. It has been suggested that the three steps represent the Trinity or Faith, Hope and Charity, though the only evidence for this appears to be anecdotal. The best example is in the churchyard at Ripley in Yorkshire.

PENNON *see* FLAGS, FUNERAL HERALDRY *and* WEATHERCOCKS AND WEATHER VANES

PENS Before the eleventh century pens were made from dried reeds. Thereafter, until the nineteenth century, the quill pen was used. This was formed from a goose feather (though feathers of swans, ravens, crows and even turkeys were also used), the hollow quill of which retained a small quantity of INK which was released by gentle downward pressure on the nib while writing. When used as pens, feathers were always stripped down to the quill, the larger end of which was carefully shaped and split with a penknife to form the nib. Metal nibs date from the mid-nineteenth century and fountain pens from the end of that century.

The pens and animal hair brushes used for producing the magnificent illuminated manuscripts of the medieval period were themselves kept in superb pen-cases: one mid-eleventh-century example at the British Museum is made from walrus ivory, obtained from Lapland through Viking traders, and carved with mounted warriors in combat with a dragon, two lions and a pair of archers in the act of shooting birds from a tree. It is likely that mouse whiskers were used for the most delicate details.

See also INK, PARCHMENT and VELLUM

PENTECOST The Greek name for the Jewish Feast of Weeks which was observed on the fiftieth day after Passover. In the Church, the name was adopted for the Feast of the Descent of the Holy Spirit upon the Apostles (see Acts 2:1) which is celebrated on the fiftieth day after EASTER and is also known as WHITSUNDAY.

See also FEAST DAYS (FIXED AND MOVABLE)

PENTECOSTALS Originally PETER'S PENCE, a tax levied on each parish church and paid to the cathedral church of the diocese. Also known as Smoke Farthings or Whitsun Farthings.

PENTECOSTARION see YEAR, LITURGICAL

PERAMBULATION (also POSSESSIONING and PROCESSIONING) Perambulation, or 'beating the bounds' (purlieu), of a PARISH is still practised in some places, though as a custom rather than of necessity. Until well into the second half of the nineteenth century, vestries were responsible for investigating the boundaries of their parishes to ensure that boundary stones and other markers had not been removed and that no new (and unrated) buildings had been erected without their knowledge. The perambulation included the incumbent and officers of the VESTRY, together with various schoolchildren and village notables, all armed with wands of office, usually willow rods, which were used to 'beat the bounds'. This annual procession replaced the ancient ROGATION ceremonies which were of eighth-century origin and contained elements of paganism and were banned following the Reformation. The willow wands are a clear remnant of these festivals and on occasions boys were also beaten or bumped on the ground so that they would '. . . well remember the bounds of the parish within which they dwell', though the original intention was that their protestations should drive away evil spirits, presumably into the neighbouring parish. Many perambulations ceased after field

enclosures which defined boundaries and made access more difficult. Those householders who by custom had been obliged to provide free 'bread and beere' en route must have been well pleased to see an end to the perambulations. CHURCH-WARDENS' ACCOUNTS often refer to expenses incurred in a perambulation: at Deptford in Kent, for example, where in 1684 the huge sum of £9 1s 0d was spent on 'a processing dinner' of meat, bread, beer, cakes and '2 bottles of Canary which we had in Peckham Lane.' In some cases, boundary disputes were aggravated by perambulations diverting from previously agreed routes, a fairly common occurrence in areas where there were no natural features which could be used for demarcation. The usual solution (once agreement was reached) was to delineate the boundary with marker stones, some of which have survived and are marked on Ordnance Survey maps. There were also instances of new curates being encouraged to take different (and advantageous) routes from those of their predecessors: one such case reached the Exchequer Court in 1616! In the nineteenth century the members of parochial 'clubs', sometimes accompanied by a village band, would often perpetuate the tradition by disporting themselves around the parish boundaries at Rogationtide before repairing to a convenient field for dancing and other festivities (see FRIENDLY SOCIETIES).

Parish BOUNDARIES are shown on nineteenth-century tithe maps (see MAPS) and many will hardly have changed for a thousand years or more. Most boundaries follow lanes, streams or hedgerows (or the lines of former hedgerows, sometimes evident in cross-field footpaths) and there may even be a path following the boundary of the parish which is still known as a Procession Way, the route taken by the villagers on their annual perambulation. Sometimes these Procession Ways are still marked by boundary stones, each inscribed with a cross or the initials of the parish, and these may be shown on Ordnance Survey maps with the letters B.S. for 'Boundary Stone' (see MERE LANE). Even in towns they may still be found embedded in walls or preserved in the edge of pavements.

See also PROCESSIONS and TRINITY SUNDAY

PERIZONIUM The cloth worn about the waist by Christ on the Cross.

PERPENDICULAR PERIOD see ARCHITECTURAL PERIODS and MEDIEVAL ARCHITECTURE

PERPETUAL CURATE A priest nominated by a lay rector to serve a parish in which there was no regular endowed vicarage. As the name suggests, perpetual curates were appointed in perpetuity and once licensed by a bishop could not be removed.

Additional seating (and income) at Tintinhull, Somerset.

PETER'S PENCE (ST. PETER'S PENCE)
Alternatively known as Pentecostals, Romescot and Smoke Penny, St. Peter's Pence was a tribute of one penny for 'every hearth or house' paid annually on Lammas Day (1 August) to the Papal See. Instituted in *c.* 787, collection was often sporadic and the tax was discontinued by statute in 1534 and the funds diverted to the Crown.
See also PENTECOSTALS

PETRA SANCTA, SYLVESTER (SYSTEM) *see* COLOURS (HERALDIC)

PEW RENTING (*CONDUCTIO SEDILIUM*)
Writing in the late eighteenth century, Gilbert White, the naturalist and antiquarian, described his church at Selborne in Hampshire: '. . . nothing can be more irregular than the pews of this church which are of all dimensions and heights, being patched up according to the fancy of the owners.' White's experience was not unusual for in the seventeenth and eighteenth centuries the order of seating in parish churches reflected a rigid social structure and was regarded as a matter of the utmost importance by those concerned (*see* EIGHTEENTH-CENTURY CHURCH *and*

SEVENTEENTH-CENTURY CHURCH). Rented accommodation varied from elaborate and often ostentatious family pews (*see* PEWS, FAMILY) to rectangular high-sided box pews, which provided comparative privacy and comfort (*see* PEWS), and benches which were reserved for particular farmsteads and tenements. Of course, additional rented accommodation resulted in additional income for the CHURCHWARDENS, often to the exclusion of those who could not afford to pay for their seats and were crowded together on makeshift forms in the aisles and galleries (*see* BENCHES AND BENCH ENDS). It is little wonder, therefore, that so many turned to the nonconformist chapels which were relatively free from social snobbery.

Inevitably, pew renting created all sorts of problems as the local establishment jostled for position. When Lord Ashburnham arrived at Ampthill, Bedfordshire, in the late seventeenth century he complained that he could not take his family to church '. . . for I have not due and proper accommodation'. Rather than invite the entire congregation to move one step down the social ladder, the churchwardens resolved their dilemma by erecting a galleried pew designed by Sir Christopher Wren and furnished with silk hangings and easy chairs with velvet cushions! In 1806 the editor of *The Royal Cornwall Gazette* complained of the inadequate seating at his local church: 'I have been nearly three years resident in this town . . . I have a pretty numerous family, eight children (with a probability of more) besides apprentices. It is my wish to bring up this numerous family [as] members of our Church Establishment, and, with this in view I have to find me room in the church. I am now again called upon for payment of the Church rate, without yet being able to get my family accommodated within its walls.' He concluded by threatening to remove his family and apprentices to the dissenting chapel where the 'doors are ever open . . .'.

In some parishes, those who rented pews were expected to maintain them and, after decades of 'do-it-yourself' repairs and decorating, the naves of many churches must have been as cluttered and 'irregular' as that of Gilbert White's Selborne. No doubt it was for this reason that in 1808 the vestry at Burton Bradstock in Dorset ordered that '. . . the present Pews and Seats be all numbered and entered on the Church Book, expressing to whom they belong, and in what Right, at the expence of the Parish, and that all persons desirous of Painting their seats shall be at liberty to do so, provided they agree to follow a uniform and regular plan to be laid down by the Minister and Church Wardens.'

The practice of pew renting was suppressed in the mid-nineteenth century and many of the old pews replaced during Victorian restorations (*see* NINETEENTH-CENTURY CHURCH). Examples which still bear the names of the farms to which they were allotted may be seen at Sutton Mallett in Somerset and West Grinstead in Sussex, while at Icklingham in Suffolk the seats are still 'graded' with the best quality pews at the front, the less comfortable ones further back and plain benches (without backs) at the rear.

PEWS Pews are enclosed benches, though the terms are considered by some to be synonymous (*see* BENCHES AND BENCH ENDS). Seventeenth- and eighteenth-century box pews were wainscotted and provided with doors to protect the occupants from drafts (*see* PEW RENTING). After the Reformation, the altar was no longer the focus of attention but the prayer-desk and pulpit and it was to these that the congregation was directed when box pews were installed. Certain 'square pews' were reserved for specific families and were upholstered and often curtained. Others were even more lavishly equipped and furnished, often with a fireplace and private doorway from the churchyard (*see* PEWS, FAMILY). Such 'parlour pews' were sometimes converted CHANTRY CHAPELS, such as that of the Long

family in Draycot Cerne church near Chippenham in Wiltshire and the Hungerford chantry in Salisbury Cathedral which was 'appropriated as a seat for mayor and bishop in sermon time' (Hutchins). Pews were often reserved for a mayor and corporation, as at Lyme Regis in Dorset where the original fittings for the mace and civic regalia are still in place.
See also SEVENTEENTH-CENTURY CHURCH

PEWS, FAMILY Family PEWS, providing private accommodation within a church, developed in England in the late sixteenth century. As symbols of superiority, they assumed the mantle of the medieval chantry chapels, indeed a number of chapels were adopted as family pews including those at Kedington, described by Betjeman as the 'Westminster Abbey of Suffolk', and Tawstock in Devon where the splendid Renaissance pew of the Earls of Bath is reminiscent of a large, canopied four-poster bed. In the seventeenth and eighteenth centuries the order of seating in parish churches reflected a rigid social structure which was regarded as a matter of the utmost importance by those

The elevated Milbanke pew at Croft, Yorkshire.

Georgian box pews at Molland, Devon.

concerned (*see* PEW RENTING). At Tibenham in Norfolk, the Buxton family pew of 1665 is approached by means of a stair in the south aisle, while at Stokesay in Shropshire there is a 'double-decker' canopied family pew dating from the mid-seventeenth century when the nave and chancel were rebuilt and the interior refurbished.

After the Reformation, the altar was replaced by the prayer-desk and pulpit as the focus of attention and seating was arranged accordingly – with the best view reserved for the family pew. At Croft-on-Tees in Yorkshire, for example, a wide balustraded staircase leads to the seventeenth-century elevated pew of the Milbanke family, an extraordinary construction which projects like a huge theatre box on columns above the north side of the nave.

Inevitably, the family pew developed into a cosy furnished apartment with upholstered armchairs, table, carpet and fireplace. These 'parlour pews' often had their own private entrance from the great house, as at Gatton in Surrey where Lord Monson's magnificent nineteenth-century parlour pew occupies the north transept, directly opposite a gallery in the south transept from which the pulpit is

suspended. Lord Ashburnham's pew at Ampthill in Bedfordshire was designed by Sir Christopher Wren and occupies an entire gallery. It was embellished with green silk, sprinkled with gold, and had easy chairs of green taffeta with gold velvet cushions. At Whitby in Yorkshire the Cholmley pew is raised on four huge columns and divides the chancel from the nave in the manner of a medieval rood loft. There are other notable examples of parlour pews at Colebrooke in Devon, Cottesbrooke in Northamptonshire, Croft in Yorkshire, Heveningham in Suffolk and Melton Constable in Norfolk.

One of the most ostentatious of family pews is that in the superb continental baroque church of St. Lawrence Whitchurch, Little Stanmore (Edgware, London) which was rebuilt by John James in 1715 for James Brydges, first Duke of Chandos (1674–1744) (*see* EIGHTEENTH-CENTURY ARCHITECTURE). The three-box pew in the west gallery is provided with painted 'curtains' held by naked cherubs and a broad oak staircase by which the Duke would ascend to take his place at services, high above the heads of the commonalty and directly facing the altar behind which was the organ on which

343

George Frideric Handel (1685–1759) accompanied his Chandos Anthems. Tradition has it that the Duke and his family occupied the centre box (with its fireplace – now concealed by panelling), his bodyguard the small box at the head of the stairs, and the servants, in their several degrees, the plain tiered seating in the box on the south side.
See also BENCHES AND BENCH-ENDS, EIGHTEENTH-CENTURY CHURCH *and* SEVENTEENTH-CENTURY CHURCH

PEWTER From the Old French *peutre*, a grey alloy: usually twenty parts of tin to three of lead and one of brass. Widely used from the Roman period to the nineteenth century for drinking vessels, plates etc.. In 1348, a number of reputable pewter-makers, anxious to maintain the standards of their craft, formed themselves into a guild which for one and a half centuries regulated the lead content in pewter. Later legislation required that each pewterer should have his own mark (*touch mark*) which was to be recorded on a *touch-plate* at the Pewterers' Hall. The original plates were lost in the Great Fire of London in 1666 but a new series was struck in 1668 and this included the marks of many of the established pewter-makers. Individual pieces of pewter may be identified by reference to: (i) a touch mark, in a variety of styles, shapes and designs, which identifies the pewterer; (ii) a hallmark, usually four punched marks, which is of no significance other than to confirm the identity of a particular pewterer (introduced in *c.* 1635); (iii) a rose and crown which, from *c.* 1566, is indicative of quality; (iv) a crowned X, believed to be a quality mark signifying use of a particularly hard pewter alloy.
For the Pewter Society *see* APPENDIX II.
See also METALS *and* PLATE
Further reading:
Hull, C., *Pewter*, Aylesbury, 1992
Peal, C., *British Pewter and Britannia Metal*, London, 1971

PEWTER TOUCHES *see* PEWTER

PHARMACY The infirmarer of a medieval religious house was expected to be skilled in the use of herbs obtained either from the community's *herbarium* or purchased elsewhere. His pharmacy was usually located within the infirmarer's chambers and most monastic libraries included reference books (*herbals*) to assist him. Sage was provided for those who had been bled (*for* PHLEBOTOMY *see* MONASTIC BUILDINGS) and monastic observances required the infirmarer always to have 'ginger, cinnamon, peony and the like', ready in his cupboard.
See also INFIRMARY

PHLEBOTOMY *see* MONASTIC BUILDINGS

PHOENIX *see* BEASTS (HERALDIC)

PHOTOGRAPHS Photographs are an essential source of information for the local historian but it should be remembered that the apparent pomposity of Victorian life as we now observe it in many early photographs is more the result of the way in which the images were recorded than of the attitudes of the subjects themselves. Until the 1870s life in photographs always had to be arranged and organized: it was rarely spontaneous. The arrival of a photographer's van was an event of considerable significance in a small community, with everyone making a point of passing that way at least once in order to watch the goings-on or even to be persuaded to pose for posterity. Many of the subjects in the earliest photographs were born well before the invention of photography. Some may have been veterans of Waterloo or were octogenarians, born when many of the states of America were still British colonies. As documentary evidence photographs have much to say of England's social history and landscape but, particularly in the nineteenth century, there is also much that is contrived. Just as today, we are presented with that which the photographer wishes to communicate, so the Victorian or Edwardian camera-man selected his subjects with care, a selection which may tell us as much about contemporary attitudes as the photographs themselves. Whether the subjects appear happier or wiser than their successors is debatable, but what is certain is that they lived very different lives: an ordered and comparatively peaceful existence that was to change forever in August 1914. There are numerous collections, mostly dating from the first decades of the present century, both in private archives and in those of county museums and record offices. Many are of villages, including innumerable churches, while others boast of Edwardian civic pride and architectural achievement. Undoubtedly the most interesting photographs of this period are those of former rural landscapes which are now buried beneath suburbia. 'Before and after' photographs of church restorations were often commissioned by churchwardens and provide evidence of the appearance of a church before restoration or even demolition (the photographic libraries of local newspapers are a useful source). In the first decades of the present century, photographs of even the most modest churches were published as postcards and these became so popular that they can still be found (often in large numbers) in most antiquarian and second-hand book shops. One of the joys of holidaying in Britain is the possibility of discovering a rare photograph of one's parish church – three hundred miles from home in a back-street book shop in Carlisle! Indeed, the chances of such a discovery increase with distance, 'local' photographs invariably being the most sought-after.

There is a major collection of early photographs at the Museum of English Rural Life at the University of Reading and the notable Fox Talbot collection is now housed at the Science Museum, London (*see* APPENDIX II).

Further reading:

Dorrell, P., *Photography in Archaeology and Conservation*, Cambridge, 1989

Oliver, G., *Photographs and Local History*, London, 1989

Riley, D., *Air Photography and Archaeology*, London, 1989

PIER A solid support of brick or masonry carrying a LINTEL or the downward thrust of an ARCH. A pier is composed of four parts: the ABACUS (from which the arch springs), the CAPITAL (immediately below the abacus), the shaft (which may be oval, rectangular or multiform), and the BASE. In MEDIEVAL ARCHITECTURE the term is synonymous with *pillar*, but it is not the same as COLUMN or PILASTER both of which have a capital and base of a CLASSICAL ORDER. An arch which springs from a pier is called a *pier arch* while a *half-pier*, which is set within a wall and carries one end of an arch, is known as a *respond*. *Fluting* is vertical channelling in the shaft and a pier which is surrounded by clusters of attached or detached shafts is a *compound* or *clustered pier*. An ENGAGED pier (also *applied* or *attached*) is one where part of its surface is in contact with a wall. A slender pier dividing a large doorway is known as a *trumeau*.
See also ARCADE *and* BAY

PIETA In religious art, a representation of the Virgin Mary lamenting over the body of Christ which she supports on her knees.

PILARETTE (PILASTERETTE) A diminutive form of the PILASTER.

PILASTER A rectangular classical column partly built into, partly projecting from, a wall.
See also LESENE

PILASTER STRIP Correctly, the term PILASTER should be applied only to classical architecture. Nevertheless, the term 'pilaster strip' is often used to describe a LESENE: a shallow pier, without capital or base, attached to a wall. Pilaster strips are a characteristic feature of ANGLO-SAXON ARCHITECTURE. There are good examples at Earl's Barton in Northamptonshire and Worth in Sussex.

PILGRIMAGE OF GRACE, THE (1536–7) Multiple insurrection in the northern counties of England motivated by widespread resentment of Thomas Cromwell's ecclesiastical, administrative and fiscal reforms. The Pilgrimage of Grace was in essence a huge and popular demonstration of disgust. It encompassed the northern lords, whose traditional independence was threatened by Cromwell's new centralised (southern) administration, and many who were oppressed by Cromwell's novel taxes and consequently distrusted the King's new 'low-born' counsellors. Above all there were those who deeply resented the religious changes, again imposed centrally, and wished to return to the customs of former times. Yet even within these forces of religious conservatism there were disparate elements: some wishing to return to Rome and others accepting the royal supremacy but seeking the restoration of their ancient practices and privileges. In particular the DISSOLUTION OF THE MONASTERIES, a highly visible operation which affected the structure of society, provided a focus for discontent. King Henry responded at first with incredulity and then with ferocity – tempered by the practicalities of the situation (there was no standing army and loyal forces were difficult to muster) and the advice of the Duke of Norfolk who had been entrusted with pacifying the North. A general pardon was granted to those north of Doncaster for all offences committed before 7 December, 1536. Even so, over two hundred rebels were eventually executed, including Robert Aske, the leader of the Yorkshire rebels.
See also REFORMATION, THE

PILGRIMAGES *see* SHRINES

PILGRIM CROSSES *see* GRAFFITI, SHRINES *and* VOTIVE CROSSES

PILGRIMS *and* **PILGRIMS' WAY** *see* HOLY WELLS *and* SHRINES

PILLAR *see* PIER

PILLAR PISCINA A free-standing PISCINA.

PINFOLD *see* POUNDS

PINNACLE A miniature spire constructed both as a decorative termination to a BUTTRESS or PARAPET and to provide additional weight in order to counteract the outward thrust of a vault or spire. Pinnacles were added to the TOWERS of many parish churches in nineteenth century, as 'Gothic' features, together with castellated parapets.

PISCINA A stone basin in which a priest rinsed the chalice and paten after MASS (*see* ABLUTIONS). A piscina is usually set within a FENESTELLA (a canopied niche) in the south wall of the PRESBYTERY and this may also contain SEDILIA (seats), a CREDENCE (shelf) and AUMBRY (cupboard). In churches where the chancel has been

lengthened there may be two piscinas, that to the west being the earlier. Evidence of piscinas elsewhere in a church (typically, at the eastern end of an aisle) is indicative of a former side-chapel and altar (*see also* SQUINT). A small number of piscinas have survived in PORCHES, though they are similar in appearance to HOLY WATER STOUPS. From the piscina a drain conveyed the water (itself sanctified through contact with the Elements) to the consecrated ground of the churchyard. Occasionally this drain is continued by means of a bracket projecting from the exterior wall: at Skelton and Skipwith in Yorkshire, for example. Having been in contact with the Elements (the Host and the wine which were believed to have been transubstantiated into the body and blood of Christ), and with the sacred vessels in which they were contained, the priest would also wash his fingers over the piscina (*see* LAVABO). Some late thirteenth- and early fourteenth-century piscinas have two basins: one for the vessels and the other for the hands, as at Cherry Hinton in Cambridgeshire, Barnston in Essex and Carleton Rode in Norfolk. There is a rare set of twelfth-century piscina, lavabo and double aumbry at Ledbury in Herefordshire, while a piscina at the early twelfth-century church at Torpenhoe in Cumbria is believed to be of Roman origin. *Angle piscinas*, cut out of the eastern jamb of a south window and with openings to the north and west, are a feature of several East Anglian churches, notably Great Snoring in Norfolk. A unique piscina at Oare in Somerset is carved in the form of a head supported by two hands. In some churches the piscina is free-standing on a pillar and is then termed a *pillar piscina*: at Finchampstead in Berkshire and Penmon Priory, Anglesey, for example. At Tirley, on the banks of the Severn in Gloucestershire, the piscina is almost at floor level, the original floor having been raised to prevent the church being flooded.
See also CHANCEL VENTILATOR

PISTRINUM *see* BAKEHOUSE

PIT MONEY A customary burial fee.

PITTANCE A modest addition to a normally frugal monastic meal, usually in celebration of a liturgical feast or some other event in the community's life.

PLACE-NAMES AND FIELD-NAMES Place-names and field-names are an indispensable source of information for those who are researching the history of a parish. They can provide clues to features of the landscape which are no longer apparent, to manorial lordships in names such as Okeford Fitzpaine and Redmarley D'Abitot, and glimpses of the people who once lived in a place – Gylla's people who occupied a Dark Age homestead

(*ham*) at Gillingham, for example. Most names were not originally given to villages, of which there were very few before the eighth century, but to earlier TOWNSHIPS and locations in which villages were later established and from which the names were devolved. It should also be remembered that names recorded in the DOMESDAY survey refer to feudal estates and not necessarily to villages.

The superficial interpretation of modern forms of place-names can be extremely misleading, for names which may appear to be derived from the same source may have originated in entirely different etymons. Highlow in Derbyshire, Highnam in Gloucestershire and Highway in Wiltshire, for example, seem to possess a common element. But Highlow is derived from the Old English *heah hlaw* meaning 'high hill', Highnam from *hiwan hamm* meaning 'the monks' meadow' and Highway from the West Saxon *hïeg* and the Old English *weg*, together meaning 'a track along which hay is carried.'

Place-names may contain linguistic elements culled from Anglo-Norman, British, East Frisian, East Saxon, Flemish, Frisian, German, Gaelic, Gaulish, Greek, Gothic, Indo-Germanic, Irish, Latin, Low German, Middle Welsh, Norwegian, Old Breton, Old British, Old Cornish, Old Danish, Old Dutch, Old English (or Anglo-Saxon), Old East Scandinavian and West Saxon sources. Add to this the distinct possibility of corruption through illiteracy, dialectal modification and selective pronunciation and one will begin to appreciate the complexity of accurate interpretation.

With the diversity of meanings which may be derived from a single element, experts will normally turn to documentary evidence in order to establish the earliest recorded form of a name and may also consider the topography of a particular area before selecting that interpretation which they believe to be most appropriate. For the amateur historian, the series of county books published by the English Place-Name Society are invaluable. Each book is devoted to a county, or to groups of hundreds within a county, and place-names, field-names, street names and the names of properties are given in considerable detail. (It is advisable to obtain a copy of Volume I which explains the methodology and abbreviations used in the other volumes. *For* address *see* APPENDIX II.)

MONASTIC AND ECCLESIASTICAL PLACE-NAMES
The extraordinary number and diversity of monastic place-names bear witness to the prosperity of the medieval Church. Most names originated in endowments of lands, for the benefit of both a religious order and the soul of the benefactor, or were granted in return for corrodies (*see* CORRODY). Some recall the sites of minor religious houses, usually dependencies or granges (*see* GRANGE), and a small number commemorate

former abbeys, as at Cerne Abbas in Dorset (*abbas*, from the Latin for 'abbot'). Typical are names such as Abbotsbury ('the manor of the abbot'), Friar Waddon ('the hill of the friars where woad grew'), Whitchurch Canonicorum ('the stone church of the canons'), Toller Fratrum ('land by the Toller stream belonging to the brethren') and Maiden Newton ('the new homestead of the sisters'), all in Dorset; White Ladies Aston ('the eastern homestead of the [Premonstratensian] Canonesses') in Worcestershire; Newton Abbot ('the new homestead of the Abbot') and Monkton ('the homestead of the monks') in Devon; two villages of Stoke Prior, one in Herefordshire and the other in Worcestershire ('the prior's place' or or possibly 'the prior's cell') and Fryerning ('the place of the brothers') in Essex. Not all are strictly monastic: the 'brothers' who dwelt at Fryerning were Knights Hospitaller and canons could be either priests in canonical orders or the secular canons of a cathedral who held prebends (*see* PREBEND). At Canons Ashby in Northamptonshire a fragment of the former priory remains in Anglican use, Nunthorpe in Yorkshire was 'the [dependent] community of the nuns', while Nunney in Somerset was 'the island of the nuns' (though an alternative interpretation is 'the island of *Nunna*'). Place-name elements such as the Welsh *llan* and the Cornish *lan* (both meaning 'church') and *clas* (the Welsh for a monastic community or college) are indicative of ancient Celtic religious sites, while *kirk* ('church'), *minster* (*see* MINSTER), and (in some instances) *stoc* ('monastery' or 'cell') and *stow(e)* ('holy place', 'hermitage' or 'monastery') have similar Anglo-Saxon connotations. *Stow(e)* in particular is often joined with a saint's name as a first element (as in Bridestowe, Edwinstowe, Felixstowe etc.) meaning 'a place dedicated to Saint Bride, Saint Edwin, Saint Felix etc.'. Minster place-names are ubiquitous: Yetminster, Wimborne Minster, Minster Lovell, Minsterworth and so on.

It should be noted, however, that many monastic and ecclesiastical place-names indicate the possession of an estate rather than the existence of a religious community, as Tooting Bec reminds us that it once formed part of the considerable possessions of the great Norman house at Bec and had a Benedictine cell while, in Dorset, the manor of Stour Provost was held by the Provost and Scholars of King's College, Cambridge who, in 1830, still maintained small lifehold tenements and pastures open to common grazing. Similarly, many feudal affixes have ecclesiastical origins: in Somerset, for example, the manor of Templecombe was held by the Knights Templar and the present parish incorporates the former manor of Abbas Combe which was held by the Abbess of Shaftesbury. (For 'Temple' place-names *see* TEMPLAR, KNIGHTS.) In Dorset, the medieval Caundle Episcopi, once held by the bishops of Sarum, became Caundle Bishop and remained so until recently when it was translated to Bishops Caundle (Latin *episcopus* = 'bishop'). But place-names can be deceptive. In the same group of villages Purse Caundle is believed to have derived from the Old English *preost*, meaning 'priest', for it was a manor of Athelney Abbey. But there is also evidence of a thirteenth-century armigerous Purse family whose Dorset ancestors are said to have held a manor of that name from 1055. Place-names can originate in local traditions which are not always accurate: in the twelfth century, the hamlet of Hermitage in Dorset was known as Rocombe and the 'hermitage' was, in fact, a minor Augustinian priory.

Street names may also afford clues to the location of a former religious house. At Bicknacre in Essex, for example, where Augustine's Way and Priory Lane refer to the former priory of Austin canons, though Monks' Mead in the same town is clearly a later (and erroneous) designation. London has many ecclesiastical street names, notably Canongate, Minories and St. Sepulchregate, while Blackfriars, Whitefriars and Greyfriars are common in many towns (*see* FRIARS). Names of individual buildings may be indicative of former ecclesiastical use: Abbey, Chantry, Grange, Hermitage, Priory are obvious examples, but they should always be approached with caution.

LATIN PLACE-NAMES

Latin prepositions used as place-name elements probably originated in medieval legal documents which were, of course, written in Latin. Deeds transferring or delineating land often distinguished between settlements which otherwise had no means of individual identity by describing them as Upper and Lower Slaughter (Gloucestershire), Great and Little Tew (Oxfordshire) and so on. Sometimes the Latin original was retained as with Minterne *Magna* (Greater) and Minterne *Parva* (Lesser), Toller Fratrum (which belonged to the brothers of Forde Abbey) and Toller Porcorum (which was apparently renowned for its pigs). Many settlements with Latin names have survived in isolation, their former neighbours having been abandoned (*see* DESERTED VILLAGES). Ryme Intrinseca (Inner Ryme), for example, was so described to distinguish it from the village of Ryme Extrinseca (Outer Ryme) of which no trace remains. All the foregoing are in Dorset, a county rich in Latinised place-names. Other common Latin place-name elements include *ambo* ('both', usually a combination of two parishes), *canonicorum* ('of the canons'), *cum* ('with', possibly combined parishes), *ducis* ('of the duke'), *episcopi* ('of the bishop'), *fratrum* ('of the brethren'), *in* ('among'), *juxta* ('alongside'), *monachorum* ('of the monks'), *regis* ('of the king'), *sororum* ('of the sisters'), *sub* ('under') and *super* ('on'). In the foregoing, 'of the . . .' may imply a manor held by feudal tenancy.

FIELD-NAMES

Rapid technological innovation in late twentieth-century agriculture has not diminished the need for field-names. Adam's Bounty, Wimberry Slade, Gallows Jack, Galloping Meadow and Partridge Place are precise locations whose characteristics are as familiar to today's solitary tractor driver as they were to his more numerous predecessors, though perhaps less intimately so. Field-names are of considerable interest to local historians, especially those who are endeavouring to locate former GLEBE or monastic holdings or to trace parish BOUNDARIES and PERAMBULATIONS. It should be remembered, however, that field boundaries have often been re-defined or removed to amalgamate fields and their names may have changed or been lost with them. Names may also have been corrupted: at Long Burton in Dorset a field described as West Hall Water in the eighteenth century was recorded as Whistle Water on the tithe map of 1842. Clearly, the commissioner had difficulty in interpreting the Dorset vernacular!

Generally, field-names are more interesting (and informative) in those areas which have remained unaffected by Parliamentary enclosures. Even so, some of the names chosen in the eighteenth and nineteenth centuries may still provide clues to the past: barrows that have been lost to the plough, demolished buildings, half-forgotten religious sites or the lingering spectres of demons and hobgoblins in some sequestered corner of a farm.

When researching field-names one should always begin with those who have actually worked the land and are able to recall workaday names from memory. These should then be compared with the field-names recorded in tithe maps, drawn as a result of the granting of tithe awards in many parishes following the Tithe Commutation Act of 1836 (*see* TITHES). Numerous estate and other maps, on which field boundaries are delineated and names given, may be found in the archives of county record offices (*see* MAPS). Many estate maps are still held in private ownership and again a county record office should be able to assist with information and guidance.

For Holywell place-names *see* HOLY WELLS.

For the English Place Names Society *see* APPENDIX II.

Further reading:

Cameron, K., *English Place Names*, London, 1988

Ekwall, E., *The Concise Oxford Dictionary of English Place-Names*, Oxford, 1980

Field, J., *English Field Names*, Newton Abbot, 1972

Gelling, M., *Signposts to the Past*, (2nd edn.) London, 1988

——, *Place Names in the Landscape*, London, 1984

Room, A., *Dictionary of Place-Names*, London, 1989

Smith, A., *English Place Name Elements*, Cambridge, 1956 (reprinted 1970)

PLAGUE During the first decades of the fourteenth century climatic changes resulted in a series of poor harvests causing starvation and malnutrition which, by the 1330s, had debilitated the peasant population of Europe. Recent evidence has shown that by 1341, eight years before the arrival of the *Black Death* in England, many villages were already depopulated and their lands left uncultivated. It is now clear, therefore, that climatic change, famine and depopulation preceded the plague and, by reducing immunity to disease, contributed to its virulence.

The Black Death of 1349/50 first arrived in Britain through ports in the West Country (traditionally Melcombe Regis in Dorset) and is generally believed to have been a form of bubonic plague, though some scholars have suggested that it was anthrax. The initial symptoms, a blackish often gangrenous pustule at the point of a flea bite, was followed by an enlargement of the lymph nodes in the armpits, groin or neck. Haemorrhaging occurred beneath the skin causing the purplish blotches called *buboes* from which the bubonic plague is named. Cells died in the nervous system, which may explain the *danse macabre* ritual which often accompanied the Black Death, and between fifty and sixty per cent of victims died. The disease was carried by fleas living in the fur of black rats (*Rattus rattus*) and would have passed to humans only when so many rats had died that the fleas were forced to adopt unfamiliar human hosts. (Female black rats were capable of producing two hundred offspring a year. In Britain the species is believed to have become extinct in the wild in 1988.)

The fourteenth-century pandemic probably originated in Mongolia in the 1320s and reached Europe by *c.* 1347. Amazingly, there was no attempt to prevent its spreading across the English Channel or even to discourage contact with the stricken Continent. Indeed two weeks before the plague's arrival the Archbishop of York was warning of its inevitability, and of 'the sins of men, whose prosperity has made them complacent and who have forgotten the generosity of God.' Presumably, he was not referring to the emaciated peasantry. When it finally struck, the only provision made by the establishment was the excavation of mass grave-pits (not to be confused with mortuary holes – *see* BURIALS). At Clerkenwell, outside the walls of London, 50,000 corpses were buried in a 13–acre cemetery established by Walter de Manny who later founded a Carthusian monastery on the site as a memorial to the dead. This later became the Charterhouse, the cloister, chapel and gatehouse of which have survived, as have the foundations of the original cemetery chapel in which penitential services were held during the Black Death. At Clerkenwell a small lead cross was placed on the chest of each victim before burial.

Estimates of the numbers who died during the Black Death vary enormously but at least twenty per cent of the population must have perished in this way and some historians have proposed figures of forty or even fifty per cent. 'To our great grief the plague carried off so vast a multitude of people that it was not possible to find anybody to carry the corpses to the cemetery,' wrote a fourteenth-century monk of Rochester in Kent, '. . . mothers and fathers carried their own children on their shoulders to the church and dropped them in the common pit . . . such a terrible stench came from these pits that hardly anyone dared to walk near the cemeteries.' The nobility and gentry, with a more reliable diet and a marginally greater perception of hygiene, fared somewhat better, though neither rank nor privilege brought immunity: at Crich in Derbyshire a local knight, William de Wakebridge, erected a tiny CHANTRY CHAPEL to the memory of his wife, father, two sisters and three brothers all of whom had been cut down by the plague in the summer of 1349. At Gloucester the terrified inhabitants barred the city gates to refugees fleeing from plague-stricken Bristol, while at Winchester the populace was urged to parade barefoot round the market place and to recite the seven penitential psalms three times a week – but to no avail, for well over half the population perished.

The effects of depopulation are evident in the commercial and agricultural decline of many communities and in a marked deterioration in craftsmanship. At Ledbury church in Herefordshire, for example, the mid-fifteenth-century decorative capitals of the north arcade are of significantly inferior workmanship to those of the south arcade which were carved in c. 1340. Many settlements became moribund, though (contrary to popular belief) only a small number of villages were abandoned as a direct result of the plague (see DESERTED VILLAGES).

Further outbreaks of bubonic and (possibly) pneumonic plague occurred until the eighteenth century, notably a virulent epidemic in London vividly described in 1665 by the diarist, John Evelyn: 'Came home, there perishing near 10,000 poor creatures weekly; however I went all along the city and suburbs from Kent Street to St. James's, a dismal passage, and dangerous to see so many coffins exposed in the streets, now thin of people, the shops shut up, and all in mournful silence, not knowing whose turn it might be next.' It was the Great Fire of September 1666 which destroyed some 13,000 rat-infested houses and finally relieved London of the 'accursed pestilence'. The name Black Death dates from 1833 and is a translation from the German.
See also CELTIC CHURCH
Further reading:
Gottfried, R., *The Black Death: Natural and Human Disaster in Medieval Europe*, London
Ziegler, P., *The Black Death*, Stroud, 1990

PLAINSONG (*also* PLAINCHANT) The term is applied to the large body of traditional ritual melody of the Latin rite and is inextricably associated with monastic worship, especially that of the BENEDICTINES. Before there was any central authority to call upon, each monastery had its own musical tradition derived entirely from the skill and experience of its singers. Consequently every 'performance' was unique. The term plainsong emphasises the unadorned nature of the music, its free rhythm depending on accentuation of the words of the liturgy, sung in unison and with a single line of melody. Plainsong is unaccompanied and its scales (*modes*) run from D, E, F and G, the only accidental being a flattened B. It was introduced into England by Augustine in 597 but was largely lost at the REFORMATION though it continued in the Versicles (*see* VERSICLE) and Responses and was to influence the development of ANGLICAN CHANT. Promoted by the OXFORD MOVEMENT, plainsong enjoyed a revival in the nineteenth century and has subsequently been used (in modified form) for the PSALMS and in the liturgy generally.

Plainsong is synonymous with *Gregorian chant*, named after Pope Gregory the Great (d. 604) during whose papacy services were reorganised, choral scholars and choirs established in the Roman churches and the plainsong repertory reviewed and expanded.
See also ANTIPHON *and* CHURCH MUSIC (ANGLICAN)
Further reading:
Scholes, P., *The Oxford Companion to Music*, Oxford, 1970

PLAISTOW (*also* PLASTOW, PLASTER *and* PLAYSTOW) Derived from the Old English *pleg-stow* meaning 'a place for sport', plaistows were medieval playing fields where a community enjoyed its recreation. Some plaistow sites may also have been meeting places of manorial and hundred courts. Many occupied ancient earthworks, others comprised an enclosure adjacent to a parish church (*see* CHURCHYARDS) or an open space defined by a road junction at the centre of a village. Some are recalled in field and place-names such as Plestor at Selborne in Hampshire, the '*locus ludorum*, or play space . . . a level area near the church of about forty-four yards by thirty-six' in which 'a vast oak, with a short, squat body, and huge horizontal arms extending almost to the extremity of the area . . . surrounded with stone steps, and seats above them . . . the delight of old and young, and a place of much resort in summer evenings.' (Gilbert White 1789).

In 1474, one John Botryght, rector of Swaffham in Norfolk, provided the people of the parish with a croft in the town for use as a recreation ground. In return, he required that annual masses should be celebrated 'for the health of my soul' and stipulated that the croft was to be held by trustees who were to gather annually in the parish church to commemorate his death in a prescribed form. The churchwardens were to lease out the croft and to use its revenues to pay for the masses, any remaining funds to be spent on the fabric of the church. Whoever leased the croft was to make the land available . . .

> for all and each of the parishioners of the same town, in which they may play games, such as involve running, shooting [archery] and carrying out those things pertaining to military drill, and other honest games which it will please them to so, for evermore.

The croft donated by Botryght is also referred to as 'camping land', camp being an old (and unlawful) form of football in which players both kicked and ran with the ball.
See also CHURCH AND COMMUNITY

PLANETA A chasuble (*see* VESTMENTS).

PLASTERWORK Medieval plaster, for both interior and outdoor use, was made from lime, sand and water together with various other materials which were added to prevent cracking and to encourage binding. These included straw and hay, animal hair, feathers, dung and blood. *Plaster of Paris* was introduced into England in *c.* 1255. This was made by burning calcium sulphate (*gypsum*, obtained from the Montmartre area of Paris) which was mixed with water to produce a hard, high quality plaster. Initially, Plaster of Paris was expensive and was used only in important buildings, but when gypsum deposits were discovered in England (notably on the Isle of Purbeck in Dorset and in the Trent and Nidd valleys) its application became more widespread.

The ornate and decorative plaster ceilings of some sixteenth-, seventeenth- and eighteenth-century churches were clearly influenced by fifteenth-century Italian Renaissance work in *stucco duro*, a malleable plaster of lime, gypsum and powdered marble which set gradually, allowing time for the design to be executed, and produced a very hard, fine finish. To this the Elizabethans added a variety of ingredients including ale, beeswax and eggs. Plasterwork in the sixteenth and early seventeenth centuries was usually confined to ceilings: in the chancel of St. Nicholas at Abbotsbury in Dorset, for example, where there is a fine seventeenth-century ornamental plaster ceiling, and at East Brent in Somerset where the plaster ceiling of the nave (dated 1637) is similar to those found in houses of the period and probably covered what was by then an unfashionable medieval timber roof.

During the 1760s neo-classical styles became fashionable and architects such as Robert Adam (1728–92) incorporated the elegant motifs of classical Rome into the plasterwork of ceilings and walls. His designs were adaptable and could be made in a studio before being assembled on site. By the end of the century, a number of patent STUCCO products were available which (it was claimed) facilitated modelling and were of superior consistency and hardness. John Nash (1725–1835) also developed a plaster of sand, brick-dust, lead oxide and powdered limestone which had the appearance of stone and was intended for exterior use. Later, cement was added for this purpose and by 1840 a number of patent gypsum plasters were available, such as Keene's Cement. In 1856, the introduction of fibrous plaster, reinforced with a layer of hessian, enabled large sections of plasterwork to be pre-cast. A characteristic feature of the 1850s was the plaster ceiling rose from which hung a gas chandelier. The 'vitiated air' of burning gas lamps was removed by means of pipes, inserted in the ceiling rose, and venting to air-bricks in an outside wall.
See also ROOFS (TIMBER)

PLATE (CHURCH PLATE) Strictly speaking, 'plate' is a metal item which is 'plated' (coated) with gold. But the term is also used generically to describe articles of gold, silver and other metals required for the administration of the BLESSED SACRAMENTS, principally BAPTISM and EUCHARIST, (*sacramental plate*) and for other liturgical purposes including altar and processional crosses, candlesticks, alms dishes and so on (*liturgical plate*). In an age when many churches have to be locked for reasons of security, it is most unusual for plate to remain on public view. Indeed, many parishes have been forced either to deposit their plate for safe-keeping or to succumb to increasing economic pressures by selling it.

PRE-REFORMATION SACRAMENTAL PLATE
(* *see also* individual entries)

Asperges, a holy water sprinkler .*
Aspergillum, a small brush with a short handle for cleaning the altar table.
Chalice, the cup containing the consecrated wine.
Chrismatory which contains the Holy Oils.*
Ciborium, a covered vessel used for storing the Host. Similar in appearance to a chalice but with a rim (*bezel*) to accommodate the cover.*
Communion Plate, held beneath the chin of a communicant as he receives the Sacrament.
Cruets in which the wine and water were brought to the altar .*
Ewer, usually a flagon containing holy water for baptism .*
Monstrance, a container used for exposing the Host for veneration.*

Seventeenth-century chalice and paten.

Paten, the cover for the chalice. Used as a plate from which the Sacrament was served during the Eucharist.

Pax for the Kiss of Peace.*

Pyx, a small receptacle in which the Host is conveyed to the sick.*

Salver, a plate (larger than a paten) from which the Sacrament is served during the Eucharist.

Spoon, for measuring the water at the mixing of the chalice.

Tabernacle, a box-like container for the ciborium.*

Tazza, a wine cup with a shallow, circular bowl mounted on a foot. Similar in appearance to some patens or salvers.

Thurible (also *Censer*) for the ceremonial burning of incense.*

Viaticum, in which communion was carried to the dying.*

Wafer Box, a box for storing wafers, usually with a removable grid.*

Inventories provide a glimpse of the extraordinary richness of pre-Reformation plate, not only in the great abbeys, priories and cathedrals but also in many parish churches. Very little survived the DISSOLUTION OF THE MONASTERIES: some fifty-five chalices and ninety-five patens (strangely, half of them in Norfolk). Medieval chalices were usually of silver-gilt, from 15 cm to 20 cm in height (6 to 8 inches) with a spreading base (*foot*), stem and bowl ornamented with mouldings and polished stones (*cabushon*). The earliest chalices had wide, shallow,

hemispherical bowls, short (often plain) stems and circular bases. But from the mid-fourteenth century the bowl was more often conical and the base hexagonal (to prevent rolling when laid on its side) and there was often a CRUCIFIX on one side of the base. Tudor chalices (prior to the Reformation) had deeper, hemispherical bowls with ornate stems and bases and were often inscribed. There is a rare leather chalice case at Cawston in Norfolk.

The paten was a small, circular cover for the chalice which also served as a plate on which the Host was placed. There is usually a double depression at the centre of a paten and this often contains a decorative motif, the design of which may assist with dating. The Lamb of God (*Agnus Dei*) and (later) the Hand of God (*Manus Dei*) were the most common medieval motifs, set within a circular or quatrefoil-shaped depression. From the late-fourteenth century this was superseded by a sixfoil which usually contained a Head of Christ (*Vernicle*) or (later) a sacred monogram, usually *IHS (see* CHRISTIAN SYMBOLS), and the rim of the paten was more often circumscribed than previously. Inscriptions are in Latin, usually engraved in plain Lombardic unsials, commencing with a cross and the words separated by lozenge motifs.

It is no longer possible (or advisable) to detail with accuracy those churches which still possess medieval plate. There are, of course, splendid collections at various museums and cathedrals, notably Gloucester.

POST-REFORMATION COMMUNION PLATE

The medieval laity had been denied the Precious Blood of Christ at the Eucharist but, following the REFORMATION, communion in both kinds (i.e. both bread and wine) was restored and consequently larger vessels were required for serving the wine. These are known as communion cups and are more secular in appearance than earlier (or later) chalices. Elizabethan communion cups have elongated bowls, shaped like an inverted bell or bucket, trumpet or baluster-shaped stems and comparatively plain, circular bases. Many surviving early communion cups are, in fact, amalgamations of components from cups of different dates. Patens were also very different: they were slightly domed and, instead of simply resting on the the mouth of the cup, they were now provided with a bezel and a handle which served also as a base when the paten was turned over (*standing paten*). The covers of standing patens (known as *paten lids*) are sometimes an inverted copy of the base and in the sixteenth century were often used as covers for communion cups. Ornament was usually restricted to a single band of engraved foliage round the body of the cup and on the paten and sometimes the name of the parish was engraved on the cup. Jacobean cups are larger and even plainer, with bowls shaped like a truncated cone and stems with narrow, projecting collars.

There followed a variety of shapes and decorative forms which tend to reflect contemporary architectural styles. Seventeenth-century communion cups, for example, are generally plain with perhaps a single Christian or heraldic motif (see below) engraved on a beaker- or goblet-shaped bowl. *Covered patterns* of the period have spool feet and covers, resembling *ciboria*. Inscriptions are usually in English and in lettering similar to that used in contemporary monuments. Eighteenth-century plate is more ornate with (for example) engraved PUTTI round the base and fluting or foliated ornament and festoons of flowers and foliage on the bowl.

With the Gothic Revival, the term chalice was re-introduced, though nineteenth-century vessels are significantly larger than their medieval predecessors and are often heavily ornamented, especially the circular stems and conical bases which may be encrusted with mouldings and faceted stones.

HERALDRY ON CHURCH PLATE

Heraldry is usually indicative of a bequest or ownership but, as with some inscriptions, it may not be contemporaneous with the item on which it is engraved. For this reason coats of arms, crests, monograms and other personal devices cannot always be relied on for dating purposes. The arms of cathedral chapters, colleges and other bodies corporate were engraved on plate both for decorative purposes and to confirm ownership. From the fourteenth century, the ATTRIBUTED ARMS of saints and other CHRISTIAN SYMBOLS were popular and these may sometimes be mistaken for heraldic devices. In the Middle Ages, heraldic decoration was usually in translucent or *champlevé* enamel (see ENAMELLING) but, from the early sixteenth century, engraving was more popular and a system of hatched lines to represent colours developed (see COLOURS, HERALDIC). Some items of church plate may have originated in private chapels and the heraldry thereon will indicate ownership. An inventory of Sir John Fastolf (d. 1459) records that he possessed 13,000 ounces of domestic silverware and a further 1,200 ounces in his private chapel. Much of this would have been embellished with Fastolf heraldry and there can be little doubt that many items would have found their way into parish churches, usually as bequests. Indeed, many church vessels were originally intended for domestic purposes: the celebrated Boleyn Cup at Cirencester in Gloucestershire, for example, which once belonged to Anne Boleyn and was later given to the church as a chalice. *See also* CANDLESTICKS, COMMUNION LINEN, FLAGON, HALLMARKS, PEWTER, RESERVATION, SACRISTY, TANKARD *and* VEILS

Further reading:

Chessyre, H., *The Identification of Coats of Arms on British Silver*, London, 1978

Oman, C., *English Engraved Silver 1150–1900*, London, 1978

——, *English Church Plate*, Oxford, 1957

PLATE GLASS *see* WINDOWS

PLATE TRACERY *see* MEDIEVAL ARCHITECTURE

PLATINUM A rare, heavy white metal used on occasions for decorative purposes and for some modern church PLATE. Markings are similar to those for sterling silver (*see* HALLMARKS) except that 'an orb surmounted by a cross and encompassed by a pentagon' is used instead of the sterling mark.

PLAYSTOW *see* PLAISTOW

PLINTH The projecting base of a wall or column, usually chamfered or moulded at the top. A base supporting a vase, statue etc.

PLOUGH ALMS In Anglo-Saxon England, a penny paid annually (within a fortnight of Easter) by each plough team to the parish priest.

PLOUGH MONDAY The first Monday after EPIPHANY notable for jollifications and the collection of money offerings for church funds.

PLURALISM The holding simultaneously of two or more benefices, offices or sinecures (*pluralities*).

PLURALITIES ACT (1838) The first of a series of acts forbidding clergymen simultaneously to hold more than one benefice (*see* PLURALISM). An exception was made with regard to livings which were of limited value and in close proximity. The acts were effectively repealed by the Pastoral Reorganisation Measure of 1949.

PODIUM A continuous projecting base or pedestal to a building.

POINTED ARCH *see* ARCH

POINTS OF THE SHIELD The heraldic term *dexter* is derived from the Latin meaning both 'right' and 'favourable' and is used to describe the right-hand side of a shield of arms (the left when viewed from the front). Those who were right-handed were considered to be dexterous and to exercise dexterity.

Sinister is similarly derived from the Latin meaning both 'left' and 'perverse' and in heraldry is used to describe the left-hand side of a shield of arms (the right side when viewed from the front). In the Middle Ages, to be left-handed was considered to be unnatural and, therefore, 'sinister'.

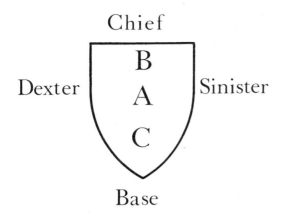

Chief

Dexter   **B**   Sinister
    A
    C

Base

Charges placed in the top portion of the shield are said to be *in chief* and those in the lower portion *in base*. There are three reference points in a shield: *fess point* at the centre (A) with *honour point* above (B) and *nobril point* below (C).
See also BLAZON

POLEYNS *see* ARMOUR

POLYCHROME In architecture, the use of different colours in a variety of materials to produce a decorative effect.

POLYPHANT STONE A grey-green Cornish potstone from quarries at Pollaphant between Bodmin and Launceton.

POMEGRANATE A popular decorative and heraldic motif. Specifically the (punning) device of Aragon which was introduced into England in 1501 by Queen Catherine (of Aragon) (1485–1536). As such it may occasionally be found in the fabric of

royal palaces and churches, despite the fact that most of Queen Catherine's devices were removed when she was supplanted in 1533 by Queen Anne (Boleyn) (*c.* 1504–36). The pomegranate is usually depicted with the skin split and the seeds showing through.

POMMEL The round end of a sword hilt, often decorated with an heraldic device (*see* ARMOUR).

PONTIFICAL The liturgical book containing the services to be performed only by bishops at confirmation, ordination etc. (*see* LITURGY).

POOR BOXES *see* ALMS BOXES

POOR CLARES A strictly contemplative order of nuns founded by St. Francis and St. Clare *c.* 1212–14. The order received its first rule in 1219 and by the fifteenth century was considered to be the most austere of all the women's orders.

POOR HOUSE Before the WORKHOUSES were built every parish owned a few cottages which were used to accommodate the poor. For the most part these were little better than hovels, damp and insanitary, with just one room and a ladder giving access to the roof space. Parishes also provided clothing, fuel and relief in cash. In 1715 Widow Fudge of Yetminster in Dorset was given five shillings to buy fuel for the winter, while at neighbouring Batcombe (where the former poor house is now an attractive cottage) the poor were permitted to remove fuel (usually furze) from a field which is still known as the Poor Lot. The parish also made provision for medical care and for burial. The Yetminster Vestry accounts record that 'Mr. Meech, apothecary of Cerne, to be paid five guineas per annum for physick and surgery except lying-in women and compound fractures'. In 1762 a grant of seven shillings and tenpence provided for a child's 'coffin, bell, grave, shroud and a drink'. Apprenticeships were also arranged for the sons of poor families, though these were not always in the immediate area and it was not uncommon for boys to be sent to London or to sea. In 1744 one James Eyles of Sherborne was indentured to Nathanial Brooks of Newfoundland, mariner, to 'learn the art and mystery of catching, curing and preserving fish.' One wonders whether he ever saw Dorset again.

POOR LAW Vagrancy was a perennial problem throughout the medieval period. From 1388 a labourer was prevented from leaving his parish without a testimonial from the local Justices, and any beggar who was unable to work could be returned to his place of birth. The *Statute of Mortmain* of 1391 required that in parishes where the rectorial tithes were held by an ecclesiastical or monastic foundation a proportion of that income was to be reserved for the relief of the poor. From 1494, able-bodied vagrants could be punished by whipping, the loss of an ear or even by hanging, and from 1530 those who were incapable of working were required to obtain a begging licence from the magistrates.

Following the DISSOLUTION OF THE MONASTERIES in 1536/39 responsibility for the maintenance of the impotent poor passed to the parishes. To discourage vagrancy, able-bodied vagrants were required to work and private alms-giving was made an offence, the penalty being a fine of ten times the amount given (though charitable donations could be solicited on Sundays by a parish priest and his wardens). In 1547 these measures were further modified so that a vagrant who refused to work could be branded with a V (for vagabond) and condemned to servitude for a period of two years. If he absconded during that time, he was adjudged a slave for life and branded with an S on his cheek. As a result many turned to outlawry (see OUTLAWS).

The Poor Law of 1563 required that 'two able persons or more shall be appointed gatherers and collectors of the charitable alms of all the residue of people inhabiting in the parish' and in 1572 the office of Overseer of the Poor was created, an elected parish official responsible for supervising endowments and charitable funds. From 1597 parishes were able to levy a poor rate: paupers were to be provided with work, and supplies of materials were kept for this purpose. In some areas the first POOR HOUSES were built as a result of this legislation. But it was the Poor Law Act which followed in 1601 which established the administrative pattern of relief for the next two centuries. Relief was to be available to three categories of person: the able-bodied (who were to be provided with work), the impotent poor and those who were unwilling to work. The churchwardens of each parish, together with two or more substantial landowners, were to act as Overseers of the Poor responsible for collecting the poor rate which was to be used:

> . . . for setting to work the children of all such whose parents shall not be thought able to maintain them'; '. . . for setting to work all such persons, married or unmarried, having no means to maintain them, and who use no ordinary or daily trade of life to get their living by'; '. . . for providing a convenient stock of flax, hemp, wood, thread, iron and other ware and stuff to set the poor on work . . . [and] 'for the necessary relief of the lame, impotent, old, blind, and such other among them being poor and not able to work.

The Law of Settlement Act of 1662 enabled overseers to remove from their parishes any stranger who was unable to persuade them of his ability to obtain work within forty days or who did not rent property worth £10 a year. A stranger could claim settlement in his adopted parish after forty days, and many parishes (known as *close parishes*) became adept at denying itinerant strangers *settlement certificates* which, once granted, entitled the holder to claim poor relief. Workers could obtain temporary employment in other parishes (at harvest time, for example) by means of certificates issued by the overseers of their home parishes which guaranteed that they would be taken back. Registers of those receiving poor relief were kept from 1691 and by the Settlement Act of 1697 paupers were required to wear a large letter P on their clothing together with the initials of their parish. The same Act enabled strangers to settle in a new parish if they could obtain a certificate from their home parish agreeing to take them back should they ever have need of poor relief.

Knatchbull's General Workhouse Act of 1723 empowered parishes, or groups of smaller parishes (*unions*), to build WORKHOUSES and by 1776 there were some 2,000 in England. At this time all paupers were generally confined to the precincts of the workhouse but Gilbert's Act of 1782 provided for the able-bodied to obtain work outside, indoor relief being available to the impotent poor. The Speenhamland System of the late eighteenth century encouraged employers to reduce wages in the knowledge that the parish would make up the difference. This resulted in a significant increase in claims for poor relief and eventually led to the Poor Law Amendment Act of 1834. This reduced greatly the provision of outdoor relief and encouraged administrators to make conditions in the workhouses as unpleasant as possible so that they should be perceived as a places of last resort.

The 1834 Act required that the Poor Law should be administered by three Commissioners, inspection being delegated to Assistant Commissioners to whom Boards of Guardians were responsible for the day-to-day management of parochial poor relief, though the vestries continued to levy the poor rate (see PARISH). These Boards of Guardians were elected locally, though the franchise was restricted to landowners and rate-payers whose incomes were assessed for the purpose, the wealthiest being allowed six votes. From 1847 the Poor Law Board was responsible for the administration of the Poor Law, though its work was carried out through civil servants, and in 1871 its duties were transferred to the newly established Local Government Board which was also responsible (among a variety of matters) for public health. Workhouses were re-named Poor Law Institutions in 1913, and in 1919 the Ministry of Health was made responsible for the Poor Law until the Local Government Act of 1929 by which the term 'pauper' was officially abolished, together with Boards of Guardians, and local authorities were encouraged to convert workhouses to infirmaries. The modern system of social security and other benefits was established in 1946.

The records of the Overseers of the Poor before 1834 were kept in vestry minutes which are now retained in the archives of county record offices where the later records of the Guardians of the Poor for individual parishes or unions may also be found. Rate books, in which payment of the poor rate was recorded, have often survived (usually from the eighteenth and nineteenth centuries) and are a particularly accurate source of information.

See also ARCHIVES *and* CHARITIES

Further reading:

Digby, A., *The Poor Law in Nineteenth-Century England and Wales*, London, 1982

Marshall, J., *The Old Poor Law 1795–1834*, London, (second edition) 1985

Wood, P., *Poverty and the Workhouse in Victorian Britain*, Stroud, 1991

POOR SOUL'S LIGHT A churchyard LANTERN in which a candle was lit to commemorate the souls of the impecunious departed. There is a rare late-thirteenth-century poor soul's light in the churchyard at Bisley in Gloucestershire.

POPERY A derogatory designation for the doctrines and practices of the Roman Catholic Church. The Declaration Against Popery (1677–1778) required all members of Parliament to denounce the Mass, the Invocation of Saints and the doctrine of transubstantiation.

POPISH PLOT, THE (1678–81) The supposed Roman Catholic (Jesuit) plot to assassinate Charles II and to place his brother James, Duke of York on the throne. Many people were executed as a consequence of false testimonies made by the conspiratorial clergyman Titus Oates (1649–1705).

POPPY HEADS Possibly derived from *puppis* meaning 'the figure head of a ship', poppy heads are ornamental finials at the tops of bench-ends. Common from the fifteenth century, in form they usually resemble a FLEUR-DE-LIS and are characteristic of bench-ends in East Anglian churches (*see* BENCHES AND BENCH-ENDS).

PORCHES Unlike the cathedrals and abbey churches with their great WEST DOORWAYS, the principal entrance to most medieval parish churches is by means of a door in the south wall of the nave and from the late twelfth century, this was almost invariably protected by a porch. Of course, there are also numerous examples of north-facing porches and many parish churches have west doors, several of which are provided with porches: at Eynsford in

Poppy head finial.

Kent and Yapton in Sussex, for example, and at Lyme Regis in Dorset where the remains of a Norman church now form the inner porch of the present building. Nevertheless, the principle of entering a church from the (consecrated) southern CHURCHYARD was well established by the eleventh century and where a fairly modest church is now entered from the north or west there is usually a historical or topographical reason for so doing. Some churches have retained both a south and a north door, the latter being provided for processional purposes, and both these may have porches (*see* PROCESSIONS). (Many north doors were blocked in the sixteenth century, though the outline may still be discernible in the masonry.)

ECCLESIASTICAL FUNCTIONS

The original purpose of the porch was to provide shelter for parishioners and to protect the church door from the weather. Consequently many early TYMPANA have been preserved (*see* MEDIEVAL ARCHITECTURE), together with several ancient SUNDIALS: that at Kirkdale in Yorkshire is nine hundred and fifty years old – though, deprived of sunlight, it no longer marks the passing of the hours. Increasingly, porches were used for liturgical purposes and as such attracted endowments so that the quality of stonework, vaulting and ornamentation is often superior to that of the church itself. BOSSES may bear the arms of the benefactor who paid for the porch, though at Cley in Norfolk the boss is carved with a boy, his trousers down, being caned: a salutary lesson for younger members of the congregation.

In the Middle Ages the traditional NEW FIRE was kindled and blessed in the porch on Holy Saturday as a symbol of spiritual renewal, and porches came to be associated with the right of sanctuary (*see* SANCTUARY, RIGHT OF). There is also evidence to suggest that, in some larger porches, a temporary gallery may have been erected from which garlands were strewn before the Palm Sunday procession: at Weston-in-Gordano in Avon, for example. Banns of marriage were announced in the porch and, providing there was no 'let or hindrance', it was there that the marriage contract was drawn up, later to be attested before the porch altar by the interested parties. A number of porch altars have survived, including one at South Poole in Devon (*see* ALTAR). Chaucer, in his Prologue to the *Canterbury Tales*, tells us that the Good Wife of Bath 'Housbones at chirche dore she hadde fyve', for at that time the first part of the marriage ceremony took place in the porch, including the placing of the ring on the bride's finger, before the couple entered the church for the wedding Mass (*see* MATRIMONY).

The CHURCHING OF WOMEN took place in the porch (women were denied admission to the church after childbirth until they had been 'churched') and the first part of the baptismal service was also held there, the priest receiving the sponsors with the infant in the porch before escorting them to the font which was usually located near the south door (*see* BAPTISM *and* FONTS). Having been met by the priest at the LICH-GATE, a funeral cortège would pause in the porch before moving to the chancel and, finally, to the committal (*see* BURIALS).

Where there were porch altars, PISCINAS would also have been provided, usually on the east wall of the porch near the inner door. Surviving porch piscinas are rare and are similar, both in appearance and location, to HOLY WATER STOUPS which were installed so that those entering the church could sign their bodies with holy water as an act of self-consecration and spiritual cleansing (*see also* GRAFFITI *and* VOTIVE CROSSES). Stoups, which are usually contained within a niche or supported on a shaft near the church door, are usually simple stone basins though there are more elaborate examples: that at Caldecote in Hertfordshire has an ornate traceried canopy.

SECULAR FUNCTIONS

There are many instances of porches which appear to be far too large for the churches to which they are attached. But their very size is indicative of their importance as centres of community life, exceeding even that of the NAVE (*see* CHURCH AND COMMUNITY). Business was transacted outside the south doorway and it was at the porch altar that contracts were signed. Executors of wills normally used the porch for distributing legacies to beneficiaries and, being the 'hub' of parochial activity, the porch was considered to be an appropriate place for the payment of debts because witnesses were readily available. On occasions, unidentified corpses would be laid out there – in the hope that someone would recognise them! Coroners' and manorial courts were often held in the church porch, as were VESTRY meetings: at Lillington in Dorset the annual (civil) parish meeting is still convened in the church porch. The stone benches which were provided for these purposes are often deeply incised where weapons and arrow-heads were sharpened in anticipation of Sunday practice at the butts (*see* ARCHERY).

Inevitably it was on the south door of the church that public notices were displayed, a tradition which persists in the publishing of electoral registers and notices of parliamentary and local government elections in church porches today. The parish stocks were sometimes stored (or even erected) in the church porch, a practice common to several Cornish churches, and occasionally the porch doubled as a village LOCK-UP. At Diss in Norfolk, the church-wardens' accounts for 1687 tell of money which was paid 'to the wench Eleanor that lay in the church porch at several times'. Eleanor was presumably a pauper, for there are many similar references to temporary lodgings being provided in church porches (*see* POOR LAW).

In order to accommodate these diverse functions, porches were sometimes constructed with an upper chamber so that business could be conducted more conveniently and cash and equipment (such as arms and armour) stored securely. The most complete strong-room (probably an armoury) is at Mendlesham in Suffolk. Many two-storey porches were built in the fourteenth and fifteenth centuries and a number of these were provided with fireplaces suggesting that they were used for a variety of purposes: by GUILDS, for example, or as school-rooms or libraries. The fifteenth-century porch at Northleach in Gloucestershire, described by Betjeman as 'the most lovely in all England', has among its many niches, turrets and pinnacles a concealed chimney flue. Others provided accom-modation for a priest, as at Guilsfield in Powys and Clun in Shropshire (a north porch) where the original priests' chambers were later used as school-rooms. Adjoining the porch at Guilsfield is a single-storey HEARSE HOUSE and therein a memorial to the churchwardens who erected it in 1739, while at Clun the porch contains a set of eighteenth-century BEQUEST BOARDS. In both cases, access to the upper storey was by means of a

The church of St. John the Baptist, Cirencester, Gloucestershire.

stair within the east wall of the porch, though at Clun only traces remain. There are splendid examples of two-storey porches at Malpas, Nantwich and Over in Cheshire and Pulham St. Mary in Norfolk, and of three-storeyed porches at Astbury in Cheshire (a west porch), Burford in Oxfordshire and Cirencester in Gloucestershire. The magnificent Cirencester porch, with its ornate traceried façade, was built as an administrative centre for the Augustinian Priory. It was later adopted by the local trade guilds as their headquarters and then as a town hall (*see* PARVIS).

There are many fine late-medieval porches in East Anglia, often with flushwork (*see* FLINT): at Beccles, Framsted, Kersey, Mendlesham and Woolpit in Suffolk, for example. In the south-east of England, where there was a plentiful supply of timber, a number of timber-framed porches have survived, mainly from the fourteenth and fifteenth centuries. In such cases the entrance was usually constructed of great arched timbers and the gabled barge-board and side openings were often skilfully carved. Notable among many are High Halden in Kent, Margaretting in Essex, West Callow and Long Wittenham in Berkshire, West Grinstead in Sussex and (finest of all) Boxford in Suffolk. In the Midlands, the two-storey, 'black and white' timbered

porch (probably a Tudor vestry) at the splendid Norman church at Berkswell is the finest of its type in Warwickshire. There are also several timber porches in the Welsh Marches: at Vowchurch in Herefordshire, for example, where a fine turned and carved wooden porch leads to an interior darkened by great timber posts supporting the roof.

Most of the liturgical functions of the church porch ceased with the Reformation but many secular traditions continued. Writing in the seventeenth century John Aubrey observed: 'It was the custom for some people that were more curious than ordinary to sit all night in the porch of their parish church on Midsummer Eve and they should see the apparitions of those that should die in the parish that year come and knock at the [church] door.' Two hundred years later, Francis Kilvert noted that at Clyro in Powys several parishioners '. . . used to go to the church door at midnight to hear the names of those who were to die within the year'.
See also GALILEE, GRAVESIDE SHELTER *and* PRIEST'S DOOR

PORCORUM *see* PLACE-NAMES

PORTICO A roofed space, open or partly enclosed, forming the entrance and centre-piece of a church. Usually a classical COLONNADE, either semi-circular or with a superimposed PEDIMENT.

PORTICUS A side-chapel or porch-like chamber entered from the main body of a church. Porticus formed the 'arms' of Saxon and Norman cruciform churches.
See also ANGLO-SAXON ARCHITECTURE, MEDIEVAL ARCHITECTURE, TOWERS *and* TRANSEPT

PORTIONISTS Persons (usually diocesan dignitaries) appointed to sinecures and granted residences near a parish church together with a right to appropriate its revenues and to appoint a vicar. Following the Reformation, portionists usually became lay rectors, though in practice they were frequently in holy orders.
See also PATRON

PORTLAND STONE The Isle of Portland, the 'Gibraltar of Wessex', was described by Hardy as a 'huge lump of freestone' jutting into the Channel from the Dorset coast: strange, bleak, almost treeless and with cliffs on every side. Its fine, hard oolitic limestone was first introduced to London by Inigo Jones in 1619 in the King's Banqueting House in Whitehall, and Christopher Wren chose Portland stone for the re-building of London after the Great Fire of 1666, notably in the new St. Paul's Cathedral and fifty-one City churches. The stone was quarried in immense blocks, trolleyed down short slipways and winched by 'slingers' onto barges to be transported along the south coast and up the River Thames. Wren's wineglass device may still be discovered on huge discarded blocks of stone in the quarries of east Portland, a few of which are worked today. Portland stone is not confined to Portland, however. Further east, the Tilly Whim Caves near Durlston were once quarried (a *whim* is a stone-miner's windlass) and the stone extracted from quarries at Chilmark in Wiltshire for the construction of Salisbury Cathedral in the thirteenth century also belongs to the Portland series. *Portland Cement*, manufactured from chalk and clay, was patented in 1824 by a Leeds brick-layer Joseph Aspdin who fancied that it bore some resemblance to the white Portland limestone.

POSTERN A small private entrance in the wall of a castle, fortified town, monastic precinct ,etc.

POSTULANT One seeking admission to a religious order. Initially, a postulant would be accommodated near the monastery gate where he would undergo testing before presenting himself on three consecutive days before the Chapter, humbly petitioning to be accepted as a NOVICE.

POT METALS *see* STAINED GLASS

POULTRY, THE *see* LARDER

POUNDS Most villages were provided with a pound (*pinfold*) within which stray animals were confined. This was usually maintained by a manor or vestry and was the responsibility of a minor official known as a *pinder*. All animals were the responsibility of their owners and were released from the pound only on payment of a fine. On occasions it would be necessary for an unclaimed beast to be 'cried' (announced) at the local market in the hope that the owner would come forward. Most medieval pounds were small fenced or hedged enclosures though later stone or brick pounds were often constructed on the sites of former medieval ones. Some of these have survived, at Leigh in Dorset, for example, and at Raskelf in Yorkshire which is an open crenellated polygonal structure with arched and barred door and window openings. Others are commemorated in local place-names such as The Pound House, Pound Lane etc. The feudal office of pinder (also *pound-keeper* or *punder*) was a necessary but unpopular one: there can have been few volunteers for a post which was often subject to abuse and occasionally to assault.

PRAEMUNIENTES A clause contained in a parliamentary summons requiring bishops to arrange for a specified number of other clergy (notably abbots) to attend at a particular session of parliament. In 1295, for example, thirty-seven Benedictine and sixty-two Cistercian abbots were summoned, though this number was exceptional and in the Parliament of 1302 the numbers were reduced to twenty-three and twenty-one respectively.

PRAYER BOOK SOCIETY, THE A society formed to promote the use of the *Book of Common Prayer* in services of the Church of England (*see* APPENDIX II).

PRAYER BOOK, THE *see* COMMON PRAYER, BOOK OF

PREACHERS, ORDER OF (THE DOMINICAN ORDER OF FRIARS PREACHER) *see* FRIARS

PREACHING CROSSES *see* CHURCHYARD CROSSES

PREBEND *see* CLERGY (CHURCH OF ENGLAND) *and* PREBENDARY

PREBENDARY The title holder of a cathedral benefice. The endowments of most medieval non-monastic cathedrals were divided into prebends, each of which was intended to support a single member of the chapter. In some cathedrals (such as Wells in Somerset) the territorial titles remain, though not the income.
See also CATHEDRALS *and* CLERGY (CHURCH OF ENGLAND)

PRECATORY SCROLL A stylised scroll containing a supplicatory prayer. Precatory scrolls are a common feature of monumental brasses where they are usually engraved near the hands or mouths of figures like the 'speech bubbles' of a modern strip cartoon (*see* LABEL).

PRECENTOR The director of music and principal CANTOR in a religious house. The precentor's duties included organising the music for the services (all of which were sung), conducting choir practices, rehearsing readers and ordering processions. He was also responsible for ensuring that the service books were properly notated and in good repair and often doubled as a community's librarian (*armarius*), annalist, archivist and chronicler. He was in absolute control of the quire: '. . . what he arranged to be sung had to be sung and what he decided to be read had to be read'. His position was to the right of the quire (hence, CANTORIS) and his deputy, the SUCCENTOR, occupied that to the left (*see* DECANI).
 The ancient office was retained in the post-Reformation cathedrals where the precentor is responsible for the direction of choral services. The

8 and 9. *All Saints church at Harewood in Yorkshire contains one of the finest collections of fifteenth- and sixteenth-century alabaster monuments in England. The illustrations show the crowded south aisle before the tomb chests and effigies were dismantled, conserved and repositioned following the transfer of the church to the Redundant Churches Fund in 1979.*

10. Jacobean bench ends at Sapperton in Gloucestershire. The Norman church of St. Kenelm was largely rebuilt in the early years of Queen Anne's reign (1702–14) when the pews, gallery and oak panelling were removed to the church from the old manor house.

11. Fifteenth-century stone 'wineglass' pulpit at Chedworth church in the Gloucestershire Cotswolds. The pulpit partially blocks the entrance to an earlier rood stair.

12. The magnificent fifteenth-century west window at Fairford in Gloucestershire. Described by Betjeman as 'a complete and perfect perpendicular church', St. Mary's contains the finest fifteenth-century glass in England. The twenty-eight windows survived the Reformation, were hidden in the Commonwealth and again during the Second World War. The huge west window depicts the Last Judgement with Christ in Majesty at the top (restored) and, below, 'a smouldering hell full of red, purple and blue horrors' (Harbison).

13. John Piper's memorial window to his friend John Betjeman (1906–84) at Farnborough, Berkshire.

14. *The tiny church of St. Michael and All Angels, dwarfed by the massive fourteenth-century walls of Croft Castle, Herefordshire.*

15. *The magnificent perpendicular church of the Holy Trinity at Long Melford, Suffolk. A giant among parish churches, it is 268 feet long and incorporates a large, three-gabled eastern lady chapel with ambulatory. The exterior is a mass of flushwork panelling and great windows, many containing fine fifteenth-century glass. The tower (Bodley, 1903) replaced an earlier eighteenth-century brick tower of somewhat mean proportions.*

office is that of a minor canon or chaplain except in cathedrals of the 'Old Foundation' where the precentor is a member of the cathedral chapter.
See also CLERGY (CHURCH OF ENGLAND)

PRECEPTORY *see* COMMANDERY

PRECES The plural of *prex* meaning 'prayer', preces are short petitions uttered by the priest and responded to by the choir or congregation. In the Church of England, those prayers which precede the Creed are called preces and those which follow it are VERSICLES.

PRECINCT The symbolic withdrawal from the world of a religious community was marked by physical boundaries defining the precinct within which the brethren lived. The precincts of medieval monasteries were extensive (that at Glastonbury Abbey in Somerset extended to 60 acres and contained, not only the abbey church and claustral buildings, but also numerous stores, barns, workshops, cattle-sheds, mill, guests' accommodation, cemetery and charnel-house. Sometimes even a monastery's orchards, vegetable gardens and vineyards were enclosed within a wall or embankment and ditch. The inner precinct, in the immediate vicinity of the abbey church and claustral buildings (the *close*), was itself surrounded by the *curia* or outer court which contained the guest-house, dairy, scullery, bakehouse, brewhouse, granary and other buildings necessary to the efficient running of the community. It was in the curia that contact was made with the outside world, though monks were not permitted to leave the claustral enclosure without permission (which was assumed in the case of certain officers). The Cistercians often had a further court, beyond the main gatehouse of the curia, in which they located noisy or offensive activities such as the smithy and tannery. Today, former precincts may be identified by reference to the delineation of later streets and house plots, to fragments of walls (notably at St. Mary's, York) and to the location of gatehouses, many of which continue to provide access to the close of a cathedral or major church.
See also FORTIFICATION *and* MONASTIC BUILDINGS

PRE-CONTRACT (*also* TROTH-PLIGHT) Medieval Canon Law differentiated between BETROTHAL and pre-contract which could be cited in cases relating to questions of inheritance, illegitimacy etc. The essential difference between pre-contract and betrothal was in the form of words used by the parties and the tense of the verb contained therein – 'I marry you' was a pre-contract whereas 'I will marry you' was a betrothal (unless it was followed by intercourse which established a presumption of 'present consent'). In the eyes of the medieval Church, the essence of marriage was consent, formalised by an interchange of personal vows. Pre-contract, therefore, was both a sacred obligation and a legally binding commitment. Consequently, a simple exchange of words was all that was required – there was no need for a priest or witnesses to be present. Inevitably, men who sought to release themselves from a marriage could seek to secure a divorce from the papal court by revealing 'evidence' of an earlier pre-contract. In the fifteenth-century *Paston Letters* we read of how the sanctity of troth-plight enabled a retainer of the great Paston family to marry his master's daughter despite furious attempts by her parents to prevent the match. In 1483 it was claimed (on behalf of the future Richard III) that the children of Edward IV were illegitimate because the king had been pre-contracted to Eleanor Butler when he married Elizabeth Woodville. In 1536, two days after the execution of Queen Anne (Boleyn), Cranmer declared that her union with Henry VIII had been invalid because she had once been 'affianced' to the earl of Northumberland.
See also BASTARDY *and* MARRIAGE LICENCES

PREDELLA (i) A platform, formed by the uppermost of the SANCTUARY steps, on which the priest stood when celebrating the Mass. (ii) A shelf behind an altar or communion table on which a REREDOS is supported or a TRIPTYCH placed.

PRELATE A high-ranking cleric in the medieval Church. In the Church of England, a bishop or archbishop.

PREMONSTRATENSIAN CANONS The 'White Canons' belonged to an order founded in 1120 by St. Norbert at Prémontré near Laon. Their rule was that of St. Augustine with additional austerities (*see* AUGUSTINIANS).

PRESBYTERIANISM The earliest organisation of the Christian churches in Palestine resembled that of the Jewish synagogues, each administered by a board of 'elders'. Similarly, Presbyterianism incorporated the principle of government by committees of *presbyters* or 'overseers' which its sixteenth- and seventeenth-century proponents regarded not as innovative but as a restoration of the New Testament model. Presbyterian churches are normally governed by a hierarchy of courts: the Kirk-Session, Presbytery, Synod and General Assembly, all of which are representative bodies of ministers and elders whose authority is based ultimately on election. Ministers are elected by the people but ordained by a presbytery which has jurisdiction over a particular area. The doctrine of Presbyterian churches is, therefore, essentially Calvinistic. The Presbyterian Church in Scotland was founded in 1560 and became the official national church in 1647. In seventeenth-century England the Presbyterian Church was unpopular and was overthrown following the Restoration of 1660. Re-established in 1876, the Presbyterian Church of England united with the greater part of the Congregational Church of England and Wales to form the United Reformed Church in 1972. The archives of the Presbyterian Church of England are maintained in the library of the United Reformed Church History Society (*see* APPENDIX II).

PRESBYTERY (i) The area of a church in the vicinity of the SANCTUARY, usually contained within a separate (and smaller) building and entered from the NAVE through an arched opening (*see* CHANCEL ARCH). In the Middle Ages the presbytery was reserved for the clergy: literally, 'the place of the presbyters', the 'elders' of the early Church. Eleventh-century presbyteries were apsidal and, in monastic churches, were often surrounded by aisles and subsidiary chapels (*see* AMBULATORY *and* MONASTIC BUILDINGS). These were generally superseded by presbyteries with square terminations in the twelfth century. At the eastern end of the presbytery was the sanctuary, a slightly raised area immediately surrounding the high altar (*see* ALTARS *and* REREDOS) and separated from the presbytery by a single Sanctuary Step (the *gradus presbyterii*). In the churches of major abbeys, priories and cathedrals there were also flights of steps separating both the presbytery and the sanctuary from the CHOIR. In parish churches, and in those of the more austere monastic orders (the Cistercians and Carthusians, for example), there was usually no architectural division between the presbytery and the NAVE. But following the Fourth Lateran Council of 1215 (which pronounced the doctrine of transubstantiation, thereby emphasising the sacredness of the MASS), it was considered necessary to enclose the presbytery of a parish church by means of a screen (*see* CHANCEL SCREEN *and* ROOD SCREEN) both to preserve the mystery of the Eucharist and to isolate the sanctuary from the secular activities of the nave (*see* CHURCH AND COMMUNITY). It is this enclosed space which is now described as the CHANCEL (from the Latin CANCELLI meaning 'lattice' or 'grating'), the term 'presbytery' being used (erroneously) as a synonym for 'sanctuary'.

Despite Victorian restorations, many medieval presbyteries have retained one or more of the architectural features which were provided for the celebration of the Mass. These may include an AUMBRY, CHANCEL VENTILATOR, CREDENCE, EASTER SEPULCHRE, FENESTELLA, PISCINA, SEDILIA and SQUINT. There may also be a small PRIEST'S DOOR in the south wall.
(ii) The residence of a Roman Catholic priest.

PRESENTATION OF CHRIST IN THE TEMPLE, THE An alternative name for the feast of Purification of the Blessed Virgin Mary (*see* Luke 2 : 21–39). Celebrated on 2 February (*see* CANDLEMAS).

PRESENTATION OF THE BLESSED VIRGIN MARY, THE Celebrated on 21 November, the feast commemorated the presentation of the Blessed Virgin Mary in the Temple when three years old. The tradition originated in the second-century apocryphal *Book of James*, one of several 'Infancy Gospels' which circulated in the early Church and contained embellished versions of Christ's birth and childhood.

PRESENTMENTS (CHURCHWARDENS') *see* VISITATIONS, ECCLESIASTICAL

PRICKET A stand with one or more upright spikes on which votive candles are fixed.
See also CANDLESTICKS and LIGHTS

PRICKING The practice of making a pattern of small holes in a sheet of parchment in order to guide the ruling of lines.
See also PARISH CLERK *and* RULING

PRIE-DIEU From the French 'pray God', a small prayer-desk for private devotions (*see* DESKS).

PRIEST Early English versions of the New Testament distinguished between *presbyter* ('elder') and *sacerdos* ('sacrificing minister') but by the eleventh century the word 'priest', which is an etymological contraction of *presbyter*, was ambiguously used for both. With the spread of Christianity, the presbyters adopted more fully the functions of priests and as the parish priest became the normal celebrant of the Eucharist, and customarily exercised the power of absolution; his supernatural functions and powers were emphasised and he acquired a position outside the feudal hierarchy while remaining subordinate to his bishop, the validity of his position being dependent on ordination. The medieval perception of the priesthood was therefore almost exclusively concerned with the Mass. This was later rejected by the Reformers though the term 'priest' was retained in the *Book of Common Prayer* apparently to ensure that deacons would not celebrate the Holy Communion. Members of religious communities were not necessarily priests. Only ordained clerks were permitted to administer the *sacraments*: baptism, absolution, confirmation (the prerogative of a bishop), ordination of clerks, matrimony, communion, unction for the sick and dying, and the casting out of evil spirits.
See also CLERGY (CHURCH OF ENGLAND) *and* HOLY ORDERS

PRIEST'S DOOR A small door, usually in the south wall of the PRESBYTERY or CHANCEL, by which the priest entered the church, either directly from the churchyard or from a SACRISTY (often described as a VESTRY). Where there is a sacristy, it is likely to be of a later date than the doorway. Priests' doors are usually very simple, though there are exceptions. At Bradford Abbas in Dorset, for example, the (north) door has an ornate fifteenth-century porch with a niche above the entrance (but no figure).

PRIESTS' HOLES Secret hiding-places incorporated into the houses of Roman Catholic families in anticipation of religious persecution. No county is richer than Worcestershire in such hiding places. Most are connected with Catholic persecution and in particular with the Gunpowder Plot of 1605, though in some cases the reason for their construction and use is obscure. The manor house at Cleeve Prior, for example, contains such a hide and yet it was occupied throughout the seventeenth century by a staunchly Protestant family, the Bushells. Nevertheless, the by-ways of this remote countryside must have witnessed many secretive comings and goings among the great recusant houses of Grafton Manor, Huddington Court, Harvington Hall, Coughton Court (in neighbouring Warwickshire) and Hindlip, the headquarters of the Jesuit mission led by Father Garnet.

Huddington Court contains two wonderful priests' holes, constructed by the legendary 'Little John' Owen, master-builder of hides and Garnet's servant who died on the rack in 1606. One hide opens into an upper storey room which was probably once the chapel. The entrance is concealed by a detachable wainscote panel and the beams of the timber framing round the entrance are chamfered to afford easier access. Typical of Owen's designs, there is also an inner hide and bolt-hole by which the priest could make his escape. Entrance to the other hide is so cunningly concealed that it was only discovered by chance in the 1940s. In the corner of an attic bedroom part of an apparently solid timber and plaster wall swings open on hidden pivots to reveal a secret chamber. The 'door' includes a substantial timber upright which appears to support an even heavier rafter.

Regrettably, of Hindlip nothing remains. Drawings show that it was an extraordinary rambling agglomeration of gables, turrets and towering chimneys whilst a writer, who visited the house shortly before its destruction in the early nineteenth century, stated:

> Its every room had a recess, a passage, a trap door, or secret stairs, the walls were in many places hollow, the ceilings false, several chimneys had double flues, one for passage of

the smoke, the second for concealment of a priest, no one – except those immediately concerned – having key or clue to the whole maze of secrets.

It is hardly surprising that Father Garnet eluded the most rigorous searches for eight days and was captured only when privation forced him to give himself up.

With the destruction of Hindlip, Harvington Hall, also in Worcestershire, contains the finest extant collection of priests' holes in England. Extended by the (Protestant) Pakington family in *c.* 1578, Harvington passed to the (Catholic) Yate family in 1631. The seven priests' holes were probably incorporated into the house at this time and were no doubt in regular use during the fresh wave of Catholic persecution which followed Titus Oates's 'Popish Plot' of 1678. All are ingenious, three particularly so. The first is entered by lifting a stair in a flight of five between the second-floor landing and the head of the great staircase. The hide itself is behind the wall of the dining hall and was contrived by lowering the ceiling of the adjacent pantry. Another, entered through a trap in the floor of a latrine, is concealed beside the chimney of the kitchen below and has a small bolt-hole opening into a shaft which extends the full height of the building and contains a pulley which once drove the kitchen spit. A third hide, discovered in 1897, is in the room known as Dr. Dodd's library where one of the seemingly substantial vertical beams in the brick and timber wall swings outwards on concealed pivots when pressed near the top to reveal the narrow entrance to the hide.

PRIESTS' HOUSES Transitional in character between the secular and the ecclesiastical, in the Middle Ages priests' houses were provided for the accommodation of parish clergy. Many priests' houses were substantial buildings: at Smallhythe in Kent, for example, where lavish use of large timbers and close studding illustrates the high standards of luxury enjoyed by certain priests immediately before the Reformation. The fourteenth-century Clergy House at Alfriston in East Sussex was designed for a small community of parish priests. Built of oak-framing, with wattle and daub walls and a thatched roof, the building contained separate apartments and a common hall for dining and recreation. Other notable examples include a thirteenth-century priest's house at Martock in Somerset which was built by the Treasurers of Wells Cathedral, a stone-built fifteenth-century priest's house at Muchelney in Somerset and a tiny lodge at Easton-on-the-Hill in Northamptonshire. Tithe BARNS, in which the rectorial TITHES were stored, were built in the vicinity of priests' houses.

See also MEDIEVAL CHURCH

Priests' house at Muchelney, Somerset.

PRIMATE The title of the bishop of 'the first see': the Archbishop of Canterbury is 'Primate of All England' and the Archbishop of York is 'Primate of England'.

PRIME Dating from *c.* 395, the first of the canonical hours observed at daybreak and sometimes followed by Prime of the Blessed Virgin Mary. Similar in structure to COMPLINE.

PRIMER (*also* PRYMER) A devotional book containing the Little Office of the Blessed Virgin Mary, the Seven Penitential Psalms, the fifteen Gradual Psalms, the Litany of the Saints and the Office for the Dead. Popular among the educated laity from the late thirteenth century.

PRIMOGENITURE The state or fact of being first-born. The custom or right of succession and inheritance by a first-born child. *Male primogeniture* further restricted inheritance to a first-born son. Primogeniture was abolished in 1925. Ultimogeniture was inheritance by the youngest son.

PRINCE BISHOP *see* PALATINATE

'PRINCE OF WALES' FEATHERS' *see* ROYAL ARMS IN CHURCHES

PRINTING Although printing was known in ancient China it probably developed independently in western Europe and emerged late in the medieval period, stimulated by an increased demand for books and a corresponding increase in manuscript production. The mechanical problems of producing 'artificial' script were resolved by the Mainz-born goldsmith Johann Gutenberg (*c.* 1400–68) whose method of printing was to remain the standard for three and a half centuries. In 1455 he completed the first printed book, the *Gutenberg Bible*, in an edition of two-hundred copies printed with hand-cut lead type-fonts on paper and vellum in the German Gothic script of contemporary manuscripts. By 1500 some sixty printing centres had developed in Germany while in England the first press was established in the precincts of Westminster Abbey in 1476 by William Caxton (*c.* 1422–91) who had learned his trade at Bruges. The first dated printed English book, *The Dictes or Sayengis of the Philosophres*, was produced in the following year. Caxton went on to produce more than eighty texts including the works of Malory, Gower and Chaucer as well as translations of Virgil's *Aeneid* and the French romances.

The structure of the printing and publishing industry in sixteenth-century England was such that it was easily regulated and therefore susceptible to political control. For example, none of Sir Thomas More's religious works was printed or reprinted between the years 1534 (the year he was committed to the Tower) and 1554, for it was not until after that date that his anti-Protestant line suited the government. There was not a total ban on More's works, however, and his *History of Richard III* was reprinted four times in this period – because (like Shakespeare's histories) it reinforced the 'official' version of the events which led to the accession of the Tudor dynasty. During the English Reformation, information technology was an instrument of government.

PRIOR *and* PRIORESS *see* PRIORY

PRIORY A religious house presided over by a prior or prioress. The head of a monastic house was either an ABBOT (abbess) or prior (prioress) and it is not always possible to draw a clear distinction between the two titles. Under the Benedictine influence the term came to denote a monk who ranked next to the abbot and acted as his deputy. It was later applied also to the heads of small houses which were dependencies of abbeys and to the heads of mendicant houses (*see* FRIARS), though in practice several priories attained religious eminence and economic prosperity which greatly exceeded that of many abbeys. All Cistercian, Premonstratensian and Victorine houses were abbeys and all Carthusian and Cluniac houses were priories, being daughter houses of the Grand Chartreuse and Cluny (though anomalously the Cluniac house of Bermondsey was an abbey). The great Benedictine foundations were abbeys, as were some Augustinian houses, but the majority of smaller houses of both these orders, and those of the Gilbertines, were priories. Furthermore, the Benedictines distinguished between *conventual priories,* which were self-governing houses, and *obedientiary priories* which were dependencies of abbeys. Where a bishop was also titular abbot, the community would be administered by a prior and its church designated as a CATHEDRAL PRIORY: at Durham and Ely, for example. At the DISSOLUTION OF THE MONASTERIES a number of priory churches were acquired for parochial use: Bolton in Yorkshire, Great Malvern in Worcestershire and Leominster in Herefordshire, for example. (*See also* ALIEN PRIORIES, CATHEDRALS, MONASTERIES *and* MONASTIC BUILDINGS)

PRISONS *see* LOCK-UP, MONASTIC BUILD-INGS *and* PORCHES

PRIVATE CHAPELS ACT (1871) An act regulating the status of Anglican chapels in institutions such as schools and hospitals and permitting diocesan bishops to license clerics to administer in such chapels.

PRIVATE MASS A mass celebrated individually by a single priest, assisted by a server or acolyte. An increasing emphasis on the propitiatory element of the eucharistic sacrifice encouraged priests in the belief that they had a duty to say a daily mass. In the monasteries this resulted in an increase in the number of monks who were also ordained priests and a proliferation of subsidiary altars. Private masses were said, in both monastic and parish churches, either at the priest's discretion and for his own purposes, or in fulfilment of obligations such as chantries (*see* CHANTRY).

PRIVILEGED ALTAR An ALTAR at which a plenary INDULGENCE could be obtained for a soul in PURGATORY through a celebration of the MASS. *See also* CHANTRY

PROBATE The official proving of a will and testament. Originally wills and testaments were separate legal documents, written in Latin and subject to CANON LAW. A will (*voluntas*) was a statement by which a person (the *testator*) regulated the disposal of his land and property. A testament was concerned with debts and the disposal of personal goods. Both were documents of binding force, revocable ('ambulatory') until the testator's death but irrevocable thereafter (*see also* CODICIL). Following the death of the testator, the *executors* appointed in the will were required to 'prove' the will before the appropriate ecclesiastical court which exercised jurisdiction over probate matters (*see also* VISITATIONS, ECCLESIASTICAL). If the testator left goods worth more than £5 (*bona notabilia*) this was usually the archdeacon's court (*see* COURTS (ECCLESIASTICAL)) though if he had estate in more than one archdeaconry jurisdiction reverted to the diocesan bishop, either through the CONSISTORY COURT or a COMMISSARY COURT. Where an estate extended over more than one diocese then probate would be granted to either the Prerogative Court of Canterbury or the Prerogative Court of York. (It has been estimated that some 36,000 wills exist for the period 1383–1528 in the Prerogative Court of Canterbury.) Peculiars exercised their own jurisdiction, known as *testamentary peculiar* (*see* PECULIAR). The executors (who usually included the wife, if she survived, or a son) had to satisfy the court that the will was an accurate expression of the last wishes of the testator. They then carried out its provisions under the court's supervision. Most wills were proved quickly and administered within a year or so, but a deathbed will disposing of large amounts of property could produce long years of litigation and its original provisions could be considerably modified. Probate records of judgements relating to contested wills usually include the words 'by decree' or 'int. dec.' (*interlocutory decree*). Once the will was proved the original copy was filed and a probate copy given to the executors which noted where and when probate was approved and to whom probate was given. If someone died *intestate* (without making a valid will) a letter of administration had to be obtained and *administrators* appointed by the court. In such cases, the personal estate usually went to the widow and children or, in the absence of children, to other relatives.

To make a will or testament, boys had to be over fourteen and girls over twelve. Married women could make a will only with their husband's consent (this was not revoked until 1882). A wife's property belonged to her husband – though she could leave a list of 'supplications' for his consideration. Widows and spinsters could make wills but inevitably the majority of surviving medieval wills were made by men. At that time it was generally only the wealthy who made wills, though there are exceptions, and felons, outlaws and traitors were unable to make wills because their property was forfeit to the crown.

Property was classified as real and personal. Personal property (*personalty*) consisted of movable goods and chattels both animate and inanimate, also the remaining years on a leasehold. Real property (*realty*) consisted of freehold land, the disposal of which was subject to manorial custom and regulation. The *Heir at Law* received all the land except a small portion which belonged to the deceased's wife by *dower right*. This often meant that a daughter might receive nothing if the heir was a male cousin, though it was possible to effect a legal solution to this problem. This was known as *enfeoffment* by which the testator enfeoffed (surrendered) his land to feoffees who were entrusted to use the lands according to the testator's wishes. Common law regarded the feoffees as the beneficial owners but they were unable to use the land for their own purposes. The personal estate had to be divided into three: one third for the widow, one third for the children and the remaining third to be disposed of according to the testator's wishes. If there were no children then it would be divided in two and if the testator made no provision for the disposition of the remaining part then it went automatically to the Church.

A will was also a religious document, intended to ease the testator's soul of any earthly burdens and to prepare him for the hereafter. Wills were usually made close to death and follow a standard format, opening with the testator committing his soul to God and affirming that he is 'of sound mind'; various saints would then be invoked and orders given for prayers and masses which, it was hoped, would expedite the soul through PURGATORY. After this, the testator would dispose of ('devise') his worldly goods and lands, making arrangements for the payment of any debts, especially those to the Church, and for bequests of money 'to pious uses'. Such bequests were intended to ensure that prayers would be said for the soul of the testator and masses celebrated in his memory (*see* CHANTRY). The rich endowed CHANTRY CHAPELS or even CHANTRY COLLEGES where prayers were offered in perpetuity by chantry priests, while others (of more modest means) were commemorated in the chapels of their GUILDS. Probate was essentially an ecclesiastical matter and it is hardly surprising, therefore, that the majority of wills were written in an incumbent's hand, or witnessed by him, and that they were so carefully scrutinised by the ecclesiastical courts.

Of course, we cannot be certain from a person's will if they really were as pious during their lifetime as the will may suggest, for a will was often made in anticipation of death and the life hereafter. It may also be difficult to ascertain whether the terms of the will were carried out precisely as the testator wished, though there is often visible evidence in his parish church, for example, or in benefactions to a religious community or the endowment of an almshouse, hospice or similar charitable institution. When considered from the opposite perspective, wills and (from 1529) the accompanying probate inventories (see below) are invaluable sources of information concerning the condition and appearance of a church at a particular time, of its furnishings and possessions (such as BOOKS, PLATE and VESTMENTS) and of altars, aisles, chapels, clerestories, porches, towers and other additions and alterations which were effected through endowments and bequests of money, goods or land. They can provide evidence of early dedications and of parochial customs and ceremonies: at Thelnetham in Suffolk, for example, where one John Cole (d. 1527) ordered that 'a new crosse to be made and sette upp where the gospell is saide upon Ascension Even'. He also left three acres of land to provide for the distribution of bread and ale at the cross during the Ascension procession.

Wills also provide evidence of changing religious attitudes, especially following the REFORMATION. At the beginning of the sixteenth century, for example, most (Catholic) testators bequeathed their souls to God and '. . . to the blessed Virgin Mary and the whole Company of Heaven'. Thereafter, a gradual change of emphasis is evident so that, by the 1560s, most (Protestant) testators dedicated themselves '. . . to Almighty God and his only son our Lord Jesus Christ, by whose precious death and passion I hope to be saved'.

The ecclesiastical courts continued to exercise jurisdiction over wills and testamentary matters until 1858. When attempting to trace an early will the researcher should first ascertain the name of the testator's parish. From this it will be possible to establish in which of the various courts the will was proved. (There is a simplified guide to the probate courts in J. Richardson's *The Local Historian's Encyclopedia.**) The archives of pre-1858 wills are usually to be found in county record offices (*see* ARCHIVES). They may include inventories of effects (*probate inventories*) which date from the period 1529–1750 and were compiled, on behalf of the executors, by two disinterested parties. Since 1858 all copies of wills and letters of administration have been deposited at the Principal Registry of the Family Division though local record offices usually have copies of the indexes.

Further reading:

Camp, A., *Wills and their Whereabouts*, London, 1974

Gibson, J., *A Simplified Guide to Probate Jurisdiction: where to look for Wills*, London, 1986

Richardson, J., *The Local Historian's Encyclopedia*, New Barnet, 1986 *

PROCESSIONAL 'BANNER' *see* FLAGS

PROCESSIONAL CROSS A cross carried on a staff before a liturgical procession.

PROCESSIONAL TORCHES *see* BIER LIGHTS

PROCESSIONS Liturgical processions, which were either festal or penitential, usually took place before the principal celebration of the Eucharist on feast days and were of such importance that they affected the architecture of churches, both large and small. In monastic communities, there was a procession of the entire convent every Sunday before High Mass. Led by the processional cross, torches, thurifer, priests and novices it visited each of the subsidiary altars in turn (including those in the claustral buildings) before returning to the choir for the singing of the High Mass. Provision had to be made for the processional route (*see* AISLE, AMBULATORY *and* WEST DOORWAY) and the stations occupied by certain participants in the procession were often marked in the church floor: at Easby Abbey in Yorkshire, for example, where traces of incised circles remain. Processions occasionally left the precincts, especially where religious houses were located in towns. At Durham the community of the cathedral priory processed through the city on St. Mark's Day to the church of St. Mary le Bow where a High Mass was celebrated. There were similar celebrations on Palm Sunday, Holy Thursday, Whitsunday and Trinity Sunday but the greatest processions were those in honour of CORPUS CHRISTI when the members of town guilds and parishes thronged the streets with their crosses, banners and relics, led by a crystal monstrance containing the Body of Christ. ROGATION days were universally marked with processions, accompanied by the singing of litanies and the 'beating of the bounds' (*see* PERAMBULATION). At York, the Rogation procession included a dragon (representing the devil) which was stored in the tower of St. Olave's, next to the gate where the procession emerged from the minster precinct.

In parish churches, processions were a regular (and popular) occurrence and provided opportunities for a congregation to participate in the ceremonial (*see* LITURGY). The fact that processions invariably signified feast days and, therefore, holidays added to their enjoyment. On leaving the chancel, the thurifer, priests, acolytes and servers would process to the south door and into the churchyard, closely followed by the churchwardens and congregation. After pausing at the CHURCH-YARD CROSS the procession would pass round the church, returning to the nave by the north door (*see* PORCHES). Once inside, it would proceed round the church by way of the aisles before passing down the nave to the rood screen through which the clergy would enter the chancel for the Mass. For the feudal peasant, the colour and richness of liturgical processions must have been an exhilarating and joyous experience, far removed from the drudgery of everyday life. The thurifer was followed by an ornate processional cross, surrounded by burning tapers, and then the priests in their embroidered vestments, the colourful banners of GUILDS and sometimes a relic carried beneath a great canopy.

See also BANNER-STAVE LOCKERS, FLAGS *and* TRIPLE CANDLESTICK

PROCTORS FOR THE CLERGY Elected representatives of the Anglican clergy who, with the members *ex officio*, constitute the Lower Houses of the CONVOCATIONS of Canterbury and York.

PROFESSION A solemn oath, including the vows of poverty, chastity and obedience required of those wishing to enter a religious order. In the Middle Ages the minimum age at which profession could be made was 18 for monks and 25 for lay brothers.

PROHIBITED DEGREES The relationships, either of blood (*consanguinity*) or of marriage (*affinity*), which render marriage unlawful. In Canon Law, such relationships are termed 'degrees' and, in the Church of England, these are listed in the Table of Kindred and Affinity.

See also AFFINITY, CONSANGUINITY *and* NULLITY

PRONE A vernacular office which followed the sermon in the High Mass. It included such matters as the announcement of banns of marriage and notices concerning fasts and feast days.

PROPHETS The notion of prophesy, and of the Messianic fulfilment of Old Testament prophesy in particular, was accepted throughout the medieval period. Indeed, it was not until the eighteenth century and the development of a critical approach to history that doubts began to be expressed concerning the validity of such claims. The figures of Old Testament prophets are occasionally found in medieval glass where they may sometimes be identified by reference to symbols (*see* CHRISTIAN SYMBOLS).

PROPRIETARY CHAPEL Since the Reformation, an Anglican chapel built and maintained by private individuals. Ministers of such chapels are required to obtain both an episcopal licence and the consent of the incumbent of the parish in which the chapel is located.
For pre-Reformation proprietary chapels *see* ANGLO-SAXON CHURCH *and* CHAPELS.

PROTESTANTISM A collective term applied to that part of Western Christendom which denies the authority of the Pope and emphasises responsibility to God rather than to the Church and its sacraments. Its chief characteristics are the acceptance of the Bible as the only source of revealed truth (the preaching and receiving of the Word is therefore considered to be of greater significance than sacramental faith and practice), the doctrine of justification by faith alone, the universal priesthood of all believers and an often austere standard of personal morality. The term is derived from the 'Protestatio' of the reforming members of the Diet of Speyer (1529) who opposed the decision of the Catholic majority and which was adopted by the followers of Martin Luther (*see* LUTHERANISM) who criticised the Roman Catholic Church for opposing reform.
The 1552 *Book of Common Prayer* marks the establishment of Protestantism in the territories of the Crown of England. It abandoned TRANSUBSTANTIATION, thereby confirming the distinction between the MASS and the communion service which is the essence of the distinction between Protestantism and Roman Catholicism. In seventeenth-century England the term 'Protestant' implied opposition to papal authority and was generally applied to members of the Established Church, even to the exclusion of Presbyterians, Quakers and Separatists. Later, it was used in contradistinction to 'Roman Catholic' and as such was viewed with disfavour by those who wished to emphasise the claim of the Anglican Church to be equally Catholic with Rome.
See also REFORMATION, THE

PROVINCE A major ecclesiastical unit of administration comprising a number of contiguous dioceses. The term originated in the provinces of the Roman Empire which provided an organisational framework for the early Church. In England, the archbishops of Canterbury and York exercise jurisdiction over their respective provinces.
See also CLERGY (CHURCH OF ENGLAND) *and* DIOCESE

PROVINCIAL EPISCOPAL VISITOR *see* CLERGY (CHURCH OF ENGLAND)

PROVOST *see* CLERGY (CHURCH OF ENGLAND)

PSALMODY *see* PSALTER

PSALMS Psalms are sacred songs accompanied by stringed instruments. The (Old Testament) *Book of Psalms*, which are used in both Jewish and Christian worship, is the oldest book of songs still in use. Some of the Psalms are accredited to particular authors (seventy-three to David, twelve to Asaph and so on) but the accreditations are more recent than the psalms themselves and some are demonstrably incorrect. The popular belief that the entire PSALTER was written by David is no longer tenable, though many of the psalms date from the early period of the monarchy in Israel and the book is most probably a collection of anthologies. They include a number of imprecatory psalms which, in whole or in part, invoke divine vengeance (e.g. Psalms 58, 69, 109 and 137). The psalms comprise the essential element of the offices of the Roman BREVIARY and, to some extent, of the Anglican services of Morning and Evening Prayer. They are sung antiphonally, either by priest (*cantor*) and choir or by the two sides of the choir (*decani* and *cantoris*), or recited responsively by the minister and congregation. The English version of the Psalms sung in churches (the 'Prayer Book Version') dates from the sixteenth century and the translations of Tyndale and Coverdale (*see* BIBLES). These were revised by Cranmer for the 'Great Bible' of 1539 and were retained in the prayer book when the Authorised Version of the Bible was issued in 1611.
See also ANGLICAN CHANT, CHURCH MUSIC (ANGLICAN) *and* PLAINSONG

PSALTER A collection of PSALMS. The psalter (or PSALTERY) so dominated the life of religious houses that the monastic hours were called *psalmodia principalis* and the lesser hours (the Hours of the Blessed Virgin Mary) the *psalmodia secundria*. The core of worship consisted of the daily recitation of the psalter during the seven divine offices (even this division was derived from the psalmist's 'Seven times a day will I worship thee

. . .') and the psalter was undoubtedly known by heart by many of the brethren.

Metrical psalters, which contain metrical versions of the psalms, were first introduced into England under Edward VI (1547–53). The *New Version of the Psalms*, a metrical psalter compiled in 1696 by Nahum Tate (1652–1715) and Nicholas Brady (1659–1726), was widely used in parish churches until the early nineteenth century. *Psalmody* is the study of the music for metrical versions of the psalms and for HYMNS.

PSALTERY (i) An ancient and medieval stringed instrument. (ii) A book containing the PSALMS and other matter for recitation at the Divine Office. Psalteries were superseded by *breviaries*, liturgical books containing not only the Psalms but also the hymns, lessons, responsories, canticles etc. used in the Divine Office. Like breviaries, medieval psalteries are often beautifully illuminated.

PUBLIC WORSHIP REGULATION ACT (1874) An act intended to suppress excessive ritualism in the Church of England (*see* NINETEENTH-CENTURY CHURCH). The act was discredited by the contumacy and imprisonment of four priests during the period 1877–82 though it was not repealed until the passing of the ECCLESIASTICAL JURISDICTION MEASURE of 1963.

PULPIT DESK *see* DESK

PULPITS A pulpit is an elevated platform (Latin: *pulpitum*) for a preacher or reader.
MEDIEVAL PULPITS
In medieval parish churches the PRESBYTERY was a mysterious *inner sanctum* in which the Mass was celebrated and from which the congregation in the nave was separated by a ROOD SCREEN. There was no seating in the nave, services were shorter than they are today and sermons were rare. Nevertheless, the growing popularity of itinerant preachers in the fourteenth century (notably the Franciscan FRIARS) is reflected in the number of pulpits erected in that period, usually (though not invariably) to the north of the CHANCEL ARCH, and in the provision in some churches of bench seating (*see* BENCHES AND BENCH-ENDS).

The earliest pulpits are from *c.* 1340 though most surviving pre-Reformation examples are from the fifteenth and early sixteenth centuries. Medieval pulpits were constructed of stone or oak and are similar in shape to a wine glass with a slender, splayed stem and tall, narrow 'drum' with traceried panels which sometimes contain carved or painted motifs depicting the likenesses of the Four Evangelists or familiar preceptors such as the Four Doctors of the Latin Church (*see* CHRISTIAN SYMBOLS). There are fine fifteenth-century

examples at Trull in Somerset and Burnham Norton, Castle Acre and Horsham St. Faith in Norfolk.

About one hundred wooden pulpits remain from the pre-Reformation period and many of these are in Norfolk and Devon churches. Of the Devon pulpits, which are characterised by rich foliage and niches, those at Coleridge, East Allington, Halberton, Holne, Ipplepen, Kenton and Chivelstone (hollowed out of a single block of oak) are the best. There are some sixty medieval stone pulpits, the finest of which are in the counties of Somerset (Barnwell), Gloucestershire (Northleach) and Devon (Bovey Tracey, Dittisham, Harberton and St. Saviour's at Dartmouth). Perhaps the finest stone pulpit, complete with its original staircase and a jolly lion on the balustrade, is at St. Peter's church, Wolverhampton in the West Midlands.
POST-REFORMATION PULPITS
Liturgical changes effected by the REFORMATION resulted in a greater emphasis on direct communication between the priest and his congregation and the pulpit acquired a more central role in worship as did the READING DESK (or *reading pew*) from

Fifteenth-century canopied pulpit at Fotheringhay, Northamptonshire. A gift of Edward IV, the royal arms and linenfold panels were repainted and gilded in the 1960s.

Early sixteenth-century pulpit at Sutcombe, Devon.

which the priest conducted the services. In 1547 Edward VI ordered that each parish should provide 'a comely and honest pulpit' and this was repeated in the Elizabethan Injunctions of 1559.

In the seventeenth and eighteenth centuries canopied pulpit and reading desk were often combined to form 'double-decker' pulpits, with the pulpit above the desk and each having its own means of access. In some churches a third tier was added to form a 'three-decker' pulpit with the parish clerk's desk (or *clerk's pew*) at the lowest level (*see* PARISH CLERK). The upper preaching tier of these great 'three-decker' pulpits towered above even the tallest box pews in the nave so that 'sermon time' must have been a formidable experience.

In the eighteenth century there was, for a time, an enthusiasm for moving the pulpit half-way down one side of the nave or directly in front of the sanctuary, and for re-arranging the seating to face the preacher. But this was short-lived and few examples of these arrangements have survived, Compton Wynyates in Warwickshire being a notable exception.

In the nineteenth century there was a change of emphasis from preaching to the administration of the sacraments (*see* NINETEENTH-CENTURY CHURCH). The priest now conducted the service from a stall in the chancel and the role of the parish clerk was much reduced. As a consequence, many reading pews and tiered pulpits were removed,

encouraged by Victorian ecclesiologists in their enthusiasm for all things medieval. Nevertheless, several triple- and double-decker pulpits have survived, notably the seventeenth-century three-tiered pulpit at Kedington in Suffolk which has retained its *tester* or overhead SOUNDING BOARD which amplified and directed the voice of the preacher, together with the iron stand for an hour-glass (see below) and even a stand for the parson's wig. There are fine tiered pulpits at St. Mary's church, Whitby in Yorkshire, Minstead in Hampshire, Old Ditton near Westbury in Wiltshire, Parracombe and Molland in Devon and Teversal in Nottinghamshire. Examples of Jacobean pulpits with tester and supporting standard or back-piece include those at Abbotsbury in Dorset, Brancepeth in County Durham, Brinkworth in Wiltshire, Croscombe in Somerset, Ivinghoe and Cheddington in Buckinghamshire, Lenham in Kent, Newport on the Isle of Wight and Stoke D'Abernon in Surrey.

The survival of seventeenth- and eighteenth-century pulpits (and other furnishings) may usually be attributed to a succession of conservative squires and rectors who preferred the old ways to the new. Where new pulpits were built they are often in the then fashionable 'Early Gothic' style for which there was no medieval precedent and, unlike their graceful fourteenth- and fifteenth-century predecessors, they are invariably ill-proportioned and singularly ugly.

HOUR GLASSES

Hour glasses may still be found in many churches, or the wrought-iron supports in which they once stood, and these are usually attached to a pillar or wall at the side of the pulpit or to the pulpit itself. Church attendance being compulsory in the seventeenth century, preachers addressed captive audiences for at least an hour (*see* SEVENTEENTH-CENTURY CHURCH). If at the end of that time the parson turned the hour glass over, the congregation knew it was in for a further hour of preaching! About 120 brackets remain but (inevitably) very few glasses: the brackets at Binfield and Hurst in Buckinghamshire are unusually ornamental, as are those at Pilton and Tawstock in Devon which are in the form of an arm with the hand holding an hour glass. Amazingly, at Earl Stonham in Suffolk no fewer than four glasses have survived, each for a different length of time! There are other examples, among them those at Amberley in Sussex, Bloxworth in Dorset, Compton Basset in Wiltshire, Earl Stonham in Suffolk and Stoke-sub-Hamdon in Somerset.
See also FRATER PULPIT *and* LECTERNS

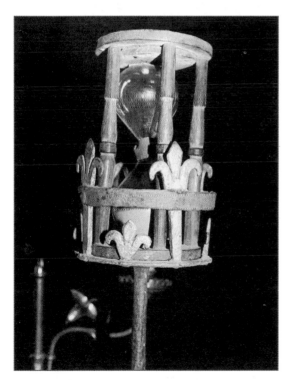

Hour glass at Bloxworth, Dorset.

PULPITUM Many of the great abbey churches and all the medieval English cathedrals once had a pulpitum: a massive transverse stone screen which separated the NAVE from the CHOIR. This usually consisted of a single wall between the piers of the CROSSING though there are several 'double' structures which occupy the depth of an entire bay: at Kirkstall Abbey in Yorkshire, for example, and at Norwich Cathedral. The position of the pulpitum varied according to the needs of the choir though it was always to the east of the ROOD SCREEN. At Malmesbury in Wiltshire the pulpitum enclosed the first bay west of the crossing (its western wall now forms a REREDOS for the altar of the parish church), while at Canterbury and Durham it connected the eastern piers of the crossing. In all cases there was a central doorway, flanked by altars in the western elevation, and a stair to the platform (*loft*) above. On occasions the loft was used as a gallery for singers, and often housed an organ (*see* ORGANS). It was also adorned with statues or paintings of historical and religious figures whose achievements were intended to inspire the beholder. The Latin *pulpitum* is a 'platform' or 'stage' suggesting that it was from here that sermons were preached before the development of the PULPIT. But monastic sermons were usually given from the president's chair in CHAPTER or choir and the main function of the pulpitum was to provide a solid screen for the RETURNED STALLS, thereby securing for the monks or canons both privacy and protection from draughts during the long hours of the divine office. The pulpitum should not to be confused with the CHANCEL SCREEN which was constructed on a very much smaller scale. The most impressive surviving examples are to be found in certain cathedrals where they often accommodate an (intrusive) organ: at Exeter, Gloucester and Lincoln, for example.
See also MEDIEVAL ARCHITECTURE *and* MONASTIC BUILDINGS

PURBECK MARBLE Used by the Romans in Britain and much favoured by the church-builders and monumental masons of thirteenth- and fourteenth-century England and Normandy, Purbeck marble is a not marble at all but a dark, fossiliferous limestone which occurs in two narrow strata in the Isle of Purbeck in Dorset. Its northern equivalent is *Frosterley marble*, a black or dark grey limestone extracted from quarries at Frosterley in County Durham.
See also TOUCH

PURGATORY Purgatory and Hell are not synonymous. Described by Eamon Duffy * as 'the out-patient department of Hell', Purgatory is 'the third place', a transient state occupied by repentant sinners who have died in grace. Hell is for the unrepentant and is a place of eternal torment (*poena sensus*) and exclusion from God's presence (*poena damni*). The concept is believed to date from the twelfth century and was intimately associated with profound social and intellectual changes, particularly attempts to introduce third orders between the powerful and the poor, the clergy and the laity. Medieval man did not believe that Purgatory held out hope of remission from Hell. Rather, Purgatory was a state of temporal punishment beyond the grave, a long and painful process of probation and expiation, preparing not-yet-worthy Christians for Heaven. Without the concept of Purgatory, the medieval practice of offering prayers and masses for the dead would have been untenable. The Reformers argued that this doctrine was unnecessary: when a sinner repented and put his faith in Jesus, he or she was immediately justified by God, adopted as a child into the heavenly Father's family and made God's friend. In the words of Paul: 'Those whom he justified he also glorified' (Romans 8: 30). God's grace short-circuited Purgatory.

See also CHANTRY, DOOM, INDULGENCES, MEDIEVAL CHURCH, PRIVILEGED ALTAR *and* WALL PAINTINGS

Further reading:

Duffy, E., *The Stripping of the Altars: Traditional Religion in England, c. 1400–c. 1580*, New Haven and London, 1992*

Le Goff, J., *The Birth of Purgatory*, Aldershot, 1984

PURIFICATION OF THE BLESSED VIRGIN MARY see CANDLEMAS *and* PRESENTATION OF CHRIST IN THE TEMPLE

PURIFICATOR *see* COMMUNION LINEN

PURITANS Members of an often extreme reforming movement dating from the reign of Henry VIII (1509–47) who, dissatisfied with the Elizabethan religious settlement, sought a further purification of the Church of England. They were particularly influential among the merchant classes and at first attacked 'unscriptual forms of worship', ornamentation, vestments and other 'trappings of the corrupted Church.' From 1570 the more extreme members began to attack the institution of the episcopacy itself. The Civil War of 1642–9 led to the temporary triumph of Puritanism but also to its proliferation into sects so that the term ceased to be appropriate after 1660.

Further reading:

Cliffe, J., *Puritans in Conflict*, Routledge, 1988

PURLIEU *see* PERAMBULATION

PURLIN A horizontal beam running parallel to the ridge of a roof and carrying the common *rafters* (*see* ROOFS (TIMBER)).

PURPURE *see* COLOURS (HERALDIC)

PUSEYITES *see* OXFORD MOVEMENT

PUTLOG HOLES Series of small square holes in which scaffolding was erected during the building of a wall or (more usually) a tower and which remain unfilled. There are examples at East Hendred in Berkshire and Great Burstead in Essex.

PUTTO *see* AMORINO

PYX A receptacle in which the reserved HOST is retained. Specifically a small silver or silver-gilt box in which the Blessed Sacrament is conveyed to the sick, wrapped in a *corporal* (*see* COMMUNION LINEN) and carried in a pyx-bag slung about the priest's neck.

See also PLATE, RESERVATION *and* TABERNACLE

PYX-SHRINE *see* TABERNACLE

QUADRAGESIMA An alternative name for the forty days of LENT and for the first Sunday in Lent.

QUADRIVIUM The four 'superior' sciences of arithmetic, astronomy, geometry and music which, together with the elementary *Trivium* of dialectic, grammar and rhetoric, comprised the Seven Liberal Arts which formed the basis of secular education in the Middle Ages. A student was required satisfactorily to complete his studies in the liberal arts before proceeding to the study of theology.

QUAKERS *see* SOCIETY OF FRIENDS

QUARE IMPEDIT An action brought by a patron in a temporal court against a bishop who refuses to institute a presentee to an ecclesiastical benefice.

QUARRY (*or* QUARREL) (i) One of a series of small diamond-shaped glass panels within a window (*see* STAINED GLASS). Stamped quarries, mass-produced and decorated with monochrome motifs, are characteristic of the nineteenth century. (ii) An unglazed floor tile (*see* TILES).

QUARTER DAYS and RENT DAYS

Lady Day	(Annunciation of the Blessed Virgin)	25 March

Michaelmas (Feast of St. Michael
and All Angels) 29 September
Christmas (Feast of the Nativity) 25 December
Midsummer Up to and including
1752 6 July
Thereafter 24 June

See also FEAST DAYS (FIXED AND MOVABLE), HOCKTIDE, LAMMAS *and* individual entries for CHRISTMAS, LADY DAY, MICHAELMAS *and* MIDSUMMER

QUARTERING (i) In HERALDRY, the method (known as MARSHALLING) whereby a shield of arms is divided to display both the paternal arms and those acquired through marriage to heraldic heiresses. (ii) Turning a bell through an angle of 90 degrees so that the clapper may strike a fresh place.

QUATREFOIL A figure with four radiating stylised 'petals' found both as an architectural motif and an heraldic device (*see* FOILS). Quatrefoils in Gothic tracery often contain heraldic shields, especially those found in the side panelling of tomb chests.

QUEEN ANNE'S BOUNTY A fund established in 1704 by Queen Anne to receive the ANNATES and tenths which had been confiscated by Henry VIII. The fund was used to augment the livings of impoverished clergymen and was later supplemented by substantial parliamentary grants and private benefactions (*see* EIGHTEENTH-CENTURY CHURCH). In 1948 the Queen Anne's Bounty was amalgamated with the Ecclesiastical Commissioners to form the Church Commissioners for England.
See also TITHES

QUEEN POST *see* KING POST *and* ROOFS

QUESTMAN A churchwarden's assistant (*see* SIDESMAN) and one who was required to attend an ecclesiastical visitation (*see* VISITATIONS, ECCLESIASTICAL).

QUINQUAGESIMA The Sunday before ASH WEDNESDAY.

QUIRE *see* CHOIR

QUOIN From the French *coin* meaning 'corner' or 'angle' a quoin is the external angle of a building and *quoins* or *quoin stones* are the dressed stones forming the angle. In Anglo-Saxon buildings, *long and short work* comprises quoins laid so that long vertical slabs alternate with short horizontal ones.
See also ANGLO-SAXON ARCHITECTURE

RAFTER Any of the sloping beams within the framework of a roof. Principal rafters are those which carry the PURLINS.
See also ROOFS

RAG *and* RAGSTONE A hard, course stone that is not FREESTONE.

RAGGLE The remains of a roof line preserved in the stonework of an adjacent building.

RAGMAN A parchment document with seals appended.

RAGWORK Rubble walling, usually a weathering face, composed of polygonal stones.
See also FACING MATERIALS *and* MASONRY

RAIL (i) A horizontal member in the framework of a panelled door.
See also BRACE, DOORS AND DOORWAYS, LEDGE, MUNTIN *and* STILE
(ii) *For* other types of rail *see* BENCHES AND BENCH-ENDS, CHANCEL SCREENS, COMMUNION RAILS, PARCLOSE *and* STAIRCASES.

RAINWATER HEAD A box-shaped metal structure (usually of lead or cast-iron) in which water from a gutter is collected and discharged into a down-pipe.

RAMPANT (i) Of an heraldic beast when standing on one hind-leg and with the other legs waving fiercely in the air. See BEASTS (HERALDIC).
(ii) *For* rampant arch *see* ARCH.

READING DESK (*also* READING PEW) A desk at the east end of the nave from which the parson conducted post-Reformation services. In the 1549 Communion Service (*see* COMMON PRAYER, BOOK OF) the people were instructed to remain in the nave until the Offertory. This part of the service (the Ante-Communion) was conducted by the priest from a reading pew in the nave, not from his old stall in the chancel. At the Offertory, priest and people moved into the chancel for the Communion, depositing their offerings of money in an oak chest provided for the purpose. The parson was also required to use the reading desk for the offices of Matins and Evensong so that the congregation could see and hear him clearly. During the seventeenth century nearly all churches acquired PULPITS and

these were often combined with reading desks to form great 'double-decker' canopied structures which towered above the congregation. In the nineteenth century, there was a return to the medieval practice of conducting services from a stall in the chancel and many fine Jacobean reading desks were relocated or dismantled. Of those which have survived, there is a splendid example of a double reading desk at Cumnor in Berkshire.
See also DESKS

REBUS A rebus is a pictorial pun on a name (*non verbis sed rebus*). Many early seals include simple rebuses and the concept therefore pre-dates heraldry. Rebuses were especially popular in medieval ecclesiastical circles and were widely used as personal devices and to decorate the fabric of buildings, chapels and tombs. At Milton Abbey in Dorset, for example, a stone corbel is carved and painted in the form of a windmill on top of a wine barrel (*tun*), the rebus of a former abbot of Milton; while at Canterbury, one Thomas Goldstone, Prior of Christchurch, used a gold flint stone ensigned with a mitre. Rebuses should not to be confused with heraldic BADGES though many badges are effectively rebuses: the talbot (hound) of the Talbots, for example, and the *hirondelle* (swallow) of the Arundels.
See also ATTRIBUTED ARMS, CYPHER, GLAZIERS' MARKS, MASONS' MARKS *and* MERCHANTS' MARKS

Rebus of Abbot William of Milton Abbey, Dorset.

RECESS *see* AUMBRY, BANNER STAVE LOCKER, BREAD OVEN, CHEST CUPBOARDS, CREDENCE, DOLE CUPBOARDS, EASTER SEPULCHRE, NICHE, PISCINA, SEDILIA *and* SQUINT

RECLUSE A religious who lives apart from the world (*see* ANCHORITE *and* COENOBITE). Not all recluses were genuinely EREMITICAL: in the medieval period, many occupied guests' rooms in religious houses and even engaged servants and private chaplains.

RECORDS *see* ARCHIVES *and* DOCUMENTARY SOURCES

RECTILINEAR TRACERY *see* MEDIEVAL ARCHITECTURE

RECTOR (i) A *clerical rector* was originally an INCUMBENT who received the 'Great Tithes': all the customary offerings and dues of his PARISH. He was responsible for the chancel and the rectory and for providing service books and vestments. In many instances, benefices were annexed by corporate bodies such as monastic or collegiate foundations who then received the Great (or Rectorial) Tithes, the Lesser (or Vicarial) Tithes going to a *vicar* who was appointed by them to administer the parish.

Following the Dissolution of the Monasteries, many monastic estates became the property of laymen (*lay rectors*) who also acquired the right to nominate vicars (subject to a bishop's approval), together with responsibility for maintaining the chancel and vicarage.

TITHES were virtually abolished in 1936 and a vicar is now appointed to all new livings, the designation rector being applicable to the incumbent of a new joint benefice or united parish or on the creation of a team ministry, even where none of the constituent parishes had a rector in the immediate past.
See also APPROPRIATION, CLERGY (CHURCH OF ENGLAND) *and* LAY RECTOR
(ii) The head of a college which may enjoy rectorial rights: as at Exeter and Lincoln colleges, Oxford.

RECTORY (i) A rectorial benefice (*see* RECTOR).
(ii) The dwelling house attached to a rectorial benefice.

RECUSANCY A recusant was one who refused to submit to the authority of the Established Church and refused to attend the services of the Church of England. By the Act of Uniformity of 1559 a recusant was fined 12 pence for each absence and in 1581 this was raised to £20 per lunar month. Legislation enacted under Elizabeth I and James I prescribed strict penalties and disabilities for recusants including the forfeiture of goods and two-thirds of his real property. The Recusant Rolls describe in detail these fines and forfeitures, though they are by no means complete. Many recusants were, of course, Roman Catholics but in some areas the majority were Puritan dissenters (the rolls do not differentiate between religious convictions). The annual rolls of the county sheriffs cover the period 1592–1691 (though some years are missing) and are deposited at the Public Record Office. The Catholic Record Society has published a number of Recusant Rolls. (*For* addresses *see* APPENDIX II). It was not until the CATHOLIC EMANCIPATION ACT of 1791 that recusancy ceased to be a crime.

See also ROMAN CATHOLIC CHURCH *and* VISITATIONS, ECCLESIASTICAL

RECUSANT ROLLS *see* RECUSANCY

RED HAND OF ULSTER *see* BARONET

RED LETTER DAYS Specific days, sometimes printed in red in the *Book of Common Prayer*, for which a proper Collect, Epistle and Gospel are provided. Important feast and saints' days were similarly printed in red in ecclesiastical calendars and came to be known as 'red letter days'.

See also RUBRIC

REDUNDANT CHURCHES *see* TWENTIETH-CENTURY CHURCHES

REFECTION SUNDAY *see* MOTHERING SUNDAY

REEDING *see* DECORATIVE MOTIFS

REFECTORIAN *see* FRATER *and* LARDER

REFECTORY *see* FRATER

REFORMATION, THE This somewhat imprecise term covers a complex series of changes which took place in the Western Church between the fourteenth and seventeenth centuries (*see* PROTESTANTISM). Reformers of Catholicism such as John Wycliffe (*c.* 1330–84), Martin Luther (1483–1546) and John Calvin (1509–64) rejected the authority of the Papacy, both religious and political, and sought authority in the original text of the Scriptures through vernacular translations (*see* ROMAN CATHOLIC CHURCH). They claimed justification (salvation) by faith, rejecting the Catholic doctrine of TRANSUBSTANTIATION and the adoration of the Virgin and the saints, and denounced malpractices and abuses within the Church such as the sale of INDULGENCES (*see* CALVINISM, LUTHERANISM *and* WYCLIFFE, JOHN).

THE REFORMATION IN ENGLAND

The Reformation was not a natural fulfilment of what had gone before but a violent disruption. In England, medieval Catholicism was neither exhausted nor decayed. Its vigour, richness and

creativity were undiminished and it retained a strong hold on the loyalty and imagination of the English people right up to the 1530s when the break with Rome occurred.

The English Reformation was a violent act of state rather than a popular movement, an insular process responsive to particular social and political forces which themselves arose from a long-standing monarchical policy of extending the sovereignty of central government. Reform was occasioned by papal procrastination concerning the 'King's Great Matter' – the dissolution of HENRY VIII's marriage with Catherine of Aragon – which led to Henry's repudiation of Papal authority in England and a series of Acts of Parliament in 1534 which severed financial, judicial and administrative links with Rome, and to the SIX ARTICLES of 1539, the first authoritative statement of the doctrines of the English Church. In particular, the Act of Supremacy of 1534 confirmed to Henry and his successors the title of 'the only supreme head in earth of the Church of England' (*see* CHURCH OF ENGLAND). It was followed by legislation intended (in Thomas Cromwell's words) to make Henry '. . . the richest Prince in Christendom'. By the Annates Acts of 1534 the Crown, as successor to the Pope, claimed the ANNATES of each benefice; acts of 1536 and 1539 authorised the DISSOLUTION OF THE MONASTERIES, in 1538 the religious SHRINES were dismantled, the relics destroyed and their treasures confiscated, and in 1547 the chantries were suppressed (*see* CHANTRY). Also in 1547, the year of the King's death, several of the traditional ceremonies of the medieval Church were abolished and an order made for the removal of all images 'from wall and window'. This resulted in the limewashing of WALL PAINTINGS (which, ironically, served to preserve them), the destruction (or defacement) of religious statues and the smashing of windows, though many escaped destruction – probably because of the cost of replacing them with clear glass.

Despite his break with Rome, Henry VIII consistently opposed the Reforming Movement and remained a convinced traditionalist in matters of doctrine and Church government, and it was not until after his death in 1547 that doctrinal Protestantism became official policy. The Act of Uniformity of 1549 required that the (first) *Book of Common Prayer* should be used in Anglican worship (*see* COMMON PRAYER, THE BOOK OF). This was followed by a second act in 1552 which authorised use of the (second) *Book of Common Prayer* and prescribed severe penalties for non-compliance and fines for non-attendance at Anglican services. The 1552 Prayer Book marks the establishment of Protestantism in the territories of the Crown of England. It abandoned transubstantiation, thereby confirming the distinction between the

MASS and the communion service which is the essence of the distinction between Protestantism and Roman Catholicism.

With the accession of Queen Mary in 1553, Roman Catholic forms of worship were restored and in 1555 there began a series of religious persecutions which acquired for the Queen the epithet 'Bloody Mary'. The fanaticism of the Queen's supporters and advisers, and the unpopularity of her marriage with the King of Spain, undoubtedly increased popular support for the objectives of the Reformers. Mary died in 1558 and a further Act of Supremacy in 1559 declared her successor, Elizabeth I (1558–1603), to be 'the only supreme governor . . . as well in all spiritual or ecclesiastical things or causes as temporal'. In the same year, the third Act of Uniformity required that a revised version of the Prayer Book should be used in all churches and weekly fines imposed for non-attandance at services. In 1563 the THIRTY-NINE ARTICLES were published and in 1593 the Conventicle Act reinforced the penalties for non-attendance and for holding secret assemblies (see CONVENTICLE).

Thus, the sixteenth century was a period of unprecedented religious upheaval, one which witnessed the dismantling of many long-established rituals of community life and presented both parishioners and clergy with acute and perplexing problems of belief and conduct. In most places, there is little evidence of hostility to the Roman Catholic Church which, in the 1530s, was still held in high regard. In early sixteenth-century wills, for example, the most common bequest was to the parish church and to the chapels of chantries and guilds which were accommodated therein. For an essentially conservative people, whose religious beliefs were focussed on the mystery of the Latin Mass, the introduction of a vernacular Bible and liturgy (see below), the destruction of familiar and comforting religious images and the prohibition of popular festivals and observances must have had a profound effect. And yet, with some notable exceptions (see PILGRIMAGE OF GRACE), most parishioners appear to have conformed to the doctrinal and liturgical changes which were imposed upon them by the combined authority of Church and State. Inevitably, a common reaction to such fundamental (and often contradictory) changes was one of helpless resignation. Documentary sources (including the lists of incumbents which are to be found in most churches) show that a remarkable number of the clergy simply shifted their position to accommodate each new change and, while a few were no doubt openly or privately cynical, most succeeded in avoiding trouble. One such was Simon Aleyn, the celebrated *Vicar of Bray*, who succeeded in retaining his Berkshire benefice through all the changes: '. . . being taxed by one for being a turncoat and an unconstant changeling, Not so, said

he, for I always kept my principle, which is this, to live and die the vicar of Bray.'

Cohabiting clerics were a phenomenon throughout medieval Europe but in 1549 the clergy of the new English Church were permitted to marry. There can be little doubt that, to the ordinary priest, respectability for his 'wife' and legitimacy for his children were above all the factors which made Protestantism acceptable to him. While in 1530 Henry VIII ruled over an essentially medieval society, by 1570 England was (outwardly, at least) whole-heartedly Protestant.

THE PARISH

The English Reformation turned the parish into a unit of local government (see VESTRY) and heaped upon its incumbent and churchwardens a whole range of new secular responsibilities. The CHURCHWARDENS bore the greatest burden – in addition to their traditional responsibilities for the maintenance of the parish church and its services and the enforcement of ecclesiastical law. But the clergy were also required actively to encourage parishioners to contribute to the relief of the poor (see POOR LAW), to attend to the punishment of 'rogues and vagabonds' and to prosecute recusants (see RECUSANCY), to administer public confessions and to lead an annual PERAMBULATION of parish boundaries. But in many ways the most dramatic effect of the English Reformation was on popular culture which hitherto had been firmly focused on the parish church – its ancient traditions and ceremonies, its calendar of festivals and religious processions and its (often boisterous) communal activities (see CHURCH AND COMMUNITY, NAVE *and* PROCESSIONS). The growth of PURITANISM in the second half of the sixteenth century engendered further criticism of activities such as CHURCH ALES, pageants, revels, play-acting and churchyard games (see also CHURCHYARDS *and* DRAMA). In their place, the Reformers promoted the benefits of preaching and attendance at sermons (see PULPITS).

The redistribution of lands and property which followed the DISSOLUTION OF THE MONASTERIES had a considerable impact on many parishes. In some, the churches of former abbeys or priories were acquired for parochial use and were often reduced in size in order to accommodate a community's needs and financial resources (see ABBEY *and* PRIORY). Others received the fittings from demolished monastic churches or even parts of their fabric: the tiny church of Hilton in Dorset, for example, has a striking series of traceried windows in the north wall which were removed from the cloister of nearby Milton Abbey in the 1530s. Impropriated parish churches (those which, in the Middle Ages, were annexed to a religious house) acquired lay patrons, members of the Tudor establishment who had received (or purchased) monastic buildings, estates and privileges at the Dissolution. Medieval abbots were often rectors (*see* RECTOR), and as such received the major revenues and tithes of impropriated parishes. These rights were also transferred to the new lay rectors (*impropriators*) who thereby assumed responsibility for maintaining the chancels of their impropriated churches and for appointing PERPETUAL CURATES to the benefices.

It was the suppression of the chantries in 1545 which resulted in the greatest impoverishment of community and civil life. Official disapproval of the doctrine of PURGATORY ('. . . vain opinions of purgatory and masses satisfactory to be done for them which be departed') led inevitably to the Chantry Act of 1547 and the confiscation of those chantry funds which had been assigned to so-called 'superstitious objects'. As a consequence, innumerable endowments, ranging from schools and hospices to the provision of wax for candles, were terminated simply because they were designed to provide perpetual masses for the souls of their founders (*see* CHANTRY *and* GUILDS). The Chantry Act was followed by a further confiscation of church possessions in 1552 (because, as the official records readily admit, 'the King's majesty had need presently of a mass of money . . .'), leaving only the bare essentials for worship. CHANTRY CHAPELS, with their altars removed, remained in the ownership of the families which endowed them and several continued in use as burial places or were adapted to serve as family pews (*see* PEWS, FAMILY).

DOCUMENTARY EVIDENCE
Surviving CHURCHWARDENS' ACCOUNTS often tell of the dramatic changes which took place in doctrine and services, in the appearance, decoration and furnishings of parish churches and in the role of the Church in the social life of communities. Sixteenth-century wills and PRO-BATE INVENTORIES are a useful guide to changing religious attitudes while DIOCESAN RECORDS, including the records of ecclesiastical visitations (*see* VISITATIONS, ECCLESIAST-ICAL), are an essential source of information. So too is the *Valor Ecclesiasticus* of 1535, an impressively comprehensive survey of clerical wealth and revenues compiled by Thomas Cromwell's administration on the eve of the English Reformation. Published in the nineteenth century by the Record Commission (*see* * *overleaf*), its six volumes include details of dioceses, archdeaconries, rural deaneries and parishes; monastic houses and their lands; rectories, vicarages and chapelries together with their revenues and the names of incumbents and chantry priests. The records of the Church courts (*see* COURTS (ECCLESIASTICAL)) are another useful source, though these are often voluminous, unsorted, unindexed and difficult to interpret. Even so, they are worthy of study because of the many aspects of daily life which fell within the courts' jurisdiction: heresy, witchcraft, the moral and spiritual condition of the clergy, stubborn adherence to the trappings of 'popery', non-attendance at church, non-payment of tithes, slander, immorality, drunkenness – all are here, for the most part recorded in the witnesses' own words and (unlike medieval ecclesiastical records) in English. *Chantry Certificates*, which were issued in 1548, are housed at the Public Record Office, together with the confiscation inventories of 1552 (*for* address *see* APPENDIX II) and many of these have been published by local history societies. They provide an invaluable source of information concerning the nature of chantries, guilds, almshouses, schools, hospitals and other charitable foundations at the close of the Middle Ages, together with details of the PLATE, VESTMENTS and other valuables which parish churches had accumulated through medieval bequests and endowments.

THE NEW LITURGY AND CHURCH FURNISHINGS
With the religious pendulum swinging first one way and then the other, there was an understandable reluctance to perpetuate the expansion of church building and refurbishment which had characterised the fifteenth and early sixteenth centuries (*see* MEDIEVAL ARCHITECTURE). Resources which had previously been used to endow chantries and to beautify churches were now diverted to more secular purposes (*see* SIXTEENTH- AND SEVENTEENTH-CENTURY ARCHITECTURE). Even before the Reformation, the classical influences of the Renaissance were increasingly apparent in architectural decoration, window glass and MONUMENTS; and HERALDRY, which emphasised the authority of the Tudor dynasty and the credentials of the post-medieval establishment, was ubiquitous – often ostentatiously so.

In 1549, the second year of Edward VI's reign (1547–53), the first English Prayer Book was issued and the revised LITURGY contained therein resulted in changes in the internal arrangement of churches. The aim of the reformers, led by Archbishop Cranmer (1489–1556), was to increase public participation in the services of the new English Church (*see* MEDIEVAL CHURCH). In the 1549 Communion service, for example, the congregation was instructed to remain in the nave until the Offertory. This part of the service (the Ante-Communion) was conducted by the priest from a reading pew in the nave, not from his old stall in the chancel. At the Offertory, priest and people moved into the chancel for the Communion, depositing their offerings of money in an oak chest provided for the purpose (*see* also PARISH CHEST *and* REGISTERS). Thus the chancel was no longer the *sanctum sanctorum* of the priests and communion was now received by the congregation in both kinds (i.e. both bread and wine). The parson was also required to use the reading desk for the revised offices of Mattins and Evensong so that the congregation could see and hear him clearly. In 1550 an order was made for the removal of the old stone ALTARS and these were replaced by wooden communion tables which were erected in the centre of the chancel so that the people could approach them from all sides. With the publication of the second Prayer Book in 1552 many of the remaining ceremonies were abolished, as were the traditional vestments, and orders were given for the removal of those 'superstitious images' which had not been taken down in accordance with earlier legislation.

Following the fanaticism and persecution of Mary's reign (see above), Queen Elizabeth attempted to reconcile the divisions within the English Church. A series of injunctions was issued which were intended to prevent extremists from taking the law into their own hands. CHANCEL SCREENS were to be retained (or rebuilt) though the figures of the ROOD were to be taken down, together with the ROOD LOFTS which, in the late medieval Church, had often accommodated a choir. These choirs, which had 'performed' the elaborate music of the period, were frowned upon by the Reformers. Congregational singing was to be encouraged, though an anthem was permitted – following the third collect at Mattins and Evensong. From this time until the nineteenth century, the PARISH CLERK led the singing of the congregation from a desk in the nave while choirs (of singers and instrumentalists) were usually located at the west end of the church, either on a raised platform or in a GALLERY which, in a number of cases, was constructed from the materials of the former rood loft (see CHURCH MUSIC). Communion tables were to be kept against the east wall of the sanctuary except during the communion service when they were moved into the centre of the chancel and turned so that the narrow ends faced east and west, thereby enabling the communicants to kneel at all four sides. Seats were sometimes provided along the chancel walls for the communicants, an arrangement which is still evident at several churches including Deerhurst and Hailes in Gloucestershire. At this time celebrations of the communion took place only once or twice a quarter (on 'Sacrament Sundays'). On other Sundays the morning service consisted of Mattins, the Litany and Ante-Communion, the sermon being of particular importance (see PULPITS). Churches were, of course, unheated and in many parishes high-sided box PEWS were erected in order to keep out draughts (see also PEWS, FAMILY and PEW RENTING). With increasing literacy, texts replaced medieval WALL PAINTINGS which the Reformers regarded as primitive and 'superstitious'. The Creed, the Lord's Prayer the Ten Commandments and other biblical texts (*sentences*), sometimes painted within a (modestly) decorative border, now adorned the walls of post-Reformation churches, instructing congregations where once pitchfork-wielding demons and gaping hell-mouths had terrified their medieval predecessors.

See also CLERGY (CHURCH OF ENGLAND), DIOCESES, INTERREGNUM, SEVENTEENTH-CENTURY CHURCH *and* THIRTY-NINE ARTICLES

Further reading:

Caley, J. and Hunter J., (eds.), *Valor Ecclesiaticus temp. Henrici VIII Auctoritate Regia Institus*, Record Commission, 1810–34 *

Chaunu, P., (ed.), *The Reformation*, Stroud, 1990

Dickens, A., *The English Reformation*, London, 1994

Duffy, E., *The Stripping of the Altars: Traditional Religion in England, c. 1400–c. 1580*, New Haven and London, 1992

Haigh, C., *English Reformations*, Oxford, 1993

REGISTERS Surviving medieval CHURCH-WARDENS' ACCOUNTS provide a rich account of community life at that time, but it was not until the mid-sixteenth century that baptisms, marriages and burials were entered into registers prescribed for that purpose. Thomas Cromwell's directive of 1538 required each parish to obtain a 'secure coffer' in which to keep its records, the parson to hold one key and the churchwardens the others (*see* PARISH CHEST). Each week, baptisms, marriages and burials were to be entered in a register by the parson, witnessed by a churchwarden and deposited in the parish chest. Most early registers contain three separate sections in the same volume though, in some, baptisms, marriages and burials are listed together and chronologically.

Further legislation, in 1598, required that all loose-leaf records were to be transcribed into books, especially those entered since the Queen's accession – which explains why so many extant records date from 1558 (see below). The Order also directed that, henceforth, both churchwardens should witness entries, that entries should be read out at Sunday services and that copies of the registers should be submitted annually to the diocesan bishops (*see* BISHOPS' TRANSCRIPTS).

From 1653, parish *registrars* were appointed to maintain the records. As a result, many parishioners deliberately avoided registration because the (sometimes illiterate) officials were authorised to charge a fee of one shilling for each entry. During the Interregnum (from 1654 to 1660), responsibility for marriages was transferred to the Justices of the Peace and consequently those couples who chose a church wedding were unable to register their marriage.

In order to finance the war with France, legislation was introduced in in 1694 which levied a tax on registration: two shillings for baptisms, two shillings and sixpence for marriages and four shillings for burials. Paupers were to be provided with free burial and there were higher rates of tax for the better-off. Furthermore, because so many children were being baptised by Dissenting ministers, all births (as distinct from baptisms) were to be notified to the parish priest and a fee of sixpence paid to compensate him for his reduced income.

Many of the earliest parish registers have not survived though, as has already been noted, instances of fragile or fragmentary registers being transcribed into new ones are not uncommon, especially from the mid-sixteenth century. These transcribed entries are usually written in the same hand on the opening pages of the new register with the signatures of the vicar (or rector) and churchwardens appended to each page.

Entries in the registers usually consist of a brief record of names and the dates of baptism, marriage or burial though, from 1644, birth dates were also noted as were dates of death. To these basic entries, were added occasional comments concerning parishioners and their everyday lives. Indeed, some clergymen treated their registers as diaries and noted significant events such as 'ruined harvest', 'heavy snowfall' and 'plague'. An act of 1711 required that proper books should be kept for registration purposes and that these should have ruled and numbered pages. In 1783, a duty of three pence was was levied on each register entry, of which the incumbent received a commission of 20 per cent (*Stamp Act 1783*).

Even the most mundane of registers can provide interesting material. In the mid-nineteenth century three-quarters of the families in a parish would have lived there for several generations, or within a few miles of its boundaries, and their names will be found time after time in the pages of registers and (from the late seventeenth century) on GRAVE-STONES in the churchyard. By studying the demography of these extended families it may be possible to discern the slow and often painful evolution of a community.

Of course, there are omissions, usually as the result of forgetfulness: many parsons and parish clerks dutifully completed their records at the week's end while others would do so only with the approach of Easter when transcripts of the registers had to be submitted to the bishop. There was also the annual PRESENTMENT when the wardens and parson were required to appear before the archdeacon (or, every third year, before the bishop) to report on the affairs of their parish.

Today, most parish registers are stored at county record offices where they are available for public inspection (*for details, see* ARCHIVES).

See also BANNS OF MARRIAGE, BURIAL IN WOOL ACTS 1667 and 1678, HARDWICKE'S MARRIAGE ACT 1754, GEORGE ROSE'S ACT 1812, MARRIAGE ACT 1836, MARRIAGE LICENCES

See also BISHOPS' REGISTERS

Further reading:

Bryant Rosier, M., *Index to Parishes in Phillimore's Marriages*, Chichester, 1991

Friar, S., *The Batsford Companion to Local History*, London, 1991

Humphery-Smith, C., *Phillimore Atlas and Index of Parish Registers*, Chichester, 1984

Richardson, J., *A Local Historian's Encyclopedia*, New Barnet, (rev. 1986)

Gibson, J., *Bishops' Transcripts and Marriage Licences*, London, 1983

Steel, D., *National Index of Parish Registers* (12 vols.), Chichester

Tate, P., *The Parish Chest*, Cambridge, 1969

Webb, C., (ed.), *The National Index of Parish Registers* (series), Chichester

REGNAL YEARS In the Middle Ages, documents were dated by reference to the year of the sovereign's reign: thus, a document of the third year of the reign of Henry VI (1422–61) would be shown as such (and in modern calendars as 3 Henry VI). In later records the *Anno Domini* year either replaced the regnal year or was given in addition to it. Regnal years began on the first day of a reign and continued until the same day twelve calendar months later. One exception is King John (1199–1216) whose rule began on Ascension Day (a movable feast): therefore each of his regnal years commences on Ascension Day and not on the calendar anniversary of his succession.

See also RULERS OF ENGLAND AND OF THE UNITED KINGDOM

REGULAR One who lives in a religious community and is bound by its rule: in contradistinction to a secular who lives in the world. As the name suggests, the life of a regular (also known as a religious) was strictly regulated so that 'Personal standing is merged in the equality of each and all, there is no inequitable mark of exemption, except the greater sanctity which is able to put one man above others.' This 'equality of each and all' applied to all members of an order: children and old men, members of the nobility and of the lower orders.

See also AUGUSTINIANS

RELICS Relics are the material remains of a saint after his death and sacred objects with which he had been in contact. The bodies of martyrs were venerated from the mid-second century and in Rome attracted cults whose members worshipped at the martyrs' tombs. The Second Council of Nicaea in 787 ordered that no church should be consecrated without them. The veneration of relics was approved for the English

Church by the Council of Constantinople in 1084 but the cult was never as popular in Britain as it was in continental Europe where its influence increased significantly during the Crusades. Nevertheless, quantities of relics, mostly spurious, were brought back from the Holy Land to be displayed in richly decorated *reliquaries* and carried before processions at religious festivals. Many gave rise to superstitious practices, vestiges of which are discernible today. In the Middle Ages, the cult acquired a theological foundation. The unique dignity of the bodies of saints as receptacles of the Holy Spirit was emphasised, together with the sanction given by God in making them the occasion of miracles. Such relics attracted innumerable pilgrims to the more famous SHRINES at which prayers of supplication were offered in the hope of salvation and cures for a multiplicity of ailments. So lucrative were these activities that it has been suggested (by G.H. Cook *) that the acquisition of shrines and relics came to be an obsession with many Benedictine abbots. The doctrine was later confirmed by the *Council of Trent*, convened at Trento in northern Italy from 1545–63, which defined the doctrines of the Church in opposition to those of the Reformation.

In England, shrines and relics were suppressed at the REFORMATION though many churches have dedications which allude to their former possessions (*see also* CHURCH SITES *and* DEDICATION, CHURCH). The church at Stanford-in-the-Vale in Berkshire, for example, still retains the reliquary which once contained a bone of St. Denys to whom the church is dedicated, while at Whitchurch Canonicorum in Dorset the shrine containing the bones of St. Wite still attracts pilgrims today. In the Middle Ages a reliquary containing the bones of St. Piran at Perranzabuloe in Cornwall was carried in procession on feast days, indeed an inventory dated 1281 also includes the saint's head – together with the teeth of St. Brendan and St. Martin!

Further reading:

Cook, G.H., *English Monasteries in the Middle Ages*, London, 1961 *

RELIC SUNDAY The third Sunday after Midsummer on which the relics kept in a church were especially venerated.

RELICT A widow (*see* MONUMENTS *and* PROBATE).

RELIGIOUS ORDERS IN THE ANGLICAN CHURCH The nineteenth-century revival of religious orders in the Anglican Communion was inspired by the OXFORD MOVEMENT and by Edward Pusey (1800–82) in particular. It was Pusey who in 1841 received the vows of Marian Hughes, the first superior of the Convent of the Holy and Undivided Trinity at Oxford (1849), and it was he who established the community at Park Village, Regent's Park in London which later merged with Priscilla Sellon's Society of the Holy Trinity at Davenport (1848) (now at Ascot Priory in Berkshire). Other communities include those of St. Mary the Virgin at Wantage in Oxfordshire (1848), St. John the Baptist at Clewer in Somerset (1852) and St. Margaret at East Grinstead in Sussex (1855). These were 'active' communities which combined a religious life with public service, notably in the slums of the great cities. The first 'closed' (contemplative) community, the Sisters of the Love of God, was founded at Fairacres, Oxford in 1907. The first religious order for men was the Society of St. John the Evangelist (the 'Cowley Fathers'), a society of mission priests and laymen founded by Richard Benson at Cowley, Oxfordshire in 1865. This was followed by the Society of the Sacred Mission at Kelham, Nottinghamshire (1891) and the Community of the Resurrection founded by Charles Gore (at Oxford, 1892) at Mirfield, Yorkshire. The English Order of St. Benedict moved from Caldey Island, Dyfed to Nashdom Abbey in Buckinghamshire (*via* Pershore in Worcestershire) when the majority of the Caldey Island community submitted to Rome in 1913. An English Franciscan order was established after the first World War at Hilfield in Dorset (1921) and was constituted as a religious community in 1931. There are now nine orders of men in the Church of England, one mixed community (the Community of the Glorious Assumption at Burton-on-Trent) and thirty-six orders of women. Most are members of the Advisory Council for Religious Communities.

Forms of address and the abbreviatory letters adopted by the various orders may be found in *Debrett's Correct Form* edited by P. Montague-Smith, Kingston-upon-Thames, 1976.

RELIQUARY A receptacle for RELICS, often made of precious metals and richly decorated.

RENDERING *see* FACING MATERIALS

RENT DAYS *see* HOCK-TIDE *and* QUARTER DAYS

REPOSE, ALTAR OF An altar on which the Host, consecrated on MAUNDY THURSDAY, was reserved for the Good Friday communion.

REPOUSSÉ (*also* EMBOSSING) Metal hammered from the back, or from within, to form raised patterns.

REQUIEM A form of MASS offered for the repose of the souls of the dead. The name is derived from the opening words of the introit which (until recently) was used at all such masses. The Requiem

Mass was popularly known as the *Black Mass* from the medieval custom of using black vestments.

RERE-ARCH An internal arch to a gothic window supporting the inner part of a wall's thickness, characteristic of thirteenth-century lancet windows.

REREBRACE *see* ARMOUR

REREDORTER The main latrine block in the conventual buildings of a religious house (*see* DORTER).

REREDOS (*also* REREDORSE *or* REREDOSS) A decorative stone or timber screen, usually supported on a shelf (*predella*) and covering the wall behind and above an altar or filling the space between two piers to the east of a sanctuary. Many late medieval reredoses were richly decorated with painted panels, set together in a wooden frame (*retable*), or tiers of ornate canopied niches each containing an alabaster figure sculpted in high relief and originally brightly coloured and gilded. Regrettably, few of these figures escaped the attentions of Cromwell's iconoclasts and most surviving reredoses contain little more than empty niches like rows of broken teeth – or are Victorian

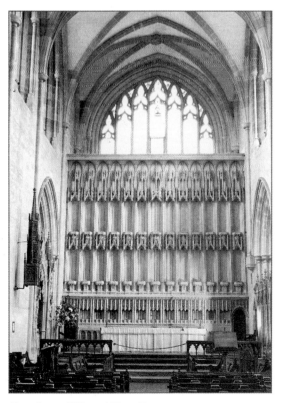

Reredos at Milton Abbey, Dorset.

replacements. A notable (and dramatic) exception is the magnificent fourteenth-century stone reredos at Christchurch Priory in Dorset which retains many original figures including a large reclining Jesse. Post-Reformation reredoses (*see* ALTARPIECE) were more austere, with the Ten Commandments, the Creed and the Lord's Prayer (and the occasional cherubim) painted on boards which were often enclosed in classical pilastered frames. The Georgian church at Tyberton in Herefordshire contains an elaborately carved reredos in dark wood with torches of life, swords, rods and scourges, crucifix, ladder, pliers and hammers, axes and faggots, all surmounted by a row of cherubim and a phoenix rising at the centre. One of the finest pieces of eighteenth-century carving in Britain, the Tyberton reredos was commissioned by the ubiquitous Duke of Chandos in the 1720s.
See also TRIPTYCH

RESERVATION The practice of reserving the Host (the consecrated bread of the Eucharist) for the purpose of Communion. In the early Church, the faithful kept the sacrament in their homes but from the fourth century it was reserved in churches, either in the SACRISTY or in a special receptacle provided for that purpose: a wall-cupboard in the sanctuary (*see* AUMBRY), a TABERNACLE suspended above the altar or a PYX on the altar. The presence of the reserved Host was signified by the burning of a lamp with a white flame (*see* LAMPS). A dispensation was made in the 1549 *Book of Common Prayer* which permitted reservation for the communion of the sick, but this was deleted from the revised Prayer Book of 1552.

RESERVED (i) A surface which is left plain to receive later decoration. (ii) *See* RESERVATION

RESIDENCE, OBLIGATION OF Clergy are obliged to reside within the ecclesiastical parish in which they are authorized to minister. This ancient obligation was reiterated in the Church of England canons of 1969.

RESONATORS *see* AMPLIFIERS

RESPOND A half-pier, bonded into a wall and carrying one end of an ARCH (*see* PIER).

RESPONSES *see* PRECES *and* VERSICLES

RESTORATION, THE *see* SEVENTEENTH-CENTURY CHURCH

RETABLE *see* ALTARS *and* REREDOS

RETARDATAIRE A piece of work executed in the style of an earlier period.

RETICULATED TRACERY *see* MEDIEVAL ARCHITECTURE

RETREAT A period spent in meditation and contemplation (and often in silence), removed from the distractions of the outside world. In the Church of England the practice was encouraged by the OXFORD MOVEMENT and remains popular today.

RETRO-CHOIR (i) In monastic churches, the space between the PULPITUM and ROOD-SCREEN where processions, which divided in order to enter by the two doors of the rood-screen, came together again before entering the CHOIR. The retro-choir was a characteristic of Cistercian churches (though not exclusively so) and usually contained two altars, one on either side of the pulpitum doorway. It also provided accommodation during the choir offices for infirm monks and those who arrived too late to enter the choir. (ii) In the later Middle Ages, the area behind (and to the east of) the high altar, often constructed to accommodate a notable shrine and the multitude of worshippers attracted to it.
See also AMBULATORY *and* MEDIEVAL ARCHITECTURE

RETURN The point at which a length of wall, moulding or pipe changes direction e.g. in the DRIPSTONE of a doorway or window opening.

RETURNED STALLS Those sections of the STALLS in the CHOIR of a monastic or collegiate church or cathedral which have their backs to a PULPITUM or CHANCEL SCREEN and therefore face east and are at right-angles to the other stalls. The return stalls were usually occupied by senior members of the community and visiting dignitaries.

REVEAL The internal side surface of an opening or recess e.g. of the aperture of a doorway or window opening between the frame and the outer surface of the wall.

REVEREND An epithet, indicative of respect, applied to the clergy since the fifteenth century and used as a title (prefixed to names in correspondence) since the seventeenth century. Some clergymen prefer 'Reverend' to be written in full but it is usually abbreviated to 'The Rev.' or (preferably) 'The Revd' – always with the definite article.
See also ADDRESS (FORMS OF)

REVET To face with masonry.

RIB *and* **RIBBED VAULT** *see* VAULTING

RIBBON (*also* **RIBAND**) (i) A decorative motif in the form of a narrow band of ornamental material,

usually depicted as a stylised bow and found in mouldings and carved stone monuments (*see* DECORATIVE MOTIFS). (ii) In HERALDRY, the shield of arms of a widow may sometimes be surrounded by a ribbon (*cordelière*).

RIDDEL CURTAINS *and* **RIDDEL POSTS** (*also* **RIDDELL**) From the French *rideau* ('curtain'), riddel curtains screened an altar on three sides or at each end. They were supported by riddel posts at the corners of an altar, each of which was often surmounted by a carved and gilded angel or ornate candle-holder. Riddel curtains were a medieval feature which was re-introduced by the ecclesiastical architect Sir Ninian Comper (1864–1960) in the early twentieth century. Riddel posts are often found *sans* curtains as a stunning decorative feature though, in one known case, the posts have been removed and the four angels placed on the window sill behind the altar!
See also ALTARS

RIDGE PIECE The principal timber running along the apex of a roof (*see* ROOFS).

RIGHTS, TAKING ONE'S The legal right of every parishioner 'devoutly and humbly desiring the same' to take communion in his or her parish church and, in the medieval church, to make confession and receive absolution.

RINGERS' FLOOR The storey of a church tower in which the BELLS are rung.

RINGS A emblem of fidelity. Since the seventh century, a ring (now usually containing an amethyst) is part of a bishop's official insignia. Wedding rings originated in the betrothal rings used by the Romans and adopted by members of the early Church. It is now common practice for rings to be exchanged during the marriage ceremony though, until recently, it was the groom who placed a ring on his bride's finger as a token of fidelity.

R.I.P. The abbreviated form of *Requiescat in Pace* meaning 'may he (or she) rest in peace' commonly found on MONUMENTS. The plural *Requiescant in Pace* ('may they rest in peace') is similarly abbreviated.
See also EPITAPHS *and* INSCRIPTIONS

RITUAL *see* LITURGY, PROCESSIONS *and* REFORMATION, THE
For the Ritualistic Movement *see* LITURGICAL MOVEMENT.

RITUAL COMMISSION, THE A Royal Commission of 1867 charged with inquiring into

Riddel posts at Mere, Wiltshire (1932),

the variations of ceremonial practice within the Church of England. It produced four reports which dealt with the Eucharistic VESTMENTS (1867), INCENSE and LAMPS (1868), the LECTIONARY (1869) and revisions of the *Book of Common Prayer* (1870) (*see* COMMON PRAYER, BOOK OF).

ROCHET *see* VESTMENTS

ROCOCO The final phase of the baroque style of architecture and decoration (*see* EIGHTEENTH-CENTURY ARCHITECTURE). In Britain, the mid-eighteenth-century rococo style is primarily a decorative one, found mainly in interiors, its delicacy and playfulness contrasting with the subdued exteriors of contemporary classical buildings. It is manifested mainly in the treatment of stucco wall decoration, doorway surrounds, chimney-pieces and MONUMENTS. Rococo work is generally in low relief, asymmetrical and abstract, and composed of ribbons, scrolls, floral wreaths, seaweed, shells, birds and animals in white and pastel tones and with only light gilding. The illuminative effect may be enhanced by the use of wall mirrors.

ROGATION The medieval festival of Rogationtide was held on the three days (*Cross Days*) preceding Ascension Day. Introduced into England during the eighth century, this festival combined pagan tradition with religious observance and practical necessity. Rogation days were prescribed days of prayer and abstinence associated especially with prayers for a bounteous harvest. The Major Rogation (25 April) was a Christianised version of the pagan *Robigalia*, a procession through the cornfields and the offering of prayers for the preservation of the crops (especially from mildew), and of the Roman feast day of Terminus, the god of fields and landmarks. Minor Rogations originated in fifth century Gaul where processional litanies were observed to protect the land against earthquakes and other perils. In the Middle Ages Rogationtide was known as 'Gang Week' from the Old Norse *gangr* meaning 'a progress'. The festival itself consisted of a perambulation during which crosses and green boughs were carried, divine blessings invoked on the land and the crops and the boundaries of the village confirmed by tracing crosses in the ground. At traditional stopping places the priest would read from the scriptures, the 'stations' being marked by an oak tree or other familiar feature. Place-names (still found in Ordnance Survey maps) such as Gospel Oak, Gospel Thorn and Amen Corner are the relics of this ancient festival and are invariably located on contemporary ecclesiastical parish boundaries (though these may subsequently have been altered). The attendant festivities were sometimes excessive and were (rightly) considered to have pagan associations so that following the Reformation the 1662 *Book of Common Prayer* ordered the observance of the three Minor Rogations as 'Days of Fasting and Abstinence' and the procession was reduced to the '*beating of the bounds*' with willow wands, a tradition which later became the formal PERAMBULATION of a parish VESTRY.

See also BOUNDARIES *and* PROCESSIONS

ROLL Strips of vellum or parchment sewn together and rolled up or bound into a book (*rotulus*).

ROLL OF HONOUR *see* WAR MEMORIALS

ROMAN CATHOLIC CHURCH That part of the Christian Church which is in communion with the Pope whose office is acknowledged to be in succession to St. Peter and the Apostles in whom Christ invested the power of the Holy Spirit. Its doctrine is characterised by a strict adherence to tradition together with a belief in the infallibility of the living voice of the Church. It has a complex hierarchical organisation of bishops and priests with the Pope at its head. Supernatural life is mediated to individual Christians by members of the hierarchy in the seven sacraments and the Mass is at the centre of liturgical life. Communion is required at Easter and attendance at Mass is obligatory on all Sundays and Feasts of Obligation.

Catholicism was the religion of England and Wales prior to the REFORMATION (*see* MEDIEVAL CHURCH), but following the Acts of Uniformity of 1552 and 1559 the political climate deteriorated and strict anti-Catholic legislation was introduced. Catholics were tolerated during the Protectorate (1653–9) but persecuted following the Restoration (1660). They were prevented from holding civil or military office by the Test Act of 1673 and from Parliament by the Test Act of 1678. In 1778, the Catholic Relief Act enabled Catholics to own land but it was received with hostility, culminating in the Gordon Riots of 1780.

The Catholic Emancipation Act of 1829 removed many constraints, such as discrimination against Catholic teachers and schools, but it was not until 1871 that Catholics were readmitted to the universities. The *Recusant Rolls* dating from 1592–1691 list many Catholics (as well as non-conformist Protestants) and are held at the Public Record Office in Chancery Lane (*see* RECUSANCY). Several have been published by the Catholic Record Society, which also publishes a journal, *Recusant History*. Catholics were obliged to register their names and land-holdings with clerks of the peace in 1771 and these records should be available in county record offices. Unofficial registers of births, marriages and deaths were maintained but few pre-date 1778 and most remain in the archives of the Church.

For the Catholic Archives Society, the Catholic Record Society, the Duke of Norfolk's Library and Archives, the Franciscan Archives (English Province) *and* the record office of the Society of Jesus *see* APPENDIX II.

Further reading:

Mullins, E., *Texts and Calendars*, Catholic Record Society, 1960

ROMANESQUE *see* ARCHITECTURAL PERIODS, ANGLO-SAXON ARCHITECTURE *and* MEDIEVAL ARCHITECTURE

ROMAN LETTERING *see* LETTERING

ROOD From the Old English *rod* meaning 'cross', a rood is a carved image of Christ crucified (a crucifix). A notable feature of Saxon religious art, roods were commonly placed above the doorways of churches, though few have survived the attentions of the iconoclasts. There are examples of Saxon roods at Bitton in Avon, Daglingworth in Gloucestershire, Headbourne Worthy and Romsey, both in Hampshire, Langford in Oxfordshire and Wormington in Worcestershire. A number of early roods have been restored to the churches from which they were 'lost' in the sixteenth century but no longer occupy their original positions. The great stone rood above the south door of the Saxon minster at Breamore in Hampshire is perhaps the best preserved, having been protected from the weather by a medieval porch. Breamore church also contains a splendid Anglo-Saxon inscription, boldly carved above the narrow archway to the south transept. In translation it reads: 'Here the covenant is revealed to you'.

The medieval *Great Rood* was a carved and painted crucifix, erected on a pedestal above the ROOD SCREEN (which separated the chancel from the nave) and flanked by the figures of the Blessed Virgin Mary and St. John the Evangelist (*see* VEILS). These figures were usually supported by a ROOD BEAM which, with the rood screen, carried a raised platform or ROOD LOFT. Others were suspended above the chancel arch or affixed to a wooden tympanum which blocked the top of the arch. Just as the death and resurrection of Christ dominates Christian theology, so the Great Rood, the symbol of Redemption, dominated the interiors of medieval churches. Of course, some were more ornate than others but there can be little doubt that nearly every church possessed a crucifix and that many were replaced by more imposing figures when walls were heightened and clerestories added in the late medieval period. There was often an elaborate gilded canopy in the ceiling above the rood (*see* ROOD CELURE) and, on the tympanum, a painting of the Last Judgement (*see* DOOM). Surviving paintings sometimes have uncoloured spaces where the great crucifix and figures were erected: at Raunds in Northamptonshire, for example.

The Great Roods were taken down and dismantled by order of the Privy Council in 1548, together with the rood lofts which supported them, though in most churches the rood screens were retained for practical purposes (*see* CHANCEL SCREENS). In some parishes, the figures of the rood were hidden – 'in anticipation of better times' – while, in others, resentful parishioners reacted to their removal by painting large crosses on the tympanum. Those roods which somehow survived the reformers' attentions in the sixteenth century were later destroyed during the iconoclastic orgies of the 1640s (*see* INTER-REGNUM). Consequently, there are now no complete medieval roods in English churches and very few fragments, those at Cartmel Fell in Lancashire and South Cerney in Gloucestershire being exceptional.

Most of the roods which are now found in churches date from the Gothic Revival of the nineteenth century (*see* NINETEENTH-CENTURY ARCHITECTURE) and from the work of ecclesiastical architects such as Sir Ninian Comper (1864–1960) whose early twentieth-century roods are sometimes flanked by attendant seraphim, as at Wimborne St. Giles in Dorset. Several 'restored' roods which have been erected on earlier screens serve to illustrate the appearance of their medieval predecessors: at Eye in Suffolk, Huttoft in Lincolnshire and Lapford in Devon, for example. Perhaps the most celebrated Victorian restoration is that of F.C. Eden at Blisland in Cornwall (1894), described by John Betjeman as shimmering in 'a blaze of red and gold and green and white', the wonderfully ornate screen, loft and rood creating '. . . an unforgettable sense of joy and mystery'.

ROOD BEAM (*also* CANDLE BEAM) A horizontal bressumer beam which extended between the piers of a CHANCEL ARCH and supported the ROOD. Together with the parallel upper rail (*head*) of the ROOD SCREEN, the rood beam also carried the superstructure of the ROOD LOFT. The size and rough-hewn nature of many of these beams is evident in a number of churches where neither the

The rood beam at Theddlethorpe church, Lincolnshire.

loft nor the cornice of the screen have survived and the original structure is exposed: at Theddlethorpe in Lincolnshire, for example. On festive occasions, the rood beam often carried candles, placed in prickets, hence the alternative name '*candle beam*'.
See also LENTEN VEIL

ROOD CELURE (*also* CEILURE) A series of ceiling panels (or the eastern bay of a nave vault) directly above a ROOD SCREEN, richly decorated in colour and gilt as a 'canopy of honour' to the ROOD.

ROOD LOFT (*also* JUBE) A projecting gallery above a ROOD SCREEN at the east end of a nave. The structure is usually carried by a ROOD BEAM and by the upper rail (*head*) of the screen itself. Parapets are often ornately carved with pierced tracery and the projecting base of the loft was usually supported on coving or fan vaulting which may have survived when the parapet was dismantled. The loft was entered by means of a *rood stair*, a flight of stone steps within an adjacent wall or turret, and provided access to the ROOD which was covered during Lent (*see* LENTEN VEIL), and to the rood beam (or *candle beam*) on which candles were lit on festive occasions. Like the PULPITUM

Late nineteenth-century rood, loft and screen at Mere, Wiltshire, incorporating medieval fragments.

in larger churches, the rood loft was sometimes used by singers and musicians, especially from the late thirteenth century when church music was becoming more elaborate.

Most rood lofts were removed at the Reformation and after 1561 singers were moved to a west gallery (*see* GALLERIES). Only a dozen medieval lofts remain in England, though there are several fine examples in Wales, notably at Llanelieu and Partrisho in Powys, Llangwm Uchaf in Gwent and Llanrwst in Denbighshire. Just across the border, the superb early sixteenth-century rood loft at St. Margaret's in Herefordshire probably survived the Reformation because of the

Late fifteenth-century rood screen and projecting loft at Swimbridge, Devon.

church's remoteness. The silvery wood is exquisitely carved with intertwined foliage, fleurs-de-lis and bosses with human faces, lion's heads and flowers. Post-Reformation paintings of the arms of the (old) English and Welsh dioceses in the panels of the medieval rood loft at Attleborough in Norfolk probably replaced earlier religious subjects, while at Flamborough in Yorkshire all the original niches have survived – but without their figures.

The rood stair was usually blocked when the loft was removed though there are several complete examples, as at Burrington in Somerset. Most medieval churches have retained at least some vestige of their former rood stairs, typically an angled recess in the masonry adjacent to a chancel arch. At Blewbury in Berkshire and Stogumber in Somerset the original rood stair doors have survived.

Most of the rood lofts which are now found in churches date from the Gothic Revival of the nineteenth century (*see* NINETEENTH-CENTURY ARCHITECTURE) and from the work of ecclesiastical architects such as Sir Ninian Comper (1864–1960). Several 'restored' rood lofts which have been erected on earlier screens serve to illustrate the appearance of their medieval predecessors (*see* ROOD).

Further reading:

Bond, F. and Camm, D. , *Rood-screens and Rood-lofts* (2 vols.), London, 1909

Bond, F., *Screens and Galleries in English Churches*, Oxford, 1908

ROODMAS *see* HOLY CROSS DAY

ROOD SCREEN In medieval churches, a decorative stone or wooden screen which separated the chancel from the nave and supported a ROOD LOFT above which was the Great Rood (*see* ROOD). Most screens were pierced with traceried lights and a central opening and gate which afforded

Painted figures in the fifteenth-century rood screen at Eye in Suffolk: Edward the Confessor, John the Evangelist, Catherine, William of Norwich, Lucy, Blaise and Cecilia.

access to the chancel. Both loft and screen were usually richly decorated with coloured and gilded carving, the panels below the tracery of the screen sometimes containing painted figures of the saints. Unlike roods and lofts, many medieval screens survived the Reformation as CHANCEL SCREENS. *See also* PULPITUM

ROOD STAIR *see* ROOD LOFT

ROOF BOSSES *see* BOSSES

ROOFING TILES *see* ROOFS (TIMBER), SLATES *and* TILES

ROOFS (TIMBER) The earliest roofs were conical structures consisting of timbers which radiated from a central pole to the ground or to a low circular wall and were covered with turf or thatch. With the development of rectangular buildings a simple tent-like roof structure was used and from this evolved the open timber-trussed roof which, until the sixteenth century, covered the majority of buildings (*for* major churches *see* VAULTING).

ROOF CONSTRUCTION

In its simplest form the medieval trussed roof consisted of a long beam (*ridge-piece*) which extended horizontally along the length of the apex of the roof and was supported at each end by the gables of the building. From either side of the ridge-piece, parallel timbers (*principal rafters* and

less substantial *common rafters*) were carried downward to timbers (*wall plates*) laid along the tops of the side walls of the building and secured by means of stone CORBELS set into the walls. Further horizontal beams (*purlins*) were incorporated at intervals between the ridge-piece and the wall plate and, to counteract the outward thrust of the roof on the wall, massive beams (*tie beams*) spanned the interior space at wall plate level. These were pinned or tenoned to the wall plates and often curve upwards at the centre where a vertical post (*king post*) or pairs of posts (*queen posts*) secured the structure to the ridge-piece. Further tie beams (*collar beams*) were sometimes incorporated above the wall plate level and curved *arch braces* or straight *struts* added for reinforcement. One of the finest (and most ornate) tie-beam roofs is at St. Mary's church, Weston Zoyland in Somerset. Each tie-beam is made from a single timber and is slightly cambered at the centre to provide additional strength. There is a splendid arch-braced roof at Llantwit Major in South Glamorgan, the underside of which may originally have been plastered (see below). *Coupled roofs* have neither tie beams nor collar beams, and *braced collar* roofs were constructed with collar beams and arch braces but no tie beams.

ROOFING MATERIALS

Horizontal rows of wooden *battens* were affixed to the outside surfaces of the rafters from which overlapping SHINGLES or SLATES were hung, or

Hammer-beam roof at Westminster Hall, London.

the roof thatched, to provide a weather-proof outer surface (*see* ANGLO-SAXON ARCHITECTURE). Roofing TILES were first introduced into Kent and East Anglia at the end of the Middle Ages and their use had spread to most other areas by the eighteenth century. The roofs of the larger (and richer) medieval churches were usually vaulted and covered with lead which was less susceptible to damage by fire and better able to accommodate the low pitch of a vaulted roof.

The pitch of a roof is determined by the materials used: thatch and pantiles require a steep pitch to throw off rainwater; Cotswold stone needs a pitch of about 45 degrees whereas sandstone roofs in northern England need only 30 degrees and lead or

slates even less. In many cases the original roof-covering has been changed: at Lillington in Dorset, for example, where the church of St. Martin was once thatched, the line (raggle) of the earlier, steeply-pitched gable is clearly visible in east wall of tower. Few thatched churches remain, those at Barsham and Bramfield in Suffolk being two of a small number of exceptions.

HAMMER-BEAM ROOFS

The celebrated hammer-beam roof evolved in the last decades of the fourteenth century. Hammer beams are abbreviated tie beams which project at wall-plate level and are supported from corbels by arch-braced *wall posts*. Vertical *hammer posts* rise from the inner ends of the hammer-beams and are secured to collar beams and purlins (*collar purlins*). This structure enables the weight of a roof to be carried across a much wider span than would otherwise be possible. At Westminster Hall in London, for example, an immense hammer-beam roof, constructed in 1399 of Sussex oak, spans a floor space measuring 88 metres (290 feet) by 21 metres (68 feet) on walls 28 metres (92 feet) high. Hammer-beam roofs and double hammer beam roofs (those with two tiers of projecting beams) reached decorative perfection in the fifteenth century, particularly in East Anglian churches such as Cotton, Gislingham and Woolpit in Suffolk and Cawston, Knapton and Swaffham in Norfolk. The projections often terminate in carved angels, sometimes exceeding one hundred in a single roof, and these may bear emblazoned shields or other heraldic devices, at Needham Market in Suffolk, for example, 'one of the most remarkable wooden roofs in England' (Harbison *). The wall plate or cornice may also be richly carved with painted and gilded figures as at Mildenhall, an immense Suffolk church which contains some of the finest medieval carving in England, its nave described as 'a cockpit of angels' by Kenneth Clark.

WAGON ROOFS

The *wagon roof* (or *barrel roof*) is a continuous timber roof of half-cylindrical section consisting of a trussed rafter structure and internal panelling in timber or plaster, often with decorative ribs and BOSSES. The closely set rafters of a wagon roof are said to resemble the inside of the canvas tilt of a wagon and are characteristic of late medieval churches in parts of the West Country. One of the finest examples is at Croscombe in Somerset.

PANELLED CEILINGS

From c. 1470 there was an increasing emphasis on domestic comfort and privacy and the provision of chambers with flat wood or wood and plaster ceilings. This was paralleled by the installation of PLASTERWORK ceilings in many churches. The first ceiling panels were supported by massive wooden beams, augmented by smaller timbers (*joists*) which spanned the spaces between beam and walls. But gradually the roof structure itself was adapted to form triangular frames of rafters, the horizontal members of which served as ceiling joists to the space below. There is a superb Tudor oak roof above the north aisle of the collegiate church of St. Peter at Ruthin in Clwyd. This was given to the church by Henry VII as a gesture to the local gentry who had supported him at Bosworth in 1485. The dark oak roof, its bosses picked out in bright paint and gilt during the 1960s, is divided into more than 400 square painted panels.

POST-REFORMATION

Perhaps the most innovative period in roof design occurred during the rebuilding which followed the destruction of over 13,000 houses in the Great Fire of London (1666). But as Isaac Ware wrote in the eighteenth century (*A Compleat Body of Archi-*

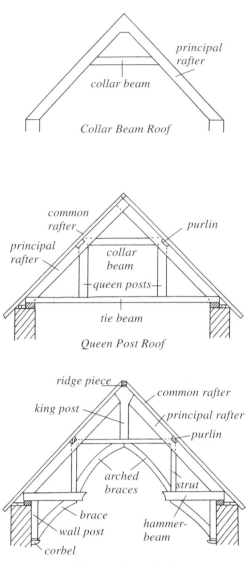

Collar Beam Roof

Queen Post Roof

Hammer-beam Roof

tecture), 'The great caution is, that the roof be neither too massy nor too light', for roof design is considerably more complex when larger spaces have to be covered and problems of stability overcome.

Many church roofs were renewed or substantially restored in the nineteenth century and (as with all Victorian restoration) the degree and quality of the work varies considerably. In some cases, architects were anxious to retain as much of the original roof as possible but often the entire structure was replaced, generally in pine and not in accordance with the original design. Where a steeply pitched early medieval roof had been replaced by one of

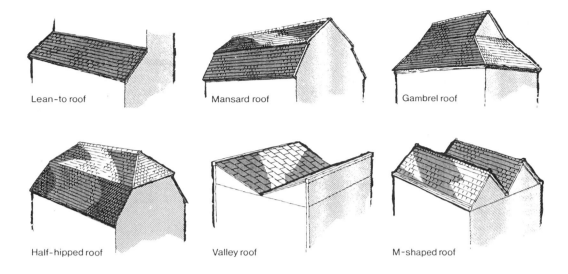

Lean-to roof · Mansard roof · Gambrel roof

Half-hipped roof · Valley roof · M-shaped roof

flatter pitch, the Victorians would often restore the original roof line. Evidence of these successive changes is sometimes apparent in the masonry of the east and west walls (*see* RAGGLE).

ROOF TYPES

Most roofs are of gabled (or *saddleback*) construction, sometimes with a lateral 'catslide' extension over an aisle. But there are three other types of roof which are commonly found in churches dating from the eighteenth and nineteenth centuries. In the M shaped roof the centre of the M is supported by a beam which spans the width of the building from front to back and is drained by means of a gutter and lead-lined trunk in the rear roof space and a downpipe at the back of the building. Named after the seventeenth-century architect François Mansard, the *mansard roof* has a double pitch with a steep slope to a height of at least 2.5 metres (8 feet) and a shallow top section to the ridge. The third type is the *valley roof* in which the rafters are set on the party walls of a terrace building forming a 'valley' at the bottom of which a gutter, on a central supporting beam, runs from front to back. Other types are the *hipped roof*, in which the ends slope outwards to a cornice instead of terminating in gables; the *half-hipped roof*, the ends of which slope immediately beneath the ridge but then finish in a gable; and the *gambrel roof*, one end of which terminates at the ridge in a small gable before sloping to a cornice.

See also CELURE *and* DOME

Further reading:

Harbison, R., *English Parish Churches*, London, 1992 *

Hewett, C.A., *Church Carpentry*, Chichester, 1982

ROOT AND BRANCH BILL (1641) *see* SEVENTEENTH-CENTURY CHURCH

ROPE MOULDING *see* CABLE MOULDING

ROSARY The devotion of the Fifteen Mysteries (the fifteen subjects of meditation) in which fifteen divisions (*decades*) are recited, each decade consisting of ten Hail Marys (*see* HAIL MARY) and each preceded by the Lord's Prayer and followed by the *Gloria Patri*. Normally, only one third of the Rosary (the *chaplet*) is said on one occasion and to assist the memory the prayers are usually counted on a string of beads (*see* BEAD).

See also INDULGENCES *and* MARY, THE BLESSED VIRGIN

ROSE SUNDAY *see* MOTHERING SUNDAY

ROSETTE A decorative motif consisting of a series of stylised roses, each of a slightly different design (*see* DECORATIVE MOTIFS).

ROSE WINDOW A circular window with a complex traceried design similar in arrangement to the petals of a rose. This type of window is often confused with the WHEEL WINDOW which is also circular but has tracery which radiates from a central hub like the spokes of a wheel. Both are commonly found in medieval cathedrals, particularly in the gable-end of nave and transepts.

See also MEDIEVAL ARCHITECTURE *and* WINDOWS

ROTULUS *see* ROLL

ROTUNDA A circular room or building, usually with a domed roof.

ROUGH-CAST *see* FACING MATERIALS

ROUND CHURCHES *see* CIRCULAR CHURCHES *and* MEDIEVAL ARCHITECTURE

ROUNDEL (i) A circular moulding usually containing a decorative motif. (ii) In HERALDRY, a flat coloured disc. A gold roundel is a *bezant* (a Byzantine coin), silver (or white) a *plate*, red a *torteau*, blue a *hurt* (bruise), green a *pomme* (apple) and black a *pellet*. When they are scattered (*semy*) they are described as *bezanty, platy, hurty, pellety* and so on. (iii) Metal plates, usually strapped to the shoulder gussets to protect the armpit (*see* ARMOUR).

ROWEL A star-shaped piece of metal which revolves at the end of a spur (*see* ARMOUR).

ROYAL ARMS (In the following *Gules* is red, *Azure* blue, *Sable* black and *Argent* silver.)
SHIELDS OF ARMS
It was during the reign of Henry I (1100–35) that the first lion was seen in England at the King's menagerie at Woodstock and it is probable that the king of beasts was adopted by him as a device. All Henry's descendants through his illegitimate children bore lions in various attitudes and sometimes combined with other devices. The coat of *Gules two Lions passant guardant Gold* is generally attributed to the Norman kings [1] and it was the first Angevin, Henry II (1154–89), who added a third lion, perhaps that of his wife Eleanor of Aquitaine who is known to have borne a single gold lion on red. A shield bearing three lions [2] later appears on the second great seal of Richard I (1195) and was used thereafter by succeeding monarchs until *c.* 1340 when Edward III adopted both the style and arms of the kings of France (*Azure semy of fleurs-de-lis Gold* – known as *France Ancient*) which he quartered with the lions of England [3] to emphasise his claim to the French throne.

These arms were modified slightly [4] in 1405 when Henry IV, following the example of Charles V of France, reduced the number of *fleurs-de-lis* to three (*France Modern*). This shield of arms continued in use until 1603 when James VI of Scotland succeeded Elizabeth I as James I of England and the arms of Scotland and Ireland (see below) were added as quarterings to those of France and England [5]. These arms were also used by Charles I, Charles II, James II and Anne. William of Orange and Mary II used the Stuart arms with the arms of Nassau (*Azure billety a Lion rampant Gold*) in pretence (at the centre of the shield) [6]. In 1707, the arms of Queen Anne were changed so that the English and Scottish coats were impaled (placed side by side) in the first and fourth quarterings with those of France and Ireland occupying the second and third [7]. From 1714 to 1801 the first three kings George placed the arms of Hanover in the fourth quarter [8]. The arms of Hanover are blazoned: *Tierced in pairle reversed* [divided into three] *1 Gules two Lions passant guardant Gold* (for Brunswick) *2 Gold semy of Hearts Gules a Lion rampant Azure* (Luneburg) *3 Gules a Horse courant Argent* (Hanover) and on an inescutcheon *Gules the Crown of Charlemagne* for the office of Arch Treasurer of the Holy Roman Empire.

From 1801 the French quartering was at last omitted and the remaining coats re-arranged: *quarterly 1 and 4 England 2 Scotland 3 Ireland and in pretence Hanover ensigned with the Electoral Bonnet* [9]. When Hanover became a kingdom in 1816 the bonnet was replaced by a crown and in 1837, because Salic Law prevented Victoria from succeeding to the throne of Hanover, the Hanoverian arms were removed entirely leaving the royal arms in their present form: *quarterly 1 and 4 England 2 Scotland and 3 Ireland* [10].
SCOTLAND AND IRELAND
In Scotland, the red lion was probably a device of William I (1165–1214) who was known as 'The Lion'. A lion rampant within a *bordure* of fleurs-de-lis first appears during the reign of his son, Alexander II (1214–49) and the arms *Gold a Lion rampant within a double Tressure flory counter flory Gules* were first used in the Great Seal of Alexander III in 1251.

Although there has never been a separate title for the King of Ireland, from the accession of James VI of Scotland as James I of England the royal arms have included a quartering for Ireland: *Azure a Harp Gold stringed Argent*. The Irish harp has occupied the third quartering since that time, even during the Commonwealth when the other quarterings were completely changed (see below). Since 1603 the royal arms of Scotland have been marshalled with England in the second quartering and Ireland in the third.
CREST AND CORONETS
From the reign of Edward III (1327–77) English sovereigns have born as a CREST a *Lion statant guardant crowned Gold*. At first this was depicted on a red and ermine cap (*chapeau*) but Edward IV encircled the chapeau with a coronet which was later changed to an arched crown by Henry VIII and has remained in that form ever since.
SUPPORTERS
Several beasts have been used as SUPPORTERS, many of which originated in the dynastic badges of magnatial families (*for* royal badges *see* BADGES). Richard II used white harts, Henry VI silver heraldic antelopes and Edward IV silver lions rampant (for Mortimer), as well as the black bull of Clarence and the white boar, a Yorkist badge which is most closely associated with Richard III, both as Duke of Gloucester and as king. Henry VII and Henry VIII used 'the red dragon of Cadwaladr' and the white greyhound of Richmond, or two greyhounds. Henry VIII also used a *Lion imperially crowned Gold* together with a red dragon. Mary I's arms were supported by *an Imperial Eagle Sable crowned Gold* for Spain and her father's English lion. Elizabeth I used Henry's lion and dragon supporters, though the dragon was often gold rather

ROYAL ARMS

Royal Arms: *1 The Norman kings (attributed); 2 1195–1337; 3 1337–1405; 4 1405–1603; 5 1603–88 and 1702–07; 6 1688–1702; 7 1707–14; 8 1714–1801; 9 1801–37; 10 1837–present.*

The royal arms of Stuart on the seventeenth-century oak screen at Abbey Dore, Herefordshire.

than red. In Scotland, unicorn supporters were adopted in 1440 and since 1603 the lion and unicorn in the English arms have remained constant.

ROYAL ARMS IN CHURCHES

The royal arms will often be found painted, and sometimes gilded, on boards affixed to the interior walls of churches. They were erected as tokens of loyalty to the Crown and obedience to the sovereign as head of the Church, and consequently all but a very small number date from after 1534 when Henry VIII assumed the title of 'Supreme Head on Earth of the Church of England' (*see* CHURCH OF ENGLAND *and* REFORMATION). Royal devices from earlier periods will also be found in glass, furnishings, memorials etc., but their function is mainly commemorative.

CHURCH WARDENS' ACCOUNTS suggest that, during the reigns of Henry VIII and Edward VI, in many churches the royal arms were erected on top of the CHANCEL SCREEN in place of the ROOD, or above the CHANCEL ARCH. But there is no known statute relating to the practice and in one instance (during the reign of Edward VI) the over-zealous curate and wardens of St. Martin's in Ironmonger Lane, London were instructed to restore the rood and take down the royal arms they had erected.

Following the succession of the Catholic Mary I, most royal arms were removed from churches, notable exceptions being those at Westerham in Kent and Rushbrooke in Suffolk. But the practice was again reversed by her successor, Elizabeth I, for whom several examples are to be found including a faded mural on the nave wall at Puddletown church in Dorset. The practice continued through the early Stuart period and in 1614 the Archbishop of Canterbury instructed a painter-stainer to 'survey and paynte in all the churches and chappells within the Realme of England, the Kinges Majesties Armes in due form, with helmet, crest, mantell, and supporters as they ought to be, together with the nobel young princes.' This directive, and its reference to the future Charles I, may have encouraged the appearance of boards bearing the 'Prince of Wales' Feathers', though that in Sherborne Abbey, Dorset, is dated 1611 and suggests that the practice existed before the directive was issued. (It should be noted that the so-called 'Prince of Wales' Feathers' device is the badge of the heir apparent to the <u>English</u> throne, not all of whom have been invested as princes of Wales.) In 1631, the Archbishop again issued instructions that the royal arms should be painted or repaired, together with the ten Commandments and '. . . other Holy sentences.'

During the Commonwealth (1649–60) many examples of the royal arms were destroyed or

The royal arms of Charles II at Milborne Port, Somerset. Erected in 1662, just two years after the Restoration, the legend is singularly apt.

defaced while others were taken down and hidden or turned round and the Commonwealth arms painted on the reverse. It seems that Protector Cromwell either shared Julius Caesar's monarchal aspirations or that he acknowledged the transitory nature of the republic and recognised that he held the monarchy in trust. Having refused the Crown, he nevertheless incorporated the symbols of sovereignty in the arms of the Commonwealth. The royal helm, crown, crest and supporter of a crowned lion were all retained, while the shield (*Quarterly 1 and 4 Argent a Cross Gules* [for England] *2 Azure a Saltire Argent* [for Scotland] *and 3 Azure a Harp Or stringed Argent* [for Ireland]) also included an inescutcheon of the Cromwell arms (*Sable a Lion rampant Argent*). Significantly, the Scottish unicorn supporter, with its Stuart associations, was replaced by the Welsh dragon. According to Sir Bernard Burke, when

Cromwell's coffin was opened it was found to contain a copper plate engraved with the royal arms of England impaling his own!

Following the restoration of Charles II in 1660, a statute requiring that the royal arms should be displayed in all churches resulted in many old boards being brought out of hiding and re-painted or new ones made. Wherever the Commonwealth arms were displayed they were to '. . . be forthwith taken down; and that the King's Majesty's Arms be set up instead thereof.'

Although the composition of the royal arms was to change several times after 1660 (see above), royal arms in churches were affected only once more by changing dynastic fortunes. So concerned were the early Hanoverians with the claims of Stuart Pretenders that nearly everywhere Stuart arms were re-painted with those of Hanover. But the work was not always accurate, with only the fourth quartering being changed, and in some cases a painted canvas of the Hanoverian arms was hastily stuck over the board, as at Cirencester in Gloucestershire.

The royal arms were usually painted on square or oblong boards or canvas (not to be confused with HATCHMENTS), though there are also examples in cast plaster, carved wood and cast iron and in a variety of other shapes. Most surviving examples date from the Hanoverian period, though all reigns from from James I to Victoria are well represented. (There are very few from the twentieth century: those to Elizabeth II at Remenham, Berkshire and Shepton Montague in Somerset, being exceptional.) Many were moved from their original positions by Victorian restorers and dating is often difficult. Many have neither dates nor initials and dating by reference to the marshalling of the various quarterings is not always conclusive: one combination was used by Queen Anne for only seven years and yet, following her death in 1714, the Hanoverian royal arms remained unchanged for eighty-seven years. Even examples with initials or dates must be treated with caution as they may have been altered: J (James) or C (Charles) were often changed to G (George) but their Stuart origins may still be evident in the floreated form of the initials. Similarly, dates may commemorate an alteration rather than the original painting and with careful examination the old date may be found painted out beneath the new. Churchwardens' accounts often provide invaluable information concerning the construction, repair and re-painting of royal arms in churches. Boards dating from the early nineteenth century are almost invariably characterised by the emasculation of the lion and unicorn supporters which, unlike their virile predecessors, are rarely *sexed, pizzled* or *coded.*

See also ARMORIAL PANELS, FUNERAL HERALDRY, MEMORIAL BOARDS *and* VISITATIONS (HERALDS)

Further reading:
Friar, S., *A New Dictionary of Heraldry*, Sherborne and London, 1987
——, *Heraldry for the Local Historian and Genealogist*, Stroud, 1992
Friar, S. and Ferguson, J., *Basic Heraldry*, London, 1993
Hasler, C., *The Royal Arms*, London, 1980
Pardoe, R., *Royal Arms in Churches: The Artists and Craftsmen*, London, 1988

ROYAL COMMISSION ON THE HISTORICAL MONUMENTS OF ENGLAND (RCHME) Of the Commission's numerous duties, three are of particular relevance to churches:
(i) Responsibility for recording listed buildings and redundant churches threatened with destruction or alteration. (ii) Responsibility for housing the NATIONAL MONUMENTS RECORD (NMR) (iii)

The compilation of inventories of historical and archaeological monuments. Traditionally these have been county based but more recent publications are arranged according to topic. The following Inventories have been published wherein all relevant churches are described, though there is a cut-off date of 1714 and in earlier volumes descriptions are brief and do not normally include detailed plans.

Hertfordshire			(1910)
Buckinghamshire	I.	South	(1912)
	II.	North	(1913)
Essex	I.	North-West	(1916)
	II.	Central & South West	(1921)
	III.	North-East	(1922)
	IV.	South-East	(1923)
Huntingdonshire			(1926)
London	I.	Westminster Abbey	(1924)
	II.	West	(1925)
	III.	The City	(1929)
	IV.	East	(1930)
Herefordshire	I.	South-West	(1931)
	II.	East	(1932)
	III.	North-West	(1934)
Westmorland			(1936)
Middlesex			(1937)
Oxford, City			(1939, reprint 1974)
Dorset	I.	West	(1952, reprint 1974)
	II.	South-East	(1970)
	III.	Central	(1970)
	IV.	North	(1972)
	V.	East	(1975)
Cambridge, City			(1959)
Cambridgeshire	I.	West	(1968)
	II.	North-East	(1972)
York	I.	The Defences	(1972)
	II.	South-West of the Ouse	(1972)
	III.	East	(1975)
	IV.	Central	(1981)
Stamford			(1977)
Salisbury	I	City (excluding the Cathedral Close)	(1980)
Northamptonshire	V	Northampton	(1985)
Churches of South-East Wiltshire			(1987)

For the Commission's address and that of the Royal Commission on Ancient and Historical Monuments (Wales) *see* APPENDIX II.

ROYAL PECULIAR *see* PECULIAR

R.R. Abbreviation for *regni Regis*, meaning 'in the —th year of King —'.

RUBBLE The term does not necessarily imply inferior construction: walls built of roughly cut stones of differing shapes and sizes, bound with lime mortar and sometimes laid in courses, are singularly durable. *See also* MASONRY

RUBRIC A textual heading, usually in red ink. In the present context, ritual or ceremonial directions in a service book which were often picked out in red ink. The celebrated 'Black Rubric' was the 'Declaration on Kneeling' which was added at the last moment, and without parliamentary authority, at the end of the Holy Communion service in the 1552 *Book of Common Prayer*. When the rubrics were later printed in red, the fact that the 'Declaration' was not authorised was indicated by printing it in black. *See also* RED LETTER DAYS

RUFF (i) Dating from the sixteenth century, a projecting starched frill worn as a collar by choristers, usually of cathedral or collegiate choirs. (ii) A similar, though more ornate, collar worn by both men and women from the sixteenth century (*see* COSTUME).

RULE (*REGULA*) The constitution which set out the principles and practices of the monastic or regular life. The fundamental rule was that of St. Benedict (*see* BENEDICTINES) which was modified and developed by later orders such as the CISTERCIANS and CLUNIACS. The Benedictine rule has been described as '. . . wholly lacking in eccentricity. It does not expect heroic virtue. It is full of provisions for exceptions, changes and relaxations in its rules; yet at the same time it insists that rules must be kept, once made. The monk must live to a timetable, and he must be doing something all the time, even if this only takes the form of eating and sleeping in order to enable him to labour afresh. The rule is classless and timeless: it is not grounded in any particular culture or geographical region, and it will fit into any society which will allow it to operate.' The other seminal rule was that of St. Augustine (*see* AUGUSTINIANS) which also provided a framework within which the Christian life might be lived to the full. *See also* MONASTICISM

RULERS OF ENGLAND AND OF THE UNITED KINGDOM

Saxon

Edwy	955	–	959
Edgar	959	–	975
Edward the Martyr	975	–	978
Ethelred the Unready	978	–	1016
Edmund Ironside			1016

Danish

Cnut	1017	–	1035
Harold I	1035	–	1040
Harthacnut	1040	–	1042

Saxon

Edward the Confessor	1042	–	1066
Harold II (Godwinson)			1066

Normandy

William I	1066	–	1087
William II	1087	–	1100
Henry I	1100	–	1135
Stephen	1135	–	1154

Plantagenet

Henry II	1154	–	1189
Richard I	1189		1199
John	1199	–	1216
Henry III	1216	–	1272
Edward I	1272	–	1307
Edward II	1307	–	1327
Edward III	1327	–	1377
Richard II	1377		1399

Lancaster

Henry IV	1399	–	1413
Henry V	1413	–	1422
Henry VI	1422	–	1461

York

Edward IV	1461	–	1483
Edward V			1483
Richard III	1483	–	1485

Tudor

Henry VII	1485	–	1509
Henry VIII	1509	–	1547
Edward VI	1547	–	1553
Mary I	1553	–	1558
Elizabeth I	1558	–	1603

Stuart

James I of England and VI of Scotland			
	1603	–	1625
Charles I	1625	–	1649

Commonwealth (declared in 1649)

Oliver Cromwell (Lord Protector)			
	1653	–	1658
Richard Cromwell	1658	–	1659

Stuart			
Charles II	1660	–	1685
James II	1685	–	1688
William III and Mary II	1689	–	1702
Anne	1702	–	1714

Hanover			
George I	1714	–	1727
George II	1727	–	1760
George III	1760	–	1820
George IV	1820	–	1830
William IV	1830	–	1837
Victoria	1837	–	1901
Saxe-Coburg-Gotha			
Edward VII	1901	–	1910

Windsor			
George V	1910	–	1936
Edward VIII			1936
George VI	1936	–	1952
Elizabeth II	1952	–	

See also REGNAL YEARS
Further reading:
Cannon, J. and Griffiths, R., *The Oxford Illustrated History of the British Monarchy*, Oxford, 1989
Delderfield, E., *Kings and Queens of England and Great Britain*, Newton Abbot, (Rev.) 1990

RULING The lines, delineated by PRICKING, which were incised or drawn on a writing surface both to guide the writing and to contain it within margins. Before the mid-twelfth century, ruling was done with the dry point of a sharp implement. Thereafter, lead was used until the beginning of the fifteenth century from which time lines were usually drawn in INK.

RUNNING DOG (also VITRUVIAN SCROLL) Any running ornament is one in which the design is continuous. Running dog consists of a series of scroll motifs, similar in appearance to stylised waves (*see* DECORATIVE MOTIFS).

RURAL DEAN *see* CLERGY (CHURCH OF ENGLAND)

RUSHLIGHT HOLDER A (now rare) form of candle consisting of a narrow trumpet-like metal receptacle containing wax and a wick of rush-pith. Generally used as slow-burning night-lights, rushlight holders may be found in clusters of three or four and attached to a hook by which they were suspended.

RUSTICATION *see* MASONRY

SABATON *see* ARMOUR

SABBATARIANISM *see* SUNDAY

SABBATH The seventh day of the Jewish week which was set apart for the worship of God and as a day of rest and recreation for man and beast. The early Church substituted the first day of the week (SUNDAY), that being the day of the Resurrection.

SABLE *see* COLOURS, HERALDIC

SACERDOTAL From the Latin *sacerdos* meaning 'priest', descriptive of priests or priestly office.

SACKCLOTH AND ASHES The penitential sackcloth of the Bible was a coarse fabric of goats' or camels' hair. To be clothed in sackcloth, and to have one's head sprinkled with ashes, was indicative of lamentation, abject penitence and humility.

SACRAMENT 'An outward and visible sign of an inward and spiritual grace given unto us, ordained by Christ himself, as a means whereby we receive the same, and a pledge to assure us thereof' (*The Book of Common Prayer*). As many as thirty Sacraments have been listed at various times but the seven Sacraments of Peter Lombard's *Sentences* (compiled 1155–8) are those which were defined by the Council of Trent in 1545–7: Baptism, Confirmation, Eucharist, Penance, Extreme Unction, Orders and Matrimony. In the Church of England, Article 25 of the THIRTY-NINE ARTICLES differentiates between Baptism and Eucharist ('two Sacraments ordained of Christ our Lord in the Gospel') and the other five ('commonly called Sacraments'). Traditional Catholic theology differentiates between the 'matter' (the material element: the bread and wine of the Eucharist and the water in Baptism) and the 'form' (the consecratory words, e.g. 'This is My Body' and 'This is My Blood' in the Eucharist).

SACRAMENTARY A liturgical book used for the celebration of the MASS until the thirteenth century. The Sacramentary contained the Canon of the Mass together with the Collects, Prefaces and other prayers, but not the Epistles or Gospels. From the tenth century sacramentaries were gradually superseded by Missals (*see* MISSAL).

SACRAMENT CERTIFICATES From 1673, a

person holding a civil or military appointment was required to furnish the Quarter Sessions with a certificate, signed by a clergyman, churchwardens and two witnesses, confirming that he had received the Sacrament within six months of taking office.

SACRAMENT HOUSE *see* TABERNACLE

'SACRAMENT SUNDAY' *see* REFORMATION, THE

SACRED HEART Devotion to the physical heart of Christ was a common feature of the medieval Church, especially among mystics. In the Roman Catholic Church it is sometimes observed on the Friday of the week following CORPUS CHRISTI. *See also* CHRISTIAN SYMBOLS

SACRILEGE Violation or profanation of anything holy whether it be a person, object or place publicly dedicated to the worship of God.

SACRING BELL *see* SANCTUS BELL

SACRIST In religious houses, the sacrist was a major obedientiary responsible for the fabric of the church: its furniture, fittings and supplies. His responsibilities included the cleanliness of the church and its repair and security, together with the design and construction of fittings, altars and windows, decoration, inscriptions and wall paintings. He was charged with the care of clocks, bells, ornaments and lights, for vestments, church plate, shrines, reliquaries and other treasures for which he kept inventories. Indeed, in the later Middle Ages, the duties of the sacrist became so wide-ranging that he was provided with a number of assistants and an office (*checker*). The sacristan usually had his own revenues derived from offerings and from monastic estates such as those at Sacristonheugh in County Durham.

SACRISTAN The person responsible for the contents of a parish church, including the church plate and vestments. In a parochial context, the term may also apply to a SEXTON.

SACRISTY A room adjacent to a PRESBYTERY or CHANCEL in which the church plate and other valuables were secured. Often entered from the presbytery by means of a PRIEST'S DOOR, the sacristy was also used for the vesting of priests and other clerics. A sacristy and VESTRY are now perceived to have similar functions but the latter is not necessarily adjacent to a presbytery and the term is more correctly applied to the body corporate of that name.
See also MEDIEVAL ARCHITECTURE

SADDLE BARS *see* WINDOWS

SADDLEBACK ROOF A gabled roof, usually of a tower (*see* TOWERS).

SAGITTARIUS *see* BEASTS (HERALDIC)

SAIL VAULT *see* DOME

ST. ANDREW'S DAY (30 November) Andrew the Apostle, the brother of Simon Peter, and (since *c.* 750) the patron saint of Scotland. The cult of St. Andrew was not confined to Scotland, however, and many English churches are dedicated to him. The tradition that he died on an X-shaped cross (*see* SALTIRE) seems to have originated in the tenth century and was particularly popular in the fourteenth. It was said that he considered himself unworthy to die on the Cross of Christ. St. Andrew is also the patron saint of elderly spinsters and fishermen ('Come, follow me, and I will make you fishers of men . . .') and may be invoked against gout and sore throats. In Christian art he is generally depicted bound to a cross, from which he is said to have preached for two days before his death, or holding a fishing net. His feast day coincides with the pagan festival of Samain which, in Scotland and the north of England, was moved to 30 November for climatic reasons. Samain was associated with the slaughtering of livestock and it was necessary to delay decisions concerning the number of beasts to be killed until the results of the harvest were known. The over-wintering of livestock depended on adequate supplies of fodder: the poorer the harvest, the greater the slaughter.
See also FEAST DAYS (FIXED AND MOVABLE)

ST. CECILIA'S DAY (22 November) Celebration of the second- or third-century Roman virgin martyr who is said to have converted her husband and his brother (who were martyred before her) and later suffered a lingering death, '. . . all the while singing in her heart for the Lord.' From the sixteenth century she was the patroness of poets, singers, music and musicians and is depicted in late medieval art holding an organ, lute or other musical instrument.

ST. CLEMENT'S DAY (23 November) Clement of Rome (d. 101) is said to have been the first of the apostolic fathers but was probably the third. According to later tradition he was banished to the Crimea where he was forced to work in the mines. Undaunted, he succeeded in creating 75 new churches and so angered the Emperor Trajan that he was lashed to an anchor and drowned in the Black Sea. Consequently St. Clement is invariably depicted holding an anchor and was adopted as the patron saint of the Guild of the Holy Trinity and St. Clement (now Trinity House). He is also the patron saint of ironworkers and as such his feast day was widely celebrated until the end of the nineteenth century. At Twyford in Hampshire, for example, local blacksmiths performed the ceremony of 'firing the anvil' by ramming gunpowder into a small hole in an anvil and igniting it. Afterwards, an effigy of the saint was carried round the village and money collected for a feast at the Bugle Inn. It seems likely that this strange ritual originated in a pagan celebration of the legendary Wayland, a Saxon smith and wizard who forged armour for the gods.

ST. DAVID'S DAY (1 March) St. Dafydd of Wales, Dewi Sant (Son of Sant) the ruler of Ceredigion (*see* CELTIC CHURCH). Known as 'The Waterman' for his abstinence and austerity, his missionary activity formed the basis of Welsh monasticism. Little is known of the historical David (*c.* 530-*c.* 589), a monk from Pembrokeshire (Dyfed) who, according to tradition, founded twelve communities including that at Menevia in Glyn Rhosyn ('the Vale of Roses'), thereafter called St. David's (Tyddewi). Like many celtic saints, David was credited with the working of innumerable miracles. Fountains were said to have burst forth from the ground at places where he miraculously healed the blind, the lame and the sick: at Ffynnon Fedyg ('the physician's well') near Aberaeron in Dyfed, for example. It is told how the members of a Church synod at Llanddewibrefi (also in Dyfed) were unable to make themselves heard above the noise of the crowd. A hill suddenly rose beneath David's feet and from its summit he was able to preach the Gospel so that all could hear. A church, dedicated to the Saint, still crowns the 'miraculous pulpit' of Llanddewibrefi ('the church of St. David on the river Brefi'). David of Wales is believed to have died at Menevia on 1 March, 589 and his cult was approved by Pope Callistus II in *c.* 1120. His relics were translated to a shrine in the cathedral of St. David's in 1131 and again at the rebuilding of the cathedral in 1275 which was largely financed from offerings at his shrine. St. David is, of course, the patron saint of Wales.

ST. GEORGE'S DAY (23 April) Martyr and patron saint of England, most of the details of George's life are based on medieval fiction. It is known that he was martyred either at Nicomedia or Lydda in Palestine before the time of Constantine (d. 337) and that he was probably a soldier in the imperial army. According to legend, George was a warrior from Cappadocia who came upon the town of Sylene (in Libya) which was being terrorised by a flesh-eating dragon. The dragon's victims were chosen by lot and on the day of George's arrival he discovered the king's daughter chained to a rock outside the city. George seized his lance, marched out and overcame the beast before leading it back to the city (using the princess's girdle as a halter) where he offered to slay it – providing the citizens of Sylene confessed the Christian faith. Not surprisingly, 15,000 men agreed to be baptised. The popularity of the cult of St. George increased significantly during the Crusades, indeed victory over the Saracens at Antioch was attributed to his intervention. He was adopted by Edward III as patron of the Order of the Garter in *c.* 1348 (*see* GARTER, MOST NOBLE ORDER OF) and he gradually superseded Edward the Confessor as the patron saint of the English. St. George was an immensely popular character in several mumming plays (*see* DRAMA) and numerous churches are dedicated to him. His ATTRIBUTED ARMS of a blood-red cross on a silver shield (*Argent a Cross Gules*) are the English national flag. He is also the patron saint of soldiers, armourers and archers and may be invoked against plagues, leprosy and syphilis.

ST. JOHN OF JERUSALEM, ORDER OF Among the many new religious orders which came into being in the eleventh and twelfth centuries were the military-religious orders of the Knights Templar and Knights Hospitaller. Both originated in the decades following the capture of the Holy City by the crusaders in 1099 and the establishing of a Christian Kingdom of Jerusalem which stretched from northern Syria to the Sinai desert (*see* CRUSADES). The Knights of the Hospital of St. John of Jerusalem provided shelter and care for the sick, poor and weary pilgrims who visited the holy places, while the Templars guarded the holy places of Jerusalem, protected travellers and lived according to the rule of Bernard of Clairvaux. Both orders were endowed with substantial revenues, property and lands in the new kingdom and throughout Catholic Europe. Within a few years of their foundation most of their brethren, while living under vows of religion, were conventual knights (their priests were known as *chaplains*) and the two orders played an increasingly significant role in the defence of the Christian settlements in Palestine and Syria and in the administration of the Kingdom of Jerusalem. They constructed and garrisoned castles and fought alongside crusading forces in the perennial wars against the Egyptians and Turks. The convent of each order was situated in the Holy Land, with dependent priories and estates throughout Europe. Each order had about fifty PRECEPTORIES or COMMANDERIES in the British Isles, many commemorated by place-names such as St. John's Jerusalem in Kent, St. John's Wood in London, Templecombe in Somerset, Temple Guiting in the Gloucestershire Cotswolds and Fryerning in Essex, 'the place of the brothers'. Driven from Palestine with the rest of the Catholics in 1291, the Hospitallers took over the island of Rhodes, off the coast of Asia Minor, which became their base for naval operations against Muslim shipping. The island was ruled as a semi-independent state until 1522 when it was seized by the Ottoman Turks and the knights removed to the island of Malta which they held as a sovereign power from 1530 until 1798. Following the persecution and papal suppression of the Templars in 1312 (*see* TEMPLAR, KNIGHTS), most of their properties were transferred to the Hospitallers. From 1312 to their dissolution by Henry VIII in 1540, the English Knights Hospitaller comprised a minor, though well-endowed, branch of an international order, drawn (as required by its statutes) from the armigerous families of the noblesse. Discipline was firm and a knight's vow of obedience to the rule was strictly observed. Chastity and poverty were also required, though in practice a successful knight could enjoy his possessions until they were claimed by the order at his death. The Hospitallers' English headquarters were at St. John's Priory, Clerkenwell in London and it was there that an aspiring knight would undertake his novitiate before travelling to Rhodes where several years of military service against the Mohammedans would normally lead to promotion to the rank of Commander. As a senior member of the order he would be responsible for the administration of its estates and finances, serve as a diplomat or be seconded into royal or magnatial service. The arms of the order were a plain white cross on red and its habit black with the badge of a white 'Maltese' cross on the shoulder.

For the Order of St. John Library and Museum *see* APPENDIX II.

Further reading:

Riley-Smith, J., *The Knights of St. John in Jerusalem and Cyprus 1050–1310*, London, 1967

ST. LUKE'S LITTLE SUMMER A period of fine weather in the late autumn, near St. Luke's Day (18 October). Fine weather on St. Martin's Day (11 November) is similarly described as St. Martin's Summer.

ST. PETER'S DAY (29 June) Simon Peter, *Cephas* 'the Rock', the 'Prince of the Apostles'. An impetuous, charismatic disciple, he began life (with his brother Andrew) as a fisherman by Lake Genesareth. In lists of the apostles, Peter is always the first named and he is mentioned more frequently than any other disciple in the gospels. After the resurrection and ascension he was acknowledged as the head of the Christian community in Jerusalem. According to tradition, he was imprisoned by Herod Agrippa in *c.* 43 and was released by an angel. Little is known of his later life but the tradition connecting him with Rome is early and substantial. The later tradition whereby he became the first bishop of Rome (an office which he is said to have held for 25 years) is less well supported. It is likely that he was

martyred under Nero in *c.* AD 64 and that his tomb at St. Peter's in Rome is authentic. He was venerated from the earliest days of the Church and is depicted in Christian art as the doorkeeper of heaven, holding a set of keys. Keys in ecclesiastical heraldry usually allude to St. Peter: in the arms of Gloucester Cathedral, for example.

St. Peter's Eve (28 June) marked the end of the English 'ritual year' and was enthusiastically celebrated throughout the land. Church porches were decorated with greenery and bonfires lit on the plaistows. Typically, in 1521, Sir Henry Willoughby provided for a St. Peter's Eve bonfire at his Warwickshire manor, giving a penny to a maiden who had handed him a garland. In Bristol, Exeter, Gloucester and Liverpool torch-bearing processions surged through the streets, while at Newcastle the guilds paid for minstrels, plays and parades.

For ST. PETER'S PENCE *see* PETER'S PENCE.

SAINTS (BRITISH) The practice of invoking and venerating the saints and martyrs has long been an element in Catholic devotion. They are perceived as being accessible as a medium of intercessionary prayer: because of their holiness they are close to God and yet they also remain close to man whose nature they share. From the eighth century, the lives of the saints were read at mattins but various councils found it necessary to curb the excesses and superstition of popular devotion. In the early Church, bishops controlled the cult of the saints in their dioceses, but the veneration of some saints spread beyond regional limits and the resulting problems sometimes required papal intervention. The first historically attested canonisation is that of Ulrich of Augsburg in 993. In *c.* 1170 it was asserted that no one should be venerated as a saint without the authority of the Roman Church and this became part of Canon Law. In the Roman Catholic Church, *canonisation* is the definitive sentence by which the Pope declares a dead person to have entered into heavenly glory and ordains that a new saint should be recognised throughout the Church. (*Beatification* is slightly different in that it permits the public veneration of a faithful Catholic in a particular church, diocese, religious order or country.) The cult of the saints was repudiated by the reformers, notably the Calvinists who objected that it was not specifically recommended in the Scriptures.

ST. AIDAN (d. 651)

Apparently of Irish origin, Aidan became a monk of Iona and bishop of Lindisfarne. When King Oswald returned to Northumbria from his Ionan exile he invited the monks to assist him in the conversion of his kingdom to Christianity. Aidan was consecrated bishop and settled at Lindisfarne which was well positioned for evangelising Oswald's northern territories. His see extended from the Forth to the

Humber but the influence of his foundation was to extend much further. Indeed, it was from the efforts of Aidan and his followers that the Christianity of most of northern and midland England sprang. According to Bede (see below), Aidan's many miracles increased his effectiveness and he wrote warmly of his personal qualities of humility, peacefulness and prayerfulness – though, being an adherent of the Roman system, he was unable to condone Aidan's Celtic observance of Easter. Aidan was accustomed to spending Lent in solitude on the island of Inner Farne (*see* St. Cuthbert, *below*) and, together with many other saints, he was known for his love of animals; in art he is often depicted in the company of a the legendary stag which he is said to have rendered invisible to protect it from its hunters. Aidan died in 651 at the church he had founded at Bamburgh (the only church dedicated to him) and Cuthbert is said to have watched from the Lammermuir Hills as his soul was transported to heaven. Aidan was buried in Lindisfarne cemetery from where his relics were later translated into the church.

ST. ALBAN (d. c. 305)

The first British martyr who probably died during the fourth-century persecutions of the Roman Emperor Diocletia or (as has recently been suggested) in the reign of Decius, a century earlier. A Roman-British soldier and leading citizen of Verulamium (now St. Albans in Hertfordshire), he was converted to Christianity by a fugitive priest who sought his protection. When his house was searched, Alban dressed himself in the priest's cloak (*amphibalus*) and was arrested. During interrogation, he refused to acknowledge pagan gods and was executed (according to Bede) on Holmhurst Hill. Alban was buried near the city and his shrine became renowned for the miracles which were performed in his name. King Offa of Mercia later founded a Benedictine abbey at the site and the cult of St. Alban continued to attract pilgrims throughout the Middle Ages.

ST. AUGUSTINE OF CANTERBURY (d. c. 604)

Described as 'The Apostle of the English', Augustine was sent by Pope Gregory I to revive the Church in England (*see* ANGLO-SAXON CHURCH). His mission landed at Thanet in Kent in 597 and was well received by King Ethelbert who was later converted to Christianity. Augustine founded the church and monastic community at Canterbury where in 597 he became the first archbishop. In the following year he created twelve DIOCESES and in 603 met with the British bishops representing the CELTIC CHURCH. But, despite his legendary powers of persuasion, they failed to reach agreement concerning differences in practice and discipline between the Roman and Celtic churches.

ST. BEDE (c. 673–735)

The Venerable Bede was born in Northumbria and spent most of his life as a monk in the monastery of Jarrow (Tyne and Wear). Described as 'The Father of English Church History', he was a student of Latin, Green and Hebrew. His scholastic and theological works were diverse and numerous though he is best known for his *Ecclesiastical History of the English People* which was completed in 731 and became a primary source for early English history. He is believed to have been the first historian to use the convention 'AD' meaning *Anno Domini*. The term 'venerable' was commonly given to priests at that time and, since monks were rarely ordained, it was attached to Bede's name in order that it might be distinguished thereby (it was formally approved by the Church in 853).

ST. COLUMBA (c. 521–97)

An Irish-born nobleman, missionary and abbot who, in c. 563, established a small religious community on the island of Iona off the west coast of Scotland. He lived there for 34 years, sending out missions and founding monastic communities in Scotland and Northumbria. The influence of Columba and his followers as factors in the development of western Christianity was considerable. The monastic traditions established by his Ionan community permeated the CELTIC CHURCH until the adoption of Roman practice and the Benedictine Rule in the late seventh century.

ST. CUTHBERT (634–87)

A monk and missionary who in 644 moved from the monastery of Melrose to Lindisfarne on the Northumbrian coast. In 676 he withdrew to the Farne Islands where he lived as a coenobite. He returned (reluctantly) to become bishop of Lindisfarne in 685 and his last two years were spent administering his diocese and caring for the victims of the plague, 'performing mysteries of healing and prophecy'. Two months before his death he finally returned to Farne where he died in March, 687. His body was buried at Lindisfarne where, after eleven years, it was exhumed and found to be incorrupt. The community abandoned Lindisfarne following Danish incursions in 875 and wandered the borders in search of a suitable site to build a new monastery. In 955 they finally settled at Durham where they erected a church over Cuthbert's shrine. His remains (apparently still incorrupt) were translated into the new Norman cathedral in 1104.

ST. DAVID OF WALES see CELTIC CHURCH and ST. DAVID'S DAY

ST. DUNSTAN (c. 925–988)

Archbishop of Canterbury who exercised a powerful influence on successive English kings. Of noble birth, Dunstan was appointed abbot of Glastonbury in c. 943 and was instrumental in reviving monasticism in England while also acting as Treasurer to King Edred (*see* ANGLO-SAXON CHURCH). Banished by Edwy in c. 956, he was restored by Edgar who appointed him bishop of Worcester and London and, in c. 960, archbishop of

Canterbury. With Ethelwold (see below), Dunstan was chiefly responsible for the revival of religious life in England.

ST. EDMUND THE MARTYR (c. 840–69)

A Christian king of East Anglia who was taken prisoner by the Danes in 869. When offered his life in exchange for half his kingdom he refused to be associated with his pagan captors and was used as a target by Danish archers and finally beheaded. His remains were translated to Bury St. Edmunds (Suffolk) in the tenth century where his shrine became a place of pilgrimage. As one might expect, his emblem is an arrow and (occasionally) a wolf which was believed to have guarded his head after decapitation. Until the mid-fourteenth century, St. Edmund was widely regarded as one of England's patron saints (see St. Edward the Confessor below).

ST. EDWARD THE CONFESSOR (c. 1003–66)

King of England (r. 1042–66), renowned for his piety, gentleness, generosity and firm government. But he became so preoccupied with religious matters (notably the building of St. Peter's Abbey at Westminster) that he failed to reconcile the conflicting interests of his Norman advisers and those of Earl Godwin (his wife's father) and his Saxon adherents. At Edward's death, Earl Godwin's son assumed control and succeeded him as Harold II. Confusion over the rival claims of Harold and William of Normandy led to the Norman Conquest of 1066. Edward was buried in his abbey of Westminster and was canonised in 1161. Edward the Confessor was regarded as the patron saint of England until he was superseded by St. George in the mid-fourteenth century (see ST. GEORGE'S DAY)

ST. ETHELWOLD (c. 908–84)

Bishop of Winchester (963) and compiler of the *Regularis Concordia*, a code of monastic observance, approved by the Synod of Winchester in c. 970. Described as Boanerges ('Son of Thunder') by one of his scribes, he was a singularly powerful and influential cleric, ecclesiastically puritanical and yet an enthusiastic patron of the tenth-century artistic renaissance. Ethelwold's reformed monastic houses evolved into one of the wealthiest and most powerful forces in England, and under his influence Winchester became the political and cultural centre of Anglo-Saxon society (see ANGLO-SAXON CHURCH).

ST. OSWALD OF NORTHUMBRIA (c. 605–42)

Forced to flee to Scotland following his father's death, Oswald was converted to Christianity by the monks of Iona before returning to claim his kingdom of Northumbria in 634. Having defeated the British king Cadwallon at Havenfelt (Heavenfield near Hexham) in 634 he began to establish Christianity in his kingdom, assisted by missionaries from Iona. Oswald succeeded in uniting the territories of Northumbria, Bernicia and Deira and his authority as overlord was acknowledged by other Anglo-Saxon rulers. In 642, at the age of 38, he was killed in battle by the pagan Penda of Mercia. His body was ritually mutilated as an offering to Woden but many of the limbs were later recovered and added to the potency of his cult. His head was buried at Lindisfarne and was later placed with the remains of St. Cuthbert at Durham.

ST. SWITHIN see ST. SWITHIN'S DAY

ST. THOMAS À BECKET OF CANTERBURY (c. 1118–70)

Thomas à Becket was an intimate and influential friend of Henry II. He became Chancellor of England in 1155 and Archbishop of Canterbury in 1162, an office which he accepted with reluctance. Having resigned the chancellorship, Becket adopted an austere mode of life and transferred his loyalty to the Church. He opposed Henry's attempts to bring the Church within the jurisdiction of the royal courts and insisted on the right of ecclesiastical courts to try the clergy (see CLARENDON, CONSTITUTIONS OF). Becket's intransigence caused considerable resentment and the Archbishop was obliged to make his escape to France in 1164. A reconciliation was effected in 1170 and he returned to Canterbury but hostility remained and Henry's ill-considered remark moved four of his knights to murder the Archbishop in his cathedral on 29 December, 1170. But his influence proved to be more potent in death than in life. Becket was canonised in 1173 and the king was forced to do public penance for his death. Becket's shrine became a major centre of pilgrimage until its destruction by Henry VIII in 1538.

ST. WILFRID (634–709)

One of the greatest figures of the Anglo-Saxon Church and chiefly responsible for introducing the Benedictine rule in Northumbria. At the Synod of Whitby (664) he attacked the Celtic Church and advocated a closer relationship with the Roman Church. He became bishop of York in 665 but did not occupy his see until 669, choosing instead to live a monastic life at Ripon. When the diocese was divided in 677 Wilfrid appealed to Rome and was restored to his bishopric though he continued to live in exile in Mercia. In 705 he returned to Northumbria and became bishop of Hexham.

See also CELTIC CHURCH, CHRISTIAN SYMBOLS, CHURCH SITES, DEDICATION OF CHURCH, FEAST DAYS (FIXED AND MOVABLE), RELICS, *and* SHRINES

Further reading:

The Book of Saints, London, 1989 (new edition)

Farmer, D., *The Oxford Dictionary of Saints*, Oxford, 1988 (new edition)

Jones, A., *A Dictionary of Saints*, Ware, 1994

Walsh, M., (ed.), *Butler's Lives of Saints*, London, 1988

SAINTS, AGE OF *see* CELTIC CHURCH

SAINTS' ATTRIBUTES *see* CHRISTIAN SYMBOLS

SAINTS DAYS AND FIXED FEAST DAYS *see* FEAST DAYS (FIXED AND MOVABLE)

ST. SIMON'S AND ST. JUDE'S DAY (28 October) In the medieval period this day acquired a reputation similar to that of ST. SWITHIN'S DAY. It is traditionally associated with the onset of Winter, a time when the fine weather finally breaks and winter gales begin.

ST. SWITHIN'S DAY (15 July) Little is actually known of Swithin's life. He was educated at the Old Minster in Winchester and in the early ninth century became personal chaplain to Egbert of Wessex. He was appointed to the bishopric of Winchester in 852 at a time when Wessex was becoming the most powerful kingdom in England. Swithin was renowned for his compassion and charity and, before his death in 862, he asked to be buried in the common cemetery of the Old Minster. But in the next century arrangements were made to translate Swithin's remains to a tomb inside the cathedral. The translation was scheduled for 15 July, 971 but was delayed by exceptionally heavy rainfall which was perceived to be a further manifestation of the saint's powers. When the translation finally took place, it was accompanied by a number of miraculous cures. Thereafter, a wet St. Swithin's Day is supposed to presage forty days of rain – in retribution for ignoring the saint's instructions.

ST. VALENTINE'S DAY (14 February) A feast day associated with courtship. Traditionally, young girls placed bay leaves beneath their pillows on Valentine's Eve in the hope that they would dream of their future husbands. A potential sweetheart or 'Valentine' was the first member of the opposite sex to be seen on the morning of St. Valentine's Day. In fact, there were two saints Valentine neither of whom had even the remotest connection with romance – indeed, both were renowned for their chastity. One Valentine was a Roman priest and doctor who was martyred under Claudius II in 350. The other was a bishop of Turni (some 60 miles from Rome) who was tortured and executed in *c.* 273 at the command of the prefect Placidus. It has been suggested that the two Valentines were, in fact, one and the same. The feast day (which they share) was also the eve of Lupercalia, the Romano-British festival of youth, when young people selected their sweethearts by lottery. But the popularity of St. Valentine's Day probably has more to do with the advent of Spring and the medieval belief that the birds began to mate on that day. The 'tradition' of sending (often anonymous) Valentine cards began in the seventeenth century. These were home-made cards with drawings and verses composed by the sender. The commercial variety, which were especially popular in the Victorian period, were often adorned with lace, flowers, feathers and moss. No British churches are dedicated to St. Valentine though he may be found in religious art with a crippled child at his feet, at his beheading or refusing to worship idols, an act of defiance for which he was martyred. He is the patron saint of beekeepers, affianced couples, travellers and the young and may be invoked against epilepsy, fainting and plague or to sustain a happy marriage.

SALAMANDER *see* BEASTS (HERALDIC)

SALIENT *see* BEASTS (HERALDIC)

SALTIRE A broad diagonal cross, familiar as the cross on which St. Andrew, the patron saint of Scotland, is said to have been crucified though its use in Celtic art clearly pre-dates Christianity. *See also* ORDINARY

SALVER *see* PLATE

SANCTORALE That section of a MISSAL or BREVIARY in which are set out the offices peculiar to particular saints' days. *See also* TEMPORALE

SANCTUARY That part of a church containing the ALTAR or, if there are several altars, the high altar. The terms sanctuary and PRESBYTERY are considered by some to be synonymous but, correctly, the former is contained within the latter and is often raised above it (*see* PREDELLA). In some churches, a separate sanctuary was added to the east of the presbytery and this may have an apsidal or square termination (*see* ANGLO-SAXON ARCHITECTURE). *See also* CHANCEL, LITURGY *and* MEDIEVAL ARCHITECTURE

SANCTUARY CROSSES Medieval roadside crosses erected to delineate the boundaries of an ecclesiastical liberty within which certain privileges were enjoyed (*see* FRANCHISE *and* SANCTUARY, RIGHT OF). There were eight such crosses around Ripon of which only one, the Sharrow Cross, survives.

SANCTUARY LAMP *see* LAMPS

SANCTUARY, RIGHT OF From the Latin *sanctus*, meaning 'inviolable', is derived the Right of

Sanctuary which, in medieval England, was of two kinds: ecclesiastical and secular.

Ecclesiastical sanctuary developed through usage from the Saxon period and originally applied only to that area in the immediate vicinity of a bishop's throne (*cathedra*) and to the precincts of certain religious houses. In 431 this was extended to include the curtilage of a church or an area defined as such. Having claimed the right of sanctuary, a fugitive could not be forcibly removed, contravention of the laws of sanctuary being a form of sacrilege punishable by excommunication. Within forty days the fugitive was permitted to take an oath before a coroner (usually at an altar in the church porch – *see* PORCHES) by which he confessed his crime, swore to *abjure the realm* (leave the country) and submit to banishment. Thereafter, dressed in a white robe or sackcloth and carrying a wooden cross, he would travel to an agreed port and board the first available ship. Such journeys had to be completed within an allotted time and by a prescribed route. This was by no means an easy task: in the fourteenth century the walk from Yorkshire to Dover had to be accomplished in nine days. The right of sanctuary could also be exercised by those who were the victims of brigandage or raids from rapacious neighbours. Indeed, entire communities were sometimes accommodated within a church tower and storage provided for their goods and cattle (*see* TOWERS). Many churches possessed sanctuary knockers (*hagodays*): brass rings, often with escutcheons in the form of some monstrous beast. By grasping the ring of the hagoday, a fugitive could claim sanctuary from his pursuers. There are surviving examples at Rhulen in Powys and Cound in Shropshire but the most celebrated sanctuary knocker is at Durham Cathedral where '. . . serten men that dyd lie alwaies in two chambers over the church dore . . . that when any such offenders dyd come and knocke, straight waie they were letten in at any our of the nyght.' Giraldus Cambrensis, writing at the end of the twelfth century, described 'The churches in Wales [which] are more quiet and tranquil than those elsewhere. Around them the cattle graze peacefully not only in the churchyards but outside too with the fences and ditches marked out and set by bishops to fix the sanctuary limits' (*see* SENTRY FIELD). In some cases, the right of sanctuary (Welsh *braint*) extended as far as '. . . the cattle go to feed in the morning and return in the evening', a privilege which was sometimes grossly abused.

Another type of ecclesiastical sanctuary, confirmed by William I in 1070, applied to twenty-two abbeys and cathedrals where sanctuary could be claimed for life. This resulted in numerous complaints of abuse, indeed the abbey of Westminster acquired an unenviable reputation as a 'base for systematic robbery'. In 1529, coroners

Sanctuary knocker on the north door of Durham Cathedral.

were instructed to ensure that those who abjured the realm should be branded with the letter A on the back of the thumb. In 1540 the right of sanctuary was abolished for those believed to be guilty of murder, rape, burglary, highway robbery or arson. James I effectively abolished the right altogether in 1623 though in some places sanctuary for debt was recognised well into the nineteenth century.

Secular sanctuary relied upon a royal grant and in theory might be applied to any franchise where a lord exercised *jura regalia*. For this reason, secular sanctuary is often confused with ecclesiastical sanctuary, for fugitives frequently sought refuge in a church in franchise, especially in ecclesiastical liberties such as Beverley and Durham. The privileges of secular sanctuary were restricted to seven cities in 1540 and were abolished in 1773.

SANCTUS BELL (*also* SACRING BELL *and* SAUNCE BELL) A bell rung at the saying of the *Sanctus* ('Holy, holy, holy . . .') at the beginning of the MASS and to focus the congregation's attention at the consecration and elevation of the Host. The sanctus bell might be a hand-bell or a small bell housed in a SANCTUS BELL-COTE and operated by means of a bellrope (usually) in the presbytery.

SANCTUS BELL-COTE An open-sided turret, usually above the chancel arch or at the eastern termination of the sanctuary, in which the SANCTUS BELL is hung (*see* BELL-COTES).

SARACEN A common charge in HERALDRY, a saracen's head is swarthy, bearded and with long dark hair. It may be 'wreathed about the temples' with a torse of twisted silk. Saracen's head crests in the arms of the Lygon, Stapleton, Warburton and Willoghby families recall crusading ancestors, but it should not be assumed that all saracen's head devices originated in this way for most examples were adopted several centuries after the event. The almost identical Moor's head crests of the Moore and Mordaunt families allude to the names and have no further significance.

SARCOPHAGUS A stone coffin, the lid of which may be decorated with a simple Christian motif. The term is also used to describe a structure on which a coffin is rested or a MONUMENT depicting the same. The original sarcophagus was a limestone used by the Greeks to make coffins and believed to consume the flesh of corpses.

SARUM, USE OF (SARUM RITE) The medieval modification of the Roman rite used in the cathedral of Salisbury in Wiltshire. Traditionally ascribed to St. Osmund, it was compiled by Bishop Richard le Poore (d. 1237) and was revised (as the New Use of Sarum) in the fourteenth century. Adopted by several other dioceses in the later Middle Ages, it formed the basis for the first *Book of Common Prayer* of 1549 (*see* USES).

SATAN *see* ATTRIBUTED ARMS, CHRISTIAN SYMBOLS, DOOM *and* WALL PAINTINGS

SAUCERY *see* LARDER

SAVAGE (*also* WILD MAN) In HERALDRY, a long-haired, bearded man, wreathed with leaves about the loins and temples, and carrying a club (*see* WODEHOUSE).

SAXON CHRISTIANITY *see* ANGLO-SAXON CHURCH

SCAGLIOLA A mixture of cement and colouring matter in imitation of marble.

SCALLOP The shell device of St. James the Apostle. More than 300 medieval English churches are dedicated to St. James and the scallop shell is frequently found depicted in stone, glass and wood in the fabric of these churches. It was also the badge worn by pilgrims returning, usually via Bordeaux, from the Saint's shrine at Santiago de Compostela in Spain, which by the twelfth century had become the most important centre of Christian pilgrimage after Jerusalem and Rome. Scallops were sewn on pilgrims' clothing or worn on their hats or shoulder bags (*scrips*) and were sometimes carved in their effigies or engraved on monumental brasses.
See also SHRINES

SCAPULAR Part of the regular monastic HABIT, a sleeveless garment worn over the shoulders at the front and back and reaching almost to the feet.

SCHISM Formal separation from the unity of the Church (*see* GREAT SCHISM). Schism was not considered to be heretical because it did not result from doctrinal differences. Priests in schism did not relinquish their authority to celebrate the Eucharist and bishops could continue to ordain priests.

SCHISM ACT (1714) Legislation which was intended to prevent nonconformists from teaching but it was entirely ineffective and was repealed in 1719.

SCHOLA CANTORUM *see* CHURCH MUSIC (ANGLICAN)

SCHOOLS Following the DISSOLUTION OF THE MONASTERIES in 1536/39, monastic and cathedral song schools were displaced, together with the small schools which were sometimes attached to medieval CHANTRIES. Their purpose had been the training of priests, and rote learning, particularly of Latin, grammar and music, predominated.
GRAMMAR SCHOOLS
The grammar schools by which they were replaced continued to teach in Latin, but there was a greater emphasis on analysis and on an understanding of classical literature, science and theology which were at that time considered to be the fount of learning. The contemporary development of printing meant that books were more readily available, though usually only for the preceptor's use, and paper also, so that the boys were able to keep journals or 'common place books' in which extracts from the texts were carefully copied and indexed.

The purpose of the 'new' secular grammar schools was to provide the sons of the emerging middle class with a suitable career. With the decline of the Church, the governance of late Tudor and Stuart England was increasingly the concern of secular administrators, drawn from the swelling ranks of well-educated young men. Latin not only continued as a necessary adjunct to the study of mathematics, medicine and the law, but was also the European language of diplomacy and trade, and classical literature provided many of the precepts for political life. Nevertheless, stimulated by the introduction of an English bible and prayer book, the use of the

English language, both in administration and in business, was increasing rapidly. Many of these sixteenth-century educational foundations remain today and are often known as the King's school, Henry VIII's School, King Edward's School and so on. Such titles do not necessarily imply that they were founded by the sovereign whose name they bear or, indeed, during that sovereign's reign. Many, including the majority of cathedral schools, were re-foundations of earlier monastic or chantry schools: King's School at Sherborne in Dorset, for example, was reputedly founded by St. Aldhelm, the first bishop of Sherborne (d. 709), and reconstituted in 1550 during the reign of Edward VI. The royal assent was sometimes required in order that the original foundation should be reconstituted, but in the majority of cases schools were re-established through public subscription or the commitment of a local benefactor.

THE SEVENTEENTH CENTURY

In order to maintain an orthodoxy of religious instruction, all teachers were required to be registered through the established Church and to obtain a licence from a diocesan bishop. Nevertheless, there were undoubtedly numerous small local schools in which boys learned the basics of reading, writing and numeracy and for which few records remain. By the seventeenth century many parish churches accommodated schools, often in a room above a porch or in a tower (see PORCHES and TOWERS) and in some places parish or charity school-rooms were built in churchyards. Many schools were short-lived, however, depending as they did on the availability and enthusiasm of a curate or suitably qualified layman. A multiplication table has survived on the Lady Chapel wall at Long Melford church in Suffolk which, in 1670, was used as 'a Publick Schoole for Melford'. Similarly, at North Cadbury in Somerset two alphabets may still be seen on the church wall. At Minchinhampton in Gloucestershire the CHURCHWARDENS' ACCOUNTS for 1651 record a payment of 6s 3d 'for stones and making a Chimnie in the Chansell for the schoole.' The Society for the Propagation of Christian Knowledge (SPCK) was founded in 1698 to provide for the spiritual and educational needs of industrial communities and by 1750 there were some 1500 schools for the poor, precursors of the Victorian charity schools, supported through voluntary subscriptions.

THE VICTORIAN ERA

Universal education slowly evolved during the Victorian era (1837–1901). In the mid-nineteenth century the sons of the establishment usually received private tuition or attended one of the old public schools which had originally been founded to provide educational opportunities for the poor. The girls were often sent to small private schools or were taught at home by governesses. Most public and grammar schools of the period were even then considered to be archaic, both in their ethos and their methods and singularly out of tune with the general tenor of Victorian philanthropy. Nevertheless a few notable headmasters, such as Thomas Arnold (1795–1842) at Rugby School, propounded and practised an educational philosophy which was emulated by their more enlightened colleagues and was to serve as a model for the later grammar schools. Smaller residential private schools, the bedrock of the Victorian middle classes, were both ubiquitous and variable: the worst being soulless institutions in which children were condemned to a life of misery and degradation. There were also numerous private *common day schools* which provided low-fee elementary education for poor children. These including the *dame schools*, elementary schools run by women, at which the fees were 3p or 4p a day.

An act of 1833 required that children in employment should also receive a basic education and several *factory schools* were established for this purpose. From 1844 the Poor Law Commissioners were empowered to send workhouse children to district schools which were sufficiently large to meet the educational needs of a group of WORKHOUSES. Many schools were provided by charitable organisations such as the nonconformist British and Foreign School Society (founded 1808) which adopted a *monitorial system* (in its 'British Schools') by which older children (who were themselves sometimes as young as eleven) taught groups of younger ones, supervised by paid teachers. By 1851 the National Society for the Education of the Poor in the Principles of the Established Church (founded 1811) controlled over 17,000 'national schools'. From 1824 both the British Schools and the National Schools received substantial government aid. Some of the best charity schools were to be found in rural areas, endowed by local congregations or benevolent land-owners. Education was not compulsory, however, and there was as yet no requirement that teachers should be trained or registered. In the heavily populated urban areas, where poverty and squalor were endemic, educational provision remained sadly neglected, though the Quakers established schools (for children and adults) in some industrial areas.

From 1833 state grants for school building were available through the churches but proved ineffective, principally because of inter-denominational intolerance. Consequently, educational opportunity in Britain was singularly inferior to that of mid-nineteenth century France, Holland or Germany despite the entreaties of many enlightened educationists and a significant body of scientists and industrialists who realised that, despite the euphoria of the new Victorian age, Britain's prosperity could not be maintained if the majority of the populace remained illiterate and uneducated. Some advances in the training of teachers and the building of schools were made in the 1860s, though the Revised Code of 1862 was attacked (by Matthew Arnold among others) for weakening the tenure and status of pupil teachers who were now employed and paid by school managers instead of being apprenticed. Consequently many young girls, for whom a career in teaching was the only alternative to domestic service, faced both arbitrary dismissal and the ruination of their careers for trivial causes. At this time, a three-year period as a pupil teacher, together with an 'unblemished' character and success in an entrance examination, were necessary qualifications for admission to a two-year course at a teacher training college. For those who could survive the harsh disciplinary regimes of such colleges, the future was bright. A newly qualified teacher in the 1860s could earn as much as £100 a year or more: sufficient to lift the sons and daughters of labouring families into an entirely different social bracket from that of their parents. Advancement was dependent both on the support of patrons and managers and on the recommendations of H.M. Inspectorate of Schools, whose ubiquitous delvings into log books, punishment books and registers and relentless testing of rote learning must have been a mortifying experience for many young teachers.

UNIVERSAL EDUCATION

It was not until W.E. Forster's Act of 1870 that educational opportunities became freely available. Forster (1819–86) was a Quaker and an enthusiastic educationist who became Vice-President of the Education Department in 1868. As a result of the Act, church schools continued to receive state funding and throughout the country district boards of education were established to provide *elementary schools* and free education for those children whose parents were unable to pay. These *board schools* were secular and undenominational and were often resented by the voluntary (church) schools which were obliged to provide adequate schooling or face being taken over by a local board. In consequence the number of church schools built in the six months following the Act was considerable.

Legislation of 1876 established the principle that all children should receive elementary education and the 1880 Education Act required attendance at school between the ages of five and ten. At that age a child could obtain a certificate which enabled him to leave school – but only if his attendance had been satisfactory. Legislation of 1891 provided for free elementary education and by the turn of the century the school-leaving age had been raised to twelve. Secondary and higher education were not provided for, however, until the Balfour Education Act of 1902 abolished the school boards and conveyed responsibility for both phases of elementary education to county and borough councils through the provision of *council schools*. Later, the 1918 Education Act raised the school-leaving age to 14 and replaced the elementary schools, which provided for children between the ages of 7 and 14, with separate junior schools (7–11) and senior schools (11–14), though these were not common until after 1926. All elementary schools, whether junior, senior or all-age, had boards of managers while grammar schools had governors. (This distinction survived until the 1980 Education Act: all English and Welsh schools now have governors which include a number of elected parents.)

THE EDUCATION ACT (1944)

Educational provision in the nineteenth century may indeed have been inequitable and diverse, but the system by which it was replaced was to establish standards by which others were assessed. In the decades following the 1944 Butler Education Act, English primary education became pre-eminent though the selective secondary system of separate grammar, technical and modern schools were less successful and, for the most part, has been replaced by comprehensive schools which provide educational opportunities for young people of varying aptitudes and abilities.

Church schools are either aided or controlled and are described as 'voluntary', having been established by voluntary bodies (such as diocesan boards of education) rather than local education authorities. *Aided schools* are voluntary schools in which the majority of the governing body comprises foundation governors whose particular duty is to ensure that the school is conducted according to the terms of the trust deed. Aided school governors employ the teachers and ancillary staff (though they are paid by the local education authority) and are responsible for the exterior maintenance and repair of the school buildings. *Controlled schools* are voluntary schools in which the governing body has been unable (or unwilling) to accept the financial responsibilities of aided status.

DOCUMENTARY RECORDS

The records of the charitable organisations mentioned above (many of which still function), of bishops' and archdeacons' visitations and church-wardens' presentments provide an extraordinarily detailed source of information as do the statutory log books, punishment books and governors' minute books which are held by all schools (*see* DOCUMENTARY SOURCES *and* MINUTES). Log books, compiled by head teachers, include inspectors' reports and details of day-to-day occurrences: absences for 'getting in the potato harvest' or 'the School closed for Pack Monday Fair at Sherborne . . .', sad tales of war-time evacuees and orphans and visits by the 'nits nurse' to check for head-lice (still a recurring problem in many schools). The maintenance of a punishment book was compulsory until the abolition of corporal punishment in 1988. Therein are the harsh realities of school life: '1913 April 28th: Mafeking and Sebastopol Cawley ages 10 and 12: Making great noise in the Boys' Lobby during dinner hour of a wet day. These boys were leaning against the door and when teacher opened the door they both fell down and evidently seemed to think it fine amusement. The teacher was not going to countenance this kind of behaviour. 3 stripes each on the hand and 1 on the back. . . . Cawley was cheeky.' For the History of Education Society *see* APPENDIX II.

See also SUNDAY SCHOOLS and UNIVERSITIES

Further reading:

Armytage, G., *Four Hundred Years of English Education*, London, 1970

Chapman, C., *The Growth of British Education and its Records*, Chichester, 1992

Sutherland, G., *Elementary Education in the Nineteenth Century*, London, 1971

SCONCE A wall-bracket holding a CANDLE-STICK.

SCOTIA A concave moulding.

SCRATCH DIALS *see* SUNDIALS

SCREENS *see* CHANCEL SCREENS, PARCLOSE, PULPITUM, REREDOS, ROOD SCREENS *and* TOWER SCREENS

SCREWS AND NAILS Early timber framing was secured by means of wooden pegs driven through holes in adjacent or interlocking timbers. For items such as doors, hand-made wrought-iron ornamental or 'clout' nails, with a variety of shaped heads, were commonly used until the mid-nineteenth century. Tapering metal screws, hand-filed and with irregular threads, were introduced in the late seventeenth century. Lathe-turned screws first appeared in the late eighteenth century and the machine-made variety in the mid-nineteenth.

SCRIPT *see* LETTERING

SCRIPTORIUM A writing-room, especially in a monastery, where documents were written (often copied), illuminated and painted (*see* MANU-SCRIPT ILLUMINATION). In Benedictine houses, the scriptorium was usually located in the south alley of the cloister where the scribes benefited from the pure, northern light. They were often provided with individual compartments (*carrels*) to reduce drafts and enhance privacy and silence (*see* CLOISTER).

SCROLL (i) A roll of parchment or paper, or an ornamental design in this shape. (ii) In heraldry, a stylised roll of parchment on which a MOTTO is written.

SCULLERY *see* LARDER

SEALS A seal (*sigil*) is a piece of wax, lead or paper, impressed with an individual design and attached to a document as a guarantee of authenticity or affixed to an envelope or receptacle to ensure that the contents may not be tampered with other than by breaking the seal. The piece of stone or metal upon which the design is engraved, and from which the impression is taken, is called a *matrix*.

Important documents carried seals before the inception of HERALDRY in the mid twelfth-century and these often bore distinctive devices which alluded to the names of their owners: a man called Swinford might use a boar (swine) on his seal, for example. Ecclesiastical bodies generally used religious symbols on their seals and these were often incorporated into later coats of arms.

The earliest recorded heraldic seal (that is, one in which the devices are depicted on a shield) dates from 1136 and this, together with a number of seals dating from the mid-twelfth century, provides evidence of the rapid spread of heraldry throughout western Europe in a comparatively short period of time. It is also apparent that the use of the same sigillary devices (those found on seals) by succeeding generations of the same family served to consolidate the hereditary nature of heraldry.

Seals are most often found singly but may also represent the parties to a contract. The normal practice in such cases was to prepare a number of copies of a document, each copy (*chirograph*) being sealed by all the parties to the agreement. The *Constitutions of Clarendon* (1164) were prepared in this way but the three identical documents were

Seal of John de la Pole, Earl of Lincoln (d. 1487).

Second seal of Richard of Bury, Bishop of Durham 1334–45.

complete with heraldic shields, horse-cloths (*caparisons*) and banners. These seals were often so large, and documents so numerous, that *privy seals* were required for administrative purposes. These were smaller and, therefore, less ornate than great seals and usually bore a simple shield within a decorative interstice and legend. A *secretum*, perhaps a signet ring, was generally used for private matters and, because of their small size, these often bore devices other than coats of arms: the bear and ragged staff badges of Richard Nevill (d. 1471), for example.

Medieval seals were usually circular in shape, pointed ovals being used by ecclesiastics, though not exclusively so. By the thirteenth century, the administrative offices of abbots, priors, bishops and cathedral chapters were producing numerous legal documents all of which required authentication by means of seals (*see* HERALDRY (ECCLESIASTICAL)). Unique among the prelates were the Prince Bishops of Durham who, as lords palatine, bore an equestrian figure on one side of their (circular) seals and a majesty on the other (see PALATINATE).

Whereas a simple shield was ideally suited to a circular seal, the elongated fourteenth-century coat of arms, with its helm and crest, created awkward spaces between the central motif and the surrounding legend. These were filled with architectural and decorative patterns (*diaper*) together with heraldic devices and the figures of beasts or chimerical creatures. These were often personal or household BADGES which, from the fifteenth century, were frequently translated into CRESTS and SUPPORTERS.

Several seals depict stylised sailing ships: that of John, Earl of Huntingdon, Admiral of England (1436), for example, in which the arms *England with a Bordure of France* cover the entire sail.

For the papal bull *see* BULLA.

Further reading:

Ellis, R., *Catalogue of Seals in the Public Record Office*, London, 1981

Friar, S., *A New Dictionary of Heraldry*, Sherborne and London, 1987

SEARCHER A person (usually a woman) appointed by a parish to verify a death, to ascertain its cause and to report any suspicious circumstances. She received a fee from the family of the deceased person and had to provide the SEXTON with a death certificate before burial could take place. The office of searcher appears never to have been recognised in law and holders were not required to have any medical knowledge.

SECCO *see* FRESCO

SECULAR (i) One who is not bound by a monastic rule (*see* REGULAR). (ii) Pertaining to matters civil in contradistinction to matters ecclesiastical. (iii) Concerned with that which is not spiritual.

never sealed. *Magna Carta* (1215) was sealed by King John's 'five-and-twenty over-kings', and one of the most remarkable surviving medieval documents, a letter to the Pope, was signed and sealed (but not delivered) by the ninety-six barons summoned to the Lincoln Parliament of Edward I in 1300.

In England, the Great Seal of the realm has always been two-sided, like the coinage, with a different device on each side. The first 'great' seal of England was probably that of Edward the Confessor (1003–66) but that which provided a model for later English monarchs was the seal of William I (1066–87) which was engraved on the reverse with the *majesty* (a depiction of the king seated in state) and on the obverse an equestrian figure, also of the king. Subsequently, the faces were reversed: the majesty becoming the obverse and the equestrian figure the reverse.

Inevitably, from the early thirteenth century, it became fashionable for the lords also to engrave their seals with equestrian figures of themselves in armour,

SECULAR ARM In CANON LAW, the term is used to describe the State or any lay authority concerned in ecclesiastical cases. Following trials for heresy, for example, condemned prisoners were usually handed over to the secular arm for punishment.

SECULAR CANONS Clergy serving a cathedral or collegiate church. Although secular canons were not members of monastic orders, and therefore did not observe a monastic rule, they nevertheless lived a quasi-monastic life of celibacy and discipline. Consequently, their accommodation tended to resemble that of the monastic orders (*see* MONASTIC BUILDINGS).

SECULAR CLERGY Priests who live in the general community as distinct from the 'regular' clergy who are members of religious orders.

SEDILIA Stone seats built within the south wall of a PRESBYTERY, often with an adjacent PISCINA. Sedilia were usually provided for the priest who celebrated the mass and for the deacon and sub-deacon who assisted him. The seats were sometimes stepped and occupied according to rank, the highest (and that nearest the altar) being for the celebrant. In some churches, nineteenth-century remodelling has raised the chancel floor so that the seats of the sedilia appear to be uncomfortably low (*see* FENESTELLA).
See also ABLUTIONS, AUMBRY, CREDENCE, LAVABO, LITURGY *and* MASS

SEE The *cathedra* (throne) of a bishop (*see* CATHEDRAL) and the jurisdiction which this represents (*see* DIOCESE).

SEGMENTAL ARCH *see* ARCH

SEIZE QUARTIERS Proof of *seize quartiers* (i.e. that all sixteen of an armiger's great-great grandparents were entitled to bear arms in their own right) was sometimes proposed as a means of defining true ancestry, 'true blood' and, therefore, undisputed gentility. In Britain, the proposal has always been regarded with considerable scepticism and has nothing to do with MARSHALLING.

SEJANT *see* BEASTS (HERALDIC)

SEMY (*also* SEMÉ) In HERALDRY, a number of small charges evenly distributed over a field to form a pattern e.g. *Azure semy of Garbs Argent* is a blue field on which are scattered a number of small silver wheatsheaves. Certain charges have their own terms e.g. *bezanty* (*semy of bezants* – gold roundels) and *estoily* (*semy of estoils* – stars).
See also FLEUR-DE-LIS

SENIORS OF THE PARISH Select vestrymen (*see* VESTRY).

SENTENCES (i) From the Latin *sententia* meaning an exposition of thought, medieval sentences were compilations of opinions which, by the thirteenth century, had evolved into accepted theological propositions. (ii) Mural texts, maxims of Christian doctrine, which often replaced earlier WALL PAINTINGS following the Reformation.

SENTRY FIELD A West Country term for a field in the vicinity of a church where at one time there was a right of sanctuary (*see* SANCTUARY, RIGHT OF).

SEPARATISTS A title applied to those who separated from the Church of England (*see* DISSENTERS).

SEPTFOIL A figure with seven radiating stylised 'petals' found both as an architectural motif and an heraldic device (*see* FOILS).

SEPTUAGESIMA The third Sunday before LENT and the ninth before EASTER. The name is derived from the seventy days remaining before the Saturday after Easter. Purple VESTMENTS are worn from Septuagesima until Holy Week.

SEPULTURE, RIGHTS OF *see* PARISH

SEQUENCE In the medieval LITURGY, a rhythm sung on prescribed days following the last reading before the Gospel.

SEQUESTRATION A legal procedure by which sequestrators are appointed to administer the emoluments of a vacant benefice for the benefit of the next incumbent.

SERAPHIM *see* ANGELS, ATTRIBUTED ARMS *and* CHRISTIAN SYMBOLS

SERGES Large 'corpse candles'.

SERMON A discourse on a religious or moral subject delivered by a clergyman during a religious service (*see* PULPITS).

SERPENT (i) In religious art, the serpent is associated with the powers of darkness. In the book of *Genesis* it is a serpent which seduces Eve into eating the forbidden fruit of the Tree of Knowledge, while in art and poetry the coils of the serpent symbolise the limitations of man's earthly experience. Snakes and serpents abound in Christian legend, perhaps most famously in the story of St. Patrick who is reputed to have banished snakes from Ireland. (ii) *See* MUSICAL INSTRUMENTS

SERVER One who assists in the sanctuary, especially at the EUCHARIST. A server's duties include the conveying of the bread and wine to the communion table and washing the celebrant's hands. He or she may also be the CRUCIFER.

SERVICES In the Middle Ages there were generally three services for the laity on Holy Days and Sundays: MATTINS and MASS in the morning and EVENSONG in the afternoon. But as the number of clergy, curates, chaplains and chantry priests increased so did the frequency of daily services which often included several celebrations of Mass. Medieval congregations took little part in the services, however, long passages of which were conducted in Latin beyond the ROOD SCREEN, and there were no hymns and only occasional sermons. Nevertheless, the regular performance of elaborate ritual and the ordered sequence of processions and feast days provided security in an otherwise wretched existence and created an intense attachment to the parish church.
See also LITURGY *and* MEDIEVAL CHURCH
For post-Reformation services *see* REFORMATION.

SETTLEMENT AND REMOVAL RECORDS The 1697 Settlement Act prevented strangers from residing in a parish unless they could demonstrate by means of a *Settlement Certificate* that their home parish would be willing to take them back if they claimed poor relief. When this occurred, *Removal Orders* were issued, records of which are now maintained in the archives of Quarter Sessions held by local record offices.
See also POOR LAW

SEVEN *see* CHRISTIAN SYMBOLS *for* SEVEN CHAMPIONS OF CHRISTENDOM, SEVEN DEADLY SINS, SEVEN JOYS OF THE VIRGIN, SEVEN SACRAMENTS (*see also* FONTS), SEVEN SPIRITS BEFORE THE THRONE, SEVEN SPIRITS OF GOD, SEVEN VIRTUES *and* SEVEN WORKS OF MERCY
See also SEVEN WORDS FROM THE CROSS

SEVEN LIBERAL ARTS *see* QUADRIVIUM *and* UNIVERSITIES

SEVENTEENTH-CENTURY ARCHITECTURE *see* SIXTEENTH- AND SEVENTEENTH-CENTURY ARCHITECTURE

SEVENTEENTH-CENTURY CHURCH Despite the manifold changes resulting from the Elizabethan Settlement of 1559 (*see* REFORMATION), in the seventeenth century the parish church continued to be the religious, social and cultural centre of a community. But, for those who could still remember the medieval forms, it was a very different Church.

Regular attendance at services was now obligatory and absence punishable in the Church courts:

> . . . all and every person and persons inhabiting within this realm or any other the Queen's Majesty's dominions shall resort to their parish church . . . upon every Sunday and other days ordained and used to be kept as Holy Days, and then and there to abide orderly and soberly during the time of Common Prayer, preachings or other service of God there to be used and ministered. (Act of Uniformity, 1559)

Enforcement was difficult, especially in urban areas and among the poor, and many were excused by virtue of old age, sickness or infirmity, or to care for their infants or 'for lack of [suitable] clothing.' Furthermore, parishioners were required to attend their own parish churches which were not necessarily those which were closest to their homes. Consequently, long journeys were often undertaken on foot, necessitating the provision of hat and coat pegs (which have occasionally survived) and notices such as that in the church porch at Hawkesbury in Avon: 'It is Desired that all Persons that come to this Church would be Careful to leave their Dogs at home and that Women would not walk in with their Pattens on.' (Pattens were wooden over-shoes.) In several instances, the need for 'parishioners sometimes to refresh themselves . . . being so far from the parish church . . . they cannot go home and come again to church . . . the same day' was cited in the courts as justification for the licensing of an alehouse.

Compulsory attendance brought together an entire parish, many of whom used the occasion to gossip or to resurrect old grievances with their neighbours. Quarrels, even fisticuffs, are attested to by the charges brought in the Church courts and many parishes were obliged to appoint beadles (or 'wakers') to keep order during services, to prod the more somnolent or inattentive members of the congregation and to eject 'such . . . children as either by crying or other noise shall be any disturbance in divine service'. Churches were, of course, unheated in winter and must have been stiflingly hot in summer when entire communities were obliged to sit through interminable sermons. One can almost hear the repressed groan of a packed, perspiring congregation as the parson paused to turn his hour glass over (*see* PULPITS) In such circumstances, a public penance must have been a welcome, though occasional, diversion.

Penance was still a common sentence of the Church courts in the seventeenth century, especially in cases of fornication and adultery. Contemporary (and not always sympathetic) reports confirm that public penance at a Sunday service was undoubtedly a humiliating ordeal, especially for women who appear to have been treated less charitably than men.

It is hardly surprising, therefore, that those who could afford to pay the considerable sums required to commute the sentence to a fine did so with alacrity. In 1640, for example, a Dorset man paid £40 to the Church court '. . . to save himself from publique shame amongst his neighbours.'

CHURCH INTERIORS

After the Reformation, the altar was no longer the focus of attention but the prayer-desk and PULPIT, and it was to these that the congregation was directed when box pews were installed. Competition for accommodation was fierce and seating arrangements reflected the rigid social divisions which existed at the time. At one end of the scale were the local gentry and their families who occupied the pews at the front while, at the back of the nave and in the aisles, sat the agricultural labourers, those with no property rights, for whom there was 'a plank for the use of the parish'. The main body of the church was usually provided with box pews which were wainscotted and fitted with doors to protect the occupants from drafts (see PEWS). The CHURCHWARDENS, always innovative fund-raisers, began charging for accommodation, the scale of fees reflecting, not only the desirability of a particular pew, but also the position of its occupants relative to other members of local society (see PEW RENTING). The lists of pews and seating plans which may survive among parish records can provide a wealth of information concerning the families in a parish and the estates, farms and cottages where they lived. In many instances they show that 'square pews' (with benches on three or four sides) were reserved for particular farms or estates and that men and women were often separated, a practice which is perpetuated at Staunton Harold Chapel in Leicestershire. Certain 'square pews' were reserved for families and were upholstered and sometimes curtained. Others were even more lavishly equipped and furnished, often with a fireplace and private doorway from the churchyard (see PEWS, FAMILY). At Ryecote in Oxfordshire, for example, two elaborate enclosed pews were erected on either side of the chancel arch, one for the Norreys family and the other for Charles I when he visited the parish in 1625. These 'parlour pews' were sometimes converted CHANTRY CHAPELS, such as that of the Long family in Draycot Cerne church near Chippenham in Wiltshire. The right to a particular seat ('pew-rights') is frequently mentioned in property leases and, on occasions, was a matter of disputation before the Church courts. Churchwardens' presentments contain numerous complaints concerning private pews which had been enlarged or rebuilt by their occupants, thereby interfering with the rights of those who could no longer hear or see the parson.

From the mid-seventeenth century it became increasingly common to erect tombs, headstones and other memorials in CHURCHYARDS. Many of the GRAVESTONES dating from this period are splendid examples of local craftsmanship, available only to the more affluent members of society who, nevertheless, were denied burial within the church because of their comparatively modest social status. These seventeenth-century memorials, with their elegant lettering and skilfully carved decorative motifs, are far removed from the banality of later centuries and from the grandiose monoliths of the aristocracy (see MONUMENTS). And, despite the Reformation, the carving often records popular medieval themes in symbolic form: the inexorable passage of Time and the brevity of human life.

SECULAR ACTIVITIES

In the decades before the Civil War (1642–9) churches and churchyards continued to be used for secular purposes (see CHURCH AND COMMUN-ITY). Annual meetings, at which churchwardens and other parochial officers were elected, and ecclesiastical and manorial courts were held in the nave while public notices were announced from the pulpit or displayed in the church porch (see PORCHES). SCHOOLS were often accommodated in churches and in accordance with the Canons of 1571 which required that only those who had been licensed by a diocesan bishop should be permitted to teach. Parish chests were used as repositories for personal papers as well as parochial and manorial documents (see PARISH CHEST) while the local trained bands (militia) mustered in the churchyard and stored their armour and weapons within the church. Fire-fighting pumps ('engines') and other equipment were also kept in the church: at Puddletown in Dorset, for example, where the long hooks for removing burning thatch are still hung beneath the west gallery, together with the community's fire buckets. Resources which, in the Middle Ages, had been expended on chantries and church building were now used to maintain and improve the church BELLS which continued in use, both as a means of communication and for the pleasure of bell-ringing.

Donations of books to church libraries were also popular, notably the 1611 translation of the Bible (see BIBLES) and copies of Erasmus's Paraphrases, Foxe's Book of Martyrs and Bishop Jewel's Apology, all of which had been authorised by the Injunctions of 1559 which required that 'parishioners may most commodiously resort to the same . . .'. Such books were highly valued and regularly appear in church inventories of the period. Several churches received handsome bequests: the 300 volumes donated by a neighbouring parson to the church of St. Wulfram at Grantham, Lincolnshire, are still stored in a room above the south porch, each volume secured by means of a long chain (see LIBRARIES).

CIVIL WAR AND THE INTERREGNUM

The Reformation, completed by 1560, had brought about fundamental doctrinal and liturgical changes in the English Church but a great deal of ceremonial was retained, particularly in the cathedrals. The administration of the Church was virtually unchanged, with power vested in the Bishops who were now responsible to the sovereign and not to the Pope. All this was anathema to the PURITANS who wished for a more radical reformation, but in the 1630s the bishops, lead by Archbishop William Laud (1573–1645) and enjoying the support of Charles I, ordered an improvement in the standards of ceremonial and a return to more traditional forms of worship (*see* LAUDIAN).

The Civil War arose from the constitutional, economic and religious differences between Charles I and the Long Parliament which he summoned in 1640. The Root and Branch Petition of the same year demanded the abolition of episcopal government in the Church and led to the *Root and Branch Bill* of 1641 which was intended to abolish the episcopy 'with all its dependencies, roots and branches.' Opposition to the bill, which only received a second reading, rallied conservative opinion behind the King. In a further attempt to reform the Church, Parliament summoned the *Westminster Assembly of Divines* in 1643. The Assembly's most significant achievement was the *Westminster Confession* of 1647 which remains the definitive statement of Presbyterian faith, though it was never fully accepted in England.

The period of republican government in Britain (known as the Commonwealth) lasted from the execution of Charles I in 1649 to the restoration of the Stuart monarchy with the return from exile of Charles II in 1660. Oliver Cromwell (1599–1658) was Lord Protector from 1653–8 and his son, Richard (1626–1712), from 1658–9. During the Civil War of 1642–9, the Church and the Monarchy were perceived by the Parliamentarians to be joint enemies of the state. Iconoclasm and desecration were rife: churches were plundered; stained glass smashed; images and tombs defaced or destroyed; organs, carved woodwork and service books burned and vestments shredded. Anything which symbolised 'Popery' was a legitimate target for the rampaging Parliamentary troops and many items of great antiquity and beauty (which had escaped destruction in the sixteenth century) were gratuitously destroyed in the name of Puritanism. Much of this desecration has subsequently been ascribed to Cromwell but, in reality, it was the inability of many of his officers to control their troops which was the real cause. Bullet holes, scars of the conflict, may still be found in the tower door at Painswick in Gloucestershire and in the pulpit of St. Nicholas' church, Abbotsbury in Dorset. Churches were often used as prisons: in 1642 Prince Rupert confined large numbers of parliamentary prisoners in Cirencester church (Gloucestershire) where the stained glass windows were broken in order that the men's relatives could supply them with food. The Dorset Clubmen, captured by Cromwell in 1645, were imprisoned in the nearby church at Iwerne Courtney (also known as Shroton) where he

haranged them from the pulpit before sending them home.

During the Civil War most of the Anglican clergy supported the royalist party and many were later removed from their benefices as 'malignants' or 'delinquents' and replaced by Puritan ministers. Indeed, a number suffered severe deprivation and even death at the hands of the Parliamentary forces. CHURCHWARDENS' ACCOUNTS, parish REGISTERS and VESTRY minutes often provide extraordinarily vivid evidence of the religious and social upheavals of the time, of the growth of non-conformity, of doctrinal disputes and liturgical change. The *Book of Common Prayer* was replaced by a *Directory* for public worship which allowed the clergy to exercise considerable latitude in the conduct of services. A second, and more systematic, attack was made on the fabric of the Church, this time sanctioned by Parliament itself. Wherever they had survived, statues, crosses and even fonts were pulled down, the royal arms removed and communion tables moved from the chancel into the midst of the congregation. Thus the Holy Communion was translated into an act of commemoration, far removed from the medieval sacrament of the Mass, and the pulpit became the focus of worship. Only the remotest churches managed to escape the attentions of the iconoclasts, many of whom exercised their authority with a fanatical enthusiasm. Perhaps the most notorious of all the iconoclasts was one William Dowsing who, in 1643–4, wreaked havoc in the counties of Cambridgeshire and Suffolk where he visited nearly one hundred churches. In such turbulent times, it is surprising to find that new churches were still being built: at Staunton Harold in Leicestershire, for example, where an inscription on the church tower recalls that

In the yeare 1653
When all things sacred were throughout ye nation
Either demollisht or profaned
Sir Robert Shirley, Barronet
Founded this church . . .

An act of 1657 required that everyone should swear an oath abjuring the papacy. Those who refused to do so were presented at Quarter Sessions.

THE RESTORATION

With the Restoration of the Monarchy in 1660 came the re-establishment of the Anglican Church and the resumption in their benefices of many of those who had been replaced by 'intruded' ministers. In 1662 the use of the *Book of Common Prayer* was revived (with minor changes), communion tables were restored to their position at the east end of the chancel and the ROYAL ARMS were erected in all churches, often with additional texts such as 'My son, fear God and the King, and meddle not with them that are given to change' (there is a splendid example at Milborne Port in Somerset). But two decades of upheaval had left their mark: nonconformity was now recognised as a fact of life and it is from this period that the lasting religious, social and political division between 'church' and 'chapel' can be dated.

In 1662 a fourth *Act of Uniformity* required that services should be conducted in accordance with the revised *Book of Common Prayer* (some two thousand clergy were removed from their livings for refusing to conform with the Act). A further *Conventicle Act* of 1664 forbade meetings of more than five persons who were not members of the same household and in 1665 the *Five Mile Act* forbade those nonconformist ministers who refused to take the non-resistance oath from coming within five miles of any city, town or parish where they had previously preached. In 1667 Roman Catholics were excluded from public office and the *Conventicle Act* of 1670 exacted severe penalties for attendance at unlawful assemblies. *The Test Act* of 1673 directed that all holders of civil and military office should receive the sacraments according to the forms of the Church of England and should take an oath repudiating the doctrine of TRANSUBSTANTIATION and affirming the monarch as head of the Church of England. A second *Test Act* of 1678 excluded Roman Catholics (other than the Duke of York) from Parliament. But the POPISH PLOT of 1678 had a salutary effect on the Establishment and, after the inevitable reprisals, the *Toleration Act* of 1689 granted nonconformists (but not Roman Catholics) the right to have their own places of worship and to engage their own preachers and teachers. Although still excluded from holding public office, they were permitted to apply for municipal office providing they could demonstrate 'occasional conformity' with Anglicanism (*see* DISSENTERS).

See also SIXTEENTH- AND SEVENTEENTH-CENTURY ARCHITECTURE

Further reading:

Bettey, J.H., *Church and Parish*, London, 1987

Hill, C., *The English Bible and the Seventeenth-Century Church*, Harmondsworth, 1994

Purvis, J.S., *An Introduction to Ecclesiastical Records*, London, 1953

Randall, G., *Church Furnishing and Decoration in England and Wales*, London, 1980

——, *The English Parish Church*, London, 1982 (Spring Books 1988)

Tate, W.E., *The Parish Chest*, Cambridge, 1960

SEVEN WORDS FROM THE CROSS The seven sentences which, according to the Gospels, were spoken by Christ on the cross:

'Father, forgive them; for they know not what they do' (Luke 23:34)

'Today shalt thou be with me in paradise' (Luke 23:43)

'Woman, behold thy son! . . . Behold thy mother!' (John 19:26ff)

'My God, my God, why hast thou forsaken me?' (Matthew 27:46)

'I thirst . . .' (John 19:28)

'It is finished' (John 19:30

'Father, into thy hands I commend my spirit' (Luke 23:46)

SEXAGESIMA The second Sunday before LENT and the eighth before EASTER. The name is derived from the fact that it falls approximately sixty days before Easter.

SEXT The monastic day office which took place at about noon ('the sixth hour') and usually followed High Mass. A simple office, similar to TERCE and NONE, it consisted of a hymn, the singing of part of Psalm CXIX, a short chapter and closing prayers which included the lesser litany, the Collect and Lord's Prayer.

SEXTON An official, assistant to the PARISH CLERK, responsible for grave-digging, bell-ringing and other jobs in and around a parish church. The sexton was appointed and paid by a parish, incumbent or churchwardens. In the Church of England a sexton may now be appointed by an incumbent and parochial church council who determine his (or her) terms of employment.

SHAFT That part of a COLUMN or PIER between the capital and base.

SHEELA-NA-GIG A grotesque female form particularly associated with Romanesque decoration (*see* MEDIEVAL ARCHITECTURE). Possibly a vestigial pagan fertility symbol or sculpted as a reminder of the fifth of the Seven Deadly Sins (lechery), there are notable examples at Kilpeck in Herefordshire, Whittlesford in Cambridgeshire and Fiddington, Somerset. The name, which derives from the Irish meaning 'Sheila of the paps', was coined by Victorian antiquaries in search of a suitable euphemism.

See also PAGAN SYMBOLS

SHEER THURSDAY A traditional name for MAUNDY THURSDAY.

SHEFFIELD PLATE Old Sheffield plate, dating from the period 1760–1840, consists of a copper layer fused between thin layers of sterling silver and rolled into sheets. Seams are dovetailed and edges rolled in order to disguise the layers. The name is derived from the city in which the process was perfected by Thomas Boulsover in *c*. 1743. Articles in Sheffield Plate became so desirable that from 1784 they were 'hallmarked', much to the irritation of the London silversmiths. Many of these marks were heraldic: the eight arrows from the arms of

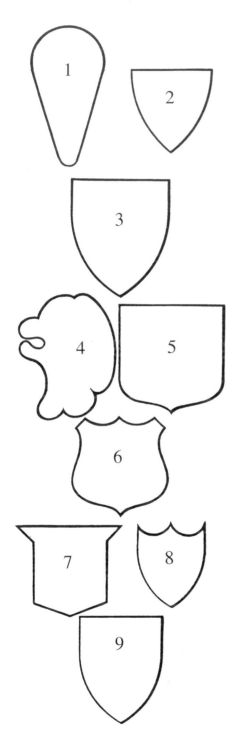

Sheffield were used by the Creswick brothers, the Hatfields used a fleur-de-lis, and the Holland Company a unicorn's head, for example. Later pieces usually bear a manufacturer's mark or name.
Further reading:
Bambery, A., *Old Sheffield Plate*, Aylesbury, 1988

SHELL *see* DECORATIVE MOTIFS *and* SCALLOP

SHIELDS The shield is the essential element of a COAT OF ARMS and, with the banner, is the principal means of heraldic display. EFFIGIES, monumental BRASSES etc. may be dated with reasonable accuracy by reference to the type of shield held by a figure or depicted elsewhere on a monument.

In the eleventh century, and at the beginning of the twelfth, shields were long, narrow and kite-shaped, covering most of the body. They had rounded tops and were made of wood covered with tough boiled leather [*see* illustration, *figure* 1]. Such shields were in use at Hastings and during the First Crusade, where raised edges, studs and bosses were often picked out in colour. During the twelfth century the tops of shields became flatter, and decoration more personal. In the thirteenth century shields became shorter and were shaped like the base of a flat-iron (called a *heater shield*) [2 and 3] and this style remained in use for heraldic purposes throughout most of the fourteenth century. But the increasing efficiency of the cross bow and long bow, and the development of plate armour, reduced the effectiveness of the shield as a means of defence and by the fifteenth century it had been abandoned by mounted knights except for heraldic purposes, notably at tournaments. It was at this time that the *à bouche* shield was most in evidence: this took a variety of forms but all had a small 'notch' cut in the side, apparently to allow for the free movement of a lance in the joust, though this may have been a stylistic affectation [4]. The sixteenth century witnessed the decline of practical heraldry and a preoccupation with heraldic display. In order to accommodate numerous acquired (or assumed) QUARTERINGS, shields of the period were almost invariably as broad as they were long [5 and 6].

From the beginning of the seventeenth century many ornate shields found their way into heraldry, few of which could ever have been used on the battlefield. For the most part, these reflect contemporary architectural styles, the most common being the eighteenth-century 'tablet' shield [7] and the popular nineteenth-century 'spade' shield [8]. A beautifully proportioned 'heater' shield [9] is that which is most often used in the present century, though the *à bouche* style is also popular.

The 'shield' in a woman's arms is conventionally depicted in the shape of a lozenge, there being an

assumption that women did not make war or participate in tournaments and therefore had no practical use for a shield. For the same reason, a lozenge is never accompanied by a helm and crest, though there are exceptions – as in a hatchment at Marnhull church in Dorset where a lozenge of the arms of Beatrix Dive (?) is surmounted with a helm bearing the family crest. In such cases it is possible that a local craftsman was unaware of armorial convention. The lozenge is such an unattractive and inconvenient shape that considerable artistic licence (and not a little ingenuity) may have been required in order to accommodate the heraldry.
See also ARMOUR, HELMETS, HERALDRY *and* POINTS OF THE SHIELD

SHINGLES Wooden tiles used for covering walls and roofs since the Roman period until the end of the Middle Ages when, because of fire hazard, they were generally replaced by clay tiles, though for structural reasons shingles were retained on a number of church spires (*see* TOWERS). Usually of oak, they measured 12.7 × 25.4 cm (5 × 10 inches) and were laid with an overlap, each tile being thicker at the lower edge.
See also ROOFS, SLATES *and* TILES

SHRINES In AD 156, the author of *The Martyrdom of Polycarp* wrote that the martyr's bones had become 'more valuable than refined gold'. But by that time the mortal remains of saints and martyrs (*see* RELICS) had already acquired a broader potency which affected all objects which themselves had been in contact with the remains or, indeed, with the tomb in which they were preserved. Christians believed that reliquaries and shrines contained the living presence of the saints and that miracles could be performed through contact with the bones or the cloths (*brandae*) which had been touched by them (*see* Acts 19: 12). Such tombs were therefore places of healing, protection, forgiveness and spiritual guidance. Palestine itself was perceived as a vast

St. Alban's shrine and watching loft at St. Albans, Hertfordshire.

relic: it became the Holy Land of Christian imagination in which certain locations were particularly venerated for their associations with Christ. Thus, pilgrims immersed themselves in the Jordan as Christ had done and plucked leaves from the palm trees of Jericho and wore them in their hats, thereby acquiring the popular name of 'palmers'. Pilgrims to the Holy land increased in number during the third and fourth centuries, many of them adding their own inventions to 'the steadily burning fire of their devotion' (Adair *). Two monks, for example, claimed to have discovered the head of John the Baptist in the ruins of Herod's palace and before long most churches in the Holy Land had acquired a 'relic' of some sort so that, by the beginning of the fifth century, pilgrimage was developing commercially, with the provision of lodgings and guided tours of the sacred sites.

THE CULT OF RELICS

By this time, Europe had also established its own centres of pilgrimage, notably at Rome where the relics of martyrs killed during the persecutions were venerated by thousands of pilgrims, including four Anglo-Saxon kings. Shrines of lesser saints and martyrs burgeoned throughout Europe and every church coveted a holy relic. In the sixth century, Pope Gregory the Great sent to Augustine and the missionaries in England 'all things necessary for the worship of the Church' including 'relics of the holy apostles and martyrs', and the second Council of Nicaea (787) ordered that no church should be consecrated without relics to be placed in or upon an altar in a *reliquary*, or in a crypt beneath. Thus, it was not only the great abbeys and cathedrals which possessed relics: the parish church of St. Denys at Stanford-in-the-Vale in Berkshire, for example, still has the reliquary which once contained one of St. Denys's bones, St. Wulfram's at Grantham in Lincolnshire possessed the relics of St. Wulfram, while at St. Edmund's, Salisbury, there was a piece of St. Wolfride's skull.

Throughout Europe the market in relics expanded rapidly: not only those of native saints but of imported items from Rome and Palestine, most of which were of extremely dubious provenance. This unsavoury trade flourished for several centuries, partly because it was believed that all relics possessed miraculous powers of self-multiplication. In Britain, Bede (d. 735) refers to shrines of native saints such as Alban, Oswald, Chad and Cuthbert which were visited from the fifth century. Not all saints were martyrs, some were *confessors* who had witnessed to the faith through suffering or by the impeccability of their lives. They were judged by the efficacy of their relics to work miracles and many were thereby acclaimed saints. In medieval Norfolk, for example, there were some seventy places of pilgrimage associated with local saints or their relics. But very few shrines acquired truly inter-national popularity. After Palestine and Rome came the shrine of St. James at Santiago de Compostela in northern Spain (*see* SCALLOP) and, in France, the shrines of St. Martin at Tours and that of the reputed head of John the Baptist at Amiens. In Germany were the relics of the Three Kings at Cologne and the shrine of the Holy Coat (the seamless robe of Christ) at Trier. Italian shrines included the tomb of St. Francis at Portiuncula near Assisi, that of St. Anthony at Padua and the Holy House of Loreto, which had miraculously been transported from Nazareth to Italy in 1295. Of contemporary English shrines only those of St. Thomas à Becket at Canterbury and Our Lady of Walsingham in Norfolk belonged to this first order, though Glastonbury in Somerset, with its mythical associations with Joseph of Arimathea and King Arthur, was also popular as were the remote shrines of St. Magnus on Orkney and Ynys Enlli (Bardsey), the 'island of innumerable saints', off the Lleyn peninsular, Gwynedd.

Not all relics are of saints and martyrs. On shelves in the crypt of the Kentish church at Hythe are stacked and arranged the remains of over four thousand people who, according to tradition, were slain in a bloody battle between the Britons and the Saxons in AD 456. Many of the skulls are cleft, suggesting that they had been struck by weapons. For some reason the relics continue to attract 'pilgrims', some of whom leave votive offerings on one or other of the assembled collection of skulls.

PENANCES AND INDULGENCES

The popularity of *pilgrimages* in the Middle Ages owed much to the practice of prescribing them as *penances*. Confession was followed by absolution which freed the repentant Christian from guilt but not from the punitive consequences of his sin. These could be commuted by performance of a penance and many of those who were convicted of serious crimes by the ecclesiastical courts undertook long pilgrimages clothed in sackcloth and ashes and with bare feet and fettered limbs. From the twelfth century, relief from purgatorial suffering could also be obtained by means of *indulgences*: certificates which stated that a period of purgatory had been remitted. Announcing the first crusade at Clermont in 1095, Pope Urban II offered a plenary indulgence to all those who confessed their sins and 'took the cross' and in the thirteenth century the Franciscans claimed a papal plenary indulgence for all pilgrims to their shrine of the Portiuncula. Papal confirmation of this concession in 1294 established a precedent which was followed by the custodians of numerous other shrines who sought partial indulgences from their bishops or from the Pope himself. Inevitably, such privileges had to be paid for, but they must have represented a sound investment for the price continued to increase throughout the fourteenth century. Many shrines acquired the right to offer indulgences associated with more famous shrines, thereby attracting pilgrims who could see little point in exposing themselves to the hazards of a long and expensive journey overseas. The sale of indulgences also enabled those who were too old or infirm to go on crusade to send a substitute and still claim the benefits of a plenary indulgence. Similarly, a substitute pilgrim could be engaged, even by a man's family after his death or as a result of a clause in a will which required prayers to be offered for the soul of the testator at a particular shrine (*see also* CHANTRY). Eventually, indulgences could be commuted to money payments and in the late medieval period *pardoners* competed with each other, and with the local shrines, in the sale of certificates.

CURATIVE SHRINES

Not all those who set out on pilgrimage did so as a means of penance, however. In an age of rudimentary medical practice many travelled to shrines whose relics were associated with miracles of healing and the relief of suffering. The Fourth Lateran Council of 1215 had declared that illness was caused, not by physical ailments, but by sin and it therefore followed that a visit to a shrine was likely to do more good than a visit to a physician. Others perceived the shrines as tangible evidence of the spiritual world of heaven, far removed from their own temporal existence but attainable through physical contact with the relics of saints and martyrs. Such places fed the medieval imagination and brought even the most sceptical of men into contact with the historical Jesus and the characters of a seemingly heroic age.

The healing powers of the seventh-century saint Melangell continue to attract pilgrims to her shrine at Pennant Melangell in Powys. Melangell came to the remote valley in 607, fleeing from a dynastic marriage arranged by her father who was a member of the ruling family in Strathclyde. Melangell (whose latin name was Monacella) founded a nunnery in the valley and became associated with the cult of the hare which, in pagan Britain, was revered as a goddess of fertility. According to legend, she gave protection to a hare which was being hunted by Brochwel, prince of Powys. When the huntsman raised his horn to urge on the hounds, it stuck to his lips and the hounds were repulsed. Medieval pilgrims prostrated themselves beneath the reliquary, sometimes remaining there all night in hope of a cure. The shrine, believed to be the oldest Romanesque reliquary in northern Europe, was removed from the church following the Reformation. But the saint's bones were preserved and placed in the restored shrine when it was reconstructed from broken fragments found in the lich-gate and walls of the church (*see also* YEW TREES).

PILGRIMAGE

The acquisition of potent and popular relics was, in medieval terms, a guarantee of financial security if not commercial success for many of the larger monastic houses, particularly those of Benedictine foundations. Hostelries such as the George and Pilgrim at Glastonbury and the George Inn at Winchcombe in Gloucestershire were built to accommodate pilgrims in the fifteenth century, as was the New Inn at Gloucester. The body of the murdered Edward II (d. 1327) had been received for burial by the Abbot of St. Peter's (now Gloucester Cathedral) in the previous century. Denied canonisation by the Pope, Edward's remains nevertheless attracted enormous numbers of pilgrims whose patronage financed the rebuilding of the superb perpendicular choir in the abbey church (1337–50). Shrine offerings (rather than money gifts) included curiosities such as griffins' eggs, elephants' teeth and unicorns' heads as well as the more usual precious stones and plate. Offerings belonged to the saints and were rarely converted into cash, even in times of crisis, and several monasteries were obliged to appoint a keeper (*tumbarius*) or Master of the FERETORY who was responsible for security (*see also* WATCHING LOFT). But not all cults were successful, indeed the majority were surprisingly short-lived. Even at Canterbury, where in 1220 (the year of the translation of the relics) offerings at Thomas à Becket's tomb had totalled no less than £1,142, annual income from pilgrims to the shrine had declined to £36 by the Dissolution.

Roads were rarely for the exclusive use of pilgrims, though causeways and bridges were often provided for their benefit, particularly where routes converged on a particular shrine. Along the more popular routes (many of which came to be known as *Pilgrims' Ways*), wayside inns, hostels, chapels and hospices developed, such as the infirmary at Castle Acre in Norfolk which was provided for ailing pilgrims on their way to Walsingham (*see also* SLIPPER CHAPEL). So numerous were the Walsingham pilgrims that in contemporary chronicles the Milky Way was sometimes referred to as 'the Walsingham Way'.

Not all shrines were located in major churches. Six miles from Hereford the church of the Nativity of the Blessed Virgin Mary at Madley was enormously popular in the Middle Ages for it housed a statue of the Virgin which (presumably) acquired a reputation for working wonders (*see* MARY, THE BLESSED VIRGIN). Chapels, a new chancel, additional naves and a crypt for the statue were all added to the original Norman church to accommodate the streams of pilgrims whose offerings enabled the church to commission several treasures – notably a rare and beautiful early thirteenth-century east window of the trial of John the Baptist.

Pilgrimage was essentially a popular and spontaneous expression of emotion: one which was never admitted as an essential of Christian duty but which was generally tolerated and, in many cases, encouraged by the Church. As the cult grew, so it became necessary for the Church to exercise control, and in some cases even to prohibit certain practices such as the veneration of HOLY WELLS, many of which were considered unsuitable for such purposes because of their pagan origins. Despite the continuing success of several major shrines, the numbers of pilgrims on the roads of England declined during the fourteenth and fifteenth centuries and, as Chaucer's *Canterbury Pilgrims* suggests, many took the journey simply for the pleasures of travel and each others' company.

For the majority of medieval society, to embark on a pilgrimage must have been the realisation of a lifetime's ambition: a unique opportunity to gain experience of the world beyond the confines of their village. Before leaving, it was necessary to obtain a priest's blessing, to make confession and, if the pilgrimage was to be a lengthy one, to make a will. Most pilgrims wore a long, course tunic known as the *sclavein* and a broad-brimmed hat turned up at the front. They travelled in bands for mutual protection and usually on foot, though in the later centuries more often on horseback. Before returning, pilgrims purchased the distinctive badge of the shrine they had visited and this was worn on their tunic or hat as proof of their pilgrimage.

THE REFORMATION AND AFTER

The English shrines were plundered in 1537–9 and most were dismantled (*see* REFORMATION, THE). At Canterbury, twenty-six wagon-loads of treasures were removed from Becket's shrine and taken to the royal mint while the bones of the saint who had opposed Henry Plantagenet were scattered by order of Henry Tudor. Nevertheless, in a severely attenuated form, pilgrimage in Britain survived the Reformation and remained a powerful image of the Christian tradition. Indeed, in the nineteenth century it enjoyed a modest revival with the emergence of the Anglo-Catholic wing of the Church of England and today Walsingham and Lourdes are as popular as ever they were in the Middle Ages. Pilgrims still leave offerings in the niches of St. Wite's tomb at Whitchurch Canonicorum in Dorset, one of the few medieval shrines in which the original relics have survived – in this case the saint's bones. The thirteenth-century shrine is a simple stone chest with three large oval openings through which pilgrims placed their afflicted limbs in the hope that close contact with the relics would cure them.

Further reading:
Adair, J., *The Pilgrims' Way*, London, 1978 *
Hole, C., *English Shrines and Sanctuaries*, London, 1954
Ohler, N., *The Medieval Traveller*, Woodbridge, 1990
Sumption, J., *Pilgrimage: an Image of Medieval Religion*, London, 1975

SHRIVE To hear CONFESSION and give ABSOLUTION, or to disburden oneself by confession and then to receive absolution.

SHROUD (i) To clothe a corpse for burial. (ii) The material used for this purpose.

Before the mid-seventeenth century not all bodies were buried in coffins but they did have shrouds. The sixteenth-century variety was a voluminous sheet, gathered at the head and feet and knotted. Those of the eighteenth century were more tailored, with sleeves and draw-strings; while in the nineteenth century they were fully fashioned.

Medieval practice varied. There is evidence, for example, that in the Low Countries corpses were often dressed in their everyday clothes at the time of burial. In England, an illustration in the *Bedford Hours* of *c.* 1423 shows a corpse closely wrapped in the manner of an Egyptian mummy, while a set of vignettes of *c.* 1480 (by Simon Marmion) shows how this was achieved. First the shroud was folded over the left-hand side of the corpse. The remainder was then drawn over the right side, with the arms folded across the body in line with the rib cage. Finally, the shroud was pinned or sewn along the centre. Little wonder that the term *'winding sheet'* was applied to the shroud used for such an operation. But by far the most common method was to place the corpse in a 'sack' which was tied at both ends. Evidence from contemporary sources (such as shroud brasses) suggests that, in the fifteenth century, shrouds were about 30 cm (12 inches) longer than the length of the body, to allow for a knot at each end, and about three times its width. A thin strip of the shroud material was formed into a cord which was used to secure the ends, though some scholars have suggested that it was the custom for chrysom cloths to be kept for this purpose.

See also BURIALS
Further reading:
Litten, J., *The English Way of Death*, London, 1991

SHROUD BRASS (SHROUDED FIGURE) *see* CADAVER

SHROVE TUESDAY (*also* PANCAKE TUESDAY) The day immediately before ASH WEDNESDAY on which it was customary to be shriven (to submit to confession and absolution) in anticipation of LENT. A pancake, a pudding or 'cake' made in a frying pan, was eaten after dinner and was intended to 'stay' the stomachs of those who were to be shriven. The Shrove Bell, which summoned the faithful to the shriving, was often referred to as the Pancake Bell. Shrovetide is Shrove Tuesday and the two preceding days.

SIDESMEN (SYNODSMEN) Persons elected as deputies to the CHURCHWARDENS. Originally, *synodsmen* (or questmen) were elected to represent their parishes at annual diocesan synods. These were convened by a diocesan bishop and archdeacon to consider the state of parishes within their jurisdiction and the synodsmen were required under oath to report, among other matters, on the behaviour of their priest. Armed with the report, the archdeacon would descend upon the parish to make his own inspection before reporting to his bishop. After the Reformation the duties of sidesmen were often combined with those of the churchwardens. Not all ecclesiastical historians have accepted the derivation of 'sidesman' from 'synodman'.

SIGLA Characters used as abbreviations.

SIGNATURES, BISHOPS AND ARCHBISHOPS
Archbishops and bishops of the Church of England and the Church in Wales sign, after a representation of the Cross, by their Christian name followed by their province or see. These are spelled normally, with the following exceptions:

ARCHBISHOPS:

Canterbury:	Cantuar
York:	Ebor
Wales:	Cambrensis

BISHOPS:

Carlisle:	Carliol
Chester:	Cestr
Chichester:	Cicestr
Durham:	Dunelm
Edinburgh:	Edenburgen
Ely:	Elien
Gloucester:	Gloucestr
London:	Londin
Norwich:	Norvic
Oxford:	Oxon
Peterborough:	Petriburg
Rochester:	Roffen
Salisbury:	Sarum
Truro:	Truron
Winchester:	Winton

See also ADDRESS (FORMS OF) *and* CLERGY (CHURCH OF ENGLAND)

SIGNS AND SYMBOLS *see* CHRISTIAN SYMBOLS, HERALDRY, *and* MARKS

SILENCE An objective of monastic and canonical communities was *summa quies* – the absence of all excitement which might detract from contemplation. It was St. Basil who wrote 'Quiet, then, is the first step in our sanctification'. The religious house was the home of silence where voices were raised only in praise or prayer or in the reading of the Scriptures in the FRATER. According to the Rule, silence accompanied even those brethren who undertook a journey together. 'Let no-one think himself a well-ordered, religious or God-fearing canon, if he get into the habit of breaking silence without urgent reason . . . for this want of control of the tongue is an evident sign of a dissolute mind and a neglected conscience. Therefore, let Canons Regular regard silence as a precious treasure since through it a remedy against so many dangers is applied. ' (*Barnwell Observances*). Noisy activities were located as far as possible from the cloister and every person within the precinct was required to be silent during the singing of the canonical hours: 'While any Hour save Compline is being sung in church, no brother shall talk to any officer of the monastery, nor within the bounds of the great court, nor even in the farmery, save for the sick who are so straitened as to be unable to keep silence for that space.' (Lanfranc: *Constitutions*). But, inevitably, it became increasingly difficult to distance the cloister from the outside world. Many monastic houses became the administrative centres of vast estates, pilgrims were actively encouraged to visit SHRINES and the hospitality of the lords spiritual often eclipsed that of the lords temporal. Originally speech was permitted only in the parlour but restricted conversation was later allowed in the cloister, providing permission had been obtained and the subject matter was of a religious nature: 'Let no one dare to ask about the gossip of the world, nor tell of it, nor speak of trifles or frivolous subjects apt to cause laughter'.

SILL The lower horizontal edge of a window.

SILVER GILT Silver covered thinly with gold.

SILVER MARKS *see* HALLMARKS

SILVER PLATE Silver-plated articles are those to which a thin coating of silver has been applied.

SILVERWARE *see* PLATE

SIMNEL SUNDAY *see* MOTHERING SUNDAY

SIMONY 'And when Simon [Magus] saw that through laying on of the apostles' hands the Holy Ghost was given, he offered them money, saying, give me also this power . . .' (Acts 8:18–19). The term simony thereby denotes the purchase or sale of matters spiritual and, in particular, benefices and ecclesiastical offices. A simoniac is one who is guilty of simony and a simonist is one who defends the practice.

SINGING BREAD Large wafers used by the priest for communion.

SINISTER *see* POINTS OF THE SHIELD

SIR (i) A reduced form of 'sire', the word is the distinctive title of address of a British baronet or knight (*see* BARONET, KNIGHT BANNERET *and* KNIGHTHOOD, ORDERS OF). (ii) At one time 'Sir' (*dominus*) was a courtesy title applied to a priest who was not *Artium Magister* and therefore could not properly be styled *Magister*. At Ledbury church in Herefordshire, for example, there is an epitaph (believed to be one of the earliest in English) to William Calwe (d. 1409), a chantry priest, which reads:

Sey pat nost [the Lord's Prayer] for sere Eillia Calwe
That loved wel god and alle hallwe [all saints].

SITES *see* CHURCH SITES

SIX ARTICLES, THE Articles enacted by Parliament in 1539 in response to the Ten Articles formulated by the Convocation of 1536 and the Bishops' Book of 1537. The Ten Articles and the Bishops' Book (entitled *The Institution of a Christian Man* and largely the work of Thomas Cranmer) dealt with various doctrinal and other matters of dispute between the Roman Catholic and English churches. The Six Articles were the first authoritative statement of the doctrine of the English Church, ostensibly enacted in the interests of moderation and uniformity but in practice savagely punitive measures intended to prevent the spread of Reformation practices and doctrines. They attempted to define those opinions which constituted heresy, defended auricular confessions and private masses, enforced clerical celibacy, confirmed monastic vows and maintained the doctrines of transubstantiation and communion in one kind. Denial of the real presence in the sacrament was to be punished by death by burning and those who denied the efficacy of private confession and private mass were to be hanged. The Six Articles represented a severe blow to the aspirations of the English reformers and served to intensify existing divisions in the English Church. Nevertheless, Henry VIII achieved popularity from the Act, shrewdly sensing that his subjects were, for the most part, '. . . more inclined to the old religion than the new opinions.'
See REFORMATION, THE *and* THIRTY-NINE ARTICLES, THE

SIXTEENTH- AND SEVENTEENTH-CENTURY ARCHITECTURE
LATE GOTHIC
Contrary to the popular view, the late fifteenth and early sixteenth centuries were a time of increasing prosperity and social stability. In 1509 there were ninety churches within the walls surrounding the square mile of the City of London, most of which had been built or extended in the boom years of the preceding century. Many of the best-known English churches date from this period: magnificent monuments to the success of commerce and, in particular, to the entrepreneurial spirit of England's wool merchants and clothiers.

It was at this time that gothic architecture reached its apogee in the truly sumptuous and audacious style known as the Perpendicular (*see* MEDIEVAL ARCHITECTURE). Perpendicular architecture is characterised by the delicate vertical tracery of windows and stone panelling (from which the term 'perpendicular' is derived) with regular horizontal divisions and slender fluted piers leading upward into an exuberance of intricate fan-shaped vaulting (*fan vaulting*) exemplified in the magnificent vaults of Sherborne Abbey, Dorset (1425–86) and the Chapel of King's College, Cambridge (1446–1515). Windows of the period are significantly wider and the arches flatter, those of the late Perpendicular and Tudor Gothic periods being of the *four-centre* type (*see* ARCHES). *Rectilinear* (or *panel*) tracery features in both windows and wall panels and is characteristic of the late Gothic period. This form of tracery incorporates both mullions and transoms thereby creating rows of small glass 'panels' (*lights*) with more complex tracery confined to the upper tiers within the arch. There are numerous wonderful examples of Perpendicular parish churches, notably St. John the Baptist at Cirencester in Gloucestershire (described by Betjeman as 'the largest and most splendid of the Cotswold 'wool' churches'), Walpole St. Peter in Norfolk ('the best of them all') and St. Mary Redcliffe at Bristol ('the most splendid parochial church in England'). The north chapel of St. Cyriac's church at Lacock in Wiltshire, described by Harbison ** as an 'explosion of gorgeousness', contains a rich sixteenth-century wall tomb (of Sir William Sharington) and a late fifteenth-century lierne vault with carved bosses, pendants and ribs 'like fruit garlands bound with ribbons' combining Gothic form and Renaissance detail. Lacock Abbey was the last monastic foundation to be suppressed at the Dissolution. It was acquired by Sir William Sharington, a talented Renaissance adventurer, and is now in the ownership of the National Trust together with 'one of the most homogeneous and architecturally distinguished villages in England.'*

It is evident that, even before the Reformation, medieval religious motifs were being superseded by secular imagery and HERALDRY in the architectural detail of late medieval churches. The nave vault at Sherborne Abbey, for example, contains numerous BOSSES many of which are carved and painted with Tudor heraldry: Tudor roses, Beaufort portcullises, lions' heads, shields of the royal arms, lion and greyhound supporters and EG cyphers for Henry VII and Elizabeth of York. The cyphers assist in dating the vault at *c.* 1486, the year of Henry's marriage. But heraldry is not always a reliable guide: the spandrels of the choir vault are also painted with shields of arms but these were added during the Victorian restoration of 1856.
ELIZABETHAN AND JACOBEAN
In 1550 some 6,000 medieval churches served a population of 3.5 million. Not surprisingly, the churchwardens of the post-Reformation period were

Folke church, Dorset.

preoccupied, not with the building of new churches, but with adapting existing ones to accommodate the liturgical and doctrinal requirements of the new English Church (*see* REFORMATION, THE). One effect of the Reformation, and of the Dissolution of the Chantries in particular, was to divert benefactions and endowments from ecclesiastical projects, such as the building of clerestories and chapels, into secular activities which ranged from the acquisition of former monastic properties to the erection of grandiose MONUMENTS. The few parish churches which were completed in the late sixteenth and early seventeenth centuries, while reflecting the doctrinal shift from altar to pulpit, continued to be built in a gothic style (sometimes known as Gothic Survival) of which the little church of St. Lawrence at Folke in Dorset is a typical example. Rebuilt in 1628, its tower could pass as Perpendicular, though its plain, triplet windows are clearly of a later date and its fine collection of screens, pews and furnishings are all in the fashionable 'Jacobean' style. Indeed, the period is characterised by English Mannerism: exuberant monuments, fittings and architectural detail, unintentionally anti-classical in

effect and often overloaded with strapwork, garlands and obelisks. Other examples of Gothic Survival churches are Leweston (1616), also in Dorset, St. Katherine Cree in London (1628–31) and Monnington-on-Wye in Herefordshire (1679, with a fifteenth-century tower).

The Reformation brought about fundamental doctrinal and liturgical changes but a great deal of ceremonial was retained, particularly in the cathedrals. The administration of the Church was virtually unchanged, with power vested in the Bishops who were now responsible to the sovereign and not to the Pope. All this was anathema to the PURITANS who wished for a more radical reformation, but in the 1630s the bishops, lead by Archbishop Laud and enjoying the support of Charles I, ordered improvements in the standards of ceremonial and a return to more traditional forms of worship (*see* LAUDIAN). This conflict is sometimes evident in the architecture and furnishings of contemporary, neighbouring churches: in Yorkshire, for example, where St. John's church, Leeds (1634) has the elaborate woodcarving, canopied pulpit and screens of the

Laudian tradition while nearby Bramhope Chapel (1649) is an unadorned, rectangular building, with simple box pews and three-decker pulpit. St. John's at Groombridge in Kent (1625) is a Gothic church with classical undertones, built in brick by John Parker to celebrate Prince Charles's return from Spain and his unsuccessful wooing of the Infanta. Even at the end of the century, the rebuilding (by Sir William Wilson in 1698–1704) of the tower, nave, aisles and transept of St. Mary's, Warwick owed more to the fifteenth century than to the seventeenth. Betjeman described Wilson's splendid vaults and arcades as an architectural *tour de force* and the church is essentially a Gothic Survival building, despite the balustrades and urns which bedeck the nave roof and the classical niches and fabulous parapets of the tower.

THE INTERREGNUM

In the pervading atmosphere of religious bigotry and iconoclasm which characterised the mid-seventeenth century it is surprising to discover that churches were still being built, though they were few in number.

At Staunton Harold in Leicestershire the royalist Shirley family built a private chapel as an Anglican gesture of defiance to the Commonwealth government. An inscription above the west door proclaims:

In the yeare 1653
When all things sacred were throughout ye nation
Either demollisht or profaned
Sir Robert Shirley, Barronet
Founded this church
Whose singular praise it is
to have done the best things in ye worst times
And
hoped them in the most callimitous
the righteous shall be had in everlasting
remembrance.

Sir Robert's faith and his audacity incensed Cromwell who announced that if a man could afford to build such a splendid chapel, he could also afford to raise a regiment. Sir Robert refused and was sent to the Tower where he died at the age of twenty-seven. At first sight, the chapel with its cruciform plan, clerestory, decorated east windows, low-pitched roofs, knobbly pinnacles and embattled parapets, conveys the impression of a late medieval building. But, on closer inspection, it is almost a Gothic self-parody and the classical west doorway, like a triumphal arch with its sculptures, coat of arms and inscription, betrays its date. The chapel, dedicated to the Holy Trinity and now in the care of the National Trust, has a wonderful iron chancel screen (by Robert Bakewell) and has retained all its seventeenth-century fittings including painted wooden ceilings and tympanum, lectern, pulpit (complete with cushions), screens, pews, altar hangings and church plate.

Another Holy Trinity, at Berwick-upon-Tweed in Northumberland, is a rare example of a Commonwealth church. Set within the star-shaped ramparts of an Elizabethan fortification, it possesses an uncomfortable mixture of gothic and classical features, its walls pierced by triple windows (half of them with round-headed central lights) and its grey stone interior dominated by Tuscan columns and a great lateral arch. A seventeenth-century gallery and canopied pulpit have survived, but awful Victorian coloured glass adds to the confusion. Other Commonwealth churches include Plaxtol in Kent (1649), a Gothic Survival church with a hammer-beam roof.

CLASSICISM

At the beginning of the seventeenth century little was known of classical harmony and proportions (*see* CLASSICAL ORDER). Post-medieval architec-ture was influenced by various classical sources but these were essentially third-hand and consequently buildings were robust, lively and well crafted but demonstrated little evidence of 'the subtle and detailed attention to proportion and line' (Yarwood ***) of true classical architecture. In Britain, the religious and social upheavals of the first three-quarters of the seventeenth century mitigated against the construction of very large buildings. Nevertheless, it was during this period that the role of the individual architect developed: church buildings were no longer designed by anonymous craftsmen but by intellectually motivated men such as Inigo Jones (1573–1652) and Christopher Wren (1632–1723).

In 1570, Andrea Palladio (1508–80) published his *I Quattro Libri dell'Architettura*, a philosophical and visual analysis of his architectural work in Italy and this was to become the main source of inspiration for the English *Palladian* movement. Inigo Jones, who had studied in Italy (*c*. 1600), was chiefly responsible for the introduction of the pure Italian Renaissance style into England. He became Surveyor-General of the Works in 1614 and thereby chief architect to the Crown. His buildings were very un-English: pure Italian with as few modifications as possible. Of his churches, Queen's Chapel at St. James's Palace in London (1623–5) survives as Marlborough House Chapel. This was his first ecclesiastical building and, there being no classical tradition in England for that type of work, he based his design on that of the antique temple – a rectangular, aisle-less interior covered by a coffered, segmental vault and lit by a large Venetian window. Jones's church of St. Paul, Covent Garden is of particular significance. Built in 1631 in a strict classical style, it has a Tuscan portico – the first of its kind in England. Inigo Jones was, of course, working to a strict set of architectural conventions and his drawings had to be interpreted accurately by masons who had previously enjoyed considerable latitude in the application of their craft. It was not until after his death that Inigo Jones's conception of classical design was to influence profoundly the development of architecture.

It is from this transitional period that many 'unsatisfactory' classical buildings date. The English climate was not conducive to the development of classical architecture: steep roofs for the clearance of snow and rainwater, massive chimneys venting numerous fireplaces and large windows, needed to maximise the fitful sunlight of an English winter, were all basic requirements which sat unhappily with the concept of classical dignity. It was *Christopher Wren* who, to a great extent, resolved the conflict between the Italian and native idioms. By a combination of extraordinary inventiveness, mathematical expertise and the use of traditional English building materials (mixing brick, Portland stone and ordinary roofing tiles, for example), Wren created buildings of considerable elegance, dignity and originality. He too was appointed Surveyor-General to the Crown and was charged with the rebuilding of London's churches following the Great Fire of 1666.

These churches were essentially buildings intended for protestant worship. Gone was the medieval sense of mystery and the barrier between priest and people. The new conception of a church was that of a large room in which as many people as possible could hear the preacher in comfort. These 'auditory' churches were rectangular or basilican in plan, usually galleried and with prominent pulpits and simple communion tables, often set within the body of the church rather than at the east end. Triforium and clerestory were replaced by classical colonnades and large, round-headed windows containing clear glass. Despite the constraints of confined sites, Wren's galleried interiors are light and beautifully proportioned with a wonderful feeling of spaciousness and tranquillity, enhanced by large, pale windows and gold and white plasterwork. Exteriors too are of simple design and usually crowned with those ingeniously constructed steeples with which Wren's churches are most readily associated: the delicate St. Mary-le-Bow and the 'wedding cake' of St. Bride, for example, '. . . all bright and glittering in the smokeless air' (Wordsworth, 1802). Of equal interest and variety are Wren's tall bell-towers and lanterns: lofty St. Magnus the Martyr, St. Margaret Lothbury, St. Martin Ludgate and St. Edmund the King. Wren varied his building materials, usually Portland stone and brick, either separately or together, to provide interest and most of his churches have lead belfries and gilded weather vanes and crosses. Wren was responsible for restoring fifty-one of the City's churches. The first, St. Mary-at-Hill, was re-opened in 1676. The last, St. Michael Cornhill, was completed in 1722 when Wren was eighty-nine.

Some churches of the period have domes, notably St. Paul's Cathedral, which was begun in 1675 and completed in 1711. Initially Wren proposed a centrally planned church with a large dome 36 metres in diameter (120 feet). This was rejected by the commissioners, who considered it to be too far removed from the English tradition, and Wren was forced to compromise, so that beneath its dome and classical shell, St. Paul's is a conventional, cruciform church with many of the characteristics of its medieval predecessor. Interestingly, Wren's early plans for St. Paul's included a long building with galleries on either side, the galleries supported by rows of shops below. Similarly, his design for St. Mary-le-Bow in the City of London had shops along Cheapside parallel to the nave.

See also EIGHTEENTH-CENTURY ARCHITECTURE

Further reading:

Harbison, R., *English Parish Churches*, London, 1992 **

Fedden, R. and Joekes, R., *The National Trust Guide*, London, 1982 *

Randall, G., *Church Furnishing and Decoration in England and Wales*, London, 1980

——, *The English Parish Church*, London, 1982 (Spring Books 1988)

Yarwood, *Encyclopaedia of Architecture*, London, 1985 ***

SIXTEENTH-CENTURY CHURCH *see* REFORMATION, THE

SKELETON BRASS *see* CADAVER

SLATES The term 'slate' was originally applied to any kind of split stone (from the Old French *esclate* meaning 'something split'). This included not only slates for roofing but also *flags* for floors and other uses such as gravestones.

Stone slates have been used for roofing since the Roman period and are commonly found on medieval churches. In the Gloucestershire Cotswolds, the production of stone slates provided income for the Knights Templar at Temple Guiting and there is evidence to suggest that their 'tile-pits' remained in almost continuous production until the beginning of the twentieth century. Since the Roman period such slates have been roughly hexagonal in shape, with a squared 'tail' and narrowing at one end. They were (and are) fastened to the battens with iron nails, though in the medieval period, when nails were expensive, oak pegs were used on less important buildings. In some districts the slates were bedded on moss (*mosseying*) which provided protection against melting snow and had to be renewed periodically (hay or straw were also used). Not all slates come from specialist quarries: most villages of the limestone belt which runs north-east from the Cotswolds through Oxfordshire and Northamptonshire had their own sources of building stone and in many cases tile-pits (*slat quarrs*) nearby. Stone for slates comes in thin layers which also provide fencing slates (*planks*) which are held together by iron clamps (these may be found enclosing some churchyards). A frosting process was probably first used at Stonesfield quarries in Oxfordshire at the end of the sixteenth century. By this method *pendles* of fissile limestone are left exposed during the winter so that the moisture in the thin films of clay between the layers freezes and expands causing the pendles to split easily into slates. Before this, quarries were chosen where stone split naturally so that the slatter's only task was to shape and trim the slates. At Stonesfield the stone was mined, with shafts descending to 20 metres (65 feet), and the pendles hauled to the surface by a windlass. When frost occurred at night the church bell was rung bringing the villagers from their beds so that the pendles could be uncovered as quickly as possible. A slatter worked in a shelter of straw-covered hurdles with a *crapping stone* between his knees. This was a narrow stone set edgewise on the ground on which he trimmed three sides of each slate with a *slat hammer* until it was of the right shape and thickness. The edges were then trimmed by battering along them with the hammer head and a peg hole made in the narrow end by tapping lightly with the point of a slat pick. Piled 'ten flat and ten edgeways', two hundred and fifty slates were considered a good day's work.

Roofing slates varied in length and were measured against a slatter's rule or *wippet stick* which, in the Cotswolds, was marked with twenty-seven notches. Each size of slate had its own name but these varied, not only from one region to another, but among individual slatters. At Stonesfield, beginning with the smallest slates at the roof ridge and working down to the largest under the eaves, they were: short, middle and long cocks; short and long cuttings; muffetts; short, middle and long becks; short and long bachelors; short and long nines; short and long wivots; short and long elevens; short and long twelves; short and long thirteens; short and long fourteens; short and long fifteens and short and long sixteens. There were numerous other names and variations such as duchesses and countesses, farwells, chilts, warnetts and wippets.

Workmanship was judged by the quality of swept valleys which were always the weakest part of a stone-tiled roof. Triangular 'valley stones' had to be cut and arranged so that they left no cracks where the water could enter. Experts at *galetting*, as the craft was called, refused to use lead for this purpose, though modern tilers have no such reservations. Roofs sometimes appear to have sagged because of the weight of the slates but this is not necessarily so for many were built in a curved fashion so that the slates held each other in place thereby reducing the risk of

being lifted by the wind. The Cotswold roofs are undoubtedly the finest, but heavy limestone slates from the Isle of Purbeck are found on churches in Dorset and Somerset and various kinds of sandstone provide roofs in many areas from the south-east of England to the Welsh border and the north country.

The term 'slate' is now commonly applied to the blue-green metamorphic rocks of Wales, Cornwall and Cumbria which, because of their formation, cleave more precisely than limestone or sandstone to produce thinner slates. This type of slate was used as a roofing material from the early medieval period but only widely so since the nineteenth century. It was cheap to extract and process and a slate roof weighed considerably less than stone, thereby reducing the need for substantial and expensive timber framing. Consequently, millions of slate roofs were constructed during the Victorian Age when the quarries of Blaenau Ffestiniog and Llanberis (Gwynedd) prospered.
See also ROOFS *and* TILES

SLAT QUARR *see* SLATES

SLIPPER CHAPEL A chapel in which pilgrims removed their shoes before approaching a shrine (*see* SHRINES). The fourteenth-century 'Shoe House' or Slipper Chapel at Houghton St. Giles in Norfolk is situated about 1.6 kilometres (1 mile) from the shrine at Walsingham. Here, the pilgrims would pause and meditate before embarking on the final stage of their journey – barefoot and penitent.

SLYPE A covered passage, usually linking the CLOISTER with the INFIRMARY or a monastic cemetery. Closed by doors at each end, a slype was often provided with seating and served as a common room or library.

SMOKE FARTHINGS *see* PENTECOSTALS

SNAKE *see* SERPENT

SOCIETY OF FRIENDS (QUAKERS) The Society of Friends originated in the activities of George Fox (1624–91), the son of a Leicestershire weaver who began preaching in 1647 and whose precept was that 'truth is the inner voice of God speaking to the soul'. The term Quaker is derived from the spiritual 'trembling' manifested at early meetings. The Society was established in 1668 and its library in 1673. Its members rejected the sacraments and were opposed to formal services and to paid ministers. They refused to take oaths or to enter into military service and before the Toleration Act of 1689 were subjected to much persecution, refusing to meet secretly and stressing the importance of outward observances in speech and plain living. Quakers have a strong commitment to pacifism and their devotion to social and educational work has earned them almost universal respect. All known Quaker registers were copied in 1837 and the originals sent to the Registrar General in 1840. These are now housed in the Public Record Office, Chancery Lane. A central repository of records is maintained in the Society of Friends Library, though many are retained locally (*see* APPENDIX II).

SOCLE A plinth at the foot of a wall.
See also HOLY WATER STOUP

SODOR AND MAN An Anglican diocese comprising the Isle of Man. The original diocese, which dates from the eleventh century, included the Hebrides and other islands off the west coast of Scotland which were detached in 1334. It is believed that the words 'and Man' were added in error during the drafting of a legal document in the seventeenth century.

SOFFIT The underside of an architectural feature.

SOLLERETS Pointed shoes, often of small overlapping and articulated steel plates, to protect the feet (*see* ARMOUR).

SORORUM Latinised place-name element meaning 'of the sisters' and suggesting that a manor was once held by a monastic foundation of nuns.
See also PLACE-NAMES

SOUL CAKE *and* SOULING *see* HALLOWE'EN

SOUL SCOT *see* MORTUARY

SOUNDING BOARD (*also* TESTER) A flat, horizontal wooden canopy above a pulpit, intended to amplify and direct a preacher's voice for the benefit of his congregation. Most surviving sounding boards have six or eight sides and were erected in the (late) sixteenth, seventeenth or eighteenth centuries. They are often found incorporated into double or three-decker PULPITS or may have been added to an earlier structure. Several sounding boards have been taken down and adapted for other purposes: the fine inlaid tester at Bradford Abbas in Dorset, for example, which is now an attractive table-top. At Lyme Regis, also in Dorset, a splendid Jacobean tester is inscribed in gold leaf with the words: 'To God's Glory Richard Harvey of London, Mercer and Merchant Adventurer 1613. Faith is by Hearing.'
See also BALDACHINO *and* ALTAR CANOPY

Oak tester adapted for use as a side table at Bradford Abbas, Dorset.

SOURCES *see* DOCUMENTARY SOURCES

SPANDREL (i) The surface between two arches in an arcade. (ii) In a vault, the surface between two adjacent ribs. (iii) The triangular area in (e.g.) an arched window or doorway framed by the horizontal and vertical lines of the dripstone and, on the third side, by the moulding of the arch. This type of spandrel is often decoratively carved.

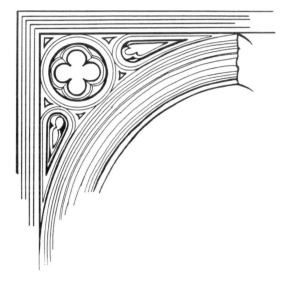

SPINSTER A seventeenth-century term for an unmarried woman. Before this time the word 'maid' had the same meaning.
See also WIDOW

SPIRELET *see* FLÈCHE

SPIRES *see* TOWERS

SPIRITUALITIES Sources of ecclesiastical income, such as TITHES, which were exempt from secular control. Conversely, TEMPORALITIES were ecclesiastical holdings which were subject to such controls.

SPITAL Medieval form of the word 'hospital', its occurrence as a place-name element is usually indicative of the site of a former HOSPICE or LAZAR HOUSE (*see* HOSPITALS).

SPLAY A sloping edge or surface, as in the embrasures of some windows which are set within thick walls.

SPOON (LITURGICAL) Church PLATE some-times includes a liturgical spoon which was used for measuring the water at the mixing of the chalice.

SPORTS, THE BOOK OF Issued in 1617 by James I, specifically for the use of magistrates in Lancashire, *The Book of Sports* defined those recreational activities which were permissible on a Sunday. These included both archery and dancing. In 1618 it was extended to include the whole country and was re-issued by Charles I in 1633. .
See also CHURCH AND COMMUNITY

SPRINGER *and* **SPRINGING LINE** *see* ARCH

SPRINGS Springs emerge on slopes where an impermeable layer of material, such as clay, prevents further downward movement of accumulated rainwater. Alternatively, they may be brought to the surface along faults in underlying rock or at a water-table, below which the ground is saturated. As reliable sources of fresh water, springs have determined the location of innumerable farmsteads and settlements from which have developed villages, towns and even cities. Chains of springs (spring-lines) often correspond with the contours of a scarp slope, as do the settlements which depend on them, or may be traced along a fault line by means of a geological map. Many springs became HOLY WELLS with both pagan and Christian associations: at St. Clether's church near Launceston in Cornwall, for example, where the waters of a spring flow beneath the stone altar of a fifteenth-century chapel which is said to stand on the site of St. Clether's cell.

Place-name elements such as -well and -wall, derived from variations of the Old English *wella* meaning 'well, spring or stream', are very common as are -font and Font- names, from the Old English *funta*, itself derived, via the British *funton*, from the Latin *fontis* meaning 'a spring.' In the north of England, -keld and Kel- elements have the same meaning, from the Old Scandinavian *kelda*.

SPUR (i) An ornamental protrusion between the circular base of a pillar or column and the square plinth on which it stands. (ii) A sloping BUTTRESS.

SPY WEDNESDAY The Wednesday before GOOD FRIDAY and that on which Judas Iscariot betrayed Jesus by agreeing to spy on behalf of the Jewish Sanhedrim (Matthew 26:14–16).

SQUINCH An arch, or a series of concentric arches, constructed within the angle between two walls to support a superstructure e.g. a spire or dome.

SQUINT (HAGIOSCOPE) Squint is a term coined by Victorian ecclesiologists to describe rectangular openings cut obliquely through masonry, usually on one or both sides of a CHANCEL ARCH, to afford a

Hagioscope in the church of St. Peter and St. Paul, Mappowder, Dorset. As in other churches where the chancel has been extended to the east, the altar is no longer visible through the opening.

limited view of the High Altar from a subsidiary altar. Hagioscopes were provided so that a CHANTRY priest could synchronise his celebration of the MASS with that at the High Altar, especially at the Elevation of the Host. Others, such as that at Loxton in Somerset, also allowed the SANCTUS BELL to be rung at precisely the right moment. Numerous medieval hagioscopes have survived, evidence of the ubiquity of chantry priests and subsidiary altars in the Middle Ages.

There is an exceptionally long squint at West Chiltington in Sussex while in Cornwall and Dyfed a number of churches have large squints which are effectively passageways. In many churches the chancel will have been extended to the east so that the altar is no longer visible through the opening. The notion that *'leper squints'* were provided for those who, because of their condition, were unable to join the congregation in the nave is almost certainly fallacious. Hermit-priests were sometimes lepers, however, and there are examples of unusual hagioscopes, the position of which suggests that they may have been provided for this purpose. Partially blocked rood stair doorways

may be mistaken for hagioscopes (*see* ROOD LOFTS), though these are rarely aligned with the altar and are usually at right angles to it.

STAFFS *see* CANDLE EXTINGUISHERS, CHURCHWARDENS' STAFFS, CROSIER *and* FLAGS

STAGS It may be that the depiction of a stag to symbolise Christ originated in a superstitious belief in the animal's ability to draw serpents by its breath from their holes and then to trample them to death. In Christian art, a stag is the attribute of St. Julian Hospitaller, St. Felix of Valois and St. Aidan (*see* SAINTS). When it has a crucifix between its horns it refers to the legendary tale of St. Hubert, the patron saint of huntsmen, who was so fond of bloodsports that he neglected his duties until one day a stag bearing a crucifix threatened him with eternal perdition unless he reformed. Thereafter, Hubert became Bishop of Liège and the apostle of Ardennes and Brabant. The majority of stags are heraldic and most are found 'at gaze', standing with the head facing the observer; or 'lodged', when sitting.
See also ANTELOPES

STAINED GLASS Before the sixteenth century, window glass was made from a mixture of wood-ash and river sand which was heated into molten form and either spun on the end of a rod into a circular sheet or blown into a long cylinder and cut longitudinally to produce a flat sheet. Although coloured glass was used in church windows from the seventh century, the earliest surviving examples in England are from the twelfth. Most medieval coloured glass was manufactured in France and Germany and imported into England where it was made into windows.
THE PAINTER-STAINER'S CRAFT
The term 'stained glass' is a misnomer. More accurately, it should be described as 'painted and stained glass'. There was, in fact, no stained glass until *c.* 1320 when silver stain was introduced (see below). Before that time powdered *pot-metal* (glass which had been deeply coloured throughout) or coloured pigment mixed with *frit* (powdered glass) was painted on to a surface, using Gum Arabic as a binder. Pot-metals were made by adding different metallic oxides to the molten clear glass: cobalt for blue, copper for ruby, manganese for violet, silver salts for yellow, iron for green or yellow, and small quantities of gold for a rose red. The colour produced also depended on the way the furnace was fired and different results were achieved by varying the level of oxidation.

The ruby and blue glasses were very dark and a technique called *flashing* was used to increase translucence, a necessary quality in England's relatively dull climate. In this process the blowpipe was first dipped into molten coloured glass and a cylindrical bubble blown in the normal way. This was then dipped into white molten glass so that, after working, the final glass panel was coated on one side with a layer of colour.

The design (*cartoon*) of the window was drawn on a whitewashed table by draughtsmen (*tracers*) and the pieces of coloured glass cut to the required shape. Before the introduction of the diamond cutter in the sixteenth century, this was done by means of a hot iron which was drawn across the glass and cold water applied, causing the glass to crack along the incision. The pieces were then trimmed with a *grozing iron* to a more precise shape, and details such as faces, hair, limbs, linen folds and foliage were painted in a mixture of metallic oxide (iron or copper), powdered glass and gum. Finally the glass sections were set out on an iron plate and covered with ash before being fired at *c.* 1,000°C (using beechwood) in a clay or dung kiln. This fused the paint onto the coloured glass.

The glass was then reassembled, adjacent pieces held together by means of lead strips (*calms*) which were soldered at the joints, and a thick, black 'putty' forced into the crevices between the lead and the glass. Lead was a most suitable material for this purpose for it was malleable when unheated and, having a low melting point, was easily cast into strips with grooves along the sides (known as H-section) to accommodate the glass.

When completed, the window was fitted into the stonework opening by means of lead strips which were attached to iron saddle-bars or, in larger window openings, set within a decorative metal framework (*armature*). As tracery became more complex in the fourteenth century, so the upper lights of windows were used to accommodate separate sections of an overall design (*see* MEDIEVAL ARCHITECTURE *and* WINDOWS).

As the craft developed, the calms were incorporated into the design itself and, from the fourteenth century, the flashed surface of coloured glass was often scraped away (*abraided*) to leave a pattern of clear glass which, when repainted with silver oxide and fired, turned to a dark yellow which passed for gold. This was particularly useful in heraldic designs when 'metal' charges (gold or silver) were depicted on a blue or red field, as in the ubiquitous royal arms of England (*Gules three Lions passant guardant Gold*).

Many heraldic devices were not of a convenient shape to be confined within strips of lead and while large charges, such as beasts, could be built up using several pieces of glass leaded together, very small or repetitive charges were often difficult to reproduce. This problem was overcome by using small pieces of coloured glass and painting around the outline of the charge with brown enamel to leave only the shape of the motif as the unpainted surface. Alternatively, a whole sheet was painted with brown enamel and the appropriate area scraped away to form the desired shape. This technique may be seen in the ancient arms of France (*Azure semy of Fleurs-de-lis Gold*) in which the small diamond-shaped panels (*quarries* or *quarrels*) bearing fleurs-de-lis alternate with strips of blue glass for the field, producing a pattern of lozenges.

THE MIDDLE AGES

Gothic buildings were conceived from the inside, the heavenward thrust of glass and stone culminating in the ethereal fragility of the Perpendicular period. The 'realm of divine and saintly imagery' which, in the windows of the great abbey churches and cathedrals, seemed to reach almost from earth into heaven, may indeed have educated and informed a largely illiterate Christian population (*see* CHRISTIAN SYMBOLS) but there can be little doubt that its principal function was a spiritual one. Windows of the twelfth and thirteenth centuries (up to *c.* 1260) were predominantly ruby and blue and created a homogeneous fabric of light which induced a sense of almost mystical contemplation. Unfortunately, little early glass remains intact in England and it is difficult for us to appreciate its effect without visiting European cathedrals such as Chartres – or the (redundant) collegiate church of St. Mary the Virgin at Shrewsbury in Shropshire where thirteenth-century glass fills the heads of four windows in the south wall.

The unearthly glow of suspended light, which characterised thirteenth-century glass, is rarely evident in windows of the fourteenth century, which inclined more to yellows and greens, and is entirely missing from the wide perpendicular windows of the fifteenth century. Of course, there are several notable examples, not least the magnificent fourteenth- and fifteenth-century glass which fills many of the vast windows of the parish church of St. Laurence at Ludlow in Shropshire. Indeed, the delicate design and fine painting of early fifteenth-century English work is considered by many to have been superior to that of any other European country, although a decline in the second half of the century caused Henry VI to engage Flemish artists to complete the great windows of his magnificent chapel at King's College, Cambridge.

From the mid-twelfth century, most windows comprised a central pictorial motif contained within a medallion and a plain or beaded border (*fillet*) next to the stonework frame (*see also* ROSE WINDOW *and* WHEEL WINDOW). The years 1260 to 1325 are notable for *grisaille glass* (from the French *gris* meaning 'grey'): large areas of clear quarries surrounded by borders of monochrome foliage decoration and occasional medallions in colour. The best-known example is the Five Sisters window in the north transept of York Minster which has an almost three-dimensional quality.

At least half the surviving medieval church glass contains an element of HERALDRY. Many late medieval windows were *donor windows*, erected both as memorials and to commemorate the generosity of those who paid for their erection.

Fifteenth-century glass commemorating Sir Thomas Clopton and his two wives in Holy Trinity church, Long Melford, Suffolk.

These often contain coats of arms or kneeling figures wearing tabards emblazoned with the benefactor's arms. But not all donors were individuals. Throughout the Middle Ages senior churchmen, magnates, guilds and fraternities endowed money for the repair of churches and, especially in the fourteenth century, groups of citizens would combine to pay for the refurbishing of their parish church. At Dorchester Abbey in Oxfordshire, for example, the south window of the chancel contains twenty-one heraldic shields recording for posterity the identity of those who financed the extension of the sanctuary in *c.* 1340. At this time, the practice of endowing chantries was particularly popular (*see* CHANTRY) and the shields or other heraldic devices in a chantry chapel window may include those of royal or magnatial patrons for whom prayers were to be said as well as those of the deceased armiger and his family.

Perhaps the greatest of all commemorative windows is the magnificent fourteenth-century east window in the choir of Gloucester Cathedral. Constructed between 1347 and 1350 it is 11.6 metres wide (38 feet) and 22 metres high (72 feet): the size of a tennis court and the largest stone traceried window in England. In the lower lights are the shields of the Gloucestershire knights who fought at the battle of Crécy in 1346.

THE POST-REFORMATION

Following the REFORMATION countless medieval windows were destroyed and replaced with glass in which no religious or allegorical subjects were permitted. The duties of the iconoclast are vividly described by Richard Culmner in *Cathedrall Newes from Canterburie* (1644): '. . . on the top of the citie ladder, near sixty steps high, with a whole pike in the hand, rattling down Becket's glassy bones from the great idolatrous window.' Heraldry was an obvious and politically acceptable alternative and one which particularly appealed to the newly created Tudor aristocracy. Anxious to prove themselves equal in blood to the old magnatial families, they erected MONUMENTS and commemorative windows which positively radiated heraldic splendour, their arms incorporating numerous acquired (or assumed) ancestral QUARTERINGS.

A fashion for secular Renaissance motifs, landscapes and classical figures, first apparent in the post-Reformation period, continued into the seventeenth, eighteenth and early nineteenth centuries and, from the late sixteenth century, transparent coloured enamels were widely used so that windows were treated as complete pictures and resembled transparent oil paintings.

THE VICTORIANS

The Gothic Revival of the nineteenth century (*see*

NINETEENTH-CENTURY ARCHITECTURE) encouraged a return to medieval methods of glass manufacture which produced irregularities, variations in thickness and striations, all of which gave early medieval glass its richness. Augustus Pugin (1812–52) and others, following more or less closely the Gothic precedent, were influential until the 1860s. Thereafter there was a massive resurgence of creative energy in the work of the Pre-Raphaelites, notably William Morris (1834–96) and Edward Burne-Jones (1833–98), whose windows in the presbytery of St. Philip's, Birmingham (now the cathedral) are particularly fine. These nineteenth-century reformers produced designs of considerable beauty and originality but, as is often the case, they became victims of their own success and their later work was often repetitive, a pastiche of the exciting originals.

One consequence of the Gothic Revival, and of the Victorians' enthusiasm for church restoration, was a demand for stained glass which outstripped the capabilities of the best designers. Inevitably, there was a corresponding increase in the number of manufacturers who were more than willing to produce stock designs from catalogues many of which were truly awful. Indeed, three-quarters of the glass in our churches belongs to this category, mass-produced diamond-shaped panes decorated with monochrome motifs (*stamped quarries*) being particularly popular.

Inspired by the writings of Morris and Ruskin, the Arts and Crafts Movement of the late nineteenth reacted against the excesses of commercialism. Together with the Art-Workers' Guild, the Arts and Crafts Exhibition Society promoted the notion that designers should be fully conversant with the techniques and materials of their craft and, where possible, involved in the execution of their designs at each stage of the manufacturing process. The foremost advocate of this philosophy was Christopher Whall (1849–1924) whose first major commissions were at St. Mary's church, Stamford in Lincolnshire and the chapel of Dorchester cemetery in Dorset. At Dorchester he used a new material called *slab glass* (also *Early English* or *Norman* glass) which can be identified by examining the exterior of a window for its irregular 'lumpy' surface texture and the interior for its uneven density of colour. Slab glass became a key ingredient in the Arts and Crafts style, together with a variety of new painting techniques and the emphatic use of the lead-line as an integral element of the design rather than a functional necessity. And while commercial studios tended to use pseudo-Gothic architectural motifs in borders and canopies, Whall and his contemporaries preferred stylised natural forms such as boughs and foliage. There is a particularly fine example of the imaginative and beautifully crafted work of the period in the east window of Littlemore

church in Oxfordshire, by Louis Davis (1861–1941) one of Whall's earliest students. Whall's influence was considerable and his book *Stained Glass Work* (1905) remains one of the most readable and inspiring treatises on the subject.

In the 1850s numerous small studios and workshops were established, though from 1850–1900 the production of stained glass in England and Wales was dominated by less than twenty firms who, between them, probably manufactured more than three-quarters of the windows of that period. The work of these firms may often be identified by a process of elimination. Reference to Pevsner's *The Buildings of England* series will usually provide a date and the name of an architect who may be associated with a particular studio. (For example, nearly all the glass in William Butterfield's churches in the 1860s was supplied by Alexander Gibbs of London.) Richly coloured glass was popular in the period 1855–70, the later Gothic revivalists of the Arts and Crafts Movement being more restrained in their use of colour. Faculties should be consulted (*see* FACULTY), together with contemporary newspaper reports of church restorations and architectural periodicals including (for the period 1842–1868) *The Ecclesiologist*. The archives of stained glass firms have rarely survived though there are exceptions, notably James Powell & Sons and C.E. Kempe & Co. (both at the Victoria and Albert Museum in London) and John Hardman & Co. (at the Birmingham Reference Library).

THE TWENTIETH CENTURY

In 1897 Mary Lowndes (1857–1929), an enthusiastic disciple of Whall, founded the firm of Lowndes and Drury to provide independent designers with facilities to carry out their commissions. The firm's purpose-built Glass House at Fulham attracted many of the most talented glass-painters of the early twentieth century and, although the style of each artist was markedly individual, all shared the same commitment to originality of design and craftsmanship of the highest quality. Other notable designers of the period include Heywood Sumner (1853–1940) and Gerald Moira (1867–1959) examples of whose work may be seen at Great Warley in Essex and Woodham, Surrey, and Robert Anning Bell (1863–1933) who produced many fine windows, as at Amberley and Hambledon in Sussex. A distinctive school of glass painting developed under the leadership of Henry Payne (1868–1940) at the Birmingham School of Art. Good examples are Payne's windows are at Hook in Worcestershire and Stokesay in Shropshire.

Described by Betjeman as 'Completely medieval minded . . . a great individualist' whose use of colour was 'dazzling yet subtle', the architect Sir Ninian Comper (1864–1960) was responsible for at least 800 windows which were singularly Gothic in

Henry Tudor at Bosworth, a detail from a window by the late pre-Raphaelite artist Walter Crane (1845–1915) at Selsey, Sussex.

character, containing much 'white space' and tabernacle work (turrets, battlements etc.). Comper learned his craft under Charles Eamer Kempe (1834–1907), an eminent member of the Arts and Crafts Movement, and his designs frequently incorporated heraldry, similar in style to the illustrations in W. St. John-Hope's book *The Stall Plates of the Knights of the Order of the Garter* (1901). There are splendid examples of Comper's work at Wimborne St. Giles in Dorset which he restored following a fire in 1908.

The influence of the Glass House reached beyond the 1950s in the work of eminent craftsmen such as Edward Payne (1906–1991) and Joseph E. Nuttgens (1892–1982), while the designs of artists such as John Piper (*b.* 1903) have made a lasting impression, though his larger commissions (such as the windows of Coventry Cathedral) are generally more successful than those in smaller churches where his strong colours tend to be overpowering.

In the nineteenth and early twentieth centuries, new windows were sometimes erected in parish churches by manorial lords and these often contain series of shields showing the arms of predecessors. This practice seems to have been popular with those who acquired manorial lordships by purchase rather than by inheritance, as at Puddletown in Dorset and at Aldermaston in Berkshire. From *c.* 1860 stained glass was often installed or refurbished as a memorial to an individual or family and small shields, military insignia and school or university arms incorporated in window designs or in tracery lights. Many of these memorials commemorate those who lost their lives in the World Wars, while others recall the achievements of local worthies. At Stinsford church in Dorset, for example, a memorial window to the poet and novelist Thomas Hardy (1840–1928) was installed in the south aisle in 1930. Designed by Douglas Strachen (1875–1950), it dramatically illustrates Hardy's favourite lines from the first Book of Kings: 'And, behold the Lord passed by, and a great and strong wind rent the mountains, and brake in pieces the rocks before the Lord; but the Lord was not in the wind; and after the wind an earthquake; but the Lord was not in the earthquake: and after the earthquake a fire; but the Lord was not in the fire: and after the fire a still small voice.' (I Kings 19: 11–12)

The lead which binds a stained glass window responds to fluctuations of temperature by expanding or contracting. Thus, in a window's flexibility lies also its durability. Even so, a stained glass window usually needs to be taken apart and reglazed in new lead approximately every two hundred years. While most stained glass remains in its original location many fragments (or even entire windows) will have been moved several times and may have been combined with glass of an entirely different period. A series of twelfth-century biblical figures at Canterbury Cathedral is surmounted by heraldic figures of the fourteenth century, while at Salisbury Cathedral there are six thirteenth-century shields at the base of the west window which is composed principally of fifteenth-century glass. Of course, glass is particularly vulnerable to vandalism and during the Gothic Revival of the nineteenth century there was a flourishing market in miscellaneous fragments from the damaged windows of restored churches. Medieval fragments are often found in haphazard clusters of 'old glass' both in church windows and illuminating the stair-wells of Victorian houses. At the extraordinary Italian Romanesque church of St. Mary and St. Nicholas at Wilton in Wiltshire (1845) is a rare example of early medieval glass (*c.* 1140) which was 'retrieved' from the abbey of St. Denis in Paris after the French Revolution.

See also GLAZIERS' MARKS

For the Birmingham Reference Library, the National Association of Fine Arts Societies *and* the Victoria and Albert Museum *see* APPENDIX II.

Further reading:
Archer, M., *English Stained Glass*, London, 1985
Cowan, P., *A Guide to Stained Glass in Britain*, London, 1985
Hall, J., *Dictionary of Subjects and Symbols in Art*, London, 1989
Harries, J., *Discovering Stained Glass*, Aylesbury, 1980
Harrison, M., *Victorian Stained Glass*, London, 1980
Lee, L., Seddon, G. and Stephens, F., *Stained Glass*, London, 1976
Marks, R., *Stained Glass in England During the Middle Ages*, London, 1993
Osborne, J., *Stained Glass in England*, Stroud, 1990
Sewter, A., *The Stained Glass of William Morris and his Circle*, Yale, 1974–5

STAIRCASES In the stair turrets of many medieval church TOWERS, or sometimes within the thickness of stone walls, spiral staircases (*turnpike stairs*) were constructed within cylindrical shafts, each identical stone step (*winder*) cut to fit precisely within the shaft and held in place by the interlocking core of the steps immediately above and below. (In medieval castles turnpike stairs usually ascend in a clockwise direction thereby facilitating the use of a weapon when facing down the stair in a defensive position but impairing its use when attempting to ascend by force.) A turnpike stair may also be described as a *vice*.

Where there is no evidence of a stone staircase, a wooden 'open tread' ladder-type staircase would have provided access between the different levels of a tower, usually by means of a single flight set against a wall or two flights at right-angles to each other. These staircases were usually built of oak and were supported by a massive pillar. The original oak stairway has survived in the Norman tower of Brabourne church in Kent, the huge timbers being more than 800 years old.

Another type of staircase commonly found in churches is the newel staircase which, like the turnpike, consists of winders ascending round a central core (*newel post*) and constructed entirely of timber. By the late sixteenth century, the *dog-leg* staircase had developed. This was of heavy construction with broad flights rising parallel to each other and connected at each level by landings. Early seventeenth-century examples have square oak newel posts at each angle, and thick supports (*balusters*) for the handrail which were often elaborately carved (*turned*) on a lathe.

From the dog-leg construction evolved the *open well* which is to be found in many Jacobean buildings of the early seventeenth century. In this type of staircase the flights ascend the walls of a square stair-well around a central space. Seventeenth-century oak staircases were particularly heavy and ornate, though from the 1670s they were less ponderous in appearance with shaped and moulded handrails and panelled BALUSTRADES and newels, carved with scrolls and foliage.

Eighteenth-century staircases were less massive and often of superb craftsmanship, though work of this quality was found only in the finest buildings. (In 1725 wood-carvers who specialised in the manufacture of staircase components could earn three shillings a day when most domestic servants earned little more than £2 a year.) From 1700 pine was widely used instead of oak which was becoming scarce, especially in the south-eastern counties, and soft-wood balusters were usually painted an off-white stone colour. From the mid-eighteenth century, staircases with wrought iron balusters and mahogany handrails became fashionable and thereafter balusters and handrails (*banisters*) became progressively lighter in construction and of more elegant appearance. Many eighteenth-century and Regency staircases had stone or marble steps and open-string balustrades with slim ornamental balusters in groups of twos or threes. They were often of cantilevered construction, with one end built into the wall, and were of circular or oval design (*geometrical stairs*).

Nineteenth-century staircases often reflected Gothic Revival influences with wrought-iron balusters, handrails and newels. But by 1900 the typical staircase of a fashionable church had a mahogany handrail and pine balusters, usually 'grained' to look like mahogany.

For rood stairs *see* ROOD LOFTS.

STAIR TURRET A circular or polygonal turret attached to the outside of a church tower (often at a corner) and containing a spiral staircase from which the various levels within the tower may be reached.

STALLS In parish churches, fixed seats in parallel rows on the north and south sides of a CHANCEL to accommodate a choir and clergy (*see* CHURCH MUSIC (ANGLICAN)).

In the Middle Ages only cathedrals and monastic and collegiate churches had stalls which, in larger churches, were located in the CHOIR between the PRESBYTERY and PULPITUM. PLAINSONG was sung by two choirs alternately, with each choir (CANTORIS and DECANI) occupying the north and south stalls respectively (*see* ANTIPHON *and* VERSICLES). Those stalls which have survived are usually separated by high projecting 'elbows' and have screens behind them and elaborately carved CANOPIES above to minimise draughts. A ledge in front of the stalls supported service books and candles and, in some cases, AMPLIFIERS provided extra resonance and amplification during the singing of plainsong. Individual seats are usually hinged and may be lifted to reveal MISERICORDS, carved brackets which provided support and relief for the

Circular stair turret on the Norman tower at Branscombe church, Devon.

quire monks or canons who were able to rest without sitting as they stood through interminable divine offices. Each monk or canon occupied a particular stall, the position of which reflected his place in the community: the longest-serving members sitting furthest from the high altar. In monastic churches, novices usually sat in less elaborate bench-like stalls at the front. In an ABBEY the abbot and prior faced the east in the RETURNED STALLS, respectively south and north of the pulpitum doorway. In a PRIORY these seats were occupied by the prior and sub-prior.

There are splendid sets of fourteenth-century stalls at Chester and Gloucester cathedrals. But in most cases, only the foundations of the medieval stalls have survived, the present structures being much-modified (usually Victorian) copies. Quite often the original seats and misericords have been incorporated into later stalls, as at Sherborne Abbey in Dorset (now the parish church). There are also several instances of

stalls having been removed to parish churches, though these have invariably been reconstructed in a much-reduced form: the fifteenth-century stalls of Easby Abbey in Yorkshire, for example, which are now in the church of St. Mary the Virgin at Richmond (the Easby canons were hanged for resisting the King's commissioners), and at Whalley in Lancashire where the richly canopied stalls of the Cistercian abbey were removed to the parish church in order to escape the iconoclasts' bonfires.

Some medieval parish churches were provided with single rows of stalls which were intended to accommodate unusually large numbers of chantry priests or the members of collegiate foundations (see CHANTRY COLLEGES *and* COLLEGIATE CHURCH). There are splendid examples of fourteenth-century canopied stalls at St. Mary's church at Lancaster, Nantwich in Cheshire and All Saints', Hereford and of fifteenth-century stalls at Ludlow in Shropshire.

It was the nineteenth-century OXFORD MOVEMENT which was principally responsible for the introduction into parish churches of male, surpliced choirs for the chanting of the responses and the psalms. This was clearly an attempt to impose on parishes a tradition which had hitherto been associated with cathedral and college choirs, even in the removal of the singers from the west gallery (see GALLERIES) to stalls erected on either side of the chancel in the collegiate fashion. The majority of choir stalls are from the late nineteenth and twentieth centuries and very few are of any artistic merit. Indeed, most medieval chancels would benefit from their removal.

Further reading:
Tracy, C., *English Gothic Choir Stalls 1200–1400,* Woodbridge, 1987

STAMP ACT (1783) A duty of 3d imposed on each entry in a parish register. An incumbent received a commission of 10 per cent.

STANCHION An upright post or support.

STANDARD *see* FLAGS

STARS *see* CHRISTIAN SYMBOLS

STATANT *see* BEASTS (HERALDIC)

STATE PRAYERS In *The Book of Common Prayer*, prayers for the Sovereign and Royal Family said towards the end of Mattins and Evensong.

STATE SERVICES Before 1859 *The Book of Common Prayer* included a number of services appointed to commemorate days of national rejoicing and deliverance. Since that time only one, the commemoration of the Sovereign's succession, has been retained.

STATIONS OF THE CROSS The fourteen incidents which occurred on Christ's last journey from Pilot's House to His entombment (*see* CHRISTIAN SYMBOLS). The Stations of the Cross may sometimes be found depicted in a series of paintings or carvings arranged round the walls of a church. During a devotion of the same name, each station is visited in turn.

STATUTE LABOUR *see* FOOTPATHS AND BRIDLEWAYS

STATUTE OF MORTMAIN (1391) This statute required that in those parishes where the rectorial TITHES were held by an ecclesiastical institution, a proportion of the income should be used for poor relief (*see* MORTMAIN).

STEEPLE A tower, especially one surmounted by a spire (*see* TOWERS). Dating from the eighteenth century, a steeplechase is a cross-country horse race of four or five miles in which steeples are used as landmarks.

STEEPLE HEADDRESS *see* COSTUME

STELE A decorative motif consisting of a rectangular slab surmounted by a low, triangular pediment.
See also MONUMENTS *and* WALL MONUMENTS

STELLAR VAULT *see* VAULTING

STERLING STANDARD Precious metal consisting of at least 92.5 per cent pure silver (*see also* BRITANNIA SILVER).

STEW PONDS *see* FISH PONDS

STIFF LEAF ORNAMENT A somewhat formal architectural ornament characteristic of the thirteenth century and especially evident in the treatment of CAPITALS and window and doorway mouldings. Unlike later NATURAL LEAF ORNAMENT, carved foliage rises stiffly from the necking and falls in stylised lobe-shaped clusters of leaves and flowers.
See also MEDIEVAL ARCHITECTURE

STIGMATA Marks resembling the wounds on Christ's body. The Stigmata Festival, observed on 16 September, is the principal public celebration of the Anglican Order of St. Francis.

STILE (i) A vertical member in the framework of a panelled door.
See also BRACE, DOORS AND DOORWAYS, LEDGE, MUNTIN *and* RAIL
(ii) The vertical outer frame members of a wooden screen (also *style*).
See also CHANCEL SCREENS

STILTED ARCH *see* ARCH

STILTS The short, vertical sections at the base of a round arch which raise its height without increasing the span.

STIPEND A salary, especially that of a clergyman.

STIR-UP SUNDAY The last Sunday after Trinity and the next before Advent, so called from the first two words of the collect 'Stir up, we beseech thee O Lord, the wills of thy faithful people . . .' and a belated reminder of the need to prepare the puddings for Christmas.

STOCK, PARISH (i) Before the Reformation, the parish stock consisted of capital, either in cash or cattle, which was lent by the churchwardens to suitable parishioners, the profits and rents accruing therefrom being paid into church funds. (ii) After the Reformation, the term was applied to the stock of 'wool, flax, hemp, wood, thread, iron and other necessary ware and stuff to set the poor on work' provided by the overseers and churchwardens at the expense of the parish.

STOCKS *see* PARISH CONSTABLE

STOLE *see* VESTMENTS

STONEWORK *see* BUILDING MATERIALS, FIGURE SCULPTURE *and* MASONRY

STOOL *see* FALDSTOOL

STOUP *see* HOLY WATER STOUP

STOVES

> The bells of waiting Advent ring,
> The Tortoise stove is lit again
> And lamp-oil light across the night
> Has caught the streaks of winter rain . . .

Alas, most of John Betjeman's coal-fired Tortoise stoves have disappeared from our churches, replaced (more often than not) by rows of forlorn electric heaters attached to pillars or suspended beneath the arches of an arcade. Installed in the nineteenth and early twentieth centuries stoves were, of course, intended to provide some respite from the chills of winter, though most were singularly inefficient. Old photographs of church interiors illustrate the range of stoves which were used for this purpose and the sometimes Heath-Robinson contraptions by which the fumes were removed. At Cameley in Somerset, for example, a crude series of pipes rose the full height of the nave from an entirely inadequate 'pillar' stove at the centre of the church.

STRAINER ARCH *see* ARCH

STRAP SCONCE A narrow ornamental bracket, secured at each end and curving outwards from a wall, on the top of which are affixed a number of candle-holders.

STRAPWORK A Renaissance form of decoration which originated in the Netherlands in *c.* 1540. Characteristic of the Elizabethan and Jacobean periods, strapwork consists of ornamental interlaced bands or straps, similar in appearance to fretwork or cut leather. In churches, it is usually executed in plaster, stone or wood in ceilings, friezes, screens, wood panelling etc.

STRETCHER A brick or piece of masonry placed lengthwise in the face of a wall.

STRING *see* BALUSTRADE

STRING COURSE A continuous projecting horizontal band or moulding in the surface of a wall.

STUCCO Plaster or cement applied to walls as a protective or decorative coating. Also plaster for moulding to form architectural decoration (*see* PLASTERWORK).

STYLE *see* STILE

STYLOBATE In classical architecture, the substructure of a row of columns.

SUBDEACON In the medieval Church, one of the three sacred ministers at High Mass whose responsibilities included that of chanting the Epistle. Until the thirteenth century, the office was considered to be one of the MINOR ORDERS. In the Church of England, the subdiaconate was dispensed with in the sixteenth century. *See also* VESTMENTS

SUBMERSION *see* AFFUSION, ASPERSION *and* BAPTISM

SUBMISSION OF THE CLERGY (1532) The act whereby the English Convocations surrendered to the demands of HENRY VIII. Confirmed by parliament in 1534, its effect was to make the Sovereign supreme in ecclesiastical causes.

SUBSCRIPTION BOOKS Diocesan records in which the beneficed clergy, curates and licensed

preachers, schoolmasters, physicians, surgeons and midwives recorded their acceptance of the THIRTY-NINE ARTICLES and acknowledged their loyalty to the Crown as required under the Act of Uniformity (1662).
See also DIOCESAN RECORDS

SUCCENTOR A minor canon in CATHEDRALS of the 'Old Foundation' where he is the deputy of the PRECENTOR.
See also CLERGY (CHURCH OF ENGLAND)

SUFFRAGAN BISHOP *see* CLERGY (CHURCH OF ENGLAND)

SUICIDES Those who take their own lives commit a mortal sin and may not be buried in consecrated ground. Before 1823 it was common practice for the corpse of one who had committed suicide to be interred ignominiously at a crossroads, without Christian rites and with a stake thrust through his body. For this reason, many lonely crossroads still attract tales of superstition and intrigue.

SUNDAY The early Church met on the 'Lord's Day' (Rev. 1:10) to commemorate Christ's Resurrection and 'to break bread' (Acts 20:7). Sunday effectively replaced the Jewish Sabbath as a day of rest and in the fourth century observance began to be regulated by ecclesiastical legislation. Attendance at MASS was obligatory from the sixth to the thirteenth centuries but thereafter dispensations became common. In seventeenth-century England, the perceived abuse of Sundays (*see* CHURCH AND COMMUNITY) led to a rigorous form of observance (*Sabbatarianism*) which was unknown elsewhere in Europe (*see* SEVENTEENTH-CENTURY CHURCH). N. Bound's *True Doctrine of the Sabbath* (1595) advocated strict enforcement in accordance with Old Testament precepts and this was followed in 1618 by James I's *Book of Sports* which defined those recreational activities which were permissible on Sunday (*see* SPORTS, BOOK OF). During the Interregnum, the Puritan Sabbath was enforced by means of parliamentary legislation but was relaxed somewhat following the Restoration in 1660. The Lord's Day Observance Act of 1781 forbade the opening on Sunday of places of entertainment for which an admission charge was made and, influenced by the Evangelical Revival, there was a further period of rigorous observance in the nineteenth century (*see* NINETEENTH-CENTURY CHURCH).

SUNDAY SCHOOLS Sunday schools, primarily (though not exclusively) for the religious instruction of children, first appeared in the mid-eighteenth century. The first Sunday school was established at Catterick in Yorkshire in 1763 but it was Robert Raikes (1735–1811) who in 1780 inspired the Sunday school movement with the foundation of a school in Gloucester. Raikes, supported by a local incumbent, engaged four women teachers to instruct the children in reading and the Catechism. The pupils were charged 1p a week. In 1775 a society was formed for the 'Establishment and Support of Sunday Schools throughout the Kingdom of Great Britain' and in 1803 the Sunday School Union, an interdenominational organisation, was founded to co-ordinate the work of Sunday schools in the London area. The founding of the Sunday School Institute in 1843 reflected concern among many Anglicans that teaching should be in accordance with the precepts of the Church of England. This became the National Sunday School Union in 1903 and the National Christian Education Council in 1966.
See also SCHOOLS

SUNDIALS Most medieval churches possessed a sundial which was usually engraved in a south wall or buttress. The function of these dials was to ensure that the bell was rung at the correct time to mark the canonical hours. But they also served other, more mundane purposes. The countryman rose with the sun and retired when it set, and during the day he was dependent on the dial, scratched on the wall of his parish church, to inform him of the passing of the hours. The traveller, anxious to reach his destination by nightfall, would have appreciated the dial of Edstone church in Yorkshire which bears the inscription *Orlogi*[um] *Viatorum*: 'hour-teller of wayfarers'. Even in the few parishes which acquired a striking clock, the sundial was the only reliable time-keeper until the introduction of railway time-tables in the nineteenth century and the adoption of Greenwich Mean Time (*see* CLOCKS).
SAXON TIDE DIALS
The Saxons divided the daylight hours into four 'tides', each of three hours, beginning at 6.00 am. and ending with sunset. Saxon dials are therefore known as *tide dials*. In their simplest form, they consist of a stone slab set into a south wall with an engraved horizontal line to represent dawn and sunset. Below this line, and at right angles to it, is a vertical line marking the noon division, and between dawn and noon and noon and sunset are two further lines, cut at 45 degrees, to mark 9.00 a.m. and 3.00 a.m.. At the intersection of these lines is a hole into which an iron style (*gnomon*) was inserted. This was set at noon on Midsummer's Day so that its shadow fell precisely on the noon line of the dial. Saxon dials were usually carved with great precision, sometimes with inscriptions added, and their divisions correspond with the times at which Mass was celebrated. Several dials have more than four divisions and, in such cases, short lines may have been cut at right angles across certain of the radii, possibly to indicate the times of services.

Saxon sundial at Welburn, Yorkshire.

Notable among the few surviving Saxon dials are those at Bishopstone in Sussex, Daglingworth in Gloucestershire and Great Edstone, Old Byland and Kirkdale in Yorkshire. The dial at St. Gregory's minster, Kirkdale, has been protected by a twelfth-century porch and is in very good condition. Divided into eight sections, it occupies the central portion of a horizontal slab, 2 metres (7 feet) in length, and is inscribed above ('This is day's Sun marker at every time'), below ('Haworth me wrought and Brand priests') and on either side ('Orm Gamal's son bought St. Gregory's Minster when it was all broken down and fallen and let it be made anew from the ground to Christ and St. Gregory, in Edward's days, the King and in Tosti's days, the Earl'). These inscriptions (which are here translated) suggest that the dial was carved in 1055 when a new church was built at Kirkdale to replace one which had been destroyed by the Danes. The Daglingworth dial was similarly rendered inoperable by the erection of a porch and was replaced by an inferior scratch dial on an outer wall, while the remains of the Saxon dial at Old Byland were crudely inserted (upside-down) into the stonework of an eighteenth-century porch. The earliest known Saxon dial is at Bewcastle in Cumbria where it is engraved on the south face of a churchyard cross, the inscription 'First year of the King of the realm, Ecgfrith' confirming the date 670. This dial is marked with twelve divisions but it is likely that some of these were added at a later date.

MEDIEVAL SCRATCH DIALS

The later, and more numerous, medieval *scratch dials* are usually circular and rather crudely inscribed with the duodecimal divisions of the day, the radial lines cut at intervals of fifteen degrees. In many examples, the line which would have been reached by the shadow of the *gnomon* at 9.00 am. is more clearly incised, this being the 'mass line' which marked the hour when mass was said on Sundays and feast days. For this reason, scratch dials are also known as *mass-dials*, though (as with their Saxon predecessors) they served other purposes. There are regional variations of style and several churches have more than one dial, each intended for use during a different season of the year. There are also several instances of dial stones being angled away from a church wall in order to compensate for the inaccurate orientation of a building. Distribution of scratch dials is extraordinarily uneven: in some areas none has survived while in others they are ubiquitous. It is difficult to account for this phenomenon at a time when a need to mark the passing of the hours must have been universal. It has been suggested that many have simply been eroded by frost and rain and it is certainly true that close scrutiny is often required to detect even vestigial traces of some medieval scratchings. But this would not account for the large numbers which have survived in southern Gloucestershire where oolitic limestone was commonly used for church buildings. There are thirty scratch dials within ten miles of Cirencester, for example, notably at Ampney Crucis, Ampney St. Mary, Ampney St. Peter, Coln St. Aldwyns, Coln Rogers, Coln St. Dennis, Eastleach Martin, Eastleach Turville, Quenington and Yanworth. Many scratch dials have been built over during subsequent restorations, suggesting that even before the Reformation they were considered to be obsolete. At Grappenhall in Cheshire the stone on which a dial was scratched was turned to face the north-west when that part of the church was rebuilt in the early sixteenth century, while at Tarvin in the same county a window cuts across the stones which once held the gnomons of three dials. A most unusual dial, carved in the timpanum of a window at the chapel of Dinmore Manor in Herefordshire (a former COMMANDERY), has fifteen radiating

Eighteenth-century sundial at Holwell, Dorset.

divisions each marked at the circumference in Roman numerals – though the XI and IX have been accidentally interchanged.

LATER DIALS

The liturgical changes effected by the Reformation meant that mass dials became obsolete and most were allowed to erode or were obscured by later buildings (*see* PORCHES). At the same time, the shafts of many CHURCHYARD CROSSES were truncated and from the mid-sixteenth century these were often capped with horizontal sundials. This was common practice in the Welsh Marches where there are good examples at several Herefordshire and Shropshire churches and especially in Cheshire, notably at Alderley, Bosley, Prestbury and Tilston.

Vertical sundials, mostly dating from the eighteenth century, are a feature of many churches. Typically, these dials consist of a square stone 'face', inscribed with radiating hourly divisions, erected on a south-facing wall or above the entrance to a porch. Quite often the dial will have been set at an angle to provide an accurate reading.

SUN IN SPLENDOUR *see* BADGES

SUPER FRONTAL A band of material, usually embroidered and fringed, overlapping the top of the FRONTAL on a communion table.
See also ALTARS

SUPERIOR One who exercised authority over others by virtue of his ecclesiastical rank. In Benedictine, Cistercian and Premonstratensian communities the superior was an ABBOT or ABBESS. In those religious communities where the church served as a cathedral the bishop was the titular abbot, though in practice it was the PRIOR who was head of the community (*see* CATHEDRAL PRIORY). The superiors of houses of Austin Canons were also priors, while the priors of Dominican houses of FRIARS, the guardians of Franciscan ones and the superiors of ALIEN PRIORIES exercised less authority than abbots.

At first, superiors occupied accommodation which was adjacent to the common DORTER, but in the later Middle Ages the feudal status of many superiors was such that they required separate lodgings in order to fulfil their obligations as hosts. In former cathedral priories, the prior's lodgings were often appropriated by a dean following the Reformation and consequently several have survived.

SUPPORTERS (HERALDIC) Figures, usually beasts, chimerical creatures or of human form, placed on either side the shield in a coat of arms to 'support' it. Unlike other elements in a coat of arms, supporters have no practical origin and cannot be traced with any certainty before the fifteenth century. Though similar devices may be found in early

SEALS, where they occupy the space between the shield and the outer decorative border, their use was almost certainly decorative. With some notable exceptions, the use of supporters is restricted to peers, knights of certain chivalric orders and major corporations.
See also BEASTS (HERALDIC)

SUPPRESSION *see* CHANTRIES, CHANTRY COLLEGES *and* DISSOLUTION OF THE MONASTERIES

SUPREMACY, ACTS OF (1534 *and* 1559) The Act confirming to HENRY VIII and his successors the 'style and title' of 'the only supreme head in earth of the Church of England' and all the prerogatives 'to the said dignity of supreme head of the same church belonging and appertaining'. It also declared the validity of the King's marriage with Queen Anne (Boleyn) together with the right of their lawful issue to succeed. Ironically, the third reading of the Act on 23 March coincided with the Pope's judgment in favour of Queen Catherine (of Aragon). Individuals were required to support the Act on oath, circumstances which presented partisans of the old order with a challenge which could not easily be resolved. Apparently, the furious Queen Catherine and her Spanish servants swore, in Spanish, that the King 'se ha hecho cabeza de Iglesia' ('has appointed himself head of the Church of England') instead of 'sea hecho . . .' ('the King may be made head . . .'). The Act of Supremacy was repealed by Queen Mary only to be replaced by a similar act in 1559 under Elizabeth I which declared the Queen to be 'the only supreme governor . . . as well in all spiritual or ecclesiastical things or causes as temporal'.

SURCOAT (i) A long coat of linen, split at the sides to facilitate movement, especially on horseback, and originally intended to protect mail from heat or rain. Dating from the Crusades of the twelfth century, the surcoat provided an obvious means of displaying heraldic devices – hence 'coat of arms'. By the middle of the fourteenth century the surcoat had been succeeded by the shorter JUPON and CYCLAS. (ii) A similar garment worn by both men and women (*see* COSTUME).

SURNAMES A name borne hereditarily by all members of a family in male-line descent. It is likely that hereditary surnames were introduced by the Normans and were used initially by those who were possessed of land and property which could be conveyed or inherited. Surnames were then inherited only by an eldest son, the practice of applying the name to all a man's children dating from the late twelfth century after which time it spread only slowly. The first legal recognition of a surname (that of de Cantebrigg) occurred in 1267. By 1400 some three-quarters of the population are believed to have borne hereditary family names and the process was completed by the mid-fifteenth century. Surnames may be changed at will (except by aliens), though in most cases a change will have been effected by Deed Poll or through a NAME AND ARMS clause in a will. There may, of course, be variations of spelling: the writer has ancestors who spelt their names variously as Friar, Frier, Frere, Fryer and Fryar.

There are eight derivation categories for surnames, the first two of which account for nearly half our English surnames:

1   Place-names (de Mowbray, Thorpe)
2   Location of abode (Attwood, Ford, Lane, Hill)
3   Occupation (Shepherd, Smith, Thatcher)
4   Status (Yeoman, Knight)
5   Creature (Fox, Bird, Bull)
6   Patronymic (Fitzwalter, Richardson)
7   Personal Name (Edwards, Williams)
8   Nickname (Friar, Longman, Smart)

It should be remembered that both the sound and spelling of many surnames will have been corrupted over the centuries and it is never safe to draw too rapid a conclusion about the origin of a modern surname, especially one which could fit into two or more categories.
Further reading:
Reaney, P., *The Origin of English Surnames*, London, 1975
——, *A Dictionary of British Surnames*, London, 1979

SURPLICE A loose, white liturgical garment with wide sleeves, usually worn over a CASSOCK by the clergy, lay readers, servers and members of a choir. The surplice is a development of the alb (*see* VESTMENTS) and from the twelfth century was worn by the lower clergy and by priests except at the celebration of MASS.
See also RUFF *and* TIPPET

SURPLICE FEES Fees paid to an incumbent at marriages and funerals, irrespective of who was officiating.

SURROGATE A clergyman or other person appointed by a bishop as his deputy to grant marriage licences without banns.

SURVEYOR OF THE HIGHWAYS *see* FOOTPATHS AND BRIDLEWAYS

SWAG Not to be confused with a FESTOON, a swag is an ornamental motif composed of draped fabric which hangs in a curve between two points. Usually of carved wood and sometimes painted or gilded (*see* DECORATIVE MOTIFS).

SWORD-RESTS Intricate metal stands in city churches to accommodate a corporation's ceremonial sword and mace during civic services. Usually of exquisite craftsmanship, sword-rests invariably incorporate civic heraldry. Perhaps the finest examples are at St. Peter Mancroft, Norwich and St. Mary Abchurch, near Cannon Street, London.

SYMBOLS AND ATTRIBUTES OF THE SAINTS AND MARTYRS *see* CHRISTIAN SYMBOLS

SYNOD A council of bishops and ecclesiastical representatives convened to regulate doctrine and discipline within the Church. Decrees emanating from oecumenical synods, assemblies of bishops of the whole Church, are considered to possess the highest authority. A synodical act (or a collection of such acts) is known as a *synodicon*.

In its present form, synodical government was introduced into the Church of England by the Synodical Government Measure of 1969. The CHURCH ASSEMBLY was replaced by the General Synod which consists of a House of Bishops and a House of Clergy (comprising the Upper and Lower Houses of the CONVOCATIONS), and a House of Laity not exceeding 250 members elected by the Houses of Laity of Deanery Synods. Doctrinal formulas and matters concerning church services and the administration of the SACRAMENTS may be proposed only by the House of Bishops. At the same time, Diocesan Conferences were replaced by Diocesan Synods consisting of a Bishop, a House of Clergy and a House of Laity. Members of the houses of Clergy and Laity are elected by the respective Houses of Deanery Synods which replaced the former Ruridecanal Conferences. Deanery Synods comprise elected members of PAROCHIAL CHURCH COUNCILS.
See also ADMINISTRATION *and* SIDESMAN

SYNODICA *see* SYNOD

T

TABARD A dress coat worn over ARMOUR from the late fifteenth century to the mid-sixteenth century. Similar to the JUPON but reaching below the thigh and with broad sleeves to the elbow, the tabard was emblazoned front and back and on the sleeves and served a purely heraldic purpose. Today, tabards of the royal arms are worn by the heralds on ceremonial occasions.
See also COSTUME

TABERNACLE (i) A canopied structure used as a portable shrine by the Israelites during their wanderings in the wilderness. It contained the Ark of the Covenant, a wooden chest in which the writings of Jewish law were kept. (ii) From this, any architectural feature or decorative motif (tabernacle work) which resembles a canopied structure (*see* FONT COVERS). (iii) Specifically, a hanging *pyx-shrine* or *sacrament house*, shaped like a tapering ornamental tower or series of towers, in which the Blessed Sacrament was reserved (*see* PYX). Very few medieval tabernacles survived the Reformation. A superbly carved oak tabernacle at Milton Abbey in Dorset is fixed to north wall of the presbytery, while that from Hessett in Suffolk is now at the British Museum. In the Middle Ages tabernacles were suspended in front of the High Altar and were raised and lowered by means of pulleys, as at West Grinstead in Sussex where the pulley socket has survived. (iv) From the sixteenth century, the term has been used to describe the box of precious metal in which the Blessed Sacrament is reserved on a communion table or GRADINE (*see* PLATE, RESERVATION *and* VEILS).

TABLET A wall-mounted panel engraved with a commemorative inscription (*see* WALL MONUMENTS).

TABLE TOMBS (ALTAR TOMBS, CASKET TOMBS *or* CHEST TOMBS) Table tomb is a generic term for the large, chest-like tombstones erected over the churchyard graves of the more prosperous members of seventeenth- and eighteenth-century society. Because of their shape, table tombs are sometimes referred to as *altar tombs*, *casket tombs* or *chest tombs* (not to be confused with TOMB CHESTS) and there are many variations of style and construction.

Seventeenth-century table tombs are usually plain and substantial with sufficient space for later burials to be commemorated on the side and end panels.

Medieval tabernacle at Milton Abbey, Dorset.

There is a fine collection of seventeenth-century tombs at Bredwardine in Herefordshire, churchyard of the clergyman diarist, Francis Kilvert (1840–79).

The *bale tomb* is a variety of table tomb surmounted by a carved stone representation of the half-cylindrical medieval hearse (*see* EFFIGIES). The term is thought (by some) to be indicative of the wealth created by the production of wool. There is a fine collection of eighteenth-century bale tombs at Burford in the Oxfordshire Cotswolds while at nearby Shipton-under-Wychwood a tomb with a bale top has been erected over an earlier table tomb.

As the name suggests, *pedestal tombs* are supported on square, circular or octagonal bases, while *ledger tombs* are effectively INCISED SLABS raised above ground level. A splendid ledger tomb in the churchyard of Sarnesfield in Herefordshire commemorates one John Abel who was buried in 1674, aged 97. This old craftsman designed his own tomb and on the lid he carved the tools of his trade: his compasses, set square and foot rule.

Many of the seventeenth- and eighteenth-century Cotswold clothiers' tombs at Painswick in Gloucestershire are elaborately carved in baroque and later rococo styles and represent the finest collection of table and pedestal tombs in Britain. Indeed, as a consequence of its prosperity, Painswick became an important centre of monumental masonry in the eighteenth century. Shapes are varied: square, circular, hexagonal and concave, sometimes with convex curves and domed caps. One tomb, shaped like a Victorian stove, is known locally as the 'tea caddy'. Decoration is similarly diverse and includes garlands, crowns, shells, torches, festoons and putti, together with skulls, skeletons and other images of mortality.
See also GRAVESTONES

TABULA (i) A monastic duty roster prepared by the PRECENTOR, read in chapter on a Saturday and published on a board in the CLOISTER. The recess in which the tabula was placed may still be seen in the cloister of Fountains Abbey in Yorkshire. (ii) A board struck with a mallet as a signal.

TACES Long strips of metal (*lames*) forming a protective 'skirt' (*see* ARMOUR).

TANKARD A drinking vessel with a handle and detachable lid.
See also EWER, FLAGON *and* PLATE

TASSETS The pair of metal plates which hang from the front of an armour skirt to protect the thighs (*see* ARMOUR).

TATE AND BRADY Nahum Tate (1652–1715) and Nicholas Brady (1659–1726), protestant Irish clergymen and co-authors of the *New Version of the Psalms*, a metrical versification of the Psalter published in 1697. The *New Version* reflected contemporary taste and was widely used until the early nineteenth century. Brady was chaplain to William III, Mary and Queen Anne while Tate, a minor poet, became Poet Laureate in 1692.
See also CHURCH MUSIC (ANGLICAN)

Table tombs in Painswick churchyard, Gloucestershire.

TAXATION (ECCLESIASTICAL) *see* ALTAR-AGE, ANNATES, APPROPRIATION, CHURCH RATES, CONDUCTION SEDILIUM, EASTER DUES, FABRIC LANDS, GODBOTE, HEARTH PENNY, LAMPLANDS, LEWN(E), MAINPORT, MORTUARY, PARSONAGE, PETER'S PENCE, PIT MONEY, PLOUGH ALMS, PROBATE, QUEEN ANNE'S BOUNTY, REGISTERS, SOUL SCOT, SPIRITUALITIES, SURPLICE FEES, TEMPORALITIES, TITHES *and* WAX SCOT

Many ecclesiastical taxation records held in the Public Record Office have been published, notably those for the thirteenth, fourteenth and sixteenth centuries. These include *Taxatio Ecclesiastica Angliae at Walliae, auctoritate Papae Nicholai IV* of *c.* 1291, a comprehensive record of 8,500 benefices valued at more than six marks ('*The Taxation of Pope Nicholas IV*', published in 1802); *Nonarum Inquisitions in Curia Scaccarii* which relates to a tax of 1341 ('*The Inquisition of the Ninths*', published in 1807); and the *Valor Ecclesiasticus, temp Henrici VIII, auctoritate regia institatus* of 1534 which was a survey of all ecclesiastical property in England immediately before the Reformation (published in six volumes from 1810 to 1834). Also in print, the '*Taxation of Norwich*' of 1254 lists the returns for the dioceses of Bangor, Durham, Ely, Lincoln, Llandaff, London, Norwich and St. Asaph.

TAZZA *see* PLATE

TE DEUM An ancient Latin hymn of praise to the Father and the Son beginning with the words *Te deum laudamus* – 'We praise thee, O God'- sung at mattins or as a thanksgiving on special occasions.

The inclusion of the *Te Deum* in the Office is mentioned in the Rule of St. Benedict.

TEMPLAR, KNIGHTS (THE POOR KNIGHTS OF CHRIST AND OF THE TEMPLE OF SOLOMON) Together, the Hospitallers, the Teutonic Knights and the Knights Templar formed the three most powerful orders of chivalry to emanate from the CRUSADES. Within a few years of their foundation most of their brethren, while living under vows of religion, were conventual knights (their priests were known as *chaplains*) and the orders played an increasingly significant role in the defence of the Christian settlements in Palestine and Syria and in the administration of the Kingdom of Jerusalem. They constructed and garrisoned castles and fought alongside crusading forces in the perennial wars against the Egyptians and Turks.

Founded in 1118/19, by Hugues de Payns and Godeffroi de St. Omer, the Order of the Poor Knights of Christ and of the Temple of Solomon was given a convent (headquarters) close to the Temple of Solomon by King Baldwin II of Jerusalem so that they should 'fight with a pure mind for the supreme and true king'. The knights, who lived according to the rule of Bernard of Clairvaux under an elected Master of the Temple, dedicated themselves to the protection of pilgrims in the Holy Land and quickly achieved the sanction of the Church.

By the end of the thirteenth century the Templars had become established in almost every European kingdom and were in receipt of enormous grants of land. But their widespread influence attracted influential enemies. Strange stories circulated about their 'secret rites' and their failure to mobilise their considerable resources in 1291 following the fall of Acre (the last Christian stronghold in the Holy Land) caused universal resentment. Eventually, in 1308, Philip IV of France moved against them. Having obtained papal support for his campaign, Philip persuaded most European rulers to suppress the Templars. The order's officers were arrested, on the grounds of alleged heresy, sorcery, sodomy and corruption, and in France at least thirty-eight Templars are known to have died during 'examination'. In 1310, sixty-seven Templars were burned at the stake, in 1312 the Pope transferred many of the order's holdings and possessions to the Hospitallers (*see* ST. JOHN OF JERUSALEM, ORDER OF) and in 1314 the Grand Master of the order was burnt alive in front of Notre Dame in Paris on the instructions of Philip the Fair. But by then, the Templars had created for themselves what was effectively a sovereign state in the Greek islands, notably at Rhodes which they eventually lost to the Ottoman Turks in 1522. The order's convent was re-established in Malta, in 1530, where it remained until 1798.

Although in several countries the order survived, in England it was suppressed, though without undue severity. Its headquarters still stand at Temple Church in Fleet Street, London, a building which was based on the Holy Sepulchre at Jerusalem. Both the Templars and the Hospitallers had about fifty preceptories or commanderies in the British Isles (*see* COMMANDERY), many commemorated by place-names such as St. John's Jerusalem in Kent, St. John's Wood in London, Temple Breuer in Lincolnshire, Templecombe in Somerset and Temple Guiting in the Gloucestershire Cotswolds. One of the most impressive Temple churches, St. Michael's at Garway on Herefordshire, was originally a circular structure (of which no sign remains internally) with a detached, fortress-like tower to the north-west (*see* TOWERS).

The habit of the order was white with a red cross of eight points worn on the left shoulder and its badges were the *Agnus Dei* and a strange device consisting of two knights riding on one horse (presumably an allusion to the original poverty of the order) which was later translated into a pegasus.

Further reading:
Burman, E., *The Templars: Knights of God*, Wellingborough, 1986

TEMPLE PLACE-NAMES *see* TEMPLAR, KNIGHTS

TEMPORALE That section of a MISSAL or BREVIARY in which are set out the variable parts of the services for the ecclesiastical year.
See also SANCTORALE.

TEMPORALITIES Secular property (known as *Church Lands*) held by the post-Reformation Church of England and largely sold off by Parliament in the 1640s (*see* BISHOPS' LANDS *and* SPIRITUAL-ITIES).

TEN ARTICLES, THE *see* SIX ARTICLES, THE

TEN COMMANDMENTS, THE The precepts revealed to Moses on Mount Sinai and engraved on two tablets of stone (*see* Exodus 20: 1–17 *and* Deuteronomy 5: 6–21). The Ten Commandments were of significance in the development of the penitential systems of the ninth century and in the popular teaching of sixteenth-century reformers (*see* REFORMATION, THE). Recitation of the Ten Commandments was introduced into the Communion office in the 1552 *Book of Common Prayer* but, since the nineteenth century, is usually replaced by the Lord's Great Commandments (*see* Matthew 22: 36–40) or the *Kyrie Eleison*, a prayer for divine mercy (Greek = 'Lord, have mercy') which, in the medieval Church, was recited at the beginning of the Mass.

TENEBRAE *see* HEARSE

TENON see MORTISE

TERCE The short office of the third hour (about nine in the morning). Similar in structure to SEXT and NONE, Terce consisted of a hymn, three psalms (or a longer psalm divided into three parts) with antiphons, a chapter or reading, the lesser litany, Lord's prayer, versicles and collect.

TERRACOTTA Unglazed earthenware material, usually brownish-red in colour, containing *grog*, previously fired earthenware which has been ground to a fine powder. Introduced to sixteenth-century Britain from Italy, where the word means 'baked earth', terracotta is harder and less porous than brick and is used as an ornamental building material and in statuary.

TERRIER see PARSONAGE

TERTIARY A member of the Third Order of a mendicant order (see FRIARS and THIRD ORDERS). A secular tertiary is one who lives in the world, whereas a regular tertiary lives in a community.

TEST ACTS (1673 and 1678) Acts designed to exclude members of churches other than the Church of England from certain positions of authority. The Test Act of 1673 required all holders of military or civil offices under the Crown to take the Oath of Supremacy, to declare their allegiance to the sovereign, to repudiate the doctrine of transubstantiation and to receive communion according to the usage of the Church of England. The 1678 Act, passed in the aftermath of the POPISH PLOT, pro-hibited Roman Catholics (with the exception of the Duke of York – the future King James II) from entering Parliament. The Acts were not repealed until 1829.
See also SEVENTEENTH-CENTURY CHURCH

TESTAMENTARY PECULIAR see PECULIAR *and* PROBATE

TESTATOR A person who has made a will (*see* PROBATE). One who has provided a valid will is said to have died testate. One who failed to make a will is said to have died intestate.

TESTER see BALDACCHINO, ALTAR CANOPY *and* SOUNDING-BOARD

TEXT (i) A passage of scripture quoted as the subject of a sermon. (ii) A religious precept or passage of scripture (such as the Ten Commandments, the Creed and the Lord's Prayer) displayed for the edification of a congregation. Such texts were often painted on post-Reformation altarpieces, for example (see ALTARPIECE). (iii) The main body of a book or page in contradistinction to notes, appendices, illustrations etc. (iv) The original words of a document, especially those prescribed for study.

THANE'S CHURCH (*also* THEGN'S CHURCH) A thane (or *thegn*) was a member of the Anglo-Saxon military élite and of a royal or noble household. Prior to the ninth century the term *gesith* had the same meaning. From the eighth century many PROPRIETARY CHAPELS were built by private landowners for the benefit of their estates and as subsidiary chapels of MINSTERS. These are sometimes described as thanes' churches.
See also ANGLO-SAXON CHURCH

THEGN'S CHURCH see THANE'S CHURCH

THIRD ORDERS Religious organisations associated with one of the mendicant orders (*see* FRIARS). Known as tertiaries, members of the Third Orders live either in the world (*Secular Tertiaries*) or in communities (*Regular Tertiaries*). They observe a rule, recite an office and may wear the habit of their order. All members of the Third Orders are under vows, as are their fully professed brothers and sisters in the First (male) and Second (female) Orders.

THIRTY-NINE ARTICLES, THE The doctrinal formulae issued by Convocation in 1563 and finally adopted by the Church of England in 1571 as a statement of its dogmatic position. Since 1865 the Anglican clergy have been required to affirm only a general assent rather than to subscribe to the Articles in every particular.
See also REFORMATION, THE *and* SIX ARTICLES, THE

THREE-DECKER PULPIT see PULPITS

THURIBLE (*also* CENSER) A metal vessel in which incense is burned (*see* PLATE). A thurible is usually suspended from chains by which it is swung during the incensation.

THURIFER The person appointed to carry the THURIBLE.

TIARA The triple-crowned, beehive-shaped head-dress which is worn by (or carried before) the Pope at important non-liturgical functions and solemn acts of jurisdiction. The papal Tiara may be found depicted in late-medieval religious art as a symbol of the Holy Father and in the vernacular imagery of the post-Reformation period where it may be worn by a pig or a monkey as a calculated insult to the Church of Rome.

TIDE DIALS see SUNDIALS

TIE-BEAM Structural timber or timbers extending horizontally from one side of a roof to the other and connecting the feet of the rafters (*see* ROOFS).

TIERCERON RIBS *see* VAULTING

TILES The floors of most medieval parish churches were of compacted earth, clay or chalk and were covered with rushes for warmth and to facilitate cleaning. Flag-stones and tiles may have been laid later, usually in the vicinity of altars, though major monastic and collegiate churches were often tiled throughout.

MANUFACTURE

Decorated floor tiles dating from the thirteenth to the sixteenth centuries may still be found in medieval churches. During the thirteenth century several methods were developed for the decoration of plain clay tiles which were normally fired with a transparent lead glaze to produce a dark red or brown colour, though green glazes were also used. A pattern could be engraved in outline on the surface of the tile or a design carved in relief or counter-relief on a wood-block which was then pressed into the tile. In both instances the tile was then glazed and fired to produce a patterned tile of one colour. A third method was to fill the matrix of a stamped tile with white pipeclay before it was glazed and fired. This produced the familiar brown and yellow *encaustic tile*. Occasionally the design was reversed with a dark pattern set into a light coloured tile. Early encaustic tiles are usually 12½–15 cm square (5–6 inches) and as much as 2½ cm thick (1 inch) with a 2 mm inlay (¹⁄₁₀ inch).

By the mid-fourteenth century a flourishing English tile manufacturing industry had been established in the Chilterns with its centre at Penn in Buckinghamshire. 'Penn' tiles were smaller, only 11½ cm square (4½ inches) and 2 cm thick (³⁄₄ inch). It seems likely that by this time the various stages of manufacture were combined in a single process: the stamp being dipped into *slip* (a fine liquid clay which could be handled like paint) before it was pushed into the malleable tile so that the slip remained in the impression when the stamp was removed. This would explain why the slip is often very thin and some edges of the inlay may be smudged or missing. The inlay was usually flush with the surface of the tile but a later development in technique resulted in the pattern being slightly concave.

DESIGNS

Early tiles were produced to decorate royal and magnatial palaces and important religious houses. During the fourteenth century their use spread to smaller churches and domestic buildings, though in many instances a commonality of design suggests that batches of tiles were 'left-overs' from large monastic commissions and had been donated by a religious house to one or more of its subsidiary churches. Most designs required four tiles to complete a pattern (some required as many as sixteen) and it is often possible to identify individual tiles from a major monastery or cathedral which have been laid down inaccurately in a parish church – possibly because insufficient tiles of each type were provided to complete a pattern or the workmen were not familiar with the original. It may be that tilers carried out smaller commissions *in situ*, constructing temporary kilns and carrying a selection of wood-blocks with them. This would explain the occurrence of identical tiles in churches many miles apart.

Many designs were used in encaustic, relief and counter-relief tiles including geometrical motifs, human and grotesque heads, CHRISTIAN SYMBOLS, REBUSES and heraldic devices associated with royal or monastic foundations or with the benefactors of a particular church or chantry chapel. The tiles at Neath Abbey in Glamorgan, for example, record graphically the dependence of the house on its Anglo-Norman patrons: the Clare earls and local settler families such as the Turbervilles and the Norreys. Heraldic tiles are a considerable aid to research (see below) but not all lions and fleurs-de-lis are of heraldic significance. Confusingly, it is not unusual to find that a heraldic design has been carved correctly on the wood-block but the resultant impression is back to front.

MEDIEVAL TILES

Examples of medieval tiles remain throughout the country, notably in the counties of Worcestershire and Devon. Often they are not in their original position but have been rescued by nineteenth-century restorers and reset somewhere else in the church. More or less complete floors have survived at Hailes in Gloucestershire and West Hendred in Berkshire and there are substantial sections of tiling at Old Cleeve and Watchet in Somerset, Cadeleigh, Haccombe and Westleigh in Devon, Launcells in Cornwall, Brook in Kent and Bredon, Great Malvern Priory and Little Malvern Priory in Worcestershire.

There can be little doubt that numerous medieval tiles await discovery beneath the floors of our ancient parish churches. At Sible Hedingham in Essex, for example, the floor-boards of a fourteenth-century sacristy were removed during a recent refurbishment to reveal a floor of eighteenth-century pammets (quarry tiles), paving bricks and medieval tiles. Several of the relief tiles bear the arms of De Vere quartering those of the dukedom of Ireland. Although the De Veres had been the principal land-owners in Hedingham since the Conquest it was Robert, ninth earl of Oxford and a favourite of Richard II, who was created Duke of Ireland in 1386 and was therefore entitled to quarter the arms of the dukedom with those of De Vere. In 1387 he led an army in support of the King against the Lords Appellant and was defeated at Radcot Bridge in Oxfordshire. In the following year he was banished

Heraldic floor tiles at Tewkesbury Abbey, Gloucestershire. Top: Despencer, Berkeley, Beauchamp. Centre: Fitzhamon. Bottom: The bear and ragged staff device of the Beauchamps and their successors as earls of Warwick.

by the Merciless Parliament and fled to flanders where he died in 1392. Thus, the tiles at Sible Hedingham may be closely dated 1386–88.

LATER TILES

Nineteenth-century Victorian reproduction encaustic tiles were manufactured in large numbers for church restorations or re-buildings. These were often based on medieval designs but are of uniform appearance and texture. Victorian tiles will also be found throughout a church while medieval examples are usually confined to the presbytery or subsidiary chapels.

Further reading:

Barnard, J., *Victorian Ceramic Tiles*, London, 1972

Eames, E., *Medieval Tiles: A Handbook*, London, 1976

——, *English Medieval Tiles*, London, 1985

——, *Medieval Craftsmen: English Tilers*, London, 1992

Herbert, T., and Huggins, K., *The Decorative Tile in Architecture and Interiors,* London, 1995

Catalogue of Medieval Lead-glazed Earthernware Tiles in the Department of Medieval and Later Antiquities in the British Museum (2 vols), 1980

For the Tiles and Architectural Ceramics Society *see* APPENDIX II.

TIME IMMEMORIAL (*or* TIME OUT OF MIND) A legal claim of 'Ancient User' was based on constant use or custom since 'time immemorial', otherwise known as 'time out of mind'. In Common Law this is deemed to be 1189 although in the Court of Chivalry it has been argued that the Norman conquest of 1066 should be regarded as the limit of legal memory. During the heralds' VISITATIONS of the seventeenth century a claim with proof of a prescriptive use of arms from the accession of Elizabeth I (1558) was considered to be sufficient.

TINCTURES *see* COLOURS (HERALDIC)

TIPPET (i) A broad black 'scarf' worn by Anglican clergy over the SURPLICE. The tippet evolved from the academic hood, the ends of which hung forward from the shoulders (*see* VESTMENTS). (ii) A long band of cloth or fur (*see* COSTUME).

TIRONIANS Members of a reformed Benedictine congregation established in the diocese of Chartres in 1114. The name was derived from the apprentices (*tirones*) who were united by its founder to pursue their trades and skills in God's service. Of the five English priories, that at St. Dogmael was autonomous, as was its cell on Caldey, the 'Island of Saints' (both in Dyfed). The parish church of St. Dogmael may once have been the external chapel of the former priory.

TITHE BARNS *see* BARNS

TITHE MAPS *see* ARCHIVES *and* MAPS

TITHES (*DECIMAE*)

> We've cheated the parson
> And we'll cheat him again
> For why should the vicar
> Have one in ten?

Tithe was a tax of one tenth, specifically a tenth part of the annual produce of land or labour, levied in a parish to support its priest, to maintain the fabric of its church and to provide for the relief of the poor. This arrangement is known as the tripartite division of tithe though there is some doubt concerning the validity of the term. Payment of tithe was made compulsory in the tenth century and could be enforced by both the civil and ecclesiastical authorities. The need to define each man's responsibility for the payment of tithes and other dues, and to determine to which church or priest such dues had to be paid, made it necessary to delineate parish boundaries precisely (*see* BOUND-ARIES *and* PARISH).

There were three types of tithe: *praedial tithes* (calculated on income from produce), *mixed tithes* (calculated on income from stock and labour combined) and *personal tithes* (calculated on income derived entirely from labour). Income from customary sources, such as woodland and waste, was exempt. Produce raised as tithe was stored in parish barns which, for the most part, were modest buildings far removed from the great monastic tithe barns which were constructed of more durable materials and have therefore survived in greater numbers (*see* BARNS).

In parishes where the RECTOR was not the incumbent, the tithes were apportioned between the rector (which might be an institution such as a collegiate or monastic foundation) and the vicar (who was appointed as a deputy to take charge of the parish) and were known respectively as the Great or *Rectorial Tithes* and Small or *Vicarial Tithes*. Vicarial Tithes were generally those raised from labour and minor produce and as such were invariably the most difficult to collect. Consequently, the income received by many vicars was inadequate and was often the cause of considerable poverty and hardship, leading inevitably to the priest augmenting his pittance by cultivating crops (in addition to the produce of his GLEBE), keeping pigeons (there is a pigeon loft for forty birds above the chancel at Elkstone church in Gloucestershire) and grazing cattle in the CHURCHYARD.

In a wealthy parish, rectorial tithes could be a valuable form of endowment and for this reason those who founded monasteries in the twelfth and thirteenth centuries often chose to provide income for their fledgling communities in the form of benefices rather than in the form of land. The new monastery would itself become the corporate rector and would thereby receive the rectorial tithes. From 1391, monastic rectors were required to set aside a proportion of their tithes for the benefit of the poor of their appropriated parishes.

With the DISSOLUTION OF THE MONASTER-IES, many monastic holdings were conveyed by the Crown into private ownership so that laymen could claim the rectorial tithes. The tithes of such impropriated parishes thereby became private property which could be freely purchased, sold or leased and were entirely divorced from the parish church and its incumbent. In the seventeenth and eighteenth centuries, assessment depended on the complex customs of a particular parish which were recorded in detail in glebe terriers (*see* PARSONAGE) and often proved a constant source of disputation between parson and parishioners.

The *Tithe Commutation Act* of 1836 permitted tithes to be commuted to rent-charges and commissioners were appointed to negotiate land values in the various parishes. Copies of the commissioners' survey records were deposited with the Public Record Office, the diocesan registries and the parochial authorities. The Royal Commission for Historical Manuscripts maintains a register of existing tithe records while the large-scale tithe maps, and the lists of land-owners and tenants which were appended to them, are now held by county record offices (*see* MAPS).

Just outside the entrance to Thornford church in Dorset is the 'tithe tomb' on which the incumbent sat to receive the tithes on St. Thomas's day. The tithe money was placed in a hollow carved out of the top of the tombstone. Francis Kilvert, vicar of Bredwardine in Herefordshire, noted in his diary on 5 February, 1878: 'Today was the tithe audit held at the vicarage. About fifty tithe-payers came, most of them very small holders, some paying as little as ninepence. As soon as they had paid their tithe [to the churchwarden] in the front hall, they retired into the back hall and regaled themselves with bread, cheese and beer, some of them eating and drinking the value of the tithe they had paid.'

An act of 1891 restricted the payment of tithes to land-owners and the *Tithe Act* of 1925 transferred tithe rent charges to the *QUEEN ANNE'S BOUNTY* fund which had been established in 1704 to receive and administer for the benefit of the poorer clergy the ecclesiastical revenues annexed by Henry VIII. Tithes were finally extinguished by the *Tithe Act* of 1936.
For addresses *see* APPENDIX II.
See also ARCHIVES *and* TAXATION
Further reading:
Evans, E., *Tithes: Maps, Apportionments and the 1836 Act*, London, 1993

TITHING A land division, originally considered to be one-tenth of a hundred which was itself an administrative division of a shire.

Tomb chest and effigy attributed to Edward, Prince of Wales (son of Richard III) at Sheriff Hutton, Yorkshire.

TITHING MAN A parochial officer, chosen at the manor court or annual VESTRY meeting, to assist the PARISH CONSTABLE.

TOKENS, COMMUNION A device for ensuring that communicants had not omitted to make their offerings towards the costs of the celebration.

TOLERATION ACT (1689) Legislation which granted freedom of worship to dissenters, other than Roman Catholics and Unitarians, subject to certain conditions (*see* SEVENTEENTH-CENTURY CHURCH).

TOMB CHEST The term is misleading for tomb chests do not contain mortal remains but are simply a form of MONUMENT. Not to be confused with TABLE TOMBS (which are also described as chest tombs), stone tomb chests first appeared in the thirteenth century, inspired by the SHRINES of saints whose bodies were often enclosed in chest-like structures above ground level. Early tomb chests were surmounted by a coped top but these were superseded by INCISED SLABS, BRASSES and EFFIGIES. Most tomb chests were free-standing though many have subsequently been moved to a side wall so that the decorative carving may be seen to continue to what is now the back of the chest. Where tomb chests were originally set against a wall they were usually placed within a low arch, the wall itself providing a canopy above. Alternatively, the tomb chest, its CANOPY, pillars and arch may be combined to form a screen between two parts of a church: the presbytery and an adjacent chapel, for example.

In the thirteenth and fourteenth centuries the decoration of the sides and ends of a chest reflected contemporary architectural styles: panels containing carved quatrefoils (or, more rarely, trefoils, hexafoils or octofoils), or miniature blind arcading, often with WEEPERS carved within the recesses (*see also* CHRISM). From the mid-thirteenth century painted and gilded shields of arms were added, either within the quatrefoils or in the recesses of the arcading, or on the spandrels on either side of the figures (shield-shapes can assist with dating, *see* SHIELDS). During the fifteenth century weepers were superseded by figures of angels, which sometimes carry shields, or the spaces in the arcading were filled entirely with heraldic devices. There is sometimes a space beneath a tomb chest and this may still contain the carved figure of a shrouded CADAVER to symbolise the transient nature of life on earth. Although difficult to see without prostrating one's self, the roofs of these compartments may be painted – with a depiction of the Annunciation or the figures of patron saints, for example.

Perhaps the finest of all medieval tomb chests, that of Richard Beauchamp, fifth earl of Warwick

(d. 1439) at St. Mary's, Warwick, was erected fifteen years after the earl's death and reflects a final flowering of several earlier styles. The Purbeck marble chest is surmounted by a magnificent life-size gilded bronze effigy and hearse, the head resting on a swan-crested helm and, at the feet, the bear and griffin devices of the earldoms of Warwick and Salisbury. Fourteen weepers, contained within canopied niches in the sides and ends of the chest, represent distinguished relatives or friends of the dead earl, each identified by its shield of arms including that of Richard Nevill, the 'King-maker' (1428–71). There are also eighteen angels each of which stands within a small, raised niche between the weepers, though for some reason these are not as finely carved (*for* illustration *see* EFFIGIES).

Following the Reformation, religious motifs were replaced by heraldic ones and Renaissance influences are evident in the gradual introduction of classical forms, both in the decoration and in the structure of the tomb chest itself. The sides of the chests were often divided into panels using balusters, pilasters and colonettes. Figures were rarely used and heraldry, both on the tomb chest and its integral canopy, became increasingly elaborate (*see* CANOPY, MONUMENTAL). From the end of the sixteenth century, many tomb chests were constructed on two levels to accommodate two or even three effigies. From the mid-seventeenth century, the tomb chest was superseded by the hanging WALL MONUMENT and it was not until the Gothic Revival of the nineteenth century that tomb chests became fashionable once again.
For the Church Monuments Society *see* APPENDIX II.

TOMBS Strictly speaking, a tomb is a grave, vault or other place where human remains have been interred. However, the term is sometimes used erroneously to describe various forms of monument which are not necessarily erected over the place of interment.
See BRASSES (MONUMENTAL), BURIAL, CANOPY (MONUMENTAL), CHURCHYARDS, EFFIGIES, GRAVESTONES, INCISED SLABS, MONUMENTS, OSSUARIES, PLAGUE, SHRINES, TABLE TOMBS, TOMB CHESTS, VAULTS *and* WALL MONUMENTS

TOMBSTONES *see* GRAVESTONES *and* MONUMENTS

TONGS *see* DOGS

TONSURE The formal shaving of the head which was introduced into the Western Church in the seventh century as 'the outward and visible mark' of a monk or cleric. The difference between the Celtic and Roman tonsure was a matter of disputation at the Synod of Whitby in 664: the former was diamond-shaped while the latter was circular (to symbolise the Crown of Thorns) and, unlike the Celtic version, the hair was cut short above the nape. In the monasteries, the tonsure was normally renewed every three weeks (and before major festivals), barbers being engaged for the purpose by the chamberlain, either from among the brethren or professionals brought in from a nearby town. The Winchester account rolls contain an entry ' . . . for 36 shavings – 4s 6d' carried out in the cloister.

TORCHÈRE A tall, ornamental candlestick. Wrought iron examples will sometimes be found adapted for use as flowerstands.

TORSE *see* WREATH

TORUS A large concave moulding, semicircular (or nearly so) in section commonly found at the base of a COLUMN.

TOUCH A black marble quarried near Tournai in Belgium (hence 'Tournai Marble') and, from the twelfth century, imported into Britain, notably in finished fonts and tomb slabs (*see* INCISED SLABS) and in decorative mouldings of the Tudor and Jacobean periods. Tournai marble is similar in appearance, though by no means identical, to PURBECK MARBLE and other cheaper 'marbles' by which it was replaced. Touchstone was also used for testing alloys.

TOUCH MARK *see* PEWTER

TOURNAI MARBLE *see* TOUCH

TOWERS Church towers are a characteristic feature of the English landscape and, even in this predominantly secular age, remain a potent symbol of community life. Most parish churches have towers at the west end of the nave, and these generally reflect both the architectural style of the period in which they were built and the affluence (or otherwise) of the communities and benefactors who erected them.

No two towers are alike, either in their construction or decoration, and there are considerable regional variations of style and materials. They may be broadly classified by reference to the arrangement of buttresses (*see* BUTTRESS), to the treatment of parapets (*see* PARAPET) and stair turrets (*see* STAIR TURRET), and to the disposition and size of windows and belfry openings.

SAXON TOWERS
Church towers originated in ninth-century Italy and first appeared in Britain a century later. Most Anglo-Saxon churches were constructed of timber but there were exceptions and it is these stone buildings which have survived (*see* ANGLO-SAXON ARCHITECTURE). Saxon towers may be recognised by LONG AND SHORT WORK, twin round-headed or triangular belfry openings (which were not recessed) and PILASTER STRIPS which were sometimes arranged in an ornamental pattern as at St. Peter's, Barton-upon-Humber, Humberside. There are notable stone-built Saxon towers at Barnack in Cambridgeshire, Bywell St. Andrew and Ovingham in Northumberland, Appleton-le-Street in Yorkshire, St. Benet's, Cambridge and St. Michael's, Oxford. The great eleventh-century tower at Sompting in Sussex has a magnificent oak-shingle Rhenish *helm roof* with four diamond-shaped sloping faces, each descending to a gable. In some instances, an existing church would be heightened at the west end to form a tower and extended to the east in a new nave, as at Barnack in Cambridgeshire. Elsewhere, a central tower may be found between the nave and the chancel and where this is flanked by PORTICUS it produces a cruciform plan more typical of the Norman period. In a few cases, such as Earl's Barton in Northamptonshire, the tower rises above the nave itself.

ENGLISH ROMANESQUE TOWERS
Early Norman towers are hardly distinguishable from late-Saxon ones: there is often no buttressing, decoration is minimal and there is usually an absence of window openings below the belfry level. Later Norman towers are characterised by their square plan, massive masonry, shallow buttressing and flat or pyramidal roofs (*see* MEDIEVAL ARCHITECTURE). From *c.* 1130 the use of decoration increased and this included blind arcading (*see* ARCADE). Twin round-headed belfry openings are usually divided by a shaft and recessed within a large, round-headed containing arch. In most cases, Norman towers were positioned above the central section of a three-cell or cruciform church (*see* axial towers *below*) and despite their solidity (or, perhaps, because of it) many collapsed. Of those which survived, that at Norwich Cathedral (1145) is the tallest and finest with a graceful spire added in 1490. There are splendidly massive Norman towers at Castor in Northamptonshire, Tewkesbury Abbey in Gloucestershire and Sandwich (St. Clement's) in Kent, and smaller, though no less impressive, examples include East Meon in Hampshire, Iffley in Oxfordshire, Old Shoreham in Sussex, Stewkley in Buckinghamshire and Weaverthorpe in Yorkshire.

DEFENSIVE TOWERS
Many communities came to appreciate the defensive advantages of having a tower in their midst, indeed the term *belfry* is of Teutonic origin and means 'a defensive place of shelter'. The name was given to the movable timber tower used in sieges and came to mean a watch-tower, beacon-tower or alarm bell-

tower. In the Welsh Marches, where raids and border disputes were a way of life, massive square towers such as those at Bosbury in Herefordshire, Clun in Shropshire and Kerry in Powys, provided refuges for an entire community. Similarly, on the Scottish borders, semi-fortified towers such as Great Salkeld and Ormside in Cumbria and Bedale in Yorkshire (where the grooves made by a portcullis have survived) were clearly intended for defensive purposes. But in most places, church towers were simply intended to accommodate a raised belfry, and where financial constraints precluded the construction of a tower, a modest BELL-COTE (bell-gable) was erected instead. Of course, towers enclosed very large spaces and it was inevitable that they should be used for other purposes: as accommodation for chantry priests, as libraries and as school rooms, for example, and several towers still contain a fireplace and even benches which were provided for these purposes.

ROUND TOWERS

Round towers are a feature of many East Anglian churches: there are one hundred and fifteen in Norfolk, forty in Suffolk and seven in Essex, nearly all located by the coast or a river. Of these, some twenty are of Saxon origin and were probably constructed as refuges from Viking incursions. They may be recognised by the location of a single doorway several metres above ground level, a ladder being required to obtain access. Those which date from the twelfth and succeeding centuries, were built as simple belfries in a country where suitable stone for constructing square-cornered towers was scarce. Haddiscoe in Norfolk is one of the finest and has retained its Saxon belfry window, as has Forncett St. Peter. At Edingthorpe and Potter Heigham in Norfolk, a later octagonal upper storey has been added.

DETACHED TOWERS

There are fifty detached church towers (correctly *detached belfries*) in England of which several are close to the Welsh border and were clearly built for defensive purposes: that at Bosbury in Herefordshire, for example, is nearly nine metres square (29 feet). The immense, fortified thirteenth-century tower of Garway church, also in Herefordshire was once detached but was linked with the main building by means of a low passage-way in the seventeenth century. Unusually (and probably because of the church's TEMPLAR origins) the tower stands at the north-west corner of the present nave and at an angle of 45 degrees to the north wall.

Fourteenth-century detached belfry at Pembridge, Herefordshire.

The thirteenth-century belfry at Ledbury in Herefordshire was built next to the church because the task of reconstructing the original building and foundations to accommodate the weight of a tower was considered excessive. It was built in three stages, a fourth being added (or possibly re-built) in 1733 when a spire was added by the well-known spire-builder Wilkinson of Worcester. The fourteenth-century tower of St. Mary Magdalene at Launceston in Cornwall was once separated from its church by a pair of cottages. These were later used for municipal purposes and eventually demolished to make way for the present vestry. At St. Feve, as elsewhere in Cornwall, a detached belfry was built on a nearby eminence because the church itself was hidden in a deep valley; while the towers of West Walton in Norfolk and Beccles in Suffolk (a huge Perpendicular structure) were erected on marshy sites which could not have supported the combined weight of church and tower. For the same reason, an extraordinary detached belfry at Brookland in Kent was built entirely of timber in three stages 'like candle-snuffers stacked one on another' (Betjeman) (*see also* BELL-CAGES).

A number of detached belfries were sited so that they would not threaten the defences of nearby fortifications, as at Berkeley in Gloucestershire (re-built 1750). Ironically it was from this tower that Parliamentary artillery terminated the three-year siege of Berkeley Castle in 1645. At Richard's Castle in Herefordshire, the free-standing bell-tower was (unusually) sited at the east end of the twelfth-century church so that it would not overlook the neighbouring castle. (*See also* CAMPANILE)

TWO-STAGE TOWERS

The magnificent fifteenth-century towers of Somerset and East Anglia (see below) and those of the famous Cotswold wool churches, celebrate in architectural splendour both God's glory and that of their builders. But not all parishes could afford to build a new tower and there are many examples of belfry storeys in the latest architectural fashion which were added to earlier towers, as at Coln St. Dennis in Gloucestershire, at Ecton and Moulton in Northamptonshire and at Little Houghton where the lower portion of the tower is Early English and the belfry storey a glorious Perpendicular addition. Quite often, the stone used for the upper storey is different from that which was used to construct the earlier tower. There are also many unfinished stone towers which have been 'capped' with a timber turret and pyramidal roof: as at Shipton in Shropshire.

Saddle-back towers, with simple tent-like roofs and gables, are often indicative of unfinished building work, as at Bagendon and Duntisbourne Abbots in the Gloucestershire Cotswolds. Of course, there are towers which were deliberately built with gabled roofs: at Ickford in Buckinghamshire, for example.

AXIAL TOWERS

From the eleventh century, many of the great English Romanesque and Gothic churches were built to a cruciform plan, with additional transept walls at right-angles to those of the nave and choir to counteract the outward thrust of massive central towers (*axial towers*), daringly constructed above the void of the crossing, and sometimes supporting spires (see below). The BELLS of these monastic and collegiate churches rang out over the fields, marking the canonical hours and summoning the brethren to services just as the bells of Sherborne Abbey in Dorset, Tewkesbury Abbey in Gloucestershire, Great Malvern Priory in Worcestershire and Portchester Priory in Hampshire now call parishioners to mattins and evensong. But primitive Cistercian usage abjured the great tower as a symbol of pride and the towers of their early churches were invariably low, as at Buildwas Abbey in Shropshire, and initially contained only a single bell. At Bolton Priory in Yorkshire, part of which remains in Anglican use, work on the construction of a great west tower ceased with the Dissolution of the Monasteries. There is a notable group of massive axial towers in east Yorkshire, at Beverley (St. Mary's), Cottingham, Hedon, Howden and, in Humberside, at Holy Trinity, Hull. The church at Purton in Wiltshire has two towers, one an axial tower with a spire and the other at the west end. In the same county, St. Andrew's church at Wanborough has a fine Perpendicular west tower and a hexagonal lantern and spire which rise ingeniously from a shortened bay at the east end of the nave.

BRICK TOWERS

The thirty old BRICK towers of Essex are a delight, especially those at Castle Hedingham, Gestingthorpe, Great Holland, Ingatestone, Rochford and Wickham St. Paul. Most date from the sixteenth century when brick was becoming fashionable. There is evidence that early brickwork was plastered to imitate stone but by the late fifteenth century it was being accepted as a facing material in its own right, leading to the ornate brickwork patterns of the Tudor period. The tower of St. Mary the Virgin at Layer Marney is a fine example, built of local yellow brick and with faint blue diapering, substantial buttressing and a pronounced corner stair turret. Essex is also a county of timber towers (eight), timber belfries (more than 80) and two detached bell-houses (at Wix and Wrabness) (*see* WEATHERBOARD).

CLASSICAL TOWERS

Seventeenth- and eighteenth-century towers usually have large, round-headed windows with projecting keystones, a classical balustrade with urns or obelisks instead of pinnacles and sometimes a cupola, as at Wimborne St. Giles in Dorset (*see* SIXTEENTH- AND SEVENTEENTH-CENTURY

Tisbury, Wiltshire. The medieval axial tower was replaced after it fell in 1762.

ARCHITECTURE *and* EIGHTEENTH-CENTURY ARCHITECTURE). The seventeenth-century tower of St. Mary's, Warwick, is Gothic in outline but its sides are peppered with classical niches and its extraordinary parapets are Jacobean in character. Unusually, the base of the tower straddles the road and forms a covered entrance to the west door. Many medieval towers acquired classical features at this time: at Leighton Bromswold in Cambridgeshire, for example, which was restored in 1627.

REGIONAL VARIATIONS

Several of the larger fifteenth-century church towers in Gloucestershire, Worcestershire and Wiltshire have ornamental panelling, as at Chipping Campden in Gloucestershire, Evesham in Worcestershire and Westwood in Wiltshire; while at Fotheringhay and Lowick in Northamptonshire and Boston in Lincolnshire there are fine examples of octagonal upper storeys. Boston's tower, the tallest of any parish church in England (88 metres or 288 feet), is facetiously known as the Stump. In west Devon and Cornwall, there are several tall fifteenth-century towers constructed of great granite blocks with heavy octagonal pinnacles (*see* PINNACLE) and crocketed spirelets, as at St. Cleer, St. Erme and Poughill in Cornwall and Widecombe in Devon. Some Devon towers taper towards the top and have a stair turret located in the middle of one of the sides, as at Ashburton and Ipplepen. Other notable fifteenth-century towers are those of Gresford in Denbigh, St. Neots in Cambridgeshire (completed 1535) and Tichmarsh in Northamptonshire, while the twin west towers of Beverley Minster in Yorkshire are undoubtedly the most perfectly proportioned Perpendicular west towers in the country.

In Kent, several Perpendicular towers have square-headed belfry windows and prominent octagonal stair turrets which project above the towers themselves (*see* BARTIZAN). Charing and Seal are good examples. There are also octagonal towers, as at Sancton in Yorkshire, North Curry in Somerset and Llanyblodwel in Shropshire, 'one of the most eccentric essays in Victorian Gothic you are ever likely to see' with a curiously convex spire. The tower at Fotheringhay in Northamptonshire has an octagonal upper storey, while the unique tower of Cartmel Priory in Lancashire consists of a square upper storey set on a larger square beneath.

A number of towers have pyramidal caps, as at Bradenham and Leckhampstead in Buckinghamshire, while a smaller version may be found on several Sussex towers, including Seaford. Large double-pyramidal roofs (i.e. one pyramid surmounting another) are a characteristic of the Welsh borders where they provided additional accommodation within a semi-fortified tower, as at Clun in Shropshire and Llanbister in Powys. A similar roof at Skenfrith in Gwent still retains the apertures of the medieval dovecot which provided food for those

who took refuge in the tower. Outside the Marches, there is a rare example of a double-pyramidal roof at Wotton in Surrey.

In the Welsh borders the principal building material is sandstone, much of it a deep red colour, though in some areas of the west Midlands a shortage of suitable building stone is evident in clusters of 'black and white' timber-framed towers, at Pirton and Warndon in Worcestershire, for example. In the east Midlands, many fine Perpendicular towers have well-proportioned belfry windows and ornamental banding, as at Great Staughton, Hamerton, Hunts and Stockerston in Bedfordshire and Warkton and Whiston in Northamptonshire.

The BELL-FLÈCHE is a characteristic of several East Anglian churches: at Burwell in Cambridgeshire and East Harling in Norfolk, for example. At Cheshunt in Hertfordshire the flèche surmounts a stair turret. After the Reformation the flèche was superseded by the CUPOLA, as at Tilty and Wivenhoe in Essex and several Middlesex churches.

Of course, not all towers are located at the west end of a parish church. At the church of St. Aldhelm, Belchalwell in Dorset, for example, a fifteenth-century tower was built against the south wall of the nave with the porch to the west and a chapel (with SQUINT) beneath. It is believed that the south wall of the present nave was originally the north wall of an earlier Saxon church and the tower was therefore erected on Saxon foundations, possibly at the west end of the earlier nave.

SOMERSET

The Perpendicular towers of Somerset, which number about sixty, are unrivalled in their composition and exquisite detail. Shepton Mallet is one of the earliest and seems to have been the prototype for others in the area. It has three parallel windows in the upper section, the flanking pair being filled with blind arcading and the central one pierced to allow the sound of the bells to escape (*see also* BELL LOUVRES). The parapet is not crenellated but is intricately pierced, as are several tower parapets in the west Mendips, notably at Axbridge, Banwell, Bleadon, Brent Knoll, Cheddar, Mark, Weare, Wedmore and Winscombe. Triple belfry windows are also a feature of an east Mendip group of churches, but here all three windows are pierced and the parapets crenellated, as at Ilminster, Leigh-on-Mendip and Mells (all of which have additional sets of 'blind' windows in the central section of the tower) and at Batcombe, Bruton, Cranmore and Weston Zoyland. With the exception of Batcombe, delicately carved, crocketed pinnacles are a prominent feature of all these towers. A further group of Somerset towers is characterised by a pair of windows in the upper section with one in the stage below, and by crenellated parapets. Bishop's Lydeard is one of the earliest, while others include Huish Episcopi, Isle Abbots, Kingsbury Episcopi,

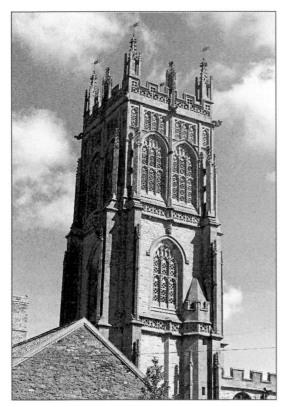

Magnificent mid-fifteenth-century tower of the church of St. John the Baptist, Glastonbury, Somerset. The elaborate parapet and panelled middle stage are reminiscent of those at Gloucester Cathedral.

Kingston St. Mary, North Petherton, Staple Fitzpaine and St. James at Taunton. The most elaborate Somerset tower, that of St. Mary Magdalene at Taunton, has pairs of windows at three levels and exceptionally ornate parapet and pinnacles, while the towers at Chewton Mendip and St. John's at Glastonbury have two windows in the two upper stories and wonderful 'filigree' parapets and pinnacles derived from the tower of Gloucester Cathedral. Several towers in south Somerset and neighbouring Dorset have pairs or clusters of pinnacles at each corner: at Crewkerne and Norton-sub-Hamdon in Somerset and Beaminster, Charminster, Dorchester, Fordington and Piddle-trenthide in Dorset, for example. (It should be remembered that, in the nineteenth century, pinnacles and castellated parapets were often added to otherwise mundane towers as 'Gothic' features, though this is certainly not true of the above examples.)

Corner stair turrets are equally varied: that at Bleadon in Somerset terminates in a cap, while at Chew Stoke, also in Somerset, and Pimperne in Dorset they are elongated into a miniature spire (*spirelet*). The turret at Crewkerne even has its own pinnacles. Outside this area only two towers are of comparable quality, though even these (at Probus in Cornwall and Chittlehampton in Devon) were clearly influenced by the Somerset masons.

Of course, there are many more modest towers in Somerset. The fifteenth-century west tower of Puxton in the Somerset Levels, for example, which lists so badly that it appears to be in imminent danger of collapse. The tower of St. Saviour's squats on a man-made pontoon of brash wood which, over the centuries, has kept it more-or-less upright on its shifting sub-strata of peat and clay, sixty feet above the Wessex bedrock.

EAST ANGLIA

There are over one thousand ancient church towers in Norfolk and Suffolk alone. They are predominantly of flint and are usually tall, those on the coast particularly so for they provided the only landmarks for shipping. There are fine examples at Covehithe, Kessingland, Southwold and Walberswick in Suffolk; Blakeney, Cromer, Happisburgh and Winterton in Norfolk and Brightlingsea in Essex. Buttresses often terminate at belfry level, thereby accentuating the graceful lines of the structure, while many have 'Norfolk air-holes', large square apertures in the centre section filled with elaborately carved tracery. The absence of ornamental parapets and pinnacles on many East Anglian churches demonstrates the difficulty (and cost) of obtaining suitable building stone, indeed it would appear that in several cases the money ran out before the work was completed, at Southwold in Suffolk and Trunch in Norfolk, for example. Where pinnacles do occur, they quite often take the form of carved beasts: as at Acle, Blofield and Filby in Norfolk. Among so many wonderful lofty towers, those at Brisley, Cawston, Great Massingham, Grimstone, Hindringham, Northrepps, Redenhall, Reedham, Sall, Southrepps in Norfolk are especially fine, as are those at Bungay, Eye, Lavenham, Stoke-by-Nayland, and Woodbridge in Suffolk. Benedictine Wymondham Abbey in Norfolk (unusually dedicated to St. Mary and St. Thomas of Canterbury) has magnificent towers at both ends of the nave: one erected for monastic purposes and the other for the benefit of the parishioners. The elegant eastern tower has octagonal upper storeys and is now roofless while the western tower rises to 43 metres (142 feet).

SPIRES

Spires are tall, tapering structures of stone or timber erected on church towers. They may be conical or polygonal in form and timber spires are usually covered with SHINGLES or lead. Their construction presented the medieval masons with a particular problem – for while most spires were octagonal, the towers on which they were constructed had only four sides. To overcome this, and to ensure that the weight of a spire was evenly distributed, a number of structural types were developed: most commonly the *broach spire* and the *parapet spire*.

Most of the early spires were of broach design. These were constructed with squinches (*see* SQUINCH) and sloping, triangular splays of masonry (*broaches*) which buttressed the spire at each corner of the tower.

As the name suggests, parapet spires (which were characteristic of the Perpendicular period) were supported by the parapet of a tower and (usually) by pinnacles erected at each corner within the spaces formed by a spire's octagonal base. Inevitably, the parapet spire was narrower than the broach type (when especially slender it is described as a *needle spire*) and was often reinforced by flying buttresses which extended from the sides of the spire to the corner pinnacles of the tower. In both types, narrow window openings were sometimes accommodated within *lucarnes*, set in the alternate faces of an octagonal spire (*see* LUCARNE).

Most medieval spires are from the early Gothic period (*see* MEDIEVAL ARCHITECTURE), the builders of Perpendicular towers preferring to compete with one another in the architectural ornamentation of pinnacles, parapets and mouldings. The most magnificent spire, that of Salisbury Cathedral, was completed in 1380 and at 121 metres (404 feet) is by far the tallest in England, though that of Old St. Paul's (destroyed by fire in 1561) was nearly 28 metres taller (93 feet). The central tower of Lincoln cathedral is 81 metres tall (271 feet) and was once crowned with a lead-covered timber spire which, at 157 metres (524 feet), is believed to have been the tallest in Europe but was destroyed in a storm in 1548.

Some of the finest medieval stone spires are to be found in Northamptonshire, a county which benefited from the raw wool trade in the fourteenth century and where there is an unusual number of cruciform churches. The grotesquely buckled fourteenth-century lead spire of St. Mary and All Saints at Chesterfield in Derbyshire leans alarmingly out of the vertical by nearly 3 metres (9 feet 5 inches). Completed in 1234, the 69 metre (228 feet) spire began to twist in *c.* 1380 as the lead warped and the unseasoned timbers dried out. At Breadsall, in the same county, the fine late fourteenth-century spire was restored after Suffragettes set fire to the church in 1915, while St. Mary's at Cleobury Mortimer in Shropshire has a wooden spire which, despite efforts to straighten it, has a pronounced twist.

There are also many examples of spires which have been added to earlier towers: the graceful seventeenth-century parapet spire of St. Mary's church at Painswick in Gloucestershire, for example, which crowns a plain fifteenth-century tower. There

are a number of shingled spires in Kent, notably at Bexley and Pembury (Old Church), while Essex has over eighty timber belfries, many with broach spires: Stock Harvard is an attractive example. The spire on the detached tower at Westbury-on-Severn in Gloucestershire glows with 60,000 tiny, silver-green shingles, while at Peterchurch, in the Golden Valley of Herefordshire, the medieval spire was replaced with a fibreglass one in 1972.

Many of the smaller churches in the Welsh border counties also have timber bell turrets, several of which have short broach spires, as at Vowchurch in Herefordshire.

The Victorians were especially fond of spires: in Dorset, for example, only three medieval spires have survived but several Victorian churches have spires including that at Bradford Peverell near Dorchester (Decimus Burton 1850), a broach spire with two tiers of lucarnes, all in the Early English-*cum*-Decorated style so beloved of the nineteenth-century Gothic Revivalists (*see* NINETEENTH-CENTURY ARCHITECTURE).

For the towers of Wren's London churches *see* SIXTEENTH- AND SEVENTEENTH-CENTURY ARCHITECTURE.

See also BELFRIES, BELLS, CARILLON, FLAGS, STAIRCASES *and* WEATHERCOCKS AND WEATHER VANES

For the Round Tower Churches Society *see* APPENDIX II.

TOWER SCREEN An ornamental screen, usually of wood, separating the nave of a church from the space beneath a tower at the west end.
See also CHANCEL SCREENS

TOWERS, DETACHED *see* TOWERS

TOWERS, FIGURE SCULPTURE ON *see* FIGURE SCULPTURE

TOWNS Most towns came into existence as the result of policy decisions made either by individuals or by institutions. While geographical and economic factors undoubtedly influenced those decisions, very few towns simply grew from settlements which happened to be in favourable locations. In the majority of cases, therefore, towns were planned and it is this which distinguished them from other types of settlement.
ANGLO-SAXON SETTLEMENTS
The popular perception of the Dark Ages is one of deserted Roman towns, dilapidated villas and a rapid reversion to barbarism. It is true that there was no discernible revival of urban affairs until the seventh century, when a number of former Roman towns were designated as the administrative centres of dioceses, notably London, Canterbury, Dorchester-on-Thames, Winchester and York. But in the late

Saxon period, several new towns were established at proto-urban settlements which, well before the end of the eighth century, had developed characteristics which marked them out from the normal agricultural settlements of the period. For the most part, they were the administrative centres of royal estates and therefore already exercised civil authority within territories which had evolved from earlier minor kingdoms and tribal units. Many possessed a MINSTER and had developed trading functions superior to those of neighbouring settlements. Significantly, most were located at or near former Roman sites, suggesting that such places had regained their status very much earlier than is generally acknowledged and that many had never been entirely deserted. Indeed, it is highly unlikely that, following the withdrawal of Rome, the entire indigenous population should suddenly abandon the towns and other Roman settlements and the network of metalled roads which radiated from them. No doubt they fell into disrepair, in the absence of a cohesive and skilled workforce, but the pattern was established which was to provide the foundation of many late Saxon towns such as Rochester in Kent, Bradford-on-Avon in Wiltshire and Dorchester in Dorset. These later towns may have been promoted by their royal or ecclesiastical owners or remodelled with regular street patterns and market places to encourage expansion, but the potential for commercial growth was already there.

Anglo-Saxon sources indicate that there were three types of town, those which developed on former Roman sites being known as *ceasters*. A defensive system of fortified *burhs* was also established in southern England during the reigns of Alfred the Great (871–99) and his Saxon successors as a direct response to the threat of Danish invasion. The third and more numerous category of Anglo-Saxon town was the *port* or commercial trading centre. These were not necessarily located on coasts or navigable rivers: many were inland market towns such as Milborne Port and Langport in Somerset. In the Danelaw several new towns were created, notably the *Five Boroughs* of Derby, Nottingham, Stamford, Leicester and Lincoln, the last two on former Roman sites.

MEDIEVAL PLANNED TOWNS

The primary role of the medieval town – the rationale for its existence and guarantee of its success – was as a centre of specialisation and exchange in what was essentially a rural, subsistence economy. From the tenth to the thirteenth centuries numerous planned towns were added to existing villages by their owners in order to encourage trade. Professor W.G. Hoskins has identified five such towns in north Oxfordshire alone, four of them (Banbury, Chipping Norton, Deddington and Woodstock) dating from the twelfth century, and the fifth (Bicester) from the thirteenth. Several were castle towns, built outside the gates of

late eleventh-century fortresses such as Alnwick in Northumberland, Ludlow in Shropshire and Chepstow in Gwent, while others were entirely new, laid out on 'green-field' sites like that at Salisbury (Sarum) in Wiltshire. The planned origins of such towns are often clearly evident in the regular grid-like pattern of their streets and the rectilinear disposition of ancient boundaries. Kingston-upon-Hull, Humberside (1293), Stratford-upon-Avon in Warwickshire (1196), Liverpool, Merseyside (1207) and Leeds in West Yorkshire (1207) are but four notable examples of early medieval planned towns, three of which developed into major cities.

In Wales, King John (1199–1216) and Henry III (1216–72) established new towns: Montgomery in Powys for example. Henry's son, Edward I (1272–1307), had seen and built new towns on a rectangular grid plan within stone walls during his time in Gascony and several of his new Welsh castles were provided with walled towns (*bastides*), inhabited by colonies of English merchants and tradespeople. The rights of burgesses were defined in their town's charter: they enjoyed a measure of self-government, legal and economic, which distanced them from the feudal world beyond their town walls. The charters of Gwynedd were versions of the charter of Rhuddlan (1277) which in turn was based on the charters of Hereford and Breteuil. As elsewhere in Europe, the boroughs were the sole centres of trade which was strictly controlled by the burgesses (*see* FAIRS AND MARKETS). About a dozen towns were created in Wales following the conquest of 1282, but none of them was particularly large. (By 1620, Carmarthen, the largest town in Wales, had a population of about 2,000.) The magnificent walls and flanking towers of Caernarfon and Conwy (both in Gwynedd) survive to this day, as do sections of several baronial bastides such as the late thirteenth-century wall of Tenby in Dyfed.

Medieval magnates, particularly those who owned castles, found it profitable to allow communities to develop nearby, both to provide for the needs of their households and to increase revenues from increased trade and commerce. Settlers were attracted by land grants, low rents and other privileges and organised trading monopolies offered economic security and the right of controlling one's own property within a town. Each freeholder had one or more plots of land with a building abutting the street in which he lived, worked and traded. More than forty English towns retain sections of their original medieval walls and several their gates which closely resemble castle gatehouses. Although originally constructed for military purposes, town walls facilitated the maintenance of law and order and effectively controlled access to a town's trading facilities which were jealously guarded by the granting of borough charters and other protective franchises and by the formation of GUILDS. But such grants were haphazard: ambitious manorial lords were able to obtain borough status for small communities in anticipation of commercial success and the historical landscape is littered with the relics of failed towns. Conversely, several substantial communities such as Ludlow in Shropshire, which possessed all the attributes of towns, were not legally defined as such until the late Middle Ages.

From the mid-thirteenth century there was a decline in the economic conditions which had previously encouraged the building of new towns but several prospered and expanded, either by ribbon development along existing streets or by the addition of new suburbs. Many *Newland* place-names in towns originated at this time.

In the early fourteenth century London probably had a population of nearly 120,000 and cities such as York, Norwich, Lincoln and Bristol each had about 20,000 inhabitants. Of a total population of five million it is now believed that at least 700,000 lived in towns. Urban society was also very well organised with medieval old peoples' homes, orphanages, hospitals, social clubs and hotels. Large numbers of social institutions were provided by wealthy benefactors (*see* CHANTRY), by ecclesiastical foundations (*see* SHRINES) and by fraternities, such as the Guild of Our Lady at Lavenham in Suffolk whose fifteenth-century meeting hall was built in part to ensure that masses were said for the souls of all paid-up members and as a social club for the town's élite, with its own resident cook and musician.

The Black Death of 1348–69 (*see* PLAGUE) effectively curtailed the creation of new towns, Bewdley, built in 1477 on the banks of the river Severn in Worcestershire, being the last medieval planned town. With the coming of the Tudor dynasty, and the growth of England's material prosperity, there was a revival of urban markets and seaports. But after the sixteenth century few new towns were established: Whitehaven in Cumbria was begun in 1660 and developed as a successful coal port and ship-building centre and the expansion of the Royal Navy resulted in new seventeenth-century towns at Chatham and Devonport in Devon, and at Portsmouth in Hampshire the suburb of Portsea was added in the early eighteenth century.

URBAN PLANNING

In the medieval period, the expansion of an urban population had usually been accommodated by subdividing plots and in-filling open spaces, particularly markets which had often outgrown their original sites. But from the mid-seventeenth century the formless conglomeration of buildings and social classes which had characterised many medieval towns was superseded by the introduction from Italy of new ideas of urban planning and architectural style which reflected more accurately the growing prosperity of the period. The concept of open circuses and squares with terraces of elegant town houses, such as Bloomsbury Square (1661), St. James' Square (1665) and Soho Square (1690) in London, was to dominate urban planning for two centuries, reaching its apotheosis in the Georgian city of Bath. But there was another side to the coin. The towns of the Industrial Revolution also had their terraces, but these were of 'tunnel-back' and 'blind-back' houses, often with inadequate sanitation, small rooms and large families. By contrast, nineteenth-century civic authorities vied with one another in the magnificence of their public buildings, and the 'dark satanic mills' of Victorian industrial magnates loomed above the regimented terraces just as the castles and abbeys of their Norman predecessors had dominated a subjugated people. Indeed, the pattern of earlier medieval fields is sometimes discernible in the disposition of blocks of nineteenth-century terraces.

Several new towns were built to serve both the canal system and the railway network. Goole in Humberside, for example, was a planned canal port founded in 1819 by the Aire and Calder Navigation Company. In Cheshire the town of Crewe was a railway town and Swindon in Wiltshire became a notable engineering centre. The railways also helped to create numerous coastal resorts while fashionable suburbs, such as Edgbaston in Birmingham, developed to accommodate a new and rapidly expanding middle class.

In the early decades of the twentieth century, a number of *garden cities* were built, such as Welwyn Garden City in Hertfordshire, and several philanthropic employers provided *model villages* for their workpeople, such as Bournville on the south-western outskirts of Birmingham, built by the Quaker Cadbury family complete with an adult education college, schools, concert hall, recreation grounds, public baths and many other facilities – but no public houses.

The most successful towns are those whose origins are least apparent. The charm of medieval Lavenham has survived only because it failed to develop after an early period of prosperity, just as Stourport in Worcestershire has retained its nineteenth-century character because of the failure of the canal system on which it was founded. In contrast, much of medieval Gloucester was destroyed in the 1960s when the developers' bulldozers moved in to reveal ancient timber-frame buildings behind Victorian façades.

Further reading:

Beresford, M., *New Towns of the Middle Ages: Town Plantation in England, Wales and Gascony*, Stroud, 1967

Grace, F., *The Late Victorian Town*, London, 1992

Haslam, J., *Anglo-Saxon Towns in Southern England*, London, 1984

Hodges, R., *The Origins of Towns*, London, 1982

Platt, C., *The English Medieval Town*, London, 1976

Reynold, S., *An Introduction to English Medieval Towns*, Oxford, 1977

West, J., *Town Records*, Chichester, 1983

TOWNSHIP (*also* **VILL**) An administrative unit within a PARISH which levied a separate poor rate and may have appointed its own petty constable. The origins of townships are unclear though most are of undoubted antiquity. When ecclesiastical parishes developed in the late Saxon and early medieval periods large numbers of townships were incorporated within the new boundaries. In the parish of Halifax in Yorkshire, for example, there were no fewer than twenty-two townships. Township communities were often scattered among neighbouring farmsteads and HAMLETS and could be administered corporately by a township assembly. Former townships may often be identified by Old English *-vill* and *-tun* place-name elements.
See also CHURCHWARDENS

TRACERS *see* STAINED GLASS

TRACERY A decorative interlaced pattern, especially ornamental stone open-work at the head of a window (*see* MEDIEVAL ARCHITECTURE *and* WINDOWS).

TRACT (i) A chant recited or sung during Lent instead of the Alleluia at Mass. (ii) A pamphlet or leaflet with a political, religious or moral purpose.

TRACTARIANISM *see* OXFORD MOVEMENT

TRADITION OF THE INSTRUMENTS *see* ORDINATION

TRANSCRIPT A duplicate of entries in parish REGISTERS furnished annually to a bishop or archdeacon by churchwardens.

TRANSCRIPTION The copying of a text into one's own handwriting. An accurate transcription would include the spelling and punctuation of the original and an indication of the places where an abbreviated form has been extended.

TRANSENNA A wall of marble pierced with holes in a decorative pattern.

TRANSEPT The transverse portion of a cruciform church, usually referred to as the north and south transept with the CROSSING between. Generally very much larger than a PORTICUS which, unlike a transept, was separated from the main body of a church and entered by means of a doorway.
See also MEDIEVAL ARCHITECTURE

TRANSFIGURATION, THE The appearance of Christ in glory, a vision witnessed by Peter, James and John and described by the Evangelists as a historical event (*see* Matthew 17: 1–13, Mark 9: 2–13 and Luke 9: 28–36). The Feast of the Transfiguration is observed on 6 August.
See also FEAST DAYS (FIXED AND MOVABLE)

TRANSLATION (i) Transferring a bishop from one see to another. Prior to the Reformation, this could only be achieved with the authority of the Pope. (ii) The removal of a saint's body or relics to a different place from that in which it originally came to rest.

TRANSOM A horizontal bar of stone or wood across a panel or the opening of a window.
See also GLAZING BARS, MULLION *and* WINDOWS

'TREACLE BIBLE' *see* BIBLES

TREE OF JESSE *see* JESSE WINDOW

TREE OF LIFE A decorative motif consisting of a stylised representation of 'the tree of life . . . in the midst of the garden' (Genesis 2: 9). In the Western Church it is a symbol of Salvation and is found, for example, in medieval WALL PAINTINGS. It can also be naturalistic in form and as such was widely depicted in Eastern art as a symbol of life and knowledge long before the time of Christ.
See also CHRISTIAN SYMBOLS

TREES *see* CHURCHYARDS, TREE OF LIFE *and* YEW TREES

TREFOIL A figure having three radiating stylised 'petals' found both as an architectural motif and an heraldic device (*see* FOILS).

TRELLIS *see* DECORATIVE MOTIFS

TRENDAL A circular candle-holder suspended before a ROOD.

TRENDEL Trendel in street names, and evident in place-names such as Trentishoe in Devon and Trull in Somerset, is derived from the Old English word meaning 'circle' and may be indicative of a former circular churchyard (*see* CHURCHYARDS).

TRENTAL A set of thirty Requiem Masses said for the repose of a soul either on a single day or successive days (*see* BURIALS *and* CHANTRY).

TRIBUNE *see* GALLERIES *and* TRIFORIUM

TRICK *see* COLOURS (HERALDIC)

TRIERS, THE Commissioners, appointed under a Commonwealth act of 1654, to approve preachers and lecturers prior to their admission to benefices.

TRIFORIUM The naves of large medieval churches usually consist of three storeys: an ARCADE of pillars separating the NAVE from the AISLES, a triforium or tribune, and a CLERESTORY which forms an upper level above the aisle roofs. Many writers erroneously refer to the triforium and tribune as though they are synonymous.

The *triforium* is an arcaded wall passage or area of blind arcading below the clerestory and above the arcade (*for* illustration *see* BAY).

The *tribune* is an arcaded gallery which extends above the stone vault of an aisle and is generally found, in place of the triforium, in larger churches where the nave was constructed before the end of the thirteenth century.

In most small churches, and in some larger ones of late-Gothic date, this middle level is omitted.
See also GALLERIES *and* MEDIEVAL ARCHITECTURE

TRIGLYPH An ornament in a frieze of the Doric order (*see* CLASSICAL ORDER) consisting of a fluted tablet. Each vertical flute or channel is a *glyph* and a panel with only two glyphs is a *diglyph*. In a frieze, triglyphs alternate with METOPES.

TRINITY, THE HOLY The central Christian mystery of the union of three persons (Father, Son and Holy Spirit) in one Godhead (*see* Matthew 28: 19, 1 Peter 1: 2, and 2 Corinthians 13: 14). In the Western Church it is held that the Holy Spirit proceeds equally from the Father and from the Son and the Trinity is therefore symbolised by a triangle.
See also CHRISTIAN SYMBOLS

TRINITY SUNDAY The first Sunday after Whitsun (Pentecost) observed as a celebration of the Triune Majesty of God (*see* TRINITY, THE HOLY). In the Western Church, the celebration dates from 1334. The *Book of Common Prayer* followed the fourteenth-century Sarum Missal in calculating Sundays after Trinity and not after Pentecost. Trinity Sunday was formerly a much more important date in the church than it is now. Traditionally, it marked the start of 'haysel', the hay harvest, and was often a day of procession, perambulations and summer fairs. *See also* FEAST DAYS (FIXED AND MOVABLE) and PERAMBULATION

TRIODION *see* YEAR, LITURGICAL

TRIPLE CANDLESTICK Until 1955, a triple candlestick was used in the Paschal Vigil Service (*see* PASCHALTIDE) to hold the candles which were lit successively during the procession to the altar.

TRIPTYCH A set of three painted and gilded panels forming an ALTARPIECE. Triptychs originated in the portable altars of the medieval nobility and may be free-standing or placed against a wall. The panels are hinged so that the outer leaves protect the centre when closed or support it when splayed. Like the DIPTYCH (which has two panels), a triptych usually depicts religious themes, though some also record genealogical and heraldic information.

One of the earliest surviving tryptichs is a remarkable fifteenth-century depiction of five of the miracles of Christ, painted on oak panels in the chapel of the Almshouse of St. John the Baptist and St. John the Evangelist in Sherborne, Dorset. Described as of the school of Van der Weyden its origin is unknown – it may be Dutch, French or even Italian, and was probably given to the brethren of the Alms House at the time of its foundation in 1437 (*see* ALMSHOUSES).

The St. John triptych at Lydiard Tregoze in Wiltshire was erected in *c.* 1615 for Sir John St. John (d. 1594) by his son, also Sir John, Bart. The reverse sides of the panels are painted with genealogical trees and the arms associated with each generation of the family. When the panels are opened, they reveal paintings of Sir John and his wife kneeling on a sarcophagus and flanked by their daughters and their son and daughter-in-law.

The unusually high (3.6 metres or 11 feet) Cornwall triptych on the north wall of Burford church in Shropshire was painted by Melchior Salabuss in 1588, the year of the Spanish Armada. On the doors are the twelve Apostles, the four Evangelists scribbling away at their books, while the inside panels are richly emblazoned with the family's heraldry. On the central panel is a tall painting of Richard Cornewall (d. 1568), his wife Janet and their son Edmund (in full armour). Edmund appears a second time – as a naked and shrouded figure, 2.2 metres in length (over 7 feet) – within an enclosed predella.

The Dwnn triptych, now at the National Gallery in

London, depicts the figures of Sir John Dwnn of Kidwelly (d. 1503) and his wife kneeling before the Virgin and Child. Commissioned from the Flemish artist Hans Memlinc (d. 1494) it is believed to be the earliest real likeness of Welsh people to have survived. Interestingly, both Sir John and his wife wear Yorkist collars of suns and white roses.

TRIVIUM *see* QUADRIVIUM

TROMPE L'OEIL Of a statue, painting, moulding etc. designed to encourage the spectator in the belief that the objects represented are real.

TROPHY A sculptured assemblage of arms and armour, used as a memorial of military victory.

TRUMEAU A slender PIER dividing a large doorway.

TRUNCHEONS (CONSTABLES') *see* CHURCH AND COMMUNITY

TRUSS (i) A framework of timbers supporting a roof. (ii) A cluster of artificial flowers or fruit.

TRUSTEES (CHURCH) Church trustees administered land or bequests belonging to a parish church. The responsibility for the church fabric or the construction of new churches was not always clearly defined in trust deeds and was often a cause for disputation between trustees and vestries (*see* VESTRY). Church trustees' records are usually deposited with county record offices though some remain with parochial church councils or (civil) parish councils.

TUDOR ARCH *see* ARCH

TUDOR ORNAMENT *see* DECORATIVE MOTIFS

TUDOR ROSE A stylised five-lobed figure of a rose which combined, in a variety of forms, the red and white rose BADGES of York and Lancaster.

Historically, the red rose has come to represent the concept of parliamentary sanction by which Henry VII acceded to the English throne. But in order that his descendants should enjoy an inalienable right of succession, he married Elizabeth of York – the heiress of the white rose. The rival roses were similarly combined in the beautiful Tudor Rose which was to become the universal symbol of the Tudor dynasty and of the new administration.
See also DECORATIVE MOTIFS

TUFA Porous rock, a type of limestone formed of lime deposited by water round lumps of vegetable matter, usually in the vicinity of mineral springs. The almost unaltered Norman church (1130) at Moccas in Herefordshire is built entirely of tufa.

TUNICLE *see* VESTMENTS

TUNNELS AND PASSAGES One of the most frequently recounted local tales is of a secret tunnel which is supposed to have been constructed as a means of escape from a church or monastery for recalcitrant priests and monks or for outlaws whose rights of sanctuary were threatened. These passages are often said to extend over the most amazing distances and beneath the most unlikely obstacles – even mountains and estuaries. If so, they would have taken decades to build and would have required such a massive investment of money and labour that they could hardly have remained 'secret' for long. In fact, the many tunnels and passages which could have been used for these purposes are comparatively short and are invariably stone-built DRAINS and sewers which were of sufficient diameter to be regularly cleaned and repaired.

TUNNEL VAULT *see* VAULTING

TURNPIKE STAIR *see* STAIRCASES *and* VICE

TUSCAN *see* CLASSICAL ORDER

TWELFTH NIGHT Either the evening before EPIPHANY (the twelfth day after CHRISTMAS) or, more recently, the evening of Epiphany itself (6 January). Traditionally Twelfth-Night marks the end of Christmas festivities, a time of merry-making when 'twelfth cakes' are eaten and Christmas decorations taken down.

TWELVE APOSTLES, THE *see* APOSTLES *and* CHRISTIAN SYMBOLS

TWELVE ARTICLES The charter of the Peasants' Revolt, adopted in 1525. The peasants' demands included the right to appoint their own pastors and control over TITHES.

TWELVE DAYS OF CHRISTMAS *see* CHRISTMAS

TWENTIETH-CENTURY CHURCHES Of the 16,000 parish churches in England more than half have been built since the seventeenth century and the majority of these are from the last or the present centuries (*see* NINETEENTH-CENTURY ARCHITECTURE).

ARCHITECTURAL TRANSITION

It was Sir Ninian Comper (1864–1960) who succeeded in refining the Gothic Revival of the nineteenth century and carrying it into the twentieth, notably in the detail of his interiors. A pupil of the architect G.F. Bodley (1827–1907), he acquired considerable expertise in a number of related disciplines, including stained glass which he studied under Kempe (*see* STAINED GLASS). Said by John Betjeman to be 'completely medieval minded . . . a great individualist', Comper's work was, in fact, a blend of Classical and Gothic. Of his restoration (1903) of St. Cyprian's church in Baker Street, London, Comper said 'The whole church has become a lantern, and the altar is the flame within it.' In 1950, the Bishop of London wrote of Comper's 'amazing versatility' which restored life to the great tradition of ecclesiastical architecture (*see* ALTARS). 'If he designed an altar frontal he knew exactly how every stitch of the embroidery should go.' But his work is not universally admired: the interior refurbishing of the parish church at Wimborne St. Giles in Dorset, for example, is described by Pevsner as 'Comper at his most wilful', wonderful or ghastly according to taste.

Comper's was not the only influence at work in the early twentieth century. E.S. Prior's massive and original church at Roker Park, Durham (1907), with its transverse arches and elementary tracery, is so simple that it might have been designed for construction in concrete rather than expensive local stone. At Great Warley in Essex, the modest roughcast exterior of Charles Harrison Townsend's church (1904) reflects a contemporary interest in vernacular architecture and conceals a tunnel-vaulted, aisleless nave and a dazzling display of Art Nouveau decoration by Sir William Reynolds Stephens.

Historicism persisted in the 'correct' English Gothic of Temple Moore: in his great brick church of St. Margaret at Leeds in Yorkshire (1908), for example. At Mile Cross, Norwich, the pale purple exterior of St. Catherine's church, designed in 1935 by A.D. Caroë and A.P. Robinson, is evocative of the English Romanesque (*see* MEDIEVAL ARCHITECTURE) while at Bournville in Birmingham the simple Byzantine church of St. Francis of Assisi has a beautifully cool, white-plastered nave, aisles and clerestory, an airy apsidal chancel and a covered 'cloister' linking church, vestry and church hall on three sides of an open quadrangle.

Described by Pevsner as 'a milestone in the history of modern church architecture', the parish church of St. Nicholas at Burnage, Manchester was designed by the firm of Welch, Cachemaille-Day and Lander in 1932. Built in yellow-grey Lincolnshire brick it has a long, low porch beside an apsidal chancel, linked to a taller baptistry and short tower. The interior is stunning, with a prominent high altar and a chapel raised on a platform at the east end. At nearby Northenden the church of St. Michael (by the same architects) is similarly impressive, as is the functional yet essentially devotional church of the Ascension at Hulme which replaced a number of Victorian churches in a heavily populated area of Manchester.

As the century wore on, architects became increasingly preoccupied with materials, rationalisation of form and structural experimentation. Interdenominational and 'community' buildings made increasing use of prefabrication and many parish churches built since 1945 seem to declare their contemporaneity both in design and furnishings. Examples include St. George's, Farnham Royal in Buckinghamshire (by H. Braddock and D. Martin-Smith), St. Paul's at Bow Common, Stepney in London (R. Maguire and K. Murray) and St. Katherine's at Woodthorpe in Yorkshire (Sir Basil Spence).

On a much larger scale, both Sir Edward Maufe's Guildford Cathedral (1961) and Sir Giles Gilbert Scott's unfinished Anglican cathedral at Liverpool are cruciform churches in the medieval monastic tradition; while at Coventry Cathedral (1962), Sir Basil Spence's nave arcade and vault, canopied choir stalls and lady chapel are twentieth-century interpretations of late Gothic themes.

Perhaps the most innovative ecclesiastical building (other than a converted semi-detached house on a seventies housing estate at Gloucester) is the Roman Catholic Metropolitan Cathedral of Christ the King at Liverpool, designed by Sir Frederick Gibberd and consecrated in 1967. The spatial handling of the interior, with its central altar and BALDACCHINO, and the use of both natural and artificial lighting, create a spiritual quality reminiscent of the great medieval cathedrals. The exterior is a circular, buttressed cone – 'like an immense marquee with a glass lantern and a metal crown above' (Yarwood *). And yet even this fine building seems somehow dated and impermanent.

Churches are still being built and many of them are both innovative and imaginative: St. Paul's at Harringay, London, for example (Peter Inskip and Peter Jenkins, 1994), which in simple planes and volumes of brick, steel and reconstituted stone, captures the idea of religious contemplation. It has the elemental qualities of a Greek temple or a cistercian abbey and the proportion and light of its interior 'conspire to quieten and elevate the rowdiest and most worldly spirit' (Jonathan Glancey).

All Saints, Taunton in Somerset.

Inevitably, the architecture of St. Paul's is not to everyone's taste but there can be no denying that it is a powerful and moving building or that it attracts worshippers to its services.

THE CHURCH OF ENGLAND

Future historians will be able to identify divergent elements in the Anglican Church at the end of the twentieth century. They will note a return to the medieval concept of the church as a community centre; the diminution of 'anachronistic' ritual and 'irrelevant' tradition; the introduction of a new liturgy (the banal *Alternative Service Book* of 1980); the ordination of women and the creation of team ministries and group parishes. They will note a rapid degeneration in the relationship of Church and State, tentative proposals for the disestablishment of the Church of England, a continuing decline in attendances (in 1992 just 2.3 per cent of the population attended a Sunday service) and interminable conflict between the traditional and progressive wings of the Church – an age of Flying Bishops, gyrating, singalong parsons and the 'outing' of homosexual priests.

There will be a plethora of documentary evidence available: from parochial church council minutes and the transcripts of synodical debates to the five-yearly reports of diocesan surveyors and architects required by the Inspection of Churches Measure of 1953. And there will be the churches themselves, many of which will have been remodelled to meet the requirements of the new liturgy: the lectern, pulpit and stalls dispensed with, pews replaced by stacking chairs to allow for 'multiple use' and the communion table moved forward into the congregation.

In his book *God With Us* (1993) the Revd. Anthony Freeman wrote 'There is nothing out there or, if there is, we can have no knowledge of it.' In a sermon he said 'The newspapers say I am an atheist. That is nonsense . . . I believe in God. God has no external existence but was a creation of the human heart and mind, a sum total of all that was good in the world.' On 31 July, 1994 the Revd. Freeman became the first parish priest this century to be sacked for his theological views. *Aqua et igni interdictus* – for proposing a definition of faith which might have rejuvenated the English Church.

REDUNDANT CHURCHES

Despite a growing popular interest in ancient buildings, demographic changes are depriving many parishes of funds for repairs. Indeed, some sections of the Church argue that money should be diverted from the maintenance of church buildings to other causes. Inevitably, it is the remote country churches and those in depopulated town centres which are under threat. The financial crisis visited upon the Church Commissioners in 1994 led to proposals for the closure of one-third of London's churches, including several of Wren's masterpieces. Every day, churches are declared redundant, mothballed or converted to workshops, recording studios, 'tele-cottages' or exclusive residential accommodation for families with a taste for the ecclesiastical.

Those churches which are included in the Department of the Environment's *Statutory Lists of Buildings of Special Architectural or Historic Interest* are exempt from the normal listed building controls so long as they remain in use for ecclesiastical purposes. But they are not exempt from local authority planning controls and are subject to the jurisdiction of the diocesan Advisory Committees for the Care of Churches (*see* FACULTY). If an advisory committee recommends demolition (or the disposal of an object of artistic or historic merit) then a diocesan chancellor is obliged to convene a CONSISTORY COURT (the equivalent of a public inquiry) at which objectors may appear and give evidence.

The *Pastoral Measure* (1968, amended 1983) and the *Redundant Churches Act* (1969) set out the procedure to be adopted once a church is no longer required for public worship. It is no longer possible for a diocesan chancellor simply to issue a faculty for the demolition of a church except in cases where a new church is to be built on the same site or closure is required under the dangerous structure provisions of the Public Health Acts. In all cases a chancellor is obliged to seek the advice of the Council for the Care of Churches and his Diocesan Advisory Committee.

The first step is the preparation of a Pastoral Scheme in which a church is declared redundant and an amalgamation of parishes or livings is recommended. This is accompanied by a report from the Council for the Care of Churches which assesses the architectural quality and historic significance of the church, its contents and curtilage. The local planning authority is then invited to comment on the proposal, though it cannot prevent it. Once the scheme has been approved by the Privy Council there are three courses of action available to the Church Commissioners following consultation with the Advisory Board for Redundant Churches. If the preservation of a church and its furnishings is considered desirable, and any alternative use would be inappropriate, then it is likely to be vested in the Churches Conservation Trust (formerly the Redundant Churches Fund), a body established under the Pastoral Measure and funded by the Church and State. If the Board considers that a church is of no architectural merit, or is beyond repair, it may agree to demolition – even though the building may be listed. Otherwise, churches which are vested in the Fund remain consecrated buildings and may be used for occasional services.

The majority of churches fall between these two categories and it is then the responsibility of the diocesan authorities to investigate alternative uses for the building. This will require planning permission for change of use and, where appropriate, listed building consent. Quite often, a churchyard will continue in use for burials and this can reduce considerably the chances of finding a suitable alternative use for the church. If, after three years, no alternative use has been established, the Church Commissioners may either vest the church in the Churches Conservation Trust or authorise demol-ition, even if the building is listed.

From the implementation of the Pastoral Measure in 1969 until the end of 1991, a total of 1317 Anglican churches were declared redundant. Of these 286 have been preserved, 302 have been demolished and 729 adapted for other purposes. During the same period, 430 new churches were consecrated in England.

For the addresses of organisations referred to in the text *and* for the Charities Aid Foundation (which publishes the *Directory of Grant-Making Trusts*) *see* APPENDIX II.

Further reading:
Yarwood, D., *Encyclopaedia of Architecture*, London, 1985 *

'TYBURN TICKET' A certificate of exemption from parochial office issued as a reward for the capture and successful prosecution of a felon.

TYGER *see* BEASTS (HERALDIC)

TYMPANUM (i) The space enclosed within a PEDIMENT or between a lintel and the arch above. The tympanum above the main entrance to a church is often ornately carved. (ii) Often the space between the top of a ROOD LOFT and the chancel arch (or the underside of the roof if there was no arch) was filled with a lath and plaster partition also known as a tympanum. Originally, this would have been painted,

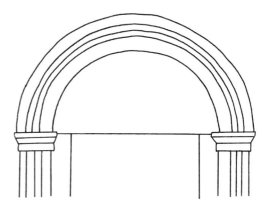

usually with a depiction of the Last Judge-ment (*see* WALL PAINTINGS), but after the Reformation this was normally painted over with biblical texts and the royal arms. Sadly, many of these tympana were removed during Victorian restorations for they were then believed to be post-medieval.
See also PORCHES and MEDIEVAL ARCHITECTURE

TYPES AND ANTITYPES In Christian art, incidents in the Old Testament (*types*) are often shown to foreshadow corresponding incidents in the New Testament (*antitypes*). For example, Jonah was confined for three days within the body of a whale just as Christ's body was confined for three days within a tomb. Jonah's escape from the whale may therefore be represented as a type of the Resurrection.

U

ULTIMOGENITURE *see* PRIMOGENITURE

UMBRACULUM *see* BALDACCHINO

UNCIAL In handwriting, letters having the large, rounded forms used in Latin and Greek manuscripts. Unlike cursive scripts, uncial letters were not joined together. The term is also applied to capital and other large letters in documents dating from the fifth to the eighth centuries.

UNCTION Anointing with oil at BAPTISM and CONFIRMATION and at the coronation of a monarch (*see* CHRISM). The word is most often applied to the Sacrament of Unction of the Sick, known as *Extreme Unction*, which in the Western Church was commonly postponed until the approach of death. In the Church of England a form of unction was included in the Order for the Visitation of the Sick in the 1549 *Book of Common Prayer* but was omitted in 1552. A 'Form of Unction and the Laying on of Hands' was approved for provisional use in 1935.

UNDERCROFT *see* CRYPT

UNDULATE BAND A continuous motif of flowers, fruit or foliage, with an undulating stem running through the design.
See also VERTEBRATE BAND

UNICORN *see* BEASTS (HERALDIC)

UNIFORMITY, ACTS OF (1549, 1552, 1559, 1662)
The 1549 Act required the exclusive use of the first *Book of Common Prayer* for all public services (*see* COMMON PRAYER, BOOK OF) and imposed penalties on the holders of benefices who failed to comply.
The 1552 Act ordered the use of the revised *Book of Common Prayer* and imposed ecclesiastical censure for failing to attend church services and imprisonment for attendance at other forms of worship.
The 1559 Act confirmed the use of the modified 1552 *Book of Common Prayer* and imposed fines for non-attendance at church services.
The 1662 Act ordered the exclusive use of the new *Book of Common Prayer* and required that all ministers should assent publicly to its use. Those ministers who had not been ordained by a bishop were deprived of their livings and consequently some 2,000 Presbyterian ministers refused to conform. The Act has since been modified, most recently by the CHURCH OF ENGLAND (WORSHIP AND DOCTRINE) MEASURE of 1974.
See also FIVE MILE ACT (1665), REFORMATION, THE *and* SEVENTEENTH-CENTURY CHURCH

UNIFORMITY, ACT OF, AMENDMENT ACT (1872)
The Act of Uniformity Amendment Act of 1872, known as the 'Shortened Services Act', provided for the optional use of shortened versions of Morning and Evening Prayer. It was repealed by the CHURCH OF ENGLAND WORSHIP AND DOCTRINE) MEASURE of 1974.

UNION FLAG *see* FLAGS

UNITARIANISM A sect, dating in England from the mid-seventeenth century, which believes in the unipersonality of God and rejects the doctrines of the Trinity and the Divinity of Christ.

UNIVERSITIES The ancient medieval universities of Oxford, Cambridge, St. Andrews, Glasgow and Aberdeen (King's College) were ecclesiastical establishments subject to international papal authority. Admission to the early universities was not a perquisite of the medieval establishment, indeed a university education was one of the few means by which the sons of commoners, or even of aspiring peasants, could rise to eminence. Most students were aged between 15 and 19 and few teachers were over 30. Today's gowns and hoods originated in the academic dress of the medieval universities where students were considered to be clerics and had their heads shaved in the style of a monk (*see* TONSURE). Oxford, the earliest university, is first mentioned in 1184 though it is likely that its foundation dates from the period 1164–69 when access to the university in Paris was disrupted during Henry II's conflict with Becket. It was enlarged by the FRIARS in the 1220s (with the support of Parisian students), and the first colleges (Balliol, Merton and University) were founded in the second half of the century (*see* CHANTRY COLLEGES). The curriculum was based on the *Quadrivium* (arithmetic, geometry, astronomy and music) which, together with the lesser *Trivium* (rhetoric, grammar and logic), formed the '*seven liberal arts*', all of which were taught in Latin. Medieval scholastic life was dominated by three apparently contradictory features: academic commitment and creativity, bureaucratic repression and sporadic lawlessness. The intellectual achievement of such Oxford scholars as Robert Grosseteste (b.*c*. 1175), Roger Bacon (1214–92) and John Wycliffe (*c*. 1330–84) was considerable, but all five universities earned a certain notoriety for petty regulation and were often viciously repressive. In the early fifteenth century a master of St. Andrews, who rejoiced in the office of Inquisitor of Heretical Depravity, ordered one of his scholars to be burned alive for his heretical views. At Aberdeen, women were not admitted to the university precincts, the students themselves were not permitted to leave without permission and all conversation had to be conducted in Latin. At Cambridge, students were forbidden from visiting the town's ale houses (and were so until 1940) and the university's regulations were enforced by Proctors' constables who, in the Middle Ages, were armed with pikes (*halberds*) which still feature in university ceremonial. It is hardly surprising that such repressive measures provoked an excessive response from the students. In 1445, Godstow Nunnery near Oxford was apparently a favourite student brothel and rioting, usually between 'town and gown', was endemic throughout the Middle Ages.

The growth of secular education following the Reformation was reflected, briefly, in the creation of several new colleges at Oxford and Cambridge and in Scotland, however the ancient English universities were generally perceived as Anglican institutions, especially following the Acts of Uniformity in 1559 and 1662, and consequently declined in popularity. Teaching was stereotyped and traditional and collegiate life more social than academic. Several medical colleges were established in London and a number of 'dissenting academies', but serious scholars turned to the European and Scottish universities, which benefited from the English malaise, and to the new university foundation of Trinity College in Dublin (1591). Despite a significant increase in population during the late sixteenth and early seventeenth centuries, there were only seven major universities in the British Isles: four in Scotland, two in England and one in Ireland.

The industrial and economic prosperity of late Victorian and Edwardian Britain, and her growing status as an international power, were reflected in the founding of a large number of new universities and colleges, particularly at the turn of the century when many 'red brick' universities were established in industrial cities such as Manchester (1895), Birmingham (1900), Leeds (1904) and Sheffield (1905).
See also OXFORD MOVEMENT *and* SCHOOLS

UPPING STOCKS As the name suggests upping stocks were used for mounting a horse and until recently were one of the most common reminders of the equestrian age and also one of the most vulnerable. They were usually positioned so that a rider could mount or dismount directly from a garden gate or churchyard without stepping into the mire of the road. A typical upping stock consists of a low square brick or stone platform with a flight of three or four steps at one side. Many were adapted and enlarged in the present century to facilitate the loading of milk churns onto the backs of lorries before the introduction of tankers. Although still numerous, countless upping stocks have been destroyed, regardless of their historical associations and quite often in contravention of regulations relating to the conservation of adjacent listed buildings of which, technically, they formed a part. It is often extremely difficult to date upping stocks: many were built during the eighteenth and nineteenth centuries and are contemporary with the buildings they served. Others may be of considerable antiquity but few, including many of medieval and Tudor origin, are listed or specifically protected. Upping stocks are also known as horse-blocks, horse-steps, horse-stones, mounting-blocks and mounting-stones.

URIEL *see* CHRISTIAN SYMBOLS

URN (i) A vase, usually with a rounded body and a foot, used especially as a receptacle for the ashes of the dead. (ii) A monumental imitation of a burial-urn.

USES Local modifications of the Roman rite (*see* LITURGY) most of which were abolished by the Council of Trent (1545–63). In England, the Use of Sarum (also the Sarum Rite or Use of Salisbury), and the fourteenth-century revision known as the New Use of Sarum, was used in many dioceses and provided material for the first *Book of Common Prayer* of 1549.
See also SARUM, USE OF

V

VAIR *see* COLOURS (HERALDIC)

VALENTINE *see* ST. VALENTINE'S DAY

VALLEY ROOF *see* ROOFS

VALOR ECCLESIASTICUS Popularly known as the 'King's Books', the *Valor Ecclesiasticus* was the official inventory of monastic and ecclesiastical properties compiled in 1534–5 as a consequence of Henry VIII's appropriation of ecclesiastical revenues (*see* DISSOLUTION OF THE MONASTERIES). *See also* REFORMATION, THE

VAMBRACE *see* ARMOUR

VAMPING HORN *see* MUSICAL INSTRUMENTS

VAULT An arched roof (*see* VAULTING *and* VAULTS (BURIAL)).

VAULTING Vaulting is the arched interior framework of a roof, usually constructed of stone or brick though some eighteenth- and nineteenth-century vaults were built in wood or plaster. Vaulted ceilings are a characteristic of MEDIEVAL ARCHITECTURE and of the nineteenth-century Gothic Revival and are normally only found in cathedrals, major churches and in the smaller components of parish churches such as a chapel or porch.

The shape of the vault follows the geometry of the ARCH and the simplest vault is, therefore, that which accompanies the semicircular arch. This is known as the *barrel vault* (also *tunnel vault* and *wagon vault*) and is commonly found in later Romanesque buildings and is so named because of its semicircular section and barrel-like appearance. Where two barrel vaults intersect at right angles they form a *groined* or *cross vault*. Because of the enormous thrust exerted on supporting walls, the barrel vault was found to be singularly unsuited to wide spans, particularly in the monastic churches of western Europe, the components of which (nave, choir, transept and aisles) were invariably of different heights and widths and could not be accommodated within a structure which was constrained by the geometry of the semicircular arch. Furthermore, the interior roofs of many early abbey churches were constructed of timber and were

a considerable fire hazard. Consequently, it was the need for stone vaulting, combined with the structural limitations of the round arch, which led to the development in the early medieval period of the *ribbed vault* and pointed arch.

Ribs are raised bands of stone or brick which spring from the wall to support and strengthen the vault. The ribbed vault consisted of a quadripartite framework (bisected by diagonal ribs), supported during construction on a temporary timber structure (*centering*). Once the spaces between the ribs (*webs* or *cells*) had been infilled with cut stone pieces the vault became self-supporting and the centering was removed.

Vaults are divided into bays by *transverse arches* and, while bays created by semicircular arches were inevitably square, the diagonals of a ribbed vault were longer than the sides and it was therefore impossible for all the ribs to be semicircular (*see* BAY). This problem was overcome by adopting the pointed arch which originated in the Middle East and, by the twelfth century, had already spread to countries such as Spain and Sicily where there was a strong north African influence. The pointed arch was ideally suited to vaulting of various heights and spans and, during the four centuries of the Gothic period, it enabled buildings of increasing complexity and architectural audacity to be constructed throughout western Europe.

The early quadripartite ribbed vault, which consisted of four compartments within each bay, formed the basis for all future designs. Stone BOSSES were added at the intersection of ribs and these were often heavily carved with gilded and painted motifs. In the fourteenth century intermediate *tierceron ribs* were added which extended from the springing of the vault (the point at which it began to splay upwards) to the *ridge rib* (at the apex of the vault) and from this developed the

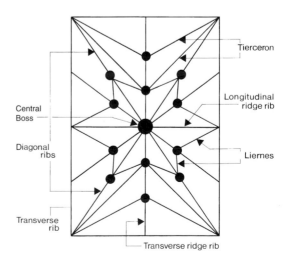

467

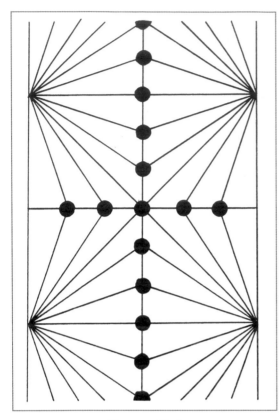

Tierceron Vault

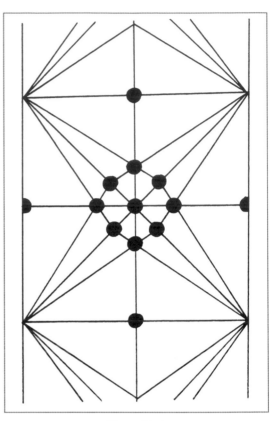

Lierne Vault

lierne vault, in which additional interlocking ribs (*liernes*) were introduced, forming elaborate patterns within the basic structural framework of ribs. A *stellar vault* is one in which the lierne ribs form a star-shaped pattern.

The final Perpendicular phase of the Gothic period is characterised by *fan vaulting* which, as the name suggests, is an ornamental vaulting of inverted half-conoids (cones with concave sides). Each pair of half-conoids just meet at the centres of their curves, all the ribs are equidistant from each other and in most cases all have the same curvature. Each section of a fan vault was carved from a stone slab and the joints between the blocks may often be seen passing across the purely decorative tracery of the ribs. Fan vaulting was an English innovation, the earliest known example being in the chantry chapel of Edward, Lord Despenser at Tewkesbury Abbey in Gloucestershire. Despenser died in 1375 and it is likely that the same mason was responsible for the magnificent fan vaulting in the cloister at nearby Gloucester Cathedral which was completed not later than 1412. Fine examples of fan vaults are those at Sherborne Abbey in Dorset (1475–1500) and King's College Chapel, Cambridge (1446–1515) (*see* CHAPELS).

In most great medieval churches, with the exception of those of the more austere monastic orders, vaulting would originally have been ablaze with brilliant colour and gilding. Although beyond the range of normal eyesight, the detail of carving and painting was faultlessly executed and was clearly intended for the greater glorification of God. It is only through the modern camera lens that we are privileged to approach such perfection for the first time.
See also ROOFS (TIMBER)

VAULTS (BURIAL)

Walls and roof were of stone, and at one end was a staircase closed by a great flat stone at the top – that same stone which I had often seen, with a ring in it, in the floor of the church above. All round the sides were stone shelves, with divisions between them like great bookcases, but instead of books there were the coffins of the Mohunes . . . .

J. Meade Falkner, *Moonfleet*

THE MIDDLE AGES
Burial vaults were the prerogative of the wealthy and were usually constructed in anticipation of

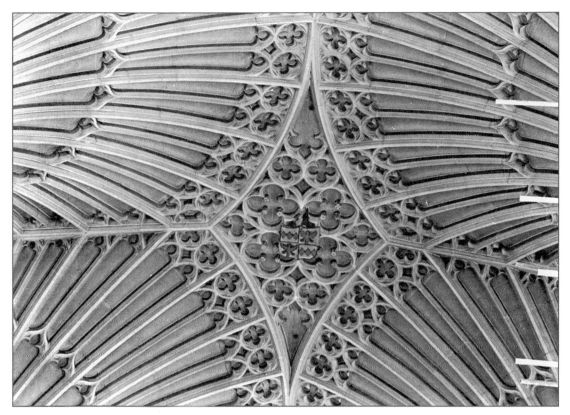

Fan vaulting at Holy Trinity, Bradford-on-Avon, Wiltshire.

death, not in response to it. It was the practice of the medieval nobility to make provision for their interment, often in a monastic or collegiate church the status of which reflected their own rank in society and where their MONUMENTS would be admired *in perpetuity*. Others were buried in their parish churches, the chancel being the most favoured position – close to the high altar where the tomb could be seen by the clergy, acolytes and worshippers during the Mass, thereby perpetuating feudal superiority even beyond the grave. Not all burial vaults were occupied by those who had built them. In *c.* 1540 Edmund Harman, one of Henry VIII's privy councillors, erected a monument at Burford in Oxfordshire 'to the Christian memory of himself and his only and most faithful wife Agnes and of the sixteen children whom, by God's mercy, she bore him'. But Edmund Harman and his wife subsequently moved to nearby Taynton where they died and were buried, Agnes in 1576 and Edmund in 1577. The family vault at Burford remained unoccupied.

POST-REFORMATION

From the third quarter of the sixteenth century increasing numbers of noble and gentry families made provision for intramural burial within their parish churches. In part this was the result of a more liberal ecclesiastical regime but it was also a consequence of the DISSOLUTION OF THE MONASTERIES. In the Middle Ages there had been a hierarchy of monastic and collegiate churches in which the great magnatial families of England had chosen to be buried. The Dissolution deprived them of this privilege. Furthermore, the suppression of the chantries (*see* CHANTRY) made intramural burial possible for those gentry families which hitherto had been unable to afford the substantial endowments necessary to maintain an altar and priest. Despite their parochial status many estate churches became private mausoleums for landowners and their families and, if space did not permit the opening of a new vault, a parish church might acquire a chapel or aisle, paid for by the families who wished to be interred therein.

Most of these early vaults were comparatively small: no more than 4.5 metres (15 feet) from north to south and 2.4 metres (8 feet) east to west. They were usually constructed with limewashed or rendered stone or brick walls and a gently curving roof and (unlike later vaults) had neither shelves nor recesses (*loculi*), the coffins being stacked on the brick or stone floor, each separated from the one beneath by wooden bearers.

INTRAMURAL BURIALS

Between the late seventeenth and early nineteenth centuries, city and town churches were heavily used by the middle class for intramural burial (*see* BURIALS). In part this was a result of overcrowded CHURCHYARDS but it was also a reaction to the increasing popularity of headstones among the lower classes. The middle class needed to reassert its superiority in death as in life and intramural burial was considered to be synonymous with social superiority. But space within the churches was at a premium. At Bristol, for example, no fewer than 107 private chambers were revealed beneath the former church of St. Augustine during excavations in 1983–4.

Chambers such as these are not vaults. A true vault is normally of not less than 1.74 metres in height (68 inches) and is capable of housing at least two coffins side by side. Furthermore, the inscriptions on mural monuments of the period may be misleading: 'In a Vault near this place . . .' may in fact refer, not to a vault, but to a brick-lined grave capped with a ledger stone (*see* INCISED SLABS).

FAMILY VAULTS

As a dynastic burial chamber, the family vault was a short-lived phenomenon, popular from the first quarter of the seventeenth century to the second quarter of the eighteenth, though there are later examples. It was unusual for a family to own more than one vault within a church; additional space was achieved by the judicious clearance of decayed coffins or by excavating additional chambers, as at the Harvey vault at Hempstead, Essex. A FACULTY was required in order to construct a vault, as was the approval of the vicar and churchwardens, and Diocesan records often contain architectural drawings and other documentary material relating to these.

There is no strict pattern of construction. The stone or brick walls and loculi may be limewashed or rendered, drainage and ventilation may have been provided and some vaults have a charnel-pit or cistern in which decayed remains were deposited (*see also* OSSUARIES).

MEMORIALS

Not all intramural burials were marked with a memorial: at Woodford in Essex, for example, where 'Sir Thomas Rowe, Lord of Mannour, was Buried in the upper end of the Chancell in the middle, his head lying part of hit vnder the Communion Table, just soo far as against the Brasse that is on Mrs. Mabs stone, and his feet lying against ye wall at the East end of the Chancell the eighth day of November, 1644' (from the church register). On the other hand, many families provided detailed information concerning access to their vaults. Thomas Raynor,

for example, who in 1618 constructed a new vault at Thaxted in Essex also erected an inscribed marker recording both the position of the entrance and the fact that 'bricks laid on end' in the floor delineated the extent of the chamber beneath. He also informed the reader that he had taken the opportunity of gathering in one place all the known remains of his ancestors from elsewhere in the church.

ENTRANCES

Steps were sometimes provided, as in the St. John vault at Lydiard Tregoze in Wiltshire, while in the churchyard at South Creake in Norfolk a large ledger stone against the south wall of the church is inscribed in huge letters 'THE MOUTH OF THE VAULT'. This is the entrance to the vault of one Davy Turner who died in 1825, though the chamber was constructed in 1811 to receive the remains of one of his adult children. In the event, all five of Turner's children predeceased their parents and all seven members of the family are buried in the vault.

The cavernous Sackville vault at Withyham in Sussex was remodelled in 1673 and is entered by means of a steep and narrow flight of steps descending from a single wooden door. In the late nineteenth century, a wooden slide with integral iron rollers was constructed down which the heavy, lead-lined coffins could be lowered into the vault. By contrast, the steps of the Poulett vault at Hinton St. George in Somerset are of sufficient width and gradient to allow bearers to descend into the chamber with the coffin on their shoulders. A blue-painted portico, entered from a stone-flagged court in the churchyard, enabled the bearers to compose themselves before making the descent.

Not all vaults are located beneath the church (*see also* MAUSOLEUM). The large and impressive Baring vault at High Beach in Essex was built in 1873 in the north-east corner of the churchyard and is sealed with a canted steel cover secured by padlocks (*see* BODY SNATCHERS). An earlier churchyard vault, erected by the Campbell family in *c*. 1650, abuts the south aisle wall of Barking church in Essex and has accommodation for thirty-eight coffins.

APPROPRIATION

It was not unknown for vaults to be appropriated. The most celebrated case concerned Sir John Boileau who, in 1835, wished to secure a prestigious site for himself and his family beneath the chancel of St. Peter's church at Ketteringham in Norfolk. Having persuaded his friend the bishop to 'turn a blind eye', he proceeded to translate the remains from the Heveningham-Atkyns vault to the churchyard and to appropriate it for his own purposes. But in the following month he received a letter from a Mr. Pemberton of Caxton which began 'I learn this morning with the deepest surprise and indignation, that you have ventured to break open the family vault . . . As one of those coffins contains the remains of my sister-in-law, I lose not a post in writing to request an immediate explanation of this most extraordinary proceeding . . .'. Consequently the coffins were disinterred from the churchyard and returned whence they came – much to the embarrassment of Sir John and his friend the bishop.

The records of Lydiard Tregoze provide an indication of the costs incurred by those who wished to maintain a family vault. Under an agreement executed in June 1645 a payment of £10 in perpetuity was made to the church so that: '. . . the Isle vault in the Church . . . called the new Isle and vault and alsoe the other Isle in the same church then called the old Isle . . . and the vault under the same Isle and all the monuments . . . might be from time to time . . . well and sufficiently repaired and maintained . . . without any charge to the said parish.'

By the close of the seventeenth century many urban churches had so little space remaining for intramural burial that vaults were excavated beneath the pews. Close family friends might be invited to share a vault and on occasions the vaults of extinct families were commandeered. It was also the custom in some city churches for a vault to be reserved for the exclusive use of the incumbent who was thereby able to augment his stipend from the rents and fees charged for burial in his vault. At St. Alphage at Greenwich no fewer than 400 coffins were admitted to Vault 16, the rector's vault, between 1718 and 1810.

COMMUNAL VAULTS

Communal vaults are a feature of several large, urban churches which were built during the eighteenth and nineteenth centuries, despite increasing concern regarding the unhealthy nature of intramural burial. Many of the new churches were raised on plinths which were architecturally dramatic and provided imposing entrances. They also allowed for a semi-subterranean space which was ideally suited to intramural burial. The bays beneath side aisles were usually partitioned for private freehold vaults, the space beneath the chancel being reserved for the incumbent and the remaining areas under the nave and portico (known as 'vestry vaults') designated for public use. The prices charged for interment in these vaults varied according to the location and the space required. In 1838 the burial fees for the church of St. Peter-le-Poor in Broad Street, London ranged from £18 5s 6d for a simple chamber to 100 guineas for a vault 'to contain 4 persons'. Parish churches were not the only places to be provided with such facilities. In the 1820s a communal vault was constructed beneath the chapel of St Thomas's Hospital at Ilford in Essex.

In 1850, the Metropolitan Interments Act forbade further intramural burials within the City of London and this was followed in 1852 by the Metropolitan Burial Act which empowered vestries of any metropolitan parish to establish a parochial cemetery (*see* CEMETERIES). In 1853 the legislation was applied to the rest of England and Wales.

Many vaults continue in use today, for the deposit of coffins and of urns containing cremated remains, providing the requirements of the Public Health Act are complied with.

Further reading:
Litten, J., *The English Way of Death*, London, 1991

VEILS (i) A headdress worn by women at confirmation and marriage. Veils were worn by Roman matrons and from the third century were presented by bishops to consecrated virgins as a symbol of their spiritual marriage with Christ. Consequently, the veil became the most important element of a nun's HABIT – hence 'taking the veil' implied that a woman had obtained admission to a nunnery. Quire nuns, who were required to make a more solemn profession, were vested with a black veil, while lay sisters wore a white one. (ii) Liturgical cloths used for covering various sacred objects. The *chalice veil* is a square silk veil of the appropriate liturgical colour used to cover the communion chalice when not in use (*see* COLOURS, LITURGICAL). The *ciborium* or *pyx veil* is a circular white linen veil beneath which the sacrament is reserved. The *monstrance veil* is of white silk, unlined and with a plain hem, and nearly twice the height of the monstrance (the vessel used for exposing the Eucharistic Host). The *humeral* or *offertory veil* is usually of cream or white silk and is worn by priests when in procession or when carrying the Sacrament (*see* VESTMENTS). A silk tabernacle veil in the liturgical colours is divided at the centre and has a hole through which the finial of the TABERNACLE protrudes. The *aumbry veil*, which may be embroidered, covers the AUMBRY and the *Lenten veil* is used to cover statues during LENT. In the pre-Reformation church, a LENTEN VEIL was used to screen the sanctuary and to cover crucifixes and religious pictures during Passiontide and later throughout Lent (*see* ROOD *and* ROOD BEAM).
See also COMMUNION LINENS *and* PLATE

VELLUM A superior form of PARCHMENT prepared by lime-washing and burnishing the skins of calves, kids or lambs. For the finest work, the skins of unborn or aborted animals were used.

VENEER A thin layer of fine wood glued to the surface of furniture for decorative effect.

VENERABLE (i) The proper address of an archdeacon. (ii) In the medieval Church, a title bestowed on a deceased person during the process of BEATIFICATION. Also used of those whose memory was considered to be worthy of veneration e.g. the Venerable Bede (*c.* 673–735).

VENETIAN WINDOW A window with three openings, the central one arched and wider than the outer ones (*see* WINDOWS).

VENITE Psalm 95, so called from the first word of its Latin version: 'Venite, Exultemus Domino' ('O Come, let us sing unto the Lord . . .'). From the early sixth century the Venite was used in the first office of the day and from the Breviary it passed into Mattins in the *Book of Common Prayer*.

VERGER From the Latin *virga* meaning 'rod', an official responsible for carrying a *verge*, a mace or wand of office, before a dignitary. The term is now commonly applied to the person or persons who (in addition to their ceremonial duties) take care of the interior fabric of a church.

VERNACULAR (i) The language or dialect of an area or of a particular indigenous class or group. (ii) Characteristics, such as building styles and materials, appertaining to a particular locality.

VERNICLE A representation of the head of Christ found, for example, as a motif on church PLATE.

VERSAL LETTER The embellished initial letter of a verse or paragraph of text (*see* MANUSCRIPT ILLUMINATION).

VERSICLES A versicle is a short sentence (e.g. from the Psalms) which is said or sung antiphonally in a Roman or Anglican service, each half of a choir or congregation responding to the other (hence 'responses'). The two 'sides' of a choir are known as CANTORIS and DECANI. The traditional Anglican settings are the ancient PLAINSONG adapted by John Merbecke (1510–85) to the English words at the time of the Reformation. Various Elizabethan composers made 'harmonised' versions of the responses, a form now generally known as Festal Responses (*see* CHURCH MUSIC, ANGLICAN). In the absence of a choir, the responses are recited by the priest and congregation (*see also* PARISH CLERK).
See also ANTIPHON, PRECES *and* STALLS

VERSO The left-hand page of an open book. Also the reverse side of a single leaf.

VERT *see* COLOURS, HERALDIC

VERTEBRATE BAND A continuous motif of flowers, fruit or foliage, with a straight stem running horizontally through the centre of the design.
See also UNDULATE BAND

VESICA PISCIS In Christian art, a *vesica piscis* (literally, 'fish's bladder') is an almond-shaped halo, consisting of two arcs each passing through the

other's centre, enclosing the body of Christ or that of the Blessed Virgin Mary.

VESPERALE (i) A cloth spread over the altar or communion table to protect the white linen altar cloths when not in use. (ii) A liturgical book containing the Psalms etc. used at VESPERS. Those of COMPLINE are usually appended.

VESPERS The Evening Office which took place in the late afternoon between NONE and COMPLINE. It consisted of a hymn, two Psalms, a New Testament canticle, a short lesson, responsary, the Magnificat and prayers. With LAUDS, Vespers is the most important of the Day Offices and is of considerable antiquity. By the fifteenth century it was often attended by devout laity. The service of Evening Prayer in the *Book of Common Prayer* was in part modelled on Vespers with additions from COMPLINE.
See also DIVINE OFFICE *and* VESPERALE

VESSELS *see* BEAKER, CRUETS, EWER, FLAGON, LAVABO, PLATE (CHURCH) *and* VIATICUM

VESTIARIUM A monastic vestry or SACRISTY in which the VESTMENTS and liturgical vessels were secured.

VESTIBULE An ante-chamber or entrance lobby next to the outer door of a church or monastic apartment. There was generally a vestibule to a CHAPTER HOUSE and those which have survived are often of considerable architectural elaboration. The INFIRMARY usually had a vestibule and the head of the night stairs may have been similarly enclosed.

VESTMENTS The dress worn by the clergy when officiating at services. Vestments originated in the secular clothing of second-century Rome and developed into a priestly costume between the fourth and ninth centuries. Use of the principal liturgical vestments was established by the tenth century, only minor changes being introduced thereafter up to the thirteenth century.

The *Eucharistic Vestments* (those worn by the celebrant at the Eucharist) include (in order of robing over the CASSOCK) the *amice*, *alb*, *girdle*, *stole*, *maniple* and *chasuble*. The Eucharistic Vestments fell into disuse after the Reformation even though the 1559 *Book of Common Prayer* ruled that the ornaments of the Church should be those in use '. . . by the authority of Parliament in the second year of the reign of King Edward VI'. Their revival in the nineteenth-century High Church caused considerable controversy (*see* NINETEENTH-CENTURY CHURCH) while their continued use is authorised by the 1969 Canons.

When depicted in monumental brasses (*see* BRASSES, MONUMENTAL), a bishop in Eucharistic Vestments wears, in addition to the foregoing, a *dalmatic*, gloves, sandals, ring and MITRE. He also carries a pastoral staff while an archbishop holds a cross-staff and wears a *pallium* over the chasuble.

Until recently the clergy wore black for non-liturgical purposes, following the usage of the Benedictines and others, as a sign of humility. The most familiar item of everyday clothing is the cassock which, before the eighteenth century, served to identified the clergy rather than the more recent Roman or clerical collar (known colloquially as a '*dog collar*').

ALB
A full-length garment of white linen reaching from the neck to the ankles, with tight-fitting sleeves and secured at the waist by a girdle. Often embroidered *apparels* on the wrists and between the feet. Worn by the celebrant at the Mass.

ALMUCE
A large cape, turned down over the shoulders, lined with fur and with two long pendants at the front. Often depicted in monumental brasses where it may be worn beneath a *cope*.

AMICE
A white linen neck-cloth with *apparel* at one edge.

APPAREL
A decorated panel applied to *albs*, *amices* and *dalmatics*.

BIRETTA
A black, purple, red or white square ridged hat worn according to rank by priests, bishops, cardinals or Pope.

CASSOCK
A full-length gown, buttoned at the front and coloured according to rank (*see* biretta).

CHASUBLE
A circular or oval cape with orphreys and a central opening for the head. The principal vestment of an officiating priest.

COPE
A semi-circular cape fastened with a *morse* and decorated with *orphreys* and a hood. Worn over the *cassock* and *surplice* in (e.g.) processions (*see* COPE CHEST).

DALMATIC
A short, wide-sleeved, open-sided over-tunic decorated with stripes (*clavi*) running from front to back over the shoulders and sometimes with *apparels*. Worn by deacons at the Eucharist and on certain occasions by bishops.

FOLDED CHASUBLE
Formerly worn by deacons and sub-deacons at the High Mass during penitential seasons, a form of *chasuble* gathered and pinned at the front.

GIRDLE
A white or coloured cord with tassels.

HOOD
A flat vestigial hood attached to a cope.

LAPPETS
A pair of ribands (*infulae*) pendant from the back of a MITRE.

MANIPLE
A decorated band worn over the arm, a vestigial napkin and purse combined.

MORSE
A metal or embroidered clasp used to fasten a *cope* across the chest.

ORPHREY
Embroidered bands on *chasubles* and *copes*.

PALLIUM
Originally a woollen vestment worn by archbishops and usually depicted as a narrow, Y-shaped strip, embroidered with crosses and descending over the shoulders and chest (*see* separate entry *and* PALL).

ROCHET
Similar to the *alb* but shorter and either sleeveless or with the sleeves gathered at the wrist.

STOLE
A decorated band of material worn over the left shoulder and under the right arm by a deacon, crossed in front of the body by a priest and uncrossed by a bishop. Usually embroidered at the ends and neck and worn beneath the *chasuble*.

SURPLICE
A white gown with long, flowing sleeves. Worn over the *cassock* and generally substituted for the *alb* (*see* separate entry).

TIPPET
A broad black band worn round the neck and over the *surplice* by Anglican clergy (*see* separate entry).

TUNICLE
Similar to the *dalmatic* but worn by a sub-deacon.

See also CLERGY (CHURCH OF ENGLAND), CROZIER, EMBROIDERY, FORTY-BUTTON MAN, RUFF *and* VEILS

Further reading:
Mayo, J., *The History of Ecclesiastical Dress*, London, 1985

VESTRY (i) A room within or attached to a church, often a former SACRISTY, in which the VESTMENTS are kept and in which the clergy prepare for divine worship. Church PLATE and current REGISTERS are often secured in the vestry. The members of a choir may have their own room which is known as the *choir vestry*.

The monastic vestry (*vestiarium*) contained the aumbries and chests for the storage of vestments which were the responsibility of the SACRIST and his assistant, though in some larger houses there was also an official called a *vesterer* who was charged with the care and maintenance of the vestments. (ii) It was in the vestry that parishioners met to administer the affairs of their parish and consequently the word came to be used for both the body of parishioners and for the meeting of which the INCUMBENT was, by custom, the chairman. An *open vestry* was a general meeting of all the ratepaying householders in a parish while a *select vestry* comprised a smaller number of members who were usually required to own property in order to qualify for co-option.

During the sixteenth and seventeenth centuries the vestry gradually assumed the functions of the manorial court as the basic unit of local government (*see* PARISH). The Local Government Act of 1894 transferred the civil functions of vestries to parish councils or parish meetings. Nevertheless, it is not uncommon for a parish meeting, which has a chairman but no other elected members, to hold its annual meeting in the parish church or, as at Lillington in Dorset, in the church porch.
See also CHURCHWARDENS' ACCOUNTS *and* MINUTES

VESTRY MINUTES *see* ARCHIVES *and* MINUTES

VIATICUM (i) From the Latin meaning 'provision for a journey', the Sacrament administered to those who are about to die in order that they should be strengthened with grace before embarking on their journey into eternity. (ii) Also the receptacle, usually of glass or precious metal, in which the consecrated elements are conveyed (*see* PLATE).

VICAR From the Latin *vicarius* meaning 'substitute' or 'deputy'. In the Middle Ages, many benefices were annexed by corporate bodies such as monastic or collegiate foundations who then received the Great (or Rectorial) Tithes, the Lesser (or Vicarial) Tithes going to a vicar who was appointed by them to administer the parish (*see* RECTOR). Following the Dissolution of the Monasteries, many monastic estates became the impropriated property of laymen (lay rectors) who also acquired the right to nominate vicars (subject to a bishop's approval), together with responsibility for maintaining the chancel and vicarage. TITHES were virtually abolished in 1936 and a vicar is now appointed to all new livings, the designation rector being applicable to the incumbent of a new joint benefice or united parish or on the creation of a team ministry. A vicar exercises precisely the same spiritual authority as a rector.
See also APPROPRIATION *and* CLERGY (CHURCH OF ENGLAND)

VICARAGE Both the residence of a VICAR and his BENEFICE. Vicars and vicarages are worthy of a book in their own right. At Morwenstow vicarage in Cornwall, the Revd. Hawker is reputed to have preached out of doors dressed as a mermaid and to have concluded his sermon with a rendition of the National Anthem. His vicarage has six chimneys, each in the form of a different church tower.
Further reading:
Wilson, A.N., *Church and Clergy*, London, 1992

VICAR CHORAL An adult male singer in a cathedral choir. The term is peculiar to the Anglican Church and both the title and the responsibilities of the office vary from one cathedral to another. At some cathedrals a vicar choral may be described as a lay clerk while at others he may be a lay vicar. The word 'vicar' indicates that the duties are really those of a canon, exercised vicariously. Indeed, at one time, every canon could call upon the services of a vicar choral or minor canon. The office, as it now exists, is one which originated in the Reformation. In the medieval church all these various 'clerks' and 'vicars' were in holy orders.
See also PARISH CLERK

VICAR GENERAL One who deputises for a bishop. In the early Church a bishop's authority could be delegated to an archdeacon but by the end of the thirteenth century the office of Vicar General was established and its duties defined. In the Church of England the office is usually committed to a diocesan Chancellor.

VICAR'S RING The ancient enclosures of a TOWNSHIP which were often tithable to a VICAR for both great and small tithe, while the great tithe of the remainder of the township went to the RECTOR.

VICE A small, turning stair or 'turnpike' within the masonry of a wall or tower (*see* STAIRCASES).

VICTORIA COUNTY HISTORY A series of volumes known collectively as *The Victoria History of the Counties of England* the compilation of which commenced in 1899 and continues today under the direction of the Institute of Historical Research of the University of London. The aim of the project's founders was to research and to record in detail the history of every English county, using original source material. The original intention was that there should be general and topographical volumes for each county, the first describing political, economic, ecclesiastical and social factors, and the second the history of individual parishes arranged in hundreds, wapentakes or wards. But in practice many county series have taken a different form: that for Dorset, for example, includes a volume devoted to *Domesday*. The *Victoria County History* is an invaluable guide to records and source material, though none of the articles of which each volume is composed should be accepted uncritically for there are inconsistencies and some entries have been superseded by more recent research.

Of equal interest is the vast collection of slip references compiled in the late nineteenth century by a team of ladies who combed manorial and parish records in the Public Record Office for information relevant to the *VCH* project. These slips are now held by the Institute of Historical Research and are available to serious researchers.

VICTORINES An order of canons regular founded in 1113 at the former abbey of St. Victor at Paris. Their English houses included Wigmore in Herefordshire and the great abbey of St. Augustine in Bristol which was reconstituted as a cathedral in 1542.

VIGIL A nocturnal act of prayer and devotion, either private or liturgical, often ending with the EUCHARIST. In the early Church, the Easter Vigil lasted throughout the night (*see* PASCHAL CANDLE) while those which preceded Sundays and other festivals normally occupied only the beginning and end of the night. From these observances evolved the offices of VESPERS, MATTINS and LAUDS (mattins was originally called *vigils*). In the Middle Ages, public vigils were subject to abuse and consequently were held before nightfall. Eventually, fast, office and Mass were anticipated and moved to the morning of the preceding day, the whole of which became a '*profestum*' (*see* WAKE). It is for this reason that Easter Eve, Christmas Eve, All Hallows Eve, etc. were of such importance in the medieval liturgical calendar.
See also LANTERN

VILLAGE HISTORIES *see* DOCUMENTARY SOURCES

VILLAGES It has been estimated that there are over ten thousand villages in Britain. Definition of the term is difficult for it has no legal or tenurial significance and is derived from the Latin *villaticus* meaning 'an assemblage of dwellings outside or pertaining to a villa.' Some authorities have defined a village as 'a nucleated rural settlement of twenty or more homesteads' while others apply the term only to those settlements which contain a parish church. Perhaps the most satisfactory definition is one which is arrived at by the consensus of those who live there: if a settlement is perceived to be the focus of parochial activity then it is invariably referred to as a village. Even in the suburbs a vestigial nucleated settlement may still be described as 'the village' by older members of the community.

During the Roman occupation the population of Britain rose to nearly five millions but by the Domesday survey of 1086 it had fallen to little more than two millions. During the intervening centuries of economic depression, political insecurity and social regression the Roman precepts of community life were effectively abandoned. It was an age, not of Anglo-Saxon conquest, but of assimilation and immigrant settlements were for the most part piecemeal and sporadic. Contrary to the traditional view, they were also small and often located on the poorest land at the periphery of indigenous communities. Many parishes still reflect this pattern of scattered Saxon farm clusters: Hazelbury Bryan in Dorset, for example, which has no obvious centre or village green and consists of a number of dispersed minor settlements, one of which (Droop) contains the parish church and school, another (Wanston) the post office and shop, and a third (Pidney) the village pub and playing field.

The development of nucleated villages began in the eighth century partly as a result of the proliferation of parish churches and, more significantly, as a consequence of the introduction of the open fields system. It is difficult to ascertain whether the churches were built to serve existing settlements or whether villages grew round their churches. What is more clear, however, is that nucleated villages were created wherever estates were sufficiently large to accommodate the so-called 'manorial system' of open fields, pasture, meadow and commons. Conversely, where the open field model was inappropriate the landscape of dispersed hamlets and farmsteads survived (*see* HAMLET).

In the late Saxon period thousands of new villages were established, a process which continued into the twelfth century. It should be noted, however, that the DOMESDAY survey recorded estates rather than villages. During the Middle Ages villages expanded, contracted, were re-sited or disappeared and it was only towards the end of this period that they began to take on a more durable form.

VILLAGE TYPES
There are four types of village: *linear settlements*

which have rows of house plots strung out along one or both sides of a street or elongated green; *enclosure settlements* in which the house plots and roads are located round the margins of an open space, often a village green or market square; and *agglomerated settlements* which conform to no obvious plan and have no apparent nucleus, the plots abutting more than one street and the dwellings set out at angles to each other. Each of these categories may be divided further into regular or irregular forms and may be found as a component of a more complex settlement pattern. In many cases, the original plan may not be apparent: where the central space of an enclosure settlement has been developed by building, for example.

The fourth category, *polyfocal villages*, are those which developed from the amalgamation of several independent settlements some of which may have declined while others prospered. Such villages may be recognised by the existence (either in the field or in documentary sources) of the several churches, manor houses and greens which were once contained within the various components and by the broken alignment of lanes or streets which mark the division of the earlier hamlets. Shrewton in Wiltshire, for example, comprises the former settlements of Elston, Maddington and Rollestone.

DEVELOPMENT AND DECLINE

Most medieval villages contained only two or three buildings of any permanence: a church, a manor house and sometimes a tithe barn. Consequently the form of a village would fluctuate as insubstantial buildings decayed and new areas were developed. Wholesale migration could result from the need to find more productive land or a more favourable site and in many cases, both in the medieval period and later, entire villages were removed by the owners of 'closed' estates, leaving the parish church in splendid isolation.

Many villages were planned as TOWNS, particularly in the early medieval period, and these may be recognised by their regular proportions, straight alignments, geometrical open spaces and house plots of roughly equal size. The acquisition of a market charter often resulted in the building of a new enclosure settlement or the extension of an existing hamlet to incorporate a new market square or green. Many of these planned villages are in fact 'failed' medieval towns where development was either ill-conceived or anticipated commercial success which was never realised.

Village populations increased rapidly in the late Saxon and early medieval periods but in the economic decline of the fourteenth century, a deteriorating climate and the debilitating effects of PLAGUE caused the contraction or abandonment of many settlements, particularly those which, because of earlier land shortages, had been established on uncompromising sites (*see* DESERTED VILLAGES).

The creation of villages continued long after the medieval period. Often these were '*model villages*', built to replace earlier settlements abandoned as the result of emparkment, or provided as accommodation for estate or factory workers.

Further reading:

Nicholson, G. and Fawcett, J., *The Village in History*, London, 1988

Rowley, T., *Villages in the Landscape*, London, 1978

Taylor, C., *Village and Farmstead*, London, 1983

West, J., *Village Records*, Chichester, 1984

VINE DECORATION A decorative motif comprising intertwined stems and vine-leaves, sometimes with fruit and often incorporating other images.

VISCOUNT *see* PEERAGE, THE

VISITATION, ECCLESIASTICAL Episcopal Visitations, periodic inspections of the temporal and spiritual affairs of dioceses, were first conducted in the sixth century and were regulated by ecclesiastical councils. From these a system of ecclesiastical visitations developed whereby bishops made three- or four-yearly inspections of their dioceses and archdeacons conducted annual inspections. The records of the visitations of bishops and archdeacons (or of their deputies), although not numerous until the mid-sixteenth century, are nevertheless an invaluable source of information.

Some medieval bishops' registers contain details of visitations and a number of bishops maintained separate records, though these have only rarely survived. Groups of laymen from each parish (*questmen*) were summoned to answer questions concerning the condition of their churches, vestments, books and equipment, the conduct of the clergy and the morals of the laity. Those whose conduct was called into question could be brought before an ecclesiastical court. In the later Middle Ages, the work of the Episcopal Visitations was conducted by bishops' commissaries and elaborate legal forms for the presentation of offenders were developed.

By the sixteenth century, the system of ecclesiastical visitations had become very much more complex and was used to enforce religious change and conformity. The Visitor first sent out a *Citation Mandate* to all incumbents in his archdeaconry (*see* CLERGY (CHURCH OF ENGLAND)) requiring them to appear before him at a specified time and place, together with their parochial officials. The Citation was then recited before the congregations of the various parishes and all those named were obliged to obtain a copy of the Visitation Articles which listed the subjects into which the Visitor was to inquire. These would normally include the church fabric and furnishings, the churchyard, the services, and an assessment of the conduct of parochial officers and of the moral and religious attitudes of the clergy and parishioners.

The Visitation began with the arrival of the Archdeacon and his Registrar who entered details of attendances, absences, communicants and fees in his Call Book and Fees Book. Those visited included rectors, vicars, chaplains, curates, licensed preachers, CHURCHWARDENS, PARISH CLERKS, schoolmasters, surgeons and midwives. The clergy were required to produce their Letters of Orders, to prove their right to their cures, together with any dispensations which enabled them to hold more than one living. Similarly, the parish clerks, surgeons, schoolmasters and midwives had to produce their licences.

The clergy and churchwardens then handed over their *presentments* which accounted for the conduct of their parishioners since the previous visitation and addressed the matters raised in the Visitation Articles. Executors or administrators of the estates of those who had recently died were also required to attend in order to prove wills or take administration, a function which at other times was performed in the ecclesiastical courts (*see* PROBATE). The presentments were then discussed and verdicts delivered on certain issues while others might be reserved for later consideration or referred to the ecclesiastical courts. The Visitation ended with the *Archdeacon's Charge*, an address to the assembled parishioners during a service.

After the Visitation, the Registrar would issue various injunctions on behalf of the Archdeacon and these would be set out in numbered paragraphs. They might include the imposition of *penances* and the incumbent and churchwardens were required to sign certificates confirming that these had been carried out. After the sixteenth century the penance was normally commuted to a *Declaration of Penance*, a public act of contrition. On occasions, the incumbent or churchwarden would provide a certificate confirming that the offender was of sufficiently good character (or social standing) to be permitted to perform his penance privately.

The Registrar also maintained the *Detecta* (accusations) and *Comperta* (revelations) volumes which contained annotated copies of presentments; copies of Citation Mandates summoning more serious offenders to appear before the Archdeacon's Court; and the Act Book, in which were recorded the findings of the Court and the penalties it imposed.

The original presentments were usually written in English on single sheets of paper. Many are of considerable interest and may include, for example, details of recusants (*see* RECUSANCY) and nonconformists, the condition of church buildings and any 'popish monuments of superstition' contained therein, PERAMBULATIONS and parish BOUNDARIES, parochial CHARITIES, the extent of GLEBE lands and the non-payment of TITHES. Almost invariably, by far the largest subject is that concerning the spiritual and moral welfare of the parishioners and their parson. Through the presentments it is possible to trace the progress of the English REFORMATION in individual parishes, the survival of old customs and festivals (*see* CHURCH AND COMMUNITY) and the extent to which statutory regulations were being observed.

Unfortunately, details of sixteenth-century visitations have not survived for all dioceses and those which remain are not necessarily informative: some parsons and churchwardens avoided further enquiry by simply reporting that all was well (*'omia bene'*).
See also ARCHIVES and DIOCESAN RECORDS

VISITATIONS (HERALDS) By the fifteenth century the use and abuse of coats of arms was becoming widespread. At that time the English kings of arms were required to survey and record the devices and pedigrees of those using arms and to correct any irregularities. Occasional tours of inquiry were held but it was not until the sixteenth century that heralds' visitations were undertaken in a regular and systematic way.

In England major visitations took place throughout the country in 1580, 1620 and 1666, minor visitations being conducted at other times. The practice was discontinued at the accession of William of Orange in 1689 when it was considered inadvisable to draw attention to those who remained loyal to 'the old ways'.

The original heralds' notebooks were used as a basis for manuscript copies, most of which have been published. These are a very useful source of early pedigrees, though it should be borne in mind that they may occasionally contain unauthorised additions or alterations which may not be immediately apparent. Many of these volumes have been published by the Harleian Society and others by county record societies. Many of the manuscripts on which the printed versions are based are held in the British Library in London. There are also good collections of printed visitation records at the Guildhall Library, London; the Society of Genealogists and the Institute of Heraldic and Genealogical Studies.
For addresses see APPENDIX II.
Further reading:
Friar, S., *A New Dictionary of Heraldry*, Sherborne and London, 1987

VISITATION OF OUR LADY The feast which originated in the thirteenth century and was celebrated on 2 July to commemorate the Blessed Virgin Mary's visit to Elizabeth (*see* Luke 1: 39–56). *See also* MARY, THE BLESSED VIRGIN

VISITATION OF THE SICK The Order for the Visitation of the Sick in the *Book of Common Prayer* provides for prayers, exhortations and blessing together with an exhortation to confession and a prescribed form of priestly absolution. The 1549 version also made provision for UNCTION but this was removed in 1552.

VISITORS' BOOKS *see* DOCUMENTARY SOURCES

VISOR The hinged, movable frontpiece of a helmet which allows the face to be revealed (*see* ARMOUR *and* HELMETS).

VITRUVIAN SCROLL (*also* RUNNING DOG) *see* DECORATIVE MOTIFS

VOLUNTAS *see* **PROBATE**

VOLUTE (i) The projecting corner termination of a classical capital in the form of a spiral scroll. A characteristic feature of Ionic capitals and, on a smaller scale, of Corinthian and Composite capitals (*see* CLASSICAL ORDER). (ii) A similar carved decorative form found in (e.g.) furniture.

VOTIVE CANDLE *see* CANDLE

VOTIVE CROSSES Small rudimentary crosses, scratched in stonework or on a church door, to commemorate the making of a vow.
See also GRAFFITI, HOLY WATER STOUP *and* PORCHES

VOUSSOIRS *see* ARCH

VOWESS (*also* AVOWESS) A widow who has avowed to live a life of chastity and obedience to God's will but has not necessarily entered a religious community. Female figures in EFFIGIES and BRASSES are often dressed in the simple white widow's veil and wimple, sideless cotehardie and kirtle of a vowess (*see* COSTUME), though many have also retained the symbols of their rank – the ducal coronet of a duchess, for example.

VULGATE The Latin version of the Bible translated mainly by St. Jerome (*c.* 342–420) with the intention of eliminating differences in the text in the Old Latin versions of the Scriptures. Work began in 382 with the revision of the Gospels which was completed in 384. Having completed his first version of the Psalter in 392 (the *Gallican Psalter*), he decided that the Old Testament could be translated satisfactorily only if he returned to the original Hebrew, a task which took him some fifteen years to complete.
See also BIBLES

WAFER BOX A small box, usually provided with a removable grill, in which the consecrated wafer of the Eucharist is kept (*see* PLATE).

WAGON ROOF A roof in which closely set rafters and arched braces have the appearance of the inside of the canvas tilt which covers a wagon. Wagon roofs may be uncovered, panelled or plastered (*ceiled*).
See also ROOFS (TIMBER)

WAGON VAULT *see* VAULTING

WAINSCOTING *see* PANELLING

WAKE Originally the procession and all-night vigil observed before certain feast days in the medieval Church. The term came to be applied to the parochial festivities on the holy day itself and specifically to the PATRONAL FESTIVAL. Although shrouded in pagan antiquity, the medieval practice of commencing celebrations on the eve of a patronal festival is not entirely extinct. After the wakeful vigil of the preceding night, the community would assemble in the parish church to celebrate Mass and this would be followed by dancing, drinking and sports on the village green or PLAISTOW or even in the churchyard itself. Many fairs originated in medieval wakes and celebrations were usually staggered so that neighbouring parishes could enjoy each others' wakes.

As a place-name element, the word usually refers to the family of Wake (as in Caundle Wake in Dorset where the Wakes were lords of the manor) but in field names the meaning is more likely to refer to the village festivities.
See also CHURCH AND COMMUNITY, MOTHERING SUNDAY *and* VIGIL

WALES, THE CHURCH IN The official title of the disestablished Anglican Church in Wales. The Church Temporalities Act of 1919 provided for the Church Commissioners to receive one million pounds from the Treasury. At the same time, the Church was to be dispossessed of ancient endowments worth £48,000 annually and these were eventually to be transferred to the University of Wales and the Welsh county councils, a complex process which was not completed until 1947.

Many Welsh Anglicans were fearful that disestablishment would isolate them from the mainstream of Anglicanism; indeed Watkin

Williams, the bishop of Bangor, expressed the hope that the legislation would be repealed. The bishops of St. Asaph and St. David's, A.G. Edwards and J. Owen, were more circumspect and acknowledged that disestablishment would lead inevitably to the creation of a Welsh province of the Anglican Communion and to the appointment of its own archbishop. Under their leadership a Representative Body was established to administer the property of the Church and a Governing Body appointed to direct its policy and doctrine. In 1920, the Welsh bishops were released from their vow of obedience to the archbishop of Canterbury and, on 1 June, A.G. Edwards was consecrated Archbishop of Wales – thereby ending a chapter which had begun with the consecration of Urban as bishop of Llandaf in 1107.

Thereafter, Monmouthshire was removed from the diocese of Llandaf to create the diocese of Monmouth in 1921 and, two years later, the counties of Brecknockshire and Radnorshire, together with the old commote of Gower, were taken from St. David's to form the new diocese of Swansea and Brecon.

See also CELTIC CHURCH, CLERGY (CHURCH OF ENGLAND), FLAGS *and* WALES, THE MEDIEVAL CHURCH IN

WALES, THE MEDIEVAL CHURCH IN

The asceticism of St. David who, according to his biographer Rhygyfarch, 'imitated the monks of Egypt and lived a life like theirs', was far removed from the self-indulgent hereditary canons of the twelfth-century Welsh *clasau* (*see* CLAS). Many of the monk-bishops of these ancient mother-churches, once the instruments of Christian conversion, had become preoccupied with protecting their property and influence. To the Normans, the *clas* with its wooden huts, its married priests and hereditary offices was a singularly corrupt and archaic institution. Furthermore, although the Welsh had accepted the Roman EASTER in 768, in almost all other matters they had remained faithful to the practices of the CELTIC CHURCH. To enthusiastic reformers, whose objective was uniformity of organisation, ritual and discipline throughout Christendom, the eccentricities of the Welsh Church were abhorrent. There were no stone churches (a particular cause of Norman contempt) and no monasteries following the Rule of St. Benedict, the most powerful of the influences which united Latin Europe. What they found was a fossilised church, badly in need of rejuvenation, and they set about the task of reform with typical Norman insensitivity.

THE BISHOPS

The reformers' first objective was to gain control of the dioceses and thereby to bring the Church in Wales within the jurisdiction of the archdiocese of Canterbury and subject to CANON LAW. Before the Conquest, each of the early kingdoms probably had its own bishop (seven bishops' houses were recorded in Dyfed) but as the kingdoms united so the number of Welsh bishoprics decreased until only three remained: those of Gwynedd, Deheubarth and Glamorgan with *cathedra* at Bangor, St. David's and Llandaf. The functions of the Welsh bishops were essentially those of their European fellows, but the organisation of their cathedrals was irregular and their diocesan boundaries indeterminate. In 1092 a Norman bishop was installed at Bangor, at Llandaf in 1107, at St. David's in 1115 and at (the newly created) St. Asaph in 1143.

In the twelfth century, diocesan and parochial BOUNDARIES began to be defined, a system of TITHES was introduced and, by the end of the thirteenth century, a judicial and administrative organisation had been established. The work was begun by Urban, bishop of Glamorgan from 1107 to 1134, the first of the Norman bishops of Wales to swear an oath of allegiance to the Archbishop of Canterbury. Anxious to keep Church property out of the hands of the rapacious Norman knights, Urban organised his diocese on the pattern of the Latin Church: he appointed a dean at his cathedral of Llandaf and divided the Vale of Glamorgan into small parishes.

At St. David's there was a growing demand that the diocese should be elevated into an archbishopric with authority over all the dioceses of Wales. It was argued that St. David himself had been an archbishop (though there is no evidence to suggest that the Celtic Church recognised such an office) and that the papacy had already endorsed the principle that every nation should have at least one archbishopric. Bishop Bernard's abortive struggle to promote St. David's (and to elevate himself) occupied the last twenty years of his life. He died in 1148 but the issue did not die with him. It was raised again in 1176 and 1179 and at the end of the century Giraldus Cambrensis (1146–1223) campaigned vigorously (but without success) for the elevation of his beloved Church of St. David.

THE BENEDICTINES

At the same time, the Norman establishment stripped most of the *clasau* of their revenues, transferring them to English monasteries or using the endowments to support new monastic communities, thereby securing control over the property of the Welsh Church. Sheltered by the invaders' fortresses, these Benedictine communities were often superior to those they replaced, for Norman monasticism itself had only recently been reformed. But the imported French-speaking monks were distrustful of the 'shaggy and wild-eyed' Welsh and concerned themselves more with the spiritual welfare of the Norman garrisons than with that of the indigenous population. In 1141 Abbot Gilbert of Gloucester urged the Benedictine community of Ewenny to surround their house with 'a good ditch and an impregnable wall'. By 1150 there were seventeen Benedictine houses in Wales, dependant cells or priories of some of the foremost monasteries of France and England. Chepstow, for example, belonged to the abbey of Cormeilles and Brecon was a dependency of Battle Abbey in Sussex.

THE AUGUSTINIAN CANONS

During the eleventh century papal reforms had hardly penetrated Wales but the situation was very different after 1100. Initially, the issue had concerned the royal control of episcopal appointments but once this had been resolved the reformers turned their attention to the localities and to the care of parish churches which, in many instances, continued to be treated by land-owners as private properties. It was determined that these were best entrusted to the care of regular canons, communities of priests who lived by the rule of St. Augustine (*see* AUGUSTINIANS). It was at Llanthony Priory, deep in the Black Mountains of Gwent, that the first of these new communities was established between 1108 and 1118. Other Anglo-Norman Augustinian priories followed at Carmarthen (before 1127) and Haverfordwest (before 1200). In many respects, the Augustinian houses were not so very different from the Celtic *clasau*; indeed, when the *clasau* of Penmon, Beddgelert and Aberdaron perceived a need for greater integration within the Latin Church they adopted the Augustinian Rule.

THE CISTERCIANS

The Benedictines were not the only monastic order in Wales. A Tironian house had been founded at St. Dogmaels in 1115 (*see* TIRONIANS) and this was followed by Savigniac houses at Neath (1130) and Basingwerk (1131) and an early Cistercian community at Tintern (1131). The Savigniacs were later integrated into the Cistercian Order, the brethren of which lived a sequestered communal life: '. . . we will follow the rule in all that pertains to the common life so that we will eat, sleep, work and perform the services of God together . . . [but] we will live as hermits in all that concerns rigorous abstinence and the total renunciation of secular concerns' (*see* CISTERCIANS).

The next Cistercian communities to reach Wales were those of Whitland (1140) and Margam (1147), both daughter houses of the Abbey of Clairvaux. After initial failures, Whitland succeeded in founding a colony at Strata Florida (Powys) which, under the patronage of the Lord Rhys (d. 1197), became the mausoleum of the princes of Deheubarth. Whitland itself was the 'stem of a new tree' and its daughter houses included Aberconwy (Gwynedd), where Llywelyn I ('The Great') was buried in 1240, and Cwmhir (Powys), the resting place of Llywelyn II, the first and only native Prince of Wales (d. 1282). Although Whitland had been founded as the result of Norman patronage, all Cistercians houses were answerable to the head of the Order at Cîteaux in Burgundy and were therefore not directly influenced by the power of the English kings. Furthermore, to the Welsh, the Cistercian rule seemed almost a re-embodiment of the principles of the ancient (and uncorrupted) Celtic Church: 'For they showed forth the discipline of Clairvaux whence they came, and by works of piety they spread the sweet savour of their mother-abbey, as it were, a strong perfume from their own house. The story spread everywhere that men of outstanding holiness and perfect religion had come from a far land; that by their virtues they had glorified the monastic name. Many were therefore moved to emulate them by joining this company whose hearts had been touched by God. Thus very soon they grew into a great company . . .' Little wonder that every Welsh ruler sought to establish a Cistercian house within his territories and that the White Monks were held in such high regard by the Welsh people.

THE LATE MIDDLE AGES

The half century which followed the Edwardian conquest of Wales (1282) is considered to be something of a golden age. In 1284 archbishop John Pecham, anxious to protect the interests of the Welsh Church and to foster the allegiance of the Welsh clergy, instituted a thorough investigation of the Church in Wales. He visited the four bishoprics and published a series of edicts for their reform, he rebuked both the monks and the clergy for their dissolute way of life and castigated those who would seek to incite the populace by glorifying the ancestry of the Welsh. Despite the archbishop's admonitions, the Welsh Church was well served by its bishops, most of whom were Welshmen or men with Welsh connections. They were also men of ability and energy who were chiefly responsible for consolidating the administrative and parochial framework of the Church, for promoting devotional prose and poetry in the Welsh language and for the construction of a number of notable ecclesiastical buildings, including the choir of St. David's cathedral and the completion of the magnificent Bishop's Palace.

There is very little evidence to suggest that at this time the Welsh clergy were critical of the system which had been imposed upon them. And yet, by the beginning of the fourteenth century, the Church in Wales was entirely under the control of the English crown. From 1294 it was taxed for the first time and there was a growing tendency for the king to reward his English officials with profitable benefices in Wales.

The most visible expression of the transformation of the local church in Wales was the building and rebuilding of its parish churches. In the early twelfth century Gwynedd 'came to shine with white-washed churches, like stars in the firmament' (the *Brut*). The churches which were built, or rebuilt, were generally small, unimpressive buildings of crude stonework, consisting of a simple square nave and smaller chancel, and without towers or aisles. Some of the major *clas* churches were also rebuilt, often to a cruciform plan, as at Twywn which came to be known as 'the glory of Meirionydd'. At the same time, the small boroughs of Anglo-Norman Wales flaunted their increasing prosperity by founding civic churches: St. Mary's at Carmarthen, for example, and at Haverfordwest where the church was rebuilt in the 1220s. Members of the princely dynasties and Norman barons sometimes provided the endowments: Gruffudd ap Cynan (he who 'had built many churches in his time') endowed Penmon Priory on Anglesey; William, earl of Gloucester (d. 1183), enlarged the church of St. Mary at Cardiff while the impressive church at Llanaber may well owe its splendour to the patronage of Hywel ap Gruffudd ap Cynan (d. 1216).

From 1350 there was a significant decline in the fortunes of the Welsh Church as a result of intellectual fatigue and economic depression. Indeed, the entire country was debilitated by recurring outbreaks of the PLAGUE and constant pressure from the English crown for resources to finance the French wars. Throughout Europe, the Church was divided: the Papacy had become little more than another state, greedy for power and wealth, and between 1379 and 1417 there were competing popes in Rome and Avignon. There was a dramatic fall in admissions to the monastic orders and no new orders were created which might have revitalised the spiritual life of the Church. As a consequence, clerics were preoccupied with safeguarding their incomes in the face of depression while the monastic houses began leasing their lands and impropriating benefices in order to profit from parochial tithes. Anti-clerical attitudes hardened while the lower clergy descended into the ranks of the proletariat and their senior colleagues sought to maintain their living standards through pluralism. Ecclesiastical appointments were made for political reasons: most of the more lucrative Welsh benefices were filled by Englishmen and the Welsh bishoprics were used as pawns in the contest between the Pope and the Prince of Wales so that able Welsh clerics could no longer expect promotion in their own country.

The economic revival which occurred in the second half of the fifteenth century is reflected in many of the MONUMENTS of the period and in the refurbishing or rebuilding of several parish churches. There are impressive town churches at Cardiff (St. John's), Wrexham in Clwyd and Tenby in Dyfed, for example, and splendid SCREENS at Llannano in Powys, Llanegryn in Gwynedd and Patrisio, Dyfed. The Vale of Clwyd is renowned for its double-aisled churches and several fine towers were constructed at

this time, notably in Gwent and north-east Clwyd. But, although not as impoverished as some historians would have us believe, the ecclesiastical institutions of Wales were poor by comparison with those of England. The combined income of the three least-endowed Welsh dioceses was less than that of the poorest English diocese, while the total wealth of the Welsh religious houses could not equal that of Glastonbury Abbey in Somerset.

THE REFORMATION

The Welsh had no representation in the English parliament and they were therefore denied an opportunity to express a view concerning the measures which terminated the link with Rome (*see* REFORMATION, THE). In 1534, Rowland Lee, the bishop of Lichfield, was appointed president of the Council of Wales and he initiated what has accurately been described as a reign of terror, intended to suppress lawlessness and to remind the Welsh of their subservience to the English crown. His strategy appears to have succeeded for, unlike the men of Yorkshire and Cornwall, the Welsh showed no inclination to challenge the power of the Tudor reformers through armed insurrection. Nevertheless, Wales was a conservative country and it is unlikely that the legislation was welcome. It was not until 1549, when fundamental changes were imposed on the parish churches, that the implication of the religious changes had any real impact on the Welsh people.

As a consequence of the DISSOLUTION OF THE MONASTERIES all but three of the major Welsh religious houses were dissolved: an appalling loss, though by that time the intellectual climate had, for a century or more, become increasingly hostile to the monastic ideal. At the Dissolution, the thirteen Cistercian monasteries of Wales had a total establishment of only eighty-five monks and the Augustinian and Benedictine houses were even emptier. The monasteries were dissolved, not because of their weakness, but because of their wealth. According to the *Valor Ecclesiasticus*, the combined income of the Welsh houses was only £3,178 even though the Church owned as much as a quarter of the land in Wales. But, as has been seen, much of this land had already been leased by gentry families, often on long leases which were confirmed at the time of the Dissolution. Thus the monastic lands passed, not to the Crown, but into the absolute possession of the gentry. Similarly, in Wales a high proportion of the ecclesiastical benefices which had been appropriated by the monasteries passed into the ownership of lay rectors where they remained impropriate until the disestablishment of the Welsh Church in 1920 (*see* WALES, THE CHURCH IN).

In 1563, the bishops of Wales and of Hereford were commanded to ensure that Welsh translations of the Bible and the *Book of Common Prayer* would be available in every parish church in Wales by St.

David's Day, 1567 and that services were to be conducted in Welsh in those parishes where the language was in general use. At the close of the sixteenth century the notion that Protestantism was 'the English religion' had almost faded, thanks to a belief, widely disseminated at the time, that the Celtic Church had been a truly Protestant Church, the purity of which had been defiled by the Romish practices of Augustine and his successors. The Welsh were returning to the faith of their forefathers: a theory which served the English reformers admirably.

See also ANGLO-SAXON CHURCH, MEDIEVAL CHURCH *and* WELSH RECORDS

Further reading:

Davies, J., *A History of Wales*, London, 1993

Davies, R., *Conquest, Coexistence and Change: Wales, 1063–1415*, Oxford, 1986

Williams, G., *Reorientation and Reformation: Wales, 1415–1642*, Oxford, 1987

WALL MONUMENT A mid-sixteenth-century development of the canopied TOMB CHEST, the wall monument was either secured to the wall (*hanging wall monument*) or supported at ground level (*standing wall monument*). Some wall monuments are quite bizarre: the seventeenth-century Allestry monument in Derby cathedral, for example, which contains a miniature coffin.

Modest versions of the wall monument are often described as *wall tablets* or *memorial tablets*: small stone panels in a variety of shapes engraved with commemorative INSCRIPTIONS.

MONUMENTS, and the inscriptions engraved thereon, are an invaluable source of information concerning a church and its community (*see also* EPITAPHS). They can tell us about contemporary artistic styles and fashions and about local society: its fluctuating economic fortunes, its social conventions and its religious observances. They can tell us about individuals and their families: how they lived, what they looked like, how they died and how they wished to be remembered by later generations. And, by interpreting the HERALDRY in a memorial, we may trace a family's genealogy and establish its position in society.

SIXTEENTH CENTURY

From *c.* 1550 the style and decoration of wall monuments followed that of the canopied tomb chest with rather stiff effigies in recumbent, kneeling or reclining postures or demi-figures. Renaissance forms and decoration superseded Gothic and were characterised by the use of STRAPWORK, ribbonwork, grotesques, allegorical figures, cherub-heads and so on. Heraldry is much in evidence and was usually concentrated in the CANOPY during the sixteenth and seventeenth centuries (in the

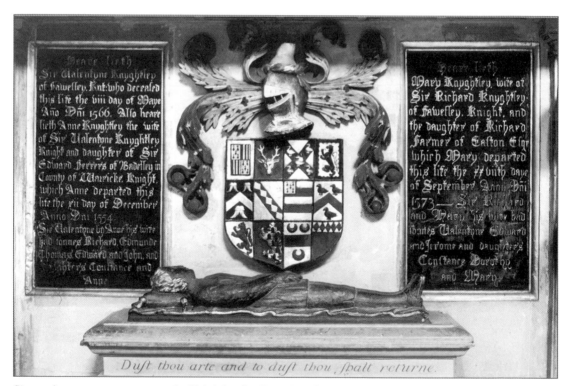

Sixteenth-century monument to the Knightley family at Fawsley, Northamptonshire.

Wall tablets for the north aisle of Bath Abbey.

eighteenth century the canopy was abandoned or reduced to an ornamental form rather than an architectural structure).

SEVENTEENTH CENTURY

In the early seventeenth century, the classical style was more refined, especially in the use of pediments on architectural canopies and frames. White and black marble was popular, as was alabaster. Figures were more finely carved and were depicted in a variety of more natural poses, usually in contemporary dress though Roman armour was popular from *c.* 1660. Pedestal busts were introduced at this time, as were medallion portraits which were carved in relief. From *c.* 1660 marble replaced alabaster, especially in baroque monuments, and recumbent or kneeling figures became increasingly rare. Allegorical figures, especially the Virtues, were common, as were symbols of mortality.

Cartouche tablets were particularly popular in the seventeenth and eighteenth centuries. These were usually made of marble and have the appearance of a sheet of paper with the sides curled up. Typically, the central section contains an inscription and, above it, a coat of arms or crest.

EIGHTEENTH CENTURY

By *c.* 1750 architectural canopies were no longer fashionable and throughout the eighteenth century wall monuments varied considerably both in size and style. Indeed, some are so large (and ostentatious) that they appear grotesquely out of place in a small, medieval church. Figures are often dressed as Romans, in armour or loosely wrapped toga-like garments, and recline against an urn or on a sarcophagus. Recumbent and kneeling effigies are rare. Many monuments of the period are finely carved with ROCOCO decoration while small portrait medallions, busts, putti, urns, cartouches and symbols of mortality are ubiquitous. Heraldry remained an important though subdued element of design with a shield or cartouche above or at the base, the arms being the only element of colour in the monument other than coloured marbles. When the deceased had enjoyed a military or naval career, or had been a prominent churchman, the monument was often flanked by guns, flags, a crosier or other appropriate devices.

Elegant neo-classical black and white tablets characterised the period 1780 to 1840 and were a

Seventeenth-century monument to members of the Bedingfeld family at Oxburgh, Norfolk.

hatchments to seven members of the Breedon family but none of their wall monuments includes heraldry.

NINETEENTH CENTURY

The restrained neo-classicism of the late eighteenth century continued into the early nineteenth. Black and white marble was still popular (white increasingly so) and figures of mourning females, leaning over an urn or sarcophagus, were especially common. So too were angels, often depicted receiving the deceased in death, and symbolism such as opium poppies (the sleep of death) and a sickle cutting a rosebud (death taking a child). Costume is mostly contemporary while military and naval figures may wear uniform. Inevitably, in the larger standing wall monuments of the Victorian period there was a significant increase in the use of alabaster and a revival of Gothic features, such as canopies, tomb chests and recumbent effigies.

The Victorians were especially fond of brass wall plates, engraved and enamelled with 'Gothic' lettering, while the wall tablets of the late nineteenth

reaction against the flamboyance of earlier baroque and rococo monuments which recited the virtues of the deceased both in their architectural and sculptural ostentation and in the banality of their inscriptions. In these tablets a panel of white marble, usually a scroll or sarcophagus bearing a dignified inscription, is set against a background of black marble with sculpture in shallow relief. The tablet may be oval, rectangular or shield-shaped and surmounted by a draped urn, a broken column, a tree of life or a figure of grief with a bowed head. The *stele* design, a rectangular slab surmounted by a low, triangular pediment, was particularly popular. Tablets were comparatively inexpensive and enabled all and sundry to elbow their way into posterity, often at the expense of architectural good taste: at Bath Abbey in Avon, for example, where the aisle walls are encrusted with tablets dating from the eighteenth and nineteenth centuries.

During this period, heraldry in wall monuments was often restricted to a CREST or was omitted entirely. Perversely, this coincided with the increasing popularity of funeral HATCHMENTS: at Pangbourne in Berkshire, for example, there are

Monument to John Alleyne (d. 1792) at North Cerney, Gloucestershire.

and twentieth centuries are for the most part restrained and unobtrusive and may contain carved and painted coats of arms and finely carved inscriptions.

See also MEMORIALS

WALL PAINTINGS In the Middle Ages the interiors of parish churches would have been very different from the quiet sober places they are today. Then, they were like immense picture books of painted plaster intended for the edification of the illiterate masses and designed to inspire fear and obedience. The walls of most pre-Reformation churches were covered with murals depicting, not only the lives of the saints and scenes from the scriptures, but also terrifying images of the inevitability of death and of divine judgment and retribution. Medieval wall paintings tell us much about popular theology and the basic teaching of the medieval Church.

THE BIBLIA PAUPERUM

In 604 St. Gregory the Great declared that the walls of parish churches were to be the *biblia pauperum*, the bible of the poor, and throughout the Middle Ages murals were considered to be the normal finish for church walls. Professional itinerant painters travelled from church to church working on newly plastered walls, wetted with lime-water and smoothed with lime putty (stiff slaked lime), using inexpensive natural colours ground and tempered with lime-water or skim-milk. Delicate work often required the use of pigments and size (*see* FRESCO). Pigments included iron oxides (which produced reds, browns, yellows and purple), lamp-black (candle soot), malachite (the green carbonate of copper), azurite (the blue carbonate of copper) and lime putty for white. Squirrel hair (from the tail) was used for the finer brushes and hog's hair for others and the pigment was often worked from scallop shells.

About 2,000 British churches retain traces of these murals and though many are fragmentary and faded some two hundred are well preserved. At Peakirk in Cambridgeshire, for example, sections of a *Life and Death* morality painting have survived in which skeletal ghosts are depicted castigating the Three Kings as they enjoy themselves in the hunt – surrounded by the maggots, beetles and flies which will one day devour those of the congregation who persist in denying their own mortality. A similar subject, the *Three Living and the Three Dead*, portrays three princes in the prime of their youth meeting with three skeletons. Such paintings echo a poem written at the court of Margaret II, the thirteenth-century queen of Flanders, in which three corpses warn the Three Kings: 'As you are, so once we were. As we are, so shall ye be'. A similar theme is evident in the Dance of Death (*Danse Macabre*) in which the figure of Death is depicted as a dancing

skeleton inviting various representatives of contemporary society to join him in the dance. This was a particularly poignant subject in the fourteenth and fifteenth centuries when involuntary movements of the body – a 'dance' – were associated with the PLAGUE.

THE LAST JUDGEMENT

More than seventy Last Judgement murals survive in Britain, mostly on tympana (*see* DOOM *and* TYMPANUM). Typically, that at Chaldon in Surrey portrays the naked figures of the damned being thrown into the caldron of Hell by a gang of dog-headed, pitchfork-wielding demons. The *Hell Mouth* often features in these paintings, a terrifying device which probably originated in the biblical story of Jonah and the whale. Medieval imagery is often sexist: gossips are invariably depicted as women, urged on by devils who sit on their shoulders and press their heads together, while symbols of the seven deadly sins are often depicted sprouting from the richly dressed (or naked) body of a woman, herself representing the fundamental evil of pride. A painting at Cameley in Somerset includes a fiendish jester while at Gussage St. Andrew in Dorset a painting of the Passion of Christ uniquely depicts the despairing Judas hanging himself from a tree.

The portrayal of the emotions as deadly sins was intended to remind the villeins of their place in feudal society and the total of a man's sins determined whether he would go to Heaven or to Hell. It was St. Michael who weighed an individual's deeds and his scales appear in wall paintings such as those at Nassington in Northamptonshire and Barton in Cambridgeshire where the judgement is depicted as a contest between the Devil, sitting in the left-hand pan of the scales, and the Virgin Mary whose rosary she has placed in the right. A number of paintings illustrate the consequences of working on a Sunday, the implements used by sinners being used to inflict pain on Christ himself. At West Chiltington in Sussex, for example, the wounded Christ is portrayed surrounded by the instruments of a variety of trades and occupations. At Michaelchurch Escley in Herefordshire's Golden Valley is another '*Christ of the Trades*'. Painted in c. 1500 it is a faded black, white and yellow figure of Christ with enormous arms and surrounded by working tools of every description including an axe, shears, spade, adze, plough, dividers and set square, wheel and flail. Further north in Shropshire the lonely Heath Chapel near Clee St. Margaret is a wonderful early Norman building, completely unrestored, the flaking plaster of its walls covering a mass of medieval wall paintings including one of St. George on a white charger above the door. Unfortunately, most of the paintings remained uncovered because of a shortage of funds for restoration.

ST. CHRISTOPHER

The regular weekly contemplation of the horrors of

Painting of St. Christopher on the north wall of Breage church, Cornwall.

the Last Judgement cannot have failed to make a profound impression on parishioners who were constantly at the mercy of plague, fire and famine. Those who could afford to do so endowed chantries, obits, lights and other benefactions in the hope of escaping the purgatorial fires (see CHANTRY). But for the commonalty, salvation must have seemed desperately unattainable. Inevitably, the medieval mind was preoccupied with death, and with the appalling possibility of endless expiation. Consequently paintings of St. Christopher were particularly popular for it was believed that merely by looking at his image, death could be delayed by a day. There are fine paintings of the saint at St. Mary's, Hayes in west London and at Albury, Surrey.

THE VIRGIN MARY

The late medieval cult of the Virgin Mary was based on the Virgin's ability, as the Mother of Mercy, to intercede on behalf of even the most wicked of sinners and at Corby Glen in Lincolnshire and Broughton, Buckinghamshire she is depicted as the *Virgin of the Mantle*, sheltering sinful souls beneath her protective cloak. The Annunciation was a popular theme, as in a mural at the delightful church of Dale Abbey in Derbyshire where there are also late thirteenth-century paintings of the Visitation and Nativity. (At Dale Abbey, the tiny church shares the roof of the adjoining farmhouse).

Godshill church on the Isle of Wight is known as the 'Church of the Lily Cross' because of a unique mural on the east wall of the south chapel. The painting (c. 1450) is of Christ crucified on a triple-branched flowering lily: the *Lily Cross*, a medieval symbol of purity. On either side are painted curtains against which statues of Our Lady and St. John would have been placed, confirming that the mural was intended as a back-drop for an altar.

'POPISH AND SUPERSTITIOUS IMAGES'

Most surviving paintings have been revealed in the past 150 years though many others were unwittingly destroyed during Victorian restorations. Most lay forgotten beneath layers of whitewash (*albacio*) applied after 1547, when the government ordered the 'obliteration' of 'popish and superstitious' images, and in 1644 when, during the Civil War, the parliamentary authorities appointed a Commissioner for the Destruction of Images. Ironically, the coatings of whitewash may have assisted in the paintings' preservation. But it should not be forgotten that, in the late Middle Ages, as the number and size of WINDOWS increased, so available wall space was reduced; while the insertion of new windows (and the enlarging of existing ones) resulted in the destruction of many earlier paintings. The later iconoclasts should not take all the blame.

There may be several layers of painting on a single wall: at the ancient church of St. Martin at Wareham in Dorset, for example, where an extraordinary series of murals above the Norman chancel arch date from the eleventh to the eighteenth century. The top layer consists of The Ten Commandments and the arms of Queen Anne (1713). These partially cover the arms of Charles I and a seventeenth-century text round the arch which reads 'Let every soul be subject unto higher powers. For there is no power but of God.' These paintings are superimposed on yet earlier murals: red stars and a masonry pattern from the thirteenth or fourteenth centuries and fragments of eleventh- or twelfth-century paintings. There is also a fine late eleventh- or twelfth-century painting of St. Martin and the beggar on the north wall of the chancel. Recent work at Llangar church in Clwyd has revealed an extraordinary series of murals, layer upon layer of paintings the finest of which is a huge image of a skeleton, probably dating from the thirteenth century, intended to remind the congregation of its mortality and the inevitability of judgement.

Of course, not all wall paintings are medieval. At the church of St. Michael at Lyme Regis in Dorset there is a large crescent-shaped mural of the 'Raising of the Cross', painted above the chancel arch in 1850.

Further reading:

Anderson, M., *Drama and Imagery in English Medieval Churches*, Cambridge, 1979

Caiger-Smith, A., *English Medieval Mural Paintings*, Oxford, 1963

Croft-Murray, E., *Decorative Painting in England 1537–1837*, London, 1962

——, E., *Decorative Painting in England: the 18th and 19th Centuries*, London, 1970

Rouse, C., *Medieval Wall Paintings*, Aylesbury, 1991

Tasker, E., *Encyclopaedia of Medieval Church Art*, London, 1994

WALLPLATE A structural timber running horizontally along the top of a wall from one end of a roof to the other (see ROOFS).

WAND see CHURCHWARDENS' STAFFS

WAR Since the Middle Ages, clerics have been expressly forbidden to shed blood (their medieval predecessors used a mace which, in theory, bruised an adversary but did not draw blood). While the Church of England continues to confirm the medieval principle, the clergy are permitted to undertake military duties when compelled to do so by the State.

WARD (i) A minor in the care of a guardian or court. (ii) The notches of a key designed to prevent duplication. (iii) An enclosed yard.

WARDEN (i) The superior of a collegiate or other quasi-monastic foundation such as an ALMS-HOUSE or HOSPITAL. The warden of such an institution was usually a priest but could be a layman. Other titles include custos, keeper, master, prior and rector. The vicar of the collegiate church of St. Peter at Ruthin in Clwyd has been addressed as 'Warden' since the fourteenth century when a small community of priests first occupied the solid two-storey cloistral buildings which still stand today. The Warden lived in the cloister until 1954 – as did the church organist. (ii) The superior responsible for a regional division (*custody*) of the Franciscan Order.

WAR MEMORIAL BOOKS *see* DOCUMENTARY SOURCES

WAR MEMORIALS Many villages possess a war memorial, usually a stone cross, obelisk or pillar with a stepped base bearing on each of its sides an engraved list of those who died in the service of their country. Often, especially in the Great War (1914–18), several members of the same family were killed and many small communities decimated. Most war memorials were erected by public subscription, usually at a crossroads or sometimes in the vicinity of a churchyard. One of the finest war memorials is at Briantspuddle in Dorset. Carved by Eric Gill it consists of a tall cross with a life-size statue of the wounded Christ on the north side and a Madonna and Child beneath a canopy on the south.

Not all memorials were placed out of doors: many were *memorial boards*, rolls of honour which were hung on the walls of parish churches, chapels and schools. It was not unusual for Church and Chapel to disagree on an appropriate location and so identical boards were painted: one for the church school and the other for the chapel. Many memorial boards have survived, often to gather dust in a school stock-cupboard or church vestry.

Other forms of war memorial include church furnishings, screens and stained glass windows. These are often accompanied by tablets on which the names of the dead are inscribed, together with regimental or naval badges.
See also CENOTAPH *and* FLAGS

WARMING HOUSE *see* CALEFACTORIUM

WASSAIL *see* CHRISTMAS

WATCHING LOFT An elevated observation post from which a sanctuary or shrine could be observed in order to prevent sacrilege or theft (*see* SHRINES). Rare examples have survived at the former Benedictine churches of St. Albans and Worcester.

WATERLEAF *see* DECORATIVE MOTIS

WATERLOO CHURCHES *see* NINETEENTH-CENTURY ARCHITECTURE

WAX SCOT A customary payment for the provision and maintenance of lights in churches.

WAYSIDE CROSSES Crosses, or stones on which crosses were engraved, were erected along tracks and highways for a multiplicity of reasons. Some commemorate events the details of which are long since forgotten. Others mark resting places along CORPSE ROADS or were intended simply to guide travellers through inhospitable terrain.

There are concentrations of such crosses on the North York Moors and on Dartmoor in Devon. Most wayside crosses are of medieval origin, are often of crude execution and may be mistaken for monastic boundary markers. But several are exquisitely carved: the huge Maen Achwyfan (the Stone of Lamentation), for example, which stands at a lonely crossroads north-east of Holywell in Clwyd. Maen Achwyfan is the tallest of all celtic crosses, nearly three metres high (11 feet), with an ornate wheel head (*see* WHEEL HEAD CROSS) and a massive shaft covered with intricate interlaced carving. Nearly a thousand years old, it is a proud symbol of the tenacity of the Celtic Church.

Inevitably, wayside crosses (especially those at crossroads) have attracted the superstitious. The Cross-in-Hand, an isolated roadside pillar on the downs above Batcombe in Dorset, is mentioned by Thomas Hardy in *Tess of the D'Urbervilles*:

Tis a thing of ill-omen . . . put up in wuld times by the relations of a malefactor who was tortured there by nailing his hand to a post and afterwards hung. The bones lie beneath. They say he sold his soul to the devil, and that he walks at times.

The origins of this 'cross' are unknown but it is possible that it was erected as a boundary marker by monks from the nearby Benedictine abbey of Cerne. *See also* CHURCHYARD CROSSES *and* ELEANOR CROSSES

WAYWARDEN (*also* WAYMAN) A parochial officer responsible for the maintenance of highways.

WEATHERBOARD (CLAPBOARD) A timber cladding consisting of lengths of board fixed to the exterior of a building, usually horizontally though sometimes vertically, to provide additional protection and insulation. Weatherboard is usually overlapping, as in a clinker-built boat, but is sometimes tongue and grooved so that it has a flat appearance. A number of church TOWERS and belfries have weatherboarded exteriors, mostly in the south-east of England: the fifteenth-century timber bell tower at Blackmore in Essex, for example, and the tower of (Saxon) St. Andrew's at Greensted in the same county.

WEATHERCOCKS *and* WEATHER VANES A weathercock is a three-dimensional, hollow metal sculpture mounted on a spire, or above a tower, and revolving easily to indicate the direction of the wind.

Cockerels symbolise vigilance and, most importantly, have tails which are ideally suited to catch the wind. They are of considerable antiquity: a weathercock was depicted in the eleventh-century Bayeux tapestry while that on the fine fourteenth-century tower of All Saints church at Oakham in Rutland is believed to be one of the oldest weathercocks in Britain.

Not all weathercocks are cockerels. Some are the emblems of patron saints, such as the gridiron of St. Lawrence on the churches of St. Lawrence, Jewry in the City of London, Ramsgate in Kent, Tidmarsh in Berkshire and Bradfield, Elmstead and Upminster in Essex. On the church of St. Mary-le-Bow, Cheapside a huge 2.7 metre (9 feet) dragon, weighing over 2 cwt., is probably a representation of the mythical Thames dragon which appears in the coat of arms of the City of London. There are other dragons at Ottery St. Mary in Devon, Sittingbourne in Kent and Upton in Norfolk and fish at Filey and Flamborough in Yorkshire and Lewes (St. John the Baptist) and Piddinghoe in Sussex. A magnificent golden galleon on the tower of Henstridge church in Somerset was the gift of Royal Navy airmen stationed at the nearby aerodrome during the second World War, while a ship at Tollesbury in Essex has red sails. A very large cockerel at Knapton in Norfolk is combined with the keys of St. Peter and the sword of St. Paul. Several churches dedicated to St. Peter have large keys instead of cocks: Cornhill in the City of London, for example, and Bedford and Brackley in Northamptonshire. The key at Aspley Guise in Bedfordshire is misleading for the church is dedicated to St. Botolph. There is a violin at Great

Late seventeenth-century weathercock at Bradford Abbas, Dorset.

Ponton in Lincolnshire, a St. Martin and the beggar at Chipping Ongar in Essex, a plough bearing an E II R cypher at Northrepps in Norfolk and a splendid Yorkist falcon and fetterlock device at Fotheringhay in Northamptonshire.

Without documentary evidence weathercocks are often very difficult to date, though CHURCH-WARDENS' ACCOUNTS may contain references to their being refurbished or replaced. One of the earliest references, a riddle in the *Exeter Book* of about 750, describes a weathercock as a hollow belly pierced by a rod. Many are of medieval appearance but are likely to have been replaced several times, though the original design may have been copied on each occasion.

Unlike weathercocks, weather vanes were intended to show both the direction of the wind and to display heraldic devices. They are effectively rigid metal flags and it has been argued (by Col. R. Gayre *) that on private houses in the medieval period the shape of a vane was dictated by the rank of its owner. The use of vanes, which probably originated in France, is evident in England from the thirteenth century and it is likely that the word is a corruption of *fane*, derived from *fannion* meaning 'banner'. Weather vanes (which are sometimes dated) are generally found on the pinnacles or stair turrets of church towers, as at Etchingham in Surrey, and on the gables of major domestic buildings, particularly those of the Tudor period. They are usually in the form of triangular or swallow-tailed *pennons* or square banners (*see* FLAGS): there are banner-shaped vanes of the Lucy family at Charlecote in Warwickshire, for example, and swallow-tailed pennons at Lambeth Palace in London. Both sets are painted with coats of arms and the borders, decorative fleurs-de-lis and 'tails' are gilded to catch the sun.

Unfortunately, most weather vanes have lost their original heraldic decoration and Victorian examples are often Gothic Revival imitations and were rarely painted.

Further reading:
Gayre, R., *Heraldic Standards and Other Ensigns*, Edinburgh, 1959 *

WEBS *see* VAULTING

WEDDINGS *see* MATRIMONY

WEDNESDAY In the early Church, Wednesday was observed as a day of fasting in remembrance of the day on which Christ was betrayed. This practice continued on EMBER DAYS.

WEEK The notion of a day of rest specially dedicated to God is derived from the Jewish Sabbath and was adopted by the early Christians who

transferred it to the first day of the week in honour of the Resurrection (*see* SUNDAY). The Jewish fasts of Tuesday and Thursday were similarly translated to WEDNESDAY (the day on which Christ was betrayed) and FRIDAY (the day of the Crucifixion). Thursday was later dedicated to the ASCENSION and Saturday to the Blessed Virgin Mary (*see* MARY, THE BLESSED VIRGIN).

WEEPERS Small stone or bronze figures set in the sides of TOMB CHESTS and other MONUMENTS as symbols of perpetual mourning. Weepers first appeared on tombs towards the end of the thirteenth century and remained popular throughout the medieval, Tudor and Jacobean periods. They usually represent a dead man's grieving family and on medieval tombs may include members of eminent and magnatial families with whom the deceased was related by inheritance or marriage. Individuals may sometimes be identified by small shields of arms placed beneath or between the niches in which they stand.

Medieval weepers were finely carved dignified figures, cloaked and hooded, their heads bowed and their hands clasped in supplication. Figures of angels were also popular from the late fourteenth century and saints in the fifteenth. Angels may be winged or clothed in albs and they often hold shields painted with coats of arms or CHRISTIAN SYMBOLS.

Elizabethan and Jacobean weepers are often crude by comparison (though there are some notable exceptions) and were sometimes painted in the form of a frieze on the front or sides of a monument. These weepers were usually separated into two groups of figures, one of sons (kneeling in descending order behind their father) and the other of daughters (similarly kneeling behind their mother who may hold an infant). Quite often there is a babe or two in swaddling-clothes (*chrisom-cloths*) bringing up the rear and it has been suggested that these represent children who died in infancy (*see* CHRISM). However, the usual custom was for those who had predeceased their parents to carry a skull. Among several Tudor monuments at Brewood in Staffordshire is one of 1556 to Sir John Giffard and his two wives in which thirteen of his eighteen children are depicted in their chrisom robes, while the seventeenth-century tomb chest of Lord Chief Justice Popham at Wellington in Somerset is surrounded by no fewer than twenty-eight carved figures.

WEEPING CROSS A stone cross marking a place of penance. The Croeswylan Stone at Oswestry in Shropshire, a large, pillow-shaped stone with a hollow in the middle, was once the base of a medieval weeping cross. During the plague of 1559, the people from the surrounding villages sold their market goods at the Croeswylan Stone without having to enter the stricken town. Tradition tells of

Weepers on the tomb chest of Ralph Fitzherbert (d. 1483) and his wife, Elizabeth, at Norbury, Derbyshire

how they would wash their coins in the hollow of the stone in the vague hope of cleansing them of the plague.

WELDON STONE A creamy, easily-cut stone quarried in Northamptonshire.

WELL DRESSING *see* HOLY WELLS

WELLS *see* HOLY WELLS

WELSH BIBLE AND PRAYER BOOK *see* BIBLES *and* COMMON PRAYER, BOOK OF

WELSH RECORDS The National Library of Wales at Aberystwyth contains court records, diocesan archives and other material relating to the Welsh Church. The Royal Commission on the Ancient and Historical Monuments of Wales has an extensive collection of plans, illustrations and photographs while the National Museum of Wales has a substantial print and photographic archive.
For addresses *see* APPENDIX II.

WEST DOORWAY The great west doors of major monastic and collegiate churches were rarely used, indeed at several abbeys (such as Brinkburn in Northumberland, Buildwas in Shropshire, Cartmel in Lancashire and Romsey in Hampshire) there is no western doorway. They were used only on ceremonial occasions such as the arrival of a new abbot, a visiting bishop or royalty and for Palm Sunday processions. Access to the nave was more usually by means of two doors from the CLOISTER which were provided for processional purposes and, in some cases, for the separate admission of the brethren and *conversi*. There may also have been a separate entrance for the public when the church was used for parochial purposes. This is sometimes on the north side of the nave but is more usually to the west beyond the cloister and was often provided with a porch in which certain lay ceremonies took place (*see* PORCHES). There are examples at Malmesbury Abbey in Wiltshire and Great Malvern Priory in Worcestershire, both of which have survived as parish churches.
See also DOORS AND DOORWAYS

WESTERN RANGE Sometimes known as the cellarer's range from the *cellarium*, the great cellar or store-room which was its principal feature, the western range of a CLOISTER consisted of a vaulted basement (which was originally sub-divided by partitions) above which was accommodation for the superior and his guests or, in Cistercian houses, the frater, dorter, rere-dorter and common room of the *conversi*.

WEST GALLERY *see* CHURCH MUSIC (ANGLICAN) *and* GALLERIES

WESTMINSTER ASSEMBLY OF DIVINES (1643) *and* WESTMINSTER CONFESSION (1647) *see* SEVENTEENTH-CENTURY CHURCH

WESTWARD POSITION The practice by which the celebrant at the EUCHARIST stands on the east side of the altar and faces the congregation. This was normal practice until the eighth or ninth centuries when the EASTWARD POSITION was introduced into the Roman Church. During the present century the Westward Position has been restored in many churches as a result of a revised liturgy (*see* COMMON PRAYER, BOOK OF).

WHEEL HEAD CROSS A form of cross, with Celtic associations, in which the cross head is contained within, or overlays, a circle. This may have evolved from the practice of bracing the arms of a wooden cross or from the Mediterranean Christian tradition of representing a cross within a circle. In HERALDRY it is described as a *Celtic Cross*.

Wheel head cross.

WHEEL WINDOW A circular window with a design of 'spokes' radiating from a central rim. This type of window is often confused with the ROSE WINDOW which is also circular but contains a more complex design. Both are commonly found in medieval cathedrals, particularly in the end walls of nave and transepts.
See also MEDIEVAL ARCHITECTURE *and* WINDOWS

WHITE FRIARS The Carmelite FRIARS.

WHITE LADIES A popular name for the MAGDALENES and for nuns of the CISTERCIANS Order.

WHITE MONKS Monks of the CISTERCIAN Order.

WHITSUNDAY Second only to EASTER in the festivals of the Church, the Feast of the Descent of the Holy Spirit upon the Apostles is observed on Whitsunday, the fiftieth day after Easter (*see* PENTECOST). The Vigil of Pentecost became one of the three great baptismal occasions of the ecclesiastical year, the white clothes traditionally required for the baptismal service providing the festival with its traditional name – White Sunday. Despite the fact that, unlike several other festivals, there were no pagan antecedents, a number of non-religious observances came to be associated with Whitsuntide. Many a churchwarden found himself organising the erection of a maypole, dancers performed on the north side of the churchyard and, on Whit Monday, the greatest church ale of the year was held to raise funds for the parish church (*see* CHURCH ALES). Of course, there were also religious traditions. In the Middle Ages, a symbolic dove was released following morning service and allowed to escape from the nave through the open door of the south porch. In many parts of the country parishioners gathered boughs of green yew or birch to decorate the church, a custom which persisted until the nineteenth century. The Rev. Francis Kilvert, writing in 1871, tells of a number of Whitsun customs which had been reported in the local newspapers: 'The hallowing of churches at the stroke of twelve, mysterious visits to the graves of friends, scattering on the graves the last blooms of May, letting loose a white pigeon in honour of the Holy Dove, maidens dressed in white, waiting in silence in church chancels as if in expectation of a celestial descent.' In Chester, Whitsuntide was marked with the annual performance of mystery plays (*see* DRAMA) in which the town's twenty five GUILDS enacted a story which began with the Creation and ended with the Last Judgment.
See also FEAST DAYS (FIXED AND MOVABLE)

WHITSUN FARTHINGS *see* PENTECOSTALS

WICKET A small gate within a larger one.

WIDOW A woman whose husband has died and who has not re-married.

WIDOWER A man whose wife has died and who has not re-married.

WIDOW'S VEIL *see* VOWESS

WIDOW'S WEEDS The deep mourning formerly worn by widows. Mourning is an expression of sorrow and the black or dark-coloured clothes are worn as a sign of bereavement.

WILLS *see* PROBATE

WIMPLE *see* COSTUME

WIND BRACES Short braces, usually arched and laid flat along the rafters, which strengthen the wind resistance of a roof area (*see* ROOFS).

WINDING SHEET (i) A linen SHROUD in which a corpse was wound. (ii) Also the dripping grease which clings to the side of a candle which is said to be similar in appearance to a shrouded corpse.

WINDOW GLASS *see* STAINED GLASS *and* WINDOWS

WINDOW MARKS *see* GLAZIERS' MARKS

WINDOW PLAN A plan of a church with the windows marked and numbered for identification. Church recorders usually mark the east window (behind the altar) 700 and work clockwise using Arabic numerals, with Roman numerals for clerestory windows and the suffix T for tower windows.

WINDOWS

> Erc I ham, booth day and nite
> To keep oot rain and let in lite.
>   (Eighteenth-century graffiti)

MEDIEVAL WINDOWS
Saxon and early medieval windows were generally small and narrow. In part this was because of the prohibitive cost of glazing, but of greater significance was the fact that contemporary builders, with a limited understanding of constructional techniques, were concerned that walls should not be weakened by large openings (*see* ARCH). Window openings were fitted with wooden shutters, but although these helped to keep out the cold air in winter they also excluded the light so that semi-transparent materials, such as horn, were often used as cheap alternatives to glass.

As building techniques improved so window openings became larger and wider. In churches, the 'seemingly ethereal fragility' of late Gothic architecture was arrived at only after centuries of experimentation and innovation. The narrow pointed lancet windows of the Early English period evolved through the mullioned and transomed lights of the Decorated and the ornate tracery of the Perpendicular to the broad, square-headed windows of the late fifteenth century.

The style of the ornamental mouldings (*tracery*) in a medieval window can be an invaluable guide to the age of a building – or, rather, to that part of the building in which the window is located (*see* MEDIEVAL ARCHITECTURE *for* illustrations). But it should be remembered that windows were frequently replaced, openings enlarged and new ones inserted into earlier masonry.

The areas of glass (*lights*) in the lower section of a medieval (or Victorian Gothic) window may be divided (horizontally) by *transoms* and (vertically) by *mullions* which, in the upper part of the window (the *head*), branch into an ornate stone framework containing a geometrical pattern of small glass panels (*tracery lights*) (*see also* STAINED GLASS). The smallest of these tracery lights are called *eyelets*. Some sections of a window (usually the lower panels) may consist of *blind tracery* which is filled, not with glass, but with stone or other solid material. In larger churches, there may also be a ROSE WINDOW or WHEEL WINDOW in the end elevation of a nave or transept.

CASEMENT WINDOWS
During the sixteenth century, windows continued to increased in size as a proportion of wall area. But large panes of glass were unable to withstand strong winds and windows were generally composed of small lozenge-shaped quarries (*leaded lights*), held together in a lattice-work of grooved lead bars (*cames*). Medieval windows were rarely intended to be opened and the cames of the leaded lights were secured by wire to iron bars (*saddle bars*) set within a stone or wood frame. Sometimes a hinged opening framework (*casement*) was provided within a window, and by the sixteenth century these had increased in size so that a large proportion of a window could be opened.

Seventeenth-century windows in the classical style were square or round-headed and had rectangular panes secured within a framework of wooden bars (*glazing bars*) which replaced the medieval lead cames. Large circular or oval windows (*bull's eye windows*) with radiating glazing bars are characteristic of churches of this period. In the eighteenth century, windows became taller, often extending the full height of a room. Semicircular *Diocletian windows* were popular during the Palladian period, as were *VENETIAN WINDOWS* (and doors) which were of tripartite design, with a central arched section between two lower flat-topped flanking lights.

SASH WINDOWS
By the end of the seventeenth century *sash windows* had largely replaced casements. A sash window

consists of two glazed frames running vertically in channels and counterbalanced by weights. When in 1597 Shakespeare wrote (in *Richard III*) 'Ere I let fall the windowes of mine eyes' he was referring to an early form of sash window which was held open, not by counter-weights, but by stays. The term itself (derived from the French *chassis* meaning 'frame') was introduced into Britain from Holland and France in 1662 and the first recorded use of counter-weights appeared in the accounts of the Office of Works for 1669. 'Double sashes' (with both top and bottom sashes sliding) are recorded in Princess Mary's closet at St. Jame's Palace, London in 1672. It is likely that window sashes were originally painted in a stone colour but from the 1770s darker colours were preferred in imitation of the oak or mahogany sashes of the best quality buildings.

As a general rule, earlier windows may be identified by thick glazing bars and substantial wooden-box framing. In London, eighteenth-century legislation required that sash frames should be concealed within the surrounding brickwork as a fire precaution. The practice became fashionable and, as a consequence, windows larger and glazing bars thinner.

As plate glass became more easily available glazing bars were removed and single sheets of plate glass fitted within each sash. But the heavier glass, and the weakening of the structure by the removal of glazing bars, often resulted in sashes collapsing so that projecting 'horns' had to be added to the upper and lower edges of the sash to increase its structural strength.
See also GLAZIERS' MARKS *and* ORIEL WINDOW

WINDOW TRACERY *see* MEDIEVAL ARCHITECTURE *and* WINDOWS

WINE Wine is one of the essential elements of the EUCHARIST. The words of administration imply that the consecrated wine conveys the Blood of Christ to the communicant, though in the medieval Church both the Body and Blood were considered to be present in each of the eucharistic species (*see* TRANSUBSTANTIATION). It has long been the custom to mix water with the eucharistic wine (*admixture*) and, although in the Church of England the practice was not ordered after 1552, it was revived in the nineteenth century.

WITCHCRAFT The majority of witch-trials arose as the result of injury for which there was no apparent explanation other than the occult activities of someone who had acquired a sinister reputation or whose behaviour or appearance was in some way unusual. Indeed the word 'sinister' (from the Latin *sinister* meaning 'left') came to be applied to those who were left-handed or in some other way

'marked-out' and therefore invited suspicion. During the Middle Ages both the Church and intellectual opinion defined a witch as a heretic who obtained his or (more usually) her powers through a pact with the Devil. It was the act itself which attracted judicial punishment and in the majority of cases, when the deed or intent was not serious, the punishment was light: confinement in the stocks or pillory (*see* PARISH CONSTABLE) or a public penance in the parish church. But charges of political intrigue, Lollardy, heresy and treason were common in the fourteenth and fifteenth centuries and, in many cases, witchcraft and necromancy were added for good measure, often securing a conviction where the prosecution of other charges had failed. A papal bull of 1484 resulted in fierce persecution which lasted for nearly one and a half centuries, the Old Testament denunciation 'Thou shalt not suffer a witch to live' (Exodus 25: 18) providing sufficient justification for more than five hundred hangings.

The Church's preoccupation with devil-worship reflected an intellectual conflict between late medieval concepts of heresy and popular superstition, and there can be little doubt that the situation was exacerbated by social pressures which encouraged allegations of witchcraft at a time when, in Protestant countries, the Church's traditional remedies (such as holy water) were no longer available. It was during the reign of Henry VIII that witchcraft (defined as a compact with the devil to commit an evil act) became a crime and although the statute was repealed in 1547 (under Edward VI) a further act of 1563 made it a felony to invoke an evil spirit for any purpose, good or bad. In 1604 James I, who wrote a book on demonology, confirmed the availability of the death penalty in such cases and widened the scope of the law to include association with an evil spirit, regardless of intent. The Devil's Mark (often a wart) was looked for as confirmation of guilt and in Scotland the use of torture often produced bizarre confessions and a multiplicity of victims. In 1645–46 a failed lawyer, Matthew Hopkins, became active as a professional witch-finder in the south-eastern counties of England, causing hysteria of epidemic proportions and using trial by ordeal to support otherwise unsustainable village prejudices and superstitions. Witchcraft was gradually rejected by informed opinion during the late seventeenth century though in rural areas it survived into the nineteenth century and beyond. The last witch was executed at Exeter in 1682 and the penalty was abolished by the Witchcraft Act of 1735. *See also* CONJUROR

WITCHES' MARKS *see* DOORS AND DOORWAYS

WODEHOUSE (WODEWOSE) A wild man of the woods, covered in green hair except where the flesh is visible in the face, elbows, knees, hands and feet. Several wodehouses are armed with clubs, as in the fifteenth-century effigy of Sir Robert Whitingham at Aldbury in Hertfordshire. They are found in STAINED GLASS and carved in the capitals of pillars and on FONTS and MISERICORDS. Although apparently derived from a combination of silvan demon and Greek satyr, wodehouses symbolise strength and wholesomeness.

See also GREEN MEN *and* PAGAN SYMBOLS

WOOD CARVING There is a wealth of surviving medieval wood-carving in the bench-ends, BOSSES, MISERICORDS, PANELLING and SCREENS of our parish churches. These carvings include symbols, both religious and secular, hagiographical, mythological and even pagan (*see* PAGAN SYMBOLS), all of which would have been familiar to contemporary congregations. The introduction of wooden seating in churches (*see* BENCHES AND BENCH-ENDS) provided opportunities for the carving of medieval imagery, though much of that which was religious was subsequently removed or defaced by the iconoclasts of the REFORMATION and Cromwell's commissioners. That which remains is, for the most part, secular and floreated in form, though there are several notable exceptions.

One consequence of the Black Death (*see* PLAGUE) was the creation of a new class of independent artisan (*see* WOODWORK). The late medieval wood-carver was a respected member of the community, highly skilled, well-versed in the iconography of his time and able to create his own own styles and designs. It is likely, therefore, that in matters of design he was his own master and this may explain the ubiquity of pagan and mythological images which reflect the folklore that was so much a part of medieval life (*see also* FIGURE CARVING).

Birds were especially popular and are to be found in a variety of stylised forms including a strange spoon-billed parrot at Stogursey in Somerset. So too are the implements of everyday life: ploughs, yokes, weavers' shuttles, teasels, hounds, horns, arrows and hawks' hoods. Even the medieval doctor is represented – as a chained monkey holding a bottle of urine. Surviving religious carvings include the Symbols of the Passion, the Five Wounds, the Paschal Lamb and numerous devices associated with the saints and martyrs (*see* CHRISTIAN SYMBOLS). Animals, both rural and heraldic, are common, though identification is sometimes difficult because medieval carvers were often asked to work from verbal descriptions of creatures they had never seen (*see* BEASTS (HERALDIC)).

Wodehouse and ragged staff devices in the effigy of Sir Robert Whitingham at Aldbury, Hertfordshire

A pelican in her piety at Hatch Beauchamp, Somerset.

Inevitably, medieval motifs were imitated by the architects and designers of the Gothic Revival (*see* NINETEENTH-CENTURY ARCHITECTURE) but, with some notable exceptions, the carving is patently mechanical and lacks the vigour and animation of the original.

Further reading:

Smith, J., *Church Woodcarvings: Misericords and Bench-ends*, Newton Abbot, 1974

WOODWORK Timber is of two types: hardwood (from deciduous trees such as oak and walnut) and softwood (from coniferous trees such as cedar and yew). Neither term is necessarily indicative of the hardness or otherwise of a particular wood, though hardwoods tend to be more suitable for exterior use.

Oak was used almost exclusively for the best quality fittings and furniture up to 1660 and continued in use to the present day. Walnut was fashionable from 1660 to 1770, mahogany from 1720 to 1770 and satinwood from 1770 to 1830. Inevitably, domestic furniture found its way into parish churches (often as bequests) and, from the late sixteenth century, exotic timbers such as ebony, lignum and rosewood from South America and the East Indies were used to embellish larger pieces of furniture. But such expensive items were generally beyond the means of most parishes who were obliged to commission work locally in hardwoods

such as elm and ash and softwoods such as redwood (Scots pine) and whitewood (spruce). Pitch pine, which was both inexpensive and easy to work, was imported in huge quantities during the great church building and restoration programme of the nineteenth and early twentieth centuries (*see* NINETEENTH-CENTURY ARCHITECTURE).

Before the fifteenth century, most church woodwork and furniture was made by the same carpenters who constructed buildings using heavy beams and wooden planks, working with tools such as the axe, saw, adze, chisel and auger. Consequently, much medieval church furniture was crude: hollowed-out logs for chests, planks supported on tripods for tables and pit-sawn boards for benches, all held together with wooden pegs or nails.

The mortise and tenon joint was introduced into English woodworking in the mid-fifteenth century (*see* MORTISE) and this enabled narrow strips of wood to be joined together to form a rigid framework, the intervening spaces filled with thin boards (*panels*). One consequence of the fourteenth-century Black Death had been the creation of a new class of independent artisan which included the joiner (as he came to be known) and wood-carver (*see* WOOD CARVING). They used more sophisticated tools to make furniture which was lighter, stronger and more durable. Many chests, chairs, tables and cupboards were commissioned for parish churches at this time and the lower sections of walls were often covered with PANELLING (*see also* LINENFOLD). Fittings, such as SCREENS and bench ends, were embellished with chamfers and with mouldings derived from contemporary architectural motifs such as the ovolo, cavetto and ogee. These were either cut from solid wood or applied separately and, in furniture, geometrical patterns of light and dark-coloured woods were inlaid within the surface of surrounding timbers (*see* INLAY).

By the mid-sixteenth century the woodturner's craft was much in evidence. As the name suggests, the woodturner spins wood on a lathe and shapes it using a variety of gouges and chisels to produce chair and table legs, the balusters of STAIRCASES, COMMUNION RAILS and other items of 'turned' woodwork including bowls and collection plates.

By 1600, upholsterers were replacing loose cushions with applied upholstery on fixed seating (*see* PEWS, FAMILY) and, from the mid-seventeenth century, the introduction of the *dovetail joint* allowed wooden boards to be joined at the corners to form rigid drawers and boxes and, eventually, chests of drawers. The development of various forms of joint enabled cabinet-makers to produce highly sophisticated pieces of furniture, the flat surfaces of cabinets and panels being ideally suited to the application of thin sheets of highly decorative (and expensive) timber (*veneer*). Floral patterns made from veneers are called *marquetry* and geometrical patterns *parquetry*.

See also BENCHES AND BENCH-ENDS, BOXES, CANOPY, CHESTS, CHAIRS (SANCTUARY), DESKS, DOORS AND DOORWAYS, FONT COVERS, GLASTONBURY CHAIR, MISERI-CORDS, PULPITS, RAILS, SCREWS, STALLS, WINDOWS *and* WOOD CARVING

Further reading:

Corkhill, T., *A Glossary of Wood*, London, 1984

Cox, C., and Harvey, A., *English Church Furniture*, London, 1973

Edwards, R., *A Shorter Dictionary of English Furniture*, London, 1964

Haywood, C., *English Period Furniture*, London, 1971

Hewett, C., *Church Carpentry*, London, 1982

——, *English Cathedral and Monastic Carpentry*, London, 1985

Howard, F., and Crossley, F., *English Church Woodwork*, London, 1927

Tracy, C., *English Medieval Furniture and Woodwork*, London, 1990

WOOL CHURCHES Churches which were built or extended as a consequence of the prosperity derived by individuals and communities from the production of wool and the manufacture of woollen cloth in the late Middle Ages.

In the fourteenth century Edward III commanded that in council his Chancellor should sit on a woolsack as a symbol of the pre-eminence of the wool trade. For more than four centuries the manufacture and export of wool cloths dominated British commerce.

The great medieval monastic houses (notably the CISTERCIANS) were 'built on wool', having acquired (usually through endowment) vast tracts of dry infertile land which, although unsuitable for arable farming, could be managed efficiently as sheep runs. Technically, the monasteries produced wool for their own needs but as these were minimal there was a massive surplus which was sold in Europe together with the produce of manorial estates. But such a trade was wasteful of resources and successive medieval governments imposed strict controls on the export of wool through taxation and the *Staple* system while encouraging the production of wool cloth by introducing advantageous trading tariffs for English merchants and the immigration to England of expert weavers from Flanders.

In the Middle Ages most wool, especially the finest from the Gloucestershire Cotswolds, passed through London to Calais. This monopoly facilitated the collection of duties and enabled governments to regulate the flow of bullion. Indeed, under the Yorkist kings the Staple effectively became a department of state responsible for the maintenance of Calais.

Each craftsman worked at home owning both equipment and materials. The weaver wove yarn bought from the spinner and sold cloth to the fuller who, having cleaned and thickened the cloth, sold it on to the merchant tailors. This independence was tempered by the craft GUILDS which, in theory, controlled wages and working methods and regulated prices and standards but in practice were often restrictive to enterprise and innovation. As a consequence, by the late Middle Ages entrepreneurs (*clothiers*) were producing wool cloth outside the incorporated towns. They purchased wool directly from the sheep farmers and sub-contracted the various processes (spinning, weaving, fulling, dyeing and finishing) to out-workers many of whom were entirely dependent on a constant supply of work and were therefore vulnerable to exploitation. John Aubrey, a Wiltshire landowner, described the clothiers as 'keeping their spinners but just alive.'

Like the capitalists of the Industrial Revolution, late medieval, Tudor and Stuart clothiers were socially ambitious. They married their children into the aristocracy, acquired coats of arms and built impressive houses for themselves, creating perhaps the most charming of all English settlements, the 'clothiers' towns' such as Painswick in the Gloucestershire Cotswolds. With the demise of the medieval guilds many clothiers accepted with alacrity the role of their predecessors, endowing numerous churches, almshouses and schools as memorials to their prosperity and benevolence.

See also MERCHANTS' MARKS

Further reading:

Tann, J., *Gloucestershire Woollen Mills*, Newton Abbot, 1967

WORDS FROM THE CROSS, THE *see* SEVEN WORDS FROM THE CROSS

WORKHOUSES Between 1723 and 1776 nearly 2,000 workhouses were built in England. These were provided by parishes and were financed out of the poor rates (*see* POOR LAW). By 1840 some 13.7 million of the 16 million inhabitants of England and Wales lived in areas where the reformed Poor Law was in force and where groups of parishes had been formed into unions to provide workhouses for the destitute. Although the 1834 Poor Law Amendment Act had administrative and financial merits it was in practice a singularly harsh piece of legislation. That 'fundamental document of Victorianism' was designed to remove from circulation those who were unable or unwilling to support themselves by refusing them outdoor relief and admitting them to the workhouse. This in turn was intended to reduce the supply of cheap labour, which had hitherto been subsidised by the rates, and to stimulate a rise in wages thereby encouraging the able-bodied to seek work.

For such a strategy to be effective it was necessary to ensure that life in the workhouse should be sufficiently unpleasant to deter the average labourer. It was not the intention of the legislation that the 'impotent and helpless poor' should be punished but in practice this is precisely what happened. Although outdoor relief remained the principal method of dealing with distress, the spectre of the workhouse inspired a pervasive dread of infirmity and destitution and many endured desperate cold and hunger before applying to a relieving officer for admission.

In the workhouse husbands and wives were rigorously separated from each other and from their children and communication was forbidden. Even at meals, which generally consisted of gruel or broth, dry bread or potatoes, silence was maintained. Relatives could only be received by special permission and in the presence of the master or matron. Honest paupers and pregnant women shared the freezing, bare wards with consumptives, imbeciles and syphilitics: no distinction was made except by sex and age, only the youngest children being permitted to remain with their mothers. The male inmates were provided with occupations such as oakum-picking, stone-breaking and bone-grinding and discipline was enforced by solitary confinement, penitential dress and a reduced diet. Although elementary education was available to the children, many of the 'teachers' were recruited from the paupers themselves and were often ineffectual and even brutal.

The paupers were not prisoners: providing they gave notice of their intention to leave the workhouse they were free to do so. But once they had passed through its doors they could not remain in the neighbourhood without any visible means of support. To do so would invite arrest and imprisonment for vagrancy.

The worst workhouses were often those which had been established before 1834 and over which the Commissioners had exercised only minimal control. Particularly bad conditions occasionally attracted publicity. At the Stockport Union near Manchester a man of seventy-two, who was suffering from a bad knee, refused to break stones and was ordered by a magistrate to spend fourteen days on the treadmill of Strangeways Prison. At Deptford in London a child of four was forced to spend three nights sleeping on the coffins in the workhouse mortuary. At St. Asaph's workhouse in Clwyd a boy was flogged so severely that he died and at Andover in Gloucestershire paupers fought over morsels of meat which still clung to the 'green' (still putrefying) bones they had been given to grind. By far the worst case was that of the notorious Infant Pauper Asylum at Tooting in London. This housed some 1,400 children of between two and fifteen years of age and

was the responsibility of a master called Drouet who made substantial profits by exploiting his captive supply of cheap labour and maintained discipline through a regime of fear and brutality. Dormitories were infested and overcrowded, meagre meals were eaten while standing and there was insufficient drinking water so that those inmates who controlled the supply extorted tolls from the others. Complaints to visiting guardians were punished with thrashings and visits by pauper parents were severely restricted. On one occasion in 1849 a mother was not informed of her child's death until several days after the funeral. Most significant was the attitude of the authorities. Official visitors, who at first expressed their outrage, subsequently 'reported most favourably' on conditions at the asylum. Perhaps Drouet was persuaded to share his profits?

One objective of the revised Poor Law was to facilitate the free movement of labour and consequently workhouses were required to accommodate 'casuals on the tramp' for one night in separate, secure premises where they could be kept firmly under control. These 'casuals' were often robust and disorderly characters who sometimes travelled in gangs and must have made life very difficult for the average rural or small-town workhouse master. In practice there was often neither proper accommodation nor the means of maintaining discipline and in the 1850s most Poor Law boards deliberately ignored their obligation to admit 'casuals', a policy which was tacitly endorsed by the central authority. Each board was acutely aware of the need to avoid acquiring a reputation for laxity which would inevitably attract 'casuals' and other itinerants including 'mouchers', a special breed of tramp which lived by scrounging, pilfering and assiduously avoiding the attentions of the constables. Parochial officers were past-masters in the art of obstruction and procrastination and it was only as a last resort that a genuinely destitute 'incomer' from another parish would be offered casual relief.

In 1913 workhouses became Poor Law Institutions and these were eventually superseded by the health and unemployment reforms which had been introduced in 1908–11, notably the National Insurance Act of 1911. Many surviving workhouse buildings have been adapted as hospitals and (the ultimate irony) as 'sheltered' retirement homes. Most are located on the outskirts of towns and are usually of an austere classical design with walled courtyards and radiating or extending wings. The earliest workhouse records are contained in vestry minutes while those of the post-1834 period will be found in the archives of the Guardians of the Poor which are usually held by county record offices.

See also POOR HOUSE

Further reading:

Longmate, N., *The Workhouse*, London, 1974

Reid, A., *The Union Workhouse*, London, 1994

WOUNDS, THE FIVE SACRED *see* FIVE WOUNDS OF CHRIST, THE

WREATH (*or* TORSE) A band of twisted strands of material worn about the medieval helmet as decoration and to conceal the base of the CREST where it was laced or bolted to the tournament helm. The wreath probably originated in the ceremonial torse of the Dark Age rulers of Western Europe and the colourful diadem of the Saracen. In HERALDRY the wreath is conventionally depicted as having six visible twists of alternate metals and colours (*see* COLOURS, HERALDIC), that to the left always being of a metal: *Or* (gold or yellow) or *Argent* (silver or white). On MONUMENTS in particular, the incorrect depiction of a wreath is invariably an indication that the heraldry has been repainted by someone who has no understanding of heraldry and the researcher should therefore be alert to the possibility of other errors in the painting of the shield and crest. A crest and wreath are often depicted above a shield without helmet or MANTLING and, for peers, with a coronet of rank (*see* CORONETS OF PEERS).

WREN CHURCHES *see* SIXTEENTH- AND SEVENTEENTH-CENTURY ARCHITECTURE

WROUGHT IRON A highly malleable and easily welded metal obtained from stirring (*puddling*) molten pig-iron (that which is first obtained from the smelting furnace). Wrought iron contains only a very small amount of other elements but particles of slag, elongated in one direction, are evident. In churches, wrought iron is widely used for decorative METALWORK.
Further reading:
Hollister-Short, G., *Discovering Wrought Iron*, Aylesbury, 1970

WYCLIFFE (*or* WYCLIF), JOHN (*c.* 1330–84) A philosopher, theologian and reformer who inspired the Lollards (*see* LOLLARDY). Born in Yorkshire he was educated at Oxford, became Master of Balliol in *c.* 1360 and Warden of Canterbury Hall in 1365. In 1374 he was appointed rector of Lutterworth in Leicestershire but until 1381 he lived mostly in Oxford. He was in the service of John of Gaunt (1340–99) and the Black Prince (1330–76) whose influence saved him from ecclesiastical censure. In his *De Divino Dominio* and *De Civili Dominio* of *c.* 1376 he argued that the Church should

neither interfere in temporal matters nor hold temporal possessions. Following the SCHISM he attacked the papacy's claims to authority, claiming that the Bible was the sole criterion of doctrine, and denied the doctrine of TRANSUBSTANTIATION. In 1381 the University of Oxford condemned his eucharistic teaching and in the following year both his doctrines and his followers were castigated by Archbishop Courtenay, though not Wycliffe himself. It was Wycliffe who is held by many to have been chiefly responsible for supervising the translation of the Bible into English (*see* BIBLES).

WYVERN *see* BEASTS (HERALDIC)

YALE *see* BEASTS (HERALDIC)

YEAR, LITURGICAL The liturgical year of the Western Church is based on the two great festivals of EASTER and CHRISTMAS. The year begins on the first SUNDAY in ADVENT and, thereafter, Sundays are traditionally numbered through Advent, after Christmas and after EPIPHANY, through LENT, after Easter and after WHITSUNDAY or TRINITY SUNDAY. In the Church of England the year is in three parts: the ten weeks before Easter (*triodion*), the paschal season (*pentecostarion*) and the remainder of the year (*octeochos*).

YEOMAN In thirteenth-century England, French and Latin terms (which had hitherto defined social class) were replaced by English ones, and those which had been founded on tenure and legal status were gradually superseded by terms indicating general social standing or economic function. Some terms were hardly affected by these changes: 'knight', for example was used more often than the French *chevalier* or the Latin *miles* but its meaning remained unchanged (*see* KNIGHT BACHELOR). Others, such as 'churl' (the Old English *ceorl*) and 'villein', disappeared altogether or retained only a literary usage.

New terms were of diverse origin: some originated in the feudal household, 'esquire', for example, which in the fourteenth century came to denote the social rank immediately below that of knight (*see* ESQUIRE). This comparatively select number of esquires was but the senior stratum of a substantial group of free land-owners (*valetti*) who, with the knights, represented their counties in parliament during the first half of the fourteenth century. Those *valetti* below the rank of esquire were, in the late fourteenth century, described as 'franklins', men of substance and of gentle birth, many of whom no doubt aspired to armigerous status (*see* FRANKLIN). But by the early fifteenth century the term 'franklin' had been superseded by two others: 'gentleman', which was applied to men of breeding who were not armigerous, and 'yeoman'.

By the mid-fifteenth century local society comprised (in descending order) knights, esquires, gentlemen, yeomen and husbandmen, though franklins still made an occasional appearance. Of these, only knights and esquires possessed armigerous qualifications and in common usage several of the other terms were evidently interchangeable despite the *Statute of Addition*s of 1413 which required that plaintiffs in personal actions should describe precisely the status of their opponents. Fifteenth-century sumptuary legislation similarly propounded a strict hierarchy and in 1445 it was determined that knights of the shire attending parliament could include 'noteable squires' and 'gentlemen of birth' but not those 'of the degree of Yeoman and bynethe.' In the context of local society, a yeoman was therefore a freeholder below the status of GENTLEMAN but above that of most other copyhold tenants and was eligible to serve on juries and to vote in county elections. However, the term *valetti* was also used in official documents to describe those officers in royal and magnatial households who, although of lower status than knights, were often drawn from gentle families. In the early fourteenth century the *valetti* included esquires, but as the esquires acquired their own distinctive armigerous status, so the term *valetti* came to be translated into English as 'yeomen'. Geoffrey Chaucer (1342–1400) was a yeoman (*valet*) of the king's chamber in 1367 before becoming an esquire.

YEW SUNDAY The medieval name for PALM SUNDAY.

YEW TREES Yews (*Taxas baccata*) are renowned both for their longevity and their mystical power. The oldest wooden weapons yet discovered are made of yew and it cannot be by chance that one of the letters of the runic alphabet is also the Old English name for the yew. Evergreen, hard-timbered and poisonous, yews prefer well-drained limestone soils and were once much more widespread than they are now. Relics of ancient yew woods may often be identified in place-names such as Uley in Gloucestershire, Ewhurst in Surrey and Iwerne Minster in Dorset. Such woods must have been singularly eerie places: even today the mist-shrouded 'primeval yews

and oaks of The Chase' (Hardy) endow Cranborne Chase on the Dorset/Wiltshire border with a character strongly evocative of the distant past.

Although legend relates how yew trees provided shelter for the first Christian missionaries, there is evidence to suggest that in England and the southern Marches of Wales the Norman clergy planted churchyard yews as they had in Normandy before the Conquest. In Ireland, yew trees have been grown in churchyards since the eighth century. The proposition that church precincts were commonly used for ARCHERY practice and that the churchyard yews provided raw material for the famous English longbow is almost certainly fallacious: bowyers much preferred Spanish or Italian yew to the native species. Only at times of emergency, such as the invasion scares of the sixteenth century, would the churchyard yews be lopped to provide makeshift weapons.

Of course, the leaves and fruit of the yew are poisonous and the prevalence of yew trees in old churchyards may be accounted for in the rebuke of a medieval Norfolk labourer: 'For, as often falls, broken were the churchyard walls. And the knight's herdsman often let his beasts into the churchyard get. . . .' Cattle, ponies and sheep graze safely in the company of yews in the New Forest and on the South Downs and yet farm stock have often been poisoned by eating yew clippings. It may be that animals recognise the growing tree as poisonous but will eat its foliage if it is found in an unaccustomed place.

But the most likely reason for the prevalence of yew trees in churchyards is that, because of their extreme age, yews were associated with ancestral burial grounds many of which had been in continuous use since pre-history (*see* CHURCH SITES). At Guilsfield in Powys, for example, there is a complete circle of yew trees surrounding the church within the boundaries of a circular churchyard (*see* CHURCHYARDS). It has been established that there was a sixth-century Christian settlement at Guilsfield on a site which had been used as a burial ground since the Bronze Age. At Pennant Melangell in the same county, the church of Saint Melangell was also built on a Bronze Age site and, again, the graveyard is surrounded by ancient yews which are reputed to be two thousand years old and, according to tradition, were planted to ward off evil spirits. Recent evidence suggests that Bronze Age round barrows were encircled with yews and this may account both for the presence of trees on these sites and for the lingering superstitions associated with them.

Thus, an ancient yew was a potent image of an earlier, pagan age and for this reason was highly valued for its evergreen foliage which was used for religious and secular festivals throughout the year, notably on PALM SUNDAY (*see* FESTIVALS AND SOCIAL CUSTOMS *and* YEW SUNDAY). Furthermore, the churchyard yew was always in leaf, drawing sustenance from the earthly remains of those who were buried at its roots. It was, therefore, not only a symbol of death but also of resurrection; a living and continuing presence within which slept the souls of a community's ancestors. Sir Thomas Browne, the distinguished seventeenth-century antiquary, observed: 'Whether the planting of yew in churchyards held not its original from ancient funeral rites or as an emblem of resurrection from its perpetual verdure, may admit conjecture.' What is beyond dispute is that medieval Christians continued to plant yew trees in newly consecrated churchyards. In 1307 Edward I ordered that yews should be planted in churchyards in order to protect the buildings from high winds and storms, a practice which was later commended by Gilbert White in the eighteenth century.

Ancient yews become extremely stout but the heartwood usually decays and it is often difficult to determine a tree's precise age. The ancient yew (now a relic) in Fortingall churchyard, Tayside, had a girth of 15 metres (50 feet) and is at least 2,000 years old, while a much healthier tree at Llangernyw in Clwyd is reputed to be 4,000 years old. The churchyard of St. Mary's, Painswick in Gloucestershire contains a magnificent collection of neatly clipped yews dating from *c.* 1779 – 'just under or just over, but never, reputedly, exactly 100 in number. . . .' (Rudder). Very few ancient churchyards are without at least a single ancient yew and many have substantial numbers: as at Adderbury in Oxfordshire, Brockenhurst, Corhampton, South Hayling and Selborne in Hampshire, Crowhurst in Sussex, Darley Dale, Doveridge and Norbury in Derbyshire, Tandridge in Surrey, Ulcombe in Kent and Woolland in Dorset.

See also CHURCHYARD CROSSES *and* YEW SUNDAY

YULE *see* CHRISTMAS

APPENDIX I

FURTHER READING

Suggestions for further reading have been appended to appropriate entries. The following are recommended as general books on parish churches and associated subjects:

Addleshaw, G., and Etchells, F., *The Architectural Setting of Anglican Worship*, London, 1948

Anderson, M., *History and Imagery in British Churches*, London, 1971

Anson, P., *Fashions in Church Furnishings*, Leighton Buzzard, 1960

Betjeman, J., *Guide to English Parish Churches* (revised N. Kerr), London, 1993

Bettey, J., *The English Parish Church and the Local Community*, London, 1985

——, *Church and Parish*, London, 1987

Bottomly, F., *The Explorer's Guide to the Abbeys, Monasteries and Churches of Great Britain*, London, 1981

Chadwick, O., (ed.), *Penguin History of the Church*, 6 vols, 1964 (reprinted 1990)

Clarke, B., *Churches the Victorians Forgot*, Ashbourne, 1989

Clifton-Taylor, A., *English Parish Churches as Works of Art*, London, 1974

Cunnington, P., *How Old is that Church?* (second ed.), Marston Magana, 1994

Dirsztay, P., *Inside Churches* (revised edition of *Church Furnishings*, 1978), London, 1989

Dunning, R., *Local History for Beginners*, Chichester, 1980

Dymond, D., *Writing a Church Guide*, London, 1986

Falkus, M. and J. Gillingham, *Historical Atlas of Great Britain*, London, 1981

Fewins, C., *Be a Church Detective* (a young person's guide to old churches), London, 1993

Foster, R., *Discovering English Churches*, London, 1981

Friar, S., *The Batsford Companion to Local History*, London, 1991

Harbison, R., *English Parish Churches*, London, 1992

Hoskins, W.G., *Local History in England*, London, 1984

——, *The Making of the English Landscape* (revised C. Taylor), London, 1989

Harries, J., *Discovering Churches*, Aylesbury, 1972

Hutton, G., and Smith, E., *English Parish Churches*, London, 1952 (new edition 1977)

Jones, L., and Tricker, R., *County Guide to English Churches*, Newbury, 1992

Lewis, P., and Darley, G., *Dictionary of Ornament*, London, 1986

Livingstone, E., *The Concise Oxford Dictionary of the Christian Church*, Oxford,1977

Mee, A. (ed.), *The King's England*, London (series: out of print and very collectable)

Munby, L.M., (ed.), *Short Guides to Records, Numbers 1–24*, First Series, Historical Association (reprinted) 1994)

Pevsner, N. (et al), *The Buildings of England* (series), London.

Randall, G., *Church Furnishings and Decoration in England and Wales*, London, 1980

——, *The English Parish Church*, London, 1982

Richardson, J., *The Local Historian's Encyclopedia*, New Barnet, 1986

Riden, P., *Local History: A Handbook for Beginners*, London, 1983

——, *Record Sources for Local History*, London, 1987

Rogers, A., *Approaches to Local History*, (second ed.), London, 1977

Salzman, L., *Building in England*, Oxford, 1967

Stafford, M., and Ware, D., *An Illustrated Dictionary of Ornament*, London, 1974

——, *The Victoria History of the Counties of England* (series), Oxford

Stephens, W., *Sources for English Local History*, Cambridge, 1981

Tate, W., *The Parish Chest*, Chichester, 1983

Thompson, K.L., (ed.), *Short Guides to Records, Numbers 25–48*, Second Series, Historical Association, 1993 onwards

Wilson, A., (ed.) *The Faber Book of Church and Clergy* (anthology), London, 1992

APPENDIX II

USEFUL ADDRESSES

Advisory Board for Redundant Churches, Fielden House, Little College Street, London SW1P 3SH
Ancient Monuments Society, St. Anne's Vestry Hall, 2 Church Entry, London EC4V 5HB
Antiquarian Booksellers Association, 31 Great Ormond Street, London WC1
Arms and Armour Society, 30 Alderney St., London SW1
Ashmolean Museum, Beaumont St., Oxford
Association for Latin Liturgy, 16 Brean Down Ave., Bristol BS9 4JF
Baptist Historical Society, 4 Southampton Row, London WC1
Barron Bell Fund, 16, Horse Grove Avenue, Ticehurst, East Sussex
Bell Ringers *see* Central Council of Church Bell Ringers
Birmingham Reference Library, Chamberlain Sq., Birmingham B3 3HQ
Bodleian Library, Oxford OX1 3BG
Bookplate Society, 20a Delorme St., London W6 8DT
Borthwick Institute of Historical Research, University of York, Peasholme Green, York Y01 2PW
British Archaeological Association, 61 Old Park Ridings, Winchmore Hill, London N21
British Archaeological Trust, 304 Eddison House, Grove End Rd., London NW8
British Architectural Library, 66 Portland Place, London W1N 4AD
British Association for Local History, Shopwyke Hall, Chichester, West Sussex PO20 6BQ
British Library, Great Russell St., London WC1B 3DG
British Museum, Great Russell St., London WC1B 3DG
British Newspaper Library, Colindale Ave., London NW9
British Record Society, Department of History, The University, Keele, Staffordshire ST5 5BG
British Records Association, Master's Court, Charterhouse Sq., London EC1M 6AU
British Trust for Conservation Volunteers, 36 St. Mary's St., Wallingford, Oxford OX10 0EU
Cadw, Brunel House, 2 Fitzalan Road, Cardiff CF2 1UY
Cambridge University Library, West Road, Cambridge, CB3 9DR
Camden Society *see* Ecclesiological Society
Canterbury and York Society, University of London, Senate House, London WC1E 7HU
Canterbury Cathedral, City and Diocesan Record Office (and library), The Precincts, Canterbury
Carlisle Cathedral Library, The Cathedral, Carlisle
Cathedrals Advisory Commission for England, 83 London Wall, London EC2M 5NA
Catholic Archives Society, Flat 7, Dawes House, High St., Burwash, Etchingham, Sussex TN19 7HD
Catholic Record Society, 114 Mount St., London WC2Y 6AH
Central Council of Church Bell Ringers, 50 Cramhurst Lane, Witley, Godalming, Surrey GU8 5QZ
Chapels Society, c/o Council for British Archaeology (Northern Office), The King's Manor, York YO1 2EP
Charities Aid Foundation, 48 Pembury Road, Tunbridge Wells, Kent
Charity Commission for England and Wales, 14 Ryder Street, London SW1Y 6AH
Church Commissioners for England, 1 Millbank, London SW1
Churches Conservation Trust (formerly the Redundant Churches Fund) 89 Fleet Street, London EC4Y 1DH
Church in Wales *see* Representative Body of the Church in Wales
Church Monuments Society, The Armouries, H.M. Tower of London, London EC3N 4AB
Church of England Record Society, c/o Selwyn College, Cambridge CB3 9DQ
Church Recorders Committee of *NADFAS*, 8 Guilford Street, London WC1N 1DT
Civic Trust, 17 Carlton House Terrace, London SW1Y 5AS
Close Society, c/o The Map Library, British Library (see above)

College of Arms, Queen Victoria St., London EC4V 4BT

Commons, Open Spaces and Footpaths Preservation Society, 166 Shaftesbury Avenue, London WC2H 8JH

Congregational Church of England and Wales, Memorial Hall, Farringdon Rd., London EC1

Connexional Archivist, Methodist Church, Central Buildings, Oldham St., Manchester

Corporation of London Records Office, Guild Hall, London EC2P 2EJ

Costume and Fashion Research Centre, 4 The Circus, Bath, Avon BA1 2EW

Council for British Archaeology (CBA), 112 Kennington Road, London SE11 6RE

Council for the Care of Churches (CCC), Fielden House, Little College St., London SW1P 3SH

Cromwell Association, Coswell Cottage, Northedge, Tupton, Chesterfield S42 6AM

Department of the Environment, 2 Marsham St., London SW1

Diocesan Advisory Committees c/o appropriate Diocesan Office

Diocesan Records Office c/o appropriate County Records Office

Duke of Norfolk's Library and Archives, Arundel Castle, Arundel, West Sussex BN18 9AB

Early English Text Society, Lady Margaret Hall, Oxford

Ecclesiastical Architects and Surveyors Association, 66 Portland Place, London W1N 4AP

Ecclesiastical History Society, Department of Medieval History, University of Glasgow, Glasgow G12 8QQ

Ecclesiological Society, St. Andrew-by-the-Wardrobe, Queen Victoria St., London EC4V 5DE

English Clergy Association, Hamstead Vicarage, Walsall Rd., Birmingham B42 1ES

English Heritage, Fortress House, 25 Saville Row, London W1X 2BT

English Place-Names Society, c/o University College, Gower St., London WC1E 6BT

Exeter Cathedral Library and Archives, Bishops Palace, Exeter, Devon

Federation of Family History Societies, The Benson Room, Birmingham and Midland Institute, Margaret St., Birmingham B3 3BS

Folklore Society, c/o University College, Gower St., London WC1E 6BT

Folly Society, 21 Beacon Road, Ware, Hertfordshire SG12 7HY

Franciscan Archives (English Province), 58 St. Anthony's Rd., London E7

Friends Historical Society, Friends House, Euston Rd., London NW1

Friends of Cathedral Music, Addington Palace, Croydon CR9 5AD

Friends of Friendless Churches, St. Anne's Vestry Hall, 2 Church Entry, London EC4V 5HB

Friends of the City Churches, 68 Battersea High St., London SW11 3HX

Furniture History Society, Victoria and Albert Museum, London SW7

General Register Office *see* Office of Population Censuses

Georgian Group, 37 Spital Square, London E1 6DY

Gloucester Cathedral Library, 6 College Green, Gloucester

Greater London Record Office, 40 Northampton Rd., London EC1

Guildhall Library, Aldermanbury, London EC2P 2EJ

Guild of Church Musicians, Hillbrow, Bletchingley, Surrey RH1 4PJ

Harleian Society, c/o College of Arms (see above)

Heraldry Society, 44/45 Museum St., London WC1A 1LY

Hereford Cathedral Library, The Cathedral, Hereford

Her Majesty's Stationery Office (HMSO), 49 High Holborn, London WC1V 6HB

Historical Association, 59a Kennington Park Rd., London SE11 4JH

Historic Buildings and Monuments Commission for England *see* English Heritage

Historic Buildings Council for Wales, Brunel House, 2 Fitzalan Road, Cardiff CF2 1UY

Historic Chapels Trust, c/o 8 Kensington Gate, London W8 5NA

Historic Churches Preservation Trust, Fulham Palace, London SW6 6EA

History of Education Society, University of London, Institute of Education, 20 Bedford Way, London WC1

House of Lords Library and Record Office, Westminster, London SW1A 0PW

Huguenot Library, University College, Gower St., London WC1E 6BT

Huguenot Society, 67 Victoria Rd., London W8

Hymn Society of Great Britain and Ireland, St. Nicholas Rectory, Glebe Fields, Curdworth, Sutton Coldfield, West Midlands B76 9ES

Incorporated Church Building Society, Fulham Palace, London SW6 6EA

Independent Methodist Churches Historical Society, Providence Independent Methodist Church, Albert Rd., Colne, Lancashire

Institute of Archaeology (Conservation of Historic Buildings), 31–34 Gordon Sq., London WC1

Institute of Heraldic and Genealogical Studies, Northgate, Canterbury, Kent CT1 1RB

Institute of Historical Research, University of London, Senate House, London WC1E 7HU

Kelly's Directories Ltd., Dorset House, Stamford St., London SE1

Lambeth Palace (and library), London SE1

Leche Trust, Christ Church, Spitalfields, Commercial Street, London E1 6LY

List and Index Society, Public Record Office, Ruskin Avenue, Kew, Surrey TW9 4DU

Local Population Studies Centre, 17 Rosebery Sq., Rosebery Ave., London EC1

Local Population Studies Society, Department of Anthropology, University of Durham, 43 Old Elvet, Durham

London Map Centre, 22–24 Caxton Rd., London SW1H 0QH

Manorial Society, 104 Kennington Rd., London SE11 6RE

Medieval Dress and Textile Society, Museum of London, London Wall, EC2T 5HN

Methodist Archives and Research Centre, John Rylands Library, University of Manchester, Deansgate, Manchester M3 3EH

Monumental Brass Society, c/o The Society of Antiquaries, Burlington House, Piccadilly, London W1V 0HS

Mothers' Union, 24 Tufton St., London SW1P 3RB

Museum of English Rural Life, University of Reading, Berkshire

National Association of Decorative and Fine Art Societies (NADFAS), 8 Guilford Street, London WC1N 1DT (*see* Church Recorders Committee)

National Inventory of War Memorials, Imperial War Museum, Lambeth Rd., London SE1 6HZ

National Library of Wales, Aberystwyth, Dyfed

National Monuments Record Centre *see* Royal Commission on the Historical Monuments of England

National Museum of Wales, Bute Street, Cardiff

National Register of Archives, Quality Court, London WC2A 1HP

National Trust, 36 Queen Anne's Gate, London SW1

Norwich Cathedral, Dean and Chapter's Library, The Close, Norwich

Office of Population Censuses and Surveys, General Register Office, St. Catherine's House, 10 Kingsway, London WC2B 6JP

Open University History Society, 7 Cliffe House Ave., Garforth, Leeds LS25 2BW

Order of St. John Library and Museum, St. John's Gate, Clerkenwell, London EC1M 4DA

Ordnance Survey, Romsey Rd., Maybush, Southampton SO9 4DH

Peterborough Cathedral (library), Prebendal House, The Precincts, Peterborough

Pewter Society, Hunters Lodge, Paddock Close, St Mary's Platt, Sevenoaks, Kent TN15 8NN

Phillimore & Co. Ltd., (local history publications) Shopwyke Manor Barn, Chichester, Sussex PO20 6BG

Pipe Roll Society, Public Record Office, Chancery Lane, London WC2 1AH

Prayer Book Society, St. James Garlickhythe, Garlick Hill, London EC4V 2AL

Principal Registry of the Family Division, Somerset House, Strand, London WC2R 1LP

Protestant Reform Society, PO Box 47, Ramsgate, Kent CT11 9XB

Public Record Office, Chancery Lane, London WC1A 2LR

Public Record Office, Ruskin Ave., Kew, Richmond, Surrey TW9 4DU

Public Record Office, Portugal St., London WC2

Pugin Guild, 157 Vicarage Rd., London E10 5DU

Redundant Churches Fund (RCF) *see* Churches Conservation Trust

Representative Body of the Church in Wales, 39 Cathedral Rd., Cardiff CF1 9XF

Round Tower Churches Society, Crabbe Hall, Burnham Market, King's Lynn, Norfolk PE31 8EN

Royal College of Organists, 7 St. Andrew St., London EC4V 3LQ

Royal Commission on Historical Manuscripts, Quality House, Quality Court, Chancery Lane, London WC2A 1HP

Royal Commission on the Ancient and Historical Monuments of Wales, Edleston House, Queens Road, Aberystwyth, Dyfed

Royal Commission on the Historical Monuments of England (RCHME), National Monuments Record Centre, Kemble Drive, Swindon, Wiltshire SN2 2GZ (NB: for London buildings: 55 Blandford Street, London)

Royal Historical Society, c/o University College, Gower St., London WC1E 6BT

Royal Institute of British Architecture, 66 Portland Place, London W1N 4AD

Royal School of Church Music, Addington Palace, Croydon CR9 5AD

St. George's Chapel (and library), Aerary, Dean's Close, Windsor Castle

St. Paul's Cathedral Library), c/o Guildhall Library, Aldermanbury, London EC2

Salisbury Cathedral, Chapter Archives, 6 The Close, Salisbury

Science Museum, Exhibition Rd., London SW7

Sharpe Trust, c/o Beech Pike, Elkstone, Gloucestershire

Society for Medieval Archaeology, c/o University College, Gower St., London WC1E 6BT

Society for Post-medieval Archaeology, The Museum of London, London Wall, London EC2

Society for the Protection of Ancient Buildings, 37 Spital Square, London E1 6DY

Society of Antiquaries, Burlington House, Piccadilly, London W1V 0HS
Society of Architectural Historians, Chesham House, 30 Warwick St., London W1
Society of Archivists, 20–24 Old St., London EC1V 9AP
Society of Friends Library, Friends House, Euston Rd., London NW1 2BJ
Society of Genealogists, 14 Charterhouse Buildings, London EC1M 7BA
Society of Jesus Record Office, 114 Mount St., London WC2Y 6AH
Society of Scribes and Illuminators, 54 Boileau Rd., London SW13 9BL
Tiles and Architectural Ceramics Society, c/o 3 Brown's Rise, Buckland Common, Tring, Hertfordshire, HP23 6NJ
Unitarian Headquarters, 1 Essex St., London WC2
United Reformed Church Historical Society, 86 Tavistock Place, London WC1H 9RT
Victoria and Albert Museum, Cromwell Road, South Kensington, London SW7 2RL
Victorian Society, 1 Priory Gardens, Bedford Park, London W4 1TT
Welsh Historic Monuments Office *see* Cadw
Wesley Historical Society, 34 Spiceman's Rd., Northfield, Birmingham
William and Jane Morris Fund, c/o Society of Antiquaries (see above)
Winchester Cathedral Library, The Close, Winchester
Worcester Cathedral (library), Worcester
York Minster Library, Dean's Park, York

INDEX OF PLACES

Page references for illustrations are given in italic; numbers given in bold refer to the colour plates. Where counties are listed the post-1974 groupings have been used, with the exception of Herefordshire and Worcestershire, which have been listed as separate counties.

INDEX